1951 Chlorpromazine, first antipsychotic drug, tested. *p. 442*

1951 Carl Rogers publishes *Client-Centered Therapy*. *p. 68*

1952 First edition of DSM published by the American Psychiatric Association. *p. 102*

1952 Sex-change operation performed on Christine Jorgensen. *p. 407*

1955 The Los Angeles Suicide Prevention Center founded. *p. 303*

1956 Family systems theory and therapy launched. *pp. 71, 75*

1958 Joseph Wolpe develops desensitization. *p. 62*

1961 Thomas Szasz publishes *The Myth of Mental Illness*. *p. 5*

1962 Albert Ellis proposes rational-emotive therapy. *pp. 64, 120*

1963 The Community Mental Health Act helps trigger deinstitutionalization in the United States. *p. 449*

1963 Antianxiety drug Valium introduced in the United States. *p. 125*

1964 U.S. Surgeon General warns that smoking can be dangerous to human health. *p. 351*

1965 Norepinephrine and serotonin theories of depression proposed. *p. 229*

1967 Aaron Beck publishes cognitive theory and therapy for depression. *pp. 234, 256*

1967 Methadone maintenance treatment begins. *p. 369*

1967 Holmes and Rahe develop Social Adjustment Rating Scale to measure life stress. *p. 178*

1970 Masters and Johnson publish *Human Sexual Inadequacy* and launch sex therapy. *p. 389*

1972 CAT scan introduced. *p. 98*

1973 DSM stops listing homosexuality as a mental disorder. *p. 404*

1973 David Rosenhan conducts study *On Being Sane in Insane Places*. *pp. 71, 432*

1975 Endorphins—natural opioids—discovered in human brain. *p. 346*

1975 U.S. Supreme Court declares that patients in institutions have right to adequate treatment. *p. 572*

1981 MRI first used as diagnostic tool. *p. 98*

1981 Researchers discover that Ritalin helps persons with ADHD. *p. 510*

1982 John Hinckley found not guilty by reason of insanity of the attempted murder of President Reagan. *p. 561*

1987 Antidepressant Prozac approved in the United States. *p. 267*

1988 American Psychological Society founded. *p. 22*

1990 Dr. Jack Kevorkian performs his first assisted suicide. *p. 302*

1990 FDA approves first atypical antipsychotic drug, *clozapine*. *p. 446*

1994 DSM-IV published. *p. 102*

1995 APA task force begins search to identify empirically supported (evidence-based) treatments. *p. 108*

1998 Viagra goes on sale in the United States. *p. 393*

1999 Killing rampage at Columbine High School stirs public concern about dangerousness in children. *p. 570*

2000 DSM-IV-TR is published and changes criteria for pedophilia, exhibitionism, voyeurism, frotteurism, and sexual sadism. *pp. 103, 401*

2000 Scientists finish mapping (i.e., sequencing) the human genome—spelling out the chemical "letters" that make up human DNA. *p. 51*

2001 Around 1,600 mental health workers mobilize to help 57,000 victims in wake of 9/11 terrorist attacks. *pp. 164, 171*

2001 Case of Andrea Yates, who drowned her five children, highlights the disorder postpartum psychosis. *pp. 426, 563*

2002 New Mexico grants prescription privileges to specially trained psychologists. *p. 575*

2003 First case of mad cow disease uncovered in the United States, further raising concerns about the disease vCJD. *p. 551*

2004 FDA orders *black box* warnings on all antidepressant drug containers, stating that the drugs "increase the risk of suicidal thinking and behavior in children." *p. 273*

2006 U.S. Supreme Court upholds Oregon's "Death with Dignity" Act, allowing doctors to assist suicides by terminally ill individuals under certain conditions. *p. 302*

Abnormal Psychology

Abnormal Psychology

SIXTH EDITION

Ronald J. Comer

Princeton University

Worth Publishers

New York

Publisher: Catherine Woods
Sponsoring Editors: Renee Altier and Kevin Feyen
Senior Marketing Manager: Katherine Nurre
Associate Managing Editor: Tracey Kuehn
Senior Media Editor: Danielle Pucci
Project Editor: Jane O'Neill
Photo Editor: Patricia Marx
Art Director and Cover/Text Designer: Barbara Reingold
Layout Designer: Paul Lacy
Cover Illustrator: Wiktor Sadowski
Production Manager: Sarah Segal
Composition: Northeastern Graphic
Printing and Binding: RR Donnelley

We gratefully acknowledge the following artists and agencies for providing the illustrations on the chapter opening pages: p. xxvi, Robert Carter/www.crackedhat.com; pp. 26, 278, 308, and 436, Wiktor Sadowski; p. 46, Brand X Pictures; p. 84, Alan Cober; pp. 114, 154, and 336, © 2006 James Steinberg c/o theispot.com; pp. 188 and 376, © 2003 Michael Gibbs; p. 222, © 2006 Scott Laumann c/o theispot.com; pp. 250 and 534, Gerard Dubois/marlenaagency.com; p. 410, Stefano Vitale/lindgrensmith.com; p. 460, Weislaw Walkuski; p. 496, David Hollenbach; p. 558, © Mark Oldroyd/arenaworks.com

Credits for timeline photos, inside front cover (by date): 1893, Sigmund Freud Copyrights/Everett Collection; 1901, W. H. Freeman & Company; 1907, Richard Falco/Black Star; 1939, Travis Amos; 1964, Greg Baker/AP Photo; 1967, Leif Skoogfors/WoodfinCamp & Associates; 1981, Pallava Bagla/Corbis; 2001, AP Photo/Ernesto Mora.

Library of Congress Control Number: 2006924436
ISBN 0-7167-6906-9
EAN 9780716769064

Printed in the United States of America

First printing

Worth Publishers
41 Madison Avenue
New York, NY 10010
www.worthpublishers.com

For Dave and Dos Slotkin
You will always be in our hearts

Ronald J. Comer has been a professor in Princeton University's Department of Psychology for the past 32 years and has served as Director of Clinical Psychology Studies for most of that time. His courses, Abnormal Psychology, Theories of Psychotherapy, Experimental Psychopathology, and Controversies in Clinical Psychology, have been among the university's most popular offerings.

Professor Comer has received the President's Award for Distinguished Teaching at the university. He is also a practicing clinical psychologist and serves as a consultant to the Eden Institute for Individuals with Autism and to hospitals and family practice residency programs throughout New Jersey.

In addition to writing *Abnormal Psychology,* Professor Comer is the author of the textbook *Fundamentals of Abnormal Psychology,* now in its fourth edition, and the co-author of *Case Studies in Abnormal Psychology.* He is the producer of several educational videos, including *Video Segments in Abnormal Psychology* and *Video Segments in Neuroscience;* and he has published numerous journal articles in clinical psychology, social psychology, and family medicine.

Professor Comer completed his undergraduate studies at the University of Pennsylvania and his graduate work at Clark University. He currently lives in Lawrenceville, New Jersey, with his wife, Marlene. From there he can keep an eye on his sons, Greg and Jon, who live in New York City, and on the frustrating Philadelphia sports teams with which he grew up.

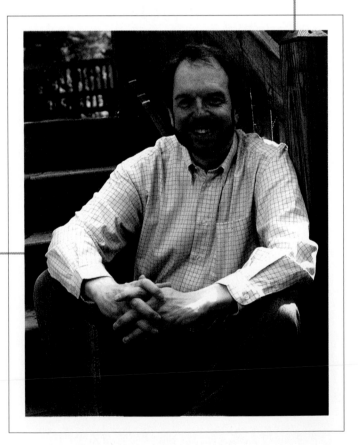

Contents in brief

Contents

I n 1981 I began writing an abnormal psychology textbook. In 1992 the first edition of *Abnormal Psychology* was published. Today, a quarter of a century later, this journey continues as I offer the sixth edition of my textbook. I don't know whether I am amazed more by the fact that I have somehow managed to write six editions of this book or by the fact that 25 years have passed so quickly.

While writing this new edition, I was faced with the same overriding challenge that I confronted in past editions—to maintain the quality and energy of the textbook. To achieve this goal, I have followed five key rules—the same rules that I followed as I wrote the previous editions: (1) Approach the new edition with the same basic goals as those of the first edition—that is, to excite students; to bring the field to life; to convey my passion for the field; and to demonstrate that behavior, including abnormal behavior, pervades our lives and our world. (2) Keep the edition current and fresh, being sure to include recent research and developments and repeatedly drawing on examples from the world around us. (3) Incorporate new pedagogical techniques that may help readers enjoy and process the material. (4) Keep listening to the feedback of my colleagues in this enterprise—the students and professors who have used this textbook over the past 15 years. And (5) don't make changes just for the sake of change: retain those techniques that have proved effective.

With these rules in mind, I believe that I have produced a new edition that will continue to excite readers and open the world of abnormal psychology to them. Let me describe what I believe to be special about this edition of *Abnormal Psychology,* although I know, and fear, that descriptions such as this always come perilously close to self-aggrandizement. For this I offer my apologies.

Changes and Features New to This Edition

The study of abnormal psychology continues to advance steadily. Similarly, the field of education is in constant motion, with new pedagogical techniques and insights emerging each day. Such developments have spurred me to include important changes and new features in the current edition.

•**EXPANDED**• **MULTICULTURAL COVERAGE** While earlier editions have certainly included ethnic, racial, gender, and other sociocultural factors, I have greatly expanded the coverage of multicultural issues in this edition, following the increased multicultural focus by clinical practitioners and researchers in the twenty-first century. The expanded multicultural coverage is particularly prominent in sections, boxes, and tables whose titles begin "Sociocultural Landscape," such as "Sociocultural Landscape: Are Hispanic Americans Prone to Stress Disorders?" (p. 163), "Sociocultural Landscape: First Dibs on Antidepressant Drugs" (p. 268), "Sociocultural Landscape: ADHD and Race" (pp. 511–512), and "Sociocultural Landscape: Race and Forensic Psychology" (p. 568).

•**EXPANDED**• **COVERAGE OF KEY DISORDERS AND TOPICS** In line with the field's (and society's) increased focus on certain psychological problems, I have greatly expanded the textbook's coverage of disorders such as borderline personality disorder (pp. 474–480), conduct disorder (pp. 499–507), ADHD (pp. 507–512), and pervasive developmental disorders, including Asperger's disorder (pp. 515–521). Similarly, I have added or expanded coverage of important topics such as the meta-worry explanations of generalized anxiety disorder (pp. 122–123), dimensional approaches to the classification of personality disorders (pp. 492–493), dialectical behavior therapy (pp. 479–480), genetics and abnormal behavior (for example, pp. 51–52), and relational psychoanalytic therapy (for example, pp. 59 and 479).

•EXPANDED• **COVERAGE OF PREVENTION AND OF THE PROMOTION OF MENTAL HEALTH** In accord with the clinical field's growing emphasis on prevention, positive psychology, and psychological wellness, I have increased the textbook's attention to these important approaches (for example, pp. 19–20, 301–305, 332–333, and 372–373).

KEY CHAPTER CHANGES In order to reflect current directions in the clinical field and to improve the flow of the textbook, I have made several key changes to some of the chapters. Chapter 15, "Treatments for Schizophrenia and Other Severe Mental Disorders," now describes treatments (and nontreatments) for a range of severe disorders, not just for schizophrenia. Chapter 16, "Personality Disorders," offers greater attention than past editions to borderline personality disorder and to alternative (dimensional) categorizations of the personality disorders. And childhood disorders that parallel adult disorders—childhood anxiety disorders and childhood depression—are now discussed within the chapters on anxiety disorders, stress disorders, and mood disorders. In turn, Chapter 17, "Disorders of Childhood and Adolescence," offers more in-depth coverage of conduct disorder, ADHD, pervasive developmental disorders, and mental retardation.

THOROUGH UPDATE In this edition I present recent theories, research, and events, including more than 2,000 new references from the years 2004–2006, as well as hundreds of new photos, tables, and figures.

•NEW!• **BOXES** A variety of new boxes have been added, such as "Can Rock and Roll Inspire Suicide?" (p. 289), "The Young and the Anxious" (p. 140), and "Depressed Children: Is Help on the Way?" (pp. 272–273).

Continuing Strengths

In this edition I have also been careful to retain the goals, themes, material, and techniques that have worked successfully and been embraced enthusiastically by past readers.

INNOVATIVE DESIGN This textbook continues to offer a unique and accessible design—a single text column with a wide margin that provides space for commentaries on the text discussion—fun facts, current events, historical notes, interesting trends, lists, and quotes.

BREADTH AND BALANCE The field's many theories, studies, disorders, and treatments are presented completely and accurately. All major models—psychological, biological, and sociocultural—receive objective, balanced, up-to-date coverage, without bias toward any single approach.

INTEGRATION OF MODELS Discussions throughout the text, particularly those headed "Putting It Together," help students better understand where and how the various models work together and how they differ.

EMPATHY The subject of abnormal psychology is people—very often people in great pain. I have therefore tried to write always with empathy and to impart this awareness to students.

INTEGRATED COVERAGE OF TREATMENT Discussions of treatment are presented throughout the book. In addition to a complete overview of treatment in the opening chapters, each of the pathology chapters includes a full discussion of relevant treatment approaches.

RICH CASE MATERIAL I integrate numerous clinical examples to bring theoretical and clinical issues to life.

TOPICS OF SPECIAL INTEREST I devote full chapters to important subjects that are of special interest to college-age readers, such as eating disorders and suicide, and I also cover controversial issues that are currently being spotlighted by the news media, including the impact of managed care, direct-to-consumer advertising, the rise in use of Ritalin, treatment over the Internet, and the right to commit suicide.

A FOCUS ON CRITICAL THINKING The textbook provides tools for thinking critically about abnormal psychology. In particular, toward the end of each chapter a section called "Critical Thoughts" poses questions that help students to analyze and apply the material they have just read.

DSM CHECKLISTS The discussion of each disorder is accompanied by a detailed checklist of the DSM-IV-TR criteria used to diagnose the disorder.

MARGIN GLOSSARY Hundreds of key words are defined in the margins of pages on which the words appear. In addition, a traditional glossary is available at the back of the book.

"PUTTING IT TOGETHER" A section toward the end of each chapter, "Putting It Together," asks whether competing models can work together in a more integrated approach and also summarizes where the field now stands and where it may be going.

"CYBERSTUDY" Each chapter ends with a "CyberStudy" section, a guide to integrating the chapter material with videos and other features found on the Student CD-ROM.

STIMULATING ILLUSTRATIONS Chapters illustrate concepts, disorders, treatments, and applications with stunning photographs, diagrams, and graphs. All graphs and tables, many new to this edition, reflect the most up-to-date data available.

ADAPTABILITY Chapters are self-contained, so they can be assigned in any order that makes sense to the professor.

Supplements

The very enthusiastic response to the supplements accompanying previous editions has been gratifying. This edition is able to retain those supplements, revising and enhancing them, and to add a number of exciting new ones.

FOR PROFESSORS

VIDEO SEGMENTS FOR *ABNORMAL PSYCHOLOGY* *Produced and Edited by Ronald Comer. Faculty Guide* included. This incomparable video series offers 100 clips that depict disorders, show historical footage, and illustrate clinical topics, pathologies, treatments, experiments, and dilemmas. Videos are available on DVD, VHS, or CD-ROM. I have also written an accompanying guide that fully describes and discusses each video clip, so that professors can make informed decisions about the use of the segments in lectures.

In addition, Nicholas Greco, College of Lake County, has written a completely new set of questions to accompany each video segment in the series. The questions have been added to the Faculty Guide (now available in the *Instructor's Resource Manual*) and are also available in PowerPoint on the companion Web site or the Instructor's Resource CD-ROM (for use with Worth Publishers' iClicker Classroom Response System).

•NEW!• CLINICAL VIDEO CASE FILE FOR *ABNORMAL PSYCHOLOGY* *Produced and Edited by Ronald Comer. Faculty Guide* included. To accompany the sixth edition of the textbook, I have created an entirely new set of *case study videos* that bring to life in a special and deeper way particularly interesting cases of psychopathology and treatment. Featuring contemporary, authentic patient interviews and therapy sessions, this new video provides students with a tangible and critical window into the world of abnormal psychology and the people who suffer from the disorders. These videos will also be available on DVD, VHS, or CD-ROM.

POWERPOINT® SLIDES *Available at www.worthpublishers.com/comer or on the Instructor's Resource CD-ROM.* These PowerPoint® slides can be used directly or customized to fit a professor's needs. There are two pre-built, customizable slide sets for each chapter of the book—one featuring chapter text, the other featuring all chapter art and illustrations.

•ENHANCED• POWERPOINT® PRESENTATION SLIDES *by Karen Clay Rhines, Seton Hall University, available at www.worthpublishers.com/comer or on the Instructor's Resource CD-ROM.* These customized slides focus on key text terms and themes, reflect the main points in significant detail, and feature tables, graphs, and figures from the book. Each set of chapter slides is accompanied by a set of student handouts. These handouts were created using the instructor slides as a base, with key points replaced as "fill-in" items. Answer keys and suggestions for use are also provided.

•NEW!• STEP UP TO *ABNORMAL PSYCHOLOGY*: A POWERPOINT® REVIEW GAME *by John Schulte, Cape Fear Community College and University of North Carolina, available at www.worthpublishers.com/comer or on the Instructor's Resource CD-ROM.* This PowerPoint®-based review adopts a game-show approach where students divide into teams to compete to climb the pyramid by answering questions related to chapter material.

•NEW!• DIGITAL PHOTO LIBRARY *Available at www.worthpublishers.com/comer or on the Instructor's Resource CD-ROM.* This collection gives you access to all of the photographs from *Abnormal Psychology,* Sixth Edition.

IMAGE AND LECTURE GALLERY *Available at www.worthpublishers.com/ILG.* The Image and Lecture Gallery is a convenient way to access electronic versions of lecture materials. Users can browse, search, and download text art, illustrations, and pre-built PowerPoint® presentation files for all Worth titles. Users can also create personal folders for easy organization of the materials.

TRANSPARENCIES Fifty full-color diagrams and graphs from the text are available for use in lectures. Additionally, there are many transparency masters of text tables and DSM-IV-TR criteria listings available in the *Instructor's Resource Manual.*

INSTRUCTOR'S RESOURCE MANUAL *by Karen Clay Rhines, Seton Hall University.* This comprehensive guide ties together the ancillary package for professors and teaching assistants. The manual includes detailed chapter outlines, lists of principal learning objectives, ideas for lectures, discussion launchers, classroom activities, extra credit projects, word search and crossword puzzles, transparency masters for every table in the text, and precise DSM-IV-TR criteria for each of the disorders discussed in the text. It also offers strategies for using the accompanying media, including the video segments series, the CD-ROM, the companion Web site, and the transparencies. Finally, it includes a comprehensive set of valuable materials that can be obtained from outside sources—items such as relevant feature films, documentaries, teaching references, and Internet sites related to abnormal psychology.

ASSESSMENT TOOLS

PRINTED TEST BANK *by Debra B. Hull, Wheeling Jesuit University, and John H. Hull, Bethany College.* A comprehensive test bank offers over 2,500 multiple-choice, fill-in-the-blank, and essay questions. Each question is graded according to difficulty, identified as factual or applied, and keyed to the topic and page in the text where the source information appears.

DIPLOMA COMPUTERIZED TEST BANK *Windows and Macintosh Dual-Platform CD-ROM.* This CD-ROM guides professors step by step through the process of creating a test and allows them to add an unlimited number of questions, edit or scramble questions, format a test, and include pictures, equations, and multimedia links. The accompanying grade book enables them to record students' grades throughout the course and includes the capacity to sort student records and view detailed analyses of test items, curve tests, generate reports, add weights to grades, and more. The CD-ROM also provides the access point for Diploma Online Testing, as well as Blackboard- and WebCT-formatted versions of the Test Bank for *Abnormal Psychology*, Sixth Edition.

ONLINE TESTING, POWERED BY DIPLOMA *at www.brownstone.net*. With Diploma, professors can create and administer secure exams over a network and over the Internet, with questions that incorporate multimedia and interactive exercises. The program also allows them to restrict tests to specific computers or time blocks and includes a suite of grade-book and result-analysis features.

ONLINE QUIZZING, POWERED BY QUESTIONMARK *Access via the companion Web site at www.worthpublishers.com/comer*. Professors can easily and securely quiz students online using prewritten multiple-choice questions for each chapter (note that questions are *not* from the Test Bank). Students receive instant feedback and can take the quizzes multiple times. Professors can view results by quiz, student, or question, or can get weekly results via e-mail.

FOR STUDENTS

ABNORMAL PSYCHOLOGY CD-ROM *Produced and Edited by Ronald Comer, Princeton University*. Upon request, this CD-ROM is free when packaged with the text. Tied directly to the *CyberStudy* sections in the text, it offers numerous intriguing videos running three to five minutes each. The Video Cases focus on an interview with a person affected by a disorder discussed in the text. Students first view the video and then answer a series of thought-provoking questions about it. Designed to promote critical thinking, each Video Exercise presents a text concept, then asks students to think about how that concept can be applied in the real world. The exercises are accompanied by a set of worksheets that can be completed and printed out for submission in class. Additionally, the CD-ROM contains multiple-choice practice test questions with built-in instructional feedback for every option.

STUDENT WORKBOOK *by Ronald Comer, Princeton University, and Gregory Comer, Princeton Academic Resources*. This student guide actively involves students in the text material, using a variety of engaging exercises. Each chapter includes a selection of practice tests and exercises, as well as key concepts, guided study questions, and section reviews.

ABNORMAL PSYCHOLOGY COMPANION WEB SITE *by Nicholas Greco, College of Lake County, and Jason Spiegelman, Community College of Baltimore County, at www.worthpublishers.com/comer*. This Web site provides students with a virtual study guide, 24 hours a day, seven days a week. These resources are free and do not require any special access codes or passwords. The tools on the site include: chapter outlines, annotated Web links, quizzes, interactive flashcards, research exercises, frequently asked questions about clinical psychology, and interactive crossword puzzles by Ann Brandt-Williams, Glendale Community College (also included in the *Instructor's Resource Manual*).

In addition, the site includes nine case studies by Elaine Cassel, Marymount University and Lord Fairfax Community College, Danae L. Hudson, Missouri State University, and Brooke L. Whisenhunt, Missouri State University. Each case describes an individual's history and symptoms and is accompanied by a set of guided questions that point to the precise DSM-IV-TR criteria for the disorder and suggest a course of treatment.

CASE STUDIES IN ABNORMAL PSYCHOLOGY *by Ethan E. Gorenstein, Behavioral Medicine Program, Columbia-Presbyterian Hospital, and Ronald Comer, Princeton University,*

2001. This casebook provides 20 case histories, each going beyond DSM-IV-TR diagnoses to describe the individual's history and symptoms, a theoretical discussion of treatment, a specific treatment plan, and the actual treatment conducted. The casebook also provides three cases without diagnoses or treatment, so that students can identify disorders and suggest appropriate therapies. In addition, case study evaluations by Ann Brandt-Williams, Glendale Community College, are available at www.worthpublishers.com/comer. Each evaluation accompanies a specific case and can be assigned to students to assess their understanding as they work through the text.

THE *SCIENTIFIC AMERICAN READER* TO ACCOMPANY *ABNORMAL PSYCHOLOGY*, SIXTH EDITION *Edited by Ronald J. Comer, Princeton University.* Upon request, this reader is free when packaged with the text. Drawn from *Scientific American,* this full-color collection of articles enhances coverage of important topics covered by the course. Keyed to specific chapters, the selections provide a preview of and discussion questions for each article.

SCIENTIFIC AMERICAN EXPLORES THE HIDDEN MIND: A COLLECTOR'S EDITION Upon request, this reader is free when packaged with the text. In this special edition, *Scientific American* provides a compilation of updated articles that explore and reveal the mysterious inner workings of our wondrous minds and brains.

MAKING SENSE OF PSYCHOLOGY ON THE WEB *(with Research Assistant, HyperFolio CD-ROM) Connie K. Varnhagen, University of Alberta.* Useful for the novice researcher as well as the experienced Internet user, this brief book helps students to become discriminating Web users and researchers. The guide includes a CD-ROM containing the award-winning *Research Assistant HyperFolio,* innovative software that enables students to clip bits and pieces of Web sites and other electronic resources (snippets of text, illustrations, video and audio clips, and more) and compile them into worksheets and an easily accessible electronic "filing cabinet."

•NEW!• iCLICKER RADIO FREQUENCY CLASSROOM RESPONSE SYSTEM Offered by Worth Publishers, in partnership with iClicker and available for fall 2006 classes, iClicker is Worth's new polling system, created by educators for educators. This radio frequency system is the hassle-free way to make your class time more interactive. The system allows you to pause to ask questions and instantly record responses, as well as take attendance, direct students through lectures, gauge your students' understanding of the material, and much more.

COURSE MANAGEMENT

•NEW!• ENHANCED COURSE MANAGEMENT SOLUTIONS: SUPERIOR CONTENT, ALL IN ONE PLACE *Available for WebCT, Blackboard, Desire2Learn, and Angel at www.bfwpub.com/lms.* As a service for adopters, Worth Publishers is launching an enhanced turnkey course for *Abnormal Psychology,* Sixth Edition. The enhanced course includes a suite of robust teaching and learning materials in one location, organized so that you can quickly customize the content for your needs, eliminating hours of work. For instructors, our Comer enhanced cartridge includes the complete Test Bank and all PowerPoint® slides. For students, we offer interactive flashcards, quizzes, crossword puzzles, chapter outlines, annotated Web links, research exercises, case studies, and more.

Acknowledgments

I am enormously grateful to the many people who have contributed to writing and producing this book. I particularly thank Marlene Comer and Marion Kowalewski for their outstanding work on the manuscript and their constant good cheer.

In addition, I am greatly indebted to Marlene Catania and Sharon Kraus for their fine work on the references. And I sincerely appreciate the superb work of the book's research assistants, including Linda Chamberlin, Jon Comer, Greg Comer, and Jami Furr.

Throughout six editions, I have received valuable feedback from academicians and clinicians who have reviewed portions of the manuscript and commented on its clarity, accuracy, and completeness. Their collective knowledge, and their willingness to share it with me, have in large part shaped the sixth edition. I am of course indebted to those who reviewed the manuscript of the new edition along with the ancilliaries that accompany it: Sonja Barcus, Rochester College; Jeffrey A. Buchanan, Minnesota State University–Mankato; Michael Connor, California State University, Long Beach; Karla Gingerich, Colorado State University; Nicholas Greco, College of Lake County; Neth Hansjoerg, Rensselaer Polytechnic Institute; Morton G. Harmatz, University of Massachusetts; Paul Hewitt, University of British Columbia; Danae Hudson, Missouri State University; Karsten Look, Columbus State Community College; Dorothy Mercer, Eastern Kentucky University; Karen Mottarella, University of Central Florida; Paul Neunuebel, Sam Houston State University; Fabian Novello, Purdue University; George Esther Rothblum, University of Vermont; Laura Scaletta, Niagara County Community College; George W. Shardlow, City College of San Francisco; Wendy E. Shields, University of Montana; Robert Sommer, University of California, Davis; Jason S. Spiegelman, Community College of Baltimore County; and Brook Whisenhunt, Missouri State University.

I also wish to thank the many professors and clinicians around the country who offered special counsel on the sixth edition, through personal communication with me during the writing of the text: Laura Burlingame-Lee, Colorado State University; Julie Carboni, San Jose College and National University; June Madsen Clausen, University of San Francisco; Jane Halonen, James Madison University; Anthony Hermann, Kalamazoo College; Futoshi Kobayashi, Northern State University; L. F. Lowenstein, Southern England Psychological Services; Robin Mogul, Queens University; Fabian Novello, Clark State Community College; Rachel Sligar, James Madison University; Amit Steinberg, Tel-Aviv University; Laura Westen, Emory University; David Yells, Utah Valley State College; and Carlos Zalaquett, University of South Florida.

I acknowledge once again the reviewers of earlier editions. Their contributions remain integral to the quality of the revision: Kent G. Bailey, Virginia Commonwealth University; Marna S. Barnett, Indiana University of Pennsylvania; Otto A. Berliner, Alfred State College; Allan Berman, University of Rhode Island; Douglas Bernstein, University of Toronto, Mississauga; Greg Bolich, Cleveland Community College; Barbara Brown, Georgia Perimeter College; Gregory M. Buchanan, Beloit College; Loretta Butehorn, Boston College; Glenn M. Callaghan, San Jose State University; E. Allen Campbell, University of St. Francis; David N. Carpenter, Southwest Texas University; Sarah Cirese, College of Marin; Victor B. Cline, University of Utah; E. M. Coles, Simon Fraser University; Frederick L. Coolidge, University of Colorado, Colorado Springs; Timothy K. Daugherty, Winthrop University; Mary Dozier, University of Delaware; S. Wayne Duncan, University of Washington, Seattle; Morris N. Eagle, York University; Anne Fisher, University of Southern Florida; William F. Flack, Jr., Bucknell University; John Forsyth, State University of New York, Albany; Alan Fridlund, University of California, Santa Barbara; Stan Friedman, Southwest Texas State University; Dale Fryxell, Chaminade University; Lawrence L. Galant, Gaston College; James Hansell, University of Michigan; Morton G. Harmatz, University of Massachusetts; David A. Hoffman, University of California, Santa Cruz; William G. Iacono, University of Minnesota; Guadalupe Vasquez King, Milwaukee Area Technical College; Bernard Kleinman, University of Missouri, Kansas City; Alan G. Krasnoff, University of Missouri, St. Louis; Robert D. Langston, University of Texas, Austin; Kimberlyn Leary, University of Michigan; Harvey R. Lerner, Kaiser-Permanente Medical Group; Arnold D. LeUnes, Texas A&M University; Michael P. Levin, Kenyon College; Mary Margaret Livingston, Louisiana Technical University; Joseph LoPiccolo, University of Missouri, Columbia; Jerald J. Marshall, University of Central Florida; Janet R. Matthews, Loyola University; Robert J. McCaffrey, State University of New York, Albany; F. Dudley McGlynn, Auburn University; Lily D. McNair, University of Georgia; Mary W. Meagher, Texas A&M University; Joni L. Mihura, University of Toledo; Karla Klein Murdock, University of Massachusetts–Boston; Sandy Naumann, Delaware Technical & Community College; Ryan Newell, Oklahoma Christian University;

Katherine M. Nicolai, Rockhurst University; Mary Ann M. Pagaduan, American Osteopathic Association; Daniel Paulson, Carthage College; Paul A. Payne, University of Cincinnati; David V. Perkins, Ball State University; Harold A. Pincus, Chair, DSM-IV, University of Pittsburgh, Western Psychiatric Institute and Clinic; Chris Piotrowski, University of West Florida; Norman Poppel, Middlesex County College; David E. Powley, University of Mobile; Max W. Rardin, University of Wyoming, Laramie; Lynn P. Rehm, University of Houston; Leslie A. Rescorla, Bryn Mawr College; R. W. Rieber, John Jay College, CUNY; Vic Ryan, University of Colorado, Boulder; Randall Salekin, Florida International University; A. A. Sappington, University of Alabama, Birmingham; Martha Sauter, McLennon Community College; Roberta S. Sherman, Bloomington Center for Counseling and Human Development; Sandra T. Sigmon, University of Maine, Orono; Janet A. Simons, Central Iowa Psychological Services; Jay R. Skidmore, Utah State University; John M. Spores, Purdue University, South Central; B. D. Stillion, Clayton College and State University; John Suler, Rider University; Thomas A. Tutko, San Jose State University; Norris D. Vestre, Arizona State University; Lance L. Weinmann, Canyon College; Doug Wessel, Black Hills State University; Joseph L. White, University of California, Irvine; Amy C. Willis, Washington, DC, Veterans Administration Medical Center; James M. Wood, University of Texas at El Paso; and Lisa Wood, University of Puget Sound.

The authors of the book's supplements package have my thanks for doing splendid jobs with their respective supplements: Debra B. Hull, Wheeling Jesuit University, and John H. Hull, Bethany College (*Test Bank*); Karen Clay Rhines, Seton Hall University (*Instructor's Resource Manual*); Gregory Comer, Princeton Academic Resources (*Student Workbook*); Nicholas Greco, College of Lake County, and Jason Spiegelman, Community College of Baltimore County (*Web Site*); John Schulte, Cape Fear Community College and University of North Carolina, Elaine Cassel, Marymount University and Lord Fairfax Community College, Danae L. Hudson, Missouri State University, and Brooke L. Whisenhunt, Missouri State University (additional material on the *Web Site*); and Ann Brandt-Williams, Glendale Community College (additional material on the *Web Site* and in the *Instructor's Resource Manual*).

I also wish to extend my deep appreciation to the core team of professionals at Worth Publishers and W. H. Freeman and Company who have worked so closely with me to produce this edition. Although the author gets most of the credit, the production of a textbook represents a collaboration by more people than one can possibly imagine. Ultimately, the book's quality reflects the ability, judgment, and dedication of these people. In my case, I was again blessed with a core team of extraordinary people—each extremely talented, each committed to excellence, each dedicated to the education of readers, each bound by a remarkable work ethic, and each a wonderful person. It is accurate to say that these people were my co-authors and co-teachers in this enterprise, and I am forever in their debt. They are, in alphabetical order: Renee Altier and Kevin Feyen, sponsoring editors; Tracey Kuehn, associate managing editor; Paul Lacy, layout designer; Patricia Marx, photo editor; Jane O'Neill, project editor; Barbara Reingold, art director; Sarah Segal, production manager; and Catherine Woods, publisher.

In addition to this core team, there are a number of other people at Worth and at Freeman to whom I am indebted. Elizabeth Widdicombe, president of Worth and Freeman, has continued to lead the companies courageously, to create a very supportive environment for my books, and to be a good friend. I am also indebted to Danny Pucci, Worth's remarkable senior media editor, who has so skillfully developed and guided the production of the extraordinary and innovative supplements package that accompanies the text. Still other professionals from Worth and Freeman to whom I am indebted are: Todd Elder, director of advertising; Barbara Salazar, copy editor; Michele Kornegay, proofreader; Ellen Brennan and Nina Isaacson, indexers; Sarah Berger and Danielle Storm, editorial assistants; Nancy Giraldo Walker, rights and permissions manager; and John Philp, for his outstanding work on the video and CD-ROM supplements.

Finally, not to be overlooked are the superb professionals at Worth and at Freeman who continuously work with remarkable energy, skill, and judgment to bring my books to the attention of professors across the world: Kate Nurre, senior marketing manager; Tom Scotty, vice president of sales and operations; and the company's wonderful sales representatives. Thank you so much.

The past year has been a difficult and strange one for my family and me. Over a short period of time, we suffered the loss of four immediate family members and a dear friend. I have been deeply saddened and, in fact, overwhelmed by these losses. When all is going well in life, it is all-too-easy to develop an inflated sense of control over one's world and even a nonchalance about one's good fortune. However, with things taking such a difficult turn over the past year, I have become keenly aware of how fortunate I have been in the past and how fortunate I continue to be in the present. Thus, at the risk of sounding like a walking cliché, let me just say, with a clarity that is now sharper and better informed than at any prior point in my life, how appreciative I am that I have a number of wonderful friends, including my closest friend, Hersh, and an extraordinary family, particularly my terrific and accomplished sons, Greg and Jon, and my wonderful wife, Marlene, whose generosity, strength, and grace have never been more on display than during the past year.

Ron Comer
Princeton University
April 2006

Abnormal Psychology: Past and Present

Alexandra cries herself to sleep every night. She is certain that the future holds nothing but misery. Indeed, this is the only thing she does feel certain about. "I'm going to die and my daughters are going to die. We're doomed. The world is ugly. I now detest every moment of my life." She has great trouble sleeping. She is afraid to close her eyes, afraid that she will never wake up, and what will happen to her daughters then? When she does drift off to sleep, her dreams are nightmares filled with blood, dismembered bodies, thunder, decay, death, destruction.

One morning Alexandra even has trouble getting out of bed. The thought of facing another day frightens and overwhelms her. She wishes that she and her daughters were dead. "Get it over with. We'd all be better off." She feels paralyzed by her depression and anxiety, too tired to move and too afraid to leave her house. She decides to stay home and to keep her daughters with her. She makes sure that all the shades in the apartment are drawn and that every conceivable entrance is secured. She is afraid of the world and afraid of life.

During the past year Brad has been hearing mysterious voices that tell him to quit his job, leave his family, and prepare for the coming invasion. These voices have brought tremendous confusion and emotional turmoil to Brad's life. He believes that they come from beings in distant parts of the universe who are somehow wired to him. Although it gives him a sense of purpose and specialness to be the chosen target of their communications, they also make him tense and anxious. He dreads the coming invasion. When he refuses an order, the voices insult and threaten him and turn his days into a waking nightmare.

Brad has put himself on a sparse diet against the possibility that his enemies may be contaminating his food. He has found a quiet apartment far from his old haunts where he has laid in a good stock of arms and ammunition. His family and friends have tried to reach out to Brad, to understand his problems, and to dissuade him from the disturbing course he is taking. Every day, however, he retreats further into his world of mysterious voices and imagined dangers.

Most of us would probably consider Alexandra's and Brad's emotions, thoughts, and behavior psychologically abnormal, the result of a state sometimes called *psychopathology, maladjustment, emotional disturbance,* or *mental illness* (see Box 1-1 on the next page). These terms have been applied to the many problems that seem closely tied to the human brain or mind. Psychological abnormality affects the famous and the obscure, the rich and the poor, the upright and the perverse. Politicians, actors, writers, and other public figures of the present and the past have struggled with it. Psychological problems can bring great suffering, but they can also be the source of inspiration and energy.

Because they are so common and so personal, these problems capture the interest of us all. Hundreds of novels, plays, films, and television programs have explored what many people see as the dark side of human nature, and self-help books

[**BOX 1-1**]

Verbal Debuts

We use words like "abnormal" and "mental disorder" so often that it is easy to forget that there was a time not that long ago when these terms did not exist. When did these and similar words (including slang terms) make their debut in print as expressions of psychological dysfunctioning? The *Oxford English Dictionary* offers the following dates.

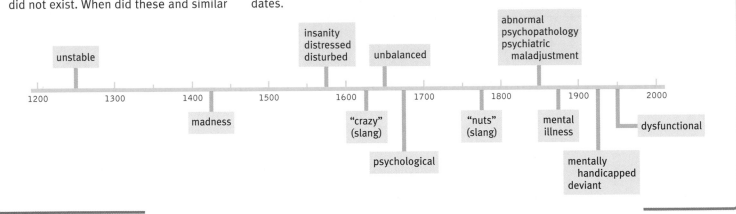

flood the market. Mental health experts are popular guests on both television and radio, and some even have their own shows.

The field devoted to the scientific study of the problems we find so fascinating is usually called **abnormal psychology.** As in any science, workers in this field, called *clinical scientists,* gather information systematically so that they may describe, predict, and explain the phenomena they study. The knowledge that they acquire is then used by *clinical practitioners,* whose role is to detect, assess, and treat abnormal patterns of functioning.

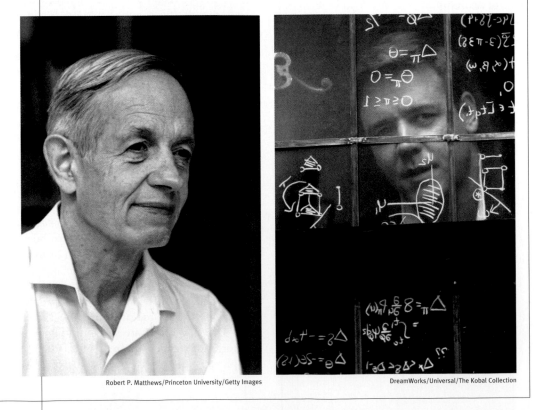

A Beautiful Mind *Psychological disorders are a popular subject in today's movies, novels, and television shows. The film* A Beautiful Mind, *for example, which presented the struggles of the mathematician John Forbes Nash against schizophrenia, received the Academy Award for best picture of the year in 2001. Nash (left) gazes out of the window of his house shortly after winning the Nobel Prize, while the actor Russell Crowe (right), who portrayed Nash in the movie, uses a window at Princeton University to work out a complex mathematical problem.*

What Is Psychological Abnormality?

Although their general goals are similar to those of other scientific professionals, clinical scientists and practitioners face problems that make their work especially difficult. One of the most troubling is that psychological abnormality is very hard to define. Consider once again Alexandra and Brad. Why are we so ready to call their responses abnormal?

Although many definitions of abnormality have been proposed over the years, none is universally accepted (Maddux & Winstead, 2005). Still, most of the definitions have certain features in common, often called "the four D's": deviance, distress, dysfunction, and danger. That is, patterns of psychological abnormality are typically *deviant* (different, extreme, unusual, perhaps even bizarre); *distressing* (unpleasant and upsetting to the person); *dysfunctional* (interfering with the person's ability to conduct daily activities in a constructive way); and possibly *dangerous*. These criteria offer a useful starting point from which to explore the phenomena of psychological abnormality. As we shall see, however, they have key limitations.

Deviance

Abnormal psychological functioning is *deviant,* but deviant from what? Alexandra's and Brad's behaviors, thoughts, and emotions are different from those that are considered normal in our place and time. We do not expect people to cry themselves to sleep each night, wish themselves dead, or obey voices that no one else hears.

In short, behavior, thoughts, and emotions are deemed abnormal when they violate a society's ideas about proper functioning. Each society establishes **norms**—explicit and implicit rules for proper conduct. Behavior that violates legal norms is called criminal. Behavior, thoughts, and emotions that violate norms of psychological functioning are called abnormal.

Judgments of abnormality vary from society to society. A society's norms grow from its particular **culture**—its history, values, institutions, habits, skills, technology, and arts. A society that values competition and assertiveness may accept aggressive behavior, whereas one that emphasizes cooperation and gentleness may consider aggressive behavior unacceptable and even abnormal. A society's values may also change over time, causing its views of what is psychologically abnormal to change as well. In Western society, for example, a woman's participation in the business world was widely considered inappropriate and strange a hundred years ago. Today the same behavior is valued.

Judgments of abnormality depend on *specific circumstances* as well as on cultural norms. What if, for example, we were to learn that the fears and desperate unhappiness of Alexandra were in fact occurring in the days following the deadly terrorist attack on the World Trade Center on September 11, 2001—an attack that killed her husband as he was at work on the 94th floor of the North Tower and wrecked the family's nearby apartment, shattering the secure and happy life they had all once known? In the ensuing weeks, as the horror and losses settled in, as she came to the conclusion that her missing husband must indeed be dead, as she and her daughters moved from one temporary location to another, Alexandra stopped expecting anything except more of the same. In this light, Alexandra's reactions do not seem quite so inappropriate. If anything is abnormal here, it is her situation. Many painful human experiences produce intense reactions—large-scale catastrophes and disasters, rape, child abuse, war, terminal illness, chronic pain (Becker-Blease & Freyd, 2005). Is there an "appropriate" way to react to such things? Should we ever call reactions to them abnormal?

Distress

Even functioning that is considered unusual does not necessarily qualify as abnormal. According to many clinical theorists, behavior, ideas, or emotions usually have to cause *distress* before they can be labeled abnormal. Consider the Ice Breakers, a group of

Carol Beckwith

Deviance and abnormality *Along the Niger River, men of the Wodaabe tribe put on elaborate makeup and costumes to attract women. In Western society, the same behavior would break behavioral norms and probably be judged abnormal.*

•**ABNORMAL PSYCHOLOGY**•The scientific study of abnormal behavior in an effort to describe, predict, explain, and change abnormal patterns of functioning.

•**NORMS**•A society's stated and unstated rules for proper conduct.

•**CULTURE**•A people's common history, values, institutions, habits, skills, technology, and arts.

people in Michigan who go swimming in lakes throughout the state every weekend from November through February. The colder the weather, the better they like it. One man, a member of the group for 17 years, says he loves the challenge of man against the elements. A 37-year-old lawyer believes that the weekly shock is good for her health. "It cleanses me," she says. "It perks me up and gives me strength." Another Ice Breaker likes the special bond the group members share. "When we get together, we know we've done something special, something no one else understands. I can't even tell most of the people I know that I'm an Ice Breaker."

Certainly these people are different from most of us, but is their behavior abnormal? Far from experiencing distress, they feel energized and challenged. Their positive feelings must cause us to hesitate before we decide that they are functioning abnormally.

Should we conclude, then, that feelings of distress must always be present before a person's functioning can be considered abnormal? Not necessarily. Some people who function abnormally maintain a positive frame of mind. What if this were the case with Brad, the young man who hears mysterious voices? Brad does experience severe distress over the coming invasion and the life changes he feels forced to make. But what if he enjoyed listening to the voices, felt honored to be chosen, and looked forward to saving the world? Shouldn't we still regard his functioning as abnormal? As we shall discover in Chapter 8, people whose behaviors are described as manic often feel just wonderful, yet still they are diagnosed as psychologically disturbed. Indeed, in many cases it is their euphoria and disproportionate sense of well-being that make them candidates for this diagnosis.

Dysfunction

Abnormal behavior tends to be *dysfunctional;* that is, it interferes with daily functioning. It so upsets, distracts, or confuses people that they cannot care for themselves properly, participate in ordinary social interactions, or work productively. Brad, for example, has quit his job, left his family, and prepared to withdraw from the productive life he once led.

Here again one's culture plays a role in the definition of abnormality. Our society holds that it is important to carry out daily activities in an effective, self-enhancing manner. Thus Brad's behavior is likely to be regarded as abnormal and undesirable, whereas that of the Ice Breakers, who continue to perform well in their jobs and enjoy fulfilling relationships, would probably be considered simply unusual.

Then again, dysfunction alone does not necessarily indicate psychological abnormality. Some people (Gandhi or César Chávez, for example) fast or in other ways deprive themselves of things they need as a means of protesting social injustice. Far from receiving a clinical label of some kind, they are widely viewed as admirable people—caring, sacrificing, even heroic.

Danger

Perhaps the ultimate in psychological dysfunctioning is behavior that becomes *dangerous* to oneself or others. Individuals whose behavior is consistently careless, hostile, or confused may be placing themselves or those around them at risk. Brad, for example, seems to be endangering himself by his diet and others by his buildup of arms and ammunition.

Although danger is often cited as a feature of abnormal psychological functioning, research suggests that it is actually the exception rather than the rule (Corrigan & Watson, 2005; Monahan, 2001, 1993, 1992). Despite popular misconceptions, most people struggling with anxiety, depression, and even bizarre thinking pose no immediate danger to themselves or to anyone else.

The Elusive Nature of Abnormality

If the concept of abnormality depends so heavily on social norms and values, it is no wonder that efforts to define psychological abnormality

A spiritual experience *In the Val d'Isère, France, students bury themselves in snow up to their necks. Far from experiencing distress or displaying abnormality, they are engaging in a Japanese practice designed to open their hearts and enlarge their spirits.*

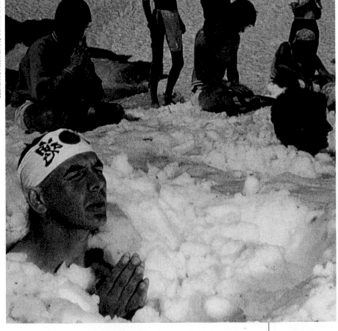

Catherine Allemande/Gamma Liaison

typically raise as many questions as they answer. Ultimately, each society selects general criteria for defining abnormality and then uses those criteria to judge particular cases.

Noting society's role in this process, one clinical theorist, Thomas Szasz (2004, 1997, 1960), argues that the whole concept of mental illness is invalid, a myth of sorts. According to Szasz, the deviations that society calls abnormal are simply "problems in living," not signs of something wrong within the person. Societies, he is convinced, invent the concept of mental illness so that they can better control or change people whose unusual patterns of functioning upset or threaten the social order.

Even if we assume that psychological abnormality is a valid concept and that it can indeed be defined, we may be unable to apply our definition consistently. If a behavior—excessive use of alcohol among college students, say—is familiar enough, the society may fail to recognize that it is deviant, distressful, dysfunctional, and dangerous. Thousands of college students throughout the United States are so dependent on alcohol that it interferes with their personal and academic lives, causes them great discomfort, jeopardizes their health, and often endangers them and the people around them. Yet their problem often goes unnoticed, certainly undiagnosed, by college administrators, other students, and health professionals. Alcohol is so much a part of the college subculture that it is easy to overlook drinking behavior that has become abnormal.

Conversely, a society may have trouble distinguishing between an abnormality that requires intervention and an *eccentricity,* or marked individuality, with which others have no right to interfere. From time to time we see or hear about people who behave in ways we consider strange, such as a man who lives alone with two dozen cats and rarely talks to other people. The behavior of such people is deviant, and it may well be distressful and dysfunctional, yet many professionals think of it as eccentric rather than abnormal (see Box 1-2 on page 7).

In short, while we may agree to define psychological abnormalities as patterns of functioning that are deviant, distressful, dysfunctional, and sometimes dangerous, we should be clear that these criteria are often vague and subjective. When is a pattern of behavior deviant, distressful, dysfunctional, and dangerous enough to be considered abnormal? The question may be impossible to answer. Few of the current categories of abnormality that we will meet in this book are as clear-cut as they may seem, and most continue to be debated by clinicians.

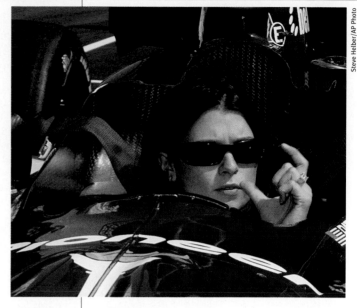

Steve Helber/AP Photo

Changing times *Two decades ago, a woman's love for race car driving would have been considered strange, perhaps even abnormal. Today Danica Patrick is one of America's finest race car drivers and is considered a role model by many.*

What Is Treatment?

Once clinicians decide that a person is indeed suffering from some form of psychological abnormality, they seek to treat it. *Treatment,* or *therapy,* is a procedure designed to change abnormal behavior into more normal behavior; it, too, requires careful definition (Compas & Gotlib, 2002). For clinical scientists, the problem is closely related to defining abnormality. Consider the case of Bill:

February: He cannot leave the house; Bill knows that for a fact. Home is the only place where he feels safe—safe from humiliation, danger, even ruin. If he were to go to work, his co-workers would somehow reveal their contempt for him. A pointed remark, a quizzical look—that's all it would take for him to get the message. If he were to go shopping at the store, before long everyone would be staring at him. Surely others would see his dark mood and thoughts; he wouldn't be able to hide them. He dare not even go for a walk alone in the woods—his heart would probably start racing again, bringing him to his knees and leaving him breathless, incoherent, and unable to get home. No, he's much better off staying in his room, trying to get through another evening of this curse called life.

>>**BY THE NUMBERS**

Not Deviant

66% People who read *Reader's Digest* in the bathroom ‹‹

50% Those who use the bathroom six times per day ‹‹

97% Those write their own name when trying out a new pen ‹‹

50% Those who regularly sneak food into movie theaters ‹‹

69% Those who eat the cake before the frosting ‹‹

57% Those who report having experienced déjà vu ‹‹

(Kanner, 1995)

July: Bill's life revolves around his circle of friends: Bob and Jack, whom he knows from the office, where he was recently promoted to director of customer relations, and Frank and Tim, his weekend tennis partners. The gang meets for dinner every week at someone's house, and they chat about life, politics, and their jobs. Particularly special in Bill's life is Janice. They go to movies, restaurants, and shows together. She thinks Bill's just terrific, and Bill finds himself beaming whenever she's around. Bill looks forward to work each day and his one-on-one dealings with customers. He is enjoying life and basking in the glow of his many activities and relationships.

Bill's thoughts, feelings, and behavior interfered with all aspects of his life in February. Yet most of his symptoms had disappeared by July. All sorts of factors may have contributed to Bill's improvement. Friends and family members may have offered support or advice. A new job or vacation may have lifted his spirits. Perhaps he changed his diet or started to exercise. Any or all of these things may have been useful to Bill, but they could not be considered treatment, or therapy. Those terms are usually reserved for special, systematic procedures that are designed to help people overcome their psychological difficulties. According to the clinical theorist Jerome Frank, all forms of therapy have three essential features:

1. A *sufferer* who seeks relief from the healer.
2. A trained, socially accepted *healer,* whose expertise is accepted by the sufferer and his or her social group.
3. A *series of contacts* between the healer and the sufferer, through which the healer, often with the aid of a group, tries to produce certain changes in the sufferer's emotional state, attitudes, and behavior.

(Frank, 1973, pp. 2–3)

Frank's definition seems straightforward enough, yet clinicians argue about how to apply it. Carl Rogers, a pioneer in the modern clinical field whom we will meet in Chapter 3, noted that "therapists are not in agreement as to their goals or aims. . . . They are not in agreement as to what constitutes a successful outcome of their work. They cannot agree as to what constitutes a failure. It seems as though the field is completely chaotic and divided."

Some clinicians view abnormality as an illness and so consider therapy a procedure that helps *cure* the illness. Others see abnormality as a problem in living and therapists as *teachers* of more functional behavior and thought. Clinicians even differ on what to call the person undergoing therapy: those who see abnormality as an illness speak of the "patient," while those who view it as a problem in living refer to the "client." Because both terms are so common, this book will use them interchangeably.

Despite their differences, most clinicians do agree that large numbers of people need therapy of one kind or another. Later we shall encounter evidence that therapy is indeed often helpful (Zarin et al., 2005; Chambless & Ollendick, 2001).

How Was Abnormality Viewed and Treated in the Past?

In any given year as many as 30 percent of the adults and 19 percent of the children and adolescents in the United States display serious psychological disturbances and are in need of clinical treatment (Kessler et al., 2005, 2004, 2001, 1994; Kazdin, 2003, 2000; Narrow et al., 2002). It is estimated that up to 18 of every 100 adults have a significant anxiety disorder, 10 suffer from profound depression, 5 display a personality disorder (inflexible and maladaptive personality traits), 1 has schizophrenia (loses touch with reality for an extended period of time), 1 experiences the brain deterioration of Alzheimer's disease, and 11 abuse alcohol or other drugs. Add to these figures as many as 600,000

>>PSYCH•LISTINGS

Top Autobiographies Recommended by Therapists

An Unquiet Mind (K. R. Jamison) ‹‹

Nobody Nowhere: The Autobiography of an Autistic (D. Williams) ‹‹

Darkness Visible: A Memoir of Madness (W. Styron) ‹‹

Out of the Depths: An Autobiographical Study of Mental Disorder and Religious Experience (A. T. Boisen) ‹‹

Girl, Interrupted (S. Kaysen) ‹‹

Too Much Anger, Too Many Tears: A Personal Triumph over Psychiatry (J. Gotkin and P. Gotkin) ‹‹

Undercurrents: A Therapist's Reckoning with Depression (M. Manning) ‹‹

Getting Better: Inside Alcoholics Anonymous (N. Robertson) ‹‹

[BOX **1-2**]

Marching to a Different Drummer: Eccentrics

Gary Holloway, an environmental planner in San Francisco, keeps a veritable stable of hobbyhorses. He is also fascinated by Martin Van Buren. . . . He discovered that Van Buren was the only U.S. president not to have a society dedicated to his memory, so he promptly founded the Van Buren Fan Club. Holloway is a lifelong devotee of St. Francis of Assisi, and frequently dresses in the habit of a Franciscan monk. "It's comfortable, fun to wear, and I like the response I get when I wear it," he explains. "People always offer me a seat on the bus."

(WEEKS & JAMES, 1995, PP. 29, 36–37)

he dictionary defines an *eccentric* as a person who deviates from common behavior patterns or displays odd or whimsical behavior. But how can we separate a psychologically healthy person who has unusual habits from a person whose oddness is a symptom of psychopathology? For years, little research was done on eccentrics, but some studies and reviews conducted over the past decade or so seem to have started the ball rolling (Pickover, 1999; Weeks & James, 1995).

For example, the researcher David Weeks studied 1,000 eccentrics over a 10-year period and estimated that as many as 1 in 5,000 persons may be "classic, full-time eccentrics." Men and women seem equally prone to such patterns. Weeks pinpointed 15 characteristics common to the eccentrics in his study: nonconformity, creativity, stong curiosity, idealism, happy obsession with hobbies, lifelong awareness of being different, high intelligence, outspokenness, noncompetitiveness, unusual eating and living habits, disinterest in others' opinions or company, mischievous sense of humor, nonmarriage, eldest or only child, poor spelling skills.

Weeks suggests that eccentrics do not typically suffer from mental disorders. Whereas the unusual behavior of persons with mental disorders is thrust upon them and usually causes them suffering, eccentricity is chosen freely and provides pleasure. In short, "Eccentrics know they're different and glory in it" (Weeks & James, 1995, p. 14). Similarly, the thought processes of eccentrics are not severely disrupted, and they do not leave them dysfunctional.

In fact, Weeks found that eccentrics actually had fewer emotional problems than the general population. Perhaps being an "original" is good for mental health. The eccentrics in his study also seemed physically healthier than others, visiting a doctor only once every eight years on average. Weeks concludes that most eccentrics, despite their deviant behavior—perhaps even because of it—are happy, well-adjusted, and joyful people.

FAMOUS ECCENTRICS

- **James Joyce** always carried a tiny pair of lady's bloomers, which he waved in the air to show approval.
- **Emily Dickinson** always wore white, never left her room, and hid her poems in tiny boxes.
- **Benjamin Franklin** took "air baths" for his health, sitting naked in front of an open window.
- **President John Quincy Adams** swam nude in the Potomac River each morning.
- **Alexander Graham Bell** covered the windows of his house to keep out the rays of the full moon. He also tried to teach his dog how to talk.
- The writer **D. H. Lawrence** enjoyed removing his clothes and climbing mulberry trees.

(ASIMOV, 1997; WEEKS & JAMES, 1995)

Howard Walker/Reuters/Corbis

Royal eccentric *Sir Richard Branson is one of England's most successful entrepreneurs. Thinking "outside the box," he has developed some of the world's most profitable and innovative businesses, including Virgin Records, Virgin Airlines, and Virgin Radio, and has been knighted for his accomplishments. But Branson is even better known for his flamboyant personal style, with loyal fans eagerly following the exploits of their favorite eccentric—for example, crossing the Atlantic by boat or by hot air balloon and crossing the English Channel by an amphibious vehicle. Here, dressed as a coachman, Branson raises his hat before successfully flying a replica of the Cayley Flyer, celebrating the 150th anniversary of the flyer's first ever manned flight.*

suicide attempts, 500,000 rapes, and 3 million cases of child abuse each year, and it becomes apparent that abnormal psychological functioning is a pervasive problem in this country. The numbers and rates in other countries are similarly high. Furthermore, most people go through periods of extreme tension, demoralization, or other forms of psychological discomfort in their lives and at such times experience at least some of the distress associated with psychological disorders.

•TREPHINATION•An ancient operation in which a stone instrument was used to cut away a circular section of the skull, perhaps to treat abnormal behavior.

•EXORCISM•The practice in early societies of treating abnormality by coaxing evil spirits to leave the person's body.

•HUMORS•According to Greek and Roman physicians, bodily chemicals that influence mental and physical functioning.

It is tempting to conclude that unique characteristics of the modern world are responsible for these numerous emotional problems—perhaps rapid technological change, the growing threats of terrorism, or a decline in religious, family, or other support systems (Schumaker, 2001). Although the special pressures of modern life probably do contribute to psychological dysfunctioning, they are hardly its primary cause. Historical records demonstrate that every society, past and present, has witnessed psychological abnormality. Perhaps, then, the proper place to begin our examination of abnormal behavior and treatment is in the past.

As we look back, we can see how each society has struggled to understand and treat psychological problems, and we can observe that many present-day ideas and treatments have roots in the past. A look backward makes it clear that progress in the understanding and treatment of mental disorders has hardly been a steady movement forward. In fact, many of the inadequacies and controversies that mark the clinical field today parallel those of the past. At the same time, looking back can help us to appreciate the significance of recent breakthroughs and the importance of the journey that lies ahead.

Ancient Views and Treatments

Most of our knowledge of prehistoric societies has been acquired indirectly and is based on inferences made from archaeological discoveries. Historians scrutinize the unearthed bones, artwork, and other remnants of ancient societies to find clues to people's customs and beliefs. Any conclusions are at best tentative and are always subject to revision in the face of new discoveries.

Thus our knowledge of how ancient societies viewed and treated people with mental disturbances is limited. Most historians believe that prehistoric societies regarded abnormal behavior as the work of evil spirits. These early societies apparently explained all phenomena as resulting from the actions of magical, sometimes sinister beings who controlled the world. In particular, they viewed the human body and mind as a battleground between external forces of good and evil. Abnormal behavior was typically interpreted as a victory by evil spirits, and the cure for such behavior was to force the demons from a victim's body.

This supernatural view of abnormality may have begun as far back as the Stone Age, a half-million years ago. Some skulls from that period recovered in Europe and South America show evidence of an operation called **trephination,** in which a stone instrument, or *trephine,* was used to cut away a circular section of the skull. Historians surmise that this operation was performed as a treatment for severe abnormal behavior—either hallucinations, in which people saw or heard things not actually present, or melancholia, characterized by extreme sadness and immobility. The purpose of opening the skull was to release the evil spirits that were supposedly causing the problem (Selling, 1940).

In recent decades, some historians have questioned whether Stone Age people actually believed that evil spirits caused abnormal behavior. Trephination may instead have been used to remove bone splinters or blood clots caused by stone weapons during tribal warfare (Maher & Maher, 1985). Either way, later societies clearly did attribute abnormal behavior to possession by demons. Egyptian, Chinese, and Hebrew writings all account for psychological deviance this way. The Bible, for example, describes how an evil spirit from the Lord affected King Saul and how David feigned madness in order to convince his enemies that he was visited by divine forces.

The treatment for abnormality in these early societies was often **exorcism.** The idea was to coax the evil spirits to leave or to make the person's body an uncomfortable place in which to live. A *shaman,* or priest, might recite prayers, plead with the evil spirits, insult them, perform magic, make loud noises, or have the person drink bitter potions. If these techniques failed, the shaman performed a more extreme form of exorcism, such as whipping or starving the person.

Greek and Roman Views and Treatments

In the years from roughly 500 B.C. to A.D. 500, in the flourishing Greek and Roman civilizations, philosophers and physicians identified a number of mental disorders. Head-

John W. Verano

Expelling evil spirits *The two holes in this skull recovered from ancient times indicate that the person underwent trephination, possibly for the purpose of releasing evil spirits and curing mental dysfunctioning.*

ing the list were *melancholia,* a condition marked by unshakable sadness; *mania,* a state of euphoria and frenzied activity; *dementia,* a general intellectual decline; *hysteria,* the presence of a physical ailment with no apparent physical cause; *delusions,* blatantly false beliefs; and *hallucinations,* the experience of imagined sights or sounds as if they were real. Although demonological interpretations of mental and physical illness were still widespread, philosophers and physicians began to offer alternative explanations during this period.

Hippocrates (460–377 B.C.), often called the father of modern medicine, taught that illnesses had natural causes. He saw abnormal behavior as a disease arising from internal physical problems. Specifically, he believed that some form of brain pathology was the culprit and that it resulted—like all other forms of disease, in his view—from an imbalance of four fluids, or **humors,** that flowed through the body: *yellow bile, black bile, blood,* and *phlegm.* An excess of yellow bile, for example, caused mania; an excess of black bile was the source of melancholia. To treat psychological dysfunctioning, Hippocrates sought to correct the underlying physical pathology. He believed, for instance, that the excess of black bile underlying melancholia could be reduced by a quiet life, a vegetable diet, temperance, exercise, celibacy, and even bleeding. Hippocrates' focus on internal causes for abnormal behavior was shared by the great Greek philosophers Plato (427–347 B.C.) and Aristotle (384–322 B.C.) and by influential Greek and Roman physicians.

Humors in action *Hippocrates believed that imbalances of the four humors affected personality. In these depictions of two of the humors, yellow bile (left) drives a husband to beat his wife, and black bile (right) leaves a man melancholic and sends him to bed.*

Europe in the Middle Ages: Demonology Returns

The enlightened views of Greek and Roman physicians and scholars did not prevent ordinary people from continuing to believe in demons. And with the decline of Rome, demonology enjoyed a strong resurgence, as a growing distrust of science spread throughout Europe.

From A.D. 500 to 1350, the period known as the Middle Ages, the power of the clergy increased greatly throughout Europe. In those days the church rejected scientific forms of investigation, and it controlled all education. Religious beliefs, which were highly superstitious and demonological at this time, came to dominate all aspects of life. Once again behavior was usually interpreted as a conflict between good and evil, God and the devil. Deviant behavior, particularly psychological dysfunctioning, was seen as evidence of Satan's influence. Although some scientists and physicians still insisted on medical explanations and treatments, their views carried little weight in this atmosphere.

The Middle Ages were a time of great stress and anxiety, of war, urban uprisings, and plagues. People blamed the devil for these troubles and feared being possessed by him. The incidence of abnormal behavior apparently increased dramatically during this period (Henley & Thorne, 2005). In addition, there were outbreaks of *mass madness,* in which large numbers of people apparently shared delusions and hallucinations. In one such disorder, *tarantism* (also known as St. Vitus's dance), groups of people would suddenly start to jump, dance, and go into convulsions (Sigerist, 1943). Some dressed oddly; others tore off their clothing. All were convinced that they had been bitten and possessed by a wolf spider, now called a tarantula, and they sought to cure their disorder by performing a dance called a tarantella. In another form of mass madness, *lycanthropy,* people thought they were possessed by wolves or other animals. They acted wolflike and imagined that fur was growing all over their bodies. Stories of lycanthropes, more popularly known as *werewolves,* have been passed down to us and continue to fire the imagination of writers, moviemakers, and their audiences.

>>**LOOKING BACK**
Historical Notes

During the Middle Ages, there was, on average, one church for every 200 people (Asimov, 1997). **‹‹**

- -

From the Middle Ages through the 1800s, *barbers* sometimes perfomed the treatments, including *bloodletting,* for both medical and mental disorders. Today's striped barber poles originated back then, when they were staffs that patients would grip while being bled by a barber. **‹‹**

- -

Most of the patients in asylums, from all classes and circumstances, were women (Barton, 2004; Gold, 1998). **‹‹**

- -

Doctors who treated people with mental disorders in the eighteenth century were called "mad-doctors." **‹‹**

- -

Before the American Revolution, only 10 percent of the 3,500 doctors in the country had any formal training. Fewer than 5 percent had medical degrees (Whitaker, 2002). **‹‹**

Not surprisingly, some of the earlier demonological treatments for psychological abnormality reemerged during the Middle Ages. Once again the key to cure was to rid the person's body of the devil that possessed it. Exorcisms were revived, and clergymen, who generally were in charge of treatment during this period, would plead, chant, or pray to the devil or evil spirit. If these techniques did not work, they had others to try, some indistinguishable from torture (see Box 1-3).

It was not until the Middle Ages drew to a close that demonology and its methods began to lose favor (Magherini & Biotti, 1998). Towns throughout Europe grew into cities, and municipal authorities gained more power and took over nonreligious activities. Among their other responsibilities, they began to run hospitals and direct the care of people suffering from mental disorders. Medical views of abnormality gained favor once again. When *lunacy trials* were held in late thirteenth-century England to determine the sanity of certain persons, it was not unusual for natural causes, such as a "blow to the head" or "fear of one's father," to be held responsible for an individual's unusual behavior (Neugebauer, 1979, 1978). During these same years, many people with psychological disturbances received treatment in medical hospitals. The Trinity Hospital in England, for example, was established to treat "madness," among other kinds of illness, and to keep the mad "safe until they are restored to reason" (Allderidge, 1979, p. 322).

Bewitched or bewildered? *A great fear of witchcraft swept Europe even during the "enlightened" Renaissance. Tens of thousands of people, mostly women, were thought to have made a pact with the devil. Some appear to have had mental disorders, which caused them to act strangely (Zilboorg & Henry, 1941). This individual is being "dunked" repeatedly until she confesses to witchery.*

The Renaissance and the Rise of Asylums

During the early part of the Renaissance, a period of flourishing cultural and scientific activity (about 1400–1700), demonological views of abnormality continued to decline. The German physician Johann Weyer (1515–1588), the first physician to specialize in mental illness, believed that the mind was as susceptible to sickness as the body. He is now considered the founder of the modern study of psychopathology.

The care of people with mental disorders continued to improve in this atmosphere. In England such individuals might be kept at home while their families were aided financially by the local parish. Across Europe religious shrines were devoted to the humane and loving treatment of people with mental disorders. The best known of these shrines was actually established centuries earlier at Gheel in Belgium, but beginning in the fifteenth century, people came to it from all over the world for psychic healing. Local residents welcomed these pilgrims into their homes, and many stayed on to form the world's first "colony" of mental patients. Gheel was the forerunner of today's *community mental health programs,* and it continues to demonstrate that people with psychological disorders can respond to loving care and respectful treatment (van Walsum, 2004; Aring, 1975, 1974). Today patients are still welcome to live in foster homes in this town, interacting with other residents, until they recover.

Bedlam *In this eighteenth-century work from* The Rake's Progress, *William Hogarth depicted London's Bethlehem Hospital, or Bedlam, as a chaotic asylum where people of fashion came to marvel at the strange behavior of the inmates.*

Unfortunately, these improvements in care began to fade by the mid-sixteenth century. By then municipal authorities had discovered that private homes and community residences could house only a small percentage of those with severe mental disorders and that medical hospitals were too few and too small. Increasingly, they converted hospitals and monasteries into **asylums,** institutions whose primary purpose was to care for people with mental illness. These institutions were founded with every intention of providing good care. Once the asylums started to overflow, however, they became virtual prisons where patients were held in filthy conditions and treated with unspeakable cruelty.

[BOX **1-3**]

Exorcism Lives

*E*xorcism has a long history as a "treatment" for persons who behave abnormally. It was particularly favored during biblical times and again during the Middle Ages. But all that is a thing of the distant past, right? Well, not completely, it turns out (Peck, 2005; Rosik, 2003).

By the 1970s exorcism had all but disappeared from Western culture (Cuneo, 2000). Then in 1973, the enormously popular book and movie *The Exorcist* spurred a rash of books and movies on demonic possession, and public interest in this procedure increased dramatically. Since then, numerous evangelical ministers and charismatics have declared themselves exorcists and performed exorcisms on people with behavioral disturbances. In most such instances, the exorcist blesses the person who is thought to be possessed, recites passages from the Bible, and commands the evil spirits to leave the body (Fountain, 2000). Often a support group is present to pray for the person while he or she cries out and perhaps even thrashes on the floor, regurgitates, or flails out (Cuneo, 2000).

During the 1990s, the techniques used by some contemporary exorcists seemed to grow more extreme, at times dangerous. The media reported cases of death by exorcism; a New York mother accidentally smothered her teenage daughter during one such procedure and a Rhode Island man jammed steel crosses down his

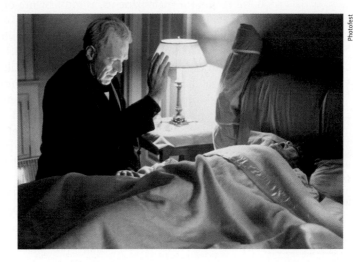

Photofest

Exorcism at the movies
In the remarkably popular horror movie The Exorcist, *an exorcist offers prayers and administers holy water to try to force the devil to leave the body of a troubled teenage girl.*

mother-in-law's throat (Fountain, 2000). In addition, a growing number of priests began to perform spiritual cleansing ceremonies not sanctioned by the Roman Catholic Church (Cuneo, 2000).

In order to regulate this growing field, both within and outside the church, and to ensure more acceptable procedures, the Roman Catholic Church in the United States has become more actively involved in exorcisms during the past decade. The number of full-time exorcists formally appointed by the church increased from 1 in 1990 to 10 in 2000 (Fountain, 2000). These officials have investigated and evaluated hundreds of cases in which individuals or their relatives or priests have sought exorcisms, determining in each case whether exorcism is appropriate. In 1999 the church issued a revised rite of exorcism

for the first time since 1614, establishing rules to be followed in making such decisions and in the exorcisms themselves. For example, a church exorcism can take place only after the church-approved exorcist consults with physicians to rule out mental or physical disorders. Also, church exorcisms must be approved by a bishop.

As a result of such rules and procedures, only a small number of potential cases actually result in church-approved exorcisms (Fountain, 2000). Even a small number of exorcisms, however, is excessive in the eyes of many mental health professionals, who see this intervention as a misguided "treatment" for psychological dysfunctioning. Given exorcism's long history and deep roots, this debate is not likely to be settled in the near future.

The first asylum had been founded in Muslim Spain in the early fifteenth century, but the idea did not gain full momentum until the 1500s. In 1547, Bethlehem Hospital was given to the city of London by Henry VIII for the sole purpose of confining the mentally ill. In this asylum patients bound in chains cried out for all to hear. During certain phases of the moon in particular, they might be chained and whipped in order to prevent violence (Asimov, 1997). The hospital even became a popular tourist attraction; people were eager to pay to look at the howling and gibbering inmates. The hospital's name, pronounced "Bedlam" by the local people, has come to mean a chaotic uproar. Similarly, in the Lunatics' Tower in Vienna, patients were herded into narrow hallways by the outer walls so that tourists outside could look up and see them. In La Bicêtre in Paris, patients were shackled to the walls of cold, dark, dirty cells with iron collars and given spoiled food that could be sold nowhere else (Selling, 1940). Such asylums remained a popular form of "care" until the late 1700s.

•ASYLUM• A type of institution that first became popular in the sixteenth century to provide care for persons with mental disorders. Most became virtual prisons.

**Treatments Used by Benjamin Rush,
Father of American Psychiatry**

Love and kindness «

- -

Bleeding «

- -

Laxatives «

- -

Emetics (substances that cause vomiting) «

- -

Scaring patient «

- -

Spinning patient «

- -

Pouring ice and cold water on shaved head «

- -

Dunking patients in ice water «

- -

Raising blisters on head and neck, then rubbing salves into them. «

- -

Restraining chair ("Tranquilizer Chair") «

The Nineteenth Century: Reform and Moral Treatment

As 1800 approached, the treatment of people with mental disorders began to improve once again (Maher & Maher, 2003). Historians usually point to La Bicêtre, an asylum in Paris for male patients, as the first site of asylum reform. In 1793, during the French Revolution, Philippe Pinel (1745–1826) was named the chief physician there. He argued that the patients were sick people whose illnesses should be treated with sympathy and kindness rather than chains and beatings (van Walsum, 2004). He unchained them and allowed them to move freely about the hospital grounds, replaced the dark dungeons with sunny, well-ventilated rooms, and offered support and advice. Pinel's approach proved remarkably successful. Patients who had been shut away for decades were now enjoying fresh air and sunlight and being treated with dignity. Many improved greatly over a short period of time and were released. Pinel later brought similar reforms to a mental hospital in Paris for female patients, La Salpetrière. Jean Esquirol (1772–1840), Pinel's student and successor, went on to help establish 10 new mental hospitals that operated on the same principles.

Meanwhile an English Quaker named William Tuke (1732–1819) was bringing similar reforms to northern England. In 1796 he founded the York Retreat, a rural estate where about 30 mental patients lived as guests in quiet country houses and were treated with a combination of rest, talk, prayer, and manual work (Borthwick et al., 2001).

THE SPREAD OF MORAL TREATMENT The methods of Pinel and Tuke, called **moral treatment** because they emphasized moral guidance and humane and respectful techniques, caught on throughout Europe and the United States. Patients with psychological problems were increasingly perceived as potentially productive human beings whose mental functioning had broken down under stress. They were considered deserving of individual care, including discussions of their problems, useful activities, work, companionship, and quiet.

The person most responsible for the early spread of moral treatment in the United States was Benjamin Rush (1745–1813), an eminent physician at Pennsylvania Hospital. Limiting his practice to mental illness, Rush developed innovative, humane approaches to treatment (Whitaker, 2002). For example, he required that the hospital hire intelligent and sensitive attendants to work closely with patients, reading and talking to them and taking them on regular walks. He also suggested that it would be therapeutic for doctors to give small gifts to their patients now and then. Rush, widely considered

Dance in a madhouse *A popular feature of moral treatment was the "lunatic ball." Hospital officials would bring patients together to dance and enjoy themselves. One such ball is shown in this painting,* Dance in a Madhouse, *by George Bellows.*

the father of American psychiatry, also wrote the first American treatise on mental illness and organized the first American course in psychiatry.

Rush's work was influential, but it was a Boston schoolteacher named Dorothea Dix (1802–1887) who made humane care a public and political concern in the United States. In 1841 Dix had gone to teach Sunday school at a local prison and been shocked by the conditions she saw there. Before long, her interest in prison conditions broadened to include the plight of poor and mentally ill people throughout the country. A powerful campaigner, Dix went from state legislature to state legislature speaking of the horrors she had observed and calling for reform. Similarly, she told the Congress of the United States that mentally ill people across the country were still being "bound with galling chains, bowed beneath fetters and heavy iron balls attached to drag chains, lacerated with ropes, scourged with rods and terrified beneath storms of execration and cruel blows" (Zilboorg & Henry, 1941, pp. 583–584).

From 1841 until 1881, Dix fought for new laws and greater government funding to improve the treatment of people with mental disorders. Each state was made responsible for developing effective public mental hospitals. Dix personally helped establish 32 of these **state hospitals,** all intended to offer moral treatment (Pomerantz, 2003; Viney, 2000). Similar hospitals were established throughout Europe.

The "crib" *Outrageous devices and techniques, such as the "crib," were used in asylums, and some continued to be used even during the reforms of the nineteenth century.*

THE DECLINE OF MORAL TREATMENT As we have observed, the treatment of abnormality has followed a crooked path. Over and over again, relative progress has been followed by serious decline. Viewed in this context, it is not surprising that the moral treatment movement began to decline toward the end of the nineteenth century.

Several factors were responsible (Bockoven, 1963). One was the speed with which the moral movement had spread. As mental hospitals multiplied, severe money and staffing shortages developed, recovery rates declined, and overcrowding in the hospitals became a major problem. Under such conditions it was often impossible to provide individual care and genuine concern. Another factor was the assumption behind moral treatment that all patients could be cured if treated with humanity and dignity. For some, this was indeed sufficient. Others, however, needed more effective treatments than any that had yet been developed. Many of these people remained hospitalized until they died. An additional factor contributing to the decline of moral treatment was the emergence of a new wave of prejudice against people with mental disorders. As more and more patients disappeared into large, distant mental hospitals, the public came to view them as strange and dangerous. In turn, people were less open-handed when it came to making donations or allocating government funds. Moreover, many of the patients entering public mental hospitals in the United States in the late nineteenth century were impoverished foreign immigrants, whom the public had little interest in helping.

By the early years of the twentieth century, the moral treatment movement had ground to a halt in both the United States and Europe. Public mental hospitals were providing only custodial care and ineffective medical treatments and were becoming more overcrowded every year. Long-term hospitalization became the rule once again.

The Early Twentieth Century: The Somatogenic and Psychogenic Perspectives

As the moral movement was declining in the late 1800s, two opposing perspectives emerged and began to vie for the attention of clinicians: the **somatogenic perspective,** the view that abnormal psychological functioning has physical causes, and the **psychogenic perspective,** the view that the chief causes of abnormal functioning are psychological. These perspectives came into full bloom during the twentieth century.

THE SOMATOGENIC PERSPECTIVE The somatogenic perspective has at least a 2,400-year history—remember Hippocrates' view that abnormal behavior resulted from brain disease and an imbalance of humors? Not until the late nineteenth century, however, did this perspective make a triumphant return and begin to gain wide acceptance.

•**MORAL TREATMENT**•A nineteenth-century approach to treating people with mental dysfunction that emphasized moral guidance and humane and respectful treatment.

•**STATE HOSPITALS**•State-run public mental institutions in the United States.

•**SOMATOGENIC PERSPECTIVE**•The view that abnormal psychological functioning has physical causes.

•**PSYCHOGENIC PERSPECTIVE**•The view that the chief causes of abnormal functioning are psychological.

Back wards *Overcrowding, limited funding, and ineffective hospital treatments led to the creation of crowded, often appalling back wards in state hospitals across the United States, which continued well into the twentieth century.*

Two factors were responsible for this rebirth. One was the work of an eminent German researcher, Emil Kraepelin (1856–1926). In 1883 Kraepelin published an influential textbook which argued that physical factors, such as fatigue, are responsible for mental dysfunction. In addition, as we shall see in Chapter 4, he also constructed the first modern system for classifying abnormal behavior. He identified various syndromes, or clusters of symptoms; listed their physical causes; and discussed their expected course (Decker, 2004; Kihlstrom, 2002). Kraepelin also measured the effects of various drugs on abnormal behavior.

New biological discoveries also triggered the rise of the somatogenic perspective. One of the most important discoveries was that an organic disease, *syphilis,* led to *general paresis,* an irreversible disorder with both physical and mental symptoms, including paralysis and delusions of grandeur. In 1897 Richard von Krafft-Ebing (1840–1902), a German neurologist, injected matter from syphilis sores into patients suffering from general paresis and found that none of the patients developed symptoms of syphilis. Their immunity could have been caused only by an earlier case of syphilis. Since all patients with general paresis were now immune to syphilis, Krafft-Ebing theorized that syphilis had been the cause of their general paresis. Finally, in 1905, Fritz Schaudinn (1871–1906), a German zoologist, discovered that the microorganism *Treponema pallida* was responsible for syphilis, which in turn was responsible for general paresis.

The work of Kraepelin and the new understanding of general paresis led many researchers and practitioners to suspect that organic factors were responsible for many mental disorders, perhaps all of them. These theories and the possibility of quick and effective medical solutions for mental disorders were especially welcomed by those who worked in mental hospitals, where patient populations were now growing at an alarming rate.

Table 1-1

Eugenics and Mental Disorders

Year	Event
1896	Connecticut became the first state in the United States to prohibit persons with mental disorders from marrying.
1896–1933	Every state in the United States passed a law prohibiting marriage by persons with mental disorders.
1907	Indiana became the first state to pass a bill calling for people with mental disorders, as well as criminals and other "defectives," to undergo sterilization.
1927	The U.S. Supreme Court ruled that eugenic sterilization was constitutional.
1907–1945	Around 45,000 Americans were sterilized under eugenic sterilization laws; 21,000 of them were patients in state mental hospitals.
1929–1932	Denmark, Norway, Sweden, Finland, and Iceland passed eugenic sterilization laws.
1933	Germany passed a eugenic sterilization law, under which 375,000 people were sterilized by 1940.
1940	Nazi Germany began to use "proper gases" to kill people with mental disorders; 70,000 or more people were killed in less than two years.

Source: Whitaker, 2002.

Despite the general optimism, biological approaches yielded largely disappointing results throughout the first half of the twentieth century. Although many medical treatments were developed for patients in mental hospitals during that time, most of the techniques failed to work. Physicians tried tooth extraction, tonsillectomy, hydrotherapy (alternating hot and cold baths), and lobotomy, a surgical cutting of certain nerve fibers in the brain. Even worse, biological views and claims led, in some circles, to proposals for immoral solutions such as eugenic sterilization (see Table 1-1). Not until the 1950s, when a number of effective medications were finally discovered, did the somatogenic perspective truly begin to pay off for patients.

THE PSYCHOGENIC PERSPECTIVE The late nineteenth century also saw the emergence of the psychogenic perspective, the view that the chief causes of abnormal functioning are often psychological. This view, too, had a long history. The Roman statesman and orator Cicero (106–43 B.C.) held that psychological disturbances could cause bodily ailments, and the Greek physician Galen believed that many mental disorders are caused by fear, disappointment in love, and other psychological events. However, the psychogenic perspective did not gain much of a following until studies of *hypnotism* demonstrated its potential.

Hypnotism is a procedure that places people in a trancelike mental state during which they become extremely suggestible. It was used to help treat psychological disorders as far back as 1778, when an Austrian physician named Friedrich Anton Mesmer (1734–1815) established a clinic in Paris. His patients suffered from *hysterical disorders,* mysterious bodily ailments that had no apparent physical basis. Mesmer had his patients sit in a darkened room filled with music; then he appeared, dressed in a flamboyant costume, and touched the troubled area of each patient's body with a special rod. A surprising number of patients seemed to be helped by this treatment, called *mesmerism.* Their pain, numbness, or paralysis disappeared. Several scientists believed that Mesmer was inducing a trancelike state in his patients and that this state was causing their symptoms to disappear. The treatment was so controversial, however, that eventually Mesmer was banished from Paris (Spiegel, 2002).

It was not until years after Mesmer died that many researchers had the courage to investigate his procedure, later called hypnotism (from *hypnos,* the Greek word for "sleep"), and its effects on hysterical disorders. By the late nineteenth century, two competing views had emerged. Because hypnosis—a technique relying on the power of suggestion—was able to alleviate hysterical ailments, some scientists concluded that hysterical disorders must be caused by the power of suggestion—that is, by the mind—in the first place. In contrast, other scientists believed that hysterical disorders had subtle physiological causes. For example, Jean Charcot (1825–1893), Paris's most eminent neurologist, argued that hysterical disorders were the result of degeneration in portions of the brain.

The experiments of two physicians practicing in the city of Nancy in France finally seemed to settle the matter. Hippolyte-Marie Bernheim (1840–1919) and Ambroise-Auguste Liébault (1823–1904) showed that hysterical disorders could actually be induced in otherwise normal subjects while they were under the influence of hypnosis. That is, the physicians could make normal people experience deafness, paralysis, blindness, or numbness by means of hypnotic suggestion—and they could remove these artificial symptoms by the same means. Thus, they established that a *mental* process—hypnotic suggestion—could both cause and cure even a physical dysfunction. Leading scientists, including Charcot, finally embraced the idea that hysterical disorders were largely psychological in origin, and the psychogenic perspective rose in popularity.

Among those who studied the effects of hypnotism on hysterical disorders was Josef Breuer (1842–1925) of Vienna. This physician discovered that his patients sometimes awoke free of hysterical symptoms after speaking candidly under hypnosis about past upsetting events. During the 1890s Breuer was joined in his work by

>>LOOKING AROUND

Literature and Abnormal Psychology

Writing during the Renaissance, William Shakespeare speculated on the nature and causes of abnormal behavior in 20 of his 38 plays and in many of his sonnets (Dalby, 1997). **<<**

- -

Although controversial in professional circles, Anton Mesmer's work attracted many persons outside the clinical field. Charles Dickens, the nineteenth-century English novelist, so strongly believed in mesmerism that he considered himself to be a doctor in this method of healing the sick (Asimov, 1997). **<<**

Hypnotism update *Hypnotism, the procedure that opened the door for the psychogenic perspective, continues to influence many areas of modern life, including the fields of psychotherapy, entertainment, and law enforcement. Here a forensic clinician uses hypnosis to help a witness recall the details of a crime. Recent research has clarified, however, that hypnotic procedures are as capable of creating false memories as they are of uncovering real memories.*

Oscar Sosa/AP Photo

another Viennese physician, Sigmund Freud (1856–1939). As we shall see in Chapter 3, Freud's work eventually led him to develop the theory of **psychoanalysis,** which holds that many forms of abnormal and normal psychological functioning are psychogenic. In particular, he believed that *unconscious* psychological processes are at the root of such functioning.

Freud also developed the *technique* of psychoanalysis, a form of discussion in which clinicians help troubled people gain insight into their unconscious psychological processes. He believed that such insight, even without hypnotic procedures, would help the patients overcome their psychological problems.

Freud and his followers applied the psychoanalytic treatment approach primarily to patients suffering from anxiety or depression, problems that did not typically require hospitalization. These patients visited therapists in their offices for sessions of approximately an hour and then went about their daily activities—a format of treatment now known as *outpatient therapy*. By the early twentieth century, psychoanalytic theory and treatment were widely accepted throughout the Western world.

The psychoanalytic approach had little effect on the treatment of severely disturbed patients in mental hospitals, however. This type of therapy requires levels of clarity, insight, and verbal skill beyond the capabilities of most such patients. Moreover, psychoanalysis often takes years to be effective, and the overcrowded and understaffed public mental hospitals could not accommodate such a leisurely pace.

Current Trends

It would hardly be accurate to say that we now live in a period of great enlightenment or dependable treatment of mental disorders (see Box 1-4 on page 18). In fact, surveys conducted during the past decade have found that 43 percent of respondents believe that people bring on mental disorders themselves, 35 percent consider such disorders to be caused by sinful behavior, and 19 percent point to a lack of willpower or self-discipline as a cause (NMHA, 1999; Murray, 1993). Nevertheless, the past 50 years have brought major changes in the ways clinicians understand and treat abnormal functioning. There are more theories and types of treatment, more research studies, more information, and, perhaps for these reasons, more disagreements about abnormal functioning today than at any time in the past. In some ways the study and treatment of psychological disorders

•**PSYCHOANALYSIS**•Either the theory or the treatment of abnormal mental functioning that emphasizes unconscious psychological forces as the cause of psychopathology.

•**PSYCHOTROPIC MEDICATIONS**•Drugs that mainly affect the brain and reduce many symptoms of mental dysfunctioning.

•**DEINSTITUTIONALIZATION**•The practice, begun in the 1960s, of releasing hundreds of thousands of patients from public mental hospitals.

•**PRIVATE PSYCHOTHERAPY**•An arrangement in which a person directly pays a therapist for counseling services.

Alternative treatment? *Tens of thousands of people with severe mental disorders are currently homeless. They receive no treatment or guidance and wind up on the streets, such as these men in San Francisco's Tenderloin district, or in public shelters.*

have made great strides, but in other respects clinical scientists and practitioners are still struggling to make a difference.

How Are People with Severe Disturbances Cared For?

In the 1950s researchers discovered a number of new **psychotropic medications**—drugs that primarily affect the brain and alleviate many symptoms of mental dysfunctioning. They included the first *antipsychotic drugs,* to correct extremely confused and distorted thinking; *antidepressant drugs,* to lift the mood of depressed people; and *antianxiety drugs,* to reduce tension and worry.

When given these drugs, many patients who had spent years in mental hospitals began to show signs of improvement. Hospital administrators, encouraged by these results and pressured by a growing public outcry over the terrible conditions in public mental hospitals, began to discharge patients almost immediately.

Since the discovery of these medications, mental health professionals in most of the developed nations of the world have followed a policy of **deinstitutionalization,** releasing hundreds of thousands of patients from public mental hospitals. On any given day in 1955, close to 600,000 people were confined in public mental institutions across the United States (see Figure 1-1). Today the daily patient population in the same kinds of hospitals is around 60,000 (Torrey, 2001).

In short, outpatient care has now become the primary mode of treatment for people with severe psychological disturbances as well as for those with more moderate problems. Today when severely impaired people do need institutionalization, they are usually given *short-term* hospitalization. Ideally, they are then given outpatient psychotherapy and medication in community programs and residences.

Chapters 3 and 15 will look more closely at this recent emphasis on community care for people with severe psychological disturbances—a philosophy called the *community mental health approach.* The approach has been helpful for many patients, but too few community programs are available to address current needs in the United States (Talbott, 2004; Torrey, 2004). As a result, hundreds of thousands of persons with severe disturbances fail to make lasting recoveries, and they shuttle back and forth between the mental hospital and the community. After release from the hospital, they at best receive minimal care and often wind up living in decrepit rooming houses or on the streets. In fact, only 40 percent of persons with severe psychological disturbances currently receive treatment of any kind (Wang et al., 2005, 2002). At least 100,000 individuals with such disturbances are homeless on any given day; another 135,000 or more are inmates of jails and prisons (Killaspy et al., 2004; Cutler et al., 2002; Torrey, 2001). Their abandonment is truly a national disgrace.

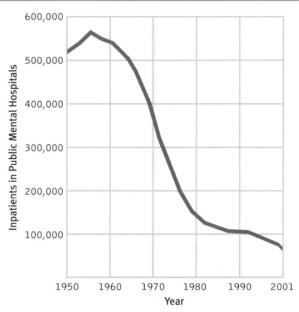

FIGURE **1-1** **The impact of deinstitutionalization**
The number of patients (60,000) now hospitalized in public mental hospitals in the United States is a small fraction of the number hospitalized in 1955. (Adapted from Torrey, 2001; Lang, 1999.)

How Are People with Less Severe Disturbances Treated?

The treatment picture for people with moderate psychological disturbances has been more positive than that for people with severe disorders. Since the 1950s, outpatient care has continued to be the preferred mode of treatment for them, and the number and types of facilities that offer such care have expanded to meet the need.

Before the 1950s, almost all outpatient care took the form of **private psychotherapy,** an arrangement by which an individual directly pays a psychotherapist for counseling services. This tended to be an expensive form of treatment, available only to the wealthy. Since the 1950s, however, most health insurance plans have expanded coverage to include private psychotherapy, so that it is now also widely available to people with modest incomes. In addition, outpatient therapy is now offered in a number of less expensive settings, such as community mental health centers, crisis intervention centers, family service centers, and other social service agencies. The new settings have spurred a dramatic increase in the number of persons seeking outpatient care for psychological problems. Nationwide surveys suggest that nearly one of every five adults in the United

[BOX 1-4]

The Moon and the Mind

Primitive societies believed that the moon had magical, mystical powers and that its changes portended events of many kinds. The moon supposedly had the power to impregnate women, to make plants grow, and to drive people crazy. Later societies also credited the power of the moon to affect behavior, and they applied the terms "lunatic" and "lunacy" to the person and the behavior to capture their lunar, or moonlike, qualities. Even today many institutions and people believe that behavior is affected by the phases of the moon (Kung & Mrazek, 2005).

Anecdotal evidence abounds: police officers have sometimes noted more violent and bizarre crimes during the full moon, and certain hospitals have claimed to experience an increase in births. One hospital even linked the full moon to the onset of ulcers and heart attacks. A Wall Street broker for years used the schedule of the full moon as a guide in giving investment advice—successfully (Gardner, 1984).

A number of scientists have advanced theories to explain a lunar effect on human behavior. Some say that since the moon causes the tides of the oceans, it is reasonable to expect that it has a similar effect on the bodily fluids of human beings, whose composition is more than 80 percent water (Thakur & Sharma, 1984). The increase in births might therefore be explained by the force of the moon on the expectant mother's amniotic fluid. Similar tidal and gravitational effects have been used to explain the apparent increase in bizarre behavior when the moon is full.

Some researchers have tried to determine whether the activity of the moon is in fact related to human behavior by calculating the precise numbers of births, crimes, and unusual behaviors that occur when the moon is full. Some of these investigators have indeed found an association between a full moon and unintentional poisonings (Oderda & Klein-Schwartz, 1983), aggression (Lieber, 1978), absenteeism (Sands & Miller, 1991), and crime (Thakur & Sharma, 1984). Other researchers, however, have found no relationship between a full moon and increases in violence in mental health settings (Owen et al., 1998), suicides (Mathew et al., 1991), car accidents (Laverty & Kelly, 1998), childhood deaths (deLeon et al., 2003), or efforts to secure relief from anxiety or depression (Kung & Mrazek, 2005; Wilkinson et al., 1997).

Skeptics have noted that even if an association exists, it may simply be due to people's expectations. That is, because certain persons expect to be influenced by a full moon, they may be more attentive and responsive to their internal sensations or desires at that time. To test this interpretation, researchers recently examined the effects of moon phases on animals, who presumably have little self-awareness. One group of researchers found a significant increase in the number of people who visited the emergency room of a small-town British hospital with animal bites on nights when the moon was full (Bhattacharjee et al., 2000), suggesting that unusual animal behavior may indeed be affected by the moon. However, when other researchers conducted studies with other animals in other towns, they found no increase in animal bites during nights of a full moon (Frangakis & Petridov, 2001; Chapman & Morrell, 2000).

And so the debate continues, as scientists and philosophers alike try to determine whether the cause of lunacy does indeed lie in the heavens or in our minds.

Silvia Otte/Photonica/Getty Images

States receives treatment for psychological disorders in the course of a year (Wang et al., 2005). The majority of clients are seen for fewer than five sessions during the year.

Outpatient treatments are also becoming available for more and more kinds of problems. When Freud and his colleagues first began to practice, most of their patients suf-

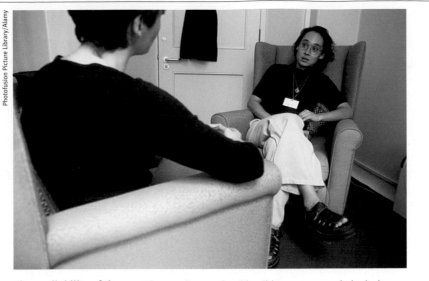

The availability of therapy *Therapy for people with mild to severe psychological disturbances is widely available in individual, group, and family formats.*

•**PREVENTION**•Interventions aimed at deterring mental disorders before they can develop.

•**POSITIVE PSYCHOLOGY**•The study and enhancement of positive feelings, traits, and abilities.

fered from anxiety or depression. These problems still dominate therapy today; almost half of all clients suffer from them. However, people with other kinds of disorders are also receiving therapy. In addition, at least 20 percent of clients enter therapy because of milder problems in living—problems with marital, family, job, peer, school, or community relationships (Wang et al., 2005).

Yet another change in outpatient care since the 1950s has been the development of programs devoted exclusively to one kind of psychological problem. We now have, for example, suicide prevention centers, substance abuse programs, eating disorder programs, phobia clinics, and sexual dysfunction programs. Clinicians in these programs have the kind of expertise that can be acquired only by concentration in a single area.

A Growing Emphasis on Preventing Disorders and Promoting Mental Health

Although the community mental health approach has often failed to address the needs of people with severe disorders, it has given rise to an important principle of mental health care—**prevention** (Knapp et al., 2005; Quinn & Poirier, 2004). Rather than wait for psychological disorders to occur, many of today's community programs try to correct the social conditions that give rise to psychological problems (poverty or violence in the community, for example) and to identify and help individuals who are at risk for developing emotional problems (for example, teenage mothers or the children of people with severe psychological disorders). As we shall see later, community prevention programs are not always successful and they often suffer from limited funding, but they have grown in number throughout the United States and Europe, offering great promise as the ultimate form of intervention. In fact, during the 1990s, the United States Secretary of Health and Human Services labeled prevention as the nation's number one health and social priority (Felner et al., 2000).

Prevention programs have been further energized in the past few years by the field of psychology's growing interest in **positive psychology** (Seligman & Steen, 2005; Kelley, 2004; Pleh, 2004). Positive psychology is the study and enhancement of positive feelings such as optimism and happiness; positive traits like perseverance and wisdom; positive abilities such as interpersonal skill and other talents; and group-directed virtues, including altruism and tolerance (see Box 1-5 on the next page).

In the clinical arena, positive psychology suggests that practitioners can help people best by *promoting* positive development and psychological wellness. While researchers study and learn more about positive psychology in the laboratory, a growing number of clinicians are already beginning to apply its principles in their work. They are teaching

>>**BY THE NUMBERS**

How Good a Life Have You Lived So Far?

13% Percentage of surveyed adults who say they have had "the best possible" life ‹‹

37% Those who believe they have led a "very good" life ‹‹

33% Those who say they have had a "good" life ‹‹

15% Those who feel they have led a "fair" life ‹‹

2% Those who say they have had a "poor" life ‹‹

(Wallis, 2005)

[BOX **1-5**]

Positive Psychology: Happiness Is All Around Us

Judging from the evening news and the spread of self-help books, one would think that happiness is rare. But there's good news. Research indicates that people's lives are, in general, more upbeat than we think. In fact, most people around the world say they're happy—including most of those who are poor, unemployed, elderly, and disabled (Wallis,

© Azita Panahpour

2005; Schimmack & Diener, 2003). Over 90 percent of people with quadriplegia say they're glad to be alive, and overall, people with spinal cord injuries report feeling only slightly less happy than other people (Diener & Diener, 1996). Men and women are equally likely to declare themselves satisfied or very happy. Wealthy people appear only slightly happier than those of modest means (Easterbrook, 2005; Diener et al., 1993). Overall, only 1 person in 10 reports being "not too happy" (Myers, 2000; Myers & Diener, 1996). And only 1 in 7 reports waking up unhappy (Wallis, 2005).

Of course, some people are indeed happier than others. Particularly happy people seem to remain happy from decade to decade, regardless of job changes, moves, and family changes (Myers & Diener, 1996). Such people adjust to negative events and return to their usual cheerful state within a few months (Diener et al., 1992).

Happiness is everywhere *As the joy in the faces of these Tibetan women illustrates, happiness is tied to factors beyond a person's economic plight, age, residence, or health.*

Conversely, unhappy people are not cheered in the long term even by positive events.

Some research indicates that happiness is dependent on personality characteristics and interpretive styles (Stewart et al., 2005; Diener, 2000). Happy people are, for example, generally optimistic, outgoing, and tender-minded; they also tend to have several close friends, possess high self-esteem, be spiritual, and have a sense of control over their lives (Sahoo et al., 2005; Diener & Seligman, 2004, 2002; Doyle & Youn, 2000). Some theorists also believe that people have a "happiness set point" to which they consistently return, despite life's ups and downs, although this notion is not always supported by research (Fujita & Diener, 2005; Lucas et al., 2004, 2003). An investigation of 2,300 twins suggested to the researchers who conducted the study that as much as half of one's sense of happiness is related to genetic factors (Lykken & Tellegen, 1996).

A better understanding of the roots of happiness is likely to emerge from the current flurry of research, perhaps providing useful solutions for those who are unhappy or even clinically depressed. In the meantime, we can take comfort in the knowledge that the human condition isn't quite so unhappy as news stories (and textbooks on abnormal psychology) may make it seem.

people coping skills that may help protect them from stress and adversity and encouraging them to become more involved in personally meaningful activities and relationships (Compas & Gotlib, 2002). In this way, the clinicians are trying to promote mental health and prevent mental disorders.

Multicultural Psychology

We are, without question, a society of multiple cultures, races, and languages. Indeed, in the coming decades, members of racial and ethnic minority groups in the United States will, collectively, outnumber white Americans (U.S. Census, 2000). This change in our society's racial and ethnic composition is due partly to shifts in immigration trends and partly to higher birth rates among minority groups in the United States. The majority of new immigrants to this country are Hispanic (34 percent) or Asian (34 percent). Moreover, while the average number of children born to white Americans is 1.7, the number born to African Americans and Hispanic Americans is 2.4 and 2.9, respectively.

In response to this growing diversity, a new area of study called **multicultural psychology** has emerged (Mio et al., 2006). Multicultural psychologists seek to understand how culture, race, ethnicity, gender, and similar factors affect behavior and thought and how people of different cultures, races, and genders may differ psychologically. The field of multicultural psychology has, in turn, begun to have a profound effect on our understanding and treatment of abnormal behavior (Alegria et al., 2004).

A number of recent studies have found, for example, that many members of ethnic and racial minority groups improve less in clinical treatment than members of majority groups (Mark et al., 2003; Sue & Sue, 2003; Lee & Sue, 2001). Similarly, studies conducted throughout the world have found that minority clients make less use of mental health services than members of majority groups (Stevens et al., 2005; Gaw, 2001). In some cases, economic factors, cultural beliefs, a language barrier, or lack of information about available services may prevent minority individuals from seeking help; in other cases, such persons may not trust the establishment, relying instead on traditional remedies that are available in their immediate social environment.

Research also indicates that members of minority groups stop therapy sooner than persons from majority groups. In the United States, African Americans, Native Americans, Asian Americans, and Hispanic Americans all have higher therapy dropout rates than white Americans (Lee & Sue, 2001). Members of these groups may stop treatment because they cannot afford to continue, do not feel they are benefiting from treatment, or feel that they cannot develop strong rapport with a therapist of a different ethnic or racial group (Stevens et al., 2005; Whaley, 1998).

How can today's clinicians be more helpful to people from minority groups? A number of studies suggest that two features of treatment can increase a therapist's effectiveness with minority clients: (1) greater sensitivity to cultural issues and (2) inclusion of cultural morals and models in treatment, especially in therapies for children and adolescents (Majumdar et al., 2004; Lee & Sue, 2001). Given such findings, some clinicians have developed **culture-sensitive therapies,** approaches that seek to address the unique issues faced by members of minority groups (Mio et al., 2006; Prochaska & Norcross, 2003). Similarly, a number of clinicians have developed therapies geared to the special pressures of being a woman in Western society, called **gender-sensitive** or **feminist therapies** (Sweeney, 2003).

The Growing Influence of Insurance Coverage

So many people now seek therapy that private insurance companies have changed their coverage for mental health patients. Today the dominant form of coverage is the **managed care program**—a program in which the insurance company determines such key issues as which therapists its clients may choose, the cost of sessions, and the number of sessions for which a client may be reimbursed (Corcoran, Gorin, & Moniz, 2005).

At least 75 percent of all privately insured persons in the United States are currently enrolled in managed care programs (Kiesler, 2000). The coverage for mental health treatment under such programs follows the same basic principles as coverage for medical treatment, including a limited pool of practitioners for patients to choose from, preapproval of treatment by the insurance company, strict standards for judging whether problems and treatments qualify for reimbursement, and ongoing reviews and assessments. In the mental health realm, both therapists and clients typically dislike the managed care programs. They fear that the programs inevitably shorten therapy (often for the worse), unfairly favor treatments whose results are not always lasting (for example, drug therapy), pose a special hardship for those with severe mental disorders, and result in treatment determined by insurance companies rather than by therapists (Mechanic, 2004; Mowbray et al., 2002).

A special problem with insurance coverage—both managed care and other kinds of insurance programs—is that reimbursements for mental disorders tend to be lower than those for medical disorders. This disparity places persons with psychological difficulties at a distinct disadvantage in their efforts to overcome their problems and inevitably affects the quality and quantity of the treatment they seek (Feldman et al., 2002). Recently the federal government and 35 states have passed so-called parity laws that direct insurance

Matthew S. Gunby/AP Photo

Positive psychology in action *Positive psychology emphasizes positive feelings and actions. Multicultural psychology examines the stressors faced by different cultural groups and their psychological impact. Often these two new fields of study work together. Here, for example, two young girls come together as one at the end of a "slave reconciliation" walk by 400 people in Maryland. The walk was intended to promote racial understanding and to help Americans overcome the lasting psychological effects of slavery.*

MULTICULTURAL PSYCHOLOGY•The field of psychology that examines the impact of culture, race, ethnicity, gender, and similar factors on our behaviors and thoughts, and also focuses on how such factors may influence the origin, nature, and treatment of abnormal behavior.

•CULTURE-SENSITIVE THERAPIES•
Approaches that address the unique issues faced by members of minority groups.

•GENDER-SENSITIVE THERAPIES•
Approaches geared to the special pressures of being a woman in Western society. Also called *feminist therapies.*

•MANAGED CARE PROGRAM•A system of health-care coverage in which the insurance company largely controls the nature, scope, and cost of medical or psychological services.

>>BY THE NUMBERS

Gender Shift

28% Psychologists in 1978 who were female **<<**

52% Psychologists today who are female **<<**

75% Current undergraduate psychology majors who are female **<<**

66% Current psychology graduate students who are female **<<**

(Gill, 2006; APA, 2005; Barber, 1999)

companies to provide equal coverage for mental and medical problems. It is not yet clear, however, whether these laws will indeed lead to better coverage and whether they will improve the treatment picture for people with psychological problems.

What Are Today's Leading Theories and Professions?

One of the most important developments in the modern understanding and treatment of abnormal psychological functioning has been the growth of numerous theoretical perspectives that now coexist in the clinical field (Compas & Gotlib, 2002). Before the 1950s, the *psychoanalytic* perspective, with its emphasis on unconscious psychological problems as the cause of abnormal behavior, was dominant. Then the discovery of effective psychotropic drugs inspired new respect for the somatogenic, or *biological,* view. As we shall see in Chapter 3, other influential perspectives that have emerged since the 1950s are the *behavioral, cognitive, humanistic-existential,* and *sociocultural* schools of thought. At present no single viewpoint dominates the clinical field as the psychoanalytic perspective once did. In fact, the perspectives often conflict and compete with one another; yet, as we shall see, in some instances they complement each other and together provide more complete explanations and treatments for psychological disorders.

In addition, a variety of professionals now offer help to people with psychological problems (Compas & Gotlib, 2002). Before the 1950s, psychotherapy was offered only by *psychiatrists,* physicians who complete three to four additional years of training after medical school (a *residency*) in the treatment of abnormal mental functioning. After World War II, however, the demand for mental health services expanded so rapidly that other professional groups stepped in to fill the need (Humphreys, 1996).

Among those other groups are *clinical psychologists*—professionals who earn a doctorate in clinical psychology by completing four years of graduate training in abnormal functioning and its treatment and also complete a one-year internship at a mental hospital or mental health agency. Before their professional responsibilities expanded into the area of treatment, clinical psychologists were principally assessors and researchers of abnormal functioning. Some of them still specialize in those activities.

Psychotherapy and related services are also provided by *counseling psychologists, educational* and *school psychologists, psychiatric nurses, marriage therapists, family therapists,* and—the largest group—*psychiatric social workers* (see Table 1-2). Each of these specialties has its own graduate training program. Theoretically, each conducts therapy in a distinctive way, but in reality clinicians from the various specialties often use similar techniques. In fact, the individual differences within a professional group are sometimes greater than the general differences between groups.

One final important development in the study and treatment of mental disorders since World War II has been a growing appreciation of the need for effective research (Goodwin, 2002). As theories and forms of treatment have increased, *clinical researchers* have tried to determine which concepts best explain and predict abnormal behavior,

Table 1-2

Profiles of Mental Health Professionals

	Degree	Began to Practice	Current Number	Percent Female
Psychiatrists	M.D., D.O.	1840s	39,056	25
Psychologists	Ph.D., Psy.D., Ed.D.	Late 1940s	88,000	52
Social workers	M.S.W., D.S.W.	Early 1950s	476,000	77
Counselors	Various	Early 1950s	175,000	50

Source: APA, 2005; Weissman, 2005, 2000; U.S. Department of Labor, 2002.

"Wow! You need professional help."

which treatments are most effective, and what kinds of changes may be required. Today well-trained clinical researchers conduct studies in universities, medical schools, laboratories, mental hospitals, mental health centers, and other clinical settings throughout the world. Their work has already produced important discoveries and changed many of our ideas about abnormal psychological functioning.

PUTTING IT together

A Work in Progress

Since ancient times, people have tried to explain, treat, and study abnormal behavior. By examining the responses of past societies to such behaviors, we can better understand the roots of our present views and treatments. In addition, a look backward helps us appreciate just how far we have come—how humane our present views, how impressive our recent discoveries, and how important our current emphasis on research.

At the same time we must recognize the many problems in abnormal psychology today. The field has yet to agree on one definition of abnormality. It is currently made up of conflicting schools of thought and treatment whose members are often unimpressed by the claims and accomplishments of the others. And clinical practice is carried out by a variety of professionals trained in different ways.

As we proceed through the topics in this book and look at the nature, treatment, and study of abnormal functioning, we must keep in mind the field's current strengths and weaknesses, the progress that has been made, and the journey that lies ahead. Perhaps the most important lesson to be learned from our look at the history of this field is that our current understanding of abnormal behavior represents a work in progress. The clinical field stands at a crossroads, with some of the most important insights, investigations, and changes yet to come.

How, then, should we proceed in our examination of abnormal psychology? To begin with, we need to learn about the basic tools and perspectives that today's scientists and practitioners find most useful. This is the task we turn to in the next several chapters. Chapter 2 describes the research strategies that are currently adding to our knowledge of abnormal functioning. Chapter 3 then examines the range of views that influence today's clinical theorists and practitioners. Finally, Chapter 4 examines how abnormal behaviors are currently being assessed, diagnosed, and treated. Later chapters present the major categories of psychological abnormality as well as the leading explanations and treatments for each of them. In the final chapter we shall see how the science of abnormal psychology and its professionals address current social issues and interact with legal, social, and other institutions in our world.

>>PSYCH•NOTES

Mental Health Finances

The total economic cost of psychological disorders, including substance abuse, in the United States—direct treatment costs, lost wages, and the like—is more than $400 billion each year (NIDA, 2000, 1998; Rice & Miller, 1998). ≪

- -

Thirty-three states in the United States mandate that every private health insurance policy must include coverage for mental health services. ≪

- -

Two-thirds of mental hospitals in the United States currently engage in "patient dumping"—denying care to patients or transferring them largely because they require costly care or are underinsured (Grinfeld, 1998; Schlesinger et al., 1997). ≪

---[**SUMMARY AND REVIEW**]---

■ **What is psychological abnormality?** Abnormal functioning is generally considered to be *deviant, distressful, dysfunctional,* and *dangerous*. Behavior must also be considered in the context in which it occurs, however, and the concept of abnormality depends on the *norms* and *values* of the society in question. *pp. 3–5*

■ **What is treatment?** *Therapy* is a systematic process for helping people overcome their psychological difficulties. It typically requires a *patient,* a *therapist,* and a *series of therapeutic contacts. pp. 5–6*

■ **How was abnormality viewed and treated in the past?** The history of psychological disorders stretches back to ancient times.

PREHISTORIC SOCIETIES Prehistoric societies apparently viewed abnormal behavior as the work of evil spirits. There is evidence that Stone Age cultures used *trephination,* a primitive form of brain surgery, to treat abnormal behavior. People of early societies also sought to drive out evil spirits by *exorcism. p. 8*

GREEKS AND ROMANS Physicians of the Greek and Roman empires offered more enlightened explanations of mental disorders. Hippocrates believed that abnormal behavior was due to an imbalance of the four bodily fluids, or *humors:* black bile, yellow bile, blood, and phlegm. Treatment consisted of correcting the underlying physical pathology through diet and lifestyle. *pp. 8–9*

THE MIDDLE AGES In the Middle Ages, Europeans returned to demonological explanations of abnormal behavior. The clergy was very influential and held that mental disorders were the work of the devil. As the Middle Ages drew to a close, such explanations and treatments began to decline, and people with mental disorders were increasingly treated in hospitals instead of by the clergy. *pp. 9–10*

THE RENAISSANCE Care of people with mental disorders continued to improve during the early part of the Renaissance. Certain religious shrines became dedicated to the humane treatment of such individuals. By the middle of the sixteenth century, however, persons with mental disorders were being warehoused in *asylums. pp. 10–11*

THE NINETEENTH CENTURY Care of those with mental disorders started to improve again in the nineteenth century. In Paris, Philippe Pinel started the movement toward *moral treatment*. Similar reforms were brought to England by William Tuke. Similarly, Dorothea Dix spearheaded a movement in the United States to ensure legal rights and protection for people with mental disorders and to establish state hospitals for their care. Unfortunately, the moral treatment movement disintegrated by the late nineteenth century, and mental hospitals again became warehouses where the inmates received minimal care. *pp. 12–13*

THE EARLY TWENTIETH CENTURY The turn of the twentieth century saw the return of the *somatogenic perspective,* the view that abnormal psychological functioning is caused primarily by physical factors. Key to this development were the work of Emil Kraepelin in the late 1800s and the finding that *general paresis* was caused by the organic disease syphilis. The same period saw the rise of the *psychogenic perspective,* the view that the chief causes of abnormal functioning are psychological. An important factor in its rise was the use of *hypnotism* to treat patients with *hysterical disorders*. Sigmund Freud's psychogenic approach, *psychoanalysis,* eventually gained wide acceptance and influenced future generations of clinicians. *pp. 13–16*

■ **Current trends** The past 50 years have brought significant changes in the understanding and treatment of abnormal functioning. In the 1950s, researchers discovered a number of new *psychotropic medications,* drugs that mainly affect the brain and reduce many symptoms of mental dysfunctioning. Their success contributed to a policy of *deinstitutionalization,* under which hundreds of thousands of patients were released from public mental hospitals. In addition, *outpatient treatment* has become the primary approach for most persons with mental disorders, both mild and severe; *prevention programs* are growing in number and influence; the field of *multicultural psy-*

chology has begun to influence how clinicians view and treat abnormality; and *insurance coverage* is having a significant impact on the way treatment is conducted. Finally, a variety of *perspectives* and *professionals* have come to operate in the field of abnormal psychology, and many well-trained *clinical researchers* now investigate the field's theories and treatments. *pp. 16–23*

>>> CRITICAL THOUGHTS <<<

1. Why are movies and novels with themes of abnormal functioning so popular? Why do actresses and actors who portray characters with psychological disorders tend to receive more awards for their performances? *pp. 1–2, 24*

2. What behaviors might fit the criteria of deviant, distressful, dysfunctional, or dangerous, yet would not be considered abnormal by most people? *pp. 3–5, 7*

3. People of the Stone Age did not leave written records, so archaeologists cannot be certain that trephination was in fact an ancient treatment for mental dysfunctioning. How else might we explain the holes found in the skulls recovered from early times? Why do you think historians have settled on mental illness as an explanation? *p. 8*

4. Have episodes of "mass madness" occurred in recent times? Might the Internet, cable television, or other forms of modern technology pose a special danger in the emergence and spread of new forms of mass madness? *p. 9*

5. In addition to the evil eye and exorcism, what other demonological explanations or treatments are still around today? Why do they persist? *pp. 9–11*

⊙─[CYBERSTUDY]──────────────────>>>

SEARCH THE *ABNORMAL PSYCHOLOGY* CD-ROM FOR

▲ Chapter 1 Video Cases and Discussions
   What did past hospital treatments for severe mental disorders look like?
   Observe the predecessors of modern electroconvulsive therapy.
   Are the early treatments behind us?

▲ Chapter 1 Practical, Research, and Decision-Making Exercises
   Comparing today's treatments to those of the past
   Tracing abnormality through the arts

▲ Chapter 1 Practice Test and Feedback

LOG ON TO THE COMER WEB PAGE FOR

▲ Suggested Web links, exercises, FAQ page, additional Chapter 1 practice test questions
   <www.worthpublishers.com/comer>

─────────────────────────────<<<

Research in Abnormal Psychology

"The brain is an organ of minor importance."

Aristotle, Greek philosopher, fourth century B.C.

"Woman may be said to be an inferior man."

Aristotle

"[Louis Pasteur's] theory of germs is a ridiculous fiction."

Pierre Pochet, professor of physiology, 1872

"Everything that can be invented has been invented."

Charles Duell, U.S. Patent Office, 1899

"The theory of relativity [is] worthless and misleading."

T. J. J. See, U.S. Government Observatory, 1924

"If excessive smoking actually plays a role in the production of lung cancer, it seems to be a minor one."

W. C. Heuper, National Cancer Institute, 1954

"Space travel is utter bilge."

Richard van der Riet Wooley, British Astronomer Royal, 1956

"There is no reason for any individual to have a computer in their home."

Ken Olson, Digital Equipment Corp., 1977

"The cloning of mammals . . . is biologically impossible."

James McGrath and Davor Solter, genetic researchers, 1984

Each of these statements was once accepted as gospel. Had their validity not been tested, had they been judged on the basis of conventional wisdom alone, had new ideas not been proposed and investigated, human knowledge and progress would have been severely limited. What enabled thinkers to move beyond such misperceptions? The answer, quite simply, is research, the systematic search for facts through the use of careful observations and investigations.

Research is as important to the field of abnormal psychology as to any other field of study. Consider, for example, schizophrenia and the treatment procedure known as the lobotomy. *Schizophrenia* is a severe disorder that causes people to lose contact with reality. Their thoughts, perceptions, and emotions become distorted and disorganized, and their behavior may be bizarre and withdrawn. For the first half of the twentieth century, this condition was attributed to inappropriate parenting. Clinicians blamed *schizophrenogenic* ("schizophrenia-causing") mothers for the disorder— women they described as cold and domineering, and impervious to their children's needs. As we will see in Chapter 14, this widely held belief turned out to be wrong.

During the same era, practitioners developed a surgical procedure that supposedly cured schizophrenia. In this procedure, called a *lobotomy,* a pointed instrument was inserted into the frontal lobe of the brain and rotated, destroying a considerable amount of brain tissue. Early reports described lobotomized patients as showing near-miraculous improvement. This impression, too, turned out to be

•**NOMOTHETIC UNDERSTANDING**•A general understanding of the nature, causes, and treatments of abnormal psychological functioning in the form of laws or principles.

•**SCIENTIFIC METHOD**•The process of systematically gathering and evaluating information through careful observations to gain an understanding of a phenomenon.

•**CASE STUDY**•A detailed account of a person's life and psychological problems.

wrong, although the mistake wasn't discovered until tens of thousands of persons had been lobotomized. Far from curing schizophrenia, lobotomies caused irreversible brain damage that left many patients withdrawn and even stuporous.

These errors underscore the importance of sound research in abnormal psychology. Theories and treatments that seem reasonable and effective in individual instances may prove disastrous to other people in other situations. Only by rigorously testing a theory or technique on representative groups of subjects can clinicians evaluate the accuracy and usefulness of their ideas and techniques. Until clinical researchers conducted relevant studies, millions of parents, already heartbroken by their children's schizophrenia, were additionally stigmatized as the primary cause of the disorder; and countless people with schizophrenia, already debilitated by their symptoms, were made permanently apathetic and spiritless by a lobotomy.

Clinical researchers face certain challenges that make their investigations particularly difficult. They must, for example, figure out how to measure such elusive concepts as unconscious motives, private thoughts, mood change, and human potential (Kazdin, 2003). They must consider the different cultural backgrounds, races, and genders of the people they select as research subjects. And, as we are reminded in Box 2-1, they must always ensure that the rights of their subjects, both human and animal, are not violated (Joy, 2005; Kapp, 2002). Despite such difficulties, research in this field has taken giant steps forward, especially during the last 35 years. In the past, most clinical researchers were limited by lack of training and a paucity of useful techniques. Now graduate clinical programs train large numbers of students to conduct appropriate studies on clinical topics. Moreover, the development of new research methods has greatly improved our understanding of psychological dysfunction.

What Do Clinical Researchers Do?

Clinical researchers, also called clinical scientists, try to discover universal laws, or principles, of abnormal psychological functioning. They search for general, or nomothetic, truths about the nature, causes, and treatments of abnormality ("nomothetic" is derived from the Greek *nomothetis,* "lawgiver") (Harris, 2003). They do not typically assess, diagnose, or treat individual clients; that is the job of clinical practitioners, who seek an idiographic, or individualistic, understanding of abnormal behavior (Saville & Buskist, 2003). We shall explore the work of practitioners in later chapters.

To gain a **nomothetic understanding** of abnormal psychology, clinical researchers, like scientists in other fields, rely primarily on the **scientific method**—that is, they systematically collect and evaluate information through careful observations. These observations in turn enable them to pinpoint and explain relationships between *variables.* Simply stated, a variable is any characteristic or event that can vary, whether from time to time, from place to place, or from person to person. Age, sex, and race are human variables. So are eye color, occupation, and social status. Clinical researchers are interested in variables such as childhood upsets, present life experiences, moods, social and occupational functioning, and responses to treatment. They try to determine whether two or more such variables change together and whether a change in one variable causes a change in another. Will the death of a parent cause a child to become depressed? If so, will a given treatment reduce that depression?

Such questions cannot be answered by logic alone, because scientists, like all human beings, make frequent errors in thinking. Thus clinical researchers must depend mainly on three methods of investigation: the *case study,* which typically focuses on one individual, and the *correlational method* and *experimental method,* approaches that usually gather information about many individuals. Each is best suited to certain kinds of circumstances and questions (Beutler et al., 1995). Collectively, these methods enable scientists to form and test *hypotheses,* or hunches, that certain variables are related in certain ways—and to draw broad conclusions as to why. More properly, a hypothesis is a tentative explanation offered to provide a basis for an investigation.

"Oh, if only it were so simple."

[BOX **2-1**]

Animals Have Rights

For years researchers have learned about abnormal human behavior from experiments with animals. Animals have sometimes been shocked, prematurely separated from their parents, and starved. They have had their brains surgically changed and they have even been killed, or "sacrificed," so that researchers could autopsy them. Are such actions always ethically acceptable?

Animal rights activists say no (Sunstein & Nussbaum, 2004). They have called the undertakings cruel and unnecessary and have fought many forms of animal research with legal protests and demonstrations. Some have even harassed scientists and vandalized their labs. In turn, some researchers accuse the activists of caring more about animals than about human beings.

In response to this controversy, a number of state courts have ruled that university researchers must publicly disclose their research proposals to help ensure the well-being of animal subjects. Similarly, government agencies and the American Psychological Association have issued rules

and guidelines for animal research (Akins et al., 2005). Still the battle goes on.

Where does the public stand on the issue? In a survey of British citizens, 64 percent of the respondents said that they disagree with animal research—71 percent of the women and 57 percent of the men (MORI, 1999). But such public disapproval appears tenuous. In the same survey, a mere reminder that animal research can

hasten clinical progress led to expressions of approval by a slim majority of the respondents. People in animal rights surveys tend to approve of experiments that use mice or rats more than those that use monkeys. Most of them disapprove of experiments that bring pain to animals, except when the investigations are seeking a cure for childhood leukemia, AIDS, or other life-threatening problems.

Paul Sukumac/AP Photo

Making a point *Members of an organization called In Defense of Animals wear monkey outfits and sit in locked cages in front of the University of California, San Francisco, to protest against the use of monkeys in research.*

The Case Study

A **case study** is a detailed and often interpretive description of a person's life and psychological problems. It describes the person's history, present circumstances, and symptoms. It may also speculate about why the problems developed, and it may describe the application and results of a particular treatment.

In his famous case study of Little Hans (1909), Sigmund Freud discusses a 4-year-old boy who has developed a fear of horses. Freud gathered his material from detailed letters sent him by Hans's father, a physician who had attended lectures on psychoanalysis, and from his own limited interviews with the child. Freud's study runs 140 pages in his *Collected Papers,* so only key excerpts are presented here.

One day while Hans was in the street he was seized with an attack of morbid anxiety. . . . [Hans's father wrote:] "He began to cry and asked to be taken home. . . . In the evening he grew visibly frightened; he cried and could not be separated from his mother. . . . [When taken for a walk the next day], again he began to cry, did not want to start, and was frightened. . . . On the way back from Schönbrunn he said to his mother, after much internal struggling: 'I was afraid a horse would bite me.' . . . In the evening he . . . had another attack similar to that of the previous evening. . . ."

But the beginnings of this psychological situation go back further still. . . . The first reports of Hans date from a period when he was not quite three years old. At that time, by means of various remarks and questions, he was showing a

>>PSYCH•NOTES

Sigmund Freud

Freud's fee for one session of therapy was $20—$160 in today's dollars. «

For almost 40 years Freud treated patients 10 hours per day, five or six days per week. «

Little Hans's father was a great admirer of Freud and not entirely objective. He communicated to Freud only those events that he knew would interest the doctor and support his theory. «

Freud's parents often favored the precociously intelligent Sigmund over his siblings—for example, by giving him his own room in which to study in peace. «

Freud did not use the term "psychoanalysis" until 1896, when he was already 40. «

(Jacobs, 2003; Gay, 1999; Asimov, 1997; Schwartz, 1993)

quite peculiarly lively interest in that portion of his body which he used to describe as his "widdler" [his word for penis]. . . .

When he was three and a half his mother found him with his hand to his penis. She threatened him in these words: "If you do that, I shall send for Dr. A. to cut off your widdler. And then what'll you widdle with?" . . . This was the occasion of his acquiring [a] "castration complex." . . .

[At the age of four, Hans entered] a state of intensified sexual excitement, the object of which was his mother. The intensity of this excitement was shown by . . . two attempts at seducing his mother. [One such attempt, occurring just before the outbreak of his anxiety, was described by his father:] "This morning Hans was given his usual daily bath by his mother and afterwards dried and powdered. As his mother was powdering round his penis and taking care not to touch it, Hans said: 'Why don't you put your finger there?' . . ."

. . . The father and son visited me during my consulting hours. . . . Certain details which I now learnt—to the effect that [Hans] was particularly bothered by what horses wear in front of their eyes and by the black round their mouths—were certainly not to be explained from what we knew. But as I saw the two of them sitting in front of me and at the same time heard Hans's description of his anxiety-horses, a further piece of the solution shot through my mind. . . . I asked Hans jokingly whether his horses wore eyeglasses, to which he replied that they did not. I then asked him whether his father wore eyeglasses, to which, against all the evidence, he once more said no. Finally I asked him whether by "the black round the mouth" he meant a moustache; and I then disclosed to him that he was afraid of his father, precisely because he was so fond of his mother. It must be, I told him, that he thought his father was angry with him on that account; but this was not so, his father was fond of him in spite of it, and he might admit everything to him without any fear. Long before he was in the world, I went on, I had known that a little Hans would come who would be so fond of his mother that he would be bound to feel afraid of his father because of it. . . .

By enlightening Hans on this subject I had cleared away his most powerful resistance. . . . [T]he little patient summoned up courage to describe the details of his phobia, and soon began to take an active share in the conduct of the analysis.

. . . It was only then that we learnt [that Hans] was not only afraid of horses biting him—he was soon silent upon that point—but also of carts, of furniture-vans, and of buses . . . , of horses that started moving, of horses that looked big and heavy, and of horses that drove quickly. The meaning of these specifications was explained by Hans himself: he was afraid of horses falling down, and consequently incorporated in his phobia everything that seemed likely to facilitate their falling down.

It was at this stage of the analysis that he recalled the event, insignificant in itself, which immediately preceded the outbreak of the illness and may no doubt be regarded as the exciting cause of the outbreak. He went for a walk with his mother, and saw a bus-horse fall down and kick about with its feet. This made a great impression on him. He was terrified, and thought the horse was dead; and from that time on he thought that all horses would fall down. His father pointed out to him that when he saw the horse fall down he must have thought of him, his father, and have wished that he might fall down in the same way and be dead. Hans did not dispute this interpretation. . . . From that time forward his behavior to his father was unconstrained and fearless, and in fact a trifle overbearing.

It is especially interesting . . . to observe the way in which the transformation of Hans's libido into anxiety was projected on to the principal object of his phobia, on to horses. Horses interested him the most of all the large animals; playing at horses was his favorite game with the older children. I had a suspicion—and this was confirmed by Hans's father when I asked him—that the first person who had served Hans as a horse must have been his father. . . . When repression had set in and brought a revulsion of feeling along with it, horses, which had till then been associated with so much pleasure, were necessarily turned into objects of fear.

[Hans later reported] two concluding phantasies, with which his recovery was rounded off. One of them, that of [a] plumber giving him a new and . . . bigger widdler, was . . . a triumphant wish-phantasy, and with it he overcame his fear of castration. . . . His other phantasy, which confessed to the wish to be married to his mother and to have many children by her . . . corrected that portion of those thoughts which was entirely unacceptable; for, instead of killing his father, it made him innocuous by promoting him to a marriage with Hans's grandmother. With this phantasy both the illness and the analysis came to an appropriate end.

(Freud, 1909)

Most clinicians take notes and keep records in the course of treating their patients, and some, like Freud, further organize such notes into a formal case study to be shared with other professionals. The clues offered by a case study may help a clinician better understand or treat the person under discussion (Stricker & Trierweiler, 1995). In addition, case studies may play nomothetic roles that go far beyond the individual clinical case (Goodwin, 2002; Beutler et al., 1995).

How Are Case Studies Helpful?

Case studies can be a source of *new ideas* about behavior and "open the way for discoveries" (Bolgar, 1965). Freud's theory of psychoanalysis was based mainly on the patients he saw in private practice. He pored over their case studies, such as the one he wrote about Little Hans, to find what he believed to be universal psychological processes and principles of development. In addition, a case study may offer *tentative support* for a theory. Freud used case studies in this way as well, regarding them as evidence for the accuracy of his ideas. Conversely, case studies may serve to *challenge a theory's assumptions* (Kratochwill, 1992).

Case studies may also inspire *new therapeutic techniques* or describe unique applications of existing techniques. The psychoanalytic principle that says patients may benefit from discussing their problems and discovering underlying psychological causes, for example, has roots in the famous case study of Anna O., presented by Freud's collaborator Josef Breuer, a case we shall explore in Chapter 3. Similarly, Freud believed that the case study of Little Hans demonstrated the therapeutic potential of a verbal approach for children as well as for adults.

Finally, case studies may offer opportunities to study *unusual problems* that do not occur often enough to permit a large number of observations (Goodwin, 2002). For years information about multiple personality disorders was based almost exclusively on case studies, such as the famous *The Three Faces of Eve,* a clinical account of a woman who displayed three alternating personalities, each having a distinct set of memories, preferences, and personal habits (Thigpen & Cleckley, 1957).

What Are the Limitations of Case Studies?

Case studies, although useful in many ways, also have limitations. First, they are reported by *biased observers,* that is, by therapists who have a personal stake in seeing their treatments succeed (Goodwin, 2002; Stricker & Trierweiler, 1995). These observers must choose what to include in a case study, and their choices may at times be self-serving. Second, case studies rely upon *subjective evidence.* Are a client's dysfunction and improvement really caused by the events that the therapist or client says are responsible? In fact, these are only a small subset of the events that may be contributing to the situation. When investigators are able to rule out all possible causes except one, a study is said to have internal accuracy, or **internal validity** (Wampold, 2006). Obviously, case studies rate low on that score.

Another problem with case studies is that they provide *little basis for generalization*. Even if we agree that Little Hans developed a dread of horses because he was terrified

Does mental dysfunctioning run in families? *One of the most celebrated case studies in abnormal psychology is a study of identical quadruplets dubbed the "Genain" sisters by researchers (after the Greek words for "dire birth"). All the sisters developed schizophrenia in their twenties.*

•**INTERNAL VALIDITY**•The accuracy with which a study can pinpoint one of various possible factors as the cause of a phenomenon.

Case study, Hollywood style *Case studies often find their way into the arts or media and capture the public's attention. Unfortunately, as this movie poster of* The Three Faces of Eve *illustrates, the studies may be trivialized or sensationalized in those venues.*

•**EXTERNAL VALIDITY**•The degree to which the results of a study may be generalized beyond that study.

•**CORRELATION**•The degree to which events or characteristics vary along with each other.

•**CORRELATIONAL METHOD**•A research procedure used to determine how much events or characteristics vary along with each other.

of castration and feared his father, how can we be confident that other people's phobias are rooted in the same kinds of causes? Events or treatments that seem important in one case may be of no help at all in efforts to understand or treat others. When the findings of an investigation can be generalized beyond the immediate study, the investigation is said to have external accuracy, or **external validity** (Wampold, 2006). Case studies rate low on external validity, too (Goodwin, 2002).

The limitations of the case study are largely addressed by two other methods of investigation: the *correlational method* and the *experimental method*. They do not offer the richness of detail that makes case studies so interesting, but they do help investigators draw broad conclusions about abnormality in the population at large. Thus they are now the preferred methods of clinical investigation. Three features of these methods enable clinical investigators to gain nomothetic insights: (1) The researchers typically observe many individuals. That way, they can collect enough information, or data, to support a conclusion. (2) The researchers apply procedures uniformly. Therefore other researchers can repeat, or *replicate,* a particular study to see whether it consistently gives the same findings. (3) The researchers use *statistical tests* to analyze the results of a study. These tests can help indicate whether broad conclusions are justified.

The Correlational Method

Correlation is the degree to which events or characteristics vary with each other. The **correlational method** is a research procedure used to determine this "co-relationship" between variables. This method can, for example, answer the question "Is there a correlation between the amount of stress in people's lives and the degree of depression they experience?" That is, as people keep experiencing stressful events, are they increasingly likely to become depressed? To test this question, researchers have collected life stress scores (for example, the number of threatening events experienced during a certain period of time) and depression scores (for example, scores on a depression survey) from individuals and have correlated these scores.

The people who are chosen for a study are its *subjects,* or *participants,* collectively called the *sample.* A sample must be representative of the larger population that the researchers wish to understand (McCready, 2006). Otherwise the relationship found in the study may not apply elsewhere in the real world—it may not have external validity. If researchers were to find a correlation between life stress and depression in a sample consisting entirely of children, for example, they could not draw clear conclusions about what, if any, correlation exists among adults.

Describing a Correlation

Suppose we use the correlational method to conduct a study of depression. We collect life stress scores and depression scores for 10 subjects, and we plot the scores on a graph, as shown in Figure 2-1. As you can see, the subject named Jim has a recent life stress score of 7, meaning seven threatening events over the past three months; he also has a depression score of 25. Thus he is "located" at the point on the graph where these two scores meet. The graph provides a visual representation of our data. Here, notice that the data points all fall roughly along a straight line that slopes upward. We draw the line so that the data points are as close to it as possible. This line is called the *line of best fit.*

The line of best fit in Figure 2-1 slopes upward and to the right, indicating that the variables under examination are increasing or decreasing together. That is, the greater someone's life stress score, the higher his or her score on the depression scale. When variables change the same way, their correlation is said to have a positive *direction* and is referred to as a *positive correlation.* Most studies of recent life stress and depression have indeed found a positive correlation between those two variables (Andrew & Wilding, 2004; Monroe & Hadjiyannakis, 2002).

Correlations can have a negative rather than a positive direction. In a *negative correlation,* the value of one variable increases as the value of the other variable decreases. Researchers have found, for example, a negative correlation between depression and activity level. The greater one's depression, the lower the number of one's activities. When the scores of a negative correlation are plotted, they produce a downward-sloping graph, like the one shown in Figure 2-2.

There is still a third possible outcome for a correlational study. The variables under study may be *unrelated,* meaning that there is no consistent relationship between them. As the measures of one variable increase, those of the other variable sometimes increase and sometimes decrease. The graph of this outcome looks like Figure 2-3. Here the line of best fit is horizontal, with no slope at all. Studies have found that depression and intelligence are unrelated, for example.

In addition to knowing the direction of a correlation, researchers need to know its *magnitude,* or strength (see Figure 2.4). That is, how closely do the two variables correspond? Does one always vary along with the other, or is their relationship less exact? When two variables are found to vary together very closely in subject after subject, the correlation is said to be high, or strong.

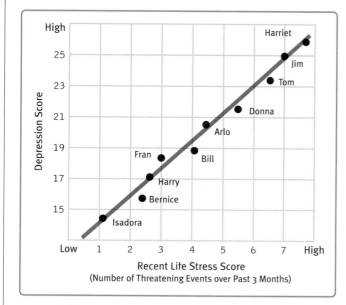

FIGURE **2-1** **Positive correlation** *The relationship between amount of recent stress and feelings of depression shown by this hypothetical sample of 10 subjects is a near-perfect "positive" correlation.*

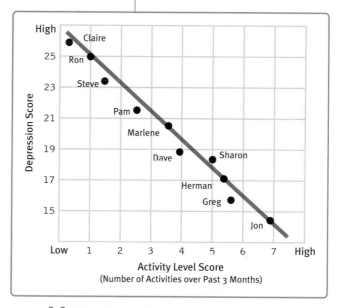

FIGURE **2-2** **Negative correlation** *The relationship between number of activities and feelings of depression shown by this hypothetical sample is a near-perfect "negative" correlation.*

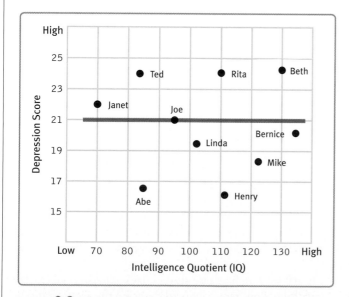

FIGURE **2-3** **No correlation** *The relationship between intelligence and feelings of depression shown by this hypothetical sample is a "near-zero" correlation.*

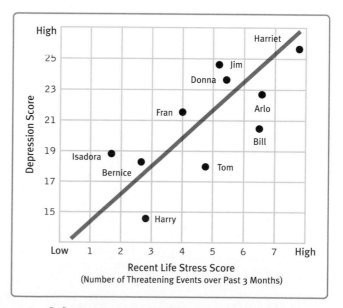

FIGURE **2-4** **Magnitude of correlation** *The relationship between amount of recent stress and feelings of depression shown by this hypothetical sample is a "moderately positive" correlation.*

•**EPIDEMIOLOGICAL STUDY**•A study that measures the incidence and prevalence of a disorder in a given population.

•**INCIDENCE**•The number of new cases of a disorder occurring in a population over a specific period of time.

•**PREVALENCE**•The total number of cases of a disorder occurring in a population over a specific period of time.

Look again at Figure 2-1. In this graph of a positive correlation between depression and life stress, the data points all fall very close to the line of best fit. Researchers can predict each person's score on one variable with a high degree of confidence if they know his or her score on the other. But what if the graph of the correlation between depression and life stress looked more like Figure 2-4? Now the data points are loosely scattered around the line of best fit rather than hugging it closely. In this case, researchers could not predict with as much accuracy a subject's score on one variable from the score on the other variable. The correlation in Figure 2-1 is stronger, or greater in magnitude, than that in Figure 2-4.

The direction and magnitude of a correlation are often calculated numerically and expressed by a statistical term called the *correlation coefficient,* symbolized by the letter *r.* The correlation coefficient can vary from +1.00, which indicates a perfect positive correlation between two variables, down to −1.00, which represents a perfect negative correlation. The *sign* of the coefficient (+ or −) signifies the direction of the correlation; the *number* represents its magnitude. An *r* of .00 reflects a zero correlation, or no relationship between variables. The closer *r* is to .00, the weaker, or lower in magnitude, the correlation. Thus correlations of +.75 and −.75 are of equal magnitude and equally strong, whereas a correlation of +.25 is weaker than either.

Everyone's behavior is changeable, and many human responses can be measured only approximately. Most correlations found in psychological research, therefore, fall short of a perfect positive or negative correlation. One study of life stress and depression, with a sample of 68 adults, found a correlation of +.53 (Miller, Ingraham, & Davidson, 1976). Although hardly perfect, a correlation of this magnitude is considered large in psychological research.

When Can Correlations Be Trusted?

Scientists must decide whether the correlation they find in a given sample of subjects accurately reflects a real correlation in the general population. Could the observed correlation have occurred by mere chance? They can never know for certain, but they can test their conclusions by a *statistical analysis* of their data, using principles of probability. In essence, they ask how likely it is that the study's particular findings have occurred by chance. If the statistical analysis indicates that chance is unlikely to account for the correlation they found, researchers may conclude that their findings reflect a real correlation in the general population.

A cutoff point helps researchers make this decision. By convention, if there is less than a 5 percent probability that a study's findings are due to chance (signified as $p < .05$), the findings are said to be *statistically significant* and are thought to reflect the larger population. In the life stress study described earlier, a statistical analysis indicated a probability of less than 5 percent that the +.53 correlation found in the sample was due to chance (Miller et al., 1976). Therefore, the researchers concluded with some confidence that among adults in general, depression does tend to rise along with the amount of recent stress in a person's life. Generally, our confidence increases with the size of the sample and the magnitude of the correlation. The larger they are, the more likely it is that a correlation will be statistically significant.

What Are the Merits of the Correlational Method?

The correlational method has certain advantages over the case study (see Table 2-1). First, it possesses high *external validity.* Because researchers measure their variables, observe large samples, and apply statistical analyses, they are in a better position to generalize their correlations to people beyond the ones they have studied. Furthermore, researchers can easily repeat correlational studies using new samples of subjects to check the results of earlier studies.

On the other hand, correlational studies, like case studies, lack *internal validity* (Field & Davey, 2005). Although correlations allow researchers to describe the relationship between two variables, they do not *explain* the relationship. When we look at the positive correlation found in many life stress studies, we may be tempted to conclude that in-

Table 2-1

Relative Strengths and Weaknesses of Research Methods

	Provides Individual Information (Idiographic)	Provides General Information (Nomothetic)	Provides Causal Information	Statistical Analysis Possible	Replicable
Case study	Yes	No	No	No	No
Correlational method	No	Yes	No	Yes	Yes
Experimental method	No	Yes	Yes	Yes	Yes

creases in recent life stress cause people to feel more depressed. In fact, however, the two variables may be correlated for any one of three reasons: (1) Life stress may cause depression. (2) Depression may cause people to experience more life stress (for example, a depressive approach to life may cause people to mismanage their money or may interfere with social relationships). (3) Depression and life stress may each be caused by a third variable, such as financial problems (Andrews & Wilding, 2004).

Although correlations say nothing about causation, they can still be of great use to clinicians. Clinicians know, for example, that suicide attempts increase as people become more depressed. Thus, when they work with severely depressed clients, they keep on the lookout for signs of suicidal thinking. Perhaps depression directly causes suicidal behavior, or perhaps a third variable, such as a sense of hopelessness, causes both depression and suicidal thoughts. Whatever the cause, just knowing that there is a correlation may enable clinicians to take measures (such as hospitalization) to help save lives.

Of course, in other instances, clinicians do need to know whether one variable causes another. Do parents' marital conflicts cause their children to be more anxious? Does job dissatisfaction lead to feelings of depression? Will a given treatment help people to cope more effectively in life? Questions about causality call for the experimental method, as we shall see later.

The impact of stress *Researchers have learned that everyday stressors, such as commuting to and from work, can often contribute to psychological problems. Moreover, when daily stress is combined with unusual traumatic stress, the personal impact is likely to be even greater. These commuters wait for a bus at Waterloo Station, London, on the morning after the London terrorist subway and bus bombings of 2005. In the days and months following the terrorist attacks, the British population displayed a rise in the onset of psychological symptoms and disorders.*

Special Forms of Correlational Research

Epidemiological studies and longitudinal studies are two kinds of correlational research used widely by clinical investigators. **Epidemiological studies** reveal the incidence and prevalence of a disorder in a particular population. **Incidence** is the number of new cases that emerge during a given period of time. **Prevalence** is the total number of cases in the population during a given time period; prevalence includes both existing and new cases. Many researchers also refer to epidemiological studies as "descriptive studies" because the goal of such investigations is largely to *describe* the incidence or prevalence of a disorder "without trying to predict or explain when or why it occurs" (Compas & Gotlib, 2002, p. 69).

Over the past 30 years clinical researchers throughout the United States have worked on the largest epidemiological study ever conducted, called the Epidemiologic Catchment Area Study. They have interviewed more than 20,000 people in five cities to determine the prevalence of many psychological disorders and the treatment programs used (Narrow et al., 2002; Regier et al., 1993). Two other large-scale epidemiological studies in the United States, the National Comorbidity Survey and the National Comorbidity Survey Replication, have questioned more than 9,000 individuals (Kessler et al., 2005,

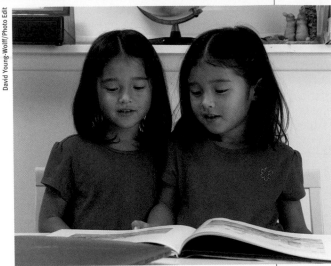

Twins, correlation, and inheritance *Correlational studies of many pairs of twins have suggested a link between genetic factors and certain psychological disorders. Identical twins (who have identical genes) display a higher correlation for some disorders than do fraternal twins (whose genetic makeup is not identical).*

2003). These studies have been further compared with epidemiological studies in other countries, to see how rates of mental disorders and treatment programs vary around the world (WHO, 2004; Alegria et al., 2000).

Such epidemiological studies have helped researchers identify groups at risk for particular disorders. Women, it turns out, have a higher rate of anxiety disorders and depression than men, while men have a higher rate of alcoholism than women. Elderly people have a higher rate of suicide than younger people. And persons in some non-Western countries (such as Taiwan) have a higher rate of mental disorders than those in Western countries. These trends may lead researchers to suspect that something unique about certain groups or settings is helping to cause particular disorders. Declining health in elderly people, for example, may make them more likely to commit suicide; cultural pressures or attitudes common in one country may be responsible for a rate of mental dysfunctioning that differs from the rate found in another country. Yet, like other forms of correlational research, epidemiological studies themselves cannot confirm such suspicions.

In **longitudinal studies** (also called *high-risk* or *developmental studies*), researchers observe the same subjects on many occasions over a long period of time. In one such study, investigators have observed the progress over the years of normally functioning children whose mothers or fathers suffered from schizophrenia (Schiffman et al., 2005, 2004; Mednick, 1971). The researchers have found, among other things, that the children of the parents with the most severe cases of schizophrenia were more likely to develop a psychological disorder and to commit crimes at later points in their development. Because longitudinal studies document the order of events, their correlations provide clues about which events are more likely to be causes and which to be the consequences. Certainly, for example, the children's problems did not cause their parents' schizophrenia. But longitudinal studies still cannot pinpoint causation (Compas & Gotlib, 2002). Did the children who developed psychological problems inherit a genetic factor? Or did their problems result from their parents' inadequate coping behaviors, the parents' long absences due to hospitalization, or some other factor? Again, only experimental studies can supply an answer.

The Experimental Method

An **experiment** is a research procedure in which a variable is manipulated and the manipulation's effect on another variable is observed. In fact, most of us perform experiments throughout our lives without knowing that we are behaving so scientifically. Suppose that we go to a party on campus to celebrate the end of midterm exams. As we mix with people at the party, we begin to notice many of them becoming quiet and depressed. It seems the more we talk, the more subdued the other guests become. As the party deteriorates before our eyes, we decide we have to do something, but what? Before we can eliminate the problem, we need to know what's causing it.

Our first hunch may be that something we're doing is responsible. Perhaps our remarks about academic pressures have been upsetting everyone. We decide to change the topic to skiing in the mountains of Colorado, and we watch for signs of depression in our next round of conversations. The problem seems to clear up; most people now smile and laugh as they chat with us. As a final check of our suspicions, we could go back to talking about school with the next several people we meet. Their dark and dismal reaction would probably convince us that our propensity to talk about school was indeed the cause of the problem.

We have just performed an experiment, testing our hypothesis about a causal relationship between our conversational gambits and the depressed mood of the people around us. We manipulated the variable that we suspected to be the cause (the topic of discussion) and then observed the effect of that manipulation on the other variable (the mood of the people around us). In scientific experiments, the manipulated variable is called the **independent variable** and the variable being observed is called the **dependent variable.**

»PSYCH•LISTINGS

Most Investigated Causal Questions in Clinical Research

Does factor X cause a disorder? **«**

- -

Is cause A more influential than cause B? **«**

- -

How does family communication and structure affect family members? **«**

- -

How does a disorder affect the quality of a person's life? **«**

- -

How does a person's disorder affect family members? **«**

- -

Does treatment X alleviate a disorder? **«**

- -

Is treatment A more helpful than treatment B? **«**

- -

Why does treatment X work? **«**

- -

Does greater therapist expertise lead to greater progress in treatment? **«**

- -

Can an intervention prevent abnormal functioning? **«**

To examine the experimental method more fully, let us consider a question that is often asked by clinicians: "Does a particular therapy relieve the symptoms of a particular disorder?" Because this question is about a causal relationship, it can be answered only by an experiment. That is, experimenters must give the therapy in question to people who are suffering from a disorder and then observe whether they improve. Here the therapy is the independent variable, and psychological improvement is the dependent variable.

If the true, or primary, cause of changes in the dependent variable cannot be separated from other possible causes, then an experiment gives us very little information. Thus, experimenters must try to eliminate all **confounds** from the study—variables other than the independent variable that may also be affecting the dependent variable. When there are confounds in an experiment, they, rather than the independent variable, may be causing the observed changes.

For example, situational variables, such as the location of the therapy office (say, a quiet country setting) or a soothing color scheme in the office, may have a therapeutic effect on participants in a therapy study. Or perhaps the participants are unusually motivated or have high expectations that the therapy will work, factors that thus account for their improvement. To guard against confounds, researchers include three important features in their experiments—a *control group, random assignment,* and a *blind design* (Wampold, 2006; Field & Davey, 2005).

The Control Group

A **control group** is a group of subjects who are not exposed to the independent variable under investigation but whose experience is similar to that of the **experimental group,** the subjects who are exposed to the independent variable. By comparing the two groups, an experimenter can better determine the effect of the independent variable.

To study the effectiveness of a particular therapy, for example, experimenters typically divide subjects into two groups after obtaining their consent to participate in the experiment (see Box 2-2 on the next page). The experimental group may come into an office and receive the therapy for an hour, while the control group may simply come into the office for an hour. If the experimenters find later that the people in the experimental group improve more than the people in the control group, they may conclude that the therapy was effective, above and beyond the effects of time, the office setting, and any other confounds. To guard against confounds, experimenters try to provide all participants, both control and experimental, with experiences that are identical in every way—except for the independent variable.

Of course, it is possible that the differences observed between an experimental group and control group have occurred simply by chance. Thus, as with correlational studies, investigators who conduct experiments must do a statistical analysis on their data and find out how likely it is that the observed differences are due to chance. If the likelihood is very low—less than 5 percent ($p < .05$)—the differences between the two groups are considered to be statistically significant, and the experimenter may conclude with some confidence that they are due to the independent variable. As a general rule, if the sample of subjects is large, if the difference observed between groups is great, and if the range of scores within each group is small, the findings of an experiment are likely to be statistically significant.

Random Assignment

Researchers must also watch out for differences in the makeup of the experimental and control groups, since those differences may also confound a study's results. In a therapy study, for example, it may happen that the experimenter has unintentionally put wealthier subjects in the experimental group and poorer subjects in the control group. This difference, rather than their therapy, could be the cause of the greater improvement later found among the experimental subjects. To reduce the effects of preexisting differences, experimenters typically use **random assignment.** This is the general term for any

•**LONGITUDINAL STUDY**•A study that observes the same subjects on many occasions over a long period of time.

•**EXPERIMENT**•A research procedure in which a variable is manipulated and the effect of the manipulation is observed.

•**INDEPENDENT VARIABLE**•The variable in an experiment that is manipulated to determine whether it has an effect on another variable.

•**DEPENDENT VARIABLE**•The variable in an experiment that is expected to change as the independent variable is manipulated.

•**CONFOUND**•In an experiment, a variable other than the independent variable that is also acting on the dependent variable.

•**CONTROL GROUP**•In an experiment, a group of subjects who are not exposed to the independent variable.

•**EXPERIMENTAL GROUP**•In an experiment, the subjects who are exposed to the independent variable under investigation.

•**RANDOM ASSIGNMENT**•A selection procedure that ensures that subjects are randomly placed either in the control group or in the experimental group.

>>**Q & A**

What is the difference between statistical significance and clinical significance in treatment studies?

Statistical significance indicates whether a subject's improvement in functioning—large or small—occurred because of treatment. **Clinical significance** indicates whether the amount of improvement is meaningful in the individual's life. Even if the moods of depressed subjects improve because of treatment, the individuals may still be too unhappy to enjoy life. Thus, although experimenters can determine *statistical* significance, only individuals and their clinicians can evaluate *clinical* significance. <<

[BOX 2-2]

Clear as a Bell?

To ensure that subjects know what they are getting into when they sign up for a study and to guarantee that subjects feel free to leave the study at any time, researchers must inform them about the nature of the study and about their rights. This principle of "informed consent," the foundation of all human research, is usually implemented with a form that spells out everything the subjects need to know.

But how clear are informed consent forms? Not very, according to some recent studies (Flory & Emanuel, 2004; Mathew & McGrath, 2002).

Many such forms are written at an advanced college level, making them incomprehensible to a large percentage of subjects. When investigators used a readability scale to compare various writing samples (higher scores indicated greater reading difficulty), they discovered the following:

An old Ann Landers column earned a score of 7.67 (75 percent of the population can understand it).

Reader's Digest magazine earned 9.95 (69 percent can understand it).

The New Yorker magazine earned 13.3 (43 percent can understand it).

Typical informed consent forms earned 15.03 (37 percent can understand them).

---

selection procedure that ensures that every subject in the experiment is as likely to be placed in one group as the other. We might, for example, try flipping a coin or picking names out of a hat.

Blind Design

A final confound problem is *bias*. Participants may bias an experiment's results by trying to please or help the experimenter (Goodwin, 2002). In a therapy experiment, for example, those who receive the treatment, knowing the purpose of the study and knowing which group they are in, might actually work harder to feel better or fulfill the experimenter's expectations. If so, subject bias rather than therapy could be causing their improvement.

To avoid this bias, experimenters can prevent participants from finding out which group they are in. This experimental strategy is called a **blind design** because subjects are blind as to their assigned group. In a therapy study, for example, control subjects could be given a *placebo* (Latin for "I shall please"), something that looks or tastes like real therapy but has none of its key ingredients. This "imitation" therapy is called **placebo therapy.** If the experimental (true therapy) subjects then improve more than the control (placebo therapy) subjects, experimenters have more confidence that the true therapy has caused their improvement.

An experiment may also be confounded by *experimenter bias* (Kazdin, 2003; Margraf et al., 1991)—that is, experimenters may have expectations that they unintentionally transmit to their subjects. This bias is sometimes referred to as the *Rosenthal effect,* after the psychologist who first identified it (Rosenthal, 1966). Experimenters can eliminate their own bias by arranging to be blind themselves. In a drug therapy study, for example, an aide could make sure that the real medication and the placebo drug look identical. The experimenter could then administer treatment without knowing which participants were receiving true medications and which were receiving false medications.

While the participants or the experimenter may be kept blind in an experiment, it is best that both be blind (a *double-blind design*). In fact, most medication

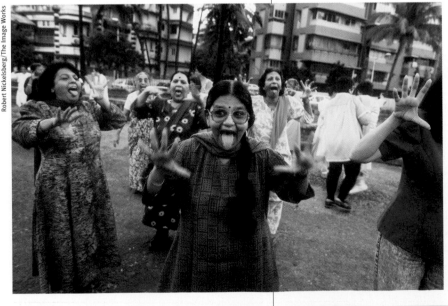

Is laughter a good medicine? *Members of this laughter club in Bombay, India, practice therapeutic laughing, or Hasyayog, a relatively new group treatment based on the belief that laughing at least 15 minutes each day will drive away depression and other ills. As many as 400 kinds of therapies are currently used for psychological problems. An experimental design is needed to determine whether this or any other form of treatment actively causes clients to improve.*

Robert Nickelsberg/The Image Works

experiments now use double-blind designs to test promising drugs (Keefe et al., 2004). Many experimenters also arrange for judges to assess the patients' improvement independently, and the judges, too, are blind to group assignments—a *triple-blind design* (Wheatley, 2004).

Alternative Experimental Designs

It is not easy to devise an experiment that is both well controlled and enlightening. Control of every possible confound is rarely attained in practice. Moreover, because psychological experiments typically use living beings, ethical and practical considerations limit the kinds of manipulations one can do (Caskey & Rosenthal, 2005) (see Box 2-3 on the next page). Thus clinical researchers must often settle for experimental designs that are less than ideal. The most common such variations are the *quasi-experimental design,* the *natural experiment,* the *analogue experiment,* and the *single-subject experiment.*

Quasi-Experimental Design

In **quasi-experiments,** or **mixed designs,** investigators do not randomly assign subjects to control and experimental groups but instead make use of groups that already exist in the world at large (Wampold, 2006). For example, because investigators of child abuse cannot actually abuse a randomly chosen group of children, they must instead compare children who already have a history of abuse with children who do not. Of course, such a strategy violates the rule of random assignment and so introduces possible confounds into the study. Children who receive physical punishment, for example, usually come from poorer and larger families than children who are punished verbally. Any differences found later in the moods or self-concepts of the two groups of children may be due to differences in wealth or family size rather than to the abuse.

Child-abuse researchers often try to address the confound problems of quasi-experiments by using *matched control subjects.* That is, they match the experimental subjects with control subjects who are similar in age, sex, race, number of children in the family, socioeconomic status, type of neighborhood, or other important characteristics. For every abused child in the experimental group, they choose an unabused child with similar characteristics to be included in the control group. When the data from studies of this kind have shown that abused children are typically sadder and think less of themselves than matched control subjects who have not been abused, the investigators have been able to conclude with some confidence that abuse is causing the differences (Kinard, 1982).

Natural Experiment

In **natural experiments** nature itself manipulates the independent variable, while the experimenter observes the effects. Natural experiments must be used for studying the psychological effects of unusual and unpredictable events such as floods, earthquakes, plane crashes, and fires. Because their subjects in those studies are selected by an accident of fate rather than by conscious design, natural experiments are actually a kind of quasi-experiment.

On February 26, 1972, a dam gave way in the town of Buffalo Creek, West Virginia, releasing 132 million gallons of black slag, mud, and water into the valley below. The disaster killed 125 people, injured hundreds more, and left thousands homeless. Eighteen months later, the researcher Goldine Gleser and her colleagues (1981) collected data from 381 survivors and from a control group of people who lived elsewhere. The survivors of the flood scored significantly higher on anxiety and

•**BLIND DESIGN**•An experiment in which subjects do not know whether they are in the experimental or the control condition.

•**PLACEBO THERAPY**•A sham treatment that the subject in an experiment believes to be genuine.

•**QUASI-EXPERIMENT**•An experiment in which investigators make use of control and experimental groups that already exist in the world at large. Also called a *mixed design.*

•**NATURAL EXPERIMENT**•An experiment in which nature, rather than an experimenter, manipulates an independent variable.

Natural experiments *A man surveys the damage wrought by a hurricane upon his home and belongings. Natural experiments conducted in the aftermath of such catastrophes have found that many survivors experience lingering feelings of anxiety and depression.*

Christopher Brown/Stock Boston

[BOX 2-3]

Human Subjects Have Rights, Too

When today's students get together and talk about studies in which they have participated, they quickly discover that their research experiences were similar: the participants were informed about the nature and foreseeable risks of the study; the experimenters obtained the consent of subjects and reminded them that they were free to leave at any time; and the experimenters debriefed the subjects about specific goals and findings at the conclusion of the study.

It is no coincidence that these and related procedures are now included in most studies involving human subjects. When the Project MK-ULTRA and Willowbrook studies (see p. 43), along with several other scandalous investigations, came to light in the 1970s, the United States Congress quickly passed the National Research Act of 1974. This law required every research institute to set up a review board to monitor and protect patients' well-being in all federally funded studies (DeVries et al., 2004). The Department of Health and Human Services created the Office for Human Research Protection to oversee the review boards and to establish rules and guidelines for all such studies. Other countries set up similar procedures and guidelines. Moreover, in the 1970s univer-

sities began to train ethicists, who conferred with philosophers, psychologists, physicians, civil rights experts, and people from all sectors of society in ongoing efforts to develop acceptable research guidelines.

These efforts have greatly improved the ethics of clinical research, but some serious problems remain (Emanuel et al., 2003; Saks et al., 2002). In fact, the clinical field was rocked just a few years ago by a new series of reports that revealed that during the 1980s and 1990s, many patients with severe mental disorders had been harmed or placed at risk in clinical studies (Emanuel et al., 2003; Kong, 1998). The studies in question typically involved antipsychotic drug treatments for patients with psychosis (loss of contact with reality). It appears that many patients in these studies had agreed to receive drug treatments (or not to receive them) without fully understanding the risks involved. In addition, the drugs used in these studies left some of the subjects with more intense psychotic symptoms. Four types of studies were cited:

- **New Drug Studies** Patients are administered an experimental drug to see whether it reduces their symptoms. The new drug is being tested

for effectiveness, safety, undesired effects, and dosage, meaning that the patients may be helped, unaffected, or damaged by the drug.

- **Placebo Studies** When a new drug is being tested on a group of experimental subjects, researchers may administer a placebo drug to a group of control subjects. The improvement of the experimental subjects is then compared with that of the placebo control subjects to determine the new drug's effectiveness. Unfortunately, in such studies, the placebo control subjects—often people with severe disorders—are receiving no treatment at all. For this reason, many researchers believe it is better to administer an established medication, rather than a placebo drug, to subjects in a control group (Baldwin et al., 2003). Improvement on the experimental drug can then be compared with improvement on the established drug to determine the merits of the new drug (LaVaque & Rossiter, 2001).

- **Symptom-Exacerbation Studies** Patients are given drugs designed to intensify their symptoms, so that researchers may learn more about the biology of their disorder. For example, people suffering from psychotic disorders have been given apomorphine,

depression measures (dependent variables) than the controls did. The survivors also experienced more difficulty falling asleep or staying asleep and had more nightmares.

Because natural experiments rely on unexpected occurrences in nature, they cannot be repeated at will. Also, because each natural event is unique in some ways, broad generalizations drawn from a single study could be incorrect. Nevertheless, catastrophes have provided opportunities for hundreds of natural experiments over the years, and certain findings have been obtained repeatedly. As a result, clinical scientists have identified patterns of reactions that often occur in such situations. We shall observe these patterns—acute stress disorders and posttraumatic stress disorders—in Chapter 6.

Analogue Experiment

There is one way in which investigators can manipulate independent variables relatively freely while avoiding many of the ethical and practical limitations of clinical research. They can induce laboratory subjects to behave in ways that seem to resemble real-life abnormal behavior and then conduct experiments on the subjects in the hope of shedding light on the real-life abnormality. This is called an **analogue experiment.**

Often analogue studies use animals as subjects. Animal subjects are easier to gather and manipulate than human subjects, and their use poses fewer ethical problems. While

•**ANALOGUE EXPERIMENT**•A research method in which the experimenter produces abnormal-like behavior in laboratory subjects and then conducts experiments on the subjects.

amphetamine, ketamine, and other drugs that lead to more delusions, hallucinations, and the like.

◆ **Medication-Withdrawal Studies**
Researchers prematurely stop medications for patients who have been symptom-free while taking the medications. The researchers then follow the patients as they relapse, in the hope of learning more about how and when patients can be taken off particular medications.

Each of these kinds of studies seeks to increase understanding of the biology of certain disorders and to improve treatment. Yet at what risk? When does the benefit to many outweigh the suffering of a few? As the clinical community and the public have grown more aware of the risks involved in these studies, they have called for better safeguards to protect research subjects with mental disorders. In 1999 the National Institute of Mental Health suspended some of its symptom-exacerbation studies, and the presidentially appointed National Bioethics Advisory Commission issued a list of recommendations. Moreover, the Office for Human Research Protection has recently undergone sweeping changes designed to make the agency more aggressive in its protection of human subjects

(DeVries et al., 2004; Emanuel et al., 2003). And Congress is currently preparing to introduce legislation that will protect the rights of human subjects in all studies, not just those receiving federal funding. Nevertheless, this important issue is far from being resolved.

How times have changed *In a 1957 study of the psychological effects of complete isolation, subjects were placed in a sound-proof box wearing dark goggles, gloves, and cardboard tubes over their hands to deprive them of hearing, sight, and touch. The 25-hour study was actually televised live throughout England, an event that probably would not be permitted today, given current human research safeguards, such as subject confidentiality, informed consent, and research review board approval and monitoring.*

the needs and rights of animal subjects must be considered, most experimenters are willing to subject animals to more discomfort than human subjects. They believe that the insights gained from such experimentation outweigh the discomfort of the animals, as long as their distress is not excessive (Gluck & Bell, 2003). In addition, experimenters can, and often do, use human subjects in analogue experiments.

As we shall see in Chapter 8, the investigator Martin Seligman has used analogue studies with great success to investigate the causes of human depression. Seligman has theorized that depression results when people believe they no longer have any control over the good and bad things that happen in their lives. To test this theory, he has produced depression-like symptoms in laboratory subjects by repeatedly giving them negative reinforcements (shocks, loud noises, task failures) over which they have no control. In these "learned helplessness" studies, the participants seem to give up, lose their initiative, and become sad—suggesting to some clinicians that human depression itself may indeed be caused by loss of control over one's reinforcements in life.

It is important to remember that the laboratory-induced learned helplessness produced in Seligman's analogue experiments is not known with certainty to be analogous to human depression. If this laboratory phenomenon is actually only superficially similar to depression, then the clinical inferences drawn from such experiments may be wrong and misleading. This, in fact, is the major limitation of all analogue research:

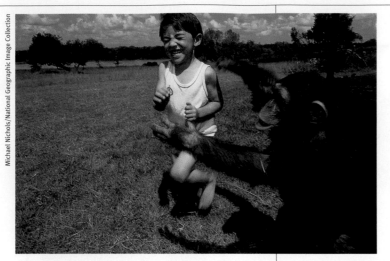

Similar enough? *Chimpanzees and human beings share more than 90 percent of their genetic material, but their brains and bodies are very different, as are their perceptions and experiences. Thus, abnormal-like behavior produced in animal analogue experiments may differ from the human abnormality under investigation.*

researchers can never be certain that the phenomena they see in the laboratory are the same as the psychological disorders they are investigating.

Single-Subject Experiment

Sometimes scientists do not have the luxury of experimenting on many subjects. They may, for example, be investigating a disorder so rare that few subjects are available. Experimentation is still possible, however, with a **single-subject experimental design.** Here a single subject is observed both before and after the manipulation of an independent variable.

Single-subject experiments first rely on baseline data—information gathered prior to any manipulations. These data set a standard with which later changes may be compared. The experimenter next introduces the independent variable and again observes the subject's behavior. Any changes in behavior are attributed to the effects of the independent variable. Common single-subject experimental designs are the *ABAB* and the *multiple-baseline designs* (Newman & Wong, 2004).

ABAB DESIGN In an *ABAB,* or *reversal, design,* a subject's reactions are measured and compared not only during a baseline period (condition A) and after the introduction of the independent variable (condition B) but also after the independent variable has been removed (condition A) and yet again after it has been reintroduced (condition B). If the subject's responses change back and forth along with changes in the independent variable, the experimenter may conclude that the independent variable is causing the shifting responses. Essentially, in an ABAB design a subject is compared with himself or herself under different conditions rather than with control subjects. Subjects, therefore, serve as their own controls (Adams et al., 2004).

One researcher used an ABAB design to determine whether the systematic use of rewards was helping to reduce a teenage boy's habit of disrupting his special education class with loud talk (Deitz, 1977). The treatment program consisted of rewarding the boy, who suffered from mental retardation, with extra teacher time whenever he went 55 minutes without interrupting the class more than three times. When observed during a baseline period, the student was found to disrupt the class frequently with loud talk. Next the boy was given a series of teacher reward sessions (the independent variable); his loud talk decreased dramatically, as expected. Then the rewards from the teacher were stopped, and the student's loud talk increased once again. Apparently the independent variable had indeed been the cause of the improvement. To be still more confident about this conclusion, the researcher had the teacher apply reward sessions yet again. Once again the subject's behavior improved.

•**SINGLE-SUBJECT EXPERIMENT**•A research method in which a single subject is observed and measured both before and after the manipulation of an independent variable.

"What if these guys in white coats who bring us food are, like, studying us and we're part of some kind of big experiment?"

MULTIPLE-BASELINE DESIGN A *multiple-baseline design* does not employ the reversals found in an ABAB design. Instead, the experimenter selects two or more behaviors (two dependent variables) displayed by a subject and observes the effect that the manipulation of an independent variable has on each behavior (Agran et al., 2005; Winn et al., 2004). Let us say that the teenage boy in the ABAB study displayed two kinds of inappropriate behavior—the disruptive talk during class and odd grimaces. In a multiple-baseline design, the experimenter would first collect baseline data on both the frequency of the boy's disruptive talk and the frequency of his facial grimaces during a 55-minute period. In the next phase of the experiment, the experimenter would reward the boy with extra teacher time whenever he cut down his verbalizations but not when he cut down his grimaces. The experimenter would then measure changes in the boy's verbal and grimacing behaviors, expecting the verbal interruptions to decrease but the grimacing to remain about the same as before. In the final phase of the experiment, the experimenter would also reward the boy with extra teacher attention whenever he reduced his grimacing, expecting that this manipulation would now reduce the grimacing as well. If the expected pattern of changes was observed, it would be reasonable to conclude that the manipulation of the independent variable (attention from the teacher), rather than some other factor, was responsible for the changes in the two behaviors.

Obviously, single-subject experiments—both ABAB and multiple-baseline designs—are similar to individual case studies in their focus on one subject. In single-subject experiments, however, the independent variable is manipulated systematically so that the investigator can confidently draw conclusions about the cause of an observed effect (Compas & Gotlib, 2002). The single-subject experiment therefore has greater internal validity than the case study. At the same time, single-subject experiments, like case studies, have only limited external validity. Because only one subject is studied, the experimenter cannot be sure that the subject's reaction to the independent variable is typical of people in general (Goodwin, 2002).

PUTTING IT together
The Use of Multiple Research Methods

We began this discussion by noting that clinical scientists look for general laws that will help them understand, prevent, and treat psychological disorders. Various obstacles interfere with their progress, however. We have already observed some of them. The most fundamental are summarized below.

1. *Clinical scientists must respect the rights of both human subjects and animal subjects.* Ethical considerations greatly limit the kinds of investigations that clinical scientists can conduct.

2. *The causes of human functioning are very complex.* Because human behavior generally results from multiple factors working together, it is difficult to pinpoint specific causes. So many factors can influence human functioning that it has actually been easier to unravel the complexities of energy and matter than to understand human sadness, stress, and anxiety.

3. *Human beings are changeable.* Moods, behaviors, and thoughts fluctuate. Is the person under study today truly the same as he or she was yesterday? Variability in a single person, let alone from person to person, limits the kinds of conclusions researchers can draw about abnormal functioning.

4. *Human self-awareness may influence the results of clinical investigations.* When human subjects know they are being studied, that knowledge influences their behavior. They may try to respond as they think researchers expect them to or to present themselves in a favorable light. Similarly, the attention they receive from investigators may itself increase their optimism and improve their mood. It is an axiom of science that the very act of measuring an object distorts the object to some degree. Nowhere is this more true than in the study of human beings.

5. *Clinical investigators have a special link to their subjects.* Clinical scientists, too, experience mood changes, troubling thoughts, and family problems. They may identify with the pain of their subjects or have personal opinions about their problems. These feelings can bias an investigator's attempts to understand abnormality.

In short, human behavior is so complex that clinical scientists must use a variety of methods to study it. Each method addresses some of the inherent problems, but no one approach overcomes them all. Case studies allow investigators to consider a broader range of causes, but experiments pinpoint causes more precisely. Similarly, correlational studies allow broad generalizations, but case studies are richer in detail. It is best to view each research method as part of a team of approaches that together may shed considerable light on abnormal human functioning. When more than one method has been used to investigate a disorder, it is important to ask whether all the results seem to point in the same direction. If they do, we are probably making progress toward understanding and treating that disorder. Conversely, if the various methods seem to produce conflicting results, we must admit that our knowledge in that particular area is still tentative.

Before accepting any research findings, however, students of the clinical field must review the details of the studies with a very critical eye. Were the variables properly controlled? Was the choice of subjects representative, was the sample large enough to be meaningful, and has bias been eliminated? Are the investigator's conclusions justified? How else might the results be interpreted? Only after painstaking scrutiny can we conclude that a truly informative investigation has taken place.

─[SUMMARY AND REVIEW]─

■ **What do clinical researchers do?** Researchers use the *scientific method* to uncover *nomothetic* principles of abnormal psychological functioning. They attempt to identify and examine relationships between variables and depend primarily on three methods of investigation. *p. 28*

■ **The case study** A *case study* is a detailed account of a person's life and psychological problems. It can serve as a source of ideas about behavior, provide support for theories, challenge theories, clarify new treatment techniques, or offer an opportunity to study an unusual problem. Yet case studies may be reported by biased observers and rely on subjective evidence. In addition, they tend to have low *internal validity* and low *external validity*. *pp. 29–32*

■ **The correlational method** Correlational studies systematically observe the degree to which events or characteristics vary together. This method allows researchers to draw broad conclusions about abnormality in the population at large.

A *correlation* may have a *positive* or *negative direction* and may be high or low in *magnitude*. It can be calculated numerically and expressed by the *correlation coefficient* (*r*). Researchers perform a *statistical analysis* to determine whether the correlation found in a study is truly characteristic of the larger population or due to chance. Correlational studies generally have high external validity but lack internal validity. Two widely used forms of the correlation method are *epidemiological studies* and *longitudinal studies*. *pp. 32–36*

■ **The experimental method** In *experiments*, researchers manipulate suspected causes to see whether expected effects will result. The variable that is manipulated is called the *independent variable*, and the variable that is expected to change as a result is called the *dependent variable*.

Confounds are variables other than the independent variable that are also acting on the dependent variable. To minimize their possible influence, experimenters use *control groups, random assignment,* and *blind designs*. The findings of experiments, like those of correlational studies, must be analyzed statistically. *pp. 36–39*

■ **Alternative experimental designs** Clinical experimenters must often settle for experimental designs that are less than ideal, including the *quasi-experiment*, the *natural experiment*, the *analogue experiment*, and the *single-subject experiment*. *pp. 39–43*

■ **The use of multiple research methods** Because human subjects have rights that must be respected, because the origins of behavior are complex, because behavior varies, and because the very act of observing a subject's behavior influences that behavior, it can be difficult to assess the findings of clinical research. Also, researchers must take into account their own biases and a study's unintended impact on subjects' usual behavior. To help address such obstacles, clinical investigators must use multiple research approaches. *pp. 43–44*

⟩⟩⟩ CRITICAL THOUGHTS ⟨⟨⟨

1. Can you think of important beliefs, beyond those stated on page 27, that were once accepted as gospel but are now considered false?

2. Even when there are credible, well-known research findings to the contrary, many people hold on to false beliefs about human behavior, particularly abnormal behavior. Why does research fail to change their views? *pp. 27–28, 43–44*

3. Which are you more likely to be influenced by in your life—a case study (or similar anecdotal offering)

or a research write-up? What features of anecdotal presentations make them particularly influential? *pp. 28–32*

4. What arguments might animal rights activists offer to support the position that the use of animals in experiments is often cruel and unnecessary? How might animal researchers counter such arguments? *p. 29*

5. Do outside restrictions on research—either animal or human—interfere with necessary investigations and

thus limit potential gains for human beings? *pp. 29, 40, 43*

6. How would you interpret the sizable correlation found between life stress and depression? How would you decide which of various possible interpretations is the most accurate? *p. 34*

7. In drug therapy studies, some control subjects who receive placebo pills actually show improvement. Why might sugar pills or other kinds of placebo treatments help people feel better? *pp. 38–39*

◉—[CYBERSTUDY]———————————⟩⟩⟩

SEARCH THE *ABNORMAL PSYCHOLOGY* CD-ROM FOR

▲ Chapter 2 Video Cases and Discussions
   How do researchers measure psychopathology?
   Observe the power of bias and expectations in research.

▲ Chapter 2 Practical, Research, and Decision-Making Exercises
   Misusing anecdotal evidence
   Testing clinical hypotheses

▲ Chapter 2 Practice Test and Feedback

LOG ON TO THE COMER WEB PAGE FOR

▲ Suggested Web links, exercises, FAQ page, additional Chapter 2 practice test questions
   ⟨www.worthpublishers.com/comer⟩

———————————————————————⟨⟨⟨

Models of Abnormality

Philip Berman, a 25-year-old single unemployed former copy editor for a large publishing house, . . . had been hospitalized after a suicide attempt in which he deeply gashed his wrist with a razor blade. He described [to the therapist] how he had sat on the bathroom floor and watched the blood drip into the bathtub for some time before he telephoned his father at work for help. He and his father went to the hospital emergency room to have the gash stitched, but he convinced himself and the hospital physician that he did not need hospitalization. The next day when his father suggested he needed help, he knocked his dinner to the floor and angrily stormed to his room. When he was calm again, he allowed his father to take him back to the hospital.

The immediate precipitant for his suicide attempt was that he had run into one of his former girlfriends with her new boyfriend. The patient stated that they had a drink together, but all the while he was with them he could not help thinking that "they were dying to run off and jump in bed." He experienced jealous rage, got up from the table, and walked out of the restaurant. He began to think about how he could "pay her back."

Mr. Berman had felt frequently depressed for brief periods during the previous several years. He was especially critical of himself for his limited social life and his inability to have managed to have sexual intercourse with a woman even once in his life. As he related this to the therapist, he lifted his eyes from the floor and with a sarcastic smirk said, "I'm a 25-year-old virgin. Go ahead, you can laugh now." He has had several girlfriends to date, whom he described as very attractive, but who he said had lost interest in him. On further questioning, however, it became apparent that Mr. Berman soon became very critical of them and demanded that they always meet his every need, often to their own detriment. The women then found the relationship very unrewarding and would soon find someone else.

During the past two years Mr. Berman had seen three psychiatrists briefly, one of whom had given him a drug, the name of which he could not remember, but that had precipitated some sort of unusual reaction for which he had to stay in a hospital overnight. . . . Concerning his hospitalization, the patient said that "It was a dump," that the staff refused to listen to what he had to say or to respond to his needs, and that they, in fact, treated all the patients "sadistically." The referring doctor corroborated that Mr. Berman was a difficult patient who demanded that he be treated as special, and yet was hostile to most staff members throughout his stay. After one angry exchange with an aide, he left the hospital without leave, and subsequently signed out against medical advice.

Mr. Berman is one of two children of a middle-class family. His father is 55 years old and employed in a managerial position for an insurance company. He perceives his father as weak and ineffectual, completely dominated by the patient's overbearing and cruel mother. He states that he hates his mother with "a passion I can barely control." He claims that his mother used to call him names like "pervert" and "sissy" when he was growing up, and that in an argument she once "kicked me in the balls." Together, he sees his parents as rich, powerful, and selfish, and, in turn, thinks that they see him as lazy, irresponsible, and a behavior problem.

When his parents called the therapist to discuss their son's treatment, they stated that his problem began with the birth of his younger brother, Arnold, when Philip was 10 years old. After Arnold's birth Philip apparently became an "ornery" child who cursed a lot and was difficult to discipline. Philip recalls this period only vaguely. He reports that his mother once was hospitalized for depression, but that now "she doesn't believe in psychiatry."

Mr. Berman had graduated from college with average grades. Since graduating he had worked at three different publishing houses, but at none of them for more than one year. He always found some justification for quitting. He usually sat around his house doing very little for two or three months after quitting a job, until his parents prodded him into getting a new one. He described innumerable interactions in his life with teachers, friends, and employers in which he felt offended or unfairly treated, . . . and frequent arguments that left him feeling bitter . . . and spent most of his time alone, "bored." He was unable to commit himself to any person, he held no strong convictions, and he felt no allegiance to any group.

The patient appeared as a very thin, bearded, and bespectacled young man with pale skin who maintained little eye contact with the therapist and who had an air of angry bitterness about him. Although he complained of depression, he denied other symptoms of the depressive syndrome. He seemed preoccupied with his rage at his parents, and seemed particularly invested in conveying a despicable image of himself. . . .

(Spitzer et al., 1983, pp. 59–61)

Philip Berman is clearly a troubled person, but how did he come to be that way? How do we explain and correct his many problems? In confronting these questions, we must first look at the wide range of complaints we are trying to understand: Philip's depression and anger, his social failures, his lack of employment, his distrust of those around him, and the problems within his family. Then we must sort through all kinds of potential causes, internal and external, biological and interpersonal, past and present. Which is having the biggest impact on his behavior?

Although we may not realize it, we all use theoretical frameworks as we read about Philip. Over the course of our lives, each of us has developed a perspective that helps us make sense of the things other people say and do. In science, the perspectives used to explain phenomena are known as **models,** or **paradigms.** Each model spells out the scientist's basic assumptions, gives order to the field under study, and sets guidelines for its investigation (Kuhn, 1962). It influences what the investigators observe as well as the questions they ask, the information they seek, and how they interpret this information (Sharf, 2000). To understand how a clinician explains or treats a specific set of symptoms, such as Philip's, we must know which model shapes his or her view of abnormal functioning.

Until recently, clinical scientists of a given place and time tended to agree on a single model of abnormality—a model greatly influenced by the beliefs of their culture. The demonological model that was used to explain abnormal functioning during the Middle Ages, for example, borrowed heavily from medieval society's concerns with religion, superstition, and warfare. Medieval practitioners would have seen the devil's guiding hand in Philip Berman's efforts to commit suicide and his feelings of depression, rage, jealousy, and hatred. Similarly, their treatments for him—from prayers to whippings—would have sought to drive foreign spirits from his body.

Today several models are used to explain and treat abnormal functioning. This variety has resulted from shifts in values and beliefs over the past half-century, as well as improvements in clinical research. At one end of the spectrum is the *biological model,* which sees physical processes as the key to human behavior. At the other end is the *sociocultural model,* which examines the effects of society and culture on individual behavior. In between are four models that focus on more psychological and personal aspects of human functioning: the *psychodynamic model* looks at people's unconscious internal processes and conflicts; the *behavioral model* emphasizes behavior and the ways in which it is learned; the *cognitive model* concentrates on the thinking that underlies behavior; and the *humanistic-existential model* stresses the role of values and choices in human functioning.

Given their different assumptions and concepts, the models are sometimes in conflict. Those who follow one perspective often scoff at the "naive" interpretations, investigations, and treatment efforts of the others. Yet none of the models are complete in themselves. Each focuses mainly on one aspect of human functioning, and none can explain all aspects of abnormality.

The Biological Model

Philip Berman is a biological being. His thoughts and feelings are the results of biochemical and bioelectrical processes throughout his brain and body. Proponents of the *biological model* believe that a full understanding of his thoughts, emotions, and behavior must therefore include an understanding of their biological basis. Not surprisingly, they believe that the most effective treatments for Philip's problems will then be biological ones.

How Do Biological Theorists Explain Abnormal Behavior?

Adopting a medical perspective, biological theorists view abnormal behavior as an illness brought about by malfunctioning parts of the organism. Typically, they point to a malfunctioning brain as the cause of abnormal behavior, focusing particularly on problems in brain anatomy or brain chemistry (Lambert & Kinsley, 2005; Andreasen, 2001).

BRAIN ANATOMY AND ABNORMAL BEHAVIOR The brain is made up of approximately 100 billion nerve cells, called **neurons,** and thousands of billions of support cells, called *glia* (from the Greek meaning "glue"). Within the brain large groups of neurons form distinct areas, or *brain regions.* To identify the regions of the brain more easily, let us imagine them as continents, countries, and states.

At the bottom of the brain is the "continent" known as the *hindbrain,* which is in turn made up of countrylike regions called the *medulla, pons,* and *cerebellum* (see Figure 3-1). In the middle of the brain is the "continent" called the *midbrain.* And at the top is the "continent" called the *forebrain,* which consists of countrylike regions called the *cerebrum* (the two cerebral hemispheres), the *thalamus,* and the *hypothalamus,* each in turn made up of statelike regions. The cerebrum, for instance, consists of the *cortex, corpus callosum, basal ganglia, hippocampus,* and *amygdala.* The neurons in each of these brain regions control important functions. The hippocampus helps control emotions and memory, for example. Clinical researchers have discovered connections between certain psychological disorders and problems in specific areas of the brain. One such disorder is *Huntington's disease,* a disorder marked by violent emotional outbursts, memory loss, suicidal thinking, involuntary body movements, and absurd beliefs. This disease has been traced to a loss of cells in the basal ganglia.

•**MODEL**•A set of assumptions and concepts that help scientists explain and interpret observations. Also called a *paradigm.*

•**NEURON**•A nerve cell.

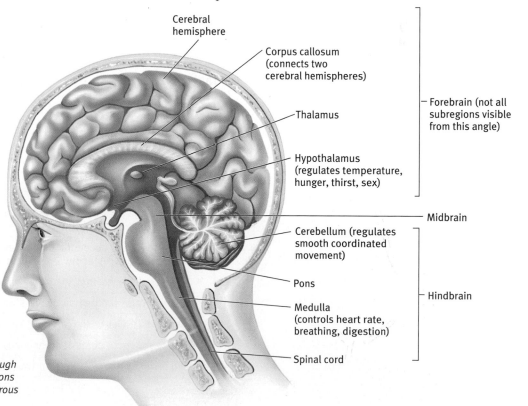

Cerebral hemisphere

Corpus callosum (connects two cerebral hemispheres)

Thalamus

Hypothalamus (regulates temperature, hunger, thirst, sex)

Forebrain (not all subregions visible from this angle)

Midbrain

Cerebellum (regulates smooth coordinated movement)

Pons

Medulla (controls heart rate, breathing, digestion)

Spinal cord

Hindbrain

FIGURE **3-1** **The human brain** *A slice through the center of the brain reveals its major divisions and regions. Each region, composed of numerous neurons, is responsible for certain functions.*

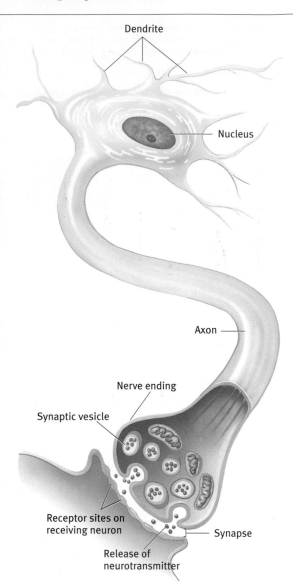

Dendrite

Nucleus

Axon

Nerve ending

Synaptic vesicle

Receptor sites on
receiving neuron

Synapse

Release of
neurotransmitter

FIGURE 3-2 **A typical neuron** *A message travels down the neuron's axon to the nerve ending, where neurotransmitters carry the message across the synaptic space to a receiving neuron. (Adapted from Bloom, Lazerson, & Hofstadter, 1985, p. 35.)*

BRAIN CHEMISTRY AND ABNORMAL BEHAVIOR Biological researchers have also learned that psychological disorders can be related to problems in the transmission of messages from neuron to neuron. Information spreads throughout the brain in the form of electrical impulses that travel from one neuron to one or more others. An impulse is first received by a neuron's *dendrites,* antenna-like extensions located at one end of the neuron. From there it travels down the neuron's axon, a long fiber extending from the neuron body. Finally, it is transmitted to other neurons through the nerve endings, at the far end of the neuron (see Figure 3-2).

But how do messages get from the nerve endings of one neuron to the dendrites of another? After all, the neurons do not actually touch each other. A tiny space, called the **synapse,** separates one neuron from the next, and the message must somehow move across that space. When an electrical impulse reaches a neuron's ending, the nerve ending is stimulated to release a chemical, called a **neurotransmitter,** that travels across the synaptic space to **receptors** on the dendrites of the adjacent neurons. Upon reception, some neurotransmitters tell the receiving neurons to "fire," that is, to trigger their own electrical impulse. Other neurotransmitters carry an inhibitory message; they tell receiving neurons to stop all firing. Obviously, neurotransmitters play a key role in moving information through the brain (see Table 3-1).

Researchers have identified dozens of neurotransmitters in the brain, and they have learned that each neuron uses only certain kinds (Delgado, 2004; Andreasen, 2001). Studies indicate that abnormal activity by certain neurotransmitters can lead to specific mental disorders. Certain anxiety disorders, for example, have been linked to low activity of the neurotransmitter *gamma-aminobutyric acid (GABA),* schizophrenia has been linked to excessive activity of the neurotransmitter *dopamine,* and depression has been linked to low activity of the neurotransmitters *serotonin* and *norepinephrine.* Perhaps low serotonin activity is responsible for Philip Berman's pattern of depression and rage.

In addition to focusing on neurons and neurotransmitters, researchers have learned that mental disorders are sometimes related to abnormal chemical activity in the body's *endocrine system.* Endocrine glands, located throughout the body, work along with neurons to control such vital activities as growth, reproduction, sexual activity, heart rate, body temperature, energy, and responses to stress. The glands release chemicals called **hormones** into the bloodstream, and these chemicals then propel body organs into action. During times of stress, for example, the *adrenal glands,* located on top of the kidneys,

Table 3-1

Brain Matters

- Around 95 percent of what is known about the brain has been learned in the past 10 years.
- A worm's brain has 23 neurons.
- An ostrich's brain is smaller than its eye.
- The average human brain weighs 3 pounds; the human liver weighs around 4 pounds.
- While the brain accounts for only about 2 percent of the total human body weight, it requires about 25 percent of the oxygen intake.
- Aristotle believed that the brain served merely as a cooling organ for the blood.
- 80 percent of the human brain is water.
- Messages travel to the brain at 224 miles per hour.
- One neuron may connect to as many as 25,000 others.
- The brain of the Neanderthal was bigger than that of the modern man.

Source: Ash, 1999; Jordon, 1997; Asimov, 1997; Roan, 1995.

secrete the hormone cortisol. Abnormal secretions of this chemical have been tied to anxiety and mood disorders.

SOURCES OF BIOLOGICAL ABNORMALITIES Why do some people have brain structures or biochemical activities that differ from the norm? A range of factors can contribute to biological dysfunctioning, from head injuries to poor nutrition to vascular diseases (which may affect the flow of blood to the brain). Three sources of biological abnormalities have received particular attention from clinical theorists in recent years—*genetics, evolution,* and *viral infections.*

GENETICS AND ABNORMAL BEHAVIOR Abnormalities in brain anatomy or chemistry are sometimes the result of genetic inheritance. Each cell in the human brain and body contains 23 pairs of *chromosomes,* with each chromosome in a pair inherited from one of the person's parents. Every chromosome contains numerous **genes**—segments that control the characteristics and traits a person inherits. Altogether, each cell contains between 30,000 and 40,000 genes (Andreasen, 2005, 2001). Scientists have known for years that genes help determine such physical characteristics as hair color, height, and eyesight. Genes can make people more prone to heart disease, cancer, or diabetes, and perhaps to possessing artistic or musical skill. In recent years, researchers have discovered that genes may also influence behavior, both normal and abnormal.

More than coincidence? *Studies of twins suggest that some aspects of behavior and personality are influenced by genetic factors. Many identical twins, like these musicians, are found to have similar tastes, behave in similar ways, and make similar life choices. Some even develop similar abnormal behaviors.*

Studies suggest that inheritance plays a part in mood disorders, schizophrenia, mental retardation, Alzheimer's disease, and other mental disorders. Yet, with few exceptions, researchers have not been able to identify the specific genes that are the culprits. Nor do they yet know the extent to which genetic factors contribute to various mental disorders. It appears that in most cases no single gene is responsible for a particular behavior or mental disorder. Instead, many genes combine to help produce our actions and reactions, both functional and dysfunctional.

The precise contributions of various genes to mental disorders should become clearer in coming years, thanks in large part to the completion of the *Human Genome Project* in 2000. In this major research undertaking, which cost billions of dollars, scientists used the tools of molecular biology to *map,* or *sequence,* all of the genes in the human body in great detail. With this information in hand, they are now trying to identify which genes help cause various human disorders—medical and psychological. They hope eventually to be able to prevent or change genes that are problematic (Andreasen, 2005, 2001).

EVOLUTION AND ABNORMAL BEHAVIOR Genes that contribute to mental disorders are typically viewed as unfortunate occurrences—almost mistakes of inheritance. The responsible gene may be a *mutation,* an abnormal form of the appropriate gene that emerges by accident. Or the problematic gene may be inherited by an individual after it has initially entered the family line as a mutation (Andreasen, 2005, 2001). According to some theorists, however, many of the genes that contribute to abnormal functioning are actually the result of normal *evolutionary* principles (Fábrega, 2004, 2002).

Evolutionary theorists argue that we can best understand why people behave the way they do—why certain genes are inherited—by examining our evolutionary history—the millions of years during which the human species evolved "from DNA sludge to upright primate" (Gilbert et al., 2000, p. 4). The theorists believe that various human reactions and the genes responsible for them have survived over the course of time because they have helped individuals to thrive and adapt. Those people who displayed such reactions in the past were usually more likely to fit in with their environment, survive, reproduce, and pass on the genes responsible for the reactions.

The evolutionary argument is straightforward with regard to many behaviors. Ancestors who had the ability to run fast, for example, or the craftiness to hide, were most able to escape predators and to reproduce. In turn, the genes responsible for effective

•**SYNAPSE**•The tiny space between the nerve ending of one neuron and the dendrite of another.

•**NEUROTRANSMITTER**•A chemical that, released by one neuron, crosses the synaptic space to be received at receptors on the dendrites of neighboring neurons.

•**RECEPTOR**•A site on a neuron that receives a neurotransmitter.

•**HORMONES**•The chemicals released by glands into the bloodstream.

•**GENE**•Chromosome segments that control the characteristics and traits we inherit.

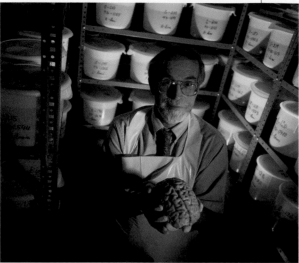

Chris Usher, Alexandria, Virginia

The brain bank *Today's researchers use a variety of methods to help determine the biological causes of abnormal functioning. One is to conduct post-mortem examinations of the brains of people who had suffered from mental disorders. Here, at a hospital "brain bank" in Washington, D.C., researcher E. Fuller Torrey holds the brain of a person who had schizophrenia. There are currently more than 100 brain banks, each preserving hundreds of brains for study by researchers around the world (Kennedy, 2004). Thirty years ago there were none.*

•**PSYCHOTROPIC MEDICATIONS**•Drugs that primarily affect the brain and reduce many symptoms of mental dysfunctioning.

•**ANTIANXIETY DRUGS**•Psychotropic drugs that help reduce tension and anxiety. Also called *minor tranquilizers* or *anxiolytics.*

•**ANTIDEPRESSANT DRUGS**•Psychotropic drugs that improve the moods of people with depression.

•**ANTIBIPOLAR DRUGS**•Psychotropic drugs that help stabilize the moods of people suffering from a bipolar mood disorder. Also called *mood stabilizers.*

•**ANTIPSYCHOTIC DRUGS**•Psychotropic drugs that help correct the confusion, hallucinations, and delusions found in psychotic disorders.

•**ELECTROCONVULSIVE THERAPY (ECT)**• A form of biological treatment, used primarily on depressed patients, in which a brain seizure is triggered as an electric current passes through electrodes attached to the patient's forehead.

•**NEUROSURGERY**•Brain surgery for mental disorders. Also called *psychosurgery.*

walking, running, or problem solving were particularly likely to be passed on from generation to generation to the present day.

The evolutionary position is less apparent, however, with regard to abnormal functioning. Why, for example, would genes that produce excessive fear responses—genes that may predispose people to anxiety disorders—be passed on from generation to generation? According to evolutionary theorists, the capacity to experience fear was, and in many instances still is, adaptive. Fear alerted individuals to dangers, threats, and losses, so that persons could avoid or escape potential problems. People who were particularly sensitive to danger—those with greater fear responses—were more likely to survive catastrophes, battles, and the like, and to reproduce, and so to pass on their fear genes. Of course, in today's world pressures and changes are more numerous, subtle, and complex than they were in the past, thus relegating many individuals with such genes to a near-endless stream of fear and arousal responses. However, say evolutionary theorists, such mismatches between genes and present-day environmental events should not hide the adaptive roots of the fear predispositions.

Actually, today's evolutionary theorists are interested in a combination of variables—adaptive behaviors of the past, genes, and the interaction between genes and current environmental events (Fabrega, 2004, 2002). Despite this broad scope, the evolutionary perspective is controversial in the clinical field and has been rejected by many biological and nonbiological theorists. Imprecise and at times impossible to research, this explanation requires leaps of faith that many scientists find unacceptable. Nevertheless, as genetic discoveries and insights have grown, interest in the possible causes of genetic differences and how they relate to current circumstances has grown as well, and evolutionary theories have received considerable attention.

VIRAL INFECTIONS AND ABNORMAL BEHAVIOR Another possible source of abnormal brain structure or biochemical dyfunctioning is *viral infections.* As we shall see in Chapter 14, for example, research suggests that *schizophrenia,* a disorder marked by delusions, hallucinations, or other departures from reality, may be related to exposure to certain viruses during childhood or *in utero,* before birth (Gourion et al., 2004; Koponen et al., 2004). Studies have found that the mothers of many individuals with this disorder contracted influenza or related viruses during their pregnancy. This and related pieces of circumstantial evidence suggest that a damaging virus may enter the fetus's brain and remain dormant there until the individual reaches puberty or young adulthood. At that time, activated by hormone changes or by another infection, the virus may produce the symptoms of schizophrenia. Interest in viral explanations of psychological disorders has been growing during the past decade, and, in fact, researchers have sometimes linked viruses to anxiety and mood disorders, as well as to psychotic disorders (Dale et al., 2004; Kim et al., 2004).

Biological Treatments

Biological practitioners look for certain kinds of clues when they try to understand abnormal behavior. Does the person's family have a history of that behavior, and hence a possible genetic predisposition to it? (Philip Berman's case history mentions that his mother was once hospitalized for depression.) Does the disorder seem to follow its own course? (Philip's depressed feelings were described as periodic; they seemed to come and go over the course of several years.) Is the behavior aggravated by factors that could have had a physiological effect? (Philip was having a drink when he flew into a jealous rage at the restaurant.)

Once the clinicians have pinpointed physical sources of dysfunctioning, they are in a better position to choose a biological course of treatment. The three leading kinds of biological treatments used today are *drug therapy, electroconvulsive therapy,* and *neurosurgery.* Drug therapy is by far the most common of these approaches; psychosurgery is infrequent.

In the 1950s, researchers discovered several effective **psychotropic medications,** drugs that mainly affect emotions and thought processes (see Figure 3-3). These drugs have greatly changed the outlook for a number of mental disorders and today are used

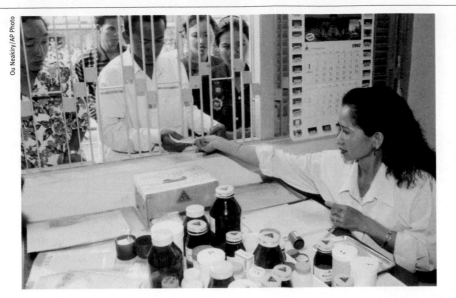

Ou Neakiry/AP Photo

Worldwide phenomenon *The psychotropic drug revolution has spread throughout the world. Here a nurse gives medications to patients at Cambodia's largest mental health facility.*

widely, either alone or with other forms of therapy. However, the psychotropic drug revolution has also produced some major problems. Many people believe, for example, that the drugs are overused. Moreover, while drugs are effective in many cases, they do not help everyone.

Four major psychotropic drug groups are used in therapy: antianxiety, antidepressant, antibipolar, and antipsychotic drugs. **Antianxiety drugs,** also called **minor tranquilizers** or **anxiolytics,** help reduce tension and anxiety. These drugs include *alprazolam* (trade name Xanax) and diazepam (Valium). **Antidepressant drugs** help improve the mood of people who are depressed. As we shall see in Chapter 9, these drugs, which include *fluoxetine* (Prozac) and *sertraline* (Zoloft), are able to help around 60 percent of those with depression. **Antibipolar drugs,** also called **mood stabilizers,** help stabilize the moods of those with a bipolar disorder, a condition marked by mood swings from mania to depression. One of the most widely used of these drugs is *lithium,* which, like the antidepressants, is helpful in approximately 60 percent of cases.

Finally, **antipsychotic drugs** help reduce the confusion, hallucinations, and delusions of *psychotic disorders,* disorders marked by a loss of contact with reality. Common antipsychotic drugs are *haloperidol* (Haldol) and *risperidone* (Risperdal). Research has shown that these drugs are more effective than any other single form of treatment for schizophrenia and other psychotic disorders, reducing symptoms in at least 65 percent of patients (Breier, 2001).

The second form of biological treatment, used primarily on depressed patients, is **electroconvulsive therapy (ECT).** Two electrodes are attached to a patient's forehead and an electrical current of 65 to 140 volts is passed briefly through the brain. The current causes a brain seizure that lasts up to a few minutes. After seven to nine ECT sessions, spaced two or three days apart, many patients feel considerably less depressed. The treatment is able to improve the mood of approximately 60 percent of depressed subjects (Pagnin et al., 2004). It is used on tens of thousands of depressed persons annually, particularly those whose depression fails to respond to other treatments.

A third form of biological treatment is **neurosurgery,** or **psychosurgery,** brain surgery for mental disorders. It is thought to have roots as far back as trephining, the prehistoric practice of chipping a hole in the skull of a person who behaved strangely. Modern procedures are derived from a technique first developed in the late 1930s by a Portuguese neuropsychiatrist, Antonio de Egas Moniz. In this procedure, known as a *lobotomy,* a surgeon cuts the connections between the brain's frontal lobes and the lower centers of the brain.

Today's brain surgery procedures are much more precise than the lobotomies of the past (Lambert & Kinsley, 2005). They have fewer unwanted effects and are apparently

Preclinical Phase (5 years)
New drug is developed and identified.
Drug is tested on animals, usually rats, to help determine its safety and efficacy.

Clinical Phase I: Safety Screening (1.5 years)
Investigators test drug on human subjects to determine its safety.
• Number of subjects: 10–100
• Typical cost: $10 million

Clinical Phase II: Preliminary Testing (2 years)
Investigators conduct studies with human subjects to determine how drug can best be evaluated and to obtain preliminary estimates of correct dosage and treatment procedures.
• Number of subjects: 50–500
• Typical cost: $20 million

Clinical Phase III: Final Testing (3.5 years)
Investigators conduct controlled studies to fully determine drug's efficacy and important side effects.
• Number of subjects: 300–30,000
• Typical cost: $45 million

Review by FDA (1.5 years)
Research is reviewed by FDA, and drug is approved or disapproved.

Postmarketing Surveillance (10 years)
Long after the drug is on the marketplace, testing continues and doctors' reports are gathered. Manufacturer must report any unexpected long-term effects and side effects.

FIGURE **3-3 How does a new drug reach the marketplace?** *It takes an average of 14 years and tens of millions of dollars for a pharmaceutical company in the United States to bring a newly discovered drug to market. The company must carefully follow steps that are mandated by law. (Adapted from Lemonick & Goldstein, 2002; Andreasen, 2001; Zivin, 2000.)*

Not that long ago *Before effective psychotropic drugs were developed, clinicians in mental institutions used techniques such as the "wet pack," designed for calming excited patients.*

helpful in some cases of severe depression, anxiety, and obsessive-compulsive disorder. Even so, they are considered experimental and are used only after certain severe disorders have continued for years without responding to any other form of treatment.

Assessing the Biological Model

Today the biological model enjoys considerable respect. Biological research constantly produces valuable new information. And biological treatments often bring great relief when other approaches have failed. At the same time, this model has its shortcomings. Some of its proponents seem to expect that all human behavior can be explained in biological terms and treated with biological methods. This view can limit rather than enhance our understanding of abnormal functioning (Kosslyn & Rosenberg, 2004). Our mental life is an interplay of biological and nonbiological factors, and it is important to understand that interplay rather than to focus on biological variables alone.

A second shortcoming is that much of the evidence for biological explanations is incomplete or inconclusive. Many brain studies, for example, are conducted on animals in whom symptoms of depression, anxiety, or some other abnormality have been produced by drugs, surgery, or experimental manipulation. Researchers can never be certain that the animals are experiencing the human disorder under investigation.

Finally, several of today's biological treatments are capable of producing significant undesirable effects. Antipsychotic drugs, for example, may produce movement problems such as severe shaking, bizarre-looking contractions of the face and body, and extreme restlessness. Clearly such costs must be addressed and weighed against the drug's benefits.

The Psychodynamic Model

The *psychodynamic model* is the oldest and most famous of the modern psychological models. Psychodynamic theorists believe that a person's behavior, whether normal or abnormal, is determined largely by underlying psychological forces of which he or she is not consciously aware. These internal forces are described as *dynamic*—that is, they interact with one another; and their interaction gives rise to behavior, thoughts, and emotions. Abnormal symptoms are viewed as the result of conflicts between these forces (Meissner, 2005).

Psychodynamic theorists would view Philip Berman as a person in conflict. They would want to explore his past experiences because, in their view, psychological conflicts are tied to early relationships and to traumatic experiences that occurred during childhood. Psychodynamic theories rest on the *deterministic* assumption that no symptom or behavior is "accidental": all behavior is determined by past experiences. Thus Philip's hatred for his mother, his memories of her as cruel and overbearing, the weakness and ineffectiveness of his father, and the birth of a younger brother when Philip was 10 may all be important to the understanding of his current problems.

The psychodynamic model was first formulated by the Viennese neurologist Sigmund Freud (1856–1939) at the turn of the twentieth century. First, Freud worked with the physician Josef Breuer (1842–1925), conducting experiments on hypnosis and hysterical illnesses—mysterious physical ailments with no apparent medical cause. In a famous case, Breuer had treated a woman he called "Anna O.," whose hysterical symptoms included paralysis of the legs and right arm, deafness, and disorganized speech. Breuer placed the woman under hypnosis, expecting that suggestions made to her in that state would help rid her of her hysterical symptoms. While she was under hypnosis, however, she began to talk about traumatic past events and to express deeply felt

Freud takes a closer look at Freud *Sigmund Freud, founder of psychoanalytic theory and therapy, contemplates a sculptured bust of himself in 1931 at his village home in Potzlein, near Vienna. As Freud and the bust go eyeball to eyeball, one can only imagine what conclusions each is drawing about the other.*

emotions. This venting of repressed memories seemed to enhance the effectiveness of the treatment. Anna referred to it as her "talking cure."

Building on this early work, Freud developed the theory of *psychoanalysis* to explain both normal and abnormal psychological functioning as well as a corresponding method of treatment, a conversational approach also called psychoanalysis. During the early 1900s, Freud and several of his colleagues in the Vienna Psychoanalytic Society—including Carl Gustav Jung (1875–1961) and Alfred Adler (1870–1937)—became the most influential clinical theorists in the Western world.

How Did Freud Explain Normal and Abnormal Functioning?

Freud believed that three central forces shape the personality—instinctual needs, rational thinking, and moral standards. All these forces, he believed, operate at the unconscious level, unavailable to immediate awareness; and he believed them to be dynamic, or interactive. Freud called the forces the *id, ego,* and *superego.*

THE ID Freud used the term **id** to denote instinctual needs, drives, and impulses. The id operates in accordance with the *pleasure principle;* that is, it always seeks gratification. Freud also believed that all id instincts tend to be sexual, noting that from the very earliest stages of life a child's pleasure is obtained from nursing, defecating, masturbating, or engaging in other activities that he considered to have sexual overtones. He further suggested that a person's *libido,* or sexual energy, fuels the id.

THE EGO During our early years we come to recognize that our environment will not meet every instinctual need. Our mother, for example, is not always available to do our bidding. A part of the id separates off and becomes the **ego.** Like the id, the ego unconsciously seeks gratification, but it does so in accordance with the *reality principle,* the knowledge we acquire through experience that it can be unacceptable to express our id impulses outright. The ego, employing reason, guides us to know when we can and cannot express those impulses.

The ego develops basic strategies, called **ego defense mechanisms,** to control unacceptable id impulses and avoid or reduce the anxiety they arouse. The most basic defense mechanism, *repression,* prevents unacceptable impulses from ever reaching consciousness. There are many other ego defense mechanisms, and each of us tends to favor some over others (see Table 3-2 on the next page).

THE SUPEREGO The **superego** grows from the ego, just as the ego grows out of the id. As we learn from our parents that many of our id impulses are unacceptable, we unconsciously adopt, or *introject,* our parents' values. Judging ourselves by their standards, we feel good when we uphold their values; conversely, when we go against them, we feel guilty. In short, we develop a *conscience.*

According to Freud, these three parts of the personality—the id, the ego, and the superego—are often in some degree of conflict. A healthy personality is one in which an effective working relationship, an acceptable compromise, has formed among the three forces. If the id, ego, and superego are in excessive conflict, the person's behavior may show signs of dysfunction.

Freudians would therefore view Philip Berman as someone whose personality forces have a poor working relationship. His ego and superego are unable to control his id impulses, which lead him repeatedly to act in impulsive and often dangerous ways—suicide gestures, jealous rages, job resignations, outbursts of temper, frequent arguments.

DEVELOPMENTAL STAGES Freud proposed that at each stage of development, from infancy to maturity, new events and pressures challenge individuals and require adjustments in their id, ego, and superego. If the adjustments are successful, they lead to personal growth. If not, the person may become **fixated,** or entrapped, at an early stage of development. Then all subsequent development suffers, and the individual may well be headed for abnormal functioning in the future. Because parents are the key environmental figures during the early years of life, they are often seen as the cause of improper development.

•**ID**•According to Freud, the psychological force that produces instinctual needs, drives, and impulses.

•**EGO**•According to Freud, the psychological force that employs reason and operates in accordance with the reality principle.

•**EGO DEFENSE MECHANISMS**•According to psychoanalytic theory, strategies developed by the ego to control unacceptable id impulses and to avoid or reduce the anxiety they arouse.

•**SUPEREGO**•According to Freud, the psychological force that represents a person's values and ideals.

•**FIXATION**•According to Freud, a condition in which the id, ego, and superego do not mature properly and are frozen at an early stage of development.

Critical training *Freud believed that toilet training is a critical developmental experience. Children whose training is too harsh may become "fixated" at the anal stage and develop an "anal character"—stubborn, contrary, stingy, or controlling.*

Laura Dwight, New York, NY

Table 3-2

Defense Mechanisms to the Rescue

Defense	Operation	Example
Repression	Person avoids anxiety by simply not allowing painful or dangerous thoughts to become conscious.	An executive's desire to run amok and attack his boss and colleagues at a board meeting is denied access to his awareness.
Denial	Person simply refuses to acknowledge the existence of an external source of anxiety.	You are not prepared for tomorrow's final exam, but you tell yourself that it's not actually an important exam and that there's no good reason not to go to a movie tonight.
Projection	Person attributes own unacceptable impulses, motives, or desires to other individuals.	The executive who repressed his destructive desires may project his anger onto his boss and claim that it is actually the boss who is hostile.
Rationalization	Person creates a socially acceptable reason for an action that actually reflects unacceptable motives.	A student explains away poor grades by citing the importance of the "total experience" of going to college and claiming that too much emphasis on grades would actually interfere with a well-rounded education.
Reaction formation	Person adopts behavior that is the exact opposite of impulses he or she is afraid to acknowledge.	A man experiences homosexual feelings and responds by taking a strong antihomosexual stance.
Displacement	Person displaces hostility away from a dangerous object and onto a safer substitute.	After your parking spot was taken, you released your pent-up anger by starting a fight with your roommate.
Intellectualization (isolation)	Person represses emotional reactions in favor of overly logical response to a problem.	A woman who has been beaten and raped gives a detached, methodical description of the effects that such attacks may have on victims.
Regression	Person retreats from an upsetting conflict to an early developmental stage at which no one is expected to behave maturely or responsibly.	A boy who cannot cope with the anger he feels toward his rejecting mother regresses to infantile behavior, soiling his clothes and no longer taking care of his basic needs.
Sublimation	Person expresses sexual and aggressive energy in ways that are acceptable to society.	Athletes, artists, surgeons, and other highly dedicated and skilled people may be reaching their high levels of accomplishment by directing otherwise potentially harmful energies into their work.

Freud named each stage of development after the body area, or erogenous zone, that he considered most important to the child at that time. For example, he referred to the first 18 months of life as the *oral stage*. During this stage, children fear that the mother who feeds and comforts them will disappear. Children whose mothers consistently fail to gratify their oral needs may become fixated at the oral stage and display an "oral character" throughout their lives, marked by extreme dependence or extreme mistrust. Such persons are particularly prone to develop depression. As we shall see in later chapters, Freud linked fixations at the other stages of development—*anal* (18 months to 3 years of age), *phallic* (3 to 5 years), *latency* (5 to 12 years), and *genital* (12 years to adulthood)—to yet other kinds of psychological dysfunction.

Like mother, like daughter *According to Freud, boys become attracted to their mothers and girls to their fathers during the phallic stage. Children repress these taboo impulses and identify instead with the parent of the same sex, acting like that parent in every way.*

How Do Other Psychodynamic Explanations Differ from Freud's?

Personal and professional differences between Freud and his colleagues led to a split in the Vienna Psychoanalytic Society early in the twentieth century. Carl Jung, Alfred Adler, and others developed new theories. Although the new theories departed from Freud's ideas in important ways, each held on to Freud's belief that human functioning is shaped by dynamic (interacting) psychological forces. Thus all such theories, including Freud's, are referred to as *psychodynamic*.

Three of today's most influential psychodynamic theories are ego theory, self theory, and object relations theory. **Ego theorists** emphasize the role of the ego and consider it a more independent and powerful force than Freud did (Sharf, 2004). **Self theorists,** in contrast, empasize the importance of developing a healthy self-interest and give greatest attention to the role of the *self*—the unified personality. They believe that the basic human motive is to strengthen the wholeness of the self (Mollon, 2003; Kohut, 2001, 1984, 1977). **Object relations theorists** propose that people are motivated mainly by a need to have relationships with others and that severe problems in the relationships between children and their caregivers may lead to abnormal development (Kernberg, 2005, 2001, 1997; Scharff & Scharff, 2005; Goldstein, 2002).

Psychodynamic Therapies

Psychodynamic therapies range from Freudian psychoanalysis to modern therapies based on self theory or object relations theory. All seek to uncover past traumas and the inner conflicts that have resulted from them. All try to help clients resolve, or settle, those conflicts and to resume personal development.

According to most psychodynamic therapists, the search for insight cannot be rushed or imposed. Therapists must subtly guide the explorations so that the patients discover their underlying problems for themselves. To aid in the process, the therapists rely on such techniques as *free association, therapist interpretation, catharsis,* and *working through.*

FREE ASSOCIATION In psychodynamic therapies, the patient is responsible for starting and leading each discussion. The therapist tells the patient to describe any thought, feeling, or image that comes to mind, even if it seems unimportant or irrelevant. This practice is known as **free association.** The therapist expects that the patient's associations will eventually uncover unconscious events and underlying dynamics. Notice how free association helps this New Yorker to discover threatening impulses and conflicts within herself:

> *Patient:* So I started walking, and walking, and decided to go behind the museum and walk through Central Park. So I walked and went through a back field and felt very excited and wonderful. I saw a park bench next to a clump of bushes and sat down. There was a rustle behind me and I got frightened. I thought of men concealing themselves in the bushes. I thought of the sex perverts I read about in Central Park. I wondered if there was someone behind me exposing himself. The idea is repulsive, but exciting too. I think of father now and feel excited. I think of an erect penis. This is connected with my father. There is something about this pushing in my mind. I don't know what it is, like on the border of my memory. (*Pause*)
>
> *Therapist:* Mm-hmm. (*Pause*) On the border of your memory?
>
> *Patient:* (*The patient breathes rapidly and seems to be under great tension*) As a little girl, I slept with my father. I get a funny feeling. I get a funny feeling over my skin, tingly-like. It's a strange feeling, like a blindness,

"I am your father, Luke." *This light-saber fight between Luke Skywalker and Darth Vader highlights the most famous, and contentious, father-son relationship in movie history. According to Sigmund Freud, however, all fathers and sons experience significant tensions and conflicts that they must work through, even in the absence of the special pressures faced by Luke and his father in the* Star Wars *series. Freud proposed, for example, that during the phallic stage (3 to 5 years of age), all boys become sexually attracted to their mothers and see their father as a rival—an unconscious conflict that must be resolved in order for the child's development to proceed satisfactorily.*

•**EGO THEORY**•The psychodynamic theory that emphasizes the role of the ego and considers it an independent force.

•**SELF THEORY**•The psychodynamic theory that emphasizes the role of the self—our unified personality.

•**OBJECT RELATIONS THEORY**•The psychodynamic theory that views the desire for relationships as the key motivating force in human behavior.

•**FREE ASSOCIATION**•A psychodynamic technique in which the patient describes any thought, feeling, or image that comes to mind, even if it seems unimportant.

•**RESISTANCE**•An unconscious refusal to participate fully in therapy.

•**TRANSFERENCE**•According to psychodynamic theorists, the redirection toward the psychotherapist of feelings associated with important figures in a patient's life, now or in the past.

•**DREAM**•A series of ideas and images that form during sleep.

•**CATHARSIS**•The reliving of past repressed feelings in order to settle internal conflicts and overcome problems.

•**WORKING THROUGH**•The psychoanalytic process of facing conflicts, reinterpreting feelings, and overcoming one's problems.

•**RELATIONAL PSYCHOANALYTIC THERAPY**• A form of psychodynamic therapy that considers therapists to be active participants in the formation of patients' feelings and reactions, and therefore calls for therapists to disclose their own experiences and feelings in discussions with patients.

> like not seeing something. My mind blurs and spreads over anything I look at. I've had this feeling off and on since I walked in the park. My mind seems to blank off like I can't think or absorb anything.
>
> *(Wolberg, 1967, p. 662)*

THERAPIST INTERPRETATION Psychodynamic therapists listen carefully as patients talk, looking for clues, drawing tentative conclusions, and sharing interpretations when they think the patient is ready to hear them. Interpretations of three phenomena are particularly important—*resistance, transference,* and *dreams.*

Patients are showing **resistance,** an unconscious refusal to participate fully in therapy, when they suddenly cannot free associate or when they change a subject to avoid a painful discussion. They demonstrate **transference** when they act and feel toward the therapist as they did or do toward important persons in their lives, especially their parents, siblings, and spouses. Consider again the woman who walked in Central Park. As she continues talking, the therapist helps her to explore her transference:

> *Patient:* I get so excited by what is happening here. I feel I'm being held back by needing to be nice. I'd like to blast loose sometimes, but I don't dare.
> *Therapist:* Because you fear my reaction?
> *Patient:* The worst thing would be that you wouldn't like me. You wouldn't speak to me friendly; you wouldn't smile; you'd feel you can't treat me and discharge me from treatment. But I know this isn't so, I know it.
> *Therapist:* Where do you think these attitudes come from?
> *Patient:* When I was nine years old, I read a lot about great men in history. I'd quote them and be dramatic. I'd want a sword at my side; I'd dress like an Indian. Mother would scold me. Don't frown, don't talk so much. Sit on your hands, over and over again. I did all kinds of things. I was a naughty child. She told me I'd be hurt. Then at fourteen I fell off a horse and broke my back. I had to be in bed. Mother told me on the day I went riding not to, that I'd get hurt because the ground was frozen. I was a stubborn, self-willed child. Then I went against her will and suffered an accident that changed my life, a fractured back. Her attitude was, "I told you so." I was put in a cast and kept in bed for months.
>
> *(Wolberg, 1967, p. 662)*

Finally, many psychodynamic therapists try to help patients interpret their **dreams** (see Table 3-3). Freud (1924) called dreams the "royal road to the unconscious." He believed that repression and other defense mechanisms operate less completely during sleep and that dreams, if correctly recalled and interpreted (see Figure 3-4), can reveal unconscious instincts, needs, and wishes. Freud identified two kinds of dream content, manifest and latent. *Manifest content* is the consciously remembered dream; *latent content* its symbolic meaning. To interpret a dream, therapists must translate its manifest content into its latent content.

CATHARSIS Insight must be an emotional as well as intellectual process. Psychodynamic therapists believe that patients must experience **catharsis,** a reliving of past repressed feelings, if they are to settle internal conflicts and overcome their problems.

WORKING THROUGH A single episode of interpretation and catharsis will not change the way a person functions. The patient and therapist must examine the same issues over and over in the course of many sessions, each time with greater clarity. This process, called **working through,** usually takes a long time, often years. When psychodynamic treatment is scheduled once a week—as most forms of it now are—it is properly known as *psychodynamic,* or *psychoanalytic, therapy.* The term *psychoanalysis,* or simply *analysis,* is reserved for therapy given on a daily basis.

>>**Q & A**

Does the unconscious differ from the subconscious?

Yes. The **unconscious** consists of deep-seated thoughts, needs, or desires that are not organized into conscious awareness. Often they are thoughts that have been repressed because the person cannot accept them. The **subconscious** consists of thoughts and needs that lie much closer to conscious awareness. They are unnoticed, rather than repressed, and can be brought to the surface relatively easily (Padwa, 1996). <<

Table 3-3

Percent of Subjects Who Have Had Common Dreams

	Men	Women
Being chased or pursued, not injured	78%	83%
Sexual experiences	85	73
Falling	73	74
School, teachers, studying	57	71
Arriving too late, e.g., for a train	55	62
On the verge of falling	53	60
Trying to do something repeatedly	55	53
A person living as dead	43	59
Flying or soaring through the air	58	44
Sensing a presence vividly	44	50
Failing an examination	37	48
Being physically attacked	40	44
Being frozen with fright	32	44
A person now dead as living	37	39
Being a child again	33	38

Source: Kantrowitz & Springen, 2004

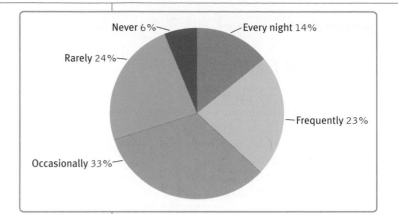

FIGURE **3-4** **Remembering our dreams** *Although most adults dream several times each night, only 14 percent of them are able to remember their dreams every night. In contrast, 30 percent rarely or never recall any of their dreams. Children recall dreams even less frequently. (Adapted from Kantrowitz & Springen, 2004; Strauch, 2004.)*

CONTEMPORARY TRENDS IN PSYCHODYNAMIC THERAPY The nature of psychodynamic therapy has continued to evolve. The past 30 years have witnessed substantial changes, especially in the way a large number of psychodynamic therapists conduct sessions. An increased demand for focused, time-limited psychotherapies has resulted in efforts to make psychodynamic therapy more efficient and cost-effective. Two contemporary psychodynamic approaches that illustrate this trend are *short-term psychodynamic therapies* and *relational psychoanalytic therapy*.

SHORT-TERM PSYCHODYNAMIC THERAPIES In several short versions of psychodynamic therapy, patients choose a single problem—a *dynamic focus*—to work on, such as difficulty getting along with other people (Charman, 2004; Hoyt, 2003). The therapist and patient focus on this problem throughout the treatment and work only on the psychodynamic issues that relate to it (such as unresolved oral needs). Only a limited number of studies have tested the effectiveness of these short-term psychodynamic therapies, but their findings do suggest that the approaches are sometimes quite helpful to patients (Muratori et al., 2005; Leichsenring et al., 2004).

RELATIONAL PSYCHOANALYTIC THERAPY Whereas Freud believed that psychodynamic therapists should take on the role of a neutral, distant expert during a treatment session, a contemporary school of psychodynamic therapy referred to as **relational psychoanalytic therapy** argues that therapists are key figures in the lives of patients—figures whose reactions and beliefs should be included in the therapy process (Levenson, 1982). In contrast to the classical psychodynamic belief that patients' feelings of transference represent distortions in their view of a neutral therapist, relational therapists see themselves as active participants in the development of the patient's reactions to the therapist (Reis, 2005; Mitchell, 1997). Thus, a key principle of relational therapy is that therapists should disclose things about themselves (their own reactions, for example) and try to establish more egalitarian relationships with patients.

Henry Martin/Cartoonbank.com

"Do you think your failure to bloom could be caused not just by improper location but also by a fear of having your blooms compared with those of other African violets?"

[BOX **3-1**]

Maternal Instincts

On an August day in 1996, a 3-year-old boy climbed over a barrier at the Brookfield Zoo in Illinois and fell 24 feet onto the cement floor of the gorilla compound. An 8-year-old 160-pound gorilla named Binti-Jua picked up the child and cradled his limp body in her arms. The child's mother, fearing the worst, screamed out, "The gorilla's got my baby!" But Binti protected the boy as if he were her own. She held off the other gorillas, rocked him gently, and carried him to the entrance of the gorilla area, where rescue workers were waiting. Within hours, the incident was seen on videotape replays around the world, and Binti was being hailed for her maternal instincts.

When Binti was herself an infant, she had been removed from her mother, Lulu, who did not have enough milk. To make up for this loss, keepers at the zoo worked around the clock to nurture Binti; she was always being held in someone's arms. When Binti became pregnant at age 6, trainers were afraid that the early separation from her mother would leave her ill prepared to raise an infant of her own. So they gave her mothering lessons and taught her to nurse and carry around a stuffed doll.

Clinical theorists have had a field day interpreting the gorilla's gentle and nurturing care for the child, each within his or her preferred theory. Many *evolutionary theorists,* for example, view the behavior as an expression of the maternal instincts that have helped the gorilla's species to survive and evolve. *Object relations theorists* suggest that the gorilla was expressing feelings of attachment and bonding, already experienced with her own 17-month-old daughter. And *behaviorists* hold that the gorilla may have been imitating the nurturing behavior that she had observed in human models during her own infancy or enacting the parenting training that she had received during her pregnancy. While the clinical field tries frantically to sort out this issue, Binti-Jua, the heroic gorilla, has returned to her relatively quiet and predictable life at the zoo.

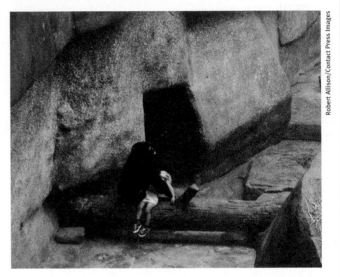

Robert Allison/Contact Press Images

•**CONDITIONING**•A simple form of learning.

•**OPERANT CONDITIONING**•A process of learning in which behavior that leads to satisfying consequences is likely to be repeated.

•**MODELING**•A process of learning in which an individual acquires responses by observing and imitating others.

•**CLASSICAL CONDITIONING**•A process of learning by temporal association in which two events that repeatedly occur close together in time become fused in a person's mind and produce the same response.

Assessing the Psychodynamic Model

Freud and his followers have helped change the way abnormal functioning is understood (Corey, 2004, 2001; Nietzel et al., 2003). Largely because of their work, a wide range of theorists today look for answers and explanations outside biological processes. Psychodynamic theorists have also helped us to understand that abnormal functioning may be rooted in the same processes as normal functioning (see Box 3-1). Psychological conflict is a common experience; it leads to abnormal functioning only if the conflict becomes excessive.

Freud and his many followers have also had a monumental impact on treatment. They were the first to apply theory and techniques systematically to treatment. They were also the first to demonstrate the potential of psychological, as opposed to biological, treatment, and their ideas have served as starting points for many other psychological treatments.

At the same time, the psychodynamic model has shortcomings. Its concepts tend to be hard to define and to research (Nietzel et al., 2003). Because processes such as id drives, ego defenses, and fixation are abstract and supposedly operate at an unconscious level, there is no way of knowing for certain if they are occurring. Not surprisingly, then, psychodynamic explanations and treatments have received limited research support, and psychodynamic theorists have been forced to rely largely on evidence provided by individual case studies (Prochaska & Norcross, 2003). Nevertheless, 19 percent of today's clinical psychologists identify themselves as psychodynamic therapists (Prochaska & Norcross, 2003). And, interestingly, many practitioners of other models report that when they seek help for their own problems, psychodynamic therapy is their choice (Norcross & Prochaska, 1984).

The Behavioral Model

Like psychodynamic theorists, behavioral theorists believe that our actions are determined largely by our experiences in life. However, the *behavioral model* concentrates wholly on *behaviors,* the responses an organism makes to its environment. Behaviors can be external (going to work, say) or internal (having a feeling or thought). In the behavioral view, people are the sum total of their learned behaviors. Behavioral theorists, therefore, base their explanations and treatments on *principles of learning,* the processes by which these behaviors change in response to the environment.

Many learned behaviors help people to cope with daily challenges and to lead happy, productive lives. However, abnormal behaviors also can be learned. Behaviorists who try to explain Philip Berman's problems might view him as a man who has received improper training: he has learned behaviors that offend others and repeatedly work against him.

Whereas the psychodynamic model had its beginnings in the clinical work of physicians, the behavioral model began in laboratories where psychologists were running experiments on **conditioning,** simple forms of learning. The researchers manipulated *stimuli* and *rewards,* then observed how their manipulations affected their subjects' responses.

During the 1950s, many clinicians became frustrated with what they viewed as the vagueness and slowness of the psychodynamic model. Some of them began to apply the principles of learning to the study and treatment of psychological problems. Their efforts gave rise to the behavioral model of abnormality.

How Do Behaviorists Explain Abnormal Functioning?

Learning theorists have identified several forms of conditioning, and each may produce abnormal behavior as well as normal behavior. In **operant conditioning,** for example, humans and animals learn to behave in certain ways as a result of receiving *rewards*—any satisfying consequences—whenever they do so. In **modeling,** individuals learn responses simply by observing other individuals and repeating their behaviors.

In a third form of conditioning, **classical conditioning,** learning occurs by *temporal association*. When two events repeatedly occur close together in time, they become fused in a person's mind, and before long the person responds in the same way to both events. If one event produces a response of joy, the other brings joy as well; if one event brings feelings of relief, so does the other. A closer look at this form of conditioning illustrates how the behavioral model can account for abnormal functioning.

Ivan Pavlov (1849–1936), a famous Russian physiologist, first demonstrated classical conditioning with animal studies. He placed a bowl of meat powder before a dog, producing the natural response that all dogs have to meat: they start to salivate (see Figure 3-5). Next Pavlov added a step: just before presenting the dog with meat powder, he sounded a metronome. After several such pairings of metronome tone and presentation of meat powder, Pavlov noted that the dog began to salivate as soon as it heard the metronome. The dog had learned to salivate in response to a sound.

FIGURE **3-5 Working for Pavlov** *In Ivan Pavlov's experimental device, the dog's saliva was collected in a tube as it was secreted, and the amount was recorded on a revolving cylinder called a kymograph. The experimenter observed the dog through a one-way glass window.*

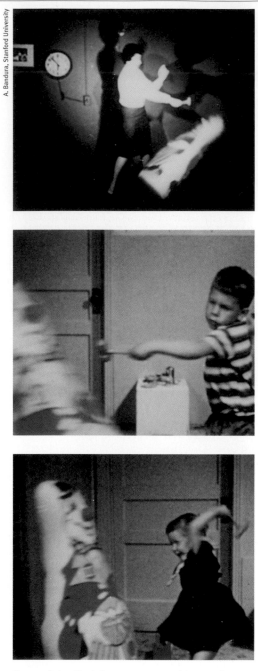

A. Bandura, Stanford University

See and do *Modeling may account for some forms of abnormal behavior. A well-known study by Albert Bandura and his colleagues (1963) demonstrated that children learned to abuse a doll by observing an adult hit it. Children who had not been exposed to the adult model did not mistreat the doll.*

•**SYSTEMATIC DESENSITIZATION**•A behavioral treatment in which clients with phobias learn to react calmly instead of with intense fear to the objects or situations they dread.

In the vocabulary of classical conditioning, the meat in this demonstration is an *unconditioned stimulus* (*US*). It elicits the *unconditioned response* (*UR*) of salivation, that is, a natural response with which the dog is born. The sound of the metronome is a *conditioned stimulus* (*CS*), a previously neutral stimulus that comes to be linked with meat in the dog's mind. As such, it too produces a salivation response. When the salivation response is produced by the conditioned stimulus rather than by the unconditioned stimulus, it is called a *conditioned response* (*CR*).

BEFORE CONDITIONING	AFTER CONDITIONING
CS: Tone → No response	CS: Tone → CR: Salivation
US: Meat → UR: Salivation	US: Meat → UR: Salivation

If, after conditioning, the conditioned stimulus is repeatedly presented alone, without being paired with the unconditioned stimulus, it will eventually stop eliciting the conditioned response. When Pavlov stopped pairing the metronome tone and meat powder, for example, the dog salivated less and less in response to the tone. The conditioned response was undergoing *extinction*.

Classical conditioning explains many familiar behaviors. The romantic feelings a young man experiences when he smells his girlfriend's perfume, say, may represent a conditioned response. Initially this perfume may have had limited emotional effect on him, but because the fragrance was present during several romantic encounters, it too came to elicit a romantic response.

Abnormal behaviors, too, can be acquired by classical conditioning. Consider a young boy who is repeatedly frightened by a neighbor's large German shepherd dog. Whenever the child walks past the neighbor's front yard, the dog barks loudly and lunges at him, stopped only by a rope tied to the porch. In this unfortunate situation, the boy's parents are not surprised to discover that he develops a fear of dogs. They are stumped, however, by another intense fear the child displays, a fear of sand. They cannot understand why he cries whenever they take him to the beach and screams in fear if sand even touches his skin.

Where did this fear of sand come from? Classical conditioning. It turns out that a big sandbox is set up in the neighbor's front yard for the dog to play in. Every time the dog barks and lunges at the boy, the sandbox is there too. After repeated pairings of this kind, the child comes to fear sand as much as he fears the dog.

Behavioral Therapies

Behavioral therapy aims to identify the behaviors that are causing a person's problems and then tries to replace them with more appropriate ones, by applying the principles of classical conditioning, operant conditioning, or modeling. The therapist's attitude toward the client is that of teacher rather than healer. A person's early life matters only for the clues it can provide to current conditioning processes.

Classical conditioning treatments, for example, may be used to change abnormal reactions to particular stimuli. **Systematic desensitization** is one such method, often applied in cases of *phobia*—a specific and unreasonable fear. In this step-by-step procedure, clients learn to react calmly instead of with intense fear to the objects or situations they dread (Wolpe, 1997, 1995, 1990). First, they are taught the skill of relaxation over the course of several sessions. Next, they construct a *fear hierarchy,* a list of feared objects or situations, starting with those that are less feared and ending with the ones that are most dreaded. Here is the hierarchy developed by a man who was afraid of criticism, especially about his mental stability:

1. Friend on the street: "Hi, how are you?"
2. Friend on the street: "How are you feeling these days?"
3. Sister: "You've got to be careful so they don't put you in the hospital."
4. Wife: "You shouldn't drink beer while you are taking medicine."
5. Mother: "What's the matter, don't you feel good?"
6. Wife: "It's just you yourself, it's all in your head."

"Virtual" exposure *In the behavioral approach of desensitization, clients overcome phobias by confronting feared objects or situations while they place themselves in a state of relaxation. In recent years, virtual reality software has enabled clients to more vividly experience the fearful objects and situations during their treatment sessions. Here an individual with a flying phobia wears a virtual reality headset that takes him on a simulated airplane flight. The computer screen mirrors what he is seeing in his headset.*

7. Service station attendant: "What are you shaking for?"
8. Neighbor borrows rake: "Is there something wrong with your leg? Your knees are shaking."
9. Friend on the job: "Is your blood pressure okay?"
10. Service station attendant: "You are pretty shaky, are you crazy or something?"

(Marquis & Morgan, 1969, p. 28)

Desensitization therapists next have their clients either imagine or actually confront each item on the hierarchy while in a state of relaxation. In step-by-step pairings of feared items and relaxation, clients move up the hierarchy until at last they can face every one of the items without experiencing fear. As we shall see in Chapter 5, research has shown systematic desensitization and other classical conditioning techniques to be effective in treating phobias (Cottraux, 2005; Wiederhold & Wiederhold, 2005).

Assessing the Behavioral Model

The number of behavioral clinicians has grown steadily since the 1950s, and the behavioral model has become a powerful force in the clinical field. Various behavioral theories have been proposed over the years, and many treatment techniques have been developed. As we can see in Figure 3-6, approximately 13 percent of today's clinical psychologists report that their approach is mainly behavioral (Prochaska & Norcross, 2003).

Perhaps the greatest appeal of the behavioral model is that it can be tested in the laboratory, whereas psychodynamic theories generally cannot. The behaviorists' basic concepts—stimulus, response, and reward—can be observed and measured. Even more important, the results of research have lent considerable support to the behavioral model. Experimenters have successfully used the principles of learning to create clinical symptoms in laboratory subjects, suggesting that psychological disorders may indeed develop in the same way. In addition, research has found that behavioral treatments can be helpful to people with specific fears, compulsive behavior, social deficits, mental retardation, and other problems (Cottraux, 2005; Clark, 2004).

At the same time, research has also revealed weaknesses in the model. Certainly behavioral researchers have produced specific symptoms in subjects. But are these symptoms *ordinarily* acquired in this way? There is still no indisputable evidence that most people with psychological disorders are victims of improper conditioning. Similarly, behavioral therapies have limitations. The improvements

FIGURE 3-6 **Theoretical orientations of today's clinical psychologists** *In one survey, 27 percent of clinical psychologists labeled themselves as "eclectic," 24 percent considered themselves "cognitive," and 19 percent called their orientation "psychodynamic." (Adapted from Prochaska & Norcross, 2003; Norcross et al., 1997.)*

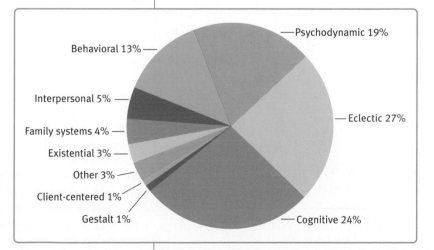

Psychodynamic 19%
Behavioral 13%
Interpersonal 5%
Family systems 4%
Existential 3%
Other 3%
Client-centered 1%
Gestalt 1%
Eclectic 27%
Cognitive 24%

Margaret Norton/AP Photo

Conditioning for fun and profit *Pet owners have discovered that they can teach animals a wide assortment of tricks by using the principles of conditioning. Only 3 percent of all dogs have learned to "sing," while 21 percent know how to sit, the most common dog trick. (Pet Food Institute.)*

The Far Side © Farworks, Inc. Reprinted with permission of Universal Press Syndicate

Stimulus, response! Stimulus, response! Don't you ever think?"

noted in the therapist's office do not always extend to real life. Nor do they necessarily last without continued therapy.

Finally, some critics hold that the behavioral view is too simplistic, that its concepts fail to account for the complexity of behavior. In 1977 Albert Bandura, the behaviorist who earlier had identified modeling as a key conditioning process, argued that in order to feel happy and function effectively people must develop a positive sense of **self-efficacy.** That is, they must know that they can master and perform needed behaviors whenever necessary. Other behaviorists of the 1960s and 1970s similarly recognized that human beings engage in *cognitive behaviors,* such as anticipating or interpreting—ways of thinking that until then had been largely ignored in behavioral theory and therapy. These individuals developed *cognitive-behavioral theories* that took unseen cognitive behaviors into greater account (Meichenbaum, 1993; Goldiamond, 1965).

Cognitive-behavioral theorists bridge the behavioral model and the cognitive model, the view we turn to next. On the one hand, their explanations are based squarely on learning principles. These theorists believe, for example, that cognitive processes are learned by classical conditioning, operant conditioning, and modeling. On the other hand, cognitive-behavioral theorists share with other kinds of cognitive theorists a belief that the ability to think is the most important aspect of human functioning.

The Cognitive Model

Philip Berman, like the rest of us, has *cognitive* abilities—special intellectual capacities to think, remember, and anticipate. These abilities can help him accomplish a great deal in life. Yet they can also work against him. As he thinks about his experiences, Philip may develop false ideas. He may misinterpret experiences in ways that lead to poor decisions, maladaptive responses, and painful emotions.

In the early 1960s two clinicians, Albert Ellis (1962) and Aaron Beck (1967), proposed that cognitive processes are at the center of behavior, thought, and emotions and that we can best understand abnormal functioning by looking to cognition—a perspective known as the *cognitive model.* Ellis and Beck claimed that clinicians must ask questions about the assumptions and attitudes that color a client's perceptions, the thoughts running through that person's mind, and the conclusions they are leading to. Other theorists and therapists soon embraced and expanded their ideas and techniques.

How Do Cognitive Theorists Explain Abnormal Functioning?

To cognitive theorists, we are all artists. We reproduce and create the world in our minds as we try to understand the events going on around us. If we are effective artists, our cognitions tend to be accurate (they agree with the perceptions of others) and useful. If we are ineffective artists, we may create a cognitive inner world that is painful and harmful to ourselves.

Abnormal functioning can result from several kinds of cognitive problems. Some people may make *assumptions* and adopt *attitudes* that are disturbing and inaccurate (Ellis, 2004; Brown & Beck, 2002). Philip Berman, for example, often seems to assume that his past history has locked him in his present situation. He believes that he was victimized by his parents and that he is now forever doomed by his past. He seems to approach all new experiences and relationships with expectations of failure and disaster.

Illogical thinking processes are another source of abnormal functioning, according to cognitive theorists. Beck (2004, 2002, 1993, 1967), for example, has found that some people consistently think in illogical ways and keep arriving at self-defeating conclusions. As we shall see in Chapter 8, he has identified a number of illogical thought processes regularly found in depression, such as *overgeneralization,* the drawing of broad negative conclusions on the basis of a single insignificant event. One depressed student couldn't remember the date of Columbus's third voyage to America during a history class. Overgeneralizing, she spent the rest of the day in despair over her invincible ignorance.

Cognitive Therapies

According to cognitive therapists, people with psychological disorders can overcome their problems by developing new, more functional ways of thinking. Because different forms of abnormality may involve different kinds of cognitive dysfunctioning, cognitive therapists have developed a number of strategies. Beck (2004, 2002, 1976, 1967), for example, has developed an approach that is widely used in cases of depression.

In Beck's approach, called simply **cognitive therapy,** therapists help clients recognize the negative thoughts, biased interpretations, and errors in logic that dominate their thinking and, according to Beck, cause them to feel depressed. Therapists also guide clients to challenge their dysfunctional thoughts, try out new interpretations, and ultimately apply the new ways of thinking in their daily lives. As we shall see in Chapter 9, people with depression who are treated with Beck's approach improve much more than those who receive no treatment.

In the excerpt that follows, a cognitive therapist guides a depressed 26-year-old graduate student to recognize the link between the way she interprets her experiences and the way she feels and to begin questioning the accuracy of her interpretations:

> *Therapist:* How do you understand it?
> *Patient:* I get depressed when things go wrong. Like when I fail a test.
> *Therapist:* How can failing a test make you depressed?
> *Patient:* Well, if I fail I'll never get into law school.
> *Therapist:* So failing the test means a lot to you. But if failing a test could drive people into clinical depression, wouldn't you expect everyone who failed the test to have a depression? . . . Did everyone who failed get depressed enough to require treatment?
> *Patient:* No, but it depends on how important the test was to the person.
> *Therapist:* Right, and who decides the importance?
> *Patient:* I do.
> *Therapist:* And so, what we have to examine is your way of viewing the test (or the way that you think about the test) and how it affects your chances of getting into law school. Do you agree?
> *Patient:* Right. . . .
> *Therapist:* Now what did failing mean?
> *Patient:* (*Tearful*) That I couldn't get into law school.
> *Therapist:* And what does that mean to you?
> *Patient:* That I'm just not smart enough.
> *Therapist:* Anything else?
> *Patient:* That I can never be happy.
> *Therapist:* And how do these thoughts make you feel?
> *Patient:* Very unhappy.
> *Therapist:* So it is the meaning of failing a test that makes you very unhappy. In fact, believing that you can never be happy is a powerful factor in producing unhappiness. So, you get yourself into a trap—by definition, failure to get into law school equals "I can never be happy."
>
> *(Beck et al., 1979, pp. 145–146)*

Assessing the Cognitive Model

The cognitive model has had very broad appeal. In addition to the behaviorists who now include cognitive concepts in their theories about learning, there are a great many clinicians who believe that thinking processes are in fact much more than conditioned reactions. Cognitive theory, research, and treatments have developed in so many interesting ways that the model is now viewed as separate from the behavioral school that gave birth to it.

Approximately 24 percent of today's clinical psychologists identify their approach as cognitive (Prochaska & Norcross, 2003). There are several reasons for the model's

•**SELF-EFFICACY**•The belief that one can master and perform needed behaviors whenever necessary.

•**COGNITIVE THERAPY**•A therapy developed by Aaron Beck that helps people recognize and change their faulty thinking processes.

>>**BY THE NUMBERS**

Attitudes toward Therapy

19% People who believe that psychotherapy is primarily for "people with serious psychological difficulties" <<

13% Those who think psychotherapy is "a waste of time" <<

49% Those who have positive feelings when they find out that an acquaintance is seeing a therapist <<

10% Those who have negative feelings when they find out that an acquaintance is seeing a therapist <<

(Fetto, 2002)

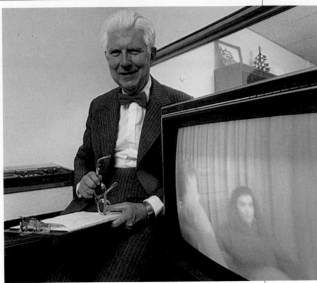

A clinical pioneer *Aaron Beck proposes that many forms of abnormal behavior can be traced to cognitive factors, such as upsetting thoughts and illogical thinking.*

popularity. First, it focuses on a process unique to human beings, the process of human thought. Just as our special cognitive abilities are responsible for so many human accomplishments, they may also be responsible for the special problems found in human functioning. Thus many theorists from varied backgrounds find themselves drawn to a model that sees thought as the primary cause of normal and abnormal behavior.

Cognitive theories also lend themselves to research. Investigators have found that people with psychological disorders often make the kinds of assumptions and errors in thinking the theorists claim (Leahy, 2004; Brown & Beck, 2002). Yet another reason for the popularity of this model is the impressive performance of cognitive therapies. They have proved very effective for treating depression, panic disorder, and sexual dysfunctions, for example (Landon & Barlow, 2004; Salkovskis, 2004). They also adapt well to new technologies (see Box 3-2).

Nevertheless, the cognitive model, too, has its drawbacks. First, although disturbed cognitive processes are found in many forms of abnormality, their precise role has yet to be determined. The cognitions seen in psychologically troubled people could well be a result rather than a cause of their difficulties. Second, although cognitive therapies are clearly of help to many people, they do not help everyone. Is it enough to change the cognitive habits of a person with a serious psychological dysfunction? Can such specific changes make a general and lasting difference in the way the person feels and behaves?

Furthermore, like the other models we have examined, the cognitive model is narrow in certain ways. Although cognition is a very special human dimension, it is still only one part of human functioning. Aren't human beings more than the sum total of their thoughts, emotions, and behaviors? Shouldn't explanations of human functioning also consider broader issues such as how people approach life, what value they extract from it, and how they deal with the question of life's meaning? This is the position of the humanistic-existential perspective.

The Humanistic-Existential Model

Philip Berman is more than the sum of his psychological conflicts, learned behaviors, or cognitions. Being human, he also has the ability to pursue philosophical goals such as self-awareness, strong values, a sense of meaning in life, and freedom of choice. According to humanistic and existential theorists, Philip's problems can be understood only in the light of such complex goals. Humanistic and existential theorists are usually grouped together—in an approach known as the *humanistic-existential model*—because of their common focus on these broader dimensions of human existence. At the same time, there are important differences between them.

Humanists, the more optimistic of the two groups, believe that human beings are born with a natural tendency to be friendly, cooperative, and constructive. People, these theorists propose, are driven to **self-actualize**—that is, to fulfill this potential for goodness and growth. They can do so, however, only if they honestly recognize and accept their weaknesses as well as their strengths and establish satisfying personal values to live by. Humanists further suggest that self-actualization leads naturally to a concern for the welfare of others and to behavior that is loving, courageous, spontaneous, and independent (Maslow, 1970).

Existentialists agree that human beings must have an accurate awareness of themselves and live meaningful—they say "authentic"—lives in order to be psychologically well adjusted. These theorists do not believe, however, that people are naturally inclined to live constructively. They believe that from birth we have total freedom, either to face up to our existence and give meaning to our lives or to shrink from that responsibility. Those who choose to "hide" from responsibility and choice will view themselves as helpless and weak and may live empty, inauthentic, and dysfunctional lives as a result.

The humanistic and existential views of abnormality both date back to the 1940s (Cain, 2002). At that time Carl Rogers (1902–1987), often considered the pioneer of the

>>**BY THE NUMBERS**
Charitable Acts

$150 BILLION	Amount contributed to charity each year in the United States ‹‹
57%	Percentage of charitable donations contributed to religious organizations ‹‹
43%	Percentage of donations directed to education, human services, health, and the arts ‹‹
75%	Percentage of incoming college freshmen who have done volunteer work in the past year ‹‹

(Kate, 1998; Reese, 1998)

[BOX **3-2**]

Cybertherapy

In this age of the Internet, it is hardly surprising that thousands of therapists are setting up on-line services, inviting persons with problems to e-mail their questions and concerns (Rosen, 2005; Rochlen et al., 2004; Heinlen et al., 2003). Such services, often called *e-therapy*, can cost as much as $2 per minute. They have raised concerns about confidentiality and the quality of care. Many e-therapists do not even have advanced clinical training.

Similarly, there are now thousands of chat groups and "virtual" support groups available around the clock on the Internet for everything from depression to substance abuse, anxiety, and eating disorders (Moskowitz, 2001). These groups provide opportunities for people with similar problems to communicate with each other, freely trading advice and empathy (Griffiths & Christensen, 2006; Landau, 2001). Of course, people who choose "chat group therapy" do not know who is on the other end of the computer connection or whether the advice they receive is at all appropriate. Distasteful or insulting messages are not uncommon (Ehrman, 1995).

Another new computer-age development is software programs that profess to offer help for emotional distress (Mortley et al., 2004; Jacobs et al., 2001). Advocates suggest that people may find it easier to reveal sensitive personal information to a computer than to a therapist. The computer offers them the freedom to express their thoughts and emotions without fear of being judged. Moreover, the computer therapist is always available, it can reach a large number of people, and its fees are modest. These are all attractive attributes in a therapist. Research indicates that some of these programs are indeed helpful

"Please dear! I need my own cyberspace."

(Lange et al., 2004; Rochlen et al, 2004; Jacobs et al., 2001).

Computers may never substitute fully for the judgment of a trained therapist. Yet, as more complex and humanlike computer programs are developed, both computer and Internet services may indeed find a place as adjuncts to other forms of treatment.

---

humanistic perspective, developed *client-centered therapy,* a warm and supportive approach that contrasted sharply with the psychodynamic techniques of the day. He also proposed a theory of personality that paid little attention to irrational instincts and conflicts.

The existential view of personality and abnormality appeared during this same period. Many of its principles came from the ideas of nineteenth-century European existential philosophers who held that human beings are constantly defining and so giving meaning to their existence through their actions (Walsh & McElwain, 2002). In the late 1950s a book titled *Existence* described a number of major existential ideas and treatment approaches and helped them gain recognition (May, Angel, & Ellenberger, 1958).

The humanistic and existential theories, and their uplifting and sometimes spiritual implications, were extremely popular during the 1960s and 1970s, years of considerable soul-searching and social upheaval in Western society. They have since lost some of their popularity, but they continue to influence the ideas and work of many clinicians.

Rogers's Humanistic Theory and Therapy

According to Carl Rogers (2000, 1987, 1951), the road to dysfunction begins in infancy. We all have a basic need to receive *positive regard* from the important people in our lives (primarily our parents). Those who receive *unconditional* (nonjudgmental) *positive regard* early in life are likely to develop *unconditional self-regard.* That is, they come to recognize their worth as persons, even while recognizing that they are not perfect. Such people are in a good position to actualize their positive potential.

Unfortunately, some children are repeatedly made to feel that they are not worthy of positive regard. As a result, they acquire *conditions of worth,* standards that tell them they are lovable and acceptable only when they conform to certain guidelines. In order

•SELF-ACTUALIZATION•The humanistic process by which people fulfill their potential for goodness and growth.

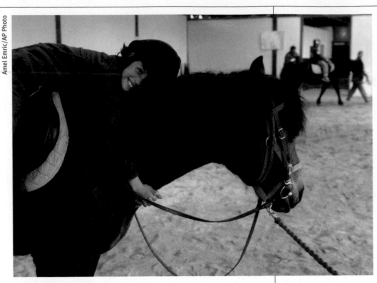

Unconditional positive regard *Carl Rogers and other humanists have argued that clients must receive unconditional positive regard in order to feel better about themselves and to overcome their psychological problems. In this spirit, a number of organizations now arrange for individuals to have close relationships with gentle and nonjudgmental animals. Here a Bosnian child hugs her horse during rehabilitation therapy at the Therapeutic and Leisure Center Kakrinje near Sarajevo.*

to maintain positive self-regard, these people have to look at themselves very selectively, denying or distorting thoughts and actions that do not measure up to their conditions of worth. They thus acquire a distorted view of themselves and their experiences. They do not know what they are truly feeling, what they genuinely need, or what values and goals would be meaningful for them. Problems in functioning are then inevitable.

Rogers might view Philip Berman as a man who has gone astray. Rather than striving to fulfill his positive human potential, he drifts from job to job, relationship to relationship, and outburst to outburst. In every interaction he is defending himself, trying to interpret events in ways he can live with, usually blaming his problems on other people. Yet his constant efforts at self-defense and self-enhancement are only partly successful. His basic negative self-image continually reveals itself. Rogers would probably link this problem to the critical ways Philip was treated by his mother throughout his childhood.

Clinicians who practice Rogers's **client-centered therapy** try to create a supportive climate in which clients feel able to look at themselves honestly and acceptingly (Raskin & Rogers, 2005; Rogers, 2000, 1992, 1957). The therapist must display three important qualities throughout the therapy—unconditional positive regard (full and warm acceptance for the client), accurate empathy (skillful listening and restatements), and genuineness (sincere communication). The following interaction shows the therapist using all these qualities to move the client toward greater self-awareness:

> *Client:* Yes, I know I shouldn't worry about it, but I do. Lots of things—money, people, clothes. In classes I feel that everyone's just waiting for a chance to jump on me.... When I meet somebody I wonder what he's actually thinking of me. Then later on I wonder how I match up to what he's come to think of me.
>
> *Therapist:* You feel that you're pretty responsive to the opinions of other people.
>
> *Client:* Yes, but it's things that shouldn't worry me.
>
> *Therapist:* You feel that it's the sort of thing that shouldn't be upsetting, but they do get you pretty much worried anyway.
>
> *Client:* Just some of them. Most of those things do worry me because they're true. The ones I told you, that is. But there are lots of little things that aren't true.... Things just seem to be piling up, piling up inside of me.... It's a feeling that things were crowding up and they were going to burst.
>
> *Therapist:* You feel that it's a sort of oppression with some frustration and that things are just unmanageable.
>
> *Client:* In a way, but some things just seem illogical. I'm afraid I'm not very clear here but that's the way it comes.
>
> *Therapist:* That's all right. You say just what you think.
>
> *(Snyder, 1947, pp. 2–24)*

•**CLIENT-CENTERED THERAPY**•The humanistic therapy developed by Carl Rogers in which clinicians try to help clients by conveying acceptance, accurate empathy, and genuineness.

•**GESTALT THERAPY**•The humanistic therapy developed by Fritz Perls in which clinicians actively move clients toward self-recognition and self-acceptance by using techniques such as role playing and self-discovery exercises.

•**EXISTENTIAL THERAPY**•A therapy that encourages clients to accept responsibility for their lives and to live with greater meaning and values.

In such an atmosphere, persons are expected to feel accepted by their therapists. They then may be able to look at themselves with honesty and acceptance—a process called *experiencing.* That is, they begin to value their own emotions, thoughts, and behaviors, and so they are freed from the insecurities and doubts that prevent self-actualization.

Client-centered therapy has not fared very well in research (Patterson, 2000; Greenberg et al., 1998, 1994). Although some studies show that people who receive this therapy improve more than control subjects, many other studies have failed to find any such advantage. All the same, Rogers's therapy has had a positive influence on clinical practice (Kirschenbaum, 2004). It was one of the first major alternatives to psychodynamic therapy, and it helped open up the field to new approaches. Rogers also helped pave the way for psychologists to practice psychotherapy; it had previously been considered the exclusive territory of psychiatrists. And his commitment to clinical research helped promote the systematic study of treatment. Approximately 1 percent of today's clinical psychologists, 2 percent of social workers, and 4 percent of counseling psychologists report that they employ the client-centered approach (Prochasca & Norcross, 2003).

Gestalt Theory and Therapy

Gestalt therapy, another humanistic approach, was developed in the 1950s by a charismatic clinician named Frederick (Fritz) Perls (1893–1970). Gestalt therapists, like client-centered therapists, guide their clients toward self-recognition and self-acceptance (Yontef & Jacobs, 2005). But unlike client-centered therapists, they often try to achieve this goal by challenging and even frustrating their clients. Some of Perls's favorite techniques were skillful frustration, role playing, and numerous rules and exercises.

In the technique of *skillful frustration,* gestalt therapists refuse to meet their clients' expectations or demands. This use of frustration is meant to help people see how often they try to manipulate others into meeting their needs. In the technique of *role playing,* the therapists instruct clients to act out various roles. A person may be told to be another person, an object, an alternative self, or even a part of the body. Role playing can become intense, as individuals are encouraged to fully express emotions. Many cry out, scream, kick, or pound. Through this experience they may come to "own" (accept) feelings that previously made them uncomfortable.

Perls also developed a list of *rules* to ensure that clients will look at themselves more closely. In some versions of gestalt therapy, for example, clients may be required to use "I" language rather than "it" language. They must say, "I am frightened" rather than "The situation is frightening." Yet another common rule requires clients to stay in the *here and now.* They have needs now, are hiding their needs now, and must observe them now.

Approximately 1 percent of clinical psychologists and other kinds of clinicians describe themselves as gestalt therapists (Prochaska & Norcross, 2003). Because they believe that subjective experiences and self-awareness cannot be measured objectively, controlled research has not often been done on the gestalt approach (Toman & Woldt, 2005; Strumpfel & Goldman, 2002).

Existential Theories and Therapy

Like humanists, existentialists believe that psychological dysfunctioning is caused by self-deception; but existentialists are talking about a kind of self-deception in which people hide from life's responsibilities and fail to recognize that it is up to them to give meaning to their lives. According to existentialists, many people become overwhelmed by the pressures of present-day society and so look to others for explanations, guidance, and authority. They overlook their personal freedom of choice and avoid responsibility for their lives and decisions (May & Yalom, 2005, 1995). Such people are left with empty, inauthentic lives. Their dominant emotions are anxiety, frustration, boredom, alienation, and depression.

Existentialists might view Philip Berman as a man who feels overwhelmed by the forces of society. He sees his parents as "rich, powerful, and selfish," and he perceives teachers, acquaintances, and employers as abusive and oppressing. He fails to appreciate his choices in life and his capacity for finding meaning and direction. Quitting becomes a habit with him—he leaves job after job, ends every romantic relationship, and flees difficult situations.

In **existential therapy** people are encouraged to accept responsibility for their lives and for their problems. They are helped to recognize their freedom so that they may choose a different course and live with greater meaning and stronger values (Schneider, 2003). For the most part, existential therapists care more about the goals of therapy than the use of specific techniques; methods vary greatly from clinician to clinician. At the same time, most do place great emphasis on the *relationship* between therapist and client and try to create an atmosphere of candor, hard work, and shared learning and growth.

Beating the blues *Gestalt therapists often guide clients to express their needs and feelings in their full intensity by banging on pillows, crying out, kicking, or pounding things. Building on these techniques, a new approach,* drum therapy, *teaches clients, such as this woman, how to beat drums in order to help release traumatic memories, change beliefs, and feel more liberated.*

> Patient:　I don't know why I keep coming here. All I do is tell you the same thing over and over. I'm not getting anywhere.
>
> Doctor:　I'm getting tired of hearing the same thing over and over, too.
>
> Patient:　Maybe I'll stop coming.
>
> Doctor:　It's certainly your choice.
>
> Patient:　What do you think I should do?
>
> Doctor:　What do you want to do?
>
> Patient:　I want to get better.
>
> Doctor:　I don't blame you.
>
> Patient:　If you think I should stay, ok, I will.
>
> Doctor:　You want me to tell you to stay?
>
> Patient:　You know what's best; you're the doctor.
>
> Doctor:　Do I act like a doctor?
>
> *(Keen, 1970, p. 200)*

Existential therapists do not believe that experimental methods can adequately test the effectiveness of their treatments (May & Yalom, 2005, 1995; Walsh & McElwain, 2002). To them, research dehumanizes individuals by reducing them to test measures or scale scores. Not surprisingly, then, very little controlled research has been devoted to the effectiveness of this approach. Nevertheless, around 3 percent of today's therapists use an approach that is primarily existential (Prochaska & Norcross, 2003).

Assessing the Humanistic-Existential Model

The humanistic-existential model appeals to many people in and out of the clinical field. In recognizing the special challenges of human existence, humanistic and existential theorists tap into an aspect of psychological life that is typically missing from the other models (Aanstoos, 2003; Seeman, 2002). Moreover, the factors that they say are essential to effective functioning—self-acceptance, personal values, personal meaning, and personal choice—are certainly lacking in many people with psychological disturbances.

The optimistic tone of the humanistic-existential model is also an attraction. Theorists who follow these principles offer great hope when they assert that despite the often overwhelming pressures of modern society, we can make our own choices, determine our own destiny, and accomplish much. Still another attractive feature of the model is its emphasis on health. Unlike clinicians from some of the other models who see individuals as patients with psychological illnesses, humanists and existentialists view them simply as people whose special potential has yet to be fulfilled.

At the same time, the humanistic-existential focus on abstract issues of human fulfillment gives rise to a major problem from a scientific point of view: these issues are difficult to research. In fact, with the notable exception of Rogers, who tried to carefully investigate his clinical methods, humanists and existentialists have traditionally rejected the use of empirical research. Typically, they have argued the merits of their views using logic, introspection, and individual case histories. In consequence, the model has received limited empirical examination or support.

This anti-research position is just now beginning to change, at least in the treatment realm. Several recent studies have been conducted by humanistic researchers to determine whether humanistic and existential therapies are in fact of help to clients. These studies, which use appropriate control groups and statistical analyses, do, in fact, suggest that such therapies can be beneficial in some cases (Cain, 2003, 2002; Elliott, 2002). This newfound interest in research by proponents of the humanistic-existential model should lead to important insights about the merits of this model in the coming years.

Acting out one's problems *These actors are participating in* drama therapy, *a treatment approach in which individuals express underlying rage and other feelings by portraying characters caught in difficult, frustrating, or painful situations. This approach combines elements from the humanistic therapies and from* psychodrama, *a form of group therapy developed in the 1920s by the famous Viennese psychiatrist Jacob Moreno.*

Kathy Siamen/AP Photo

The Sociocultural Model

Philip Berman is also a social being. He is surrounded by people and by institutions, he is a member of a family and a society, and he participates in both social and professional relationships. Thus social forces are always operating upon Philip, setting boundaries and expectations that guide and at times pressure him, helping to shape his behavior, thoughts, and emotions.

According to the *sociocultural model,* abnormal behavior is best understood in light of the social and cultural forces that influence an individual. What are the norms of the society? What roles does the person play in the social environment? What kind of cultural background or family structure is the person a part of? And how do other people view and react to him or her?

How Do Sociocultural Theorists Explain Abnormal Functioning?

Because behavior is shaped by social forces, sociocultural theorists hold, we must examine a person's social and cultural surroundings if we are to understand abnormal behavior (Tyrer & Steinberg, 2005). Sociocultural explanations focus on *societal labels and rules, social networks, family structure and communication, cultural influences, and religious factors.*

SOCIETAL LABELS AND ROLES Many sociocultural theorists believe that abnormal functioning is influenced greatly by the labels and roles assigned to troubled people (Link et al., 2004, 2001; Szasz, 2000, 1970; Scheff, 1999). When people stray from the norms of their society, the society calls them deviant and, in many cases, "mentally ill." Such labels tend to stick. Moreover, when people are viewed in particular ways, reacted to as "crazy," and perhaps even encouraged to act sick, they gradually learn to accept and play the assigned role. Ultimately the label seems appropriate.

A famous study by the clinical investigator David Rosenhan (1973) supports this position. Eight normal people presented themselves at various mental hospitals, complaining that they had been hearing voices say the words "empty," "hollow," and "thud." On the basis of this complaint alone, each was diagnosed as having schizophrenia and admitted. As the sociocultural model would predict, the "pseudopatients" had a hard time convincing others that they were well once they had been given the diagnostic label. Their hospitalizations ranged from 7 to 52 days, even though they behaved normally as soon as they were admitted. In addition, the label kept influencing the way the staff viewed and dealt with them. For example, one pseudopatient who paced the corridor out of boredom was, in clinical notes, described as "nervous." Finally, the pseudopatients reported that the staff's behavior toward them and other patients was often authoritarian, limited, and counterproductive. Overall, the pseudopatients came to feel powerless, invisible, and bored.

SOCIAL NETWORKS AND SUPPORTS Sociocultural theorists are typically concerned with the social networks in which people operate, including their social and professional relationships. How well do they communicate with others? What kind of signals do they send to or receive from others? Researchers have often found ties between deficiencies in social networks and a person's functioning (Paykel et al., 2003; Segrin et al., 2003; Segrin, 2001). They have noted, for example, that people who are isolated and lack social support or intimacy in their lives are more likely to become depressed when under stress and to remain depressed longer than are people with supportive spouses or warm friendships.

FAMILY STRUCTURE AND COMMUNICATION Of course, one of the important social networks for an individual is his or her family. According to **family systems theory,** the family is a system of interacting parts—the family members—who interact with one another in consistent ways and conform to rules unique to each family (Goldenberg & Goldenberg, 2005). The parts interact in ways that enable the system to maintain itself

•FAMILY SYSTEMS THEORY• A theory that views the family as a system of interacting parts whose interactions exhibit consistent patterns and unstated rules.

>>BY THE NUMBERS

Greater Father Involvement

57% Persons who believe that today's fathers bathe their children and change diapers more than fathers did 20 years ago. **<<**

53% Those who believe that today's fathers play with their children more than fathers of the past. **<<**

53% Those who believe that today's fathers help more with homework. **<<**

53% Those who believe that today's fathers are more involved in caring for their sick children. **<<**

(Fetto, 2002)

Today's TV families *Unlike television viewers of the 1950s, when problem-free families like the Nelsons (Ozzie & Harriet) ruled the airwaves, today's viewers prefer more complex, even dysfunctional, families, like the Fishers, whose trials and tribulations were displayed in HBO's series* Six Feet Under *for five years.*

and survive—a state known as *homeostasis.* Family systems theorists believe that the structure and communication patterns of some families actually force individual members to behave in a way that otherwise seems abnormal. If the members were to behave normally, they would severely strain the family's homeostasis and usual manner of operation and would actually increase their own and their family's turmoil.

Family systems theory holds that certain family systems are particularly likely to produce abnormal functioning in individual members. Some families, for example, have an *enmeshed* structure in which the members are grossly overinvolved in each other's activities, thoughts, and feelings. Children from this kind of family may have great difficulty becoming independent in life (Santisteban et al., 2001). Some families display *disengagement,* which is marked by very rigid boundaries between the members. Children from these families may find it hard to function in a group or to give or request support (Corey, 2004, 2001).

In the sociocultural model, Philip Berman's angry and impulsive personal style might be seen as the product of a disturbed family structure. According to family systems theorists, the whole family—mother, father, Philip, and his brother Arnold—relate in such a way as to maintain Philip's behavior. Family theorists might be particularly interested in the conflict between Philip's mother and father and the imbalance between their parental roles. They might see Philip's behavior as both a reaction to and stimulus for his parents' behaviors. With Philip acting out the role of the misbehaving child, or scapegoat, his parents may have little need or time to question their own relationship.

Family systems theorists would also seek to clarify the precise nature of Philip's relationship with each parent. Is he enmeshed with his mother and/or disengaged from his father? They would look too at the rules governing the sibling relationship in the family, the relationship between the parents and Philip's brother, and the nature of parent-child relationships in previous generations of the family.

CULTURE *Culture* refers to the set of values, attitudes, beliefs, history, and behaviors shared by a group of people and communicated from one generation to the next (Cole, 2005; Matsumoto, 1994). In Chapter 1 we observed that culture often influences which behaviors are considered abnormal and how other people react to such behaviors. If, for example, a person's friends and family value and encourage drinking large quantities of alcoholic beverages, the individual may be more inclined to turn to alcohol at times of stress and to drift into a pattern of alcohol abuse; relatives and friends may be less able to recognize a pattern of problem drinking; and interventions for such a pattern may be avoided.

Today's theorists use the term **multicultural perspective,** or **culturally diverse perspective,** to describe the view that each culture within a larger society has a particular set of values, beliefs, and the like, and that each culture has its own strengths and limitations, all of which help account for individual behavior (Mio et al., 2006; Sue & Sue, 2003). The multicultural model is different from past—less enlightened—cultural models: it does not imply that members of racial, ethnic, and other minority groups are in some way inferior or culturally deprived in comparison with a majority population (Sue & Sue, 2003). Rather, the perspective holds that an individual's behavior, whether normal or abnormal, is best understood when examined in the light of that individual's unique cultural context, from the values of that culture to the special external pressures faced by members of the culture.

The groups in the United States that have received the most attention from multicultural researchers are ethnic and racial minority groups (African American, Hispanic American, Native American, and Asian American groups) and groups such as economically disadvantaged persons, women, and homosexual individuals. Of course, membership in these groups often overlaps. Each of these groups is subjected to special pressures

•**MULTICULTURAL PERSPECTIVE**•The view that each culture within a larger society has a particular set of values and beliefs, as well as special external measures, that help account for the behavior and functioning of its members. Also called *culturally diverse perspective.*

in American society that may contribute to feelings of stress and, in some cases, to abnormal functioning. Researchers have learned, for example, that psychological abnormality, especially severe psychological abnormality, is indeed more common among poorer people than among wealthier people (Byrne et al., 2004; Draine et al., 2002). Perhaps the special pressures of poverty explain this relationship. The higher rates of crime, unemployment, overcrowding, and homelessness; the inferior medical care; and the limited educational opportunities typically experienced by poor persons may place great stress on many members of minority groups.

Multicultural researchers have also noted that the prejudice and discrimination faced by many minority groups may contribute to certain forms of abnormal functioning (Jackson et al., 2004; Nelson, 2006). Women in Western society receive diagnoses of anxiety and depressive disorders at least twice as often as men (McSweeney, 2004). Similarly, African Americans experience unusually high rates of anxiety disorders (Blazer et al., 1991). Hispanic Americans, particularly young men, have higher rates of alcoholism than members of most other ethnic groups (Helzer, Burnman, & McEvoy, 1991). And Native Americans display exceptionally high alcoholism and suicide rates (Beals et al., 2005; Kinzie et al., 1992). Although many factors may combine to produce these differences, racial and sexual prejudice and the problems they pose may contribute to abnormal patterns of tension, unhappiness, low self-esteem, and escape (Nelson, 2006; McSweeney, 2004; Winston, 2004).

Of course, significant cultural differences occur not only *within* countries, but *across* countries, and sociocultural researchers have examined these differences as well. Indeed, they have learned that some of the disorders we shall be observing in this textbook—anorexia nervosa, agoraphobia, borderline personality disorder—are much less common in non-Western countries (Anderson-Fye, 2004; Cooper, 2001; Paris, 2001). It may be that key Western values—such as the importance of a thin appearance, emphasis on high mobility, and endorsement of emotional expression—help set the stage for such disorders.

RELIGION AND SPIRITUALITY Although religious beliefs are often tied to a particular culture, it is also the case that members of different cultural groups may practice the same religion or at least share similar degrees of spirituality. Thus, in recent years many sociocultural theorists have paid particular attention to the role of religion in psychological functioning and mental health. For most of the twentieth century, clinical scientists viewed religion as a negative—or at best neutral—factor in mental health (Richards & Bergin, 2004, 2000). Anxious to distance themselves from the demonological explanations and treatments offered by the clergy during the Middle Ages and beyond, many twentieth-century theorists and clinicians held that religious beliefs were potentially damaging.

In the early 1900s, for example, Freud argued that religious beliefs were defense mechanisms, "born from man's need to make his helplessness tolerable" (1961, p. 23). Subsequently, clinical theorists proposed that people with strong religious beliefs were more suspicious, irrational, guilt-ridden, and unstable than others, and less able to cope with life's difficulties. Correspondingly, spiritual principles and issues were considered a taboo topic in most forms of therapy.

The alienation between the clinical field and religion now seems to be ending. During the past decade, numerous articles and books linking spiritual issues to clinical treatment have been published, and the ethical codes of psychologists, psychiatrists, and counselors have each concluded that religion is a type of diversity that mental health professionals are obligated to respect (Richards & Bergin, 2004, 2000). Researchers have systematically studied possible links between religious faith and mental health and have learned that spirituality can, in fact, be of psychological benefit to people. In particular,

Liss Steve/Corbis Sygma

Victims of hate *This memorial service for Matthew Shepard, brutally beaten to death in 1998 because of his gay orientation, is a powerful reminder of the prejudice, discrimination, and even danger that members of minority groups can confront in our society. Culture-sensitive therapies seek to address the special impact of such stressors upon individuals, as well as other psychological issues.*

>>BY THE NUMBERS

Prayer and Health

84% Percentage of Americans who believe that praying for the sick improves their chance of recovery

70% Those who say they pray often for the health of a family member

65% Precentage of prayers about health that actually relate to mental health

(Sheler, 2004; Kalb, 2003)

Religion and mental health *A Thai Buddhist monk speaks during a psychological session at a school in Bang Niang Camp. In Thailand, people recovering from personal problems often go to their local temple seeking consolation through prayer and meditation.*

studies have examined the mental health of people who are devout and who view God as warm, caring, helpful, and dependable. Repeatedly, these individuals are found to be less lonely, pessimistic, depressed, or anxious than people without any religious beliefs or those who view God as cold and unresponsive (Koenig, 2002; Bergin & Richards, 2001; Clay, 1996). Such individuals also seem to cope better with major life stressors—from illness to war—and to attempt suicide less often. In addition, they are less likely to abuse drugs.

In line with such findings, many therapists now make a point of focusing on spiritual issues when they treat religious clients (Serlin, 2005; Shafranske & Sperry, 2005; Richards & Bergin, 2004, 2000). At the very least, they try to identify and respect how religious beliefs and values are affecting their clients' lives and psychological functioning and to include such beliefs in their therapy discussions. Some therapists further encourage clients to use their spiritual resources to help them cope with current stresses and dysfunctioning.

Sociocultural Treatments

As we have just seen, the apparent links between religion and mental health have led some therapists to focus on spiritual issues when they treat certain clients. Similarly, the sociocultural theories that we have been examining have helped spur the growth of several treatment approaches, including *culture-sensitive therapy, group therapy, family* and *couple therapy,* and *community treatment.* Therapists of any orientation may work with clients in these various formats, applying the techniques and principles of their preferred models. In such instances the therapy approach is not purely sociocultural. However, more and more of the clinicians who use these formats believe that psychological problems emerge in a social setting and are best treated in such a setting, and they include special sociocultural strategies in their work.

CULTURE-SENSITIVE THERAPY A number of recent studies have found that many members of ethnic and racial minority groups improve less in clinical treatment than members of majority groups (Mio et al., 2006; Smedley & Smedley, 2005; Lee & Sue, 2001). Similarly, studies conducted throughout the world have found that minority clients use mental health services less often than members of majority groups (Kung, 2004; Sue, 2003; Gaw, 2001). In some cases, cultural beliefs, a language barrier, or lack of information about available services prevents minority individuals from seeking help; in other cases, such persons may not be able to afford quality treatment. And in still other cases minority individuals may not trust the establishment, relying instead on traditional remedies that are available in their immediate social environment (Smedley & Smedley, 2005).

Research also indicates that members of minority groups stop therapy sooner than persons from majority groups. In the United States, African Americans, Native Americans, Asian Americans, and Hispanic Americans all have higher therapy dropout rates than white Americans (Lee & Sue, 2001). Members of such groups may stop treatment because they do not feel they are benefiting from it or because ethnic and racial differences prevent the development of a strong rapport with their therapist (Kung, 2004; Whaley, 1998).

How can clinicians be more helpful to people from minority groups? A number of studies suggest that two features of treatment can increase a therapist's effectiveness with minority clients: (1) greater sensitivity to cultural issues and (2) inclusion of cultural morals and models in treatment, especially in therapies for children and adolescents (Caldwell & White, 2005; Carrasco, 2005; Gil & Drewes, 2005). Given such findings, clinicians have developed **culture-sensitive therapies,** approaches that seek to address the unique issues faced by members of minority groups (Mio et al., 2006). These ap-

>>BY THE NUMBERS
Pressures of Poverty

90 Number of victims of violent crime per 1,000 poor persons «

50 Number of victims per 1,000 middle-income people «

40 Number of victims per 1,000 wealthy people «

(U.S. Bureau of Justice Statistics)

proaches often include such features as (1) helping minority-group clients understand the impact of the dominant culture and of their own culture on their views of themselves and on their behaviors, (2) helping clients to express suppressed anger and pain, and (3) helping clients to make choices that work for them and to achieve a bicultural balance that feels right for them. Therapies geared to the special pressures of being a woman in Western society, called **gender-sensitive,** or **feminist, therapies,** follow similar principles.

GROUP THERAPY Thousands of therapists specialize in **group therapy,** a format in which a therapist meets with a group of clients who have similar problems. Indeed, one survey of clinical psychologists revealed that almost one-third of them devoted some portion of their practice to group therapy (Norcross et al., 1993). Typically, members of a therapy group meet together with a therapist and discuss the problems of one or more of the people in the group. Together they develop important insights, build social skills, strengthen feelings of self-worth, and share useful information or advice (Vinogradov, Cox, & Yalom, 2003). Many groups are created with particular client populations in mind; for example, there are groups for people with alcoholism and other kinds of substance abuse, for those who are physically handicapped, and for people who are divorced, abused, or bereaved.

Research suggests that group therapy is of help to many clients, often as helpful as individual therapy (Dies, 2003; McDermut et al., 2001). The group format has also been used for purposes that are educational rather than therapeutic, such as "consciousness raising" and spiritual inspiration.

A format similar to group therapy is the **self-help group** (or **mutual help group**). Here people who have similar problems (bereavement, substance abuse, illness, unemployment, divorce) come together to help and support one another without the direct leadership of a professional clinician (Munn-Giddings & Borkman, 2005; Weiss et al., 2005; Wituk et al., 2002). According to estimates, there are now between 500,000 and 3 million such groups in the United States alone, attended each year by 3 to 4 percent of the population (see Box 3 3 on page 78). Indeed, it is estimated that 25 million Americans will participate in self-help groups at some point in their lives (Davison et al., 2000). Self-help groups tend to offer more direct advice than is provided in group therapy and to encourage more exchange of information or "tips."

FAMILY THERAPY **Family therapy** was first introduced in the 1950s. A therapist meets with all members of a family, points out problem behaviors and interactions, and helps the whole family to change (Goldenberg & Goldenberg, 2005; Minuchin, 1997; Bowen, 1960). Here, the entire family is viewed as the unit under treatment, even if only one of the members receives a clinical diagnosis. The following is a typical interaction between family members and a therapist:

Tommy sat motionless in a chair gazing out the window. He was fourteen and a bit small for his age. . . . Sissy was eleven. She was sitting on the couch between her Mom and Dad with a smile on her face. Across from them sat Ms. Fargo, the family therapist.

Ms. Fargo spoke. "Could you be a little more specific about the changes you have seen in Tommy and when they came about?"

Mrs. Davis answered first. "Well, I guess it was about two years ago. Tommy started getting in fights at school. When we talked to him at home he said it was none of our business. He became moody and disobedient. He wouldn't do anything that we wanted him to. He began to act mean to his sister and even hit her."

"What about the fights at school?" Ms. Fargo asked.

This time it was Mr. Davis who spoke first. "Ginny was more worried about them than I was. I used to fight a lot when I was in school and I think it is normal. . . . But I was very respectful to my parents, especially my Dad. If I ever got out of line he would smack me one."

"Have you ever had to hit Tommy?" Ms. Fargo inquired softly.

"Sure, a couple of times, but it didn't seem to do any good."

•**CULTURE-SENSITIVE THERAPIES**•
Approaches that seek to address the unique issues faced by members of minority groups.

•**GENDER-SENSITIVE THERAPIES**•
Approaches geared to the special pressures of being a woman in Western society. Also called *feminist therapies.*

•**GROUP THERAPY**•A therapy format in which a group of people with similar problems meet together with a therapist to work on those problems.

•**SELF-HELP GROUP**•A group made up of people with similar problems who help and support one another without the direct leadership of a clinician. Also called a *mutual help group.*

•**FAMILY THERAPY**•A therapy format in which the therapist meets with all members of a family and helps them to change in therapeutic ways.

•**COUPLE THERAPY**•A therapy format in which the therapist works with two people who share a long-term relationship. Also called *marital therapy.*

All at once Tommy seemed to be paying attention, his eyes riveted on his father. "Yeah, he hit me a lot, for no reason at all!"

"Now, that's not true, Thomas." Mrs. Davis has a scolding expression on her face. "If you behaved yourself a little better you wouldn't get hit. Ms. Fargo, I can't say that I am in favor of the hitting, but I understand sometimes how frustrating it may be for Bob."

"You don't know how frustrating it is for me, honey." Bob seemed upset. "You don't have to work all day at the office and then come home to contend with all of this. Sometimes I feel like I don't even want to come home."

Ginny gave him a hard stare. "You think things at home are easy all day? I could use some support from you. You think all you have to do is earn the money and I will do everything else. Well, I am not about to do that anymore." . . .

Mrs. Davis began to cry. "I just don't know what to do anymore. Things just seem so hopeless. Why can't people be nice in this family anymore? I don't think I am asking too much, am I?"

Ms. Fargo spoke thoughtfully. "I get the feeling that people in this family would like things to be different. Bob, I can see how frustrating it must be for you to work so hard and not be able to relax when you get home. And, Ginny, your job is not easy either. You have a lot to do at home and Bob can't be there to help because he has to earn a living. And you kids sound like you would like some things to be different too. It must be hard for you, Tommy, to be catching so much flack these days. I think this also makes it hard for you to have fun at home too, Sissy."

She looked at each person briefly and was sure to make eye contact. "There seems to be a lot going on. . . . I think we are going to need to understand a lot of things to see why this is happening. . . ."

(Sheras & Worchel, 1979, pp. 108–110)

Family therapists may follow any of the major theoretical models, but more and more of them are adopting the sociocultural principles of family systems theory. Today 4 percent of all clinical psychologists, 13 percent of social workers, and 1 percent of psychiatrists identify themselves mainly as *family systems therapists* (Prochaska & Norcross, 2003).

As we observed earlier, family systems theory holds that each family has its own rules, structure, and communication patterns that shape the individual members' behavior. In one family systems approach, *structural family therapy,* therapists try to change the family power structure, the roles each person plays, and the alliances between members (Wetchler, 2003; Minuchin, 1997, 1987, 1974). In another, *conjoint family therapy,* therapists try to help members recognize and change harmful patterns of communication (Innes, 2002; Satir, 1987, 1967, 1964).

Family therapies of various kinds are often helpful to individuals, although rsesearch has not yet clarified how helpful (Goldenberg & Goldenberg, 2005; Sexton & Alexander, 2002). Some studies have found that as many as 65 percent of individuals treated with family approaches improve, while other studies suggest much lower success rates. Nor has any one type of family therapy emerged as consistently more helpful than the others (Alexander et al., 2002; Diamond & Diamond, 2002).

COUPLE THERAPY In **couple therapy,** or **marital therapy,** the therapist works with two individuals who are in a long-term relationship. Often they are husband and wife, but the couple need not be married or even living together. Like family therapy, couple therapy often focuses on the structure and communication patterns occurring in the relationship (Harway, 2005; Baucom et al., 2005, 2000). A couple approach may also be employed when a child's psychological problems are traced to problems in the parents' relationship.

Although some degree of conflict exists in any long-term relationship (see Table 3-4), many adults in our society experience serious marital discord. The divorce rate in Canada, the United States, and Europe is now close to 50 percent of the marriage rate

Henry Martin/Cartoonbank.com

"What do you mean we don't communicate? I sent you e-mail on Monday."

Desperate relationships? *Marital discord is an all too common problem in our society, explaining, in part, the extraordinary popularity of the television series* Desperate Housewives. *Millions of viewers tune in each week to follow the relationship difficulties of Bree, Susan, Lynette, Gabrielle, and Edie, identifying, in a small way at least, with the pressures, complexities, and temptations that each of the characters faces.*

(Lewin, 2004; NCHS, 2000, 1999). Many couples who live together without marrying apparently have similar levels of difficulty (Harway, 2005).

Couple therapy, like family and group therapy, may follow the principles of any of the major therapy orientations. *Behavioral couple therapy,* for example, uses many techniques from the behavioral perspective (Shadish & Baldwin, 2005; Byrne et al., 2004; Gurman, 2003). Therapists help spouses recognize and change problem behaviors largely by teaching specific problem-solving and communication skills. A broader, more sociocultural version, called *integrative couple therapy,* further helps partners accept behaviors that they cannot change and embrace the whole relationship nevertheless (Christensen et al., 2004; Gollan & Jacobson, 2001). Partners are asked to see such behaviors as an understandable result of basic differences between them.

Couples treated by couple therapy seem to show greater improvement in their relationships than couples with similar problems who fail to receive treatment, but no one form of couple therapy stands out as superior to others (Snyder & Castellani, 2006; Harway 2005; Gollan & Jacobson, 2002). Although two-thirds of treated couples experience improved marital functioning by the end of therapy, fewer than half of those who are treated achieve "distress-free" or "happy" relationships. Moreover, one-third of successfully

---

Table **3-4**

Couple Trouble

- Annual marriage rate in the United States: 51 per 1,000 unmarried women
- Annual divorce rate: 20 per 1,000 married women
- Highest marriage rate: Nevada
- Highest divorce rate: Nevada
- Sources of marital bickering: money (29 percent), television selections (28 percent), time together (21 percent), child discipline (20 percent)
- Almost 40 percent of persons wish they could ask their spouse for more affection
- Almost 40 percent of persons report having kept a secret from their spouse
- Length of silent treatment after a spousal fight: one week (3 percent), one day (21 percent), one hour (31 percent), five minutes (19 percent)

Source: Henry & Miller, 2004; Yin, 2002; Uretsky, 1999; Kanner, 1998, 1995; *Time,* 1998; NCHS, 1998; Roper Reports, 1998.

[**BOX 3-3**]

Self-Help Groups: Too Much of a Good Thing?

Self-help groups are widely accepted in our society, by consumers and clinicians alike (Isenberg et al., 2004). Indeed, one survey of mental health professionals revealed that almost 90 percent of all therapists in the United States often recommend such groups to their clients as a supplement to therapy (Clifford et al., 1998).

Small wonder that the number, range, and appeal of such groups have grown rapidly over the past several decades and that 25 million persons in the United States alone are estimated to attend self-help groups over the course of their lives. The self-help group movement and its impact on our society are brought to life in the following notice that was posted in a Colorado church in 1990 (Moskowitz, 2001), listing support groups that would be meeting at the church during the coming week:

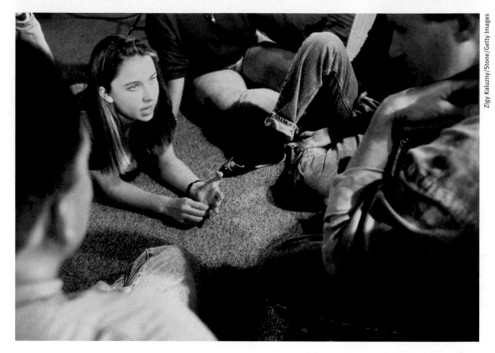

Zigy Kaluzny/Stone/Getty Images

Sunday

12:00 noon	Cocaine Anonymous, main floor
5:30 p.m.	Survivors of Incest, main floor
6:00 p.m.	Al-Anon, 2nd floor
6:00 p.m.	Alcoholics Anonymous, basement

Monday

5:30 p.m.	Debtors Anonymous, basement
6:30 p.m.	Codependents of Sex Addicts Anonymous, 2nd floor
7:00 p.m.	Adult Children of Alcoholics, 2nd floor
8:00 p.m.	Alcoholics Anonymous, basement
8:00 p.m.	Al-Anon, 2nd floor
8:00 p.m.	Alateen, basement
8:00 p.m.	Cocaine Anonymous, main floor

Tuesday

8:00 p.m.	Survivors of Incest Anonymous, basement

Wednesday

5:30 p.m.	Sex & Love Addicts Anonymous, basement
7:30 p.m.	Adult Children of Alcoholics, 2nd floor
8:00 p.m.	Cocaine Anonymous, main floor

Thursday

7:00 p.m.	Codependents of Sex Addicts Anonymous, 2nd floor
7:00 p.m.	Women's Cocaine Anonymous, main floor

Friday

5:30 p.m.	Sex & Love Addicts Anonymous, basement
5:45 p.m.	Adult Overeaters Anonymous, 2nd floor
7:30 p.m.	Codependents Anonymous, basement
7:30 p.m.	Adult Children of Alcoholics, 2nd floor
8:00 p.m.	Cocaine Anonymous, main floor

Saturday

10:00 a.m.	Adult Children of Alcoholics, main floor
12:00 p.m.	Self-Abusers Anonymous, 2nd floor

•**COMMUNITY MENTAL HEALTH TREAT-MENT**•A treatment approach that emphasizes community care.

treated couples may relapse within two years after therapy. Couples who are younger, well adjusted, and less rigid in their gender roles tend to have the best results.

COMMUNITY TREATMENT Following sociocultural principles, **community mental health treatment** programs allow clients, particularly those with severe psychological difficulties, to receive treatment in familiar surroundings as they try to recover. In 1963 President Kennedy called for such a "bold new approach" to the treatment of mental disorders—a community approach that would enable most people with psychological

The dysfunctional society *The pressures and uncertainty of living in a war-torn environment may contribute to the development of psychological problems. The environment's ongoing violence may leave some individuals feeling numb and confused. This child seemed hardly to notice the burning bombed truck behind him as he bicycled through a street in Northern Ireland several years ago.*

problems to receive services from nearby agencies rather than distant facilities or institutions. Congress passed the Community Mental Health Act soon after, launching the community mental health movement across the United States. A number of other countries have launched similar movements.

As we observed in Chapter 1, a key principle of community treatment is prevention. Here clinicians actively reach out to clients rather than wait for them to seek treatment. Research suggests that such efforts are often very successful (Harper & Dwivedi; 2004; Oxley, 2000). Community workers recognize three types of prevention, which they call *primary, secondary,* and *tertiary.*

Primary prevention consists of efforts to improve community attitudes and policies. Its goal is to prevent psychological disorders altogether. Community workers may lobby for better community recreational programs or child-care facilities, consult with a local school board to help develop a curriculum, or offer health fairs or public workshops on stress reduction (LeCroy, 2005; Oldenberg & Burton, 2004).

Secondary prevention consists of identifying and treating psychological disorders in the early stages, before they become serious. Community workers may work with schoolteachers, ministers, or police to help them recognize the early signs of psychological dysfunction and teach them how to help people find treatment (Hafner et al., 2004; Molina et al., 2005).

Secondary prevention in action *Community mental health professionals sometimes work with police and other public servants, teaching them how to address the psychological needs of people who are under extreme stress and upset. This 8-year-old had to call the police when he saw his father attacking his mother with a knife. The child's rage, frustration, and emotional pain are apparent.*

>>BY THE NUMBERS

**Marital Infidelity
over the Past Decade**

22% Percentage of married men who
confessed in 1991 to having had an
extramarital affair <<

- -

22% Married men who confessed in 2002 to
an extramarital affair <<

- -

10% Married women who confessed in 1991
to having had an extramarital affair <<

- -

15% Married women who confessed in 2002
to an extramarital affair <<

(National Opinion Research, 2005;
Ali & Miller, 2004)

The goal of *tertiary prevention* is to provide effective treatment as soon as it is needed so that moderate or severe disorders do not become long-term problems. Today community agencies across the United States do successfully offer tertiary care for millions of people with moderate psychological problems, but, as we also observed in Chapter 1, they often fail to provide the services needed by hundreds of thousands with severe disturbances (Weisman, 2004). One of the reasons for this failure is lack of funding, an issue that we shall return to in later chapters (Weisman, 2004; Humphreys & Rappaport, 1993).

Assessing the Sociocultural Model

The sociocultural model has added greatly to the understanding and treatment of abnormal functioning. Today most clinicians take family, cultural, social, and societal issues into account, factors that were overlooked just 30 years ago. In addition, clinicians have become more aware of the impact of clinical and social labels. Finally, as we have just observed, sociocultural treatment formats sometimes succeed where traditional approaches have failed.

At the same time, the sociocultural model, like the other models, has certain problems. To begin with, sociocultural research findings are often difficult to interpret. Research may reveal a relationship between certain sociocultural factors and a particular disorder yet fail to establish that they are its cause. Studies show a link between family conflict and schizophrenia, for example, but that finding does not necessarily mean that family dysfunction causes schizophrenia. It is equally possible that family functioning is disrupted by the tension and conflict created by the schizophrenic behavior of a family member (Madianos et al., 2004).

Another limitation of the model is its inability to predict abnormality in specific individuals. For example, if societal conditions such as prejudice and discrimination are key causes of anxiety and depression, why do only some of the people subjected to such forces experience psychological disorders? Are still other factors necessary for the development of the disorders?

Given these limitations, most clinicians view sociocultural explanations as operating in conjunction with biological or psychological explanations. They agree that sociocultural factors may create a climate favorable to the development of certain disorders. They believe, however, that biological or psychological conditions or both must also be present in order for the disorders to evolve.

PUTTING IT together

Integration of the Models

Today's leading models vary widely (see Table 3-5). They look at behavior differently, begin with different assumptions, arrive at different conclusions, and apply different treatments. Yet none of the models has proved consistently superior. Each helps us appreciate a key aspect of human functioning, and each has important strengths as well as serious limitations.

With all their differences, the conclusions and techniques of the various models are often compatible. Certainly our understanding and treatment of abnormal behavior are more complete if we appreciate the biological, psychological, and sociocultural aspects of a person's problem rather than only one of them. Not surprisingly, then, a growing number of clinicians are formulating explanations of abnormal behavior that consider more than one kind of cause at a time. These explanations, sometimes called **biopsychosocial theories,** state that abnormality results from the interaction of genetic, biological, developmental, emotional, behavioral, cognitive, social, cultural, and societal influences (Gatchel, 2005; Suls & Rothman, 2004). If so, the task facing researchers and clinicians is to identify the relative importance of each factor and learn how the factors work together to produce abnormal functioning. A case of depression, for example, might best be explained by pointing collectively to an individual's inheritance of unfavorable genes, traumatic losses during childhood, negative ways of thinking, and social isolation.

•**BIOPSYCHOSOCIAL THEORIES**•Explanations that attribute the cause of abnormality to an interaction of genetic, biological, developmental, emotional, behavioral, cognitive, social, and societal influences.

Table 3-5

Comparing the Models

	Biological	Psychodynamic	Behavioral	Cognitive	Humanistic	Existential	Socio-Cultural
Cause of dysfunction	Biological malfunction	Underlying conflicts	Maladaptive learning	Maladaptive thinking	Self-deceit	Avoidance of responsibility	Family or social stress
Research support	Strong	Modest	Strong	Strong	Weak	Weak	Moderate
Consumer designation	Patient	Patient	Client	Client	Patient or client	Patient or client	Client
Therapist role	Doctor	Interpreter	Teacher	Persuader	Observer	Collaborator	Social facilitator
Key therapist technique	Biological intervention	Free association and interpretation	Conditioning	Reasoning	Reflection	Varied	Social intervention
Therapy goal	Biological repair	Broad psychological change	Functional behaviors	Adaptive thinking	Self-actualization	Authentic life	Effective family or social system

Some biopsychosocial theorists favor a *diathesis-stress* explanation of how the various factors work together to cause abnormal functioning ("diathesis" means a vulnerability or a predisposed tendency). According to this theory, people must first have a biological, psychological, or sociocultural predisposition to develop a disorder and must then be subjected to episodes of severe stress. In a case of depression, for example, we might find that unfavorable genes and related biochemical abnormalities predispose the individual to develop the disorder, while the loss of a loved one actually triggers its onset.

Other biopsychosocial theorists favor a *reciprocal effects* explanation of abnormal functioning. They believe that some key factors help produce abnormal functioning by influencing other key factors—that is, by increasing the likelihood or intensity of the other factors (Saudino et al., 2004, 1997; Kendler et al., 1995). Say, for example, a man inherits a genetic tendency to be timid and awkward. Because of his timidity and awkwardness, this individual may accept unpleasant partners in his life more readily than most other people would, thus increasing his chances of experiencing stressful relationships, breakups, or periods of isolation in his life—each a factor conducive to depression. In addition, his experiences of interpersonal stress may lower his serotonin activity, another factor conducive to depression. In short, by profoundly affecting each other, a variety of relevant factors may collectively drive an individual toward depression.

In a similar quest for integration, many therapists are now combining treatment techniques from several models. In fact, 27 percent of today's clinical psychologists, 34 percent of social workers, and 53 percent of psychiatrists describe their approach as "eclectic" or "integrative" (Prochaska & Norcross, 2003). Studies confirm that clinical problems often respond better to combined approaches than to any one therapy alone. For example, as we shall see, drug therapy combined with cognitive therapy is sometimes the most effective treatment for depression (TADS, 2005, 2004).

Given the recent rise in biopsychosocial theories and combination treatments, our examination of abnormal behavior throughout this book will take two directions. As different disorders are presented, we will be interested in how today's models explain each disorder, how clinicians who endorse each model treat people with the disorder, and how well these explanations and treatments are supported by research. Just as important, however, we will also be observing how the explanations and treatments may build upon and strengthen each other, and we will examine current efforts toward integration of the models.

>>LOOKING BACK

Beliefs about Dreams

Ancient Egypt	Dreams were considered messages from the gods «
Bible	Dreams were often believed to be prophetic «
Ancient Greece	Aristotle considered dreams to be products of the mind, not of the gods «
Middle Ages	Dreams were viewed as works of the Devil «
Early 20th century	Freud considered dreams to be expressions of repressed needs and conflicts «
1953	The discovery that people dream during the phase of sleep called *rapid eye movement* (*REM*) opened the door to various neuroscience explanations of dreams. «

(Domhoff, 2005; Solms, 2005; Hobson, 2004; Winson, 2004; Kantrowitz & Springen, 2004; Van de Castle, 1993)

[SUMMARY AND REVIEW]

■ **Models of psychological abnormality** Scientists and clinicians use *models,* or *paradigms,* to understand and treat abnormal behavior. The principles and techniques of treatment used by clinical practitioners correspond to their preferred models. *pp. 47–49*

■ **The biological model** Biological theorists look at the biological processes of human functioning to explain abnormal behavior, pointing to *anatomical* or *biochemical* problems in the brain and body. Such abnormalities are sometimes the result of *genetic inheritance of abnormalities, normal evolution,* or *viral infections.* Biological therapists use physical and chemical methods to help people overcome their psychological problems. The leading ones are *drug therapy, electroconvulsive therapy,* and, on rare occasions, *psychosurgery. pp. 49–54*

■ **The psychodynamic model** Psychodynamic theorists believe that an individual's behavior, whether normal or abnormal, is determined by underlying psychological forces. They consider psychological conflicts to be rooted in early parent-child relationships and traumatic experiences. The psychodynamic model was formulated by Sigmund Freud, who said that three dynamic forces—the *id, ego,* and *superego*—interact to produce thought, feeling, and behavior. Other psychodynamic theories are *ego theory, self theory,* and *object relations theory.* Psychodynamic therapists help people uncover past traumas and the inner conflicts that have resulted from them. They use a number of techniques, including *free association* and interpretations of psychological phenomena such as *resistance, transference,* and *dreams.* The leading contemporary psychodynamic approaches include short-term psychodynamic therapies and relational psychoanalytic therapy. *pp. 54–60*

■ **The behavioral model** Behaviorists concentrate on *behaviors* and propose that they develop in accordance with the *principles of learning.* These theorists hold that three types of conditioning—*classical conditioning, operant conditioning,* and *modeling*—account for all behavior, whether normal or dysfunctional. The goal of the behavioral therapies is to identify the client's problematic behaviors and replace them with more appropriate ones, using techniques based on one or more of the principles of learning. The classical conditioning approach of *systematic desensitization,* for example, has been effective in treating phobias. *pp. 61–64*

■ **The cognitive model** According to the cognitive model, we must understand human thought to understand human behavior. When people display abnormal patterns of functioning, cognitive theorists point to cognitive problems, such as *maladaptive assumptions* and *illogical thinking processes.* Cognitive therapists try to help people recognize and change their faulty ideas and thinking processes. Among the most widely used cognitive treatments is Beck's *cognitive therapy. pp. 64–66*

■ **The humanistic-existential model** The humanistic-existential model focuses on the human need to successfully confront philosophical issues such as self-awareness, values, meaning, and choice in order to be satisfied in life.

Humanists believe that people are driven to *self-actualize.* When this drive is interfered with, abnormal behavior may result. One group of humanistic therapists, *client-centered therapists,* try to create a very supportive therapy climate in which people can look at themselves honestly and acceptingly, thus opening the door to self-actualization. Another group, *gestalt therapists,* use more active techniques to help people recognize and accept their needs.

According to existentialists, abnormal behavior results from hiding from life's responsibilities. Existential therapists encourage people to accept *responsibility* for their lives, to recognize their *freedom to choose* a different course, and to choose to live with greater meaning. *pp. 66–70*

■ **The sociocultural model** The sociocultural model looks outward to the social forces that affect members of a society. Some sociocultural theorists focus on *societal labels* and *roles;* they hold that society calls certain people "mentally ill" and that the label itself may influence how a person behaves and is responded to. Still others emphasize the *family system,* believing that a family's structure or communication patterns may force members to behave in abnormal ways. In addition, many socio-cultural theorists look at *social networks* and *support, cultural background,* or *spirituality* to determine what roles these factors play in psychological functioning.

Special sociocultural principles are often on display in *culture-sensitive, group, family,* and *couple therapies.* Research indicates that these approaches are useful for some problems and under some circumstances. In *community treatment,* therapists try to work with people in settings close to home, school, and work. Their goal is either *primary, secondary,* or *tertiary prevention. pp. 71–80*

>>> CRITICAL THOUGHTS <<<

1. What might the enormous popularity of psychotropic drugs suggest about the needs and coping styles of individuals today and about problem solving in our technological society? *pp. 52–53*

2. In *Paradise Lost* Milton wrote, "The mind . . . can make a heaven of hell, a hell of heaven." Which model(s) of abnormal functioning would agree with this statement? *pp. 54–60; 64–70*

3. Although Freud argued that psychoanalytic therapy needs to be long-term and in depth, he himself sometimes practiced a short-term version of the approach. Why might Freud have chosen to break his own rules of conduct in certain cases? Can you think of other pioneers, in or out of the clinical field, whose actual work sometimes departed from their theories? *pp. 57–60*

4. Twenty-one percent of Americans say they are regularly "bored out of their mind" (Kanner, 1999). How might humanistic-existential theorists explain the phenomenon of severe boredom and such reactions to it? *pp. 66–70*

5. In *Anna Karenina* the writer Leo Tolstoy wrote, "All happy families resemble one another; every unhappy family is unhappy in its own fashion." Would family systems theorists agree with Tolstoy? *pp. 71–72; 75–78*

6. Why might positive religious beliefs be linked to mental health? Why have so many clinicians been suspicious of religious beliefs for so long? *pp. 73–74*

7. What might be the advantages and disadvantages of self-help groups in comparison with professional treatment? *pp. 75, 78*

⊙—[CYBERSTUDY] ——————————————— >>>

SEARCH THE *ABNORMAL PSYCHOLOGY* CD-ROM FOR

▲ Chapter 3 Video Cases and Discussions
   Observe the biological, psychodynamic, and sociocultural models in operation.
   How do treatments vary?
   Are dreams the "royal road to the unconscious"?

▲ Chapter 3 Practical, Research, and Decision-Making Exercises
   Detecting past models in today's theories
   Sorting out today's models
   Recognizing Freud's wide-ranging influence

▲ Chapter 3 Practice Test and Feedback

LOG ON TO THE COMER WEB PAGE FOR

▲ Suggested Web links, exercises, FAQ page, additional Chapter 3 practice test questions
   <www.worthpublishers.com/comer>

——————————————————————————— <<<

Clinical Assessment, Diagnosis, and Treatment

Angela Savanti was 22 years old, lived at home with her mother, and was employed as a secretary in a large insurance company. She . . . had had passing periods of "the blues" before, but her present feelings of despondency were of much greater proportion. She was troubled by a severe depression and frequent crying spells, which had not lessened over the past two months. Angela found it hard to concentrate on her job, had great difficulty falling asleep at night, and had a poor appetite. . . . Her depression had begun after she and her boyfriend Jerry broke up two months previously.

(Leon, 1984, p. 109)

Her feelings of despondency led Angela Savanti to make an appointment with a therapist at a local counseling center. The first step the clinician took was to learn as much as possible about Angela and her disturbance. Who is she, what is her life like, and what precisely are her symptoms? The answers might help to reveal the causes and probable course of her present dysfunction and suggest what kinds of strategies would be most likely to help her. Treatment could then be tailored to Angela's needs and particular pattern of abnormal functioning.

In Chapters 2 and 3 we saw how researchers in abnormal psychology build a *nomothetic,* or *general,* understanding of abnormal functioning. Clinical practitioners apply this general information in their work, but their main focus when faced with a new client is to gather **idiographic,** or individual, information about their clients. To help a particular client overcome his or her problems, a practitioner must have the fullest possible understanding of that person and know the circumstances under which the problems arose. Only after thoroughly examining the person can the therapist effectively apply relevant nomothetic information. Clinicians use the procedures of *assessment* and *diagnosis* to gather individual information about a client. Then they are in a position to apply *treatment.*

Clinical Assessment: How and Why Does the Client Behave Abnormally?

Assessment is simply the collecting of relevant information in an effort to reach a conclusion. It goes on in every realm of life. We make assessments when we decide what cereal to buy or which presidential candidate to vote for. College admissions officers, who have to select the "best" of the students applying to their college, depend on academic records, recommendations, achievement test scores, interviews, and application forms to help them decide. Employers, who have to predict which applicants are most likely to be effective workers, collect information from résumés, interviews, references, and perhaps on-the-job observations.

Clinical assessment is used to determine how and why a person is behaving abnormally and how that person may be helped. It also enables clinicians to evaluate people's progress after they have been in treatment for a while and decide whether the treatment should be changed. The specific tools that are used to do an assessment depend on the clinician's theoretical orientation (see Box 4-1). Psychodynamic clinicians, for example, use methods that assess a client's personality and probe for any unconscious conflicts he or she may be experiencing. This kind of assessment, called a *personality assessment,* enables them to piece together a clinical picture in accordance with the principles of their model. Behavioral and cognitive clinicians are more likely to use assessment methods that reveal specific dysfunctional behaviors and cognitions. The goal of this kind of assessment, called a *behavioral assessment,* is to produce a *functional analysis* of the person's behaviors—an analysis of how the behaviors are learned and reinforced (Fox & Davis, 2005; Haynes & Heiby, 2004).

The hundreds of clinical assessment techniques and tools that have been developed fall into three categories: *clinical interviews, tests,* and *observations.* To be useful, these tools must be *standardized* and have clear *reliability* and *validity.*

Characteristics of Assessment Tools

All clinicians must follow the same procedures when they use a particular technique of assessment. To **standardize** a technique is to set up common steps to be followed whenever it is administered. Similarly, clinicians must standardize the way they interpret the results of an assessment tool in order to be able to understand what a particular score means. They may standardize the scores of a test, for example, by first administering it to a group of subjects whose performance will then serve as a common standard, or norm, against which later individual scores can be measured. The group that initially takes the test is called the *standardization sample.* This sample must be typical of the larger population for whom the test is intended. If an aggressiveness test meant for the public at large were standardized on a group of marines, for example, the resulting "norm" might turn out to be misleadingly high.

Reliability refers to the *consistency* of assessment measures. A good assessment tool will always yield the same results in the same situation (Aiken & Groth-Marnat, 2006; Hempel, 2005). An assessment tool has high *test–retest reliability,* one kind of reliability, if it yields the same results every time it is given to the same people. If a woman's responses on a particular test indicate that she is generally a heavy drinker, the test should produce the same result when she takes it again a week later. To measure test–retest reliability, subjects are tested on two occasions and the two scores are correlated. The higher the correlation, the greater the test's reliability (see Chapter 2).

An assessment tool shows high *interrater* (or *interjudge*) *reliability,* another kind of reliability, if different judges independently agree on how to score and interpret it. True–false and multiple-choice tests yield consistent scores no matter who evaluates them, but other tests require that the evaluator make a judgment. Consider a test that requires the person to draw a copy of a picture, which a judge then rates for accuracy. Different judges may give different ratings to the same drawing.

Finally, an assessment tool must have **validity:** it must *accurately* measure what it is supposed to measure (Aiken & Groth-Marnat, 2006; Hersen, 2004). Suppose a weight scale reads 12 pounds every time a 10-pound bag of sugar is placed on it. Although the scale is reliable because its readings are consistent, those readings are not valid, or accurate.

A given assessment tool may appear to be valid simply because it makes sense and seems reasonable. However, this sort of validity, called *face validity,* does not by itself mean that the instrument is trustworthy. A test for depression, for example, might include questions about how often a person cries. Because it makes sense that depressed people would cry, these test questions would have face validity. It turns out, however, that many people cry a great deal for reasons other than depression, and some extremely depressed people fail to cry at all. Thus an assessment tool should not be used unless it meets more exacting criteria of validity, such as high predictive or concurrent validity.

Predictive validity is a tool's ability to predict future characteristics or behavior. Let us say that a test has been developed to

Unreliable assessments *On* American Idol, *the popular TV show, the performances of competing singers are assessed each week by judges Randy Jackson (left), Simon Cowell (center), and Paula Abdul. Typically, Cowell's assessment is negative (even insulting at times), Abdul's is positive, and Jackson's falls somewhere in between. Such low interrater reliability may reflect evaluator bias or defects in the scoring procedure.*

[BOX **4-1**]

Assessing Van Gogh

Vincent van Gogh led a tortured and unhappy life. In a legendary incident the artist cut off one of his ears. Later he was admitted to a mental institution, and ultimately he committed suicide at the age of 37. Van Gogh wrote a great deal about his pain and anguish, describing mental and physical torment and hallucinations. For years clinicians speculated that the artist suffered from a mood disorder, schizophrenia, or both. Recently, however, these assessments have been challenged (Hyams, 2003; Blumer, 2002).

A Harvard neurologist, for example, has suggested that van Gogh in fact suffered from *Geschwind's syndrome,* technically known as *interictal personality disorder,* caused by brain seizure disorder, or epilepsy. Van Gogh displayed many of

its symptoms, including excessive drawing (hypergraphia), hyperreligiosity, and aggression (Hochman, 2000; Trotter, 1985).

In contrast, medical specialists in Colorado have concluded that van Gogh suffered from an extreme form of Menière's syndrome, a disorder marked by an excessive buildup of fluid in the inner ear. The enormous pressure may produce nausea, dizziness, poor balance, pain, deafness, and constant buzzing or ringing sensations. Perhaps van Gogh cut off his ear in an effort to reduce the pain. And perhaps his other problems and pains arose from the severe secondary psychological problems that can accompany Menière's syndrome (Hochman, 2000; Scott, 1990).

Courtesy of the Fogg Art Museum, Harvard University Art Museums

Vincent van Gogh, a self-portrait

identify elementary school children who are likely to take up cigarette smoking in junior high school. The test gathers information about the children's parents—their personal characteristics, smoking habits, and attitudes toward smoking—and on that basis identifies high-risk children. To establish the test's predictive validity, we could administer it to a group of elementary school students, wait until they were in junior high school, and then check to see which children actually did become smokers.

Concurrent validity is the degree to which the measures gathered from one tool agree with measures gathered from other assessment techniques. Subjects' scores on a new test designed to measure anxiety, for example, should correlate highly with their scores on other anxiety tests or with their behavior during clinical interviews.

Before any assessment technique can be fully useful, it must meet the requirements of standardization, reliability, and validity. No matter how insightful or clever a technique may be, clinicians cannot profitably use its results if they are uninterpretable, inconsistent, or inaccurate. Unfortunately, more than a few clinical assessment tools fall short, suggesting that at least some clinical assessments, too, miss their mark.

Clinical Interviews

Most of us feel instinctively that the best way to get to know people is to meet with them face to face. Under these circumstances, we can see them react to what we do and say, observe as well as listen as they answer, watch them observing us, and generally get a sense of who they are. A **clinical interview** is just such a face-to-face encounter (Sommers-Flanagan & Sommers-Flanagan, 2003). If during a clinical interview a man looks as happy as can be while describing his sadness over the recent death of his mother, the clinician may suspect that the man actually has conflicting emotions about this loss. Almost all practitioners use interviews as part of the assessment process.

CONDUCTING THE INTERVIEW The interview is often the first contact between client and clinician. Clinicians use it to collect detailed information about the person's problems and feelings, lifestyle and relationships, and other personal history. They may also ask about the person's expectations of therapy and motives for seeking it. The clinician who worked with Angela Savanti began with a face-to-face interview:

•**IDIOGRAPHIC UNDERSTANDING**•An understanding of the behavior of a particular individual.

•**ASSESSMENT**•The process of collecting and interpreting relevant information about a client or subject.

•**STANDARDIZATION**•The process in which a test is administered to a large group of persons whose performance then serves as a common standard or norm against which any individual's score can be measured.

•**RELIABILITY**•A measure of the consistency of test or research results.

•**VALIDITY**•The accuracy of a test's or study's results; that is, the extent to which the test or study actually measures or shows what it claims.

•**CLINICAL INTERVIEW**•A face-to-face encounter in which clinicians ask questions of clients, weigh their responses and reactions, and learn about them and their psychological problems.

Angela was dressed neatly when she appeared for her first interview. She was attractive, but her eyes were puffy and ringed with dark circles. She answered questions and related information about her life history in a slow, flat tone of voice, which had an impersonal quality to it. She sat stiffly in her chair. . . .

The client stated that the time period just before she and her boyfriend terminated their relationship had been one of extreme emotional turmoil. She was not sure whether she wanted to marry Jerry, and he began to demand that she decide either one way or the other. Mrs. Savanti [Angela's mother] did not seem to like Jerry and was very cold and aloof whenever he came to the house. Angela felt caught in the middle and unable to make a decision about her future. After several confrontations with Jerry over whether she would marry him or not, he told her he felt that she would never decide, so he was not going to see her anymore. . . .

Angela stated that her childhood was a very unhappy period. Her father was seldom home, and when he was present, her parents fought constantly. . . .

Angela recalled feeling very guilty when Mr. Savanti left. . . . She revealed that whenever she thought of her father, she always felt that she had been responsible in some way for his leaving the family. . . .

Angela described her mother as the "long-suffering type" who said that she had sacrificed her life to make her children happy, and the only thing she ever got in return was grief and unhappiness. . . . When Angela and [her sister] began dating, Mrs. Savanti . . . would make disparaging remarks about the boys they had been with and about men in general. . . .

Angela revealed that she had often been troubled with depressed moods. During high school, if she got a lower grade in a subject than she had expected, her initial response was one of anger, followed by depression. She began to think that she was not smart enough to get good grades, and she blamed herself for studying too little. Angela also became despondent when she got into an argument with her mother or felt that she was being taken advantage of at work. . . .

The intensity and duration of the [mood change] that she experienced when she broke up with Jerry were much more severe. She was not sure why she was so depressed, but she began to feel it was an effort to walk around and go out to work. Talking with others became difficult. Angela found it hard to concentrate, and she began to forget things she was supposed to do. . . . She preferred to lie in bed rather than be with anyone, and she often cried when alone.

(Leon, 1984, pp. 110–115)

Beyond gathering basic background data of this kind, clinical interviewers give special attention to whatever topics they consider most important. Psychodynamic interviewers try to learn about the person's needs and memories of past events and relationships. Behavioral interviewers try to pinpoint the precise nature of the abnormal responses, including information about the stimuli that trigger such responses and their consequences. Cognitive interviewers try to discover assumptions and interpretations that influence the person. Humanistic clinicians ask about the person's self-evaluation, self-concept, and values. Biological clinicians look for signs of biochemical or brain dysfunction. And sociocultural interviewers ask about the family, social, and cultural environments.

Interviews can be either unstructured or structured (Aiken & Groth-Marnat, 2006; Theinemann, 2004). In an *unstructured interview,* the clinician asks open-ended questions, perhaps as simple as "Would you tell me about yourself?" The lack of structure allows the interviewer to follow interesting leads and explore relevant topics that could not be anticipated before the interview.

In a *structured interview,* clinicians ask prepared questions. Sometimes they use a published *interview schedule*—a standard set of questions designed for all interviews. Many structured interviews include a **mental status exam,** a set of questions and observations that systematically evaluate the client's awareness, orientation with regard to time and place, attention span, memory, judgment and insight, thought content and processes, mood, and appearance (Salloway et al., 2006; Powsner & Powsner, 2005). A structured format ensures that clinicians will cover the same kinds of important issues in all their interviews and enables them to compare the responses of different individuals (Grant et al., 2004; Shear et al., 2001).

Although most clinical interviews have both unstructured and structured portions (Fylan, 2005; Kulic, 2005), many clinicians favor one kind over the other. Unstructured interviews typically appeal to psychodynamic and humanistic clinicians, while structured formats are widely used by behavioral and cognitive clinicians, who need to pinpoint behaviors, attitudes, or thinking processes that may underlie abnormal behavior (Hersen, 2004; Thienemann, 2004).

WHAT ARE THE LIMITATIONS OF CLINICAL INTERVIEWS? Although interviews often produce valuable information about people, there are limits to what they can accomplish (Hersen, 2004; Meyer et al., 2001). One problem is that they sometimes lack validity, or accuracy. Individuals may intentionally mislead in order to present themselves in a positive light or to avoid discussing embarrassing topics. Or people may be unable to give an accurate report in their interview. Individuals who suffer from depression, for example, take a pessimistic view of themselves and may describe themselves as poor workers or inadequate parents when that isn't the case at all.

Interviewers too may make mistakes in judgments that slant the information they gather. They usually rely too heavily on first impressions, for example, and give too much weight to unfavorable information about a client (Meehl, 1996, 1960). Interviewer biases, including gender, race, and age biases, may also influence the interviewers' interpretations of what a client says (McFarland et al., 2004; Plante, 1999).

Interviews, particularly unstructured ones, may also lack reliability (Wood et al., 2002; Wiens et al., 2001). People respond differently to different interviewers, providing less information to a cold interviewer than to a warm and supportive one (Black, 2005; Eisenthal, Koopman, & Lazare, 1983). Similarly, a clinician's race, sex, age, and appearance may influence a client's responses (Caplan & Cosgrove, 2004; Paurohit, Dowd, & Cottingham, 1982).

Because different clinicians can obtain different answers and draw different conclusions, even when they ask the same questions of the same person, some researchers believe that interviewing should be discarded as a tool of clinical assessment. As we shall see, however, the two other kinds of clinical assessment methods also have serious limitations.

Clinical Tests

Tests are devices for gathering information about a few aspects of a person's psychological functioning, from which broader information about the person can be inferred (Gregory, 2004). On the surface, it may look easy to design an effective test. Every month, magazines and newspapers present new tests that supposedly tell us about our personalities, our relationships, our sex lives, our reactions to stress, our ability to succeed. Such tests might sound convincing, but most of them lack reliability, validity, and standardization. That is, they do not yield consistent, accurate information or say anything meaningful about where we stand in comparison with others.

More than 500 clinical tests are currently in use throughout the United States. The ones that clinicians use most often are of six kinds: *projective tests, personality inventories, response inventories, psychophysiological tests, neurological and neuropsychological tests,* and *intelligence tests.*

PROJECTIVE TESTS **Projective tests** require that subjects interpret vague stimuli, such as inkblots or ambiguous pictures, or follow open-ended instructions such as "Draw a person." Theoretically, when clues and instructions are so vague, subjects will "project" aspects of their personality into the task. Projective tests are used primarily by psychodynamic clinicians to help assess the unconscious drives and conflicts they believe to be

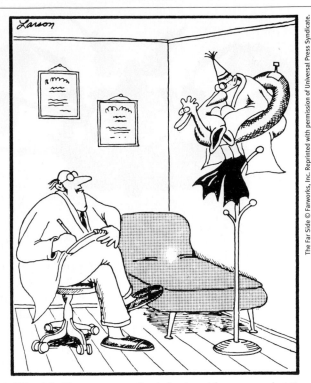

"So, Mr. Fenton, . . . Let's begin with your mother."

The Far Side © Farworks, Inc. Reprinted with permission of Universal Press Syndicate.

•**MENTAL STATUS EXAM**•A set of interview questions and observations designed to reveal the degree and nature of a client's abnormal functioning.

•**TEST**•A device for gathering information about a few aspects of a person's psychological functioning from which broader information about the person can be inferred.

•**PROJECTIVE TEST**•A test consisting of ambiguous material that people interpret or respond to.

FIGURE 4-1 *An inkblot similar to those used in the Rorschach*

at the root of abnormal functioning (Heydebrand & Wetzel, 2005; McGowen, 2001). The most widely used projective tests are the *Rorschach test,* the *Thematic Apperception Test, sentence-completion tests,* and *drawings.*

RORSCHACH TEST In 1911 Hermann Rorschach, a Swiss psychiatrist, experimented with the use of inkblots in his clinical work. He made thousands of blots by dropping ink on paper and then folding the paper in half to create a symmetrical but wholly accidental design, such as the one shown in Figure 4-1. Rorschach found that everyone saw images in these blots. In addition, the images a viewer saw seemed to correspond in important ways with his or her psychological condition. People diagnosed with schizophrenia, for example, tended to see images that differed from those described by people suffering from depression.

Rorschach selected 10 inkblots and published them in 1921 with instructions for their use in assessment. This set was called the *Rorschach Psychodynamic Inkblot Test.* Rorschach died just eight months later, at the age of 37, but his work was continued by others, and his inkblots took their place among the most widely used projective tests of the twentieth century.

Clinicians administer the "Rorschach," as it is commonly called, by presenting one inkblot card at a time and asking respondents what they see, what the inkblot seems to be, or what it reminds them of. In the following exchange, a tense 32-year-old woman who complains of feeling unworthy and lacking in confidence responds to one Rorschach inkblot:

Subject: Oh, dear! My goodness! O.K. Just this [upper] part is a bug. Something like an ant—one of the social group which is a worker, trying to pull something. I think this is some kind of food for the rest of the ants. It's a bee because it has wings, a worker bee bringing up something edible for the rest of the clan. . . . Here is the bee, the mouth and the wings. I don't think bees eat leaves but it looks like a leaf or a piece of lettuce.

Clinician: What makes it look like a piece of lettuce?

Subject: Its shape and it has a vein up the middle. It is definitely a bee.

(Klopfer & Davidson, 1962, p. 164)

In the early years, Rorschach testers paid special attention to the *themes* and *images* that the inkblots evoked, called the *thematic content* (Weiner, 2004, 2000). Testers now also pay attention to the *style* of the responses: Do the subjects view the design as a whole or see specific details? Do they focus on the blots or on the white spaces between them? Do they use or do they ignore the shadings and colors in several of the cards? Do they see human movement in the designs, or animal movement? Here is how the clinician interpreted the bug responses of the woman just quoted:

The bee may reflect the image she has of herself as a hard worker (a fact noted by her supervisor). In addition, the "bee bringing up something edible for the rest of the clan" suggests that she feels an overwhelming sense of responsibility toward others.

This card frequently evokes both masculine and feminine sexual associations, either in direct or symbolic form. Apparently [this woman] is not able to handle such material comfortably either overtly or in a more socialized manner, and so both sexual symbols are replaced by the oral symbolism of providing food.

(Klopfer & Davidson, 1962, pp. 182–183)

>>LOOKING BACK

Believe It or Not

By a strange coincidence, Hermann Rorschach's young schoolmates gave him the nickname Klex, a variant of the German *Klecks,* which means "inkblot" (Schwartz, 1993). **<<**

THEMATIC APPERCEPTION TEST The *Thematic Apperception Test (TAT)* is a pictorial projective test (Masling, 2004; Morgan & Murray, 1935). People who take the TAT are commonly shown 30 black-and-white pictures of individuals in vague situations and are asked to make up a dramatic story about each card. They must tell what is happening in the picture, what led up to it, what the characters are feeling and thinking, and what the outcome of the situation will be.

Clinicians who use the TAT believe that people always identify with one of the characters on each card, called the *hero*. The stories are thought to reflect the individuals' own circumstances, needs, emotions, and sense of reality and fantasy. For example, a female client seems to be revealing her own feelings in this story about the TAT picture shown in Figure 4-2, one of the few TAT pictures permitted for display in textbooks:

> This is a woman who has been quite troubled by memories of a mother she was resentful toward. She has feelings of sorrow for the way she treated her mother, her memories of her mother plague her. These feelings seem to be increasing as she grows older and sees her children treating her the same way that she treated her mother.
>
> *(Aiken, 1985, p. 372)*

SENTENCE-COMPLETION TEST The *sentence-completion test,* first developed in the 1920s (Payne, 1928), asks people to complete a series of unfinished sentences, such as "I wish _____" or "My father _____." The test is considered a good springboard for discussion and a quick and easy way to pinpoint topics to explore.

DRAWINGS On the assumption that a drawing tells us something about its creator, clinicians often ask clients to draw human figures and talk about them. Evaluations of these drawings are based on the details and shape of the drawing, solidity of the pencil line, location of the drawing on the paper, size of the figures, features of the figures, use of background, and comments made by the respondent during the drawing task. In the *Draw-a-Person (DAP) Test,* the most popular of the drawing tests, subjects are first told to draw "a person" and then are instructed to draw another person of the opposite sex.

WHAT ARE THE MERITS OF PROJECTIVE TESTS? Until the 1950s, projective tests were the most common technique for assessing personality. In recent years, however, clinicians and researchers have relied on them largely to gain "supplementary" insights (Westen et al., 1999). One reason for this shift is that practitioners who follow the newer models have less use for the tests than psychodynamic clinicians do. Even more important, the tests have not consistently demonstrated much reliability or validity (Wood et al., 2002).

In reliability studies, different clinicians have tended to score the same person's projective test quite differently. To address this problem and improve scoring consistency, several standardized procedures for administering and scoring the tests have been developed (Masling & Bornstein, 2005). For example, the *Rorschach Comprehensive System* (Exner, 2003) is a highly regarded scoring system that has often yielded impressive reliability scores among clinicians who are trained in its use and application (Meyer, Mihura, & Smith, 2005). However, only a minority of projective test administrators actually use such standardized procedures.

Research has also challenged the validity of projective tests. When clinicians try to describe a client's personality and feelings on the basis of responses to projective tests, their conclusions often fail to match the self-report of the client, the view of the psychotherapist, or the picture gathered from an extensive case history (Wood et al., 2002). Another validity problem is that projective tests are sometimes biased against minority ethnic groups (Dana, 2005) (see Table 4-1 on the next page). For example, people are supposed to identify with the characters in the Thematic Apperception Test (TAT) when they make

FIGURE 4-2 *A picture used in the Thematic Apperception Test*

Drawing test *Drawing tests are commonly used to assess the functioning of children. A popular one is the Kinetic Family Drawing test, in which children draw their household members performing some activity ("kinetic" means "active").*

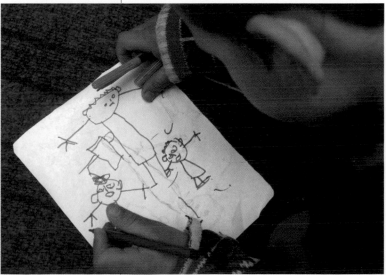

AP Photo/Suzanne Plunkett

Table 4-1

Multicultural Hot Spots in Assessment and Diagnosis

Cultural Hot Spot	Effect on Assessment or Diagnosis
• Immigrant client	**• Dominant-culture assessor**
Homeland culture may differ from current country's dominant culture	May misread culture-bound reactions as pathology
May have left homeland to escape war or oppression	May overlook client's vulnerability to posttraumatic stress
May not have strong support systems in this country	May overlook client's heightened vulnerability to stressors
Lifestyle (wealth and occupation) in this country may fall below lifestyle in homeland	May overlook client's sense of loss and frustration

May refuse or be unable to learn dominant language
  —May not understand questions
  —May not express complex feelings
	May misunderstand client's assessment responses
	May overlook or misdiagnose client's symptoms

• Ethnic-minority client	**• Dominant-culture assessor**
May reject dominant culture and identify only with own culture	May misread client's culture-bound responses as pathology
May distrust members of dominant culture, including assessor	May experience little rapport with client May misinterpret client's distrust as pathology
May be uncomfortable with dominant culture's values (e.g., assertiveness), making it hard to apply clinician's recommendations	May view client as unmotivated
May be bicultural (identifies with both own culture and dominant culture)	May misread client's expressions of ambivalence during assessment
May manifest stress in culture-bound ways (e.g., stress is expressed in somatic terms, such as stomachaches)	May misinterpret symptom patterns
May conflict with family members over cultural identity (e.g., teenagers may not share parents' cultural values)	May overlook family tensions
May hold cultural beliefs that seem strange to dominant culture (e.g., belief in communication with dead)	May misinterpret cultural responses as pathology (e.g., a delusion)
• Dominant-culture assessor	**• Ethnic-minority client**
May be unknowledgeable about ethnic minority culture	Cultural differences may be pathologized Symptoms may be overlooked
May hold cultural biases or stereotypes	Cultural differences may be pathologized Symptoms may be overlooked
May be unaware of client's discomfort	Discomfort level may rise unabated
May nonverbally convey own discomfort to ethnic minority client	May become tense and anxious
• Assessment/diagnostic tool	**• Ethnic-minority client**
Assessment tasks or questions may largely reflect dominant culture	May not relate to questions as dominant-culture clients do May experience discomfort or distrust May perform more poorly on test May offer answers that seem pathological
Minority cultures may be poorly represented in a test's standardization group	May perform more poorly on test May offer answers that seem pathological
• Classification system	**• Dominant-culture assessor**
May omit disorders that are unique to certain cultures (e.g., *koro* among Chinese, *ghost sickness* among Native Americans)	May overlook client's culture-bound disorders
May fail to recognize that symptoms of disorders sometimes vary by culture (e.g., delusions may differ from culture to culture)	May misread or overlook client's symptoms
May include categories of abnormality that reflect gender or cultural differences rather than clear research support	May pathologize gender or cultural differences (e.g., homosexuality was considered a mental disorder until 1973)

Source: Dana, 2005, 1998; Westermeyer, 2004, 2001, 1993; Sue, 2002, 2001; Sue & Sue, 2003; Sue et al., 1998; Lopez & Guarnaccia, 2005, 2000; Kirmayer, 2003, 2002, 2001; Tsai et al., 2001; Thakker & Ward, 1998.

The art of assessment *Clinicians often view works of art as informal projective tests in which artists reveal their conflicts and mental stability. The sometimes bizarre cat portraits of the early-twentieth-century artist Louis Wain, for example, have been interpreted as reflections of the psychosis with which he struggled for many years. Others believe such interpretations are incorrect, however, and note that the decorative patterns in some of his later paintings were actually based on textile designs.*

up stories about them, yet no members of minority groups are in the TAT pictures. In response to this problem, some clinicians have developed other TAT-like tests with African American or Hispanic figures (Dana, 2005; Costantino et al., 2001).

PERSONALITY INVENTORIES An alternative way to collect information about individuals is to ask them to assess themselves. The **personality inventory** asks respondents a wide range of questions about their behavior, beliefs, and feelings. In the typical personality inventory, individuals indicate whether or not each of a long list of statements applies to them. Clinicians then use the responses to draw conclusions about the person's personality and psychological functioning.

By far the most widely used personality inventory is the *Minnesota Multiphasic Personality Inventory* (*MMPI*) (Graham, 2006; Greene & Clopton, 2004). Two adult versions are available—the original test, published in 1945, and the *MMPI-2,* a 1989 revision. A special version of the test for adolescents, the *MMPI-A,* is also used widely.

The MMPI consists of more than 500 self-statements, to be labeled "true," "false," or "cannot say." The statements describe physical concerns; mood; morale; attitudes toward religion, sex, and social activities; and psychological symptoms, such as fears or hallucinations. The inventory was originally constructed by a method called *criterion keying.* The authors asked 724 "normal" people (hospital visitors) and 800 hospitalized mental patients to indicate whether or not each of hundreds of self-statements was true for them. Only statements that differentiated the hospitalized subjects from the normal subjects were incorporated into the inventory.

The items in the MMPI make up 10 clinical scales:

Hypochondriasis (HS) Items showing abnormal concern with bodily functions ("I have chest pains several times a week.")

Depression (D) Items showing extreme pessimism and hopelessness ("I often feel hopeless about the future.")

Hysteria (Hy) Items suggesting that the person may use physical or mental symptoms as a way of unconsciously avoiding conflicts and responsibilities ("My heart frequently pounds so hard I can feel it.")

Psychopathic deviate (PD) Items showing a repeated and gross disregard for social customs and an emotional shallowness ("My activities and interests are often criticized by others.")

•**PERSONALITY INVENTORY**•A test designed to measure broad personality characteristics, consisting of statements about behaviors, beliefs, and feelings that people evaluate as either characteristic or uncharacteristic of them.

>>**PSYCH•NOTES**

MMPI Preferences

According to surveys, 80 percent of professionals who administer an MMPI in their work use the MMPI-2, 37 percent the MMPI, and 40 percent the MMPI-A. <<

Around 68 percent of professionals who administer the MMPI today use computerized scoring, and 44 percent use computerized interpretations of the scores. <<

(Downey et al., 1998)

Masculinity-femininity (Mf) Items that are thought to distinguish male and female respondents ("I like to arrange flowers.")

Paranoia (Pa) Items that show abnormal suspiciousness and delusions of grandeur or persecution ("There are evil people trying to influence my mind.")

Psychasthenia (Pt) Items that show obsessions, compulsions, abnormal fears, and guilt and indecisiveness ("I save nearly everything I buy, even after I have no use for it.")

Schizophrenia (Sc) Items that show bizarre or unusual thoughts or behavior, including extreme withdrawal, delusions, or hallucinations ("Things around me do not seem real.")

Hypomania (Ma) Items that show emotional excitement, overactivity, and flight of ideas ("At times I feel very 'high' or very 'low' for no apparent reason.")

Social introversion (Si) Items that show shyness, little interest in people, and insecurity ("I am easily embarrassed.")

Scores for each scale can range from 0 to 120. When people score above 70, their functioning on that scale is considered deviant. When the scores are connected on a graph, a pattern called the *profile* takes shape, indicating the person's general personality and underlying emotional needs. Figure 4-3 shows the MMPI profile of John, a depressed 27-year-old man. It indicates that he is very depressed, feels anxious and threatened, is socially withdrawn, and is prone to physical complaints. In addition to such clinical measures, questions have been built into the MMPI to detect whether respondents are lying, defensive, or careless in their answers (Graham, 2006; Butcher, 2000).

The MMPI-2, the newer version of the MMPI, contains 567 items—many identical to those in the original, some rewritten to reflect current language ("upset stomach," for instance, replaces "acid stomach"), and others that are new. This version was developed partly because the language of the original MMPI was growing out of date and partly because the designers of the original scale had used a narrow standardization sample that did not represent the diverse populations that now mark Western societies. To better ensure the MMPI-2's validity and generalizability, the scale's designers sampled 2,600 persons who more properly represented various geographical regions; racial, cultural, and gender groups; occupations; educational levels; and treatment and nontreatment setttings. In turn, the MMPI-2 is a more valid indicator of personality and abnormal functioning than the original version (Graham, 2006; Gotts & Knudsen, 2005; Greene & Clopton, 2004).

The MMPI and other personality inventories have several advantages over projective tests (Wood et al., 2002). Because they are paper-and-pencil (or computerized) tests, they do not take much time to administer, and they are objectively scored. Like the MMPI, most personality inventories are standardized, so one person's scores can be compared to those of many others. Moreover, they often display greater test–retest reliability than projective tests. For example, people who take the MMPI a second time after a period of less than two weeks receive approximately the same scores (Graham, 2006).

Personality inventories also appear to have greater validity, or accuracy, than projective tests (Selbom et al., 2005; Wood et al., 2000). However, they can hardly be considered *highly* valid. When clinicians have used these tests alone, they have not typically been able to judge a respondent's personality accurately (Johnson et al., 1996). One problem is that the personality traits that the tests seek to measure cannot be examined directly. How can we fully know a person's character, emotions, and needs from self-reports alone?

Another problem is that despite the more diverse sampling of standardization groups conducted by the MMPI-2 designers, this and other personality tests retain certain cultural limitations. In particular, they often fail to allow for cultural differences in people's responses (Dana, 2005). Responses indicative of a psychological disorder in one culture may be normal responses in another (Dana, 2005, 2000). In Puerto Rico, for example, where it is common to practice spiritualism, it would be normal to answer "true" to the MMPI item "Evil spirits possess me at times." In other populations, that response could indicate psychopathology (Rogler, Malgady, & Rodriguez, 1989).

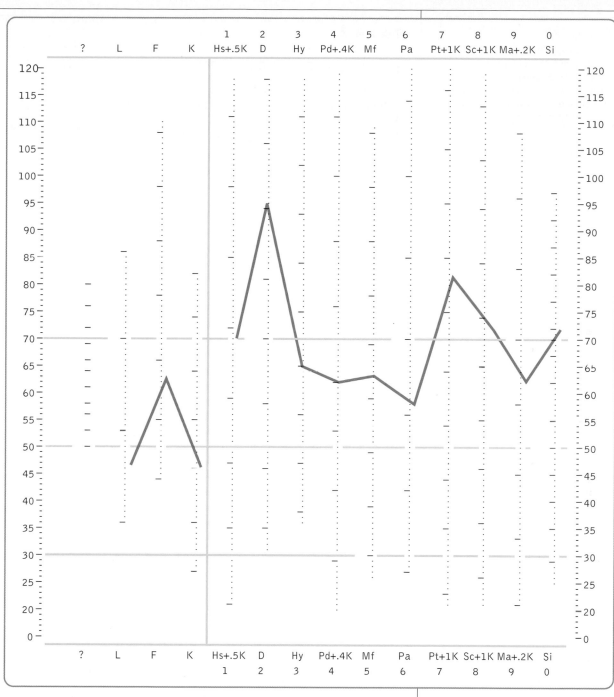

| | ? | L | F | K | 1
Hs+.5K | 2
D | 3
Hy | 4
Pd+.4K | 5
Mf | 6
Pa | 7
Pt+1K | 8
Sc+1K | 9
Ma+.2K | 0
Si | |

FIGURE **4-3** **An MMPI profile** *The profile of John, a 27-year-old man, suggests that he is depressed. He also appears to be anxious, prone to physical complaints, indecisive, introverted, and insecure. (From Graham, 1977, p. 164.)*

Despite their limited validity, personality inventories continue to be popular (Greene & Clopton, 2004; Kamphaus & Frick, 2002). Research indicates that they can help clinicians learn about people's personal styles and disorders as long as they are used in combination with interviews or other assessment tools.

RESPONSE INVENTORIES Like personality inventories, **response inventories** ask people to provide detailed information about themselves, but these tests focus on one specific area of functioning. For example, one such test may measure affect (emotion), another social skills, and still another cognitive processes. Clinicians can use them to determine the role such factors play in a person's disorder.

Affective inventories measure the severity of such emotions as anxiety, depression, and anger (Wilson et al., 2004; Beidel et al., 2000, 1995). In one of the most widely used affective inventories, the Beck Depression Inventory, shown in Table 4-2 on the next page, people rate their level of sadness and its effect on their functioning. *Social skills inventories,* used particularly by behavioral and sociocultural clinicians, ask respondents to

•**RESPONSE INVENTORIES**•Tests designed to measure a person's responses in one specific area of functioning, such as affect, social skills, or cognitive processes.

>>**LOOKING AROUND**

Spotting Depression Family physicians recognize fewer than one-third of all cases of clinical depression that they encounter among their patients. Most of the undetected cases are mild (Coyne et al., 1995). <<

Treatment Delay Most individuals with mood, anxiety, or addictive disorders fail to contact a therapist until at least six years after the initial onset of their symptoms (Kessler et al., 1998). <<

College Counseling At least 8 percent of all college students seek psychotherapy at their college's counseling center. The percentage is higher at small, private colleges and prestigious schools (Gallagher, 1998). <<

Table 4-2

Sample Items from the Beck Depression Inventory

Items	Inventory	
Suicidal ideas	0	I don't have any thoughts of killing myself.
	1	I have thoughts of killing myself but I would not carry them out.
	2	I would like to kill myself.
	3	I would kill myself if I had the chance.
Work inhibition	0	I can work about as well as before.
	1	It takes extra effort to get started at doing something.
	2	I have to push myself very hard to do anything.
	3	I can't do any work at all.
Loss of libido	0	I have not noticed any recent change in my interest in sex.
	1	I am less interested in sex than I used to be.
	2	I am much less interested in sex now.
	3	I have lost interest in sex completely.

indicate how they would react in a variety of social situations (Deniz, Hamarta, & Ari, 2005). *Cognitive inventories* reveal a person's typical thoughts and assumptions and can uncover counterproductive patterns of thinking that may be at the root of abnormal functioning (Glass & Merluzzi, 2000). They are, not surprisingly, often used by cognitive therapists and researchers.

Because response inventories collect information directly from the clients themselves, they have strong face validity. Thus both the number of these tests and the number of clinicians who use them have increased steadily in the past 25 years (Black, 2005). At the same time, however, these inventories have major limitations. Unlike the personality inventories, they rarely include questions to indicate whether people are being careless or inaccurate in their accounts. Moreover, with the notable exceptions of the Beck Depression Inventory and a few others, response inventories have generally not been subjected to careful standardization, reliability, and validity procedures (Kamphaus & Frick, 2002; Canals et al., 2001). Often they are improvised as a need arises, without being tested for accuracy and consistency.

PSYCHOPHYSIOLOGICAL TESTS Clinicians may also use **psychophysiological tests,** which measure physiological responses as possible indicators of psychological problems (Allen, 2002). This practice began three decades ago after several studies suggested that states of anxiety are regularly accompanied by physiological changes, particularly increases in heart rate, body temperature, blood pressure, skin reactions (*galvanic skin response*), and muscle contraction. The measuring of physiological changes has since played a key role in the assessment of certain psychological disorders.

One psychophysiological test is the *polygraph,* popularly known as a *lie detector* (Vrij, 2004; Kleiner, 2002). Electrodes attached to various parts of a person's body detect changes in breathing, perspiration, and heart rate while the individual answers questions. The clinician observes these functions while the subject answers yes to *control questions*—questions whose answers are known to be yes, such as "Are your parents both alive?" Then the clinician observes the same physiological functions while the person answers *test questions,* such as "Did you commit this robbery?" If breathing, perspiration, and heart rate suddenly increase, the subject is suspected of lying.

Like other kinds of clinical tests, psychophysiological tests have their drawbacks. Many require expensive equipment that must be carefully tuned and maintained. In addition, psychophysiological measurements can be inaccurate and unreliable (see Box 4-2).

•**PSYCHOPHYSIOLOGICAL TEST**•A test that measures physical responses (such as heart rate and muscle tension) as possible indicators of psychological problems.

•**NEUROLOGICAL TEST**•A test that directly measures brain structure or activity.

[BOX 4-2]

The Truth, the Whole Truth, and Nothing but the Truth

In movies, criminals being grilled by the police reveal their guilt by sweating, shaking, cursing, or twitching. When they are hooked up to a polygraph (a lie detector), the needles bounce all over the paper. This image has been with us since World War I, when some clinicians developed the theory that people who are telling lies display systemic changes in their breathing, perspiration, and heart rate (Marston, 1917).

The danger of relying on polygraph tests is that, according to researchers, they do not work as well as we would like (Vrij, 2004; Raskin & Honts, 2002). The public did not pay much attention to this inconvenient fact until the mid-1980s, when the American Psychological Association officially reported that polygraphs were often inaccurate and the United States Congress voted to restrict their use in criminal prosecution and employment screening (Krapohl, 2002). Research clarifies that 8 out of 100 truths, on average, are called lies in polygraph testing (Raskin & Honts, 2002; MacLaren, 2001). Imagine, then, how many innocent people might be convicted

Polygraph, a test that lies?

of crimes if polygraph findings were taken as valid evidence in criminal trials.

Given such findings, polygraphs are less trusted and less popular today than they once were. For example, few courts now admit results from such tests as evidence of criminal guilt (Daniels, 2002). Polygraph testing has by no means disappeared, however. The FBI uses it exten-

sively in counterintelligence work; parole boards and probation offices routinely use it to help evaluate sex offenders and to help decide whether to release convicted offenders; and in public-sector hiring (such as for police officers), the use of polygraph screening may actually be on the increase (Kokish et al., 2005; Krapohl, 2002).

The laboratory equipment itself—impressive, unusual, and sometimes frightening—may arouse a subject's nervous system and thus change his or her physical responses. Physiological responses may also change when they are measured repeatedly in a single session. Galvanic skin responses, for example, often decrease during repeated testing.

NEUROLOGICAL AND NEUROPSYCHOLOGICAL TESTS Some problems in personality or behavior are caused primarily by damage to the brain or changes in brain activity. Head injury, brain tumors, brain malfunctions, alcoholism, infections, and other disorders can all cause such impairment. If a psychological dysfunction is to be treated effectively, it is important to know whether its primary cause is a physical abnormality in the brain.

A number of techniques may help pinpoint brain abnormalities. Some procedures, such as brain surgery, biopsy, and X ray, have been used for many years. More recently, scientists have developed a number of **neurological tests,** designed to measure brain structure and activity directly. One neurological test is the *electroencephalogram (EEG),* which records *brain waves,* the electrical activity taking place within the brain as a result of neurons firing. In this procedure, electrodes placed on the scalp send brain-wave impulses to a machine, called an oscillograph, which records them. When the electroencephalogram reveals an abnormal brain-wave pattern, or *dysrhythmia,* clinicians suspect the existence of brain injuries, tumors, seizures, or other brain abnormalities, and they turn to more precise and sophisticated techniques to ascertain the nature and scope of the problem.

The EEG *Electrodes pasted to a person's scalp detect electrical impulses from the brain. The electroencephalogram (EEG), used here to measure the brain waves of a 4-month-old being stimulated with toys, is only a gross indicator of the brain's activity.*

Scanning *The leading neuroimaging techniques—the MRI, CAT, and PET scans—take pictures of the living brain. The machinery for each of these techniques is bulky and imposing, much like the MRI machine shown at left. However, the scans produced by the machines are very different. Here, an MRI scan (above left) reveals a large tumor, colored in orange; a CAT scan (above center) reveals a subdural hemotoma, a mass of blood within the brain; and a PET scan (above right) shows which areas of the brain are active (those colored in red, orange, and yellow) when an individual is stimulated.*

•**NEUROIMAGING TECHNIQUES**•Neurological tests that provide images of brain structure or activity, such as CT scans, PET scans, and MRIs.

•**NEUROPSYCHOLOGICAL TEST**•A test that detects brain impairment by measuring a person's cognitive, perceptual, and motor performances.

•**INTELLIGENCE TEST**•A test designed to measure a person's intellectual ability.

•**INTELLIGENCE QUOTIENT (IQ)**•A score derived from intelligence tests that is considered to represent a person's overall level of intelligence.

•**NATURALISTIC OBSERVATION**•A method for observing behavior in which clinicians or researchers observe people in their everyday environments.

•**ANALOG OBSERVATION**•A method for observing behavior in which people are observed in artificial settings such as clinicians' offices or laboratories.

•**SELF-MONITORING**•A technique for observing behavior in which clients observe themselves.

Other neurological tests actually take "pictures" of brain structure or brain activity. These tests, called **neuroimaging techniques,** include *computerized axial tomography* (*CAT scan* or *CT scan*), in which X rays of the brain's structure are taken at different angles; *positron emission tomography* (*PET scan*), a computer-produced motion picture of chemical activity throughout the brain; and *magnetic resonance imaging* (*MRI*), a procedure that uses the magnetic property of certain atoms in the brain to create a detailed picture of the brain's structure and activity (Anderson et al., 2005; Bigler, 2005).

Though widely used, these various techniques are sometimes unable to detect subtle brain abnormalities. Clinicians have therefore developed less direct but sometimes more revealing **neuropsychological tests** that measure cognitive, perceptual, and motor performances on certain tasks and interpret abnormal performances as an indicator of underlying brain problems (Pelham & Lovell, 2005). Brain damage is especially likely to affect visual perception, memory, and visual-motor coordination, and so neuropsychological tests focus particularly on these areas.

The *Bender Visual-Motor Gestalt Test* (Bender, 1938), a widely used neuropsychological test, consists of nine cards, each displaying a simple design (see Figure 4-4). Patients look at the designs one at a time and copy each one on a piece of paper. Later they try to redraw the designs from memory. By the age of 12, most people can remember and redraw the designs accurately. Notable errors in accuracy are thought to reflect organic brain impairment. To achieve greater precision and accuracy in their assessments of brain abnormalities, clinicians often use a *battery,* or series, of neuropsychological tests, each targeting a specific skill area (Reitan & Wolfson, 2001, 1996).

INTELLIGENCE TESTS An early definition of intelligence described it as "the capacity to judge well, to reason well, and to comprehend well" (Binet & Simon, 1916, p. 192). Because intelligence is an *inferred* quality rather than a specific physical process, it can be measured only indirectly. In 1905 the French psychologist Alfred Binet and his associate Theodore Simon produced an **intelligence test** consisting of a series of tasks requiring people to use various verbal and nonverbal skills. The general score derived from this and subsequent intelligence tests is termed an **intelligence quotient,** or **IQ,** so called because initially it represented the ratio of a person's "mental" age to his or her "chronological" age, multiplied by 100.

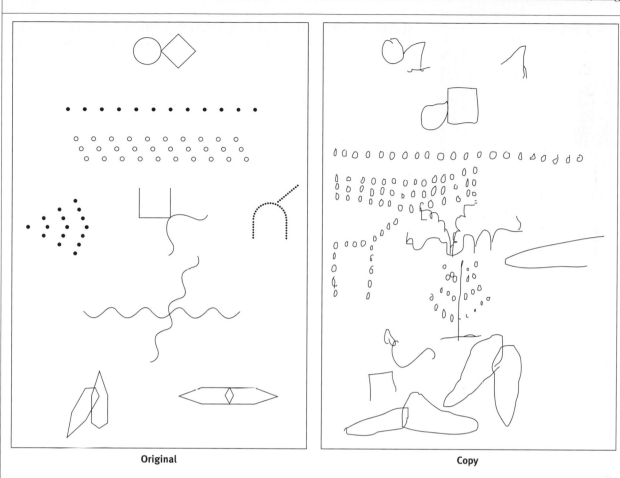

Original   **Copy**

There are now more than 100 intelligence tests available, including the widely used *Wechsler Adult Intelligence Scale, Wechsler Intelligence Scale for Children,* and *Stanford-Binet Intelligence Scale.* As we shall see in Chapter 17, intelligence tests play a key role in the diagnosis of mental retardation, but they can also help clinicians identify other problems (Sternberg, 2004).

Intelligence tests are among the most carefully produced of all clinical tests (Gott-fredson, 2005). Because they have been standardized on large groups of subjects, clinicians have a good idea how each individual's score compares with the performance of the population at large. These tests have also shown very high reliability: people who repeat the same IQ test years later receive approximately the same score. Finally, the major IQ tests appear to have fairly high validity: children's IQ scores often correlate with their performance in school, for example.

Nevertheless, intelligence tests have some key shortcomings. Factors that have nothing to do with intelligence, such as low motivation and high anxiety, can greatly influence a performance (Gregory, 2004). In addition, IQ tests may contain cultural biases in their language or tasks that place people of one background at an advantage over those of another (Shuttleworth-Edwards et al., 2004). Similarly, members of some minority groups may have little experience with this kind of test, or they may be uncomfortable with test examiners of a majority ethnic background. Either way, their performances may suffer.

Clinical Observations

In addition to interviewing and testing people, clinicians may systematically observe their behavior. In one technique, called **naturalistic observation,** clinicians observe clients in their everyday environments. In another, **analog observation,** they observe them in an artificial setting, such as a clinical office or laboratory. Finally, in **self-monitoring,** clients are instructed to observe themselves.

FIGURE 4-4 The Bender Visual-Motor Gestalt Test *Individuals copy each of nine designs on a piece of paper, then produce them again from memory. Sizable errors in a drawing (as in the one on the right, which was done by a person with brain damage) may reflect organic brain dysfunction. (Adapted from Lacks, 1984, p. 33.)*

The Wechsler Adult Intelligence Scale-Revised (WAIS-R) *This widely used intelligence test has 11 subtests, which cover such areas as factual information, memory, vocabulary, arithmetic, design, and eye-hand coordination.*

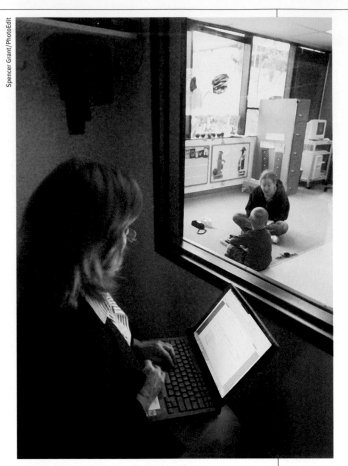

Spencer Grant/PhotoEdit

An ideal observation *Using a one-way mirror, a clinical observer is able to view a mother interacting with her child without distracting the duo or influencing their behaviors.*

NATURALISTIC AND ANALOG OBSERVATIONS Naturalistic clinical observations usually take place in homes, schools, institutions such as hospitals and prisons, or community settings. Most of them focus on parent-child, sibling-child, or teacher-child interactions and on fearful, aggressive, or disruptive behavior (Murdock et al., 2005). Often such observations are made by *participant observers,* key persons in the client's environment, and reported to the clinician.

When naturalistic observations are not practical, clinicians may resort to analog observations, often aided by special equipment such as a videotape recorder or one-way mirror (Haynes, 2001). Analog observations have often focused on children interacting with their parents, married couples attempting to settle a disagreement, speech-anxious people giving a speech, and fearful people approaching an object they find frightening.

Although much can be learned from actually witnessing behavior, clinical observations have certain disadvantages (Pine, 2005). For one thing, they are not always reliable. It is possible for various clinicians who observe the same person to focus on different aspects of behavior, assess the person differently, and arrive at different conclusions. Careful training of observers and the use of observer checklists can help reduce this problem.

Similarly, observers may make errors that affect the validity, or accuracy, of their observations (Aiken & Groth-Marnat, 2006; Pine, 2005). The observer may suffer from *overload* and be unable to see or record all the important behaviors and events. Or the observer may experience *observer drift,* a steady decline in accuracy as a result of fatigue or of a gradual unintentional change in the standards used when an observation continues for a long period of time. Another possible problem is *observer bias*—the observer's judgments may be influenced by information and expectations he or she already has about the person.

A client's *reactivity* may also limit the validity of clinical observations; that is, his or her behavior may be affected by the very presence of the observer (Kamphaus & Frick, 2002). If schoolchildren are aware that someone special is watching them, for example, they may change their usual classroom behavior, perhaps in the hope of creating a good impression.

Finally, clinical observations may lack *cross-situational,* or *external, validity.* A child who behaves aggressively in school is not necessarily aggressive at home or with friends after school. Because behavior is often specific to particular situations, observations in one setting cannot always be applied to other settings (Haynes, 2001).

SELF-MONITORING As we saw earlier, personality and response inventories are tests in which persons report their own behaviors, feelings, or cognitions. In a related assessment procedure, *self-monitoring,* people observe themselves and carefully record the frequency of certain behaviors, feelings, or cognitions as they occur over time (Stevens & Munoz, 2004). How frequently, for instance, does a drug user have an urge for drugs or a headache sufferer have a headache? What kinds of circumstances bring those feelings about?

Self-monitoring is especially useful in assessing behavior that occurs so infrequently it is unlikely to be seen during other kinds of observations. It is also useful for behaviors that occur so frequently that any other method of observing them in detail would be impossible—for example, smoking, drinking, or other drug use. Third, self-monitoring may be the only way to observe and measure private thoughts or perceptions.

Like all other clinical assessment procedures, however, self-monitoring has drawbacks (Achenbach et al., 2005). Here too validity is often a problem. People do not always receive proper instruction in this form of observation, nor do they always try to record their observations accurately. Furthermore, when people monitor themselves, they may change their behaviors unintentionally (Otten, 2004; Plante, 1999). Smokers, for example, often smoke fewer cigarettes than usual when they are monitoring themselves, drug users take drugs less frequently, and teachers give more positive and fewer negative comments to their students.

•**DIAGNOSIS**•A determination that a person's problems reflect a particular disorder.

•**SYNDROME**•A cluster of symptoms that usually occur together.

Diagnosis: Does the Client's Syndrome Match a Known Disorder?

Clinicians use the information from interviews, tests, and observations to construct an integrated picture of the factors that are causing and maintaining a client's disturbance, a construction sometimes known as a *clinical picture* (Choca, 2004). Although research suggests that systematic statistical analyses of assessment data yield the most accurate clinical judgments, clinicians typically follow their own implicit rules of logic to form clinical pictures (Wood et al., 2002; Grove et al., 2000). Such pictures are also influenced by the clinicians' theoretical orientation (Wood et al., 2002) (see Box 4-3 on the next page). The psychologist who worked with Angela Savanti held a cognitive-behavioral view of abnormality and so produced a picture that emphasized modeling and reinforcement principles and Angela's expectations, assumptions, and interpretations:

> Angela was rarely reinforced for any of her accomplishments at school, but she gained her mother's negative attention for what Mrs. Savanti judged to be poor performance at school or at home. Mrs. Savanti repeatedly told her daughter that she was incompetent, and any mishaps that happened to her were her own fault. . . . When Mr. Savanti deserted the family, Angela's first response was that somehow she was responsible. From her mother's past behavior, Angela had learned to expect that in some way she would be blamed. At the time that Angela broke up with her boyfriend, she did not blame Jerry for his behavior, but interpreted this event as a failing solely on her part. As a result, her level of self-esteem was lowered still more.
>
> The type of marital relationship that Angela saw her mother and father model remained her concept of what married life is like. She generalized from her observations of her parents' discordant interactions to an expectation of the type of behavior that she and Jerry would ultimately engage in. . . .
>
> Angela's uncertainties intensified when she was deprived of the major source of gratification she had, her relationship with Jerry. Despite the fact that she was overwhelmed with doubts about whether to marry him or not, she had gained a great deal of pleasure through being with Jerry. Whatever feelings she had been able to express, she had shared with him and no one else. Angela labeled Jerry's termination of their relationship as proof that she was not worthy of another person's interest. She viewed her present unhappiness as likely to continue, and she attributed it to some failing on her part. As a result, she became quite depressed.
>
> *(Leon, 1984, pp. 123–125)*

With the assessment data and clinical picture in hand, clinicians are ready to make a **diagnosis** (from Greek for "a discrimination")—that is, a determination that a person's psychological problems constitute a particular disorder. When clinicians decide, through diagnosis, that a client's pattern of dysfunction reflects a particular disorder, they are saying that the pattern is basically the same as one that has been displayed by many other people, has been observed and investigated in a variety of studies, and perhaps has responded to particular forms of treatment. They can then apply what is generally known about the disorder to the particular individual they are trying to help. They can, for example, better predict the future course of the person's problem and the treatments that are likely to be helpful (Black, 2005).

Classification Systems

The principle behind diagnosis is straightforward. When certain symptoms regularly occur together—a cluster of symptoms is called a **syndrome**—and follow a particular course, clinicians agree that those symptoms make up a particular mental disorder. When people display this particular pattern of symptoms, diagnosticians assign them to that

>>Q & A
What is a nervous breakdown?

The term "nervous breakdown" is used by laypersons, not clinicians. Most people use it to refer to a *sudden* psychological disturbance that *incapacitates* a person, perhaps requiring hospitalization. Some people use the term simply to connote the onset of any psychological disorder (Padwa, 1996). ‹‹

>>Q & A
What happened to neurosis?

One of Freud's most famous concepts was **neurosis**, his term for any disorder in which a person's ego defense mechanisms repeatedly failed to reduce the anxiety aroused by unconscious conflicts. In some neurotic disorders the uncontrolled anxiety was apparent, while in others it was hidden. Because the DSM now defines disorders by symptoms and not causes, the term "neurosis" has been dropped from the diagnostic system. Disorders in which anxiety is particularly apparent are now categorized as *anxiety disorders*. The other former neurotic disorders are now labeled *mood disorders, somatoform disorders,* and *dissociative disorders*. ‹‹

Sociocultural Landscape: Culture-Bound Abnormality

Red Bear sits up wild-eyed, his body drenched in sweat, every muscle tensed. The horror of the dream is still with him; he is choked with fear. Fighting waves of nausea, he stares at his young wife lying asleep on the far side of the wigwam, illuminated by the dying embers.

His troubles began several days before, when he came back from a hunting expedition empty-handed. Ashamed of his failure, he fell prey to a deep, lingering depression. Others in the village, noticing a change in Red Bear, watched him nervously, afraid that he was becoming bewitched by a windigo. Red Bear was frightened too. The signs of windigo were all there: depression, lack of appetite, nausea, sleeplessness and, now, the dream. Indeed, there could be no mistake.

He had dreamed of the windigo—the monster with a heart of ice—and the dream sealed his doom. Coldness gripped his own heart. The ice monster had entered his body and possessed him. He himself had become a windigo, and he could do nothing to avert his fate.

Suddenly, the form of Red Bear's sleeping wife begins to change. He no longer sees a woman, but a deer. His eyes flame. Silently, he draws his knife from under the blanket and moves stealthily toward the motionless figure. Saliva drips from the corners of his mouth, and a terrible hunger twists his intestines. A powerful desire to eat raw flesh consumes him.

With the body of the "deer" at his feet, Red Bear raises the knife high, preparing the strike. Unexpectedly, the deer screams and twists away. But the knife flashes down, again and again. Too late, Red Bear's kinsmen rush into the wigwam. With cries of outrage and horror, they drag him outside into the cold night air and swiftly kill him.

(LINDHOLM & LINDHOLM, 1981, P. 52)

Red Bear was suffering from *windigo,* a disorder once common among Algonquin Indian hunters. They believed in a supernatural monster that ate human beings and had the power to bewitch them and turn them into cannibals. Red Bear was among the few afflicted hunters who actually did kill and eat members of their households.

Windigo is but one of several unusual mental disorders discovered around the world, each unique to a particular culture, each apparently growing from that culture's pressures, history, institutions, and ideas (Glazer et al., 2004; Sarro & Sarro, 2004; Gaw, 2001; Lindholm & Lindholm, 1981). Such disorders remind us that the classifications and diagnoses applied in one culture may not always be appropriate in another.

Susto, a disorder found among members of Indian tribes in Central and South America and Hispanic natives of the Andean highlands of Peru, Bolivia, and Colombia, is most likely to occur in infants and young children. The symptoms are extreme anxiety, excitability, and depression, along with loss of weight, weakness, and rapid heartbeat. The culture holds that this disorder is caused by contact with supernatural beings or with frightening strangers or by bad air from cemeteries and other supposedly dangerous places.

People affected with *amok,* a disorder found in Malaysia, the Philippines, Java, and some parts of Africa, jump around violently, yell loudly, grab knives or other

---

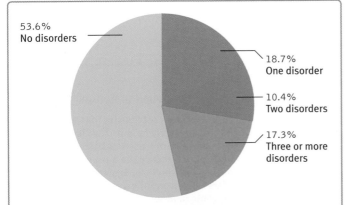

FIGURE 4-5 How many people in the United States qualify for a DSM diagnosis during their lives? *Almost half, according to one survey. Some of them even experience two or more different disorders, an occurrence known as comorbidity. (Adapted from Kessler et al., 2005.)*

diagnostic category. A list of such categories, or disorders, with descriptions of the symptoms and guidelines for assigning individuals to the categories, is known as a **classification system.**

In 1883 Emil Kraepelin developed the first modern classification system for abnormal behavior (see Chapter 1). His categories have formed the foundation for the psychological part of the *International Classification of Diseases (ICD),* the classification system now used by the World Health Organization. They have also influenced the *Diagnostic and Statistical Manual of Mental Disorders (DSM),* a classification system developed by the American Psychiatric Association. The DSM, like the ICD, has been changed over time. First published in 1952, the DSM underwent major revisions in 1968 (DSM-II), 1980 (DSM-III), 1987 (DSM-IIIR), and 1994 (DSM-IV).

DSM-IV lists approximately 400 mental disorders (see Figure 4–5). Each entry describes the criteria for diagnosing the disorder and its key clinical features. The system also describes related features, which are often but not always present. The classification system is further accompanied by *text information* (that is, background information) such as research indications; age, culture, or gender trends; and each disorder's prevalence and risk, course, complications, predisposing factors, and family patterns.

weapons, and attack any people and objects they encounter. Within the culture, amok is thought to be caused by stress, severe shortage of sleep, alcohol consumption, and extreme heat.

Koro is a pattern of anxiety found in Southeast Asia in which a man suddenly becomes intensely fearful that his penis will withdraw into his abdomen and that he will die as a result. Cultural lore holds that the disorder is caused by an imbalance of "yin" and "yang," two natural forces believed to be the fundamental components of life. Accepted forms of treatment include having the individual keep a firm hold on his penis until the fear passes, often with the assistance of family members or friends, and clamping the penis to a wooden box.

Latah is a disorder found in Malaysia, usually among uneducated middle-aged or elderly women. Certain circumstances (hearing someone say "snake" or being tickled, for example) trigger a fright reaction that is marked by repeating the words and acts of other people, uttering obscenities, and doing the opposite of what others ask.

Western abnormality? *For years, theorists believed that eating disorders were culture-bound problems caused by Western society's emphasis on female thinness. However, as Western fashions, ads, and the like have spread, these disorders have become more prevalent in countries everywhere. Here teenagers in Buenos Aires walk in front of a clothing store that features ultra-thin models and tiny-sized outfits. Argentine officials have recently encouraged retailers and the fashion industry to highlight and sell larger sizes to teens in that country, which now has one of the highest rates of eating disorders in the world.*

In 2000, the American Psychiatric Association published an update of the text information that accompanies DSM-IV. This update, called the *DSM-IV Text Revision* (*DSM-IV-TR*), also changed the *diagnostic criteria* for a few disorders (certain sexual disorders), as we shall observe in Chapter 13. Because DSM-IV-TR did in fact make changes to the DSM-IV categories and criteria, few though they were, many clinicians cite DSM-IV-TR as the current edition of the DSM, a trend that will be followed throughout this textbook. Other clinicians continue to point to DSM-IV as the current edition. Either way, it is important to be clear that almost all of DSM-IV-TR's criteria were in fact introduced in 1994 with the publication of DSM-IV.

DSM-IV-TR

DSM-IV-TR is the most widely used classification system in the United States (APA, 2000). It requires clinicians to evaluate a client's condition on five separate *axes,* or branches of information, when making a diagnosis. First, they must decide whether the person is displaying one or more of the disorders found on *Axis I,* an extensive list of clinical syndromes that typically cause significant impairment. Some of the most frequently diagnosed disorders listed on this axis are the anxiety disorders and mood disorders—problems we shall discuss later:

•CLASSIFICATION SYSTEM•A list of disorders, along with descriptions of symptoms and guidelines for making appropriate diagnoses.

Anxiety disorders People with anxiety disorders may experience general feelings of anxiety and worry (*generalized anxiety disorder*), anxiety centered on a specific situation or object (*phobias*), periods of panic (*panic disorder*), persistent thoughts or repetitive behaviors or both (*obsessive-compulsive disorder*), or lingering anxiety reactions to unusually traumatic events (*acute stress disorder* and *posttraumatic stress disorder*).

Mood disorders People with mood disorders feel extremely sad or elated for long periods of time. These disorders include *major depressive disorder* and *bipolar disorders* (in which episodes of mania alternate with episodes of depression).

Next, diagnosticians must decide whether the person is displaying one of the disorders listed on *Axis II,* which includes long-standing problems that are frequently overlooked in the presence of the disorders on Axis I. There are only two groups of Axis II disorders: *mental retardation* and *personality disorders.* We will also examine these patterns in later chapters:

Mental retardation People with this disorder display significantly subaverage intellectual functioning and poor adaptive functioning by 18 years of age.

Personality disorders People with these disorders display a very rigid maladaptive pattern of inner experience and outward behavior that has continued for many years. People with *antisocial personality disorder,* for example, persistently disregard and violate the rights of others. People with *dependent personality disorder* are persistently dependent on others, clinging, obedient, and very afraid of separation.

Although people usually receive a diagnosis from *either* Axis I or Axis II, they may receive diagnoses from both axes. Angela Savanti would first receive a diagnosis of *major depressive disorder* from Axis I (a mood disorder). Let us suppose that the clinician judged that Angela also displayed a life history of dependent behavior. She might then also receive an Axis II diagnosis of *dependent personality disorder.*

The remaining axes of DSM-IV-TR guide diagnosticians in reporting other factors. *Axis III* asks for information concerning relevant general medical conditions from which the person is currently suffering. *Axis IV* asks about special psychosocial or environmental problems the person is facing, such as school or housing problems. And *Axis V* requires the diagnostician to make a *global assessment of functioning* (*GAF*), that is, to rate the person's psychological, social, and occupational functioning overall.

If Angela Savanti had diabetes, for example, the clinician might include that under Axis III information. Angela's recent breakup with her boyfriend would be noted on Axis IV. And because she seemed fairly dysfunctional at the time of diagnosis, Angela's GAF would probably be around 55 on Axis V, indicating a moderate level of dysfunction. The complete diagnosis for Angela Savanti would then be:

Axis I: Major depressive disorder

Axis II: Dependent personality disorder

Axis III: Diabetes

Axis IV: Problem related to the social environment (termination of engagement)

Axis V: GAF = 55 (current)

Because DSM-IV-TR uses several kinds of diagnostic information, each defined by a different "axis," it is known as a *multiaxial system.* The diagnoses arrived at under this classification system are thought to be more informative and more carefully considered than those derived from the early DSMs.

Is DSM-IV-TR an Effective Classification System?

A classification system, like an assessment method, is judged by its reliability and validity. Here *reliability* means that different diagnosticians are likely to agree on the diagnosis when they use the system to diagnose the same client. Early versions of the DSM were at best moderately reliable (Spiegel, 2005; Malik & Beutler, 2002; Kirk & Kutchins, 1992). In the early 1960s, for example, four clinicians, each relying on DSM-I, indepen-

>>PSYCH•LISTINGS

Rock Bands with Psychological Labels

Bad Brains ‹‹

Placebo ‹‹

The Dissociatives ‹‹

Mood Elevator ‹‹

Neurosis ‹‹

Disturbed ‹‹

Widespread Panic ‹‹

10,000 Maniacs ‹‹

Moody Blues ‹‹

Grupo Mania ‹‹

Suicidal Tendencies ‹‹

Xanax 25 ‹‹

Mental as Anything ‹‹

The Insane Clown Posse ‹‹

Unsane ‹‹

Jane's Addiction ‹‹

Therapy? ‹‹

dently interviewed 153 patients (Beck et al., 1962). Only 54 percent of their diagnoses were in agreement. Because all four clinicians were experienced diagnosticians, their failure to agree suggested deficiencies in the classification system.

DSM-IV-TR appears to have greater reliability than the early DSMs (Black, 2005; Reeb, 2000). The framers of DSM-IV conducted extensive reviews of research to pinpoint which categories in past DSMs had been too vague and unreliable. In turn, they developed a number of new diagnostic criteria and categories, and then ran *field trials* to make sure that the new criteria and categories were in fact reliable (Malik & Beutler, 2002). They had many clinicians and researchers use the new criteria in their work, and found that, in most cases, the same clients or kinds of clients were receiving the same diagnoses.

When it was first published in 1994, DSM-IV was heralded as a *highly* reliable classification system. However, clinical use and research conducted over the past decade indicate that DSM-IV (and likewise DSM-IV-TR) does contain certain reliability problems (Black, 2005; Beutler & Malik, 2002). Many clinicians, for example, have difficulty distinguishing one kind of anxiety disorder from another. The disorder of a particular client may be classified as generalized anxiety disorder by one clinician, agoraphobia (fear of traveling outside of one's home) by another, and social phobia (fear of social situations) by yet another. Moreover, many anxious clients receive multiple (*comorbid*) diagnoses: they may receive, for example, a diagnosis of *both* agoraphobia *and* social phobia.

It may be that the criteria for certain categories overlap too much in the current DSM. For example, an excessive fear of embarrassment or humiliation is listed as a criterion for both agoraphobia and social phobia. Alternatively, it may simply be that people with one anxiety disorder are highly prone to develop another anxiety disorder as well. Either way, diagnostic confusion of this kind has spurred serious concerns about DSM-IV-TR's reliability.

The *validity* of a classification system is the accuracy of the information that its diagnostic categories provide. Categories are of most use to clinicians when they demonstrate *predictive validity*—that is, when they help predict future symptoms or events. A common symptom of major depressive disorder, for example, is either insomnia or excessive sleep. When clinicians give Angela Savanti a diagnosis of major depressive disorder, they expect that she may eventually develop sleep problems even if none are present now. In addition, they expect her to respond to treatments that are effective for other depressed persons. The more often such predictions are accurate, the greater a category's predictive validity.

The framers of DSM-IV tried to ensure the validity of their new version of the DSM by again conducting extensive reviews of research and running many field studies. As a result, its criteria and categories initially appeared to have stronger validity than those of the earlier versions of the DSM (Reeb, 2000; Nathan & Lagenbucher, 1999). Yet, again, since 1994 many clinical theorists have argued persuasively that at least some of the criteria and categories in DSM-IV (and carried over to DSM-IV-TR) are based on weak research and that others reflect gender or racial bias (Dosen, 2005; Faravelli et al., 2005; Cosgrove & Riddle, 2004) (see Box 4-4 on the next page).

Beyond these concerns about the reliability and validity of certain categories, a growing number of clinical theorists believe that two fundamental problems weaken the current edition of the DSM (Widiger & Simonsen, 2005). One problem is DSM-IV-TR's basic assumption that clinical disorders are *qualitatively* different from normal behavior. Perhaps this assumption is incorrect. It may be, for example, that the feelings of dejection occasionally experienced by everyone differ from mild clinical depression in *degree* only and, similarly, that mild clinical depression differs from severe depression in degree rather than kind. In support of this notion, some studies find that the early features and

The power of labeling *When looking at this late-nineteenth-century photograph of a baseball team at the State Homeopathic Asylum for the Insane in Middletown, New York, most observers assume that the players are patients. As a result, they tend to "see" depression or confusion in the players' faces and posture. In fact, the players are members of the asylum staff, some of whom even sought their jobs for the express purpose of playing for the hospital team.*

>>BY THE NUMBERS

1 Number of categories of psychological dysfunctioning listed in the 1840 U.S. census ("idiocy/insanity") ‹‹

7 Number of categories listed in the 1880 census ‹‹

60 Number of categories listed in DSM-I in 1952 ‹‹

400 Number of categories listed in DSM-IV-TR today ‹‹

[BOX 4-4]

The Battle over Premenstrual Dysphoric Disorder

Some categories of mental dysfunctioning are much more controversial than others, causing clinicians and the public alike to battle over their appropriateness. After long and heated discussions two decades ago, for example, DSM-III dropped homosexuality as a category of mental dysfunctioning, citing a lack of evidence for including it and a concern about the social implications of calling a sexual orientation abnormal.

One of the biggest controversies in the development of DSM-IV centered on the category *premenstrual dysphoric disorder* (*PMDD*) (Offman & Kleinplatz, 2004). A DSM work group recommended in 1993 that PMDD be formally listed as a new and distinct kind of depressive disorder. The category was to be applied when a woman was regularly impaired by at least 5 of 11 symptoms during the week before her menses: sad or hopeless feelings;

tense or anxious feelings; marked mood changes; frequent irritability or anger and increased interpersonal conflicts; decreased interest in her usual activities; lack of concentration; lack of energy; changes in appetite; insomnia or sleepiness; a subjective feeling of being overwhelmed or out of control; and physical symptoms such as swollen breasts, headaches, muscle pain, a "bloated" sensation, or weight gain.

This recommendation set off an uproar. Many clinicians (including some dissenting members of the work group), several national organizations, interest groups, and the media warned that this diagnostic category would "pathologize" severe cases of *premenstrual syndrome,* or *PMS,* the premenstrual discomforts that are common and normal, and might cause women's behavior in general to be attributed largely to "raging hormones" (a stereotype that

society is finally rejecting). They also argued that there were insufficient data to include the new category (Caplan, 2004; Chase, 1993).

The DSM solution? A compromise. PMDD is not currently listed as a formal category in DSM-IV or DSM-IV-TR, but the pattern is listed in the DSM appendix, with the suggestion that it be studied more thoroughly in the coming years. Of course, an "in-between" status of this kind can be confusing to the public. In fact, in recent years pharmaceutical companies, hoping that consumers will purchase psychotropic medications that the companies have developed for PMDD, have tried to promote public awareness of this "disorder" through high-profile television commercials detailing its symptoms (Mitchell, 2004; Moynihan, 2004). Naturally, such advertisements have alarmed critics of the category all the more.

predictors of mild depression are almost identical to those of severe depression (Akiskal, 2005; Judd et al., 2004, 2003, 2002, 1997). If certain psychological disorders actually differ from normal behavior and from each other in degree rather than kind, many of today's criteria and categories are, at the very least, misleading.

Another (related) criticism centers on DSM-IV-TR's use of *discrete* diagnostic categories, with each category of pathology considered to be separate from all the others. Some critics believe that certain of its categories reflect, in fact, variations of a single, fundamental *dimension* of functioning rather than separate disorders. Let us consider the dimension of *negative affect,* for example. Perhaps this dimension should be used when describing abnormal patterns. When an individual's negative affect is extreme and maladaptive and takes on a particular character, the person may appear highly anxious. Alternatively, a person with extreme negative affect may appear highly depressed, or, indeed, seem both anxious *and* depressed. In short, rather than distinguish two kinds of disorders—an anxiety disorder and a depressive disorder—the classification should list each pattern as a variation of a key dimension, negative affect. If this dimensional view is appropriate, the DSM-IV-TR is, once again, misleading clinicians when it asks them to determine whether persons are suffering from an anxiety disorder *or* a mood disorder. Small wonder that clinicians often find high anxiety levels among people with a major depressive disorder, or very depressed feelings among clients with an anxiety disorder. There is growing evidence that fundamental dimensions do indeed cut across different DSM categories and that this may be the reason that multiple diagnoses so often need to be assigned to the same client.

Given such concerns, there is no question that DSM-V, the next edition of DSM, will include some key changes, including at least some dimensional, rather than categorical, forms of classification. Indeed, a series of research planning conferences have already taken place to consider what kinds of changes might be appropriate for DSM-V (Widiger & Simonsen, 2005). Nevertheless, the debut of DSM-V is not imminent. DSM-V work groups will not convene until 2007 at the earliest, and DSM-V itself will not be completed until 2012 or later. In the meantime, clinicians continue to rely on DSM-IV-TR, a classification system that is superior to its predecessors, but, at the same time, filled with important limitations and questions.

Can Diagnosis and Labeling Cause Harm?

Even with trustworthy assessment data and reliable and valid classification categories, clinicians will sometimes arrive at a wrong conclusion (Rohrer, 2005; Wood et al., 2002). Like all human beings, they are flawed information processors. Studies show that they are influenced disproportionately by information gathered early in the assessment process (Meehl, 1996, 1960). They sometimes pay too much attention to certain sources of information, such as a parent's report about a child, and too little to others, such as the child's point of view (McCoy, 1976). Finally, their judgments can be distorted by any number of personal biases—gender, age, race, and socioeconomic status, to name just a few (Kress et al., 2005; Winstead & Sanchez, 2005).

Given the limitations of assessment tools, assessors, and classification systems, it is small wonder that studies sometimes uncover shocking errors in diagnosis, especially in hospitals (Chen, Swann, & Burt, 1996). In one study a clinical team was asked to reevaluate the records of 131 patients at a mental hospital in New York, conduct interviews with many of these persons, and arrive at a diagnosis for each one (Lipton & Simon, 1985). The researchers then compared the team's diagnoses with the original diagnoses for which the patients were hospitalized. Although 89 of the patients had originally received a diagnosis of schizophrenia, only 16 received it upon reevaluation. And whereas 15 patients originally had been given a diagnosis of mood disorder, 50 received it now. It is obviously important for clinicians to be aware that such huge disagreements can occur.

Beyond the potential for misdiagnosis, the very act of classifying people can lead to unintended results (see Box 4-5 on page 109). As we observed in Chapter 3, for example, many sociocultural theorists believe that diagnostic labels can become self-fulfilling prophecies. When people are diagnosed as mentally disturbed, they may be viewed and reacted to correspondingly. If others expect them to take on a sick role, they may begin to consider themselves sick as well and act that way. Furthermore, our society attaches a stigma to abnormality (Corrigan, 2005, 2004; Link et al., 2004, 2001). People labeled mentally ill may find it difficult to get a job, especially a position of responsibility, or to be welcomed into social relationships. Once a label has been applied, it may stick for a long time.

Because of these problems, some clinicians would like to do away with diagnoses (Gurman & Messer, 2003). Others disagree. They believe we must simply work to increase what is known about psychological disorders and improve diagnostic techniques (Cunningham-Owens, 2000). They hold that classification and diagnosis are critical to understanding and treating people in distress.

Treatment: How Might the Client Be Helped?

Over the course of 10 months, Angela Savanti was treated for depression and related symptoms. She improved considerably during that time, as the following report describes.

Angela's depression eased as she began to make progress in therapy. A few months before the termination of treatment, she and Jerry resumed dating. Angela discussed with Jerry her greater comfort in expressing her feelings and her hope that Jerry would also become more expressive with her. They discussed the reasons why Angela was ambivalent about getting married, and they began to talk again about the possibility of marriage. Jerry, however, was not making demands for a decision by a certain date, and Angela felt that she was not as frightened about marriage as she previously had been. . . .

Toby Talbot/AP Photo

Insensitive labeling *Recognizing that glib labels can contribute to negative stereotypes and to the stigmatization of people with psychological disorders, mental health advocacy groups recently protested the production and sale of "Crazy for You" bears, a new line of Vermont Teddy Bears. The teddy bear company subsequently agreed to cease the production and marketing of those bears.*

>>BY THE NUMBERS
The Stigma Continues

67% Percentage of Americans who would not tell their employer that they were seeking mental health treatment «

51% Americans who would hesitate to see a psychotherapist if a diagnosis were required «

41% Americans who believe they should be able to handle psychological problems on their own. «

37% Americans who would be reluctant to seek treatment because of confidentiality concerns «

33% Americans who would not seek counseling for fear of being labeled "mentally ill" «

(Opinion Research Corporation, 2004)

Treatment outreach *To increase the availability and effectiveness of therapy, especially in rural areas, a number of health care agencies and therapists have begun to offer video teleconferencing, or* telehealth. *Here, a 13-year-old boy has a session with a physician and psychologist, who are actually in an office located far from the child's hometown.*

Nati Harnik/AP Photo

> Psychotherapy provided Angela with the opportunity to learn to express her feelings to the persons she was interacting with, and this was quite helpful to her. Most important, she was able to generalize from some of the learning experiences in therapy and modify her behavior in her renewed relationship with Jerry. Angela still had much progress to make in terms of changing the characteristic ways she interacted with others, but she had already made a number of important steps in a potentially happier direction.
>
> *(Leon, 1984, pp. 118, 125)*

Clearly, treatment helped Angela, and by its conclusion she was a happier, more functional person than the woman who had first sought help 10 months earlier. But how did her therapist decide on the treatment program that proved to be so helpful? And was the effectiveness of Angela's therapy typical of that offered by other therapists to other clients with other problems?

Treatment Decisions

Angela's therapist began, like all therapists, with assessment information and diagnostic decisions (Beutler et al., 2004). Knowing the specific details and background of Angela's problem (*idiographic data*), and combining this information with established information about the nature and treatment of depression (*nomothetic data*), the clinician could arrive at a treatment plan for her.

Yet therapists may also be influenced by other factors when they make treatment decisions. Their treatment plans typically reflect their theoretical orientations and how they have learned to conduct therapy (Mahrer, 2003, 2000). As therapists apply a favored model in case after case, they become more and more familiar with its principles and treatment techniques and tend to use them in work with still other clients.

Current research may also play a role. Most clinicians say that they value research as a guide to practice (Beutler et al., 1995). However, not all of them actually read research articles, so they cannot be directly influenced by them. Research articles tend to be written for other researchers, in technical language that is not typically accessible to clinicians or other kinds of readers. In fact, according to surveys, today's therapists actually gather most of their information about the latest developments in the field from colleagues, professional newsletters, workshops, conferences, books, and the like (Corrie & Callanan, 2001; Goldfried & Wolfe, 1996). Unfortunately, the accuracy and usefulness of these sources vary widely.

To help clinicians become more familiar with and apply research findings, there is currently a movement afoot in the United States, the United Kingdom, and elsewhere called *empirically supported,* or *evidence-based, treatment* (Davidson et al., 2004; Kazdin, 2004; Chambless, 2002; Chambless & Ollendick, 2001). Proponents of this approach have formed task forces that seek to identify those therapies that have received clear research support, conduct new therapy research, develop treatment guidelines, and spread such information to clinicians. Critics of the approach worry that efforts to distinguish effective from ineffective treatments have thus far been simplistic, biased, and, at times, misleading (Mahrer, 2005; Westen et al., 2005). However, the movement has been gaining momentum in recent years.

How much, in fact, do we currently know about treatment and treatment effectiveness? And how can researchers best examine such questions? We turn to this set of questions next.

The Effectiveness of Treatment

Altogether, as many as 400 forms of therapy are currently practiced in the clinical field (Prochaska & Norcross, 2003). Naturally, the most important question to ask about each of them is whether it does what it is supposed to do. Does a particular treatment really help people

[BOX 4-5]

Oppression and Mental Health: The Politics of Labeling

Throughout history governments have applied the label of mental illness as a way of controlling or changing people whose views threaten the social order. This was a common practice in the former Soviet Union. There, political dissent was considered a symptom of abnormal mental functioning, and many dissidents were committed to mental hospitals.

In a more subtle process, a country's cultural values often influence the clinical assessments made by its practitioners. The historians Lynn Gamwell and Nancy Tomes (1995) have noted, for example, the widespread clinical belief in the nineteenth-century United States that freedom would drive such "primitive" people as Native Americans insane. Medical experts of that time went so far as to claim that the forcible movement of tribal groups onto reservations was in their best interest because it would save them from the madness that awaited them in free society. The medical officer who supervised the "removal" of the Cherokees from their homeland to Oklahoma was later pleased to report that during the whole time he oversaw the migration of 20,000 Cherokees (over 4,000 of whom died), he had not observed a single case of insanity.

Slave owners, too, liked to believe that slaves were psychologically comfortable with their subservience and that those who tried to escape either were or would soon become insane. Secretary of State John Calhoun of South Carolina pointed to the 1840 census, conducted by his office,

as evidence: it identified almost no insanity among slaves in the South but many cases among former slaves living in the North. Calhoun asserted: "The data on insanity revealed in this census is unimpeachable. From it our nation must conclude that the abolition of slavery would be to the African a curse instead of a blessing."

The work of clinicians at that time lent support to this belief. One specialist claimed that several kinds of mental disorders were unique to African Americans, including *drapetomania* (from the Latin *drapeta*, "fugitive")—an obsessive desire for freedom that drove some slaves to try to flee. Any slave who tried to run away more than twice was considered insane.

Drapetomania is long forgotten, but cultural views continue to influence psychological assessments and categories. Many clinicians have argued that categories such as "homosexuality," "sexual frigidity," and "masochistic personality"—each an established clinical category during much of the twentieth century—show all too well the impact of cultural beliefs on clinical categorizations and diagnoses.

Francis G. Meyer/Corbis

A ride for liberty *Eastman Johnson's 1862 painting,* A Ride for Liberty—The Fugitive Slaves, *demonstrates the courage and clear-mindedness slaves needed to escape, in stark contrast to the mental instability of which they were accused.*

overcome their psychological problems? On the surface, the question may seem simple. In fact, it is one of the most difficult questions for clinical researchers to answer.

The first problem is how to *define* "success" (Erwin, 2000; Strupp, 1996, 1989). If, as Angela's therapist suggests, she still has much progress to make at the conclusion of therapy, should her recovery be considered successful? The second problem is how to *measure* improvement (Luborsky, 2004; Luborsky et al., 2003, 2002, 1999). Should researchers give equal weight to the reports of clients, friends, relatives, therapists, and teachers? Should they use rating scales, inventories, therapy insights, observations, or some other measure?

Perhaps the biggest problem in determining the effectiveness of treatment is the *variety* and *complexity* of the treatments currently in use. People differ in their problems, personal styles, and motivations for therapy. Therapists differ in skill, experience, orientation, and personality. And therapies differ in theory, format, and setting. Because an individual's progress is influenced by all these factors and more, the findings of a particular study will not always apply to other clients and therapists.

Proper research procedures address some of these problems. By using control groups, random assignment, matched subjects, and the like, clinicians can draw certain conclusions about various therapies. Even in studies that are well designed, however, the variety and complexity of treatment limit the conclusions that can be reached (Kazdin, 2004, 1994).

Despite these difficulties, the job of evaluating therapies must be done, and clinical researchers have plowed ahead with it. Investigators have, in fact, conducted thousands of *therapy outcome studies,* studies that measure the effects of various treatments. The studies typically ask one of three questions:

1. Is therapy *in general* effective?
2. Are *particular* therapies generally effective?
3. Are *particular* therapies effective for *particular* problems?

IS THERAPY GENERALLY EFFECTIVE? Studies suggest that therapy is often more helpful than no treatment or than placebos. A pioneering review examined 375 controlled studies, covering a total of almost 25,000 people seen in a wide assortment of therapies (Smith, Glass, & Miller, 1980; Smith & Glass, 1977). The reviewers combined the findings of these studies by using a special statistical technique called *meta-analysis.* They rated the level of improvement in each person treated and in each untreated control subject and measured the average difference between the two groups. According to this statistical analysis, the average person who received treatment was better off than 75 percent of the untreated control subjects (see Figure 4-6). Other meta-analyses have found similar relationships between treatment and improvement (Bickman, 2005).

Some clinicians have concerned themselves with an important related question: Can therapy be harmful? In his book *My Analysis with Freud,* the psychoanalyst Abraham Kardiner (1977) wrote, "Freud was always infuriated whenever I would say to him that you could not do harm with psychoanalysis. He said: 'When you say that, you also say it cannot do any good. Because if you cannot do any harm, how can you do good?'" In agreement with Freud, a number of studies have found that more than 5 percent of patients actually seem to get worse because of therapy (Nolan et al., 2004; Lambert & Bergin, 1994). Their symptoms may become more intense, or the individuals may develop new ones, such as a sense of failure, guilt, reduced self-concept, or hopelessness, because of their inability to profit from therapy (Lambert, Shapiro, & Bergin, 1986; Hadley & Strupp, 1976).

ARE PARTICULAR THERAPIES GENERALLY EFFECTIVE? The studies we have looked at so far have lumped all therapies together to consider their general effectiveness. Many researchers, however, consider it wrong to treat all therapies alike. One critic suggests that these studies are operating under a *uniformity myth*—a false belief that all therapies are equivalent despite differences in the therapists' training, experience, theoretical orientations, and personalities (Kiesler, 1995, 1966).

Thus, an alternative approach examines the effectiveness of *particular* therapies (Bickman, 2005). Most research of this kind shows each of the major forms of therapy to be superior to no treatment or to placebo treatment (Prochaska & Norcross, 2003, 1999, 1994). A number of other studies have compared particular therapies with one another and found that no one form of therapy generally stands out over all others (Luborsky et al., 2003, 2002, 1975).

If different kinds of therapy have similar successes, might they have something in common? A **rapprochement movement** has tried to identify a set of common strategies that may run through the work of all effective therapists, regardless of the clinicians' particular orientation (Bickman, 2005; Luborsky et al., 2003, 2002). A survey of

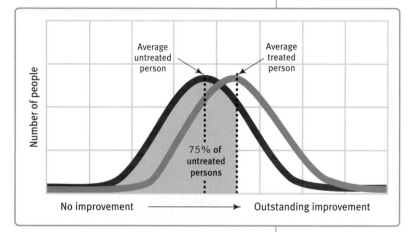

FIGURE **4-6** **Does therapy help?** *Combining subjects and results from hundreds of studies, investigators have determined that the average person who receives psychotherapy experiences greater improvement than do 75 percent of all untreated people with similar problems. (Adapted from Prochaska & Norcross, 2003; Lambert, Weber, & Sykes, 1993; Smith, Glass, & Miller, 1980.)*

•**RAPPROCHEMENT MOVEMENT**•An effort to identify a set of common strategies that run through the work of all effective therapists.

•**PSYCHOPHARMACOLOGIST**•A psychiatrist who primarily prescribes medications. Also known as a *pharmacotherapist.*

highly successful therapists suggests, for example, that most give feedback to patients, help patients focus on their own thoughts and behavior, pay attention to the way they and their patients are interacting, and try to promote self-mastery in their patients. In short, effective therapists of any type may practice more similarly than they preach (Korchin & Sands, 1983).

ARE PARTICULAR THERAPIES EFFECTIVE FOR PARTICULAR PROBLEMS? People with different disorders may respond differently to the various forms of therapy. Gordon Paul, an influential clinical theorist, said some years back that the most appropriate question regarding the effectiveness of therapy may be "*What* specific treatment, by *whom,* is most effective for *this* individual with *that* specific problem, and under *which* set of circumstances?" (Paul, 1967, p. 111). Researchers have investigated how effective particular therapies are at treating particular disorders, and they have often found sizable differences among the various therapies. Behavioral therapies, for example, appear to be the most effective of all in treating phobias (Tryon, 2005), whereas drug therapy is the single most effective treatment for schizophrenia (Weiden & Kane, 2005).

As we observed previously, studies also show that some clinical problems may respond better to *combined* approaches (Marder & Kane, 2005; TADS, 2004). Drug therapy is sometimes combined with certain forms of psychotherapy, for example, to treat depression. In fact, it is now common for clients to be seen by two therapists—one of them a **psychopharmacologist,** a psychiatrist who primarily prescribes medications, and the other a psychologist, social worker, or other therapist who conducts psychotherapy.

Obviously, knowledge of how particular therapies fare with particular disorders can help therapists and clients alike make better decisions about treatment (Beutler et al., 2004; Beutler, 2002, 2000, 1991) (see Figure 4-7). It can also lead researchers to a better understanding of why therapy works and ultimately of abnormal functioning. Thus this is a question to which we shall keep returning as we examine the disorders the therapies have been devised to combat.

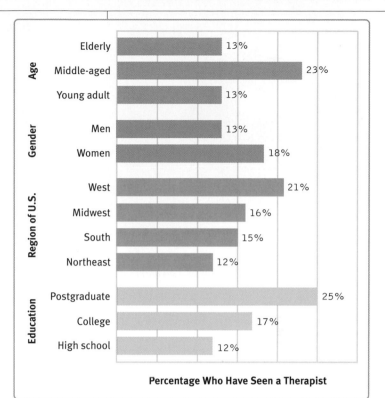

Percentage Who Have Seen a Therapist

FIGURE **4-7** **Who seeks therapy?** *According to surveys conducted in the United States, people who are middle-aged, female, from Western states, and highly educated are the most likely to have been in therapy at some point in their lives. (Adapted from Fetto, 2002.)*

PUTTING IT together
Renewed Respect Collides with Economic Pressure

In Chapter 3 we observed that today's leading models of abnormal behavior often differ widely in their assumptions, conclusions, and treatments. It should not surprise us, then, that clinicians also differ considerably in their approaches to assessment and diagnosis or that those who prefer certain assessment techniques sometimes scoff at those who use other approaches. Yet when all is said and done, no assessment technique stands out as superior to the rest. Each of the hundreds of available tools has major limitations, and each produces at best an incomplete picture of how a person is functioning and why.

In short, even though some assessment procedures have received more research support than others (and clinicians should pay close attention to such findings when they are deciding which ones to use), the present state of assessment and diagnosis argues against relying exclusively on any one approach. As a result, more and more clinicians now use batteries of assessment tools in their work (Nillson et al., 2005; Meyer et al., 2003, 2001). Such batteries are already providing invaluable guidance in the assessment of Alzheimer's disease and certain other disorders that are particularly difficult to diagnose, as we shall see later.

Attitudes toward clinical assessment have shifted back and forth over the past several decades. Before the 1950s, assessment was a highly regarded part of clinical practice. As the number of clinical models grew during the 1960s and 1970s, however, followers of each model favored certain tools over others, and the practice of assessment became

>>Q & A
What is the difference between treatment efficacy and treatment effectiveness?

Many writers use the terms "treatment efficacy" and "treatment effectiveness" interchangeably. Technically, however, efficacy research determines whether a treatment can work under ideal conditions (for example, with therapists who are given special training for the study), while effectiveness research examines whether a treatment works well in the real world (for example, as offered by practicing therapists). <<

"This is getting us nowhere!"

fragmented. Meanwhile, research began to reveal that a number of tools were inaccurate or inconsistent. In this atmosphere, many clinicians lost confidence in systematic assessment and diagnosis, and some came to approach these tasks casually.

Today respect for assessment and diagnosis is on the rise once again. One reason for the renewal of interest is the development of more precise diagnostic criteria, as presented in DSM-IV-TR. Another is the drive by researchers for more rigorous tests to help them select appropriate subjects for clinical studies. Still another factor is the clinical field's growing awareness that certain disorders can be properly identified only after careful assessment procedures.

Along with heightened respect for assessment and diagnosis has come increased research. Every major kind of assessment tool—from projective tests to personality inventories—is now undergoing careful scrutiny. This work is helping many clinicians perform their work with more accuracy and consistency—welcome news for people with psychological problems.

Ironically, just as today's clinicians and researchers are rediscovering systematic assessment, powerful economic forces have emerged to work against the use of assessment tools. In particular, managed care insurance plans, which emphasize cost containment and shorter treatments, often refuse to provide coverage for extensive clinical testing or observations (Wood et al., 2002). Indeed, in one survey of psychologists, half of the respondents reported spending less time giving clinical tests than they had done previously, using fewer tests, or discontinuing such tests altogether—all because of managed care policies (Piotrowski et al., 1998). Which of these forces will ultimately have a greater influence on clinical assessment and diagnosis—promising research or economic pressure? We shall find out in the coming years.

⊣[SUMMARY AND REVIEW]⊢

- **The practitioner's task** Clinical practitioners are interested primarily in gathering *idiographic* information about their clients. They seek an understanding of the specific nature and origins of a client's problems through *clinical assessment* and *diagnosis. pp. 85–86*

- **Clinical assessment** To be useful, assessment tools must be *standardized, reliable,* and *valid.* Most clinical assessment methods fall into three general categories: *clinical interviews, tests,* and *observations.* A clinical interview permits the practitioner to interact with a client and generally get a sense of who he or she is. It may be either *unstructured* or *structured.* Types of clinical tests include *projective, personality, response, psychophysiological, neurological, neuropsychological,* and *intelligence* tests. Types of observation include *naturalistic observation* and *analog observation.* Practitioners also employ *self-monitoring:* subjects observe themselves and record designated behaviors, feelings, or cognitions as they occur. *pp. 86–100*

- **Diagnosis** After collecting assessment information, clinicians form a *clinical picture* and decide upon a *diagnosis.* The diagnosis is chosen from a *classification system.* The system used most widely in the United States is the *Diagnostic and Statistical Manual of Mental Disorders (DSM). pp. 101–103*

- **DSM-IV-TR** The most recent version of the DSM, known as *DSM-IV-TR,* lists approximately 400 disorders. Clinicians must evaluate a client's condition on five axes, or categories of information. The reliability and validity of DSM-IV-TR continue to receive broad clinical review and criticism. *pp. 103–107*

- **Dangers of diagnosis and labeling** Even with trustworthy assessment data and reliable and valid classification categories, clinicians will not always arrive at the correct conclusion. They are human and so fall prey to various biases, misconceptions, and expectations. Another problem related to diagnosis is the prejudice that labels arouse, which may be damaging to the person who is diagnosed. *p. 107*

≫LOOKING AROUND

The Power of Observation Everyday observations are more prone to error than clinical observations and often more damaging. Mistaken eyewitness testimony is the primary cause of the conviction of innocent people (Wells et al., 1998). ≪

Believing Is Seeing Persons' beliefs often wrongly influence their observations and recollections. Most moviegoers recall seeing Bambi's mother die in the snow and a knife slash Janet Leigh in the shower in *Psycho,* and hearing Tarzan say, "Me Tarzan, you Jane," and Humphrey Bogart say, "Play it again, Sam," in *Casablanca.* Yet none of these events took place in their respective movies. ≪

■ **Treatment** The *treatment decisions* of therapists may be influenced by assessment information, the diagnosis, the clinician's theoretical orientation and familiarity with research, and the field's state of knowledge. Determining the *effectiveness of treatment* is difficult because therapists differ in their ways of defining and measuring success. The variety and complexity of today's treatments also present a problem. *Therapy outcome studies* have led to three general conclusions: (1) people in therapy are usually better off than people with similar problems who receive no treatment; (2) the various therapies do not appear to differ dramatically in their general effectiveness; (3) certain therapies or combinations of therapies do appear to be more effective than others for certain disorders. Some therapists currently advocate *empirically supported treatment,* the active identification, promotion, and teaching of those interventions that have received clear research support. *pp. 107–111*

>>> CRITICAL THOUGHTS <<<

1. How would you grade the tests you take in school? That is, how reliable and valid are they? How about the tests you see in magazines? *pp. 86–87, 89–99*

2. Would people react to van Gogh's work differently if they thought of him as having had an ear disorder rather than a psychological disorder? Why do people find it fascinating to assess famous people, particularly those in the arts, long after their death? *p. 87*

3. How might IQ scores be misused by school officials, parents, or other individuals? Why do you think our society is so preoccupied with the concept of intelligence and with IQ scores? *pp. 98–99*

4. Many people argue for a "people first" approach to clinical labeling. For example, they recommend using the phrase "a person with schizophrenia" rather than "a schizophrenic" (Foderaro, 1995). Why might this approach to labeling be preferable? *pp. 101–107*

5. A newspaper columnist has observed, "Newspapers usually take great care not to mention the race of those accused of violent crimes. But how many times have you seen the sentence, 'He had a history of mental illness'?" What does this double standard suggest about the status and rights of people with psychological disorders? *p. 107*

6. How can persons make wise decisions about therapists and treatment approaches when they are seeking treatment? *pp. 107–111*

7. One of every five persons surveyed still does not believe that people with psychological disorders can be treated and can improve (National Mental Health Association, 1999). Why do such beliefs persist despite research evidence to the contrary? *pp. 107–111*

⊙—[CYBER**STUDY**]————————>>>

SEARCH THE *ABNORMAL PSYCHOLOGY* CD-ROM FOR

▲ Chapter 4 video cases and discussions
   How do clinicians arrive at a diagnosis?
   See neuroimaging in action.
   What causes aggression and violence?

▲ Chapter 4 Practical, Research, and Decision-Making Exercises
   Assessing and labeling in everyday life
   Uncovering the effects of expectations on observations

▲ Chapter 4 Practice Test and Feedback

LOG ON TO THE COMER WEB PAGE FOR

▲ Suggested Web links, exercises, FAQ page, additional Chapter 4 practice test questions
   <www.worthpublishers.com/comer>

<<<

Anxiety Disorders

Bob Donaldson was a 22-year-old carpenter referred to the psychiatric outpatient department of a community hospital. . . . During the initial interview Bob was visibly distressed. He appeared tense, worried, and frightened. He sat on the edge of his chair, tapping his foot and fidgeting with a pencil on the psychiatrist's desk. He sighed frequently, took deep breaths between sentences, and periodically exhaled audibly and changed his position as he attempted to relate his story:

> *Bob:* It's been an awful month. I can't seem to do anything. I don't know whether I'm coming or going. I'm afraid I'm going crazy or something.
> *Doctor:* What makes you think that?
> *Bob:* I can't concentrate. My boss tells me to do something and I start to do it, but before I've taken five steps I don't know what I started out to do. I get dizzy and I can feel my heart beating and everything looks like it's shimmering or far away from me or something—it's unbelievable.
> *Doctor:* What thoughts come to mind when you're feeling like this?
> *Bob:* I just think, "Oh, Christ, my heart is really beating, my head is swimming, my ears are ringing—I'm either going to die or go crazy."
> *Doctor:* What happens then?
> *Bob:* Well, it doesn't last more than a few seconds, I mean that intense feeling. I come back down to earth, but then I'm worrying what's the matter with me all the time, or checking my pulse to see how fast it's going, or feeling my palms to see if they're sweating.
> *Doctor:* Can others see what you're going through?
> *Bob:* You know, I doubt it. I hide it. I haven't been seeing my friends. You know, they say "Let's stop for a beer" or something after work and I give them some excuse—you know, like I have to do something around the house or with my car. I'm not with them when I'm with them anyway—I'm just sitting there worrying. My friend Pat said I was frowning all the time. So, anyway, I just go home and turn on the TV or pick up the sports page, but I can't really get into that either.

Bob went on to say that he had stopped playing softball because of fatigability and trouble concentrating. On several occasions during the past two weeks he was unable to go to work because he was "too nervous."

(Spitzer et al., 1983, pp. 11–12)

One does not need to be as troubled as Bob Donaldson to experience fear and anxiety. Think about a time when your breathing quickened, your muscles tensed, and your heart pounded with a sudden sense of dread. Was it when your car almost skidded off the road in the rain? When your professor announced a pop quiz? What about when the person you were in love with went out with someone else, or your boss suggested that your job performance ought to improve? Any time you face what seems to be a serious threat to your well-being, you may react with the state of immediate alarm known as **fear.** Sometimes you cannot pinpoint a specific cause for your alarm, but still you feel tense and edgy, as if you expected something

•**FEAR**•The central nervous system's physiological and emotional response to a serious threat to one's well-being.

•**ANXIETY**•The central nervous system's physiological and emotional response to a vague sense of threat or danger.

•**GENERALIZED ANXIETY DISORDER**•A disorder marked by persistent and excessive feelings of anxiety and worry about numerous events and activities.

unpleasant to happen. The vague sense of being in danger is usually termed **anxiety,** and it has the same features—the same increase in breathing, muscular tension, perspiration, and so forth—as fear (Barlow, 2002).

Although everyday experiences of fear and anxiety are not pleasant, they often have an adaptive function: they prepare us for action—for "fight or flight"—when danger threatens. They may lead us to drive more cautiously in a storm, keep up with our reading assignments, treat our dates more sensitively, and work harder at our jobs. Unfortunately, some people suffer such disabling fear and anxiety that they cannot lead normal lives. Their discomfort is too severe or too frequent; it lasts too long; or it is triggered too easily. These people are said to have an *anxiety disorder* or a related kind of disorder.

Anxiety disorders are the most common mental disorders in the United States. In any given year 18.1 percent of the adult population suffer from one or another of the six anxiety disorders identified by DSM-IV-TR, while close to 29 percent of all people develop one of the disorders at some point in their lives (Kessler et al., 2005). Only around one-fifth of these individuals seek treatment (Wang et al., 2005). The disorders cost society at least $42 billion each year in health care expenses, lost wages, and lost productivity (Dozois & Westra, 2004; Greenberg et al., 1999).

People with *generalized anxiety disorder* experience general and persistent feelings of worry and anxiety. People with *phobias* experience a persistent and irrational fear of a specific object, activity, or situation. Individuals with *panic disorder* have recurrent attacks of terror. Those with *obsessive-compulsive disorder* feel overrun by recurrent thoughts that cause anxiety or by the need to perform repetitive actions to reduce anxiety. And those with *acute stress disorder* and *posttraumatic stress disorder* are tormented by fear and related symptoms well after a traumatic event (military combat, rape, torture) has ended. As we observed in the previous chapter, most individuals with one anxiety disorder suffer from a second one as well (Angst et al, 2005; Rapee & Spence, 2004) (see Figure 5-1). Bob Donaldson, for example, experiences the excessive worry found in generalized anxiety disorder and the repeated attacks of terror that mark panic disorder.

In this chapter we shall look at generalized anxiety disorder, phobias, panic disorder, and obsessive-compulsive disorder. The other anxiety disorders—acute and posttraumatic stress disorders—will be examined in the next chapter, when we consider the special effects that intense or ongoing stress have on both our psychological and physical functioning.

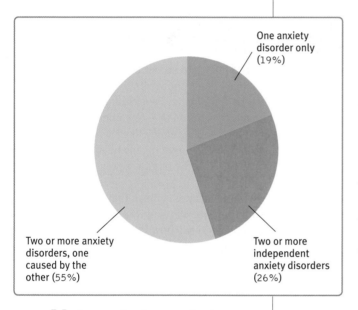

One anxiety disorder only (19%)

Two or more anxiety disorders, one caused by the other (55%)

Two or more independent anxiety disorders (26%)

FIGURE **5-1** **Does anxiety beget anxiety?** *People with one anxiety disorder usually experience another as well, either simultaneously or at another point in their lives. One study of persons with anxiety disorders found that 81 percent actually suffered from multiple disorders. (Adapted from Rodriguez et al., 2004; Hunt & Andrews, 1995.)*

Generalized Anxiety Disorder

People with **generalized anxiety disorder** experience excessive anxiety under most circumstances and worry about practically anything. In fact, their problem is sometimes described as *free-floating anxiety.* Like the young carpenter Bob Donaldson, they typically feel restless, keyed up, or on edge; tire easily; have difficulty concentrating; suffer from muscle tension; and have sleep problems (see Table 5-1). The symptoms last at least six months. Nevertheless, most people with the disorder are able, with some difficulty, to carry on social relationships and job activities.

Generalized anxiety disorder is common in Western society. Surveys suggest that 3.1 percent of the U.S. population have the symptoms of this disorder in any given year, a rate that holds across Canada, Britain, and other Western countries (Kessler et al., 2005). Altogether, close to 6 percent of all people develop generalized anxiety disorder sometime during their lives. It may emerge at any age, but usually it first appears in childhood or adolescence. Women diagnosed with the disorder outnumber men 2 to 1. Around one-quarter of individuals with generalized anxiety disorder are currently in treatment (Wang et al., 2005).

A variety of factors have been cited to explain the development of this disorder. Here we shall observe the views and treatments offered by the sociocultural, psychodynamic, humanistic, cognitive, and biological models. The behavioral perspective will be examined when we turn to phobias later in the chapter because that model approaches generalized anxiety disorder and phobias in basically the same way.

The Sociocultural Perspective

According to sociocultural theorists, generalized anxiety disorder is most likely to develop in people who are faced with societal conditions that are truly dangerous. Studies have found that people in highly threatening environments are indeed more likely to develop the general feelings of tension, anxiety, and fatigue; the exaggerated startle reactions; and the sleep disturbances found in this disorder (Andrews & Wilding, 2004; Kendler, Karkowski, & Prescott, 1998).

Take, for example, the psychological impact of living near the Three Mile Island nuclear power plant after the nuclear reactor accident of March 1979 (Wroble & Baum, 2002; Bromet & Litcher, 2002; Bromet et al., 1984, 1982). In the months following the accident, local mothers of preschool children were found to display five times as many anxiety or depression disorders as mothers living elsewhere. Although the number of disorders decreased during the next year, the Three Mile Island mothers still displayed high levels of anxiety or depression a year later.

One of the most powerful forms of societal stress is poverty. People without financial means are likely to live in run-down communities with high crime rates, have fewer educational and job opportunities, and run a greater risk for health problems. As sociocultural theorists would predict, such people also have a higher rate of generalized anxiety disorder. In the United States, the rate is twice as high among people with low incomes as among those with higher incomes (Kessler et al., 2005; Hastings, 2001; Blazer et al., 1991). As wages decrease in this country, the rate of generalized anxiety disorder steadily increases (see Table 5-2 on the next page).

Since race is closely tied to income and job opportunity in the United States, it is also tied to the prevalence of generalized anxiety disorder. In any given year, approximately 6 percent of all African Americans suffer from this disorder, compared to 3.1 percent of white Americans. African American women, perhaps the country's most socially stressed group, have the highest rate of all—6.6 percent.

Although poverty and other societal pressures may create a climate in which generalized anxiety disorder is more likely to develop, sociocultural variables are not the only factors at work. After all, most people in poor, war-torn, politically oppressed, or dangerous environments do not develop this anxiety disorder. Even if sociocultural factors play a broad role, theorists still must explain why some people develop the disorder and others do not. The psychodynamic, humanistic-existential, cognitive, and biological schools of thought have all tried to explain why and have offered corresponding treatments.

The Psychodynamic Perspective

Sigmund Freud (1933, 1917) believed that all children experience some degree of anxiety as part of growing up, and all use ego defense mechanisms to help control such anxiety (see p. 55). Children experience *realistic anxiety* when they face actual danger; *neurotic anxiety* when they are repeatedly prevented, by parents or by circumstances, from expressing their id impulses; and *moral anxiety* when they are punished or threatened for expressing their id impulses. According to Freud, some children experience particularly high levels of such anxiety, or their defense mechanisms are particularly inadequate, and these individuals may, in turn, develop generalized anxiety disorder.

PSYCHODYNAMIC EXPLANATIONS: WHEN CHILDHOOD ANXIETY GOES UNRESOLVED According to Freud, some children are overrun by neurotic or moral anxiety, thus setting the stage for generalized anxiety disorder. Early developmental experiences may produce an unusually high level of anxiety in these children. Say that a boy is spanked every time he cries for milk as an infant, messes his pants as a 2-year-old, and explores his genitals as a toddler. He may eventually come to believe that his various id impulses are very dangerous, and he may experience overwhelming anxiety whenever he has such impulses.

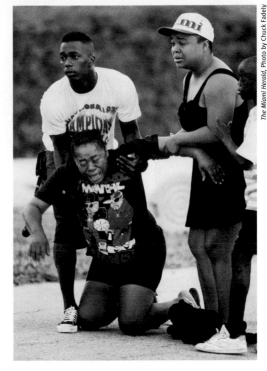

The Miami Herald, Photo by Chuck Fadely

The role of society *Upon learning that her son was a victim of a drive-by shooting, a woman collapses in the arms of relatives at the scene. People who live in dangerous environments experience greater anxiety and have a higher rate of generalized anxiety disorder than those residing in other settings.*

Table **5-1** DSM Checklist

GENERALIZED ANXIETY DISORDER

1. Excessive or ongoing anxiety and worry, for at least six months, about numerous events or activities.
2. Difficulty controlling the worry.
3. At least three of the following symptoms: restlessness • easy fatigue • irritability • muscle tension • sleep disturbance.
4. Significant distress or impairment.

Based on APA, 2000.

Table 5-2

Sociocultural Landscape: Anxiety Disorders

Prevalence of Anxiety Disorders (Compared to Rate in Total Population)

	Female	Low income	African American	Hispanic American	Elderly
Generalized anxiety disorder	Higher	Higher	Higher	Same	Higher
Specific phobias	Higher	Higher	Higher	Higher	Lower
Social phobia	Higher	Higher	Higher	Same	Lower
Panic disorder	Higher	Higher	Same	Same	Lower
Obsessive-compulsive disorder	Same	Higher	Same	Same	Lower

Relevant Sociocultural Factors

Women, minority groups, and poor persons tend to have less equality, less power, greater vulnerability, and greater risk of loss—each a source of anxiety.

Women, minority groups, and poor persons are more often victims of crime and abuse—common sources of anxiety.

Women acknowledge anxiety symptoms more readily than men.

Men with anxiety symptoms self-medicate (e.g., drink alcohol) more readily than women.

Anxiety disorders may impair the ability of persons to hold onto jobs and so lower their income level.

Some individuals overcome their anxiety disorders before reaching old age.

People with severe anxiety disorders have an elevated mortality risk.

Culture-Bound Anxiety Disorders

Nervios ("nerves"): disorder of chronic worrying and negative thinking, manifested in Latino cultures. Includes expressions of anger, headaches, and other somatic ailments. Tied to poverty and poor education.

Taijin kyofusho: social phobia-like disorder, manifested in Japan. Unlike Westerners who have social phobias, however, persons with this disorder fear that they will offend or embarrass others.

Ataque de nervios ("attack of nerves"): panic-like attacks, dominated by somatic symptoms such as trembling, heart palpitations, numbness, and the like; manifested in Latino cultures. Tied to stress or spiritual causes.

Shen-k'vei: pattern of severe anxiety or panic, accompanied by bodily complaints, manifested in China. Supposedly tied to excessive semen loss after frequent masturbation or intercourse, a loss believed to endanger the individual's vital essence. Similar to *dhat,* a disorder found in India.

Source: Kessler et al., 2005; Lopez & Guarnaccia, 2005, 2000; Glazer et al., 2004; Antony & Barlow, 2002; Roemer et al., 2002; Steketee & Barlow, 2002; APA, 2000; Friedman, 1994; Blazer et al., 1991; Eaton et al., 1991; Karno & Golding, 1991; Burnam et al., 1988; Chambless et al., 1987.

Alternatively, a child's ego defense mechanisms may be too weak to cope with even normal levels of anxiety. Overprotected children, shielded by their parents from all frustrations and threats, have little opportunity to develop effective defense mechanisms. When they face the pressures of adult life, their defense mechanisms may be too weak to cope with the resulting anxieties.

Today's psychodynamic theorists often disagree with specific aspects of Freud's explanation for generalized anxiety disorder. Most continue to believe, however, that the disorder can be traced to inadequacies in the early relationships between children and their parents (Scharff, 2001). Researchers have tested the psychodynamic explanations in various ways. In one strategy, they have tried to show that people with generalized anxiety disorder are particularly likely to use defense mechanisms. For example, one team of investigators examined the early therapy transcripts of patients with this diagnosis and found that the patients often reacted defensively. When asked by therapists to discuss upsetting experiences, they would quickly forget (*repress*) what they had just been talking about, change the direction of the discussion, or deny having negative feelings (Luborsky, 1973).

In another line of research, investigators have studied people who as children suffered extreme punishment for id impulses. As psychodynamic theorists would predict, these people have higher levels of anxiety later in life (Chiu, 1971). In cultures where children are regularly punished and threatened, for example, adults seem to have more fears and anxieties (Whiting et al., 1966). In addition, several studies have supported the psychodynamic position that extreme protectiveness by parents may often lead to high levels of anxiety in their children (Hudson & Rapee, 2004; Jenkins, 1968; Eisenberg, 1958).

Although these studies are consistent with psychodynamic explanations, some scientists question whether they show what they claim to show. When people have difficulty talking about upsetting events early in therapy, for example, they are not necessarily repressing those events. They may be purposely focusing on the positive aspects of their lives, or they may be too embarrassed to share personal negative events until they develop trust in the therapist.

Another problem is that some research studies and clinical reports have actually contradicted the psychodynamic explanations. In one, 16 people with generalized anxiety disorder were interviewed about their upbringing (Raskin et al., 1982). They reported relatively little of the excessive discipline or disturbed childhood environments that psychodynamic therapists might expect for people with this disorder.

PSYCHODYNAMIC THERAPIES Psychodynamic therapists use the same general techniques to treat all psychological problems: *free association* and the therapist's interpretations of *transference, resistance,* and *dreams. Freudian psychodynamic therapists* use these methods to help clients with generalized anxiety disorder become less afraid of their id impulses and more successful in controlling them. Other psychodynamic therapists, particularly *object relations therapists,* use them to help anxious patients identify and settle the childhood relationship problems that continue to produce anxiety in adulthood (Nolan, 2002).

Controlled studies have typically found psychodynamic treatments to be of only modest help to persons with generalized anxiety disorder (Goisman et al., 1999). An exception to this trend is *short-term psychodynamic therapy* (see Chapter 3), which has in some cases significantly reduced the levels of anxiety, worry, and social difficulty of patients with this disorder (Crits-Christoph et al., 2004; Crits-Christoph, 2002).

The Humanistic Perspective

Humanistic theorists propose that generalized anxiety disorder, like other psychological disorders, arises when people stop looking at themselves honestly and acceptingly. Repeated denials of their true thoughts, emotions, and behavior make these people extremely anxious and unable to fulfill their potential as human beings.

The humanistic view of why people develop this disorder is best illustrated by Carl Rogers's explanation. As we saw in Chapter 3, Rogers believed that children who fail to receive *unconditional positive regard* from others may become overly critical of themselves and develop harsh self-standards, what Rogers called *conditions of worth.* They try to meet these standards by repeatedly distorting and denying their true thoughts and experiences. Despite such efforts, however, threatening self-judgments keep breaking through and causing them intense anxiety. This onslaught of anxiety sets the stage for generalized anxiety disorder or some other form of psychological dysfunctioning.

Practitioners of Rogers's treatment approach, **client-centered therapy,** try to show unconditional positive regard for their clients and to empathize with them. The therapists hope that an atmosphere of genuine acceptance and

•**CLIENT-CENTERED THERAPY**•The humanistic therapy developed by Carl Rogers in which clinicians try to help clients by being accepting, empathizing accurately, and conveying genuineness.

No judgment allowed *According to* client-centered therapists, *individuals can overcome their psychological problems only if they feel accepted and understood by their therapists.*

"Don't make me come over there."

•**BASIC IRRATIONAL ASSUMPTIONS**•The inaccurate and inappropriate beliefs held by people with various psychological problems, according to Albert Ellis.

caring will help clients feel secure enough to recognize their true needs, thoughts, and emotions. When clients eventually are honest and comfortable with themselves, their anxiety or other symptoms will subside. In the following excerpt, Rogers describes the progress made by a client with anxiety and related symptoms:

> Therapy was an experiencing of herself, in all its aspects, in a safe relationship. At first it was her guilt and her concern over being responsible for the maladjustments of others. Then it was her hatred and bitterness toward life for having cheated and frustrated her in so many different areas, particularly the sexual, and then it was the experiencing of her own hurt, of the sorrow she felt for herself for having been so wounded. But along with these went the experiencing of self as having a capacity for wholeness . . . a self that cared about others. This last followed . . . the realization that the therapist cared, that it really mattered to him how therapy turned out for her, that he really valued her. She experienced the soundness of her basic directions. She gradually became aware of the fact that, though she had searched in every corner of herself, there was nothing fundamentally bad, but rather, at heart she was positive and sound.
>
> *(Rogers, 1954, pp. 261–264)*

In spite of such optimistic case reports, controlled studies have failed to offer strong support for this approach. Although research does suggest that client-centered therapy is usually more helpful to anxious clients than no treatment, the approach is only sometimes superior to placebo therapy (Prochaska & Norcross, 2003; Grawe et al., 1998). In addition, researchers have found, at best, only limited support for Rogers's explanation of generalized anxiety disorder and other forms of abnormal behavior. Nor have other humanistic theories and treatment received much research support.

The Cognitive Perspective

Proponents of the cognitive model suggest that psychological problems are often caused by dysfunctional ways of thinking (see Box 5-1). Given that excessive worry—a cognitive symptom—is a key characteristic of generalized anxiety disorder (see Figure 5-2), it is not surprising that cognitive theorists have had much to say about the causes of and treatments for this particular disorder (Holaway, Rodebaugh, & Heimberg, 2006).

MALADAPTIVE ASSUMPTIONS Initially, cognitive theorists suggested that generalized anxiety disorder is primarily caused by *maladaptive assumptions,* a notion that continues to be influential. Albert Ellis, for example, proposed that many people are guided by irrational beliefs that lead them to act and react in inappropriate ways (Ellis, 2005, 2002, 1977, 1962). Ellis called these **basic irrational assumptions,** and he claimed that people with generalized anxiety disorder often hold the following ones:

> "It is a dire necessity for an adult human being to be loved or approved of by virtually every significant other person in his community."

> "It is awful and catastrophic when things are not the way one would very much like them to be."

> "If something is or may be dangerous or fearsome, one should be terribly concerned about it and should keep dwelling on the possibility of its occurring."

> "One should be thoroughly competent, adequate, and achieving in all possible respects if one is to consider oneself worthwhile."

> *(Ellis, 1962)*

When people who make these assumptions are faced with a stressful event, such as an exam or a blind date, they are likely to interpret it as dangerous and threatening, to

FIGURE 5-2 How long do your worries last? *In one survey, 62 percent of college students said they spend less than 10 minutes at a time worrying about something. In contrast, 20 percent worry for more than an hour (Adapted from Tallis et al., 1994).*

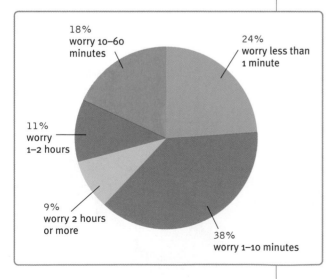

- 18% worry 10–60 minutes
- 24% worry less than 1 minute
- 11% worry 1–2 hours
- 9% worry 2 hours or more
- 38% worry 1–10 minutes

[BOX **5-1**]

Fears, Shmears: The Odds Are Usually on Our Side

People with anxiety disorders have many unreasonable fears, but millions of other people, too, worry about disaster every day. Most of the catastrophes they fear are not probable. Perhaps the ability to live by laws of *probability* rather than *possibility* is what separates the fearless from the fearful. What are the odds, then, that commonly feared events will happen? The range of probability is wide, but the odds are usually heavily in our favor.

A city resident will be a victim of a violent crime . . . 1 in 60

A suburbanite will be a victim of a violent crime . . . 1 in 1,000

A small-town resident will be a victim of a violent crime . . . 1 in 2,000

A child will suffer a high-chair injury this year . . . 1 in 6,000

The IRS will audit you this year . . . 1 in 100

You will be murdered this year . . . 1 in 12,000

You will be killed on your *next* bus ride . . . 1 in 500 million

You will be hit by a baseball at a major-league game . . . 1 in 300,000

You will drown in the tub this year . . . 1 in 685,000

Your house will have a fire this year . . . 1 in 200

Your carton will contain a broken egg . . . 1 in 10

Build with care *The chance of a construction worker being injured at work during the year is 1 in 27.*

You will develop a tooth cavity . . . 1 in 6

You will contract AIDS from a blood transfusion . . . 1 in 100,000

You will die in a tsunami . . . 1 in 500,000

You will be attacked by a shark . . . 1 in 4 million

You will receive a diagnosis of cancer this year . . . 1 in 8,000

A woman will develop breast cancer during her lifetime . . . 1 in 9

A piano player will eventually develop lower back pain . . . 1 in 3

You will be killed on your *next* automobile outing . . . 1 in 4 million

Condom use will eventually fail to prevent pregnancy . . . 1 in 10

An IUD will eventually fail to prevent pregnancy . . . 1 in 10

Coitus interruptus will eventually fail to prevent pregnancy . . . 1 in 5

You will die as a result of a collision between an asteroid and the earth . . . 1 in 500,000

You will die as a result of a lightning strike . . . 1 in 84,000

(ADAPTED FROM BRITT, 2005; KRANTZ, 1992)

overreact, and to experience fear. As they apply the assumptions to more and more events, they may begin to develop generalized anxiety disorder (Warren, 1997).

Similarly, the cognitive theorist Aaron Beck argued that people with generalized anxiety disorder constantly hold silent assumptions (for example, "A situation or a person is unsafe until proven to be safe" or "It is always best to assume the worst") that imply they are in imminent danger (Beck & Weishaar, 2005; Beck & Emery, 1985). Since the time of Ellis's and Beck's initial proposals, researchers have repeatedly found that people with generalized anxiety disorder do indeed hold maladaptive assumptions, particularly about dangerousness (Riskind & Williams, 2005; Wells, 2005; Beck et al., 1974).

What kinds of people are likely to have exaggerated expectations of danger? Some cognitive theorists point to those whose lives have been filled with *unpredictable negative events*. These individuals become generally fearful of the unknown and always wait for the boom to drop. To avoid being blindsided, they keep trying to predict negative events.

Fearful delights *Many people enjoy the feeling of fear as long as it occurs under controlled circumstances, as when they are safely watching the tension grow in the popular movie* The Ring.

They look everywhere for signs of danger, and they wind up seeing danger everywhere, thus setting up a life of anxiety. In support of this idea, studies have demonstrated that people with generalized anxiety symptoms pay unusually close attention to threatening cues (Mogg & Bradley, 2005). In addition, research finds that both animal and human subjects respond more fearfully to unpredictable negative events than to predictable ones and that people with generalized anxiety disorder are much more uncomfortable with uncertainty than other people are and worry more about the future (Mineka & Zinberg, 2006; Coles & Heimberg, 2005; Dugas et al., 2005, 2002).

SECOND-GENERATION COGNITIVE EXPLANATIONS In recent years, two promising explanations, sometimes called the *second-generation cognitive explanations,* have emerged. One is the *metacognitive theory,* the other the *avoidance theory.* Both explanations build on the work of Ellis and Beck and their special emphasis on danger (Riskind, 2005).

The *metacognitive theory of generalized anxiety disorder,* developed by the researcher Adrian Wells (2005), holds that the most problematic assumptions at work in generalized anxiety disorder are the individual's beliefs about worrying itself. Wells argues that people with this disorder implicitly hold both positive and negative beliefs about worrying. On the positive side, they believe that worrying is a useful way of appraising and coping with threats in life. And so they look for and examine all possible signs of danger—that is, they worry incessantly.

At the same time, Wells argues, individuals with generalized anxiety disorder also hold negative beliefs about worrying, and these negative attitudes are the ones that really open the door to the disorder. Because society teaches them that worrying is a bad thing, the individuals come to believe that their repeated worrying is in fact harmful (mentally and physically) and uncontrollable. Now they further worry about the fact that they always seem to be worrying (so-called *metaworries*) (see Table 5-3). The net effect of all this worrying: generalized anxiety disorder.

This explanation has received considerable research support. Studies indicate that individuals with generalized anxiety disorder do indeed consider worrying to have a positive value (Wells, 2005; Borkovec & Roemer, 1995), that people who generally hold both positive and negative beliefs about worrying are particularly prone to develop generalized anxiety disorder (Wells, 2005; Wells & Papagerorgiou, 1998), and that repeated metaworrying (negative worrying) is a particularly powerful predictor of developing the disorder (Wells & Carter, 1999).

The *avoidance theory of generalized anxiety disorder,* developed by the researcher Thomas Borkovec, also holds that worrying serves a "positive" function for individuals with this disorder. However, the function that Borkevec cites is different from the one that Wells points to. Borkovec begins by suggesting that people with generalized anxiety disorder have greater bodily arousal (higher heart rate, perspiration, respiration) than other people and he further asserts that worrying actually serves to *reduce* this bodily arousal.

In breakthrough studies, Borkovec and other researchers have found that for all people, cognitive activity temporarily reduces emotional bodily arousal. It is as if our cognitive functioning temporarily distracts us from our somatic arousal. It may be then that people with generalized anxiety disorder worry repeatedly in order to reduce or avoid their states of heightened somatic arousal. When, for example, they find themselves in an uncomfortable job situation or social relationship, they implicitly choose to intellectualize (that is, worry about) losing their job or losing their friend, rather than having to stew in a state of intense negative arousal. In short, individuals with generalized anxiety disorder may turn to worrying as a quick, though ultimately maladaptive, way of coping with unpleasant states of emotional arousal.

Borkovec's explanation has been supported in numerous studies. Research with laboratory subjects has found, for example, that worrying does indeed temporarily reduce heart rate and other forms of bodily arousal. In

---

Table 5-3

Worrying about Worrying: Items from the Meta-Worry Questionnaire

I am going crazy with worry.

My worrying will escalate and I'll cease to function.

I'm making myself ill with worry.

I'm abnormal for worrying.

My mind can't take the worrying.

I'm losing out in life because of worrying.

My body can't take the worrying.

Source: Wells, 2005.

addition, clinical studies have revealed that people with generalized anxiety disorder experience particularly fast and intense bodily reactions across various situations; find bodily and emotional arousal highly confusing, overwhelming, and unpleasant; have great difficulty managing or coping with such emotional arousal; worry more than other people upon becoming somatically and emotionally aroused; and successfully reduce their arousal whenever they worry (Mennin et al., 2005, 2004, 2002; Roemer et al., 2005; Turk et al., 2005; Borkovec & Sharpless, 2004).

COGNITIVE THERAPIES Two kinds of cognitive approaches are used in cases of generalized anxiety disorder (Waters & Craske, 2005). In one, based on the pioneering work of Ellis and Beck, therapists help clients change the maladaptive assumptions and related dysfunctional thinking that characterize their disorder. In the other, therapists help clients to understand the special role that worrying may play in the disorder and to change their views about and reactions to worrying.

CHANGING MALADAPTIVE ASSUMPTIONS In Ellis's technique of **rational-emotive therapy,** practitioners point out the irrational assumptions held by clients, suggest more appropriate assumptions, and assign homework that gives the individuals practice at challenging old assumptions and applying new ones (Ellis, 2005, 2002, 2001). Research has been limited, but studies do suggest that this approach brings at least modest relief to persons suffering from anxiety (Ellis, 2005; Cowan & Brunero, 1997). The approach is illustrated in the following discussion between Ellis and an anxious client who fears failure and disapproval at work, especially over a testing procedure that she has developed for her company:

> *Client:* I'm so distraught these days that I can hardly concentrate on anything for more than a minute or two at a time. My mind just keeps wandering to that damn testing procedure I devised, and that they've put so much money into; and whether it's going to work well or be just a waste of all that time and money. . . .
>
> *Ellis:* Point one is that you must admit that you are telling yourself something to start your worrying going, and you must begin to look, and I mean really look, for the specific nonsense with which you keep reindoctrinating yourself. . . . The false statement is: "If, because my testing procedure doesn't work and I am functioning inefficiently on my job, my co-workers do not want me or approve of me, then I shall be a worthless person." . . .
>
> *Client:* But if I want to do what my firm also wants me to do, and I am useless to them, aren't I also useless to me?
>
> *Ellis:* No—not unless you think you are. You are frustrated, of course, if you want to set up a good testing procedure and you can't. But need you be desperately unhappy because you are frustrated? And need you deem yourself completely unworthwhile because you can't do one of the main things you want to do in life?
>
> *(Ellis, 1962, pp. 160–165)*

Beck's similar but more systematic approach, called, simply, *cognitive therapy,* is an adaptation of his influential and very effective treatment for depression (which is discussed in Chapter 9). Researchers have found that, like Ellis's rational emotion therapy, it often helps reduce generalized anxiety to more tolerable levels (Tafet et al., 2005).

FOCUSING ON WORRYING In light of the recent findings about worrying and its special role in generalized anxiety disorder, some cognitive therapists now try to guide clients with this disorder to recognize and change their dysfunctional use of worrying (Waters & Craske, 2005; Leahy, 2004; Mennin, 2004). The therapists often begin treatment with psycho-education about worrying and generalized anxiety disorder. After repeated educational discussions and self-monitoring of their somatic arousal and cognitive responses, the clients

---

>>LOOKING AROUND

**Modern Anxiety:
Top Computer Worries**

Computer crash <<

Server overload <<

Computer viruses <<

Lack of computer privacy/computer security <<

Identity theft <<

Internet child predators <<

Cyberstalking <<

Cybercrime/computer hoaxes and scams <<

Internet misinformation <<

Cyberterrorism <<

•**RATIONAL-EMOTIVE THERAPY**•A cognitive therapy developed by Albert Ellis which helps clients to identify and change the irrational assumptions and thinking that help cause their psychological disorder.

"No, no, that's not a sin, either. My goodness, you must have worried yourself to death."

come to appreciate the triggers of their worrying, their misconceptions about worrying, and their misguided efforts to control and predict their emotions and their lives by worrying. As therapy proceeds, the clients become increasingly skilled at identifying their heightened states of arousal and their counterproductive uses of worry to reduce such arousal. As such insights and skills grow, clients are expected to see the world as less threatening (and so less emotionally arousing); to try out and adopt more constructive ways of dealing with emotional arousal; and, in general, to worry less about the fact that they worry so much.

Currently, the precise procedures for changing worry-related attitudes and behaviors vary from clinician to clinician. Some therapists stay strictly within the cognitive realm, while others supplement their cognitive approaches with tools such as behavior modification, relaxation training, and medication. Such variations aside, research has begun to indicate that a concentrated focus on worrying is a very helpful addition to the traditional cognitive treatment for generalized anxiety disorder (Hollon et al., 2006; Waters & Craske, 2005; Mennin, 2004).

The Biological Perspective

Biological theorists believe that generalized anxiety disorder is caused chiefly by biological factors. For years this claim was supported primarily by **family pedigree studies,** in which researchers determine how many and which relatives of a person with a disorder have the same disorder. If biological tendencies toward generalized anxiety disorder are inherited, people who are biologically related should have similar probabilities of developing this disorder. Studies have in fact found that biological relatives of persons with generalized anxiety disorder are more likely than nonrelatives to have the disorder too (Wetherell et al., 2006; Hettema et al., 2001). Approximately 15 percent of the relatives of people with the disorder display it themselves—much more than the 6 percent lifetime prevalence rate found in the general population. And the closer the relative (an identical twin, for example, as opposed to a fraternal twin or other sibling), the greater the likelihood that he or she will also have the disorder (APA, 2000).

Of course, investigators cannot have full confidence in biological interpretations of such findings. Because relatives are likely to share aspects of the same environment, their shared disorders may reflect similarities in environment and upbringing rather than similarities in biological makeup. And, indeed, the closer the relatives, the more similar their environmental experiences are likely to be. Because identical twins are more physically alike than fraternal twins, they may even experience more similarities in their upbringing.

BIOLOGICAL EXPLANATIONS: GABA INACTIVITY In recent decades important discoveries by brain researchers have offered more direct evidence that generalized anxiety disorder is related to biological factors. One of the first such discoveries occurred in the 1950s, when researchers determined that **benzodiazepines,** the family of drugs that includes *diazepam* (Valium) and *alprazolam* (Xanax), provide relief from anxiety. At first, no one understood why benzodiazepines reduce anxiety. Eventually, however, the development of radioactive techniques enabled researchers to pinpoint the exact sites in the brain that are affected by benzodiazepines (Mohler & Okada, 1977). Apparently certain neurons have receptors that receive the benzodiazepines, just as a lock receives a key.

Investigators soon discovered that these benzodiazepine receptors ordinarily receive **gamma-aminobutyric acid (GABA),** a common and important neurotransmitter in the brain (Dawson et al., 2005; Gorman, 2005). As we observed in Chapter 3, neurotransmitters are chemicals that carry messages from one neuron to another. GABA carries *inhibitory* messages: when GABA is received at a receptor, it causes the neuron to stop firing.

On the basis of such findings, biological researchers eventually pieced together several scenarios of how fear reactions may occur. One of the leading ones began with the notion that in normal fear reactions, key neurons throughout the brain fire more rapidly, triggering the firing of still more neurons and creating a general state of excitability

•**FAMILY PEDIGREE STUDY**•A research design in which investigators determine how many and which relatives of a person with a disorder have the same disorder.

•**BENZODIAZEPINES**•The most common group of antianxiety drugs, which includes Valium and Xanax.

•**GABA**•The neurotransmitter gamma-aminobutyric acid, whose low activity has been linked to generalized anxiety disorder.

•**SEDATIVE-HYPNOTIC DRUGS**•Drugs that calm people at lower doses and help them to fall asleep at higher doses.

throughout the brain and body. Perspiration, breathing, and muscle tension increase. This state is experienced as fear or anxiety. After neuron firing continues for a while, it triggers a feedback system—that is, brain and body activities that reduce the level of excitability. Some neurons throughout the brain release the neurotransmitter GABA, which then binds to GABA receptors on certain neurons and instructs those neurons to stop firing. The state of excitability ceases, and the experience of fear or anxiety subsides (Ator, 2005; Costa, 1985, 1983).

A number of researchers concluded that a malfunction in this feedback system can cause fear or anxiety to go unchecked (Roy-Byrne, 2005). In fact, when some investigators reduced GABA's ability to bind to GABA receptors, they found that animal subjects reacted with a rise in anxiety (Costa, 1985; Mohler, Richards, & Wu, 1981). This finding suggested that people with generalized anxiety disorder may have ongoing problems in their anxiety feedback system. Perhaps they have too few GABA receptors, or their GABA receptors do not readily capture the neurotransmitter.

This explanation was certainly promising and it continues to have many supporters, but it has problems. One is that recent biological discoveries have complicated the picture. It has been found, for example, that other neurotransmitters and receptors may also play important roles in anxiety and generalized anxiety disorder, acting alone or in conjunction with GABA (Wetherell et al., 2006; Meyer & Quenzer, 2005; Hennig, 2004). Another problem is that much of this research on the biology of anxiety has been done on laboratory animals. When researchers produce fear responses in animals, they assume that the animals are experiencing something similar to human anxiety, but it is impossible to be certain. The animals may be experiencing a high level of arousal that is quite different from human anxiety.

Finally, biological theorists are faced with the problem of establishing a causal relationship. Although studies have tied physiological functioning to generalized anxiety disorder, they have not established that the physiological events *cause* the disorder. The biological responses of anxious persons may be the result, rather than the cause, of their anxiety disorders. Perhaps long-term anxiety eventually leads to poorer GABA reception, for example.

BIOLOGICAL TREATMENTS The leading biological approach to treating generalized anxiety disorder is to prescribe *antianxiety drugs,* known popularly as tranquilizers (see Table 5-4). Other biological interventions are *relaxation training,* in which people learn to relax the muscles throughout their bodies, and *biofeedback,* in which clients learn to control underlying biological processes voluntarily.

ANTIANXIETY DRUGS Before the 1950s, a family of drugs labeled *barbiturates* were the major biological treatment for anxiety disorders (Meyer & Quenzer, 2005). Because these drugs were used in low doses to calm people and in higher doses to help them fall asleep, they were generally known as **sedative-hypnotic drugs.** However, barbiturates created serious problems. They made people very drowsy, too high a dose could lead to death, and those who took them over a long period could become physically dependent on them. In the late 1940s, a drug called *meprobamate* was developed and later released as a new kind of sedative-hypnotic medication under the brand name Miltown. This drug was less dangerous and less addictive than barbiturates, but it still caused great drowsiness. Finally, in the late 1950s another group of antianxiety drugs called *benzodiazepines* was marketed. These drugs did not seem to produce as much tiredness as the others and were quickly embraced by both doctors and patients.

Only years later did investigators come to understand the reasons for the drugs' effectiveness. As we have observed, researchers eventually learned that there are specific neuron sites in the brain that receive benzodiazepines (Mohler & Okada, 1977) and that these same receptor sites ordinarily receive the neurotransmitter GABA. Apparently, when benzodiazepines bind to these neuron receptor sites, particularly those receptors known as *GABA-A receptors,* they increase the ability of GABA to bind to them as well, and so improve GABA's ability to stop neuron firing and reduce anxiety (Dawson et al., 2005).

Do monkeys experience anxiety? *Clinical researchers must be careful in interpreting the reactions of animal subjects. This infant monkey was considered "fearful" after being separated from its mother. But perhaps it was feeling depressed or experiencing a level of arousal that does not correspond to either fear or depression.*

Table 5-4

Drugs That Reduce Anxiety, by Class

Generic Name	Trade Name
Benzodiazepines	
Alprazolam	Xanax
Chlorazepate	Tranxene
Chlordiazepoxide	Librium
Clonazepam	Klonopin
Diazepam	Valium
Estazolam	ProSom
Halazepam	Paxipam
Lorazepam	Ativan
Midazolam	Versed
Oxazepam	Serax
Prazepam	Centrax
Temazepam	Rostoril
Others	
Buspirone	BuSpar
Propranolol	Inderal
Atenolol	Tenormin

Studies indicate that benzodiazepines sometimes provide temporary and modest relief for people with generalized anxiety disorder (Julien, 2005; Davidson, 2004). However, clinicians have come to realize the potential dangers of these drugs. First, when the medications are stopped, many persons' anxieties return as strong as ever. Second, we now know that people who take benzodiazepines in large doses for an extended time can become physically dependent on them. Third, the drugs can produce undesirable effects such as drowsiness, lack of coordination, memory loss, depression, and aggressive behavior. Finally, the drugs mix badly with certain other drugs or substances. For example, if people on benzodiazepines drink even small amounts of alcohol, their breathing can slow down dangerously, sometimes fatally (Meyer & Quenzer, 2005).

In recent years, still other kinds of antianxiety drugs have become available for people with generalized anxiety disorder (Julien, 2005). One of these drugs, *buspirone* (trade name BuSpar), has gained particular popularity. Binding to a different set of receptors in the brain, this drug is often just as effective as benzodiazepines and is less likely to lead to physical dependence. In addition, certain *antidepressant* medications have proved to be of help to many people with generalized anxiety disorder. In fact, a number of clinicians have come to believe that these antidepressant drugs represent the most effective biological intervention for this disorder (Ball et al., 2005; Liebowitz et al., 2005; Weizhen et al., 2005).

Modern relaxation *At the Brain Mind Gym, business executives receive pulsations of light and sound from goggles and headphones, which are meant to lull their brains into deep relaxation.*

RELAXATION TRAINING A nonchemical biological technique commonly used to treat generalized anxiety disorder is **relaxation training.** The notion behind this approach is that physical relaxation will lead to a state of psychological relaxation. In one version, therapists teach clients to identify individual muscle groups, tense them, release the tension, and ultimately relax the whole body. With continued practice, they can bring on a state of deep muscle relaxation at will, reducing their state of anxiety.

Research indicates that relaxation training is more effective than no treatment or placebo treatment in cases of generalized anxiety disorder. The improvement it produces, however, tends to be modest (Leahy, 2004; Butler et al., 1991), and other techniques that are known to relax people, such as *meditation,* often seem to be equally effective (Bourne et al., 2004; Kabat-Zinn et al., 1992). Relaxation training is of greatest help to people with generalized anxiety disorder when it is combined with cognitive therapy or with biofeedback (Lang, 2004; Brown et al., 2001).

BIOFEEDBACK In **biofeedback,** therapists use electrical signals from the body to train people to control physiological processes such as heart rate or muscle tension. Clients are connected to a monitor that gives them continuous information about their bodily activities. By attending to the therapist's instructions and the signals from the monitor, they may gradually learn to control even seemingly involuntary physiological processes.

The most widely applied method of biofeedback for the treatment of anxiety uses a device called an **electromyograph (EMG),** which provides feedback about the level of muscular tension in the body. Electrodes are attached to the client's muscles—usually the forehead muscles—where they detect the minute electrical activity that accompanies muscle tension (see Figure 5-3). The device then converts electric potentials coming from the muscles into an image, such as lines on a screen, or into a tone whose pitch changes along with changes in muscle tension. Thus clients "see" or "hear" when their muscles are becoming more or less tense. Through repeated trial and error, the individuals become skilled at voluntarily reducing muscle tension and, theoretically, at reducing tension and anxiety in everyday stressful situations.

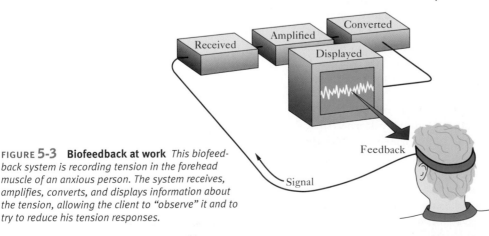

FIGURE **5-3** **Biofeedback at work** *This biofeedback system is recording tension in the forehead muscle of an anxious person. The system receives, amplifies, converts, and displays information about the tension, allowing the client to "observe" it and to try to reduce his tension responses.*

Research finds that, in most cases, EMG biofeedback, like relaxation training, has only a modest effect on a person's anxiety level (Brambrink, 2004; Brown et al., 2001, 1992). As we shall see in the next chapter, this and other forms of biofeedback have had their greatest impact when they play *adjunct* roles in the treatment of certain medical problems, including headaches, back pain, gastrointestinal disorders, seizure disorders, and neuromuscular disorders such as cerebral palsy (Astin, 2004; Engel et al., 2004).

Phobias

Most of us are none too eager to confront a spider or to be caught in a thunderstorm, but few of us have such dread as Marianne or Trisha:

Marianne Seeing a spider makes me rigid with fear, hot, trembling and dizzy. I have occasionally vomited and once fainted in order to escape from the situation. These symptoms last three or four days after seeing a spider. Realistic pictures can cause the same effect, especially if I inadvertently place my hand on one.

(Melville, 1978, p. 44)

Trisha At the end of March each year, I start getting agitated because summer is coming and that means thunderstorms. I have been afraid since my early twenties, but the last three years have been the worst. I have such a heartbeat that for hours after a storm my whole left side is painful. . . . I say I will stay in the room, but when it comes I am a jelly, reduced to nothing. I have a little cupboard and I go there, I press my eyes so hard I can't see for about an hour, and if I sit in the cupboard over an hour my husband has to straighten me up.

(Melville, 1978, p. 104)

A **phobia** (from the Greek for "fear") is a persistent and unreasonable fear of a particular object, activity, or situation (see Box 5-2 on page 130). People with a phobia become fearful if they even think about the object or situation they dread, but they usually remain comfortable as long as they avoid the object or thoughts about it. Most are well aware that their fears are excessive and unreasonable.

We all have our areas of special fear, and it is normal for some things to upset us more than other things, perhaps even different things at different stages of our lives (Antony & Barlow, 2002). A survey of residents of a community in Burlington, Vermont, found that fears of crowds, death, injury, illness, and separation were more common among people in their sixties than in other age groups (Agras, Sylvester, & Oliveau, 1969). Among 20-year-olds, fears of snakes, heights, storms, enclosures, and social situations were much more common.

How do these common fears differ from phobias? DSM-IV-TR indicates that a phobia is more intense and persistent and the desire to avoid the object or situation is greater (APA, 2000). People with phobias often feel so much distress that their fears may interfere dramatically with their lives.

Most phobias technically fall under the category of **specific phobias,** DSM-IV-TR's label for a marked and persistent fear of a specific object or situation. In addition, there are two broader kinds of phobias: **social phobia,** a fear of social or performance situations in which embarrassment may occur, and *agoraphobia,* a fear of venturing into public places, especially when one is alone. Because agoraphobia is usually, perhaps always, experienced in conjunction with *panic attacks,* unpredictable attacks of terror, we shall examine that phobia later within our discussion of panic disorders.

Specific Phobias

As we have observed, a specific phobia is a persistent fear of a specific object or situation (see Table 5-5 on the next page). When sufferers are exposed to the object or situation,

Sprinkle lightly *In the early twentieth century, drug companies did not have to prove the safety or value of their products. Brain Salt, a patent medicine for anxiety and related difficulties, promised to cure nervous disability, headaches, indigestion, heart palpitations, and sleep problems.*

•**RELAXATION TRAINING**•A treatment procedure that teaches clients to relax at will so they can calm themselves in stressful situations.

•**BIOFEEDBACK**•A treatment technique in which a client is given information about physiological reactions as they occur and learns to control the reactions voluntarily.

•**ELECTROMYOGRAPH (EMG)**•A device that provides feedback about the level of muscular tension in the body.

•**PHOBIA**•A persistent and unreasonable fear of a particular object, activity, or situation.

•**SPECIFIC PHOBIA**•A severe and persistent fear of a specific object or situation (other than agoraphobia and social phobia).

•**SOCIAL PHOBIA**•A severe and persistent fear of social or performance situations in which embarrassment may occur.

Table 5-5 DSM Checklist

SPECIFIC PHOBIA

1. Marked and persistent fear of a specific object or situation that is excessive or unreasonable, lasting at least six months.
2. Immediate anxiety usually produced by exposure to the object.
3. Recognition that the fear is excessive or unreasonable.
4. Avoidance of the feared situation.
5. Significant distress or impairment.

Based on APA, 2000.

they typically experience immediate fear. Common specific phobias are intense fears of specific animals or insects, heights, enclosed spaces, thunderstorms, and blood. Earlier, Marianne and Trisha described their specific phobias of spiders and thunderstorms. Here, Andrew talks about his phobic fear of flying:

> We got on board, and then there was the take-off. There it was again, that horrible feeling as we gathered speed. It was creeping over me again, that old feeling of panic. I kept seeing everyone as puppets, all strapped to their seats with no control over their destinies, me included. Every time the plane did a variation of speed or route, my heart would leap and I would hurriedly ask what was happening. When the plane started to lose height, I was terrified that we were about to crash.
>
> *(Melville, 1978, p. 59)*

Each year 8.7 percent of all people in the United States have the symptoms of a specific phobia (Kessler et al., 2005). More than 12 percent of individuals develop such phobias at some point during their lives, and many people have more than one at a time. Women with the disorder outnumber men by at least 2 to 1. For reasons that are not clear, the prevalence of specific phobias also differs among racial and ethnic minority groups. Hispanic Americans, for example, report twice as many of them as white Americans (Antony & Barlow, 2002).

The impact of a specific phobia on a person's life depends on what arouses the fear. People whose phobias center on dogs, insects, or water will keep encountering the objects they dread. Their efforts to avoid them must be elaborate and may greatly restrict their activities. Urban residents with snake phobias have a much easier time. The vast majority of people with a specific phobia do not seek treatment. They try instead to avoid the objects they fear (Roth & Fonagy, 2005; Wang et al., 2005).

Social Phobias

Many people worry about interacting with others or talking or performing in front of others. A number of entertainers, from the singer Barbra Streisand to the actor Sir Laurence Olivier to the football player Ricky Williams, have described major bouts of anxiety before performing. Social fears of this kind are unpleasant and inconvenient, but usually the people who have them manage to function adequately, some at a very high level.

People with a social phobia, by contrast, have severe, persistent, and irrational fears of social or performance situations in which embarrassment may occur (see Table 5-6). A social phobia may be *narrow,* such as a fear of talking in public or writing in front of others, or it may be *broad,* such as a general fear of functioning poorly in front of others. In both forms, people repeatedly judge themselves as performing less adequately than they actually do.

A social phobia can interfere greatly with one's life. A person who is unable to interact with others or speak in public may fail to perform important responsibilities. One who cannot eat in public may reject dinner invitations and other social opportunities. Since most people with this phobia keep their fears secret, their social reluctance is often misinterpreted as snobbery, lack of interest, or hostility.

Surveys indicate that 6.8 percent of people in the United States and other Western countries—around three women for every two men—experience a social phobia in any given year (Kessler et al., 2005) (see Table 5-7). Around 12 percent develop this problem at some point in their lives (Wetherell et al., 2006; Kessler et al., 2005). It often begins in late childhood or adolescence and may continue into adulthood (APA, 2000).

What Causes Phobias?

Each of the models offers explanations for phobias. Evidence tends to support the behavioral explanations. Behaviorists believe that people with phobias first learn to fear certain objects, situations, or events through conditioning (Wolfe, 2005; King et al.,

Table 5-6 DSM Checklist

SOCIAL PHOBIA

1. Marked and persistent fear of social or performance situations involving exposure to unfamiliar people or possible scrutiny by others, lasting at least six months. Concern about humiliating or embarrassing oneself.
2. Anxiety usually produced by exposure to the social situation.
3. Recognition that the fear is excessive or unreasonable.
4. Avoidance of feared situations.
5. Significant distress or impairment.

Based on APA, 2000.

Table 5-7

Anxiety Disorders Profile

	One-Year Prevalence	Female to Male Ratio	Typical Age at Onset	Prevalence among Close Relatives	Percentage Currently Receiving Clinical Treatment
Generalized anxiety disorder	3.1%	2:1	0–20 years	Elevated	25.5%
Specific phobia	8.7%	2:1	Variable	Elevated	19.0%
Social phobia	6.8%	3:2	10–20 years	Elevated	24.7%
Panic disorder	2.7%	5:2	15–35 years	Elevated	34.7%
Obsessive-compulsive disorder	1.0%	1:1	4–25 years	Elevated	41.3%

Source: Kessler et al., 2005, 1999, 1994; Wang et al., 2005; Regier et al., 1993.

2004). Once the fears are acquired, the individuals avoid the dreaded object or situation, permitting the fears to become all the more entrenched.

HOW ARE FEARS LEARNED? Behaviorists propose **classical conditioning** as a common way of acquiring phobic reactions. Here, two events that occur close together in time become closely associated in a person's mind, and, as we saw in Chapter 3, the person then reacts similarly to both of them. If one event triggers a fear response, the other may also.

In the 1920s a clinician described the case of a young woman who apparently acquired a phobia of running water through classical conditioning (Bagby, 1922). As a child of 7 she went on a picnic with her mother and aunt and ran off by herself into the woods after lunch. While she was climbing over some large rocks, her feet were caught between two of them. The harder she tried to free herself, the more trapped she became. No one heard her screams, and she grew more and more terrified. In the language of behaviorists, the entrapment was eliciting a fear response.

Entrapment → Fear response

As she struggled to free her feet, the girl heard a waterfall nearby. The sound of the running water became linked in her mind to her terrifying battle with the rocks, and she developed a fear of running water as well.

Running water → Fear response

Eventually the aunt found the screaming child, freed her from the rocks, and comforted her; but the psychological damage had been done. From that day forward, the girl was terrified of running water. For years family members had to hold her down to bathe her. When she traveled on a train, friends had to cover the windows so that she would not have to look at any streams. The young woman had apparently acquired a phobia through classical conditioning.

In conditioning terms, the entrapment was an *unconditioned stimulus* (US) that understandably elicited an *unconditioned response* (UR) of fear. The running water represented a *conditioned stimulus* (CS), a formerly neutral stimulus that became associated with entrapment in the child's mind and came also to elicit a fear reaction. The newly acquired fear was a *conditioned response* (CR).

US: Entrapment → UR: Fear

CS: Running water → CR: Fear

Another way of acquiring a fear reaction is through **modeling,** that is, through observation and imitation (Bandura & Rosenthal, 1966). A person may observe that others are

•**CLASSICAL CONDITIONING**•A process of learning in which two events that repeatedly occur close together in time become tied together in a person's mind and so produce the same response.

•**MODELING**•A process of learning in which a person observes and then imitates others. Also, a therapy approach based on the same principle.

[BOX 5-2]

Phobias, Familiar and Not So Familiar

Animals—*zoophobia*

Beards—*pogonophobia*

Being afraid—*phobophobia*

Blood—*hematophobia*

Books—*bibliophobia*

Churches—*ecclesiaphobia*

Corpses—*necrophobia*

Crossing a bridge—*gephyrophobia*

Crowds—*ochlophobia*

Darkness—*achluophobia, nyctophobia*

Demons or devils—*demonophobia*

Dogs—*cynophobia*

Dolls—*pediophobia*

Drugs—*pharmacophobia*

Enclosed spaces—*claustrophobia*

Eyes—*ommatophobia*

Feces—*coprophobia*

Fire—*pyrophobia*

Flood—*antlophobia*

Flowers—*anthophobia*

Flying—*aerophobia*

Fog—*homichlophobia*

Fur—*doraphobia*

Germs—*spermophobia*

Ghosts—*phasmophobia*

God—*theophobia*

Graves—*taphophobia*

Heat—*thermophobia*

Heights—*acrophobia*

Homosexuality—*homophobia*

Horses—*hippophobia*

Ice, frost—*cryophobia*

Insects—*entomophobia*

Machinery—*mechanophobia*

Marriage—*gamophobia*

Meat—*carnophobia*

Mice—*musophobia*

Mirrors—*eisoptrophobia*

Money—*chrometrophobia*

Night—*nyctophobia*

Noise or loud talking—*phonophobia*

Odors—*osmophobia*

Pleasure—*hedonophobia*

Poison—*toxiphobia*

Poverty—*peniaphobia*

Pregnancy—*maieusiophobia*

Railways—*siderodromophobia*

Rain—*ombrophobia*

Rivers—*potamophobia*

Robbers—*harpaxophobia*

Satan—*Satanophobia*

Sexual intercourse—*coitophobia, cypridophobia*

Shadows—*sciophobia*

Sleep—*hypnophobia*

Snakes—*ophidiophobia*

Snow—*chionophobia*

Speed—*tachophobia*

Spiders—*arachnophobia*

Stings—*cnidophobia*

Strangers—*xenophobia*

Sun—*heliophobia*

Surgery—*ergasiophobia*

Teeth—*odontophobia*

Travel—*hodophobia*

Trees—*dendrophobia*

Wasps—*spheksophobia*

Water—*hydrophobia*

Wind—*anemophobia*

Worms—*helminthophobia*

Wounds, injury—*traumatophobia*

(MELVILLE, 1978, PP. 196–202)

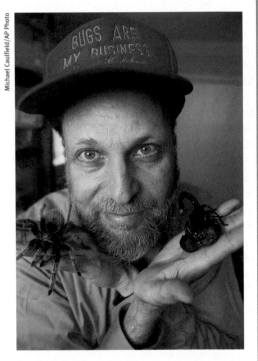

Michael Caulfield/AP Photo

Arachnophobia, not *While many people experience arachnophobia, a fear of spiders, a hardy few actually enjoy these and other kinds of bugs. Here, Steve Kutcher, a bug wrangler, holds a Chilean rose tarantula (left) and an Emperor scorpion. He has turned his childhood fascination with bugs into a lucrative business, making his many creepy crawlers available to the movies.*

afraid of certain objects or events and develop fears of the same things. Consider a young boy whose mother is afraid of illnesses, doctors, and hospitals. If she frequently expresses those fears, before long the boy himself may fear illnesses, doctors, and hospitals.

Why should one upsetting experience develop into a long-term phobia? Shouldn't the trapped girl later have seen that running water would bring her no harm? Shouldn't the boy later see that illnesses are temporary and doctors and hospitals helpful? Behaviorists believe that after acquiring a fear response, people try to *avoid* what they fear. Whenever they find themselves near a fearsome object, they quickly move away. They may also plan ahead to ensure that such encounters will not occur. Remember that the girl had friends cover the windows on trains so that she could avoid looking at streams.

People with phobias do not get close to the dreaded objects often enough to learn that they are really quite harmless.

Behaviorists also propose that specific learned fears will blossom into a generalized anxiety disorder when a person acquires a large number of them. This development is presumed to come about through **stimulus generalization:** responses to one stimulus are also elicited by similar stimuli. The fear of running water acquired by the girl in the rocks could have generalized to such similar stimuli as milk being poured into a glass or even the sound of bubbly music. Perhaps a person experiences a series of upsetting events, each event produces one or more feared stimuli, and the person's reactions to each of these stimuli generalize to yet other stimuli. That person may then build up a large number of fears and eventually develop generalized anxiety disorder.

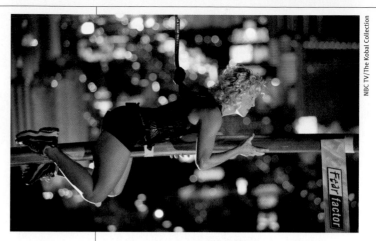

NBC TV/The Kobal Collection

Fear Factor: **Helpful, harmful, or just horrible?** *The popular reality show* Fear Factor *has raised a mild controversy in the clinical field. When contestants on the television series are forced to crawl on a pole high above Times Square, slurp mouthfuls of roaches and beetles, or swim in a barrel of live rats, what effect do these stunts have on viewers? Do they produce phobias? Do they show viewers that feared objects and situations are actually quite harmless? Or do they simply "gross out" viewers? The clinical verdict is still out.*

HOW HAVE BEHAVIORAL EXPLANATIONS FARED IN RESEARCH? Some laboratory studies have found that animals and humans can indeed be taught to fear objects through classical conditioning (Miller, 1948; Mowrer, 1947, 1939). In one famous report, the psychologists John B. Watson and Rosalie Rayner (1920) described how they taught a baby boy called Little Albert to fear white rats. For weeks Albert was allowed to play with a white rat and appeared to enjoy doing so. One time when Albert reached for the rat, however, the experimenter struck a steel bar with a hammer, making a very loud noise that upset and frightened Albert. The next several times that Albert reached for the rat, the experimenter again made the loud noise. Albert acquired a fear and avoidance response to the rat. As Watson (1930) described it, "The instant the rat was shown, the baby began to cry . . . and . . . crawl away" (p. 161).

Research has also supported the behavioral position that fears can be acquired through modeling. The psychologists Albert Bandura and Theodore Rosenthal (1966), for example, had human subjects observe a person apparently being shocked by electricity whenever a buzzer sounded. The victim was actually the experimenter's accomplice—in research terminology, a *confederate*—who pretended to experience pain by twitching and yelling whenever the buzzer went on. After the unsuspecting subjects had observed several such episodes, they themselves experienced a fear reaction whenever they heard the buzzer.

Although these studies support behaviorists' explanations of phobias, other research has called those explanations into question (Ressler & Davis, 2003; Antony & Barlow, 2002). Several laboratory studies with children and adults have failed to condition fear reactions. In addition, although most case studies trace phobias to possible incidents of classical conditioning or modeling, quite a few fail to do so. So, although it appears that a phobia *can* be acquired by classical conditioning or modeling, researchers have not established that the disorder is *ordinarily* acquired in this way.

A BEHAVIORAL-EVOLUTIONARY EXPLANATION Some phobias are much more common than others (see Figure 5-4 on the next page). Phobic reactions to animals, heights, and darkness are more common than phobic reactions to meat, grass, and houses. Theorists often account for these differences by proposing that human beings, as a species, have a predisposition to develop certain fears (Mineka & Ohman, 2002; Seligman, 1971). This idea is referred to as **preparedness** because human beings, theoretically, are "prepared" to acquire some phobias and not others. The following case makes the point:

A four-year-old girl was playing in the park. Thinking that she saw a snake, she ran to her parents' car and jumped inside, slamming the door behind her. Unfortunately, the girl's hand was caught by the closing car door, the results of which were severe pain and several visits to the doctor. Before this, she may have been afraid of snakes, but not phobic. After this experience, a phobia developed, not of cars or car doors, but of snakes. The snake phobia persisted into adulthood, at which time she sought treatment from me.

(Marks, 1977, p. 192)

•STIMULUS GENERALIZATION• A phenomenon in which responses to one stimulus are also produced by similar stimuli.

•PREPAREDNESS• A predisposition to develop certain fears.

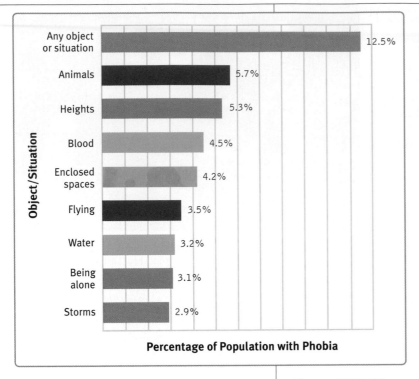

FIGURE 5-4 How common are the specific phobias? *Over the course of their lives, 12.5 percent of people in the United States develop a specific phobia. The most common ones are fears of certain animals and of heights. Most sufferers experience more than one specific phobia. (Adapted from Curtis et al., 1998.)*

•**EXPOSURE TREATMENTS**•Behavioral treatments in which persons are exposed to the objects or situations they dread.

•**SYSTEMATIC DESENSITIZATION**•A behavioral treatment that uses relaxation training and a fear hierarchy to help clients with phobias react calmly to the objects or situations they dread.

•**FEAR HIERARCHY**•A list of objects or situations that frighten a person, starting with those that are slightly feared and ending with those that are feared greatly.

•**FLOODING**•A treatment for phobias in which clients are exposed repeatedly and intensively to a feared object and made to see that it is actually harmless.

In a series of studies on preparedness, the psychologist Arne Ohman and his colleagues have conditioned different kinds of fears in two groups of human subjects (Lundqvist & Ohman, 2005; Ohman & Soares, 1993; Ohman et al., 1975). In one study they showed all subjects slides of faces, houses, snakes, and spiders. One group received electric shocks whenever they observed the slides of faces and houses, while the other group received shocks when they looked at snakes and spiders. Were subjects more prepared to fear snakes and spiders? Using skin reactions, or *galvanic skin responses (GSRs)*, as a measure of fear, the experimenters found that both groups learned to fear the intended objects after repeated shock pairings. But then they noted an interesting distinction: after a short shock-free period, the persons who had learned to fear faces and houses stopped registering high GSRs in the presence of those objects, while the persons who had learned to fear snakes and spiders continued to show high GSRs in response to them for a long while. One interpretation is that animals and insects are stronger candidates for human phobias than faces or houses.

Researchers do not know whether human predispositions to fear are the result of evolutionary or environmental factors (Ohman & Mineka, 2003; Mineka & Ohman, 2002; Clum & Febbraro, 2001). Those who propose an *evolutionary* explanation argue that a predisposition to fear has been transmitted genetically through the evolutionary process. Among our ancestors, the ones who more readily acquired a fear of animals, darkness, heights, and the like were more likely to survive long enough to reproduce. Proponents of an *environmental* explanation argue instead that experiences teach us early in life that certain objects are legitimate sources of fear, and this training predisposes many people to acquire corresponding phobias.

How Are Phobias Treated?

Surveys reveal that around 19 percent of individuals with specific phobias and 25 percent of those with social phobia are currently in treatment (Wang et al., 2005). Every theoretical model has its own approach to treating phobias, but behavioral techniques are more widely used than the rest, particularly for specific phobias. Research has shown such techniques to be highly effective and to fare better than other approaches in most head-to-head comparisons. Thus we shall focus primarily on the behavioral interventions.

TREATMENTS FOR SPECIFIC PHOBIAS Specific phobias were among the first anxiety disorders to be treated successfully in clinical practice. The major behavioral approaches to treating them are *desensitization, flooding,* and *modeling.* Together, these approaches are called **exposure treatments** because in all of them individuals are exposed to the objects or situations they dread.

People treated by **systematic desensitization,** a technique developed by Joseph Wolpe (1997, 1987, 1969), learn to relax while gradually facing the objects or situations they fear. Since relaxation and fear are incompatible, the new relaxation response is thought to substitute for the fear response. Desensitization therapists first offer *relaxation training* to clients, teaching them how to bring on a state of deep muscle relaxation at will. In addition, the therapists help clients create a **fear hierarchy,** a list of feared objects or situations, ordered from mildly to extremely upsetting.

Then clients learn how to pair relaxation with the objects or situations they fear. While the client is in a state of relaxation, the therapist has the client face the event at the bottom of his or her hierarchy. This may be an actual confrontation, a process called *in vivo desensitization.* A person who fears heights, for example, may stand on a chair or climb a stepladder. Or the confrontation may be imagined, a process called *covert desensitization.* In this case, the person imagines the frightening event while the therapist describes it. The client moves through the entire list, pairing his or her relaxation responses with each feared item. Because the first item is only mildly frightening, it is usually only a short while before the person is able to relax totally in its presence. Over the course of several sessions, clients move up the ladder of their fears until they reach and overcome the one that frightens them most of all.

Another behavioral treatment for specific phobias is **flooding.** Flooding therapists believe that people will stop fearing things when they are exposed to them repeatedly and made to see that they are actually quite harmless. Clients are forced to face their feared objects or situations without relaxation training and without a gradual buildup. The flooding procedure, like desensitization, can be either in vivo or covert.

When flooding therapists guide clients in imagining feared objects or situations, they often exaggerate the description so that the clients experience intense emotional arousal. In the case of a woman with a snake phobia, the therapist had her imagine the following scene, among others:

> Close your eyes again. Picture the snake out in front of you, now make yourself pick it up. Reach down, pick it up, put it in your lap, feel it wiggling around in your lap, leave your hand on it, put your hand out and feel it wiggling around. Kind of explore its body with your fingers and hand. You don't like to do it, make yourself do it. Make yourself do it. Really grab onto the snake. Squeeze it a little bit, feel it. Feel it kind of start to wind around your hand. Let it. Leave your hand there, feel it touching your hand and winding around it, curling around your wrist.
>
> *(Hogan, 1968, p. 423)*

In *modeling,* or *vicarious conditioning,* it is the therapist who confronts the feared object or situation while the fearful person observes (Bandura, 2004, 1977, 1971; Bandura, Adams, & Beyer, 1977). The behavioral therapist acts as a model to demonstrate that the person's fear is groundless. After several sessions many clients are able to approach the objects or situations calmly. In one version of modeling, *participant modeling,* the client is actively encouraged to join in with the therapist.

Clinical researchers have repeatedly found that each of the exposure treatments helps people with specific phobias (Wolfe, 2005; Pull, 2005). The key to success in all these therapies appears to be *actual* contact with the feared object or situation (van Hout & Emmelkamp, 2002). In vivo desensitization is more effective than covert desensitization, in vivo flooding more effective than covert flooding, and participant modeling more helpful than strictly observational modeling. Many behavioral therapists now combine features of each of the exposure approaches. In addition, a growing number of therapists are using *virtual reality*—3D computer graphics that simulate real-world objects and situations—as a useful exposure tool (Winerman, 2005).

TREATMENTS FOR SOCIAL PHOBIAS Only in recent years have clinicians been able to treat social phobias successfully (Cottraux, 2005; Kearney, 2005). Their newfound success is due in part to the growing recognition that social phobias have two distinct features that may feed upon each other: (1) people with the phobias may have overwhelming social fears, and (2) they may lack skill at starting conversations, communicating their needs, or meeting the needs of others. Armed with this insight, clinicians now treat social phobias by trying to reduce social fears, by providing training in social skills, or both.

Conquering coasterphobia *Missing out on thousands of dollars each year because many persons are afraid of roller coasters and the new wave of amusement park horror rides, some parks offer behavioral programs to help customers overcome their fears. After "treatment," some clients are able to ride the rails with the best of them. For others, it's back to the relative calm of the Ferris wheel.*

Participant modeling *Employing the exposure technique of participant modeling, therapist Pete Cohen treats clients who manifest* ophidiophobia *(fear of snakes) by first handling a snake himself, then encouraging the clients to handle it.*

HOW CAN SOCIAL FEARS BE REDUCED? Unlike specific phobias, which do not typically respond to psychotropic drugs, social fears are often reduced through medication (Julien, 2005). Somewhat surprisingly, it is *antidepressant medications* that seem to be the drugs of most help for this disorder, often more helpful than benzodiazepines or other kinds of antianxiety medications (Davidson, 2004).

At the same time, several types of psychotherapy have proved to be at least as effective as medication at reducing social fears, and people helped by such psychological treatments appear less likely to relapse than those treated with medications alone (Rodebaugh, Holaway, & Heimberg, 2004). This finding suggests to some clinicians that the psychological approaches should always be included in the treatment of social fears.

One psychological approach is *exposure therapy,* the behavioral intervention so effective with specific phobias. Exposure therapists guide, encourage, and persuade clients with social fears to expose themselves to the dreaded social situations and to remain until their fears subside (Rodebaugh et al., 2004). Usually the exposure is gradual, and it often includes homework assignments that are carried out in social situations. In addition, group therapy offers an ideal setting for exposure treatments by allowing people to face social situations in an atmosphere of support and caring (Turk et al., 2001). In one group, for example, a man who was afraid that his hands would tremble in the presence of other people had to write on a blackboard in front of the group and serve tea to the other members (Emmelkamp, 1982).

Cognitive therapies have also been widely used to treat social fears, often in combination with behavioral techniques (Hollon et al., 2006; Ledey & Heimberg, 2005). In the following discussion, Albert Ellis uses rational-emotive therapy to help a man who fears he will be rejected if he speaks up at gatherings. The discussion took place after the man had done a homework assignment in which he was to observe his self-defeating social expectations and force himself to say anything he had on his mind in social situations, no matter how stupid it might seem to him:

> After two weeks of this assignment, the patient came into his next session of therapy and reported: "I did what you told me to do. . . . [Every] time, just as you said, I found myself retreating from people, I said to myself: 'Now, even though you can't see it, there must be some sentences. What are they?' And I finally found them. And there were many of them! And they all seemed to say the same thing."
>
> "What thing?"
>
> "That I, uh, was going to be rejected. . . . [If] I related to them I was going to be rejected. And wouldn't that be perfectly awful if I was to be rejected. And there was no reason for me, uh, to take that, uh, sort of thing, and be rejected in that awful manner." . . .
>
> "And did you do the second part of the homework assignment?"
>
> "The forcing myself to speak up and express myself?"
>
> "Yes, that part."
>
> "That was worse. That was really hard. Much harder than I thought it would be. But I did it."
>
> "And?"
>
> "Oh, not bad at all. I spoke up several times; more than I've ever done before. Some people were very surprised. Phyllis was very surprised, too. But I spoke up." . . .
>
> "And how did you feel after expressing yourself like that?"
>
> "Remarkable! I don't remember when I last felt this way. I felt, uh, just remarkable—good, that is. It was really something to feel! But it was so hard. I almost didn't make it. And a couple of other times during the week I had to force myself again. But I did. And I was glad!"
>
> *(Ellis, 1962, pp. 202–203)*

Studies show that rational-emotive therapy and other cognitive approaches do indeed help reduce social fears (Hollon et al., 2006; Ledley & Heimberg, 2005; Rodebaugh et al., 2004). And these reductions typically persist for years. On the other hand, research also suggests that in most cases cognitive therapy, like drug therapy and exposure therapy, fails to eliminate social phobias fully (Hofmann & Barlow, 2002). It may reduce social fear, but it does not consistently help people perform effectively in social settings. This is where social skills training has come to the forefront.

HOW CAN SOCIAL SKILLS BE IMPROVED? In **social skills training,** therapists combine several behavioral techniques in order to help people improve their social skills. They usually model appropriate social behaviors for clients and encourage the individuals to try them out. The clients then role-play with the therapists, rehearsing their new behaviors until they become more effective. Throughout the process, therapists provide frank *feedback* and *reinforce* (praise) the clients for effective performances.

Reinforcement from other people with similar social difficulties is often more powerful than reinforcement from a therapist alone. In *social skills training groups* and *assertiveness training groups,* members try out and rehearse new social behavior with other group members. The group can also provide guidance on what is socially appropriate.

Social skills training has helped many people perform better in social situations (Fisher et al., 2004). Some people, however, continue to experience uncomfortable levels of fear despite such treatments. In fact, research indicates that no single approach—drug therapy, exposure treatment, cognitive therapy, or social skills training—consistently causes social phobias to disappear (Rodebaugh et al., 2004). Yet each is helpful, and when the approaches are combined, the results have often been encouraging (Julien, 2005; Heimberg, 2003).

Metallica: Some Kind of Monster *An unusual example of group therapy, particularly social skills training groups, is presented in the 2004 documentary film* Metallica: Some Kind of Monster. *In the film, a group therapist works with members of the heavy metal band as they try to record the album* St. Anger, *encouraging the band members to express resentments and feelings that they have bottled up for years. The band's therapy sessions are credited with preventing a meltdown and perhaps saving the band.*

Panic Disorder

Sometimes an anxiety reaction takes the form of a smothering, nightmarish panic in which people lose control of their behavior and, in fact, are practically unaware of what they are doing. Anyone can react with panic when a real threat looms up suddenly. Some people, however, experience **panic attacks**—periodic, short bouts of panic that occur suddenly, reach a peak within 10 minutes, and gradually pass.

The attacks feature at least four of the following symptoms of panic: palpitations of the heart, tingling in the hands or feet, shortness of breath, sweating, hot and cold flashes, trembling, chest pains, choking sensations, faintness, dizziness, and a feeling of unreality (see Table 5-8 on the next page). Small wonder that during a panic attack many people fear they will die, go crazy, or lose control.

I was inside a very busy shopping precinct and all of a sudden it happened: in a matter of seconds I was like a mad woman. It was like a nightmare, only I was awake; everything went black and sweat poured out of me—my body, my hands and even my hair got wet through. All the blood seemed to drain out of me; I went as white as a ghost. I felt as if I were going to collapse; it was as if I had no control over my limbs; my back and legs were very weak and I felt as though it were impossible to move. It was as if I had been taken over by some stronger force. I saw all the people looking at me—just faces, no bodies, all merged into one. My heart started pounding in my head and in my ears; I thought my heart was going to stop. I could see black and yellow lights. I could hear the voices of the people but from a long way off. I could not think of anything except the way I was feeling and that now I had to get out and run quickly or I would die. I must escape and get into the fresh air.

(Hawkrigg, 1975)

•**SOCIAL SKILLS TRAINING**•A therapy approach that helps people learn or improve social skills and assertiveness through role playing and rehearsing of desirable behaviors.

•**PANIC ATTACKS**•Periodic, short bouts of panic that occur suddenly, reach a peak within minutes, and gradually pass.

Table 5-8 DSM Checklist

PANIC ATTACK

A discrete period of intense fear in which at least four of the following symptoms develop suddenly and reach a peak within 10 minutes:

- Palpitations, pounding heart, or accelerated heart rate
- Sweating
- Trembling or shaking
- Sensations of shortness of breath or smothering
- A feeling of choking
- Chest pain or discomfort
- Nausea or abdominal distress
- Feeling dizzy, unsteady, light-headed, or faint
- Derealization or depersonalization
- Fear of losing control or going crazy
- Fear of dying
- Numbness or tingling sensations
- Chills or hot flashes

Based on APA, 2000.

Table 5-9 DSM Checklist

PANIC DISORDER

1. Recurrent unexpected panic attacks.
2. A month or more of one of the following after at least one of the attacks.
   (a) Persistent concern about having additional attacks.
   (b) Worry about the implications or consequences of the attack.
   (c) Significant change in behavior related to the attacks.

Based on APA, 2000.

People with any of the anxiety disorders (or, for that matter, people without an anxiety disorder) may experience a panic attack when they are faced with something they dread. Some people, however, have panic attacks repeatedly and unexpectedly without apparent reason. They may be suffering from **panic disorder.** In addition to the panic attacks, people who are diagnosed with panic disorder experience dysfunctional changes in their thinking or behavior as a result of the attacks for a period of a month or more (see Table 5-9). For example, they may worry persistently about having another attack, have concerns about what such an attack means ("Am I losing my mind?"), or plan their behavior around the possibility of a future attack.

Panic disorder is often accompanied by **agoraphobia,** one of the three categories of phobia mentioned earlier. People with agoraphobia (from the Greek for "fear of the marketplace") are afraid to leave the house and travel to public places or other locations where escape might be difficult or help unavailable should panic symptoms develop. The intensity of agoraphobia may fluctuate. In severe cases, people become virtual prisoners in their own homes. Their social life dwindles, and they cannot hold a job.

Until recently, clinicians failed to recognize the close link between agoraphobia and panic attacks. They now realize that panic attacks, or at least some panic-like symptoms, typically set the stage for agoraphobia (Wilson & Hayward, 2005): after experiencing one or more unpredictable attacks, certain individuals become fearful of having new attacks in public places where help or escape might be difficult. Anne Watson's plight illustrates a typical onset of agoraphobia:

> Ms. Watson reported that until the onset of her current problems two years ago, she had led a normal and happy life. At that time an uncle to whom she had been extremely close in her childhood died following a sudden unexpected heart attack. . . . Six months after his death she was returning home from work one evening when suddenly she felt that she couldn't catch her breath. Her heart began to pound, and she broke out into a cold sweat. Things began to seem unreal, her legs felt leaden, and she became sure she would die or faint before she reached home. She asked a passerby to help her get a taxi and went to a nearby hospital emergency room. The doctors there found her physical examination, blood count and chemistries, and electrocardiogram all completely normal. . . .
>
> Four weeks later Ms. Watson had a second similar attack while preparing dinner at home. She made an appointment to see her family doctor, but again, all examinations were normal. She decided to put the episodes out of her mind and continue with her normal activities. Within the next several weeks, however, she had four attacks and noticed that she began to worry about when the next one would occur. . . .
>
> She then found herself constantly thinking about her anxieties as attacks continued; she began to dread leaving the house alone for fear she would be stranded, helpless and alone, by an attack. She began to avoid going to movies, parties, and dinners with friends for fear she would have an attack and be embarrassed by her need to leave. When household chores necessitated driving she waited until it was possible to take her children or a friend along for the ride. She also began walking the twenty blocks to her office to avoid the possibility of being trapped in a subway car between stops when an attack occurred.
>
> *(Spitzer et al., 1983, pp. 7–8)*

Not everyone with panic disorder develops agoraphobia, but many such persons do. Thus DSM-IV-TR distinguishes *panic disorder without agoraphobia* from *panic disorder with agoraphobia*. Around 2.7 percent of all people in the United States suffer from one or the other of these patterns in a given year; close to 5 percent develop one of the patterns at some point in their lives (Kessler et al., 2005; Julien, 2005). Both kinds of panic disorder are likely to develop in late adolescence or early adulthood and are at least twice as common among women as among men (APA, 2000). Surveys indicate that around 35 percent of individuals with panic disorder are currently in treatment (Wang et al., 2005).

The Biological Perspective

In the 1960s, clinicians made the surprising discovery that panic disorder was helped less by benzodiazepine drugs, the drugs useful in treating generalized anxiety disorder, than by certain *antidepressant drugs,* drugs that are usually used to reduce the symptoms of depression (Klein, 1964; Klein & Fink, 1962). This observation led to the first biological explanations and treatments for panic disorder.

WHAT BIOLOGICAL FACTORS CONTRIBUTE TO PANIC DISORDER? To understand the biology of panic disorder, researchers worked backward from their understanding of the antidepressant drugs that seemed to control it. They knew that many of the antidepressant drugs change the activity of **norepinephrine,** one of the neurotransmitters that carry messages from neuron to neuron in the brain. If the drugs also eliminated panic attacks, researchers wondered, might panic disorder be caused in the first place by abnormal norepinephrine activity?

Several studies produced evidence that norepinephrine activity is indeed irregular in people who suffer from panic attacks. For example, the **locus ceruleus** is a brain area rich in neurons that use norepinephrine. When this area is electrically stimulated in monkeys, the monkeys have a panic-like reaction, suggesting that panic reactions may be related to changes in norepinephrine activity in the locus ceruleus (Redmond, 1981, 1979, 1977) (see Figure 5-5). Similarly, in another line of research, scientists were able to induce panic attacks in human beings by injecting them with chemicals known to affect the activity of norepinephrine (Bourin et al., 1995; Charney et al., 1990, 1987).

These findings strongly tied norepinephrine and the locus ceruleus to panic attacks. However, research conducted in recent years indicates that the root of panic attacks is probably more complicated than a single neurotransmitter or single brain area. Researchers have determined that emotional reactions of various kinds are tied to brain *circuits*—networks of brain structures that work together, triggering each other into action and producing a particular kind of emotional reaction. It turns out that the circuit that produces panic reactions includes brain areas such as the *amygdala, ventromedial nucleus of the hypothalamus, central gray matter,* and *locus ceruleus* (Ninan & Dunlop, 2005; Mezzasalma et al., 2004). When a person confronts a frightening object or situation, the amygdala is stimulated, and it in turn stimulates the other brain areas in the circuit, setting into motion an "alarm-and-escape" response (increased heart rate, respiration, blood pressure, and the like) that is very similar to a panic reaction (Gray & McNaughton, 1996). Normally, such a reaction is countered by the activity of other brain regions so that the individual can calm down and cope with the situation at hand.

While most of today's researchers agree that this brain circuit probably functions improperly in people who experience panic disorder, they disagree as to where in the circuit the problem lies. Some researchers continue to believe that the locus ceruleus and the neurotransmitter norepinephrine are the key culprits (Bailey et al., 2003). However, other investigators argue that dysfunctioning by other brain structures or neurotransmitters in the circuit is primarily responsible for panic disorder (Maron et al., 2004; Bellodi et al., 2003; Gorman, 2003).

It is worth noting that the brain circuit responsible for panic reactions appears to be different from the circuit responsible for *anxiety* reactions (reactions that are more diffuse, ongoing, and worry-dominated than panic reactions), although some of the brain areas and neurotransmitters in the two circuits do overlap—particularly the *amygdala,* which is at the center of each circuit. The finding that the panic brain circuit and the anxiety brain circuit differ has further convinced researchers that panic disorder is biologically different from generalized anxiety disorder, and, for that matter, from other kinds of anxiety disorders.

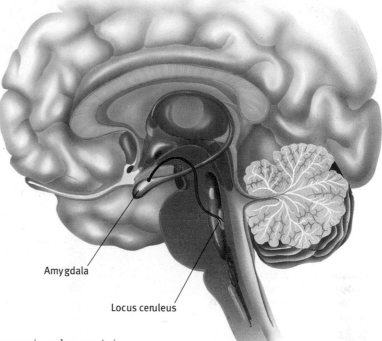

Amygdala

Locus ceruleus

FIGURE 5-5 The biology of panic *As part of an important brain circuit, the locus ceruleus receives and sends messages from and to the amygdala, a brain region tied to emotional reactions. Many neurons in the locus ceruleus use norepinephrine, a neurotransmitter implicated in panic disorder and in depression.*

•**PANIC DISORDER**•An anxiety disorder marked by recurrent and unpredictable panic attacks.

•**AGORAPHOBIA**•An anxiety disorder in which a person is afraid to be in places or situations from which escape might be difficult (or embarrassing) or help unavailable if panic-like symptoms were to occur.

•**NOREPINEPHRINE**•A neurotransmitter whose abnormal activity is linked to panic disorder and depression.

•**LOCUS CERULEUS**•A small area of the brain that seems to be active in the regulation of emotions. Many of its neurons use norepinephrine.

The Scream: **The rest of the story** *Edvard Munch's* The Scream *is one of the most famous paintings in the world, but few people know the story behind this work of art. While walking on a bridge at sunset with two friends, the artist stopped to admire the view. Munch's friends kept walking, however, and when he realized that they were gone, he experienced a panic attack, which he immortalized with the painting.*

Why might some people have abnormalities in norepinephrine activity, locus ceruleus functioning, or other parts of their panic brain circuit? One possibility is that a predisposition to develop such abnormalities is inherited (Maron et al., 2005; Stein, Jang, & Livesley, 1999; Torgersen, 1990, 1983). Once again, if a genetic factor is indeed at work, close relatives should have higher rates of panic disorder than more distant relatives. One study did find that among identical twins (twins who share all of their genes), if one twin had panic disorder, the other twin had the same disorder in 24 percent of cases. Among fraternal twins (who share only some of their genes), if one twin had panic disorder, the other twin had the same disorder in only 11 percent of cases (Kendler et al., 1995, 1993).

DRUG THERAPIES In 1962 it was discovered that certain antidepressant drugs could prevent panic attacks or reduce their frequency. As we have seen, this finding was a surprise at first. Since then, however, studies across the world have repeatedly confirmed this observation (Julien, 2005; Pollack, 2005). In fact, these drugs seem to be helpful whether or not the panic disorder is accompanied by depressive symptoms.

It appears that many of these antidepressant drugs restore proper activity of norepinephrine or other neurotransmitters that operate in the panic brain circuit (Pollack, 2005; Redmond, 1985). The drugs bring at least some improvement to 80 percent of patients who have panic disorder. Approximately half recover markedly or fully, and the improvements can last indefinitely, as long as the drugs are continued (McNally, 2001). In recent years *alprazolam* (Xanax) and other powerful benzodiazepine drugs have also proved very effective (Julien, 2005; Pollack, 2005).

Clinicians have also found these antidepressant drugs or powerful benzodiazepines to be helpful in most cases of panic disorder with agoraphobia (Clum & Febbraro, 2001). As the drugs eliminate or reduce a sufferer's panic attacks, he or she becomes confident enough to journey out into public places once again. Some people with this disorder, however, need a combination of medication and behavioral exposure treatment to fully overcome their agoraphobic fears (Wolfe, 2005; Antony & Swinson, 2000).

The Cognitive Perspective

Cognitive theorists and practitioners have come to recognize that biological factors are only part of the cause of panic attacks. In their view, full panic reactions are experienced only by people who further *misinterpret* the physiological events that are occurring within their bodies. Cognitive treatments are aimed at correcting such misinterpretations.

THE COGNITIVE EXPLANATION: MISINTERPRETING BODILY SENSATIONS

Cognitive theorists believe that panic-prone people may be very sensitive to certain bodily sensations; when they unexpectedly experience such sensations, they misinterpret them as signs of a medical catastrophe (Casey et al., 2004; Ley, 2004). Rather than understanding the probable cause of their sensations as "something I ate" or "a fight with the boss," the panic-prone grow increasingly upset about losing control, fear the worst, lose all perspective, and rapidly plunge into panic. For example, many people with panic disorder seem to "overbreathe," or hyperventilate, in stressful situations. The abnormal breathing makes them think that they are in danger of suffocation, so they panic (Dratcu, 2000). Such individuals further develop the belief that these and other "dangerous" sensations may return at any time and so set themselves up for future panic attacks.

In **biological challenge tests,** researchers produce hyperventilation or other biological sensations by administering drugs or by instructing subjects to breathe, exercise, or simply think in certain ways. As one might expect, people with panic disorder experience greater upset during these tests than people without the disorder, particularly when they believe that their bodily sensations are dangerous or out of control (Masdrakis & Papaskostas, 2004; Antony & Barlow, 2002).

•**BIOLOGICAL CHALLENGE TEST**•A procedure used to produce panic in subjects or clients by having them exercise vigorously or perform some other potentially panic-inducing task in the presence of a researcher or therapist.

•**ANXIETY SENSITIVITY**•A tendency to focus on one's bodily sensations, assess them illogically, and interpret them as harmful.

Why might some people be prone to such misinterpretations? One possibility is that panic-prone individuals generally experience, through no fault of their own, more frequent or more intense bodily sensations than other people do (Nardi et al., 2001). In fact, the kinds of sensations that are most often misinterpreted in panic disorders seem to be carbon dioxide increases in the blood, shifts in blood pressure, and rises in heart rate—bodily events that are controlled in part by the locus ceruleus and other regions of the panic brain circuit.

Still other clinical theorists suggest that people are more prone to misinterpret bodily sensations (and, in turn, to experience panic attacks) if they have poor coping skills or lack social support. Perhaps their childhoods were filled with unpredictable events, lack of control, chronic illnesses in the family, or parental overreactions to their children's bodily symptoms (Stewart et al., 2001) (see Box 5-3 on the next page).

Whatever the precise causes, research suggests that panic-prone individuals generally have a high degree of what is called **anxiety sensitivity;** that is, they focus on their bodily sensations much of the time, are unable to assess them logically, and interpret them as potentially harmful (Wilson & Hayward, 2005). One study found that people who scored high on an anxiety sensitivity survey were five times more likely than other subjects to develop panic disorder (Maller & Reiss, 1992). Other studies have found that individuals with panic disorder typically earn higher anxiety sensitivity scores that other people do (Dattilio, 2001; McNally, 2001b).

"I'm sorry, I didn't hear what you said, I was listening to my body."

COGNITIVE THERAPY Cognitive therapists try to correct people's misinterpretations of their body sensations (McCabe & Antony, 2005). The first step is to educate clients about the general nature of panic attacks, the actual causes of bodily sensations, and the tendency of clients to misinterpret their sensations. The next step is to teach clients to apply more accurate interpretations during stressful situations, thus short-circuiting the panic sequence at an early point. Therapists may also teach clients to cope better with anxiety—for example, by applying relaxation and breathing techniques—and to distract themselves from their sensations, perhaps by striking up a conversation with someone.

Cognitive therapists may also use biological challenge procedures (called *interoceptive exposure* when applied in therapy) to induce panic sensations, so that clients can apply their new skills under watchful supervision (Meuret et al., 2005). Individuals whose attacks are typically triggered by a rapid heart rate, for example, may be told to jump up and down for several minutes or to run up a flight of stairs. They can then practice interpreting the resulting sensations appropriately and not dwelling on them.

According to research, cognitive treatments often help people with panic disorder (Otto & Deveney, 2005; Hollon et al., 2006). In international studies, 85 percent of subjects given these treatments were free of panic for as long as two years or more, compared to only 13 percent of control subjects. As with drug therapy, cognitive treatments are only sometimes sufficient for persons whose panic disorders are accompanied by agoraphobia. For many such individuals, therapists add exposure techniques to the cognitive treatment program—an addition that has produced high success rates.

Cognitive therapy has proved to be at least as helpful as antidepressant drugs or alprazolam in the treatment of panic disorder, sometimes even more so (McCabe & Antony, 2005). In view of the effectiveness of both cognitive and drug treatments, many clinicians have tried combining them (Julien, 2005; Biondi & Picardi, 2003). It is not yet clear, however, whether this strategy is more effective than cognitive therapy alone.

Joy turns to panic *Anyone is capable of experiencing panic in the face of a fast-moving and severe threat. Celebrations of soccer victories have led to several famous outbursts of panic in which thousands of fans have been injured or killed by stampeding crowds. Mindful of such tragedies, police now intervene at the earliest signs of loss of control or panic by crowd members, as we see here in the aftermath of the 2002 World Cup game in Saitama, Japan.*

[BOX **5-3**]

The Young and the Anxious

According to DSM-IV-TR, children may suffer from any of the anxiety disorders described in this chapter. But is childhood anxiety the same as adult anxiety? Not always.

Anxiety is, to a degree, a normal and common part of childhood. Since children have had fewer experiences than adults, their world is often new and scary. They may be frightened by common events, such as the beginning of school, or by special upsets, such as moving to a new house or becoming seriously ill. In addition, each generation of children is confronted by new sources of anxiety. Today's children, for example, are repeatedly warned, both at home and at school, about the dangers of child abduction, drugs, and terrorism. They are bombarded by violent images in television shows, movies, and news programs. Even fairy tales and nursery rhymes contain frightening images that upset many children.

Because they are highly dependent on their parents for emotional support and guidance, children may also be greatly affected by parental inadequacies (Mufson et al., 2002). If, for example, parents typically react to events with high levels of anxiety or overprotect their child, the child may be more likely to respond to the world with anxiety (Barrett & Shortt, 2003; Barrett et al., 1996). Similarly, if parents repeatedly reject, disappoint, or avoid their children, the world may seem an unpleasant and anxious place for them.

For some children, such anxieties become chronic and debilitating, interfering with their daily lives and their ability to function appropriately. These children may be suffering from an anxiety disorder (Beidel & Turner, 2005). Some such anxiety disorders are remarkably similar to their adult counterparts. When specific phobias are experienced by chidren, for example, they usually look and operate just like the phobias of adulthood. Indeed, a number of untreated childhood phobias grow into adult ones.

More often, however, the anxiety disorders of childhood take on a somewhat different character from that of adult anxiety disorders. Consider *generalized anxiety disorder,* marked by constant worrying, and *social phobia,* marked by fears of embarrassing oneself in front of others. In order to have such disorders, individuals must be able to anticipate future negative events (losing one's job, having a car accident, fainting in front of others), to take on the perspective of other people, and/or to recognize that the thoughts and beliefs of others differ from their own (Vasey, 1993). These cognitive skills are simply beyond the capacity of very young children, and so the symptoms of generalized anxiety disorder and social phobia do not appear in earnest until children are 7 years old or older. In short, odd as it may sound, some patterns of anxiety cannot fully unfold until children are afforded the "benefits" of cognitive, physical, and emotional growth (Bengtsson, 2005; Selman, 1980).

What, then, do the anxiety disorders of young children look like? Typically they are dominated by behavioral and somatic symptoms rather than cognitive ones—symptoms such as clinging, sleep difficulties, and stomach pains (Kendall & Pimentel, 2003). They tend to center on specific, sometimes imaginary, objects and events, such as monsters, ghosts, or thunderstorms, rather than broad concerns about the future or one's place in the world. And they are more often than not triggered by current events and situations.

Not surprisingly, one of the most common childhood anxiety disorders, *separation anxiety disorder,* follows this profile. This disorder is unique to childhood, begins as early as the preschool years, and is displayed by 4 percent of all children (Beidel & Turner, 2005; APA, 2000). Sufferers feel extreme anxiety, often panic, whenever they are separated from home or a parent. They have great trouble traveling away from their family, and they often refuse to visit friends' houses, go on errands, or attend camp or school. Many cannot even stay alone in a room and cling to their parent around the house. Some also have temper tantrums, cry, or plead to keep their parents from leaving them. As long as the children are near their parents and not threatened by separation, they may function quite normally. At the first hint of separation, however, the dramatic pattern of symptoms may be set in motion.

Clearly, childhood is not always the carefree and happy time that most parents would like it to be. And for some children, it can be especially frightening and upsetting. Thus, it is important for parents (as well as teachers, coaches, and other key figures in the lives of children) to keep this in mind, and also to recognize that the fears and anxieties of such children typically reflect the unique experiences and mental life of childhood.

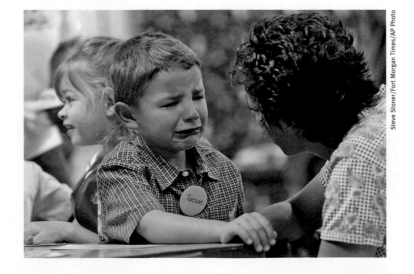

Steve Stoner/Fort Morgan Times/AP Photo

Oh, that first day! *The first day of kindergarten is overwhelming for this child and perhaps also for his mother, who tries her best to comfort him. Such anxiety reactions to the beginning of school and to being temporarily separated from one's parents are common among young children. However, 4 percent of children have broader fears and display separation anxiety disorder.*

Obsessive-Compulsive Disorder

Obsessions are persistent thoughts, ideas, impulses, or images that seem to invade a person's consciousness. **Compulsions** are repetitive and rigid behaviors or mental acts that people feel they must perform in order to prevent or reduce anxiety. As Figure 5-6 indicates, minor obsessions and compulsions are familiar to almost everyone. We may find ourselves filled with thoughts about an upcoming performance or exam, worry that we forgot to turn off the stove or lock the door, or be haunted for days by the same song or melody. We may feel better when we avoid stepping on cracks, turn away from black cats, or arrange our closets in a particular manner.

Minor obsessions and compulsions can play a helpful role in life. Distracting tunes or little rituals often calm us during times of stress. A person who repeatedly hums a tune or taps his or her fingers during a test may be releasing tension and thus improving performance. Many people find it comforting to repeat religious or cultural rituals, such as touching a mezuzah, sprinkling holy water, or fingering rosary beads.

According to DSM-IV-TR, a diagnosis of **obsessive-compulsive disorder** may be called for when obsessions or compulsions feel excessive or unreasonable, cause great distress, consume considerable time, or interfere with daily functions (see Table 5-10 on the next page). Obsessive-compulsive disorder is classified as an anxiety disorder because the victims' obsessions cause intense anxiety, while their compulsions are aimed at preventing or reducing anxiety. In addition, their anxiety rises if they try to resist their obsessions or compulsions.

Georgia, a woman with this disorder, observed: "I can't get to sleep unless I am sure everything in the house is in its proper place so that when I get up in the morning, the house is organized. I work like mad to set everything straight before I go to bed, but, when I get up in the morning, I can think of a thousand things that I ought to do. . . . I can't stand to know something needs doing and I haven't done it" (McNeil, 1967, pp. 26–28). Georgia's family was no less affected by her rigid pattern, as these comments by her husband indicate:

"Sometimes I think she never sleeps. I got up one night at 4 a.m. and there she was doing the laundry downstairs. . . . If I forget to leave my dirty shoes outside the back door she gives me a look like I had just crapped in the middle of an operating room. I stay out of the house a lot and I'm about half-stoned when I do have to be home. She even made us get rid of the dog because she said he was always filthy. When we used to have people over for supper she would jitterbug around everybody till they couldn't digest their food. I hated to call them up and ask them over because I could always hear them hem and haw and make up excuses not to come over. Even the kids are walking down the street nervous about getting dirt on them. I'm going out of my mind but you can't talk to her. She just blows up and spends twice as much time cleaning things. We have guys in to wash the walls so often I think the house is going to fall down from being scrubbed all the time."

(McNeil, 1967, pp. 26–27)

Between 1 and 2 percent of the people in the United States and other countries throughout the world suffer from obsessive-compulsive disorder in any given year (Wetherell et al., 2006; Kessler et al., 2005). Between 2 and 3 percent develop the disorder at some point during their lives. It is equally common in men and women and among people of different races and ethnic groups. The disorder usually begins by young adulthood and typically persists for many years, although its symptoms and their sever-

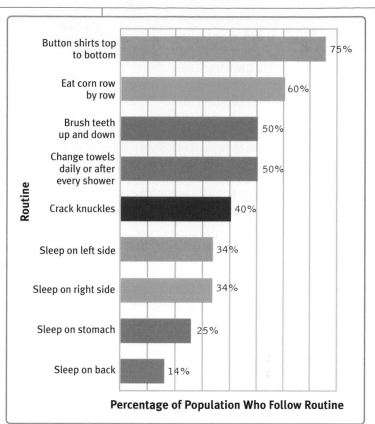

FIGURE 5-6 Normal routines *Most people find it comforting to follow set routines when they carry out everyday activities, and, in fact, 40 percent become irritated if they are forced to depart from their routines. (Adapted from Kanner, 1998, 1995.)*

•**OBSESSION**•A persistent thought, idea, impulse, or image that is experienced repeatedly, feels intrusive, and causes anxiety.

•**COMPULSION**•A repetitive and rigid behavior or mental act that a person feels driven to perform in order to prevent or reduce anxiety.

•**OBSESSIVE-COMPULSIVE DISORDER**•A disorder in which a person has recurrent and unwanted thoughts, a need to perform repetitive and rigid actions, or both.

Table 5-10 DSM Checklist

OBSESSIVE-COMPULSIVE DISORDER

1. Recurrent obsessions or compulsions.
2. Past or present recognition that the obsessions or compulsions are excessive or unreasonable.
3. Significant distress or impairment, or disruption by symptoms for more than one hour a day.

Based on APA, 2000.

ity may fluctuate over time (Angst et al., 2004). It is estimated that more than 40 percent of people with obsessive-compulsive disorder seek treatment (Kessler et al., 1999, 1994; Regier et al., 1993).

What Are the Features of Obsessions and Compulsions?

Obsessions are thoughts that feel both intrusive ("ego dystonic") and foreign ("ego alien") to the people who experience them. Attempts to ignore or resist these thoughts may arouse even more anxiety, and before long they come back more strongly than ever. Like Georgia, people with obsessions are quite aware that their thoughts are excessive.

Obsessions often take the form of obsessive *wishes* (for example, repeated wishes that one's spouse would die), *impulses* (repeated urges to yell out obscenities at work or in church), *images* (fleeting visions of forbidden sexual scenes), *ideas* (notions that germs are lurking everywhere), or *doubts* (concerns that one has made or will make a wrong decision). In the following excerpt, a clinician describes a 20-year-old college junior who was plagued by obsessive doubts.

He now spent hours each night "rehashing" the day's events, especially interactions with friends and teachers, endlessly making "right" in his mind any and all regrets. He likened the process to playing a videotape of each event over and over again in his mind, asking himself if he had behaved properly and telling himself that he had done his best, or had said the right thing every step of the way. He would do this while sitting at his desk, supposedly studying; and it was not unusual for him to look at the clock after such a period of rumination and note that, to his surprise, two or three hours had elapsed.

(Spitzer et al., 1981, pp. 20–21)

Certain basic themes run through the thoughts of most people troubled by obsessive thinking (Ryan, 2004; APA, 2000). The most common theme appears to be dirt or contamination (see Box 5-4). Other common ones are violence and aggression, orderliness, religion, and sexuality.

Compulsions are similar to obsessions in many ways. For example, although compulsive behaviors are technically under voluntary control, the people who feel they must

Kazuhiro Nogi/AFP/Getty Images

Cultural rituals *Rituals do not necessarily reflect compulsions. Indeed, cultural and religious rituals often give meaning and comfort to their practitioners. Here, for example, Buddhist monks splash water over themselves during their annual winter prayers at a temple in Tokyo. This cleansing ritual, performed to pray for good luck, is a far cry from the cleaning compulsions found in many cases of obsessive-compulsive disorder.*

[BOX **5-4**]

Terror behind the Smile

*M*any of today's college students grew up watching *Double Dare* and *Family Double Dare,* two of the messiest game shows in television history. Young contestants were regularly splattered with goo and dunked in slime and muck (Summers, 1996). All the while, the host, Marc Summers, seemed to be having a great time, especially when the kids picked him up and threw him into the mess as well. In 1996, however, Summers revealed that his years on the show had been a personal nightmare because he had an obsessive-compulsive disorder.

Steve Labadessa/Outline

Summers says that his disorder dates back to the age of 8. He remembers cleaning his room for hours, removing and dusting every book in his bookcase. When he got the offer to host *Double Dare,* he couldn't turn down the career opportunity. But the price was high. After the shows, he would spend hours in the shower. "It was the most uncomfortable feeling in the world—a feeling of physical revulsion." Only later did Summers recognize his disorder and receive successful treatment for it.

do them have little sense of choice in the matter. Most of these individuals recognize that their behavior is unreasonable, but they believe at the same time something terrible will happen if they don't perform the compulsions. After performing a compulsive act, they usually feel less anxious for a short while. For some people the compulsive acts develop into detailed *rituals.* They must go through the ritual in exactly the same way every time, according to certain rules.

Like obsessions, compulsions take various forms. *Cleaning compulsions* are very common. Like Georgia, people with these compulsions feel compelled to keep cleaning themselves, their clothing, or their homes. The cleaning may follow ritualistic rules and be repeated dozens or hundreds of times a day. People with *checking compulsions* check the same items over and over—door locks, gas taps, important papers—to make sure that all is as it should be. Another common compulsion is the constant effort to seek *order* or *balance.* People with this compulsion keep placing certain items (clothing, books, foods) in perfect order in accordance with strict rules.

> Ted is a 13-year-old referred to a Midwestern inpatient psychiatric research ward because of "senseless rituals and attention to minutiae." He can spend 3 hours centering the toilet paper roll on its holder or rearranging his bed and other objects in his room. When placing objects down, such as books or shoelaces after tying them, he picks them up and replaces them several times until they seem "straight." Although usually placid, he becomes abusive with family members who try to enter his room for fear they will move or break his objects. When he is at school, he worries that people may disturb his room. He sometimes has to be forced to interrupt his routine to attend meals. Last year he hid pieces of his clothing around the house because they wouldn't lie straight in his drawers. Moreover, he often repeats to himself, "This is perfect; you are perfect."
>
> *(Spitzer et al., 1983, p. 15)*

Touching, verbal, and *counting* compulsions are also common. People with touching compulsions repeatedly touch or avoid touching certain items. Individuals with verbal rituals feel compelled to repeat expressions, phrases, or chants. And those with counting compulsions constantly count things they see around them.

Although some people with obsessive-compulsive disorder experience obsessions only or compulsions only, most of them experience both. In fact, compulsive acts are often a response to obsessive thoughts (Foa & Franklin, 2001). One study found that in

>>PSYCH•NOTES

An Obsession That Changed the World The experiments that led Louis Pasteur to the pasteurization process may have been driven in part by his obsession with contamination and infection. Apparently he would not shake hands and regularly wiped his glass and plate before dining (Asimov, 1997). **<<**

Losing Battle People who try to avoid all contamination and rid themselves and their world of all germs are fighting a losing battle. While talking, the average person sprays 300 microscopic saliva droplets per minute, or 2.5 per word. **<<**

"Is the Itsy Bitsy Spider obsessive-compulsive?"

most cases, compulsions seemed to represent a *yielding* to obsessive doubts, ideas, or urges (Akhtar et al., 1975). A woman who keeps doubting that her house is secure may yield to that obsessive doubt by repeatedly checking locks and gas jets. Or a man who obsessively fears contamination may yield to that fear by performing cleaning rituals. The study also found that compulsions sometimes serve to help *control* obsessions. A teenager describes how she tried to control her obsessive fears of contamination by performing counting and verbal rituals:

> **Patient:** If I heard the word, like, something that had to do with germs or disease, it would be considered something bad, and so I had things that would go through my mind that were sort of like "cross that out and it'll make it okay" to hear that word.
>
> **Interviewer:** What sort of things?
>
> **Patient:** Like numbers or words that seemed to be sort of like a protector.
>
> **Interviewer:** What numbers and what words were they?
>
> **Patient:** It started out to be the number 3 and multiples of 3 and then words like "soap and water," something like that; and then the multiples of 3 got really high, and they'd end up to be 124 or something like that. It got real bad then.
>
> *(Spitzer et al., 1981, p. 137)*

Many people with obsessive-compulsive disorder worry that they will act out their obsessions. A man with obsessive images of wounded loved ones may worry that he is but a step away from committing murder; or a woman with obsessive urges to yell out in church may worry that she will one day give in to them and embarrass herself. Most such concerns are unfounded. Although many obsessions lead to compulsive acts—particularly to cleaning and checking compulsions—they do not usually lead to violence or immoral conduct.

Obsessive-compulsive disorder was once among the least understood of the psychological disorders. In recent years, however, researchers have begun to learn more about it. The most influential explanations and treatments come from the psychodynamic, behavioral, cognitive, and biological models.

The Psychodynamic Perspective

As we have observed, psychodynamic theorists believe that an anxiety disorder develops when children come to fear their own id impulses and use ego defense mechanisms to lessen the resulting anxiety. What distinguishes obsessive-compulsive disorder from

---

>>LOOKING AROUND

Penny-Wise and Pound-Foolish

In 2004, an Ohio man cashed in the last of his record-setting collection of pennies—$14,075.50 worth, accumulated over 34 years (Cauchon, 2004). Since 1970 he had gathered around 112 pennies per day, inspecting each one, separating them by year and mint location, and wrapping them in 28,851 rolls. Protesting that his behavior did not represent a compulsion, the individual said that he found organizing and wrapping the coins to be very relaxing. **<<**

other anxiety disorders, in their view, is that here the battle between anxiety-provoking id impulses and anxiety-reducing defense mechanisms is not buried in the unconscious but is played out in dramatic thoughts and actions. The id impulses usually take the form of obsessive thoughts, and the ego defenses appear as counterthoughts or compulsive actions. A woman who keeps imagining her mother lying broken and bleeding, for example, may counter those thoughts with repeated safety checks throughout the house.

According to psychodynamic theorists, three ego defense mechanisms are particularly common in obsessive-compulsive disorder: *isolation, undoing,* and *reaction formation.* People who resort to **isolation** simply disown their unwanted thoughts and experience them as foreign intrusions. People who engage in **undoing** perform acts that are meant to cancel out their undesirable impulses. Those who wash their hands repeatedly, for example, may be symbolically undoing their unacceptable id impulses. People who develop a **reaction formation** take on a lifestyle that directly opposes their unacceptable impulses. A person may live a life of compulsive kindness and devotion to others in order to counter unacceptably aggressive impulses.

Sigmund Freud believed that during the *anal stage* of development (occurring at about 2 years of age) some children experience intense rage and shame that fuel the battle between id and ego. He theorized that children at this stage get pleasure from their bowel movements. When their parents try to toilet train them, the children must learn to delay their anal pleasure. If parents are premature or too harsh in their toilet training, the children may feel such rage that they develop *aggressive id impulses*—antisocial impulses that repeatedly seek expression. They may soil their clothes all the more frequently and become generally destructive, messy, or stubborn.

If parents handle the child's aggressiveness by further pressure and embarrassment, the child may also feel ashamed, guilty, and dirty. The aggressive impulses will now compete with a strong desire to control them; the child who wants to soil will also have a desire to retain. If this conflict between the id and the ego continues, it may eventually blossom into obsessive-compulsive disorder.

Not all psychodynamic theorists agree with Freud's explanation. Some believe, for example, that the aggressive impulses of people with this disorder are rooted in feelings of insecurity rather than poor toilet-training experiences (Erikson, 1963; Sullivan, 1953; Horney, 1937). Even these theorists, however, agree with Freud that people with the disorder have strong aggressive impulses and a competing need to control them. Overall, research has not clearly supported the various psychodynamic theories (Fitz, 1990).

When treating patients with obsessive-compulsive disorder, psychodynamic therapists try to help the individuals uncover and overcome their underlying conflicts and defenses, using the customary techniques of free association and therapist interpretation. Research has offered little evidence, however, that a traditional psychodynamic approach is of much help (Bram & Bjorgvinsson, 2004; Foa & Franklin, 2004). Thus some psychodynamic therapists now prefer to treat these patients with short-term psychodynamic therapies, which, as we observed in Chapter 3, are more direct and action-oriented than the classical techniques.

The Behavioral Perspective

Behaviorists have concentrated on explaining and treating compulsions rather than obsessions. They propose that people happen upon their compulsions quite randomly. In a fearful situation, they happen just coincidentally to wash their hands, say, or dress a certain way. When the threat lifts, they link the improvement to that particular action. After repeated accidental associations, they believe that the action is bringing them good luck or actually changing the situation, and so they perform the same actions again and again in similar situations. The act becomes a key method of avoiding or reducing anxiety (Frost & Steketee, 2001).

The famous clinical scientist Stanley Rachman and his associates have shown that compulsions do appear to be rewarded by a reduction in anxiety. In one of their experiments, for example, 12 people with compulsive hand-washing rituals were placed in contact with objects that they considered contaminated (Hodgson & Rachman, 1972). As behaviorists would predict, the hand-washing rituals of these subjects seemed to

•**ISOLATION**•An ego defense mechanism in which people unconsciously isolate and disown undesirable and unwanted thoughts, experiencing them as foreign intrusions.

•**UNDOING**•An ego defense mechanism whereby a person unconsciously cancels out an unacceptable desire or act by performing another act.

•**REACTION FORMATION**•An ego defense mechanism whereby a person suppresses an unacceptable desire by taking on a lifestyle that expresses the opposite desire.

>>**LOOKING BACK**
Origins of Superstitions

Avoid walking under a ladder: Egypt (3000 B.C.) «

Knock on wood: North America (2000 B.C.) «

Carry a rabbit's foot: Western Europe (pre-600 B.C.) «

Break a wishbone: Italy (pre-400 B.C.) «

Cross fingers: Western Europe (pre-100 B.C.) «

Avoid broken mirrors: Rome (first century) «

Hang a horseshoe: Greece (fourth century) «

Avoid black cats: England (Middle Ages) «

(Panati, 1987)

•**EXPOSURE AND RESPONSE PREVENTION**•A behavioral treatment for obsessive-compulsive disorder that exposes clients to anxiety-arousing thoughts or situations and then prevents them from performing their compulsive acts. Also called *exposure and ritual prevention*.

•**NEUTRALIZING**•A person's attempt to eliminate unwanted thoughts by thinking or behaving in ways that put matters right internally, making up for the unacceptable thoughts.

•**HABITUATION TRAINING**•A therapeutic technique in which a therapist tries to call forth a client's obsessive thoughts again and again, with the expectation that the thoughts will eventually lose their power to frighten and thus to cause anxiety.

lower their anxiety. Of course, although such investigations suggest that compulsions may eventually be rewarded by a reduction in anxiety, they do not show that compulsions are acquired in the first place as a result of such reductions.

If people keep performing compulsive behaviors in order to prevent bad outcomes and ensure positive outcomes, can't they be taught that such behaviors are not really serving this purpose? In a behavioral treatment called **exposure and response prevention** (or **exposure and ritual prevention**), first developed by the psychiatrist Victor Meyer (1966), clients are repeatedly exposed to objects or situations that produce anxiety, obsessive fears, and compulsive behaviors, but they are told to *resist* performing the behaviors they feel so bound to perform. Because people find it very difficult to resist such behaviors, therapists may set an example first.

Many behavioral therapists now use exposure and response prevention in both individual and group therapy formats. Some of them also have people carry out *self-help* procedures at home (Foa et al., 2005). That is, they assign homework in exposure and response prevention, such as these assignments given to a woman with a cleaning compulsion:

◆ Do not mop the floor of your bathroom for a week. After this, clean it within three minutes, using an ordinary mop. Use this mop for other chores as well without cleaning it.

◆ Buy a fluffy mohair sweater and wear it for a week. When taking it off at night do not remove the bits of fluff. Do not clean your house for a week.

◆ You, your husband, and children all have to keep shoes on. Do not clean the house for a week.

◆ Drop a cookie on the contaminated floor, pick the cookie up and eat it.

◆ Leave the sheets and blankets on the floor and then put them on the beds. Do not change these for a week.

(Emmelkamp, 1982, pp. 299–300)

Eventually this woman was able to set up a reasonable routine for cleaning herself and her home.

Between 55 and 85 percent of clients with obsessive-compulsive disorder have been found to improve considerably with exposure and response prevention, improvements that often continue indefinitely (Hollon et al., 2006; Franklin, Riggs, & Pai, 2005). The

Getting down and dirty *The principle behind exposure and response prevention is to place clients in anxiety-provoking situations while preventing them from performing their usual compulsive acts. Clients with cleaning compulsions, for example, might be instructed to do heavy-duty gardening and then to resist washing their hands or taking a shower. They may never go so far as to participate in and enjoy mud wrestling, like these delightfully filthy individuals at the annual Mud Day event in Westland, Michigan, but you get the point.*

Bill Pugliano/Getty Images

effectiveness of this approach suggests that people with obsessive-compulsive disorder are like the superstitious man in the old joke who keeps snapping his fingers to keep elephants away. When someone points out, "But there aren't any elephants around here," the man replies, "See? It works!" One review concludes, "With hindsight, it is possible to see that the obsessional individual has been snapping his fingers, and unless he stops (response prevention) and takes a look around at the same time (exposure), he isn't going to learn much of value about elephants" (Berk & Efran, 1983, p. 546).

At the same time, research has revealed certain limitations in exposure and response prevention. Few clients who receive the treatment overcome all their symptoms, and as many as one-quarter fail to improve at all (Foa et al., 2005; Frost & Steketee, 2001). Also, the approach is of limited help to those who have obsessions but no compulsions (Hohagen et al., 1998; Jenike, 1992).

The Cognitive Perspective

The cognitive explanation for obsessive-compulsive disorder begins by pointing out that everyone has repetitive, unwanted, and intrusive thoughts. Anyone might have thoughts of harming others or being contaminated by germs, for example, but most people dismiss or ignore them with ease (Baer, 2001). Those who develop this disorder, however, typically blame themselves for such thoughts and expect that somehow terrible things will happen (Shafran, 2005; Salkovskis, 1999, 1989, 1985). To avoid such negative outcomes, they try to **neutralize** the thoughts—thinking or behaving in ways meant to put matters right or to make amends (Salkovskis et al., 2003).

Neutralizing acts might include requesting special reassurance from others, deliberately thinking "good" thoughts, washing one's hands, or checking for possible sources of danger. When a neutralizing effort of some kind brings about a temporary reduction in discomfort, it is reinforced and will likely be repeated. Eventually the neutralizing thought or act is used so often that it becomes, by definition, an obsession or compulsion. At the same time, the individual becomes more and more convinced that his or her unpleasant intrusive thoughts are dangerous. As the person's fear of such thoughts increases, the thoughts begin to occur more frequently and they, too, become obsessions.

In support of this explanation, studies have found that people who have obsessive-compulsive disorder experience intrusive thoughts more often than other people, resort to more elaborate neutralizing strategies, and experience reductions in anxiety after using neutralizing techniques (Shafran, 2005; Salkovskis et al., 2003).

Although everyone sometimes has undesired thoughts, only some people develop obsessive-compulsive disorder. Why do these individuals find such normal thoughts so disturbing to begin with? Researchers have found that this population tends (1) to be more depressed than other people (Hong et al., 2004); (2) to have exceptionally high standards of conduct and morality (Rachman, 1993); (3) to believe that their intrusive negative thoughts are equivalent to actions and capable of causing harm to themselves or others (Steketee et al., 2003); and (4) generally to believe that they should have perfect control over all their thoughts and behaviors (Coles et al., 2005; Frost & Steketee, 2002, 2001).

COGNITIVE THERAPY Cognitive therapists focus treatment on the cognitive processes that help produce and maintain obsessive thoughts and compulsive acts. Initially, they provide psychoeducation, teaching clients about their misinterpretations of unwanted thoughts, excessive sense of responsibility, and neutralizing acts. They then move on to help the clients identify, challenge, and change their distorted cognitions. Many cognitive therapists also include **habituation training** in their sessions, directing clients to call forth their obsessive thoughts again and again. The clinicians expect that with such repetitions, the obsessive thoughts will lose their power to frighten or threaten the clients, and thus will produce less anxiety and trigger fewer new obsessive thoughts and compulsive acts (Franklin et al., 2002; Salkovskis & Westbrook, 1989). In one version of habituation training, clients are simply instructed to summon obsessive thoughts or images to mind and hold them for a while. In another version, clients spend up to an hour once or twice a day listening to their own voices on tape stating their obsessive thoughts

Reverse the curse *Although mild and harmless, superstitious beliefs and acts are similar in certain respects to obsessions and compulsions. In fact, superstitions, obsessions, and compulsions may also have similar origins, according to some psychologists. A widely shared superstition was the 84-year-old belief by Boston Red Sox fans that their team was suffering the* Curse of the Bambino *and would never again win a World Series title—a curse supposedly triggered by the Red Sox's 1920 trade of Babe Ruth to the New York Yankees. In an effort to reverse the curse, Red Sox fans performed various superstitious acts game after game, year after year, such as displaying signs written backward (above). When the Red Sox finally won a World Series title in 2004 (right), many of the fans were forced to acknowledge that there had never really been a curse. Others, however, concluded that their backward signs and the like had finally done the job.*

again and again. Such cognitive techniques have indeed helped reduce the number and impact of obsessions and compulsions (Rufer et al., 2005; Eddy et al., 2004).

COGNITIVE-BEHAVIORAL THERAPY While the behavioral approach (exposure and response prevention) and the cognitive approach have each been of help to clients with obsessive-compulsive disorder, research suggests that a combination of the two approaches is often more effective than either intervention alone (Franklin et al., 2005; March, Franklin, & Foa, 2005; Clark, 2004). Typically such cognitive-behavioral treatments begin with psychoeducation about the nature of obsessions and compulsions and an explanation of the rationale behind exposure and response prevention (Foa et al., 2005). Treatment then moves on to numerous exposure-and-response-prevention exercises both in the office and at home, repeated sessions of habituation training, and ongoing therapy discussions about the reductions in anxiety that result from such exercises and training. Increasingly, clients become able to distinguish realistic concerns from obsessive ones, and their repeated thoughts and rituals decrease.

The Biological Perspective

Family pedigree studies provided the earliest hints that obsessive-compulsive disorder may be linked in part to biological factors (Lambert & Kinsley, 2005). Studies of twins found that if one identical twin manifests obsessive-compulsive disorder, the other twin also develops it in at least 53 percent of cases. In contrast, among fraternal twins (twins who share half rather than all their genes) both twins manifest the disorder in only 23 percent of cases. In short, the more similar the gene composition of two individuals, the more likely both are to experience obsessive-compulsive disorder, if indeed one of them manifests the disorder. Currently, more direct genetic studies are being conducted to try to pinpoint the gene or combination of genes that may predispose some individuals to develop this disorder (Miguel et al., 2005, 1997; Delorme et al., 2004).

•**SEROTONIN**•A neurotransmitter whose abnormal activity is linked to depression, obsessive-compulsive disorder, and eating disorders.

•**NEUROMODULATOR**•A neurotransmitter that helps modify or regulate the effect of other neurotransmitters.

•**ORBITOFRONTAL CORTEX**•A region of the brain in which impulses involving excretion, sexuality, violence, and other primitive activities normally arise.

•**CAUDATE NUCLEI**•Structures in the brain, within the region known as the basal ganglia, that help convert sensory information into thoughts and actions.

Additional evidence that biological factors play a role in obsessive-compulsive disorder has been uncovered in recent years, and promising biological treatments for the disorder have been developed as well. The most compelling explanations point to (1) abnormally low activity of the neurotransmitter *serotonin* and (2) abnormal functioning in key regions of the brain.

ABNORMAL SEROTONIN ACTIVITY Serotonin, like GABA and norepinephrine, is a brain chemical that carries messages from neuron to neuron. The first clue to its role in obsessive-compulsive disorder was the surprising finding by clinical researchers that two antidepressant drugs, *clomipramine* and *fluoxetine* (Anafranil and Prozac), reduce obsessive and compulsive symptoms (Julien, 2005; Zohar et al., 2004). Since these particular drugs also increase serotonin activity, some researchers concluded that the disorder is caused by low serotonin activity. In fact, only those antidepressant drugs that increase serotonin activity help in cases of obsessive-compulsive disorder; antidepressants that mainly affect other neurotransmitters typically have no effect on it (Jenike, 1992).

Although serotonin is currently the neurotransmitter most often cited in explanations of obsessive-compulsive disorder, recent studies have suggested that other neurotransmitters, particularly *glutamate, GABA,* and *dopamine,* may also play important roles in the development of this disorder (Lambert & Kinsley, 2005). Some researchers even argue that, with regard to obsessive-compulsive disorder, serotonin may act largely as a **neuromodulator,** a chemical whose primary function is to increase or decrease the activity of other key neurotransmitters.

ABNORMAL BRAIN STRUCTURE AND FUNCTIONING Another line of research has linked obsessive-compulsive disorder to abnormal brain functioning in specific regions of the brain, particularly the **orbitofrontal cortex** (just above each eye) and the **caudate nuclei** (structures located within the brain region known as the *basal ganglia*). As it turns out, these regions are part of a brain circuit that converts sensory information into thoughts and actions (Chamberlain et al., 2005). The circuit begins in the orbitofrontal cortex, where sexual, violent, and other primitive impulses normally arise. These impulses next move on to the caudate nuclei, which act as filters that send only the most powerful impulses on to the *thalamus,* the next stop on the circuit (see Figure 5-7). If impulses reach the thalamus, the person is driven to think further about them and perhaps to act. Many theorists now believe that either the orbitofrontal cortex or the caudate nuclei of some people are too active, leading to a constant eruption of troublesome thoughts and actions (Lambert & Kinsley, 2005; Rosenberg et al., 2005). Additional parts of this brain circuit have also been identified in recent years, including the *cingulate cortex* and, once again, the *amygdala.* Of course, it may turn out that these regions also play key roles in obsessive-compulsive disorder.

In support of this brain circuit explanation, medical scientists have observed for years that obsessive-compulsive symptoms do sometimes arise or subside after the orbitofrontal cortex, caudate nuclei, or other regions in the circuit are damaged by accident or illness (Coetzer, 2004; Berthier et al., 2001). In one highly publicized case, a patient with obsessive-compulsive disorder tried to commit suicide by shooting himself in the head. Although he survived the shot, he did considerable damage to the brain areas in question. Perhaps as a result of the injury, his obsessive and compulsive symptoms declined dramatically. Similarly, neuroimaging studies, which offer pictures of brain functioning and structure, have shown that the caudate nuclei and the orbitofrontal cortex of patients with obsessive-compulsive disorder are more active than those of control subjects (Chamberlain et al., 2005; Baxter et al., 2001, 1990).

The serotonin and brain circuit explanations may themselves be linked. It turns out that serotonin—along with the neurotransmitters glutamate, GABA, and dopamine—plays a key role in the operation of the orbitofrontal cortex, caudate nuclei, and other parts of the brain circuit; certainly abnormal activity by one or more of these neurotransmitters could be contributing to the improper functioning of various parts of the circuit.

>>PSYCH•NOTES

Obsessive Love

One team of researchers found that the serotonin activity of subjects who claimed to be newly in love was about as low as that of subjects with obsessive-compulsive disorder (Marazziti et al., 1999; Asimov, 1997). **<<**

Basal ganglia

Putamen and globus pallidus

Caudate nucleus

Orbital frontal cortex

Thalamus

FIGURE 5-7 The biology of obsessive-compulsive disorder *A three-dimensional view of the brain shows some of the regions that have been linked to obsessive-compulsive disorder. These areas may be too active in people with the disorder. (Adapted from Rapoport, 1989, p. 85.)*

BIOLOGICAL THERAPIES As we have seen, researchers have learned that certain antidepressant drugs are very useful in the treatment of obsessive-compulsive disorder (Julien, 2005). Not only do the drugs increase brain serotonin activity, but they also produce more normal activity in the orbitofrontal cortex and caudate nuclei (Baxter et al., 2000, 1992). Studies have found that clomipramine (Anafranil), fluoxetine (Prozac), fluvoxamine (Luvox), and similar antidepressant drugs bring improvement to between 50 and 80 percent of those with obsessive-compulsive disorder (Julien, 2005; Lambert & Kinsley, 2005; Bareggi et al., 2004). The obsessions and compulsions do not usually disappear totally, but on average they are cut almost in half within eight weeks of treatment (DeVeaugh-Geiss et al., 1992). People who are treated with such drugs alone, however, tend to relapse if the medication is stopped.

More and more individuals with obsessive-compulsive disorder are now being treated by a combination of behavioral, cognitive, and drug therapies. According to research, such combinations often yield higher levels of symptom reduction and bring relief to more clients than do each of the approaches alone—improvements that often last for years (Kordon et al., 2005; Rufer et al., 2005). At the very least, these treatment combinations appear to yield better outcomes than drug therapy alone (Foa et al., 2005).

Thus the treatment picture for obsessive-compulsive disorder, like that for panic disorder, has improved greatly over the past 15 years. Once a very stubborn problem, this disorder is now helped by several forms of treatment, often used in combination. In fact, at least two studies suggest that the behavioral, cognitive, and biological approaches may ultimately have the same effect on the brain. In these investigations, both subjects who responded to cognitive-behavioral treatment and those who responded to antidepressant drugs showed marked reductions in activity in the caudate nuclei (Schwartz & Begley, 2002; Baxter et al., 2000, 1992).

PUTTING IT together
Diathesis-Stress in Action

Clinicians and researchers have developed many ideas about generalized anxiety disorder, phobias, panic disorder, and obsessive-compulsive disorder. At times, however, the sheer quantity of concepts and findings makes it difficult to grasp what is and what is not really known about the disorders.

Overall, it is fair to say that clinicians currently know more about the causes of phobias, panic disorder, and obsessive-compulsive disorder than about generalized anxiety disorder, even though the latter problem has been studied the longest of all the anxiety disorders. It is worth noting that the insights about panic disorder and obsessive-compulsive disorder—once among the field's most puzzling patterns—did not emerge until clinical theorists took a look at the disorders from more than one perspective and integrated those views. Today's cognitive explanation of panic disorder, for example, builds squarely on the biological idea that the disorder begins with abnormal brain activity and unusual physical sensations. Similarly, the cognitive explanation of obsessive-compulsive disorder takes its lead from the biological position that some persons are predisposed to experience more unwanted and intrusive thoughts than other persons.

It may be that a better understanding of generalized anxiety disorder awaits a similar integration of the various models. In fact, such an integration has already begun to unfold. Some of the new cognitive explanations for generalized anxiety disorder have, for example, linked the cognitive process of worrying to heightened somatic arousal in individuals with the disorder (Riskind, 2005). More generally, a growing number of theorists are coming to believe that people develop generalized anxiety disorder only when biological, psychological, and sociocultural factors are *all* at work (Heimberg et al., 2004). Adopting a *diathesis-stress* perspective, these theorists suggest that certain individuals have a biological vulnerability toward experiencing heightened somatic arousal and that this sets the stage for the disorder. Consistent with this notion, genetic investigators have discovered that certain genes may determine whether a person reacts to life's stressors calmly or in a tense manner, and developmental researchers have found that even during the earliest stages of life some infants become particularly aroused when stimulated (Lonigan et al., 2004; Hettema et al., 2001; Kalin, 1993). Perhaps these easily aroused infants have inherited defects in GABA functioning or other biological characteristics that predispose them to generalized anxiety disorder. If, over the course of their lives, the individuals also face intense societal pressures, learn to interpret the world as a dangerous place, or come to regard worrying as a useful tool, they may indeed be candidates for developing generalized anxiety disorder.

An integration of insights from the various models may also shed light on phobias. Although today's leading phobia theories—especially the behavioral ones—are enlightening, combining them with genetic explanations may help us better predict who will and who will not develop phobias. Indeed, in one study, almost a third of subjects with a specific phobia had close relatives with a similar phobia (Fyer et al., 1995, 1990). And in a related vein, several studies suggest that certain infants are born with a style of social inhibition or shyness that may increase their risk of developing a social phobia (Smoller et al., 2003; Kagan & Snidman, 1999, 1991). Perhaps people must have both a genetic predisposition and unfortunate conditioning experiences if they are to develop particular phobias.

In the treatment realm, integration of the models is already on display for each of the anxiety disorders. Therapists have discovered, for example, that treatment is at least sometimes more effective when medications are combined with cognitive techniques to treat panic disorder and when medications are combined with cognitive-behavioral techniques to treat obsessive-compulsive disorder. Similarly, cognitive techniques are now often combined with relaxation training or biofeedback in the treatment of generalized anxiety disorder—a package known as a **stress management program** (Taylor, 2006). And treatment programs for social phobias often include a combination of medications, exposure therapy, cognitive therapy, and social skills training. For the millions of people who suffer from these various anxiety disorders, such treatment combinations are a welcome development.

—[**SUMMARY AND REVIEW**]————————————————

■ **Generalized anxiety disorder** People with *generalized anxiety disorder* experience excessive anxiety and worry about a wide range of events and activities. The various explanations and treatments for this anxiety disorder have received only limited research support, although recent cognitive and biological approaches seem to be promising.

According to the *sociocultural* view, increases in *societal dangers* and *pressures* create a climate in which cases of generalized anxiety disorder are more likely to develop.

In the original *psychodynamic* explanation, Freud said that generalized anxicty disorder may develop when anxiety is excessive and defense mechanisms break down and function poorly. Psychodynamic therapists use free association, interpretation, and related psychodynamic techniques to help people overcome this problem.

Carl Rogers, the leading *humanistic* theorist, believed that people with generalized anxiety disorder fail to receive *unconditional positive regard* from significant others during their childhood and so become overly critical of themselves. He treated such individuals with *client-centered therapy.*

Cognitive theorists believe that generalized anxiety disorder is caused by *maladaptive assumptions* and *beliefs* that lead people to view most life situations as dangerous. Many cognitive theorists further believe that implicit beliefs about the power and value of *worrying* are particularly important in the development and maintenance of this disorder. Cognitive therapists help their clients to change such thinking and to find more effective ways of coping during stressful situations.

Biological theorists hold that generalized anxiety disorder results from low activity of the neurotransmitter *GABA.* A common biological treatment is *antianxiety drugs,* particularly *benzodiazepines. Relaxation training* and *biofeedback* are also applied in many cases. *pp. 116–127*

•**STRESS MANAGEMENT PROGRAM**•An approach to treating generalized and other anxiety disorders that teaches clients techniques for reducing and controlling stress.

>>**LOOKING AROUND**

Insecurity, Adult Style

Children may cling to blankets or cuddly toys to feel more secure. Adults, too, may hug a beloved object in order to relax: 1 in 5 adult women and 1 in 20 men admit to sleeping with a stuffed animal on a regular basis (Kanner, 1995). <<

Phobias A phobia is a severe, persistent, and unreasonable fear of a particular object, activity, or situation. There are three main categories of phobias: *specific phobias, social phobias,* and *agoraphobia.* Behavioral explanations of phobias, particularly specific phobias, are the most influential today. Behaviorists believe that phobias are learned from the environment through *classical conditioning* or through *modeling,* and then are maintained by avoidance behaviors.

Specific phobias have been treated most successfully with behavioral *exposure techniques* by which people are led to confront the objects they fear. The exposure may be gradual and relaxed (*desensitization*), intense (*flooding*), or vicarious (*modeling*).

Therapists who treat social phobias typically distinguish two components of this disorder: *social fears* and *poor social skills.* They try to reduce social fears by drug therapy, exposure techniques, group therapy, various cognitive approaches, or a combination of these interventions. They may try to improve social skills by *social skills training. pp. 127–135*

Panic disorder *Panic attacks* are periodic, discrete bouts of panic that occur suddenly. Sufferers of *panic disorder* experience panic attacks repeatedly and unexpectedly and without apparent reason. When panic disorder leads to *agoraphobia,* it is termed *panic disorder with agoraphobia.*

Some biological theorists believe that abnormal *norepinephrine* activity in the brain's *locus ceruleus* may be the key to panic disorder. Others believe that related neurotransmitters and brain regions may also play key roles. Biological therapists use certain *antidepressant drugs* or powerful *benzodiazepines* to treat people with this disorder. Patients whose panic disorder is accompanied by agoraphobia may need a combination of drug therapy and behavioral *exposure treatment.*

Cognitive theorists suggest that panic-prone people become preoccupied with some of their bodily sensations, misinterpret them as signs of medical catastrophe, panic, and in some cases develop panic disorder. Such persons have a high degree of *anxiety sensitivity* and also experience greater anxiety during *biological challenge tests.* Cognitive therapists teach patients to interpret their physical sensations more accurately and to cope better with anxiety. In cases of panic disorder with agoraphobia, practitioners may combine a cognitive approach with behavioral exposure techniques. *pp. 135–140*

Obsessive-compulsive disorder People with *obsessive-compulsive disorder* are beset by *obsessions,* perform *compulsions,* or display both. Common themes in obsessions are contamination and violence. Compulsions commonly center on cleaning or checking. Other common compulsions involve touching, verbal rituals, or counting. Compulsions are often a response to a person's obsessive thoughts.

According to the psychodynamic view, obsessive-compulsive disorder arises out of a battle between id impulses, which appear as obsessive thoughts, and ego defense mechanisms, which take the form of counterthoughts or compulsive actions. Behaviorists believe that compulsive behaviors develop through chance associations. The leading behavioral treatment combines prolonged *exposure* with *response prevention.* Cognitive theorists believe that obsessive-compulsive disorder grows from a normal human tendency to have *unwanted and unpleasant thoughts.* The efforts of some people to understand, eliminate, or avoid such thoughts actually lead to obsessions and compulsions. Cognitive therapy for this disorder includes *habituation training,* during which therapists encourage clients to summon their obsessive thoughts to mind for a prolonged period, expecting that the repetition of such thoughts will cause the thoughts to feel less threatening and to generate less anxiety. While the behavioral and cognitive therapies are each helpful to clients with obsessive-compulsive disorder, research suggests that a combined *cognitive-behavioral approach* may be more effective than either therapy alone.

Biological researchers have tied obsessive-compulsive disorder to low *serotonin* activity and abnormal functioning in the *orbitofrontal cortex* and in the *caudate nuclei.* Antidepressant drugs that raise serotonin activity are a useful form of treatment. *pp. 141–150*

>>> CRITICAL THOUGHTS <<<

1. The word "worry" initially meant "to choke." Dogs that attack sheep are still said to "worry" them; otherwise, the term no longer connotes outward aggression (Ash, 1999). What connections do you see between the word's original meaning and its present one? *p. 116*

2. Why might people whose childhoods were marked by unpredictable or uncontrollable events or by chronic family illnesses be inaccurate interpreters of their bodily sensations? *pp. 121–122*

3. How might antianxiety drugs be administered so as to take advantage of their helpful effects yet minimize their undesired effects? *pp. 125–126*

4. Why do so many professional performers seem particularly prone to social anxiety? Wouldn't their repeated exposure to audiences lead to a reduction in fear? *pp. 128, 134*

5. Today's human-subject review boards probably would not permit Watson and Rayner to conduct their study on Little Albert. What concerns might they raise about the procedure? Do these concerns outweigh the insights gained from this study? *p. 131*

6. Can you think of instances when you instinctively tried a simple version of exposure and response prevention in order to stop behaving in certain ways? Were your efforts successful? *pp. 146–147*

●—[CYBERSTUDY]————————————>>>

SEARCH THE *ABNORMAL PSYCHOLOGY* CD-ROM FOR

▲ Chapter 5 video cases and discussions
> **How does worrying affect psychological functioning?**
> **How disruptive are obsessions and compulsions?**
> **Observe treatments for anxiety disorders.**

▲ Chapter 5 practical, research, and decision-making exercises
> **Identifying and correcting irrational assumptions**
> **Distinguishing bothersome fears from phobias**
> **Detecting superstitions and habits in everyday life**

▲ Chapter 5 practice test and feedback

LOG ON TO THE COMER WEB PAGE FOR

▲ Suggested Web links, exercises, FAQ page, additional Chapter 5 practice test questions
‹www.worthpublishers.com/comer›

————————————————————<<<

Stress Disorders

Mark remembers his first "firefight" and encountering the VC [Viet Cong] for the first time. He lost all bladder and bowel control—in a matter of a few minutes. In his own words, "I was scared and literally shitless; I pissed all over myself, and shit all over myself too. Man, all hell broke loose. I tell you, I was so scared, I thought I would never make it out alive. I was convinced of that. Charlie had us pinned down and [was] hitting the shit out of us for hours. We had to call in the napalm and the bombing." During the first fight, Mark, an infantryman, experienced gruesome sights and strange sounds in battle. He witnessed headless bodies. "One guy said to me, 'Hey, Mark, new greenhorn boy, you saw that head go flying off that gook's shoulder. Isn't that something?' " Within 2 weeks Mark saw the head of a running comrade blown off his shoulders, the headless body moving for a few feet before falling to the ground. Mark, nauseous and vomiting for a long time, couldn't see himself surviving much longer: "I couldn't get that sight out of my head; it just kept on coming back to me in my dreams, nightmares. Like clockwork, I'd see R's head flying, and his headless body falling to the ground. I knew the guy. He was very good to me when I first got to the unit. Nobody else seemed to give a damn about me; he broke me in. It's like I would see his head and body, you know, man, wow!" Mark often found himself crying during his first weeks of combat. "I wanted to go home. I was so lonely, helpless, and really scared. But I knew I could not go home until my year was up."

(Brende & Parson, 1985, pp. 23–24)

Mark's reaction to the horror of combat is normal and understandable. During battle, soldiers often become highly anxious and depressed and physically ill. And, indeed, for many the effects of such extraordinary stress continue well beyond the combat experience itself.

But it is not just combat soldiers who are affected by stress. Nor does stress have to rise to the level of combat trauma to have a profound effect on psychological and physical functioning. Stress comes in all sizes and shapes, and we are all greatly affected by it.

We feel some degree of stress whenever we are faced with demands or opportunities that require us to change in some manner. The state of stress has two components: a **stressor,** the event that creates the demands, and a **stress response,** the person's reactions to the demands. The stressors of life may include annoying everyday hassles, such as rush-hour traffic or the appearance of unexpected company; turning-point events, such as college graduation or marriage; long-term problems, such as poverty, poor health, or overcrowded living conditions; or traumatic events, such as major accidents, assaults, tornadoes, or military combat (Gold et al., 2005). Our response to such stressors is influenced by the way we *appraise* both the events and our capacity to react to them in an effective way (Folkman & Moskowitz, 2004; Lazarus & Folkman, 1984). People who sense that they have the ability and the resources to cope are more likely to take stressors in stride and to respond constructively.

When we appraise a stressor as threatening, a natural reaction is arousal and a sense of fear—a response frequently on display in Chapter 5. As we observed in

•**STRESSOR**•An event that creates a sense of threat by confronting a person with a demand or opportunity for change.

•**STRESS RESPONSE**•A person's particular reactions to stress.

•**AUTONOMIC NERVOUS SYSTEM (ANS)**• The network of nerve fibers that connect the central nervous system to all the other organs of the body.

•**ENDOCRINE SYSTEM**•The system of glands located throughout the body that help control important activities such as growth and sexual activity.

Risky business *The modern world offers many opportunities for stress. Here, a currency dealer shouts orders during trading at the Paris Stock Exchange. The stresses of working in high-pressure environments apparently increase one's risk of developing both psychological and medical disorders.*

that chapter, fear is actually a package of responses—*physical, emotional,* and *cognitive.* Physically, we perspire, our breathing quickens, our muscles tense, and our hearts beat faster. Turning pale, developing goose bumps, and feeling nauseated are other physical reactions. Emotional responses to extreme threats include horror, dread, and even panic, while in the cognitive realm fear can disturb our ability to concentrate and distort our view of the world. We may exaggerate the harm that actually threatens us or remember things incorrectly after the threat has passed.

Stress reactions, and the sense of fear they produce, are often at play in psychological disorders. People who experience a large number of stressful events are particularly vulnerable to the onset of the anxiety disorders that we examined in Chapter 5. Similarly, increases in stress have been linked to the onset of depression, schizophrenia, sexual dysfunctioning, and yet other psychological problems.

In addition, stress plays a more central role in certain psychological and physical disorders. In such disorders, the features of stress become severe and debilitating, linger for a long period of time, and may make it impossible for the individual to live a normal life. The key psychological stress disorders are *acute stress disorder* and *posttraumatic stress disorder.* DSM-IV-TR technically lists these patterns as anxiety disorders, but as we shall see, their features extend far beyond the symptoms of anxiety. The physical stress disorders are typically called *psychophysiological disorders,* problems that DSM-IV-TR now lists

Different strokes for different folks *Some individuals are exhilarated by the opportunity to chase bulls through the streets of Pamplona, Spain, during the annual "running of the bulls" (left), while others are terrified by such a prospect. Conversely, certain individuals find it exciting to engage tamer animals, for example, ostriches, during the "running of the ostriches" fiesta (right) in Irurzun, Spain, while others are more than a little bored by such activities. Individual reactions of this kind represent differences in situation, or state, anxiety.*

under the heading *psychological factors affecting medical condition*. These psychological and physical stress disorders are the focus of this chapter. Before examining them, however, we need to understand just how the brain and body react to stress.

Stress and Arousal: The Fight-or-Flight Response

The features of arousal and fear are set in motion by the brain area called the *hypothalamus*. When our brain interprets a situation as dangerous, neurotransmitters in the hypothalamus are released, triggering the firing of neurons throughout the brain and the release of chemicals throughout the body. In particular, the hypothalamus activates two important systems—the *autonomic nervous system* and the *endocrine system*. The **autonomic nervous system (ANS)** is the extensive network of nerve fibers that connect the *central nervous system* (the brain and spinal cord) to all the other organs of the body. These fibers help regulate the *involuntary* activities of the organs—breathing, heartbeat, blood pressure, perspiration, and the like (see Figure 6-1). The **endocrine system** is the network of *glands* located throughout the body. (As we observed in Chapter 3, glands release *hormones* into the bloodstream and on to the various body organs.) The autonomic nervous system and the endocrine system often overlap in their responsibilities and activities. There are two pathways, or routes, by which these systems produce arousal and fear reactions—the *sympathetic nervous system* pathway and the *hypothalamic-pituitary-adrenal* pathway.

FIGURE 6-1 **The autonomic nervous system (ANS)** *When the sympathetic division of the ANS is activated, it stimulates some organs and inhibits others. The result is a state of general arousal. In contrast, activation of the parasympathetic division leads to an overall calming effect.*

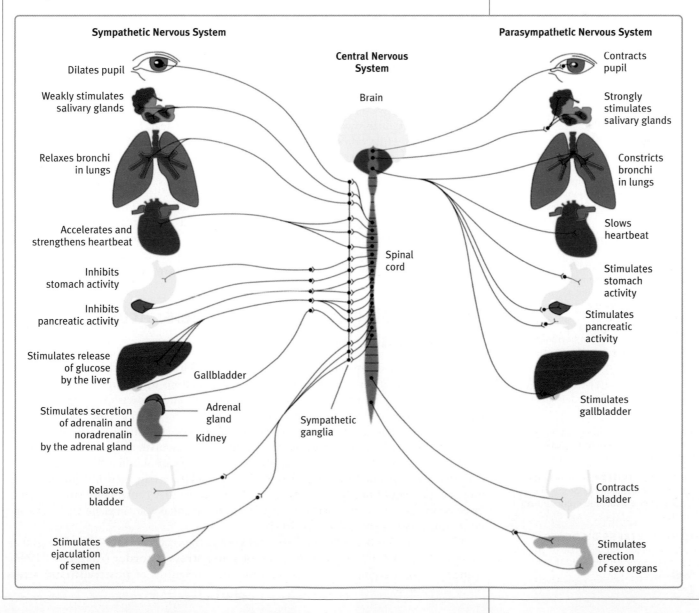

Sympathetic Nervous System

- Dilates pupil
- Weakly stimulates salivary glands
- Relaxes bronchi in lungs
- Accelerates and strengthens heartbeat
- Inhibits stomach activity
- Inhibits pancreatic activity
- Stimulates release of glucose by the liver
- Stimulates secretion of adrenalin and noradrenalin by the adrenal gland
- Relaxes bladder
- Stimulates ejaculation of semen

Central Nervous System

- Brain
- Spinal cord
- Sympathetic ganglia
- Gallbladder
- Adrenal gland
- Kidney

Parasympathetic Nervous System

- Contracts pupil
- Strongly stimulates salivary glands
- Constricts bronchi in lungs
- Slows heartbeat
- Stimulates stomach activity
- Stimulates pancreatic activity
- Stimulates gallbladder
- Contracts bladder
- Stimulates erection of sex organs

When we face a dangerous situation, the hypothalamus first excites the **sympathetic nervous system,** a special group of autonomic nervous system fibers that work to quicken our heartbeat and produce the other changes that we experience as fear or anxiety. These nerves may stimulate the organs of the body directly—for example, they may directly stimulate the heart and increase heart rate. The nerves may also influence the organs indirectly, by stimulating the *adrenal glands* (glands located on top of the kidneys), particularly the inner layer of these glands, an area called the *adrenal medulla.* When this layer of the adrenal glands is stimulated, the chemicals *epinephrine* (adrenaline) and *norepinephrine* (*noradrenaline*) are released. We have already observed that these chemicals are important neurotransmitters when they operate in the brain (pp. 137–138). When released from the adrenal medulla, however, they act as hormones and travel through the bloodstream to various organs and muscles, further producing arousal and fear.

When the perceived danger passes, a second group of autonomic nervous system fibers, called the **parasympathetic nervous system,** helps return our heartbeat and other body processes to normal. Together the sympathetic and parasympathetic nervous systems help control our arousal and fear reactions.

The second pathway by which arousal and fear reactions are produced is the **hypothalamic-pituitary-adrenal (HPA) pathway** (see Figure 6-2). When we are confronted by stressors, the hypothalamus also signals the *pituitary gland,* which lies nearby, to secrete the *adrenocorticotropic hormone* (*ACTH*), sometimes called the body's "major stress hormone." ACTH, in turn, stimulates the outer layer of the adrenal glands, an area called the *adrenal cortex,* triggering the release of a group of stress hormones called **corticosteroids,** including the hormone *cortisol.* These corticosteroids travel to various body organs where they further generate arousal and fear reactions. Eventually the corticosteroids signal the *hippocampus,* the brain part that seems to control emotional memories, and the hippocampus helps turn off the body's arousal.

The reactions on display in these two pathways are collectively referred to as the *fight-or-flight* response, precisely because they arouse our body and prepare us for a response to danger. We all have particular patterns of autonomic and endocrine functioning and so particular ways of experiencing arousal and fear. Some people are almost always relaxed, while others typically feel some tension, even when no threat is apparent. A person's general level of arousal and anxiety is sometimes called **trait anxiety,** because it seems to be a general trait that each of us brings to the events in our lives (Spielberger, 1985, 1972, 1966). Psychologists have found that differences in trait anxiety appear soon after birth (Leonardo & Hen, 2006; Kagan, 2003).

People also differ in their sense of which situations are threatening (Fisher et al., 2004). Walking through a forest may be fearsome for one person but relaxing for another. Flying in an airplane may arouse terror in some people and boredom in others. Such variations are called differences in **situation,** or **state, anxiety.**

The Psychological Stress Disorders: Acute and Posttraumatic Stress Disorders

At the beginning of this chapter we observed Mark's reaction to the stress of combat and noted that it is common for persons in such situations to become anxious and depressed. For some, however, the symptoms of anxiety and depression, as well as other kinds of symptoms, persist well after the situation is over. These people may be suffering from *acute stress disorder* or *posttraumatic stress disorder,* patterns that arise in reaction to a psychologically traumatic event. The event usually involves actual or threatened serious injury to the person or to a family member or friend. Unlike the anxiety disorders that we examined in Chapter 5, which typically are triggered by situations that most people would not find threatening, the situations that cause acute stress disorder or posttraumatic stress disorder—combat, rape, an earthquake, an airplane crash—would be traumatic for anyone (Corales, 2005).

If the symptoms begin within four weeks of the traumatic event and last for less than a month, DSM-IV-TR assigns a diagnosis of **acute stress disorder** (APA, 2000, 1994). If the symptoms continue longer than a month, a diagnosis of **posttraumatic stress**

•**SYMPATHETIC NERVOUS SYSTEM**•The nerve fibers of the autonomic nervous system that quicken the heartbeat and produce other changes experienced as arousal and fear.

•**PARASYMPATHETIC NERVOUS SYSTEM**• The nerve fibers of the autonomic nervous system that help maintain normal organ functioning. They also slow organ functioning after stimulation and return other bodily processes to normal.

•**HYPOTHALAMIC-PITUITARY-ADRENAL (HPA) PATHWAY**•One route by which the brain and body produce arousal and fear. At times of stress, the hypothalamus signals the pituitary gland, which in turn signals the adrenal glands. Stress hormones are then released to various body organs.

•**CORTICOSTEROIDS**•A group of hormones, including cortisol, released by the adrenal glands at times of stress.

•**TRAIT ANXIETY**•The general level of anxiety that a person brings to the various events in his or her life.

•**SITUATION ANXIETY**•The level of anxiety produced in a person by a particular situation. Also called *state anxiety.*

•**ACUTE STRESS DISORDER**•An anxiety disorder in which fear and related symptoms are experienced soon after a traumatic event and last less than a month.

•**POSTTRAUMATIC STRESS DISORDER**•An anxiety disorder in which fear and related symptoms continue to be experienced long after a traumatic event.

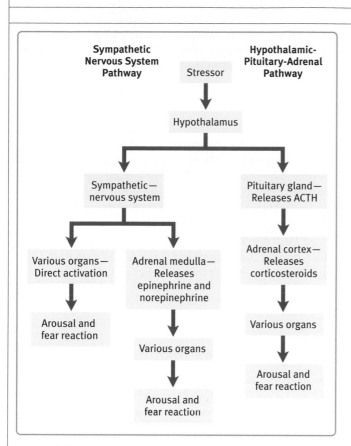

FIGURE 6-2 Pathways of arousal and fear *When we are confronted by a stressor, our bodies produce arousal and fear reactions through two pathways. In one, the hypothalamus sends a message to the sympathetic nervous system, which then activates key body organs, either directly or by causing the adrenal medulla to release epinephrine and norepinephrine into the bloodstream. In the other pathway, the hypothalamus sends a message to the pituitary gland, which then signals the adrenal cortex to release corticosteroids—the stress hormones—into the bloodstream.*

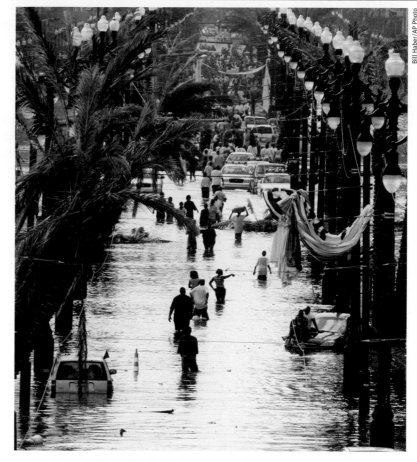

Mother Nature's other side *Although a range of situations may trigger acute or post-traumatic stress disorders, natural disasters are among the most common causes. Here, residents of New Orleans walk through the floodwaters on Canal Street the day after Hurricane Katrina devastated the Louisiana and Mississippi coasts in 2005. The storm and its lingering aftermath led to a significant rise in the rate of acute and post-traumatic stress disorders among residents of these states.*

disorder is given. The symptoms of posttraumatic stress disorder may begin either shortly after the traumatic event or months or years afterward (see Table 6-1 on the next page). Studies indicate that as many as 80 percent of all cases of acute stress disorder develop into posttraumatic stress disorder (Bryant et al., 2005). Aside from the differences in onset and duration, the symptoms of these two disorders are almost identical:

Reexperiencing the traumatic event People may be battered by recurring thoughts, memories, dreams, or nightmares connected to the event (Clark, 2005; Michael et al., 2005). A few relive the event so vividly in their minds (flashbacks) that they think it is actually happening again.

Avoidance People will usually avoid activities that remind them of the traumatic event and will try to avoid related thoughts, feelings, or conversations (Marx & Sloan, 2005; Asmundson et al., 2004).

Reduced responsiveness People feel detached from other people or lose interest in activities that once brought enjoyment. Some experience symptoms of *dissociation*, or psychological separation (Marx & Sloan 2005): they feel dazed, have trouble remembering things, have a sense of derealization (feeling that the environment is unreal or strange), or experience depersonalization (their thoughts or body feel unreal or foreign to them).

Increased arousal, anxiety, and guilt People with these disorders may feel overly alert (hyperalertness), be easily startled, have trouble concentrating, and develop sleep

>>PSYCH•NOTES

Returning Home

One-quarter of the 1.5 million combat soldiers who returned from Vietnam were arrested within two years of their return (Williams, 1983). ‹‹

problems (Breslau et al., 2005; Feuer, Nishith, & Resick, 2005). They may feel extreme guilt because they survived the traumatic event while others did not. Some also feel guilty about what they may have had to do to survive.

We can see these symptoms in the recollections of a Vietnam combat veteran years after he returned home:

> I can't get the memories out of my mind! The images come flooding back in vivid detail, triggered by the most inconsequential things, like a door slamming or the smell of stir-fried pork. Last night I went to bed, was having a good sleep for a change. Then in the early morning a storm-front passed through and there was a bolt of crackling thunder. I awoke instantly, frozen in fear. I am right back in Vietnam, in the middle of the monsoon season at my guard post. I am sure I'll get hit in the next volley and convinced I will die. My hands are freezing, yet sweat pours from my entire body. I feel each hair on the back of my neck standing on end. I can't catch my breath and my heart is pounding. I smell a damp sulfur smell.
>
> *(Davis, 1992)*

What Triggers a Psychological Stress Disorder?

An acute or posttraumatic stress disorder can occur at any age, even in childhood, and can affect one's personal, family, social, or occupational life (Matthews, 2005). People with these stress disorders may also experience depression or substance abuse or become suicidal (Holtzheimer et al., 2005). Surveys indicate that 3.5 percent of people in the United States experience one of the stress disorders in any given year; almost 7 percent suffer from one of them during their lifetimes (Kessler et al., 2005). Around two-thirds of these individuals seek treatment at some point in their lives, but only 7 percent do so when they first develop the disorder (Wang et al., 2005).

Women are at least twice as likely as men to develop stress disorders: around 20 percent of women who are exposed to a serious trauma may develop one, compared to 8 percent of men (Khouzam et al., 2005). Although many clinicians believe that the prevalence and appearance of stress disorders probably differs from race to race and cultural group to cultural group, researchers are just now beginning to shed light on this issue (see Box 6-1 on page 163).

Any traumatic event can trigger a stress disorder; however, some are particularly likely to do so. Among the most common are combat, disasters, and abuse and victimization.

COMBAT AND STRESS DISORDERS For years clinicians have recognized that many soldiers develop symptoms of severe anxiety and depression *during* combat. It was called "shell shock" during World War I and "combat fatigue" during World War II and the Korean War (Figley, 1978). Not until after the Vietnam War, however, did clinicians learn that a great many soldiers also experience serious psychological symptoms *after* combat (Khouzam et al., 2005).

By the late 1970s, it became apparent that many Vietnam combat veterans were still experiencing war-related psychological difficulties (Roy-Byrne et al., 2004). We now know that as many as 29 percent of all Vietnam veterans, male and female, suffered an acute or posttraumatic stress disorder, while another 22 percent suffered from at least some stress symptoms (Weiss et al., 1992). In fact, 10 percent of the veterans of this war still experience posttraumatic stress symptoms, including flashbacks, night terrors, nightmares, and persistent images and thoughts.

Table **6-1 DSM Checklist**

POSTTRAUMATIC STRESS DISORDER

1. A history of having experienced, witnessed, or confronted event(s) involving death, serious injury, or threat to the physical integrity of self or others. Reaction of intense fear, helplessness, or horror produced by event.

2. Event persistently reexperienced in at least one of the following ways:
   (a) Recurrent distressing recollections.
   (b) Recurrent distressing dreams, illusions, flashbacks, or a sense of reliving the experience.
   (c) Distress caused by reminders of event.
   (d) Physical arousal produced by reminders of event.

3. Persistent avoidance of reminders of the event and a subjective sense of numbing, detachment, or emotional unresponsiveness.

4. At least two marked symptoms of increased arousal:
   (a) Difficulty sleeping.
   (b) Irritability.
   (c) Poor concentration.
   (d) Hypervigilance.
   (e) Exaggerated startle response.

5. Significant distress or impairment, with symptoms lasting at least one month.

Based on APA, 2000.

DISASTERS AND STRESS DISORDERS Acute and post-traumatic stress disorders may also follow natural and accidental disasters such as earthquakes, floods, tornadoes, fires, airplane crashes, and serious car accidents (see Table 6-2). In fact, because they occur more often, civilian traumas have been implicated in stress disorders at least 10 times as often as combat traumas (Bremner, 2002). Studies have found, for example, that as many as one-third of victims—adult or child—of serious traffic accidents may develop posttraumatic stress disorder within a year of the accident (Wiederhold & Wiederhold, 2005; Ursano et al., 1999).

Similarly, several studies found stress reactions among the survivors of Hurricane Andrew, the storm that ravaged Florida and other parts of the southeastern United States and Mexico in 1992 (Ibanez et al., 2004; Vernberg et al., 1996). By a month after the storm the number of calls received by the domestic violence hot line in Miami and the number of women applying for police protection had doubled (Treaster, 1992). By six months after the storm it was apparent that many elementary-school-age children were also victims of posttraumatic stress disorder; their symptoms ranged from misbehavior in school to failing grades and problems with sleep (Vernberg et al., 1996).

VICTIMIZATION AND STRESS DISORDERS People who have been abused, victimized, or terrorized often experience lingering stress symptoms (Logan et al., 2006). Research suggests that more than one-third of all victims of physical or sexual assault develop posttraumatic stress disorder (Jaycox & Foa, 2001). Similarly, as many as half of all civilians who are directly exposed to terrorism or torture may develop this disorder.

SEXUAL ASSAULT A common form of victimization in our society today is sexual assault. **Rape** is forced sexual intercourse or another sexual act committed against a nonconsenting person or intercourse with an underage person. Surveys suggest that in the United States more than 400,000 persons are victims of rape or attempted rape each year (Rennison, 2002). Most rapists are men and most victims are women. Around one

Table 6-2

Worst Natural Disasters of the Past 100 Years

Disaster	Year	Location	Number Killed
Flood	1931	Huang He River, China	3,700,000
Tsunami	2004	South Asia	280,000
Earthquake	1976	Tangshan, China	242,419
Heat wave	2003	Europe	35,000
Volcano	1985	Nevado del Ruiz, Colombia	23,000
Hurricane	1998	(Mitch) Central America	18,277
Landslide	1970	Yungay, Peru	17,500
Avalanche	1916	Italian Alps	10,000
Blizzard	1972	Iran	4,000
Tornado	1989	Shaturia, Bangladesh	1,300

Adapted from CNN, 2005; Gorman, 2005; Wikipedia, 2005; Ash, 2001, 1999, 1998.

Preventing the trauma *One way to reduce the rate of posttraumatic stress disorders is to prevent the occurrence of traumatic events. In 2001, a Tokyo railway designated a "Women Only" rail car for female commuters who needed to travel late at night. Designation of special cars of this kind was spurred by a sharp increase in late-night sexual assaults in Japan's commuter trains.*

•**RAPE**•Forced sexual intercourse or another sexual act committed against a nonconsenting person or intercourse with an underage person.

>>LOOKING AROUND
Reporting Rape

Since 1975, sweeping changes have been made in rape laws, including the legal definition of rape and the kind of evidence required to establish that it occurred. «

- -

Rapes are more likely to be reported to police today than they were before 1975. «

- -

Only one-third of rapes and attempted rapes are currently reported to police. «

- -

Rapes are more likely to be reported if they are "aggravated rapes"— unknown assailant, multiple assailants, use of a weapon, or severe injury to the victim. «

- -

Rapes are more likely to be reported if additional degrading acts were inflicted during the sexual assault. «

- -

Married and highly educated rape victims are more likely to report the sexual assault. «

- -

(Clay-Warner & Burt, 2005; Rennison, 2002)

>>LOOKING AROUND
Rape: Country by Country

The United States has the highest rate of rape of any industrialized nation—4 times higher than Germany's, 12 times higher than England's, and 20 times higher than Japan's. «

(Rozee, 2005)

in seven women is raped at some time during her life (Rozee, 2005). Surveys also suggest that most rape victims are young: 29 percent are under 11 years old, 32 percent are between the ages of 11 and 17, and 29 percent are between 18 and 29. Approximately 70 percent of the victims are raped by acquaintances or relatives (Rennison, 2002).

The psychological impact of rape on a victim is immediate and may last a long time (Koss, 2005, 1993; Koss & Kilpatrick, 2001). Rape victims typically experience enormous distress during the week after the assault. Stress continues to rise for the next 3 weeks, maintains a peak level for another month or so, and then starts to improve. In one study, 94 percent of rape victims fully qualified for a clinical diagnosis of acute stress disorder when they were observed around 12 days after the assault (Rothbaum et al., 1992). Although most rape victims improve psychologically within 3 or 4 months, the effects may persist for up to 18 months or longer. Victims typically continue to have higher than average levels of anxiety, suspiciousness, depression, self-esteem problems, self-blame, flashbacks, sleep problems, and sexual dysfunction (Logan et al., 2006; Cling, 2004). The lingering psychological impact of rape is apparent in the following case description:

Mary Billings is a 33-year-old divorced nurse, referred to the Victim Clinic at Bedford Psychiatric Hospital for counseling by her supervisory head nurse. Mary had been raped two months ago. The assailant gained entry to her apartment while she was sleeping, and she awoke to find him on top of her. He was armed with a knife and threatened to kill her and her child (who was asleep in the next room) if she did not submit to his demands. He forced her to undress and repeatedly raped her vaginally over a period of 1 hour. He then admonished her that if she told anyone or reported the incident to the police he would return and assault her child.

After he left, she called her boyfriend, who came to her apartment right away. He helped her contact the Sex Crimes Unit of the Police Department, which is currently investigating the case. He then took her to a local hospital for a physical examination and collection of evidence for the police (traces of sperm, pubic hair samples, fingernail scrapings). She was given antibiotics as prophylaxis against venereal disease. Mary then returned home with a girlfriend who spent the remainder of the night with her.

Over the next few weeks Mary continued to be afraid of being alone and had her girlfriend move in with her. She became preoccupied with thoughts of what had happened to her and the possibility that it could happen again. Mary was frightened that the rapist might return to her apartment and therefore had additional locks installed on both the door and the windows. She was so upset and had such difficulty concentrating that she decided she could not yet return to work. When she did return to work several weeks later, she was still clearly upset, and her supervisor suggested that she might be helped by counseling.

During the clinic interview, Mary was coherent and spoke quite rationally in a hushed voice. She reported recurrent and intrusive thoughts about the sexual assault, to the extent that her concentration was impaired and she had difficulty doing chores such as making meals for herself and her daughter. She felt she was not able to be effective at work, still felt afraid to leave her home, to answer her phone, and had little interest in contacting friends or relatives.

. . . [Mary] talked in the same tone of voice whether discussing the assault or less emotionally charged topics, such as her work history. She was easily startled by an unexpected noise. She also was unable to fall asleep because she kept thinking about the assault. She had no desire to eat, and when she did attempt it, she felt nauseated. Mary was repelled by the thought of sex and stated that she did not want to have sex for a long time, although she was willing to be held and comforted by her boyfriend.

(Spitzer et al., 1983, pp. 20–21)

Although many rape victims are severely injured by their attacker or experience other physical problems as a result of their assault, only half receive the kind of formal

[BOX 6-1]

Sociocultural Landscape: Are Hispanic Americans Prone to Stress Disorders?

For years many clinical theorists have expected the rates of posttraumatic stress disorder (PTSD) to differ from ethnic group to ethnic group in the United States. After all, vulnerability to this disorder is related to factors such as a person's coping style, general attitudes, sense of control, economic status, childhood experiences, and social support system, and these factors frequently vary from culture to culture.

However, the overall rate of PTSD has been surprisingly stable from group to group. Granted, twice as many women as men in the United States experience this disorder. However, time and again, white Americans, African Americans, Hispanic Americans, and Asian Americans have seemed to display the same rate for PTSD—3.5 percent in any given year.

But now the wind is shifting. It appears that there may indeed be important cultural differences in the occurrence of posttraumatic stress disorder—differences that clinicians previously missed. In particular, *Hispanic Americans* may have a greater vulnerability to the disorder than other cultural groups (Pole et al., 2005).

Some cases in point: (1) A study of Vietnam combat veterans has revealed that the current rate of posttraumatic stress disorder among Hispanic American veterans is higher than that among white American and African American veterans (Kulka et al., 1990). (2) Research suggests that Hispanic American combat veterans

with PTSD have, on average, more severe symptoms than veterans of other ethnic or racial groups (Rosenheck & Fontana, 1996). (3) In surveys of police officers, Hispanic officers typically report more severe duty-related stress symptoms than their non-Hispanic counterparts (Pole et al., 2001). (4) A careful look at past data on Hurricane Andrew victims reveals that Hispanic victims had a significantly higher rate of PTSD than victims of all other ethnic groups (Perilla et al., 2002). (5) Surveys of New York City residents, conducted in the months following the terrorist attacks of September 11, 2001, reveal that 14 percent of Hispanic American residents developed posttraumatic stress disorder, compared to 9 percent of African American residents and 7 percent of white American residents (Galea et al., 2002).

Why might Hispanic Americans be more vulnerable to posttraumatic stress disorder than other racial or ethnic groups? Several explanations have been suggested. One centers on the initial reactions of Hispanic Americans to traumatic events. Recent research has indicated that an early dissociative reaction (altered state of consciousness) is one of the stongest predictors that an individual will go on to develop posttraumatic stress disorder (Ozer et al., 2003). Moreover, it is known from research in Latin America that dissociative symptoms are very common in a number of culture-bound Latin psychological disorders (Escobar, 1995). If

Hispanic Americans are more likely than other individuals to react to traumatic events with dissociative symptoms, they may be particularly prone to develop PTSD (Pole et al., 2005).

Another explanation holds that as part of their cultural belief system, many Hispanic Americans tend to view traumatic events as inevitable and unalterable, a coping response that may heighten their risk for posttraumatic stress disorder (Perilla et al., 2002).

And still another explanation suggests that their culture's emphasis on social relationships and social support may place Hispanic victims at special risk when traumatic events deprive them—temporarily or permanently—of important relationships and support systems. Indeed, a study conducted more than two decades ago found that among Hispanic Vietnam combat veterans with stress disorders, those with poor family and social relationships suffered the most severe symptoms (Escobar et al., 1983).

Whether these or other explanations have much merit remains to be seen. Now that this cultural difference has been uncovered, clinical researchers are faced with the important task of clarifying its nature and causes and turning their insights into effective prevention and treatment programs for those Hispanic Americans who come face to face with extraordinary stressors.

medical care afforded Mary (Logan et al., 2006; Rennison, 2002). Between 4 and 30 percent of victims develop a sexually transmitted disease (Koss, 1993; Murphy, 1990) and 5 percent become pregnant (Beebe, 1991; Koss et al., 1991), yet surveys reveal that 60 percent of rape victims fail to receive pregnancy testing, preventive measures, or testing for exposure to HIV (National Victims Center, 1992).

Female victims of rape and other crimes are also much more likely than other women to suffer serious long-term health problems (Leserman et al., 1996; Koss & Heslet, 1992). Interviews with 390 women revealed that such victims had poorer physical well-being for at least five years after the crime and made twice as many visits to physicians.

As we shall see in Chapter 17, ongoing victimization and abuse in the family—specifically child and spouse abuse—may also lead to psychological stress disorders. Because these forms of abuse may occur over the long term and violate family trust, many victims develop other symptoms and disorders as well (Borger, Cox, & Asmundson, 2005; Woods, 2005).

[BOX 6-2]

September 11, 2001: The Psychological Aftermath

Spencer Platt/Getty Images

On September 11, 2001, the United States experienced the most catastrophic act of terrorism in history when four commercial airplanes were hijacked and three of them were crashed into the twin towers of the World Trade Center in New York City and the Pentagon in Washington, D.C. The attacks resulted in mass casualties and injuries, affecting not only the immediate victims and survivors but the entire nation, as millions witnessed the resulting death and destruction on television. Studies conducted since that fateful day have confirmed what psychologists knew all too well would happen—that in the aftermath of September 11, many individuals experienced immediate and long-term psychological and physical effects, ranging from brief stress reactions, such as shock, fear, and anger, to enduring psychological disorders, such as posttraumatic stress disorder (Blanchard et al., 2005; Callahan et al., 2005; Hoven et al., 2005; Lengua et al., 2005).

In a survey conducted the week after the terrorist attacks, 560 randomly selected adults across the United States were interviewed. Forty-four percent of them reported substantial stress symptoms; 90 percent reported at least some increase in stress (Schuster et al., 2001). Moreover, individuals closest to the disaster site experienced the greatest stress reactions: 61 percent of adults living within 100 miles of the World Trade Center had substantial stress symptoms, compared to 36 percent of those living over 1,000 miles from the site.

A later survey of close to 2,000 individuals revealed that many Americans were still feeling the psychological effects of September 11 five months after the terrorist attacks (Bossolo & Lichtenstein, 2002). Nearly 25 percent of Americans reported that they continued to feel more depressed or anxious since the time of the attacks, and 77 percent said that they were still trying to gain perspective on their lives and to reprioritize their goals. A related study indicated that people who had experienced a greater number of traumas in the past were more likely than others to develop stress symptoms and disorders in the aftermath of September 11 (Pugh, 2003).

Research focusing specifically on New Yorkers indicated that they were almost twice as likely as those living elsewhere to develop depressive, anxiety, or posttraumatic stress disorders (Galea & Resnick, 2005; Bossolo & Lichtenstein, 2002). In addition, 40 percent of New York residents (twice the national average) reported extreme nervousness and anxiety at the sound of sirens or the sight of airplanes flying above.

Still other studies have been conducted in recent years, each looking at a particu-

AP Photo/Suzanne Plunkett

TERRORISM People who are victims of terrorism or who live under the threat of terrorism often experience posttraumatic stress symptoms (Galea & Resnick, 2005; Hoven et al., 2005). Unfortunately, this source of traumatic stress is on the rise in our society. Few will ever forget the events of September 11, 2001, when hijacked airplanes crashed into and brought down the World Trade Center in New York City and partially destroyed the Pentagon in Washington, D.C., killing thousands of victims and rescue workers and forcing thousands more to desperately run, crawl, and even dig their way to lar aspect of the September 11 attack and its enormous psychological impact. Presented here are some notable findings from these studies, each serving in its own way to build a more complete understanding of this trauma and its lingering effects, and each helping clinicians to better serve the victims of both this disaster and other kinds of disasters.

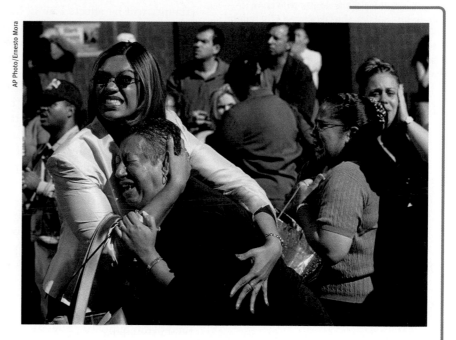

AP Photo/Ernesto Mora

During the First Week

What percentage of the population had substantial stress reactions?

Adults	44%
Children	35
Women	50
Men	37
Nonwhite Americans	62
White Americans	41
Residents within 100 miles of attack	61
Residents beyond 100 miles of attack	36

(Schuster et al., 2001)

Two Months Later

What percentage of the population developed posttraumatic stress disorder?

Adults who live in New York City	11%
Adults who live in Washington, D.C.	3
Adults who live in the United States	4
Children who live in the United States	8
College students in the United States	7
College students in New York State	11

(Lengua et al., 2005; Blanchard et al., 2004; Schlenger et al., 2002)

Six Months Later and Beyond

What percentage of the population continue to have terrorism-related concerns and problems?

Adults who report high terrorism fear	42%
New Yorkers who report high terrorism fear	70
Adults who report drinking more alcohol	15
Adults who feel less safe in homes	23
U.S. adults with PTSD	4
New York adults with PTSD	9
Pentagon staff members with PTSD	23
U.S. college students with PTSD	7
New York college students with PTSD	8
U.S. children with PTSD	4
New York children with PTSD	11

(Adams & Boscarino, 2005; Blanchard et al., 2005; Hoven et al., 2005; Connelly & Dutton, 2002; Boscarino et al., 2004; Fetto, 2002; Gardyn, 2002; Lord, 2002; Time Poll, 2002).

safety. One of the many legacies of this infamous event is the lingering psychological effect that it has had on those people who were immediately affected and their family members, and on tens of millions of others who were traumatized simply by watching images of the disaster on their television sets as the day unfolded. A number of studies clarify that stress reactions were common among victims and observers in the days following the terrorist attacks, and that these posttraumatic symptoms will, in many cases, linger for years (Simeon et al., 2005) (see Box 6-2).

Why Do People Develop a Psychological Stress Disorder?

Clearly, extraordinary trauma can cause a stress disorder. The stressful event alone, however, may not be the entire explanation. Certainly, anyone who experiences an unusual trauma will be affected by it, but only some people develop a disorder (Engelhard & Arntz, 2005). To understand the development of stress disorders more fully, researchers have looked to the survivors' biological processes, personalities, childhood experiences, and social support systems and to the severity of the traumas.

BIOLOGICAL AND GENETIC FACTORS Investigators have learned that traumatic events trigger physical changes in the brain and body that may lead to severe stress reactions and, in some cases, to stress disorders. They have, for example, found abnormal activity of the hormone *cortisol* and the neurotransmitter/hormone *norepinephrine* in the urine, blood, and saliva of combat soldiers, rape victims, concentration camp survivors, and survivors of other severe stresses (Delahanty et al., 2005; Neylan et al., 2005; Duval et al., 2004).

There is also evidence that once a stress disorder sets in, individuals experience further biochemical arousal and this continuing arousal may eventually damage key brain areas (Mirzaei et al., 2005). Two areas in particular seem to be affected—the *hippocampus* and the *amygdala*. Normally, the hippocampus plays a major role both in memory and in the regulation of the body's stress hormones. Clearly, a dysfunctional hippocampus may help produce the intrusive memories and ongoing arousal that characterize posttraumatic stress disorder (Bremner et al., 2005; Shin et al., 2005). Similarly, as we observed in Chapter 5, the amygdala helps control emotional responses, including anxiety and panic responses. The amygdala also works with the hipppocampus to produce the emotional components of memory. A dysfunctional amygdala may help produce the repeated emotional symptoms and intense emotional memories experienced by persons with posttraumatic stress disorder (Protopopescu et al., 2005; Shin et al., 2005). In short, the excessive arousal generated by extraordinary traumatic events may lead to stress disorders in some people, and the stress disorders may produce yet further brain abnormalities, locking in the disorders all the more firmly.

It may be that people whose biochemical reactions to stress are particularly strong are more likely than others to develop acute and posttraumatic stress disorders. But why would certain people be prone to such strong biological reactions? One possibility is that the propensity is inherited. A study of approximately 4,000 pairs of twins who had served in the Vietnam War found that if one twin developed stress symptoms after combat, an identical twin was more likely than a fraternal twin to develop the same problems (True & Lyons, 1999; True et al., 1993). We must remember, however, that the similarities seen in identical twins do not always reflect genetic influences: childhood experiences, personalities, and support systems may also be more similar in identical twins than in fraternal twins and explain the greater similarity in their reactions to stress. Thus, more direct genetic studies are currently under way to determine whether a particular gene or combination of genes predisposes individuals to posttraumatic stress disorder (Bachmann et al., 2005).

PERSONALITY Some studies suggest that people with certain personality profiles, attitudes, and coping styles are particularly likely to develop stress disorders (Chung et al., 2005; Knezevic et al., 2005). In the aftermath of Hurricane Hugo in 1989, for example, children who had been highly anxious before the storm were more likely than other children to develop severe stress reactions (Hardin et al., 2002; Lonigan et al., 1994). Similarly, the victims who are most likely to develop stress disorders after being raped are the ones who had psychological problems before they were raped or who were struggling with stressful life situations (Darvres-Bornoz et al., 1995). The same is true of war veterans who had psychological problems before they went into combat (Dikel et al., 2005; Orsillo et al., 1996).

Research has also found that people who generally view life's negative events as beyond their control tend to develop more severe stress symptoms after sexual or other kinds of criminal assaults than people who feel greater control over their lives (Bremner, 2002; Regehr et al., 1999). Similarly, individuals who generally find it difficult to derive

Protection by personality *Millions react to hurricanes and other disasters with dread and panic, but some laid-back individuals seem to thrive on all the excitement. For example, this 38-year-old man awaited the imminent arrival of Hurricane Isabel in 2003 by swinging on a pier in Atlantic Beach, North Carolina. Researchers believe that the "hardy" (although occasionally foolish) personality styles of such people may help protect them from the development of stress disorders.*

AP Photo

anything positive from unpleasant situations adjust more poorly after traumatic events than people who find a way to greet aversive situations with positive emotions of one kind or another (gratitude, interest, love) (Bonanno, 2004; Fredrickson et al., 2003). These findings coincide with another discovery: that many people respond to stress with a set of positive attitudes, collectively called *resiliency* or *hardiness,* that enables them to carry on their lives with a sense of fortitude, control, and commitment (Bonanno, 2004; Oulette, 1993).

CHILDHOOD EXPERIENCES A recent wave of studies have found that certain childhood experiences seem to leave some people at risk for later acute and posttraumatic stress disorders. People whose childhoods have been marked by poverty appear more likely to develop these disorders in the face of later trauma. So do people whose family members suffered from psychological disorders; who experienced assault, abuse, or catastrophe at an early age; or who were younger than 10 when their parents separated or divorced (Koopman et al., 2004; Shephard, 2004; Ozer et al., 2003).

Such childhood experiences may help produce the personality styles or attitudes that have been linked to stress disorders. Perhaps their early situations teach children that the world is an unpredictable and dangerous place. In Chapter 5 we observed that such a worldview may help set the stage for generalized anxiety disorder. Similarly, it may lead people to react more hopelessly and fearfully to extraordinary trauma, and so increase their risk of developing a stress disorder.

SOCIAL SUPPORT It has been found that people whose social and family support systems are weak are also more likely to develop a stress disorder after a traumatic event (Ozer, 2005; Simeon et al., 2005; Ozer et al., 2003). Rape victims who feel loved, cared for, valued, and accepted by their friends and relatives recover more successfully. So do those treated with dignity and respect by the criminal justice system (Murphy, 2001; Davis et al., 1991; Sales et al., 1984). In contrast, clinical reports have suggested that poor social support has contributed to the development of posttraumatic stress disorder in some combat veterans (Dirkzwager, Bramsen, & van der Ploeg, 2005; Figley & Leventman, 1990).

SEVERITY OF TRAUMA As one might expect, the severity and nature of traumatic events help determine whether one will develop a stress disorder. Some events can override even a nurturing childhood, positive attitudes, and social support (Dikel, Engdahl, & Eberly, 2005) (see Table 6-3). One study examined 253 Vietnam War prisoners five years after their release. Some 23 percent qualified for a clinical diagnosis, though all had been evaluated as well adjusted before their imprisonment (Ursano et al., 1981).

Generally, the more severe the trauma and the more direct one's exposure to it, the greater the likelihood of developing a stress disorder (Chung et al., 2005). Among the Vietnam prisoners of war, for example, the men who had been imprisoned longest and treated most harshly had the highest percentage of disorders. Mutilation and severe physical injury in particular seem to increase the risk of stress reactions, as does witnessing the injury or death of other people (Koren et al., 2005; Ursano et al., 2003). It is, as a survivor of trauma once said, "hard to be a survivor" (Kolff & Doan, 1985, p. 45).

How Do Clinicians Treat the Psychological Stress Disorders?

Treatment can make a major difference to a person who has been overwhelmed by traumatic events (Bradley et al., 2005) (see Box 6-3 on page 169). One survey found that posttraumatic stress symptoms lasted an average of three years with treatment but five and a half years without it (Kessler & Zhao, 1999; Kessler et al.,

Table 6-3

Initial Reactions to 1963 Kennedy Assassination and 2001 Terrorist Attacks (percent)

Symptom	Kennedy Assassination	Terrorist Attacks
Felt anger	44%	65%
Felt very nervous and tense	68	51
Felt sort of dazed and numb	57	46
Cried	53	60
Had trouble getting to sleep	48	50
Didn't feel like eating	43	29
Felt more tired than usual	42	36
Kept forgetting things	34	19
Had rapid heartbeats	26	16
Had headaches	25	20
Had an upset stomach	22	35
Hands sweat, felt clammy	17	9
Felt dizzy at times	12	8
Felt ashamed that this could happen in the United States	50	22

(Smith & Rasinski, 2002)

Victimization and posttraumatic stress disorder
Many survivors of Nazi concentration camps faced a long road back to psychological health (Joffe et al., 2003). Because knowledge of posttraumatic stress disorder was nonexistent until recent years, most survivors had to find their way back without professional help.

The horror continues *Even with the clinical field's improved understanding and treatment of posttraumatic stress disorder, some individuals fail to overcome the psychological effects of extraordinary traumatic experiences. Fifty years after his release from a concentration camp, this survivor stands in a ray of light at Tirat Hacarmel's Medical Center for Mental Health. One-fifth of Israel's long-term patients at mental hospitals are concentration camp survivors.*

1995). Today's treatment procedures for troubled survivors typically vary from trauma to trauma. Was it combat, sexual molestation, or a major accident? Yet all the programs share basic goals: they try to help survivors put an end to their stress reactions, gain perspective on their painful experiences, and return to constructive living (Bryant et al., 2005; Ehlers et al., 2005). Programs for combat veterans who suffer from posttraumatic stress disorder illustrate how these issues may be addressed.

TREATMENT FOR COMBAT VETERANS Therapists have used a variety of techniques to reduce veterans' posttraumatic symptoms. Among the most common are *drug therapy, exposure techniques, insight therapy, family therapy,* and *group therapy.* Typically the approaches are combined, as no one of them successfully reduces all the symptoms (Lombardo & Gray, 2005; Wiederhold & Wiederhold, 2005).

Antianxiety drugs help control the tension that many veterans experience. In addition, antidepressant medications may reduce the occurrence of nightmares, panic attacks, flashbacks, and feelings of depression (Davidson et al., 2005; Bremner & Vermetten, 2004; McNamara, 2004).

Behavioral exposure techniques, too, have helped reduce specific symptoms, and they have often led to improvements in overall adjustment. In fact, some studies indicate that exposure treatment is the single most helpful intervention for persons with stress disorders, irrespective of the precipitating trauma (Turner et al., 2005; Wiederhold & Wiederhold, 2005). This finding suggests to many clinical theorists that exposure of one kind or another should always be part of the treatment picture. In one case, the exposure technique of *flooding,* along with relaxation training, helped rid a 31-year-old veteran of frightening flashbacks and nightmares (Fairbank & Keane, 1982). The therapist and the veteran first singled out combat scenes that the man had been reexperiencing frequently. The therapist then helped the veteran to imagine one of these scenes in great detail and urged him to hold on to the image until his anxiety stopped. After each of these flooding exercises, the therapist had the veteran switch to a positive image and led him through relaxation exercises.

A relatively new form of exposure therapy is **eye movement desensitization and reprocessing (EMDR),** in which clients move their eyes in a *saccadic,* or rhythmic,

•EYE MOVEMENT DESENSITIZATION AND REPROCESSING (EMDR)•A behavioral exposure treatment in which clients move their eyes in a saccadic (rhythmic) manner from side to side while flooding their minds with images of objects and situations they ordinarily avoid.

[BOX 6-3]

Adjustment Disorders: A Category of Compromise?

Some people react to a major stressor in their lives with extended and excessive feelings of anxiety, depressed mood, or antisocial behaviors. The symptoms do not quite add up to acute stress disorder or posttraumatic stress disorder, nor do they reflect an anxiety or mood disorder, but they do cause considerable distress or interfere with the person's job, schoolwork, or social life. Should we consider such reactions normal? No, says DSM-IV-TR. Somewhere between effective coping strategies and stress disorders lie the *adjustment disorders* (APA, 2000).

DSM-IV-TR lists several types of adjustment disorders, including *adjustment disorder with anxiety* and *adjustment disorder with depressed mood*. People receive such diagnoses if they develop their symptoms within three months of the onset of a stressor. If the stressor is long-term, such as a medical condition, the adjustment disorder may last indefinitely.

Almost any kind of stressor may trigger an adjustment disorder. Common ones are the breakup of a relationship, marital problems, business difficulties, and living in a crime-ridden neighborhood. The disorder may also be triggered by developmental events such as going away to school, getting married, or retiring from a job.

Up to 30 percent of all people in outpatient therapy receive this diagnosis; it accounts for far more treatment claims submitted to insurance companies than any other (APA, 2000). However, some experts doubt that adjustment disorders are as common as this figure suggests. Rather, the diagnosis seems to be a favorite among clinicians—it can easily be applied to a range of problems yet is less stigmatizing than many other categories.

The Museum of Modern Art Film Stills Archive

manner from side to side while flooding their minds with images of the objects and situations they ordinarily try to avoid. Case studies and controlled studies suggest that this treatment can often be helpful to persons with posttraumatic stress disorder (Gonzalez-Brigmardello & Vasquez, 2004; Jaycox & Foa, 2001). Many theorists argue that it is the exposure feature of EMDR, rather than the eye movement, that accounts for its success with the disorder (Foa et al., 2003).

Although drug therapy and exposure techniques bring some relief, most clinicians believe that veterans with posttraumatic stress disorder cannot fully recover with these approaches alone: they must also come to grips in some way with their combat experiences and the impact those experiences continue to have. Thus clinicians often try to help veterans bring out deep-seated feelings, accept what they have done and experienced, become less judgmental of themselves, and learn to trust and relate effectively with other people once again (Turner et al., 2005; Resick & Calhoun, 2001).

Similarly, cognitive therapists help individuals with posttraumatic stress disorder to systematically examine and change the dysfunctional attitudes and styles of interpretation that have emerged as a result of the traumatic event (Ehlers et al., 2005; Taylor et al., 2005). In research along these lines, the psychologist James Pennebaker has found that talking (or even writing) about traumatic experiences can reduce lingering anxiety and tension, particularly if individuals try to develop perspective and growth in their discussions or writings (Cohen et al., 2004; Smyth & Pennebaker, 2001).

People who have a psychological stress disorder may be further helped in a couple or family therapy format (Johnson, 2005; Monson et al., 2005; Rodgers et al., 2005).

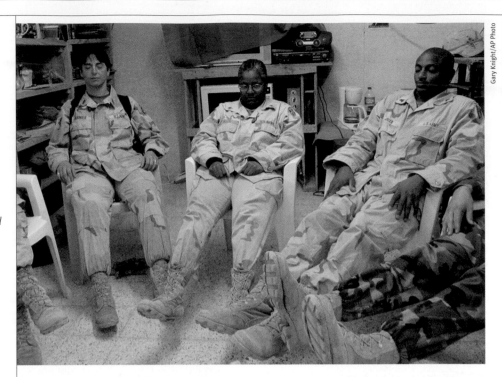

Gary Knight/AP Photo

Combat stress relief *According to research, 13 percent of U.S. troops experience significant psychological problems while fighting in combat zones in the Iraq war, and a total of 30 percent of combat veterans develop stress symptoms and disorders within four months after returning home from Iraq. To reduce stress reactions, the U.S. military has set up combat stress control teams that meet with soldiers throughout Iraq, talk with them soon after battles, and try to diagnose troops who have special mental health needs. Here, members of one combat stress control team give a class in stress relief to soldiers in Iraq in 2003.*

The symptoms of posttraumatic stress disorder tend to be particularly apparent to family members, who may be directly affected by the client's anxieties, depressive mood, or angry outbursts (Dekel et al., 2005; Beckerman, 2004). With the help and support of their family members, individuals may come to recognize their feelings, examine their impact on others, learn to communicate better, and improve their problem-solving skills.

Veterans may also benefit from **rap groups,** where they meet with others like themselves to share experiences and feelings, develop insights, and give mutual support (Lifton, 2005; Ford & Stewart, 1999). One of the major issues rap groups deal with is *guilt*—guilt about things the members may have done to survive or about the very fact that they did survive while close friends died. These groups may also focus on the rage many combat veterans feel.

Today hundreds of small *Veteran Outreach Centers* across the country, as well as treatment programs in Veterans Administration hospitals and mental health clinics, specialize in rap groups (Batres, 2003; Ford & Stewart, 1999). These agencies also offer individual

Cris Bouroncle/AFP/Getty Images

Combat stress relief: The informal version *One way of trying to reduce stress is to take breaks and engage in pleasant and uplifting activities. Here, for example, a U.S. army soldier joins Iraqi children in a foosball game. The respite from danger is brief—for both the soldier and his young co-players—and the broader situation remains frightening, but spontaneous breaks of this kind help protect the psychological and physical health of many individuals who face ongoing and severe danger.*

therapy, counseling for the spouses and children, family therapy, and aid in seeking jobs, education, and benefits. Clinical reports suggest that these programs offer a necessary, sometimes life-saving treatment opportunity. Julius's search for help upon his return from Vietnam was, unfortunately, an ordeal that many veterans of that war shared:

> When I got back from the 'Nam, I knew I needed psychotherapy or something like that. I just knew that if I didn't get help I was going to kill myself or somebody else. . . . I went to see this doctor; he barely looked at me. I felt he "saw me coming" and knew all about my sickness. I was the "sicky" to him. He just kept on asking me all that bullshit about how many children I had killed and was I guilty and depressed about it. He asked how it felt to kill people. He also kept on asking me about my brothers and sisters. But he never asked me about what my experiences were like in Vietnam. He never did. I saw him for treatment for about a month—about three visits, but I quit because we weren't getting anywhere. . . . He just kept on giving me more and more medications. I could've set up my own pharmacy. I needed someone to talk to about my problems, my real problems, not some bullshit about my childhood. I needed someone who wanted to help. The clinic later referred me to another shrink. . . . I guess she thought she was being honest with me, by telling me that she was not a veteran, was not in Vietnam, and did not know what was wrong with me. She also told me that she had no experience working with Vietnam veterans, and that I should go to the Veterans Administration for help. . . .
>
> It was only in the last 3 years when my wife made an important phone call to a local Veterans Outreach Center that I started feeling I had hope, that something could be done for me. I received the help that I have always needed. Finally, I found it easier to hold a job and take care of my family. My nightmares are not as frightening or as frequent as they used to be. Things are better now; I am learning to trust people and give more to my wife and children.
>
> *(Brende & Parson, 1985, pp. 206–208)*

PSYCHOLOGICAL DEBRIEFING: THE SOCIOCULTURAL MODEL IN ACTION People who are traumatized by disasters, victimization, or accidents profit from many of the same treatments that are used to help survivors of combat. In addition, because their traumas occur in their own community, where mental health resources are close at hand, these individuals may, according to many clinicians, further benefit from immediate community interventions. The leading such approach is called **psychological debriefing,** or **critical incident stress debriefing.**

Psychological debriefing is actually a form of crisis intervention that has victims of trauma talk extensively—a session typically lasts 3 to 4 hours—about their feelings and reactions within days of the critical incident (Mitchell, 2003, 1983; Mitchell & Everly, 2000). Because such sessions are expected to prevent or reduce stress reactions, they are commonly applied to victims who have not yet manifested any symptoms at all, as well as those who have. During the sessions, often conducted in a group format, counselors guide the individuals to vividly describe the details of the recent trauma and the thoughts that had accompanied the unfolding event, to vent and relive the emotions provoked at the time of the event, and to express their lingering reactions. The clinicians then clarify to the victims that their reactions are perfectly normal responses to a terrible event, offer stress management tips, and, when necessary, refer the victims to professionals who can provide long-term counseling.

Thousands of counselors, both professionals and nonprofessionals, are now trained in psychological debriefing each year and the intense approach has been applied in the aftermath of countless traumatic events (McNally, 2004). When the traumatic incident affects numerous individuals, debriefing-trained counselors may come from far and wide to gather at the scene of the incident and conduct debriefing sessions with the victims. For example, 1,600 counselors were mobilized to counsel people during the days and weeks following the World Trade Center attack in 2001 (Pepe, 2002).

•**RAP GROUP**•A group that meets to talk about and explore members' problems in an atmosphere of mutual support.

•**PSYCHOLOGICAL DEBRIEFING** •A form of crisis intervention in which victims are helped to talk about their feelings and reactions to traumatic incidents. Also called *critical incident stress debriefing.*

>>LOOKING AROUND

The Tsunami: Sociocultural Fallout

Since late 2004, tourism in South Asia has been way down, due largely to fears about the occurrence of another tsunami. However, hordes of Asian vacationers are also staying away from Asian beaches for another reason: they believe the Chinese superstition that if bodies are not recovered and buried properly, the spirits may wander the world restlessly and perhaps even drag living beings into their land of spiritual limbo (Foreman, 2005). **<<**

Everyone is affected *A fire captain cradles 1-year-old Baylee Almon, a child killed in the bombing of the Oklahoma City federal building. This famous photograph reminds us that rescue workers are themselves subjected to enormous stress and trauma during disasters (Bryant & Harvey, 1995).*

>>PSYCH•NOTES

"It Could Have Been Sammy"

Disaster workers who deal with the remains of deceased victims are more likely to develop a stress disorder if they identify with the victims—"It could have been my family" (Ursano et al., 1999). ‹‹

One of the largest mobilization programs of this kind is the *Disaster Response Network (DRN)*, developed in 1991 by the American Psychological Association and the American Red Cross. The network is made up of more than 2,000 volunteer psychologists who offer free emergency mental health services at disaster sites throughout North America (Daw, 2002, 2001). They have been mobilized for such disasters as earthquakes in California, the 1995 Oklahoma City bombing, the 1999 shooting of 23 persons at Columbine High School in Colorado, the 2001 World Trade Center attack, and the floods caused by Hurricane Katrina in 2005. In addition, some members of the Disaster Response Network traveled to South Asia to work with victims of the devastating tsunami that occurred in late 2004 and to aid in the worldwide mobilization of counseling services for people in that area (APA, 2005).

In such community-wide mobilizations, the counselors may knock on doors or approach victims at shelters and service centers. Although victims from all socioeconomic groups may be engaged, some theorists argue that those who live in poverty are in particular need of such community-level interventions. These victims may experience more psychological distress after community traumas than survivors with higher incomes (Gibbs, 1989), partly because they cannot afford private counseling and are less likely to know where to seek counseling.

Relief workers, too, can become overwhelmed by the traumas they witness (Creamer & Liddle, 2005; Simons et al., 2005). During the 1992 Los Angeles riots, for example, a key responsibility of many community counselors was to help Red Cross workers vent and accept their own feelings as well as teach them about stress disorders and how to identify victims who needed further treatment. Many counselors who live in a disaster area may need counseling themselves, since they, too, are survivors.

DOES PSYCHOLOGICAL DEBRIEFING WORK? Obviously, rapid mobilization programs for disaster victims personify the sociocultural model in action. Moreover, research and personal testimonials for these programs have often been favorable (Watson & Shalev, 2005; Mitchell, 2003; Raphael & Wilson, 2000). Nevertheless, a number of studies have called into question the effectiveness of these kinds of interventions (McNally, 2004; McNally et al., 2003).

An investigation conducted over a decade ago was among the first to raise concerns about the disaster mental health programs (Bisson & Deahl, 1994). Crisis counselors offered debriefing sessions to 62 British soldiers whose job during the Gulf War was to handle and identify the bodies of individuals who had been killed. Despite such sessions, half of the soldiers displayed posttraumatic stress symptoms when interviewed nine months later, a finding that led some theorists to conclude that disaster intervention programs may not really make much difference.

In a properly controlled study conducted a few years later on hospitalized burn victims, researchers separated the victims into two groups (Bisson et al., 1997). One group received a single one-on-one debriefing session within 2 to 19 days of their burn accidents, while the other (control) group of burn victims received no such intervention. Three months later, it was found that the debriefed and the control patients had similar rates of posttraumatic stress disorder, suggesting once again that psychological debriefing may not prevent or reduce stress reactions.

A follow-up to this particular study was even more disturbing. Thirteen months after the debriefing sessions, the rate of posttraumatic stress disorder was, in fact, *higher* among the debriefed burn victims (26 percent) than among the control victims (9 percent). Several other studies, focusing on yet other kinds of disasters, have yielded similar patterns of findings (Van Emmerik et al., 2002; Rose et al., 2001). Obviously, these studies raise serious questions about this widespread and highly regarded approach. Some clinicians believe that the early intervention programs may encourage victims to dwell too long on the traumatic events that they have experienced. And a number worry that early disaster counseling may inadvertently "suggest" problems to victims, thus helping to produce stress disorders in the first place (McNally, 2004; McClelland, 1998).

Finally, questions have been raised about the *cultural competence* of the crisis counselors in these community interventions. When hundreds of clinicians were mobilized in New York City after the attacks of September 11, 2001, for example, many wound up working with residents of the Chinatown neighborhood, located near the World Trade Center. It is not clear that the counseling techniques of these clinicians were fully appropriate for a population that prefers to speak Cantonese and whose culture is often uncomfortable with the kinds of openness that characterize Western therapy (Stoil, 2001).

The current clinical climate continues to favor disaster counseling, and research may indeed eventually clarify that such programs are as helpful as many clinicians believe. However, the concerns that have been raised merit serious consideration. We are reminded here, as elsewhere, of the constant need for careful research in the field of abnormal psychology.

Essential or excessive? *A relief worker comforts the family member of a victim of Egypt Air Flight 990, the plane that crashed off Nantucket Island in 1999 under mysterious circumstances, killing all 217 aboard.*

The Physical Stress Disorders: Psychophysiological Disorders

As we have seen, stress can greatly affect our psychological functioning (see Figure 6-3). It can also have enormous impact on our physical functioning, contributing in some cases to the development of medical problems (Asmundson & Taylor, 2005). The idea that stress and related psychosocial factors may contribute to somatic illnesses has ancient roots, yet it had few supporters before the twentieth century. The seventeenth-century French philosopher René Descartes went so far as to claim that the mind, or soul, is separate from the body—a position called **mind-body dualism.**

Not until the twentieth century were medical scientists persuaded that stress and related psychosocial factors can sometimes contribute greatly to physical illness. This belief

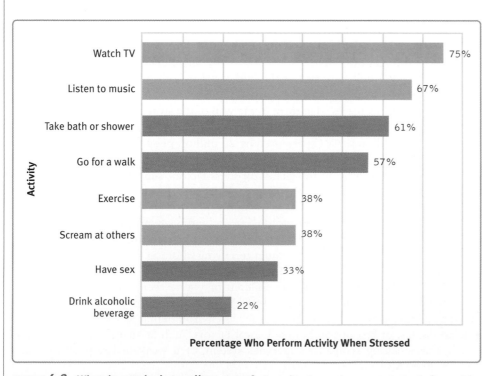

FIGURE **6-3** **What do people do to relieve stress?** *According to one large survey, most of us watch television or listen to music (Kanner, 1995).*

•**MIND-BODY DUALISM**•René Descartes's position that the mind is separate from the body.

Treating asthma *Children who suffer from asthma may use an aerochamber, or inhaler, to help them inhale helpful medications. With the aid of such devices, many asthmatic children are able to lead active and relatively normal lives.*

•**PSYCHOPHYSIOLOGICAL DISORDERS**•
Illnesses that result from an interaction of psychosocial and organic factors. Also known as *psychosomatic disorders.*

•**ULCER**•A lesion that forms in the wall of the stomach or of the duodenum.

•**ASTHMA**•A medical problem marked by narrowing of the trachea and bronchi, which results in shortness of breath, wheezing, coughing, and a choking sensation.

•**INSOMNIA**•Difficulty falling or staying asleep.

•**MUSCLE CONTRACTION HEADACHE**•A headache caused by a narrowing of muscles surrounding the skull. Also known as *tension headache.*

•**MIGRAINE HEADACHE**•A very severe headache that occurs on one side of the head, often preceded by a warning sensation and sometimes accompanied by dizziness, nausea, or vomiting.

•**HYPERTENSION**•Chronic high blood pressure.

•**CORONARY HEART DISEASE**•Illness of the heart caused by blocking of the coronary arteries.

> ### Table 6-4 DSM Checklist
>
> **PSYCHOLOGICAL FACTORS AFFECTING GENERAL MEDICAL CONDITION**
>
> 1. The presence of a general medical condition.
> 2. Psychological factors adversely affecting the general medical condition in one of the following ways:
>   (a) Influencing the course of the general medical condition.
>   (b) Interfering with the treatment of the general medical condition.
>   (c) Posing additional health risks.
>   (d) Stress-related physiological responses precipitating or exacerbating the general medical condition.
>
> Based on APA, 2000.

began to take hold about 80 years ago, when clinicians first identified a group of physical illnesses that seemed to result from an *interaction* of biological, psychological, and sociocultural factors (Dunbar, 1948; Bott, 1928). Early versions of the DSM labeled these illnesses **psychophysiological,** or **psychosomatic, disorders,** but DSM-IV-TR labels them *psychological factors affecting medical condition* (see Table 6-4). We shall use the more familiar term "psychophysiological" in discussing them.

It is important to recognize that psychophysiological disorders bring about *actual* physical damage. They are different from "apparent" physical illnesses—*factitious disorders* or *somatoform disorders*—disorders that are accounted for entirely by factors such as hidden needs, repression, or reinforcement. We shall be examining those kinds of problems in the next chapter. Consistent with our current interest in stress and its direct role in certain psychological and physical disorders, we shall focus here only on psychophysiological disorders.

Traditional Psychophysiological Disorders

Before the 1970s, clinicians believed that only a limited number of illnesses were psychophysiological. The best known and most common of these disorders were ulcers, asthma, insomnia, chronic headaches, high blood pressure, and coronary heart disease. Recent research, however, has shown that many other physical illnesses—including bacterial and viral infections—may also be caused by an interaction of psychosocial and physical factors. We will look first at the traditional psychophysiological disorders and then at the newer illnesses in this category.

Ulcers are lesions (holes) that form in the wall of the stomach or of the duodenum, resulting in burning sensations or pain in the stomach, occasional vomiting, and stomach bleeding. This disorder is experienced by 20 million people in the United States at some point during their lives and is responsible for more than 6,000 deaths each year. Ulcers are often caused by an interaction of stress factors, such as environmental pressure or intense feelings of anger or anxiety, and physiological factors, such as the bacteria *H. pylori* (Carr, 2001).

Asthma causes the body's airways (the trachea and bronchi) to narrow periodically, making it hard for air to pass to and from the lungs. The resulting symptoms are shortness of breath, wheezing, coughing, and a terrifying choking sensation. Some 20 million people in the United States currently suffer from asthma, twice as many as 25 years ago (AAAAI, 2005). Most victims are children or young teenagers at the time of the first attack (Melamed, Roth, & Fogel, 2001). Seventy percent of all cases appear to be caused by an interaction of stress factors, such as environmental pressures, troubled family relationships, or anxiety, and physiological factors, such as allergies to specific substances, a slow-acting sympathetic nervous system, or a weakened respiratory system (NCHS, 2005; Melamed et al., 2001).

Insomnia, difficulty falling asleep or maintaining sleep, plagues 35 percent of the population each year (Taylor, 2006). Although many of us have temporary bouts of insomnia that last a few nights or so, a large number of people experience insomnia that lasts months or years. They feel as though they are almost constantly awake. Chronic insomniacs are often very sleepy during the day and may have difficulty functioning. Their problem may be caused by a combination of psychosocial factors, such as high levels of anxiety or depression, and physiological problems, such as an overactive arousal system or certain medical ailments (Thase, 2005; VandeCreek, 2005).

Chronic headaches are frequent intense aches of the head or neck that are not caused by another physical disorder. There are two major types. **Muscle contraction,** or **tension, headaches** are marked by pain at the back or front of the head or the back of the neck. These occur when the muscles surrounding the skull tighten, narrowing the blood vessels. Approximately 40 million Americans suffer from such headaches. **Migraine headaches** are extremely severe, often near-paralyzing aches located on one side of the head. They are often preceded by a warning sensation called an *aura* and are sometimes accompanied by dizziness, nausea, or vomiting. Migraine headaches are thought by some medical theorists to develop in two phases: (1) blood vessels in the brain narrow, so that the flow of blood to parts of the brain is reduced, and (2) the same blood vessels later expand, so that blood flows through them rapidly, stimulating many neuron endings and causing pain. Migraines are suffered by about 23 million people in the United States.

Research suggests that chronic headaches are caused by an interaction of stress factors, such as environmental pressures or general feelings of helplessness, anger, anxiety, or depression, and physiological factors, such as abnormal activity of the neurotransmitter serotonin, vascular problems, or muscle weakness (Andrasik & Walch, 2003; McGrath & Hillier, 2001).

Hypertension is a state of chronic high blood pressure. That is, the blood pumped through the body's arteries by the heart produces too much pressure against the artery walls. Hypertension has few outward symptoms, but it interferes with the proper functioning of the entire cardiovascular system, greatly increasing the likelihood of stroke, coronary heart disease, and kidney problems. It is estimated that 65 million people in the United States have hypertension, 14,000 die directly from it annually, and millions more perish because of illnesses caused by it (Kalb, 2004; Kluger, 2004; NCHS, 1999). Around 10 percent of all cases are caused by physiological abnormalities alone; the rest result from a combination of psychosocial and physiological factors and are called *essential hypertension* (Taylor, 2006). Some of the leading psychosocial causes of essential hypertension are constant stress, environmental danger, and general feelings of anger or depression. Physiological factors include obesity, smoking, poor kidney regulation of salt and fluid levels, and a high proportion of *collagen* rather than elastic tissue in an individual's blood vessels (Taylor, 2006; Kluger, 2004).

Coronary heart disease is caused by a blocking of the *coronary arteries,* the blood vessels that surround the heart and are responsible for carrying oxygen to the heart muscle. The term actually refers to several problems, including *angina pectoris,* extreme chest pain caused by a partial blockage of the coronary arteries; *coronary occlusion,* a complete blockage of a coronary artery that halts the flow of blood to various parts of the heart muscle; and *myocardial infarction* (a "heart attack"). Nearly 14 million people in the United States suffer from some form of coronary heart disease (AHA, 2005a). It is the leading cause of death in men over the age of 35 and of women over 40 in the United States, accounting for close to 1 million deaths each year, around 40 percent of all deaths in the nation (AHA, 2005a, 2003). The majority of all cases of coronary heart disease are related to an interaction of psychosocial factors, such as job stress or high levels of anger or depression, and physiological factors, such as a high level of cholesterol, obesity, hypertension, smoking, or lack of exercise (AHA, 2005b; Wang et al., 2004).

Over the years, clinicians have identified a number of variables that may generally contribute to the development of psychophysiological disorders (see Figure 6-4). It should not surprise us

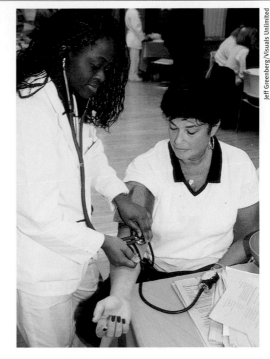

The silent killer *High blood pressure, a psychophysiological disorder with few outward signs, kills tens of thousands of people each year, prompting health professionals to provide free blood pressure checks in the workplace or other community settings.*

FIGURE **6-4** **Stress at home** *In our high-tech world, even the operation of everyday home devices may present problems and produce stress. In a survey of 3,000 American adults, the majority of respondents admitted that they often have difficulty operating their cell phones, home computers, and security systems. (Adapted from NFO World Group, 2002.)*

Home Device

Device	Percentage
Cell phone	56%
Computer	56%
Security system	55%
VCR	40%
Answering machine	27%
Stereo	23%
Microwave	22%
TV	18%

Adults Who Have Problems Operating Device

•**TYPE A PERSONALITY STYLE**•A personality pattern characterized by hostility, cynicism, drivenness, impatience, competitiveness, and ambition.

•**TYPE B PERSONALITY STYLE**•A personality pattern in which persons are more relaxed, less aggressive, and less concerned about time.

Stress-resistant temperament? *Developmental psychologists have learned that even during the earliest stages of life some infants are generally calm while others consistently become physically and psychologically aroused whenever they are stimulated. Many suspect that the easily aroused individuals are more likely candidates for posttraumatic stress disorders and/or psychophysiological disorders throughout their lives.*

that several of these variables are the same as those that contribute to the onset of the psychological stress disorders—acute and posttraumatic stress disorders. The variables may be grouped as sociocultural, psychological, and biological factors.

SOCIOCULTURAL FACTORS The stressful demands placed on people by their culture or social group may set the stage for psychophysiological disorders (see Box 6-4). The stress may be wide-ranging, such as that produced by wars or natural disasters. After a 1979 nuclear accident at Three Mile Island in Pennsylvania, for example, people who lived near the nuclear plant experienced a high number of psychophysiological disorders, and they continued to do so for years (Wroble & Baum, 2002; Baum et al., 1983). Alternatively, local social conditions may produce persistent feelings of tension, such as living in a crime-ridden neighborhood or working in an unsatisfying or stressful job (Landsbergis et al., 2003, 1994). For example, hypertension is 43 percent more common among African Americans than among white Americans (Kluger, 2004). Although physiological factors may largely explain this difference, some theorists believe that it is also linked to the dangerous environments in which so many African Americans live, the unsatisfying jobs at which so many must work, and the racial discrimination most face (Cozier-D'Amico, 2004; Peters, 2004).

PSYCHOLOGICAL FACTORS According to many theorists, certain needs, attitudes, emotions, or coping styles may cause people to overreact repeatedly to stressors, and so increase their chances of developing psychophysiological disorders (Chung et al., 2005). Researchers have found, for example, that men with a *repressive coping style* (a reluctance to express discomfort, anger, or hostility) tend to experience a particularly sharp rise in blood pressure and heart rate when they are stressed (Pauls & Stemmler, 2003; Coy, 1998).

Another personality style that may contribute to psychophysiological disorders is the **Type A personality style,** an idea introduced by two cardiologists, Meyer Friedman and Raymond Rosenman (1959). People with this style are said to be consistently angry, cynical, driven, impatient, competitive, and ambitious. They interact with the world in a way that, according to Friedman and Rosenman, produces continual stress and often leads to coronary heart disease. People with a **Type B personality style,** by contrast, are thought to be more relaxed, less aggressive, and less concerned about time. They are less likely to experience cardiovascular deterioration. In reality, of course, most people fall between these two extremes, tending toward one or the other but showing features of both.

The link between the Type A personality style and coronary heart disease has been supported by many studies. In one well-known investigation of more than 3,000 people, Friedman and Rosenman (1974) separated healthy men in their forties and fifties into Type A and Type B categories and then followed their health over the next eight years. More than twice as many Type A men developed coronary heart disease. Later studies found that Type A functioning correlates similarly with heart disease in women (Haynes, Feinleib, & Kannel, 1980).

In recent studies the link found between the Type A personality style and heart disease has not been as strong as the earlier studies suggest. They do show, nevertheless, that some of the characteristics that supposedly make up the Type A style, particularly *hostility* and *time urgency,* are very likely to be related to heart disease (Taylor, 2006; Boyle et al., 2004).

BIOLOGICAL FACTORS We saw earlier that one way in which the brain activates body organs is through the operation of the *autonomic nervous system* (*ANS*), the network of nerve fibers that connect the central nervous system to the body's organs. Hans Selye (1976, 1974) was one of the first researchers to describe the relationship between stress and the ANS. He proposed that people typically respond to stress in three stages, which he called, collectively, the *general adaptation syndrome.* In the presence of threat, the sympathetic nervous system increases its activity and arouses responses throughout the body (*alarm stage*). The parasympathetic nervous system next attempts to counteract these responses (*resistance stage*). Finally, if exposure to stress continues, the resistance may fail and organs controlled by the ANS may become overworked and break down (*exhaustion stage*).

[BOX 6-4]

Working with Death

One of the least pleasant jobs in our society is that of tying up loose ends after a disaster or murder. Yet the work must be done, regardless of the toll it may take on the workers. It turns out that reactions to such responsibilities vary widely.

In 1993, 83 persons died in the fire at the Branch Davidian compound in Waco, Texas, when federal agents tried to end a 51-day standoff between the Branch Davidian sect and the FBI. Thirty-one dentists had to examine the dental remains of the dead. A study later revealed that these dentists went on to develop more psychological and physical symptoms of severe stress than did a control

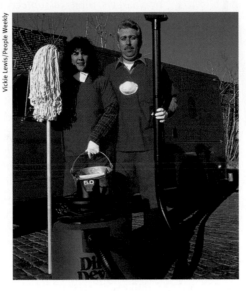

Vickie Lewis/People Weekly

group of other dentists (McCarroll et al., 1996).

Then there are Ray and Louise Barnes (see photo), who run a business called Crime Scene Clean-Up. They and their staffers are hired by police departments, funeral homes, and grieving families to clean up after homicides, suicides, and accidents. They use latex gloves, mops, respirators, and other tools of the trade to "scrub away the detritus of human disaster" (Howe & Nugent, 1996). While hardly indifferent to the grisly scenes, Ray Barnes says that he has grown somewhat used to them, and he and his wife have built a thriving business.

Because the ANS is one of the body systems responsible for "normal" stress reactions, defects in this system are believed to contribute to the development of psychophysiological disorders (Hugdahl, 1995). If one's ANS is stimulated too easily, for example, it may overreact to situations that most people find only mildly stressful, eventually damaging certain organs and causing a psychophysiological disorder (Boyce et al., 1995).

Other more specific biological problems may also contribute to psychophysiological disorders. A person with a weak gastrointestinal system, for example, may be a prime candidate for an ulcer, whereas someone with a weak respiratory system may develop asthma readily. In a related vein, people may display favored biological reactions that raise their chances of developing psychophysiological disorders. Some individuals perspire in response to stress, others develop stomachaches, and still others experience a rise in blood pressure (Fahrenberg, Foerster, & Wilmers, 1995). Although such variations are perfectly normal, the repeated overuse of a single system may wear it down and eventually help cause a psychophysiological disorder. Research has indicated, for example, that some individuals are particularly likely to experience temporary rises in blood pressure when stressed (Gianaros et al., 2005). It may be that they are prone to develop hypertension. Similarly, some infants produce much more gastric acid under stress than other infants (Weiner, 1977; Mirsky, 1958). Perhaps, over the years, this physical reaction wears down the lining of the stomach or duodenum, leaving the individuals more vulnerable to ulcers.

Clearly, sociocultural, psychological, and biological variables combine to produce psychophysiological disorders. In fact, the interaction of psychosocial and physical factors is now considered the rule of bodily functioning, not the exception, and, as the years have passed, more and more illnesses have been added to the list of traditional psychophysiological disorders. Let us turn next to the "new" psychophysiological disorders.

New Psychophysiological Disorders

Since the 1960s, researchers have found many links between psychosocial stress and a wide range of physical illnesses. Let us look first at how these links were established and then at *psychoneuroimmunology,* the area of study that ties stress and illness to the body's immune system.

>>BY THE NUMBERS

Traffic Stress

46 Average number of hours American motorists spend in rush-hour traffic each year «

93 Average number of hours that Los Angeles motorists spend in rush-hour traffic «

67 Average number of hours that Washington, D.C., drivers spend in rush-hour traffic «

50 Average number of hours that New York City drivers spend in rush-hour traffic «

5.7 billion Gallons of fuel used in the United States each year while automobiles idle in traffic «

(Reuters, 2004)

FIGURE **6-5** **Catastrophic stress** *Paul and Gerald Adams (1984) found that during the months immediately after the eruption of Mount St. Helens on May 18, 1980, there was a 34 percent increase in emergency room visits and a 19 percent rise in deaths in nearby Othello, Washington.*

ARE PHYSICAL ILLNESSES RELATED TO STRESS? In 1967 two researchers, Thomas Holmes and Richard Rahe, developed the *Social Adjustment Rating Scale,* which assigns numerical values to the stresses that most people experience at some time in their lives (see Table 6-5). Answers given by a large sample of subjects indicated that the most stressful event on the scale should be the death of a spouse, which receives a score of 100 *life change units* (*LCUs*). Lower on the scale is retirement (45 LCUs), and still lower is a minor violation of the law (11 LCUs). Even positive events, such as an outstanding personal achievement (28 LCUs), are somewhat stressful. This scale gave researchers a yardstick for measuring the total amount of stress a person faces over a period of time. If, for example, in the course of a year a businesswoman started a new business (39 LCUs), sent her son off to college (29 LCUs), moved to a new house (20 LCUs), and experienced the death of a close friend (37 LCUs), her stress score for the year would be 125 LCUs, a considerable amount of stress for such a period of time.

With the Social Adjustment Rating Scale in hand, the researchers were able to examine the relationship between life stress and the onset of illness. They found that the LCU scores of sick people during the year before they fell ill were much higher than those of healthy people (Holmes & Rahe, 1989, 1967). If a person's life changes totaled more than 300 LCUs over the course of a year, that person was particularly likely to develop a serious health problem.

The Social Adjustment Rating Scale has been updated and revised by various researchers over the years (Hobson et al., 1998; Miller & Rahe, 1997). Using either the original or the revised scales, studies have linked stresses of various kinds to a wide range of physical conditions, from trench mouth and upper respiratory infection to cancer (Cohen, 2005; Taylor, 2004). Overall, the greater the amount of life stress, the greater the likelihood of illness (see Figure 6-5). Researchers even have found a relationship between traumatic stress and death. Widows and widowers, for example, display an increased risk of death during their period of bereavement (Rees & Lutkin, 1967; Young et al., 1963). A particularly striking instance of death after the loss of a loved one is seen in the following case:

> Charlie and Josephine had been inseparable companions for 13 years. In a senseless act of violence Charlie, in full view of Josephine, was shot and killed in a melee with police. Josephine first stood motionless, then slowly approached his prostrate form, sunk to her knees, and silently rested her head on the dead and bloody body. Concerned persons attempted to help her away, but she refused to move. Hoping she would soon surmount her overwhelming grief, they let her be. But she never rose again; in 15 minutes she was dead. Now the remarkable part of the story is that Charlie and Josephine were llamas in the zoo! They had escaped from their pen during a snow storm and Charlie, a mean animal to begin with, was shot when he proved unmanageable. I was able to establish from the zoo keeper that to all intents and purposes Josephine had been normally frisky and healthy right up to the moment of the tragic event.
>
> *(Engel, 1968)*

One shortcoming of Holmes and Rahe's Social Adjustment Rating Scale is that it does not take into consideration the particular life stress reactions of specific populations. For example, in their development of the scale, the researchers sampled white Americans predominantly. Less than 5 percent of the subjects were African Americans. But since their ongoing life experiences often differ in significant ways, might not African Americans and white Americans differ in their stress reactions to various kinds of life events? One study indicates that indeed they do (Komaroff, Masuda, & Holmes, 1989, 1986). Both white and African Americans rank death of a spouse as the single most stressful life event, but African Americans experience greater stress than white Americans from such events as a major personal injury or illness, a major change in work

>>LAB•NOTES

Calming the Savage Beast

As most pet owners will tell you, dogs, like people, have preferences in music. In one study, 50 dogs were exposed to different types of music—four hours for each type. The dogs were calmer—they rested, sat more, and were quieter—when listening to classical music. In contrast, they spent more time barking when exposed to heavy metal music. The effects of other kinds of auditory stimulation—human conversation and pop music—fell somewhere in the middle. **<<**

(Wells et al., 2002)

Table 6-5

Most Stressful Life Events

Adults: Social adjustment rating scale*

1. Death of spouse	12. Pregnancy
2. Divorce	13. Sex difficulties
3. Marital separation	14. Gain of new family member
4. Jail term	15. Business readjustment
5. Death of close family member	16. Change in financial state
6. Personal injury or illness	17. Death of close friend
7. Marriage	18. Change to different line of work
8. Fired at work	19. Change in number of arguments with spouse
9. Marital reconciliation	20. Mortgage over $10,000
10. Retirement	21. Foreclosure of mortgage or loan
11. Change in health of family member	22. Change in responsibilities at work

*Full scale has 43 items.
Source: Holmes & Rahe, 1967.

Students: Undergraduate stress questionnaire[†]

1. Death (family member or friend)	12. Went into a test unprepared
2. Had a lot of tests	13. Lost something (especially wallet)
3. It's finals week	14. Death of a pet
4. Applying to graduate school	15. Did worse than expected on test
5. Victim of a crime	16. Had an interview
6. Assignments in all classes due the same day	17. Had projects, research papers due
7. Breaking up with boy-/girlfriend	18. Did badly on a test
8. Found out boy-/girlfriend cheated on you	19. Parents getting divorce
9. Lots of deadlines to meet	20. Dependent on other people
10. Property stolen	21. Having roommate conflicts
11. You have a hard upcoming week	22. Car/bike broke down, flat tire, etc.

[†]Full scale has 83 items.
Source: Crandall et al., 1992.

responsibilities, or a major change in living conditions. Similarly, studies have shown that women and men differ in their reactions to certain life changes on the scale (Miller & Rahe, 1997). Women, for example, tend to experience more stress than men when faced with the death of a close family member, loss of a job, a major injury or illness, a decrease in income, credit problems, or a change in residence.

Finally, college students may face stressors that are different from those listed in the Social Adjustment Rating Scale. Instead of having marital difficulties, being fired, or applying for a job, a college student may have trouble with a roommate, fail a course, or apply to graduate school. When researchers developed special scales to measure life events more accurately in this population (see bottom half of Table 6-5), they found the expected relationships between stressful events and illness (Crandall et al., 1992).

PSYCHONEUROIMMUNOLOGY How do stressful events result in a viral or bacterial infection? An area of study called **psychoneuroimmunology** seeks to answer this question by uncovering the links between psychosocial stress, the immune system, and health (Taylor, 2006; Miller & Cohen, 2005).

The **immune system** is the body's network of activities and cells that identify and destroy **antigens**—foreign invaders, such as bacteria, viruses, fungi, and parasites—and cancer cells. Immune cells are located in the bone marrow, thymus, lymph nodes, spleen, tonsils, appendix, and small intestine. Among the most important cells in this system are billions of **lymphocytes,** white blood cells that circulate through the lymph system and the bloodstream. When stimulated by antigens, lymphocytes spring into action to help the body overcome the invaders.

•**PSYCHONEUROIMMUNOLOGY**•The study of the connections between stress, the body's immune system, and illness.

•**IMMUNE SYSTEM**•The body's network of activities and cells that identify and destroy antigens and cancer cells.

•**ANTIGEN**•A foreign invader of the body, such as a bacterium or virus.

•**LYMPHOCYTES**•White blood cells that circulate through the lymph system and bloodstream, helping the body identify and destroy antigens and cancer cells.

Killer T-cells at work *These killer T-cells surround a larger cancer cell and destroy it, thus helping to prevent the spread of cancer.*

One group of lymphocytes, called *helper T-cells,* identify antigens and then multiply and trigger the production of other kinds of immune cells. Another group, *natural killer T-cells,* seek out and destroy body cells that have already been infected by viruses, thus helping to stop the spread of a viral infection. A third group of lymphocytes, *B-cells,* produce *antibodies,* protein molecules that recognize and bind to antigens, mark them for destruction, and prevent them from causing infection.

Researchers now believe that stress can interfere with the activity of lymphocytes, slowing them down and thus increasing a person's susceptibility to viral and bacterial infections (Lutgendorf et al., 2005; Benight et al., 2004; Ader et al., 2001). In a landmark study, R. W. Bartrop and his colleagues (1977) in New South Wales, Australia, compared the immune systems of 26 people whose spouses had died eight weeks earlier with those of 26 matched control subjects whose spouses had not died. Blood samples revealed that lymphocyte functioning was much lower in the bereaved people than in the controls. Still other studies have shown slow immune functioning in persons who are exposed to long-term stress. For example, researchers have found poorer immune functioning among people who face the challenge of providing ongoing care for a relative with Alzheimer's disease (Vitaliano et al., 2005; Redwine et al., 2004; Kiecolt-Glaser et al., 2002, 1996).

These studies seem to be telling a remarkable story. During periods when healthy individuals happened to experience unusual levels of stress, they remained healthy on the surface, but their experiences apparently slowed their immune systems so that they became susceptible to illness. If stress affects our capacity to fight off illness, it is no wonder that researchers have repeatedly found a relationship between life stress and illnesses of various kinds. But why and when does stress interfere with the immune system? Several factors influence whether stress will result in a slowdown of the system, including *biochemical activity, behavioral changes, personality style,* and *degree of social support.*

BIOCHEMICAL ACTIVITY We observed earlier that abnormal activity of *norepinephrine* and of the *corticosteroids* may contribute to the development of acute and posttraumatic stress disorders. Similarly, these chemicals have been implicated in slowdowns of the immune system during prolonged periods of stress. Remember that stress leads to increased activity by the sympathetic nervous system, including an increase in the release of norepinephrine throughout the brain and body. It appears that, beyond supporting the activity of the sympathetic nervous system, this chemical eventually helps slow the functioning of the immune system (Lekander, 2002). During low stress or early stages of stress, norepinephrine travels to certain lymphocyte receptors and gives a message for the lymphocytes to increase their activity. As the stress continues or rises, however, the chemical travels to yet other receptors on the lymphocytes and gives them an *inhibitory message* to stop their activity. Thus, while the release of norepinephrine improves immune functioning at low levels of stress, it actually slows down immune functioning at higher levels.

Similarly, the corticosteroids—cortisol and other so-called stress hormones—contribute to poorer immune system functioning during periods of prolonged stress. Remember that when a person is under stress, the adrenal glands release these corticosteroids. At first the release of such hormones stimulates body organs to greater activity. After stress continues for 30 minutes or more, however, the stress hormones travel to certain receptor sites in the body and give *inhibitory messages,* which help calm down the overstressed body (Manuck et al., 1991). One such group of receptor sites is located on the lymphocytes. When the corticosteroids bind to these receptors, their inhibitory messages actually slow down the activity of the lymphocytes (Bauer, 2005; Bellinger et al., 1994). Thus, again, the very chemicals that initially help people to deal with stress eventually serve to slow the immune system.

Recent research has further indicated that one of the actions of the corticosteroids is to trigger an increase in the production of *cytokines,* proteins that bind to receptors throughout the body. At early and moderate levels of stress, the cytokines, another key player in the immune system, help combat infection. But as stress continues and more corticosteroids are released, the growing production and spread of cytokines lead to

---

›› LAB•NOTES

The Immune System at Work

Virtues of Laughter After watching a humorous video, subjects who had laughed at and enjoyed the film showed decreases in stress and improvements in natural killer cell activity (Bennett, 1998). ‹‹

- -

Direct Impact Studies indicate that the abnormal biochemical activity that accompanies depression also directly disrupts lymphocyte activity (Azar, 1996). Correspondingly, the immune systems of depressed people do not function as well as those of other people (Schleifer et al., 1999, 1996). ‹‹

- -

Marital Stress During and after marital spats, women typically experience a greater release of stress hormones than men, and so a greater decrease in immune functioning (Kiecolt-Glaser et al., 1996). ‹‹

chronic inflammation throughout the body. Among other activities, the cytokines travel to the liver and induce increased production of *C-reactive protein,* or *CRP,* a protein that enters the bloodstream, spreads throughout the body, and, over time, contributes to heart disease, stroke, and other illnesses (Grippo et al., 2005; Suarez, 2004; McEwen, 2002).

BEHAVIORAL CHANGES Stress may set in motion a series of behavioral changes that indirectly affect the immune system. Some people under stress may, for example, become anxious or depressed, perhaps even develop an anxiety or mood disorder. As a result, they may sleep badly, eat poorly, exercise less, or smoke or drink more—behaviors known to slow down the immune system (Irwin & Cole, 2005; Kiecolt-Glaser & Glaser, 2002, 1999).

PERSONALITY STYLE An individual's personality may also play a role in determining how much the immune system is slowed down by stress (Chung et al., 2005; Sarid et al., 2004). According to research, people who generally respond to life stress with optimism, constructive coping, and resilience—that is, people who welcome challenge and are willing to take control in their daily encounters—experience better immune system functioning and are better prepared to fight off illness (Taylor, 2006, 2004). Some studies find, for example, that people with "hardy" or resilient personalities remain healthy after stressful events, while those whose personalities are less hardy seem more susceptible to illness (Bonanno, 2004; Oulette & DiPlacido, 2001). One study even discovered that men with a general sense of hopelessness die at above-average rates from heart disease and other causes (Everson et al., 1996) (see Figure 6-6). Similarly, a growing body of research suggests that people who are spiritual tend to be healthier than individuals without spiritual beliefs, and a few studies have linked spirituality to better immune system functioning (Thoresen & Plante, 2005; Lutgendorf et al., 2004).

In related work, some studies have noted a relationship between certain personality characteristics and recovery from cancer (Hjerl et al., 2003; Greer, 1999). They have found that patients with certain forms of cancer who display a helpless coping style and who cannot easily express their feelings, particularly anger, tend to have less successful recoveries than patients who do express their emotions. Other studies, however, have found no relationship between personality and cancer outcome (Urcuyo et al., 2005; Garssen & Goodkin, 1999).

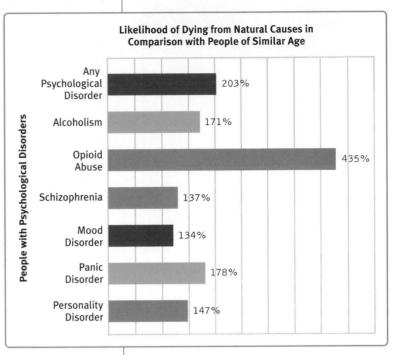

FIGURE **6-6** **Warning: psychological disorders may be dangerous to your health** *Psychological disorders are themselves a source of stress that can lead to medical problems. People with such disorders are twice as likely to die of natural causes (medical illnesses) as people in the same age group without psychological difficulties. (Adapted from Harris & Barraclough, 1998.)*

Everyone needs a break *Stress affects everyone, from humans to animals, and indeed everyone needs to find ways to overcome and cope with the pressures of their lives. These monkeys who live in a valley in Yamanouchi, Japan, fight stress and find relaxation by bathing regularly in one of the valley's hot springs.*

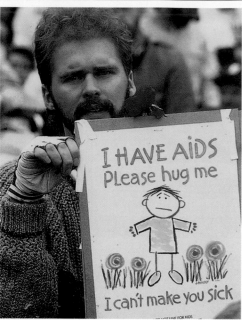

In need of support *AIDS is a disease in which certain immune cells become infected by the* human immunodeficiency virus (HIV), *which launches a full-scale attack on the immune system. Studies reveal that victims who receive positive social support are better able to fight off the disease than are those who are stigmatized and discriminated against (Schneiderman, 1999).*

Relaxation, the hard way *While dangling from Alaska's Mount Barrile, a climber uses "Tranquilite" sleep goggles, which are supposed to produce relaxation with blue light and a soothing "pink sound."*

SOCIAL SUPPORT Finally, people who have few social supports and feel lonely seem to display poorer immune functioning in the face of stress than people who do not feel lonely (Curtis et al., 2004; Cohen, 2002). In one study, medical students were given the *UCLA Loneliness Scale* and then divided into "high" and "low" loneliness groups (Kiecolt-Glaser et al., 1984). The high-loneliness group showed lower lymphocyte responses during a final exam period.

Other studies have found that social support and affiliation may actually help protect people from stress, poor immune system functioning, and subsequent illness, or help speed up recovery from illness or surgery (Taylor, 2006; Cohen, 2002; Kiecolt-Glaser et al., 2002, 1998, 1991). Similarly, some studies have suggested that patients with certain forms of cancer who receive social support in their personal lives or supportive therapy often have better immune system functioning and, in turn, more successful recoveries than patients without such supports (Taylor, 2006; Spiegel & Fawzy, 2002) (see Box 6-5 on page 184).

Psychological Treatments for Physical Disorders

As clinicians have discovered that stress and related psychosocial factors may contribute to physical disorders, they have applied psychological treatments to more and more medical problems (Antoni, 2005; Gatchel & Maddrey, 2004). The most common of these interventions are relaxation training, biofeedback, meditation, hypnosis, cognitive interventions, insight therapy, and support groups. The field of treatment that combines psychological and physical approaches to treat or prevent medical problems is known as **behavioral medicine.**

RELAXATION TRAINING As we saw in Chapter 5, people can be taught to relax their muscles at will, a process that sometimes reduces feelings of anxiety. Given the positive effects of relaxation on anxiety and the nervous system, clinicians believe that **relaxation training** can help prevent or treat medical illnesses that are related to stress.

Relaxation training, often in combination with medication, has been widely used in the treatment of high blood pressure (Stetter & Kupper, 2002). One study assigned hypertensive subjects to one of three forms of treatment: medication, medication plus relaxation training, or medication plus supportive psychotherapy (Taylor et al., 1977). Those who received relaxation training in combination with medication showed the greatest reduction in blood pressure. Relaxation training has also been of some help in treating headaches, insomnia, asthma, diabetes, pain after surgery, certain vascular diseases, and the undesirable effects of cancer treatments (Devineni & Blanchard, 2005; Carmichael, 2004).

BIOFEEDBACK As we also have seen in Chapter 5, patients given **biofeedback training** are connected to machinery that gives them continuous readings about their involuntary body activities. This information enables them gradually to gain control over those activities. Somewhat helpful in the treatment of anxiety disorders, the procedure has also been applied to a growing number of physical disorders.

In one study, *electromyograph (EMG)* feedback was used to treat 16 patients who were experiencing facial pain caused in part by tension in their jaw muscles (Dohrmann & Laskin, 1978). In an EMG procedure, electrodes are attached to a person's muscles so that the muscle contractions are detected and converted into a tone for the individual to hear (pp. 126–127). Changes in the pitch and volume of the tone indicate changes in muscle tension. After "listening" to EMG feedback repeatedly, the 16 patients in this study learned how to relax their jaw muscles at will and later reported a reduction in facial pain. In contrast, 8 control subjects, who were wired to similar equipment but not given biofeedback training, showed little improvement in muscle tension or their experience of pain.

EMG feedback has also been used successfully in the treatment of headaches and muscular disabilities caused by strokes or accidents. Still other forms of biofeedback training have been of some help in the treatment of heartbeat irregularities, asthma, migraine headaches, high blood pressure, stuttering, and pain from burns (Martin, 2002; Moss, 2002; Gatchel, 2001).

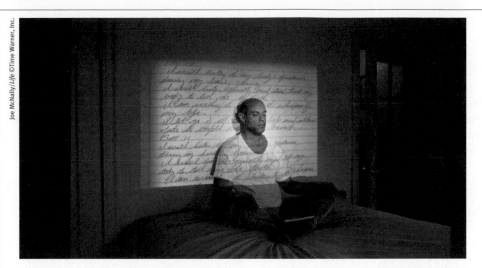

Fighting HIV on all fronts *As part of his treatment at the Wellness Center in San Francisco, this man meditates and writes letters to his HIV virus.*

MEDITATION Although meditation has been practiced since ancient times, Western health care professionals have only recently become aware of its effectiveness in relieving physical distress. **Meditation** is a technique of turning one's concentration inward, achieving a slightly changed state of consciousness, and temporarily ignoring all stressors. In the most common approach, meditators go to a quiet place, assume a comfortable posture, utter or think a particular sound (called a *mantra*) to help focus their attention, and allow their minds to turn away from all outside thoughts and concerns (Dass & Levine, 2002).

Many people who meditate regularly report feeling more peaceful, engaged, and creative. Meditation has been used to help manage pain in cancer patients and to help treat high blood pressure, heart problems, asthma, skin disorders, diabetes, insomnia, and even viral infections (Stein, 2003; Andresen, 2000).

HYPNOSIS As we discussed in Chapter 1, individuals who undergo **hypnosis** are guided by a hypnotist into a sleeplike, suggestible state during which they can be directed to act in unusual ways, experience unusual sensations, remember seemingly forgotten events, or forget remembered events. With training some people are even able to induce their own hypnotic state (*self-hypnosis*). Hypnosis is now used as an aid to psychotherapy and to help treat many physical conditions (Shenefelt, 2003).

Hypnosis seems to be particularly helpful in the control of pain (Kiecolt-Glaser et al., 1998). One case study describes a patient who underwent dental surgery under hypnotic suggestion: after a hypnotic state was induced, the dentist suggested to the patient that he was in a pleasant and relaxed setting listening to a friend describe his own success at undergoing similar dental surgery under hypnosis. The dentist then proceeded to perform a successful 25-minute operation (Gheorghiu & Orleanu, 1982). Although only some people are able to undergo surgery while anesthetized by hypnosis alone, hypnosis combined with chemical forms of anesthesia is apparently helpful to many patients (Fredericks, 2001). Beyond its use in the control of pain, hypnosis has been used successfully to help treat such problems as skin diseases, asthma, insomnia, high blood pressure, warts, and other forms of infection (Modlin, 2002; Hornyak et al., 2000).

COGNITIVE INTERVENTIONS People with physical ailments have sometimes been taught new attitudes or cognitive responses toward their ailments as part of treatment (Devineni & Blanchard, 2005; Kiecolt-Glaser et al., 2002, 1998). For example, an approach called **self-instruction training** has helped patients cope with severe pain (Allison & Friedman, 2004; Meichenbaum, 1997, 1993, 1977, 1975). In self-instruction training therapists teach people to identify and eventually rid themselves of unpleasant thoughts that keep emerging during pain episodes (so-called *negative self-statements* such as "Oh, no, I can't take this pain"), and to replace them with *coping self-statements* instead ("When pain comes, just pause; keep focusing on what you have to do").

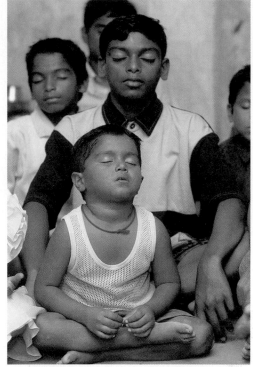

Meditation at any age *To help survivors of the 2004 tsunami overcome their traumatic and life-changing ordeal, the Art and Living Foundation organized meditation sessions throughout Asia. In this session, a 4-year-old Indian child, along with several older survivors, learns how to meditate, with the hope that this technique, among others, will help him cope better and maintain his psychological and physical health.*

•**BEHAVIORAL MEDICINE**•A field of treatment that combines psychological and physical interventions to treat or prevent medical problems.

•**RELAXATION TRAINING**•A treatment procedure that teaches clients to relax at will.

•**BIOFEEDBACK TRAINING**•A treatment technique in which a client is given information about physiological reactions as they occur and learns to control the reactions voluntarily.

•**MEDITATION**•A technique of turning one's concentration inward and achieving a slightly changed state of consciousness.

•**HYPNOSIS**•A sleeplike suggestible state during which a person can be directed to act in unusual ways, to experience unusual sensations, to remember seemingly forgotten events, or to forget remembered events.

•**SELF-INSTRUCTION TRAINING**•A cognitive treatment that teaches clients to use coping self-statements at times of stress or discomfort.

[**BOX 6-5**]

Sharing the Pain

A few years ago, 13 fifth-grade boys in San Marcos, California, went to a barbershop and proceeded to have their heads shaved. The purpose of this seemingly strange group action? To show support and compassion for their 11-year-old friend and classmate Ian O'Gorman. Ian was undergoing chemotherapy for cancer at the time and was beginning to lose his hair. His friends didn't want him to feel left out or further traumatized, so they undertook this selfless display of support. Their teacher, who had his head shaved, too, said that the idea came from the boys, who nicknamed themselves the Bald Eagles. All parents gave their blessings to the group action. Ian gratefully reported, "What my friends did really made me feel stronger. It helped me get through all this. . . . I was really amazed that they would do something like this for me."

No doubt the generous behavior of his friends had an enormous impact on Ian's state of mind. Just as important, the growing body of research in psychoneuroimmunology suggests that such acts may have had a positive effect on his health and recovery as well. Clearly, our society is more sensitive today than in the past to the psychosocial issues at work in illnesses such as Ian's.

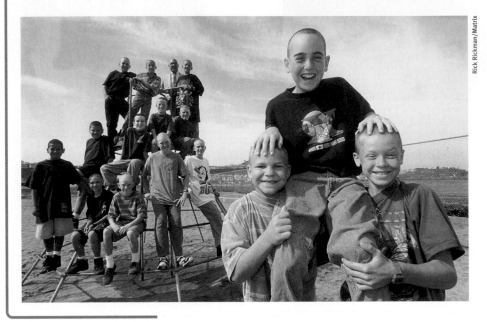

Rick Rickman/Matrix

INSIGHT THERAPY AND SUPPORT GROUPS If anxiety, depression, anger, and the like contribute to a person's physical ills, therapy to reduce these negative emotions should help reduce the ills (Antoni, 2005; Hawkins, 2004). In such cases, physicians may recommend insight therapy, support groups, or both to help patients overcome their medical difficulties (Antoni, 2005). Research suggests that the discussion of past and present upsets may indeed help improve a person's health, just as it may help one's psychological functioning (Smyth & Pennebaker, 2001). In one study, asthma and arthritis patients who simply wrote down their thoughts and feelings about stressful events for a handful of days showed lasting improvements in their conditions. Similarly, stress-related writing was found to be beneficial for patients with HIV infections (Petrie et al., 2004). In addition, as we have seen, recovery from cancer and certain other illnesses is sometimes improved by participation in support groups (Antoni, 2005; Spiegel & Fawzy, 2002).

COMBINATION APPROACHES Studies have found that the various psychological interventions for physical problems tend to be equal in effectiveness (Devineni & Blanchard, 2005; Brauer, 1999). Relaxation and biofeedback training, for example, are equally helpful (and more helpful than placebos) in the treatment of high blood pressure, headaches, and asthma. Psychological interventions are, in fact, often of greatest help when they are combined with other psychological interventions and with medical treatments (Suinn, 2001). In one study, ulcer patients who were given relaxation, self-instruction, and assertiveness training along with medication were found to be less anxious and more comfortable, have fewer symptoms, and have a better long-term outcome than patients who received medication only (Brooks & Richardson, 1980).

Combination interventions have also been helpful in changing Type A patterns and in reducing the risk of coronary heart disease among Type A people (Williams, 2001; Cohen et al., 1997). In one study, 862 patients who had suffered a heart attack within the previous six months were assigned to one of two groups (Friedman et al., 1984). The control group was given three years of cardiological counseling (diet, exercise, and

>>LOOKING AROUND

Recovery from Illness

Surgical Risk People who experience more fear or stress before surgery tend to experience more pain and more complications after surgery and stay longer in the hospital (Kiecolt-Glaser et al., 1998). «

Room with a View According to one hospital's records of individuals who underwent gallbladder surgery, those in rooms with a good view from their window had shorter hospitalizations and needed fewer pain medications than those in rooms without a good view (Ulrich, 1984). «

medical advice). The experimental group received the same counseling *plus* Type A behavioral counseling. They were taught about the Type A personality style and to recognize their excessive physiological, cognitive, and behavioral responses in stressful situations. They were also trained in relaxation and taught to change counterproductive attitudes.

The addition of the Type A behavioral counseling led to major differences in lifestyle and health. Type A behavior was reduced in almost 80 percent of the patients who received both Type A counseling and cardiological counseling for three years, compared to only 50 percent of those who received cardiological counseling alone. Moreover, fewer of those who received the combined counseling suffered another heart attack—only 7 percent, compared to 13 percent of the subjects in the control group.

Clearly, the treatment picture for physical illnesses has been changing dramatically. While medical treatments continue to dominate, today's medical practitioners are traveling a course far removed from the mind-body dualism of centuries past.

PUTTING IT together
Expanding the Boundaries of Abnormal Psychology

The concept of stress is familiar to everyone, yet only in recent decades have clinical scientists and practitioners had much success in understanding and treating it and recognizing its pervasive impact on our functioning; now that the impact of stress has been identified, however, research efforts in this area are moving forward at near-lightning speed. What researchers once saw as a vague connection between stress and psychological dysfunctioning or between stress and physical illness is now understood as a complex interaction of many variables. Such factors as life changes, individual psychological and bodily reactions, social support, biochemical activity, and slowing of the immune system are all recognized as contributors to psychological and physical stress disorders.

Insights into the treatment of the various stress disorders have been accumulating just as rapidly. In recent years clinicians have learned that a combination of approaches—from drug therapy to behavioral techniques to community interventions—may be of help to people with acute and posttraumatic stress disorders. Similarly, psychological approaches such as relaxation training and cognitive therapy are being applied to various physical ills, usually in combination with traditional medical treatments. Small wonder that many practitioners are convinced that such treatment combinations will eventually be the norm in treating the majority of physical ailments.

One of the most exciting aspects of these recent developments is the field's growing emphasis on the *interrelationship* of the social environment, the brain, and the rest of the body. Researchers have observed repeatedly that mental disorders are often best understood and treated when sociocultural, psychological, and biological factors are all taken into consideration. They now know that this interaction also helps explain medical problems. We are reminded that the brain is part of the body and that both are part of a social context. For better and for worse, the three are inextricably linked.

Another exciting aspect of this work on stress and its wide-ranging impact is the interest it has sparked in *illness prevention* and *health promotion* (Compas & Gotlib, 2002; Kaplan, 2000). If stress is indeed key to the development of both psychological and physical disorders, perhaps such disorders can be prevented by eliminating or reducing stress—for example, by helping people to cope better generally or by better preparing their bodies for stress's impact. With this notion in mind, illness prevention and health promotion programs are now being developed around the world. Clinical theorists have, for example, designed school-curriculum programs to help promote *social competence* in children (Weissberg, 2000) and teach children more *optimistic ways of thinking* (Gillham et al., 2000, 1995). Similarly, prevention programs have been developed that teach *coping skills* to children whose parents are divorcing and *conflict-reduction skills* to the parents themselves (Wolchick et al., 2000). And in the realm of acute and posttraumatic stress disorders, one team of clinical researchers has developed a program that *immediately* offers rape victims a combination of relaxation training, exposure techniques, cognitive interventions, and education about rape's impact, all before the onset of psychological or physical symptoms (Foa et al., 1995). Research indicates that women who receive

Jeffery Blitz/The Kobal Collection

All in good fun? *Competition is considered healthy, rewarding, and character-building in Western society, so parents often encourage their children to participate in competitive activities ranging from sports to beauty pageants to spelling bees. But many clinical researchers worry that competitive activities place too much pressure on certain children—pressure that may heighten their chances of developing stress-related ailments. This child's facial expression reflects the extraordinary level of stress he is experiencing as he struggles to spell a word in a spelling competition featured in the 2002 film documentary* Spellbound.

"It's got to come out, of course, but that doesn't address the deeper problem."

Sometimes the body trumps the mind *Many experts have come to believe that all medical ailments have at least some psychological dimensions. However, a number of clinicians worry that too much emphasis is now being placed on the role of psychological factors and caution that the precise contributions of such factors vary greatly from ailment to ailment and from patient to patient.*

>>**LOOKING AROUND**
Stress in Japan

The Japanese term *karoshi* means "death from overwork." It suggests that the high stress and heavy work conditions that Japan is so proud of in terms of productivity can lead to an increase of sudden death by promoting cardiovascular and cerebrovascular disease. This has been a controversial issue in Japan since the 1970s. <<

such preventive measures do indeed develop fewer stress symptoms in the months following their attacks than do other rape victims.

Amidst these exciting and rapidly unfolding developments also lies a cautionary tale. When problems are studied heavily, it is common for the public, as well as some researchers and clinicians, to draw conclusions that may be too bold. In the psychological realm, for example, many individuals—perhaps too many—are now receiving diagnoses of posttraumatic stress disorder partly because the symptoms of the disorder are many, a variety of life events can be considered traumatic, and the disorder has received so much attention. Similarly, given the growing body of work on psychophysiological disorders and psychoneuroimmunology, some people, including a number of clinicians, are all too quick to explain medical problems by pointing simplistically to psychosocial factors such as counterproductive attitudes, too little faith, or lack of social support. Explanations of this kind reflect a misapplication of the complex research that has been unfolding in the study of stress and health. We shall see such potential problems again when we look at other problems that are currently receiving great focus, such as attention deficit hyperactivity disorder, repressed memories of childhood abuse, and multiple personality disorder. The line between enlightenment and overenthusiasm is often thin.

┤[SUMMARY AND REVIEW]├

■ **Effects of stress** When we appraise a *stressor* as threatening, we often experience a *stress response* consisting of arousal and a sense of fear. The features of arousal and fear are set in motion by the *hypothalamus,* a brain area that activates the *autonomic nervous system* and the *endocrine system.* There are two pathways by which these systems produce arousal and fear—the *sympathetic nervous system* pathway and the *hypothalamic-pituitary-adrenal* pathway. *pp. 155–158*

■ **Psychological stress disorders** People with *acute stress disorder* or *posttraumatic stress disorder* react with anxiety and related symptoms after a traumatic event, including reexperiencing the traumatic event, avoiding related events, being markedly less responsive than normal, and experiencing increased arousal, anxiety, and guilt. The traumatic event may be *combat experience,* a *disaster,* or *victimization.* The symptoms of *acute stress disorder* begin soon after the trauma and last less than a month. Those of *posttraumatic stress disorder* may begin at any time (even years) after the trauma, and may last for months or years.

In attempting to explain why some people develop a psychological stress disorder and others do not, researchers have focused on *biological factors, personality, childhood experiences, social support,* and the *severity of the traumatic event.* Techniques used to treat the stress disorders include drug therapy and behavioral exposure techniques. Clinicians may also use insight therapy, family therapy, and group therapy (including *rap groups* for combat veterans) to help sufferers develop insight and perspective. Rapidly mobilized *community therapy,* such as that offered by the *Disaster Response Network,* follows the principles of *critical incident stress debriefing.* It often seems helpful after large-scale disasters; however, some studies have raised questions about the usefulness of this approach. *pp. 158–173*

■ **Psychophysiological disorders** *Psychophysiological disorders* are those in which psychosocial and physiological factors interact to cause a physical problem. Factors linked to these disorders are sociocultural factors, such as society-wide stressors or persistent social conditions; psychological factors, such as particular needs, attitudes, or personality styles; and biological factors, such as defects in the autonomic nervous system or particular organs.

For years clinical researchers singled out a limited number of physical illnesses as psychophysiological. These traditional psychophysiological disorders include *ulcers, asthma, insomnia, chronic headaches, hypertension,* and *coronary heart disease.* Recently many other psychophysiological disorders have been identified. Scientists have linked many physical illnesses to stress and have developed a new area of study called *psychoneuroimmunology. pp. 173–179*

■ **Psychoneuroimmunology** The body's *immune system* consists of *lymphocytes* and other cells that fight off *antigens*—bacteria, viruses, and other foreign invaders—and cancer cells. Stress can slow *lymphocyte* activity, thereby interfering with the immune system's ability to protect against illness during times of stress. Factors that seem to affect immune functioning include *norepinephrine and corticosteroid activity, behavioral changes, personality style,* and *social support. pp. 179–182*

■ **Psychological treatments for physical disorders** *Behavioral medicine* combines psychological and physical interventions to treat or prevent medical problems. Psychological approaches such as *relaxation training, biofeedback training, meditation, hypnosis, cognitive techniques, insight therapy,* and *support groups* are increasingly being included in the treatment of various medical problems. *pp. 182–185*

■ **Illness prevention and health promotion** In recent years clinicians have increasingly designed programs that aim to eliminate or reduce stress by helping people generally to cope better or to prepare their bodies for stress's impact. The logic behind such programs is that the better people handle stress, the less likely they will be to develop the psychological and physical disorders that often result from stress. *pp. 185–186*

>>> CRITICAL THOUGHTS <<<

1. What types of events in modern society might trigger acute and post-traumatic stress disorders? What kinds of factors might serve to relieve the stresses of modern society? *pp. 160–165*

2. Do you think the vivid images seen daily on television, in movies, in rock videos, and the like would make people more vulnerable to developing psychological stress disorders or less vulnerable? Why? *pp. 160–167*

3. How might physicians, police, the courts, and other agents better meet the psychological needs of rape victims? *pp. 161–164*

4. Have you, a friend, or a relative ever reacted to stress in ways that might suggest a diagnosis of "adjustment disorder"? Is this category too vague or too easily applied? *p. 169*

5. What jobs in our society might be particularly stressful and traumatizing? *p. 177*

6. Some observers fear that today there may be too much emphasis on psychosocial factors in explaining physical illness. What problems might result from an overemphasis on the role of psychosocial factors? *pp. 177–185*

7. Holmes and Rahe's Social Adjustment Rating Scale has been criticized for assigning a specific stress score to each major life event. Why might such a number fail to be a good indicator of the amount of stress the event actually causes for a particular individual? *pp. 178–179*

⊙—[CYBERSTUDY]————————————>>>

SEARCH THE *ABNORMAL PSYCHOLOGY* CD-ROM FOR

▲ Chapter 6 video cases and discussions
  How might stress and anxiety affect performance?
  Observe "fight-or-flight" reactions in operation.
  How do physical, psychological, and sociocultural factors affect health?

▲ Chapter 6 Practical, Research, and Decision-Making Exercises
  Linking modern-day pressures to psychological symptoms
  Examining the connection between life changes and health

▲ Chapter 6 Practice Test and Feedback

LOG ON TO THE COMER WEB PAGE FOR

▲ Suggested Web links, exercises, FAQ page, additional Chapter 6 practice test questions
  <www.worthpublishers.com/comer>

————————————————————— <<<

Somatoform and Dissociative Disorders

Brian was spending Saturday sailing with his wife, Helen. The water was rough but well within what they considered safe limits. They were having a wonderful time and really didn't notice that the sky was getting darker, the wind blowing harder, and the sailboat becoming more difficult to control. After a few hours of sailing, they found themselves far from shore in the middle of a powerful and dangerous storm.

The storm intensified very quickly. Brian had trouble controlling the sailboat amidst the high winds and wild waves. He and Helen tried to put on the safety jackets they had neglected to wear earlier, but the boat turned over before they were finished. Brian, the better swimmer of the two, was able to swim back to the overturned sailboat, grab the side, and hold on for dear life, but Helen simply could not overcome the rough waves and reach the boat. As Brian watched in horror and disbelief, his wife disappeared from view.

After a time, the storm began to lose its strength. Brian managed to right the sailboat and sail back to shore. Finally he reached safety, but the personal consequences of this storm were just beginning. The next days were filled with pain and further horror: the Coast Guard finding Helen's body . . . conversations with friends . . . self-blame . . . grief . . . and more.

Compounding this horror, the accident had left Brian with a severe physical impairment—he could not walk properly. He first noticed this terrible impairment when he sailed the boat back to shore, right after the accident. As he tried to run from the sailboat to get help, he could hardly make his legs work. By the time he reached the nearby beach restaurant, all he could do was crawl. Two patrons had to lift him to a chair, and after he told his story and the authorities were alerted, he had to be taken to a hospital.

At first Brian and the hospital physician assumed that he must have been hurt during the accident. One by one, however, the hospital tests revealed nothing—no broken bones, no spinal damage, nothing. Nothing that could explain such severe impairment.

By the following morning, the weakness in his legs had become near paralysis. Because the physicians could not pin down the nature of his injuries, they decided to keep his activities to a minimum. He was not allowed to talk long with the police. Someone else had to inform Helen's parents of her death. To his deep regret, he was not even permitted to attend Helen's funeral.

The mystery deepened over the following days and weeks. As Brian's paralysis continued, he became more and more withdrawn, unable to see more than a few friends and family members and unable to take care of the many unpleasant tasks attached to Helen's death. He could not bring himself to return to work or get on with his life. Almost from the beginning, Brian's paralysis had left him self-absorbed and drained of emotion, unable to look back and unable to move forward.

Annie Wells/©The New Press Democrat, Santa Rosa, CA

Deliverance from danger *As a creek's wild waters rage around her, a young woman is saved from drowning. Unfortunately, for some people deliverance from a life-threatening event, such as a boating accident, combat, a flood, or a tornado, is the beginning rather than the end of their trauma. Somatoform disorders (particularly conversion disorders) and dissociative disorders may emerge during or shortly after such stressful events.*

In the previous two chapters, we have seen how stress and anxiety can negatively affect functioning. Indeed, anxiety is the key feature of disorders such as generalized anxiety disorder, phobias, panic disorder, and obsessive-compulsive disorder. And stress can produce the lingering reactions seen in acute stress disorder, posttraumatic stress disorder, and psychophysiological disorders.

Two other kinds of disorders are commonly linked to stress and anxiety—somatoform disorders and dissociative disorders. *Somatoform disorders* are problems that appear to be medical but are actually due to psychosocial factors. Unlike psychophysiological disorders, in which psychosocial factors interact with physical ailments, the somatoform disorders are psychological disorders masquerading as physical problems. Brian may have been suffering from a somatoform disorder. *Dissociative disorders* are syndromes that feature major losses or changes in memory and identity—losses that are due almost entirely to psychosocial factors rather than physical ones.

The somatoform and dissociative disorders have much in common. Both, for example, may occur in response to severe stress, and both have traditionally been viewed as forms of escape from that stress. In addition, a number of individuals suffer from both a somatoform and a dissociative disorder (Sar et al., 2004). Indeed, theorists and clinicians often explain and treat the two groups of disorders in similar ways. Because of such similarities, the two groups of disorders are commonly discussed together, as in this chapter.

Somatoform Disorders

Think back to Brian, the young man whose tragic boating accident left him unable to walk. As medical test after test failed to explain his paralysis, physicians became convinced that the cause of his problem lay elsewhere.

When a physical ailment has no apparent medical cause, doctors may suspect a **somatoform disorder,** a pattern of physical complaints with largely psychosocial causes (Mayou et al., 2005). People with such disorders do not consciously want or purposely produce their symptoms; like Brian, they almost always believe that their problems are genuinely medical (Abbey, 2005). In some somatoform disorders, known as *hysterical somatoform disorders,* there is an actual change in physical functioning. In others, the *preoccupation somatoform disorders,* people who are healthy mistakenly worry that there is something physically wrong with them.

What Are Hysterical Somatoform Disorders?

People with **hysterical somatoform disorders** suffer actual changes in their physical functioning. These somatoform disorders are often hard to distinguish from genuine medical problems (Fink et al., 2004). In fact, it is always possible that a diagnosis of hysterical disorder is a mistake and that the patient's problem has an undetected organic cause (Merskey, 2004). The tools of medical science are too imprecise to eliminate physical factors completely. DSM-IV-TR lists three hysterical somatoform disorders: *conversion disorder, somatization disorder,* and *pain disorder associated with psychological factors.*

CONVERSION DISORDER In **conversion disorder,** a psychosocial conflict or need is converted into dramatic physical symptoms that affect voluntary motor or sensory functioning (see Table 7-1 on page 192). Brian, the man with the unexplained paralysis, would probably receive this particular diagnosis. The symptoms often seem neurological, such as paralysis, blindness, or loss of feeling (*anesthesia*), and so may be called "pseudoneurological" (APA, 2000). One woman developed dizziness in apparent response to her unhappy marriage:

A 46-year-old married housewife . . . described being overcome with feelings of extreme dizziness, accompanied by slight nausea, four or five nights a week. During these attacks, the room around her would take on a "shimmering" appearance, and she would have the feeling that she was "floating" and unable to keep her balance. Inexplicably, the attacks almost always occurred at about 4:00 P.M. She usually had to lie down on the couch and often did not feel better until 7:00 or 8:00 P.M. After recovering, she generally spent the rest of the evening watching TV; and more often than not, she would fall asleep in the living room, not going to bed in the bedroom until 2:00 or 3:00 in the morning.

The patient had been pronounced physically fit by her internist, a neurologist, and an ear, nose, and throat specialist on more than one occasion. Hypoglycemia had been ruled out by glucose tolerance tests.

When asked about her marriage, the patient described her husband as a tyrant, frequently demanding and verbally abusive of her and their four children. She admitted that she dreaded his arrival home from work each day, knowing that he would comment that the house was a mess and the dinner, if prepared, not to his liking. Recently, since the onset of her attacks, when she was unable to make dinner he and the four kids would go to McDonald's or the local pizza parlor. After that, he would settle in to watch a ballgame in the bedroom, and their conversation was minimal. In spite of their troubles, the patient claimed that she loved her husband and needed him very much.

(Spitzer et al., 1981, pp. 92–93)

Most conversion disorders begin between late childhood and young adulthood; they are diagnosed at least twice as often in women as in men (Abbey, 2005; APA, 2000). They usually appear suddenly, at times of extreme stress, and last a matter of weeks. Some research suggests that people who develop this disorder tend to be generally suggestible; many are highly susceptible to hypnotic procedures, for example (Roelofs et al., 2002). Conversion disorders are thought to be quite rare, occurring in at most 5 of every 1,000 persons.

SOMATIZATION DISORDER Sheila baffled medical specialists with the wide range of her symptoms:

Sheila reported having abdominal pain since age 17, necessitating exploratory surgery that yielded no specific diagnosis. She had several pregnancies, each with severe nausea, vomiting, and abdominal pain; she ultimately had a hysterectomy for a "tipped uterus." Since age 40 she had experienced dizziness and "blackouts," which she eventually was told might be multiple sclerosis or a brain tumor. She continued to be bedridden for extended periods of time, with weakness, blurred vision, and difficulty urinating. At age 43 she was worked up for a hiatal hernia because of complaints of bloating and intolerance of a variety of foods. She also had additional hospitalizations for neurological, hypertensive, and renal workups, all of which failed to reveal a definitive diagnosis.

(Spitzer et al., 1981, pp. 185, 260)

Like Sheila, people with **somatization disorder** have many long-lasting physical ailments that have little or no organic basis (see again Table 7-1). This hysterical pattern, first described by Pierre Briquet in 1859, is also known as *Briquet's syndrome*. To receive this diagnosis, a person must have a range of ailments, including several pain symptoms (such as headaches and chest pain), gastrointestinal symptoms (such as nausea and diarrhea), a sexual symptom (such as erectile or menstrual difficulties), and a neurological symptom (such as double vision or paralysis) (APA, 2000). People with somatization disorder usually go from doctor to doctor in search of relief. They often describe their

•SOMATOFORM DISORDER• A physical illness or ailment that is explained largely by psychosocial causes, in which the patient experiences no sense of wanting or guiding the symptoms.

•HYSTERICAL SOMATOFORM DISORDERS• Somatoform disorders in which people suffer actual changes in their physical functioning.

•CONVERSION DISORDER• A somatoform disorder in which a psychosocial need or conflict is converted into dramatic physical symptoms that affect voluntary motor or sensory function.

•SOMATIZATION DISORDER• A somatoform disorder marked by numerous recurring physical ailments without an organic basis. Also known as *Briquet's syndrome*.

>>IN THEIR WORDS

"A cheerful heart is a good medicine, but a downcast spirit dries up the bones." <<
Proverbs 17:22

- -

"Pain is increased by attending to it." <<
Charles Darwin, *Expression of Emotions in Man and Animals* (1872)

- -

"It's no longer a question of staying healthy. It's a question of finding a sickness you like." <<
Jackie Mason, comedian

> ### Table 7-1 DSM Checklist
>
> **CONVERSION DISORDER**
>
> 1. One or more physical symptoms or deficits affecting voluntary motor or sensory function that suggest a neurological or other general medical condition.
> 2. Psychological factors judged to be associated with the symptom or deficit.
> 3. Symptom or deficit not intentionally produced or feigned.
> 4. Symptom or deficit not fully explained by a general medical condition or a substance.
> 5. Significant distress or impairment.
>
> **SOMATIZATION DISORDER**
>
> 1. A history of many physical complaints, beginning before the age of 30, that occur over a period of several years and result in treatment being sought or in significant impairment.
> 2. Physical complaints over the period include all of the following:
>   (a) Four different kinds of pain symptoms.
>   (b) Two gastrointestinal symptoms.
>   (c) One sexual symptom.
>   (d) One neurological-type symptom.
> 3. Physical complaints not fully explained by a known general medical condition or a drug, or extending beyond the usual impact of such a condition.
> 4. Symptoms not intentionally produced or feigned.
>
> **PAIN DISORDER ASSOCIATED WITH PSYCHOLOGICAL FACTORS**
>
> 1. Significant pain as the primary problem.
> 2. Psychological factors judged to have the major role in the onset, severity, exacerbation, or maintenance of the pain.
> 3. Symptom or deficit not intentionally produced or feigned.
> 4. Significant distress or impairment.
>
> Based on APA, 2000.

Mind over matter *The opposite of hysterical disorders—though again demonstrating the power of psychological processes—are instances in which people "ignore" pain or other physical symptoms. Despite incurring a number of significant injuries each season, Philadelphia 76ers basketball player Allen Iverson misses very few games and plays night after night at an extremely high level of accomplishment. Fans, fellow players, and sports writers alike marvel at his ability to put his various pains out of his mind during each game.*

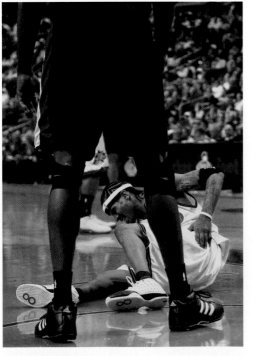

George Widman/AP Photo

many symptoms in dramatic and exaggerated terms. Most also feel anxious and depressed (Fink et al., 2004; APA, 2000).

Between 0.2 and 2.0 percent of all women in the United States may experience a somatization disorder in any given year, compared to less than 0.2 percent of men (Eifer & Zvolensky, 2005; North, 2005; APA, 2000). The disorder often runs in families; 10 to 20 percent of the close female relatives of women with the disorder also develop it. It usually begins between adolescence and young adulthood.

A somatization disorder lasts much longer than a conversion disorder, typically for many years. The symptoms may fluctuate over time but rarely disappear completely without therapy (Abbey, 2005; Smith, Rost, & Kashner, 1995). Two-thirds of individuals with this disorder in the United States receive treatment for their physical ailments from a medical or mental health professional in any given year (Regier et al., 1993).

PAIN DISORDER ASSOCIATED WITH PSYCHOLOGICAL FACTORS When psychosocial factors play a central role in the onset, severity, or continuation of pain, patients may receive a diagnosis of **pain disorder associated with psychological factors** (see again Table 7-1). Patients with a conversion or somatization disorder may also experience pain, but it is the key symptom in this disorder (Abbey, 2005).

Although the precise prevalence has not been determined, pain disorder associated with psychological factors appears to be fairly common (de Waal et al., 2004). The disorder may begin at any age, and women seem more likely than men to experience it (APA, 2000). Often it develops after an accident or during an illness that has caused genuine pain, which then takes on a life of its own. Laura, a 36-year-old woman, reported pains that went far beyond the usual symptoms of her tubercular disease, called sarcoidosis:

Before the operation I would have little joint pains, nothing that really bothered me that much. After the operation I was having severe pains in my chest and in my ribs, and those were the type of problems I'd been having after the operation, that I didn't have before. . . . I'd go to an emergency room at night, 11:00, 12:00, 1:00 or so. I'd take the medicine, and the next day it stopped hurting, and I'd go back again. In the meantime this is when I went to the other doctors, to complain about the same thing, to find out what was wrong; and they could never find out what was wrong with me either. . . .

. . . At certain points when I go out or my husband and I go out, we have to leave early because I start hurting. . . . A lot of times I just won't do things because my chest is hurting for one reason or another. . . . Two months ago when the doctor checked me and another doctor looked at the x-rays, he said he didn't see any signs of the sarcoid then and that they were doing a study now, on blood and various things, to see if it was connected to sarcoid. . . .

(Green, 1985, pp. 60–63)

HYSTERICAL VS. MEDICAL SYMPTOMS As we have observed, it can be difficult to distinguish hysterical somatoform disorders from "true" medical problems. Studies across the world suggest that as many as one-fifth of all patients who seek medical care from primary care physicians may actually suffer from somatoform disorders (deWaal et al., 2004; Fink et al., 2004). Because hysterical somatoform disorders are so similar to "genuine" medical ailments, physicians sometimes rely on oddities in the patient's medical picture to help distinguish the two (Abbey, 2005; Roelofs et al., 2002). The symptoms of a hysterical disorder may, for example, be at odds with the way the nervous system is known to work (APA, 2000). In a conversion symptom called *glove anesthesia,* numbness begins sharply at the wrist and extends evenly right to the fingertips. As Figure 7-1 shows, real neurological damage is rarely as abrupt or equally distributed.

The physical effects of a hysterical disorder may also differ from those of the corresponding medical problem. For example, when paralysis from the waist down, or paraplegia, is caused by damage to the spinal cord, a person's leg muscles may *atrophy,* or waste away, unless physical therapy is applied. People whose paralysis is the result of a conversion disorder, in contrast, do not usually experience atrophy. Perhaps they exercise their muscles without being aware that they are doing so. Similarly, people with conversion blindness have fewer accidents than people who are organically blind, an indication that they have at least some vision even if they are unaware of it.

HYSTERICAL VS. FACTITIOUS SYMPTOMS Hysterical somatoform disorders are different from patterns in which individuals are purposefully producing or faking medical symptoms. A patient may, for example, *malinger*—intentionally fake illness to achieve some external gain, such as financial compensation or deferment from military service. Or a patient may intentionally produce or fake physical symptoms simply out of a wish to be a patient; that is, the motivation for assuming the sick role may be the role itself. Physicians would then decide that the patient is displaying a **factitious disorder.**

A 29-year-old female laboratory technician was admitted to the medical service via the emergency room because of bloody urine. The patient said that she was being treated for lupus erythematosus by a physician in a different city. She also mentioned that she had had Von Willebrand's disease (a rare hereditary blood disorder) as a child. On the third day of her hospitalization, a medical student mentioned to the resident that she had seen this patient several weeks before at a different hospital in the area, where the patient had been admitted for the same problem. A search of the patient's belongings revealed a cache of anticoagulant medication. When confronted with this information she refused to discuss the matter and hurriedly signed out of the hospital against medical advice.

(Spitzer et al., 1981, p. 33)

•PAIN DISORDER ASSOCIATED WITH PSYCHOLOGICAL FACTORS•A somatoform disorder marked by pain, with psychosocial factors playing a central role in the onset, severity, or continuation of the pain.

•FACTITIOUS DISORDER•An illness with no identifiable physical cause, in which the patient is believed to be intentionally producing or faking symptoms in order to assume a sick role.

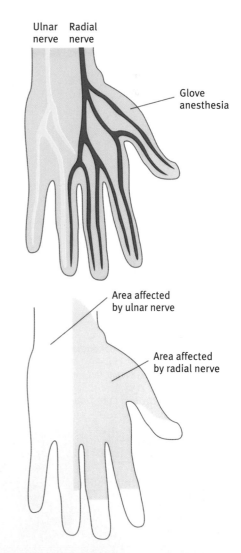

FIGURE **7-1 Glove anesthesia** *In this conversion symptom the entire hand, extending from the fingertips to the wrist, becomes numb. Actual physical damage to the ulnar nerve, in contrast, causes anesthesia in the ring finger and little finger and beyond the wrist partway up the arm; and damage to the radial nerve causes loss of feeling only in parts of the ring, middle, and index fingers and the thumb and partway up the arm. (Adapted from Gray, 1959.)*

•MUNCHAUSEN SYNDROME•The extreme and chronic form of factitious disorder.

•MUNCHAUSEN SYNDROME BY PROXY•A factitious disorder in which parents make up or produce illnesses in their children. Also known as *factitious disorder by proxy.*

•PREOCCUPATION SOMATOFORM DISORDERS•Disorders in which people misinterpret and overreact to minor, even normal, bodily symptoms or features.

•HYPOCHONDRIASIS•A disorder in which people mistakenly fear that minor changes in their physical functioning indicate a serious disease.

•BODY DYSMORPHIC DISORDER•A disorder marked by excessive worry that some aspect of one's physical appearance is defective. Also known as *dysmorphophobia.*

An extreme case of *hypochondriasis?* *Not necessarily. After the 1918 flu epidemic killed 20 million people, people in Japan started wearing a masuku to protect them from stray germs. Some, like this commuter, continue the tradition during cold and flu season.*

Torlin Boyd Photo, Tokyo, Japan

People with a factitious disorder often go to extremes to create the appearance of illness (Ford, 2005; Phillips, 2001). Many give themselves medications secretly. Some, like the woman just described, inject drugs to cause bleeding. High fevers are especially easy to create. In one study of patients with prolonged mysterious fever, more than 9 percent were eventually diagnosed with factitious disorder (Feldman, Ford, & Reinhold, 1994). People with a factitious disorder often research their supposed ailments and are impressively knowledgeable about medicine. When confronted with evidence that their symptoms are factitious, they typically deny the charges and go to another doctor or hospital.

Clinical researchers have had a hard time determining the prevalence of factitious disorder, since patients hide the true nature of their problem. Overall, the pattern is apparently more common in women than men (Ford, 2005; APA, 2000). Severe cases, however, seem to be more frequent among men. The disorder usually begins during early adulthood.

Factitious disorder seems to be most common among people who (1) as children received extensive medical treatment for a true physical disorder; (2) experienced family disruptions or physical or emotional abuse in childhood; (3) carry a grudge against the medical profession; (4) have worked as a nurse, laboratory technician, or medical aide; or (5) have an underlying personality problem such as extreme dependence (Ford, 2005; APA, 2000; Feldman et al., 1994). They often have limited social support, few enduring social relationships, and little family life.

Psychotherapists and medical practitioners often become angry at people with a factitious disorder, feeling that these individuals are, among other issues, wasting their time. Yet people with this disorder, like most persons with psychological disorders, feel they have no control over their problem, and they often experience great distress.

Munchausen syndrome is the extreme and long-term form of factitious disorder. It is named after Baron Munchausen, an eighteenth-century cavalry officer who journeyed from tavern to tavern in Europe telling fantastical tales about his supposed military adventures (Ford, 2005; Feldman, 2004). In a related disorder, **Munchausen syndrome by proxy,** or **factitious disorder by proxy,** parents make up or produce physical illnesses in their children, leading in some cases to repeated painful diagnostic tests, medication, and surgery (see Box 7-1).

What Are Preoccupation Somatoform Disorders?

Hypochondriasis and *body dysmorphic disorder* are **preoccupation somatoform disorders.** People with these problems misinterpret and overreact to bodily symptoms or features no matter what friends, relatives, and physicians may say. Although preoccupation disorders also cause great distress, their impact on one's life differs from that of hysterical disorders.

HYPOCHONDRIASIS People who suffer from **hypochondriasis** unrealistically interpret bodily symptoms as signs of a serious illness (see Table 7-2 on page 196). Often their symptoms are merely normal bodily changes, such as occasional coughing, sores, or sweating. Although some patients recognize that their concerns are excessive, many do not.

Hypochondriasis can present a picture very similar to that of somatization disorder (Fink et al., 2004; Noyes, 2003, 2001, 1999). Each typically involves numerous physical symptoms and frequent visits to doctors, and each causes considerable upset. If the anxiety is great and the bodily symptoms are relatively minor, a diagnosis of hypochondriasis is probably in order; if the symptoms overshadow the patient's anxiety, they may indicate somatization disorder.

Although hypochondriasis can begin at any age, it starts most often in early adulthood, among men and women in equal numbers. Between 1 and 5 percent of all people experience the disorder (Abbey, 2005; Eifert & Zvolensky, 2005; APA, 2000). As with pain disorder associated with psychological factors, physicians report seeing many cases (Mitchell, 2004). As many as 5 percent of all patients seen by primary care physicians may display hypochondriasis (Fink et al., 2004). For most patients, the symptoms rise and fall over the years.

[BOX **7-1**]

Munchausen Syndrome by Proxy

I *[Jennifer] had been hospitalized 200 times and undergone 40 operations. Physicians removed her gallbladder, her appendix and part of her intestines, and inserted tubes into her chest, stomach and intestines. [The 9-year-old from Florida] was befriended by the Florida Marlins and served as a poster child for health care reform, posing with Hillary Rodham Clinton at a White House rally. Then police notified her mother that she was under investigation for child abuse. Suddenly, Jennifer's condition improved dramatically. In the next nine months, she was hospitalized only once, for a viral infection. . . . Experts said Jennifer's numerous baffling infections were "consistent with someone smearing fecal matter" into her feeding line and urinary catheter.* **I**

(KATEL & BECK, 1996)

Christopher Wood Gallery, London, Bridgeman/Art Resource, NY

Convalescent, *1994, by Frank Holl*

ases like Jennifer's have horrified the public and called attention to *Munchausen syndrome by proxy,* a pattern first identified in 1977. This disorder is caused by a caregiver who uses various techniques to induce symptoms in a child—giving the child drugs, tampering with medications, contaminating a feeding tube, or even smothering the child, for example. The illness can take almost any form, but the most common symptoms are bleeding, seizures, asthma, comas, diarrhea, vomiting, "accidental" poisonings, infections, fevers, and sudden infant death syndrome (Feldman, 2004; Plunkett & Southall, 2001; Boros et al., 1995).

Between 6 and 30 percent of the victims of Munchausen syndrome by proxy die as a result of their symptoms, and 8 percent of those who survive are permanently disfigured or physically impaired

(Mitchell, 2001; Von Burg & Hibbard, 1995). Psychological, educational, and physical development are also affected (Libow & Schreier, 1998; Libow, 1995). Jennifer missed so much school that at age 9 she could barely read or write.

The syndrome is very hard to diagnose and may be more common than clinicians once thought (Feldman, 2004; Rogers, 2004). The parent (usually the mother) seems to be so devoted and caring that others sympathize with and admire her (Abdulhamid, 2002). Yet the physical problems disappear when child and parent are separated. In many cases siblings of the sick child have also been victimized (Skau & Mouridsen, 1995).

What kind of parent carefully inflicts pain and illness on her own child? The typical Munchausen mother is emotionally needy: she craves the attention and praise she receives for her devoted care of her sick child (Noeker, 2004). She may have little social support outside the medical

system. Many of these mothers are intelligent; often they have a medical background of some kind—perhaps having worked formerly in a doctor's office. Typically they deny their actions, even in the face of clear evidence, and refuse to undergo therapy. In fact, to date, successful treatment has been uncommon (Bluglass, 2001; Ayoub et al., 2000).

Law enforcement authorities are reluctant to consider Munchausen syndrome by proxy a psychological disorder and instead approach it as a crime—a carefully planned form of child abuse (Mart, 2004). They almost always require that the child be separated from the mother (Ayoub et al., 2000). At the same time, a parent who resorts to such actions is obviously experiencing serious psychological disturbance and greatly needs clinical help. Thus clinical researchers and practitioners must now work to develop clearer insights and more effective treatments for such parents and for their small victims.

BODY DYSMORPHIC DISORDER People who experience **body dysmorphic disorder,** also known as **dysmorphophobia,** become deeply concerned about some imagined or minor defect in their appearance (see again Table 7-2). Most often they focus on wrinkles, spots on the skin, excessive facial hair, swelling of the face, or a misshapen nose, mouth, jaw, or eyebrow (Veale, 2004). Some worry about the appearance of their feet, hands, breasts, penis, or other body parts (see Box 7-2 on page 197). Still others are concerned about bad odors coming from sweat, breath, genitals, or the rectum (Phillips & Castle, 2002). Here we see such a case:

Table 7-2 DSM Checklist

HYPOCHONDRIASIS

1. Preoccupation with fears or beliefs that one has a serious disease, based on misinterpretation of bodily symptoms, lasting at least six months.
2. Persistence of preoccupation despite appropriate medical evaluation and reassurance.
3. Absence of delusions.
4. Significant distress or impairment.

BODY DYSMORPHIC DISORDER

1. Preoccupation with an imagined or exaggerated defect in appearance.
2. Significant distress or impairment.

Based on APA, 2000.

Frown lines disappear *A plastic surgeon injects* Botox (Botulinum Toxin Type A) *into the muscles between a patient's eyebrows, hoping to eliminate her so-called frown lines. A cautionary note: as many as 15 percent of people who seek help from cosmetic surgery or dermatologists are believed to have body dysmorphic disorder (APA, 2000).*

A woman of 35 had for 16 years been worried that her sweat smelled terrible. The fear began just before her marriage when she was sharing a bed with a close friend who said that someone at work smelled badly, and the patient felt that the remark was directed at her. For fear that she smelled, for 5 years she had not gone out anywhere except when accompanied by her husband or mother. She had not spoken to her neighbors for 3 years because she thought she had overheard them speak about her to some friends. She avoided cinemas, dances, shops, cafes, and private homes. . . . Her husband was not allowed to invite any friends home; she constantly sought reassurance from him about her smell. . . . Her husband bought all her new clothes as she was afraid to try on clothes in front of shop assistants. She used vast quantities of deodorant and always bathed and changed her clothes before going out, up to 4 times daily.

(Marks, 1987, p. 371)

It is common in our society to worry about appearance. Many teenagers and young adults worry about acne, for instance. The concerns of people with body dysmorphic disorder, however, are extreme. Sufferers may severely limit contact with other people, be unable to look others in the eye, or go to great lengths to conceal their "defects"—say, always wearing sunglasses to cover their supposedly misshapen eyes (Phillips, 2005; Veale, 2004). As many as half of people with this disorder seek plastic surgery or dermatology treatment, and often they feel worse rather than better afterward (Miller, 2005). One study found that 30 percent of subjects with body dysmorphic disorder were housebound and 17 percent had attempted suicide (Phillips et al., 1993).

Most cases of the disorder begin during adolescence. Often, however, people don't reveal their concerns for many years. Up to 2 percent of people in the United States—4 percent of college students—suffer from body dysmorphic disorder (Miller, 2005; Ovsiew, 2006; Bohne et al., 2002). Clinical reports suggest that it may be equally common among men and women (APA, 2000).

What Causes Somatoform Disorders?

Theorists typically explain the preoccupation somatoform disorders much as they do anxiety disorders (Miller, 2004; Noyes, 2003, 2001, 1999). Behaviorists, for example, believe that the fears found in hypochondriasis and body dysmorphic disorder are acquired through classical conditioning or modeling (see Figure 7-2 on the facing page and Table 7-3 on page 198). Cognitive theorists suggest that people with the disorders are so sensitive to and threatened by bodily cues that they come to misinterpret them.

In contrast, the hysterical somatoform disorders—conversion, somatization, and pain disorders—are widely considered unique and in need of special explanations. The ancient Greeks believed that only women had hysterical disorders. The uterus of a sexually

≫PSYCH•LISTINGS:

Leading Cosmetic Procedures in the United States Annually

Nonsurgical procedures
• Botox injection (2,837,346 procedures)
• Laser hair removal (1,411,899)
• Chemical peel (1,110,401)
• Microdermabrasion (1,098,316)
• Hyaluronic acid (882,469) ≪

Surgical procedures
• Liposuction (478,251)
• Breast augmentation (334,052)
• Eyelid surgery (290,343)
• Rhinoplasty (reshape nose) (166,187)
• Facelift (157,061) ≪

(American Society for Aesthetic Plastic Surgery, 2004)

[BOX **7-2**]

Beauty Is in the Eye of the Beholder (and the Culture)

People almost everywhere want to be attractive, and they tend to worry about how they appear in the eyes of others. At the same time, these concerns take different forms in different cultures.

Whereas people in Western society worry in particular about their body size and facial features, women of the Padaung tribe in Burma focus on the length of their neck and wear heavy stacks of brass rings to try to extend it. Many of them seek desperately to achieve what their culture has taught them is the perfect neck size. Said one, "It is most beautiful when the neck is really long. The longer it is, the more beautiful it is. I will never take off my rings . . . I'll be buried in them" (Mydans, 1996).

Similarly, for centuries women of China, in response to the preferences and demands of men in that country, worried greatly about the size and appearance of their feet and practiced *foot binding* to stop the growth of these extremities (Wang Ping, 2000). In this procedure, which began in the year 900 and was widely practiced until it was outlawed in 1911, young girls were instructed to tightly wrap a long bandage around their feet each day, forcing the four toes under the sole of the foot. The procedure, which was carried out for about two years, caused the feet to become narrower and smaller. Typically the practice led to serious medical problems and poor mobility, but it did produce the small feet that were considered attractive.

Western culture is far from immune to such cultural influences. Past decades have witnessed staggering increases in such procedures as *rhinoplasty* (reshaping of the nose), *breast augmentation,* and *body piercing*—all reminders that cultural values greatly influence each person's ideas about and concerns about beauty, and in some cases may set the stage for body dysmorphic disorder.

Steve McCurry/Magnum Photos

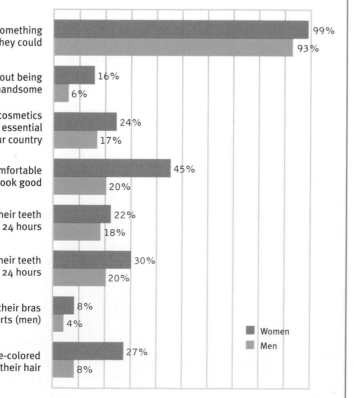

People who would change something about their appearance if they could — 99% / 93%

People who daydream about being beautiful or handsome — 16% / 6%

People who think that the cosmetics industry is very important or essential to our country — 24% / 17%

People who wear uncomfortable shoes because they look good — 45% / 20%

People who have brushed their teeth twice in the last 24 hours — 22% / 18%

People who have flossed their teeth in the last 24 hours — 30% / 20%

People who have stuffed their bras (women) or shorts (men) — 8% / 4%

People who have bottle-colored their hair — 27% / 8%

■ Women
■ Men

FIGURE 7-2 "Mirror, mirror, on the wall . . ." *People with body dysmorphic disorder are not the only ones who have concerns about their appearance. Surveys find that in our appearance-conscious society, large percentages of people regularly think about and try to change the way they look (Noonan, 2003; Kimball, 1993; Poretz & Sinrod, 1991; Weiss, 1991; Simmon, 1990).*

•**PRIMARY GAIN**•In psychodynamic theory, the gain achieved when hysterical symptoms keep internal conflicts out of awareness.

•**SECONDARY GAIN**•In psychodynamic theory, the gain achieved when hysterical symptoms elicit kindness from others or provide an excuse to avoid unpleasant activities.

Table 7-3

When Did Body and Beauty Aids Make Their Debuts?

4000 B.C.	Egypt produces the first eye glitter, blue and black lipstick, rouge, and other cosmetics for women and men.
3000 B.C.	Fingernail paint originates in China. Creams, oils, and moisturizers are developed in Egypt. The art of wigmaking is developed in Egypt. Sumerians (in Mesopotamia) and Egyptians make the transition from incense to perfumes.
1500 B.C.	Assyria perfects the art of hair styling.
303 B.C.	The first professional barbers, formed into guilds, open shops in Rome.
A.D. 157	The Greek physician Galen develops the first cold cream.
1600–1700	Beauty patches (shaped like stars, crescent moons, hearts) are purchased throughout Europe to cover up scars left by smallpox.
1709	The Italian barber Jean-Baptiste Farina concocts an alcohol-based blend of fruits in Cologne, Germany—a product thereafter known by the name of the city.
1882	The Dutch immigrant Andrew Jergens forms a company to make prestigious toilet soap and later best-selling Jergens lotion.
1886	The door-to-door salesman David McConnell launches Avon Calling in New York State.
1909	The French chemist Eugène Schueller develops the first safe commercial hair dye.

ungratified woman was supposed to wander throughout her body in search of fulfill-ment, producing a physical symptom wherever it lodged. Thus Hippocrates suggested marriage as the most effective treatment for such disorders.

Work by Ambroise-Auguste Liébault and Hippolyte Bernheim in the late nine-teenth century set the stage for today's prevailing opinion that psychosocial factors cause hysterical disorders. These researchers founded the Nancy School in Paris for the study and treatment of mental disorders. There they were able to produce hysterical symp-toms in normal people—deafness, paralysis, blindness, and numbness—by hypnotic sug-gestion, and they could remove the symptoms by the same means (see Chapter 1). If hypnotic suggestion could both produce and reverse physical dysfunctioning, they con-cluded, hysterical disorders might themselves be caused by psychological processes.

Today's leading explanations for hysterical somatoform disorders come from the psy-chodynamic, behavioral, and cognitive models. None have received much research sup-port, however, and the disorders are still poorly understood (Eifert & Zvolensky, 2005; Kirmayer et al., 2004, 1994).

THE PSYCHODYNAMIC VIEW As we observed in Chapter 1, Freud's theory of psy-choanalysis began with his efforts to explain hysterical symptoms. Indeed, he was one of the few clinicians of his day to treat patients with these symptoms seriously, as peo-ple with a genuine problem. After studying hypnosis in Paris and becoming acquainted with the work of Liébault and Bernheim, Freud became interested in the work of an older physician, Josef Breuer (1842–1925). Breuer had successfully used hypnosis to treat a woman he called Anna O., who suffered from hysterical deafness, disorganized speech, and paralysis. Critics have since questioned whether Anna's ailments were entirely hys-terical and whether Breuer's treatment helped her as much as he claimed (Ellenberger, 1972). But on the basis of this and similar cases, Freud (1894) came to believe that hys-terical disorders represented a *conversion* of underlying emotional conflicts into physical symptoms.

>>**PSYCH•NOTES**

Diagnostic Confusion

Many medical problems with vague or con-fusing symptoms—**hyperparathyroidism, multiple sclerosis, lupus, and chronic fatigue syndrome** are examples—are frequently misdiagnosed as hysterical somatoform dis-orders. In the past, **whiplash** was regularly diagnosed as hysteria (Nemecek, 1996; Merskey, 1986). <<

Observing that most of his patients with hysterical disorders were women, Freud centered his explanation of hysterical disorders on the needs of girls during their *phallic stage* (ages 3 through 5). At that time in life, he believed, all girls develop a pattern of desires called the *Electra complex:* each girl experiences sexual feelings for her father and at the same time recognizes that she must compete with her mother for his affection. However, aware of her mother's more powerful position and of cultural taboos, the child typically represses her sexual feelings and rejects these early desires for her father.

Freud believed that if a child's parents overreact to her sexual feelings—with strong punishments, for example—the Electra conflict will be unresolved and the child may reexperience sexual anxiety throughout her life. Whenever events trigger sexual feelings, she may experience an unconscious need to hide them from both herself and others. Freud concluded that some women hide their sexual feelings by unconsciously converting them into physical symptoms.

Most of today's psychodynamic theorists take issue with Freud's explanation of hysterical disorders, particularly his notion that the disorders can always be traced to an unresolved Electra conflict (Hess, 1995; Scott, 1995). They continue to believe, however, that sufferers of these disorders have unconscious conflicts carried forth from childhood which arouse anxiety and that the individuals convert this anxiety into "more tolerable" physical symptoms (Brown et al., 2005; Hawkins, 2004). Consistent with this belief, studies have found that people with the disorders often have childhood histories of trauma, abuse, or neglect (Sar et al., 2004; Noyes et al., 2002).

Psychodynamic theorists propose that two mechanisms are at work in hysterical somatoform disorders—primary gain and secondary gain (van Egmond, 2003). People achieve **primary gain** when their hysterical symptoms keep their internal conflicts out of awareness. During an argument, for example, a man who has underlying fears about expressing anger may develop a conversion paralysis of the arm, thus preventing his feelings of rage from reaching consciousness. People achieve **secondary gain** when their hysterical symptoms further enable them to avoid unpleasant activities or to receive kindness or sympathy from others. When, for example, a conversion paralysis allows a soldier to avoid combat duty or conversion blindness prevents the breakup of a relationship, secondary gain may be operating. Similarly, the conversion paralysis of Brian, the man who lost his wife in the boating accident, seemed to help him avoid many painful duties after the accident, from telling his wife's parents of her death to attending her funeral and returning to work. In short, primary gains initiate hysterical symptoms; secondary gains are by-products of the symptoms. Both forms of gain help to lock in the conversion symptoms, according to psychodynamic theorists.

THE BEHAVIORAL VIEW Behavioral theorists propose that the physical symptoms of hysterical disorders bring *rewards* to sufferers (see Table 7-4 on the next page). Perhaps the symptoms remove the individuals from an unpleasant work situation or relationship or bring attention from other people (Whitehead et al., 1994). In response to such rewards, the sufferers learn to display the symptoms more and more prominently. Behaviorists also hold that people who are familiar with an illness will more readily adopt its physical symptoms (Garralda, 1996). In fact, studies find that many sufferers develop their hysterical symptoms after they or their close relatives or friends have had similar medical problems (Stuart & Noyes, 1999).

The behavioral focus on rewards is similar to the psychodynamic idea of secondary gains. The key difference is that psychodynamic theorists view the gains as indeed secondary—that is, as rewards that come only after underlying conflicts produce the disorder. Behaviorists view them as the primary cause of the development of the disorder.

Like the psychodynamic explanation, the behavioral view of hysterical disorders has received little research support. Even clinical case reports only occasionally support this position. In many cases the pain and upset that surround the disorders seem to outweigh any rewards the symptoms may bring.

Electra complex goes awry *Freud argued that a hysterical disorder may result when parents overreact to their daughter's early displays of affection for her father. The child may go on to exhibit sexual repression in adulthood and convert sexual feelings into physical ailments.*

>>**LOOKING AROUND**

Trying to Gain on Pain

Around 1 in 6 Americans suffers from chronic or recurrent pain. ‹‹

According to studies, half of Americans with chronic or recurrent pain have not found a satisfying solution for the pain. ‹‹

Chronic pain is the leading cause of lost workdays. ‹‹

The leading pain-management clinics in the world typically include four elements: pain medications, injection treatments, physical therapy and exercise, and psychological techniques such as relaxation training, biofeedback, and psychotherapy. ‹‹

Insurers are more willing to reimburse the physical treatments for pain than the psychological ones. Thus, many pain patients at pain-management centers must pay out of pocket for the psychological elements of their treatment. ‹‹

(Wallis, 2005)

Phantom limb syndrome *While hiking in Utah, Aron Ralston's arm became pinned under a boulder and he had to amputate it himself. People who have lost their limbs often continue to feel pain and other sensations where their limbs used to be. Initially, such "phantom" pain was thought to reflect a somatoform pain disorder. However, neuroscientists have since discovered that even after amputation, brain areas that used to trigger sensations in the limbs remain intact and may sometimes produce sensations where the missing limbs used to be.*

Table 7-4

Disorders That Have Physical Symptoms

Disorder	Voluntary Control of Symptoms?	Symptoms Linked to Psychosocial Factor?	An Apparent Goal?
Malingering	Yes	Maybe	Yes
Factitious disorder	Yes	Yes	No*
Somatoform disorder	No	Yes	Maybe
Psychophysiological disorder	No	Yes	Maybe
Physical illness	No	Maybe	No

*Except for medical attention.
Source: Adapted from Hyler & Spitzer, 1978.

THE COGNITIVE VIEW Some cognitive theorists propose that hysterical disorders are forms of *communication,* providing a means for people to express emotions that would otherwise be difficult to convey (Mitchell, 2004). Like their psychodynamic colleagues, these theorists hold that the emotions of patients with hysterical disorders are being converted into physical symptoms. They suggest, however, that the purpose of the conversion is not to defend against anxiety but to communicate extreme feelings—anger, fear, depression, guilt, jealousy—in a "physical language" that is familiar and comfortable for the patient (Koh et al., 2005; Fry, 1993).

According to this view, people who find it particularly hard to recognize or express their emotions are candidates for a hysterical disorder. So are those who "know" the language of physical symptoms through firsthand experience with a genuine physical malady. Because children are less able to express their emotions verbally, they are particularly likely to develop physical symptoms as a form of communication (Dhossche et al., 2002). Similarly, members of certain ethnic groups, where somatic reactions are accepted and even valued, may be particularly likely to display physical symptoms in the face of stress (see Box 7-3). Like the other explanations, this cognitive view has not been widely tested or supported by research.

A POSSIBLE ROLE FOR BIOLOGY Although hysterical somatoform disorders are, by definition, thought to result largely from psychosocial factors, the impact of biological processes should not be overlooked (Ovsiew, 2006; Gatchel & Maddrey, 2004). To understand this point, consider first what researchers have learned about *placebos* and the *placebo effect.*

For centuries physicians have observed that patients suffering from many kinds of illnesses, from seasickness to angina, often find relief from **placebos,** substances that have no known medicinal value (Sauro & Greenberg, 2005; Brody, 2000). Some reviews have raised questions about the actual number of patients helped by placebos (Hrobjartsson & Goltzsche, 2001), but it is generally agreed that such "pretend" treatments do bring help to many people.

Why do placebos have a medicinal effect? Theorists used to believe that they operated in purely psychological ways—that the power of suggestion worked almost magically upon the body. More recently, however, researchers have found that a belief or expectation can trigger certain chemicals throughout the body into action, and these chemicals then may produce a medicinal effect (Sauro & Greenberg, 2005). The body chemicals most often implicated are *hormones* and *lymphocytes,* chemicals that we observed at work in Chapter 6, and *endorphins,* natural opioid substances that we shall examine in Chapter 12. Howard Brody, a leading theorist on the subject, compares the placebo effect to visiting a pharmacy:

•**PLACEBO**•A sham treatment that a patient believes to be genuine.

[BOX 7-3]

Sociocultural Landscape: Somatization and Coping

*S*omatization, the development of somatic symptoms in response to personal distress, is typically considered inappropriate in Western countries (Escobar, 2004). Indeed, many sociocultural theorists argue that a bias exists in Western clinical circles against somatization—a bias that views somatic symptoms as an inferior way of dealing with emotions and psychological coping mechanisms as a superior response to traumatic events (Moldavsky, 2004; Fabrega, 1990).

In fact, however, the transformation of personal distress into somatic complaints is the norm in most non-Western cultures (Escobar, 2004; Kleinman, 1987). Not only is somatization common in such cultures; it is usually viewed as a socially and medically correct—and less stigmatizing—reaction to life's stressors (Shorter 1994).

International studies have detected very high rates of somatization in non-Western medical practices thoughout the world, with patients in Latin countries displaying the largest number of such symptoms (Escobar, 2004, 1995; Escobar et al., 1998, 1992; Gureje et al., 1997). Even within the United States, people from Hispanic cultures display more somatic symptoms in the face of stress than do other populations.

In Chapter 6 we observed that posttraumatic stress disorder may be more common among Hispanic Americans than among other ethnic groups in the United States (see page 163). Interestingly, research clarifies that this trend exists only among Hispanic Americans who were born in the United States or have lived in the United States for a number of years

(Escobar, 2004, 1998). In fact, *recent* Latin and other immigrants in the United States display a *lower* rate of posttraumatic stress disorder than do other individuals thoughout the country. It may be that recent immigrants, not yet influenced by the Western bias against somatization, deal with traumatic events by expressing their overwhelming feelings largely through familiar somatic symptoms.

The lesson to be learned from all this is not that somatic reactions to stress are superior to psychological ones or vice versa, but rather that reactions to life's stressors are influenced in large part by one's culture. Overlooking this point can lead to knee-jerk mislabels or misdiagnoses.

Our bodies are capable of producing many substances that can heal a wide variety of illnesses, and make us feel generally healthier and more energized. When the body simply secretes these substances on its own, we have what is often termed "spontaneous healing." Some of the time, our bodies seem slow to react, and a message from outside can serve as a wake-up call to our inner pharmacy. The placebo response can thus be seen as the reaction of our inner pharmacies to that wake-up call.

(Brody, 2000, p. 61)

If placebos can "wake up" our inner pharmacies in this way, perhaps traumatic events and related concerns or needs are doing the same thing (although in a negative way) in cases of conversion disorder, somatization disorder, or pain disorder associated with psychological factors. That is, such events and reactions may, in fact, be triggering our inner pharmacies and setting in motion the bodily symptoms of hysterical somatoform disorders.

How Are Somatoform Disorders Treated?

People with somatoform disorders usually seek psychotherapy only as a last resort. They fully believe that their problems are medical and at first reject all suggestions to the contrary (Barsky, 2005; Miller, 2005). When a physician tells them that their problems have no physical basis, they often go to another physician. Eventually, however, many patients with these disorders do consent to psychotherapy, psychotropic drug therapy, or both.

Individuals with preoccupation somatoform disorders typically receive the kinds of treatment that are applied to generalized anxiety disorder or obsessive–compulsive disorder (Barksy & Ahern, 2004; Miller, 2004). Studies reveal, for example, that many patients with body dysmorphic disorder improve considerably when treated with the particular *antidepressant drugs*

"If this doesn't help you don't worry, it's a placebo."

Worldwide influence *A lingerie advertisement in a center city subway station in Shanghai, China, displays a woman in a push-up bra. As West increasingly meets East, Asian women have been bombarded by ads and TV shows encouraging them to undergo Western-like cosmetic surgery, from facial changes (the most common procedures) to changes in other body parts. The number of Asian women who pursue cosmetic surgery has increased about sevenfold during the past 20 years, and over one-third of Asian women now say that they would like to have cosmetic surgery (Hakuhodo Institute of Life and Living, 2001).*

•**MEMORY**•The faculty for recalling past events and past learning.

•**DISSOCIATIVE DISORDERS**•Disorders marked by major changes in memory that do not have clear physical causes.

that are also helpful in cases of obsessive-compulsive disorder (Ovsiew, 2006; Phillips, 2005; Fallon, 2004). Similarly, in one study, 17 patients with body dysmorphic disorder were treated with *exposure and response prevention*—the behavioral approach that often helps persons with obsessive-compulsive disorder. Over the course of four weeks, the clients were repeatedly reminded of their perceived physical defects and prevented from doing anything (for example, checking their appearance) to help reduce their discomfort (Neziroglu et al., 1996). By the end of treatment, they were less concerned with their "defects" and spent less time checking their body parts, looking in the mirror, and avoiding social interactions. Increasingly, this kind of behavioral approach is being combined with a cognitive approach that further helps clients identify, test, and change their distorted thoughts about their appearance and their social impact (Geremia & Neziroglu, 2001). The effectiveness of these various treatments, however, has yet to be tested widely (Fallon, 2004; Looper & Kirmayer, 2002).

Treatments for hysterical somatoform disorders—conversion, somatization, and pain disorders—focus either on the *cause* of the disorder (the trauma or anxiety behind the physical symptoms) or the physical *symptoms* themselves. Clinicians who address the cause use the same kinds of techniques used in cases of posttraumatic stress disorder, particularly insight, exposure, and drug therapies. Psychodynamic therapists, for example, try to help individuals become conscious of and resolve their underlying fears and anxiety-arousing conflicts, thus eliminating the need to convert anxiety into physical symptoms (Hawkins, 2004; Milrod, 2002). Alternatively, behavioral therapists use exposure treatments: they have clients think about or actually approach features of the traumatic events that have triggered their physical symptoms. With increasing exposure, the individuals are expected to become less anxious and, in turn, more able to face the upsetting events directly rather than through physical channels (Ciano-Federoff & Sperry, 2005). And biological therapists use antianxiety drugs or certain antidepressant drugs to help reduce the clients' anxiety (Turkington et al., 2002). Of course, clients will not usually agree to such approaches until they entertain the possibility that their physical ailments are rooted in trauma and anxiety.

Therapists who concentrate on the physical symptoms of hysterical disorders typically use techniques involving *suggestion, reinforcement,* or *confrontation.* Those who employ *suggestion* offer emotional support to patients and tell them persuasively that their physical symptoms will soon disappear (Anooshian et al., 1999), or they suggest the same thing to them under hypnosis (Moene et al., 2002). Therapists who take a *reinforcement* approach arrange the removal of rewards for a client's "sick" behaviors and an increase of rewards for healthy behaviors (North, 2005). And therapists who take a *confrontational* approach try to force patients out of the sick role by straightforwardly telling them that their symptoms are without medical basis (Sjolie, 2002).

Researchers have not systematically evaluated the effects of these various approaches on hysterical disorders (Ciano-Federoff & Sperry, 2005; Moene et al., 2002). Case studies suggest, however, that conversion disorder and pain disorder respond better to therapy than does somatization disorder and that approaches using a confrontational strategy are less helpful than the other kinds of intervention (Miller, 2004).

Dissociative Disorders

Most of us experience a sense of wholeness and continuity as we interact with the world. We perceive ourselves as being more than a random collection of isolated sensory experiences, feelings, and behaviors. In other words, we have an *identity,* a sense of who we are and where we fit in our environment. Others recognize us and expect certain things of us. But more important, we recognize ourselves and have our own expectations, values, and goals.

Memory is a key to this sense of identity, the link between our past, present, and future. Our recall of past experiences, although not always precisely accurate, helps us react to present events and guides us in making decisions about the future. We recognize our friends and relatives, teachers and employers, and respond to them in appropriate ways. Without a memory, we would always be starting over; with it, life moves forward.

People sometimes experience a major disruption of their memory, identity, or consciousness. They may, for example, lose their ability to remember new information they just learned or old information they once knew well. When such changes in memory lack a clear physical cause, they are called **dissociative disorders.** In such disorders, one part of the person's memory typically seems to be *dissociated,* or separated, from the rest.

There are several kinds of dissociative disorders. The primary symptom of *dissociative amnesia* is an inability to recall important personal events and information. A person with *dissociative fugue* not only forgets the past but also travels to a new location and may assume a new identity. Individuals with *dissociative identity disorder* (also known as *multiple personality disorder*) have two or more separate identities that may not always be aware of each other's thoughts, feelings, and behavior.

Several memorable books and movies have portrayed dissociative disorders. Two of the best known are *The Three Faces of Eve* and *Sybil,* each about a woman with multiple personalities. The topic is so fascinating that most television drama series seem to include at least one case of dissociation every season, creating the impression that the disorders are very common. Many clinicians, however, believe that they are rare.

DSM-IV-TR also lists *depersonalization disorder* as a dissociative disorder. People with this problem feel as though they have become detached from their own mental processes or body and are observing themselves from the outside. This listing is controversial because the memories and identities of people with depersonalization disorder seem to remain intact. It is their sense of self that changes: their mental processes or bodies feel unreal or foreign to them. We shall examine this disorder at the close of the chapter. Outside of that discussion, however, "dissociative disorders" will refer to those problems that involve clear changes in memory and identity: dissociative amnesia, dissociative fugue, and dissociative identity disorder.

As you read this chapter, keep in mind that dissociative symptoms are often found in cases of acute or posttraumatic stress disorder. Recall from Chapter 6 that sufferers of those disorders may feel dazed, have trouble remembering things, or experience a sense of unreality. When such symptoms occur as part of a stress disorder, they do not necessarily indicate a dissociative disorder—a pattern in which the dissociative symptoms dominate. On the other hand, research suggests that a number of people with one of these disorders also develop the other as well. A study of Vietnam combat veterans, for example, found that the majority of individuals with posttraumatic stress disorder further qualified for a diagnosis of a dissociative disorder (Bremner, 2002; Bremner & Brett, 1997).

Dissociative Amnesia

At the beginning of this chapter we met the unfortunate man named Brian. As you will recall, Brian developed a conversion disorder after a traumatic boating accident in which his wife was killed. To help us examine dissociative amnesia, let us now revisit that case, but change the reactions and symptoms that Brian develops in the aftermath of the traumatic event.

Brian was spending Saturday sailing with his wife, Helen. The water was rough but well within what they considered safe limits. They were having a wonderful time and really didn't notice that the sky was getting darker, the wind blowing harder, and the sailboat becoming more difficult to control. After a few hours of

"The motion has been made and seconded that we stick our heads in the sand."

Mischa Richter/Cartoonbank.com

At risk *The stunned looks on the faces of these soldiers suggest confusion, shock, and exhaustion. Combat soldiers are particularly vulnerable to amnesia and other dissociative reactions. They may forget specific horrors, personal information, or even their identities.*

Bettmann/Corbis

sailing, they found themselves far from shore in the middle of a powerful and dangerous storm.

The storm intensified very quickly. Brian had trouble controlling the sailboat amidst the high winds and wild waves. He and Helen tried to put on the safety jackets they had neglected to wear earlier, but the boat turned over before they were finished. Brian, the better swimmer of the two, was able to swim back to the overturned sailboat, grab the side, and hold on for dear life, but Helen simply could not overcome the rough waves and reach the boat. As Brian watched in horror and disbelief, his wife disappeared from view.

After a time, the storm began to lose its strength. Brian managed to right the sailboat and sail back to shore. Finally he reached safety, but the personal consequences of this storm were just beginning. The next days were filled with pain and further horror: the Coast Guard finding Helen's body . . . discussions with authorities . . . breaking the news to Helen's parents . . . conversations with friends . . . self-blame . . . grief . . . and more. On Wednesday, five days after that fateful afternoon, Brian collected himself and attended Helen's funeral and burial. It was the longest and most difficult day of his life. Most of the time, he felt as though he were in a trance.

Soon after awakening on Thursday morning, Brian realized that something was terribly wrong with him. Try though he might, he couldn't remember the events of the past few days. He remembered the accident, Helen's death, and the call from the Coast Guard after they had found her body. But just about everything else was gone, right up through the funeral. At first he had even thought that it was now Sunday, and that his discussions with family and friends and the funeral were all ahead of him. But the newspaper, the funeral guestbook, and a phone conversation with his brother soon convinced him that he had lost the past four days of his life.

In this revised scenario, Brian is reacting to his traumatic experience with symptoms of **dissociative amnesia.** People with this disorder are unable to recall important information, usually of an upsetting nature, about their lives (APA, 2000). The loss of memory is much more extensive than normal forgetting and is not caused by organic factors (see Table 7–5). Very often an episode of amnesia is directly triggered by a specific upsetting event (McLeod, Byrne & Aitken, 2004).

Dissociative amnesia may be *localized, selective, generalized,* or *continuous.* Any of these kinds of amnesia can be triggered by a traumatic experience such as Brian's, but each represents a particular pattern of forgetting. Brian was suffering from *localized,* or *circumscribed, amnesia,* the most common type of dissociative amnesia, in which a person loses all memory of events that took place within a limited period of time, almost always beginning with some very disturbing occurrence. Recall that Brian awakened on the day after the funeral and could not recall any of the events of the past difficult days, beginning after the boating tragedy. He remembered everything that happened up to and including the accident. He could also recall everything from the morning after the funeral onward, but the days in between remained a total blank. The forgotten period is called the *amnestic episode.* During an amnestic episode, people may appear confused; in some cases they wander about aimlessly. They are already experiencing memory difficulties, but seem unaware of them. In the revised case, for example, Brian felt as though he were in a trance on the day of Helen's funeral.

People with *selective amnesia,* the second most common form of dissociative amnesia, remember some, but not all, events that occurred during a period of time. If Brian had selective amnesia, he might remember certain of his conversations with friends but perhaps not the funeral itself.

In some cases the loss of memory extends back to times long before the upsetting period. Brian might awaken after the funeral and find that, in addition to forgetting events of the past few days, he could not remember events that occurred earlier in his life. In this case, he would be experiencing *generalized amnesia.* In extreme cases, Brian might not even remember who he was and might fail to recognize relatives and friends.

In the forms of dissociative amnesia discussed so far, the period affected by the amnesia has an end. In *continuous amnesia,* however, forgetting continues into the present. Brian might forget new and ongoing experiences as well as what happened before and during the tragedy. Continuous forgetting of this kind is actually quite rare in cases of dissociative amnesia, but, as we shall see in Chapter 18, not in cases of organic amnesia.

All of these forms of dissociative amnesia are similar in that the amnesia interferes mostly with *episodic memory*—a person's memory of personal material. *Semantic memory*—memory for abstract or encyclopedic information—usually remains intact. People with dissociative amnesia are as likely as anyone else to know the name of the president of the United States and how to write, read, or drive a car.

Clinicians do not know how common dissociative amnesia is, but they do know that many cases seem to begin during serious threats to health and safety, as in wartime and natural disasters (Witztum et al., 2002). Combat veterans often report memory gaps of hours or days, and some forget personal information, such as their names and addresses (Bremner, 2002). It appears that childhood abuse, particularly child sexual abuse, can also sometimes trigger dissociative amnesia; indeed, the 1990s witnessed many reports in which adults claimed to recall long-forgotten experiences of childhood abuse (see Box 7-4 on the next page). In addition, dissociative amnesia may occur under more ordinary circumstances, such as the sudden loss of a loved one through rejection or death or guilt over certain actions (for example, an extramarital affair) (Koh et al., 2000).

The personal impact of dissociative amnesia depends on how much is forgotten. Obviously, an amnestic episode of two years is more of a problem than one of two hours. Similarly, an amnestic episode during which a person's life changes in major ways causes more difficulties than one that is quiet.

Dissociative Fugue

People with a **dissociative fugue** not only forget their personal identities and details of their past lives but also flee to an entirely different location (see again Table 7-5). Some individuals travel but a short distance and make few social contacts in the new setting

---

>>PSYCH•LISTINGS
Most Common Forgotten Matters

Where keys were left ‹‹

Where the remote control was left ‹‹

Phone numbers ‹‹

Names ‹‹

Dream content ‹‹

Birthdays/anniversaries ‹‹

Saving a computer document ‹‹

Mathematical principles ‹‹

Where reading glasses were left ‹‹

Where a wallet was left ‹‹

Details of TV shows, movies, or music ‹‹

Table 7-5 DSM Checklist

DISSOCIATIVE AMNESIA

1. One or more episodes of inability to recall important personal information, usually of a traumatic or stressful nature, that is too extensive to be explained by ordinary forgetfulness.
2. Significant distress or impairment.

DISSOCIATIVE FUGUE

1. Sudden, unexpected travel away from home or one's customary place of work, with inability to recall one's past.
2. Confusion about personal identity, or the assumption of a new identity.
3. Significant distress or impairment.

DISSOCIATIVE IDENTITY DISORDER (MULTIPLE PERSONALITY DISORDER)

1. The presence of two or more distinct identities or personality states.
2. Control of the person's behavior recurrently taken by at least two of these identities or personality states.
3. An inability to recall important personal information that is too extensive to be explained by ordinary forgetfulness.

Based on APA, 2000.

•**DISSOCIATIVE AMNESIA**•A dissociative disorder marked by an inability to recall important personal events and information.

•**DISSOCIATIVE FUGUE**•A dissociative disorder in which a person travels to a new location and may assume a new identity, simultaneously forgetting his or her past.

Repressed Childhood Memories or False Memory Syndrome?

Throughout the 1990s, reports of *repressed childhood memory of abuse* attracted much public attention. Adults with this type of *dissociative amnesia* seemed to recover buried memories of sexual and physical abuse from their childhood. A woman might claim, for example, that her father had sexually molested her repeatedly between the ages of 5 and 7. Or a young man might remember that a family friend had made sexual advances on several occasions when he was very young. Often the repressed memories surfaced during therapy for another problem, perhaps for an eating disorder or depression.

Although the number of such claims currently seems to be declining, experts remain split on this issue (McNally et al., 2005; McNally, 2003, 2001; Leavitt, 2002, 2001). Some believe that recovered memories are just what they appear to be—horrible memories of abuse that have been buried for years in the person's mind. Other experts believe that the memories are actually illusions—false images created by a mind that is confused. In fact, an organization called the False Memory Syndrome Foundation assists people who claim to be falsely charged with abuse.

Opponents of the repressed memory concept hold that the details of childhood sexual abuse are often remembered all too well, not completely wiped from memory (McNally et al., 2004; Loftus, 2000,

1993). They also point out that memory in general is hardly foolproof (Lindsay et al., 2004). Even when recalling events as dramatic as the Kennedy assassination or the terrorist attack on the World Trade Center, people give inaccurate accounts of where they were at the time of the event or who first told them about it. Moreover, false memories of various kinds can be created in the laboratory by tapping into subjects' imaginations (Marsh & Bower, 2004; Thomas & Loftus, 2002). If memory in general is so flawed, questions certainly can be raised about the accuracy of recovered memories.

If the alleged recovery of childhood memories is not what it appears to be, what is it? According to opponents of the concept, it may be a powerful case of suggestibility (Loftus, 2003, 2001, 1997). These theorists hold that the attention paid to the phenomenon by both clinicians and the public has led some therapists to make the diagnosis without sufficient evidence (Frankel, 1993). The therapists may actively search for signs of early sexual abuse in clients and even encourage clients to produce repressed memories (Gardner, 2004). Certain therapists in fact use special memory recovery techniques, including hypnosis, regression therapy, journal writing, dream interpretation, and interpretation of bodily symptoms (Madill & Holch, 2004; Lindsay, 1996, 1994). Perhaps some clients respond to the tech-

niques by unknowingly forming false memories of abuse (Hyman & Loftus, 2002). The apparent memories may then become increasingly familiar to them as a result of repeated therapy discussions of the alleged incidents. In short, recovered memories may actually be *iatrogenic*—unintentionally caused by the therapist.

Of course, repressed memories of childhood sexual abuse do not emerge only in clinical settings (Leavitt, 2002, 2001). Many individuals come forward on their own. Opponents of the repressed memory concept explain these cases by pointing to various books, articles, and television shows that seem to validate repressed memories of childhood sexual abuse (Loftus, 1993). Several books even tell readers how to diagnose repression in themselves, often listing symptoms that are actually rather common—not clinical symptoms at all (Tavris, 1993). Readers with a number of these symptoms may begin a search for repressed memories of childhood abuse. Still other opponents of the repressed memory concept believe that, for biological or other reasons, some individuals are more prone than others to experience false memories—either of childhood abuse or of other kinds of events (McNally et al., 2005).

It is important to recognize that the experts who question the recovery of repressed childhood memories do not in any way deny the problem of child sexual abuse (Chu, 2000; Knapp & Vande Creek, 2000). In fact, proponents and opponents alike are greatly concerned that the public may take this debate to mean that clinicians have doubts about the scope of the problem of child sexual abuse. Whatever may be the final outcome of the repressed memory debate, the problem of childhood sexual abuse appears to be all too real and all too common.

Early recall *Research suggests that our memories of early childhood may be influenced by the reminiscences of family members, our dreams, television and movie plots, and our present self-image.*

(APA, 2000). Their fugue may be brief—a matter of hours or days—and end suddenly. In other cases, however, the person may travel far from home, take a new name, and establish a new identity, new relationships, and even a new line of work. Such people may also display new personality characteristics; often they are more outgoing (APA, 2000). This pattern is seen in the case of the Reverend Ansel Bourne, described by the famous psychologist William James at the end of the nineteenth century:

> On January 17, 1887, [the Reverend Ansel Bourne, of Greene, R.I.] drew 551 dollars from a bank in Providence with which to pay for a certain lot of land in Greene, paid certain bills, and got into a Pawtucket horsecar. This is the last incident which he remembers. He did not return home that day, and nothing was heard of him for two months. He was published in the papers as missing, and foul play being suspected, the police sought in vain his whereabouts. On the morning of March 14th, however, at Norristown, Pennsylvania, a man calling himself A. I. Brown who had rented a small shop six weeks previously, stocked it with stationery, confectionery, fruit and small articles, and carried on his quiet trade without seeming to any one unnatural or eccentric, woke up in a fright and called in the people of the house to tell him where he was. He said that his name was Ansel Bourne, that he was entirely ignorant of Norristown, that he knew nothing of shop-keeping, and that the last thing he remembered—it seemed only yesterday—was drawing the money from the bank, etc. in Providence. . . . He was very weak, having lost apparently over twenty pounds of flesh during his escapade, and had such a horror of the idea of the candy-store that he refused to set foot in it again.
>
> The first two weeks of the period remained unaccounted for, as he had no memory, after he had once resumed his normal personality, of any part of the time, and no one who knew him seems to have seen him after he left home. The remarkable part of the change is, of course, the peculiar occupation which the so-called Brown indulged in. Mr. Bourne has never in his life had the slightest contact with trade. "Brown" was described by the neighbors as taciturn, orderly in his habits, and in no way queer. He went to Philadelphia several times; replenished his stock; cooked for himself in the back shop, where he also slept; went regularly to church; and once at a prayer-meeting made what was considered by the hearers a good address, in the course of which he related an incident which he had witnessed in his natural state of Bourne.
>
> *(James, 1890, pp. 391–393)*

Approximately 0.2 percent of the population experience dissociative fugue. Like dissociative amnesia, a fugue usually follows a severely stressful event (APA, 2000). Some adolescent runaways may be in a state of fugue (Loewenstein, 1991). Like cases of dissociative amnesia, fugues usually affect personal (*episodic*) memories rather than encyclopedic or abstract (*semantic*) knowledge (Glisky et al., 2004; Kihlstrom, 2001).

Fugues tend to end abruptly. In some cases, as with Reverend Bourne, the person "awakens" in a strange place, surrounded by unfamiliar faces, and wonders how he or she got there. In other cases, the lack of personal history may arouse suspicion. Perhaps a traffic accident or legal problem leads police to discover the false identity; at other times friends search for and find the missing person. When people are found before their state of fugue has ended, therapists may find it necessary to ask them many questions about the details of their lives, repeatedly remind them who they are, and even initiate psychotherapy before they recover their memories. As these people recover their past, some forget the events of the fugue period (APA, 2000).

The majority of people who experience dissociative fugue regain most or all of their memories and never have a recurrence. Since fugues are usually brief and totally reversible, individuals tend to experience

Lost and found *Cheryl Ann Barnes is helped off a plane by her grandmother and stepmother upon arrival in Florida in 1996. The 17-year-old high school honor student had disappeared from her Florida home and was found one month later in a New York City hospital listed as Jane Doe, apparently suffering from fugue.*

Peter Cosgrove/AP Photo

few aftereffects. People who have been away for months or years, however, often do have trouble adjusting to the changes that have occurred during their flights. In addition, some people commit illegal or violent acts in their fugue state and later must face the consequences.

Dissociative Identity Disorder (Multiple Personality Disorder)

Dissociative identity disorder is both dramatic and disabling, as we see in the case of Eric:

Dazed and bruised from a beating, Eric, 29, was discovered wandering around a Daytona Beach shopping mall on Feb. 9. . . . Transferred six weeks later to Daytona Beach's Human Resources Center, Eric began talking to doctors in two voices: the infantile rhythms of "young Eric," a dim and frightened child, and the measured tones of "older Eric," who told a tale of terror and child abuse. According to "older Eric," after his immigrant German parents died, a harsh stepfather and his mistress took Eric from his native South Carolina to a drug dealers' hideout in a Florida swamp. Eric said he was raped by several gang members and watched his stepfather murder two men.

One day in late March an alarmed counselor watched Eric's face twist into a violent snarl. Eric let loose an unearthly growl and spat out a stream of obscenities. "It sounded like something out of *The Exorcist,*" says Malcolm Graham, the psychologist who directs the case at the center. "It was the most intense thing I've ever seen in a patient." That disclosure of a new personality, who insolently demanded to be called Mark, was the first indication that Graham had been dealing with a rare and serious emotional disorder: true multiple personality. . . .

Eric's other manifestations emerged over the next weeks: quiet, middle-aged Dwight; the hysterically blind and mute Jeffrey; Michael, an arrogant jock; the coquettish Tian, whom Eric considered a whore; and argumentative Phillip, the lawyer. "Phillip was always asking about Eric's rights," says Graham. "He was kind of obnoxious. Actually, Phillip was a pain."

To Graham's astonishment, Eric gradually unfurled 27 different personalities, including three females. . . . . They ranged in age from a fetus to a sordid old man who kept trying to persuade Eric to fight as a mercenary in Haiti. In one therapy session, reports Graham, Eric shifted personality nine times in an hour. "I felt I was losing control of the sessions," says the psychologist, who has eleven years of clinical experience. "Some personalities would not talk to me, and some of them were very insightful into my behavior as well as Eric's."

(Time, October 25, 1982, p. 70)

•**DISSOCIATIVE IDENTITY DISORDER**•A dissociative disorder in which a person develops two or more distinct personalities. Also known as *multiple personality disorder.*

•**SUBPERSONALITIES**•The two or more distinct personalities found in individuals suffering from multiple personality disorder, each with a unique set of memories, behaviors, thoughts, and emotions. Also known as *alternate personalities.*

A person with **dissociative identity disorder,** or **multiple personality disorder,** develops two or more distinct personalities, often called **subpersonalities** or **alternate personalities,** each with a unique set of memories, behaviors, thoughts, and emotions (see again Table 7-5 on page 205). At any given time, one of the subpersonalities takes center stage and dominates the person's functioning. Usually one subpersonality, called the *primary,* or *host, personality,* appears more often than the others.

The transition from one subpersonality to another, called *switching,* is usually sudden and may be dramatic (APA, 2000). Eric, for example, twisted his face, growled, and yelled obscenities while changing personalities. Switching is usually triggered by a stressful event, although clinicians can also bring about the change with hypnotic suggestion (APA, 2000).

Cases of multiple personality disorder were first reported almost three centuries ago (Rieber, 2002). Many clinicians consider the disorder to be rare, but some reports suggest that it may be more common than was once thought (Lilienfeld & Lynn, 2003; APA, 2000). Most cases are first diagnosed in late adolescence or early adulthood, but, more often than not, the symptoms actually began in early childhood after episodes of abuse (often sexual abuse), perhaps even before the age of 5 (van der Hart et al., 2005;

Ross et al., 1991). Women receive this diagnosis at least three times as often as men (APA, 2000).

HOW DO SUBPERSONALITIES INTERACT? How subpersonalities relate to or recall one another varies from case to case. Generally, however, there are three kinds of relationships. In *mutually amnesic relationships,* the subpersonalities have no awareness of one another (Ellenberger, 1970). Conversely, in *mutually cognizant patterns,* each subpersonality is well aware of the rest. They may hear one another's voices and even talk among themselves. Some are on good terms, while others do not get along at all.

In *one-way amnesic relationships,* the most common relationship pattern, some subpersonalities are aware of others, but the awareness is not mutual (Huntjens et al., 2005). Those that are aware, called *co-conscious subpersonalities,* are "quiet observers" who watch the actions and thoughts of the other subpersonalities but do not interact with them. Sometimes while another subpersonality is present, the co-conscious personality makes itself known through indirect means, such as auditory hallucinations (perhaps a voice giving commands) or "automatic writing" (the current personality may find itself writing down words over which it has no control).

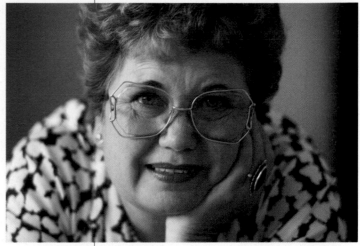

"I'm Eve" *In 1975 Chris Sizemore revealed that she had been the subject of the book and the film* The Three Faces of Eve. *A fully integrated personality for more than 30 years, Ms. Sizemore is now an accomplished author, artist, and mental health spokesperson.*

Investigators used to believe that most cases of multiple personality disorder involved two or three subpersonalities. Studies now suggest, however, that the average number of subpersonalities per patient is much higher—15 for women and 8 for men (APA, 2000; Ross et al., 1989). In fact, there have been cases in which 100 or more subpersonalities were observed (APA, 2000). Often the subpersonalities emerge in groups of two or three at a time.

In the case of "Eve White," made famous in the book and movie *The Three Faces of Eve,* a woman had three subpersonalities—Eve White, Eve Black, and Jane (Thigpen & Cleckley, 1957). Eve White, the primary personality, was quiet and serious; Eve Black was carefree and mischievous; and Jane was mature and intelligent. According to the book, these three subpersonalities eventually merged into Evelyn, a stable personality who was really an integration of the other three.

The book was mistaken, however; this was not to be the end of Eve's dissociation. In an autobiography 20 years later, she revealed that altogether 22 subpersonalities had come forth during her life, including 9 subpersonalities after Evelyn. Usually they appeared in groups of three, and so the authors of *The Three Faces of Eve* apparently never knew about her previous or subsequent subpersonalities. She has now overcome her disorder, achieving a single, stable identity, and has been known as Chris Sizemore for over 30 years (Sizemore, 1991).

HOW DO SUBPERSONALITIES DIFFER? As in Chris Sizemore's case, subpersonalities often exhibit dramatically different characteristics. They may also have their own names and different *vital statistics, abilities and preferences,* and even *physiological responses.*

VITAL STATISTICS The subpersonalities may differ in features as basic as age, sex, race, and family history, as in the famous case of Sybil Dorsett. Sybil's multiple personality disorder has been described in fictional form (in the novel *Sybil*) but is based on a real case from the practice of the psychiatrist Cornelia Wilbur (Schreiber, 1973). Sybil displayed 17 subpersonalities, all with different identifying features. They included adults, a teenager, and a baby named Ruthie; two were male, named Mike and Sid. Sybil's subpersonalities each had particular images of themselves and of each other. The subpersonality named Vicky, for example, saw herself as an attractive blonde, while another, Peggy Lou, was described as a pixie with a pug nose. Mary was plump with dark hair, and Vanessa was a tall redhead with a willowy figure.

ABILITIES AND PREFERENCES Although memories of abstract or encyclopedic information are not usually affected in dissociative amnesia or fugue, they are often disturbed in dissociative identity disorder. It is not uncommon for the different subpersonalities to have different abilities: one may be able to drive, speak a foreign language, or play a

>>LOOKING AROUND

Major Impact Before the publication of *Sybil* in 1973, only 100 cases of multiple personality disorder had been published. Since then, an estimated 40,000 diagnoses have been made, most of them in North America (Acocella, 1999; Miller & Kantrowitz, 1999). **<<**

- -

The Beginnings of Sybilization Several colleagues who worked closely with the author of *Sybil* and with the therapist claim that Sybil was actually highly hypnotizable, extremely suggestible, and eager to please her therapist, and that her disorder was in fact induced by the treatment techniques of hypnosis and sodium pentothal (Rieber, 2002, 1999; Miller & Kantrowitz, 1999). **<<**

Early beginnings *Chris Sizemore's multiple personality disorder developed long before this photograph of her was taken at age 10. It emerged during her preschool years after she experienced several traumas (witnessing two deaths and a horrifying accident) within a three-month period.*

musical instrument, while the others cannot (Coons & Bowman, 2001; Coons et al., 1988). Their handwriting can also differ. In addition, the subpersonalities usually have different tastes in food, friends, music, and literature. Chris Sizemore ("Eve") later pointed out, "If I had learned to sew as one personality and then tried to sew as another, I couldn't do it. Driving a car was the same. Some of my personalities couldn't drive" (1977, p. 4).

PHYSIOLOGICAL RESPONSES Researchers have discovered that subpersonalities may have physiological differences, such as differences in autonomic nervous system activity, blood pressure levels, and allergies (Putnam, Zahn, & Post, 1990). One study looked at the brain activities of different subpersonalities by measuring their *evoked potentials*—that is, brain-response patterns recorded on an electroencephalograph (Putnam, 1984). The brain pattern a person produces in response to a specific stimulus (such as a flashing light) is usually unique and consistent. However, when an evoked potential test was administered to four subpersonalities of each of 10 people with dissociative identity disorder, the results were dramatic. The brain-activity pattern of each subpersonality was unique, showing the kinds of variations usually found in totally different people.

The evoked potential study also used control subjects who pretended to have different subpersonalities. These normal individuals were instructed to create and rehearse alternate personalities. The brain-reaction patterns of these subjects, in contrast to those of real patients, did not vary as they shifted from subpersonality to subpersonality, suggesting that simple faking cannot produce the variations in brain reaction found in cases of multiple personality.

HOW COMMON IS DISSOCIATIVE IDENTITY DISORDER? As we have seen, dissociative identity disorder has traditionally been thought of as rare. Some researchers even argue that many or all cases are **iatrogenic**—that is, unintentionally produced by practitioners (Miller, 2005; Piper & Merskey, 2004a). They believe that therapists create this disorder by subtly suggesting the existence of other personalities during therapy or by explicitly asking a patient to produce different personalities while under hypnosis. In addition, they believe, a therapist who is looking for multiple personalities may reinforce these patterns by displaying greater interest when a patient displays symptoms of dissociation.

These arguments seem to be supported by the fact that many cases of dissociative identity disorder first come to attention while the person is already in treatment for a less serious problem. But such is not true of all cases; many people seek treatment because they have noticed time lapses throughout their lives or because relatives and friends have observed their subpersonalities (Putnam, 2000, 1988, 1985).

The number of people diagnosed with dissociative identify disorder has been increasing (Casey, 2001). Although the disorder is still uncommon, thousands of cases have now been diagnosed in the United States and Canada alone. Two factors may account for this increase. First, a growing number of today's clinicians believe that the disorder does exist and are willing to diagnose it (Lalonde et al., 2002, 2001). Second, diagnostic procedures tend to be more accurate today than in past years. For much of the twentieth century, schizophrenia was one of the clinical field's most commonly applied diagnoses. It was applied, often incorrectly, to a wide range of unusual behavioral patterns, perhaps including dissociative identity disorder (Turkington & Harris, 2001). Under the stricter criteria of recent editions of the DSM, clinicians are now more accurate in diagnosing schizophrenia, allowing more cases of dissociative identity disorder to be recognized (Welburn et al., 2003). In addition, several diagnostic tests have been developed to help detect dissociative identity disorder (Somer & Dell, 2005; Mann, 1995). Despite such changes, however, many clinicians continue to question the legitimacy of this category (Lalonde et al., 2002, 2001).

How Do Theorists Explain Dissociative Disorders?

A variety of theories have been proposed to explain dissociative disorders. Older explanations, such as those offered by psychodynamic and behavioral theorists, have not

•**IATROGENIC DISORDER**•A disorder that is unintentionally caused by a practitioner.

received much investigation. However, newer viewpoints, which combine cognitive, behavioral, and biological principles and highlight such factors as *state-dependent learning* and *self-hypnosis,* have captured the interest of clinical scientists.

THE PSYCHODYNAMIC VIEW Psychodynamic theorists believe that dissociative disorders are caused by *repression,* the most basic ego defense mechanism: people fight off anxiety by unconsciously preventing painful memories, thoughts, or impulses from reaching awareness. Everyone uses repression to a degree, but people with dissociative disorders are thought to repress their memories excessively (Fayek, 2002).

In the psychodynamic view, dissociative amnesia and fugue are *single episodes* of massive repression. In each of these disorders, a person unconsciously blocks the memory of an extremely upsetting event to avoid the pain of facing it (Turkington & Harris, 2001). Repressing may be their only protection from overwhelming anxiety.

In contrast, dissociative identity disorder is thought to result from a *lifetime* of excessive repression (Brenner, 1999; Reis, 1993). Psychodynamic theorists believe that continuous use of repression is motivated by traumatic childhood events, particularly abusive parenting. Young Sybil, for example, was repeatedly subjected to unspeakable tortures by her disturbed mother, Hattie:

> A favorite ritual . . . was to separate Sybil's legs with a long wooden spoon, tie her feet to the spoon with dish towels, and then string her to the end of a light bulb cord, suspended from the ceiling. The child was left to swing in space while the mother proceeded to the water faucet to wait for the water to get cold. After muttering, "Well, it's not going to get any colder," she would fill the adult-sized enema bag to capacity and return with it to her daughter. As the child swung in space, the mother would insert the enema tip into the child's urethra and fill the bladder with cold water. "I did it," Hattie would scream triumphantly when her mission was accomplished. "I did it." The scream was followed by laughter, which went on and on.
>
> *(Schreiber, 1973, p. 160)*

According to psychodynamic theorists, children who experience such traumas may come to fear the dangerous world they live in and take flight from it by pretending to be another person who is safely looking on from afar. Abused children may also come to fear the impulses that they believe are the reasons for their excessive punishments. Whenever they experience "bad" thoughts or impulses, they unconsciously try to disown and deny them by assigning them to other personalities.

Most of the support for the psychodynamic position is drawn from case histories, which report such brutal childhood experiences as beatings, cuttings, burnings with cigarettes, imprisonment in closets, rape, and extensive verbal abuse. Yet some individuals with dissociative identity disorder do not seem to have experiences of abuse in their background (Bliss, 1980). Moreover, child abuse appears to be far more common than dissociative identity disorder. Why might only a small fraction of abused children develop this disorder?

THE BEHAVIORAL VIEW Behaviorists believe that dissocation grows from normal memory processes such as drifting of the mind or forgetting (see Box 7-5 on the next page). Specifically, they hold that dissociation is a response learned through operant conditioning (Casey, 2001). People who experience a horrifying event may later find temporary relief when their minds drift to other subjects. For some, this momentary forgetting, leading to a drop in anxiety, increases the likelihood of future forgetting. In short, they are reinforced for the act of forgetting and learn—without being aware that they are learning—that such acts help them escape anxiety. Thus, like psychodynamic theorists, behaviorists see dissociation as escape behavior. But behaviorists believe that a reinforcement process rather than a hardworking unconscious is keeping the individuals unaware that they are using dissociation as a means of escape.

Movie madness *One of the cinema's best-known fictional sufferers of multiple personality disorder, Norman Bates, is horrified to discover that his mother (actually his subpersonality) has stabbed a woman to death in the shower in the movie* Psycho.

The Kobal Colection

[BOX 7-5]

Peculiarities of Memory

Usually memory problems must interfere greatly with a person's functioning before they are considered a sign of a disorder. Peculiarities of memory, on the other hand, fill our daily lives. Memory investigators have identified a number of these peculiarities—some familiar, some useful, some problematic, but none abnormal (Brown, 2004, 2003; Turkington & Harris, 2001; Noll & Turkington, 1994).

◆ **Absentmindedness** Often we fail to register information because our thoughts are focusing on other things. If we haven't absorbed the information in the first place, it is no surprise that later we can't recall it.

◆ **Déjà vu** Almost all of us have at some time had the strange sensation of recognizing a scene that we happen upon for the first time. We feel sure we have been there before.

◆ **Jamais vu** Sometimes we have the opposite experience: a situation or scene that is part of our daily life seems suddenly unfamiliar. "I knew it was my car, but I felt as if I'd never seen it before."

◆ **The tip-of-the-tongue phenomenon** To have something on the tip of the tongue is an acute "feeling of knowing": we are unable to recall some piece of information, but we know that we know it.

◆ **Eidetic images** Some people experience visual afterimages so vividly that they can describe a picture in detail after looking at it just once. The images may be memories of pictures, events, fantasies, or dreams.

◆ **Memory while under anesthesia** Some anesthetized patients may process enough of what is said in their presence during surgery to affect their recovery. In such cases, the ability to understand language has continued under anesthesia, even though the patient cannot explicitly recall it.

◆ **Memory for music** Even as a small child, Mozart could memorize and reproduce a piece of music after having heard it only once. While no one yet has matched the genius of Mozart, many musicians can mentally hear whole pieces of music, so that they can rehearse anywhere, far from their instruments.

◆ **Visual memory** Most people recall visual information better than other kinds of information: they can easily bring to their mind the appearance of places, objects, faces, or the pages of a book. They almost never forget a face, yet they may well forget the name attached to it. Other people have stronger verbal memories: they remember sounds or words particularly well, and the memories that come to their minds are often puns or rhymes.

◆ **Prenatal memory** Some North American medicine men claim to remember parts of a prenatal existence, an ability they believe is lost to "common" people. Many practicing Buddhists also claim to remember past lives. A few—such as Buddha himself—claim to remember their very first existence.

© The New Yorker Collection 1998, Mick Stevens, from Cartoonbank.com

Like psychodynamic theorists, behaviorists have relied largely on case histories to support their view of dissociative disorders. Such descriptions do often support this view, but they are equally consistent with other kinds of explanations as well: a case that seems to show reinforcement of forgetting can usually also be interpreted as an instance of unconscious repression. In addition, the behavioral explanation fails to explain precisely how temporary and normal escapes from painful memories grow into a complex disorder or why more people do not develop dissociative disorders.

STATE-DEPENDENT LEARNING If people learn something when they are in a particular situation or state of mind, they are likely to remember it best when they are again in that same condition. If they are given a learning task while under the influence of alcohol, for example, their later recall of the information may be strongest under the influence of alcohol (Overton, 1966). Similarly, if they smoke cigarettes while learning, they may later have better recall when they are again smoking.

This link between state and recall is called **state-dependent learning.** It was initially observed in experimental animals who were given certain drugs and then taught to perform certain tasks. Researchers repeatedly found that the animals' subsequent test performances were best in the same drug states (Vakili et al., 2004; Overton, 1966, 1964). Research with human subjects later showed that state-dependent learning can be associated with mood states as well: material learned during a happy mood is recalled best when the subject is again happy, and sad-state learning is recalled best during sad states (de l'Etoile, 2002; Bower, 1981) (see Figure 7-3).

What causes state-dependent learning? One possibility is that *arousal* levels are an important dimension of learning and memory. That is, a particular level of arousal will have a set of remembered events, thoughts, and skills attached to it. When a situation produces that particular level of arousal, the person is more likely to recall the memories linked to it.

Although people may remember certain events better in some arousal states than in others, most can recall events under a variety of states. However, perhaps people who are prone to develop dissociative disorders have state-to-memory links that are extremely rigid and narrow. Maybe each of their thoughts, memories, and skills is tied *exclusively* to a particular state of arousal, so that they recall a given event only when they experience an arousal state almost identical to the state in which the memory was first acquired. When such people are calm, for example, they may forget what occurred during stressful times, thus laying the groundwork for dissociative amnesia or fugue. Similarly, in dissociative identity disorder, different arousal levels may produce entirely different groups of memories, thoughts, and abilities—that is, different subpersonalities (Putnam, 1992). This could explain why personality transitions in dissociative identity disorder tend to be sudden and stress-related.

SELF-HYPNOSIS As we first saw in Chapter 1, people who are *hypnotized* enter a sleeplike state in which they become very suggestible. While in this state, they can behave, perceive, and think in ways that would ordinarily seem impossible. They may, for example, become temporarily blind, deaf, or insensitive to pain. Hypnosis can also help people remember events that occurred and were forgotten years ago, a capability used by many psychotherapists. Conversely, it can make people forget facts, events, and even their personal identities—an effect called *hypnotic amnesia*.

Most studies of hypnotic amnesia follow similar formats. Subjects are asked to study a word list or other material until they are able to repeat it correctly. Under hypnosis, they are then directed to forget the material until they receive a *cancellation signal* (such as the snap of a finger), at which time they will suddenly recall the learned material. Repeatedly these experiments have found the subjects' memories to be poor during the period of hypnotic amnesia and then restored after the cancellation signal is given.

The parallels between hypnotic amnesia and dissociative disorders are striking. Both are conditions in which people forget certain material for a period of time yet later remember it. And in both, the people forget without any insight into why they are forgetting or any awareness that something is being forgotten. These parallels have led some theorists to conclude that dissociative disorders may be a form of **self-hypnosis** in which people hypnotize themselves to forget unpleasant events (Maldonado & Spiegel, 2003; Bryant et al., 2001; Bliss, 1985, 1980). Dissociative amnesia may occur, for example, in people who, consciously or unconsciously, hypnotize themselves into forgetting horrifying experiences that have recently occurred in their lives. If the self-induced amnesia covers all memories of a person's past and identity, that person may undergo a dissociative fugue.

Self-hypnosis might also be used to explain dissociative identity disorder. On the basis of several investigations, some theorists believe that this disorder often begins between the ages of 4 and 6, a time when children are generally very suggestible and excellent hypnotic subjects (Kluft, 2001, 1987; Bliss, 1985, 1980) (see Figure 7-4 on the next page). These theorists argue that some children who experience abuse or other horrifying

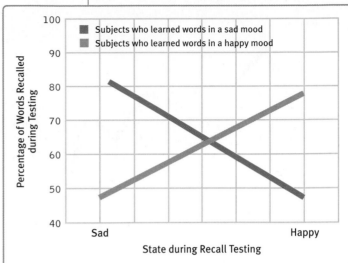

FIGURE **7-3** **State-dependent learning** *In one study, subjects who learned a list of words while in a hypnotically induced happy state remembered the words better if they were in a happy mood when tested later than if they were in a sad mood. Conversely, subjects who learned the words when in a sad mood recalled them better if they were sad during testing than if they were happy (Bower, 1981).*

•**STATE-DEPENDENT LEARNING**•Learning that becomes associated with the conditions under which it occurred, so that it is best remembered under the same conditions.

•**SELF-HYPNOSIS**•The process of hypnotizing oneself, sometimes for the purpose of forgetting unpleasant events.

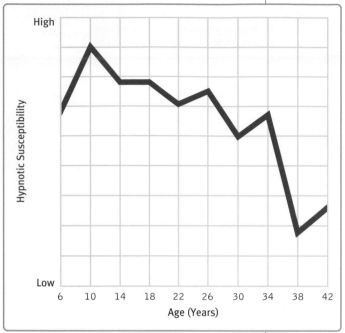

FIGURE **7-4** **Hypnotic susceptibility and age**
Multiple personality disorder often seems to begin between the ages of 4 and 6, when a child's hypnotic susceptibility is on the rise. A person's hypnotic susceptibility increases until just before adolescence, then generally declines. (Adapted from Morgan & Hilgard, 1973.)

events manage to escape their threatening world by self-hypnosis, mentally separating themselves from their bodies and fulfilling their wish to become some other person or persons. One patient with multiple personalities observed, "I was in a trance often [during my childhood]. There was a little place where I could sit, close my eyes and imagine, until I felt very relaxed just like hypnosis" (Bliss, 1980, p. 1392).

There are different schools of thought about the nature of hypnosis (Kihlstrom, 2005). Some theorists see hypnosis as a *special process,* an out-of-the-ordinary kind of functioning (Hilgard, 1992, 1987, 1977). Accordingly, these theorists contend that people with dissociative disorders place themselves in internal trances during which their conscious functioning is significantly altered. Other theorists believe that hypnotic behaviors, and hypnotic amnesia in particular, are produced by *common social and cognitive processes,* such as high motivation, focused attention, role enactment, and self-fulfilling expectations (Sarbin, 2002; Spanos & Coe, 1992). According to this point of view, hypnotized people are simply highly motivated individuals performing tasks that are asked of them, while believing all along that the hypnotic state is doing the work for them. Common-process theorists hold that people with dissociative disorders provide themselves (or are provided by others) with powerful suggestions to forget and that social and cognitive mechanisms then put the suggestions into practice. Whether hypnosis consists of special or common processes, hypnosis research effectively demonstrates the power of our normal thought processes, and so renders the notion of dissociative disorders somewhat less remarkable.

How Are Dissociative Disorders Treated?

As we have seen, people with dissociative amnesia and fugue often recover on their own. Only sometimes do their memory problems linger and require treatment. In contrast, people with dissociative identity disorder usually require treatment to regain their lost memories and develop an integrated personality. Treatments for dissociative amnesia and fugue tend to be more successful than those for dissociative identity disorder, probably because the former disorders are less complex.

HOW DO THERAPISTS HELP PEOPLE WITH DISSOCIATIVE AMNESIA AND FUGUE? The leading treatments for dissociative amnesia and fugue are *psychodynamic therapy, hypnotic therapy,* and *drug therapy,* although support for these interventions comes largely from case studies rather than controlled investigations (Maldonado & Spiegel, 2003). Psychodynamic therapists guide patients with these disorders to search their unconscious in the hope of bringing forgotten experiences back to consciousness (Bartholomew,

Hypnotic recall *Northwood University students react while under hypnosis to the suggestion of being on a beach in Hawaii and needing suntan lotion. Many clinicians use hypnotic procedures to help clients recall past events. Research reveals, however, that such procedures are as capable of creating false memories as they are of uncovering real memories.*

2000; Loewenstein, 1991). The focus of psychodynamic therapy seems particularly well suited to the needs of people with these disorders. After all, the patients need to recover lost memories, and the general approach of psychodynamic therapists is to try to uncover memories—as well as other psychological processes—that have been repressed. Thus many theorists, including some who do not ordinarily favor psychodynamic approaches, believe that psychodynamic therapy may be the most appropriate treatment for these disorders.

Another common treatment for dissociative amnesia and fugue is **hypnotic therapy,** or **hypnotherapy** (see Table 7-6). Therapists hypnotize patients and then guide them to recall forgotten events (Degun-Mather, 2002). Experiments have repeatedly indicated that hypnotic suggestion can help elicit forgotten memories, and experience has shown that people with dissociative disorders are usually highly susceptible to hypnosis (Maldonado & Spiegel, 2003). Given the possibility that dissociative amnesia and fugue may each be a form of self-hypnosis, hypnotherapy may be a particularly useful intervention. It has been applied both alone and in combination with other approaches.

Sometimes intravenous injections of barbiturates such as *sodium amobarbital* (Amytal) or *sodium pentobarbital* (Pentothal) are used to help patients with dissociative amnesia and fugue regain lost memories. The drugs are often called "truth serums," but the key to their success is their ability to sedate people and free their inhibitions, thus helping them to recall anxiety-producing events (Fraser, 1993; Kluft, 1988). These drugs do not always work, however, and if used at all, they are likely to be combined with other treatment approaches (Spiegel, 1994).

HOW DO THERAPISTS HELP INDIVIDUALS WITH DISSOCIATIVE IDENTITY DISORDER? Unlike victims of amnesia and fugue, people with dissociative identity disorder do not typically recover without treatment (Maldonado & Spiegel, 2003; Spiegel, 1994). Treatment for this pattern is complex and difficult, much like the disorder itself. Therapists usually try to help the clients (1) recognize fully the nature of their

•**HYPNOTIC THERAPY**•A treatment in which the patient undergoes hypnosis and is then guided to recall forgotten events or perform other therapeutic activities. Also known as *hypnotherapy.*

Table 7-6

Myths about Hypnosis
Michael Nash (2001)

Myth	Reality
Hypnosis is all a matter of having a good imagination.	Ability to imagine vividly is unrelated to hypnotizability.
Relaxation is an important feature of hypnosis.	Hypnosis has been induced during vigorous exercise.
It's a matter of willful faking.	Physiological responses indicate that hypnotized subjects are not lying.
It is dangerous.	Standard hypnotic procedures are no more distressing than lectures.
It has something to do with a sleeplike state.	Hypnotized subjects are fully awake.
Responding to hypnosis is like responding to a placebo.	Placebo responsiveness and hypnotizability are not correlated.
People who are hypnotized lose control of themselves.	Subjects are perfectly capable of saying no or terminating hypnosis.
Hypnosis can enable people to "relive" the past.	Age-regressed adults behave like adults play-acting as children.
When hypnotized, people can remember more accurately.	Hypnosis may actually muddle the distinction between memory and fantasy and may artificially inflate confidence.
Hypnotized people can be led to do acts that conflict with moral standards.	Hypnotized subjects fully adhere to their usual values.
Hypnotized people spontaneously forget what happened during the session.	Posthypnotic amnesia does not occur spontaneously.
Hypnosis can enable people to perform otherwise impossible feats of strength, endurance, learning, and sensory acuity.	Performance following hypnotic suggestions for increased muscle strength, learning, and sensory acuity does not exceed what can be accomplished by motivated subjects outside hypnosis.

disorder, (2) recover the gaps in their memory, and (3) integrate their subpersonalities into one functional personality (North & Yutzy, 2005; Kihlstrom, 2001).

RECOGNIZING THE DISORDER Once a diagnosis of dissociative identity disorder is made, therapists typically try to bond with the primary personality and with each of the subpersonalities (Kluft, 1999, 1992). As bonds are formed, therapists try to educate patients and help them to recognize fully the nature of their disorder (Krakauer, 2001; Allen, 1993). Some therapists actually introduce the subpersonalities to one another under hypnosis, and some have patients look at videotapes of their other personalities (Ross & Gahan, 1988; Sakheim, Hess, & Chivas, 1988). Many therapists have also found that group therapy helps to educate patients (Fine & Madden, 2000). Being with a group of people who all have multiple personalities helps relieve a person's feelings of isolation. Family therapy may also be used to help educate spouses and children about the disorder and to gather helpful information about the patient (Kluft, 2001, 2000; Porter et al., 1993).

RECOVERING MEMORIES To help patients recover the missing pieces of their past, therapists use many of the approaches applied in other dissociative disorders, including psychodynamic therapy, hypnotherapy, and drug treatment (Kluft, 2001, 1991, 1985). These techniques work slowly for patients with dissociative identity disorder, as some subpersonalities may keep denying experiences that the others recall (Lyon, 1992). One of the subpersonalities may even assume a "protector" role, to prevent the primary personality from suffering the pain of recollecting traumatic experiences. Some patients become self-destructive and violent during this phase of treatment (Kelly, 1993).

INTEGRATING THE SUBPERSONALITIES The final goal of therapy is to merge the different subpersonalities into a single, integrated identity. Integration is a continuous process that occurs throughout treatment until patients "own" all of their behaviors, emotions, sensations, and knowledge. **Fusion** is the final merging of two or more subpersonalities. Many patients distrust this final treatment goal, and their subpersonalities are likely to see integration as a form of death (Kluft, 2001, 1999, 1991). As one subpersonality said, "There are too many advantages to being multiple. Maybe we're being sold a bill of goods by therapists" (Hale, 1983). Therapists have used a range of approaches to help merge subpersonalities, including psychodynamic, supportive, cognitive, and drug therapies (Goldman, 1995; Fichtner et al., 1990).

Once the subpersonalities are integrated, further therapy is typically needed to maintain the complete personality and to teach social and coping skills that may help prevent later dissociations (Kihlstrom, 2001). In case reports, some therapists note high success rates (Coons & Bowman, 2001; Kluft, 2001, 1999, 1993), but others find that patients continue to resist full and final integration. A few therapists have in fact questioned the need for full integration. The limited number of reported cases generally prevents researchers from gathering samples that are large enough to conduct enlightening research on the treatment of this disorder.

In Sybil's case, the progress toward full integration was slow and halting and required 11 years of therapy. Her progress can be traced in the following excerpts from different stages of her treatment (Schreiber, 1973):

1957 Integration? Far from it. As the past flooded back, there was all the more reason to regress into the other selves, defenses against the past. (p. 270)

1958 Peggy Lou's memories were becoming Sybil's. By responding to Peggy Lou's memory as if it were her own, . . . Sybil had been able to recall an incident from the childhood of the alternating self. And all at once Sybil realized that at that moment she felt not merely *like* Peggy Lou: she was *one* with her. (p. 272)

1962 "Am I going to die?" each of the selves asked Dr. Wilbur. For some of the selves integration seemed synonymous with death. The doctor's assurances that, although one with Sybil, the individual selves would not cease to be seemed at best only partly convincing. "There are many things I have to do," Vanessa told Marcia. "You see, I won't be here very long." (p. 316)

1965 Sybil's attitude toward these selves . . . had completely changed, from initial denial to hostility to acceptance—even to love. Having learned to love these parts of herself, she had in effect replaced self-derogation with self-love. This replacement was an important measure of her integration and restoration. . . . Dr. Wilbur hypnotized Sybil and called for Vicky Antoinette. "How are things going, Vicky?" the doctor asked. "What progress is there underneath?" "I'm part of Sybil now, you know," Vicky replied. "She always wanted to be like me. Now we are one." (p. 337)

•**FUSION**•The final merging of two or more subpersonalities in multiple personality disorder.

•**DEPERSONALIZATION DISORDER**•A disorder marked by a persistent and recurrent feeling of being detached from one's own mental processes or body.

Depersonalization Disorder

As we observed earlier, DSM-IV-TR categorizes **depersonalization disorder** as a dissociative disorder, even though it is quite different from the other dissociative patterns (APA, 2000). Its central symptom is persistent and recurrent episodes of *depersonalization,* a change in one's experience of the self in which one's mental functioning or body feels unreal or foreign.

A 24-year-old graduate student sought treatment because he felt he was losing his mind. He had begun to doubt his own reality. He felt he was living in a dream in which he saw himself from without, and did not feel connected to his body or his thoughts. When he saw himself through his own eyes, he perceived his body parts as distorted—his hands and feet seemed quite large. As he walked across campus, he often felt the people he saw might be robots; he began to ruminate about his dizzy spells—did this mean that he had a brain tumor? . . . He often noted that he spent so much time thinking about his situation that he lost contact with all feelings except a pervasive discomfort about his own predicament.

In his second session, he was preoccupied with his perception that his feet had grown too large for his shoes, and fretted over whether to break up with his girlfriend because he doubted the reality of his feelings for her, and had begun to perceive her in a distorted manner. He said he had hesitated before returning for his second appointment, because he wondered whether his therapist was really alive. He was very pessimistic that he could be helped, and had vague suicidal ideation. A thorough medical and neurological evaluation found no organic etiology.

(Kluft, 1988, p. 580)

Like this graduate student, people with depersonalization disorder feel as though they have become separated from their body and are observing themselves from outside. Occasionally their mind seems to be floating a few feet above them—a sensation known as *doubling.* Their body parts seem foreign to them, the hands and feet smaller or bigger than usual. Many sufferers describe their emotional state as "mechanical," "dreamlike," or "dizzy." Throughout the whole depersonalization experience, however, they are aware that their perceptions are distorted, and in that sense they remain in contact with reality.

In some cases this sense of unreality also extends to other sensory experiences and behavior. People may, for example, experience distortions in their sense of touch or smell or their judgments of time or space, or they may feel that they have lost control over their speech or actions.

Depersonalization is often accompanied by an experience of *derealization*—the feeling that the external world, too, is unreal and strange. Objects may seem to change shape or size; other persons may seem removed, mechanical, or even dead. The graduate student, for example, began to perceive his girlfriend in a distorted manner, and he hesitated to return for a second session of therapy because he wondered whether his therapist was really alive.

Depersonalization experiences by themselves do not indicate a depersonalization disorder. Transient depersonalization reactions are fairly common, while a depersonalization

>>**IN THEIR WORDS**

"I was trying to daydream, but my mind kept wandering." <<

Steven Wright, comedian

Depersonalization and development *Psychologists have observed that children may occasionally experience depersonalization, feelings that their thoughts and words are foreign and unreal, while developing their capacity for self-awareness. Similarly, half of all adults experience at least one episode of depersonalization. Such transient feelings are normal. In contrast, depersonalization disorder is marked by persistent or recurrent experiences of detachment that cause significant distress or impairment.*

disorder is not (Miller, 2005; APA, 2000). One-third of all people say that on occasion they have felt as though they were watching themselves in a movie. Similarly, one-third of individuals who confront a life-threatening danger experience feelings of depersonalization or derealization. People sometimes have feelings of depersonalization after practicing meditation, and individuals who travel to new places often report a temporary sense of depersonalization. Young children may also experience depersonalization from time to time as they are developing their capacity for self-awareness. In most such cases, the individuals are able to compensate for the distortion, and continue to function with reasonable effectiveness until the temporary episode eventually ends.

The symptoms of a depersonalization disorder, in contrast, are persistent or recurrent, cause considerable distress, and interfere with social relationships and job performance (Simeon et al., 2003). The disorder occurs most frequently in adolescents and young adults, hardly ever in people over 40 (APA, 2000). It usually comes on suddenly, triggered by experiences such as extreme fatigue, physical pain, intense stress, anxiety, depression, or recovery from substance abuse. Survivors of traumatic experiences or people caught in life-threatening situations, such as hostages or kidnap victims, seem to be particularly vulnerable (APA, 2000). The disorder tends to be long-lasting; the symptoms may improve and even disappear for a time, only to return or intensify during times of severe stress. Like the graduate student in our case discussion, many people with the disorder fear that they are losing their minds and become preoccupied with worry about their symptoms.

Like other dissociative symptoms, feelings of depersonalization and derealization may appear in other disorders, including ones that we observed earlier. Sufferers of panic disorder, for example, commonly experience some feelings of unreality. Similarly, people with acute and posttraumatic stress disorders often have a sense of derealization (Simeon et al., 2003; Bremner, 2002).

Relatively few theories have been offered to explain depersonalization disorder and little research has been conducted on the problem. In recent times some investigators have used brain scan techniques, such as PET and MRI scans, to determine whether the disorder is accompanied by particular changes in brain activity (Phillips et al., 2001; Simeon et al., 2000). However, clear biological factors have yet to emerge. Similarly, treatments for this disorder have not received much study, although a range of approaches, including psychodynamic, cognitive, hypnotic, and drug therapies, have been tried (Sierra et al., 2001).

PUTTING IT together
Disorders Rediscovered

Somatoform and dissociative disorders are among the clinical field's earliest identified psychological disorders. Indeed, as we observed in Chapter 1, they were key to the development of the psychogenic perspective. Recall, for example, that Anton Mesmer developed the procedure of *hypnotism* (*mesmerism*) in the late eighteenth century by working with people who displayed hysterical somatoform disorders. Similarly, Freud's development of the psychoanalytic model in the late nineteenth century drew largely from his work with patients who displayed hysterical and dissociative disorders.

Despite this early impact, the clinical field stopped paying much attention to these disorders during the middle part of the twentieth century. The feeling among many clinical theorists was that the number of such cases was shrinking. And more than a few questioned the legitimacy of these diagnoses.

Much of that thinking has changed in the past two decades. The field's keen interest in the impact of stress upon health and physical illness has, by association, reawakened interest in somatoform disorders. Similarly, as we shall see in Chapter 18, the field has

>>Q & A
Why "a memory like an elephant's"?

The popular belief that elephants have long memories is based on the observation that the animals effortlessly find their way back home even after traveling more than 30 miles to find water. <<

Columbia/The Kobal Collection

Close encounters of a false kind? *In the popular 1977 movie* Close Encounters of the Third Kind, *Earth was visited by space aliens, and in a subsequent release of the film, humans actually got to enter the aliens' space ship. Simple science fiction entertainment for most people, but it turns out that some 3 million Americans believe that they have in fact had encounters with space aliens (Grierson, 2003). Research reveals that these people demonstrate the same kinds of lingering stress reactions experienced by people who recall more worldly traumatic events, such as combat experiences (Warner, 2004). Many clinical theorists believe that recollections of alien abductions are actually false memories. The theorists point out that the recollections of such abductions are often "recovered" memories, brought out by hypnosis or other unreliable memory-retrieval techniques, and that many people who believe they were abducted by aliens are particularly likely to experience alterations in consciousness, to have rich fantasy lives, and to endorse unconventional beliefs (Warner, 2004).*

greatly intensified its efforts to understand and treat Alzheimer's disease in recent years, and that work has sparked a broad interest in the operation and wonder of memory, including an interest in dissociative disorders.

Over the past 20 years there has been an explosion of research seeking to help clinicians recognize, understand, and treat unexplained physical and memory disorders. Although this research has yet to yield clear insights or highly effective treatments, it has already suggested that the disorders may be more common than clinical theorists had come to believe. Moreover, there is growing evidence that the disorders may be rooted in processes that are already well known from other areas of study, such as overattentiveness to bodily processes, cognitive misinterpretations, state-dependent learning, and self-hypnosis. Given this new wave of research enthusiasm, we may witness significant growth in our understanding and treatment of these disorders in the coming years.

Researchers' growing interest in these disorders has been accompanied by intense public interest as well. Moreover, it has sparked a greater belief in somatoform and dissociative disorders among many clinicians. More and more therapists are now identifying patients with multiple personalities, for example, and they are trying to provide corresponding treatments.

With this heightened interest and work come new problems (Mayou et al., 2005). Many of today's clinicians worry that the focus on somatoform and dissociative disorders is swinging too far—that the high degree of interest in them may be creating a false impression of their prevalence or importance (Piper & Merskey, 2004b). Some clinicians note, for example, that physicians are often quick to assign the label "somatoform" to elusive medical problems such as chronic fatigue syndrome, Gulf War syndrome, and lupus—clearly a disservice to patients with such severe problems and to the progress of medical science. Similarly, a number of clinicians worry that at least some of the many legal defenses based on dissociative identity disorder or other dissociative disorders are contrived or inaccurate. Of course, such possibilities serve to highlight even further the importance of continued investigations into all aspects of the disorders.

⟦ SUMMARY AND REVIEW ⟧

■ **Somatoform disorders** Patients with *somatoform disorders* have physical complaints whose causes are largely psychosocial. Nevertheless, the individuals genuinely believe that their illnesses are organic.

Hysterical somatoform disorders involve an actual loss or change of physical functioning. They include *conversion disorder, somatization disorder* (or *Briquet's syndrome*), and *pain disorder associated with psychological factors.* Diagnosticians are sometimes able

≫LOOKING AROUND
Gender Confusion

In some cultures, fathers follow the custom of *couvade:* they feel ill and stay in bed before and during the deliveries of their children. They may even show some symptoms of pregnancy and experience the pangs of childbirth (Kahn & Fawcett, 1993). ≪

>>LOOKING BACK
Strictly a Coincidence?

On February 17, 1673, the French actor-playwright Molière collapsed onstage and died while performing in *Le Malade Imaginaire* (*The Hypochondriac*) (Ash, 1999). ‹‹

to distinguish hysterical somatoform disorders from "true" medical problems by observing oddities in the patient's medical picture. They must also distinguish hysterical somatoform disorders from *malingering* and *factitious disorders.*

Freud developed the initial *psychodynamic view* of hysterical somatoform disorders, proposing that the disorders represent a conversion of underlying emotional conflicts into physical symptoms. According to *behaviorists,* the physical symptoms of these disorders bring rewards to the sufferer, and such reinforcement helps maintain the symptoms. Some *cognitive theorists* propose that the disorders are forms of *communication* and that people express their emotions through their physical symptoms. *Biological factors* may also help explain these disorders, as we are reminded by recent studies of *placebos.* Treatments for hysterical disorders emphasize either *insight, suggestion, reinforcement,* or *confrontation.*

People with *preoccupation somatoform disorders* are preoccupied with the notion that something is wrong with them physically. In this category are *hypochodriasis* and *body dysmorphic disorder.* Theorists explain preoccupation somatoform disorders much as they do anxiety disorders. Treatment for the disorders includes medications, exposure and response prevention, and other treatments originally developed for anxiety disorders. *pp. 190–202*

■ **Dissociative disorders** Memory plays a key role in our functioning by linking our past, present, and future. People with *dissociative disorders* experience major changes in memory, consciousness, and identity that are not due to clear physical causes. Typically, one part of the memory is *dissociated,* or separated, from the rest. People with *dissociative amnesia* are suddenly unable to recall important personal information or past events in their lives. Those with *dissociative fugue* not only fail to remember their personal identities but also flee to a different location and may establish a new identity.

In another dissociative disorder, *dissociative identity disorder (multiple personality disorder),* people display two or more distinct *subpersonalities.* The subpersonalities often have complex relationships with one another and usually differ in *vital statistics, abilities and preferences,* and even *physiological responses.* A *primary personality* appears more often than the others. The number of people diagnosed with multiple personality disorder has increased in recent years. *pp. 202–210*

■ **Explanations of dissociative disorders** The dissociative disorders are not well understood. Among the processes that have been cited to explain them are *extreme repression, operant conditioning, state-dependent learning,* and *self-hypnosis.* The latter two phenomena, in particular, have excited the interest of clinical scientists. The state-dependent learning explanation suggests that the thoughts, memories, and skills of people who develop dissociative disorders are tied exclusively to specific states of arousal, that is, to whatever mental state or emotion the people were experiencing when they first acquired the thoughts, memories, or skills. The self-hypnosis explanation proposes that people with these disorders have hypnotized themselves to forget horrifying experiences in their lives. *pp. 210–214*

■ **Treatments for dissociative disorders** Dissociative amnesia and fugue may end on their own or may require treatment. Dissociative identity disorder typically requires treatment. Approaches commonly used to help people with dissociative amnesia and fugue recover their lost memories are *psychodynamic therapy, hypnotic therapy,* and *sodium amobarbital* or *sodium pentobarbital.* Therapists who treat people with multiple personality disorder use the same approaches but focus on trying to help the clients *recognize the nature and scope of their disorder, recover the gaps in their memory,* and *integrate their subpersonalities into one functional personality. pp. 214–217*

■ **Depersonalization disorder** People with *depersonalization disorder* feel as though they have become detached from their own mental processes or body and are observing themselves from the outside. Some also experience *derealization.* Transient depersonalization experiences seem to be relatively common, while depersonalization disorder is not. People who experience traumatic events seem particularly vulnerable to this disorder. *pp. 217–218*

>>LOOKING BACK
Hypochondriasis through the Ages

Fourth Century B.C. Ancient Greeks used the term *hypochondria* to describe ailments such as melancholia and indigestion, because they believed those problems to start in the *hypochondrium,* a section under the rib cage. ‹‹

Fifteenth Century A.D. Hypochondria was associated with witchcraft and treated with potions and chants. ‹‹

Seventeenth Century A.D. Hypochondria was treated with bloodletting, vomiting, and sweating. ‹‹

Eighteenth Century A.D. Hypochondriasis was called the "English malady" because it occurred mainly in the English aristocracy. ‹‹

Nineteenth Century A.D. Hypochondriasis was treated with fresh air, spas, and relaxation. ‹‹

(Mitchell, 2004)

>>> CRITICAL THOUGHTS <<<

1. Why do the terms "hysteria" and "hysterical" currently have such negative connotations in our society, as in "mass hysteria" and "hysterical personality"? *pp. 190–194*

2. If parents who harm their children are clearly disturbed, as in cases of Munchausen syndrome by proxy, how should society react to them? Which is more appropriate—treatment or punishment? *p. 195*

3. How might a culture help create individual cases of body dysmorphic disorder? Why do some people in a society carry a culture's aesthetic ideals to an extreme, while others stay within normal bounds? *pp. 195–197*

4. Most people have had odd memory lapses such as forgetting why they are doing something, arriving at a destination without remembering any details of the drive there, forgetting an important appointment or occasion, having trouble remembering the name of a person or where they know someone from, or forgetting an event everyone else seems to remember. What kinds of explanations can you think of for each of these cases? *pp. 202–205*

5. Women are much more likely to receive a diagnosis of dissociative identity disorder than men. What might be some reasons for this difference? *pp. 208–214*

6. Some accused criminals claim that they have dissociative identity disorder and that their crimes were committed by one of their subpersonalities. If such claims are accurate, what would be an appropriate verdict? *p. 210*

7. Hypnosis is often used by therapists to help uncover hidden memories, motives, and needs. But hypnotic therapists can also use this suggestive technique to create desires, emotions, and behaviors. How can hypnotists know when they are *uncovering* a person's state of mind rather than *creating* it? *pp. 213–216*

⊙—[CYBER**STUDY**]————————————>>>

SEARCH THE *ABNORMAL PSYCHOLOGY* CD-ROM FOR

▲ Chapter 7 Video Cases and Discussions
   When do somatoform symptoms impair functioning and endanger sufferers?
   Why is it important to distinguish somatoform symptoms from factitious or true medical symptoms?
   Observe an individual with multiple personality disorder, and see "switches" from subpersonality to subpersonality.

▲ Chapter 7 Practical, Research, and Decision-Making Exercises
   Observing and measuring the power of suggestion
   Manufacturing memories

▲ Chapter 7 Practice Test and Feedback

LOG ON TO THE COMER WEB PAGE FOR

▲ Suggested Web links, exercises, FAQ page, additional Chapter 7 practice test questions
   <www.worthpublishers.com/comer>

————————————————————————————————<<<

Mood Disorders

F or . . . a six-month period, her irritability bordered on the irrational. She screamed in anger or sobbed in despair at every dirty dish left on the coffee table or on the bedroom floor. Each day the need to plan the dinner menu provoked agonizing indecision. How could all the virtues or, more likely, vices of hamburgers be accurately compared to those of spaghetti? . . . She had her whole family walking on eggs. She thought they would be better off if she were dead.

Beatrice could not cope with her job. As a branch manager of a large chain store, she had many decisions to make. Unable to make them herself, she would ask employees who were much less competent for advice, but then she could not decide whose advice to take. Each morning before going to work, she complained of nausea. . . .

Beatrice's husband loved her, but he did not understand what was wrong. He thought that she would improve if he made her life easier by taking over more housework, cooking, and child care. His attempt to help only made Beatrice feel more guilty and worthless. She wanted to make a contribution to her family. She wanted to do the chores "like normal people" did but broke down crying at the smallest impediment to a perfect job. . . . Months passed, and Beatrice's problem became more serious. Some days she was too upset to go to work. She stopped seeing her friends. She spent most of her time at home either yelling or crying. Finally, Beatrice's husband called the psychiatrist and insisted that something was seriously wrong.

(Lickey & Gordon, 1991, p. 181)

Most people's moods come and go. Their feelings of elation or sadness are understandable reactions to daily events and do not affect their lives greatly. The moods of people with mood disorders, in contrast, tend to last a long time. As in Beatrice's case, the mood colors all of their interactions with the world and interferes with normal functioning.

Depression and mania are the key emotions in mood disorders. **Depression** is a low, sad state in which life seems dark and its challenges overwhelming. **Mania,** the opposite of depression, is a state of breathless euphoria, or at least frenzied energy, in which people may have an exaggerated belief that the world is theirs for the taking. Most people with a mood disorder suffer only from depression, a pattern called **unipolar depression.** They have no history of mania and return to a normal or nearly normal mood when their depression lifts. Others experience periods of mania that alternate with periods of depression, a pattern called **bipolar disorder.** One might logically expect a third pattern of mood disorder, *unipolar mania,* in which people suffer from mania only, but this pattern is uncommon (Harish et al., 2005; APA, 2000, 1994).

Mood disorders have always captured people's interest, in part because so many famous people have suffered from them. The Bible speaks of the severe depressions of Nebuchadnezzar, Saul, and Moses. Queen Victoria of England and Abraham Lincoln seem to have experienced recurring depressions. Mood disorders also have plagued such writers as Ernest Hemingway, Eugene O'Neill, Virginia

•**DEPRESSION**•A low, sad state marked by significant levels of sadness, lack of energy, low self-worth, guilt, or related symptoms.

•**MANIA**•A state or episode of euphoria or frenzied activity in which people may have an exaggerated belief that the world is theirs for the taking.

•**UNIPOLAR DEPRESSION**•Depression without a history of mania.

•**BIPOLAR DISORDER**•A disorder marked by alternating or intermixed periods of mania and depression.

Woolf, and Sylvia Plath. Their mood problems have been shared by millions, and today the economic costs (work loss, treatment, hospitalization) amount to more than $80 billion each year (Sullivan et al., 2004; Greenberg et al., 2003). Of course, the human suffering that the disorders cause is beyond calculation.

Unipolar Depression

Whenever we feel particularly unhappy, we are likely to describe ourselves as "depressed." In all likelihood, we are merely responding to sad events, fatigue, or unhappy thoughts. This loose use of the term confuses a perfectly normal mood swing with a clinical syndrome. All of us experience dejection from time to time, but only some experience unipolar depression.

Normal dejection is seldom so severe as to influence daily functioning significantly or to persist very long. Such downturns in mood can even be beneficial (Keller & Nesse, 2005). Periods spent in contemplation can lead us to explore our inner selves, our values, and our way of life, and we often emerge with a sense of greater strength, clarity, and resolve.

Clinical depression, on the other hand, has no redeeming characteristics. It brings severe and long-lasting psychological pain that may intensify as time goes by (Isacson et al., 2005). Those who suffer from it may lose their will to carry out the simplest of life's activities; some even lose their will to live.

How Common Is Unipolar Depression?

Almost 7 percent of adults in the United States suffer from a severe unipolar pattern of depression in any given year, while as many as 5 percent suffer from mild forms (Kessler et al., 2005; Waraich et al., 2004). The prevalence is similar in Canada, England, France, and many other countries (WHO, 2004; Smith & Weissman, 1992) (see Table 8-1). Around 17 percent of all adults may experience an episode of severe unipolar depression at some point in their lives (Kessler et al., 2005, 2003, 2002). A worldwide research project suggests that the risk of experiencing this problem has steadily increased since 1915. Although unipolar depression may begin at any age, the median age for its onset, now 34 in the United States, has dropped with each generation (Drevets & Todd, 2005; Weissman et al., 1992, 1991).

In almost all countries, women are at least twice as likely as men to experience episodes of severe unipolar depression (McSweeney, 2004). As many as 26 percent of women may have an episode at some time in their lives, compared with 12 percent of men. Among children, the prevalence of unipolar depression is similar for girls and boys (Garber & Horowitz, 2002).

All of these rates hold steady across the various socioeconomic classes. Similarly, few differences in prevalence of unipolar depression have been found among ethnic groups. In the United States, middle-aged white Americans have a somewhat higher rate than middle-aged African Americans, but the rates for younger and older adults are the same in both populations (Weissman et al., 1991). Approximately half of people with unipolar depression recover within six weeks and 90 percent recover within a year, some without treatment (Kessler, 2002; Kendler et al., 1997). However, most of them have at least one other episode of depression later in their lives (Boland & Keller, 2002).

What Are the Symptoms of Depression?

The picture of depression may vary from person to person. Earlier we saw how Beatrice's indecisiveness, uncontrollable sobbing, and feelings of despair, anger, and worthlessness brought her job and social life to a standstill. Other depressed people have symptoms that are less severe. They manage to function, although their depression typically robs them of much effectiveness or pleasure, as we see in the case of Derek:

Musical remedy *Feeling blue is a normal part of life and should not be confused with clinical depression. Indeed it is much easier to fight off the blues than to eliminate depression. More than half of all people say, for example, that just listening to music effectively lifts their spirits when they are feeling down. Small wonder that iPods have become one of the twenty-first century's most popular electronic devices.*

Jeff Chiu/AP Photo

Derek has probably suffered from depression all of his adult life but was unaware of it for many years. Derek called himself a night person, claiming that he could not think clearly until after noon even though he was often awake by 4:00 A.M. He tried to schedule his work as editorial writer for a small town newspaper so that it was compatible with his depressed mood at the beginning of the day. Therefore, he scheduled meetings for the mornings; talking with people got him moving. He saved writing and decision making for later in the day.

. . . Derek's private thoughts were rarely cheerful and self-confident. He felt that his marriage was a mere business partnership. He provided the money, and she provided a home and children. Derek and his wife rarely expressed affection for each other. Occasionally, he had images of his own violent death in a bicycle crash, in a plane crash, or in a murder by an unidentified assailant.

Derek felt that he was constantly on the edge of job failure. He was disappointed that his editorials had not attracted the attention of larger papers. He was certain that several of the younger people on the paper had better ideas and wrote more skillfully than he did. He scolded himself for a bad editorial that he had written ten years earlier. Although that particular piece had not been up to his usual standards, everyone else on the paper had forgotten it a week after it appeared. But ten years later, Derek was still ruminating over that one editorial. . . .

Derek brushed off his morning confusion as a lack of quick intelligence. He had no way to know that it was a symptom of depression. He never realized that his death images might be suicidal thinking. People do not talk about such things. For all Derek knew, everyone had similar thoughts.

(Lickey & Gordon, 1991, pp. 183–185)

Table 8-1

Across the World: What Percentage of Adults Suffer from Mood Disorders Each Year?

United States	9.6%
Mexico	4.8%
Colombia	6.8%
France	8.5%
Germany	3.6%
Italy	3.8%
Spain	4.9%
Lebanon	6.6%
Japan	3.1%

Note: Mood disorders considered are major depressive disorder, dysthymic disorder, and bipolar disorder.
Source: WHO, 2004.

As the cases of Beatrice and Derek indicate, depression has many symptoms other than sadness. The symptoms, which often exacerbate one another, span five areas of functioning: emotional, motivational, behavioral, cognitive, and physical.

EMOTIONAL SYMPTOMS Most people who are depressed feel sad and dejected. They describe themselves as feeling "miserable," "empty," and "humiliated." They report getting little pleasure from anything, and they tend to lose their sense of humor. Some also experience anxiety, anger, or agitation (Benazzi et al., 2004). This sea of misery may lead to crying spells.

MOTIVATIONAL SYMPTOMS Depressed people typically lose the desire to pursue their usual activities. Almost all report a lack of drive, initiative, and spontaneity. They may have to force themselves to go to work, talk with friends, eat meals, or have sex. This state has been described as a "paralysis of will" (Beck, 1967). One individual recalls, "I didn't want to do anything—just wanted to stay put and be let alone" (Kraines & Thetford, 1972, p. 20).

Suicide represents the ultimate escape from life's challenges. As we shall see in Chapter 10, many depressed people become uninterested in life or wish to die; others wish they could kill themselves, and some actually do. It has been estimated that between 6 and 15 percent of people who suffer from severe depression commit suicide (Newman, 2005; Stolberg et al., 2002). More than one-quarter at least attempt suicide (Julien, 2005).

BEHAVIORAL SYMPTOMS Depressed people are usually less active and less productive. They spend more time alone and may stay in bed for long periods. One man recalls, "I'd awaken early, but I'd just lie there—what was the use of getting up to a miserable day?" (Kraines & Thetford, 1972, p. 21). Depressed people may also move and even speak more slowly (Joiner, 2002).

COGNITIVE SYMPTOMS Depressed people hold extremely negative views of themselves. They consider themselves inadequate, undesirable, inferior, perhaps evil. They also blame themselves for nearly every unfortunate event, even things that have nothing to do with them, and they rarely credit themselves for positive achievements.

Non-Western depression *Depressed people in non-Western countries tend to have fewer cognitive symptoms, such as self-blame, and more physical symptoms, such as fatigue, weakness, and sleep disturbances.*

Mirii Forsyth/Monkmeyer

"I usually wake up screaming at six-thirty, and I'm in my office by nine."

Another cognitive symptom of depression is pessimism. Sufferers are usually convinced that nothing will ever improve, and they feel helpless to change any aspect of their lives. Because they expect the worst, they are likely to procrastinate. Their sense of hopelessness and helplessness makes them especially vulnerable to suicidal thinking.

People with depression frequently complain that their intellectual ability is poor. They feel confused, unable to remember things, easily distracted, and unable to solve even the smallest problems. In laboratory studies, depressed subjects do perform more poorly than nondepressed subjects on some tasks of memory, attention, and reasoning (Bremner et al., 2004). It may be, however, that these difficulties sometimes reflect motivational problems rather than cognitive ones.

PHYSICAL SYMPTOMS People who are depressed frequently have such physical ailments as headaches, indigestion, constipation, dizzy spells, and general pain (Fishbain, 2000). In fact, many depressions are misdiagnosed as medical problems at first (Simon & Katzelnick, 1997). Disturbances in appetite and sleep are particularly common (Genchi et al., 2004). Most depressed people eat less, sleep less, and feel more fatigued than they did prior to the disorder. Some, however, eat and sleep excessively.

Diagnosing Unipolar Depression

According to DSM-IV-TR, a *major depressive episode* is a period marked by at least five symptoms of depression and lasting for two weeks or more (see Table 8-2). In extreme cases, the episode may include psychotic symptoms, ones marked by a loss of contact

---

Table **8-2** DSM Checklist:

MAJOR DEPRESSIVE EPISODE

1. The presence of at least five of the following symptoms during the same two-week period: • depressed mood most of the day, nearly every day • markedly diminished interest or pleasure in almost all activities most of the day, nearly every day • significant weight loss or weight gain, or decrease or increase in appetite nearly every day • insomnia or hypersomnia nearly every day • psychomotor agitation or retardation nearly every day • fatigue or loss of energy nearly every day • feelings of worthlessness or excessive guilt nearly every day • reduced ability to think or concentrate, or indecisiveness, nearly every day • recurrent thoughts of death or suicide, a suicide attempt, or a specific plan for committing suicide.
2. Significant distress or impairment.

MAJOR DEPRESSIVE DISORDER

1. The presence of a major depressive episode.
2. No history of a manic or hypomanic episode.

DYSTHYMIC DISORDER

1. Depressed mood for most of the day, for more days than not, for at least two years.
2. Presence, while depressed, of at least two of the following: • poor appetite or overeating • insomnia or hypersomnia • low energy or fatigue • low self-esteem • poor concentration or difficulty making decisions • feelings of hopelessness.
3. During the two-year period, symptoms not absent for more than two months at a time.
4. No history of a manic or hypomanic episode.
5. Significant distress or impairment.

Based on APA, 2000.

>>LOOKING AROUND

Campus Depression

Common Experience In a survey by the American College Health Association, more than 40 percent of students reported feeling "so depressed, it was difficult to function" at least once during the year (McGinn & Depasquale, 2004). **<<**

- -

Deconstructive Criticism College students who seek and receive negative feedback from their roommates feel more depressed than students who do not receive such feedback (Joiner, 1995).**<<**

with reality, such as *delusions*—bizarre ideas without foundation—or *hallucinations*—perceptions of things that are not actually present. A depressed man with psychotic symptoms may imagine that he can't eat "because my intestines are deteriorating and will soon stop working," or he may believe that he sees his dead wife.

People who experience a major depressive episode without having any history of mania receive a diagnosis of **major depressive disorder.** The disorder may be additionally categorized as *recurrent* if it has been preceded by previous episodes; *seasonal* if it changes with the seasons (for example, if the depression recurs each winter); *catatonic* if it is marked by either immobility or excessive activity; *postpartum* if it occurs within four weeks of giving birth (see Box 8-1 on the next page); or *melancholic* if the person is almost totally unaffected by pleasurable events (APA, 2000). It sometimes turns out that an apparent case of major depressive disorder is, in fact, a depressive episode occurring within a larger pattern of bipolar disorder—a pattern in which the individual's manic episode has not yet appeared. When the person experiences a manic episode at a later time, the diagnosis is changed to bipolar disorder (Angst et al., 2005; Bowden, 2005).

People who display a longer-lasting (at least two years) but less disabling pattern of unipolar depression may receive a diagnosis of **dysthymic disorder.** When dysthymic disorder leads to major depressive disorder, the sequence is called *double depression* (Dunner, 2005).

What Causes Unipolar Depression?

Episodes of unipolar depression often seem to be triggered by stressful events (Henn & Vollmayr, 2005; Paykel, 2003). In fact, researchers have found that depressed people experience a greater number of stressful life events during the month just before the onset of their disorder than do other people during the same period of time (Kendler et al., 2004, 1999; Monroe & Hadjiyannakis, 2002). Of course, stressful life events also precede other psychological disorders, but depressed people report more such events than anybody else.

Some clinicians consider it important to distinguish a *reactive (exogenous) depression,* which follows clear-cut stressful events, from an *endogenous depression,* which seems to be a response to internal factors (Kessing, 2004). But can one ever know for certain whether a depression is reactive or not? Even if stressful events occurred before the onset of depression, that depression may not be reactive. The events could actually be a coincidence (Paykel, 2003). Thus, today's clinicians usually concentrate on recognizing both the situational and the internal aspects of any given case of unipolar depression.

The current explanations of unipolar depression point to biological, psychological, and sociocultural factors. Just as clinicians now recognize both internal and situational features in each case of depression, many believe that the various explanations should be viewed collectively in order for unipolar depression to be fully understood.

The Biological View

Medical researchers have been aware for years that certain diseases and drugs produce mood changes. Could unipolar depression itself have biological causes? Evidence from genetic and biochemical studies suggests that often it does.

GENETIC FACTORS Four kinds of research—family pedigree, twin, adoption, and molecular biology gene studies—suggest that some people inherit a predisposition to unipolar depression. *Family pedigree studies* select people with unipolar depression as *probands* (the proband is the person who is the focus of a genetic study), examine their relatives, and see whether depression also afflicts other members of the family. If a predisposition to unipolar depression is inherited, a proband's relatives should have a higher rate of depression than the population at large. Researchers have in fact found that as many as 20 percent of those relatives are depressed (see Table 8-3 on page 229), compared with fewer than 10 percent of the general population (Harrington et al., 1993).

•**MAJOR DEPRESSIVE DISORDER**•A severe pattern of depression that is disabling and is not caused by such factors as drugs or a general medical condition.

•**DYSTHYMIC DISORDER**•A mood disorder that is similar to but longer-lasting and less disabling than a major depressive disorder.

Lincoln's private war *In 1841 Abraham Lincoln wrote to a friend, "I am now the most miserable man living. If what I feel were equally distributed to the whole human family, there would be not one cheerful face on earth."*

George P. A. Healy, 1887, The National Portrait Gallery, Smithsonian Institution

Sadness at the Happiest of Times

Women usually expect the birth of a child to be a happy experience. But for 10 to 30 percent of new mothers, the weeks and months after childbirth bring clinical depression (Rubertsson et al., 2005; Grace et al., 2003; O'Hara, 2003). Postpartum depression typically begins within four weeks after the birth of a child (APA, 2000), and it is far more severe than simple "baby blues." It is also different from other postpartum syndromes such as *postpartum psychosis,* a problem that we shall examine in Chapter 14.

The "baby blues" are so common—as many as 80 percent of women experience them—that most researchers consider them normal. As new mothers try to cope with the wakeful nights, rattled emotions, and other stresses that accompany the arrival of a new baby, they may experience crying spells, fatigue, anxiety, insomnia, and sadness. These symptoms usually disappear within days or weeks (Horowitz et al., 2005, 1995; Najman et al., 2000).

In postpartum depression, however, depressive symptoms continue and may last up to a year (Terry et al., 1996). The symptoms include extreme sadness, despair, tearfulness, insomnia, anxiety, intrusive thoughts, compulsions, panic attacks, feelings of inability to cope, and suicidal thoughts (Lindahl et al., 2005; Stevens et al., 2002). The mother-infant relationship and the health of the child may suffer as a result (Monti et al., 2004; Weinberg et al., 2001). Women who experience postpartum depression have a 25 to 50 percent chance of developing it again with a subsequent birth (Stevens et al., 2002; Wisner et al., 2001).

Many clinicians believe that the hormonal changes accompanying childbirth trigger postpartum depression (Parry, 1999). All women experience a kind of hormone "withdrawal" after delivery, as estrogen and progesterone levels, which rise as much as 50 times above normal during pregnancy, now drop sharply to levels far below normal (Horowitz et al., 2005, 1995). The levels of thyroid hormones, prolactin, and cortisol also change (Abou-Saleh et al., 1999). Perhaps some women are particularly influenced by these dramatic hormone changes. Still other theorists suggest a genetic predisposition to postpartum depression. A woman with a family history of mood disorders appears to be at high risk, even if she herself has not previously had a mood disorder (APA, 2000; Steiner & Tam, 1999).

At the same time, psychological and sociocultural factors may play important roles in the disorder. The birth of a baby brings enormous psychological and social change (Gjerdingen & Center, 2005; Nicolson, 1999). A woman typically faces changes in her marital relationship, daily routines, and social roles. Sleep and relaxation are likely to decrease and financial pressures may increase. Perhaps she feels the added stress of giving up a career—or of trying to maintain one. This pileup of stress may heighten the risk of depression (Horowitz et al., 2005; Swendsen & Mazure, 2000; Terry et al., 1996). Mothers whose infants are sick or temperamentally "difficult" may experience yet additional pressure.

Fortunately, treatment can make a big difference for most women with postpartum depression. Self-help support groups have proved extremely helpful for many women with the disorder (O'Hara, 2003; Stevens et al., 2002; Honikman, 1999). In addition, many respond well to the same approaches that are applied to other forms of depression—antidepressant medications, cognitive therapy, interpersonal psychotherapy, or a combination of these approaches (O'Hara, 2003; Stuart et al., 2003; Stowe et al., 1995).

However, many women who would benefit from treatment do not seek help because they feel ashamed about being sad at a time that is supposed to be joyous or they are concerned about being judged harshly (APA, 2000, 1994). For them, and for the spouses and family members close to them, a large dose of education is in order. Even positive events can be stressful and upsetting if they also bring major change to one's life. Recognizing and addressing such upsets are in everyone's best interest.

Paramount/The Kobal Collection

And Down Came the Rain *Brooke Shields's professional life was forever changed when she starred in the critically acclaimed 1978 movie* Pretty Baby. *In her recent book,* And Down Came the Rain, *Shields describes how her personal life was profoundly changed when she gave birth to her daughter, Rowan, in 2003. The birth triggered an episode of postpartum depression, which was successfully treated by a combination of support, counseling, and antidepressant drugs.*

Table 8-3

Mood Disorders Profile

	One-year Prevalence (Percent)	Female to Male Ratio	Typical Age at Onset (Years)	Prevalence among First-Degree Relatives	Percentage Currently Receiving Treatment
Major depressive disorder	6.7%	2:1	24–29	Elevated	32.9%
Dysthymic disorder	1.5–5.0	Between 3:2 and 2:1	10–25	Elevated	36.8
Bipolar I disorder	1.6	1:6	15–44	Elevated	33.8
Bipolar II disorder	1.0	1:1	15–44	Elevated	33.8
Cyclothymic disorder	0.4	1:1	15–25	Elevated	Unknown

Source: Kessler et al., 2005, 1994; APA, 2000, 1994; Regier et al., 1993; Weissman et al., 1991

If a predisposition to unipolar depression is inherited, we would also expect to find a particularly large number of cases among the close relatives of a proband. *Twin studies* have supported this expectation (Richard & Lyness, 2006; Kalidindi & McGuffin, 2003). One study looked at nearly 200 pairs of twins. When a monozygotic (identical) twin had uni-polar depression, there was a 46 percent chance that the other twin would have the same disorder. In contrast, when a dizygotic (fraternal) twin had unipolar depression, the other twin had only a 20 percent chance of developing the disorder (McGuffin et al., 1996).

Adoption studies have also implicated a genetic factor, at least in cases of severe unipolar depression. One study looked at the families of adopted persons who had been hospitalized for this disorder in Denmark. The biological parents of these adoptees turned out to have a higher incidence of severe depression (but not mild depression) than did the biological parents of a control group of nondepressed adoptees (Wender et al., 1986). Some theorists interpret these findings to mean that severe depression is more likely than mild depression to be caused by genetic factors.

Finally, today's scientists have at their disposal techniques from the field of molecular biology to help them directly identify genes and determine whether certain gene abnormalities are related to depression. Using such techniques, a number of researchers have found that individuals who are depressed often have an abnormality of their *5-HTT* gene, the gene responsible for the brain's transportation of the neurotransmitter serotonin (Hecimovic & Gilliam, 2006). As we have seen, neurotransmitters are the brain chemicals that carry messages from one nerve cell to another. And, as we shall observe in the next section, low activity of serotonin is closely tied to depression (Brody et al., 2005; Murphy et al., 2004; Caspi et al, 2003).

BIOCHEMICAL FACTORS Low activity of two neurotransmitter chemicals, **norepinephrine** and **serotonin,** has been strongly linked to unipolar depression. In the 1950s, several pieces of evidence began to point to this relationship. First, medical researchers discovered that *reserpine* and other medications for high blood pressure often caused depression (Ayd, 1956). As it turned out, some of these medications lowered norepinephrine activity and others lowered serotonin. A second piece of evidence was the discovery of the first truly effective antidepressant drugs. Although these drugs were discovered by accident, researchers soon learned that they relieve depression by increasing either norepinephrine or serotonin activity.

For years it was thought that low activity of *either* norepinephrine or serotonin was capable of producing depression, but researchers now believe that their relation to depression is more complicated than that (Drevets & Todd, 2005). Investigations suggest that interactions between serotonin and norepinephrine activity, or between these neurotransmitters and yet other neurotransmitters in the brain, rather than the operation of

•NOREPINEPHRINE•A neurotransmitter whose abnormal activity is linked to depression and panic disorder.

•SEROTONIN•A neurotransmitter whose abnormal activity is linked to depression, obsessive-compulsive disorder, and eating disorders.

[BOX 8-2]

The Rhythms of Depression

Our lives are structured by cycles and rhythms—daily, monthly, seasonal, and yearly. The 24-hour day provides the cycle to which we adapt our most common activities—sleeping, eating, working, and socializing. Although our daily rhythms are affected by our environment, they are also driven by a kind of internal clock, consisting of recurrent biological fluctuations, called *circadian rhythms,* which must be coordinated with one another and with changes in the environment (Loros et al., 2004).

One of these circadian rhythms is strong and consistent, and it rigidly controls regular changes in body temperature, hormone secretions, and *rapid eye movement (REM)* sleep—the near-awake phase of sleep during which we dream. Another, more flexible rhythm controls the sleep-wake cycle and activity-rest cycle. Most people can go to sleep late one night and early the next and have no trouble falling asleep quickly and sleeping soundly; but during this period their body temperature will rigidly follow its usual pattern, peaking at the same time each afternoon and bottoming out each morning.

SLEEP AND DEPRESSION

A series of revealing studies begun in the 1980s suggests that depression is often the result of an imbalance, or *desynchronization,* between the body's circadian rhythms and the rhythms of the environment (Bunney & Bunney, 2000). For example, the sleep cycle, the most basic rhythm in our lives, apparently is reversed in depressed people (Wilson & Nutt, 2005; Thase et al., 2002). They move into REM sleep more quickly than nondepressed people after falling asleep, experience longer stretches of REM sleep during the early parts of the sleep cycle and shorter stretches toward the morning, display more frequent rapid eye movements during REM sleep, and enjoy less deep sleep overall (Wichniak et al., 2000). Thus some theorists think that the body's circadian rhythms, the rigid one that is in control of REM sleep and the flexible one in control of the sleep-wake cycle, may be out of harmony for depressed people.

If the sleep-wake cycle is disturbed for depressed people, and if their body rhythms are indeed out of harmony, might it not be helpful to change their sleep patterns? This is, in fact, a strategy sometimes used on depressed people who do not respond to more conventional forms of treatment. In a number of sleep laboratories, clinicians have deprived depressed patients of partial or full episodes of sleep. Their findings? The moods and functioning of many such patients improve markedly (Danilenko & Putilov, 2005; Koorengevel et al., 2003, 2002).

PUTTING A GOOD LIGHT ON DEPRESSION

The hormone *melatonin* plays a major role in the operation of our circadian rhythms. For animals and humans alike, this hormone is released by the brain's *pineal gland* when environmental surroundings are dark, but not when they are light. In animals the hormone helps to control hibernation, activity levels, and the reproductive cycle. As nights grow longer during the fall, animals release more and more melatonin, which has the effect of slowing them down and preparing them for an extended rest over the winter. When daylight hours lengthen in the spring, melatonin secretions decline, raising energy levels.

Although they do not produce hibernation in humans, the heightened melatonin secretions of winter do apparently cause us to slow down, have less energy, and need more rest (Wetterberg, 1999). While most people adjust to such changes, some individuals seem so sensitive to winter's heightened secretions that they find it impossible to carry on with business as

---

any one neurotransmitter alone, may account for unipolar depression. Some studies hint, for example, that depressed people have an overall imbalance in the activity of the neurotransmitters serotonin, norepinephrine, dopamine, and acetylcholine (Thase et al., 2002). In a variation of this theory, some researchers believe that serotonin is, as we observed on page 149, actually a *neuromodulator,* a chemical whose primary function is to increase or decrease the activity of other key neurotransmitters. If so, perhaps low serotonin activity serves to disrupt the activity of the other neurotransmitters, thus leading to depression.

Biological researchers have also learned that the body's *endocrine system* may play a role in unipolar depression (see Box 8-2). As we have seen, endocrine glands throughout the body release *hormones,* chemicals that in turn spur body organs into action (see Chapter 6). People with unipolar depression have been found to have abnormal levels of *cortisol,* one of the hormones released by the adrenal glands during times of stress (Neumeister et al., 2005; Holsboer, 2001). This relationship is not all that surprising, given that stressful events often seem to trigger depression. Another hormone that has been tied to depression is *melatonin,* sometimes called the "Dracula hormone" because it is released only in the dark.

usual. Their slowdown takes the form of depression each winter, a pattern called *seasonal affective disorder,* or *SAD* (Neto et al., 2004; Waterhouse & DeCoursey, 2004; Rosenthal & Blehar, 1989). SAD is less common in locations closer to the equator—that is, in areas where daylight hours vary little throughout the year and melatonin secretions do not increase appreciably in the winter months (Teng et al., 1995; Ito et al., 1992). Certain people with SAD are also very sensitive to the drop in melatonin secretions that occurs during the longer days of summer; some even become overenergized and manic every summer (Faedda et al., 1993).

If in fact darkness is the problem in SAD, the answer may be light. One of the most effective treatments for SAD turns out to be *light therapy,* or *phototherapy,* exposure to extra amounts of artificial light throughout the winter. When seasonally depressed patients sit under special lights for several hours every winter day, their depression is often reduced or eliminated (Golden et al., 2005; Gitlin, 2002).

Of course, there are more natural ways to get extra light. Some researchers have found that SAD patients are helped by morning walks outside (Wirz-Justice et al., 1996). Similarly, clinicians often recommend taking a winter vacation in a sunny place. Some go so far as to suggest that people with wintertime blues, and certainly those with SAD, should spend a week or two just before winter begins in a location approximately 3 to 4 degrees north or south of the equator, where 70 percent more sunlight is available each day. The effectiveness of this form of "treatment" has yet to be investigated systematically.

Clinicians are also searching for simpler ways to change the melatonin levels of people with SAD. One possibility is the enormously popular *melatonin pills.* Research suggests that melatonin pills, given at key times in the day, might help readjust patients' secretions of their own melatonin and reduce depression (Leppamaki et al., 2003; Hätönen, Alila, & Laakso, 1996). Thus far, however, the optimal dosage and timing of such pills have proved elusive.

The importance of light
These children, who live 200 miles north of the Arctic Circle, receive a daily dose of ultraviolet light to compensate for the lack of midwinter sun. Clinicians now know that light is important to both physical and psychological health.

Mark S. Wexler, Chicago

Still other biological researchers are starting to believe that unipolar depression is tied more closely to what happens *within* neurons than to the chemicals that carry messages from neuron to neuron (Julien, 2005). They believe that activity by key neurotransmitters or hormones ultimately leads to deficiencies of important proteins and other chemicals within neurons, particularly to deficiencies of a chemical called *brain-derived neurotrophic factor (BDNF)* (Julien, 2005; Duman, 2004; Wallace et al., 2004). Such chemical deficiencies within neurons may impair the health of the neurons and lead, in turn, to depression.

The biological explanations of unipolar depression have produced much enthusiasm, but research in this area has certain limitations. Some of it has relied on *analogue studies,* which create depression-like symptoms in laboratory animals. Researchers cannot be certain that these symptoms do in fact reflect the human disorder. Similarly, until recent years, technology was limited, and biological studies of human depression had to measure brain activity indirectly. As a result, investigators could never be certain of the biological events that were occurring in the brain. Current studies using newer technology, such as PET and MRI scans, are helping to eliminate such uncertainties about brain activity.

>>LAB•NOTES
Mutual Damage

Investigators have long known that physical decline in the elderly can lead to depression. Studies also reveal that depression itself often causes physical decline and physical impairment in the elderly (Callahan et al., 1998; Penninx et al., 1998). <<

Psychological Views

The psychological models that have been most widely applied to unipolar depression are the psychodynamic, behavioral, and cognitive models. The psychodynamic explanation has not been strongly supported by research, and the behavioral view has received only modest support. In contrast, cognitive explanations have received considerable research support and have gained a large following.

THE PSYCHODYNAMIC VIEW Sigmund Freud (1917) and his student Karl Abraham (1916, 1911) developed the first psychodynamic explanation of depression. They began by noting the similarity between clinical depression and grief in people who lose loved ones: constant weeping, loss of appetite, difficulty sleeping, loss of pleasure in life, and general withdrawal.

According to Freud and Abraham, a series of unconscious processes is set in motion when a loved one dies. Unable to accept the loss, mourners at first regress to the *oral stage* of development, the period of total dependency when infants cannot distinguish themselves from their parents. By regressing to this stage, the mourners merge their own identity with that of the person they have lost, and so symbolically regain the lost person. In this process, called *introjection,* they direct all their feelings for the loved one, including sadness and anger, toward themselves.

For most mourners, introjection is temporary. For some, however, grief worsens over time. They feel empty, they continue to avoid social relationships, and their sense of loss increases. They become depressed. Freud and Abraham believed that two kinds of people are particularly likely to become clinically depressed in the face of loss: those whose parents failed to nurture them and meet their needs during the oral stage and those whose parents gratified those needs excessively. Infants whose needs are inadequately met remain overly dependent on others throughout their lives, feel unworthy of love, and have low self-esteem. Those whose needs are excessively gratified find the oral stage so pleasant that they resist moving on to subsequent stages. Either way, the individuals may devote their lives to others, desperately in search of love and approval (Busch et al., 2004; Bemporad, 1992). They are likely to feel a greater sense of loss when a loved one dies.

Of course, many people become depressed without losing a loved one. To explain why, Freud proposed the concept of **symbolic,** or **imagined, loss,** in which persons equate other kinds of events with loss of a loved one. A college student may, for example, experience failure in a calculus course as the loss of her parents, believing that they love her only when she excels academically.

Although many psychodynamic theorists have parted company with Freud and Abraham's theory of depression, it continues to influence current psychodynamic thinking (Busch et al., 2004). For example, *object relations theorists,* the psychodynamic theorists who emphasize relationships, propose that depression results when people's relationships leave them feeling unsafe and insecure (Allen et al., 2004; Blatt, 2004). People whose parents pushed them toward either excessive dependence or excessive self-reliance are more likely to become depressed when they later lose important relationships.

The following therapist description of a depressed middle-aged woman illustrates the psychodynamic concepts of dependence, loss of a loved one, symbolic loss, and introjection:

Homer Sykes/Woodfin Camp & Associates

Early loss *Research has found that people who lose their parents as children have an increased likelihood of experiencing depression as adults.*

•**SYMBOLIC LOSS**•According to Freudian theory, the loss of a valued object (for example, a loss of employment) which is unconsciously interpreted as the loss of a loved one. Also called *imagined loss.*

•**ANACLITIC DEPRESSION**•A pattern of depressed behavior found among very young children that is caused by separation from one's mother.

> Mrs. Marie Carls . . . had always felt very attached to her mother. As a matter of fact, they used to call her "Stamp" because she stuck to her mother as a stamp to a letter. She always tried to placate her volcanic mother, to please her in every possible way. . . .
>
> After marriage [to Julius], she continued her pattern of submission and compliance. Before her marriage she had difficulty in complying with a volcanic mother, and after her marriage she almost automatically assumed a submissive role. . . .

Several months after beginning treatment, the patient reported a dream. Ignatius and she had decided not to see each other again. She would have to leave him forever. I asked who Ignatius was, because I had not heard the name until then. The patient replied almost with surprise, "But the first time I came to see you, I told you that in the past I had had an infatuation." She then told me that when she was thirty years old . . . [she] and her husband invited Ignatius, who was single, to come and live with them. Ignatius and the patient soon discovered that they had an attraction for each other. They both tried to fight that feeling; but when Julius had to go to another city for a few days, the so-called infatuation became much more than that. There were a few physical contacts. . . . There was an intense spiritual affinity. . . . A few months later everybody had to leave the city. . . . Nothing was done to maintain contact. Two years later, approximately a year after the end of the war, Marie heard that Ignatius had married. She felt terribly alone and despondent. . . .

Her suffering had become more acute as she realized that old age was approaching and she had lost all her chances. Ignatius remained as the memory of lost opportunities. . . . Her life of compliance and obedience had not permitted her to reach her goal. . . . When she became aware of these ideas, she felt even more depressed. . . . She felt that everything she had built in her life was false or based on a false premise.

(Arieti & Bemporad, 1978, pp. 275–284)

>>LOOKING AROUND

World Count Around 122,865,000 new cases of mood disorder emerge each year worldwide (World Health Organization). **<<**

Popular Search Depression is the most common health care topic searched for on the Internet each year (19 percent of searches), followed by allergies/sinuses (16 percent), bipolar disorder (14 percent), and arthritis/rheumatism (10 percent) (Harris Poll). **<<**

Studies have offered general support for the psychodynamic idea that depression may be triggered by a major loss. In a famous study of 123 infants who were placed in a nursery after being separated from their mothers, René Spitz (1946, 1945) found that 19 of the infants became very weepy and sad upon separation and withdrew from their surroundings—a pattern called **anaclitic depression.** Studies of infant monkeys who are separated from their mothers have noted a similar pattern of apparent depression (Harlow & Zimmermann, 1996; Harlow & Harlow, 1965).

Other research, involving both human and animal subjects, suggests that losses suffered early in life may set the stage for later depression (Pryce et al., 2005; Lara & Klein, 1999). When, for example, a depression scale was administered to 1,250 medical patients during visits to their family physicians, the patients whose fathers had died during their childhood scored higher on depression (Barnes & Prosen, 1985).

Related research supports the psychodynamic idea that people whose childhood needs were improperly met are particularly likely to become depressed after experiencing loss (Goodman, 2002). In some studies, depressed subjects have filled out a scale called the Parental Bonding Instrument, which indicates how much care and protection people feel they received as children. Many have identified their parents' child-rearing style as "affectionless control," consisting of a mixture of low care and high protection (Martin et al., 2004; Narita et al., 2000; Parker et al., 1995).

These studies offer some support for the psychodynamic view of unipolar depression, but this support has key limitations. First, although the findings indicate that losses and inadequate parenting *sometimes* relate to depression, they do not establish that such factors are *typically* responsible for the disorder. In the studies of young children and young monkeys, for example, only some of the subjects who were separated from their mothers showed depressive reactions. In fact, it is estimated that less than 10 percent of all people who experience major losses in life actually become depressed (Bonanno, 2004; Paykel & Cooper, 1992; Paykel, 1982). Second, many findings are inconsistent. Though some studies find evidence of a relationship between childhood loss and later depression, others do not (Parker, 1992). Finally, certain features of the psychodynamic explanation are nearly impossible to test. Because symbolic loss is said to operate at an unconscious level, for example, it is difficult for researchers to determine if and when it is occurring.

Across the species *Researcher Harry Harlow and his colleagues found that infant monkeys reacted with apparent despair to separation from their mothers. Even monkeys raised with surrogate mothers—wire cylinders wrapped with foam rubber and covered with terry cloth—formed an attachment to them and mourned their absence.*

University of Wisconsin Primate Laboratory, Madison

Mark Lennihan/AP Worldwide Photos

Saying goodbye *As highlights of his glorious career appear on a screen, Wayne Gretsky announces his retirement from ice hockey. According to behaviorists, the reduction in rewards brought about by retirement places sports stars and other high achievers at risk for depression unless they can develop a healthy perspective about the change and add new sources of gratification to their lives.*

>>PSYCH•LISTINGS

Laughter, a Good Medicine

55% Percentage of adults in the United States who say they laugh at least once an hour **‹‹**

- -

75% Young adults who laugh at least once an hour **‹‹**

- -

36% Elderly people who laugh at least once an hour **‹‹**

- -

(Kanner, 1998)

THE BEHAVIORAL VIEW Behaviorists believe that unipolar depression results from significant changes in the number of rewards and punishments people receive in their lives. During the 1970s and 1980s, the clinical researcher Peter Lewinsohn developed one of the leading behavioral explanations (Lewinsohn et al., 1990, 1984). He suggested that the positive rewards in life dwindle for some persons, leading them to perform fewer and fewer constructive behaviors. The rewards of campus life, for example, disappear when a young woman graduates from college and takes a job; and an aging baseball player loses the rewards of high salary and adulation when his skills deteriorate. Although many people manage to fill their lives with other forms of gratification, some become particularly disheartened. The positive features of their lives decrease even more, and the decline in rewards leads them to perform still fewer constructive behaviors. In this manner, the individuals spiral toward depression.

In a series of studies, Lewinsohn and his colleagues found that the number of rewards people receive in life is indeed related to the presence or absence of depression. Not only did depressed subjects in his studies report fewer positive rewards than nondepressed subjects, but when their rewards began to increase, their mood improved as well (Lewinsohn, Youngren, & Grosscup, 1979). Similarly, more recent investigations have found a strong relationship between positive life events and feelings of life satisfaction and happiness (Lu, 1999).

Lewinsohn and other behaviorists further proposed that *social* rewards are particularly important in the downward spiral of depression (Peterson, 1993; Lewinsohn et al., 1984). This claim has been supported by research showing that depressed persons experience fewer social rewards than nondepressed persons and that as their mood improves, their social rewards increase. Although depressed people are sometimes the victims of social circumstances, it may also be that their dark mood and flat behaviors help produce a decline in social rewards (Joiner, 2002; Coyne, 2001).

Behaviorists have done an admirable job of compiling data to support this theory, but this research, too, has limitations. It has relied heavily on the self-reports of depressed subjects, and as we saw in Chapter 4, measures of this kind can be biased and inaccurate; depressed people's reports may be influenced heavily by a gloomy mood and negative outlook. Moreover, the behavioral studies have been largely correlational and do not establish that decreases in rewarding events are the initial cause of depression. As we just noted, for example, a depressed mood in itself may lead to negative behaviors and decreases in activities and hence to fewer rewards.

COGNITIVE VIEWS Cognitive theorists believe that people with unipolar depression persistently view events in negative ways and that such perceptions lead to their disorder. The two most influential cognitive explanations are the *theory of negative thinking* and the *theory of learned helplessness.*

NEGATIVE THINKING Aaron Beck (2002, 1991, 1967) believes that negative thinking, rather than underlying conflicts or a reduction in positive rewards, lies at the heart of depression. Other cognitive theorists—Albert Ellis, for one—also point to maladaptive thinking as a key to depression, but Beck's theory is the one most often associated with the disorder. According to Beck, *maladaptive attitudes,* a *cognitive triad,* errors in thinking, and *automatic thoughts* combine to produce unipolar depression.

Beck believes that some people develop *maladaptive attitudes* as children, such as "My general worth is tied to every task I perform" or "If I fail, others will feel repelled by me." The attitudes result from their own experiences, their family relationships, and the judgments of the people around them (see Figure 8-1). Many failures are inevitable in a full, active life, so such attitudes are inaccurate and set the stage for all kinds of negative thoughts and reactions. Beck suggests that later in these people's lives, upsetting situations may trigger an extended round of negative thinking. That thinking typically takes three forms, which he calls the **cognitive triad:** the individuals repeatedly interpret (1) their *experiences,* (2) *themselves,* and (3) their *futures* in negative ways that lead them to feel depressed. The cognitive triad is at work in the thinking of this depressed person:

> I can't bear it. I can't stand the humiliating fact that I'm the only woman in the world who can't take care of her family, take her place as a real wife and mother, and be respected in her community. When I speak to my young son Billy, I know I can't let him down, but I feel so ill-equipped to take care of him; that's what frightens me. I don't know what to do or where to turn; the whole thing is too overwhelming. . . . I must be a laughing stock. It's more than I can do to go out and meet people and have the fact pointed up to me so clearly.
>
> *(Fieve, 1975)*

According to Beck, depressed people also make *errors in their thinking.* In one common error of logic, they draw *arbitrary inferences*—negative conclusions based on little evidence. A man walking through the park, for example, passes a woman who is looking at nearby flowers, and he concludes, "She's avoiding looking at me." Similarly, depressed people often *minimize* the significance of positive experiences or *magnify* that of negative ones. A college student receives an A on a difficult English exam, for example, but concludes that the grade reflects the professor's generosity rather than her own ability (minimization). Later in the week the same student must miss an English class and is convinced that she will be unable to keep up the rest of the semester (magnification).

Finally, depressed people experience **automatic thoughts,** a steady train of unpleasant thoughts that keep suggesting to them that they are inadequate and that their situation is hopeless. Beck labels these thoughts "automatic" because they seem to just happen, as if by reflex. In the course of only a few hours, depressed people may be visited by hundreds of such thoughts: "I'm worthless. . . . I'll never amount to anything. . . . I let everyone down. . . . Everyone hates me. . . . My responsibilities are overwhelming. . . . I've failed as a parent. . . . I'm stupid. . . . Everything is difficult for me. . . . Things will never change." One therapist said of a depressed client, "By the end of the day, she is worn out, she has lived a thousand painful accidents, participated in a thousand deaths, mourned a thousand mistakes" (Mendels, 1970).

Many studies have produced evidence in support of Beck's explanation. Several of them confirm that depressed people hold maladaptive attitudes, and the more of these maladaptive attitudes they hold, the more depressed they tend to be (Evans et al., 2005;

•**COGNITIVE TRIAD**•The three forms of negative thinking that Aaron Beck theorizes lead people to feel depressed. The triad consists of a negative view of one's experiences, oneself, and the future.

•**AUTOMATIC THOUGHTS**•Numerous unpleasant thoughts that help to cause or maintain depression, anxiety, or other forms of psychological dysfunction.

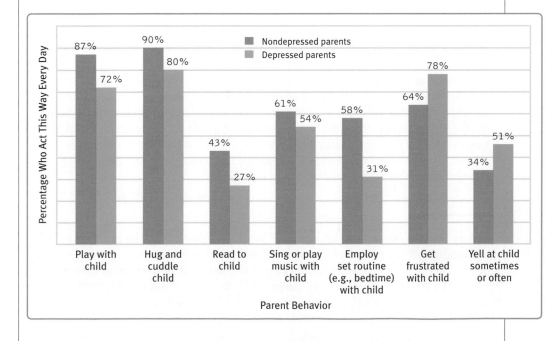

FIGURE **8-1** **How depressed parents and their children interact** *Depressed parents are less likely than nondepressed parents to play with, hug, read to, or sing to their young children each day or to employ the same routine each day. They are also more likely to get frustrated with their children on a daily basis. (Adapted from Princeton Survey Research Associates, 1996.)*

Arnie Levin/Cartoonbank.com

"I have trouble keeping in touch with my silver lining."

Whisman & McGarvey, 1995). Still other research has found the cognitive triad at work in depressed people (Ridout et al., 2003). In various studies, depressed subjects seem to recall unpleasant experiences more readily than positive ones, rate their performances on laboratory tasks lower than nondepressed subjects do, and select pessimistic statements in storytelling tests (for example, "I expect my plans will fail").

Beck's claims about errors in logic have also received research support (Cole & Turner, 1993). In one study, female subjects—some depressed, some not—were asked to read and interpret paragraphs about women in difficult situations. Depressed subjects made more errors in logic (such as arbitrary inference) in their interpretations than nondepressed women did (Hammen & Krantz, 1976).

Finally, research has supported Beck's claim that automatic thoughts are tied to depression. In several studies, nondepressed subjects who are tricked into reading negative automatic-thought-like statements about themselves become increasingly depressed (Bates, Thompson, & Flanagan, 1999; Strickland, Hale, & Anderson, 1975). In a related line of research, it has been found that people who generally make *ruminative responses* during their depressed moods—that is, repeatedly dwell mentally on their mood without acting to change it—experience dejection longer and are more likely to develop clinical depression later in life than people who avoid such ruminations (Nolen-Hoeksema & Corte, 2004; Nolen-Hoeksema, 2002, 1998, 1995).

This body of research shows that negative thinking is indeed linked to depression, but it fails to show that such patterns of thought are the cause and core of unipolar depression. It could be that a central mood problem leads to thinking difficulties that then take a further toll on mood, behavior, and physiology.

LEARNED HELPLESSNESS Feelings of helplessness fill this account of a young woman's depression:

> Mary was 25 years old and had just begun her senior year in college. . . . Asked to recount how her life had been going recently, Mary began to weep. Sobbing, she said that for the last year or so she felt she was losing control of her life and that recent stresses (starting school again, friction with her boyfriend) had left her feeling worthless and frightened. Because of a gradual deterioration in her vision, she was now forced to wear glasses all day. "The glasses make me look terrible," she said, and "I don't look people in the eye much any more." Also, to her dismay, Mary had gained 20 pounds in the past year. She viewed herself as overweight and unattractive. At times she was convinced that with enough money to buy contact lenses and enough time to exercise she could cast off her depression; at other times she believed nothing would help. . . . Mary saw her life deteriorating in other spheres, as well. She felt overwhelmed by schoolwork and, for the first time in her life, was on academic probation. . . . In addition to her dissatisfaction with her appearance and her fears about her academic future, Mary complained of a lack of friends. Her social network consisted solely of her boyfriend, with whom she was living. Although there were times she experienced this relationship as almost unbearably frustrating, she felt helpless to change it and was pessimistic about its permanence. . . .
>
> *(Spitzer et al., 1983, pp. 122–123)*

Mary feels that she is "losing control of her life." According to the psychologist Martin Seligman (1975), such feelings of helplessness are at the center of her depression. Since the mid-1960s Seligman has developed the **learned helplessness** theory of depression. It holds that people become depressed when they think (1) that they no longer have control over the reinforcements (the rewards and punishments) in their lives and (2) that they themselves are responsible for this helpless state.

•**LEARNED HELPLESSNESS**•The perception, based on past experiences, that one has no control over one's reinforcements.

Seligman's theory first began to take shape when he was working with laboratory dogs. In one procedure, he strapped dogs into an apparatus called a hammock, in which they received shocks periodically no matter what they would do. The next day each dog was placed in a *shuttle box,* a box divided in half by a barrier over which the animal could jump to reach the other side (see Figure 8-2). Seligman applied shocks to the dogs in the box, expecting that they, like other dogs in this situation, would soon learn to escape by jumping over the barrier. However, most of these dogs failed to learn anything in the shuttle box. After a flurry of activity, they simply "lay down and quietly whined" and accepted the shock.

Seligman decided that while receiving inescapable shocks in the hammock the day before, the dogs had learned that they had no control over unpleasant events (shocks) in their lives. That is, they had learned that they were helpless to do anything to change negative situations. Thus, when later they were placed in a new situation (the shuttle box) where they could in fact control their fate, they continued to believe that they were generally helpless. Seligman noted that the effects of learned helplessness greatly resemble the symptoms of human depression, and he proposed that people in fact become depressed after developing a general belief that they have no control over reinforcements in their lives.

In numerous human and animal studies, subjects who undergo helplessness training have displayed reactions similar to depressive symptoms. When, for example, human subjects are exposed to uncontrollable negative events, they later score higher than other subjects on a depressive mood survey (Miller & Seligman, 1975). Similarly, helplessness-trained animal subjects lose interest in sexual and social activities—a common symptom of human depression (Lindner, 1968). Finally, uncontrollable negative events result in lower norepinephrine and serotonin activity in rats (Wu et al., 1999). This, of course, is similar to the neurotransmitter activity found in the brains of people with unipolar depression.

The learned helplessness explanation of depression has been revised somewhat over the past two decades. According to a new version of the theory, the *attribution-helplessness theory,* when people view events as beyond their control, they ask themselves why this is so (Mezulis et al., 2004; Abramson et al., 2002, 1989, 1978). If they attribute their present lack of control to some *internal* cause that is both *global* and *stable* ("I am inadequate at everything and I always will be"), they may well feel helpless to prevent future negative outcomes and they may experience depression. If they make other kinds of attributions, this reaction is unlikely (see Table 8-4).

Consider a college student whose girlfriend breaks up with him. If he attributes this loss of control to an internal cause thIat is both global and stable—"It's my fault [internal], I ruin everything I touch [global], and I always will [stable]"—he then has reason to expect similar losses of control in the future and may generally experience a sense of

FIGURE 8-2 Jumping to safety *Experimental animals learn to escape or avoid shocks that are administered on one side of a shuttle box by jumping to the other (safe) side.*

Table 8-4

Internal and External Attributions
Event: "I failed my psych test today."

	INTERNAL		EXTERNAL	
	Stable	**Unstable**	**Stable**	**Unstable**
Global	"I have a problem with test anxiety."	"Getting into an argument with my roommate threw my whole day off."	"Written tests are an unfair way to assess knowledge."	"No one does well on tests that are given the day after vacation."
Specific	"I just have no grasp of psychology."	"I got upset and froze when I couldn't answer the first two questions."	"Everyone knows that this professor enjoys giving unfair tests."	"This professor didn't put much thought into the test because of the pressure of her book deadline."

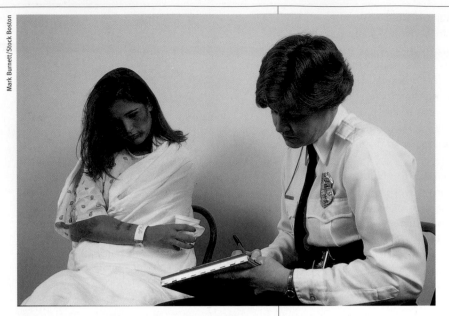

Spouse abuse: victimization and learned helplessness *Spouse abuse occurs in at least 4 million American homes each year (National Crime Victimization Survey). Psychologists believe that many victims of spouse abuse develop feelings of helplessness over the course of their ordeal, thus explaining their "decision" to stay with their abusive husbands. Many such women come to believe that nothing they can do will stop the repeated episodes of violence, that they have no economic alternatives, and that the criminal justice system will be unable to protect them. In turn, they typically develop feelings of depression, low self-esteem, and self-blame.* **«**

Mark Burnett/Stock Boston

>>**LOOKING AROUND**

The Color of Depression

In Western society, **black** is often the color of choice in describing depression. The British prime minister Winston Churchill called his recurrent episodes a "black dog always waiting to bare its teeth." The American novelist Ernest Hemingway referred to his bouts as "black-assed" days. And the Rolling Stones sing about depressive thinking: "I see a red door and I want to paint it black." **«**

helplessness. According to the learned helplessness view, he is a prime candidate for depression. If the student had instead attributed the breakup to causes that were more *specific* ("The way I've behaved the past couple of weeks blew this relationship"), *unstable* ("I don't know what got into me—I don't usually act like that"), or *external* ("She never did know what she wanted"), he might not expect to lose control again and would probably not experience helplessness and depression.

Hundreds of studies have supported the relationship between styles of attribution, helplessness, and depression (Yu & Seligman, 2002; Kinderman & Bentall, 1997). In one, depressed persons were asked to fill out an *Attributional Style Questionnaire* both before and after successful therapy. Before therapy, their depression was accompanied by the internal/global/stable pattern of attribution. At the end of therapy and again one year later, their depression was improved and their attribution styles were less likely to be limited to internal, global, and stable ones (Seligman et al., 1988).

Some theorists have refined the helplessness model yet again in recent years. They suggest that attributions are likely to cause depression only when they further produce a sense of *hopelessness* in an individual (Abela et al., 2004; Abramson et al., 2002, 1989). By taking this factor into consideration, clinicians are often able to predict depression with still greater precision (Robinson & Alloy, 2003).

Although the learned helplessness theory of unipolar depression has been very influential, it too has imperfections. First, laboratory helplessness does not parallel depression in every respect. Uncontrollable shocks in the laboratory, for example, almost always produce anxiety along with the helplessness effects (Seligman, 1975), but human depression is not always accompanied by anxiety. Second, much of the learned helplessness research relies on animal subjects (Henn & Vollmayr, 2005). It is impossible to know whether the animals' symptoms do in fact reflect the clinical depression found in humans. Third, the attributional feature of the theory raises difficult questions. What about the dogs and rats who learn helplessness? Can animals make attributions, even implicitly?

The Sociocultural View

Sociocultural theorists propose that unipolar depression is greatly influenced by the social structure in which people live. Their belief is supported by the finding, discussed earlier, that this disorder is often triggered by outside stressors. In addition, researchers have found ties between depression and factors such as culture, gender, race, and social support.

HOW ARE CULTURE AND DEPRESSION RELATED? On the one hand, depression is a worldwide phenomenon: persons in all countries and cultures are at risk for it (WHO, 2004). On the other hand, the precise picture of depression varies from culture to culture (Tsai & Chentsova-Dutton, 2002; Manson & Good, 1993). Depressed people in non–Western countries, for example, are more likely to be troubled by physical symptoms such as fatigue, weakness, sleep disturbances, and weight loss. Depression in these countries is less often marked by such psychological symptoms as self-blame, low self-esteem, and guilt. As these countries have become more Westernized, depression there has taken on the more psychological character it has in the West.

HOW DO GENDER AND RACE RELATE TO DEPRESSION? The rates of unipolar depression also vary from subgroup to subgroup within a society. As we have already seen, the rate of depression is much higher among women than among men. One sociocultural theory holds that the social pressures and complexities of women's roles in society leave them particularly prone to depression (see Box 8-3 on page 240).

Similarly, although few differences in the *overall* rate of unipolar depression have been found among white Americans, African Americans, and Hispanic Americans, researchers sometimes find striking differences when they look at specific ethnic populations living under special circumstances (Ayalon & Young, 2003). A study of one Native American village in the United States, for example, showed that the lifetime risk of developing depression was 37 percent among women, 19 percent among men, and 28 percent overall, much higher than the risk in the general United States population (Kinzie et al., 1992). High prevalence rates of this kind may be linked to the terrible social and economic pressures faced by the people who live on Native American reservations. Similarly, in a recent survey of Hispanic and African Americans who were residing in public housing, almost half of the respondents reported that they were suffering from depression (Bazargan et al., 2005). Within these minority populations, the likelihood of being depressed rose along with the individual's degree of poverty, family size, and number of health problems.

Of course, each minority group itself comprises persons of varied backgrounds and cultural values. Thus, it is not surprising that depression is distributed unevenly across some of the groups. As with certain anxiety disorders (see p. 201), depression is much more common among U.S.-born Hispanic and African Americans than among Hispanic and African American immigrants (Miranda et al., 2005). Moreover, within the Hispanic American population, Puerto Ricans display a significantly higher rate of depression than do Mexican Americans or Cuban Americans (Oquendo et al., 2004), while among African Americans, individuals whose families originally arrived in the United States directly from Africa and those whose families came by way of a Caribbean island experience similar rates of depression (Miranda et al., 2005).

HOW DOES SOCIAL SUPPORT RELATE TO DEPRESSION? The availability of social support seems to influence the likelihood of depression (Kendler et al., 2005). As we see in Figure 8-3, across the United States, people who are separated or divorced display three times the depression rate of married or widowed persons and double the rate of people who have never been married (Weissman et al., 1991). In some cases, the spouse's depression may contribute to marital discord, a separation, or divorce, but often the interpersonal conflicts and low social support found in troubled relationships seem to lead to depression (Highet et al., 2005; Franchi, 2004; Whisman, 2001).

People whose lives are isolated and without intimacy seem particularly likely to become depressed at times of stress (Kendler et al., 2005; Nezlek et al., 2000). Some highly publicized studies conducted in England a couple of decades ago showed that women who had three or more young children, lacked a close confidante, and had no outside employment were more likely than other women to become depressed after experiencing stressful events (Brown et al., 1995; Brown & Harris, 1978). Studies have also found that depressed people who lack social support remain depressed longer than those who have a supportive spouse or warm friendships (Moos & Cronkite, 1999).

Special companionship *Social support of various kinds helps reduce or prevent depression. Indeed, the companionship and warmth of dogs and other pets have been found to prevent loneliness and isolation and, in turn, to help alleviate or prevent depression.*

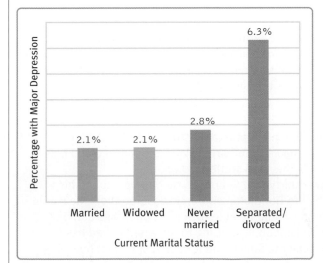

FIGURE **8-3 Marital status and major depressive disorder** *Currently separated or divorced people are three times more likely to be depressed than people who currently are married. (Adapted from Weissman et al., 1991.)*

>>BY THE NUMBERS

Single ≠ Lonely in Germany

80% Percentage of unmarried German women who say they are perfectly content to live alone **‹‹**

36% German women who say they opt to stay single because it is more fun **‹‹**

36% German women who say they like single life because they do not have to endure watching sports on television with a male spouse **‹‹**

2% Single German women who report that they do not enjoy their solitary lifestyle **‹‹**

(Stern, 2004)

Sociocultural Landscape: Depressing News for Women

omen in places as far apart as Paris, Sweden, Lebanon, New Zealand, and the United States are at least twice as likely as men to receive a diagnosis of unipolar depression (Whiffen & Demidenko, 2006; McSweeney, 2004; Pajer, 1995). Women also appear to be younger when depression strikes, to have more frequent and longer-lasting bouts, and to respond less successfully to treatment. Why the huge difference between the sexes? Several theories have been offered (Nolen-Hoeksema, 2002, 1995, 1990, 1987).

The artifact theory One theory holds that women and men are equally prone to depression but that clinicians often fail to detect depression in men (Brommelhoff et al., 2004). Perhaps men find it less socially acceptable to admit feeling depressed or to seek treatment. Perhaps depressed women display more emotional symptoms, such as sadness and crying, which are easily diagnosed, while depressed men mask their depression behind traditionally "masculine" symptoms such as anger. This explanation lacks consistent research support (McSweeney, 2004). It turns out that women are actually no more willing or able than men to identify their de-

pressive symptoms and seek treatment (Nolen-Hoeksema, 1990).

The hormone theory Another theory holds that hormone changes trigger depression in many women (Parker & Brotchie, 2004; Dunn & Steiner, 2000). A woman's biological life from her early teens to middle age is marked by frequent changes in hormone levels. Gender differences in rates of depression also span these same years. It is unlikely, however, that hormone changes alone are responsible for the high levels of depression in women (Whiffen & Demidenko, 2006). Important social and life events that occur at puberty, pregnancy, and menopause could likewise have an effect. Hormone explanations have also been criticized as sexist, since they imply that a woman's normal biology is flawed.

The quality-of-life theory Perhaps women in our society experience more stress than men (Hankin & Abramson, 2001). On average they face more poverty, more menial jobs, less adequate housing, and more discrimination than men—all factors that have been linked to depression (Maciejewski et al., 2001; Brems, 1995). And in many homes, women bear a disproportionate

share of responsibility for child care and housework.

The societal pressure theory Almost from birth, females in Western society are taught to seek a low body weight and slender body shape—goals that are unreasonable, unhealthy, and often unattainable. The cultural standard for males is much more lenient. As girls approach adolescence, peer pressure may produce greater and greater dissatisfaction with their weight and body, increasing the likelihood of depression. Consistent with this theory, gender differences in depression do indeed first appear during adolescence (Galambos et al., 2004; Nolen-Hoeksema & Girgus, 1995) and persons with eating disorders often experience high levels of depression (Paxton & Diggens, 1997). However, it is not clear that eating and weight concerns actually cause depression; they may instead be the result of depression.

The lack-of-control theory According to this theory, women are more prone to depression because they feel less control over their lives. Studies have, in fact, confirmed that women are more prone to develop learned helplessness in the laboratory than men (Le Unes,

Bipolar Disorders

People with a *bipolar disorder* experience both the lows of depression and the highs of mania. Many describe their life as an emotional roller coaster, as they shift back and forth between extreme moods. A number of sufferers eventually become suicidal (Newman, 2005). Their roller coaster ride and its impact on relatives and friends are seen in the following case study:

In his early school years he had been a remarkable student and had shown a gift for watercolor and oils. Later he had studied art in Paris and married an English girl he had met there. Eventually they had settled in London.

Ten years later, when he was thirty-four years old, he had persuaded his wife and only son to accompany him to Honolulu, where, he assured them, he would be considered famous. He felt he would be able to sell his paintings at many times the prices he could get in London. According to his wife, he had been in an accelerated state, but at that time the family had left, unsuspecting, believing

Edvard Munch, *Melancholia, Laura*, 1899. Oslo kommunes kunstsamlinger Munch-Museet

Female melancholy *Edvard Munch's painting* Melancholy (Laura) *was inspired by his sister's bouts of severe depression.*

Nation, & Turley, 1980). In addition, it has been found that victimization of any kind, from burglary to rape, often produces a general sense of helplessness and increases the symptoms of depression; and women in our society are more likely than men to be victims, particularly of sexual assault and child abuse (Whiffen & Demidenko, 2006; Nolen-Hoeksema, 2002).

The self-blame theory Past research often indicated that women are more likely than men to blame their failures on lack of ability and to attribute their successes to luck—an attribution style that has also been linked to depression (Abramson et al., 2002; Wolfe & Russianoff, 1997). However, several more recent studies suggest that today's women and men may not differ as much as they used to in their levels of self-esteem and self-blame (Kling et al., 1999).

The rumination theory *Rumination* is the tendency to repeatedly focus on one's feelings when depressed and repeatedly consider the causes and consequences of that depression. "Why am I so down. . . . I won't be able to finish my work if I keep going like this. . . ." Research shows that people who tend to ruminate whenever they feel sad are more likely to become depressed and stay depressed longer. It turns out that women are more likely than men to ruminate when their moods darken, perhaps making them more vulnerable to the onset of clinical depression (Nolen-Hoeksema & Corte, 2004; Nolen-Hoeksema, 2002, 2000).

Each of these explanations for the gender difference in unipolar depression offers food for thought. Each has gathered just enough supporting evidence to make it interesting and just enough evidence to the contrary to raise questions about its usefulness. Thus, at present, the gender difference in depression remains one of the most talked-about but least understood phenomena in the clinical field.

with the patient in their imminent good fortune. When they arrived they found almost no one in the art world that he was supposed to know. There were no connections for sales and deals in Hawaii that he had anticipated. Settling down, the patient began to behave more peculiarly than ever. After enduring several months of the patient's exhilaration, overactivity, weight loss, constant talking, and unbelievably little sleep, the young wife and child began to fear for his sanity. None of his plans materialized. After five months in the Pacific, with finances growing thin, the patient's overactivity subsided and he fell into a depression.

During that period he refused to move, paint, or leave the house. He lost twenty pounds, became utterly dependent on his wife, and insisted on seeing none of the friends he had accumulated in his manic state. His despondency became so severe that several doctors came to the house and advised psychiatric hospitalization. He quickly agreed and received twelve electroshock treatments, which relieved his depressed state. Soon afterward he began to paint again and to sell his work modestly. Recognition began to come from galleries and critics in the Far East. Several reviews acclaimed his work as exceptionally brilliant.

>>LOOKING BACK

Frenzied Masterpiece

George Frideric Handel wrote his *Messiah* in less than a month during a manic episode (Roesch, 1991). **<<**

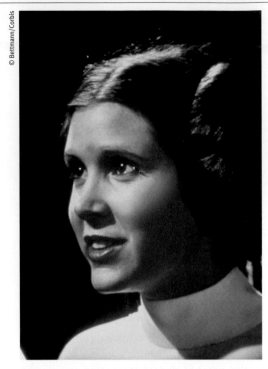

© Bettmann/Corbis

War of a different kind *While starring as Princess Leia, the invincible heroine in the* Star Wars *movies from 1977 to 1983, the actress Carrie Fisher received a diagnosis of bipolar disorder. The disorder is now under control with the help of medication, and Fisher says, "I don't want peace [in my life], I just don't want war" (Epstein, 2001, p. 36).*

This was the beginning of the lifelong career of his moodswing. In 1952, while still in Honolulu, he once again became severely depressed. . . . Four years later he returned to London in a high. . . . When this manic period subsided and he surveyed the wreckage of his life, an eight-month interval of normal mood followed, after which he again switched into a profound depression.

(Fieve, 1975, pp. 64–65)

What Are the Symptoms of Mania?

Unlike people sunk in the gloom of depression, those in a state of mania typically experience dramatic and inappropriate rises in mood. The symptoms of mania span the same areas of functioning—*emotional, motivational, behavioral, cognitive,* and *physical*—as those of depression, but mania affects those areas in an opposite way.

A person in the throes of mania has active, powerful emotions in search of an outlet. The mood of euphoric joy and well-being is out of all proportion to the actual happenings in the person's life. One person with mania explained, "I feel no sense of restriction or censorship whatsoever. I am afraid of nothing and no one" (Fieve, 1975, p. 68). Not every person with mania is a picture of happiness, however. Some instead become irritable and angry—especially when others get in the way of their exaggerated ambitions—like this man:

All by himself, he had been building a magnificent swimming pool for his country home in Virginia, working eighteen hours a day at it. He decided to make the pool public and open a concession stand at one end to help defray the mounting costs of the project. When his wife suggested that he might be going overboard, he became furious and threatened to leave her for another woman. Soon afterward, when his wife was out, he took many valuables from the house—his share, he claimed—and sold or pawned them. Complaining that his wife was a stick in the mud, he decided to throw a round-the-clock party, and he invited to the house almost everyone he passed on the street.

(Fieve, 1975, p. 148)

In the motivational realm, people with mania seem to want constant excitement, involvement, and companionship. They enthusiastically seek out new friends and old, new interests and old, and have little awareness that their social style is overwhelming, domineering, and excessive:

He was interested in everything and everyone around him. He talked familiarly to patients, attendants, nurses, and physicians. He took a fancy to the woman physician on duty in the admission building, calling her by her first name and annoying her with letters and with his familiar, ill mannered, and obtrusive attentions. . . . He made many comments and asked many questions about other patients and promised that he would secure their discharge. He interfered with their affairs and soon received a blow on the jaw from one patient and a black eye from another.

(Kolb, 1973, p. 372)

The behavior of people with mania is usually very active. They move quickly, as though there were not enough time to do everything they want to do. They may talk rapidly and loudly, their conversations filled with jokes and efforts to be clever or, conversely, with complaints and verbal outbursts. Flamboyance is not uncommon: dressing in flashy clothes, giving large sums of money to strangers, or even getting involved in dangerous activities. Several of these qualities are evident in the monologue delivered by Joe to the two policemen who escorted him to a mental hospital:

•**BIPOLAR I DISORDER**•A type of bipolar disorder marked by full manic and major depressive episodes.

•**BIPOLAR II DISORDER**•A type of bipolar disorder marked by mildly manic (hypomanic) episodes and major depressive episodes.

You look like a couple of bright, alert, hardworking, clean-cut, energetic go-getters and I could use you in my organization! I need guys that are loyal and enthusiastic about the great opportunities life offers on this planet! It's yours for the taking! Too many people pass opportunity by without hearing it knock because they don't know how to grasp the moment and strike while the iron is hot! You've got to grab it when it comes up for air, pick up the ball and run! You've got to be decisive! decisive! decisive! No shilly-shallying! Sweat! Yeah, sweat with a goal! Push, push, push, and you can push over a mountain! Two mountains, maybe. It's not luck! Hell, if it wasn't for bad luck I wouldn't have any luck at all! Be there firstest with the mostest! My guts and your blood! That's the system! I know, you know, he, she or it knows it's the only way to travel! Get 'em off balance, baby, and the rest is leverage! Use your head and save your heels! What's this deal? Who are these guys? Have you got a telephone and a secretary I can have instanter if not sooner? What I need is office space and the old LDO [long-distance operator].

(McNeil, 1967, p. 147)

>>PSYCH•NOTES

Clinical Oversight

The National Mental Health Association estimates that as many as 80 percent of people with a bipolar disorder may be misdiagnosed or not diagnosed at all. **<<**

In the cognitive realm, people with mania usually show poor judgment and planning, as if they feel too good or move too fast to consider possible pitfalls. Filled with optimism, they rarely listen when others try to slow them down, interrupt their buying sprees, or prevent them from investing money unwisely. They may also hold an inflated opinion of themselves, and sometimes their self-esteem approaches grandiosity. During severe episodes of mania, some have trouble remaining coherent or in touch with reality.

Finally, in the physical realm, people with mania feel remarkably energetic. They typically get little sleep yet feel and act wide awake (Gupta et al., 2004). Even if they miss a night or two of sleep, their energy level may remain high.

Diagnosing Bipolar Disorders

People are considered to be in a full *manic episode* when for at least one week they display an abnormally high or irritable mood, along with at least three other symptoms of mania (see Table 8-5). The episode may even include psychotic features such as delusions or hallucinations. When the symptoms of mania are less severe (causing little impairment), the person is said to be experiencing a *hypomanic episode* (Bowden, 2005; APA, 2000, 1994).

DSM-IV-TR distinguishes two kinds of bipolar disorders —bipolar I and bipolar II. People with **bipolar I disorder** have full manic and major depressive episodes. Most of them experience an *alternation* of the episodes; for example, weeks of mania followed by a period of wellness, followed, in turn, by an episode of depression. Some people, however, have *mixed* episodes, in which they swing from manic to depressive symptoms and back again on the same day (Berk et al., 2005). In **bipolar II disorder,** hypomanic—that is, mildly manic—episodes alternate with major depressive episodes over the course of time (Akiskal, 2005). Some people with this pattern accomplish huge amounts of work during their mild manic periods (see Box 8-4 on the next page).

Without treatment, the mood episodes tend to recur for people with either type of bipolar disorder (Julien, 2005). If people experience four or more episodes within a one-year period, their disorder is further classified as *rapid cycling*. If their episodes vary with the seasons, the disorder is further classified as *seasonal*.

Table 8-5 DSM Checklist

MANIC EPISODE

1. A period of abnormally and persistently elevated, expansive, or irritable mood, lasting at least one week.
2. Persistence of at least three of the following: • inflated self-esteem or grandiosity • decreased need for sleep • more talkativeness than usual, or pressure to keep talking • flight of ideas or the experience that thoughts are racing • distractibility • increase in activity or psychomotor agitation • excessive involvement in pleasurable activities that have a high potential for painful consequences.
3. Significant distress or impairment.

BIPOLAR I DISORDER

1. The presence of a manic, hypomanic, or major depressive episode.
2. If currently in a hypomanic or major depressive episode, history of a manic episode.
3. Significant distress or impairment.

BIPOLAR II DISORDER

1. The presence of a hypomanic or major depressive episode.
2. If currently in a major depressive episode, history of a hypomanic episode. If currently in a hypomanic episode, history of a major depressive episode. No history of a manic episode.
3. Significant distress or impairment.

Based on APA, 2000.

[BOX **8-4**]

Abnormality and Creativity: A Delicate Balance

Up to a point, states of depression, mania, anxiety, and even confusion can be useful. This may be particularly true in the arts. The ancient Greeks believed that various forms of "divine madness" inspired creative acts, from poetry to performance (Ludwig, 1995). In the eighteenth century, romantic notions of the "mad genius" led asylum superintendents to encourage their patients to write; the patients' creations were published in asylum literary journals (Gamwell & Tomes, 1995).

Even today many people expect "creative geniuses" to be psychologically disturbed. A popular image of the artist includes a glass of liquor, a cigarette, and a tormented expression. Classic examples include the writer William Faulkner, who suffered from alcoholism and received electroconvulsive therapy for depression; the poet Sylvia Plath, who experienced depression most of her life and eventually committed suicide; and the dancer Vaslav Nijinsky, who suffered from schizophrenia and spent many years in institutions. In fact, a number of studies indicate that artists and writers are somewhat more likely than others to suffer from mental disorders, particularly mood disorders (Lauronen et al., 2004; Jamison, 1995; Ludwig, 1995, 1994).

Why might creative people be prone to psychological disorders? Some may be predisposed to such disorders long before they begin their artistic careers; the careers may simply bring attention to their emotional struggles (Ludwig, 1995). Indeed, creative people often have a family history of psychological problems. A number also have experienced intense psychological trauma during childhood. The English novelist and essayist Virginia Woolf, for example, endured sexual abuse as a child.

Another reason for the creativity link may be that creative endeavors create emotional turmoil that is overwhelming. Truman Capote said that writing his famous book *In Cold Blood* "killed" him psychologically. Before writing this account of the brutal murders of a family, he considered himself "a stable person. . . . Afterward something happened to me" (Ludwig, 1995).

Yet a third explanation for the link between creativity and psychological disorders is that the creative professions offer a welcome climate for those with psychological disturbances. In the worlds of poetry, painting, and acting, for example, emotional expression and personal turmoil are valued as sources of inspiration and success (Ludwig, 1995).

Much remains to be learned about the relationship between emotional turmoil and creativity, but work in this area has already clarified two important points. First, psychological disturbance is hardly a requirement for creativity. Many "creative geniuses" are, in fact, psychologically stable and happy throughout their entire lives (Schlesinger & Ismail, 2004). Second, *mild* psychological disturbances relate to creative achievement much more strongly than severe disturbances do. For example, mild patterns of mania, or *hypomania,* often produce sharpened and creative thinking and greater productivity (Jamison, 1995). Extreme disturbance, however, such as severe mania, depression, or anxiety, or a pattern of alcoholism, tends to reduce the quality and quantity of creative work and often ruins careers (Ludwig, 1995). The nineteenth-century composer Robert Schumann produced 27 works during one hypomanic year but next to nothing during years when he was severely depressed and suicidal (Jamison, 1995).

Some artists worry that their creativity would disappear if their psychological suffering were to stop. In fact, however, research suggests that successful treatment for severe psychological disorders more often than not improves the creative process (Jamison, 1995; Ludwig, 1995). Romantic notions aside, severe mental dysfunctioning has little redeeming value, in the arts or anywhere else (Rothenberg, 1990).

The price of creativity? *The influential English novelist and essayist Virginia Woolf (1882–1941) suffered major episodes of depression and mania at the ages of 13, 22, 28, and 30, and less severe mood swings throughout the rest of her life. She took her own life by drowning at the age of 59 during a depressive episode, fearing that she was "going mad again."*

Regardless of their particular pattern, individuals with a bipolar disorder tend to experience depression more than mania over the years (Lambert & Kindsley, 2005; Post, 2005; Fu et al., 2004). In most cases, their depressive episodes occur three times as often as manic ones, and the depressive episodes also last longer.

Surveys from around the world indicate that between 1.0 and 2.6 percent of all adults suffer from a bipolar disorder at any given time (Kessler et al., 2005). As many as

•CYCLOTHYMIC DISORDER• A disorder marked by numerous periods of hypomanic symptoms and mild depressive symptoms.

4.0 percent experience one of the bipolar disorders over the course of their lives. Bipolar I disorder seems to be a bit more common than bipolar II disorder (Rihmer & Angst, 2005; Kessler et al., 1994). The disorders appear to be equally common in women and men and among all socioeconomic classes and ethnic groups (Shastry, 2005; APA, 2000). However, women may experience more depressive episodes and more rapid cycling than men (Curtis, 2005; Papadimitiou et al., 2005). Onset usually occurs between the ages of 15 and 44 years. In most untreated cases of bipolar disorder, the manic and depressive episodes eventually subside, only to recur at a later time (APA, 2000, 1994). Generally, when episodes recur, the intervening periods of normality grow shorter and shorter (Goodwin & Jamison, 1984). It also appears that over time people with bipolar disorders develop more medical ailments than the rest of the population (Kupfer, 2005).

When a person experiences numerous periods of hypomanic symptoms and mild depressive symptoms, DSM-IV-TR assigns a diagnosis of **cyclothymic disorder.** The symptoms of this milder form of bipolar disorder continue for two or more years, interrupted occasionally by normal moods that may last for only days or weeks. This disorder, like bipolar I and bipolar II disorders, usually begins in adolescence or early adulthood and is equally common among women and men. At least 0.4 percent of the population develops cyclothymic disorder (APA, 2000). In some cases, the milder symptoms eventually blossom into a bipolar I or II disorder.

"Those? Oh, just a few souvenirs from my bipolar-disorder days."

What Causes Bipolar Disorders?

Throughout the first half of the twentieth century, the search for the cause of bipolar disorders made little progress. Various explanations were proposed, but research did not support their validity. Psychodynamic theorists, for example, suggested that mania, like depression, emerges from the loss of a love object. Whereas some people introject the lost object and become depressed, others deny the loss and become manic. To avoid the terrifying conflicts generated by the loss, they escape into a dizzying round of activity (Lewin, 1950). Although case reports sometimes fit this explanation (Krishnan et al., 1984; Cohen et al., 1954), only a few controlled studies have found a relationship between loss early or later in life and the onset of manic episodes (Tsuchiya et al., 2005; Furukawa et al., 1999).

More recently, biological research has produced some promising clues. The biological insights have come from research into *neurotransmitter activity, ion activity, brain structure,* and *genetic factors.*

NEUROTRANSMITTERS Could overactivity of norepinephrine be related to mania? This was the expectation of several clinicians back in the 1960s after investigators first found a relationship between low norepinephrine activity and unipolar depression (Schildkraut, 1965). One study did indeed find the norepinephrine activity of persons with mania to be higher than that of depressed or control subjects (Post et al., 1980, 1978). In another study patients with a bipolar disorder were given *reserpine,* the blood pressure drug known to reduce norepinephrine activity in the brain, and the manic symptoms of some subsided (Telner et al., 1986).

Because serotonin activity often parallels norepinephrine activity in unipolar depression, theorists at first expected that mania would also be related to high serotonin activity, but no such relationship has been found. Instead, research suggests that mania, like depression, may be linked to *low* serotonin activity (Shastry, 2005; Sobczak et al., 2002). Perhaps low activity of serotonin, acting again as a neuromodulator, opens the door to a mood disorder and *permits* the activity of norepinephrine (or perhaps other neurotransmitters) to define the particular form the disorder will take. That is, low serotonin activity accompanied by low norepinephrine activity may lead to depression; low serotonin activity accompanied by high norepinephrine activity may lead to mania.

Bipolar disorder and the brain *These PET scans of the brain of a person with bipolar disorder were taken over the course of 10 days. The scans show the individual shifting from depression (top row) to mania (middle row) and back to depression (bottom row). As in all PET scans, red, orange, and yellow colors indicate higher levels of brain activity, while blue and green colors indicate lower levels.*

>>Q & A
What is hypergraphia?

Hypergraphia refers to a compulsive need to write. During severe episodes, individuals with this rare problem write constantly, not only filling up notebooks or computer screens, but feverishly finding unusual writing surfaces, including their own skin. The problem has been linked to several disorders, including bipolar disorders, temporal lobe epilepsy, and schizophrenia. There is speculation that some famous writers and artists worked under the sway of hypergraphia, such as the prolific author Fyodor Dostoyevski and the painter Vincent van Gogh, who produced an endless stream of paintings and letters (Martineau, 2004). <<

ION ACTIVITY On both sides of the cell membrane of each neuron sit positively charged *sodium ions.* The ions play a critical role in sending incoming messages down the neuron to the nerve endings. When the neuron is at *rest,* most of the sodium ions sit on the outer side of the membrane. When the neuron is stimulated by an incoming message at its receptor site, however, the sodium ions from the outer side of the membrane travel across to the inner side. This movement, in turn, starts a wave of electrochemical activity that continues down the length of the neuron and results in its "firing." Afterward, a flow of *potassium ions* from the inside to the outside of the neuron helps it to return to its original resting state (see Figure 8-4).

If brain messages are to be sent and received appropriately, the ions must travel properly back and forth between the outside and the inside of the neural membrane. Some theorists believe that improper transport of these ions may cause neurons to fire too easily (resulting in mania) or to stubbornly resist firing (resulting in depression) (Li & El-Mallakh, 2004; El-Mallakh & Huff, 2001). Not surprisingly, investigators have found membrane defects in the neurons of persons with bipolar disorders and have observed abnormal functioning in the proteins that help transport ions across a neuron's membrane (Sassi & Soares, 2002; Wang et al., 1999; Meltzer, 1991).

Even if bipolar disorders are not the direct result of disturbed ion transportation within neurons, it may be that such disturbances produce abnormal chemical activities within neurons—activities that help produce a bipolar disorder. A growing number of researchers believe, for example, that people with bipolar disorders have deficiencies of key proteins or other chemicals within many of their neurons, and that these deficiencies lead to poor cell health and, ultimately, bipolar disorders (Julien, 2005; Gray et al., 2003).

BRAIN STRUCTURE Brain imaging and postmortem studies have identified a number of abnormal brain structures in people with bipolar disorders (Lambert & Kinsley, 2005; Shastry, 2005; Baumann & Bogerts, 2001; Stoll et al., 2000). In particular, the basal ganglia and cerebellum of these individuals tend to be smaller than those of other people. In addition, their dorsal raphe nucleus, striatum, amygdala, and prefontal cortex have structural abnormalities. It is not clear what role such structural abnormalities play in bipolar disorders (Monkul et al., 2005). It may be that they help produce the neurotransmitter and ion abnormalities that we observed earlier. The dorsal raphe nucleus, for example, is one of the brain sites where serotonin is produced. Alternatively, the structural problems may simply be the result of the neurotransmitter or ion abnormalities or of the medications that many patients with bipolar disorders now take.

GENETIC FACTORS Many experts believe that people inherit a biological predisposition to develop bipolar disorders. Family pedigree studies support this idea (Maier et al., 2005; Shastry, 2005; Gershon & Nurnberger, 1995). Identical twins of persons with a bipolar disorder have a 40 percent likelihood of developing the same disorder, and fraternal twins, siblings, and other close relatives of such persons have a 5 to 10 percent likelihood, compared to the 1 to 2.6 percent prevalence rate in the general population.

Researchers have also conducted *genetic linkage* studies to identify possible patterns in the inheritance of bipolar disorders. They select large families that have

Extended families and genetic research *Closely knit families in which there is little intermarriage across generations are attractive candidates for genetic linkage studies, which seek to identify possible patterns in the inheritance of disorders. The possible genetic patterns of bipolar disorders have, for example, been studied in some Amish families in Pennsylvania.*

had high rates of a disorder over several generations, observe the pattern of distribution of the disorder among family members, and determine whether it closely follows the distribution pattern of a known genetically transmitted family trait (called a *genetic marker*), such as color blindness, red hair, or a particular medical syndrome.

After studying the records of Israeli, Belgian, and Italian families that had shown high rates of bipolar disorders across several generations, one team of researchers seemed for a while to have linked bipolar disorders to genes on the X chromosome (Mendlewicz et al., 1987, 1980). Other research teams, however, later used techniques from *molecular biology* to examine genetic patterns in large families, and they linked bipolar disorders to genes on chromosomes 1, 4, 6, 10, 11, 12, 13, 15, 18, 21, and 22 (Maier et al., 2005; Baron, 2002). Such wide-ranging findings suggest that a number of genetic abnormalities probably combine to help bring about bipolar disorders (Payne, Potash, & DePaulo, 2005).

PUTTING IT together
Making Sense of All That Is Known

With mood disorders so prevalent in all societies, it is no wonder that they have been the focus of so much research. Great quantities of data about these disorders have been gathered. Still, clinicians have yet to understand fully all that they know.

Several factors have been closely tied to unipolar depression, including biological abnormalities, a reduction in positive reinforcements, negative ways of thinking, a perception of helplessness, and life stress and other sociocultural influences. Indeed, more contributing factors have been associated with unipolar depression than with most other psychological disorders. Precisely how all of these factors relate to unipolar depression, however, is unclear (Meyer et al., 2003). Several relationships are possible:

1. *One of the factors* may be the key cause of unipolar depression. That is, one theory may be more useful than any of the others for predicting and explaining how unipolar depression occurs. If so, cognitive or biological factors are leading candidates, for these kinds of factors have each been found, at times, to precede and predict depression.

2. *Different factors* may be capable of initiating unipolar depression in different persons. Some people may, for example, begin with low serotonin activity, which predisposes them to react helplessly in stressful situations, interpret events negatively, and enjoy fewer pleasures in life. Others may first suffer a severe loss, which triggers helplessness reactions, low serotonin activity, and reductions in positive rewards. Regardless of the initial cause, these factors may merge into a "final common pathway" of unipolar depression.

3. An *interaction between two or more specific factors* may be necessary to produce unipolar depression (Klocek, Oliver, & Ross, 1997). Perhaps people will become depressed only if they have low levels of serotonin activity, feel helpless, *and* repeatedly blame themselves for negative events.

4. The *various factors may play different roles* in unipolar depression. Some may cause the disorder, some may result from it, and some may keep it going. Peter Lewinsohn and his colleagues (1988) assessed more than 500 nondepressed persons on the various factors linked to depression. They then assessed the subjects again eight months later to see who had in fact become depressed and which of the factors had predicted depression. Negative thinking, self-dissatisfaction, and life stress were found to precede and predict depression; poor social relationships and reductions in positive rewards did not. The researchers concluded that the former factors help cause unipolar depression, while the latter simply accompany or result from depression, and perhaps help maintain it.

As with unipolar depression, clinicians and researchers have learned much about bipolar disorders during the past 30 years. But bipolar disorders appear to be best explained by

FIGURE **8-4** **Ions and the firing of neurons** *Neurons relay messages in the form of electrical impulses that travel down the axon toward the nerve endings. As an impulse travels along the axon, sodium ions (Na^+), which had been resting on the outside of the neuron's membrane, flow to the inside, causing the impulse to continue down the axon. Once sodium ions flow in, potassium ions (K^+) flow out, thus helping the membrane's electrical balance to return to its resting state, ready for the arrival of a new impulse. (Adapted from Snyder, 1986, p. 7.)*

>>PSYCH•NOTES
Paternal Postpartum Depression

Considerable research has already indicated that a mother's postpartum depression can lead to disturbances in her child's social, behavioral, and cognitive development. Recent research suggests that a father's postpartum depression can have similar effects and may also set the stage for later conduct problems in boys (Ramchandani et al., 2005). ‹‹

The biochemical culprits *Computer-drawn molecules of the neurotransmitters* norepinephrine *(top) and* serotonin *(bottom). According to research, these chemicals are clearly linked to unipolar depression and may play roles in bipolar disorders.*

a focus on *one* kind of variable—biological factors. The evidence suggests that biological abnormalities, perhaps inherited and perhaps triggered by life stress, cause bipolar disorders. Whatever roles other factors may play, the primary one appears to lie in this realm.

Thus we see that one kind of mood disorder may result from multiple causes, while another may result largely from a single factor. Although today's theorists are increasingly looking for intersecting factors to explain various psychological disorders, this is not always the most enlightening course. It depends on the disorder. What is important is that the cause or causes of a disorder be recognized. Scientists can then invest their energies more efficiently and clinicians can better understand the persons with whom they work.

There is no question that investigations into the mood disorders have been fruitful, and valuable insights should continue to unfold in the years ahead. Now that clinical researchers have gathered so many important pieces of the puzzle, they must put the pieces together into a still more meaningful picture that will suggest even better ways to predict, prevent, and treat these disorders (Munoz et al., 2002).

⊣[SUMMARY AND REVIEW]⊢

■ **Mood disorders** People with mood disorders have mood problems that tend to last for months or years, dominate their interactions with the world, and disrupt their normal functioning. *Depression* and *mania* are the key moods in these disorders. *pp. 223–224*

■ **Unipolar depression** People with *unipolar depression,* the most common pattern of mood disorder, suffer exclusively from depression. The symptoms of depression span five areas of functioning: emotional, motivational, behavioral, cognitive, and physical. Depressed people are also at greater risk for suicidal thinking and behavior. Women are at least twice as likely as men to experience severe unipolar depression. *pp. 224–227*

■ **Explanations of unipolar disorder** Each of the leading models has offered explanations for unipolar depression. The biological, cognitive, and sociocultural views have received the greatest research support.

According to the *biological view,* low activity of two neurotransmitters, *norepinephrine* and *serotonin,* helps cause depression. *Hormonal factors* may also be at work. So too may deficiencies of key proteins and other chemicals *within* certain neurons. These biological problems may be linked to *genetic factors.* According to the *psychodynamic view,* certain people who experience *real or imagined losses* may *regress* to an earlier stage of development, *introject* feelings for the lost object, and eventually become depressed.

The *behavioral view* says that when people experience a large reduction in their positive rewards in life, they may display fewer and fewer positive behaviors. This response leads to a still lower rate of positive rewards and eventually to depression. The leading *cognitive explanations* of unipolar depression focus on *negative thinking* and *learned helplessness.* According to Beck's theory of negative thinking, *maladaptive attitudes,* the *cognitive triad, errors in thinking,* and *automatic thoughts* help produce unipolar depression. According to Seligman's learned helplessness theory, people become depressed when they believe that they have lost control over the reinforcements in their lives and when they attribute this loss to causes that are *internal, global,* and *stable.*

Sociocultural theorists propose that unipolar depression is influenced by social factors. In support of this position, research finds that stressful events often seem to trigger depression; the character and prevalence of depression can vary by culture, gender, and race; and a low level of social support is linked to unipolar depression. *pp. 227–239*

■ **Bipolar disorders** In *bipolar disorders,* episodes of mania alternate or intermix with episodes of depression. These disorders are much less common than unipolar depression. They may take the form of *bipolar I, bipolar II,* or *cyclothymic disorder. pp. 240–245*

>>PSYCH•LISTINGS

Medical Problems and Depression

50% Percentage of stroke victims who experience clinical depression ‹‹

- -

17% Heart attack victims who become depressed ‹‹

- -

30% Cancer patients who experience depression ‹‹

- -

18% People with diabetes who are depressed ‹‹

- -

(Simpson, 1996)

■ **Explanations of bipolar disorders** Mania may be related to *high norepinephrine activity along with a low level of serotonin activity.* Some researchers have also linked bipolar disorders to *improper transport of ions* back and forth between the outside and the inside of a neuron's membrane. Still other investigators have focused on deficiencies of key proteins and other chemicals within certain neurons. Genetic studies suggest that people may *inherit* a predisposition to these biological abnormalities. *pp. 245–247*

>>> | CRITICAL THOUGHTS | <<<

1. Almost every day we experience ups and downs in mood. How can we distinguish the everyday blues from clinical depression? *pp. 224–227*

2. In one study, students who listened to a sad song became more depressed than those who listened to a happy song (Stratton & Zalanow, 1999, 1994). Yet the sad-song students reported "enjoying" their musical experience more than the happy-song students. What might be going on here? *pp. 224–227*

3. Can you remember instances when a stressful event or period in your life triggered depressed feelings? Can you think of other times in your life when a similar event did not lead to depressed feelings? What was different about you or about this period of time that prevented a negative reaction? *pp. 227–239*

4. Many comedians report that they have grappled with depression. Is there something about performing that might improve their mood? Is there something about being depressed that might make them more skilled at thinking or acting funny? *pp. 227–239*

5. One-third of people who felt unhappy as children continue to feel unhappy as adults. In contrast, fewer than one-tenth of those who were happy as children become unhappy adults (Freeman et al., 1999). How might different theorists explain this correlation between childhood and adult happiness? *pp. 227–239*

6. Why might depression feature more physical symptoms in non-Western cultures and more psychological symptoms in Western cultures? *pp. 238–239*

●—[CYBER**STUDY**]————————————————>>>

SEARCH THE *ABNORMAL PSYCHOLOGY* CD-ROM FOR

▲ Chapter 8 Video Cases and Discussions
   See the symptoms of mood disorders in operation.
   How do negative thoughts contribute to depression?

▲ Chapter 8 Practical, Research, and Decision-Making Exercises
   Observing the power of mood
   Cheering oneself up and bringing oneself down
   Creating depression in the laboratory

▲ Chapter 8 Practice Test and Feedback

LOG ON TO THE COMER WEB PAGE FOR

▲ Suggested Web links, exercises, FAQ page, additional Chapter 8 practice test questions
   <www.worthpublishers.com/comer>

————————————————————<<<

Treatments for Mood Disorders

"I think depression has made me a stronger person somehow. I mean in learning to handle this kind of thing. I think that I've had to develop skills and abilities that I wouldn't otherwise. And sensitivities too. I think it's made me more compassionate. I think, because of it, I know what it's like to go through something like that and I'm more curious about other people and what they're going through. [I'm also] more intent in trying to make some meaning out of the whole thing [life]. . . ."
Anonymous (in Karp, 1996, p. 130)

"I will take Zoloft for the rest of my life. I'm quite content to do it."
Mike Wallace, television news journalist (in Biddle et al., 1996)

"In my case, ECT [electroconvulsive therapy] was miraculous. My wife was dubious, but when she came into my room afterward, I sat up and said, 'Look who's back among the living.' It was like a magic wand."
Dick Cavett, talk show host (in People, *1992)*

". . . the hospital was my salvation, and it is something of a paradox that in this austere place with its locked and wired doors and desolate green hallways . . . I found the repose, the assuagement of the tempest in my brain, that I was unable to find in my quiet farmhouse. . . . For me the real healers were seclusion and time."
William Styron, novelist (in Styron, 1990, pp. 68–69)

"Because I thought I ought to be able to handle my increasingly violent mood swings by myself, for the first ten years I did not seek any kind of treatment. Even after my condition became a medical emergency, I still intermittently resisted the medications. . . . Having finally cottoned onto the disastrous consequences of starting and stopping lithium, I took it faithfully and found that life was a much stabler and more predictable place than I had ever reckoned. My moods were still intense and my temperament rather quick to the boil, but I could make plans with far more certainty and the periods of absolute blackness were fewer and less extreme. . . . I am [now] too frightened that I will again become morbidly depressed or virulently manic—either of which would, in turn, rip apart every aspect of my life, relationships, and work that I find most meaningful—to seriously consider any change in my medical treatment."
Kay Redfield Jamison, clinical researcher (in Jamison, 1995, pp. 5, 153, 212)

Each of these persons suffered from and overcame a severe mood disorder. And, clearly, all believe that the treatment they received was the key to their improvement—the key that opened the door to a normal, stable, and productive life. Yet the treatments that seemed to help them differed greatly. Psychotherapy

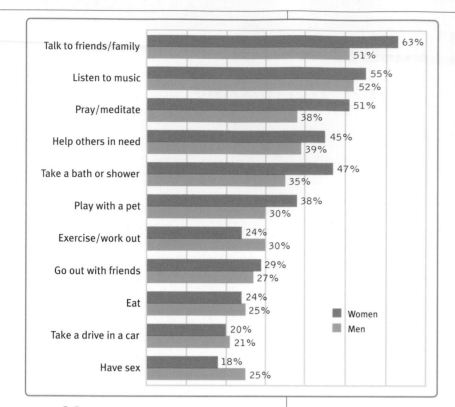

FIGURE **9-1** **What do people do to improve their mood?** *Almost two-thirds of women talk to friends and family members, half listen to music, and half pray or meditate. Around half of men talk to friends and family members, half listen to music, one-third take a bath or shower, and one-quarter have sex (Wallis, 2005).*

helped bring control, compassion, and meaning back to the life of the first individual. Electroconvulsive therapy, popularly known as shock treatment, lifted Dick Cavett from the black hole of severe unipolar depression. Hospitalization and its temporary retreat was the answer for William Styron, and antidepressant drugs were the key for Mike Wallace. Kay Jamison escaped the roller-coaster ride of bipolar disorders with the help of lithium, a common, inexpensive element found in mineral salts.

How could such diverse therapies be so helpful to people suffering from the same or similar disorders? As this chapter will show, mood disorders—as painful and disabling as they tend to be—respond more successfully to more kinds of treatment than do most other forms of psychological dysfunction (see Figure 9-1). This diversity of successful treatments has affected individuals with depression in both negative and positive ways. On the negative side, it has led to intense competition in the treatment marketplace, marked by a flood of consumer ads and the like (see Box 9-1 on page 254). On the positive side, the range of treatment options has been a source of reassurance and hope for the millions of people who desire desperately to regain some measure of control over their moods (Lewis & Hoofnagle, 2005).

Treatments for Unipolar Depression

Around one-third of persons with unipolar depression (major depressive or dysthymic disorder) receive treatment from a mental health professional each year (Wang et al., 2005). In addition, many other people in therapy experience depressed feelings as part of another disorder, such as an eating disorder, or in association with general problems that they are encountering in life. Thus much of the therapy being administered today is for unipolar depression.

A variety of treatment approaches are currently in widespread use for unipolar depression. We shall look first at the psychological approaches, focusing on the psychodynamic, behavioral, and cognitive therapies. We will then turn to the sociocultural approaches, including a highly regarded intervention called interpersonal psychotherapy. Last, we will consider two effective biological approaches—electroconvulsive therapy and antidepressant drugs. In the process, it will become evident that unipolar patterns of depression are indeed among the most successfully treated of all psychological disorders.

Psychological Approaches

The psychological treatments used most often to combat unipolar depression come from the psychodynamic, behavioral, and cognitive schools of thought. Psychodynamic therapy, the oldest of all modern psychotherapies, continues to be used widely for depression even though research has not offered strong evidence of its effectiveness. Behavioral therapy, effective primarily for mild or moderate depression, is practiced less often today than it was in past decades. Cognitive therapy has performed so well in research that it has a large and growing following among clinicians.

PSYCHODYNAMIC THERAPY Believing that unipolar depression results from unconscious grief over real or imagined losses, compounded by excessive dependence on other people, psychodynamic therapists seek to help clients bring these underlying issues to consciousness and work them through. Using the arsenal of basic psychodynamic procedures, they encourage the depressed client to associate freely during therapy; suggest interpretations of the client's associations, dreams, and displays of resistance and transference; and help the person review past events and feelings (Busch et al., 2004). Free

≫Q & A

Where do depressed persons first seek treatment?

Therapists are not necessarily the first health professionals to be contacted when depression strikes. Initially, 41 percent of persons with this disorder go to a physician with complaints of feeling generally ill: 37 percent of them complain of pain and 12 percent report general tiredness and fatigue (Katon & Walker, 1998). ≪

association, for example, helped one man recall the early experiences of loss that, according to his therapist, had set the stage for his depression:

> Among his earliest memories, possibly the earliest of all, was the recollection of being wheeled in his baby cart under the elevated train structure and left there alone. Another memory that recurred vividly during the analysis was of an operation around the age of five. He was anesthetized and his mother left him with the doctor. He recalled how he had kicked and screamed, raging at her for leaving him.
>
> *(Lorand, 1968, pp. 325–326)*

In the following excerpt, the therapist interpreted a depressed client's dream and traced his mood problem to early dependence and to real and symbolic losses:

> The patient reported a dream in which he was at his father's gravesite, in which his dead father was lying. In the dream the patient was crying and others were trying to comfort him. He had the feeling that everyone close to him was sick. He woke from the dream crying. In his associations this patient remembered the actual death of his father, stating that at the time, "I felt as if my purpose in life had been extinguished." The patient had had a quasi-symbiotic relationship with his father, who had preferred him over the other children. He followed his father's orders to the letter, in return for which his father lavished praise on him and gave him substantial sums of money. He never dared to cross his father since he had the experience of witnessing what had occurred to his brothers when they disagreed even slightly with the father. This patient had grown up in a rural area where the father, a wealthy and influential businessman, had ruled over a large estate like a small monarch. Although he had slavishly followed his father's instructions, the patient often had been irresponsible in his own affairs, and had lost moderate sums of money because of his naiveté. He had the dream after losing a considerable sum of money at cards. The dream may have represented an awareness that he was now on his own, yet there remained within him a desperate desire to be taken care of once again by a powerful other. The dream showed his characteristic turning to others to make things right, as his father had done in the past whenever he was in trouble.
>
> *(Arieti & Bemporad, 1978, p. 300)*

Psychodynamic therapists expect that in the course of treatment depressed clients will eventually become less dependent on others, cope with losses more effectively, and make corresponding changes in their daily lives. The transition of a therapeutic insight into a real-life change is seen in the case of a middle-aged executive:

> The patient's father was still living and in a nursing home, where the patient visited him regularly. On one occasion, he went to see his father full of high expectations, as he had concluded a very successful business transaction. As he began to describe his accomplishments to his father, however, the latter completely ignored his son's remarks and viciously berated him for wearing a pink shirt, which he considered unprofessional. Such a response from the father was not unusual, but this time, as a result of the work that had been accomplished in therapy, the patient could objectively analyze his initial sense of disappointment and deep feeling of failure for not pleasing the older man. Although this experience led to a transient state of depression, it also revealed to the patient his whole dependent lifestyle—his use of others to supply him with a feeling of worth. This experience added a dimension of immediate reality to the insights that had been achieved in therapy and gave the patient the motivation to change radically his childhood system of perceiving himself in relation to paternal transference figures.
>
> *(Bemporad, 1992, p. 291)*

A place for laughter *Many comedians have histories of depression. Drew Carey, for example, suffered from severe depression for much of his life. He reports that he has been able to successfully overcome this mood disorder by developing a positive outlook—through reading psychology books, listening to tapes on positive thinking, and, of course, generating and communicating humorous thoughts.*

Steve Labadessa/Outline

[BOX 9-1]

"And Remember to Ask Your Doctor about This Medication"

"Maybe you are suffering from depression" . . . "Ask your doctor about Zoloft" . . . "There is no need to suffer any longer." Anyone who watches television is familiar with phrases such as these. They are at the heart of *direct-to-consumer (DTC)* drug advertising—advertisements in which pharmaceutical companies appeal directly to consumers, coaxing them to ask their physicians to prescribe particular drugs for them. Research shows that consumers are, on average, familiar with 4 of every 10 drug ads (Wilkes et al., 2000). DTC drug ads on television are so commonplace that it is easy to forget they have been a major part of our viewing pleasure for only a few years. It was not until 1997, when the U.S. Food and Drug Administration (FDA) relaxed the rules of pharmaceutical advertising, that these ads really took off.

Antidepressants are among the leading drugs to receive DTC television advertising, along with oral antihistamines, cholesterol reducers, and anti-ulcer drugs (Rosenthal et al., 2002; Pines, 1999). Sales of antidepressants now total around $13 billion each year, and at least some of the success of these drugs is due to DTC ads.

Altogether, pharmaceutical companies now spend more than $2.5 billion a year on American television advertising, around seven times the amount spent in 1997 (Fetto, 2002; Rosenthal et al., 2002; Kaiser Family Foundation, 2001). In fact, 30 percent of adults say they have asked their doctors about specific medications that they saw advertised, and half of these individuals report that their doctors gave them a prescription for the advertised drug (Kaiser Family Foundation, 2001). With results like that, it is small wonder that the pharmaceutical companies are increasing their DTC expenditures by at least 33 percent each year (Fetto, 2002).

But how did we get here? Where did this tidal wave of advertising come from? And what's with those endless "side effects" that are blurted out so rapidly on each and every commercial? It's a long and complex story (Curtiss, 2002), but here are some of the key plot twists that helped set the stage for the emergence of DTC television drug advertising.

1938: FOOD, DRUG, AND COSMETIC ACT

Congress passed the *Food, Drug, and Cosmetic Act,* which gave the FDA jurisdiction over the labels on prescriptions and over-the-counter drugs and over most related forms of drug advertising (Kessler & Pines, 1990).

1962: KEFAUVER-HARRIS DRUG AMENDMENTS

In the spirit of consumer protection, Congress passed a law requiring that all pharmaceutical drugs be proved safe and effective. The law also transferred still more authority for prescription drug ads from the Federal Trade Commission (which regulates most other kinds of advertising) to the FDA (Wilkes et al., 2000).

Finally, and perhaps most important, the law set up rules that companies were required to follow in their drug advertisements, including a detailed summary of the drug's contraindications, side effects, and effectiveness, and a "fair balance" coverage of risks and benefits.

1962–1981: DRUG ADS FOR PHYSICIANS

For the next two decades, pharmaceutical companies targeted their ads to the physicians who were writing the prescriptions. As more and more *psychotropic* drugs were developed, psychiatrists were included among those targeted.

1981: FIRST PITCH

The pharmaceutical drug industry proposed shifting the advertising of drugs di-

Despite successful case reports such as this (Karon, 2005; Busch et al., 2004), researchers have found that long-term psychodynamic therapy is only occasionally helpful in cases of unipolar depression (APA, 1993; Prochaska, 1984). Two features of the approach may help limit its effectiveness. First, depressed clients may be too passive and feel too weary to join fully into the subtle therapy discussions (Widloecher, 2001). Second, they may become discouraged and end treatment too early when this long-term approach is unable to provide the quick relief that they desperately seek. Generally, psychodynamic therapy seems to be of greatest help in cases of depression that clearly involve a history of childhood loss or trauma, a long-standing sense of emptiness, feelings of perfectionism, and extreme self-criticism (Blatt, 1999, 1995). Short-term psychodynamic therapies have performed better than the traditional approaches (Leichsenring, 2001; Jefferson & Greist, 1994).

BEHAVIORAL THERAPY Peter Lewinsohn, whose theory of depression tied mood to the rewards in a person's life, also developed a behavioral treatment for unipolar depression in the 1970s. In this approach, therapists (1) reintroduce clients to pleasurable events rectly to consumers—an approach previously inconceivable because of the paternalized role of physicians (Curtiss, 2002; Wilkes et al., 2000). The argument was based on the notion that such advertising would protect consumers by directly educating them about those drugs that were available.

1983: FIRST DTC DRUG AD

The first direct-to-consumer drug ad appeared. In turn, the FDA imposed a voluntary moratorium on such ads until it could develop a formal policy (Pines, 1999).

1985: LIFTING THE BAN

The FDA lifted the moratorium and allowed DTC drug ads as long as the ads adhered to the physician-directed promotion standards. That is, each consumer-oriented ad also had to include a summary of the drug's side effects, contraindications, and effectiveness; avoid false advertising; and offer a fair balance in its information about effectiveness and risks (Curtiss, 2002; Ostrove, 2001; Pines, 1999).

Because so much background information was required in each ad, the companies effectively were forced to limit their DTC ads primarily to magazines and ad brochures.

1997: FDA MAKES TELEVISION-FRIENDLY CHANGES

Recognizing that its previous guidelines could not readily be applied to brief TV ads, which may run for only 30 seconds, the FDA changed its guidelines for DTC television drug ads. It passed a *Draft Guidance,* which ruled that DTC television advertisements must simply mention a drug's important risks and must indicate where consumers can get further information about the drug. The company must also make available such information by providing a toll-free phone number and a Web site. In addition, it must refer consumers to a magazine ad or other printed material that contains more detailed information, and it must recommend that consumers speak with a doctor about the drug (Wilkes et al., 2000).

"I think the dosage needs adjusting. I'm not nearly as happy as the people in the ads."

Barbara Smaller/Cartoonbank.com

and activities, (2) appropriately reinforce their depressive and nondepressive behaviors, and (3) help them improve their social skills (Lewinsohn et al., 1990, 1982).

First, the therapist selects activities that the client considers pleasurable, such as going shopping or taking photographs, and encourages the person to set up a weekly schedule for engaging in them. Studies have shown that adding positive activities to a person's life can indeed lead to a better mood (Leenstra, Ormel, & Giel, 1995). The following case description exemplifies this process:

This patient was a forty-nine-year-old housewife whose children were grown and no longer living at home. Her major interest in life was painting, and indeed she was an accomplished artist. She developed a depression characterized by apathy, self-derogation, and anxiety while she was incapacitated with a severe respiratory infection. She was unable to paint during her illness and lost interest and confidence in her art work when she became depressed. Her therapist thought that she could reinstitute her sources of "reinforcement" if she could be motivated to return to the easel. After providing a supportive relationship for a month, the therapist scheduled a home visit to look at her paintings and to watch and talk with her while she picked up her brush and put paint to canvas. By the time he arrived, she had already begun to paint and within a few weeks experienced a gradual lessening of her depression.

(Liberman & Raskin, 1971, p. 521)

Stretching one's emotions *Although formal treatment is typically needed for severe depression, personal efforts such as going on vacation or spending time with friends can often make a significant difference for people who are struggling with mild depression. Research shows, for example, that regular exercise can help prevent or reduce feelings of depression as well as other psychological symptoms (Dunn et al., 2005).*

While reintroducing pleasurable events into a client's life, the therapist makes sure that the person's various behaviors are rewarded correctly. Behaviorists have argued that when people become depressed, their negative behaviors—crying, complaining, or self-depreciation—keep others at a distance, reducing chances for rewarding experiences and interactions. To change this pattern, the therapist may use a *contingency management approach,* systematically ignoring a client's depressive behaviors while praising or otherwise rewarding constructive statements and behavior, such as going to work. Sometimes family members and friends are recruited to help with this feature of treatment (Liberman & Raskin, 1971).

Finally, behavioral therapists may train clients in effective social skills (Segrin, 2000; Hersen et al., 1984). In group therapy programs, for example, members may work together to improve eye contact, facial expression, posture, and other behaviors that send social messages.

These behavioral techniques seem to be of only limited help when just one of them is applied. In one study, for example, depressed people who were instructed to increase their pleasant activities showed no more improvement than those in a control group who were told simply to keep track of their activities (Hammen & Glass, 1975). However, when two or more behavioral techniques are combined, much as Lewinsohn had envisioned, behavioral treatment does appear to reduce depressive symptoms, particularly if the depression is mild (Jacobson et al., 1996; Teri & Lewinsohn, 1986). It is worth noting that Lewinsohn himself has combined behavioral techniques with cognitive strategies in recent years, in an approach similar to the cognitive treatment that we shall turn to next (Clarke et al., 1999; Lewinsohn & Clarke, 1999).

COGNITIVE THERAPY In Chapter 8 we saw that Aaron Beck views unipolar depression as resulting from a pattern of negative thinking that may be triggered by current upsetting situations (see Box 9-2). *Maladaptive attitudes* lead people to repeatedly view themselves, their world, and their future in negative ways—the so-called *cognitive triad.* Such biased views combine with *illogical thinking* to produce *automatic thoughts,* unrelentingly negative thoughts that flood the mind and produce the symptoms of depression.

"You're sad about the wrong things, Albert."

[BOX **9-2**]

The Grieving Process

Each year tens of millions of people experience the death of a close relative or friend. Reactions to such painful losses can be so similar to clinical depression that Freud and Abraham based the psychoanalytic explanation of depression on them. But mourning is a natural process that allows us eventually to come to grips with our loss and resume our lives.

Unfortunately, there are many common misconceptions about grieving. The most common is the belief that there is a set timetable for mourning (Becvar, 2003, 2001; Doka, 2002, 1999). Friends and acquaintances often allow the mourner only a few weeks to return to normal life. In fact, it is sometimes many months before a person is ready to do so. The amount of time needed depends on such factors as the relationship of the mourner to the deceased, the age of the mourner, and the mourner's gender or personality (Stroebe et al., 2005, 2000; Carr et al., 2001, 2000; Doka & Martin, 2001).

The bereavement process is also experienced differently in different cultural groups (Stroebe & Schut, 2005; Morgan & Laungani, 2002; Stroebe et al., 1992). Japanese Buddhists believe in maintaining contact with dead ancestors, and almost all homes have an altar dedicated to them. Offering food and speaking to the dead are common practices. The Hopi Indians, though, believe that contact with death brings pollution, so they quickly rid the home of all reminders of their deceased relatives. Muslims in Egypt believe that the bereaved should dwell on their loss and surround themselves with others who share their sorrow, but Muslims in Bali are taught to contain their grief, to laugh and be joyful (Wikan, 1991).

Western society tends to view bereavement as an interference in the daily routine, a troublesome, debilitating emotional response that one must overcome as quickly and efficiently as possible (Becvar, 2003). This view was not always the norm in the West. In the mid-nineteenth century,

for example, communication with the dead through séances and mediums was popular. The amount of grief one felt after the death of a loved one was held to indicate the relationship's strength and significance, and the bereaved were expected to focus on a reunion with the deceased in heaven.

Despite individual variations, many mourners in Western society today go through a predictable sequence of emotions (Clayton, 2004; Osterweis & Townsend, 1988). The bereavement process may begin with *shock:* the survivor has difficulty believing that the person has died. This is frequently followed by a sense of *loss and separation,* a feeling that sometimes leads to misperceptions and illusions—glimpses of the dead person in the street or dreams that the person is alive. Once the mourner fully accepts the fact that the deceased is not coming back, despair may set in. Depression, irritability, guilt, spiritual doubts, and anger are natural responses at this stage (Doka, 2002). Social relationships may

deteriorate at this time, and some mourners may suffer from medical problems (Arnette, 1996).

Once the mourning process is complete, it becomes possible to think of the deceased person without being overwhelmed by despair and a sense of loss. At this point, one is prepared to get on with one's life, although anniversaries and other special dates may cause flare-ups of mourning for many years to come.

Whatever a culture's or individual's reaction to grief may be, research suggests that social support plays an important role during the bereavement process (Hullett, 2005; Becvar, 2003, 2001). Thus, it is not surprising that numerous self-help bereavement groups have emerged across the world, giving mourners opportunities to gather with others who have lost loved ones and discuss the emotional and practical problems they all face. These groups, which are apparently helpful for many mourners, allow a necessary process to proceed as it should—without pressure, misinterpretation, or judgment.

Matt Dunham/AP Photo

Mass grief *After widespread catastrophes or when famous people die, it is now common for hundreds, or even thousands, of people to come together to mourn the loss of life and to build extemporaneous memorial sites consisting of flowers, candles, notes, drawings, and other personal items. Here a British police officer lays flowers in Tavistock Square, near the scene where a bus exploded during the London terrorist bombings of 2005.*

	Monday	Tuesday	Wednesday	Thursday	Fr
9-10		Go to grocery store	Go to museum	Get ready to go out	
10-11		Go to grocery store	Go to museum	Drive to doctor's appointment	
11-12	Doctor's appointment	Call friend	Go to museum	Doctor's appointment	
12-1	Lunch	Lunch	Lunch at museum		
1-2	Drive home	Clean front room	Drive home		
2-3	Read novel	Clean front room	Washing		
3-4	Clean bedroom	Read novel	Washing		
4-5	Watch TV	Watch TV	Watch TV		
5-6	Fix dinner	Fix dinner	Fix dinner		
6-7	Eat with family	Eat with family	Eat with family		
7-8	Clean kitchen	Clean kitchen	Clean kitchen		
8-12	Watch TV, read novel, sleep	Call sister, watch TV, read novel, sleep	Work on rug, read novel, sleep		

FIGURE **9-2** **Increasing activity** *In the early stages of cognitive therapy for depression, the client and therapist prepare an activity schedule such as this. Activities as simple as watching television and calling a friend are specified. (Adapted from Beck et al., 1979, p. 122.)*

•**COGNITIVE THERAPY**•A therapy developed by Aaron Beck that helps people identify and change the maladaptive assumptions and ways of thinking that help cause their psychological disorders.

•**INTERPERSONAL PSYCHOTHERAPY (IPT)**•
A treatment for unipolar depression that is based on the belief that clarifying and changing one's interpersonal problems will help lead to recovery.

Beck's **cognitive therapy,** the leading cognitive treatment for unipolar depression, is designed to help clients recognize and change their negative cognitive processes and thus to improve both their mood and their counterproductive behaviors (Beck & Weishaar, 2005; Beck, 2002, 1985, 1967). The approach is similar to Albert Ellis's *rational-emotive therapy* (discussed in Chapters 3 and 5), but it is tailored to the specific cognitive errors found in depression. Beck's approach follows four phases and usually requires fewer than 20 sessions (see Table 9-1).

Phase 1: Increasing activities and elevating mood Using behavioral techniques to set the stage for cognitive treatment, therapists first encourage individuals to become more active and confident. Clients spend time during each session preparing a detailed schedule of hourly activities for the coming week (see Figure 9-2). As they become more active from week to week, their mood is expected to improve. Inasmuch as this early stage of treatment incorporates behavioral techniques, Beck's approach should probably be considered a cognitive-behavioral approach rather than a purely cognitive intervention (Hollon, Haman, & Brown, 2002).

Phase 2: Challenging automatic thoughts Once people are more active and feeling some emotional relief, cognitive therapists begin to educate them about their negative automatic thoughts. The individuals are instructed to recognize and record automatic thoughts as they occur and bring their lists to each session. Therapist and client then test the reality behind the thoughts, often concluding that they are groundless. Beck offers the following exchange as an example of this sort of review:

Therapist: Why do you think you won't be able to get into the university of your choice?

Patient: Because my grades were really not so hot.

Therapist: Well, what was your grade average?

Patient: Well, pretty good up until the last semester in high school.

Therapist: What was your grade average in general?

Patient: A's and B's.

Therapist: Well, how many of each?

Patient: Well, I guess, almost all of my grades were A's but I got terrible grades my last semester.

Therapist: What were your grades then?

Patient: I got two A's and two B's.

Therapist: Since your grade average would seem to me to come out to almost all A's, why do you think you won't be able to get into the university?

Patient: Because of competition being so tough.

Therapist: Have you found out what the average grades are for admission to the college?

Patient: Well, somebody told me that a B+ average would suffice.

Therapist: Isn't your average better than that?

Patient: I guess so.

(Beck et al., 1979, p. 153)

Phase 3: Identifying negative thinking and biases As people begin to recognize the flaws in their automatic thoughts, cognitive therapists show them how illogical thinking processes are contributing to these thoughts. The depressed student, for example, was using *dichotomous* (all-or-nothing) thinking when she concluded that any grade lower than A was "terrible." The therapists also guide clients to recognize that almost all their interpretations of events have a negative bias and to change that style of interpretation.

Phase 4: Changing primary attitudes Therapists help clients change the maladaptive attitudes that set the stage for their depression in the first place. As part of the process,

Table 9-1

Mood Disorders and Treatment

Disorder	Most Effective Treatment	Average Length of Initial Treament (weeks)	Percent Improved by Treatment
Major depressive disorder	Cognitive or interpersonal psychotherapy	20	60%
	Antidepressant drugs	20	60
	ECT	2	60
Dysthymic disorder	Cognitive or interpersonal psychotherapy	20	60
	Antidepressant drugs	20	60
Bipolar I disorder	Antibipolar drugs	Indefinite	60
Bipolar II disorder	Antibipolar drugs	Indefinite	60
Cyclothymic disorder	Psychotherapy or antibipolar drugs	20 to indefinite	Unknown

therapists often encourage clients to test their attitudes, as in the following therapy discussion:

Therapist: On what do you base this belief that you can't be happy without a man?

Patient: I was really depressed for a year and a half when I didn't have a man.

Therapist: Is there another reason why you were depressed?

Patient: As we discussed, I was looking at everything in a distorted way. But I still don't know if I could be happy if no one was interested in me.

Therapist: I don't know either. Is there a way we could find out?

Patient: Well, as an experiment, I could not go out on dates for a while and see how I feel.

Therapist: I think that's a good idea. Although it has its flaws, the experimental method is still the best way currently available to discover the facts. You're fortunate in being able to run this type of experiment. Now, for the first time in your adult life you aren't attached to a man. If you find you can be happy without a man, this will greatly strengthen you and also make your future relationships all the better.

(Beck et al., 1979, pp. 253–254)

Over the past three decades, hundreds of studies have shown that cognitive therapy helps with unipolar depression. Depressed adults who receive this therapy improve much more than those who receive placebos or no treatment at all (Hollon et al., 2006, 2005, 2002; DeRubeis et al., 2005). Around 50 to 60 percent show a near-total elimination of their symptoms. In view of this strong research support, many therapists have adopted the cognitive approach, some offering it in a group therapy format (Petrocelli, 2002).

Sociocultural Approaches

As we observed in Chapter 8, sociocultural theorists trace the causes of unipolar depression to the broader social structure in which people live and the roles they are required to play. The most effective sociocultural approaches to treating depression are *interpersonal psychotherapy* and *couple therapy*. The techniques used in these approaches often borrow from the other models, but they are used in cases of depression to help persons overcome the social difficulties that may underlie their disorder.

INTERPERSONAL PSYCHOTHERAPY Developed during the 1980s by the clinical researchers Gerald Klerman and Myrna Weissman, **interpersonal psychotherapy (IPT)** holds that any of four interpersonal problem areas may lead to depression and must be

>>LOOKING AROUND
Self-Help Goes Awry

In 1991 the Gloucester branch of *Depressives Anonymous* ejected several members because they were too cheerful. Said the group chairperson, "Those with sensitive tender feelings have been put off by more robust members who have not always been depressives" (Shaw, 2004). **<<**

Tom Moran

Role transition *Major life changes such as marriage, the birth of a child, or divorce can present difficulties in role transition, one of the interpersonal problem areas addressed by IPT therapists in their work with depressed clients.*

>>PSYCH•NOTES

Clinical Bias?

In one study, a third of all poor people who reported feeling depressed said that a physician had never diagnosed their condition (Bazargan et al., 2005). ‹‹

addressed: interpersonal loss, interpersonal role dispute, interpersonal role transition, and interpersonal deficits (Weissman & Markowitz, 2002; Klerman & Weissman, 1992). Over the course of around 16 sessions, IPT therapists address these areas.

First, depressed persons may, as psychodynamic theorists suggest, be experiencing a grief reaction over an *interpersonal loss,* the loss of an important loved one. In such cases, IPT therapists encourage clients to explore their relationship with the lost person and express any feelings of anger they may discover. Eventually clients develop new ways of remembering the lost person and also seek new relationships.

Second, depressed people may find themselves in the midst of an *interpersonal role dispute.* Role disputes occur when two people have different expectations of their relationship and of the role each should play. IPT therapists help clients examine whatever role disputes they may be involved in and then develop ways of resolving them.

Depressed people may also be experiencing an *interpersonal role transition,* brought about by major life changes such as divorce or the birth of a child. They may feel overwhelmed by the role changes that accompany the life change. In such cases IPT therapists help them develop the social supports and skills the new roles require.

Finally, some depressed people display *interpersonal deficits,* such as extreme shyness, or social awkwardness, which prevent them from having intimate relationships. IPT therapists may help such individuals recognize their deficits and teach them social skills and assertiveness in order to improve their social effectiveness. In the following discussion, the therapist encourages a depressed man to recognize the effect his behavior has on others:

> **Client:** (*After a long pause with eyes downcast, a sad facial expression, and slumped posture*) People always make fun of me. I guess I'm just the type of guy who really was meant to be a loner, damn it. (*Deep sigh*)
>
> **Therapist:** Could you do that again for me?
>
> **Client:** What?
>
> **Therapist:** The sigh, only a bit deeper.
>
> **Client:** Why? (*Pause*) Okay, but I don't see what . . . okay. (*Client sighs again and smiles*)
>
> **Therapist:** Well, that time you smiled, but mostly when you sigh and look so sad I get the feeling that I better leave you alone in your misery, that I should walk on eggshells and not get too chummy or I might hurt you even more.
>
> **Client:** (*A bit of anger in his voice*) Well, excuse me! I was only trying to tell you how I felt.
>
> **Therapist:** I know you felt miserable, but I also got the message that you wanted to keep me at a distance, that I had no way to reach you.
>
> **Client:** (*Slowly*) I feel like a loner, I feel that even you don't care about me—making fun of me.
>
> **Therapist:** I wonder if other folks need to pass this test, too?
>
> *(Young & Beier, 1984, p. 270)*

Studies suggest that IPT and related interpersonal treatments for depression have a success rate similar to that of cognitive therapy (Weissman & Markowitz, 2002; Swartz, 1999). That is, symptoms almost totally disappear in 50 to 60 percent of clients who receive treatment. After IPT, clients not only experience a reduction of depressive symptoms but also function more effectively in their social and family interactions. Not surprisingly, IPT is considered especially useful for depressed people who are struggling with social conflicts or undergoing changes in their careers or social roles (Weissman & Markowitz, 2002; APA, 1993).

COUPLE THERAPY As we have seen, depression can result from marital discord, and recovery from depression is often slower for people who do not receive support from their spouse (Franchi, 2004; Bruce & Kim, 1992). In fact, as many as half of all depressed clients may be in a dysfunctional relationship. Thus it is not surprising that many cases of depression have been treated by **couple therapy,** the approach in which a therapist works with two people who share a long-term relationship.

Therapists who offer *behavioral marital therapy* help spouses change harmful marital behavior by teaching them specific communication and problem-solving skills (see Chapter 3). When the depressed person's marriage is filled with conflict, this approach and similar ones may be as effective as individual cognitive therapy, interpersonal psychotherapy, or drug therapy in helping to reduce depression (Snyder & Castellani, 2006; Franchi, 2004; Denton, 2003). In addition, depressed clients who receive couple therapy are more likely than those in individual therapy to be more satisfied with their marriage after treatment.

Richard Nowitz/Photo Researchers

Shared responsibility *Couple therapy has proved to be an effective treatment for depression when the client's disorder occurs within the context of a troubled marriage or relationship.*

Biological Approaches

Like several of the psychological and sociocultural therapies, biological treatments can bring great relief to people with unipolar depression. Usually biological treatment means *antidepressant drugs* or popular herbal supplements (see Box 9-3 on page 264), but for severely depressed persons who do not respond to other forms of treatment, it sometimes means *electroconvulsive therapy.* Many people are surprised to learn that electroconvulsive therapy is, in fact, a highly effective approach for treating unipolar depression.

ELECTROCONVULSIVE THERAPY One of the most controversial forms of treatment for depression is **electroconvulsive therapy,** or **ECT.** One patient describes his experience:

> Strapped to a stretcher, you are wheeled into the ECT room. The electroshock machine is in clear view. It is a solemn occasion; there is little talk. The nurse, the attendant, and the anesthetist go about their preparation methodically. Your psychiatrist enters. He seems quite matter-of-fact, businesslike—perhaps a bit rushed. "Everything is going to be just fine. I have given hundreds of these treatments. No one has ever died." You flinch inside. Why did he say that? But there is no time to dwell on it. They are ready. The electrodes are in place. The long clear plastic tube running from the bottle above ends with a needle in your vein. An injection is given. Suddenly—terrifyingly—you can no longer breathe; and then . . . You awaken in your hospital bed. There is a soreness in your legs and a bruise on your arm you can't explain. You are confused to find it so difficult to recover memories. Finally, you stop struggling in the realization that you have no memory for what has transpired. You were scheduled to have ECT, but something must have happened. Perhaps it was postponed. But the nurse keeps coming over to you and asking, "How are you feeling?" You think to yourself: "It must have been given"; but you can't remember. Confused and uncomfortable, you begin to dread the return to the ECT room. You have forgotten, but something about it remains. You are frightened.
>
> *(Taylor, 1975)*

Clinicians and patients alike vary greatly in their opinions of ECT. Some consider it a safe biological procedure with minimal risks (Bolwig, 2005); others believe it to be an extreme measure that can cause troublesome memory loss and even neurological damage. Despite the heat of this controversy, ECT is used frequently, largely because it is an effective and fast-acting intervention for unipolar depression (APA, 1993).

THE TREATMENT PROCEDURE In an ECT procedure, two electrodes are attached to the patient's head, and an electric current of 65 to 140 volts is sent through the brain for half a second or less. The current causes a *brain seizure* that lasts from 25 seconds to a few minutes. After 6 to 12 such treatments, spaced over two to four weeks, most patients feel

•**COUPLE THERAPY**•A therapy format in which the therapist works with two people who share a long-term relationship.

•**ELECTROCONVULSIVE THERAPY (ECT)**• A treatment for depression in which electrodes attached to a patient's head send an electrical current through the brain, causing a convulsion.

less depressed (Gitlin, 2002; Fink, 2001, 1992). In *bilateral ECT* one electrode is applied to each side of the forehead and a current passes through both sides of the brain. In *unilateral ECT,* the electrodes are placed so that the current passes through only one side.

THE ORIGINS OF ECT The discovery that electric shock can be therapeutic was made by accident. In the 1930s, clinical researchers mistakenly came to believe that brain seizures, or the *convulsions* (severe body spasms) that accompany them, could cure schizophrenia and other psychotic disorders. They observed that people with psychosis rarely suffered from *epilepsy* (*brain seizure disorder*) and that people with epilepsy rarely were psychotic, and so concluded that brain seizures or convulsions somehow prevented psychosis. We now know that the observed correlation between seizures and lack of psychotic symptoms does not necessarily imply that one event caused the other. Nevertheless, swayed by faulty logic, clinicians in the 1930s searched for ways to induce seizures as a treatment for patients with psychosis.

A Hungarian physician named Joseph von Meduna gave the drug *metrazol* to patients suffering from psychosis, and a Viennese physician named Manfred Sakel gave them large doses of insulin (*insulin coma therapy*). These procedures produced the desired brain seizures, but each was quite dangerous and sometimes even caused death. Finally, an Italian psychiatrist named Ugo Cerletti discovered that he could produce seizures more safely by applying electric currents to patients' heads, and he and his colleague Lucio Bini soon developed electroconvulsive therapy as a treatment for psychosis (Cerletti & Bini, 1938). As one might expect, much uncertainty and confusion accompanied their first clinical application of ECT. Did experimenters have the right to impose such an untested treatment against a patient's will?

> The schizophrenic arrived by train from Milan without a ticket or any means of identification. Physically healthy, he was bedraggled and alternately was mute or expressed himself in incomprehensible gibberish made up of odd neologisms. The patient was brought in but despite their vast animal experience there was great apprehension and fear that the patient might be damaged, and so the shock was cautiously set at 70 volts for one-tenth of a second. The low dosage predictably produced only a minor spasm, after which the patient burst into song. Cerletti suggested another shock at a higher voltage, and an excited and voluble discussion broke out among the spectators. . . . All of the staff objected to a further shock, protesting that the patient would probably die. Cerletti was familiar with committees and knew that postponement would inevitably mean prolonged and possibly permanent procrastination, and so he decided to proceed at 110 volts for one-half second. However, before he could do so, the patient who had heard but so far not participated in the discussion sat up and pontifically proclaimed in clear Italian without hint of jargon, "Non una seconda! Mortifera!" (Not again! It will kill me!). Professor Bini hesitated but gave the order to proceed. After recovery, Bini asked the patient "What has been happening to you?" and the man replied "I don't know; perhaps I've been asleep." He remained jargon-free and gave a complete account of himself, and was discharged completely recovered after 11 complete and 3 incomplete treatments over a course of 2 months.
>
> *(Brandon, 1981, pp. 8–9)*

ECT soon became popular and was tried out on a wide range of psychological problems, as new techniques so often are. Its effectiveness with severe depression in particular became apparent. Ironically, however, doubts were soon raised concerning its usefulness for psychosis, and many researchers have since judged it ineffective for most psychotic disorders (Taylor & Carroll, 1987).

CHANGES IN ECT PROCEDURES Although Cerletti gained international fame for his procedure, eventually he abandoned ECT and spent his later years seeking other treatments for mental disorders (Karon, 1985). The reason: he abhorred the broken bones and dislocations of the jaw or shoulders that sometimes resulted from ECT's severe

AP Photo

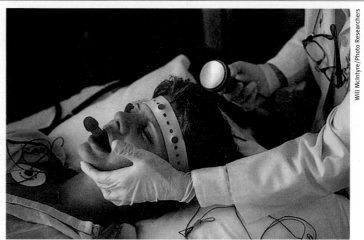

Will McIntyre/Photo Researchers

ECT: Past and present *The techniques for administering ECT have changed significantly since the treatment's early days. In the 1930s and 1940s (left), patients were awake and held down by attendants throughout the procedure. Today (right), patients are given drugs to help them sleep, muscle relaxants to prevent severe jerks of the body and broken bones, and oxygen to guard against brain damage.*

convulsions, as well as the memory loss, confusion, and brain damage that the seizures could cause. Other clinicians have stayed with the procedure, however, and have changed it over the years to reduce its undesirable consequences. Today's practitioners give patients strong *muscle relaxants* to minimize convulsions, thus eliminating the danger of fractures or dislocations. They also use *anesthetics* (*barbiturates*) to put patients to sleep during the procedure, reducing their terror. With these precautions, ECT is medically more complex than it used to be, but also less dangerous and somewhat less disturbing (Gitlin, 2002).

Patients who receive ECT, particularly bilateral ECT, typically have difficulty remembering the events immediately before and after their treatments. In most cases, this memory loss clears up within a few months (Calev et al., 1995, 1991; Squire & Slater, 1983). Some patients, however, experience gaps in more distant memory, and this form of amnesia can be permanent (Squire, 1977). Understandably, these individuals may be left embittered by the procedure.

EFFECTIVENESS OF ECT ECT is clearly effective in treating unipolar depression. Studies find that between 60 and 70 percent of ECT patients improve (Richard & Lyness, 2006; Fink, 2001). The procedure seems to be particularly effective in severe cases of depression that include delusions. It has been difficult, however, to determine why ECT works so well (Lambert & Kinsley, 2005). After all, this procedure delivers a broad insult to the brain that causes neurons all over the brain to fire and all kinds of neurotransmitters to be released, and it affects many other systems throughout the body as well.

Although ECT is effective and ECT techniques have improved, its use has generally declined since the 1950s. It is estimated that more than 100,000 patients a year underwent ECT in the United States during the 1940s and 1950s. Today as few as 50,000 per year are believed to receive it (Cauchon, 1999). Two of the reasons for this decline are the memory loss caused by ECT and the frightening nature of the procedure. Another is the emergence of effective *antidepressant drugs.*

ANTIDEPRESSANT DRUGS Two kinds of drugs discovered in the 1950s reduce the symptoms of depression: *monoamine oxidase* (*MAO*) *inhibitors* and *tricyclics.* These drugs have been joined in recent years by a third group, the so-called *second-generation antidepressants* (see Table 9-2 on page 267).

MAO INHIBITORS The effectiveness of **MAO inhibitors** as a treatment for unipolar depression was discovered accidentally. Physicians noted that *iproniazid,* a drug being tested on patients with tuberculosis, had an interesting effect: it seemed to make the patients

•**MAO INHIBITOR**•An antidepressant drug that prevents the action of the enzyme monoamine oxidase.

[BOX 9-3]

Nature's Way

Today more than one-quarter of all Americans take "herbal" supplements and "natural" hormones to help combat ills ranging from depression to arthritis (Fetto, 2001; Harris Interactive, 2001). Such supplements—collectively called *dietary supplements* or *nutraceuticals*—are experiencing a remarkable growth in popularity, but they are hardly new. Chinese healers compiled the first of their 11,000 medicinal herb formulas as far back as 3000 B.C.

Dietary supplements are a $20 billion industry in the United States, with sales increasing by about $1 billion each year (NBJ, 2001). This sales explosion can be traced to the 1994 passage of the Dietary Supplement Health and Education Act, which provides that dietary supplements are not bound by the same legal requirements as medicinal drugs. To receive approval for a drug, its manufacturer must prove it safe and effective through a testing process that costs manufacturers hundreds of millions of dollars. Dietary supplements, in contrast, are assumed to be safe unless the U.S. Food and Drug Administration can prove them harmful. In the wake of this law, 4,000 manufacturers have rushed dietary supplements into the marketplace, typically without research and often with a number of extraordinary claims about their healing powers.

Many other countries—including Canada, Germany, and China—regulate supplements more stringently than the United States, requiring prescriptions by physicians and encouraging ongoing research. In fact, most of the research on supplements has been conducted outside the United States. Over the past several years, however, the United States has begun to increase its research on supplements (Miller et al., 2004). In 1998, for example, Congress established the National Center for Complementary and Alternative Medicine to sponsor such research. The center has funded rigorous studies of supplements such as *Saint-John's-wort* and *gingko biloba* (Berman, 2004; NCCAM, 2002). Nevertheless, research on supplements remains modest in comparison with the extensive investigations conducted on medicinal drugs, and there remains a serious shortage of knowledge about the effectiveness of most supplements, as well as their safety, proper dosages, unintended effects, and interactions with other substances.

Compounding these research problems is the reluctance of patients to discuss their use of supplements with their therapists or physicians. As many as three-quarters of those who use unconventional therapies fail to tell their health care provider about them (Sibinga et al., 2004; Kessler, 2002). Yet nutraceuticals can be potent and may interact dangerously with conventional medications (Zhou et al., 2004; Schwartz, 2000). In addition, patients often take nutraceuticals incorrectly, partly because they learn about them primarily from friends or from the Internet, where misinformation on this subject abounds (Walji et al., 2004). The supplement gingko biloba, for instance, does offer patients with Alzheimer's disease the possibility of some improved cognitive functioning (Sommer & Schatzberg, 2002), but it does not work immediately (Maher et al., 2002). People who expect instant results from the herb may be disappointed and discontinue its use before they have had time to receive its therapeutic benefits.

Despite such drawbacks, a number of nutraceuticals do appear to offer considerable promise as treatments for psychological disorders. Gingko biloba's potential benefits for patients with Alzheimer's disease have already been noted. Here are some others:

SAM-e In 1999, *s-adenosylmethionine,* or *SAM-e* (pronounced "Sammy"), entered the United States marketplace after more than 20 years of use in Italy and 13 other countries. A common molecule produced by all living cells, this compound is used in cases of depression. It has the advantages of taking effect in about a week and producing relatively few undesired effects. In contrast, pharmaceutical antidepressants take about a month to be of help and often produce at least inconvenient effects (Brown, Gerbarg, & Bottiglieri, 2002). At the same time, SAM-e itself has certain drawbacks, including its price—it costs several dollars a day for a therapeutic dose.

happier (Sandler, 1990). It was found to have the same effect on depressed patients (Kline, 1958; Loomer, Saunders, & Kline, 1957). What this and several related drugs had in common biochemically was that they slowed the body's production of the enzyme *monoamine oxidase (MAO)*. Thus they were called MAO inhibitors.

Normally, brain supplies of the enzyme MAO break down, or degrade, the neurotransmitter norepinephrine. MAO inhibitors block MAO from carrying out this activity and thereby stop the destruction of norepinephrine. The result is a rise in norepinephrine activity and, in turn, a reduction of depressive symptoms. Approximately half of depressed patients who take MAO inhibitors are helped by them (Thase, Trivedi, & Rush, 1995). There is, however, a potential danger with regard to these drugs. People who take them will experience a dangerous rise in blood pressure if they eat foods containing the chemical *tyramine,* including such common foods as cheeses, bananas, and certain wines. Thus people on MAO inhibitors must stick to a rigid diet. In recent years, a new MAO

Matias Costa/Panos

Special water *In Hungary, a popular alternative treatment for both psychological and physical problems is to visit the historic Rudas Turkish bath and immerse oneself in its soothing water along with hundreds of other people. Hungary's thermal waters lie remarkably near the surface, producing more than 1,000 hot springs throughout the country. Given their high concentration of dissolved minerals, the waters are renowned for their medicinal effect.*

Saint-John's-wort Research suggests that this common flower can be quite helpful in cases of mild depression (Linde et al., 2005). Moreover, it is relatively inexpensive and produces few undesired effects. However, it does not appear to benefit people with severe depression.

DHEA This compound seems to sometimes help improve cognitive functioning in cases of Alzheimer's disease and other forms of dementia. DHEA is not a recent discovery; published reports on its therapeutic potential first appeared in 1952 (Wolkowitz & Reus, 2002).

Black cohosh This herb shows some promise as a treatment for the symptoms of premenstrual syndrome and menopause (Dentali, 2002). A host of other herbs have also been touted for these conditions, including *evening primrose oil, wild yam,* and *chaste berry* (Chavez & Spitzer, 2002).

Zinc People with the eating disorder anorexia nervosa sometimes benefit from dietary supplements of zinc. Studies show that this mineral helps produce weight gain in such individuals and may also help decrease their levels of anxiety and depression (Su & Birmingham, 2002).

Melatonin This hormone, which is secreted naturally by the brain's pineal gland, has been touted to do everything from alleviating depression to improving sexual performance and even increasing the life span. However, the hormone has not received clear research support in most of these realms. It has received modest research support as a treatment for certain sleep difficulties (Armour & Paton, 2004). It can also help reduce jet lag by resetting the body's internal clock, tricking the body into believing that it is still nighttime. And melatonin can be useful for night-shift workers and blind or elderly people (including Alzheimer's patients), whose circadian rhythms may be out of sync (Lewy et al., 2004; Mahlberg et al., 2004).

Other minerals, vitamins, and nutrients An intriguing study was recently conducted on young adult prisoners (Gesch et al., 2002). Noting that criminal offenders tended to have diets lacking in essential nutrients (vitamins, minerals, and essential fatty acids), the researchers hypothesized that such deficits might be contributing to their antisocial behavior. They proceeded to give 231 prisoners either nutritional supplements or a placebo. After two weeks, those who received the supplements committed an average of 26 percent fewer disciplinary offenses; in contrast, the placebo subjects showed no such improvement.

inhibitor has become available in the form of a *skin patch* that allows for slow, continuous absorption of the drug into the client's body (Julien, 2005; Amsterdam, 2003). Because the doses absorbed across the skin are low, dangerous food interactions do not appear to be as common a problem with this kind of MAO inhibitor.

TRICYCLICS The discovery of **tricyclics** in the 1950s was also accidental. Researchers who were looking for a new drug to combat schizophrenia ran some tests on a drug called *imipramine* (Kuhn, 1958). They discovered that imipramine was of no help in cases of schizophrenia, but it did relieve unipolar depression in many people. The new drug (trade name Tofranil) and related ones became known as tricyclic antidepressants because they all share a three-ring molecular structure.

In hundreds of studies, depressed patients taking tricyclics have improved much more than similar patients taking placebos, although the drugs must be taken for at least

•**TRICYCLIC**•An antidepressant drug such as imipramine that has three rings in its molecular structure.

10 days before such improvements take hold (Julien, 2005; APA, 1993). About 60 to 65 percent of patients who take tricyclics are helped by them (Gitlin, 2002; Hirschfeld, 1999). The case of Derek, whom we met in Chapter 8, is typical:

One winter Derek signed up for an evening course called "The Use and Abuse of Psychoactive Drugs" because he wanted to be able to provide accurate background information in future newspaper articles on drug use among high school and college students. The course covered psychiatric as well as recreational drugs. When the professor listed the symptoms of affective mood disorders on the blackboard, Derek had a flash of recognition. Perhaps he suffered from depression with melancholia.

Derek then consulted with a psychiatrist, who confirmed his suspicion and prescribed imipramine. A week later, Derek was sleeping until his alarm went off. Two weeks later, at 9:00 A.M. he was writing his column and making difficult decisions about editorials on sensitive topics. He started writing some feature stories on drugs just because he was interested in the subject. Writing was more fun than it had been in years. His images of his own violent death disappeared. His wife found him more responsive. He conversed with her enthusiastically and answered her questions without . . . long delays.

(Lickey & Gordon, 1991, p. 185)

If depressed people stop taking tricyclics immediately after obtaining relief, they run a high risk of relapsing within a year (Montgomery et al., 1993). If, however, they continue taking the drugs for five months or more after being free of depressive symptoms—a practice called "continuation therapy"—their chances of relapse decrease considerably (Kessler, 2002). Certain studies further suggest that patients who take these antidepressant drugs for three or more years after initial improvement—a practice called "maintenance therapy"—may reduce the risk of relapse even more. As a result, clinicians often keep patients on the antidepressant drugs indefinitely.

Most researchers have concluded that tricyclics reduce depression by acting on neurotransmitter "reuptake" mechanisms (Julien, 2005). We have seen that messages are carried from one neuron across the synaptic space to a receiving neuron by a neurotransmitter, a chemical released from the nerve ending of the sending neuron. However, there is a complication in this process. While the nerve ending is releasing the neurotransmitter, a pumplike mechanism in the same ending is trying to recapture it. The purpose of this mechanism is to prevent the neurotransmitter from remaining in the synapse too long and repeatedly stimulating the receiving neuron. Perhaps this pumplike reuptake mechanism is too successful in some people, reducing norepinephrine or serotonin activity too much. The reduced activity of these neurotransmitters may, in turn, result in clinical depression. Apparently tricyclics *block* this reuptake process, thus increasing neurotransmitter activity (see Figure 9-3).

If tricyclics act immediately to increase norepinephrine and serotonin activity and efficiency, why do the symptoms of depression continue for 10 or more days after drug therapy begins? There is growing evidence that when tricyclics are ingested, they initially slow down the activity of the neu-

FIGURE **9-3** **Reuptake and antidepressants** *(Left) When a neuron releases norepinephrine or serotonin from its endings, a pumplike reuptake mechanism immediately starts to recapture the neurotransmitters before they are received by the postsynaptic (receptor) neuron. (Right) Tricyclic and most second-generation antidepressant drugs block this reuptake process, enabling more norepinephrine or serotonin to reach the postsynaptic neuron. (Adapted from Snyder, 1986, p. 106.)*

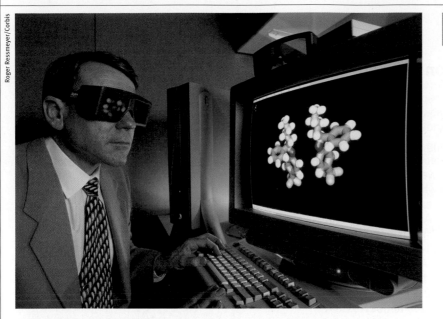

The antidepressant revolution *A clinical scientist studies the molecular structure of Prozac. Sales of antidepressant drugs now total $13 billion each year.*

Table 9-2

Drugs That Reduce Unipolar Depression

Class/Generic Name	Trade Name
Monoamine oxidase inhibitors	
Isocarboxazid	Marplan
Phenelzine	Nardil
Tranylcypromine	Parnate
Selegiline	Eldepril
Tricyclics	
Imipramine	Tofranil
Amitriptyline	Elavil
Doxepin	Adapin; Sinequan
Trimipramine	Surmontil
Desipramine	Norpramin; Pertofrane
Nortriptyline	Aventil; Pamelor
Protriptyline	Vivactil
Second-generation antidepressants	
Maprotiline	Ludiomil
Amoxapine	Asendin
Trazodone	Desyrel
Clomipramine	Anafranil
Fluoxetine	Prozac
Sertraline	Zoloft
Paroxetine	Paxil
Venlafaxine	Effexor
Fluvoxamine	Generic only
Nefazodone	Generic only
Bupropion	Wellbutrin
Mirtazapine	Remeron
Citalopram	Celexa
Escitalopram	Lexapro
Duloxetine	Cymbalta
Reboxetine	Unavailable in the U.S.
Atomoxetine	Strattera

(Julien, 2005)

rons that use norepinephrine and serotonin (Lambert & Kinsley, 2005; Blier & de Montigny, 1994). Granted, the reuptake mechanisms of these cells are immediately corrected, thus allowing more efficient transmission of the neurotransmitters, but the neurons themselves respond to the change by releasing smaller amounts of the neurotransmitters. After a week or two, the neurons finally adapt to the tricyclic drugs and go back to releasing normal amounts of the neurotransmitters. Now the corrections in the reuptake mechanisms begin to have the desired effect: the neurotransmitters reach the receptor neurons in greater numbers, hence triggering more neural firing and producing a decrease in depression.

Tricyclics are currently prescribed more often than MAO inhibitors. They do not require restrictions of the person's diet as MAO inhibitors do, and persons taking tricyclics typically show higher rates of improvement than those taking MAO inhibitors. On the other hand, some individuals respond better to MAO inhibitors than to either tricyclics or the new antidepressants described next, and they continue to be given these drugs (Julien, 2005; Parker et al., 2001).

SECOND-GENERATION ANTIDEPRESSANTS A third group of effective antidepressant drugs, structurally different from the MAO inhibitors and tricyclics, has been developed during the past few decades. Most of these second-generation antidepressants are labeled **selective serotonin reuptake inhibitors (SSRIs)** because they increase serotonin activity specifically, without affecting norepinephrine or other neurotransmitters. The SSRIs include *fluoxetine* (trade name Prozac) and *sertraline* (Zoloft). Newly developed *selective norepinephrine reuptake inhibitors* (which increase norepinephrine activity only) and *serotonin-norepinephrine reuptake inhibitors* (which increase both serotonin and norepinephrine activity) are also now available (DeRubeis et al., 2005, Julien, 2005; Rivas-Vazquez, 2001).

In effectiveness and speed of action the second-generation antidepressant drugs are about on a par with the tricyclics (Julien, 2005), yet their sales have skyrocketed. Clinicians often prefer the new antidepressants because it is harder to overdose on them than on the other kinds of antidepressants. In addition, they do not pose the dietary problems of the MAO inhibitors or produce some of the unpleasant effects of the tricyclics, such as dry mouth and constipation. At the same time, the new antidepressants can result in undesired effects of their own. Some people experience a reduction in their sex drive, for example (Julien, 2005). Decisions about which kinds of antidepressants are

•SELECTIVE SEROTONIN REUPTAKE INHIBITORS (SSRIs)• A group of second-generation antidepressant drugs that increase serotonin activity specifically, without affecting other neurotransmitters.

[BOX **9-4**]

Sociocultural Landscape: First Dibs on Antidepressant Drugs?

In our society, the likelihood of being treated for depression and the types of treatment received by clients often differ greatly from ethnic group to ethnic group. In a recent Medicaid study, researchers closely examined the antidepressant prescriptions written for 2,349 Medicaid recipients who had met the criteria for a diagnosis of depression (Melfi et al., 2005). The following patterns emerged:

◆ Almost 40 percent of depressed individuals were seen by a mental health provider, irrespective of gender, race, or ethnic group.

◆ African Americans, Hispanic Americans, and Native Americans were half as likely as white Americans to be prescribed antidepressant medications on their initial therapy visits.

◆ Although African Americans were less likely to receive antidepressant drugs, clinical trials suggest that they may be more likely than white Americans to respond to proper antidepressant medications (Lawson, 1996, 1986).

◆ Research indicates that African Americans on Medicaid also receive fewer

prescriptions than white Americans for most nonpsychiatric disorders (Khandker & Simoni-Wastila, 1998).

◆ Among those individuals prescribed antidepressant drugs, African Americans were significantly more likely than white Americans to receive tricyclic antidepressant drugs, while white Americans were more likely than African Americans to receive second-generation antidepressant drugs. At the time of the study, tricyclics tended to be less expensive for insurance providers than second-generation antidepressants.

◆ Although African Americans were more likely to receive tricyclic antidepressants, clinical trials suggest that they may be more susceptible than

white Americans to the undesired effects of those kinds of drugs (Sramek, 1996; Strickland et al., 1991).

◆ Depressed individuals in the study who were older or who also had comorbid psychological disorders were more likely than other depressed subjects to receive antidepressant medications, regardless of gender, race, or ethnic group.

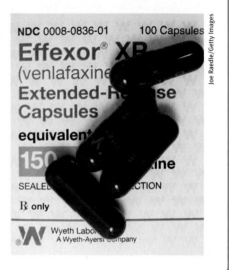

Preferential treatment? *Venlafaxine (brand name Effexor) is a second-generation antidepressant. Studies reveal that, on average, depressed African American patients who are insured by Medicaid are less likely than white American patients to be prescribed second-generation antidepressants and more likely to be prescribed the cheaper tricyclic antidepressants.*

---

prescribed for patients can also be influenced by other factors, such as insurance coverage or financial means (see Box 9-4).

How Do the Treatments for Unipolar Depression Compare?

For most kinds of psychological disorders, no more than one or two treatments or combinations of treatments, if any, emerge as highly successful. Unipolar depression seems to be an exception. One of the most treatable of all abnormal patterns, it may respond to any of several approaches. During the past 20 years researchers have conducted a number of treatment outcome studies, revealing some important trends:

1. Cognitive, interpersonal, and biological therapies are all highly effective treatments for unipolar depression, from mild to severe (DeRubeis et al., 2005; Hollon et al., 2005, 2002). In most head-to-head comparisons, they seem to be equally effective at reducing depressive symptoms; however, there are indications that some populations of depressed patients respond better to one therapy than to another (Weissman & Markowitz, 2002; Thase et al., 2000).

   One of the most ambitious studies of depression therapy was a six-year investigation sponsored by the National Institute of Mental Health (Elkin, 1994; Elkin et al., 1989, 1985). Experimenters separated 239 moderately and severely depressed people into four treatment groups. One group was treated with 16 weeks of Beck's cognitive therapy, another with 16 weeks of interpersonal psychotherapy, and a third group with the antidepressant drug imipramine. The fourth group received a placebo. A total of 28 therapists conducted these treatments.

Using a depression assessment instrument called the *Hamilton Rating Scale for Depression,* the investigators found that each of the three therapies almost completely eliminated depressive symptoms in 50 to 60 percent of the subjects who completed treatment, whereas only 29 percent of those who received the placebo showed such improvement—a trend that also held, although somewhat less powerfully, when other assessment measures were used. These findings are consistent with those of most other comparative outcome studies (Hollon et al., 2006, 2005, 2002).

The study found that drug therapy reduced depressive symptoms more quickly than the cognitive and interpersonal therapies did, but these psychotherapies had matched the drugs in effectiveness by the final four weeks of treatment. In addition, some recent studies suggest that cognitive therapy may be more effective than drug therapy at preventing recurrences of depression except when drug therapy is continued for an extended period of time (Hollon et al., 2006, 2005, 2002). Despite the comparable or even superior showing of cognitive therapy, the past few decades have witnessed a significant increase in the number of physicians prescribing antidepressants. The number of antidepressant prescriptions has grown from 2.5 million in 1980 to 4.7 million in 1990 to tens of millions today (Holden, 2004; Henderson, 2004; Olfson & Klerman, 1993).

2. Although the cognitive and interpersonal therapies may lower the likelihood of relapse, they are hardly relapse-proof. Some studies suggest that as many as 30 percent of the depressed patients who respond to these approaches may, in fact, relapse within a few years after the completion of treatment (Weissman & Markowitz, 2002; Cameron et al., 1999; Shea et al., 1992). In an effort to head off relapse, some of today's cognitive and interpersonal therapists continue to offer treatment, perhaps on a less frequent basis and sometimes in group or classroom formats, after the depression lifts—an approach similar to the "continuation" or "maintenance" approaches used with antidepressant drugs. Early indications are that treatment extensions of this kind do in fact reduce the rate of relapse among successfully treated patients (Hollon et al., 2005; Kuehner, 2005). In fact, some research now suggests that persons who have recovered from depression are less likely to relapse if they receive continuation or maintenance therapy in either drug or psychotherapy form, irrespective of which kind of therapy they originally received (Reynolds et al., 1999).

3. When persons with unipolar depression experience significant discord in their marriages, couple therapy tends to be as helpful as cognitive, interpersonal, or drug therapy.

4. In head-to-head comparisons, depressed people who receive strictly behavioral therapy have shown less improvement than those who receive cognitive, interpersonal, or biological therapy. Behavioral therapy has, however, proved more effective than placebo treatments or no attention at all (Emmelkamp, 1994; Shaw, 1977, 1976). Also, as we have seen, behavioral therapy is of less help to people who are severely depressed than to those with mild or moderate depression.

5. Most studies suggest that psychodynamic therapies are less effective than these other therapies in treating all levels of unipolar depression (Svartberg & Stiles, 1991; McLean & Hakstian, 1979). Many psychodynamic clinicians argue, however, that this system of therapy simply does not lend itself to empirical research, and its effectiveness should be judged more by therapists' reports of individual recovery and progress (Busch et al., 2004).

>>LOOKING AROUND
Drugs on the Rise

Antidepressant medications are now the second most prescribed class of drugs, just behind drugs for high blood pressure. ‹‹

Currently 3 of the 12 most prescribed drugs of any kind in the United States are antidepressants (Gitlin, 2002). ‹‹

With so many medications now available, many of them bearing similar names, mistakes by pharmacists are on the increase. Prescriptions for the antidepressant Celexa (citalopram), for example, are often confused with those for the arthritis drug Celebrex and the seizure drug Cerebyx (Hendren, 1999). ‹‹

"Of course your daddy loves you.
He's on Prozac—he loves everybody."

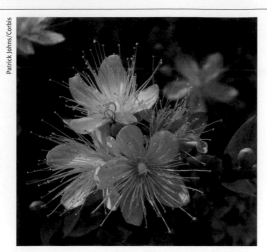

Flower power *Extracts from* Hypericum perforatum, *popularly known as Saint-John's-wort, are currently among the hottest-selling treatments for depression. Saint- John's-wort is a low, wild-growing shrub with yellow flowers that has been used for 2,400 years in folk and herbal remedies.*

6. Studies have found that a combination of psychotherapy (usually cognitive or interpersonal) and drug therapy is modestly more helpful to depressed people than either treatment alone (Hollon et al., 2002).

7. These various trends do not always carry over to the treatment of depressed children and adolescents (see Box 9-5 on page 272). For example, a broad six-year project called the *Treatment for Adolescents with Depression Study (TADS)* indicates that a combination of cognitive and drug therapy may be *much* more helpful to depressed teenagers than either treatment alone (Apter et al., 2005; TADS, 2004).

8. Among biological treatments, antidepressant drugs and ECT appear to be equally effective for reducing depression, although ECT seems to act more quickly (Fogel, 1986). Half of patients treated by either intervention, however, relapse within a year unless the initial treatment is followed up by continuing drug treatment or by psychotherapy (Gitlin, 2002; Fink, 2001, 1992).

When clinicians today choose a biological treatment for mild to severe unipolar depression, they generally prescribe one of the antidepressant medications. Alternatively, some may suggest one of the popular herbal supplements now in the marketplace (Kessler, 2002). They are not likely to refer patients for ECT unless the depression is severe and has been unresponsive to all other forms of treatment, such as unipolar depression accompanied by delusions (Gitlin, 2002). ECT appears to be helpful for 50 to 80 percent of the severely depressed patients who do not respond to antidepressant drugs (APA, 1993; Avery & Lubrano, 1979). If depressed persons seem to be at high risk for suicide, clinicians sometimes refer them for ECT treatment more readily (Gitlin, 2002; Fink, 2001, 1992). Although ECT clearly has a beneficial effect on suicidal behavior in the short run, studies have not clearly indicated that it has a long-term effect on suicide rates (Prudic & Sackeim, 1999).

Treatments for Bipolar Disorders

Until the latter part of the twentieth century, people with bipolar disorders were destined to spend their lives on an emotional roller coaster. Psychotherapists reported almost no success, and antidepressant drugs were of limited help (Prien et al., 1974). In fact, the drugs sometimes triggered a manic episode (Post, 2005; Suppes et al., 2005). ECT, too, only occasionally relieved either the depressive or the manic episodes of bipolar disorders (Jefferson & Greist, 1994).

Lithium Therapy

The use of **lithium** has so dramatically changed this gloomy picture that many people view the silvery-white element—found in various simple mineral salts throughout the natural world—as a true miracle drug. Anna started taking lithium in the 1960s, when lithium was still considered an experimental drug. Her experience shows the extraordinary impact it can have.

•**LITHIUM**•A metallic element that occurs in nature as a mineral salt and is an effective treatment for bipolar disorders.

Anna was a 21-year-old college student. Before she became ill, Anna was sedate and polite, perhaps even a bit prim. During the fall of her sophomore year at college, she had an episode of mild depression that began when she received a C on a history paper she had worked quite hard on. The same day she received a sanctimonious letter from her father reminding her of the financial hardships he was undergoing to send her to college. He warned her to stick to her books and not to play around with men. Anna became discouraged. She doubted that she deserved her parents' sacrifice. Anna's depression did not seem unusual to her roommate, to her other friends, or even to Anna herself. It seemed a natural reaction to her father's unreasonable letter and her fear that she could not live up to the standards he set. In retrospect, this mild depression was the first episode of her bipolar illness.

Several months later, Anna became restless, angry, and obnoxious. She talked continuously and rapidly, jumping from one idea to another. Her speech was filled with rhymes, puns, and sexual innuendoes. During Christmas vacation, she made frequent and unwelcome sexual overtures to her brother's friend in the presence of her entire family. When Anna's mother asked her to behave more politely, Anna began to cry and then slapped her mother across the mouth. Anna did not sleep that night. She sobbed. Between sobs she screamed that no one understood her problems, and no one would even try. The next day, Anna's family took her to the hospital. . . . When she was discharged two weeks later, she was less angry and no longer assaultive. But she was not well and did not go back to school. Her thought and speech were still hypomanic. She had an exaggerated idea of her attractiveness and expected men to fall for her at the first smile. She was irritated when they ignored her attentions. Depressive symptoms were still mixed with the manic ones. She often cried when her bids for attention were not successful or when her parents criticized her dress or behavior.

Anna returned to school the following fall but suffered another depressive episode, followed by another attack of mania within seven months. She had to withdraw from school and enter the hospital. This time . . . the psychiatrists diagnosed her illness as bipolar disorder [and] began treatment with . . . lithium. . . . After seventeen days on lithium, Anna's behavior was quite normal. She was attractively and modestly dressed for her psychiatric interviews. Earlier, she had been sloppily seductive; hair in disarray, half-open blouse, smeared lipstick, bright pink rouge on her cheeks, and bright green make-up on her eyelids. With the help of lithium, she gained some ability to tolerate frustration. During the first week of her hospital stay, she had screamed at a nurse who would not permit her to read late into the night in violation of the ward's 11:00 P.M. "lights out" policy. On lithium, Anna was still annoyed by this "juvenile" rule, but she controlled her anger. She gained some insight into her illness, recognizing that her manic behavior was destructive to herself and others. She also recognized the depression that was often mixed with the mania. . . . She admitted, "Actually, when I'm high, I'm really feeling low. I need to exaggerate in order to feel more important."

Because Anna was on a research ward, the effectiveness of lithium had to be verified by removal of the drug. When she had been off lithium for four to five days, Anna began to show symptoms of both mania and depression. She threatened her psychiatrist, and as before, the threats were grandiose with sexual overtones. In a slinky voice, she warned, "I have ways to put the director of this hospital in my debt. He crawled for me before and he'll do it again. When I snap my fingers, he'll come down to this ward and squash you under his foot." Soon afterward, she threatened suicide. She later explained, "I felt so low last night that if someone had given me a knife or gun, POW." By the ninth day off lithium, Anna's speech was almost incomprehensible: "It's sad to be so putty, pretty, so much like water dripping from a faucet. . . ." Lithium therapy was reinstituted, and within about sixteen days, Anna again recovered and was discharged on lithium.

(Lickey & Gordon, 1991, pp. 236–239)

>>LOOKING AROUND
Cause for Admission

Up to 40 percent of all bipolar patients admitted to a psychiatric facility are in the midst of a *mixed* bipolar episode (Kruger et al., 2005). <<

Determining the correct lithium dosage for a given patient is a delicate process, requiring regular analyses of blood and urine samples and other laboratory tests (Julien, 2005). Too low a dose will have little or no effect on the bipolar mood swings, but too high a dose can result in lithium *intoxication* (literally, poisoning), which can cause nausea, vomiting, sluggishness, tremors, dizziness, slurred speech, seizures, kidney dysfunction, and even death. With the correct dose, however, lithium often produces a noticeable change, as it did for Anna. Some patients respond better to other mood stabilizing drugs, such as the antiseizure drugs *carbamazepine* (Tegretol) or *valproate* (Depakote), or to a combination of such drugs (Bowden & Singh, 2005; Singh et al., 2005). And still others respond best to a combination of lithium and *atypical antipsychotic drugs,* medications that we shall examine more closely in Chapter 15 (Dunner, 2005; Kasper, 2005).

>>PSYCH•NOTES
Taking the Lead

In 1998 *valproate (Depakote)* surpassed lithium to become the drug most prescribed for treating mania in bipolar disorders (UTMB, 1999). <<

[BOX **9-5**]

Depressed Children: Is Help on the Way?

*L*ike adults, children may experience a depressive disorder. Bobby is one such child:

In observing Bobby in the playroom it was obvious that his activity level was well below that expected for a child of 10. He showed a lack of interest in the toys that were available to him, and the interviewer was unable to get him interested in any play activity for more than a few minutes. In questioning him about home and school, Bobby indicated that he didn't like school because he didn't have any friends, and he wasn't good at playing games like baseball and soccer like the other kids were, stating "I'm not really very good at anything." . . . When asked what he would wish for if he could have any three wishes granted he indicated, "I would wish that I was the type of boy my mother and father want, I would wish that I could have friends, and I would wish that I wouldn't feel sad so much."

In speaking with the parents, the mother reported that she and her husband had become increasingly concerned about their son during the past year. She indicated that he always seemed to look sad and cried a lot for no apparent reason and that he appeared to have lost interest in most of the things that he used to enjoy doing. The mother confirmed Bobby's statements that he had no friends, indicating that he had become more and more of a loner during the past 6 to 9 months. She stated that his schoolwork had also suffered in that he is unable to concentrate on school assignments and seems to have "just lost interest." The mother notes, however, that her greatest concern is that he has recently spoken more and more frequently about "killing himself," saying that the parents would be better off if he wasn't around.

(SCHWARTZ & JOHNSON, 1985, P. 214)

Between 2 and 4 percent of children under 17 years of age experience major depressive disorder (Phares, 2003; Kazdin, 1994). The rate is around 8 percent among adolescents alone. Indeed, as many as 15 percent of adolescents experience at least one depressive episode (Apter et al., 2005).

As with anxiety disorders, very young children lack some of the cognitive skills that help produce clinical depression, thus accounting for the low rate of depression among the very young. For example, in order to experience the sense of hopelessness typically found in depressed adults, children must demonstrate an ability to hold expectations about the future, a skill rarely in full bloom before the age of 7 (Piaget & Inhelder, 1966; Wallace & Rabin, 1960).

Nevertheless, if life situations or biological predispositions are significant enough, even very young children sometimes experience severe and enduring downward turns of mood (Najman et al., 2005). Depression in the young may be triggered by negative life events (particularly losses), major changes, rejection, or ongoing abuse (Molnar et al., 2001). Some of the features of childhood depression differ from those that characterize adult depression. For example, as in Bobby's case, a depressed child's inability to experience pleasure (*anhedonia*) is typically expressed as a disinterest in toys and games, as opposed to a reduced desire for sex in depressed adults (Weiss & Garber, 2003). In addition, childhood depression is more commonly characterized by such symptoms as headaches, stomach pain, and irritability (Garber & Horowitz, 2002).

Clinical depression is much more common among teenagers than among young children. Adolescence is, under the best of circumstances, a difficult and confusing time, marked by angst, hormonal and bodily changes, mood changes, and complex relationships. And for some teens the "normal" upsets of adolescence cross the line into clinical depression. In fact, as we shall observe in Chapter 10, suicidal thoughts and attempts are particularly common among adolescents—one in five teens considers suicide each year—and depression is the leading cause of such thoughts and attempts (Anderson, 2002; Grunbaum et al., 2002).

Interestingly, while there is no difference between the rates of depression in boys and girls before the age of 13, girls are twice as likely as boys to be depressed by the age of 16 (Hankin & Abramson, 2001, 1999). Why this gender shift? Several factors have been pointed to. One of the leading ones appears to be teenage girls' growing dissatisfaction with their bodies. Whereas boys tend to like the increase in muscle mass and other body changes that accompany puberty, girls often detest the increases in body fat and weight gain that they experience during puberty and beyond. Raised in a society that values and demands extreme thinness as the aesthetic female ideal, many adolescent girls feel imprisoned by their own bodies, experience low self-esteem, and become depressed (Allgood-Merten et al., 1990). Many also develop eating disorders, as we shall see in Chapter 11.

Throughout the 1990s it was generally believed that childhood and teenage depression would respond well to the same treatments that have been of help to depressed adults—cognitive therapy, interpersonal approaches, and antidepressant drugs (Kaslow et al., 2002). In addition, family therapy was often applied. Some recent studies and events, however, have raised questions about these expectations, and many of today's therapists are beginning to change their strategies for treating childhood and adolescent depression.

First, the National Institute of Mental Health recently sponsored a six-year, 13-site study called the *Treatments for Adolescents with Depression Study (TADS)*, which compared the effectiveness of cognitive therapy alone, antidepressant therapy alone, cognitive and antidepressant therapy combined, and placebo therapy for teenage depression (Apter et al., 2005; TADS, 2004). Three major surprises emerged from this highly regarded study. First, neither antidepressants alone nor cognitive therapy alone was as effective for teenage depression as a combination of antidepressants and cognitive therapy. Second, antidepressants alone tended to be significantly more helpful to depressed teens than cognitive therapy alone. And third, cognitive therapy alone was barely more helpful than placebo therapy. Such findings contrast sharply with the adult depression literature. Adults are helped greatly and equally by either antidepressants or cognitive therapy. Moreover, a combination of the two approaches provides little, if any, extra benefit for depressed adults.

It may turn out that certain peculiarities in the subject population of the TADS study were responsible for this unexpected pattern of findings (Apter et al., 2005). Or it may in fact be that many teens respond less well to cognitive therapy than adults do and that most teens require a combination of antidepressants and psychotherapy to best combat their

depression. The clinical community is currently trying to sort out these important issues.

A second development in recent years has been the discovery that antidepressant drugs may be highly dangerous for some depressed children and teenagers. Throughout the 1990s, most psychiatrists believed that second-generation antidepressants were safe and effective for children and adolescents, and they prescribed them readily (Holden, 2004). However, after reviewing a large number of clinical reports and studying 3,300 patients on antidepressants, the United States Food and Drug Administration (FDA) concluded in 2004 that the drugs produce a real, though small, increase in the risk of suicidal behavior for certain children and adolescents, especially during the first few months of treatment, and it ordered that all antidepressant containers carry "black box" warnings stating that the drugs "increase the risk of suicidal thinking and behavior in children."

Although many clinicians have been pleased by this FDA order, others worry that it may be misleading. They argue that while the drugs may indeed increase the risk of suicidal thoughts and attempts in as many as 2 to 3 percent of young patients, the overall risk of suicide is actually reduced in the vast majority of children who take the drugs (Henderson, 2005). To support this argument, they point out that suicides among children and teenagers have, in fact, decreased by 25 percent across the country in the last decade, as the number of antidepressant prescriptions provided to children and teenagers have soared.

Initially, the heightened suicidal risk posed by antidepressant drugs was thought to be unique to children and teens—perhaps tied to the metabolic processes of a select number of young persons. However, the FDA went on to reanalyze hundreds of antidepressant drug studies in 2004 and 2005, and it eventually concluded that the drugs may pose the same kind of threat to a small group of adults. Thus, the federal agency has since issued repeated public health advisories encouraging doctors and patients alike to watch closely for worsening depression or suicidal thinking in either adult or child patients who take antidepressant drugs.

These recent developments—the TADS findings and the antidepressant drug warnings—highlight once again the importance of research, particularly in the treatment realm (Diller, 2005). Treatments that seem to work for individuals of a certain age, gender, race, or ethnic background may be ineffective or even dangerous for other groups of individuals. The clinical community must always be on the lookout for possible differences between individuals of different groups and must be ever vigilant when applying adult treatments to children. Certainly, one of the best forms of vigilance is careful and systematic research.

Loss and childhood depression *Edvard Munch's painting* The Dead Mother and the Little Girl *captures the devastating impact the death of a parent can have on a child. The loss of a parent and other significant personal losses often trigger childhood depression.*

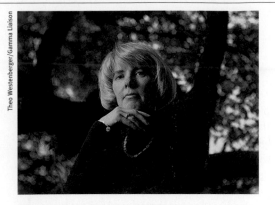

Theo Westenberger/Gamma Liaison

Personal expertise *Kay Redfield Jamison, one of the world's most productive researchers on bipolar disorders, has herself suffered from the disorder throughout her adult life. Despite her expertise, she resisted taking lithium for years, fearing that the medication would stifle her sense of freedom and her creativity. After repeated destructive bipolar episodes, however, she now adheres to a proper medication regimen, saying "freedom from the control imposed by medication loses its meaning when the only alternatives are death and insanity" (Jamison, 1995).*

Given the effectiveness of lithium and its counterparts, around one-third of all persons with a bipolar disorder now seek treatment from a mental health professional in any given year. Another 15 percent are treated or monitored by family physicians (Wang et al., 2005).

ORIGINS OF LITHIUM TREATMENT The discovery that lithium effectively reduces bipolar symptoms was, like so many other medical discoveries, quite accidental. In 1949 an Australian psychiatrist, John Cade, hypothesized that manic behavior is caused by a toxic level of uric acid in the body. He set out to test this theory by injecting guinea pigs with uric acid, but first he combined it with lithium to increase its solubility.

To Cade's surprise, the guinea pigs became not manic but quite lethargic after their injections. Cade suspected that the lithium had produced this effect. When he later administered lithium to 10 human beings who had mania, he discovered that it calmed and normalized their mood. Although many countries began using lithium for bipolar disorders soon after, it was not until 1970 that the U.S. Food and Drug Administration approved it.

EFFECTIVENESS OF LITHIUM All manner of research has attested to lithium's effectiveness in treating *manic* episodes (Grof, 2005). More than 60 percent of patients with mania improve on this medication. In addition, most of them experience fewer new episodes as long as they continue taking lithium (Carney & Goodwin, 2005). One study found that the risk of relapse is 28 times greater if patients stop taking lithium (Suppes et al., 1991). These findings suggest that lithium is also a prophylactic drug, one that actually helps prevent symptoms from developing (Julien, 2005). Thus, today's clinicians usually continue patients on some level of lithium even after their manic episodes subside (Swann, 2005; Cusack, 2002).

Lithium also helps those with bipolar disorder overcome their *depressive* episodes, though to a lesser degree than it helps with their manic episodes (Hlastala et al., 1997). Given lithium's less powerful impact on depressive episodes, many clinicians use a combination of certain antidepressant drugs and lithium to treat bipolar depression (Swann, 2005; Grunze, 2005). In addition, continued doses of lithium (or lithium combined with antidepressant drugs) apparently reduce the risk of future depressive episodes and future suicide attempts, just as they seem to prevent the return of manic episodes (Carney & Goodwin, 2005).

These findings have led researchers to wonder whether lithium might also be helpful in cases of unipolar depression. Here the results have been mixed. A few studies suggest that lithium does help some patients with unipolar depression (Lenox et al., 1998) and occasionally prevents recurrences of that pattern (Abou-Saleh, 1992). Of course, it is possible that the "unipolar" depressed patients helped by lithium actually have a bipolar disorder whose manic episode has yet to appear (Post, 2005; Sharma et al., 2005; Suppes et al., 2005).

In the same vein, lithium often seems to enhance the effectiveness of antidepressant drugs prescribed for unipolar depression (Fava, 2000). In one study, up to two-thirds of "tricyclic nonrespondent" patients were converted to "responders" when lithium was added to their antidepressant drug therapy (Joffe et al., 1993).

LITHIUM'S MODE OF OPERATION Researchers do not fully understand how lithium operates (Lambert & Kinsley, 2005). They suspect that it changes synaptic activity in neurons, but in a way different from that of antidepressant drugs. The firing of a neuron actually consists of several phases that ensue at lightning speed. When the neurotransmitter binds to a receptor on the receiving neuron, a series of changes occur *within* the receiving neuron to set the stage for firing. The substances in the neuron that carry out those changes are often called **second messengers** because they relay the original message from the receptor site to the firing mechanism of the neuron. (The neurotransmitter itself is considered the *first messenger.*) Whereas antidepressant drugs affect a neuron's initial reception of neurotransmitters, lithium appears to affect a neuron's second messengers (Julien, 2005).

Different second-messenger systems are at work in different neurons (Andreasen, 2001). In one of the most important systems, chemicals called *phosphoinositides* are pro-

•**SECOND MESSENGERS**•Chemical changes within a neuron just after the neuron receives a neurotransmitter message and just before it responds.

duced once neurotransmitters are received. Lithium apparently affects this particular messenger system (Manji et al., 1999). Lithium may in fact affect the activity of any neuron that uses this second-messenger system and in so doing may correct the biological abnormalities that lead to bipolar disorders.

In a similar vein, it has been found that lithium and other antibipolar drugs also increase the activity of key proteins and other chemicals that operate within certain neurons. In so doing, the drugs may increase the health and functioning of those cells and, in turn, reduce bipolar symptoms (Gray et al., 2003; Ren et al., 2003).

Alternatively, it may be that lithium corrects bipolar functioning by directly changing sodium and potassium ion activity in neurons (Swonger & Constantine, 1983). In Chapter 8 we noted the theory that bipolar disorders are triggered by unstable alignments of ions along the membranes of certain neurons in the brain. If this instability is the key to bipolar problems, lithium would be expected to have some kind of effect on the ion activity. Several studies in fact suggest that lithium ions often substitute, although imperfectly, for sodium ions (Lambert & Kinsley, 2005; Baer et al., 1971), and other research suggests that lithium changes the transport mechanisms that move ions back and forth across the neural membrane (Soares et al., 1999; Lenox et al., 1998).

"Now that I've swung back to depression, I'm truly sorry for what I did when I was manic."

Adjunctive Psychotherapy

Psychotherapy alone is rarely helpful for persons with bipolar disorders. At the same time, clinicians have learned that lithium therapy alone is not always sufficient either. Thirty percent or more of patients with these disorders may not respond to lithium or a related drug, may not receive the proper dose, or may relapse while taking it. In addition, a number of patients stop taking lithium on their own because they are bothered by the drug's unwanted effects, feel too well to recognize the need for it, miss the euphoria felt during manic episodes, or worry about becoming less productive when they take the drug (Julien, 2005; Lewis, 2005).

In view of these problems, many clinicians now use individual, group, or family therapy as an *adjunct* to lithium treatment (Leahy, 2005; Newman, 2005; Vieta, 2005). Most often, therapists use these formats to emphasize the importance of continuing to take medications; to improve social skills and relationships that may be affected by bipolar episodes; to educate patients and families about bipolar disorders; to help patients solve the special family, school, and occupational problems caused by their disorder; and to help prevent patients from attempting suicide. Few controlled studies have tested the effectiveness of such adjunctive therapy, but those that have been done, along with numerous clinical reports, suggest that it helps reduce hospitalization, improves social functioning, and increases patients' ability to obtain and hold a job (Scott & Colom, 2005; Vieta, 2005; Colom et al., 2003). Psychotherapy plays a more central role in the treatment of cyclothymic disorder, the mild bipolar pattern that was described in Chapter 8. In fact, patients with this problem typically receive psychotherapy, alone or in combination with lithium (Klerman et al., 1994).

PUTTING IT together

With Success Come New Questions

Mood disorders are among the most treatable of all psychological disorders. The choice of treatment for bipolar disorders is narrow and simple: drug therapy, perhaps accompanied by psychotherapy, is the single most successful approach. The picture for unipolar depression is more varied and complex, although no less promising. Cognitive therapy, interpersonal psychotherapy, and antidepressant drugs are all helpful in cases of any severity; couple therapy is helpful in select cases; behavioral therapy helps in mild to moderate cases; and ECT is useful and effective in severe cases.

Why should several very different approaches be highly effective in the treatment of unipolar depression? Two explanations have been proposed. First, if many factors contribute

>>LAB•NOTES

Race and Noncompliance

A recent study of bipolar outpatients found that half of the African American patients and half of the white American patients failed to take their antibipolar medications as prescribed (Fleck et al., 2005). Why? Patients of both races were equally likely to point to the medications' undesired effects. However, the African American patients were more likely than the white American patients to further cite a fear of becoming addicted to the drugs and a concern that the drugs symbolized severe illness. **<<**

>>BY THE NUMBERS
Choice of Treatment

74% Percentage of patients with unipolar depression who currently use antidepressant drugs as all or part of treatment **<<**

37% Depressed patients whose treatment included antidepressant drugs 12 years ago **<<**

60% Depressed patients who currently receive psychotherapy as all or part of treatment **<<**

71% Depressed patients whose treatment included psychotherapy 12 years ago **<<**

(Boyles, 2002)

>>PSYCH•NOTES
Splitting the Pill

The cost of filling a medication prescription tends to be based on the number of pills more than on the dosage of the pills. Thus, two clever clinical researchers have suggested that clients should be given prescriptions for double-dose (noncapsule) antidepressant drugs and should simply split the pills in half when they take their medications. The estimated savings that this strategy would yield is $1.7 billion in the United States alone. **<<**

(Cohen & Cohen, 2002)

to unipolar depression, it is plausible that the removal of any one of them could improve all areas of functioning. In fact, studies have sometimes found that when one kind of therapy is effective, clients tend to function better in all spheres. When certain antidepressant drugs are effective, for instance, clients make the same improvements in their thinking and social functioning that cognitive and interpersonal therapy would bring about (Meyer et al., 2003; Weissman, 2000).

A second explanation suggests that there are various kinds of unipolar depression, each of which responds to a different kind of therapy. There is evidence that interpersonal psychotherapy is more helpful in depressions brought on by social problems than in depressions that seem to occur spontaneously (Weissman & Markowitz, 2002; Thase et al., 1997). Similarly, antidepressant medications seem more helpful than other treatments in cases marked by appetite and sleep problems, sudden onset, and a family history of depression (McNeal & Cimbolic, 1986).

Whatever the ultimate explanation, the treatment picture is very promising both for people with unipolar depression and for those with bipolar disorders. The odds are that one or a combination of the therapies now in use will relieve their symptoms. Yet the sobering fact remains that as many as 40 percent of people with a mood disorder do not improve under treatment and must suffer their mania or depression until it has run its course (Gitlin, 2002).

⊣[SUMMARY AND REVIEW]⊢

■ **Treatments for mood disorders** More than 60 percent of people with mood disorders can be helped by treatment. *pp. 251–252*

■ **Treatments for unipolar depression** Various treatments have been used with unipolar depression. *Psychodynamic therapists* try to help depressed persons become aware of and work through their real or imagined losses and their excessive dependence on others. *Behavioral therapists* reintroduce clients to events and activities that they once found pleasurable, reinforce nondepressive behaviors, and teach interpersonal skills. *Cognitive therapists* help depressed persons identify and change their dysfunctional cognitions. *pp. 252–259*

Sociocultural theorists trace unipolar depression to such factors as social structure and social roles. One sociocultural approach, *interpersonal psychotherapy,* is based on the premise that depression stems from social problems, and so therapists try to help clients develop insight into their interpersonal problems, change them and the conditions that are causing them, and learn skills to protect themselves in the future. Another sociocultural approach, *couple therapy,* may be used when depressed people are in a dysfunctional relationship. *pp. 259–261*

Most biological treatments consist of antidepressant drugs, but electroconvulsive therapy is still used to treat some severe cases of depression. *Electroconvulsive therapy (ECT)* remains a controversial procedure, although it is a fast-acting intervention that is particularly effective when depression is severe, unresponsive to other kinds of treatment, or characterized by delusions. *Antidepressant drugs* include three classes: MAO inhibitors, tricyclics, and second-generation antidepressants. *MAO inhibitors* block the degradation of norepinephrine, allowing the levels of this neurotransmitter to build up and relieve depressive symptoms. People taking MAO inhibitors must be careful to avoid eating foods with tyramine. *Tricyclics* improve depression by blocking neurotransmitter *reuptake* mechanisms, thereby increasing the activity of norepinephrine and serotonin. The *second-generation antidepressants* include *selective serotonin reuptake inhibitors,* or *SSRIs,* drugs that selectively increase the activity of serotonin. These drugs are as effective as tricyclics and have fewer undesired effects. *pp. 261–268*

■ **Comparing treatments for unipolar depression** The cognitive, interpersonal, and biological therapies appear to be the most successful for mild to severe depression. Couple therapy is helpful when the individual's depression is accompanied by significant marital discord. Behavioral therapy is helpful in mild to moderate cases.

And ECT is effective in severe cases. Combinations of psychotherapy and drug therapy tend to be modestly more helpful than any one approach on its own. *pp. 268–270*

■ **Treatments for bipolar disorders** Lithium (or, alternatively, *carbamazepine* or *valproate*) has proved to be very effective in alleviating and preventing both the manic and the depressive episodes of bipolar disorders. It is helpful in 60 percent or more of cases. This drug may reduce bipolar symptoms by affecting the activity of *second-messenger* systems or key proteins or other chemicals in certain neurons throughout the brain. Alternatively, lithium may directly change the activity of *sodium and other ions* in neurons, for example, by altering the transportation of the ions across neural membranes.

In recent years clinicians have learned that patients may fare better when lithium is supplemented by adjunctive psychotherapy. The issues most often addressed by psychotherapists are medication management, social skills and relationships, education of patients, and solving the family, school, and occupational problems caused by bipolar episodes. *pp. 270–275*

>>> **CRITICAL THOUGHTS** <<<

1. What kinds of transference issues might psychodynamic therapists expect to arise in treatment with depressed persons? *pp. 252–254*

2. Friends and family members try, with limited success, to convince depressed people that their gloom-and-doom view of things is wrong. How does the successful cognitive approach to unipolar depression differ from such efforts at friendly persuasion? *pp. 256–259*

3. Some people argue that antidepressant drugs serve to curb useful behavior, destroy individuality, and blunt people's concerns about societal ills. Are such concerns justified? *pp. 263–268*

4. A growing number of troubled pets are now being treated with Prozac. Are such uses of psychotropic drugs appropriate? What other human treatments (psychological or medical) have been applied to pets? *pp. 263–268*

5. If antidepressant drugs are highly effective, why would people seek out herbal supplements, such as Saint-John's-wort or melatonin, for depression? *pp. 264–265*

6. What issues of lifestyle, family and social relationships, and other areas of functioning might need to be addressed in adjunctive psychotherapy for persons with a bipolar disorder? *p. 275*

⊙—[**CYBER**STUDY]————————————————————>>>

SEARCH THE *ABNORMAL PSYCHOLOGY* CD-ROM FOR

▲ **Chapter 9 Video Cases and Discussions**
   Observe psychological and biological treatments for mood disorders at work.
   How has ECT changed over the years?

▲ **Chapter 9 Practical, Research, and Decision-Making Exercises**
   Distinguishing mood fluctuations from mood disorders
   Choosing the right treatment for depression

▲ **Chapter 9 Practice Test and Feedback**

LOG ON TO THE COMER WEB PAGE FOR

▲ Suggested Web links, exercises, FAQ page, additional Chapter 9 practice test questions
   <www.worthpublishers.com/comer>

————————————————————————<<<

Suicide

I had done all I could and I was still sinking. I sat many hours seeking answers, and all there was was a silent wind. The answer was in my head. It was all clear now: Die. . . .

The next day a friend offered to sell me a gun, a .357 magnum pistol. I bought it. My first thought was: What a mess this is going to make. That day I began to say goodbye to people: not actually saying it but expressing it silently.

Friends were around, but I didn't let them see what was wrong with me. I could not let them know lest they prevent it. My mind became locked on my target. My thoughts were: Soon it will all be over. I would obtain the peace I had so long sought. The will to survive and succeed had been crushed and defeated. I was like a general on a battlefield being encroached on by my enemy and its hordes: fear, hate, self-depreciation, desolation. I felt I had to have the upper hand, to control my environment, so I sought to die rather than surrender. . . .

I was only aware of myself and my plight. Death swallowed me long before I pulled the trigger. The world through my eyes seemed to die with me. It was like I was to push the final button to end this world. I committed myself to the arms of death. There comes a time when all things cease to shine, when the rays of hope are lost.

I placed the gun to my head. Then, I remember a tremendous explosion of lights like fireworks. Thus did the pain become glorious, an army rallied to the side of death to help destroy my life, which I could feel leaving my body with each rushing surge of blood. I was engulfed in total darkness.

(Shneidman, 1987, p. 56)

Salmon spawn and then die, after an exhausting upstream swim to their breeding ground. Lemmings rush to the sea and drown. But only humans knowingly take their own lives. The actions of salmon and lemmings are instinctual responses that may even help their species survive in the long run. Only in the human act of suicide do beings act for the specific purpose of putting an end to their lives.

Suicide has been recorded throughout history. The Old Testament described King Saul's suicide: "There Saul took a sword and fell on it." The ancient Chinese, Greeks, and Romans also provided examples. More recently, twentieth-century suicides by such celebrated individuals as the writer Ernest Hemingway, the actress Marilyn Monroe, and the rock star Kurt Cobain have both shocked and fascinated the public (see Box 10-1 on the next page). Even more disturbing are mass suicides such as those of the Heaven's Gate cult in 1997.

Before you finish reading this page, someone in the United States will try to kill himself. At least 60 Americans will have taken their own lives by this time tomorrow. . . . Many of those who attempted will try again, a number with lethal success.

(Shneidman & Mandelkorn, 1983)

[BOX 10-1]

Suicide in the Family

On July 1, 1996, the model and actress Margaux Hemingway killed herself by taking an overdose of barbiturates. She was the fifth person in four generations of her family to commit suicide. Her death came almost 35 years to the day after the suicide of her famous grandfather, the novelist Ernest Hemingway, by shotgun. Severely depressed about his progressive physical illness, he had failed

Karsh/Woodfin Camp & Associates

to respond to two series of electroconvulsive shock treatments.

Margaux Hemingway had suffered from severe depression, alcoholism, and bulimia nervosa. She had had a successful modeling and acting career in the 1970s, but in later years her work consisted primarily of infomercials and low-budget movies. According to friends, she had tried for years to handle her anguish and setbacks with grace. "I was taught it was Hemingwayesque to take your blows and walk stoically through them."

Famous cases such as this remind us that suicide sometimes runs in families. One study found that 11 percent of the subjects who committed suicide had a close relative who had done the same, compared to none of the control subjects, people who died of natural causes (Maris, 2001). But, as with other family-linked disorders, we cannot be certain whether genetic factors, environmental factors, or both produce family patterns of suicide. Indeed, for members of celebrity families, the family name itself may

add considerable stress to their lives. Just as Margaux Hemingway believed that she had to attempt to be "Hemingwayesque," members of celebrity families may feel trapped by the instant recognition, close scrutiny, and high expectations that go along with their family name.

Marc C. Biggins/Gamma Liaison

>>PSYCH•NOTES

Most Common Killings

More suicides (31,000) than homicides (23,000) are committed in the United States each year. <<

Today suicide is one of the leading causes of death in the world. It has been estimated that 700,000 or more people may die by it each year, more than 31,000 in the United States alone (Stolberg et al., 2002; Clark & Goldney, 2000) (see Table 10-1). Millions of other people throughout the world—600,000 in the United States—make unsuccessful attempts to kill themselves; such attempts are called **parasuicides** (Welch, 2001). Actually, it is difficult to obtain accurate figures on suicide, and many investigators believe that estimates are often low. For one thing, suicide can be difficult to distinguish from unintentional drug overdoses, automobile crashes, drownings, and other accidents (Wertheimer, 2001; Lester, 2000). Many apparent "accidents" were probably intentional. For another, suicide is frowned on in our society, so that relatives and friends often refuse to acknowledge that loved ones have taken their own lives.

Suicide is not classified as a mental disorder by DSM-IV-TR, but clinicians are aware of the high frequency with which psychological dysfunctioning—a breakdown of coping skills, emotional turmoil, a distorted view of life—plays a role in this act. Although suicide is frequently linked to depression, around half of all suicides result from other mental disorders, such as schizophrenia or alcohol dependence, or involve no clear psychological disorder at all (Maris, 2001).

Many people are misinformed about the symptoms and causes of suicide. A generation ago, when researchers gave a suicide "fact test" to several hundred undergraduates, the average score was only 59 percent correct (McIntosh, Hubbard, & Santos, 1985). As suicide has become a major focus of the clinical field, however, people's insights are improving, and more recent scores on a similar test by students in both Canada and the United States were higher (Leenaars & Lester, 1992).

Table 10-1

Most Common Causes of Death in the United States

Rank	Cause	Deaths Per Year	Percentage of Total Deaths
1	Heart disease	696,947	28.5%
2	Cancer	557,271	22.8
3	Stroke	162,672	6.7
4	Chronic respiratory diseases	124,816	5.1
5	Accidents	106,742	4.4
6	Diabetes	73,249	3.0
7	Pneumonia and influenza	65,681	2.7
8	Alzheimer's	58,866	2.4
9	Kidney disease	40,974	1.7
10	Septicemia	33,965	1.4
11	**Suicide**	**31,655**	**1.3**

Source: U.S. National Center for Health Statistics, *National Vital Health Statistics Report* (2004).

Dr. Andrew C. Mason, Section of Neurobiology & Behavior, Cornell University

Fatal attraction *A tiny male redback spider prepares to be eaten by his large female partner during copulation and even aids in his own death. While placing his intromittent organ into his partner, he also spins around and dangles his enticing abdomen in front of her mouth. The male may be shortsighted, but he is not intending to die. In fact, by keeping his partner busy eating him, he can deposit a maximum amount of sperm, thus increasing the chances of reproduction and the birth of an offspring with similar tendencies (Andrade, 1996).*

What Is Suicide?

Not every self-inflicted death is a suicide. A man who crashes his car into a tree after falling asleep at the steering wheel is not trying to kill himself. Thus Edwin Shneidman (2005, 1993, 1981, 1963), one of the most influential writers on this topic, defines **suicide** as an intentioned death—a self-inflicted death in which one makes an intentional, direct, and conscious effort to end one's life.

Intentioned deaths may take various forms. Consider the following examples. All three of these people intended to die, but their motives, concerns, and actions differed greatly.

Dave was a successful man. By the age of 50 he had risen to the vice presidency of a small but profitable office machine firm. He had a devoted wife and two teenage sons who respected him. They lived in an upper-middle-class neighborhood, had a spacious house, and enjoyed a life of comfort.

In August of his fiftieth year, everything changed. Dave was fired. Just like that, after many years of loyal and effective service. The firm's profits were down and the president wanted to try new, fresher marketing approaches. He wanted to try a younger person in Dave's position.

Dave was shocked. The experience of rejection, loss, and emptiness was overwhelming. He looked for another position, but found only low-paying jobs for which he was overqualified. Each day as he looked for work Dave became more depressed, anxious, and desperate. He was convinced that his wife and sons would not love him if he could not maintain their lifestyle. Even if they did, he could not love himself under such circumstances. He kept sinking, withdrew from others, and became increasingly hopeless.

Six months after losing his job, Dave began to consider ending his life. The pain was too great, the humiliation unending. He hated the present and dreaded the future. Throughout February he went back and forth. On some days he was sure he wanted to die. On other days, an enjoyable evening or uplifting conversation might change his mind temporarily. On a Monday late in February he heard about a job possibility, and the anticipation of the next day's interview seemed

•PARASUICIDE• A suicide attempt that does not result in death.

•SUICIDE• A self-inflicted death in which the person acts intentionally, directly, and consciously.

to lift his spirits. But Tuesday's interview did not go well. It was clear to him that he would not be offered the job. He went home, took a recently purchased gun from his locked desk drawer, and shot himself.

Billy never truly recovered from his mother's death. He was only 7 years old and unprepared for such a loss. His father sent him to live with his grandparents for a time, to a new school with new kids and a new way of life. In Billy's mind, all these changes were for the worse. He missed the joy and laughter of the past. He missed his home, his father, and his friends. Most of all he missed his mother.

He did not really understand her death. His father said that she was in heaven now, at peace, happy; that she had not wanted to die or leave Billy; that an accident had taken her life. Billy's unhappiness and loneliness continued day after day and he began to put things together in his own way. He believed he would be happy again if he could join his mother. He felt she was waiting for him, waiting for him to come to her. These thoughts seemed so right to him; they brought him comfort and hope. One evening, shortly after saying good night to his grandparents, Billy climbed out of bed, went up the stairs to the roof of their apartment house, and jumped to his death. In his mind he was joining his mother in heaven.

Margaret and Bob had been going together for a year. It was Margaret's first serious relationship; it was her whole life. Thus when Bob told her that he no longer loved her and was leaving her for someone else, Margaret was shocked and shaken.

As the weeks went by, Margaret was filled with two competing feelings— depression and anger. Several times she called Bob, begged him to reconsider, and pleaded for a chance to win him back. At the same time, she hated him for putting her through such misery.

Margaret's friends became more and more worried about her. At first they sympathized with her pain, assuming it would soon lift. But as time went on, her depression and anger worsened, and Margaret began to act strangely. She started to drink heavily and to mix her drinks with all kinds of pills. She seemed to be flirting with danger.

One night Margaret went into her bathroom, reached for a bottle of sleeping pills, and swallowed a handful of them. She wanted to make her pain go away, and she wanted Bob to know just how much pain he had caused her. She continued swallowing pill after pill, crying and swearing as she gulped them down. When she began to feel drowsy, she decided to call her close friend Cindy. She was not sure why she was calling, perhaps to say good-bye, to explain her actions, or to make sure that Bob was told; or perhaps to be talked out of it. Cindy pleaded and reasoned with Margaret and tried to motivate her to live. Margaret was trying to listen, but she became less and less coherent. Cindy hung up the phone and quickly called Margaret's neighbor and the police. When reached by her neighbor, Margaret was already in a coma. Seven hours later, while her friends and family waited for news in the hospital lounge, Margaret died.

While Margaret seemed to have mixed feelings about her death, Dave was clear in his wish to die. Whereas Billy viewed death as a trip to heaven, Dave saw it as an end to his existence. Such differences can be important in efforts to understand and treat suicidal persons. Accordingly, Shneidman has distinguished four kinds of people who intentionally end their lives: the *death seeker, death initiator, death ignorer,* and *death darer.*

Death seekers clearly intend to end their lives at the time they attempt suicide (Harriss & Hawton, 2005). This singleness of purpose may last only a short time. It can change to confusion the very next hour or day, and then return again in short order. Dave, the middle-aged executive, was a death seeker. He had many misgivings about suicide and was ambivalent about it for weeks, but on Tuesday night he was a death seeker—clear in his desire to die and acting in a manner that virtually guaranteed a fatal outcome.

Death initiators also clearly intend to end their lives, but they act out of a belief that the process of death is already under way and that they are simply hastening the process. Some expect that they will die in a matter of days or weeks. Many suicides among the elderly and very sick fall into this category. The robust novelist Ernest Hemingway was profoundly concerned about his failing body—a concern that some observers believe was at the center of his suicide.

Death ignorers do not believe that their self-inflicted death will mean the end of their existence. They believe they are trading their present lives for a better or happier existence. Many child suicides, like Billy's, fall into this category, as do those of adult believers in a hereafter who commit suicide to reach another form of life. In 1997, for example, the world was shocked to learn that 39 members of an unusual cult named Heaven's Gate had committed suicide at an expensive house outside San Diego. It turned out that these members had acted out of the belief that their deaths would free their spirits and enable them to ascend to a "Higher Kingdom."

Death darers experience mixed feelings, or ambivalence, in their intent to die even at the moment of their attempt, and they show this ambivalence in the act itself. Although to some degree they wish to die, and they often do die, their risk-taking behavior does not guarantee death. The person who plays Russian roulette—that is, pulls the trigger of a revolver randomly loaded with one bullet—is a death darer. Many death darers are as interested in gaining attention, making someone feel guilty, or expressing anger as in dying per se (Brent et al., 1988). Margaret might be considered a death darer. Although her unhappiness and anger were great, she was not sure that she wanted to die. Even while taking pills, she called her friend, reported her actions, and listened to her friend's pleas.

When individuals play *indirect, covert, partial,* or *unconscious* roles in their own deaths, Shneidman (2001, 1993, 1981) classifies them in a suicide-like category called **subintentional death.** Seriously ill people who consistently mismanage their medicines may belong in this category. In related work, the influential clinical theorist Karl Menninger (1938) distinguished a category called *chronic suicide.* These people behave in life-endangering ways over an extended period of time, perhaps consuming excessive alcohol, abusing drugs, or indulging in risky activities or occupations. Although their deaths may represent a form of suicide, their true intent is unclear, and so these individuals are not included in the discussions of this chapter.

How Is Suicide Studied?

Suicide researchers face a major obstacle: their subjects are no longer alive. How can investigators draw accurate conclusions about the intentions, feelings, and circumstances of people who can no longer explain their actions? Two research methods attempt to deal with this problem, each with only partial success.

One strategy is **retrospective analysis,** a kind of psychological autopsy in which clinicians and researchers piece together data from the suicide victim's past (Wetzel & Murphy, 2005). Relatives, friends, therapists, or physicians may remember past statements, conversations, and behavior that shed light on a suicide. Retrospective information may also be provided by the suicide notes that some victims leave behind (Leenaars et al., 2001) (see Box 10-2 on the next page).

However, such sources of information are not always available. Around half of all suicide victims have never been in psychotherapy (Stolberg et al., 2002), and less than one-third leave notes (Maris, 2001; Black, 1993). Nor is retrospective information necessarily valid. A grieving, perhaps guilt-ridden relative or a distraught therapist may be incapable of objective recollections (Carrier, 2004; Wertheimer, 2001).

Because of these limitations, many researchers also use a second strategy—*studying people who survive their suicide attempts.* It is estimated that there are 8 to 20 nonfatal suicide attempts for every fatal suicide (Maris, 2001). However, it may be that people who

Death darers? *A sky surfer tries to ride the perfect cloud over Sweden. Are thrill-seekers daredevils searching for new highs, as many of them claim, or are some actually death darers?*

•**DEATH SEEKER**•A person who clearly intends to end his or her life at the time of a suicide attempt.

•**DEATH INITIATOR**•A person who attempts suicide believing that the process of death is already under way and that he or she is simply hastening the process.

•**DEATH IGNORER**•A person who attempts suicide without recognizing the finality of death.

•**DEATH DARER**•A person who is ambivalent about the wish to die even as he or she attempts suicide.

•**SUBINTENTIONAL DEATH**•A death in which the victim plays an indirect, hidden, partial, or unconscious role.

•**RETROSPECTIVE ANALYSIS**•A psychological autopsy in which clinicians and researchers piece together information about a person's suicide from the person's past.

[BOX 10-2]

Suicide Notes

Bill: I am sorry for causing you so much trouble. I really didn't want to and if you would have told me at the first time the truth probably both of us would be very happy now. Bill I am sorry but I can't take the life any more, I don't think there is any goodness in the world. I love you very very much and I want you to be as happy in your life as I wanted to make you. Tell your parents I am very sorry and please if you can do it don't ever let my parents know what happened.

Please, don't hate me Bill, I love you. Mary

(LEENAARS, 1991)

Many suicides go undetected or unconfirmed because the only people who could tell us the truth are gone from the world. Many other people who commit suicide, however—an estimated 12 to 33 percent—leave notes that reveal their intentions and psychological state only hours or minutes before they died (Girdhar et al., 2004; Maris, 2001; Lester, 2000).

Each suicide note is a personal document, unique to the writer and the circumstances (Leenaars, 2002, 1989). Some are barely a single sentence; others run several pages. People who leave notes clearly wish to send a powerful message to those they leave behind, whether it be "a cry for help, an epitaph, or a last will and testament" (Frederick, 1969, p. 17). Most suicide notes are addressed to specific individuals.

Survivors' reactions to suicide notes vary (Wertheimer, 2001; Leenaars, 1989). A note can clarify the cause of death, thus saving relatives the ordeal of a legal investigation. Friends and relatives may find that it eases their grief to know the person's reasons for committing suicide. Yet some suicide notes, especially ones that are passive-aggressive or outright hostile, add to the confusion, guilt, or horror that

survivors experience, as in the following case:

Rather than permit his wife to leave him, twenty-year-old Mr. Jefferson hanged himself in the bathroom, leaving a note on the front door for his wife, saying, "Cathy I love you. You're right, I am crazy . . . and thank you for trying to love me. Phil." Mrs. Jefferson felt and frequently insisted that she "killed Phil." She attempted suicide herself a week after.

(WALLACE, 1981, P. 79)

Clinical researchers have tried to improve their understanding of suicide by studying differences between genuine and fake suicide notes; the age, culture, and sex of note writers; the grammar of notes; the type and frequency of words used; conscious and unconscious contents; handwriting; and emotional, cognitive, and motivational themes (Lester et al., 2004; O'Connor & Leenaars, 2004; Black & Lester, 2003). One important finding is that suicide notes vary significantly with age. Younger persons express more hostility toward themselves and cite more interpersonal problems in their notes; those between 40 and 49 report being unable to cope with life; those between 50 and 59 tend not to cite a reason for their suicide; and those over 60 are motivated by such problems as illness, pain, disability, and loneliness (Lester et al., 2004; Lester, 1998).

A number of studies have also been conducted on writings that are similar to suicide notes. For example, one team of investigators compared poems by nine poets who committed suicide to those written by nine poets who did not commit suicide (Stirman & Pennebaker, 2001). The poets who committed suicide used more first-person self-references in their works, such as "I" and "me," as well as more words associated with death. In addition,

the poets who committed suicide used fewer communication terms (such as "talk" and "listen") in the poems they had written close to the time of their suicides, while the nonsuicidal poets actually increased their use of such words during this same period of time. Thus, it may be that people who are contemplating suicide tend to use language in distinct ways—ways that may eventually help clinicians identify a person's risk for suicide.

Of course, we must keep in mind that the writers of suicide notes themselves may not be fully aware of their motives; their desperate thinking may prevent them from being truly insightful. Thus, suicide notes are "not the royal road to an easy understanding of suicidal phenomena" (Shneidman, 1973, p. 380). Nevertheless, in combination with other sources they can point clinicians and researchers in the right direction (Black, 1995).

The suicide note left by Paul Bern to his wife, the famed actress Jean Harlow, in 1932.

survive suicide differ in important ways from those who do not (Cutler et al., 2001; Diekstra et al., 1995). Many of them may not really have wanted to die, for example. Nevertheless, suicide researchers have found it useful to study survivors of suicide; and we shall consider those who attempt suicide and those who commit suicide as more or less alike.

Patterns and Statistics

Suicide happens within a larger social setting, and researchers have gathered many statistics regarding the social contexts in which such deaths take place. They have found, for example, that suicide rates vary from country to country (Humphrey, 2006; Lester, 2000). Russia, Hungary, Germany, Austria, Finland, Denmark, China, and Japan have very high rates, more than 20 suicides annually per 100,000 persons; conversely, Egypt, Mexico, Greece, and Spain have relatively low rates, fewer than 5 per 100,000. The United States and Canada fall in between, each with a suicide rate of around 12 per 100,000 persons, and England has a rate of 9 per 100,000.

Religious affiliation and beliefs may help account for these national differences (Brown, 2002). For example, countries that are largely Catholic, Jewish, or Muslim tend to have low suicide rates. Perhaps in these countries, strict prohibitions against suicide or a strong religious tradition deter many people from committing suicide. Yet there are exceptions to this tentative rule. Austria, a predominantly Roman Catholic country, has one of the highest suicide rates in the world.

Research is beginning to suggest that religious doctrine may not help prevent suicide as much as the degree of an individual's *devoutness*. Regardless of their particular persuasion, very religious people seem less likely to commit suicide (Thio, 2006; Garroutte et al., 2004; Jahangir et al., 1998). Similarly, it seems that people who hold a greater reverence for life are less prone to consider or attempt self-destruction (Lee, 1985).

The suicide rates of men and women also differ (see Figure 10-1). Three times as many women attempt suicide as men, yet men succeed at more than three times the rate of women (Humphrey, 2006; Maris, 2001). Around the world 19 of every 100,000 men kill themselves each year; the suicide rate for women is 4 per 100,000 (Miller, 2003).

One reason for these differing rates appears to be the different methods used by men and women (Ayd & Palma, 1999). Men tend to use more violent methods, such as shooting, stabbing, or hanging themselves, whereas women use less violent methods, such as drug overdose. Guns are used in nearly two-thirds of the male suicides in the United States, compared to 40 percent of the female suicides (Maris, 2001; Canetto & Lester, 1995).

Suicide is also related to social environment and marital status (Thio, 2006). In one study, around half of the subjects who had committed suicide were found to have no close friends (Maris, 2001). Fewer still had close relationships with parents and other family members. In a related vein, research has revealed that divorced persons have a higher suicide rate than married or cohabitating individuals (Stolberg et al., 2002).

Retrospective analysis *Efforts to understand the reasons behind the suicide of the rock star Kurt Cobain have continued since the day of his death in 1994. This very public retrospective analysis was given new impetus in 2002 with the publication of his personal diaries—800 pages written over several years—which include Cobain's descriptions of his thoughts and concerns, bouts with depression, and drug addiction.*

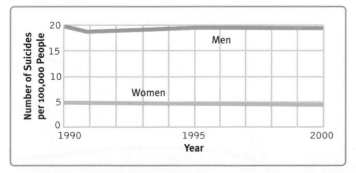

FIGURE **10-1** **Suicide's gender gap** *The suicide rates of men and women have remained approximately the same over the years. In 1990, 20 out of every 100,000 men in the United States committed suicide each year, around four times the rate of women (5 per 100,000). At the turn of the twenty-first century, the suicide rate was 19 per 100,000 among men and 4 per 100,000 among women (Miller, 2003).*

>>**LOOKING AROUND**

The China Profile

China's 300,000 annual suicides, 10 times the United States' toll, represent 40 percent of all suicides in the world. China is the only country in which female suicides are more common than male suicides, accounting for half of suicides by women worldwide (Kaplan, 1999; Phillips et al., 1999; Schmidtke et al., 1999). «

Finally, in the United States at least, suicide rates seem to vary according to race (see Figure 10-2). The suicide rate of white Americans, 12 per 100,000 persons, is almost twice as high as that of African Americans, Hispanic Americans, and members of other racial groups (Oquendo et al., 2005; Stolberg et al., 2002). A major exception to this pattern is the very high suicide rate of Native Americans, which overall is one and a half times the national average (Humphrey, 2006; Garroutte et al., 2003). Although the extreme poverty of many Native Americans may partly explain such trends, studies show that such factors as alcohol use, modeling, and the availability of guns may also play a role (Berman & Jobes, 1995, 1991; Young, 1991). Studies of Native Americans in Canada yield similar results (Strickland, 1997; Bagley, 1991).

Some of these statistics on suicide have been questioned in recent years. One analysis suggests that the actual rate of suicide may be 15 percent higher for African Americans and 6 percent higher for women than usually reported (Phillips & Ruth, 1993). People in these groups are more likely than others to use methods of suicide that can be mistaken for causes of accidental death, such as poisoning, drug overdose, single-car crashes, and pedestrian accidents.

FIGURE **10-2** **Current U.S. suicide rates** *(A) People over the age of 65 are more likely to commit suicide than those in any other age group; (B) males commit suicide at higher rates than females of corresponding ages; (C) white Americans commit suicide at higher rates than African Americans of corresponding ages; (D) elderly white American men have the highest risk of suicide. (Adapted from Stillion & McDowell, 1996; U.S. Bureau of the Census, 1994, 1990; McIntosh, 1991, pp. 62–63.)*

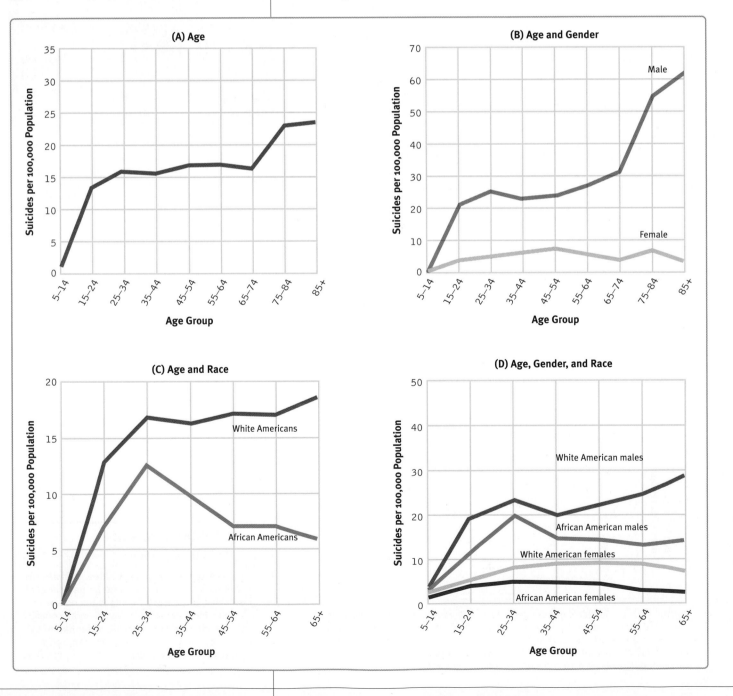

What Triggers a Suicide?

Suicidal acts may be connected to recent events or current conditions in a person's life. Although such factors may not be the basic motivation for the suicide, they can precipitate it. Common triggering factors include *stressful events, mood and thought changes, alcohol and other drug use, mental disorders,* and *modeling.*

Stressful Events and Situations

Researchers have counted more stressful events in the recent lives of suicide attempters than in the lives of matched control subjects (Hendin et al., 2001). In one study, suicide attempters reported twice as many stressful events in the year before their attempts as nonsuicidal depressed patients or patients with other kinds of psychological problems (Cohen-Sandler et al., 1982). Common forms of *immediate stress* seen in cases of suicide are the loss of a loved one through death, divorce, or rejection (Jacobs et al., 1999); loss of a job (Yamasaki et al., 2005); and the stress associated with hurricanes or other natural disasters, even among very young children (Cytryn & McKnew, 1996). A suicide attempt may also be precipitated by a series of recent events that have a combined impact, rather than by a single event, as in the following case:

> Sally's suicide attempt took place in the context of a very difficult year for the family. Sally's mother and stepfather separated after 9 years of marriage. After the father moved out, he visited the family erratically. Four months after he moved out of the house, the mother's boyfriend moved into the house. The mother planned to divorce her husband and marry her boyfriend, who had become the major disciplinarian for the children, a fact that Sally intensely resented. Sally also complained of being "left out" in relation to the closeness she had with her mother. Another problem for Sally had been two school changes in the last 2 years which left Sally feeling friendless. In addition, she failed all her subjects in the last marking period.
>
> *(Pfeffer, 1986, pp. 129–130)*

People may also attempt suicide in response to long-term rather than recent stress. Three *long-term stressors* are particularly common—serious illness, an abusive environment, and occupational stress.

SERIOUS ILLNESS People whose illnesses cause them great pain or severe disability may try to commit suicide, believing that death is unavoidable and imminent (Erlangsen et al., 2005; Hendin, 2002, 1999). They may also believe that the suffering and problems caused by their illnesses are more than they can endure. One study found that 37 percent of the subjects who died by suicide had been in poor physical health (Conwell, Caine, & Olsen, 1990); other studies tell a similar story. Illness-linked suicides have become more common, and controversial, in recent years (Leenaars et al., 2001). Although physicians can now keep seriously ill people alive much longer, they often fail to extend the quality and comfort of the patients' lives (Werth, 1995).

ABUSIVE ENVIRONMENT Victims of an abusive or repressive environment from which they have little or no hope of escape sometimes commit suicide. For example, prisoners of war, inmates of concentration camps, abused spouses, abused children, and prison inmates have tried to end their lives (Thio, 2006; Akyuz et al., 2005; Way et al., 2005) (see Figure 10-3). Like those who have serious illnesses, these people may have felt that they could endure no more suffering and believed that there was no hope for improvement in their condition.

FIGURE **10-3** **Suicide in prisons** *Approximately 107 of every 100,000 inmates in U.S. jails commit suicide each year, many times the national prevalence. Most such suicides occur during the first day of incarceration. (Adapted from Dahle et al., 2005; Bonner, 1992; Hayes & Rowan, 1988.)*

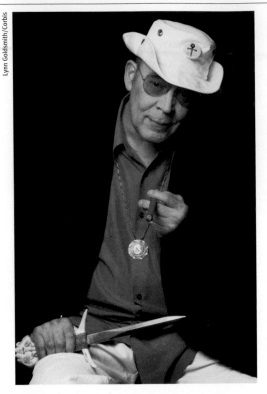

Lynn Goldsmith/Corbis

Multiple risks *People who experience multiple suicide factors are at particular risk for self-destruction (Wunderlich et al., 1998). In 2005, the famous writer Hunter S. Thompson, the pioneer of so-called Gonzo journalism and author of the book* Fear and Loathing in Las Vegas, *shot himself to death. Thompson's suicide is thought to have been motivated by a combination of chronic pain (due to medical problems) and depression.*

OCCUPATIONAL STRESS Some jobs create feelings of tension or dissatisfaction that may precipitate suicide attempts. Research has found particularly high suicide rates among psychiatrists and psychologists, physicians, nurses, dentists, lawyers, farmers, and unskilled laborers (Schernhammer, 2005; Stack, 2005; Wertheimer, 2001). Such correlations do not necessarily mean that occupational pressures directly cause suicidal actions. Perhaps unskilled workers are responding to financial insecurity rather than job stress when they attempt suicide (Wasserman & Stack, 2000). Similarly, rather than reacting to the emotional strain of their work, suicidal psychiatrists and psychologists may have long-standing emotional problems that stimulated their career interest in the first place (Johnson, 1991).

Clinicians once believed that married women who held jobs outside the home had higher suicide rates than other women, perhaps because of conflicts between the demands of their families and their jobs (Stack, 1987; Stillion, 1985). However, recent studies call these notions into question and some even suggest that work outside the home may be linked to lower suicide rates among women, just as it is among men (Stack, 1998; Yang & Lester, 1995).

Mood and Thought Changes

Many suicide attempts are preceded by a change in mood (see Box 10-3). The change may not be severe enough to warrant a diagnosis of a mental disorder, but it does represent a significant shift from the person's past mood. The most common change is an increase in sadness (Werth, 2004; Hendin et al., 2001). Also common are increases in feelings of anxiety, tension, frustration, anger, or shame. In fact, Shneidman (2005, 2001) suggests that the key to suicide is "psychache," a feeling of psychological pain that seems intolerable to the person.

Suicide attempts may also be preceded by shifts in patterns of thinking. Individuals may become preoccupied with their problems, lose perspective, and see suicide as the only effective solution to their difficulties (Shneidman, 2005, 2001, 1999, 1987). They often develop a sense of **hopelessness**—a pessimistic belief that their present circumstances, problems, or mood will not change. Some clinicians believe that a feeling of hopelessness is the single most likely indicator of suicidal intent, and they take special care to look for signs of hopelessness when they assess the risk of suicide (Wen-Hung et al., 2004).

Many people who attempt suicide fall victim to **dichotomous thinking,** viewing problems and solutions in rigid either/or terms (Shneidman, 2005, 2001, 1993; Weishaar, 2000). Indeed, Schneidman has said that the "four-letter word" in suicide is "only," as in "suicide was the *only* thing I could do" (Maris, 2001). In the following statement a woman who survived her leap from a building describes her dichotomous thinking at the time. She saw death as the only alternative to her pain:

> I was so desperate. I felt, my God, I couldn't face this thing. Everything was like a terrible whirlpool of confusion. And I thought to myself: There's only one thing to do. I just have to lose consciousness. That's the only way to get away from it. The only way to lose consciousness, I thought, was to jump off something good and high. . . .
>
> *(Shneidman, 1987, p. 56)*

Alcohol and Other Drug Use

Studies indicate that as many as 70 percent of the people who attempt suicide drink alcohol just before the act (McCloud et al., 2004; Lester, 2000). Autopsies reveal that about one-fourth of these people are legally intoxicated (Flavin et al., 1990). In fact, since coroners are more likely to classify deaths as accidental when they detect high alcohol levels (Crompton, 1985), the excessive use of alcohol just before suicide is probably much higher. It may be that the use of alcohol lowers the individuals' fears of committing sui-

•**HOPELESSNESS**•A pessimistic belief that one's present circumstances, problems, or mood will not change.

•**DICHOTOMOUS THINKING**•Viewing problems and solutions in rigid either/or terms.

[BOX **10-3**]

Can Rock and Roll Inspire Suicide?

Parents frequently worry about the influence of rock and roll on their teenage children. In fact, such concerns have led to a music rating system which informs consumers (and their parents) about the kinds of language and themes that will appear on the CDs or tapes they are about to buy.

One of the greatest parental concerns is that rock and roll lyrics may encourage and lead to suicide. Two famous cases have brought this concern into public awareness.

One case involved the music of the rocker Ozzy Osbourne, leader of the band Black Sabbath. In the early days of Black Sabbath, Osbourne and the band centered much of their music on psychological themes, and the band's music was even perceived by many as having a "satanic" bent. The band's 1970 album *Paranoid* became its biggest success.

Osbourne departed the band for a solo career between 1979 and the late 1990s. During this solo period, his music was blamed for three suicides. In 1984 a 19-year-old boy shot himself in the head while listening to Osbourne's song "Suicide Solution." A lawyer for the boy's family and lawyers for two other families whose children committed suicide claimed that the theme of the song encouraged suicide as an acceptable solution to one's problems. The lawyers also claimed that the song contained tones known as "hemi-sync" (a process that uses sound waves to influence an individual's mental state) and that these tones left the suicidal boys unable to resist what was being said in the song. Finally, the lawyers claimed that the song had *subliminal* lyrics—words sung much faster than the normal rate of speech and unrecognizable to first-time listeners. Supposedly, the subliminal lyrics in the song were "Why try, why try? Get the gun and try it! Shoot, Shoot, Shoot." Osbourne's lawyers claimed that all of this was nonsense and further argued that the musician had a First Amendment right to write about anything he wanted. The court agreed and dismissed all three cases by 1986.

A second famous case involved the music of the heavy metal band Judas Priest. In 1985 two boys shot themselves in the head with a shotgun; one of them died immediately and the other boy three years later. The boys had been drunk and on drugs and shot themselves in a "suicide pact" after listening to a Judas Priest album for hours. Lawyers for the boys' families claimed that Judas Priest's 1977 song "Better by You, Better than Me" contained, when played backward, the subliminal message "Do it" as well as "Try suicide" and "Let's be dead." The band's lawyers countered that any song played backward might seem to have a hidden message. The trial judge agreed, and in 1990, after a month-long trial featuring various audio experts, he dismissed the $6.2 million lawsuit. He ruled that

Glen Wexler Studio, Inc.

even if the lyrics conveyed subliminal messages, such messages had been unintentional.

If the music in these cases did not itself lead to suicide, what did? According to many experts, other nonmusical factors were probably to blame. A number of clinicians have argued that the individuals in these cases were probably suffering from several kinds of factors typically linked to suicide—depression, stress, and the like.

Of course, the dismissal of these suits has not necessarily put to rest the concerns of parents, and their concerns grow still greater whenever they read about a teenager who commits suicide while listening to a death-themed rock song. While such events are not common in our society, they do, sadly, occur on occasion.

cide, releases underlying aggressive feelings, or impairs their judgment and problem-solving ability. Research shows that the use of other kinds of drugs may have a similar tie to suicide, particularly in teenagers and young adults (Darke et al., 2005; Lester, 2000). A high level of heroin, for example, was found in the blood of Kurt Cobain at the time of his suicide in 1994 (Colburn, 1996).

Mental Disorders

Although people who attempt suicide may be troubled or anxious, they do not necessarily have a psychological disorder as defined in DSM-IV-TR. Nevertheless, the majority

Table **10-2**

Common Predictors of Suicide

1. Depressive disorder and certain other mental disorders
----
2. Alcoholism and other forms of substance abuse
----
3. Suicide ideation, talk, preparation; certain religious ideas
----
4. Prior suicide attempts
----
5. Lethal methods
----
6. Isolation, living alone, loss of support
----
7. Hopelessness, cognitive rigidity
----
8. Impulsivity and risk-taking behavior
----
9. Being an older white male
----
10. Modeling, suicide in the family, genetics
----
11. Economic or work problems; certain occupations
----
12. Marital problems, family pathology
----
13. Stress and stressful events
----
14. Anger, aggression, irritability
----
15. Psychosis
----
16. Physical illness
----
17. Repetition and combination of factors 1 to 16

Source: Adapted from Papolos et al., 2005; Maris, 1992.

Mass suicide *In 1997 the world was shocked to learn of the bizarre beliefs held by the Heaven's Gate cult when 39 of its members committed suicide in a suburban San Diego house. Influenced by the cult's leader, Marshall Herff Applewhite (pictured above), the members believed that their bodies were "containers" for higher heavenly spirits and that their deaths would free them to fly to a higher kingdom on a UFO.*

of all suicide attempters do display such a disorder (Carrier & Ennis, 2004; Stolberg et al., 2002). In fact, research suggests that as many as half of all suicide victims had been experiencing severe *depression,* 20 percent *chronic alcoholism,* and 10 percent *schizophrenia* (see Table 10-2). Correspondingly, as many as 15 percent of people with each of these disorders try to kill themselves. People who are both depressed and dependent on alcohol seem particularly prone to suicidal impulses (Sher et al., 2005). Certain anxiety disorders, including posttraumatic stress disorder and panic disorder, have also been linked to suicide, but in most cases of suicide these disorders occur in conjunction with depression, a substance-related disorder, or schizophrenia (Oquendo et al., 2005; Sareen et al., 2005). It is also the case that many people with borderline personality disorder, a broad pattern that we shall be observing in Chapter 16, try to harm themselves or make suicidal gestures as part of their disorder (Stanley & Brodsky, 2005; Black et al., 2004). The special issues that these individuals are grappling with and the treatments to which they respond are often quite different from those of other suicidal persons. Thus, we shall put off examining the suicidal features and treatments of borderline personality disorder until Chapter 16.

As we observed in Chapter 8, people with major depressive disorder often experience suicidal thoughts (Wetzel & Murphy, 2005). Those whose depression includes a very strong sense of hopelessness seem particularly likely to attempt suicide (Fawcett et al., 1987). One program in Sweden was able to reduce the community suicide rate by teaching physicians how to recognize and treat depression at an early stage (Rihmer, Rutz, & Pihlgren, 1995). Even when depressed people are showing improvements in mood, however, they may remain high suicide risks. In fact, among those who are severely depressed, the risk of suicide may actually increase as their mood improves and they have more energy to act on their suicidal wishes.

Severe depression also may play a key role in suicide attempts by persons with serious physical illnesses (Chochinov & Schwartz, 2002). A study of 44 patients with terminal illnesses revealed that fewer than one-quarter of them had thoughts of suicide or wished for an early death and that those who did were all suffering from major depressive disorder (Brown et al., 1986).

A number of the people who drink alcohol or use drugs just before a suicide attempt actually have a long history of abusing such substances (Cottler et al., 2005; Preuss et al., 2003). The basis for the link between substance-related disorders and suicide is not clear. Perhaps the tragic lifestyle of many persons with these disorders or their sense of being hopelessly trapped by a substance leads to suicidal thinking. Alternatively, a third factor—psychological pain, for instance, or desperation—may cause both substance abuse and suicidal thinking (Sher et al., 2005; Frances & Franklin, 1988). Such people may be caught in a downward spiral: they are driven toward substance use by psychological pain or loss, only to find themselves caught in a pattern of substance abuse that aggravates rather than solves their problems (Maris, 2001; Downey, 1991).

People with schizophrenia, as we shall see in Chapter 14, may hear voices that are not actually present (hallucinations) or hold beliefs that are clearly false and perhaps bizarre (delusions). There is a popular notion that when such persons kill themselves, they must be responding to an imagined voice commanding them to do so or to a delusion that suicide is a grand and noble gesture. Research indicates, however, that suicides by people with schizophrenia more often reflect feelings of *demoralization* or the like (Wetzel & Murphy, 2005; Kim et al., 2003). For example, many young and unemployed sufferers who have had relapses over several years come to believe that the disorder will forever disrupt their lives (see Box 10-4). Still others seem to be disheartened by their unfortunate, sometimes dreadful living conditions. Suicide is the leading cause of premature death in this population (Pompili et al., 2004).

Gamma Liaison

[BOX 10-4]

"I'm All Traveled Out"

On October 5, 1998, Margaret Mary Ray knelt down in front of an oncoming 105-car coal train in Hotchkiss, Colorado, and brought her life to an immediate end. Ms. Ray, 46, had suffered from schizophrenia for years, holding delusions that she was in intimate relationships with famous people and even stalking them in their residences. Like a number of other people with schizophrenia, she eventually grew weary and hopeless about the chances that her disorder would ever improve. In a suicide note sent to her mother, she said, "I'm all traveled out. . . . I choose a painless and instantaneous way to end my life. . . ."

One difference between Ms. Ray and most other people with schizophrenia is that millions of people knew something about her dysfunction. She gained notoriety during her last decade as the woman who believed that she was romantically involved with the television comedian David Letterman, repeatedly breaking into his home, sleeping on his tennis court, and on one occasion stealing his car. Her delusion first came to light in 1988 when she was arrested while driving Letterman's car at the entrance to the Lincoln Tunnel in New York City. When she was unable to pay the toll, she identified herself as Letterman's wife and her son as his son. Over the next decade, she was arrested repeatedly for trespassing and was forced to spend a total of 10 months in prison and 14 months in a state hospital. Newspaper accounts usually described her exploits in a lighthearted way, and readers generally considered her to be a strange and comical character.

Not until Ms. Ray killed herself did most people become aware of just how disturbed she was. In fact, two of her three brothers had also suffered from schizophrenia and killed themselves years earlier. Her adult life consisted of sudden trips across the country, strange ideas, and impulsive and erratic behavior that extended well beyond her focus on Letterman. Her surviving brother remembers times when she spoke in sentences that made no sense and warm days when she wore three layers of clothing (Bruni, 1998). Medications often seemed to help her, but

A weary Margaret Ray faces charges of stalking in 1997.

she usually stopped taking them outside of prison or the state hospital.

Letterman himself recognized the seriousness of Ms. Ray's problem and grappled with how best to handle things. He rarely talked about her, never mentioned her name on the air, and often declined to press charges against her. After her death, he recalled that she had sent him many letters between her uninvited house visits, and it had been apparent in each letter whether she was taking her medications (Bruni, 1998). "When she was on them, it was like hearing from your aunt. When she was off them, it was like hearing from your aunt on Neptune." On the day after her death, he observed, "This is a sad end to a confused life."

Modeling: The Contagion of Suicide

It is not unusual for people, particularly teenagers, to try to commit suicide after observing or reading about someone else who has done so (Stack 2005, 2003; Wertheimer, 2001). Perhaps these people have been struggling with major problems and the other person's suicide seems to reveal a possible solution; or they have been thinking about suicide and the other person's suicide seems to give them permission or finally persuades them to act. Either way, one suicidal act apparently serves as a *model* for another. Suicides by celebrities, other highly publicized suicides, and suicides by co-workers or colleagues are particularly common triggers.

CELEBRITIES Research suggests that suicides by entertainers, political figures, and other well-known persons are regularly followed by unusual increases in the number of suicides across the nation (Stack, 2005, 1987; Tousignant et al., 2005). During the week after the suicide of Marilyn Monroe in 1963, for example, the national suicide rate rose 12 percent (Phillips, 1974).

OTHER HIGHLY PUBLICIZED CASES Suicides with bizarre or unusual aspects often receive intense coverage by the news media (Wertheimer, 2001). Such highly publicized accounts may lead to similar suicides (Gould, 2001). During the year after a widely publicized, politically motivated suicide by self-burning in England, for example, 82 other people set themselves on fire, with equally fatal results (Ashton & Donnan, 1981). Inquest reports revealed that most of those people had histories of emotional problems and that none of the suicides had the political motivation of the publicized suicide. The imitators seemed to be responding to their own problems in a manner triggered by the suicide they had observed or read about.

Dealing with the pain *In the days following the suicide of Nirvana's Kurt Cobain, some 5,000 people, including these two fans, attended a candlelight vigil in Seattle. To help address the trauma experienced by many fans of celebrities who have recently taken their own lives and to help prevent "copycat" suicides, "postvention" approaches are often used, including counseling sessions in schools and special media programs.*

Even a media program that is clearly intended to educate and help viewers may have the paradoxical effect of spurring imitators. One study found a dramatic increase in the rate of suicide among West German teenagers after the airing of a television documentary showing the suicide of a teenager who jumped under a train (Schmidtke & Häfner, 1988). The number of railway suicides by male teenagers increased by 175 percent after the program was aired.

Some clinicians argue that more responsible reporting could reduce this frightening impact of highly publicized suicides (Bailey, 2003; Gould, 2001; Wertheimer, 2001). A careful approach to reporting was seen in the media's coverage of the suicide of Kurt Cobain. MTV's repeated theme on the evening of the suicide was "Don't do it!" In fact, thousands of young people called MTV and other radio and television stations in the hours after Cobain's death, upset, frightened, and in some cases suicidal. Some of the stations responded by posting the phone numbers of suicide prevention centers, presenting interviews with suicide experts, and offering counseling services and advice directly to callers. Perhaps because of such efforts, the usual rate of suicide both in Seattle, Cobain's hometown, and elsewhere held steady during the weeks that followed (Colburn, 1996).

CO-WORKERS AND COLLEAGUES The word-of-mouth publicity that attends suicides in a school, workplace, or small community may trigger suicide attempts. The suicide of a recruit at a U.S. Navy training school, for example, was followed within two weeks by another and also by an attempted suicide at the school. To head off what threatened to become a suicide epidemic, the school began a program of staff education on suicide and group therapy sessions for recruits who had been close to the suicide victims (Grigg, 1988). The kinds of postsuicide programs put into action by this school and by MTV in the aftermath of Kurt Cobain's death are often referred to by clinicians as *postvention*.

What Are the Underlying Causes of Suicide?

Most people faced with difficult situations never try to kill themselves. In an effort to understand why some people are more prone to suicide than others, theorists have proposed more fundamental explanations for self-destructive action than the immediate triggers considered in the previous section. The leading theories come from the psychodynamic, sociocultural, and biological perspectives. As a group, however, these hypotheses have received limited research support and fail to address the full range of suicidal acts. Thus the clinical field currently lacks a satisfactory understanding of suicide.

The Psychodynamic View

Many psychodynamic theorists believe that suicide results from depression and from anger at others that is redirected toward oneself. This theory was first stated by Wilhelm

>>**LOOKING AROUND**

Suicides by Musicians: Post–Kurt Cobaine

Jason Thirsk, punk band Pennywise (1996) «

Faron Young, country music (1996) «

Michael Hutchence, INXS (1997) «

Rob Pilatus, Milli Vanilli (1998) «

Wendy O. Williams, rock singer (1998) «

Screaming Lord Sutch, British rock singer (1999) «

Susannah McCorkle, jazz singer (2001) «

Herman Brood, Dutch rock singer (2001) «

Leslie Cheung, Chinese singer (2003) «

Elliott Smith, rock singer (2003) «

Stekel at a meeting in Vienna in 1910, when he proclaimed that "no one kills himself who has not wanted to kill another or at least wished the death of another" (Shneidman, 1979). Some years later Sigmund Freud (1920) wrote, "No neurotic harbors thoughts of suicide which he has not turned back upon himself from murderous impulses against others." Agreeing with this notion, Karl Menninger called suicide "murder in the 180th degree."

As we saw in Chapter 8, Freud (1917) and Abraham (1916, 1911) proposed that when people experience the real or symbolic loss of a loved one, they come to "introject" the lost person; that is, they unconsciously incorporate the person into their own identity and feel toward themselves as they had felt toward the other. For a short while, negative feelings toward the lost loved one are experienced as self-hatred. Anger toward the loved one may turn into intense anger against oneself and finally into depression. Suicide is thought to be an extreme expression of this self-hatred. The following description of a suicidal patient demonstrates how such forces may operate:

> A 27-year-old conscientious and responsible woman took a knife to her wrists to punish herself for being tyrannical, unreliable, self-centered, and abusive. She was perplexed and frightened by this uncharacteristic self-destructive episode and was enormously relieved when her therapist pointed out that her invective described her recently deceased father much better than it did herself.
>
> *(Gill, 1982, p. 15)*

In support of Freud's view, researchers have often found a relationship between childhood losses—real or symbolic—and later suicidal behaviors (Read et al., 2001; Kaslow et al., 1998). One study of 200 family histories found that early parental loss was much more common among suicide attempters (48 percent) than among nonsuicidal control subjects (24 percent) (Adam, Bouckoms, & Streiner, 1982). Common forms of loss were death of the father and divorce or separation of the parents.

Late in his career, Freud proposed that human beings have a basic "death instinct." He called this instinct *Thanatos,* and said that it opposes the "life instinct." According to Freud, while most people learn to redirect their death instinct, by aiming it toward others, suicidal people, caught in a web of self-anger, direct it squarely upon themselves.

Sociological findings are consistent with this explanation of suicide. National suicide rates have been found to drop in times of war (Maris, 2001), when, one could argue, people are encouraged to direct their self-destructive energy against "the enemy." In addition, societies with high rates of homicide tend to have low rates of suicide, and vice versa (Somasundaram & Rajadurai, 1995). However, research has failed to establish that suicidal people are in fact dominated by intense feelings of anger. Although hostility is an important element in some suicides (Sher et al., 2005), several studies find that other emotional states are even more prevalent (Castrogiovanni, Pieraccini, & DiMuto, 1998).

By the end of his career, Freud himself expressed dissatisfaction with his theory of suicide. Other psychodynamic theorists have also challenged his ideas over the years, yet themes of loss and self-directed aggression generally remain at the center of most psychodynamic explanations (King, 2003; Maltsberger, 1999).

The Sociocultural View

Toward the end of the nineteenth century, Emile Durkheim (1897), a sociologist, developed a broad theory of suicidal behavior. Today this theory continues to be influential. According to Durkheim, the probability of suicide is determined by how attached a person is to such social groups as the family, religious institutions, and community. The more thoroughly a person belongs, the lower the risk of suicide. Conversely, people who have poor relationships with their society are at greater risk of killing themselves. He defined several categories of suicide, including *egoistic, altruistic,* and *anomic* suicide.

Paramount/The Kobal Collection

"Never was a story of more woe ..." *Two of the most famous suicides in English literature are those of Shakespeare's star-crossed lovers Romeo and Juliet. They each end their own life when confronted by the unbearable loss of a loved one. After observing Juliet in a potion-induced coma and mistakenly believing that she is dead, Romeo drinks poison. Upon awakening and seeing that Romeo is dead, Juliet stabs herself fatally with his dagger.*

In the service of others *According to Durkheim, people who intentionally sacrifice their lives for others are committing altruistic suicide. Betsy Smith, a heart transplant recipient who was warned that she would probably die if she did not terminate her pregnancy, elected to have the baby and died giving birth.*

Egoistic suicides are committed by people over whom society has little or no control. These people are not concerned with the norms or rules of society, nor are they integrated into the social fabric. According to Durkheim, this kind of suicide is more likely in people who are isolated, alienated, and nonreligious. The larger the number of such people living in a society, the higher that society's suicide rate.

Altruistic suicides, in contrast, are committed by people who are so well integrated into the social structure that they intentionally sacrifice their lives for its well-being. Soldiers who threw themselves on top of a live grenade to save others, Japanese kamikaze pilots who gave their lives in air attacks, and Buddhist monks and nuns who protested the Vietnam War by setting themselves on fire may have been committing altruistic suicide (Leenaars, 2004; Stack, 2004). According to Durkheim, societies that encourage altruistic deaths and deaths to preserve one's honor (as Far Eastern societies do) are likely to have higher suicide rates.

Anomic suicides, another category proposed by Durkheim, are those committed by people whose social environment fails to provide stable structures, such as family and religion, to support and give meaning to life. Such a societal condition, called *anomie* (literally, "without law"), leaves individuals without a sense of belonging. Unlike egoistic suicide, which is the act of a person who rejects the structures of a society, anomic suicide is the act of a person who has been let down by a disorganized, inadequate, often decaying society.

Durkheim argued that when societies go through periods of anomie, their suicide rates increase. Historical trends support this claim. Periods of economic depression may bring about some degree of anomie in a country, and national suicide rates tend to rise during such times (Maris, 2001). Periods of population change and increased immigration, too, tend to bring about a state of anomie, and again suicide rates rise (Burvill, 1998; Ferrada et al., 1995).

A major change in an individual's immediate surroundings, rather than general societal problems, can also lead to anomic suicide. People who suddenly inherit a great deal of money, for example, may go through a period of anomie as their relationships with social, economic, and occupational structures are changed. Thus Durkheim predicted that societies with greater opportunities for change in individual wealth or status would have higher suicide rates, and this prediction, too, is supported by research (Cutright & Fernquist, 2001; Lester, 2000, 1985). Conversely, people who are removed from society and sent to a prison environment may experience anomie. As we observed earlier, research confirms that such individuals have a heightened suicide rate (Tartaro & Lester, 2005).

Although today's sociocultural theorists do not always embrace Durkheim's particular ideas, most agree that social structure and cultural stress often play major roles in suicide (Hassan, 1998) (see Box 10-5). In fact, the sociocultural view pervades the study

Altruistic suicide? *Rescue workers sort through the remains of a crowded bus that was destroyed by a "suicide bomber" in the Middle East, killing dozens of people. Some sociologists believe that the acts of today's suicide bombers, like those of Japanese kamikaze pilots in World War II, fit Durkheim's definition of altruistic suicide. They argue that at least some of the bombers believe they are sacrificing their lives for the ultimate well-being of their society. However, many other theorists strongly disagree with this interpretation (Humphrey, 2006). They point out that many such bombers seem indifferent to the innocent lives and families they are destroying and categorize the bombers instead as mass murderers who are motivated by revenge or hatred rather than feelings of altruism.*

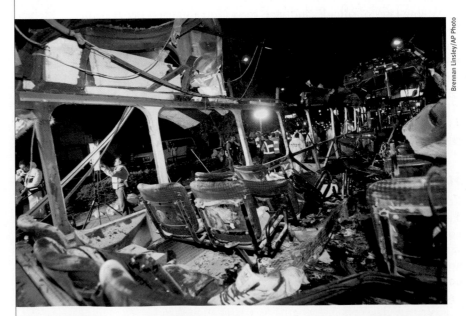

[BOX 10-5]

Sociocultural Landscape: Suicide among the Japanese

According to a comparison of American and Japanese medical students, Americans tend to regard suicide as an expression of anger or aggression, whereas the Japanese view it as normal, reasonable behavior (Domino & Takahashi, 1991). The sociologist Mamoru Iga (2001, 1993) holds that this difference reflects the cultures' religious and philosophical understandings of life and death.

The Shinto and Buddhist traditions stress eternal change and the transience of life. In the Buddhist view, life is sorrowful, and death is a way of freeing oneself from illusion and suffering. Furthermore, the highest aim of many Japanese is complete detachment from earthly concerns, total self-negation. Within this framework, death can be seen as positive, as an expression of sincerity (*makoto*) or an appropriate reaction to shame. Thus, according to Iga, "In Japan, suicide has traditionally been an accepted, if not a welcomed, way of solving a serious problem. . . . Suicide is not a sin in Japan; it is not punishable by God. Suicide is not viewed as a social or national issue but a personal problem."

Many of the factors that trigger suicide in the West—physical illness, alcohol abuse, mental disorders—are also at work in Japanese suicides (Fushimi et al., 2005; Lester & Saito, 1999). However, the different attitudes of the two cultures toward death and suicide may help explain the sizable difference between the rates of suicide in Japan (26 per 100,000 persons) and the United States (12 per 100,000).

Iga and other theorists also point to the absence of a humanistic tradition in Japan. Self-expression, self-love, and self-enhancement are prominent values in the West, and out of such a tradition comes the impulse to prevent suicide. Japanese society, however, values the subjugation of the individual to the social order (Young, 2002) and stresses harmony between humanity and nature: humans must bow to nature. Thus no deep-rooted principle in Japan requires that people be stopped from taking their own lives.

Finally, Iga points to several other sociocultural factors that may contribute to the high rate of suicide in Japan. One is the long-standing, pervasive sexism in Japanese culture. Others are increasing academic pressure on young people and increasing work pressure on middle-aged men. Nor should economic pressure in Japan be overlooked (Fushimi et al., 2005; Yamasaki et al., 2005, 2004). During the country's severe recession of the late 1990s, the number of suicides increased by more than one-third.

Of course, in today's world East and West meet regularly, and in fact interactions between the cultures have had an impact on Japanese attitudes in respect to one facet of suicide—*suicide prevention*. After visiting the Los Angeles Suicide Prevention Center, some Japanese psychologists and psychiatrists opened the first suicide prevention center in Japan in 1971. They worried at first that shame would deter the Japanese from seeking help, but the center was so successful that by 1990 it was operating branches in 33 Japanese cities. Still other efforts at suicide prevention have followed (Shiho et al., 2005; Ueda & Matsumoto, 2003).

Stress *The students in this classroom are participating in summer* juku, *a Japanese camp where they receive remedial help, extra lessons, and exam practice 11 hours a day.*

of suicide. We saw its impact earlier when we observed the many studies linking suicide to broad factors such as religious affiliation, marital status, gender, race, and societal stress. We will also see it when we consider the ties between suicide and age.

Despite the influence of sociocultural theories, they cannot by themselves explain why some people who experience particular societal pressures commit suicide whereas the majority do not. Durkheim himself concluded that the final explanation probably lies in the interaction between societal and individual factors.

Words of despair *The poet and author Sylvia Plath committed suicide in 1963 at age 31. One of her poems reads: "I saw the years of my life spaced along a road in the form of telephone poles, threaded together by wires. I counted one, two, three . . . nineteen poles, and then the wires dangled into space. . . . I couldn't see a single pole beyond the nineteenth."*

>>LOOKING AROUND
Left Behind

It is estimated that each suicide victim leaves behind an average of six close survivors who may be left confused, guilt-ridden, and traumatized by the suicidal act (Hoyert et al., 2001). **<<**

The Biological View

For years biological researchers relied largely on family pedigree studies to support their position that biological factors contribute to suicidal behavior. They have repeatedly found higher rates of suicide among the parents and close relatives of suicidal people than among those of nonsuicidal people (Brent & Mann, 2003; Maris, 2001). Indeed, one study found that over one-third of teenage subjects who committed suicide had a relative who had attempted suicide (Gould, Shaffer, & Davies, 1990). Such findings may suggest that genetic, and so biological, factors are at work.

Studies of twins also have supported this view of suicide. Researchers who studied twins born in Denmark between 1870 and 1920, for example, located 19 identical pairs and 58 fraternal pairs in which at least one twin had committed suicide (Juel-Nielsen & Videbech, 1970). In four of the identical pairs the other twin also committed suicide (21 percent), while none of the other twins among the fraternal pairs had done so.

As with all family and twin research, there are nonbiological interpretations for these findings as well (Maris, 2001). Psychodynamic clinicians might argue that children whose close relatives commit suicide are prone to depression and suicide because they have lost a loved one at a critical stage of development. Behavioral theorists might emphasize the modeling role played by parents or close relatives who attempt suicide.

In the past two decades, laboratory research has offered more direct support for a biological view of suicide. The activity level of the neurotransmitter serotonin has often been found to be low in people who commit suicide (Chen et al., 2005; Mann et al., 2001, 1999). An early hint of this relationship came from a study by the psychiatric researcher Marie Asberg and her colleagues (1976). They studied 68 depressed patients and found that 20 of the patients had particularly low levels of serotonin activity. It turned out that 40 percent of the low-serotonin people attempted suicide, compared with 15 percent of the higher-serotonin subjects. The researchers interpreted this to mean that low serotonin activity may be "a predictor of suicidal acts." Later studies found that suicide attempters with low serotonin activity are 10 times more likely to make a repeat attempt and succeed than are suicide attempters with higher serotonin activity (Roy, 1992).

Studies that examine the autopsied brains of suicide victims point in the same direction (Boldrini et al., 2005; Mann & Arango, 1999; Stanley et al., 1986, 1982). Some of these studies have found, for example, that people who commit suicide tend to have fewer receptor sites on neurons that normally receive serotonin than do people who do not commit suicide.

At first glance, these and related studies may appear to tell us only that depressed people often attempt suicide. After all, depression is itself related to low serotonin activity. On the other hand, there is evidence of low serotonin activity even among suicidal subjects who have no history of depression (Van Praag, 1983). That is, low serotonin activity seems also to have a role in suicide separate from depression.

How, then, might low serotonin activity increase the likelihood of suicidal behavior? One possibility is that it contributes to aggressive behavior. It has been found, for example, that serotonin activity is lower in aggressive men than in nonaggressive men and that serotonin activity is often low in those who commit such aggressive acts as arson and murder (Stanley et al., 2000; Bourgeois, 1991). Moreover, other studies have found that depressed patients with lower serotonin activity try to commit suicide more often, use more lethal methods, and score higher in hostility on various personality inventories than do depressed patients with relatively higher serotonin activity (Malone et al., 1996; Van Praag, 1986). Such findings suggest that low serotonin activity helps produce aggressive feelings and perhaps impulsive behavior (Mann et al., 2001). In people who are clinically depressed, low serotonin activity may produce aggressive tendencies that cause them to be particularly vulnerable to suicidal thoughts and acts. Even in the absence of a depressive disorder, however, people with low serotonin activity may develop such aggressive feelings that they, too, are dangerous to themselves or to others.

Is Suicide Linked to Age?

The likelihood of committing suicide generally increases with age, although people of all ages may try to kill themselves. Recently clinicians have paid particular attention to self-destructive behavior in three age groups: *children, adolescents,* and the *elderly*. Although the features and theories of suicide discussed throughout this chapter apply to all age groups, each group faces unique problems that may play key roles in the suicidal acts of its members.

Children

> Tommy [age 7] and his younger brother were playing together, and an altercation arose that was settled by the mother, who then left the room. The mother recalled nothing to distinguish this incident from innumerable similar ones. Several minutes after she left, she considered Tommy strangely quiet and returned to find him crimson-faced and struggling for air, having knotted a jumping rope around his neck and jerked it tight.
>
> *(French & Berlin, 1979, p. 144)*

> Dear Mom and Dad,
>   I love you. Please tell my teacher that I cannot take it anymore. I quit. Please don't take me to school anymore. Please help me. I will run away so don't stop me. I will kill myself. So don't look for me because I will be dead. I love you. I will always love you. Remember me.
>   Help me.
>   Love Justin [age 10]
>
> *(Pfeffer, 1986, p. 273)*

Although suicide is infrequent among children, it has been increasing over the past several decades (Pfeffer, 2000). Approximately 500 children under 14 years of age in the United States now commit suicide each year—around 0.9 per 100,000 in this age group, nearly 8 times the rate of 1950 (Goldman & Beardslee, 1999; Stillion & McDowell, 1996). Boys outnumber girls by as much as 5 to 1. In addition, it has been estimated that one of every 100 children tries to harm him- or herself, and many thousands of children are hospitalized each year for deliberately self-destructive acts, such as stabbing, cutting, burning, overdosing, jumping from high places, or shooting themselves (Cytryn & McKnew, 1996).

Researchers have found that suicide attempts by the very young are commonly preceded by such behavioral patterns as running away from home; accident-proneness; aggressive acting out; temper tantrums; self-criticism; social withdrawal and loneliness; extreme sensitivity to criticism by others; low tolerance of frustration; dark fantasies, daydreams, or hallucinations; marked personality change; and overwhelming interest in death and suicide (Papolos et al., 2005; Cytryn & McKnew, 1996; McGuire, 1982). Studies have further linked child suicides to the recent or anticipated loss of a loved one, family stress and a parent's unemployment, abuse by parents, and a clinical level of depression (Pfeffer, 2000; Goldman & Beardsley, 1999).

Most people find it hard to believe that children fully comprehend the meaning of a suicidal act. They argue that because a child's thinking is so limited, children who attempt suicide fall into Shneidman's category of "death ignorers," like Billy, who sought to join his mother in heaven (Fasko & Fasko, 1991). Many child suicides, however, appear to be based on a clear understanding of death and on a clear wish to die (Carlson et al., 1994, 1991; Pfeffer, 1993, 1986). In addition, suicidal thinking among even normal children is apparently more common than most people once believed (Kovacs et al., 1993; Pfeffer et al., 1984). Clinical interviews with schoolchildren have revealed that between 6 and 33 percent have thought about suicide (Culp, Clyman, & Culp, 1995; Jacobsen et al., 1994).

>>LOOKING AROUND

Sources of Information

Interviews indicate that elementary school children learn about suicide most often from television and discussions with other children, and rarely discuss suicide with adults (Mishara, 1999). <<

>>PSYCH•NOTES

Lingering Impact of Child Abuse

Adults who were sexually or physically abused in childhood harm themselves, think about suicide, and attempt suicide more than do adults without this history (Read et al., 2001; Dinwiddie et al., 2000). <<

Adolescents

Dear Mom, Dad, and everyone else,
   I'm sorry for what I've done, but I loved you all and I always will, for eternity. Please, please, please don't blame it on yourselves. It was all my fault and not yours or anyone else's. If I didn't do this now, I would have done it later anyway. We all die some day, I just died sooner.
   Love,
    John

(Berman, 1986)

The suicide of John, age 17, was not an unusual occurrence. Suicidal actions become much more common after the age of 14 than at any earlier age. According to official records, over 2,000 teenagers, or 11 of every 100,000, commit suicide in the United States each year. In addition, as many as 500,000 teenagers may make attempts (Popenhagen & Qualley, 1998). Because fatal illnesses are uncommon among the young, suicide has become the third leading cause of death in this age group, after accidents and homicides. Furthermore, as many as half of all teenagers have thought about killing themselves (Goldman & Beardslee, 1999).

Although young white Americans are more prone to suicide than young African Americans, the rates of the two groups are becoming closer (Washington & Teague, 2005; Willis et al., 2002). The white American rate was 157 percent greater than the African American rate in 1980; today it is only 42 percent greater. This trend may reflect increasingly similar pressures on young African Americans and young white Americans— competition for grades and college opportunities, for example, is now intense for both groups. The growing suicide rate for young African Americans may also be linked to rising unemployment among them, the many anxieties of inner-city life, and the rage felt by many young African Americans over racial inequities in our society (Willis et al., 2002; Burr et al., 1999).

About half of teenage suicides, like those of people in other age groups, have been tied to clinical depression, low self-esteem, and feelings of hopelessness, but many teenagers who try to kill themselves also appear to struggle with anger and impulsiveness (King & Apter, 2003; Sheras, 2001) or to have serious alcohol or drug problems (Maris, 2001). In addition, some have deficiencies in their ability to sort out and solve problems (Brent, 2001).

Teenagers who consider or attempt suicide are often under great stress. They may experience long-term pressures such as poor (or missing) relationships with parents, family conflict, inadequate peer relationships, and social isolation (Brent & Mann, 2003; Houston et al., 2001; Sourander et al., 2001). Alternatively, their actions also may be triggered by more immediate stress, such as a parent's unemployment or medical illness, financial setbacks for the family, or problems with a boyfriend or girlfriend (Fergusson et al., 2000). Stress at school seems to be a particularly common problem for teenagers who attempt suicide (Ho et al., 1995). Some have trouble keeping up at school, while others may be high achievers who feel pressured to be perfect and to stay at the top of the class (Delisle, 1986; Leroux, 1986).

Some theorists believe that the period of adolescence itself produces a stressful climate in which suicidal actions are more likely (King & Apter, 2003; Goldman & Beardslee, 1999). As we observed in Chapter 9 (pp. 272–273), adolescence is a period of rapid growth and it is often marked by conflicts, depressed feelings, tensions, and difficulties at home and school. Adolescents tend to react to events more sensi-

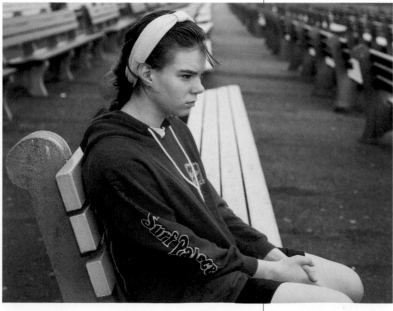

Difficult years *The angst, confusion, conflict, and impulsivity that typically characterize adolescence provide fertile ground for the growth of suicidal thoughts and attempts at suicide.*

Jeff Isaac Greenberg/Photo Researchers

tively, angrily, dramatically, and impulsively than individuals in other age groups; thus the likelihood of suicidal acts during times of stress is increased (Taylor & Stansfeld, 1984). Finally, the suggestibility of adolescents and their eagerness to imitate others, including others who attempt suicide, may set the stage for suicidal action (Hazell & Lewin, 1993). One study found that 93 percent of adolescent suicide attempters had known someone who had attempted suicide (Conrad, 1992).

Far more teenagers attempt suicide than actually kill themselves—the ratio may be as high as 200 to 1. The unusually large number of unsuccessful suicides may mean that teenagers are less certain than older persons who make such attempts. While some do indeed wish to die, many may simply want to make others understand how desperate they are, get help, or teach others a lesson (Leenaars et al., 2001; Boergers et al., 1998). Up to half of teenage attempters make new suicide attempts in the future, and as many as 14 percent eventually die by suicide (Diekstra et al., 1995; Diekstra, 1989).

Why is the rate of suicide attempts so high among teenagers (as well as among young adults)? Several explanations, most pointing to societal factors, have been proposed. First, as the number and proportion of teenagers and young adults in the general population have risen, the competition for jobs, college positions, and academic and athletic honors has intensified for them, leading increasingly to shattered dreams and ambitions (Holinger & Offer, 1993, 1991, 1982). Other explanations point to weakening ties in the family (which may produce feelings of alienation and rejection in many of today's young people) and to the easy availability of alcohol and other drugs and the pressure to use them among teenagers and young adults (Brent, 2001; Cutler et al., 2001).

The mass media coverage of suicide attempts by teenagers and young adults may also contribute to the high rate of suicide attempts among the young (Grossman & Kruesi, 2000). The detailed descriptions of teenage suicide that the media and the arts often offer may serve as models for young people who are contemplating suicide (Wertheimer, 2001). Within days of the highly publicized suicides of four adolescents in one New Jersey town in 1987, dozens of teenagers across the United States took similar actions (at least 12 of them fatal)—two in the same garage just one week later. Similarly, a 1986 study found that the rate of adolescent suicide rose about 7 percent in New York City during the week following a television film on suicide, in contrast to a 0.5 percent increase in the adult suicide rate during the same week (Maris, 2001).

The Elderly

Rose Ashby walks to the dry cleaner's to pick up her old but finest dinner dress. Although shaken at the cost of having it cleaned, Rose tells the sympathetic girl behind the counter, "Don't worry. It doesn't matter. I won't be needing the money any more."

Walking through the streets of St. Petersburg, Florida, she still wishes it had been Miami. The west coast of the fountain-of-youth peninsula is not as warm as the east. If only Chet had left more insurance money, Rose could have afforded Miami. In St. Petersburg, Rose failed to unearth de León's promised fount.

Last week, she told the doctor she felt lonely and depressed. He said she should perk up. She had everything to live for. What does he know? Has he lost a husband like Chet and his left breast to cancer all in one year? Has he suffered arthritis all his life? Were his ovaries so bad he had to undergo a hysterectomy? Did he have to suffer through menopause just to end up alone without family or friends? Does he have to live in a dungeon? Is his furniture worn, his carpet threadbare? What does he know? Might his every day be the last one for him?

As Rose turns into the walk to her white cinderblock apartment building, fat Mrs. Green asks if she is coming to the community center that evening. Who needs it? The social worker did say Rose should come. Since Rose was in such good health, she could help those not so well as she.

Help them do what? Finger-paint like little children? Make baskets like insane people? Sew? Who can see to sew? Besides, who would appreciate it? Who would thank her? Who could she tell about her troubles? Who cares?

When she told the doctor she couldn't sleep, he gave her the prescription but said that all elderly people have trouble sleeping. What does he know? Does he have a middle-aged daughter who can only think about her latest divorce, or grandchildren who only acknowledge her birthday check by the endorsement on the back? Are all his friends dead and gone? Is all the money from his dead husband's insurance used up? What does he know? Who could sleep in this dungeon?

Back in her apartment, Rose washes and sets her hair. It's good she has to do it herself. Look at this hair. So thin, so sparse, so frowsy. What would a hairdresser think?

Then make-up. Base. Rouge. Lipstick. Bright red. Perfume? No! No cheap perfume for Rose today. Remember the bottles of Joy Chet would buy for her? He always wanted her to have the best. He would boast that she had everything, and that she never had to work a day in her life for it.

"She doesn't have to lift her little finger," Chet would say, puffing on his cigar. Where is the Joy now? Dead and gone. With Chet. Rose manages a wry laugh at the play on words.

Slipping into her dinner dress, she looks into the dresser mirror. "It's good you can't see this face now, Chet. How old and ugly it looks."

Taking some lavender notepaper from the drawer, she stands at the dresser to write. Why didn't anyone warn her that growing old was like this? It is so unfair. But they don't care. People don't care about anyone except themselves.

Leaving the note on the dresser, she suddenly feels excited. Breathing hard now, she rushes to the sink—who could call a sink in the counter in the living room a kitchen?—and gets a glass of water.

Trying to relax, Rose arranges the folds in her skirt as she settles down on the chaise. Carefully sipping the water as she takes all the capsules so as to not smear her lipstick, Rose quietly begins to sob. After a lifetime of tears, these will be her last. Her note on the dresser is short, written to no one and to everyone.

You don't know what it is like to have to grow old and die.

(Gernsbacher, 1985, pp. 227–228)

In Western society the elderly are more likely to commit suicide than people in any other age group. About 19 of every 100,000 persons over the age of 65 in the United States commit suicide (McIntosh, 1995, 1992). Elderly persons commit over 19 percent of all suicides in the United States, yet they account for only 12 percent of the total population (Conwell & Duberstein, 2001).

Many factors contribute to this high suicide rate (Oyama et al., 2005; Peter et al., 2004; Pearson, 2000). As people grow older, all too often they become ill, lose close friends and relatives, lose control over their lives, and lose status in our society. Such experiences may result in feelings of hopelessness, loneliness, depression, or inevitability among aged persons and so increase the likelihood that they will attempt suicide. In one study, 44 percent of elderly people who committed suicide gave some indication that their act was prompted by the fear of being placed in a nursing home (Loebel et al., 1991). Another study found that two-thirds of elderly subjects (above 80 years old) who committed suicide had experienced a medical hospitalization within two years preceding the suicide (Erlangen et al., 2005). Also, the suicide rate of elderly people who have recently lost a spouse is relatively high (Duberstein, Conwell, & Cox, 1998). The risk is greatest during the first year of bereavement, but it remains high in later years as well.

Elderly persons are typically more determined than younger persons in their decision to die and they give fewer warnings, so their success rate is much higher (DeLeo et al.,

The power of respect *Elderly persons are held in high esteem in many traditional societies because of the store of knowledge they have accumulated. Perhaps not so coincidentally, suicides among the elderly seem to be less common in these cultures than in those of many modern industrialized nations.*

Lawrence Migdale

2001; Clark, 1999). Apparently one of every four elderly persons who attempts suicide succeeds. Given the resolve of aged persons and their physical decline, some people argue that older persons who want to die are clear in their thinking and should be allowed to carry out their wishes (see Box 10-6 on the next page). However, clinical depression appears to play an important role in as many as 60 percent of suicides by the elderly, suggesting that more elderly persons who are suicidal should be receiving treatment for their depressive disorders (Awata et al., 2005; Peter et al., 2004).

The suicide rate among the elderly in the United States is lower in some minority groups (Kettl, 1998). Although Native Americans have the highest overall suicide rate, for example, the rate among elderly Native Americans is relatively low (NIH, 1999; McIntosh & Santos, 1982). The aged are held in high esteem by Native Americans and looked to for the wisdom and experience they have acquired over the years, and this may help account for their low suicide rate. Such high regard is in sharp contrast to the loss of status often experienced by elderly white Americans (Butler, 1975).

Similarly, the suicide rate is only one-third as high among elderly African Americans as among elderly white Americans (McIntosh, 1992). One reason for this low suicide rate may be the pressures faced by African Americans: "only the strongest survive" (Seiden, 1981). Those who reach an advanced age have overcome great adversity and often feel proud of what they have accomplished. Because reaching old age is not in itself a form of success for white Americans, their attitude toward aging is more negative. Another possible explanation is that aged African Americans have successfully overcome the rage that prompts many suicides in younger African Americans.

Treatment and Suicide

Treatment of suicidal people falls into two major categories: *treatment after suicide has been attempted* and *suicide prevention*. While treatment may also be beneficial to relatives and friends, whose feelings of loss, guilt, and anger after a suicide fatality or attempt can be intense (Wertheimer, 2001; Provini et al., 2000), the discussion here is limited to the treatment afforded suicidal people themselves.

What Treatments Are Used after Suicide Attempts?

After a suicide attempt, most victims need medical care. Some are left with severe injuries, brain damage, or other medical problems. Once the physical damage is treated, psychotherapy or drug therapy may begin, on either an inpatient or outpatient basis.

Unfortunately, even after trying to kill themselves, many suicidal people fail to receive systematic follow-up care (Goldney, 2003; Beautrais, Joyce, & Mulder, 2000). In a random survey of several hundred teenagers, 9 percent were found to have made at least one suicide attempt, and of those only half had received later psychological treatment (Harkavy & Asnis, 1985). Similarly, in another study, one-third of adolescent attempters reported that they had not received any help after trying to end their lives (Larsson & Ivarsson, 1998). In some cases, health care professionals are at fault. In others, the person who has attempted suicide refuses follow-up therapy (Piacentini et al., 1995).

The goals of therapy are to keep people alive, help them achieve a nonsuicidal state of mind, and guide them to develop better ways of handling stress (Wetzel & Murphy, 2005; Shneidman, 2001, 1999). Various therapies have been employed, including drug, psychodynamic, cognitive, group, and family therapies (Hawton, 2001; Rudd et al., 2001). Treatment appears to help. Studies have found that 30 percent of suicide attempters who do not receive treatment try again, compared with 16 percent of patients in treatment (Nordstrom et al., 1995; Allard et al., 1992). It is not clear, however, whether any one approach is more effective than the others.

What Is Suicide Prevention?

During the past 50 years, emphasis around the world has shifted from suicide treatment to suicide prevention (Kerkhof, 2005). In some respects this change is most appropriate: the last opportunity to keep many potential suicide victims alive comes before the first attempt.

>>BY THE NUMBERS
Doctor Visits

83% Percentage of suicide victims who had seen a family doctor in the previous year, typically for vague physical symptoms ≪

66% Those who had visited a doctor in the previous month ≪

40% Those who had seen a doctor in the previous week ≪

20% Those who had visited a doctor within the past day ≪

(Pirkis & Burgess, 1998; Hirschfeld & Russell, 1997)

>>PSYCH•NOTES
Still at Risk

Approximately 4 percent of all suicides are committed by people who are inpatients at mental hospitals or other psychiatric facilities. ≪

(Cassells et al., 2005)

[BOX **10-6**]

The Right to Commit Suicide

In the fall of 1989, a Michigan doctor, Jack Kevorkian, built a "suicide device." A person using it could, at the touch of a button, change a saline solution being fed intravenously into the arm to one containing chemicals that would bring unconsciousness and a swift death. The following June, under the doctor's supervision, Mrs. J. Adkins took her life. She left a note explaining: "This is a decision taken in a normal state of mind and is fully considered. I have Alzheimer's disease and I do not want to let it progress any further. I do not want to put my family or myself through the agony of this terrible disease." Mrs. Adkins believed that she had a right to choose death. Michigan authorities promptly prohibited further use of Kevorkian's device, but the physician continued to assist in the suicides of medically ill persons throughout the 1990s.

(ADAPTED FROM BELKIN, 1990; MALCOLM, 1990)

In 1999 Dr. Kevorkian was convicted of second-degree murder and sentenced to prison for an assisted suicide that he had conducted, filmed, and aired on the television news show *Sixty Minutes*. He will be eligible for parole in 2007. However, his many court battles have helped bring an important question to the public's attention: Do individuals have a right to commit suicide, or does society have the right to stop them (Strate et al., 2005)?

The ancient Greeks valued physical and mental well-being in life and dignity in death. Therefore, individuals with a grave illness or mental anguish were permitted to commit suicide. Citizens could obtain official permission from the Senate to take their own lives, and judges were allowed to give them hemlock (Humphry & Wickett, 1986).

Western traditions, in contrast, discourage suicide, on the basis of belief in the "sanctity of life" (Eser, 1981). We speak of "committing" suicide, as though it were a criminal act (Wertheimer, 2001; Barrington, 1980), and we allow the state to use force, including involuntary commitment to a mental hospital, to prevent it. But times and attitudes are changing. Today the ideas of a "right to suicide" and "rational suicide" are receiving more support from the public, psychotherapists, and physicians (Leenaars et al., 2001). In fact, surveys suggest that half of today's physicians believe that suicide can be rational in some circumstances (Ganzini et al., 2000; Duberstein et al., 1995).

Public support for a right to suicide seems strongest in connection with great pain and terminal illness (Werth, 2004, 2000, 1999, 1996). Studies show that about half or more of all Americans believe that terminally ill persons should be free to take their lives or to seek a physician's assistance to do so (Duberstein et al., 1995). In line with this belief, the state of Oregon in 1997 passed the "Death with Dignity" Act, allowing a doctor to assist a suicide (by administering a lethal dose of drugs) if two physicians determine that the patient has less than six months to live and is not basing the decision to die on depression or another mental disorder. More than 170 people have used this law to end their lives since 1998 (Yen, 2005). In 2006, after an extended legal battle between the federal government and Oregon, the U.S. Supreme Court upheld the law by a 6-to-3 vote, ruling that individual states have the constitutional right to pass such legislation. Other states are currently considering similar laws.

Critics of the Oregon law and the right-to-suicide movement argue that the suicidal acts of patients with severe or fatal illnesses may often spring largely from psychological distress (Foley & Hendin, 2002; Akechi et al., 2001). Indeed, a number of studies suggest that half or more of severely ill patients who are suicidal may be clinically depressed (Werth, 2004; Chochinov & Schwartz, 2002). Thus, in some cases, it may be more beneficial to help individuals come to terms with a fatal illness than to offer them a license to end their lives. On the other hand, according to yet other research, decisions to seek physician-assisted suicide are often made in the absence of clinical depression (Rosenfeld, 2004).

Some clinicians also worry that the right to suicide could be experienced more as a "duty to die" than as the ultimate freedom (Foley & Hendin, 2003; Brock, 2001). Elderly people might feel selfish in expecting relatives to support and care for them when suicide is a socially approved alternative (Sherlock, 1983). Moreover, as care for the terminally ill grows ever more costly, might suicide be subtly encouraged among the poor and disadvantaged? Could assisted suicide become a form of medical cost control (Brock, 2001)? In the Netherlands, where physician-assisted suicide and euthanasia were approved by law in 2001 after years of informal acceptance, euthanasia is clearly on the increase (Rurup et al., 2005). Around 2.6 percent of all deaths in that country are now the result of physician-assisted suicide and voluntary euthanasia (Hendin, 2002). In fact, almost 1 percent of deaths are the result of *involuntary* euthanasia—the termination of life without an explicit request from the patient.

How are these issues to be resolved? Understanding and preventing suicide remain challenges for the future, and so do questions about whether and when we should stand back and do nothing. Whatever one's position on this issue, it is a matter of life and death.

KEYT-TV/AP Photo

KEYT**3** Santa Barbara

A right to die? *Multiple sclerosis patient Rebecca Badger conducts a TV interview from her bed in 1996, just two days before she committed suicide, with the assistance of Dr. Jack Kevorkian. Badger stated that the constant pain and torment of immobility caused by her illness eventually made her long for death.*

The first **suicide prevention program** in the United States was founded in Los Angeles in 1955; the first in England, called the *Samaritans,* was started in 1953. There are now hundreds of suicide prevention centers in the United States and in England. In addition, many of today's mental health centers, hospital emergency rooms, pastoral counseling centers, and poison control centers include suicide prevention programs among their services (Dorwart & Ostacher, 1999).

There are also hundreds of *suicide hot lines* in the United States, 24-hour-a-day telephone services. Callers reach a counselor, typically a *paraprofessional,* a person trained in counseling but without a formal degree, who provides services under the supervision of a mental health professional (Neimeyer & Bonnelle, 1997).

Suicide prevention programs and hot lines respond to suicidal people as individuals *in crisis*—that is, under great stress, unable to cope, feeling threatened or hurt, and interpreting their situations as unchangeable. Thus the programs offer **crisis intervention:** they try to help suicidal people see their situations more accurately, make better decisions, act more constructively, and overcome their crises (Frankish, 1994). Because crises can occur at any time, the centers advertise their hot lines and also welcome people who walk in without appointments.

Working with suicide *An individual breaks free from police and falls from a bridge in New York City. The scene reminds us that many kinds of professionals face suicidal behavior. Police departments typically provide special crisis intervention training so that officers can develop the skills to address suicidal individuals.*

Today suicide prevention takes place not only in special settings, but also in therapists' offices. Suicide experts encourage all therapists to look for and address signs of suicidal thinking and behavior in their clients, regardless of the broad reasons that the clients are seeking treatment. With this in mind, a number of guidelines have been developed to help therapists effectively uncover, assess, prevent, and treat suicidal thinking and behavior in their daily work with clients (Fawcett, 2004; Shea, 2004, 1999, 1998).

Although specific techniques vary from threrapist to therapist or from prevention center to prevention center, the general approach used by the Los Angeles Suicide Prevention Center reflects the goals and techniques of many clinicians and organizations. During the initial contact at the center, the counselor has several tasks (Shneidman & Farberow, 1968):

Establishing a positive relationship As callers must trust counselors in order to confide in them and follow their suggestions, counselors try to set a positive and comfortable tone for the discussion. They convey that they are listening, understanding, interested, nonjudgmental, and available.

Understanding and clarifying the problem Counselors first try to understand the full scope of the caller's crisis and then help the person see the crisis in clear and constructive terms. In particular, they try to help callers see the central issues and the transient nature of their crises and recognize the alternatives to suicide.

Assessing suicide potential Crisis workers at the Los Angeles Suicide Prevention Center fill out a questionnaire, often called a *lethality scale,* to estimate the caller's potential for suicide. It helps them determine the degree of stress the caller is under, relevant personality characteristics, how detailed the suicide plan is, the severity of symptoms, and the coping resources available to the caller.

Assessing and mobilizing the caller's resources Although they may view themselves as ineffectual and helpless, people who are suicidal usually have many strengths and resources, including relatives and friends. It is the counselor's job to recognize, point out, and activate those resources.

Formulating a plan Together the crisis worker and caller develop a plan of action. In essence, they are agreeing on a way out of the crisis, an alternative to suicidal action. Most plans include a series of follow-up counseling sessions over the next few days or weeks, either in person at the center or by phone. Each plan also requires the caller

•**SUICIDE PREVENTION PROGRAM**•A program that tries to identify people who are at risk of killing themselves and to offer them crisis intervention.

•**CRISIS INTERVENTION**•A treatment approach that tries to help people in a psychological crisis to view their situation more accurately, make better decisions, act more constructively, and overcome the crisis.

to take certain actions and make certain changes in his or her personal life. Counselors usually negotiate a *no-suicide contract* with the caller—a promise not to attempt suicide, or at least a promise to reestablish contact if the caller again considers suicide. Although such contracts are popular, their usefulness has been called into question in recent years (Miller et al., 1998). In addition, if callers are in the midst of a suicide attempt, counselors will try to find out their whereabouts and get medical help to them immediately.

Although crisis intervention may to be sufficient treatment for some suicidal people, longer-term therapy is needed for most (Stolberg et al., 2002; Rudd, 2000). If a crisis intervention center does not offer this kind of therapy, its counselors will refer the clients elsewhere.

As the suicide prevention movement spread during the 1960s, many clinicians came to believe that crisis intervention techniques should also be applied to problems other than suicide. Crisis intervention has emerged during the past three decades as a respected form of treatment for such wide-ranging problems as teenage confusion, drug and alcohol abuse, rape victimization, and spouse abuse.

Yet another way to help prevent suicide may be to reduce the public's access to common means of suicide (Daigle, 2005; Leenaars et al., 2003). In 1960, for example, around 12 of every 100,000 persons in Britain killed themselves by inhaling coal gas (which contains carbon monoxide). In the 1960s Britain replaced coal gas with natural gas (which contains no carbon monoxide) as an energy source, and by the mid-1970s the rate of coal gas suicide fell to zero (Maris, 2001; Diekstra et al., 1995). In fact, England's overall rate of suicide, at least for older people, dropped as well. On the other hand, the Netherlands' drop in gas-induced suicides was compensated for by an increase in other methods, particularly drug overdoses. Thus, while it is hoped that such measures as gun control, safer medications, and car emission controls may lower suicide rates, there is no guarantee that they will (Brent, 2001).

Do Suicide Prevention Programs Work?

It is difficult for researchers to measure the effectiveness of suicide prevention programs (DeLeo & Evans, 2004; Goldney, 1998). There are many kinds of programs, each with its own procedures and serving populations that vary in number, age, and the like. Communities with high suicide risk factors, such as a high elderly population or economic problems, may continue to have higher suicide rates than other communities regardless of the effectiveness of their local prevention centers.

Do suicide prevention centers reduce the number of suicides in a community? Clinical researchers do not know (DeLeo & Evans, 2004; Canetto, 1995). Studies comparing local suicide rates before and after the establishment of community prevention centers have yielded different findings. Some find a decline in a community's suicide rates, others no change, and still others an increase (DeLeo & Evans, 2004; Leenaars & Lester, 2004; Dew et al., 1987). Of course, even an increase may represent a positive impact, if it is lower than the larger society's overall increase in suicidal behavior. One investigator found that although suicide rates did increase in certain cities with prevention programs, they increased even more in cities without such programs (Lester, 1991, 1974).

Do suicidal people contact prevention centers? Apparently only a small percentage do. Moreover, the typical caller to an urban prevention center appears to be young, African American, and female, whereas the greatest number of suicides are committed by older white men (Maris, 2001; Canetto, 1995; Lester, 2000, 1989, 1972). A key problem is that people who are suicidal do not necessarily admit or talk about their feelings in discussions with others, even with professionals (Stolberg et al., 2002). In fact, one study discovered that more than half of the depressed patients in a mental hospital who killed themselves had previously denied having suicidal thoughts or had, at most, admitted to vague thoughts about it (Fawcett, 1988).

Prevention programs do seem to reduce the number of suicides among those high-risk people who do call. One study identified 8,000 high-risk individuals who contacted the Los Angeles Suicide Prevention Center (Farberow & Litman, 1970). Approximately 2 percent of these callers later committed suicide, compared to the 6 percent suicide rate usually found in similar high-risk groups. Clearly, centers need to be more visible and available to people who are thinking of suicide. The growing number of advertisements and announcements in newspapers and on television, radio, and billboards indicate a movement in this direction.

Partly because of the many suicide prevention programs and the data they have generated, today's clinicians have a better understanding of suicide and greater ability to assess its risk than those of the past (Clum & Yang, 1995; McIntosh et al., 1985). Studies reveal that the professionals who are most knowledgeable about suicide are psychologists, psychiatrists, and personnel who actually work in prevention programs (Domino & Swain, 1986). Other professionals whom suicidal persons might contact, such as members of the clergy, are sometimes less well informed (Leane & Shute, 1998; Domino & Swain, 1986).

Several theorists have called for more effective public education about suicide as the ultimate form of prevention, and at least some *suicide education* programs—most of them concentrating on teachers and students—have begun to emerge (Leenaars et al., 2005; Kalafat & Ryerson, 1999). The curriculum for such programs has been the subject of much debate (Dorwart & Ostacher, 1999), but clinicians typically agree with the goals behind them and, more generally, with Shneidman when he states:

Raising public awareness *In order to better educate the public about suicide's far reach, many states now hold special remembrances and offer informative programs about suicide. Here a police officer looks at a large quilt dedicated to those who committed suicide in 2004 during a gathering to commemorate Suicide Awareness Week in Montgomery, Alabama's Capitol building.*

> The primary prevention of suicide lies in education. The route is through teaching one another and . . . the public that suicide can happen to anyone, that there are verbal and behavioral clues that can be looked for . . . , and that help is available. . . .
>
> In the last analysis, the prevention of suicide is everybody's business.
>
> *(Shneidman, 1985, p. 238)*

PUTTING IT together
Psychological and Biological Insights Lag Behind

Once a mysterious and hidden problem, hardly acknowledged by the public and barely investigated by professionals, suicide today is the focus of much attention. During the past 30 years in particular, investigators have learned a great deal about this life-or-death problem.

In contrast to most other problems covered in this textbook, suicide has received much more examination from the sociocultural model than from any other. Sociocultural theorists have, for example, highlighted the importance of societal change and stress, national and religious affiliation, marital status, gender, race, and the mass media. The insights and information gathered by psychological and biological researchers have been more limited.

Although sociocultural factors certainly shed light on the general background and triggers of suicide, they typically leave us unable to predict that a given person will attempt suicide. When all is said and done, clinicians do not yet fully understand why some people kill themselves while others in similar circumstances manage to find better ways of addressing their problems. Psychological and biological insights must catch up to the sociocultural insights if clinicians are truly to explain and understand suicide.

Treatments for suicide also pose some difficult problems. Clinicians have yet to develop clearly successful therapies for suicidal persons. Although suicide prevention programs certainly show the clinical field's commitment to helping people who are suicidal, it is not yet clear how much such programs actually reduce the overall risk or rate of suicide.

At the same time, the growth in the amount of research on suicide offers great promise. And perhaps most promising of all, clinicians are now enlisting the public in the fight against this problem. They are calling for broader public education about suicide—

>>BY THE NUMBERS
Murder-Suicides

3.5% Percentage of suicides in which someone else—a spouse, intimate friend, or relative—is murdered at the same time ‹‹

5% Individuals who attempt suicide soon after committing a homicide ‹‹

20% Persons who attempt suicide soon after killing a child ‹‹

(Stolberg et al., 2002)

programs aimed at both young and old. It is reasonable to expect that the current commitment will lead to a better understanding of suicide and to more successful interventions. Such goals are of importance to everyone. Although suicide itself is typically a lonely and desperate act, the impact of such acts is very broad indeed.

┤ SUMMARY AND REVIEW ├

■ **What is suicide?** *Suicide* is a self-inflicted death in which one makes an intentional, direct, and conscious effort to end one's life. Four kinds of people who intentionally end their lives have been distinguished: the *death seeker,* the *death initiator,* the *death ignorer,* and the *death darer. pp. 279–283*

■ **Research strategies** Two major strategies are used in the study of suicide: *retrospective analysis* (a psychological autopsy) and the *study of people who survive suicide attempts,* on the assumption that they are similar to those who commit fatal suicides. Each strategy has limitations. *pp. 283–284*

■ **Patterns and statistics** Suicide ranks among the top 10 causes of death in Western society. Rates vary from country to country. One reason seems to be cultural differences in *religious affiliation, beliefs,* or *degree of devoutness.* Suicide rates also vary according to *race, gender,* and *marital status. pp. 285–286*

■ **Factors that trigger suicide** Many suicidal acts are triggered by the current events or conditions in a person's life. The acts may be triggered by *recent stressors,* such as loss of a loved one and job loss, or *long-term stressors,* such as serious illness, an abusive environment, and job stress. They may also be preceded by *changes in mood or thought,* particularly increases in one's sense of *hopelessness.* In addition, the *use of alcohol or other kinds of substances, mental disorders,* or *news of another's suicide* may precede suicide attempts. *pp. 287–292*

■ **Explanations** The leading explanations for suicide come from the psychodynamic, sociocultural, and biological models. Each has received only limited support. *Psychodynamic* theorists believe that suicide usually results from depression and self-directed anger. Emile Durkheim's *sociocultural* theory defines three categories of suicide based on the person's relationship with society: *egoistic, altruistic,* and *anomic* suicides. And *biological* theorists suggest that the activity of the neurotransmitter serotonin is particularly low in individuals who commit suicide. *pp. 292–296*

■ **Suicide in different age groups** The likelihood of suicide varies with age. It is uncommon among *children,* although it has been increasing in that group during the past several decades. Suicide by *adolescents,* a more common occurrence, is also on the increase. In particular, *suicide attempts* by this age group are numerous. Adolescent suicide has been linked to clinical depression, anger, impulsiveness, major stress, and adolescent life itself. The rising suicide rate among adolescents and young adults may be related to the growing number and proportion of young people in the general population, the weakening of family ties, the increased availability and use of drugs among the young, and the broad media coverage of suicide attempts by the young.

In Western society the *elderly* are more likely to commit suicide than people in any other age group. The loss of health, friends, control, and status may produce feelings of hopelessness, loneliness, depression, or inevitability in this age group. *pp. 297–301*

■ **Treatment and suicide** Treatment may *follow* a suicide attempt. In such cases, therapists seek to help the person achieve a nonsuicidal state of mind and develop better ways of handling stress and solving problems.

Over the past 30 years, emphasis has shifted to *suicide prevention.* Suicide prevention programs include 24-hour-a-day hot lines and walk-in centers staffed largely by *paraprofessionals.* During their initial contact with a suicidal person, counselors seek to establish a positive relationship, to understand and clarify the problem, to assess the potential for suicide, to assess and mobilize the caller's resources, and to formulate a plan for overcoming the crisis. Beyond such *crisis intervention,* most suicidal people also need *longer-term therapy.* In a still broader attempt at prevention, *suicide education programs* for the public are beginning to appear. *pp. 301–305*

>>> CRITICAL THOUGHTS <<<

1. As we observed in the case of Margaux Hemingway and Ernest Hemingway, suicide sometimes runs in families. Why might this be the case? *p. 280*

2. Why might people in past times have been inclined to punish those who committed suicide and their surviving relatives? Why do most people take a different view today? *p. 282*

3. A person's wish to die is often ambivalent. In addition, most people who think about suicide do not act. How, then, should clinicians decide whether to hospitalize a person who is considering suicide or even one who has made an attempt? *pp. 282–283, 301–305*

4. Suicide rates vary widely from country to country. What factors besides religion might help account for the differences? *pp. 285–286*

5. Often people view the suicide of an elderly or chronically sick person as less tragic than that of a young or healthy person. Why might they think this way, and is their reasoning valid? *pp. 287, 299–301*

6. Why do people tend to overlook or dismiss the psychological pain of people with bizarre ideas or erratic behaviors, such as those of Margaret Ray? How might such oversights contribute to the suffering or symptoms of such individuals? *pp. 289–290, 291*

7. Some schools are reluctant to offer suicide education programs, especially if they have never experienced a suicide attempt by one of their students. What might be their concerns? How valid is their position? *p. 305*

⊙—[CYBER**STUDY**]———————————————»»»

SEARCH THE *ABNORMAL PSYCHOLOGY* CD-ROM FOR

▲ Chapter 10 Video Cases and Discussions
 Observe the behaviors, thought processes, and feelings of suicidal persons.
 What roles might alcohol, weapon availability, or other variables play in suicide?

▲ Chapter 10 Practical, Research, and Decision-Making Exercises
 Assessing suicidal risk
 Determining helpful and appropriate interventions for people at risk

▲ Chapter 10 Practice Test and Feedback

LOG ON TO THE COMER WEB PAGE FOR

▲ Suggested Web links, exercises, FAQ page, additional Chapter 10 practice test questions
 ‹www.worthpublishers.com/comer›

————————————————————————«««

Eating Disorders

Janet Caldwell was . . . five feet, two inches tall and weighed 62 pounds. . . . Janet began dieting at the age of 12 when she weighed 115 pounds and was chided by her family and friends for being "pudgy." She continued to restrict her food intake over a two-year period, and as she grew thinner, her parents became increasingly more concerned about her eating behavior. . . .

Janet . . . felt that her weight problem began at the time of puberty. She said that her family and friends had supported her efforts to achieve a ten-pound weight loss when she first began dieting at age 12. Janet did not go on any special kind of diet. Instead, she restricted her food intake at meals, generally cut down on carbohydrates and protein intake, tended to eat a lot of salads, and completely stopped snacking between meals. At first, she was quite pleased with her progressive weight reduction, and she was able to ignore her feelings of hunger by remembering the weight loss goal she had set for herself. However, each time she lost the number of pounds she had set for her goal she decided to lose just a few more pounds. Therefore she continued to set new weight goals for herself. In this manner, her weight dropped from 115 pounds to 88 pounds during the first year of her weight loss regimen.

Janet felt that, in her second year of dieting, her weight loss had continued beyond her control. . . . She became convinced that there was something inside of her that would not let her gain weight. . . . Janet commented that although there had been occasions over the past few years when she had been fairly "down" or unhappy, she still felt driven to keep on dieting. As a result, she frequently went for walks, ran errands for her family, and spent a great deal of time cleaning her room and keeping it in a meticulously neat and unaltered arrangement.

When Janet's weight loss continued beyond the first year, her parents insisted that she see their family physician, and Mrs. Caldwell accompanied Janet to her appointment. Their family practitioner was quite alarmed at Janet's appearance and prescribed a high-calorie diet. Janet said that her mother spent a great deal of time pleading with her to eat, and Mrs. Caldwell planned various types of meals that she thought would be appealing to Janet. Mrs. Caldwell also talked a great deal to Janet about the importance of good nutrition. Mr. Caldwell, on the other hand, became quite impatient with these discussions and tended to order Janet to eat. Janet then would try to eat something, but often became tearful and ran out of the room because she could not swallow the food she had been ordered to eat. The youngster said that she often responded to her parents' entreaties that she eat by telling them that she indeed had eaten but they had not seen her do so. She often listed foods that she said she had consumed which in fact she had flushed down the toilet. She estimated that she only was eating about 300 calories a day.

(Leon, 1984, pp. 179–184)

It has not always done so, but Western society today equates thinness with health and beauty (see Figure 11-1). In fact, in the United States thinness has become a national obsession. Most of us are as preoccupied with how much we eat as with

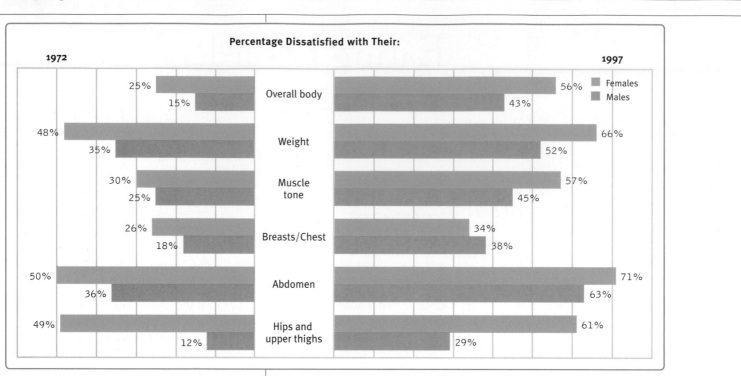

Percentage Dissatisfied with Their:

1972 — 1997

	1972 Females	1972 Males	1997 Females	1997 Males
Overall body	25%	15%	56%	43%
Weight	48%	35%	66%	52%
Muscle tone	30%	25%	57%	45%
Breasts/Chest	26%	18%	34%	38%
Abdomen	50%	36%	71%	63%
Hips and upper thighs	49%	12%	61%	29%

FIGURE **11-1** **Body dissatisfaction on the rise**
According to surveys on body image, people in our society are much more dissatisfied with their bodies now than they were a generation ago. Women are still more dissatisfied than men, but today's men are more dissatisfied with their bodies than the men of a generation past. (Adapted from Garner, Cooke, & Marano, 1997, p. 42; Rodin, 1992, p. 57.)

the taste and nutritional value of our food. Thus it is not surprising that during the past three decades we have also witnessed an increase in two eating disorders that have at their core a morbid fear of gaining weight. Sufferers of *anorexia nervosa,* like Janet Caldwell, are convinced that they need to be extremely thin, and they lose so much weight that they may starve themselves to death. People with *bulimia nervosa* go on frequent eating binges, during which they uncontrollably consume large quantities of food, then force themselves to vomit or take other extreme steps to keep from gaining weight.

The news media have published many reports about anorexic or bulimic behavior. One reason for the surge in public interest is the frightening medical consequences that can result. The death in 1983 of Karen Carpenter, a popular singer and entertainer, from medical problems related to anorexia nervosa serves as a reminder (see Box 11-1). Another reason for concern is the disproportionate prevalence of these disorders among adolescent girls and young women (Russell, 1995).

Clinicians now understand that the similarities between anorexia nervosa and bulimia nervosa can be as important as the differences between them (Serpell & Treasure, 2002). For example, many people with anorexia nervosa binge as they persist in losing dangerous amounts of weight; some later develop bulimia nervosa (Tozzi et al., 2005; APA, 2000). Conversely, people with bulimia nervosa sometimes develop anorexia nervosa as time goes on.

Anorexia Nervosa

Janet Caldwell, 14 years old and in the eighth grade, displays many symptoms of **anorexia nervosa:** she refuses to maintain more than 85 percent of her normal body weight, intensely fears becoming overweight, has a distorted view of her weight and shape, and has stopped menstruating (see Table 11-1).

Like Janet, at least half of the people with anorexia nervosa reduce their weight by restricting their intake of food, a pattern called *restricting-type anorexia nervosa.* At first they tend to cut out sweets and fattening snacks and then, increasingly, other foods (APA, 2000, 1994). Eventually people with this kind of anorexia nervosa show almost no variability in diet. Others, however, lose weight by forcing themselves to vomit after meals or by abusing laxatives or diuretics, and they may even engage in eating binges, a pattern called *binge-eating/purging-type anorexia nervosa,* which we shall observe in more detail when we turn to bulimia nervosa (APA, 2000, 1994).

Table **11-1** DSM Checklist

ANOREXIA NERVOSA

1. Refusal to maintain body weight above a minimally normal weight for age and height.
2. Intense fear of gaining weight, even though underweight.
3. Disturbed body perception, undue influence of weight or shape on self-evaluation, or denial of the seriousness of the current low weight.
4. In postmenarcheal females, amenorrhea.

Based on APA, 2000.

[BOX 11-1]

We've Only Just Begun

Given the hard-living, substance-abusing, risk-taking image cultivated by many pop music artists, we are no longer shocked to read about the untimely death of one of them, from Elvis Presley, Jimi Hendrix, or Sid Vicious to Kurt Cobain, Tupac Shakur, Notorious B.I.G., or Russell Jones (Ol' Dirty Bastard). The 1983 death of Karen Carpenter, from the effects of anorexia nervosa, in contrast, stunned the country. Karen, the 32-year-old velvet-voiced lead singer of the soft-rock brother-and-sister duo The Carpenters, did not drink, take drugs, drive fast cars, or tear up the roadside on a motorcycle. She never appeared in the pages of the tabloids. Until her late twenties—well into her fame—she even continued to live at home with her parents and brother, Richard, in suburban Downey, California. Indeed, she and Richard were icons of unrebellious, quiet youthful virtue.

The pressure to maintain this wholesome image may have contributed to Karen's destruction. After reading an early concert review describing her as "chubby," Karen began a downward spiral into anorexia nervosa. Always a dutiful family member and content to let Richard make all the management and artistic decisions for their group, Karen seemed to have little control over her fame. One friend and fellow sufferer later said about Karen's eating disorder, "When you start denying yourself food, and begin feeling you have control over a life that has been pretty

much controlled for you, it's exhilarating" (O'Neill, as cited in Levin, 1983).

For nine years Karen starved herself, abused laxatives and thyroid pills, and purged by repeatedly swallowing drugs that induce vomiting. Her weight dropped from a high of 140 pounds at the beginning of her singing career to a devastating low of 80 pounds. Ironically, in the last year of her life, it looked as though she had gotten a handle on her disorder. She had increased her weight to an almost-normal 108 pounds after a year of therapy. Yet on a visit home to her parents' house in California, on February 4, 1983, she collapsed. Paramedics could not revive her, and she died an hour later of cardiac arrest. Traces of a vomit-inducing drug were found in her bloodstream.

Until Karen's death, the public knew little about anorexia nervosa, and what it knew did not sound serious—more like the latest celebrity fad diet than a dangerous, potentially fatal condition. But that lighthearted view changed dramatically with her death, as scores of articles in newspapers and magazines detailed not only the tragically short life of Karen Car-

penter but also the disorder that killed her. Anorexia nervosa was no longer something to be taken casually. Since then numerous other famous personalities in diverse fields have gone public about their own struggles with eating disorders.

Approximately 90 to 95 percent of all cases of anorexia nervosa occur in females (Freeman, 2005). Although the disorder can appear at any age, the peak age of onset is between 14 and 18 years (APA, 2000). Between 0.5 and 2 percent of all females in Western countries develop the disorder in their lifetime, and many more display at least some of its symptoms (Kjelsas et al., 2004; Favaro et al., 2003). It seems to be on the increase in North America, Europe, and Japan.

Typically the disorder begins after a person who is slightly overweight or of normal weight has been on a diet. The escalation toward anorexia nervosa may follow a stressful event such as separation of parents, a move away from home, or an experience of personal failure (Wilson et al., 2003; Gowers et al., 1996). Although most victims recover, between 2 and 6 percent of them become so seriously ill that they die, usually from medical problems brought about by starvation or from suicide (Millar et al., 2005; Nielsen et al., 1998; Slade, 1995).

•ANOREXIA NERVOSA•A disorder marked by the pursuit of extreme thinness and by extreme loss of weight.

Laboratory starvation *Thirty-six conscientious objectors who were put on a semistarvation diet for six months developed many of the symptoms seen in anorexia nervosa and bulimia nervosa (Keys et al., 1950).*

The Clinical Picture

Becoming thin is the key goal for people with anorexia nervosa, but *fear* provides their motivation (Russell, 1995). People with this disorder are afraid of becoming obese, of giving in to their growing desire to eat, and more generally of losing control over the size and shape of their bodies. In addition, despite their focus on thinness and the severe restrictions they may place on their food intake, people with anorexia are *preoccupied with food*. They may spend considerable time thinking and even reading about food and planning their limited meals (King, Polivy, & Herman, 1991). Many report that their dreams are filled with images of food and eating (Schredl & Montasser, 1999; Levitan, 1981).

This preoccupation with food may in fact be a result of food deprivation rather than its cause. In a famous "starvation study" conducted in the late 1940s, 36 normal-weight conscientious objectors were put on a semi-starvation diet for six months (Keys et al., 1950). Like people with anorexia nervosa, the volunteers became preoccupied with food and eating. They spent hours each day planning their small meals, talked more about food than about any other topic, studied cookbooks and recipes, mixed food in odd combinations, and dawdled over their meals. Many also had vivid dreams about food.

Persons with anorexia nervosa also *think in distorted ways.* They usually have a low opinion of their body shape, for example, and consider themselves unattractive (Kaye et al., 2002). In addition, they are likely to overestimate their actual proportions. While most women in Western society overestimate their body size, the estimates of those with anorexia nervosa are particularly high. A 23-year-old patient said:

> I look in a full-length mirror at least four or five times daily and I really cannot see myself as too thin. Sometimes after several days of strict dieting, I feel that my shape is tolerable, but most of the time, odd as it may seem, I look in the mirror and believe that I am too fat.
>
> *(Bruch, 1973)*

This tendency to overestimate body size has been tested in the laboratory (Farrell, Lee, & Shafran, 2005). In a popular assessment technique, subjects look at a photograph of themselves through an adjustable lens. They are asked to adjust the lens until the image that they see matches their actual body size. The image can be made to vary from 20 percent thinner to 20 percent larger than actual appearance. In one study, more than half of the subjects with anorexia nervosa were found to overestimate their body size, stopping the lens when the image was larger than they actually were.

The distorted thinking of anorexia nervosa also takes the form of certain maladaptive attitudes and misperceptions (Gilo et al., 2005; Garner & Bemis, 1985, 1982). Sufferers tend to hold such beliefs as "I must be perfect in every way"; "I will become a better person if I deprive myself"; and "I can avoid guilt by not eating." Gertrude, who recovered from anorexia nervosa, recalls that at age 15 "my thought processes became very unrealistic. I felt I had to do something I didn't want to do for a higher purpose. That took over my life. It all went haywire" (Bruch, 1978, p. 17).

People with anorexia nervosa also display certain *psychological problems,* such as depression and anxiety and low self-esteem (Godart et al., 2005; O'Brien & Vincent, 2003). Some also experience insomnia or other sleep disturbances. A number grapple with substance abuse. And many display obsessive-compulsive patterns. They may set rigid rules for food preparation or even cut food into specific shapes. Broader obsessive-compulsive patterns are common as well (Sansone et al., 2005; Shafran, 2002). In one study, people with anorexia nervosa and others with obsessive-compulsive disorder scored equally high for obsessiveness and compulsiveness (Bastiani et al.,

Seeing is deceiving *In one research technique, people look at photographs of themselves through a special lens and adjust the lens until they see what they believe is their actual image. A subject may change her actual image (left) from 20 percent thinner (middle) to 20 percent larger (right).*

1996). Finally, persons with anorexia nervosa tend to be perfectionistic, a characteristic that typically precedes the onset of the disorder (Rousset et al., 2004; Shafran, Cooper, & Fairburn, 2002).

Medical Problems

The starvation habits of anorexia nervosa cause medical problems (Katzman, 2005; Tyre, 2005). Women develop **amenorrhea,** the absence of menstrual cycles. Other problems include lowered body temperature, low blood pressure, body swelling, reduced bone mineral density, and slow heart rate. Metabolic and electrolyte imbalances also may occur and can lead to death by heart failure or circulatory collapse (Froelich et al., 2001). The poor nutrition of people with anorexia nervosa may also cause skin to become rough, dry, and cracked; nails to become brittle; and hands and feet to be cold and blue. Some people lose hair from the scalp and some grow lanugo (the fine, silky hair that covers some newborns) on their trunk, extremities, and face.

Clearly, people with this disorder are caught in a vicious cycle. Their fear of obesity and distorted body image lead them to starve themselves. Starvation in turn leads to a preoccupation with food, increased anxiety and depression, and medical problems, causing them to feel even more afraid that they will lose control over their weight, their eating, and themselves. They then try still harder to achieve thinness by not eating.

Bulimia Nervosa

People with **bulimia nervosa**—a disorder also known as **binge-purge syndrome**—engage in repeated episodes of uncontrollable overeating, or **binges.** A binge occurs over a limited period of time, often an hour, during which the person eats much more food than most people would eat during a similar time span (APA, 2000, 1994). In addition, people with this disorder repeatedly perform inappropriate *compensatory behaviors,* such as forcing themselves to vomit; misusing laxatives, diuretics, or enemas; fasting; or exercising excessively (see Table 11-2). If the compensatory behaviors regularly include forced vomiting or misuse of laxatives, diuretics, or enemas, the specific diagnosis is *purging-type bulimia nervosa.* If individuals instead compensate by fasting or exercising frantically, the specific diagnosis is *nonpurging-type bulimia nervosa.* A married woman with the former pattern, since recovered, describes a morning during her disorder:

Today I am going to be really good and that means eating certain predetermined portions of food and not taking one more bite than I think I am allowed. I am very careful to see that I don't take more than Doug does. I judge by his body. I can feel the tension building. I wish Doug would hurry up and leave so I can get going!

As soon as he shuts the door, I try to get involved with one of the myriad of responsibilities on the list. I hate them all! I just want to crawl into a hole. I don't want to do anything. I'd rather eat. I am alone, I am nervous, I am no good, I always do everything wrong anyway, I am not in control, I can't make it through the day, I just know it. It has been the same for so long.

I remember the starchy cereal I ate for breakfast. I am into the bathroom and onto the scale. It measures the same, BUT I DON'T WANT TO STAY THE SAME! I want to be thinner! I look in the mirror, I think my thighs are ugly and deformed looking. I see a lumpy, clumsy, pear-shaped wimp. There is always something wrong with what I see. I feel frustrated trapped in this body and I don't know what to do about it.

I float to the refrigerator knowing exactly what is there. I begin with last night's brownies. I always begin with the sweets. At first I try to make it look like nothing is missing, but my appetite is huge and I resolve to make another batch of brownies. I know there is half of a bag of cookies in the bathroom, thrown out the night before, and I polish them off immediately. I take some milk so my vomiting will be smoother. I like the full feeling I get after downing a big glass. I get

•AMENORRHEA• The cessation of menstrual cycles.

•BULIMIA NERVOSA• A disorder marked by frequent eating binges that are followed by forced vomiting or other extreme compensatory behaviors to avoid gaining weight. Also known as *binge-purge syndrome.*

•BINGE• An episode of uncontrollable eating during which a person ingests a very large quantity of food.

Table 11-2 DSM Checklist

BULIMIA NERVOSA

1. Recurrent episodes of binge eating.
2. Recurrent inappropriate compensatory behavior in order to prevent weight gain.
3. Symptoms continuing, on average, at least twice a week for three months.
4. Undue influence of weight or shape on self-evaluation.

Based on APA, 2000.

out six pieces of bread and toast one side in the broiler, turn them over and load them with patties of butter and put them under the broiler again till they are bubbling. I take all six pieces on a plate to the television and go back for a bowl of cereal and a banana to have along with them. Before the last toast is finished, I am already preparing the next batch of six more pieces. Maybe another brownie or five, and a couple of large bowlfuls of ice cream, yogurt or cottage cheese. My stomach is stretched into a huge ball below my ribcage. I know I'll have to go into the bathroom soon, but I want to postpone it. I am in never-never land. I am waiting, feeling the pressure, pacing the floor in and out of the rooms. Time is passing. Time is passing. It is getting to be time.

I wander aimlessly through each of the rooms again tidying, making the whole house neat and put back together. I finally make the turn into the bathroom. I brace my feet, pull my hair back and stick my finger down my throat, stroking twice, and get up a huge pile of food. Three times, four and another pile of food. I can see everything come back. I am glad to see those brownies because they are SO fattening. The rhythm of the emptying is broken and my head is beginning to hurt. I stand up feeling dizzy, empty and weak. The whole episode has taken about an hour.

(Hall, 1980, pp. 5–6)

Like anorexia nervosa, bulimia nervosa usually occurs in females, again in 90 to 95 percent of the cases (Freeman, 2005) (see Box 11-2 on page 316). It begins in adolescence or young adulthood (most often between 15 and 21 years of age) and often lasts for several years, with periodic letup. The weight of people with bulimia nervosa usually stays within a normal range, although it may fluctuate markedly within that range (APA, 2000, 1994). Some people with this disorder, however, become seriously underweight and may eventually qualify for a diagnosis of anorexia nervosa instead (see Figure 11-2). Clinicians have also observed that certain people, a number of them overweight, display a pattern of binge eating without vomiting or other inappropriate compensatory behaviors. This pattern, often called *binge-eating disorder,* is not yet listed in the DSM, although it is being considered for inclusion in the next edition (Striegel-Moore et al., 2005; Wilson, 2005). Between 2 and 7 percent of the population and as many as one-quarter of severely overweight people are thought to have this disorder (Pull, 2004; Hoek & van Koeken, 2003).

Many teenagers and young adults go on occasional eating binges or experiment with vomiting or laxatives after they hear about these behaviors from their friends or the media (McDermott & Jaffa, 2005; Pyle, 1999). In one study, half of the college students surveyed reported periodic binges, 6 percent had tried vomiting, and 8 percent had experimented with laxatives at least once (Mitchell et al., 1982). Only some of these individuals, however, qualify for a diagnosis of bulimia nervosa. Surveys in several Western countries suggest that as many as 5 percent of women develop the full syndrome (Kjelsas et al, 2004; Favaro et al., 2003).

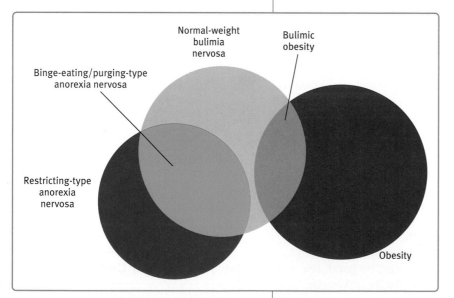

FIGURE **11-2** **Overlapping patterns of anorexia nervosa, bulimia nervosa, and obesity** *Some people with anorexia nervosa binge and purge their way to weight loss, and some obese persons binge-eat. However, most people with bulimia nervosa are not obese, and most overweight people do not binge-eat. (Adapted from APA, 2000, 1994; Garner & Fairburn, 1988; Russell, 1979.)*

Binges

People with bulimia nervosa may have 2 to 40 binge episodes per week, although the number is usually closer to 10 (Mizes, 1995, 1993). In most cases, the binges are carried out in secret. The person eats massive amounts of food very rapidly, with minimal chewing—usually sweet, high-calorie foods with a soft texture, such as ice cream, cookies, doughnuts, and sandwiches. The food is hardly tasted or thought about. Binge-eaters commonly consume more than 1,000 calories (often more than 3,000) during an episode (Guertin, 1999; Agras, 1995).

Binges are usually preceded by feelings of great tension (Crowther et al., 2001). The person feels irritable, "unreal," and powerless to control an overwhelming need to eat "forbidden" foods. During the binge, the person feels unable to stop eating. Although the binge itself may be experienced as pleasurable in the sense that it relieves the unbearable tension, it is followed by feelings of extreme self-blame, shame, guilt, and depression, as well as fears of gaining weight and being discovered (Hayaki et al., 2002).

Compensatory Behaviors

After a binge, people with bulimia nervosa try to compensate for and undo its effects. Many resort to vomiting. But vomiting actually fails to prevent the absorption of half of the calories consumed during a binge. Furthermore, repeated vomiting affects one's general ability to feel satiated; thus it leads to greater hunger and more frequent and intense binges (Wooley & Wooley, 1985). Similarly, the use of laxatives or diuretics largely fails to undo the caloric effects of bingeing (Garner et al., 1985).

Vomiting and other compensatory behaviors may temporarily relieve the uncomfortable physical feelings of fullness or reduce the feelings of anxiety and self-disgust attached to binge eating. Over time, however, a cycle develops in which purging allows more bingeing, and bingeing necessitates more purging. The cycle eventually causes people with this disorder to feel powerless and disgusted with themselves (Hayaki et al., 2002). Most recognize fully that they have an eating disorder. The woman we met earlier recalls how the pattern of bingeing, purging, and self-disgust took hold while she was a teenager in boarding school:

> Every bite that went into my mouth was a naughty and selfish indulgence, and I became more and more disgusted with myself. . . .
> The first time I stuck my fingers down my throat was during the last week of school. I saw a girl come out of the bathroom with her face all red and her eyes puffy. She had always talked about her weight and how she should be dieting even though her body was really shapely. I knew instantly what she had just done and I had to try it. . . .
> I began with breakfasts which were served buffet-style on the main floor of the dorm. I learned which foods I could eat that would come back up easily. When I woke in the morning, I had to make the decision whether to stuff myself for half an hour and throw up before class, or whether to try and make it through the whole day without overeating. . . . I always thought people noticed when I took huge portions at mealtimes, but I figured they assumed that because I was an athlete, I burned it off. . . . Once a binge was under way, I did not stop until my stomach looked pregnant and I felt like I could not swallow one more time.
> That year was the first of my nine years of obsessive eating and throwing up. . . . I didn't want to tell anyone what I was doing, and I didn't want to stop. . . . [Though] being in love or other distractions occasionally lessened the cravings, I always returned to the food.
>
> *(Hall, 1980, pp. 9–12)*

As with anorexia nervosa, a bulimic pattern typically begins during or after a period of intense dieting, often one that has been successful and earned praise from family members and friends (Helgeson, 2002). Research has found that normal subjects placed on very strict diets also develop a tendency to binge. Some of the subjects in the conscientious objector "starvation study," for example, later binged when they were allowed to return to regular eating, and a number of them continued to be hungry even after

Eating for sport *Many people go on occasional eating binges, particularly teenagers and young adults. In fact, sometimes binges are officially endorsed, as we see in this photo from the World Pizza Eating Championships in New York City. However, individuals are considered to have an eating disorder only when the binges recur and the pattern endures, and the issues of weight or shape dominate self-evaluation.*

Rosaria Esposito/AP Photo

>>LOOKING AROUND

Dietary Triggers Although most dieters do not develop an eating disorder, female teenagers who follow a severely restrictive diet are 18 times more likely than nondieters to develop an eating disorder within one year of the diet (Patton et al., 1999). <<

The Diet Business Americans spend $31 billion each year on weight-reduction products and services, including $500 million on prescription and over-the-counter diet drugs (National Task Force on the Prevention and Treatment of Obesity). <<

[BOX 11-2]

Not for Women Only

The number of young men with eating disorders appears to be on the rise, and more men are now seeking treatment for these disorders (Drummond, 2002; Robb & Dadson, 2002). Nevertheless, males account for only 5 to 10 percent of all cases of eating disorders. The reasons for this striking gender difference are not entirely clear.

One possible explanation is that men and women are subject to different sociocultural pressures (Toro et al., 2005). For example, a survey of college men found that the majority selected "muscular, strong and broad shoulders" to describe the ideal male body and "thin, slim, slightly underweight" to describe the ideal female body (Kearney-Cooke & Steichen-Ash, 1990). A second reason for the different rates of eating disorders may be the different methods of weight loss favored by men and women. According to some clinical observations, men are more likely to use exercise to lose weight, whereas women more often diet (Toro et al. 2005; Braun, 1996; Mickalide, 1990).

And dieting often precedes the onset of eating disorders.

Perhaps a third reason for the difference in reported cases is that eating disorders in men may be underdiagnosed (Freeman, 2005). Some men do not want to admit that they have what many consider a "female problem." In addition, it may be more difficult for clinicians to identify eating disorders in men because the clinical manifestations are different. For example, amenorrhea, an obvious symptom of anorexia nervosa among females, does not occur in men.

Why do men develop eating disorders? For some the disorder is linked to the *requirements and pressures of a job or sport* (Thompson & Sherman, 1993). In fact, such factors are more likely to trigger eating disorders in men than in women. According to one study, 37 percent of males with eating disorders had jobs or played sports for which weight control was important, compared to 13 percent of women (Braun, 1996). The highest rates have been found among jockeys, wrestlers,

distance runners, body builders, and swimmers. Jockeys commonly spend hours before a race in a sauna, shedding up to seven pounds of weight, and may restrict their food intake, abuse laxatives and diuretics, and force vomiting (King & Mezey, 1987). Similarly, male wrestlers in high school and college commonly restrict their food for up to three days before a match in order to "make weight." Some lose up to five pounds of water weight by practicing or running in several layers of warm or rubber clothing before weighing in for a match (Thompson & Sherman, 1993).

Whereas most women with eating disorders are obsessed with thinness at all times, wrestlers and jockeys are usually preoccupied with weight reduction only during their active season. After "making weight," many wrestlers go on eating and drinking binges in order to gain strength for the upcoming match, only to return to a weight-loss strategy after the match in preparation for the next weigh-in. A cycle of losing and regaining weight each season changes metabolic activity and jeopar-

---

large meals (Keys et al., 1950). A later study examined the binge-eating behavior of subjects at the end of a very low-calorie weight-loss program (Telch & Agras, 1993). Immediately after the program, 62 percent of the subjects, who had not previously been binge eaters, reported binge-eating episodes, although the episodes did decrease during the three months after treatment stopped.

Schindler Family Photo/AP Photo

Was bulimia nervosa the cause? *One of the most publicized and tragic cases of 2005 was that of Terri Schiavo, shown in this photo shortly after she collapsed and suffered an apparent heart attack in 1990. After experiencing cardiac arrest, she suffered extensive brain damage and was left in what was termed a "persistent vegetative state." Following a series of legal battles, a court ordered in 2005 that Schiavo's feeding tube be removed, and she died a week later. One question at the center of this case was whether Schiavo's heart dysfunction had been the result of bulimia nervosa. Blood tests revealed that she had a potassium deficiency (a dangerous medical complication of bulimia nervosa); her weight had fluctuated significantly during the years prior to her collapse; a number of friends reported observing bulimia-like patterns of behavior; and, in fact, a jury eventually awarded Schiavo more than $1 million in a malpractice suit against the obstetrician who had been treating her for infertility prior to her collapse, contending that he had failed to test her for or diagnose an eating disorder. On the other hand, Schiavo's autopsy offered no direct proof of an eating disorder, and alternative explanations for her collapse and cardiac arrest have been proposed.*

The weigh-in *Although this jockey does not have an eating disorder, his prerace weigh-in illustrates the weight standards and pressures to which such athletes are subjected.*

dizes the person's health and future efforts at weight control (Mickalide, 1990; Steen et al., 1988).

Beyond job or sport pressures, *body image* appears to be a strong predictor of eating disorders in men, just as it is in women. Some men who develop eating disorders report that they want a "lean, toned, thin" shape similar to the ideal female body, rather than the muscular, broad-shouldered shape of the typical male ideal (Kearney-Cooke & Steichen-Ash, 1990). However, those who aspire to the typical male ideal are also at risk. A study of 548 males—both young and old—revealed that 43 percent of them were dissatisfied with their bodies to some degree, with many of them expressing a desire to increase their muscle mass, especially in their abdomen and chest (Garner & Kearney-Cooke, 1997). The most dissatisfied men were those in their 30s and 50s; the least dissatisfied were men in their 20s.

Given such concerns, it may not be surprising that a new kind of eating disorder has been emerging, found almost exclusively among men, called *reverse anorexia nervosa* or *muscle dysmorphobia*. This disorder is displayed by men who are very muscular but still see themselves as scrawny and small and therefore continue to strive for a perfect body through extreme measures such as excessive weight lifting or the abuse of steroids (Robb & Dadson, 2002; Olivardia, Pope, & Phillips, 2000). Individuals with muscle dysmorphobia typically experience shame about their body image, and many have a history of depression, anxiety, or self-destructive compulsive behavior. About one-third of them also display related dysfunctional behaviors such as bingeing.

As the number of males with eating disturbances increases, researchers are increasing their efforts to understand both the similarities and the differences between males and females with these disorders. Since eating disturbances cause problems for both men and women, investigators must unravel the important factors that operate across the gender divide.

Bulimia Nervosa vs. Anorexia Nervosa

Bulimia nervosa is similar to anorexia nervosa in many ways. Both disorders typically begin after a period of dieting by people who are fearful of becoming obese; driven to become thin; preoccupied with food, weight, and appearance; and struggling with feelings of depression, anxiety, and the need to be perfect (Thompson-Brenner & Westen, 2005; Fairburn et al., 2003). Individuals with either of the disorders have a heightened risk of self-harm or attempts at suicide (Ruuska et al., 2005; Levitt et al., 2004). Substance abuse may accompany either disorder, perhaps beginning with the excessive use of diet pills. People with either disorder believe that they weigh too much and look too heavy regardless of their actual weight or appearance (Kaye et al., 2002). And both disorders are marked by disturbed attitudes toward eating.

Yet the two disorders also differ in important ways (see Table 11–3 on the next page). Although people with either disorder worry about the opinions of others, those with bulimia nervosa tend to be more concerned about pleasing others, being attractive to others, and having intimate relationships (Striegel-Moore, Silberstein, & Rodin, 1993). They also tend to be more sexually experienced and active than people with anorexia nervosa. On the positive side, people with bulimia nervosa display fewer of the obsessive qualities that drive people with restricting-type anorexia nervosa to control their caloric intake so rigidly (Halmi, 1995; Andersen, 1985). On the negative side, they are more likely to have long histories of mood swings, become easily frustrated or bored, and have trouble coping effectively or controlling their impulses (Claes et al., 2002; APA, 2000). Individuals with bulimia nervosa also tend to be ruled by strong emotions and

>>**LOOKING BACK**

Poetic Concerns

The famed poet Lord Byron (1788–1824), author of *Don Juan,* wrote: "A woman should never be seen eating and drinking unless it be lobster salad and champagne." Friends of Byron noted that the poet himself had "a horror of fat." He regularly abstained from eating, believing that he would lose his creativity if he ate normally (Brumberg, 1988). <<

Table 11-3

Anorexia Nervosa vs. Bulimia Nervosa

Restricting-type Anorexia Nervosa	Bulimia Nervosa
Refusal to maintain a minimum body weight for healthy functioning	Underweight, normal weight, near-normal weight, or overweight
Hunger and disorder denied; often proud of weight management and more satisfied with body	Intense hunger experienced; binge-purge experienced as abnormal; greater body dissatisfaction
Less antisocial behavior	Greater tendency to antisocial behavior and alcohol abuse
Amenorrhea of at least 3 months' duration common	Irregular menstrual periods common; amenorrhea uncommon unless body weight is low
Mistrust of others, particularly professionals	More trusting of people who wish to help
Tend to be obsessional	Tend to be dramatic
Greater self-control, but emotionally overcontrolled, with problems experiencing and expressing feelings	More impulsivity and emotional instability
More likely to be sexually immature and inexperienced	More sexually experienced and sexually active
Females more likely to reject traditional feminine role	Females more likely to embrace traditional feminine role
Age of onset often around 14–18	Age of onset around 15–21
Greater tendency for maximum pre-disorder weight to be near normal for age	Greater tendency for maximum pre-disorder weight to be slightly greater than normal
Lesser familial predisposition to obesity	Greater familial predisposition to obesity
Greater tendency toward pre-disorder compliance with parents	Greater tendency toward pre-disorder conflict with parents
Tendency to deny family conflict	Tendency to perceive intense family conflict

Source: APA, 2000, 1994; Levine, 1987; Andersen, 1985; Garner et al., 1985; Neuman & Halvorson, 1983.

may change friends and relationships frequently. And more than one-third of them display the characteristics of a personality disorder, particularly borderline personality disorder, which we shall examine more closely in Chapter 16 (Sansone, Levitt, & Sansone, 2005; Maranon et al., 2004).

Another difference is the nature of the medical complications that accompany the two disorders (Birmingham & Beaumont, 2004; Mickley, 2001). Only half of women with bulimia nervosa are amenorrheic or have very irregular menstrual periods, compared to almost all of those with anorexia nervosa (Crow et al., 2002). On the other hand, repeated vomiting bathes teeth and gums in hydrochloric acid, leading some women with bulimia nervosa to experience serious dental problems, such as breakdown of enamel and even loss of teeth (Helgeson, 2002; Casper, 1995). Moreover, frequent vomiting or chronic diarrhea (from the use of laxatives) can cause dangerous potassium deficiencies, which may lead to weakness, intestinal disorders, kidney disease, or heart damage (Turner et al., 2000; Halmi et al., 1994).

What Causes Eating Disorders?

Most of today's theorists and researchers use a **multidimensional risk perspective** to explain eating disorders. That is, they identify several key factors that place individuals at risk for these disorders (Rousset et al., 2004; Lyon et al., 1997). The more of these factors that are present, the greater the likelihood that a person will develop an eating disorder. The factors cited most often include sociocultural conditions (societal and family pressures), psychological problems (ego, cognitive, and mood disturbances), and biological factors.

•MULTIDIMENSIONAL RISK PERSPECTIVE•
A theory that identifies several kinds of risk factors that are thought to combine to help cause a disorder. The more factors present, the greater the risk of developing the disorder.

Societal Pressures

Many theorists believe that the current Western standards of female attractiveness have contributed to increases in eating disorders (Jambor, 2001). These standards have changed throughout history, with a noticeable shift toward preference for a thin female frame in recent decades (Gilbert et al., 2005). One study that tracked the height, weight, and age of contestants in the Miss America Pageant from 1959 through 1978 found an average decline of 0.28 pound per year among the contestants and 0.37 pound per year among winners (Garner et al., 1980). The researchers also examined data on all *Playboy* magazine centerfold models over the same time period and found that the average weight, bust, and hip measurements of these women had decreased steadily. More recent studies of Miss America contestants and *Playboy* centerfolds indicate that these trends have continued (Rubinstein & Caballero, 2000; Wiseman et al., 1992).

Because thinness is especially valued in the subcultures of fashion models, actors, dancers, and certain athletes, members of these groups are likely to be particularly concerned about their weight (Taylor & Ste-Marie, 2001). As sociocultural theorists would predict, studies have found that people in these professions are more prone than others to eating disorders (Thompson & Sherman, 2005, 1999). In fact, many famous young women from these fields have publicly acknowledged grossly disordered eating patterns in recent years. One survey of 1,443 athletes at 10 colleges around the United States revealed that more than 9 percent of female college athletes suffer from an eating disorder and another 50 percent admit to eating behaviors that put them at risk for such disorders (Johnson, 1995). A full 20 percent of the gymnasts surveyed had an eating disorder (see Figure 11-3).

Attitudes toward thinness may also help explain economic and racial differences in the rates of eating disorders (see Box 11-3 on the next page). In the past, white American women in the upper socioeconomic classes expressed more concern about thinness and dieting than African American women or white American women of the lower socioeconomic classes (Margo, 1985; Stunkard, 1975). Correspondingly, eating disorders were more common among white American women higher on the socioeconomic scale (Foreyt et al., 1996; Rosen et al., 1991). In more recent years, however, dieting and preoccupation with thinness have increased to some degree in all classes and minority groups, as has the prevalence of eating disorders (Germer, 2005; Striegel-Moore et al., 2005).

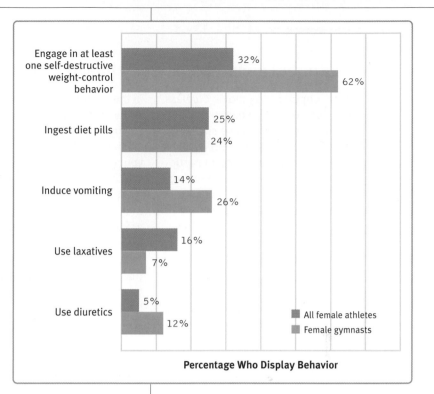

Percentage Who Display Behavior

FIGURE 11-3 Dangerous shortcuts *According to surveys, in sports ranging from field hockey to gymnastics, numerous female athletes engage in one or more self-destructive behaviors to control their weight (Taylor & Ste-Marie, 2001). One study found that close to two-thirds of female college gymnasts engage in at least one such behavior. (Adapted from Rosen & Hough, 1988; Rosen et al., 1986.)*

curvy thighs, bigger bums, rounder stomachs. What better way to test our firming range?

new Dove Firming Range
Gel Cream - Body Wash - Lotion

Image courtesy of The Advertising Archives

The ad! *An advertising campaign that created an enormous stir in 2005 was the "Dove girls" ad. The manufacturer of Dove Firming products recruited six young women with no prior modeling experience, had them pose in their underwear, and displayed the ad in magazines and on billboards across the country. Many people praised Dove for "courageously" using less than perfectly shaped women in the ad, while others had a decidedly less positive reaction. The point that both sides overlooked is that the women, while not ultra-thin models, were far from overweight, with dress sizes ranging from 6 to 12 (the average American woman is size 14). Thus, the controversy reflected once again the predominant belief in Western society that extreme—typically unattainable—thinness is the aesthetic ideal for women.*

[BOX **11-3**]

Sociocultural Landscape: Is Body Image a Matter of Race?

In the popular 1995 movie *Clueless*, Cher and Dionne, wealthy teenage friends of different races, have similar tastes, beliefs, and values about everything from boys to schoolwork. In particular, they have the same kinds of eating habits and beauty ideals, and they are even similar in weight and physical form. But does the story of these young women reflect the realities of white and African American females in our society?

In the early 1990s, the answer to this question appeared to be a resounding no. Most studies conducted up to the time of the movie's release indicated that the eating behaviors, values, and goals of young African American women were considerably healthier than those of young white American women (Lovejoy, 2001; Cash & Henry, 1995; Parker et al., 1995). However, it turns out that the movie and the later television show of the same name were in fact clued in to changes occurring in the United States. Most studies conducted *since* 1995 suggest that African American women, as well as women of other minority groups, are becoming more and more like white American women in their worries about weight and appearance, their inclination to diet, and their vulnerability to eating disorders.

Let's look first at the situation before 1995 and then at the clinical picture that has been unfolding since then.

PRE-1995

A widely publicized 1995 study at the University of Arizona offered findings and conclusions consistent with other research in the early 1990s (Parker et al., 1995). The study found that the eating behaviors and attitudes of young African American women were more positive than those of young white American women. It found, specifically, that nearly 90 percent of the white respondents were dissatisfied with their weight and body shape, compared to around 70 percent of the African American teens. The African American teens expressed satisfaction regardless of their actual weight; even those who were overweight described themselves as happy.

The study also suggested that white and African American adolescent girls had very different ideals of beauty. The white teens, asked to define the "perfect girl," described a girl of 5'7" weighing between 100 and 110 pounds—proportions that mirror those of so-called supermodels. Attaining a perfect weight, many said, was the key to being "totally happy," and they indicated that thinness was a requirement for popularity.

In contrast, the African American respondents tended to emphasize personality traits over physical characteristics when they described the ideal girl. They defined the "perfect" African American girl as smart, fun, easy to talk to, not conceited, and funny; she did not necessarily need to be "pretty," as long as she was well groomed. The body dimensions the African American teens described were more attainable for the typical girl; they favored fuller hips, for example. In addition, two-thirds of them defined beauty as "the right attitude." Given such definitions of beauty, it was not surprising that the

African American subjects were less likely than the white American respondents to diet for extended periods.

Despite the findings of this and related studies in the early 1990s, the University of Arizona investigators and other clinical theorists warned that problems might lie ahead for young African American women in the areas of self-image and eating behaviors. They observed, "It remains to be seen whether they will be able to maintain these self-perceptions. . . . [They] may be more likely to deemphasize their black identities in order to get ahead. . . . Will this translate into body discipline in the form of dieting to obtain a thin body by girls who aspire to make it?" (Parker et al., 1995, p. 111).

POST-1995

Unfortunately, the concerns of the University of Arizona investigators seem to have been borne out in the years since their study. Research conducted over the past decade suggests that body image concerns, dysfunctional eating patterns, and eating disorders are on the upswing among young African American women as well as among women of other minority groups. Here are some of the most striking findings:

Surveys conducted by *Essence*, the largest-circulation African American magazine, and by several teams of researchers have found that African American women today have about the same risk for developing eating disorders as white American women, along with similar attitudes regarding body image, weight, and eating (Walcott et al., 2003; Mulholland & Mintz,

Cultural differences may also help explain the striking gender gap for eating disorders. Our society's emphasis on a thin appearance is aimed at women much more than men. Some theorists believe that this double standard has made women much more inclined to diet and more prone to eating disorders (Cole & Daniel, 2005; Rand & Kuldau, 1991).

Western society not only glorifies thinness but creates a climate of prejudice against overweight people. Whereas slurs based on ethnicity, race, and gender are considered unacceptable, cruel jokes about obesity are standard fare on television and in movies, books,

Courtesy of Everett Collection

Fact or fiction? *In the movie* Clueless, *best friends Dionne and Cher think, act, dress, and look alike and hold identical values and concerns. Here they talk to each other on cell phones while walking side by side.*

2001; Pumariega et al., 1994). In the *Essence* survey, 65 percent of African American respondents reported dieting behavior, 39 percent said that food controlled their lives, 19 percent avoided eating when hungry, 17 percent used laxatives, and 4 percent vomited to lose weight.

African American women may be at particular risk for binge eating. In one study, African American women reported more bingeing than did white American women when they tried to lose weight through extreme methods (Striegel-Moore et al., 2000). Many African American subjects also reported using overeating to fill an emotional void in their lives, to cope with hardships such as racism, and to deal with fear and anger in their daily lives.

In a study of more than 2,000 girls aged 9 to 10 years, 40 percent of the respondents—African American and white American subjects in equal measure—reported wanting to lose weight (Schreiber et al., 1996).

The shift in the eating behaviors and eating problems of African American women appears to be partly related to their *acculturation* (Striegel-Moore & Smolak, 1997). One study compared African American women at a predominately white university with those at a predominately African American university. Those at the former school had significantly higher depression scores, and those scores were positively correlated with eating problems (Ford, 2000).

Studies indicate that Hispanic American women also engage in disordered eating behaviors and express body dissatisfaction at rates similar to those of white American women (Germer, 2005; Granillo et al., 2005). Moreover, one study found that Hispanic American subjects who were dissatisfied with their weight tended to display more severe binge-eating behavior than white American or African American subjects with similar concerns (Fitzgibbon et al., 1998).

Eating disorders also appear to be on the increase among young Asian American women and young women in several Asian countries (Pike & Borovoy, 2004; Walcott et al., 2003; Efron, 1997). Indeed, a study in Taiwan surveyed 843 schoolgirls, aged 10 to 14 years, and found that 8 percent were severely underweight and 10 percent were somewhat underweight (Wong & Huang, 2000). Around 65 percent of the underweight girls nevertheless wished they were thinner. Altogether, 38 percent of the participants had intentionally tried to lose weight, including 13 percent of underweight girls and 35 percent of girls whose weight was appropriate for their height.

Clearly the "protections" of race or culture that once seemed to operate in the realms of weight control and eating disorders no longer apply.

and magazines (Gilbert et al., 2005). Research indicates that the prejudice against obese people is deep-rooted (Tiggeman & Wilson-Barrett, 1998). Prospective parents who were shown pictures of a chubby child and a medium-weight or thin child rated the former as less friendly, energetic, intelligent, and desirable than the latter. In another study, preschool children who were given a choice between a chubby and a thin rag doll chose the thin one, although they could not say why. It is small wonder that as many as half of elementary school girls have tried to lose weight and 61 percent of middle school girls are currently dieting (Stewart, 2004; Shisslak et al., 1998; Hunnicut & Newman, 1993).

Donna Terek, *Michigan* magazine, *The Detroit News/Free Press*

Models and mannequins *Mannequins were once made extra-thin to show the lines of the clothing for sale to best advantage. Today the shape of the ideal woman is indistinguishable from that of a mannequin, and a growing number of young women try to achieve this ideal.*

Family Environment

Families may play an important role in the development of eating disorders (Reich, 2005; Moorhead et al., 2003). Research suggests that as many as half of the families of people with eating disorders have a long history of emphasizing thinness, physical appearance, and dieting. In fact, the mothers in these families are more likely to diet themselves and to be generally perfectionistic than are the mothers in other families (Woodside et al., 2002; Pike & Rodin, 1991). Abnormal interactions and forms of communication within a family may also set the stage for an eating disorder (Reich, 2005; Vidovic et al., 2005). Family systems theorists argue that the families of people who develop eating disorders are often dysfunctional to begin with and that the eating disorder of one member is a reflection of the larger problem (Rowa et al., 2001). The influential family theorist Salvador Minuchin, for example, believes that what he calls an **enmeshed family pattern** often leads to eating disorders (Minuchin, Rosman, & Baker, 1978).

In an enmeshed system, family members are overinvolved in each other's affairs and overconcerned with the details of each other's lives. On the positive side, enmeshed families can be affectionate and loyal. On the negative side, they can be clingy and foster dependency. Parents are too involved in the lives of their children, allowing little room for individuality and independence. Minuchin argues that adolescence poses a special problem for these families. The teenager's normal push for independence threatens the family's apparent harmony and closeness. In response, the family may subtly force the child to take on a "sick" role—to develop an eating disorder or some other illness. The child's disorder enables the family to maintain its appearance of harmony. A sick child needs her family, and family members can rally to protect her. Some case studies have supported such family systems explanations, but systematic research fails to show that particular family patterns consistently set the stage for the development of eating disorders (Wilson et al., 2003, 1996). In fact, the families of people with either anorexia nervosa or bulimia nervosa vary widely.

Ego Deficiencies and Cognitive Disturbances

Hilde Bruch, a pioneer in the study and treatment of eating disorders, developed a theory built on both psychodynamic and cognitive notions. She argued that disturbed mother–child interactions lead to serious *ego deficiencies* in the child (including a poor sense of independence and control) and to severe *cognitive disturbances* that jointly help produce disordered eating patterns (Bruch, 2001, 1991, 1982, 1962).

According to Bruch, parents may respond to their children either effectively or ineffectively. *Effective parents* accurately attend to their children's biological and emotional needs, giving them food when they are crying from hunger and comfort when they are crying out of fear. *Ineffective parents,* by contrast, fail to attend to their children's needs, deciding that their children are hungry, cold, or tired without correctly interpreting the children's actual condition. They may feed the children at times of anxiety rather than hunger, or comfort them at times of tiredness rather than anxiety. Children who receive such parenting may grow up confused and unaware of their own internal needs, not knowing for themselves when they are hungry or full and unable to identify their own emotions.

Pierre August Renoir, *Seated Bather*, 1903–1906, Detroit Institute of the Arts, bequest of Robert H. Tannahill

Changing times *Seated Bather, by Pierre-Auguste Renoir (1841–1919), shows that the aesthetically ideal woman of the past was considerably larger than today's ideal.*

Unable to rely on internal signals, these children turn instead to external guides, such as their parents. They seem to be "model children," but they fail to develop genuine self-reliance and "experience themselves as not being in control of their behavior, needs, and impulses, as not owning their own bodies" (Bruch, 1973, p. 55). Adolescence increases their basic desire to establish independence, yet they feel unable to do so. To overcome their sense of helplessness, they seek excessive control over their body size and shape and over their eating habits. Helen, an 18-year-old, describes her experience:

> There is a peculiar contradiction—everybody thinks you're doing so well and everybody thinks you're great, but your real problem is that you think that you are not good enough. You are afraid of not living up to what you think you are expected to do. You have one great fear, namely that of being ordinary, or average, or common—just not good enough. This peculiar dieting begins with such anxiety. You want to prove that you have control, that you can do it. The peculiar part of it is that it makes you feel good about yourself, makes you feel "I can accomplish something." It makes you feel "I can do something nobody else can do."
>
> *(Bruch, 1978, p. 128)*

Clinical reports and research have provided some support for Bruch's theory (Pearlman, 2005). Clinicians have observed that the parents of teenagers with eating disorders do tend to define their children's needs rather than allow the children to define their own needs (Ihle et al., 2005; Steiner et al., 1991). When Bruch interviewed the mothers of 51 children with anorexia nervosa, many proudly recalled that they had always "anticipated" their young child's needs, never permitting the child to "feel hungry" (Bruch, 1973).

Research has also supported Bruch's belief that people with eating disorders perceive internal cues, including emotional cues, inaccurately (Bydlowski et al., 2005; Speranza et al., 2005). When subjects with an eating disorder are anxious or upset, for example, many of them mistakenly think they are also hungry (see Figure 11-4), and they respond as they might respond to hunger—by eating. Finally, studies support Bruch's argument that people with eating disorders rely excessively on the opinions, wishes, and views of others. They are more likely than other people to worry about how

•**ENMESHED FAMILY PATTERN**•A family system in which members are overinvolved with each other's affairs and overconcerned about each other's welfare.

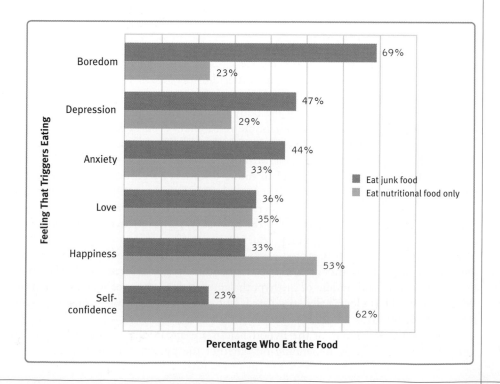

FIGURE **11-4** **When do people seek junk food?** *Apparently, when they feel bad. People who eat junk food when they are feeling bad outnumber those who eat nutritional food under similar circumstances. In contrast, more people seek nutritional food when they are feeling good. (Adapted from Lyman, 1982.)*

Unfair game *As we are reminded by one of the leading characters in the highly successful film* Austin Powers 2: The Spy Who Shagged Me, *overweight people in Western society are typically treated with insensitivity. They are the targets of humor in magazines, books, television shows, and movies.*

>>**BY THE NUMBERS**

Weighing In

5% Percentage of Americans who weigh themselves more than once per day «

8% Those who weigh in once per day «

10% Those who weigh in twice per week «

36% Those who weigh themselves twice per month «

75% Percentage of scale-checkers who are women «

(Kanner, 1995)

others view them, to seek approval, to be conforming, and to feel a lack of control over their lives (Button & Warren, 2001; Walters & Kendler, 1995).

Mood Disorders

Many people with eating disorders, particularly those with bulimia nervosa, experience symptoms of depression (Speranza et al., 2005; LeGrange & Lock, 2002). This finding has led some theorists to suggest that mood disorders set the stage for eating disorders.

Their claim is supported by four kinds of evidence. First, many more people with an eating disorder qualify for a clinical diagnosis of major depressive disorder than do people in the general population (Duncan et al., 2005; Brewerton et al., 1995). Second, the close relatives of people with eating disorders seem to have a higher rate of mood disorders than do close relatives of people without such disorders (Moorhead et al., 2003; APA, 2000). Third, as we shall see, many people with eating disorders, particularly bulimia nervosa, have low activity of the neurotransmitter serotonin, similar to the serotonin abnormalities found in depressed people. And finally, people with eating disorders are often helped by some of the same antidepressant drugs that reduce depression.

Although such findings suggest that depression may be linked to eating disorders, other explanations are possible (Stice & Bearman, 2001). For example, the pressure and pain of having an eating disorder may *cause* a mood disorder. Whatever the correct interpretation, many people struggling with eating disorders also suffer from depression, among other psychological problems.

Biological Factors

Biological theorists suspect that certain genes may leave some persons particularly susceptible to eating disorders (Kaplan, 2005; Steiger et al., 2005; Vink et al., 2001). Consistent with this idea, relatives of people with eating disorders are up to six times more likely than other individuals to develop the disorders themselves (Strober et al., 2001, 2000; Gorwood et al., 1998). Moreover, if one identical twin has bulimia nervosa, the other twin also develops the disorder in 23 percent of cases; in contrast, the rate for fraternal twins, who are genetically less similar, is 9 percent (Kendler et al., 1995, 1991). Although such family and twin findings do not rule out environmental explanations, they have encouraged biological researchers to look further still for specific biological causes.

One factor that has interested investigators is the possible role of *serotonin*. Several research teams have found a link between eating disorders and the genes responsible for the production of this neurotransmitter, and still others have measured low serotonin activity in many people with eating disorders (Kuhn et al., 2004; Enoch et al., 1998; Carrasco et al., 2000). Given serotonin's role in depression and obsessive-compulsive disorder—problems that often accompany eating disorders—it is possible that low serotonin activity has more to do with those other disorders than with the eating disorders per se. On the other hand, perhaps low serotonin activity contributes directly to eating disorders—for example, by causing the body to crave and binge on high-carbohydrate foods (Kaye et al., 2005, 2002, 2000). Some researchers even believe that persons with eating disorders are born with excessively *high* levels of serotonin activity, which they instinctively try to reduce by starving or purging themselves (Kaye et al., 2005, 1998).

Other biological researchers explain eating disorders by pointing to the **hypothalamus,** a part of the brain that regulates many bodily functions (Uher & Treasure, 2005; Leibowitz & Hoebel, 1998). Researchers have located two separate areas in the hypothalamus that help control eating. One, the **lateral hypothalamus (LH),** consisting of the side areas of the hypothalamus, produces hunger when it is activated. When the LH of a laboratory animal is stimulated electrically, the animal eats, even if it has been fed recently. In contrast, another area, the **ventromedial hypothalamus (VMH),** consisting of the bottom and middle of the hypothalamus, reduces hunger when it is activated. When the VMH is electrically stimulated, laboratory animals stop eating (Duggan & Booth, 1986) (see Box 11-4 on page 326).

These different centers of the hypothalamus are apparently activated by chemicals from the brain and body, depending on whether the person is eating or fasting. One such brain chemical is *glucagon-like peptide-1* (*GLP-1*), a natural appetite suppressant. When a team of researchers collected and injected GLP-1 into the brains of rats, the chemical traveled to receptors in the hypothalamus and caused the rats to reduce their food intake almost entirely even though they had not eaten for 24 hours (Turton et al., 1996). Conversely, when "full" rats were injected with a substance that blocked the reception of GLP-1 in the hypothalamus, they more than doubled their food intake.

Some researchers believe that the LH and VMH and chemicals such as GLP-1, working together, comprise a "weight thermostat" of sorts in the body, responsible for keeping an individual at a particular weight level called the **weight set point** (Hallschmid et al. 2004; Garner et al., 1985; Keesey & Corbett, 1983). Genetic inheritance and early eating practices seem to determine each person's weight set point. When a person's weight falls below his or her particular set point, the LH is activated and seeks to restore the lost weight by producing hunger and lowering the body's *metabolic rate,* the rate at which the body expends energy. When a person's weight rises above his or her set point, the VMH is activated, and it seeks to remove the excess weight by reducing hunger and increasing the body's metabolic rate.

According to the weight set point theory, when people diet and fall to a weight below their weight set point, their brain starts trying to restore the lost weight. Hypothalamic activity produces a preoccupation with food and a desire to binge. It also triggers bodily changes that make it harder to lose weight and easier to gain weight, however little is eaten (Spalter et al., 1993; Hill & Robinson, 1991). Once the brain and body begin conspiring to raise weight in this way, dieters actually enter into a battle against themselves. Some people apparently manage to shut down the inner "thermostat" and control their eating almost completely. These people move toward restricting-type anorexia nervosa. For others, the battle spirals toward a binge-purge pattern. Although the weight set point explanation has received considerable debate in the clinical field, it remains widely accepted by theorists and practitioners (Pinel et al., 2000).

Laboratory obesity *By electrically stimulating parts of a rodent's hypothalamus, researchers can induce overeating and massive weight gain.*

How Are Eating Disorders Treated?

Today's treatments for eating disorders have two goals. The first is to correct as quickly as possible the dangerous eating pattern. The second is to address the broader psychological and situational factors that have led to and now maintain the eating problem. Family and friends can also play an important role in helping to overcome the disorder.

Treatments for Anorexia Nervosa

The immediate aims of treatment for anorexia nervosa are to help individuals regain their lost weight, recover from malnourishment, and eat normally again. Therapists must then help them to make psychological and perhaps family changes to lock in those gains.

HOW ARE PROPER WEIGHT AND NORMAL EATING RESTORED? A variety of treatment methods are used to help patients with anorexia nervosa gain weight quickly and return to health within weeks. In the past, treatment almost always took place in a hospital, but now it is often offered in outpatient settings (Gowers et al., 2000; Pyle, 1999).

In life-threatening cases, clinicians may need to force *tube and intravenous feedings* on a patient who refuses to eat (Tyre, 2005). Unfortunately, this use of force may breed distrust in the patient (Robb et al., 2002; Treasure, Todd, & Szmuckler, 1995). In contrast, behavioral weight-restoration approaches have clinicians use *rewards* whenever patients eat properly or gain weight and offer no rewards when they eat improperly or fail to gain weight (Tacon & Caldera, 2001; Griffiths et al., 1998).

Perhaps the most popular weight-restoration technique of recent years has been a combination of *supportive nursing care,* nutritional counseling, and a relatively high-calorie diet (Sorrentino et al., 2005; Roloff, 2001; Treasure et al., 1995). Here nurses *gradually* increase a patient's diet over the course of several weeks to more than 2,500 calories a day (Herzog et al., 2004). The nurses educate patients about the program, track their progress, provide encouragement, and help them recognize that their weight gain

•**HYPOTHALAMUS**•A part of the brain that helps regulate various bodily functions, including eating and hunger.

•**LATERAL HYPOTHALAMUS (LH)**•A brain region that produces hunger when activated.

•**VENTROMEDIAL HYPOTHALAMUS (VMH)**•A brain region that depresses hunger when activated.

•**WEIGHT SET POINT**•The weight level that a person is predisposed to maintain, controlled in part by the hypothalamus.

[BOX **11-4**]

Obesity: To Lose or Not to Lose

By medical standards, one-third of adults in the United States and Canada weigh at least 20 percent more than people of their height should (Hilbert et al., 2005; Birmingham et al., 2003). In fact, despite the public's focus on thinness, obesity has become increasingly common in these and many other countries (Johnston, 2004). Being overweight is not a mental disorder, nor in most cases is it the result of abnormal psychological processes. Nevertheless, it causes great anguish, and not just because of its physical effects. The media, people on the streets, and even many health professionals treat obesity as shameful. Obese people are often the unrecognized victims of discrimination in efforts to gain admission to college, jobs, and promotions (Rothblum, 1992).

Mounting evidence indicates that overweight persons are not to be sneered at as weak and that obesity results from multiple factors (Hilbert et al., 2005). First, genetic and biological factors seem to play large roles. Researchers have found that children of obese biological parents are more likely to be obese than children whose biological parents are not obese,

whether or not the people who raise those children are obese (Stunkard et al., 1986). Other researchers have identified several genes that seem to be linked to obesity (Nagle et al., 1999; Halaas et al., 1995). And still others have identified chemicals in the body, including a hormone called *leptin* and a protein called *glucagon-like peptide-1* (*GLP-1*), that apparently act as natural appetite suppressants (Costa et al., 2002). Suspicion is growing that the brain receptors for these chemicals may be defective in overweight persons.

Environment also plays a causal role in obesity. Studies have shown that people eat

Never too young? *A Head Start teacher leads two preschoolers in a yoga exercise as part of a pilot program aimed at preventing childhood obesity.*

is under control and will not lead to obesity. Studies find that patients in nursing-care programs usually gain the necessary weight over 8 to 12 weeks (Treasure et al., 1995).

HOW ARE LASTING CHANGES ACHIEVED? Clinical researchers have found that individuals with anorexia nervosa must overcome their underlying psychological problems in order to achieve lasting improvement. Therapists typically provide both therapy and education to achieve this broader goal, using a combination of individual, group, and family approaches (Hechler et al., 2005; Kalodner & Coughlin, 2004).

BUILDING INDEPENDENCE AND SELF-AWARENESS One focus of treatment is to help patients with anorexia nervosa recognize their need for independence and teach them more appropriate ways to exercise control (Dare & Crowther, 1995; Robin et al., 1995). Therapists may also teach them to better identify and trust their internal sensations and feelings (Kaplan & Garfinkel, 1999). In the following session, a therapist tries to help a 15-year-old client recognize and share her feelings:

> *Patient:* I don't talk about my feelings; I never did.
> *Therapist:* Do you think I'll respond like others?
> *Patient:* What do you mean?
> *Therapist:* I think you may be afraid that I won't pay close attention to what you feel inside, or that I'll tell you not to feel the way you do—that it's

more when they are in the company of others, particularly if the other people are eating (Logue, 1991). In addition, research finds that people in low socioeconomic environments are more likely to be obese than those of high socioeconomic background (Ernst & Harlan, 1991).

HEALTH RISK?

Do mildly to moderately obese people have a greater risk of coronary disease, cancer, or other disease? Investigations into this question have produced conflicting results (Bender et al., 1999; Lean, Han, & Seidell, 1999). One long-term study found that while moderately overweight subjects had a 30 percent higher risk of early death, underweight subjects had a low likelihood of dying at an early age as long as their thinness could not be attributed to smoking or illness (Manson et al., 1995). However, another study found that the mortality rate of underweight subjects was as high as that of overweight subjects regardless of smoking behavior or illness (Troiano et al., 1996). These findings suggest that the jury is still out on this issue.

DOES DIETING WORK?

There are scores of diets and diet pills. There is almost no evidence, however, that any diet yet devised can ensure long-term weight loss (Wilson, 1994). In fact, long-term studies reveal a *rebound effect,* a net gain in weight in obese people who have lost weight on very low-calorie diets. Research also suggests that the feelings of failure that accompany diet rebounds may lead to dysfunctional eating patterns, including binge eating (Venditti et al., 1996).

Efforts are now under way to develop new kinds of drugs that will operate directly on the genes, hormones, proteins, and brain regions that have been linked to obesity (Marchione, 2005; Carek & Dickerson, 1999). Theoretically, these drugs will counteract the bodily reactions that undermine efforts at dieting. Whether such interventions can provide safe and permanent weight loss remains to be seen.

WHAT IS THE PROPER GOAL?

Some researchers argue that attempts to reduce obesity should focus less on weight loss and more on improving general health and attitudes (Painot et al., 2001; Rosen et al., 1995). If poor eating habits can be corrected, if a poor self-concept and distorted body image can be improved, and if overweight people can be educated about the myths and truths regarding obesity, perhaps everyone will be better off.

Most experts agree that extreme obesity is indeed a clear health hazard and that weight loss is advisable in such cases. For these individuals, the most promising path to long-term weight loss may be to set realistic, attainable goals rather than unrealistic ideals (Brownell & O'Neil, 1993; Brownell & Wadden, 1992). As for people who are mildly and even moderately overweight, a growing number of experts now suggest that perhaps they should be left alone, or, at the very least, encouraged to set more modest and realistic goals (Butryn & Wadden, 2005). In addition, it is critical that the public overcome its prejudice against people who are overweight and come to appreciate that obesity is, at worst, a problem that requires treatment, and perhaps simply another version of the normal human condition.

---

foolish to feel frightened, to feel fat, to doubt yourself, considering how well you do in school, how you're appreciated by teachers, how pretty you are.

Patient: (*Looking somewhat tense and agitated*) Well, I was always told to be polite and respect other people, just like a stupid, faceless doll. (*Affecting a vacant, doll-like pose*)

Therapist: Do I give you the impression that it would be disrespectful for you to share your feelings, whatever they may be?

Patient: Not really; I don't know.

Therapist: I can't, and won't, tell you that this is easy for you to do. . . . But I can promise you that you are free to speak your mind, and that I won't turn away.

(*Strober & Yager, 1985, pp. 368–369*)

CORRECTING DISTURBED COGNITIONS Another focus of treatment is to help people with anorexia nervosa change their attitudes about eating and weight (McFarlane, Carter, & Olmsted, 2005; Garner & Magana, 2002) (see Table 11-4 on the next page). Using cognitive approaches, therapists may guide clients to identify, challenge, and change maladaptive assumptions, such as "I must always be perfect" or "My weight and shape

Table 11-4

Sample Items from the Eating Disorder Inventory

For each item, decide if the item is true about you ALWAYS (A), USUALLY (U), OFTEN (O), SOMETIMES (S), RARELY (R), or NEVER (N). Circle the letter that corresponds to your rating.

A	U	O	S	R	N	I think that my stomach is too big.
A	U	O	S	R	N	I eat when I am upset.
A	U	O	S	R	N	I stuff myself with food.
A	U	O	S	R	N	I think about dieting.
A	U	O	S	R	N	I think that my thighs are too large.
A	U	O	S	R	N	I feel extremely guilty after overeating.
A	U	O	S	R	N	I am terrified of gaining weight.
A	U	O	S	R	N	I get confused about what emotion I am feeling.
A	U	O	S	R	N	I feel inadequate.
A	U	O	S	R	N	I have gone on eating binges where I felt that I could not stop.
A	U	O	S	R	N	I have trouble expressing my emotions to others.
A	U	O	S	R	N	I get confused as to whether or not I am hungry.
A	U	O	S	R	N	I think my hips are too big.
A	U	O	S	R	N	If I gain a pound, I worry that I will keep gaining.
A	U	O	S	R	N	I have the thought of trying to vomit in order to lose weight.
A	U	O	S	R	N	I think my buttocks are too large.
A	U	O	S	R	N	I eat or drink in secrecy.
A	U	O	S	R	N	I would like to be in total control of my bodily urges.

Source: Garner, 2005; Garner, Olmsted, & Polivy, 1991, 1984.

determine my value" (Lask & Bryant–Waugh, 2000; Freeman, 1995). Therapists may also educate clients about the body distortions typical of anorexia nervosa and help them see that their own assessments of their size are incorrect (Wegner & Wegner, 2001). Even if a client never learns to judge her body shape accurately, she may at least reach a point where she says, "I know that a key feature of anorexia nervosa is a misperception of my own size, so I can expect to feel fat regardless of my actual size."

CHANGING FAMILY INTERACTIONS Family therapy is often part of the treatment program for anorexia nervosa (Lock & le Grange, 2005; Reich, 2005). As in other family therapy situations, the therapist meets with the family as a whole, points out troublesome family patterns, and helps the members make appropriate changes. In particular, family therapists may try to help the person with anorexia nervosa separate her feelings and needs from those of other family members. Although the role of family in the development of anorexia nervosa is not yet clear, research strongly suggests that family therapy (or at least parent counseling) can be helpful in the treatment of this disorder (McDermott & Jaffa, 2005; Robin, 2003).

>>IN THEIR WORDS

"Girls should be encouraged to take an interest in their appearance when they are very young." <<

Ladies' Home Journal, 1940

"All philosophy in two words—sustain and abstain." <<

Epictetus (A.D. c. 55–c. 135)

"To be born woman is to know—Although they do not speak of it at school—Women must labor to be beautiful." <<

W. B. Yeats

Mother: I think I know what [Susan] is going through: all the doubt and insecurity of growing up and establishing her own identity. *(Turning to the patient, with tears)* If you just place trust in yourself, with the support of those around you who care, everything will turn out for the better.

Therapist: Are you making yourself available to her? Should she turn to you, rely on you for guidance and emotional support?

Mother:	Well, that's what parents are for.
Therapist:	(*Turning to patient*) What do you think?
Susan:	(*To mother*) I can't keep depending on you, Mom, or everyone else. That's what I've been doing, and it gave me anorexia. . . .
Therapist:	Do you think your mom would prefer that there be no secrets between her and the kids—an open door, so to speak?
Older sister:	Sometimes I do.
Therapist:	(*To patient and younger sister*) How about you two?
Susan:	Yeah. Sometimes it's like whatever I feel, she has to feel.
Younger sister:	Yeah.

(Strober & Yager, 1985, pp. 381–382)

WHAT IS THE AFTERMATH OF ANOREXIA NERVOSA? The use of combined treatment approaches has greatly improved the outlook for people with anorexia nervosa, although the road to recovery can be difficult and research findings are sometimes mixed (Fairburn, 2005). The course and outcome of this disorder vary from person to person, but researchers have noted certain trends.

On the positive side, weight is often quickly restored once treatment for the disorder begins (McDermott & Jaffa, 2005), and treatment gains may continue for years (Haliburn, 2005; Ro et al., 2005). In one study, 83 percent of patients continued to show improvement when they were interviewed several years or more after their initial recovery: around 33 percent were fully recovered and 50 percent partially improved (Herzog et al., 1999; Treasure et al., 1995). Other studies have found that most individuals perform effectively at their jobs and express job satisfaction years after their recovery (Fombonne, 1995; Theander, 1970).

Another positive note is that most females with anorexia nervosa menstruate again when they regain their weight (Fombonne, 1995; Crisp, 1981), and other medical improvements follow (Iketani et al., 1995). Also encouraging is that the death rate from anorexia nervosa seems to be declining (Neumarker, 1997; Treasure & Szmuklcr, 1995). Earlier diagnosis and safer and faster weight-restoration techniques may account for this trend. Deaths that do occur are usually caused by suicide, starvation, infection, gastrointestinal problems, or electrolyte imbalance.

On the negative side, close to 20 percent of persons with anorexia nervosa remain seriously troubled for years (Haliburn, 2005; Steinhausen, 2002; APA, 2000). Furthermore, recovery, when it does occur, is not always permanent (Richard et al., 2005). Anorexic behavior recurs in at least one-third of recovered patients, usually triggered by new stresses, such as marriage, pregnancy, or a major relocation (Fennig et al., 2002; Lay et al., 2002). Even years later, many recovered individuals continue to express concerns about their weight and appearance. Some continue to restrict their diets to a degree,

>>LOOKING AROUND

The Lure of "Ana"

Eating disorder specialists are concerned about a widespread underground movement that actively promotes self-starvation, often using the fictitious character "Ana" to give advice on the Web about what to eat and to mock people who do not lose weight. Many followers of Ana (short for anorexia) wear red Ana bracelets, follow the "Ana creed" of control and self-starvation, and offer each other words of "thinspiration" on Web pages and blogs. A Stanford University survey of teens with eating disorders found that 40 percent had visited Web sites that promote eating disorders (Irvine, 2005). **<<**

Les Stone/Sygma

Harmful advertising *When Calvin Klein posed young teenagers in sexually suggestive clothing ads in 1995, the public protested and the ads were halted. However, what some researchers consider even more damaging—the use of very thin young models who influence the body ideals and dietary habits of millions of teenage girls—continued uninterrupted.*

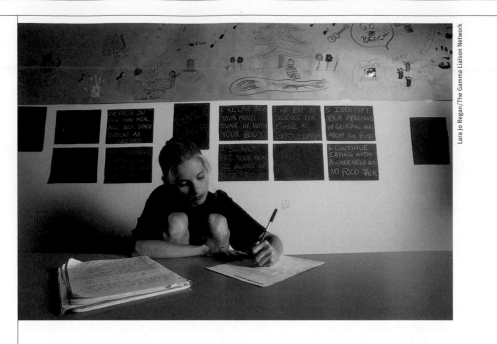

Daily record *A teenager with anorexia nervosa writes in her journal as part of an inpatient treatment program. The writing helps her identify the fears, emotions, and needs that have contributed to her disorder.*

experience anxiety when they eat with other people, or hold some distorted ideas about food, eating, and weight (Fichter & Pirke, 1995).

About half of those who have suffered from anorexia nervosa continue to experience certain emotional problems—particularly depression, social anxiety, and obsessiveness—years after treatment. Such problems are particularly common in those who have not succeeded in reaching a fully normal weight (Steinhausen, 2002; Halmi, 1995).

The more weight persons have lost and the more time that has passed before they entered treatment, the poorer the recovery rate (Richard, 2005; Finfgeld, 2002). Individuals who had psychological or sexual problems before the onset of the disorder tend to have a poorer recovery rate than those without such a history (Finfgeld, 2002; Lewis & Chatoor, 1994). Teenagers seem to have a better recovery rate than older patients (Richard, 2005; Steinhausen et al., 2000). Females have a better recovery rate than males.

Treatments for Bulimia Nervosa

Treatment programs for bulimia nervosa are often offered in eating disorder clinics. Such programs share the immediate goal of helping clients to eliminate their binge-purge patterns and establish good eating habits and the more general goal of eliminating the underlying causes of bulimic patterns. The programs emphasize education as much as therapy (Davis et al., 1997; Button, 1993). Like programs for anorexia nervosa, they often combine several treatment strategies, including individual insight therapy, behavioral therapy, antidepressant drug therapy, and group therapy (Wilson, 2005; Narash-Eisikovits et al., 2002; Tobin, 2000).

INDIVIDUAL INSIGHT THERAPY The insight approach that is now receiving the most attention in cases of bulimia nervosa is *cognitive therapy,* which tries to help clients recognize and change their maladaptive attitudes toward food, eating, weight, and shape (McFarlane et al., 2005; Wilson, 2005; Mitchell et al., 2002). Cognitive therapists typically teach the individuals to identify and challenge the negative thoughts that regularly precede their urge to binge—"I have no self-control," "I might as well give up," "I look fat" (Fairburn, 1985). They may also guide clients to recognize, question, and eventually change their perfectionistic standards, sense of helplessness, and low self-concept (see Box 11-5). Cognitive therapy seems to help as many as 65 percent of patients to stop bingeing and purging (Mitchell et al., 2002).

Because of its effectiveness in the treatment of bulimia nervosa, cognitive therapy is often tried first, before other individual insight therapies are considered. If clients do not respond to the cognitive approach, approaches with promising but less impressive track records may then be tried. A common alternative is *interpersonal psychotherapy,* the treat-

>>LOOKING BACK

Saintly Restraint

During the Middle Ages, restrained eating, prolonged fasting, or purging by a number of female saints was greatly admired and was even counted among their miracles. Catherine of Siena sometimes pushed twigs down her throat to bring up food; Mary of Oignes and Beatrice of Nazareth vomited from the mere smell of meat; and Columba of Rieti died of self-starvation (Brumberg, 1988). <<

[BOX **11-5**]

And She Lived Happily Ever After?

In May 1996 Alicia Machado, a 19-year-old woman from Venezuela, was crowned Miss Universe. Then her problems began. During the first eight months of her reign, her weight rose from 118 to 160 pounds, angering pageant officials and sparking rumors that she was about to be relieved of her crown. The "problem" received broad newspaper and television coverage and much ridicule on talk radio programs around the world.

Ms. Machado explained, "I was a normal girl, but my life has had big changes. I travel to many countries, eat different foods." Nevertheless, in response to all the pressure, she undertook a special diet

Marcus/Sipa Press

and an extensive exercise program to lose at least some of the weight she had gained. Her trainer claimed that a weight of 118 pounds was too low for her frame and explained that she had originally attained it by taking diet pills.

In the meantime, the whole episode served to demonstrate once again the powerful role of society in defining female beauty, acceptable weight, and "proper" eating. Ironically, many of the individuals who harshly criticized Ms. Machado or made fun of her—that is, the female critics—are themselves victims of the demanding and unrealistic standards of Western cultures that drive so many individuals toward dysfunctional patterns of eating.

ment that seeks to improve interpersonal functioning (Phillips et al., 2003; Mitchell et al., 2002). A number of clinicians also suggest *self-care manuals* for clients, which describe numerous education and treatment strategies for sufferers (Wilson, 2005; Palmer et al., 2002). *Psychodynamic therapy* has also been used in cases of bulimia nervosa, but only a few research studies have tested and supported its effectiveness (Valbak, 2001; Zerbe, 2001).

BEHAVIORAL THERAPY Behavioral techniques are often applied in cases of bulimia nervosa, particularly as a supplement to cognitive therapy (Wilson, 2005; Mizes & Bonifazi, 2002). Clients may, for example, be asked to keep diaries of their eating behavior, changes in sensations of hunger and fullness, and the ebb and flow of other feelings (Latner & Wilson, 2002). This helps them to observe their eating patterns more objectively and recognize the emotions that trigger their desire to binge.

Some behaviorists use the technique of *exposure and response prevention* to help break the binge–purge cycle. As we saw in Chapter 5, this approach consists of exposing people to situations that would ordinarily raise anxiety and then preventing them from performing their usual compulsive responses until they learn that the situations are actually harmless and their compulsive acts unnecessary. For bulimia nervosa, the therapists require clients to eat particular kinds and amounts of food and then prevent them from vomiting, to show that eating can be a harmless and even constructive activity that needs no undoing (Toro et al., 2003; Rosen & Leitenberg, 1985, 1982). Typically the therapist sits with the client during the eating of forbidden foods and stays until the urge to purge

Aynsley Floyd/AP Photo

New dolls for a new generation *After nearly 50 years of Barbie and her extremely thin waistline dominating the doll industry, a number of manufacturers are now introducing very different-looking dolls to the marketplace. The new dolls, such as these "Get Real Girls" dolls, often emphasize fitness and health, multicultural appearance, and sports, business, and other professional roles for females. Observers hope that such products will have a positive effect on the body satisfaction, self-image, and goals of young girls and also help prevent eating disorders.*

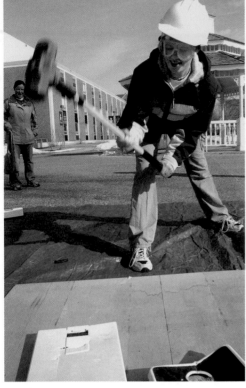

New efforts at prevention *A number of innovative educational programs have been developed in recent years to help promote healthy body images and prevent eating disorders among females ranging from preteens to young adults. (Above) An instructor helps two 11-year-old girls with their stretching exercises as part of "Girls in Motion," a nutrition and exercise program offered by Southern Methodist University. (Left) A Winona State University freshman swings a maul over her shoulder and into bathroom scales, as part of Eating Disorders Awareness Week. The scale smashing is an annual event.*

has passed. Studies find that this treatment often helps reduce eating-related anxieties, bingeing, and vomiting (Bulik et al., 1998).

ANTIDEPRESSANT MEDICATIONS During the past decade, antidepressant drugs such as *fluoxetine,* or Prozac, have been used to help treat bulimia nervosa (Sloan et al., 2004; Mitchell, 2001). According to research, the drugs help as many as 40 percent of patients, reducing their binges by an average of 67 percent and vomiting by 56 percent. Once again, drug therapy seems to work best in combination with other forms of therapy. Alternatively, some therapists wait to see whether cognitive therapy or another insight approach is effective before trying antidepressants (Wilson, 2005; Mitchell et al., 2002).

GROUP THERAPY Finally, bulimia nervosa programs now often feature group therapy, including self-help groups to give clients an opportunity to share their concerns and experiences with one another (Kalodner & Coughlin, 2004; Riess, 2002). Group members learn that their disorder is not unique or shameful, and they receive support from one another, along with honest feedback and insights. In the group they can also work directly on underlying fears of displeasing others or being criticized. Research suggests that group therapy is at least somewhat helpful in as many as 75 percent of bulimia nervosa cases, particularly when it is combined with individual insight therapy (Valbak, 2001; McKisack & Waller, 1997).

THE AFTERMATH OF BULIMIA NERVOSA Left untreated, bulimia nervosa can last for years, sometimes improving temporarily but then returning (APA, 2000). Treatment, however, produces immediate, significant improvement in approximately 40 percent of clients: they stop or greatly reduce their bingeing and purging, eat properly, and maintain a normal weight (Richard, 2005). Another 40 percent show a moderate response—at least some decrease in bingeing and purging. As many as 20 percent show little immediate improvement (Keel & Mitchell, 1997; Button, 1993). Follow-up studies suggest that by 10 years after treatment, 89 percent of persons with bulimia nervosa have recovered either fully (70 percent) or partially (19 percent) (Herzog et al., 1999; Keel et al., 1999). Those with partial recoveries continue to have recurrent binges or purges.

Relapse can be a problem even among people who respond successfully to treatment (Olmsted et al., 2005; Herzog et al., 1999). As with anorexia nervosa, relapses are

>>Q & A

Is prevention possible?

Apparently so. In a psychoeducation program, 11- to 13-year-old girls who were extremely worried about gaining weight were taught that female weight gain after puberty is normal and that excessive restriction of food can actually lead to weight gain. The concerns of the girls lessened markedly, in contrast to those of similar subjects who did not receive the instruction (Killen, 1996; Killen et al., 1994). **<<**

usually triggered by a new life stress, such as an upcoming exam, job change, marriage, or divorce (Abraham & Llewellyn-Jones, 1985). One study found that close to one-third of persons who had recovered from bulimia nervosa relapsed within two years of treatment, usually within six months (Olmsted, Kaplan, & Rockert, 1994). Relapse is more likely among persons who had longer histories of bulimia nervosa before treatment, had vomited more frequently during their disorder, had histories of substance abuse, made slower progress in the early stages of treatment, and continue to be lonely or to distrust others after treatment (Fairburn et al., 2004; Stewart, 2004; Keel et al., 2002, 2000, 1999).

Research also indicates that treatment helps many, but not all, people with bulimia nervosa attain lasting improvements in their overall psychological and social functioning (Keel et al., 2002, 2000; Stein et al., 2002). Follow-up studies find former patients to be less depressed than they had been at the time of diagnosis (Halmi, 1995). Approximately one-third of former patients interact in healthier ways at work, at home, and in social settings, while another third interact effectively in two of these areas (Hsu & Holder, 1986).

PUTTING IT together
A Standard for Integrating Perspectives

We have observed throughout this book that it is often useful to consider sociocultural, psychological, and biological factors jointly when one tries to explain or treat various forms of abnormal functioning. Nowhere is the argument for combining these perspectives more powerful than in the case of eating disorders. According to the multidimensional risk perspective, embraced by many theorists, varied factors act together to encourage the development of eating disorders. One case may be the result of societal pressures, autonomy problems, the changes of adolescence, and hypothalamic overactivity, while another case may result from family pressures, depression, and the effects of dieting. No wonder that the most helpful treatment programs for eating disorders combine sociocultural, psychological, and biological approaches. When the multidimensional risk perspective is applied to eating disorders, it demonstrates that scientists and practitioners who follow very different models can work together productively in an atmosphere of mutual respect.

Today's many investigations of eating disorders keep revealing new surprises that force clinicians to adjust their theories and treatment programs. For example, in recent times researchers have learned that people with bulimia nervosa sometimes feel strangely positive about their symptoms (Serpell & Treasure, 2002). A recovered patient said, "I still miss my bulimia as I would an old friend who has died" (Cauwels, 1983, p. 173). Only when feelings like these are understood will treatment become fully effective—another reason why the cooperative efforts of different kinds of theorists, clinicians, and researchers are so important.

While clinicians and researchers seek more answers about eating disorders, clients themselves have begun to take an active role. A number of patient-run organizations now provide information, education, and support through national telephone hot lines, Web sites, professional referrals, newsletters, workshops, and conferences. For example, the National Eating Disorders Association, the American Anorexia and Bulimia Association, and the National Association of Anorexia Nervosa and Associated Disorders help fight the feelings of isolation and shame experienced by people with eating disorders. They show countless sufferers that they are hardly alone or powerless.

[SUMMARY AND REVIEW]

■ **Eating disorders** Rates of eating disorders have increased dramatically as thinness has become a national obsession. The two leading disorders in this category, *anorexia nervosa* and *bulimia nervosa,* share many similarities, as well as key differences. *pp. 309–310*

■ **Anorexia nervosa** People with anorexia nervosa pursue extreme thinness and lose dangerous amounts of weight. They may follow a pattern of *restricting-type anorexia*

>>LOOKING AROUND
A small step in the right direction?

The manufacturer of *king-sized* Mars and Snickers chocolate bars, oversized snacks weighing as much as 3.5 ounces and containing 387 calories, recently decided to re-package the snacks in "two shareable portions." The decision came as a result of Britain's Food and Drink Federation's manifesto to the food industry to reduce portion sizes (Reuters, 2004). **<<**

nervosa or *binge-eating/purging-type anorexia nervosa.* The central features of anorexia nervosa are a drive for thinness, fear of weight, preoccupation with food, cognitive disturbances, psychological problems such as depressed feelings or obsessive functioning, and consequent medical problems, including *amenorrhea.*

Approximately 90 to 95 percent of all cases of anorexia nervosa occur among females. Typically the disorder begins after a person who is slightly overweight or of normal weight has been on a diet. *pp. 310–313*

■ **Bulimia nervosa** Individuals with bulimia nervosa go on frequent *eating binges* and then force themselves to vomit or perform other inappropriate *compensatory behaviors.* They may follow a pattern of *purging-type bulimia nervosa* or *nonpurging-type bulimia nervosa.* The binges often occur in response to increasing tension and are followed by feelings of guilt and self-blame. Compensatory behavior is at first reinforced by the temporary relief from uncomfortable feelings of fullness or the reduction of feelings of anxiety, self-disgust, and loss of control attached to bingeing. Over time, however, people come to feel generally disgusted with themselves, depressed, and guilty.

People with bulimia nervosa may experience mood swings or have difficulty controlling their impulses. Some display a personality disorder. Around half are amenorrheic, a number develop dental problems, and some develop a potassium deficiency.

Clinicians have also observed that certain people display a pattern of binge eating without vomiting or other inappropriate compensatory behaviors. This pattern, often called *binge-eating disorder,* is not yet listed in the DSM, although it is being considered for inclusion in the next edition. *pp. 313–318*

■ **Explanations** Most theorists now apply a *multidimensional risk perspective* to explain eating disorders and identify several key contributing factors. Principal among these are *society's emphasis on thinness and bias against obesity; family environment,* including, perhaps, an *enmeshed family pattern; ego and cognitive disturbances,* including a poor sense of *autonomy and control,* the result, perhaps, of parents incorrectly identifying and reacting to their young children's internal needs and cues; a *mood disorder;* and *biological factors,* such as activity of the *hypothalamus, biochemical activity,* and the body's *weight set point. pp. 318–325*

■ **Treatments** Therapists aim first to help people with eating disorders resume normal eating and regain their health; then they tackle the broader problems that led to the disorder. The first step in treating *anorexia nervosa,* for example, is to increase calorie intake and quickly restore the person's weight, using a strategy such as *supportive nursing care.* The second step is to deal with the underlying psychological and family problems, often using a combination of *individual, group,* and *family approaches,* and *education.* Therapists try to help clients build independence and self-awareness, correct their disturbed cognitions, and change dysfunctional family interactions, among other goals. About 83 percent of people who receive successful treatment for anorexia nervosa continue to show full or partial improvements years later. However, some of them relapse along the way, many continue to worry about their weight and appearance, and half continue to experience some emotional or family problems. Most menstruate again when they regain weight. Most of those who recover are later found to enjoy work and perform effectively at their jobs and to marry or have intimate relationships at the usual rates. *pp. 325–330*

Treatments for *bulimia nervosa* focus first on stopping the binge-purge pattern and then on addressing the underlying causes of the disorder. Often several treatment strategies are combined, including *individual insight therapy* (particularly cognitive therapy and, at times, interpersonal psychotherapy, self-care manuals, and psychodynamic therapy), *group therapy* (including self-help groups), *behavioral therapy* (including exposure and response prevention and keeping a food intake diary), and *antidepressant medications.* Approximately 89 percent of those who receive treatment eventually improve either fully or partially. While relapse can be a problem and may be precipitated by a new stress, treatment leads to lasting improvements in psychological and social functioning for many individuals. *pp. 330–333*

>>> CRITICAL THOUGHTS <<<

1. Many, perhaps most, women in Western society feel as if they are dieting or between diets their entire adult lives. Is it possible to be a woman in this society and not struggle with at least some issues of eating and appearance? Who is responsible for the standards and pressures that affect so many women? *pp. 309–310, 319–321*

2. The most successful of today's fashion models, often referred to as supermodels, have a celebrity status that was not conferred upon models in the past. Why do you think the fame and status of models have risen in this way? *pp. 319–324*

3. The prevalence of eating disorders is particularly low in cultures that restrict female social roles and reduce a woman's freedom to make decisions about her life (Miller & Pumariega, 1999; Bemporad, 1997). How might you explain this relationship? *pp. 319–324*

4. Relapse is a problem for some people who recover from anorexia nervosa and bulimia nervosa. Why might people remain vulnerable even after recovery? How might they and their therapists reduce the chances of relapse? *pp. 325–333*

5. What does the 1996 Miss Universe flap suggest about the role of societal factors in the development of eating problems? Why do you think so many people held such strong, often critical, opinions about Ms. Machado's weight? *p. 331*

⊙—[CYBERSTUDY]————————————————>>>

SEARCH THE *ABNORMAL PSYCHOLOGY* CD-ROM FOR

▲ Chapter 11 Video Cases and Discussions
   Witness the feelings behind bingeing and purging.
   How does an eating disorder begin?
   How do individuals feel toward their eating disorders?

▲ Chapter 11 Practical, Research, and Decision-Making Exercises
   Uncovering attitudes toward eating, food, and weight
   Tracing the media's role in eating behaviors and disorders

▲ Chapter 11 Practice Test and Feedback

LOG ON TO THE COMER WEB PAGE FOR

▲ Suggested Web links, exercises, FAQ page, additional Chapter 11 practice test questions
   <www.worthpublishers.com/comer>

————————————————————<<<

Substance-Related Disorders

"I am Duncan. I am an alcoholic." The audience settled deeper into their chairs at these familiar words. Another chronicle of death and rebirth would shortly begin [at] Alcoholics Anonymous. . . .

. . . "I must have been just past my 15th birthday when I had that first drink that everybody talks about. And like so many of them . . . it was like a miracle. With a little beer in my gut, the world was transformed. I wasn't a weakling anymore, I could lick almost anybody on the block. And girls? Well, you can imagine how a couple of beers made me feel like I could have any girl I wanted. . . .

"Though it's obvious to me now that my drinking even then, in high school, and after I got to college, was a problem, I didn't think so at the time. After all, everybody was drinking and getting drunk and acting stupid, and I didn't really think I was different. . . . I guess the fact that I hadn't really had any blackouts and that I could go for days without having to drink reassured me that things hadn't gotten out of control. And that's the way it went, until I found myself drinking even more—and more often—and suffering more from my drinking, along about my third year of college.

. . . "My roommate, a friend from high school, started bugging me about my drinking. It wasn't even that I'd have to sleep it off the whole next day and miss class, it was that he had begun to hear other friends talking about me, about the fool I'd made of myself at parties. He saw how shaky I was the morning after, and he saw how different I was when I'd been drinking a lot—almost out of my head was the way he put it. And he could count the bottles that I'd leave around the room, and he knew what the drinking and carousing was doing to my grades. . . . [P]artly because I really cared about my roommate and didn't want to lose him as a friend, I did cut down on my drinking by half or more. I only drank on weekends—and then only at night. . . . And that got me through the rest of college and, actually, through law school as well. . . .

"Shortly after getting my law degree, I married my first wife, and . . . for the first time since I started, my drinking was no problem at all. I would go for weeks at a time without touching a drop. . . .

"My marriage started to go bad after our second son, our third child, was born. I was very much career-and-success oriented, and I had little time to spend at home with my family. . . . My traveling had increased a lot, there were stimulating people on those trips, and, let's face it, there were some pretty exciting women available, too. So home got to be little else but a nagging, boring wife and children I wasn't very interested in. My drinking had gotten bad again, too, with being on the road so much, having to do a lot of entertaining at lunch when I wasn't away, and trying to soften the hassles at home. I guess I was putting down close to a gallon of very good scotch a week, with one thing or another.

"And as that went on, the drinking began to affect both my marriage and my career. With enough booze in me and under the pressures of guilt over my failure to carry out my responsibilities to my wife and children, I sometimes got kind of rough physically with them. I would break furniture, throw things around, then

•**SUBSTANCE ABUSE**•A pattern of behavior in which people rely on a drug excessively and regularly, bringing damage to their relationships, functioning poorly at work, or putting themselves or others in danger.

•**SUBSTANCE DEPENDENCE**•A pattern of behavior in which people organize their lives around a drug, possibly building a tolerance to it or experiencing withdrawal symptoms when they stop taking it, or both. Also called *addiction*.

•**TOLERANCE**•The adjustment that the brain and the body make to the regular use of certain drugs so that ever larger doses are needed to achieve the earlier effects.

•**WITHDRAWAL**•Unpleasant, sometimes dangerous reactions that may occur when people who use a drug regularly stop taking or reduce their dosage of the drug.

•**ALCOHOL**•Any beverage containing ethyl alcohol, including beer, wine, and liquor.

FIGURE **12-1** **Sociocultural landscape: How do races differ in substance abuse and dependence?** *In the United States, Native Americans (age 12 years and older) are much more likely than members of other ethnic cultural groups to abuse or be dependent on substances. Conversely, Asian Americans are considerably less likely than members of other groups to display substance abuse or dependence (NSDUH, 2005).*

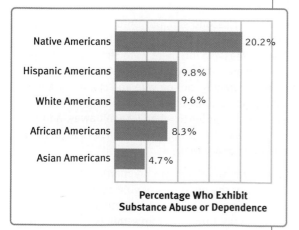

Native Americans 20.2%
Hispanic Americans 9.8%
White Americans 9.6%
African Americans 8.3%
Asian Americans 4.7%

Percentage Who Exhibit Substance Abuse or Dependence

---

rush out and drive off in the car. I had a couple of wrecks, lost my license for two years because of one of them. Worst of all was when I tried to stop. By then I was totally hooked, so every time I tried to stop drinking, I'd experience withdrawal in all its horrors . . . with the vomiting and the "shakes" and being unable to sit still or to lie down. And that would go on for days at a time. . . .

"Then, about four years ago, with my life in ruins, my wife given up on me and the kids with her, out of a job, and way down on my luck, [Alcoholics Anonymous] and I found each other. . . . I've been dry now for a little over two years, and with luck and support, I may stay sober. . . ."

(Spitzer et al., 1983, pp. 87–89)

Human beings enjoy a remarkable variety of foods and drinks. Every substance on earth probably has been tried by someone, somewhere, at some time. We also have discovered substances that have interesting nonnutritive effects—both medical and pleasurable—on our brains and the rest of our bodies. We may swallow an aspirin to quiet a headache, an antibiotic to fight an infection, or a tranquilizer to calm us down. We may drink coffee to get going in the morning or wine to relax with friends. We may smoke cigarettes to soothe our nerves. However, many of the substances we consume can harm us or disrupt our behavior or mood. The misuse of such substances has become one of society's biggest problems; it has been estimated that the cost of drug misuse is a staggering $414 billion each year in the United States alone (RWJF, 2001).

A *drug* is defined as any substance other than food that affects our bodies or minds. It need not be a medicine or be illegal. The term "substance" is now frequently used in place of "drug," in part because many people fail to see that such substances as alcohol, tobacco, and caffeine are drugs, too. When a person ingests a substance—whether it be alcohol, cocaine, marijuana, or some form of medication—trillions of powerful molecules surge through the bloodstream and into the brain (Nash, 1997). Once there, the molecules set off a series of biochemical events that disturb the normal operation of the brain and body. Not surprisingly, then, substance misuse may lead to various kinds of abnormal functioning.

Drugs may cause *temporary* changes in behavior, emotion, or thought. As Duncan found out, for example, an excessive amount of alcohol may lead to *intoxication* (literally, "poisoning"), a temporary state of poor judgment, mood changes, irritability, slurred speech, and poor coordination. Drugs such as LSD may produce a particular form of intoxication, sometimes called *hallucinosis,* which consists of perceptual distortions and hallucinations.

Some substances can also lead to *long-term* problems. People who regularly ingest them may develop maladaptive patterns of behavior and changes in their body's physical responses (APA, 2000). In one such pattern, called **substance abuse,** they rely on the drug excessively and chronically and in so doing damage their family and social relationships, function poorly at work, or put themselves and others in danger (see Figure 12-1).

A more advanced pattern, **substance dependence,** is also known as **addiction.** In this pattern, people not only abuse the drug but also center their lives on it and perhaps acquire a physical dependence on it, marked by a *tolerance* for it, *withdrawal* symptoms, or both (see Table 12-1). When people develop **tolerance,** they need increasing doses of a drug in order to keep getting the desired effect. **Withdrawal** consists of unpleasant and even dangerous symptoms—cramps, anxiety attacks, sweating, nausea—that occur when individuals suddenly stop taking or cut back on the drug.

Duncan, who described his problems to fellow members at an Alcoholics Anonymous meeting, was caught in a pattern of alcohol dependence. When he was a college student and later a lawyer, alcohol damaged his family, social, academic, and work life. He also built up a tolerance for the substance over time and experienced withdrawal symptoms such as vomiting and shaking when he tried to stop using it. In any given year, 9.4 percent of all adults in the United States, around 22 million people, display a pattern of substance abuse or dependence

(NSDUH, 2005). Only 26 percent of them receive treatment from a mental health professional (Wang et al., 2005).

Many drugs are available in our society, and new ones are introduced almost every day. Some are harvested from nature, others derived from natural substances, and still others produced in the laboratory. Some, such as antianxiety drugs and barbiturates, require a physician's prescription for legal use. Others, such as alcohol and nicotine, are legally available to adults. Still others, such as heroin, are illegal under all circumstances. In 1962 only 4 million people in the United States had ever used marijuana, cocaine, heroin, or another illegal substance; today the number has climbed to more than 94 million (NSDUH, 2005). In fact, 28 million people have used illegal substances within the past year, and 19 million are using one currently. Almost one-quarter of all high school seniors have used an illegal drug within the past month (Johnston et al., 2005).

The substances people misuse fall into several categories: *depressants,* such as alcohol and opioids, which slow the central nervous system; *stimulants* of the central nervous system, such as cocaine and amphetamines; *hallucinogens,* such as LSD, which cause delusions, hallucinations, and other powerful changes in sensory perception; and *cannabis* substances, such as marijuana, which cause a mixture of hallucinogenic, depressant, and stimulant effects. Many people take more than one of these substances at a time, a practice known as *polydrug use.* In this chapter we shall look at some of the most problematic substances and the abnormal patterns they may produce. After first examining the substances separately, we shall consider the causes and treatments of substance-related disorders together as a group.

Heroin chic *Over the years, different substances may rise and fall and rise again in popularity. In the 1990s, heroin's popularity rose greatly. For a time the drug even defined a new look in the fashion industry—"heroin chic"—and it was prominently featured in movies such as* Trainspotting.

Depressants

Depressants slow the activity of the central nervous system. They reduce tension and inhibitions and may interfere with a person's judgment, motor activity, and concentration. The three most widely used groups of depressants are *alcohol, sedative-hypnotic drugs,* and *opioids.*

Alcohol

The World Health Organization estimates that 2 billion people worldwide consume alcohol. In the United States two-thirds of all residents at least from time to time drink beverages that contain **alcohol** (CDC, 2004). Purchases of beer, wine, and liquor amount to tens of billions of dollars each year in the United States alone. Nearly 7 percent of persons over 11 years of age are heavy drinkers, consuming at least five drinks on at least five occasions each month (NSDUH, 2005). Among heavy drinkers, males outnumber females by more than three to one, around 9 percent to 3 percent.

When people consume five or more drinks on a single occasion, it is called a *binge-drinking* episode. Fifty million people in the United States over the age of 11 binge-drink each year (NSDUH, 2005). Over the past decade, the number of binge-drinking episodes per person has increased by 35 percent—by 25 percent among drinkers over 25 years of age and by 56 percent among underage drinkers (Naimi et al., 2003). Men account for 81 percent of binge-drinking episodes.

All alcoholic beverages contain *ethyl alcohol,* a chemical that is quickly absorbed into the blood through the lining of the stomach and the intestine. The ethyl alcohol immediately begins to take effect as it is carried in the bloodstream to the central nervous system (the brain and spinal cord), where it acts to depress, or slow, functioning by binding to various neurons. One important group of neurons to which ethyl alcohol binds are those that normally receive the neurotransmitter GABA. As we observed

Table 12-1 DSM Checklist

SUBSTANCE ABUSE

1. A maladaptive pattern of substance use leading to significant impairment or distress
2. At least one of the following features occurring within one year:
   (a) Recurrent substance use, resulting in failure to fulfill major role obligations at work, school, or home
   (b) Recurrent substance use in situations in which it is physically hazardous
   (c) Recurrent substance-related legal problems
   (d) Substance use that continues despite its causing or increasing persistent social or interpersonal problems

SUBSTANCE DEPENDENCE

1. A maladaptive pattern of substance use leading to significant impairment or distress
2. At least three of the following:
   (a) Tolerance
   (b) Withdrawal
   (c) Substance often taken in larger amounts over a longer period than was intended
   (d) Persistent desire for substance or unsuccessful efforts to control substance use
   (e) Considerable time spent trying to obtain, use, or recover from the substance
   (f) Substance use in place of important activities
   (g) Substance use that continues despite its causing or increasing persistent physical or psychological problems

Based on APA, 2000, 1994.

>>LOOKING BACK

Founding Fathers

George Washington brewed beer at Mount Vernon before the Revolutionary War and strongly rebuked the Continental Congress during the war for scrimping on beer rations (a quart a day) for his soldiers. <<

(Wells, 2004)

in Chapter 5, GABA carries an *inhibitory* message—a message to stop firing—when it is received at certain neurons. When alcohol binds to receptors on those neurons, it apparently helps GABA to shut down the neurons, thus helping to relax the drinker (Grilly, 2006; Staley et al., 2005).

At first ethyl alcohol depresses the areas of the brain that control judgment and inhibition; people become looser, more talkative, and often more friendly. As their inner control breaks down, they may feel relaxed, confident, and happy. When more alcohol is absorbed, it slows down additional areas in the central nervous system, leaving the drinkers less able to make sound judgments, their speech less careful and less coherent, and their memory weaker. Many people become highly emotional and perhaps loud and aggressive.

Motor difficulties increase as drinking continues, and reaction times slow. People may be unsteady when they stand or walk and clumsy in performing even simple activities. They may drop things, bump into doors and furniture, and misjudge distances. Their vision becomes blurred, particularly peripheral, or side, vision, and they have trouble hearing. As a result, people who have drunk too much alcohol may have great difficulty driving or solving simple problems.

The extent of the effect of ethyl alcohol is determined by its *concentration,* or proportion, in the blood. Thus a given amount of alcohol will have less effect on a large person than on a small one (see Table 12-2). Gender also affects the concentration of alcohol in the blood. Women have less of the stomach enzyme *alcohol dehydrogenase,* which breaks down alcohol in the stomach before it enters the blood. Thus, women become more intoxicated than men on equal doses of alcohol, and women may be at greater risk for physical and psychological damage from alcohol than men who drink similar quantitites of alcohol (Nolen-Hoeksema, 2004).

Levels of impairment are closely related to the concentration of ethyl alcohol in the blood. When the alcohol concentration reaches 0.06 percent of the blood volume, a person usually feels relaxed and comfortable. By the time it reaches 0.09 percent, however,

Table 12-2

Relationships between Sex, Weight, Oral Alcohol Consumption, and Blood Alcohol Level

Absolute Alcohol (oz.)	Beverage Intake*	Blood Alcohol Level (percent)					
		Female (100 lb.)	Male (100 lb.)	Female (150 lb.)	Male (150 lb.)	Female (200 lb.)	Male (200 lb.)
1/2	1 oz. spirits[†] 1 glass wine 1 can beer	0.045	0.037	0.03	0.025	0.022	0.019
1	2 oz. spirits 2 glasses wine 2 cans beer	0.090	0.075	0.06	0.050	0.045	0.037
2	4 oz. spirits 4 glasses wine 4 cans beer	0.180	0.150	0.12	0.100	0.090	0.070
3	6 oz. spirits 6 glasses wine 6 cans beer	0.270	0.220	0.18	0.150	0.130	0.110
4	8 oz. spirits 8 glasses wine 8 cans beer	0.360	0.300	0.24	0.200	0.180	0.150
5	10 oz. spirits 10 glasses wine 10 cans beer	0.450	0.370	0.30	0.250	0.220	0.180

*In 1 hour.
[†]100-proof spirits.
Source: Ray & Ksir, 1993, p. 194.

Aris Messinis/AP Photo

Alcohol and sports fans *A problem that has received growing attention in recent years is excessive drinking (and accompanying violence) by fans at sporting events. While two soccer players were jumping for a high ball at this 2002 playoff game in Athens, Greece, fans of the rival teams—many of them inebriated—ripped out plastic seats, threw flares on the field, and hurled coins and rocks at the players.*

the drinker crosses the line into intoxication. If the level goes as high as 0.55 percent, death will probably result. Most people, however, lose consciousness before they can drink enough to reach this level.

The effects of alcohol subside only when the alcohol concentration in the blood declines. Most of the alcohol is broken down, or *metabolized,* by the liver into carbon dioxide and water, which can be exhaled and excreted. The average rate of this metabolism is 13 percent of an ounce per hour, but different people's livers work at different speeds; thus rates of "sobering up" vary. Despite popular belief, only time and metabolism can make a person sober. Drinking black coffee, splashing cold water on one's face, or "pulling oneself together" cannot hurry the process.

ALCOHOL ABUSE AND DEPENDENCE Though legal, alcohol is actually one of the most dangerous of recreational drugs, and its reach extends across the life span. In fact, around 10 percent of elementary school students admit to some alcohol use, while nearly 50 percent of high school seniors drink alcohol each month (most to the point of intoxication) and 3.6 percent report drinking every day (Johnston et al., 2005; NIDA, 1995). Similarly, alcohol misuse is a major problem on college campuses (Doweiko, 2006; Sharma, 2005) (see Box 12-1 on the next page).

In any given year, 6.6 percent of the world population fall into a long-term pattern of alcohol abuse or dependence, either of which is known in popular terms as *alcoholism,* and 13.2 percent experience one of the patterns sometime during their lifetime (Somers et al., 2004). Similarly, surveys indicate that over a one-year period, 7.7 percent of all adults in the United States display an alcohol use disorder (NSDUH, 2005). Between 9 and 18 percent of the nation's adults display such a disorder at some time in their lives, with men outnumbering women by at least 2 to 1 (Kessler et al., 2005; NSDUH, 2005). Many teenagers also experience alcohol abuse or dependence (Johnston et al., 2005).

The prevalence of alcoholism in a given year is around the same (7 to 10 percent) for white Americans, African Americans, and Hispanic Americans (NSDUH, 2005; APA, 2000; Anthony et al., 1995; Helzer et al., 1991). The men in these groups, however, show strikingly different age patterns. For white and Hispanic American men, the rate of alcoholism is highest—over 18 percent—during young adulthood, compared to 8 percent among African American men in that age group. For African American men, the rate is highest during late middle age, 15 percent compared to 8 percent among white and Hispanic American men in that age group.

Native Americans, particularly men, tend to display a higher rate of alcohol abuse and dependence than any of these groups, although their specific prevalence rates differ across the various Native American reservation communities (Beals et al., 2005).

>>LOOKING AROUND
Fatal Victory

In March 2005, the 21-year-old winner of a competition to drink the most tequila at a Dominican Republic discotheque died within hours of his victory. The young man, who was awarded $330 after drinking more than 50 shots of tequila, apparently died from heart failure brought on by alcohol poisoning (Associated Press, 2005). **<<**

[BOX 12-1]

College Binge Drinking: An Extracurricular Crisis

Drinking large amounts of alcohol in a short time, or *binge drinking*, is a serious problem on college campuses, as well as in many other settings (Vicary & Karshin, 2002). Studies show that 43.4 percent of college students binge-drink at least once each year, around half of them six times or more per month (Sharma, 2005; NSDUH, 2005; Wechsler et al., 2004, 2000, 1997, 1994). These are higher rates than those displayed by people of the same age who are not in college. In many circles, alcohol use is an accepted part of college life. Are we as a society taking the issue too lightly? Consider some of the following statistics:

◆ Alcohol is a factor in nearly 40 percent of academic problems and 28 percent of all college dropouts (Anderson, 1994).

◆ Although 84 percent of incoming freshmen consider heavy alcohol use to be a problem on campus, 68 percent drink during their first semester, at least half of them during their first week on campus (Harvard School of Public Health, 1995).

◆ Alcohol affects not only those who drink but also those who do not; approximately 600,000 students each year are physically or emotionally traumatized or sexually assaulted by a student drinker (Hingson et al., 2002).

◆ Binge drinking has been linked to severe health problems and serious injury, auto crashes, unplanned and unprotected sex, aggressive behaviors, and various psychological problems (Wechsler & Wuethrich, 2002). Binge drinking by college students has been associated with an estimated 1,400 deaths, 500,000 injuries, and 70,000 cases of sexual assault, including date rape, every year (Wechsler et al., 2000).

◆ Teenagers who begin binge drinking at age 13 and continue through adolescence are nearly four times more likely than non-binge-drinking peers to be overweight or have high blood pressure at age 24 (Oesterle et al., 2004).

◆ The number of female binge drinkers among college students increased 31 percent from 1993 to 2001.

These findings have led some educators to describe binge drinking as "the No. 1 public health hazard" for full-time college students, and many researchers and clinicians have turned their attention to it. Henry Wechsler and his colleagues (1995) at the Harvard School of Public Health mailed a questionnaire about drinking patterns to students at 140 college campuses around the United States and received close to 18,000 replies. According to the responses, people most likely to binge-drink were those who lived in a fraternity or sorority house, pursued a party-centered lifestyle, and engaged in high-risk behaviors such as smoking marijuana, having multiple sex partners, and smoking cigarettes. The study also found that students who were binge drinkers in high school were more likely to binge-drink in college.

Efforts to change such patterns have begun to make a difference. For example, some universities now provide substance-free dorms: 36 percent of the residents in such dorms were binge drinkers, according to one study, compared to 75 percent of those who lived in a fraternity or sorority house (Wechsler et al., 2002).

The results of such studies are based on self-administered questionnaires, and subjects' responses may have been biased. Perhaps binge drinkers are more (or less) likely than nondrinkers to respond to such questionnaires. Still, the implications are clear: college drinking, certainly binge drinking, may be more common and more harmful than was previously believed. At the very least, it is a problem whose research time has come.

Andrew Lichtenstein/Corbis Sygma

Testing the limits *Binge drinking, similar to this display at a college campus party, has led to a number of deaths in recent years.*

Generally, Asians in the United States and elsewhere have lower rates of alcoholism than do people from other cultures. As many as one-half of these individuals have a deficiency of alcohol dehydrogenase, the chemical responsible for breaking down alcohol, so they react quite negatively to even a modest intake of alcohol. Such reactions in turn prevent extended use (Wall et al., 2001; APA, 2000).

ALCOHOL ABUSE Generally speaking, people who abuse alcohol drink large amounts regularly and rely on it to enable them to do things that would otherwise make them anxious. Eventually the drinking interferes with their social behavior and ability to think and work. They may have frequent arguments with family members or friends, miss work repeatedly, and even lose their jobs. MRI scans of chronic heavy drinkers have revealed damage in various regions of their brains and, correspondingly, impairments in their short-term memory, speed of thinking, attention skills, and balance (Grilly, 2006; Meyerhoff et al., 2004).

Individually, people vary in their patterns of alcohol abuse. Some drink large amounts of alcohol every day and keep drinking until intoxicated. Others go on periodic binges of heavy drinking that can last weeks or months. They may remain intoxicated for days and later be unable to remember anything about the period. Still others may limit their excessive drinking to weekends or evenings, or both. The actor Dick Van Dyke commented:

> I didn't miss work ever because of drinking. And I never drank at work. Never drank during the day—only at home and only in the evenings. . . . I never craved a drink during the day. I was never a morning drinker—I didn't want one then. The idea made me as sick as it would make anyone else. But evening drinking is a form of alcoholism, just like periodic drinking is a form of alcoholism. . . .
>
> *(HEW, 1976, p. 76)*

ALCOHOL DEPENDENCE For many people, the pattern of alcohol misuse includes dependence. Their bodies build up a tolerance for alcohol and they need to drink ever greater amounts to feel its effects. They also experience withdrawal when they stop drinking. Within hours their hands, tongue, and eyelids begin to shake; they feel weak and nauseated; they sweat and vomit; their heart beats rapidly; and their blood pressure rises. They may also become anxious, depressed, unable to sleep, or irritable (APA, 2000).

A small percentage of people who are dependent on alcohol experience a particularly dramatic withdrawal reaction called **delirium tremens ("the DTs")**, or **alcohol withdrawal delirium.** It consists of terrifying visual hallucinations that begin within three days after they stop or reduce their drinking. Some people see small, frightening animals chasing or crawling on them or objects dancing about in front of their eyes. Mark Twain gave a classic picture of delirium tremens in Huckleberry Finn's description of his father:

> I don't know how long I was asleep, but . . . there was an awful scream and I was up. There was Pap looking wild, and skipping around every which way and yelling about snakes. He said they was crawling up on his legs; and then he would give a jump and scream, and say one had bit him on the cheek—but I couldn't see no snakes. He started and run round . . . hollering "Take him off! he's biting me on the neck!" I never see a man look so wild in the eyes. Pretty soon he . . . fell down panting; then he rolled over . . . kicking things every which way, and striking and grabbing at the air with his hands, and screaming . . . there was devils a-hold of him. He wore out by and by. . . . He says . . .
>
> "Tramp-tramp-tramp: that's the dead; tramp-tramp-tramp; they're coming after me; but I won't go. Oh, they're here; don't touch me. . . . They're cold; let go. . . ."
>
> Then he went down on all fours and crawled off, begging them to let him alone. . . .
>
> *(Twain, 1885)*

Like most other alcohol withdrawal symptoms, the DTs usually run their course in two to three days. However, people who experience severe withdrawal reactions such as this may also have seizures, lose consciousness, suffer a stroke, or even die. Today certain medical procedures can help prevent or reduce such extreme reactions (Doweiko, 2006).

•DELIRIUM TREMENS (DTs)• A dramatic withdrawal reaction experienced by some people who are alcohol-dependent. It consists of confusion, clouded consciousness, and terrifying visual hallucinations. Also called *alcohol withdrawal delirium.*

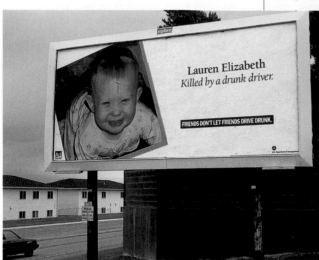

Spreading the word *Educating the public with billboard, television, and radio ads about the dangers of alcohol has helped reduce the number of alcohol-related automobile deaths by over 25 percent in recent years (CDC, 1997).*

•**KORSAKOFF'S SYNDROME**•An alcohol-related disorder marked by extreme confusion, memory impairment, and other neurological symptoms.

•**FETAL ALCOHOL SYNDROME**•A cluster of problems in a child, including low birth weight, irregularities in the head and face, and intellectual deficits, caused by excessive alcohol intake by the mother during pregnancy.

•**SEDATIVE-HYPNOTIC DRUG**•A drug used in low doses to reduce anxiety and in higher doses to help people sleep. Also called *anxiolytic drug.*

•**BARBITURATES**•Addictive sedative-hypnotic drugs that reduce anxiety and help produce asleep.

•**BENZODIAZEPINES**•The most common group of antianxiety drugs, which includes Valium and Xanax.

•**OPIOID**•Opium or any of the drugs derived from opium, including morphine, heroin, and codeine.

•**OPIUM**•A highly addictive substance made from the sap of the opium poppy.

•**MORPHINE**•A highly addictive substance derived from opium that is particularly effective in relieving pain.

•**HEROIN**•One of the most addictive substances derived from opium.

WHAT IS THE PERSONAL AND SOCIAL IMPACT OF ALCOHOLISM? Alcoholism destroys millions of families, social relationships, and careers (Murphy et al., 2005; Nace, 2005). Medical treatment, lost productivity, and losses due to deaths from alcoholism cost society as much as $200 billion annually (Brick, 2004). The disorder also plays a role in more than one-third of all suicides, homicides, assaults, rapes, and accidental deaths, including 41 percent of all fatal automobile accidents in the United States (Doweiko, 2006; NSDUH, 2005; CDC, 2002). Altogether, intoxicated drivers are responsible for 19,000 deaths each year. More than 32 million adults (13.5 percent) have driven while intoxicated at least once in the past year (NSDUH, 2005).

Alcoholism has serious effects on the 30 million children of persons with this disorder. Home life for these children is likely to include much conflict and perhaps sexual or other forms of abuse. In turn, the children themselves have higher rates of psychological problems such as anxiety, depression, phobias, conduct disorder, attention-deficit disorder, and substance-related disorders during their lifetimes (Hall & Webster, 2002; Mylant et al., 2002). Many have low self-esteem, poor communication skills, poor sociability, and marital problems (Watt, 2002; Lewis-Harter, 2000).

Long-term excessive drinking can also seriously damage one's physical health (Grilly, 2006; Nace, 2005). It so overworks the liver that people may develop an irreversible condition called *cirrhosis,* in which the liver becomes scarred and dysfunctional. Cirrhosis accounts for some 27,000 deaths each year (CDC, 2004). Alcohol abuse and dependence may also damage the heart and lower the immune system's ability to fight off cancer and bacterial infections and to resist the onset of AIDS after infection.

Long-term excessive drinking also causes major nutritional problems. Alcohol makes people feel full and lowers their desire for food, yet it has no nutritional value. As a result, chronic drinkers become malnourished, weak, and prone to disease. Their vitamin and mineral deficiencies may also cause problems. An alcohol-related deficiency of vitamin B (thiamine), for example, may lead to **Korsakoff's syndrome,** a disease marked by extreme confusion, memory loss, and other neurological symptoms (Doweiko, 2006). People with Korsakoff's syndrome cannot remember the past or learn new information and may make up for their memory losses by *confabulating*—reciting made-up events to fill in the gaps.

Finally, women who drink during pregnancy place their fetuses at risk. Excessive alcohol use during pregnancy may cause a baby to be born with **fetal alcohol syndrome,** a pattern of abnormalities that can include mental retardation, hyperactivity, head and face deformities, heart defects, and slow growth (Grilly, 2006; Hankin, 2002). It has been estimated that in the overall population 1 of every 1,000 babies is born with this syndrome (May & Gossage, 2001; Ray & Ksir, 1993). The rate may increase to as many as 29 of every 1,000 babies of women who are problem drinkers. In addition, heavy drinking early in pregnancy often leads to a miscarriage. According to surveys, 11.2 percent of pregnant American women have drunk alcohol during the past month and 4.5 percent of pregnant women had binge-drinking episodes (NSDUH, 2005).

Sedative-Hypnotic Drugs

Sedative-hypnotic drugs, also called **anxiolytic** (meaning "anxiety-reducing") **drugs,** produce feelings of relaxation and drowsiness. At low dosages, the drugs have a calming or sedative effect. At higher dosages, they are sleep inducers, or hypnotics. The sedative-hypnotic drugs include *barbiturates* and *benzodiazepines.*

BARBITURATES First discovered in Germany more than 100 years ago, **barbiturates** were widely prescribed in the first half of the twentieth century to fight anxiety and to help people sleep. Although still prescribed by some physicians, these drugs have been largely replaced by benzodiazepines, which are generally safer drugs. Barbiturates can cause many problems, not the least of which are abuse and dependence. Several thousand deaths a year are caused by accidental or suicidal overdoses.

Barbiturates are usually taken in pill or capsule form. In low doses they reduce a person's level of excitement in the same way that alcohol does, by attaching to receptors on the neurons that receive the inhibitory neurotransmitter GABA and by helping GABA operate at those neurons (Grilly, 2006; Gao & Greenfield, 2005; Mazarakis & Nestoros, 2001). People can get intoxicated from large doses of barbiturates, just as they do from alcohol. And, like alcohol, barbiturates are broken down in the liver (Nishino et al., 1995). At high doses, barbiturates also depress the *reticular formation,* the part of the brain that normally keeps people awake, thus causing the person to get sleepy. At too high a level, the drugs can halt breathing, lower blood pressure, and lead to coma and death.

Repeated use of barbiturates can quickly result in a pattern of abuse (Dupont & Dupont, 2005). Users may spend much of the day intoxicated, irritable, and unable to do their work. Dependence can also result. The user organizes his or her life around the drug and needs increasing amounts of it to calm down or fall asleep. A great danger of barbiturate dependence is that the lethal dose of the drug remains the same even while the body is building up a tolerance for its sedating effects (Landry, 1994; Gold, 1986). Once the prescribed dose stops reducing anxiety or inducing sleep, the user is all too likely to increase it without medical supervision and eventually may ingest a dose that proves fatal. Those caught in a pattern of barbiturate dependence may also experience withdrawal symptoms such as nausea, anxiety, and sleep problems. Barbiturate withdrawal is particularly dangerous because it can cause convulsions.

BENZODIAZEPINES Chapter 5 described **benzodiazepines,** the antianxiety drugs developed in the 1950s, as the most popular sedative-hypnotic drugs available. Xanax and Valium are just two of the dozens of these compounds in clinical use. Like alcohol and barbiturates, they calm people by binding to receptors on the neurons that receive GABA and by increasing GABA's activity at those neurons (Gao & Greenfield, 2005). These drugs, however, relieve anxiety without making people as drowsy as other kinds of sedative-hypnotics. They are also less likely to slow a person's breathing, so they are less likely to cause death in the event of an overdose (Nishino et al., 1995).

When benzodiazepines were first discovered, they seemed so safe and effective that physicians prescribed them generously, and their use spread. Eventually it became clear that in high enough doses the drugs can cause intoxication and lead to abuse or dependence (Dupont & Dupont, 2005). As many as 1 percent of the adults in the United States abuse or become physically dependent on these antianxiety drugs at some point in their lives (APA, 2000; Anthony et al., 1995) and thus become subject to some of the same dangers that researchers have identified in barbiturate misuse.

Opioids

Opioids include opium—taken from the sap of the opium poppy—and the drugs derived from it, such as heroin, morphine, and codeine. **Opium** itself has been in use for thousands of years. In the past it was used widely in the treatment of medical disorders because of its ability to reduce both physical and emotional pain. Eventually, however, physicians discovered that the drug was physically addictive.

In 1804 a new substance, **morphine,** was derived from opium. Named after Morpheus, the Greek god of sleep, this drug relieved pain even better than opium did and initially was considered safe. However, wide use of the drug eventually revealed that it, too, could lead to addiction. So many wounded soldiers in the United States received morphine injections during the Civil War that morphine dependence became known as "soldiers' disease."

In 1898 morphine was converted into yet another new pain reliever, **heroin.** For several years heroin was viewed as a wonder drug and was used as a cough medicine and for other medical purposes. Eventually, however, physicians learned that heroin is even more addictive than the other opioids. By 1917 the U.S. Congress had concluded that all drugs derived from opium were addictive (see Table 12-3 on the next page), and it passed a law making opioids illegal except for medical purposes.

Purer blend *In the past, heroin was usually injected. However, heroin, derived from poppies such as these in Mexico, is purer today than it was in the 1980s (65 percent pure vs. 5 percent), so that users can heighten the impact of the drug considerably by snorting or smoking it.*

Rodolfo Valtierra/Corbis Sygma

Brennan Linsley/AP Photo

Injecting heroin *Opioids may be taken by mouth, inhaled, snorted, injected just beneath the surface of the skin, or injected intravenously. Here, one addict injects another with heroin inside one of the many so-called shooting galleries where addicts gather in downtown San Juan, Puerto Rico.*

Still other drugs have been derived from opium, and *synthetic* (laboratory-blended) opioids such as *methadone* have also been developed. All these opioid drugs—natural and synthetic—are known collectively as *narcotics.* Each drug has a different strength, speed of action, and tolerance level. Morphine and *codeine* are medical narcotics usually prescribed to relieve pain. Heroin is illegal in the United States under all circumstances.

Narcotics are smoked, inhaled, snorted, injected by needle just beneath the skin ("skin popped"), or injected directly into the bloodstream ("mainlined"). Injection seems to be the most common method of narcotic use, although the other techniques have been used increasingly in recent years (NSDUH, 2005). An injection quickly brings on a *rush*—a spasm of warmth and ecstasy that is sometimes compared with orgasm. The brief spasm is followed by several hours of a pleasant feeling called a *high* or *nod.* During a high, the drug user feels relaxed, happy, and unconcerned about food, sex, or other bodily needs.

Opioids create these effects by depressing the central nervous system, particularly the centers that help control emotion. The drugs attach to brain receptor sites that ordinarily receive **endorphins**—neurotransmitters that help relieve pain and reduce emotional tension (Grilly, 2006; Snyder, 1991, 1986). When neurons at these receptor sites receive opioids, they produce pleasurable and calming feelings just as they would do if they were receiving endorphins. In addition to reducing pain and tension, opioids cause nausea, narrowing of the pupils ("pinpoint pupils"), and constipation—bodily reactions that can also be brought about by releases of endorphins in the brain.

HEROIN ABUSE AND DEPENDENCE Heroin use exemplifies the kinds of problems posed by opioids. After taking heroin repeatedly for just a few weeks, users may become caught in a pattern of abuse: the drug interferes significantly with their social and occupational functioning. In most cases, heroin abuse leads to a pattern of dependence as well, and users soon center their lives on the substance, build a tolerance for it, and experience a withdrawal reaction when they stop taking it (Dilts & Dilts, 2005). At first the withdrawal symptoms are anxiety, restlessness, sweating, and rapid breathing; later they include severe twitching, aches, fever, vomiting, diarrhea, loss of appetite, high blood pressure, and weight loss of up to 15 pounds (due to loss of bodily fluids). These symptoms usually peak by the third day, gradually subside, and disappear by the eighth day. A person in withdrawal can either wait out the symptoms or end withdrawal by taking heroin again.

Table 12-3

Risks and Consequences of Drug Misuse

	Potential Intoxication	Dependency Potential	Risk of Organ Damage or Death	Risk of Severe Social or Economic Consequences	Risk of Severe or Long-Lasting Mental and Behvioral Change
Opioids	High	High	Low	High	Low to moderate
Sedative-hypnotics					
Barbiturates	Moderate	Moderate to high	Moderate to high	Moderate to high	Low
Benzodiazepines	Moderate	Low	Low	Low	Low
Stimulants (cocaine, amphetamines)	High	High	Moderate	Low to moderate	Moderate to high
Alcohol	High	Moderate	High	High	High
Cannabis	High	Low to moderate	Low	Low to moderate	Low
Mixed drug classes	High	High	High	High	High

Source: APA, 2000, 1994; Gold, 1986, p. 28.

People who are dependent on heroin soon need the drug just to avoid going into withdrawal, and they must continually increase their doses in order to achieve even that relief. The temporary high becomes less intense and less important. The individuals may spend much of their time planning their next dose, in many cases turning to criminal activities, such as theft and prostitution, to support the expensive "habit" (Allen, 2005).

Surveys suggest that close to 1 percent of adults in the United States become addicted to heroin or other opioids at some time in their lives (APA, 2000, 1994). The rate of addiction dropped considerably during the 1980s, rose in the early 1990s, fell in the late 1990s, and now seems to be relatively high once again (NSDUH, 2005). The number of persons currently addicted to these drugs is estimated to be as much as 270,000 (NSDUH, 2005). The actual number may be even higher, however, given the reluctance of many people to admit an illegal activity.

WHAT ARE THE DANGERS OF HEROIN ABUSE? The most immediate danger of heroin use is an overdose, which closes down the respiratory center in the brain, almost paralyzing breathing and in many cases causing death. Death is particularly likely during sleep, when a person is unable to fight this effect by consciously working to breathe. People who resume heroin use after having avoided it for some time often make the fatal mistake of taking the same dose they had built up to before. Because their bodies have been without heroin for some time, however, they can no longer tolerate this high level. Each year approximately 2 percent of persons dependent on heroin and other opioids die under the drug's influence, usually from an overdose (Theodorou & Haber, 2005; APA, 2000).

Users run other risks as well. Often pushers mix heroin with a cheaper drug or even a deadly substance such as cyanide or battery acid. In addition, dirty needles and other unsterile equipment spread infections such as AIDS, hepatitis, and skin abscesses (Kennedy et al., 2005; Ferrando, 2001). In some areas of the United States the HIV infection rate among persons dependent on heroin is reported to be as high as 60 percent (APA, 2000, 1994).

Stimulants

Stimulants are substances that increase the activity of the central nervous system, resulting in increased blood pressure and heart rate, greater alertness, and speeded-up behavior and thinking. Among the most troublesome stimulants are *cocaine* and *amphetamines*, whose effects on people are very similar. When users report different effects, it is often because they have ingested different amounts of the drugs. Two other widely used and legal stimulants are *caffeine* and *nicotine* (see Box 12-2 on page 351).

Cocaine

Cocaine—the central active ingredient of the coca plant, found in South America—is the most powerful natural stimulant now known. The drug was first separated from the plant in 1865. Native people of South America, however, have chewed the leaves of the plant since prehistoric times for the energy and alertness the drug offers. Processed cocaine (*hydrochloride powder*) is an odorless, white, fluffy powder. For recreational use, it is most often snorted so that it is absorbed through the mucous membrane of the nose. Some users prefer the more powerful effects of injecting cocaine intravenously or smoking it in a pipe or cigarette.

Sherlock Holmes took his bottle from the corner of the mantelpiece, and his hypodermic syringe from its neat morocco case. With his long white nervous fingers, he adjusted the delicate needle and rolled back his left shirtcuff. For some little time his eyes rested thoughtfully upon the sinewy forearm and wrist, all dotted and scarred with innumerable puncture-marks. Finally, he thrust the sharp point home, pressed down the tiny piston, and sank back into the velvet-lined armchair with a long sigh of satisfaction.

•**ENDORPHINS**• Neurotransmitters that help relieve pain and reduce emotional tension. They are sometimes referred to as the body's own opioids.

•**COCAINE**• An addictive stimulant obtained from the coca plant. It is the most powerful natural stimulant known.

>>PSYCH•NOTES

Freud's Folly Early in his career, Sigmund Freud was a staunch advocate of cocaine use. He proclaimed, "Cocaine brings about an exhilaration and lasting euphoria . . . an increase in self-control and . . . more vitality and capacity for work. . . . In other words, you are simply normal." **<<**

(Freud, 1885)

Cardiac Risk During the first hour after taking cocaine, a user's risk of heart attack increases nearly 24 times. **<<**

(Mittleman et al., 1999)

Three times a day for many months I had witnessed this performance, but custom had not reconciled my mind to it. . . .

"Which is it today," I asked, "morphine or cocaine?"

He raised his eyes languidly from the old black-letter volume which he had opened.

"It is cocaine," he said, "a seven-per-cent solution. Would you care to try it?"

"No, indeed," I answered brusquely. "My constitution has not got over the Afghan campaign yet. I cannot afford to throw any extra strain upon it."

He smiled at my vehemence. "Perhaps you are right, Watson," he said. "I suppose that its influence is physically a bad one. I find it, however, so transcendently stimulating and clarifying to the mind that its secondary action is a matter of small moment."

"But consider!" I said earnestly. "Count the cost! Your brain may, as you say, be roused and excited, but it is a pathological and morbid process which involves increased tissue-change and . . . a permanent weakness. You know, too, what a black reaction comes upon you. Surely, the game is hardly worth the candle."

(Doyle, 1938, pp. 91–92)

For years people believed that cocaine posed few problems aside from intoxication and, on occasion, temporary psychosis. Like Sherlock Holmes, many felt that the benefits outweighed the costs. Only later did researchers come to appreciate its many dangers. Their insights came after society witnessed a dramatic increase in the drug's popularity and in problems related to its use. In the early 1960s an estimated 10,000 persons in the United States had tried cocaine. Today 28 million people have tried it, and 2 million—most of them teenagers or young adults—are using it currently (NSDUH, 2005). In fact, more than 5 percent of all high school seniors have used cocaine within the past year (Johnston et al., 2005). Altogether, close to 3 percent of the population become dependent on cocaine at some point in their lives (Anthony et al., 1995).

Cocaine brings on a euphoric rush of well-being and confidence. Given a high enough dose, this rush can be almost orgasmic, like the one produced by heroin. At first cocaine stimulates the higher centers of the central nervous system, making users feel excited, energetic, talkative, and even euphoric. As more is taken, it stimulates other centers of the central nervous system, producing a faster pulse, higher blood pressure, faster and deeper breathing, and further arousal and wakefulness.

Cocaine apparently produces these effects largely by increasing supplies of the neurotransmitter *dopamine* at key neurons throughout the brain (Messas et al., 2005) (see Figure 12-2). More precisely, cocaine prevents the neurons that release dopamine from reabsorbing it, as they normally would do. So excessive amounts of dopamine travel to receiving neurons throughout the central nervous system and overstimulate them. In addition, cocaine appears to increase the activity of the neurotransmitters *norepinephrine* and *serotonin* in some areas of the brain (Hall et al., 2004; Quiñones-Jenab, 2001).

High doses of the drug produce *cocaine intoxication,* whose symptoms are poor muscle coordination, grandiosity, bad judgment, anger, aggression, compulsive behavior, anxiety, and confusion. Some people experience hallucinations or delusions, or both, a condition known as *cocaine-induced psychotic disorder* (APA, 2000).

FIGURE 12-2 **Biochemical euphoria** *The subjective experiences of euphoria after a cocaine injection closely parallel cocaine's action at dopamine-using neurons. The peak experience of euphoria seems to occur around the same time as the peak of neuron activity (Fowler, Volkow, & Wolf, 1995, p. 110; Cook, Jeffcoat, & Perez-Reyes, 1985).*

A young man described how, after free-basing, he went to his closet to get his clothes, but his suit asked him, "What do you want?" Afraid, he walked toward the door, which told him, "Get back!" Retreating, he then heard the sofa say, "If you sit on me, I'll kick your ass." With a sense of impending doom, intense anxiety, and momentary panic, the young man ran to the hospital where he received help.

(Allen, 1985, pp. 19–20)

As the stimulant effects of cocaine subside, the user experiences a depression-like letdown, popularly called *crashing,* a pattern that may also include headaches, dizziness, and fainting (Doweiko, 2002). For occasional users, the aftereffects usually disappear within 24 hours, but they may last longer for people who have taken a particularly high dose. These individuals may sink into a stupor, deep sleep, or, in some cases, coma (Coambs & McAndrews, 1994).

COCAINE ABUSE AND DEPENDENCE Regular use of cocaine may lead to a pattern of abuse in which the person remains under its effects much of each day and functions poorly in social relationships and at work. Regular drug use may also cause problems in short-term memory or attention (Kubler et al., 2005). Dependence may also develop, so that cocaine dominates the person's life, higher doses are needed to gain the desired effects, and stopping it results in depression, fatigue, sleep problems, irritability, and anxiety (Acosta et al., 2005; APA, 2000). These withdrawal symptoms may last for weeks or even months after drug use has ended.

Wonder drug *Legal in the United States until 1914, cocaine was an ingredient in over-the-counter medicines, such as Cocaine Toothache Drops. This 1885 ad shows that it was used to treat children as well as adults. Cocaine was also part of Coca-Cola's formula until 1903.*

In the past, cocaine use and impact were limited by the drug's high cost. Moreover, cocaine was usually snorted, a form of ingestion that has less powerful effects than either smoking or injection. Since 1984, however, the availability of newer, more powerful, and sometimes cheaper forms of cocaine has produced an enormous increase in abuse and dependence. Currently, close to 1 percent of all people in the United States manifest cocaine abuse or dependence (NSDUH, 2005). Altogether one user in five falls into such a pattern. Many people now ingest cocaine by **free-basing,** a technique in which the pure cocaine basic alkaloid is chemically separated, or "freed," from processed cocaine, vaporized by heat from a flame, and inhaled through a pipe.

Millions more people use **crack,** a powerful form of free-base cocaine that has been boiled down into crystalline balls. It is smoked with a special pipe and makes a crackling sound as it is inhaled (hence the name). Crack is sold in small quantities at a fairly low cost, a practice that has resulted in crack epidemics among people who previously could not have afforded cocaine, primarily those in poor urban areas (Acosta et al., 2005). Approximately 2.3 percent of high school seniors report having used crack within the past year, up from 1.5 percent in 1993, yet down from a peak of 2.7 percent just a few years ago (Johnston et al., 2005).

WHAT ARE THE DANGERS OF COCAINE? Aside from cocaine's harmful effects on behavior, the drug poses serious physical dangers (Doweiko, 2006). Its growing use in powerful forms has caused the annual number of cocaine-related emergency room incidents in the United States to multiply 44 times since 1982, from around 4,000 cases to 175,000 (NCHS, 2002). In addition, cocaine use has been linked to as many as 20 percent of all suicides by men under 61 years of age (Garlow, 2002; Marzuk et al., 1992).

Smoking crack *Crack, a powerful form of free-base cocaine, is produced by boiling cocaine down into crystalline balls and is smoked with a special crack pipe.*

•**FREE-BASE**•A technique for ingesting cocaine in which the pure cocaine basic alkaloid is chemically separated from processed cocaine, vaporized by heat from a flame, and inhaled with a pipe.

•**CRACK**•A powerful, ready-to-smoke free-base cocaine.

•AMPHETAMINE•A stimulant drug that is manufactured in the laboratory.

•METHAMPHETAMINE•A powerful amphetamine drug that has experienced a surge in popularity in recent years, posing major health and law enforcement problems.

Prenatal concerns *This baby, born prematurely to a woman dependent on cocaine, lived only a few months. The use of cocaine, alcohol, or other drugs during pregnancy greatly increases the risk of miscarriage, premature birth, and child abnormalities.*

The greatest danger of cocaine use is an overdose. Excessive doses have a strong effect on the respiratory center of the brain, at first stimulating it and then depressing it, to the point where breathing may stop. Cocaine can also create major, even fatal, heart irregularities or brain seizures that bring breathing or heart functioning to a sudden stop (Doweiko, 2006). In addition, pregnant women who use cocaine run the risk of having a miscarriage and of having children with abnormalities in immune functioning, attention and learning, thyroid size, and dopamine and serotonin activity in the brain (Grilly, 2006; Delaney-Black et al., 2004; Ness et al., 1999).

Amphetamines

The **amphetamines** are stimulant drugs that are manufactured in the laboratory. Some common examples are amphetamine (Benzedrine), dextroamphetamine (Dexedrine), and methamphetamine (Methedrine). **Methamphetamine**, in particular, has had a surge in popularity in recent years. First produced in the 1930s to help treat asthma, these drugs soon became popular among people trying to lose weight; athletes seeking an extra burst of energy; soldiers, truck drivers, and pilots trying to stay awake; and students studying for exams through the night. Physicians now know the drugs are far too dangerous to be used so casually (Liu et al., 2002), and they prescribe them much less freely.

Amphetamines are most often taken in pill or capsule form, although some people inject the drugs intravenously for a quicker, more powerful effect. Others take the drugs in such forms as "ice" and "crank," counterparts of free-base cocaine and crack, respectively. Like cocaine, amphetamines increase energy and alertness and reduce appetite when taken in small doses; produce a rush, intoxication, and psychosis in high doses; and cause an emotional letdown as they leave the body. Also like cocaine, amphetamines stimulate the central nervous system by increasing the release of the neurotransmitters dopamine, norepinephrine, and serotonin throughout the brain, although the actions of amphetamines differ somewhat from those of cocaine (Doweiko, 2006, 1999).

Tolerance to amphetamines builds very quickly, so users are at great risk of becoming dependent (Acosta et al., 2005; Liu et al., 2002). People who start using the drug to reduce their appetite and weight, for example, may soon find they are as hungry as ever and increase their dose in response. Athletes who

Methamphetamine dependence: spreading the word *This powerful ad shows the degenerative effects of methamphetamine addiction on a woman over a four-year period—from age 36 in the top photo to age 40 in the bottom one.*

[BOX 12-2]

Tobacco, Nicotine, and Addiction

Almost one-quarter of all Americans over the age of 12, around 70 million people, regularly smoke tobacco (Oslin, 2006). Surveys also suggest that nearly 30 percent of all high school seniors have smoked within the past month, more than half of them on a regular basis (Johnston et al., 2005). At the same time, 430,000 persons in the United States die each year as a result of smoking (Ruedrich et al., 2003). Smoking is directly tied to high blood pressure, coronary heart disease, lung disease, cancer, strokes, and other deadly medical problems (Hymowitz, 2005; De Laune & Schmitz, 2004; NCHS, 2002). Nonsmokers who inhale cigarette smoke from their environment have a higher risk of lung cancer and other diseases (Report of the Surgeon General, 1987). And pregnant women who smoke are more likely than nonsmokers to deliver premature and underweight babies (Hasman & Holm, 2004; NCHS, 2002).

Research suggests that smoking may actually increase stress levels (Parrott, 2000, 1999), and most smokers know that smoking is unhealthy, so why do they continue to smoke? Because *nicotine,* the active substance in tobacco and a stimulant of the central nervous system, is as addictive as heroin, perhaps even more so (Report of the Surgeon General, 1988). Indeed, the World Health Organization estimates that 1.1 billion people worldwide are addicted to nicotine (Hasman & Holm, 2004). Regular smokers develop a tolerance for nicotine and must smoke more and more in order to achieve the same results (Hymowitz, 2005). When they try to stop smoking, they experience withdrawal symptoms—irritability, increased appetite, sleep disturbances, slower metabolism, cognitive difficulties, and cravings to smoke (Dodgen, 2005; APA, 2000). Nicotine acts on the same neurotransmitters and reward center in the brain as amphetamines and cocaine (Grilly, 2006; McGehee et al., 1995). Inhaling a puff of cigarette smoke delivers a dose of nicotine to the brain faster than it could be delivered by injection into the bloodstream.

The declining acceptability of smoking in our society has created a market for products and techniques to help people kick the habit. Most of these methods do not work very well. Self-help kits, commercial programs, and support groups are of limited help. Smokers who do quit permanently tend to be successful only after several failed attempts (Spanier et al., 1996).

One fairly successful behavioral treatment for nicotine addiction is *aversion therapy.* In one version of this approach, known as *rapid smoking,* the smoker sits in a closed room and puffs quickly on a cigarette, as often as once every six seconds, until he or she begins to feel ill and cannot take another puff. The feelings of illness become associated with smoking, and the smoker develops an aversion to cigarettes (Spiegler & Guevremont, 2003).

Several biological treatments have also been developed. A common one is the use of *nicotine gum,* which contains a high level of nicotine that is released as the smoker chews. Theoretically, people who obtain nicotine by chewing will no longer feel a need to smoke. A similar approach is the *nicotine patch,* which is attached to the skin like a Band-Aid. Its nicotine is absorbed through the skin throughout the day, supposedly easing withdrawal and reducing the smoker's need for nicotine. Studies find that both nicotine gum and the nicotine patch help people to abstain from smoking (Grilly, 2006; O'Brien & McKay, 2002; Shiffman et al., 2002). Combining the two techniques has also shown promise. *Nicotine nasal spray,* a relatively new biological approach, delivers nicotine much more rapidly than other methods. It can be used several times an hour, whenever the urge to smoke arises. Finally, the antidepressant drug *bupropion* (brand names Zyban and Wellbutrin) has demonstrated some success as a treatment for cigarette smoking (Watts et al., 2002).

The more one smokes, the harder it is to quit. On the positive side, however, former smokers' risk of disease and death decreases steadily the longer they continue to avoid smoking (Goldstein, 1994; Jaffe, 1985). This assurance may be a powerful motivator for many smokers, and, in fact, around 46 percent of regular smokers want to stop and are eventually able to stop permanently (NSDUH, 2005). In the meantime, more than 1,000 people die of smoking-related diseases each day.

Greg Baker/AP Photo

Genetics of modeling? *A man smokes a cigarette while reading to his daughter under an overpass in Beijing, China. The tendency to smoke tobacco and become dependent on nicotine often runs in families. Researchers have found that both genetics and environment play key roles in such family trends (Rende et al., 2005).*

>>LOOKING AROUND
The Methamphetamine Boom

In a survey of 500 law enforcement agencies, 58 percent said that methamphetamine is the leading drug that they battle today. Nineteen percent pointed instead to cocaine, 17 percent to marijuana, and 3 percent to heroin. «

More than 12 million Americans have tried methamphetamine (5 percent of the population above 12 years of age), and 1.5 million are regular users. «

Methamphetamine makes users feel hyper-sexual and uninhibited. In Los Angeles one-third of all men who tested positive for HIV last year reported using this drug. «

Increases in crimes over the past four years linked to methamphetamine use: *domestic violence* (increase of 62%), *assault* (53%), and *robbery* (70%). «

(Jefferson, 2005)

use amphetamines to increase their energy may also find before long that larger and larger amounts of the drug are needed. So-called speed freaks, who pop pills all day for days at a time, have built a tolerance so high that they now take as much as 200 times their initial amphetamine dose. When people who depend on the drug stop taking it, they plunge into a deep depression and extended sleep identical to the withdrawal from cocaine. Less than 0.5 percent of the population display amphetamine abuse or dependence each year (NSDUH, 2005). Around 1.5 to 2 percent become dependent on amphetamines at some point in their lives (APA, 2000; Anthony et al., 1995).

Caffeine

Caffeine is the world's most widely used stimulant. Around 80 percent of the world's population consumes it daily (Rogers, 2005). Most of this caffeine is taken in the form of coffee (from the coffee bean); the rest is consumed in tea (from the tea leaf), cola (from the kola nut), chocolate (from the cocoa bean), and numerous prescription and over-the-counter medications, such as Excedrin (Nehlig, 2004).

Around 99 percent of ingested caffeine is absorbed by the body and reaches its peak concentration within an hour. It acts as a stimulant of the central nervous system, again producing a release of the neurotransmitters dopamine, serotonin, and norepinephrine in the brain (Cauli & Morelli, 2005). Thus it increases arousal and motor activity and reduces fatigue. It can also disrupt mood, fine motor movement, and reaction time and may interfere with sleep (Judelson et al., 2005; Nehlig, 2004; Thompson & Keene, 2004). Finally, it increases the rate of breathing and gastric acid secretions in the stomach (Benowitz, 1990; Levitt, 1975).

More than two to three cups of brewed coffee (250 milligrams of caffeine) can produce caffeine intoxication, which may include such symptoms as restlessness, nervousness, anxiety, stomach disturbances, twitching, and increased heart rate (Paton & Beer, 2001; APA, 2000). Grand mal seizures and fatal respiratory failure or circulatory failure can occur at doses greater than 10 grams of caffeine (about 100 cups of coffee).

Many people who suddenly stop or cut back on their usual intake of caffeine experience withdrawal symptoms—even some individuals whose regular consumption is low (two and a half cups of coffee daily or seven cans of cola). One study had adult subjects consume their usual caffeine-filled drinks and foods for two days, then abstain from all caffeine-containing foods for two days while taking placebo pills that they thought contained caffeine, and then abstain from such foods for two days while taking actual caffeine pills (Silverman et al., 1992). More subjects experienced headaches (52 percent), depression (11 percent), anxiety (8 percent), and fatigue (8 percent) during the two-day placebo period than during the caffeine periods. In addition, subjects reported using more unauthorized medications (13 percent) and performed experimental tasks more slowly during the placebo period than during the caffeine periods.

Investigators often assess caffeine's impact by measuring coffee consumption, yet coffee also contains other chemicals that may be dangerous to one's health. Thus, although some studies hint at links between caffeine and cancer (particularly pancreatic cancer), the evidence is not conclusive. Similarly, studies demonstrating correlations between high doses of caffeine and heart rhythm irregularities (arrhythmias) or high cholesterol levels are not fully reliable (Nehlig, 2004; Hirsch et al., 1989; Rosmarin, 1989). Caffeine does, however, appear to cause at least a slight increase in blood pressure over time in regular users and a larger but short-lived increase during the first few days of consumption by new users (Thompson & Keene, 2004; Lane, 1999). As public awareness of these possible health risks has increased, caffeine consumption has declined over the past few decades, although some evidence suggests that it may currently be on the rise once again (CRI, 2001; Grimm, 2001; Chou, 1992).

"No thanks, I'm fine."

Hallucinogens, Cannabis, and Combinations of Substances

Other kinds of substances may also cause problems for their users and for society. *Hallucinogens* produce delusions, hallucinations, and other sensory changes. *Cannabis substances* produce sensory changes, but they also have depressant and stimulant effects, and so they are considered apart from hallucinogens in DSM-IV-TR. And many individuals take *combinations of substances.*

Hallucinogens

Hallucinogens are substances that cause powerful changes in sensory perception, from strengthening a person's normal perceptions to inducing illusions and hallucinations. They produce sensations so out of the ordinary that they are sometimes called "trips." The trips may be exciting or frightening, depending on how a person's mind interacts with the drugs. Also called **psychedelic drugs,** the hallucinogens include LSD, mescaline, psilocybin, and MDMA (Ecstasy) (see Box 12-3 on the next page). Many of these substances come from plants or animals; others are laboratory-produced.

LSD (lysergic acid diethylamide), one of the most famous and most powerful hallucinogens, was derived by the Swiss chemist Albert Hoffman in 1938 from a group of naturally occurring drugs called *ergot alkaloids.* During the 1960s, a decade of social rebellion and experimentation, millions of persons turned to the drug as a way of expanding their experience. Within two hours of being swallowed, LSD brings on a state of *hallucinogen intoxication,* sometimes called *hallucinosis,* marked by a general strengthening of perceptions, particularly visual perceptions, along with psychological changes and physical symptoms. People may focus on small details—the pores of the skin, for example, or individual blades of grass. Colors may seem enhanced or take on a shade of purple. Illusions may be experienced in which objects seem distorted and may appear to move, breathe, or change shape. A person under the influence of LSD may also hallucinate—seeing people, objects, or forms that are not actually present.

Hallucinosis may also cause one to hear sounds more clearly, feel tingling or numbness in the limbs, or confuse the sensations of hot and cold. Some people have been badly burned after touching flames that felt cool to them under the influence of LSD. The drug may also cause different senses to cross, an effect called *synesthesia.* Colors, for example, may be "heard" or "felt."

LSD can also induce strong emotions, from joy to anxiety or depression. The perception of time may slow dramatically. Long-forgotten thoughts and feelings may resurface. Physical symptoms can include sweating, palpitations, blurred vision, tremors, and poor coordination. All these effects take place while the user is fully awake and alert, and they wear off in about six hours.

It seems that LSD produces these symptoms primarily by binding to some of the neurons that normally receive the neurotransmitter *serotonin,* changing the neurotransmitter's activity at those sites (Appel, West, & Buggy, 2004; Jacobs, 1994, 1984). These neurons ordinarily help the brain send visual information and control emotions (as we observed in Chapter 8); thus LSD's activity there produces various visual and emotional symptoms.

More than 14 percent of all persons in the United States have used LSD or another hallucinogen at some point in their lives (NSDUH, 2005). Around 1.6 percent have used such drugs within the past year. Although people do not usually develop tolerance to LSD or have withdrawal symptoms when they stop taking it, the drug poses dangers for both one-time and long-term users. It is so powerful that any dose, no matter how small, is likely to produce enormous perceptual, emotional, and behavioral reactions. Sometimes the reactions are extremely unpleasant—an experience called a "bad trip." Reports of LSD users who injure themselves or others usually involve a reaction of this kind:

Bettmann/Corbis

Early LSD research *In the 1950s, researchers came to believe that LSD produced a "model psychosis" and that studying its effects might offer insights into schizophrenia. Not yet recognizing how powerful and dangerous this drug can be, however, early investigators sometimes conducted LSD research in a naïve and casual manner. This 1955 photo shows one researcher administering LSD to another in Emory University's Pharmacological Department.*

•**CAFFEINE**•The world's most widely used stimulant, most often consumed in coffee.

•**HALLUCINOGEN**•A substance that causes powerful changes primarily in sensory perception, including strengthening perceptions and producing illusions and hallucinations. Also called *psychedelic drug.*

•**LSD (LYSERGIC ACID DIETHYLAMIDE)**•A hallucinogenic drug derived from ergot alkaloids.

[BOX **12-3**]

X Marks the (Wrong) Spot

You probably know of the drug MDMA (3,4-methylenedioxy-methamphetamine) by its common street name, *Ecstasy*. It is also known as X, Adam, hug, beans, and love drug. This laboratory-produced drug is technically a *stimulant,* similar to amphetamines, but it also produces hallucinogenic effects and so is often considered a *hallucinogenic* drug. MDMA was developed as far back as 1910, but only in the past two decades has it gained life as a "club drug"—the drug of choice for all-night techno-dance parties known as "raves." Today, in the United States alone, consumers collectively take hundreds of thousands of doses of MDMA weekly (McDowell, 2005; Holland, 2001).

What is Ecstasy's allure? As a stimulant and hallucinogen, it helps to raise the mood of many partygoers and provides them with an energy boost that enables them to keep dancing and partying. However, it also turns out to be a dangerous drug, particularly when taken repeatedly, and so in 1985 the federal government banned its use (Murray, 2001). However, as with many drugs, this taboo status seemed only to make it more attractive to many consumers. Altogether, 8 million Americans have tried it at least once in their lifetimes (NHSDA, 2002). Around 4 percent of all high school seniors have used it within the past year, and more than 1.2 percent of seniors have used it within the past month (Johnston et al., 2005). Use of the drug is even more widespread among 18-to-25-year-olds (NSDUH, 2005).

WHAT ARE THE DANGERS OF USING ECSTASY?

The mood and energy lift produced by MDMA comes at a high price. The problems that the drug may cause include the following:

- ◆ Immediate psychological problems such as confusion, depression, sleep difficulties, severe anxiety, and paranoid thinking. These symptoms may also continue for weeks after ingestion of MDMA (NIDA, 2002).
- ◆ Significant impairment of memory and other cognitive skills (Reneman et al., 2000).

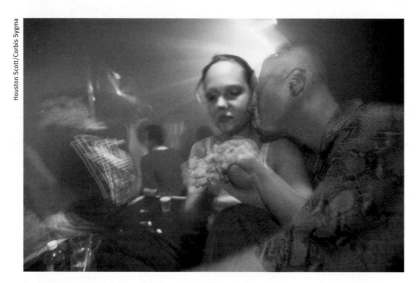

Feeling the effects *Shortly after taking MDMA, this couple manifests a shift in mood, energy, and behavior. Although this drug can feel pleasurable and energizing, often it produces undesired immediate effects, including confusion, depression, anxiety, sleep difficulties, and paranoid thinking.*

A 21-year-old woman was admitted to the hospital along with her lover. He had had a number of LSD experiences and had convinced her to take it to make her less constrained sexually. About half an hour after ingestion of approximately 200 microgm., she noticed that the bricks in the wall began to go in and out and that light affected her strangely. She became frightened when she realized that she was unable to distinguish her body from the chair she was sitting on or from her lover's body. Her fear became more marked after she thought that she would not get back into herself. At the time of admission she was hyperactive and laughed inappropriately. Her stream of talk was illogical and affect labile. Two days later, this reaction had ceased.

(Frosch, Robbins, & Stern, 1965)

>>LOOKING BACK
Linguistic Roots
The term *hallucinogen* comes from the Latin for "wander in mind." **‹‹**

Another danger is the long-term effect that LSD may have. Some users eventually develop psychosis or a mood or anxiety disorder. About one-quarter of users have *flashbacks*—a recurrence of the sensory and emotional changes after the LSD has left

◆ Physical symptoms such as muscle tension, nausea, blurred vision, faintness, and chills or sweating (NIDA, 2002). MDMA also causes many people to clench and grind their teeth for hours at a time (Milosevic et al., 1999; Redfearn, Agrawal, & Mair, 1998).

◆ Increases in heart rate and blood pressure, which place people with heart disease at special risk (NIDA, 2002).

◆ Reduced sweat production. At a hot, crowded dance party, taking Ecstasy can even cause heat stroke, or *hyperthermia* (Pedersen & Blessing, 2001). Users generally try to remedy this problem by drinking lots of water, but since the body cannot sweat under the drug's influence, the excess fluid intake can result in an equally perilous condition known as *hyponatremia,* or "water intoxication" (Braback & Humble, 2001; Holmes et al., 1999).

◆ Potential liver damage (De Carlis et al., 2001; Garbino et al., 2001). This may happen when users take MDMA in combination with other drugs that are broken down by the same liver enzyme, such as the cheaper compound *DXM,* which is commonly mixed in with Ecstasy by pushers (Malberg & Bonson, 2001).

HOW DOES MDMA OPERATE IN THE BRAIN?

MDMA works by causing the neurotransmitters *serotonin* and (to a lesser extent) *dopamine* to be released all at once throughout the brain, at first increasing and then depleting a person's overall supply of the neurotransmitters (Malberg & Bonson, 2001). MDMA also interferes with the body's ability to produce new supplies of serotonin, reducing the availability of the neurotransmitter still further. With chronic use, the brain eventually produces less and less serotonin and shuts down the neuron receptors to which it normally binds (Baggot & Mendelson, 2001).

Ecstasy's impact on these neurotransmitters accounts for its various psychological effects—and associated problems. High levels of serotonin, such as those produced after one first ingests MDMA, produce feelings of well-being, sociability, and even euphoria. Remember, though, that MDMA also increases levels of dopamine. As we shall observe in Chapter 14, very high levels of that neurotransmitter can produce paranoid—even psychotic—thinking (Jansen, 2001).

Conversely, abnormally low serotonin levels are associated with depression and anxiety (Jansen, 2001). This is why "coming down" off a dose of Ecstasy often produces those psychological symptoms (Malberg & Bonson, 2001). Moreover, because repeated use of Ecstasy leads to long-term serotonin deficits, the depression and anxiety may be long-lasting. Finally, serotonin is linked to our ability to concentrate; thus the repeated use of Ecstasy may produce problems in memory and learning (Heffernan et al., 2001; Rodgers, 2000).

END OF THE HONEYMOON?

The dangers of MDMA do not yet seem to outweigh its pleasures in the minds of some individuals. In fact, use of the drug is now expanding to many social settings beyond raves, dance clubs, and college scenes (NIDA, 2002). Clearly, the honeymoon for this drug is not yet over. MDMA emergency room visits are on the rise, as is the number of deaths caused by the drug, for reasons ranging from kidney failure (the result of heat stroke) to liver failure to a heart attack. Like other dangerous drugs over the years, it will eventually lose its popularity, but obviously not before it has taken a considerable toll.

---

the body (Doweiko, 2006; APA, 2000). Flashbacks may occur days or even months after the last LSD experience. Although they typically become less severe and disappear within several months, some people report flashbacks a year or more after taking the drug.

Cannabis

Cannabis sativa, the hemp plant, grows in warm climates throughout the world. The drugs produced from varieties of hemp are, as a group, called **cannabis.** The most powerful of them is *hashish;* the weaker ones include the best-known form of cannabis, **marijuana,** a mixture derived from the buds, crushed leaves, and flowering tops of hemp plants. Each of these drugs is found in various strengths because the potency of a cannabis drug is greatly affected by the climate in which the plant is grown, the way it was prepared, and the manner and duration of its storage. Of the several hundred active chemicals in cannabis, **tetrahydrocannabinol (THC)** appears to be the one most responsible for its effects. The greater the THC content, the more powerful the cannabis: hashish contains a large portion, while marijuana's is small.

•**CANNABIS DRUGS**•Drugs produced from the varieties of the hemp plant *Cannabis sativa*. They cause a mixture of hallucinogenic, depressant, and stimulant effects.

•**MARIJUANA**•One of the cannabis drugs, derived from buds, leaves, and flowering tops of the hemp plant *Cannabis sativa*.

•**TETRAHYDROCANNABINOL (THC)**•The main active ingredient of cannabis substances.

The source of marijuana *Marijuana is made from the leaves of the hemp plant,* Cannabis sativa. *The plant is an annual herb, reaches a height of between 3 and 15 feet, and is grown in a wide range of altitudes, climates, and soils.*

When smoked, cannabis produces a mixture of hallucinogenic, depressant, and stimulant effects. At low doses, the smoker typically has feelings of joy and relaxation and may become either quiet or talkative. Some smokers, however, become anxious, suspicious, or irritated, especially if they have been in a bad mood or are smoking in an upsetting environment. Many smokers report sharpened perceptions and fascination with the intensified sounds and sights around them. Time seems to slow down, and distances and sizes seem greater than they actually are. This overall "high" is technically called *cannabis intoxication*. Physical changes include reddening of the eyes, fast heartbeat, increases in blood pressure and appetite, dryness in the mouth, and dizziness. Some people become drowsy and may fall asleep.

In high doses, cannabis produces odd visual experiences, changes in body image, and hallucinations (McDowell, 2005). Smokers may become confused or impulsive. Some worry that other people are trying to hurt them. Most of the effects of cannabis last three to six hours. The changes in mood, however, may continue longer (Chait, Fishman, & Schuster, 1985).

MARIJUANA ABUSE AND DEPENDENCE Until the early 1970s, the use of marijuana, the weak form of cannabis, rarely led to a pattern of abuse or dependence. Today, however, many people, including large numbers of high school students, are caught in a pattern of marijuana abuse, getting high on marijuana regularly and finding their social and occupational or academic lives greatly affected. Many regular users also become physically dependent on marijuana. They develop a tolerance for it and may experience flu-like symptoms, restlessness, and irritability when they stop smoking (Chen et al., 2005; Smith, 2002; Kouri & Pope, 2000). Around 1.9 percent of all persons in the United States have displayed marijuana abuse or dependence in the past year; between 4 and 5 percent fall into one of these patterns at some point in their lives (NSDUH, 2005; APA, 2000; Anthony et al., 1995).

Why have patterns of marijuana abuse and dependence increased in the last three decades? Mainly because the drug has changed (Doweiko, 2006). The marijuana widely available in the United States today is at least four times more powerful than that used in the early 1970s (see Figure 12-3). The THC content of today's marijuana is, on average, 8 percent, compared to 2 percent in the late 1960s (APA, 2000). Marijuana is now grown in places with a hot, dry climate, which increases the THC content.

IS MARIJUANA DANGEROUS? As the strength and use of marijuana have increased, researchers have discovered that smoking it may pose certain dangers. It occasionally causes panic reactions similar to the ones caused by hallucinogens, and some smokers may fear they are losing their minds (Doweiko, 2006; APA, 2000). Typically such reactions end in three to six hours, along with marijuana's other effects.

Because marijuana can interfere with the performance of complex sensorimotor tasks and with cognitive functioning, it has caused many automobile accidents (Kauert & Iwersen-Bergmann, 2004). Furthermore, people on a marijuana high often fail to remember information, especially anything that has been recently learned, no matter how hard they try to concentrate; thus heavy marijuana smokers are at a serious disadvantage at school or work (Lundqvist, 2005; Ashton, 2001).

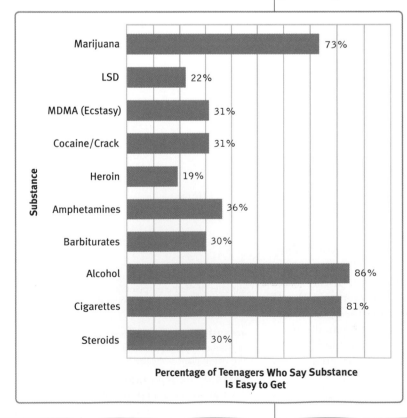

FIGURE **12-3 How easy is it for teenagers to acquire substances?** *According to the vast majority of surveyed tenth graders, it is very easy in the case of cigarettes, alcohol, and marijuana. In addition, around one-third of the students say it is easy to get Ecstasy, amphetamines, steroids, and barbiturates (Johnston et al., 2005).*

A recent study compared blood flow in the brain arteries of chronic marijuana users and nonusers (Herning et al., 2005). After one month of abstinence from smoking marijuana, chronic users continued to display higher blood flow than nonusers. Though still higher than normal, the blood flow of light marijuana users (fewer than 16 smokes per week) and of moderate users (fewer than 70 smokes per week) did improve somewhat over the course of the abstinence month. The blood flow of heavy users, however, showed no improvement. This lingering effect may help explain the memory and thinking problems of chronic heavy users of marijuana.

There are indications that regular marijuana smoking may also lead to long-term health problems (Deplanque, 2005). It may, for example, contribute to lung disease. Studies show that marijuana smoking reduces the ability to expel air from the lungs (Grilly, 2002) even more than tobacco smoking does (NIDA, 2002; Nahas et al., 1999). In addition, marijuana smoke contains more tar and benzopyrene than tobacco smoke. Both of these substances have been linked to cancer. Another concern is the effect of regular marijuana smoking on human reproduction. Studies since the late 1970s have discovered lower sperm counts in men who are chronic smokers of marijuana, and abnormal ovulation has been found in female smokers (Nahas et al., 1999).

Efforts to educate the public about the growing dangers of repeated marijuana use appeared to have paid off throughout the 1980s. The percentage of high school seniors who smoked the substance on a daily basis decreased from 11 percent in 1978 to 2 percent in 1992 (Johnston et al., 1993). Furthermore, in 1992 about 77 percent of high school seniors believed that regular marijuana smoking poses a serious health risk, a much higher percentage than that in earlier years. However, marijuana use among the young jumped up again during the 1990s. Today nearly 6 percent of high school seniors smoke marijuana daily, and fewer than 55 percent believe that regular use can be harmful (Johnston et al., 2005, 2002) (see Figure 12-4).

>>**LOOKING AROUND**

Popular Potsicles

Always on the lookout for new products and profits, a number of manufacturers are now producing marijuana-flavored lollipops with such names as Purple Haze, Acapulco Gold, Rasta, and Kronic Kandy. The candies, which are appearing on the shelves of convenience stores around the country, are legal because they are made with hemp oil, a common ingredient in health food. Many drug experts and government officials have expressed outrage and deep concern about the message that such products give, especially to children (Gross, 2005). **<<**

FIGURE **12-4** **Teenagers and substance use** *The overall percentage of high school seniors who admitted to using substances illicitly at least once within the previous 30 days rose in the 1970s, declined in the 1980s, rose again in the early 1990s, and has been declining slightly since 1997 (Johnston et al., 2005). In addition to the drugs shown in this figure, other drugs used by high school seniors within the past month include MDMA, or Ecstasy (1.2 percent); inhalants (1.5 percent); methamphetamine (1.4 percent); and steroids (1.6 percent).*

>>LOOKING AROUND

Pot Potency

The tetrahydrocannabinol (THC) content of cannabis is 6 to 8 percent in most countries, a potency that has remained steady over the past several years. **<<**

- -

The major exception is the Netherlands, where THC content is 16 percent, largely because of supplies of intensively produced home-grown cannabis. **<<**

- -

(European Monitoring Center for Drugs and Drug Addictions, 2004)

CANNABIS AND SOCIETY: A ROCKY RELATIONSHIP For centuries cannabis played a respected role in medicine. It was recommended as a surgical anesthetic by Chinese physicians 2,000 years ago and was used in other lands to treat cholera, malaria, coughs, insomnia, and rheumatism. When cannabis entered the United States in the early twentieth century, mainly in the form of marijuana, it was likewise used for various medical purposes. Soon, however, more effective medicines replaced it, and the favorable view of cannabis began to change. Marijuana began to be used as a recreational drug, and its illegal distribution became a law enforcement problem. Authorities assumed it was highly dangerous and outlawed the "killer weed."

But marijuana didn't go away. During the 1960s, a time of disillusionment, protest, and self-exploration, young people discovered the pleasures of getting high from smoking marijuana. By the end of the 1970s, 16 million people reported using it at least once, and 11 percent of the population were recent users.

In the 1980s researchers developed precise techniques for measuring THC and for extracting pure THC from cannabis; they also developed laboratory forms of THC. These inventions opened the door to new medical applications for cannabis (Mack & Joy, 2001; Watson et al., 2000), such as its use in treating glaucoma, a severe eye disease. Cannabis was also found to help patients with chronic pain or asthma, to reduce the nausea and vomiting of cancer patients in chemotherapy, and to improve the appetites of AIDS patients and so combat weight loss in people with that disorder.

In light of these findings, several interest groups campaigned during the late 1980s for the *medical legalization* of marijuana, which operates on the brain and body more quickly than the THC capsules developed in the laboratory. In 1992, however, the Drug Enforcement Administration opposed this measure and the Food and Drug Administration stopped reviewing requests for the "compassionate use" of marijuana (Karel, 1992). They held that prescriptions for pure THC served all needed medical functions.

Advocates of the medical use of marijuana challenged the government position again during the elections of 1996. Voter referendums, which have the force of law, were passed in California and Arizona, giving physicians the right to prescribe marijuana for "seriously ill" or "terminally ill" patients. Voters in nine other states followed suit in subsequent years. But the federal government responded by threatening to revoke the prescription-writing privilege of any physician who prescribed marijuana and even to prosecute such physicians. Angered by the government's position on this complex issue, many more physicians openly joined the battle, and in 1997 the *New England Journal of Medicine,* one of the world's most prestigious medical publications, published an editorial favoring the medical use of marijuana. Unfazed, the federal government continued to fight and punish the production and distribution of marijuana for medical purposes. Finally, in 2005, the United States Supreme Court ruled 6 to 3 that medically ill marijuana smokers and those who help them grow or obtain marijuana can be prosecuted, even if

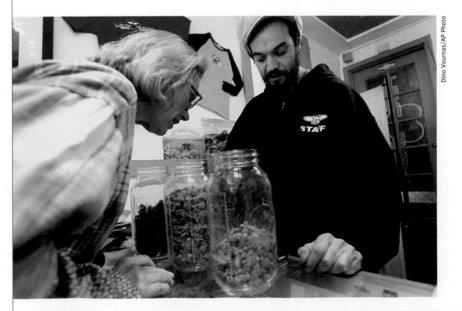

Medicinal use *Prior to the 2005 Supreme Court ruling that even medically ill marijuana smokers can be prosecuted for use of the substance, a number of medicinal cannabis shops were opening throughout the United States. Here, for example, a medical marijuana patient (left), assisted by a volunteer, smells the different offerings at the Love Shack medicinal cannabis shop in San Francisco. It is not yet clear how the 2005 Supreme Court ruling will affect medical users of marijuana or shops such as this.*

Dino Vournas/AP Photo

their physicians prescribed it and even if they live in states where medical marijuana use is legal (Henderson, 2005). Although this ruling was considered a severe blow to the medical marijuana cause, proponents of the medical use of marijuana appear to be fighting on; many are following the advice of Supreme Court Justice John Paul Stevens, who, writing for the majority, suggested that users of medical marijuana look to Congress to overturn the laws against medical marijuana and meanwhile pursuade lawmakers to restrain the Justice Department from spending money to prosecute medical users in the states that permit it.

The Canadian government has taken a different tack. In 2003 Canada's health minister announced an interim policy allowing eligible medical sufferers to buy marijuana from the government until that country's *medical marijuana research program* has reached a clear conclusion regarding this complex issue. Some 900 Canadian citizens are now authorized to use medical marijuana. Moreover, in 2005, Health Canada, the country's health care regulator, announced plans to sell medical marijuana in select pharmacies beginning in 2006, making Canada the second country in the world, after the Netherlands, to do so.

Combinations of Substances

Because people often take more than one drug at a time, a pattern called *polysubstance use,* researchers have studied the ways in which drugs interact with one another. Two important discoveries have emerged from this work: the phenomena of *cross-tolerance* and *synergistic effects.*

Sometimes two or more drugs are so similar in their actions on the brain and the body that as people build a tolerance for one drug, they are simultaneously developing a tolerance for the other, even if they have never taken the latter. Correspondingly, users who display such **cross-tolerance** can reduce the symptoms of withdrawal from one drug by taking the other. Alcohol and antianxiety drugs are cross-tolerant, for example, so it is sometimes possible to reduce the alcohol withdrawal reaction of delirium tremens by administering benzodiazepines, along with vitamins and electrolytes (Doweiko, 2006; Franz et al., 2001).

When different drugs are in the body at the same time, they may multiply, or potentiate, each other's effects. The combined impact, called a **synergistic effect,** is often greater than the sum of the effects of each drug taken alone: a small dose of one drug mixed with a small dose of another can produce an enormous change in body chemistry (Cichewicz, 2004).

One kind of synergistic effect occurs when two or more drugs have *similar actions.* For instance, alcohol, benzodiazepines, barbiturates, and opioids—all depressants—may severely depress the central nervous system when mixed (Miller & Gold, 1990). Combining them, even in small doses, can lead to extreme intoxication, coma, and even death (Nishino et al., 1995). A young man may have just a few alcoholic drinks at a party, for

•CROSS-TOLERANCE• Tolerance for a substance one has not taken before as a result of using another substance similar to it.

•SYNERGISTIC EFFECT• In pharmacology, an increase of effects that occurs when more than one substance is acting on the body at the same time.

Continuing problem *A number of popular performers have been victims of polysubstance abuse. The 1982 death of John Belushi (left), comedic actor and founding member of the Blues Brothers, was attributed to a mixture of cocaine and heroin. Similarly, the 2004 death of popular rap musician Russell Jones (right), known to fans as Ol' Dirty Bastard, was attributed to a lethal mixture of cocaine and pain medication.*

•POLYSUBSTANCE-RELATED DISORDER•
A long-term pattern of maladaptive behavior centered on abuse of or dependence on a combination of drugs.

example, and shortly afterward take a moderate dose of barbiturates to help him fall asleep. He believes he has acted with restraint and good judgment—yet he may never wake up.

A different kind of synergistic effect results when drugs have *opposite,* or *antagonistic, actions.* Stimulant drugs, for example, interfere with the liver's usual disposal of barbiturates and alcohol. Thus people who combine barbiturates or alcohol with cocaine or amphetamines may build up toxic, even lethal, levels of the depressant drugs in their systems. Students who take amphetamines to help them study late into the night and then take barbiturates to help them fall asleep are unknowingly placing themselves in serious danger.

Each year tens of thousands of people are admitted to hospitals with a multiple-drug emergency, and several thousand of them die (DAWN, 2002). Sometimes the cause is carelessness or ignorance. Often, however, people use multiple drugs precisely because they enjoy the synergistic effects. In fact, **polysubstance-related disorders** are becoming as common as individual substance-related disorders in the United States, Canada, and Europe (Rosenthal & Levounis, 2005; Wu et al., 2005; Schuckit et al., 2001). As many as 90 percent of persons who use one illegal drug are also using another to some extent. A look-in on a group therapy session for users of crack reveals that several of the group members have used other substances in addition:

> *Therapist:* Okay. Now, can you give me a list of all the drugs you've used? Gary?
> *Gary:* Pot. Coke. Crack. Mescaline. Acid. Speed. Crystal meth. Smack. Base dust. Sometimes alcohol.
> *Dennis:* Alcohol. Pot. Coke. Mescaline. LSD. Amyl nitrate. Speed and Valium.
> *Davy:* Coke. Crack. Reefer. Alcohol. Acid. Mescaline. Mushrooms. Ecstasy. Speed. Smack.
> *Rich:* Alcohol. Pot. Ludes [Quaaludes]. Valium. Speed. Ups [amphetamines]. Downs [barbiturates]. Acid. Mescaline. Crack. Base. Dust. That's about it.
> *Carol:* Alcohol. Pot. Cocaine. Mescaline. Valium. Crack.
>
> *(Chatlos, 1987, pp. 30–31)*

Fans still mourn the deaths of many celebrities who have been the victims of polysubstance use. Elvis Presley's delicate balancing act of stimulants and depressants eventually killed him. Janis Joplin's mixtures of wine and heroin were ultimately fatal. And John Belushi's and Chris Farley's liking for the combined effect of cocaine and opioids ("speedballs") also ended in tragedy.

What Causes Substance-Related Disorders?

Clinical theorists have developed sociocultural, psychological, and biological explanations for why people abuse or become dependent on various substances. No single explanation, however, has gained broad support. Like so many other disorders, excessive and chronic drug use is increasingly viewed as the result of a combination of these factors.

The Sociocultural View

A number of sociocultural theorists propose that people are most likely to develop patterns of substance abuse or dependence when they live under stressful socioeconomic conditions. In fact, studies have found that regions with higher levels of unemployment have higher rates of alcoholism. Similarly, lower socioeconomic classes have substance-abuse rates that are higher than those of the other classes (Franklin & Markarian, 2005; Khan, Murray, & Barnes, 2002).

Other sociocultural theorists propose that substance abuse and dependence are more likely to appear in families and social environments where substance use is valued, or at least accepted. Researchers have, in fact, found that problem drinking is more common

>>PSYCH•LISTINGS

Celebrities Who Have Died of Drug Overdose

Ol' Dirty Bastard, rapper, Wu-Tang Clan (polydrug, 2004) «

Shannon Hoon, rock singer, Blind Melon (cocaine, 1995) «

Ken Caminiti, baseball player (cocaine, 2004) «

Rick James, singer (cocaine, 2004) «

Glenn Quinn, actor (heroin, 2002) «

Chris Farley, comedian (polydrug, 1998) «

River Phoenix, actor (polydrug, 1993) «

Janis Joplin, singer (heroin, 1970) «

Sid Vicious, musician, Sex Pistols (heroin, 1979) «

Dee Dee Ramone, musician, The Ramones (heroin, 2002) «

Howie Epstein, musician, Heartbreakers (heroin, 2003) «

Jim Morrison, singer, The Doors (heroin, 1971) «

Elvis Presley, singer (polydrug, 1977) «

Jimi Hendrix, singer (barbiturates, 1970) «

John Belushi, comedian (polydrug, 1982) «

among teenagers whose parents and peers drink, as well as among teenagers whose family environments are stressful and unsupportive (Legrand et al., 2005; Lieb et al., 2002; Wills et al., 1996). Moreover, lower rates of alcohol abuse are found among Jews and Protestants, groups in which drinking is typically acceptable only as long as it remains within clear limits, whereas alcoholism rates are higher among the Irish and Eastern Europeans, who do not, on average, draw as clear a line (Ledoux et al., 2002; Vaillant & Milofsky, 1982).

The Psychodynamic View

Psychodynamic theorists believe that people who abuse substances have powerful *dependency* needs that can be traced to their early years (Stetter, 2000; Shedler & Block, 1990). They claim that when parents fail to satisfy a young child's need for nurturance, the child is likely to grow up depending excessively on others for help and comfort, trying to find the nurturance that was lacking during the early years. If this search for outside support includes experimentation with a drug, the person may well develop a dependent relationship with the substance.

Some psychodynamic theorists also believe that certain people respond to their early deprivations by developing a *substance abuse personality* that leaves them particularly prone to drug abuse. Personality inventories and patient interviews have in fact indicated that people who abuse or depend on drugs tend to be more dependent, antisocial, impulsive, novelty-seeking, and depressive than other people (Legrand et al., 2005; Coffey et al., 2003; Cox et al., 2001). These findings are correlational, however, and do not clarify whether such personality traits lead to drug use or whether drug use causes people to be dependent, impulsive, and the like.

In an effort to establish clearer causation, one longitudinal study measured the personality traits of a large group of nonalcoholic young men and then kept track of each man's development (Jones, 1971, 1968). Years later, the traits of the men who developed alcohol problems in middle age were compared with the traits of those who did not. The men who developed alcohol problems had been more impulsive as teenagers and continued to be so in middle age, a finding suggesting that impulsive men are indeed more prone to develop alcohol problems. Similarly, in one laboratory investigation, "impulsive" rats—those that generally had trouble delaying their rewards—were found to drink more alcohol when offered it than other rats (Poulos, Le, & Parker, 1995).

A major weakness of this line of argument is the wide range of personality traits that have been tied to substance abuse and dependence. In fact, different studies point to different "key" traits. Inasmuch as some people with a drug addiction appear to be dependent, others impulsive, and still others antisocial, researchers cannot presently conclude

Steven Rubin/The Image Works

Common substance, uncommon danger *A 13-year-old boy sniffs glue as he lies dazed near a garbage heap. In the United States, at least 6 percent of all people have tried to get high by inhaling the hydrocarbons found in common substances such as glue, gasoline, paint thinner, cleaners, and spray-can propellants (APA, 2000). Such behavior may lead to* inhalant abuse *or* dependence *and poses a number of serious medical dangers.*

that any one personality trait or group of traits stands out in substance-related disorders (Chassin et al., 2001; Rozin & Stoess, 1993).

The Behavioral and Cognitive Views

According to behaviorists, *operant conditioning* may play a key role in substance abuse (Higgins et al., 2004). They argue that the temporary reduction of tension or raising of spirits produced by a drug has a rewarding effect, thus increasing the likelihood that the user will seek this reaction again (Rutledge & Sher, 2001). Similarly, the rewarding effects of a substance may eventually lead users to try higher dosages or more powerful methods of ingestion (see Table 12-4). Cognitive theorists further argue that such rewards eventually produce an *expectancy* that substances will be rewarding, and this expectation helps motivate individuals to increase drug use at times of tension (Chassin et al., 2001).

In support of these views, studies have found that many subjects do in fact drink more alcohol or seek heroin when they feel tense (Ham et al., 2002; Cooper, 1994). In one study, as subjects worked on a difficult anagram task, a confederate planted by the researchers unfairly criticized and belittled them (Marlatt, Kosturn, & Lang, 1975). The subjects were then asked to participate in an "alcohol taste task," supposedly to compare and rate alcoholic beverages. The subjects who had been harassed drank more alcohol during the taste task than did the control subjects who had not been criticized. A third group of subjects were harassed while doing the anagrams but were given an opportunity to retaliate against their critics. These subjects drank relatively little during the tasting. Their retaliatory behavior had apparently reduced their tension and lessened their need for alcohol.

In a manner of speaking, the behavioral and cognitive theorists are arguing that many people take drugs to "medicate" themselves when they feel tense. If so, one would expect higher rates of drug abuse among people who suffer from anxiety, depression, or intense anger. In fact, substance abuse and dependence do appear to be fairly common among people with mood disorders (Grant et al., 2004; McDowell & Clodfelter, 2001).

Table 12-4

Methods of Taking Substances

Method	Route	Time to Reach Brain
Inhaling	Drug in vapor form is inhaled through mouth and lungs into circulatory system.	7 seconds
Snorting	Drug in powdered form is snorted into the nose. Some of the drug lands on the nasal mucous membranes, is absorbed by blood vessels, and enters the bloodstream.	4 minutes
Injection	Drug in liquid form directly enters the body through a needle. Injection may be intravenous or intramuscular (subcutaneous).	
	intravenous	20 seconds
	intramuscular	4 minutes
Oral ingestion	Drug in solid or liquid form passes through esophagus and stomach and finally to the small intestines. It is absorbed by blood vessels in the intestines.	30 minutes
Other routes	Drugs can be absorbed through areas that contain mucous membranes. Drugs can be placed under the tongue, inserted anally and vaginally, and administered as eyedrops.	Variable

Source: Landry, 1994, p. 24.

One study of 835 clinically depressed patients found that more than one-fourth abused drugs during episodes of depression (Hasin, Endicott, & Lewis, 1985). Similarly, higher-than-usual rates of drug abuse have been found among people with posttraumatic stress disorder, eating disorders, schizophrenia, antisocial personality disorder, histories of being abused, and other psychological problems (Doweiko, 2006; Aalto-Setala & Marttunen, 2003; Brown et al., 2003).

Of course, not all drug users find drugs pleasurable or reinforcing when they first take them. Many people report that they did not get high the first time they smoked marijuana, for example, and some opioid users were unaffected or sickened by their initial experiences with opioids. Moreover, even when drugs do initially produce pleasant feelings and rewards, a user's response to them tends to change over time. A number of people become anxious and depressed as they take more and more drugs (Roggla & Uhl, 1995; Vaillant, 1993). Why, then, do users keep on taking drugs?

Some theorists use Richard Solomon's *opponent-process theory* to answer this question. Solomon (1980) held that the brain is structured in such a way that pleasurable emotions, such as drug-induced euphoria, inevitably lead to opponent processes—negative aftereffects—that leave the person feeling worse than usual. People who continue to use pleasure-giving drugs inevitably develop opponent aftereffects, such as cravings for more of the drug, an increasing need for the drug, and withdrawal responses. According to Solomon, the opponent processes eventually dominate, and avoidance of the negative aftereffects replaces pursuit of pleasure as the primary factor in drug taking. Although a highly regarded theory, the opponent-process explanation has not received systematic research support.

Still other behaviorists have proposed that *classical conditioning* may play a role in substance abuse and dependence (Drobes, Saladin, & Tiffany, 2001). Objects present at the time drugs are taken may act as classically conditioned stimuli and come to produce some of the same pleasure brought on by the drugs themselves. Just the sight of a hypodermic needle or a regular supplier, for example, has been known to comfort people who abuse heroin or amphetamines and to relieve their withdrawal symptoms. In a similar manner, objects that are present during withdrawal distress may produce withdrawal-like symptoms. One man who had formerly been dependent on heroin experienced nausea and other withdrawal symptoms when he returned to the neighborhood where he had gone through withdrawal in the past—a reaction that led him to start taking heroin again (O'Brien et al., 1975). Although classical conditioning may in fact be at work in particular cases or aspects of drug abuse and dependence, it has not received widespread research support as a major factor in such patterns (Drobes et al., 2001).

The Biological View

In recent years researchers have come to suspect that drug misuse may have biological causes. Studies on genetic predisposition and specific biochemical processes have provided some support for these suspicions.

GENETIC PREDISPOSITION For years breeding experiments have been conducted to see whether certain animals are genetically predisposed to become dependent on drugs (Li, 2000; Kurtz et al., 1996). In several studies, for example, investigators have first identified animals that prefer alcohol to other beverages and then mated them to one another. Generally, the offspring of these animals have been found to also display an unusual preference for alcohol (Melo et al., 1996).

Similarly, some research with human twins has suggested that people may inherit a predisposition to abuse substances. One classic study found an alcohol abuse *concordance* rate of 54 percent in a group of identical twins; that is, if one identical twin abused alcohol, the other twin also abused alcohol in 54 percent of the cases. In contrast, a group of fraternal twins had a concordance rate of only 28 percent (Kaij, 1960). Other studies have found similar twin patterns (Legrand et al., 2005; Tsuang et al., 2001; Kendler et al., 1994, 1992). As we have observed, however, such findings do not rule out other interpretations (Walters, 2002). For one thing, the parenting received by two identical twins may be more similar than that received by two fraternal twins.

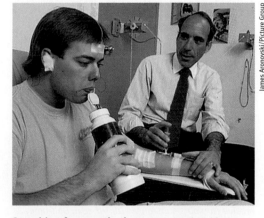

Searching for genetic clues *A research subject drinks various substances to help determine whether the effects of alcohol and causes of alcohol abuse are linked to genetic factors.*

A stronger indication that genetics may play a role in substance abuse and dependence comes from studies of alcoholism rates in people adopted shortly after birth (Walters, 2002; Cadoret et al., 1995; Goldstein, 1994). These studies have compared adoptees whose biological parents are dependent on alcohol with adoptees whose biological parents are not. By adulthood, the individuals whose biological parents are dependent on alcohol typically show higher rates of alcohol abuse than those with nonalcoholic biological parents.

Genetic linkage strategies and *molecular biology* techniques provide more direct evidence in support of a genetic explanation. One line of investigation has found an abnormal form of the so-called *dopamine-2 (D2) receptor gene* in a majority of subjects with alcohol dependence and half of subjects with cocaine dependence, but in less than 20 percent of nondependent subjects (Connor et al., 2002; Blum et al., 1996, 1990). Other studies have tied still other genes to substance-related disorders (Doweiko, 2006; Legrand et al., 2005).

BIOCHEMICAL FACTORS Over the past few decades, investigators have pieced together several biological explanations of drug tolerance and withdrawal symptoms (Kosten et al., 2005; Wise, 1996). According to one of the leading explanations, when a particular drug is ingested, it increases the activity of certain neurotransmitters whose normal purpose is to calm, reduce pain, lift mood, or increase alertness. When a person keeps on taking the drug, the brain apparently makes an adjustment and reduces its own production of the neurotransmitters. Because the drug is increasing neurotransmitter activity or efficiency, action by the brain is less necessary. As drug intake increases, the body's production of the neurotransmitters continues to decrease, leaving the person in need of more and more of the drug to achieve its effects. In this way, drug takers build tolerance for a drug, becoming more and more reliant on it rather than on their own biological processes to feel comfortable, happy, or alert. If they suddenly stop taking the drug, their supply of neurotransmitters will be low for a time, producing the symptoms of withdrawal. Withdrawal continues until the brain resumes its normal production of the necessary neurotransmitters.

Which neurotransmitters are affected depends on the drug used. A chronic and excessive use of alcohol or benzodiazepines may lower the brain's production of the neurotransmitter GABA; regular use of opioids may reduce the brain's production of endorphins; and regular use of cocaine or amphetamines may lower the brain's production of dopamine (Volkow et al., 2004, 1999). In addition, researchers have identified neurotransmitters called *cannabinoids* that operate much like THC; excessive use of marijuana may reduce the production of these neurotransmitters (Hitti, 2004; Johns, 2001).

This theory helps explain why people who regularly take substances experience tolerance and withdrawal reactions. But why are drugs so rewarding, and why do certain people turn to them in the first place? A number of brain-imaging studies suggest that many, perhaps all, drugs eventually activate a single **reward center,** or "pleasure pathway," in the brain (Oslin, 2006; Schultz, 2006). This reward center apparently extends from the brain area called the *ventral tegmental area* (in the midbrain) to an area known as the *nucleus accumbens* and on to the *frontal cortex.* A key neurotransmitter in this pleasure pathway appears to be *dopamine* (Volkow et al., 2004). When dopamine is activated there, a person experiences pleasure. Music may activate dopamine in the reward center. So may a hug or a word of praise. And so may drugs. Some researchers believe that other neurotransmitters may also play important roles in the reward center.

Certain drugs apparently stimulate the reward center directly. Remember that cocaine, amphetamines, and caffeine directly increase dopamine activity. Other drugs seem to stimulate it in roundabout ways. The biochemical reactions triggered by alcohol, opioids, and marijuana probably set in motion a series of chemical events that eventually lead to increased dopamine activity in the reward center.

A number of theorists suspect that people who abuse drugs suffer from a **reward-deficiency syndrome:** their reward center is not readily activated by the usual events in their lives (Blum et al., 2000; Nash, 1997) so they turn to drugs to stimulate this pleasure pathway, particularly at times of stress. Abnormal genes, such as the abnormal D2 receptor gene, have been cited as a possible cause of this syndrome (Finckh, 2001; Lawford et al., 1997).

C/B Productions/The Stock Market

Addicted to chocolate? *Recent studies suggest that a craving for chocolate may be more than just a state of mind. Apparently some chemicals in chocolate may bind to the same neuron receptors that receive cannabis substances (di Tomaso, Beltramo, & Piomelli, 1996). At the same time, however, a person would have to eat 25 pounds of chocolate in one sitting to experience a cannabis-like effect. Then again, for chocolate lovers . . .*

How Are Substance-Related Disorders Treated?

Many approaches have been used to treat substance-related disorders, including psychodynamic, behavioral, cognitive-behavioral, biological, and sociocultural therapies. Although these treatments sometimes meet with great success, more often they are only moderately helpful (Frances et al., 2005, 2001; Prendergast et al., 2002). Today the treatments are typically used in combination on both an outpatient and an inpatient basis (Carroll, 2005).

The value of a treatment for substance abuse or dependence can be difficult to determine (Babor et al., 2000). After all, different substance-related disorders pose different treatment problems. Moreover, some people recover without any intervention at all, while others recover and then relapse (Miller, 2000). Finally, different criteria are used by different clinical researchers. How long, for example, must a person refrain from substance use in order to be called a treatment success? And is total abstention the only criterion, or is a reduction of drug use acceptable?

Psychodynamic Therapies

Psychodynamic therapists first guide clients to uncover and work through the underlying needs and conflicts that they believe have led to the disorder. The therapists then try to help the individuals change their substance-related styles of living (Dodes & Khantzian, 2005; Stetter, 2000). Although often applied, this approach has not been found to be particularly effective in cases of substance-related disorders (Cornish et al., 1995; Holder et al., 1991). It may be that drug abuse or dependence, regardless of its causes, eventually becomes a stubborn independent problem that must be the direct target of treatment if people are to become drug-free. Psychodynamic therapy tends to be of greater help when it is combined with other approaches in a multidimensional treatment program (Galanter & Brooks, 2001).

Behavioral Therapies

A widely used behavioral treatment for substance-related disorders is **aversion therapy,** an approach based on the principles of classical conditioning. Individuals are repeatedly presented with an unpleasant stimulus (for example, an electric shock) at the very moment that they are taking a drug. After repeated pairings, they are expected to react negatively to the substance itself and to lose their craving for it.

Aversion therapy has been applied to alcohol abuse and dependence more than to other substance-related disorders. In one version of this therapy, drinking behavior is paired with drug-induced nausea and vomiting (Owen-Howard, 2001; Welsh & Liberto, 2001). Another version, *covert sensitization,* requires people with alcoholism to imagine extremely upsetting, repulsive, or frightening scenes while they are drinking (Cautela, 2000; Kassel et al., 1999). The pairing of the imagined scenes with liquor is expected to produce negative responses to liquor itself. Here are the kinds of scenes therapists may guide a client to imagine:

I'd like you to vividly imagine that you are drinking and tasting (beer, whiskey, etc.). You are in a (restaurant, pub, etc.) where others are drinking. 'See' yourself there, having a drink. Capture the exact taste of it, the color and the smell. Use all of your senses. Imagine that you are actually drinking it, tasting it, swallowing it, feel the glass in your hand; and be aware of its temperature, taste and smell, but especially the taste.

As you swallow the drink, a man sitting not far from you gives a low groan, replaces his glass on the table and pushes it away. His head remains lowered as he grasps his stomach with both hands and continues moaning. His eyes are closed now as he grimaces and slowly shakes his head. His face has become a sickly pale color, and his hands are trembling as he starts to make quick swallowing motions. He opens his eyes and claps both hands over his mouth, but he

•**REWARD CENTER**•A dopamine-rich pathway in the brain that produces feelings of pleasure when activated.

•**REWARD-DEFICIENCY SYNDROME**•A condition, suspected to be present in some individuals, in which the brain's reward center is not readily activated by the usual events in their lives.

•**AVERSION THERAPY**•A treatment in which clients are repeatedly presented with unpleasant stimuli while performing undesirable behaviors such as taking a drug.

>>**LOOKING BACK**

Drastic Measure

In one early form of aversion therapy, people with alcoholism were injected with *succinyl-choline,* a drug that actually paralyzed their bodies while they tasted alcoholic beverages (Sanderson et al., 1963). Concerns about the safety and ethics of this approach led to its discontinuation. **<<**

cannot hold it in and the vomit bursts out. You can see it so clearly. Pieces of food run down his face, soaking his clothes and even reaching his glass. He continues to throw up and particles of his last meal stick to his chin and the hot sticky smell of alcohol reaches you. He really is a disgusting sight. He's got the dry heaves now, there's nothing left to bring up, but his face is still pale and he continues moaning.

I'd like you to vividly imagine that you are tasting the (beer, whiskey, etc.). See yourself tasting it, capture the exact taste, color and consistency. Use all of your senses. After you've tasted the drink you notice that there is something small and white floating in the glass—it stands out. You bend closer to examine it more carefully, your nose is right over the glass now and the smell fills your nostrils as you remember exactly what the drink tastes like. Now you can see what's in the glass. There are several maggots floating on the surface. As you watch, revolted, one manages to get a grip on the glass and, undulating, creeps up the glass. There are even more of the repulsive creatures in the glass than you first thought. You realise that you have swallowed some of them and you're very aware of the taste in your mouth. You feel very sick and wish you'd never reached for the glass and had the drink at all.

(Clarke & Saunders, 1988, pp. 143–144)

A behavioral approach that has been effective in the short-term treatment of people who abuse cocaine and some other drugs is *contingency management,* which makes incentives (such as program privileges) contingent on the submission of drug-free urine specimens (Katz et al., 2001; Petry, 2000). In one study, 68 percent of cocaine abusers who completed a six-month contingency training program achieved at least eight weeks of continuous abstinence (Higgins et al., 1993).

Behavioral interventions for substance abuse and dependence have usually had only limited success when they are the sole form of treatment (Carroll & Rounsaville, 1995). A major problem is that the approaches can be effective only when individuals are motivated to continue with them despite their unpleasantness or demands. Generally, behavioral treatments work best in combination with either biological or cognitive approaches (Grilly, 2006; Kassel et al., 1999).

Fighting drug abuse while in prison *Inmates enrolled in the substance abuse program at a prison in Alabama participate in a group therapy session to help address their drug problems. The group sessions highlight psychoeducation and a mixture of insight-oriented, behavioral, and sociocultural interventions, and they typically include candid, sometimes confrontational, discussions.*

>>**PSYCH•NOTES**

Spontaneous Remission

Between 20 and 30 percent of all people with substance-related disorders apparently recover within 10 years without treatment (Schuckit, 1999). **<<**

[BOX **12-4**]

Controlled Drug Use vs. Abstinence

Is total abstinence the only cure for drug abuse and dependence, or can people with substance-related disorders learn to keep drug use under control? This issue has been debated for years, especially when the drug in question is alcohol (Grilly, 2006; Adelson, 2005).

Some cognitive-behavioral theorists believe that people can continue to drink in moderation if they learn to set appropriate drinking limits. They argue that demanding strict abstinence of people may in fact cause them to lose self-control entirely if they have a single drink (Marlatt et al., 2001; Peele, 1989; Heather et al.,

1982). In contrast, those who view alcoholism as a disease take the AA position of "Once an alcoholic, always an alcoholic," and argue that people with alcoholism are in fact more likely to relapse when they believe that they can safely take one drink (Pendery et al., 1982). This misguided belief, they hold, will sooner or later open the door to alcohol once again and lead back to uncontrollable drinking.

Feelings run so strongly that the people on one side have at times challenged the motives and honesty of those on the other (Sobell & Sobell, 1984, 1973; Pendery et

al., 1982). Research indicates, however, that both controlled drinking and abstinence may be useful treatment goals, depending on the individual's personality and on the nature of the particular drinking problem. Studies suggest, for example, that abstinence is a more appropriate goal for people who have a long-standing dependence on alcohol, while controlled drinking can be helpful to younger drinkers whose pattern does not include physical dependence. The latter individuals may in fact need to be taught a nonabusive form of drinking (Foxhall, 2001; Peele, 1992; Marlatt, 1985). Studies also suggest that abstinence is appropriate for people who believe that abstinence is the only answer for them (Rosenberg, 1993). These individuals are indeed more likely to relapse after having just one drink.

Generally speaking, both abstinence and controlled drinking are extremely difficult for persons with alcoholism to achieve. Although treatment may help them to improve for a while, many of them relapse (Adelson, 2005; Allsop et al., 2000). Such statistics serve as a harsh reminder that substance abuse and dependence remain among society's most disabling problems.

AP Photo

Failure of forced abstinence *Although individual efforts at voluntary abstinence from alcohol are often successful, broad social programs that try to force individuals to abstain from drinking usually meet with failure. During the period of "prohibition" in the United States (1920–1933), for example, the consumption of alcohol initially decreased but then soon increased, contributing to the repeal of "the noble experiment" in 1933. During this social ban on alcohol, people developed ingenious techniques for concealing and transporting this substance. Here, for example, a tube of liquor was hidden in the heel of a shoe available in shoe stores throughout the country.*

Cognitive-Behavioral Therapies

Two popular approaches combine cognitive and behavioral techniques to help people gain *control* over their substance-related behaviors. In one, **behavioral self-control training (BSCT),** applied to alcoholism in particular, therapists first have clients keep track of their own drinking behavior (Adelson, 2005; Miller et al., 1992; Miller, 1983). Writing down the times, locations, emotions, bodily changes, and other circumstances of their drinking, they become more aware of the situations that place them at risk for excessive drinking. They are then taught coping strategies to use when such situations arise. They learn, for example, to set limits on their drinking (see Box 12-4), to recognize when the limits are being approached, to control their rate of drinking (perhaps by spacing their drinks or by sipping them rather than gulping), and to practice relaxation techniques, assertiveness skills, and other coping behaviors in situations in which they would otherwise be drinking. Approximately 70 percent of the people who complete this training apparently show some improvement, particularly those who are young and not physically dependent on alcohol (Walters, 2000; Hester, 1995).

In a related cognitive-behavioral approach, **relapse-prevention training,** heavy drinkers are assigned many of the same tasks as clients in BSCT (Adelson, 2005; Gray & Gibson, 2004; Witkiewitz & Marlatt, 2004). They are also taught to plan ahead of time

•**BEHAVIORAL SELF-CONTROL TRAINING (BSCT)**•A cognitive-behavioral approach to treating alcohol abuse and dependence in which clients are taught to keep track of their drinking behavior and to apply coping strategies in situations that typically trigger excessive drinking.

•**RELAPSE-PREVENTION TRAINING**•An approach to treating alcohol abuse that is similar to BSCT and also has clients plan ahead for risky situations and reactions.

how many drinks are appropriate, what to drink, and under what circumstances. The approach often lowers the frequency of intoxication, although the majority of clients achieve success only after repeated relapse prevention treatments (Witkiewitz & Marlatt, 2004). The approach has also been used, with some success, in the treatment of marijuana and cocaine abuse as well as with other kinds of disorders such as sexual paraphilias (see Chapter 13).

Biological Treatments

Biological approaches may be used to help people withdraw from substances, abstain from them, or simply maintain their level of use without further increases (McCance-Katz & Kosten, 2005). As with the other forms of treatment, biological approaches alone rarely bring long-term improvement, but they can be helpful when combined with other approaches.

DETOXIFICATION **Detoxification** is systematic and medically supervised withdrawal from a drug. Some detoxification programs are offered on an outpatient basis. Others are located in hospitals and clinics and may also offer individual and group therapy, a "full-service" institutional approach that has become popular. One detoxification approach is to have clients withdraw gradually from the substance, taking smaller and smaller doses until they are off the drug completely (Wright & Thompson, 2002). A second detoxification strategy is to give clients other drugs that reduce the symptoms of withdrawal (Oslin, 2006). Antianxiety drugs, for example, are sometimes used to reduce severe alcohol withdrawal reactions such as delirium tremens and seizures. Detoxification programs seem to help motivated people withdraw from drugs (Zhao et al., 2001; Allan et al., 2000). However, relapse rates tend to be high for those who fail to receive a follow-up form of treatment—psychological, biological, or sociocultural—after successful detoxification.

ANTAGONIST DRUGS After successfully stopping a drug, people must avoid falling back into a pattern of abuse or dependence. As an aid to resisting temptation, some people with substance-related disorders are given **antagonist drugs,** which block or change the effects of the addictive drug (McCance-Katz & Kosten, 2005). *Disulfiram* (Antabuse), for example, is often given to people who are trying to stay away from alcohol. By itself a low dose of this drug seems to have few negative effects, but a person who drinks alcohol while taking disulfiram will experience intense nausea, vomiting, blushing, faster heart rate, dizziness, and perhaps fainting. People taking disulfiram are less likely to drink alcohol because they know the terrible reaction that awaits them should they have even one drink. Disulfiram has proved helpful, but again only with people who are motivated to take it as prescribed (Grilly, 2006).

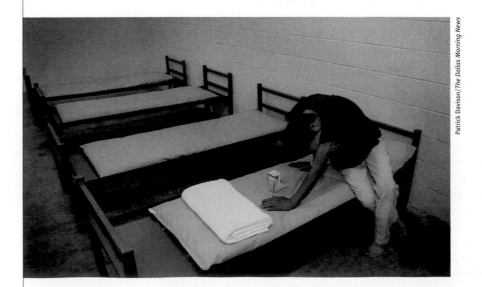

Forced detoxification *Abstinence is not always medically supervised, nor is it necessarily planned or voluntary. This sufferer of alcoholism begins to experience symptoms of withdrawal soon after being imprisoned for public intoxication.*

Patrick Davison/*The Dallas Morning News*

Several other antagonist drugs are now being tested as possible treatments for people who abuse alcohol (Ehrenfeld, 2005). Unlike disulfiram, these drugs do not make the individuals ill when mixed with alcohol, but they do alter the brain's release of GABA, the neurotransmitter affected by alcohol use, and, in turn, seem to reduce the individuals' cravings for alcohol. One of the leading such drugs under study is *topiramate* (Topamax), a medication that has been used for years to help treat people with brain seizure disorder.

In the realm of opioid dependence, several *narcotic antagonists,* such as *naloxone* and *naltrexone,* are used to treat people who are addicted to drugs of that kind (Kirchmayer et al., 2002). These antagonists attach to *endorphin* receptor sites throughout the brain and make it impossible for the opioids to have their usual effect. Without the rush or high, continued drug use becomes pointless. Although narcotic antagonists have been helpful—particularly in emergencies, to rescue people from an overdose of opioids—some clinicians consider them too dangerous for regular treatment of opioid dependence. These antagonists must be given very carefully because of their ability to throw a person with an addiction into severe withdrawal (Roozen et al., 2002; Ling, Huber, & Rawson, 2001). In recent years, so-called *partial antagonists,* narcotic antagonists that produce less severe withdrawal symptoms, have been developed (Amass et al., 2000).

Recent studies indicate that narcotic antagonists may also be useful in the treatment of alcohol and cocaine dependence (Oslin, 2006; O'Brien & McKay, 2002). In some studies, for example, the narcotic antagonist naltrexone has helped reduce cravings for alcohol (O'Malley et al., 2000, 1996, 1992). Why should narcotic antagonists, which operate at the brain's endorphin receptors, help with alcoholism, which has been tied largely to activity at GABA sites? The answer may lie in the reward center of the brain (Gianoulakis, 2001). If various drugs eventually stimulate the same pleasure pathway, it seems reasonable that antagonists for one drug may, in a roundabout way, affect the impact of other drugs as well.

DRUG MAINTENANCE THERAPY A drug-related lifestyle may be a greater problem than the drug's direct effects. Much of the damage caused by heroin addiction, for example, comes from overdoses, unsterile needles, and an accompanying life of crime. Thus clinicians were very enthusiastic when **methadone maintenance programs** were developed in the 1960s to treat heroin addiction (Dole & Nyswander, 1967, 1965). In these programs, people with an addiction are given the laboratory opioid *methadone* as a substitute for heroin. Although they then become dependent on methadone, their new addiction is maintained under safe medical supervision. Unlike heroin, methadone can be taken by mouth, thus eliminating the dangers of needles, and needs to be taken only once a day.

At first, methadone programs seemed very effective, and many of them were set up throughout the United States, Canada, and England (Payte, 1989). These programs became less popular during the 1980s, however, because of the dangers of methadone itself. Many clinicians came to believe that substituting one addiction for another is not an acceptable "solution" for substance dependence, and many persons with an addiction complained that methadone addiction was creating an additional drug problem that simply complicated their original one (McCance-Katz & Kosten, 2005; Cornish et al., 1995). In fact, methadone is sometimes harder to withdraw from than heroin, because the withdrawal symptoms can last nearly twice as long (Backmund et al., 2001; Kleber, 1981). Moreover, pregnant women maintained on methadone have the added concern of the drug's effect on their fetus (DeCubas & Field, 1993).

Despite such concerns, maintenance treatment with methadone (or with *buprenorphine,* a newly developed substitute drug) has again sparked interest among clinicians in recent years, partly because of new research support (Gossop et al., 2001; Ritter, 2001) and partly because of the rapid spread of the HIV virus among intravenous drug abusers and their sex partners and children (Cornish et al., 1995). More than one-quarter of AIDS cases reported in the early 1990s were directly tied to drug abuse, and intravenous drug abuse is the indirect cause in 60 percent of childhood AIDS cases (Brown, 1993; NIDA, 1995). Not only is methadone treatment safer than street opioid use, but many methadone programs now include AIDS education and other health instructions in their

•**DETOXIFICATION**•Systematic and medically supervised withdrawal from a drug.

•**ANTAGONIST DRUGS**•Drugs that block or change the effects of an addictive drug.

•**METHADONE MAINTENANCE PROGRAM**•An approach to treating heroin dependence in which clients are given legally and medically supervised doses of a substitute drug, methadone.

Shawn Patrick Ouelette/Maine Sunday Telegram/AP Photo

Pros and cons of methadone treatment *People sometimes forget that methadone itself is a narcotic that can be as dangerous as other opioids when not taken under safe medical supervision. Here a husband and wife protest against a proposed methadone treatment facility in Maine. The couple's 19-year-old daughter, who was not an opioid addict, had died months earlier after taking methadone to get high.*

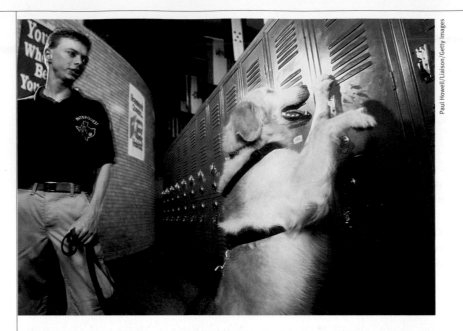

Paul Howell/Liaison/Getty Images

Sniffing for drugs *An increasingly common scene in schools, airports, storage facilities, and similar settings is that of trained dogs sniffing for marijuana, cocaine, opioids, and other substances. Here one such animal sniffs lockers at a school in Texas to see whether students have hidden any illegal substances among their books or other belongings.*

services (Sorensen & Copeland, 2000). Research suggests that methadone maintenance programs are most effective when they are combined with education, psychotherapy, family therapy, and employment counseling (O'Brien & McKay, 2002; Woody et al., 1998). Today more than 900 methadone clinics across the United States dispense the drug to as many as 160,000 patients at an average cost of $13 a day (ONDCP, 2002, 2000; Marks, 1998).

Sociocultural Therapies

As we have seen, sociocultural theorists believe that psychological problems emerge in a social setting and are best treated in a social context. Three sociocultural approaches have been applied to substance-related disorders: (1) *self-help programs;* (2) *culture- and gender-sensitive programs;* and (3) *community prevention programs.*

SELF-HELP AND RESIDENTIAL TREATMENT PROGRAMS Many people who abuse drugs have organized among themselves to help one another recover without professional assistance. The drug self-help movement dates back to 1935, when two Ohio men suffering from alcoholism met and wound up discussing alternative treatment possibilities. The first discussion led to others and to the eventual formation of a self-help group whose members discussed alcohol-related problems, traded ideas, and provided support. The organization became known as **Alcoholics Anonymous (AA)** (see Box 12-5).

Today AA has more than 2 million members in 100,000 groups across the United States and 150 other countries (AA World Services, 2005). It offers peer support along with moral and spiritual guidelines to help people overcome alcoholism. Different members apparently find different aspects of AA helpful. For some it is the peer support (Galanter et al., 2005, 1990); for others it is the spiritual dimension (Swora, 2001). Meetings take place regularly, and members are available to help each other 24 hours a day.

By offering guidelines for living, the organization helps members abstain "one day at a time," urging them to accept as "fact" the idea that they are powerless over alcohol and that they must stop drinking entirely and permanently if they are to live normal lives. Related self-help organizations, *Al-Anon* and *Alateen,* offer support for people who live with and care about persons with alcoholism. Self-help programs such as *Narcotics Anonymous* and *Cocaine Anonymous* have been developed for other substance-related disorders.

Many self-help programs have expanded into **residential treatment centers,** or **therapeutic communities**—such as *Daytop Village* and *Phoenix House*—where people formerly dependent on drugs live, work, and socialize in a drug-free environment while undergoing individual, group, and family therapies and making a transition back to community life (Doweiko, 2006).

•**ALCOHOLICS ANONYMOUS (AA)**•A self-help organization that provides support and guidance for persons with alcohol abuse or dependence.

•**RESIDENTIAL TREATMENT CENTER**•A place where people formerly dependent on drugs live, work, and socialize in a drug-free environment. Also called a *therapeutic community.*

[BOX **12-5**]

"In the Beginning"

In the summer of 1935, Bill W. sat defeated in a hotel room far from home, longing for a drink.

Six months earlier, this high-risk stock analyst had climbed on the wagon of sobriety and managed to convince his long-suffering employer to give him one more chance. The New York brokerage firm for which he worked reluctantly agreed to let him lead a proxy fight at an annual stockholders' meeting in Akron, Ohio. But Bill failed at this task, and he now felt as if his last hope for restoring his career and his dignity had vanished. In such moments of misery, his usual action would be to reach for a bottle of gin.

This time, however, Bill picked up a phone book and dialed a church at random. He asked the minister who answered if there were any other "hopeless drunks" he could talk to. The minister directed him to a counselor who, in turn, hooked Bill up with Dr. Bob, a local physician who was "drying out" and making his umpteenth attempt to stop drinking. Bill and Dr. Bob shared their stories for several hours. The two men began searching for other "alcoholics" to talk to, and before long they were holding regular meetings in their homes, where recovering individuals would join together to tell their stories and exchange thoughts and advice about the road to sobriety.

From such humble beginnings *Alcoholics Anonymous (AA)* was born, a movement with the singular purpose of helping fellow problem drinkers reclaim their lives. The philosophy of the group is simple: AA members gather to share their experiences with anyone who desires to stop drinking.

For an international organization with more than 2 million members, AA is remarkably decentralized. It works steadfastly to remain "nonprofessional" and strives to create a low-key, humble, and quiet atmosphere. There are no dues for membership, local and national leadership rotates regularly, and bureaucracy is kept to a minimum. AA does not actively solicit members, sponsor research or education, or provide any social services, such as medical or financial help, for persons struggling with alcoholism. It does not officially take any position on alcohol-related issues such as "driving under the influence" or minimum-drinking-age laws. It makes little effort to publicize its activities, and it even refuses outside donations, funding itself solely by passing the hat at meetings and by selling its literature to members.

It wasn't always so. Flush with AA's early successes, Bill W. envisioned alcoholic hospitals and recovery centers across the country, paid missionaries who would seek out excessive drinkers and urge them to recover, and the publication of books that would generate millions of dollars for the cause. To do all this, however, the organization needed a considerable amount of seed money. Knowing that John D. Rockefeller Jr. was impressed by the fledgling organization, Bill W. persuaded the industrialist to sponsor a dinner with 75 of New York's wealthiest and most influential citizens, where he could describe AA and its aspirations. After Bill W. confidently delivered his pitch, Rockefeller's son Nelson (later to become vice president of the United States) lauded AA and announced,

"Gentlemen, you can all see that this is a work of good will. Its power lies in the fact that one member carries the good message to the next, without any thought of financial income or reward. Therefore, it is our belief that Alcoholics Anonymous should be self-supporting so far as money is concerned. It needs only our good will" (Bill W., 1957/1975, pp. 184–185).

After several funding disappointments of this kind, AA decided to make its corporate poverty and its narrow goal into a strength. At an international convention in 1950, the membership agreed that "an AA group ought never endorse, finance or lend the AA name to any related facility or outside purpose, lest problems of money, property and prestige divert us from our primary purpose." Since then, the self-supporting, modest, and single-minded nature of AA has, in the view of many, become central to its mission, its message, and its success. The organization's yearly revenues from member donations and book sales represent but a small fraction of the billions of dollars that America spends more generally on treatment for alcohol abuse and dependence.

Layne Kennedy, Minneapolis

Spreading the word *The AA message to accept one's powerlessness over alcohol and abstain from drinking "one day at a time" has been embraced by all kinds of people in all kinds of places. Here, for example, sober bikers get together at the Dry Gulch, a favorite spot in St. Paul, Minnesota.*

The evidence that keeps self-help and residential treatment programs going comes largely in the form of individual testimonials. Many tens of thousands of persons have revealed that they are members of these programs and credit them with turning their lives around (Gleick, 1995). Studies of the programs have also had favorable findings, but their numbers have been limited (Galanter et al., 2005; Tonigan, 2001; Timko et al., 2000).

CULTURE- AND GENDER-SENSITIVE PROGRAMS Many persons who abuse substances live in a poor and perhaps violent setting. A growing number of today's treatment programs try to be sensitive to the special sociocultural pressures and problems faced by drug abusers who are poor, homeless, or members of minority groups (Franklin & Markarian, 2005). Therapists who are sensitive to their clients' life challenges can do more to address the stresses that often lead to relapse.

Similarly, therapists have become more aware that women often require treatment methods different from those designed for men (Blume & Zilberman, 2005; Weisner, 2005). Women and men often have different physical and psychological reactions to drugs, for example. In addition, treatment of women who abuse substances may be complicated by the impact of sexual abuse, the possibility that they may become pregnant while taking drugs, the stresses of raising children, and the fear of criminal prosecution for abusing drugs during pregnancy. Thus many women with such disorders feel more comfortable seeking help at gender-sensitive clinics or residential programs; some such programs also allow children to live with their recovering mothers (Clark, 2001).

COMMUNITY PREVENTION PROGRAMS Perhaps the most effective approach to substance-related disorders is to prevent them (Gottfredson & Wilson, 2003). The first drug-prevention efforts were conducted in schools. Today prevention programs are also offered in workplaces, activity centers, and other community settings, and even through the media (NSDUH, 2005). Some prevention programs argue for total abstinence from drugs, while others teach responsible use. Some seek to interrupt drug use; others try to delay the age at which people first experiment with drugs. Programs may also differ in whether they offer drug education, teach alternatives to drug use, try to change the psychological state of the potential user, seek to change relationships with peers, or combine these techniques.

Prevention programs may focus on the *individual* (for example, by providing education about unpleasant drug effects), the *family* (by teaching parenting skills), the *peer group*

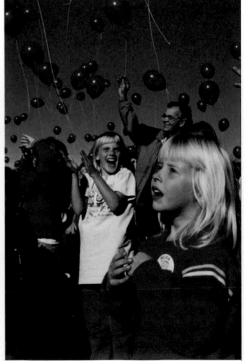

Before it begins *Community prevention programs for substance-related disorders often target very young children. (Left) A kindergarten student smiles as he puts his footprints on a giant sign reading "Stomp Out Drugs." He and his classmates were performing this activity as part of Red Ribbon Week, an annual celebration devoted to creating drug- and alcohol-free communities for children throughout the United States. (Right) Children pledge abstinence from drug and alcohol use during Red Ribbon Week by releasing balloons.*

(by teaching resistance to peer pressure), the *school* (by setting up firm enforcement of drug policies), or the *community* at large (by public service announcements such as the "Just say no" campaign of the 1980s and 1990s). The most effective prevention efforts focus on several of these areas to provide a consistent message about drug abuse in all areas of individuals' lives (Smith, 2001; Wagenaar et al., 2000). Some prevention programs have even been developed for preschool children (Hall & Zigler, 1997).

PUTTING IT together
New Wrinkles to a Familiar Story

In some respects the story of the misuse of drugs is the same today as in the past. Substance use is still rampant, often creating damaging psychological disorders. New drugs keep emerging, and the public goes through periods of believing, naively, that they are "safe." Only gradually do people learn that these drugs, too, pose dangers. And treatments for substance-related disorders continue to have only limited effect.

Yet there are important new wrinkles in this familiar story. Researchers have begun to develop a clearer understanding of how drugs act on the brain and body. In treatment, self-help groups and rehabilitation programs are flourishing. And preventive education to make people aware of the dangers of drug misuse is also expanding and seems to be having an effect. One reason for these improvements is that investigators and clinicians have stopped working in isolation and are instead looking for intersections between their own work and that from other models. The same kind of integrated efforts that have helped with other psychological disorders are bringing new promise and hope to the study and treatment of substance-related disorders.

Perhaps the most important insight to be gained from these integrated efforts is that several of the models were already on the right track. Social pressures, personality characteristics, rewards, and genetic predispositions all seem to play roles in substance-related disorders, and in fact to operate together. For example, some people may inherit a malfunction of the biological reward center and so may need special doses of external stimulation—say, intense relationships, an abundance of certain foods, or drugs—to stimulate their reward center. Their pursuit of external rewards may take on the character of an addictive personality (Ebstein & Kotler, 2002). Such individuals may be especially prone to experimenting with drugs, particularly when their social group makes the drugs available or when they are faced with intense social and personal stress.

Just as each model has identified important factors in the development of substance-related disorders, each has made important contributions to treatment. As we have seen, the various forms of treatment seem to work best when they are combined with approaches from the other models, making integrated treatment the most productive approach.

These recent developments are encouraging. At the same time, however, enormous and increasing levels of drug use continue. New drugs and drug combinations are discovered almost daily, and with them come new problems, new questions, and the need for new research and new treatments. Perhaps the most valuable lesson is an old one: there is no free lunch. The pleasures derived from these substances come with high psychological and biological costs, some not yet even known.

┤ SUMMARY AND REVIEW ├

■ **Substance misuse** The misuse of *substances* (or *drugs*) may lead to temporary changes in behavior, emotion, or thought, including *intoxication*. Chronic and excessive use can lead to *substance abuse* or *substance dependence*. People who become dependent on a drug may develop a *tolerance* for it or experience unpleasant *withdrawal symptoms* when they abstain from it, or both. *pp. 337–339*

■ **Depressants** *Depressants* are substances that slow the activity of the central nervous system. Each of the major depressants presents certain problems and dangers. Chronic and excessive use of these substances can lead to a pattern of abuse or dependence.

>>LOOKING AROUND
Nonmedical Use of Pain Relievers

In the United States, the largest increase in illicit drug use during the past year centered on the nonmedical use of pain relievers. <<

- -

Around 4.4 million persons currently use pain relievers nonmedically. <<

- -

During the past year, 2.4 million persons used pain relievers nonmedically for the first time. <<

- -

The average age of first-time users of pain relief drugs for nonmedical purposes is 23 years. <<

- -

(NSDUH, 2005)

>>LOOKING BACK
Blinded by the Sun?

In 1967 major news services throughout the United States reported that four California college students had suffered permanent vision loss after staring at the sun while under the influence of LSD. The students were said to have suffered damage to their retinas. Eight months later another news report surfaced saying that six Pennsylvania college students had suffered total and permanent blindness after, again, staring at the sun during LSD trips. The stories were seized upon by medical and government officials as clear evidence of the destructive power of LSD. One problem: the stories turned out to be hoaxes. However, retractions of the stories were few and far between, and the incidents continued to be widely believed for decades. <<

Alcoholic beverages contain *ethyl alcohol,* which is carried by the blood to the central nervous system, depressing its function. Intoxication occurs when the concentration of alcohol in the bloodstream reaches 0.09 percent. Among other actions, alcohol increases the activity of the neurotransmitter GABA at key sites in the brain. Excessive use has been tied to accidents, health problems, and certain psychological disorders. The *sedative-hypnotic drugs,* which produce feelings of relaxation and drowsiness, include *barbiturates* and *benzodiazepines.* These drugs also increase the activity of GABA.

Opioids include *opium* and drugs derived from it, such as *morphine* and *heroin,* as well as laboratory-made opioids. They all reduce tension and pain and cause other reactions. Opioids operate by binding to neurons that ordinarily receive *endorphins.* *pp. 339–347*

■ **Stimulants** *Stimulants* are substances that increase the activity of the central nervous system. They may lead to intoxication, abuse, and dependence, including a withdrawal pattern marked by depression, fatigue, and irritability. *Cocaine, amphetamines,* and *caffeine* (less potent but more widely used) produce their effects by increasing the activity of dopamine, norepinephrine, and serotonin in the brain. *pp. 347–352*

■ **Hallucinogens** *Hallucinogens,* such as *LSD,* are substances that cause powerful changes primarily in sensory perception. Perceptions are intensified and illusions and hallucinations can occur. LSD apparently causes such effects by disturbing the release of the neurotransmitter serotonin. LSD is extremely potent, and it may lead to a "bad trip" or to *flashbacks. pp. 353–355*

■ **Cannabis** The main ingredient of *Cannabis sativa,* a hemp plant, is *tetrahydrocannabinol (THC). Marijuana,* the most popular form of cannabis, is more powerful today than it was in years past. It can cause intoxication, and regular use can lead to abuse and dependence. *pp. 355–359*

■ **Combinations of substances** Many people take more than one drug at a time, and the drugs interact. The use of two or more drugs at the same time—*polysubstance use*—has become increasingly common. Similarly, *polysubstance-related disorders* have also become a major problem. *pp. 359–360*

■ **Explanations for substance-related disorders** Several explanations for substance abuse and dependence have been put forward. No single one of them has gained unqualified research support, but together they are beginning to shed light on the disorders. According to the *sociocultural* view, the people most likely to abuse drugs are those living in socioeconomic conditions that generate stress or whose families value or tolerate drug use. In the *psychodynamic view,* people who turn to substance abuse have excessive *dependency* needs traceable to the early stages of life. Some psychodynamic theorists also believe that certain people have a *substance abuse personality* that makes them prone to drug use. The leading *behavioral* view proposes that drug use is reinforced initially because it reduces tensions and raises spirits. According to *cognitive* theorists, such reductions may also lead to an *expectancy* that drugs will be comforting and helpful.

The *biological* explanations are supported by twin, adoptee, genetic linkage, and molecular biology studies, suggesting that people may inherit a predisposition to substance dependence. Researchers have also learned that drug tolerance and withdrawal symptoms may be caused by cutbacks in the brain's production of particular neurotransmitters during excessive and chronic drug use. Finally, biological studies suggest that many, perhaps all, drugs may ultimately lead to increased *dopamine* activity in the brain's *reward center. pp. 360–364*

■ **Treatments for substance-related disorders** Treatments for substance abuse and dependence vary widely. Usually several approaches are combined. *Psychodynamic* therapies try to help clients become aware of and correct the underlying needs and conflicts that may have led to their use of drugs. A common *behavioral* technique is *aversion therapy,* in which an unpleasant stimulus is paired with the drug that the person is abusing. *Cognitive* and *behavioral* techniques have been combined in such forms as *behavioral self-control training* (BSCT) and *relapse-prevention training*. *Biological* treatments include *detoxification, antagonist drugs,* and *drug maintenance therapy. Sociocultural* treatments approach substance-related disorders in a social context by means of *self-help groups* (for example, *Alcoholics Anonymous*), *culture-* and *gender-sensitive treatments,* and *community prevention programs. pp. 365–373*

>>> CRITICAL THOUGHTS <<<

1. What effects might the use of drugs by some rock performers have on teenagers and young adults? Who has the greater impact on the drug behaviors of teenagers and young adults: rock performers who speak out against drugs or rock performers who praise the virtues of drugs? *pp. 359–360*

2. What different kinds of issues might be confronted by drug abusers of different ethnic groups or genders that, in turn, might influence their efforts at recovery? *pp. 360–361*

3. Different ethnic, religious, and national groups have different rates of alcohol abuse. What social factors might help explain this observation? Can we be certain that biological factors are not involved? *pp. 360–364*

4. Only one-third of the $15 billion the U.S. government spends on drug abuse goes to prevention and treatment. Does the focus on the criminalization of drugs ultimately add to the stigma of drug abuse and, in turn, make effective treatment more difficult (Nash, 1997)? *pp. 365–373*

5. In 1995, the popular talk show host Oprah Winfrey revealed, with great emotion, that she had been physically dependent on cocaine in the mid-1970s. What impact might admissions like Winfrey's have on people's willingness to seek treatment for substance abuse? *pp. 365–373*

6. Since the major dangers of heroin come from overdose, unsterilized needles, and criminal lifestyle, society has periodically tried legal, medically supervised use of heroin (in Great Britain) or of a heroin substitute (in the United States) to combat this drug problem. Generally, such approaches have had limited effectiveness. Why? *pp. 369–370*

⊙—[CYBER**STUDY**]————————————>>>

SEARCH THE *ABNORMAL PSYCHOLOGY* CD-ROM FOR

▲ Chapter 12 Video Cases and Discussions
    Why do some people develop substance-related disorders?
    How does substance abuse affect personal, family, and occupational functioning?
    What triggers a user's cravings?

▲ Chapter 12 Practical, Research, and Decision-Making Exercises
    Choosing between abstinence and moderation
    Examining the impact of peers in substance use and misuse

▲ Chapter 12 Practice Test and Feedback

LOG ON TO THE COMER WEB PAGE FOR

▲ Suggested Web links, exercises, FAQ page, additional Chapter 12 practice test questions
    ‹www.worthpublishers.com/comer›

<<<

Sexual Disorders and Gender Identity Disorder

Robert, a 57-year-old man, came to sex therapy with his wife because of his inability to get erections. He had not had a problem with erections until six months earlier, when they attempted to have sex after an evening out, during which he had had several drinks. They attributed his failure to get an erection to his being "a little drunk," but he found himself worrying over the next few days that he was perhaps becoming impotent. When they next attempted intercourse, he found himself unable to get involved in what they were doing because he was so intent on watching himself to see if he would get an erection. Once again he did not, and they were both very upset. His failure to get an erection continued over the next few months. Robert's wife was very upset and . . . frustrated, accusing him of having an affair, or of no longer finding her attractive. Robert wondered if he was getting too old, or if his medication for high blood pressure, which he had been taking for about a year, might be interfering with erection. . . . When they came for sex therapy, they had not attempted any sexual activity for over two months.

(LoPiccolo, 1992, p. 492)

Sexual behavior is a major focus of both our private thoughts and public discussions. Sexual feelings are a crucial part of our development and daily functioning, sexual activity is tied to the satisfaction of our basic needs, and sexual performance is linked to our self-esteem. Most people are fascinated by the abnormal sexual behavior of others and worry about the normality of their own sexuality.

Experts recognize two general categories of sexual disorders: sexual dysfunctions and paraphilias. People with *sexual dysfunctions* experience problems with their sexual responses. Robert, for example, had a dysfunction known as erectile disorder, a repeated failure to attain or maintain an erection during sexual activity. People with *paraphilias* have repeated and intense sexual urges or fantasies in response to objects or situations that society deems inappropriate, and they may behave inappropriately as well. They may be aroused by the thought of sexual activity with a child, for example, or of exposing their genitals to strangers, and they may act on those urges. In addition to the sexual disorders, DSM includes a diagnosis called *gender identity disorder,* a sex-related disorder in which people persistently feel that they have been assigned to the wrong sex and in fact identify with the other gender.

Sexual Dysfunctions

Sexual dysfunctions, disorders in which people cannot respond normally in key areas of sexual functioning, make it difficult or impossible to enjoy sexual intercourse. A large study suggests that as many as 31 percent of men and 43 percent of women in the United States suffer from such a dysfunction during their lives (Heiman, 2002; Laumann et al., 1999, 1994). Sexual dysfunctions are typically very distressing, and they often lead to sexual frustration, guilt, loss of self-esteem, and interpersonal problems (Basson et al., 2001). Often these dysfunctions are interrelated, so that many patients with one experience another as well. Sexual dysfunctioning

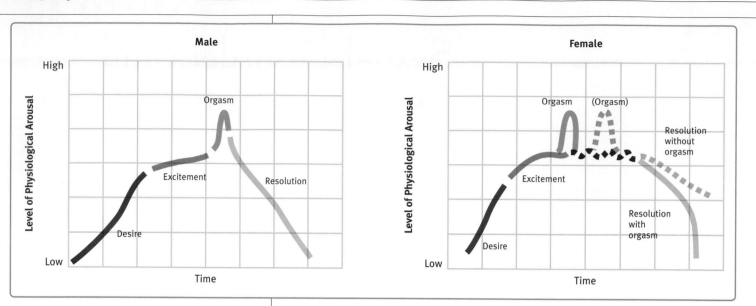

FIGURE 13-1 The normal sexual response cycle
Researchers have found a similar sequence of phases in both males and females. Sometimes, however, women do not experience orgasm; in that case, the resolution phase is less sudden. And sometimes women experience two or more orgasms in succession before the resolution phase. (Adapted from Kaplan, 1974; Masters & Johnson, 1970, 1966.)

will be described here for heterosexual couples, the majority of couples seen in therapy. Homosexual couples have the same dysfunctions, however, and therapists use the same basic techniques to treat them (LoPiccolo, 2004, 1995).

The human sexual response can be described as a *cycle* with four phases: *desire, excitement, orgasm,* and *resolution* (see Figure 13-1). Sexual dysfunctions affect one or more of the first three phases. Resolution consists simply of the relaxation and reduction in arousal that follow orgasm. Some people struggle with a sexual dysfunction their whole lives (labeled *lifelong type* in DSM-IV-TR); in other cases, normal sexual functioning preceded the dysfunction (*acquired type*). In some cases the dysfunction is present during all sexual situations (*generalized type*); in others it is tied to particular situations (*situational type*) (APA, 2000, 1994).

Disorders of Desire

The **desire phase** of the sexual response cycle consists of an urge to have sex, sexual fantasies, and sexual attraction to others (see Figure 13-2). Two dysfunctions—*hypoactive sexual desire* and *sexual aversion*—affect the desire phase. A client named Ms. Bryarton experiences both of these disorders:

Mr. and Ms. [Bryarton] have been married for 14 years and have three children, ages 8 through 12. They [complain that Ms. Bryarton] has never enjoyed [sex] since they have been married.

Before their marriage, although they had intercourse only twice, Ms. Bryarton had been highly aroused by kissing and petting and felt she used her attractiveness to "seduce" her husband into marriage. She did, however, feel intense guilt about their two episodes of premarital intercourse; during their honeymoon, she began to think of sex as a chore that could not be pleasing. Although she periodically passively complied with intercourse, she had almost no spontaneous desire for sex. She never masturbated, had never reached orgasm, thought of all variations such as oral sex as completely repulsive, and was preoccupied with a fantasy of how disapproving her family would be if she ever engaged in any of these activities.

Ms. Bryarton is almost totally certain that no woman she respects in any older generation has enjoyed sex, and that despite the "new vogue" of sexuality, only sleazy, crude women let themselves act like "animals." These beliefs have led to a pattern of regular, but infrequent, sex that at best is accommodating and gives little or no pleasure to her or her husband. Whenever Ms. Bryarton comes close to having a feeling of sexual arousal, numerous negative thoughts come into her mind, such as "What am I, a tramp?" "If I like this, he'll just want it more

•**SEXUAL DYSFUNCTION**•A disorder marked by a persistent inability to function normally in some area of the human sexual response cycle.

•**DESIRE PHASE**•The phase of the sexual response cycle consisting of an urge to have sex, sexual fantasies, and sexual attraction to others.

•**HYPOACTIVE SEXUAL DESIRE DISORDER**• A disorder marked by a lack of interest in sex and hence a low level of sexual activity.

•**SEXUAL AVERSION DISORDER**•A disorder characterized by an aversion to and avoidance of genital sexual interplay.

often." Or "How could I look myself in the mirror after something like this?" These thoughts almost inevitably are accompanied by a cold feeling and an insensitivity to sensual pleasure. As a result, sex is invariably an unhappy experience. Almost any excuse, such as fatigue or being busy, is sufficient for her to rationalize avoiding intercourse.

Yet, intellectually Ms. Bryarton wonders, "Is something wrong with me?"

(Spitzer et al., 1994, p. 251)

Hypoactive sexual desire is a lack of interest in sex and, in turn, a low level of sexual activity (see Table 13-1). Nevertheless, when people with hypoactive sexual desire do have sex, their physical responses may be normal and they may enjoy the experience. While our culture portrays men as wanting all the sex they can get, hypoactive sexual desire may be found in as many as 16 percent of men, and the number seeking therapy has increased during the past decade (Heiman, 2002; Laumann et al., 1999). It may also be found in 33 percent of women. A number of people experience normal sexual interest and arousal but choose, as a matter of lifestyle, not to engage in sexual relations. These individuals are not diagnosed as having hypoactive sexual desire.

DSM-IV-TR defines hypoactive sexual desire as "deficient or absent sexual fantasies and desire for sexual activity," but it does not specify what a "deficient" level is. In fact, this criterion is difficult to define (LoPiccolo, 2004, 1995; Bach, Wincze, & Barlow, 2001). Age, number of years married, education, social class, race, and other factors may all influence the frequency of sex (see Box 13-1 on page 381). In one survey, 93 happily married couples were asked to report how often they desire sexual encounters. Almost all of them said that they desire sex at least once every two weeks, and around 85 percent reported a desire rate of several times a week or more. On the basis of this survey, sexual desire would be considered hypoactive only when a person desires sex less frequently than once every two weeks.

People with **sexual aversion** find sex distinctly unpleasant or repulsive. Sexual advances may sicken, disgust, or frighten them. Some people are repelled by a particular aspect of sex, such as penetration of the vagina; others experience a general aversion to all sexual stimuli, including kissing or touching. Aversion to sex seems to be quite rare in men and somewhat more common in women (Heiman, 2002).

A person's sex drive is determined by a combination of biological, psychological, and sociocultural factors, and any of them may reduce sexual desire (Heard-Davison,

Table 13-1 DSM Checklist

HYPOACTIVE SEXUAL DESIRE DISORDER

1. Persistent or recurrent deficiency of sexual fantasies and desire for sexual activity.
2. Significant distress or interpersonal difficulty.

SEXUAL AVERSION DISORDER

1. Persistent or recurrent extreme aversion to, and avoidance of, almost all genital contact with a sexual partner.
2. Significant distress or interpersonal difficulty.

Based on APA, 2000, 1994.

FIGURE 13-2 Normal female sexual anatomy
Changes in the female anatomy occur during the different phases of the sexual response cycle. (Adapted from Hyde, 1990, p. 200.)

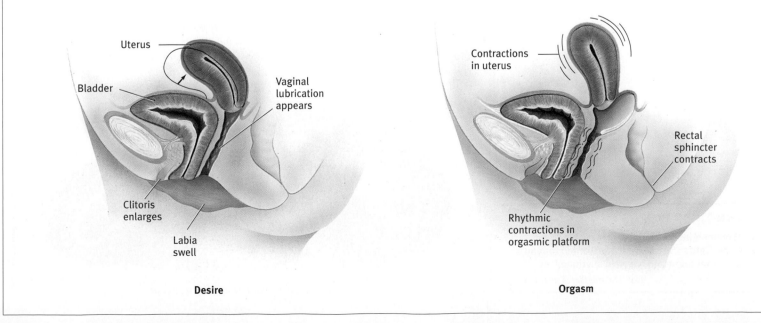

Desire

Orgasm

Heiman, & Briggs, 2004). Most cases of low sexual desire or sexual aversion are caused primarily by sociocultural and psychological factors, but biological conditions can also lower sex drive significantly.

BIOLOGICAL CAUSES A number of hormones interact to produce sexual desire and behavior, and abnormalities in their activity can lower the sex drive (Hyde, 2005; Davis, 2001; Rosen & Leiblum, 1995). In both men and women, a high level of the hormone *prolactin,* a low level of the male sex hormone *testosterone,* and either a high or low level of the female sex hormone *estrogen* can lead to low sex drive. Low sex drive has been linked to the high levels of estrogen contained in some birth control pills, for example. Conversely, it has also been tied to the low level of estrogen found in many post-menopausal women or women who have recently given birth. Long-term physical illness can also lower the sex drive (Kalayjian & Morrell, 2000). The low drive may be a direct result of the illness or an indirect result due to stress, pain, or depression brought on by the illness.

Sex drive can be lowered by some pain medications, certain psychotropic drugs, and a number of illegal drugs such as cocaine, marijuana, amphetamines, and heroin (Stahl, 2001; Segraves, 1995). Low levels of alcohol may enhance the sex drive by lowering a person's inhibitions, yet high levels will reduce it (Roehrich & Kinder, 1991).

PSYCHOLOGICAL CAUSES A general increase in anxiety or anger may reduce sexual desire in both men and women (Westheimer & Lopater, 2005; Beck & Bozman, 1996). Frequently, as cognitive theorists have noted, people with hypoactive sexual desire and sexual aversion have particular attitudes, fears, or memories that contribute to their dysfunction, such as a belief that sex is immoral or dangerous (LoPiccolo, 2004, 1995). Other people are so afraid of losing control over their sexual urges that they try to resist them completely. And still others fear pregnancy.

Certain psychological disorders may also contribute to hypoactive sexual desire and sexual aversion. Even a mild level of depression can interfere with sexual desire, and some people with obsessive-compulsive symptoms find contact with another person's body fluids and odors to be highly unpleasant (LoPiccolo, 2004, 1995).

SOCIOCULTURAL CAUSES The attitudes, fears, and psychological disorders that contribute to hypoactive sexual desire and sexual aversion occur within a social context, and thus certain sociocultural factors have also been linked to these dysfunctions. Many sufferers are feeling situational pressures—divorce, a death in the family, job stress, infertility difficulties, having a baby (Burns, 1995; Letourneau & O'Donohue, 1993). Others may be having problems in their relationships. People who are in an unhappy relationship, have lost affection for their partner, or feel powerless and dominated by their partner can lose interest in sex (Westheimer & Lopater, 2005; Metz & Epstein, 2002). Even in basically happy relationships, if one partner is a very unskilled, unenthusiastic lover, the other can begin to lose interest in sex. And sometimes partners differ in their needs for closeness. The one who needs more personal space may develop hypoactive sexual desire as a way of keeping distance (LoPiccolo, 2004, 1997, 1995).

"You're wasting your time. I'm asexual."

© 2000, Robert Mankoff, from cartoonbank.com

[BOX 13-1]

Lifetime Patterns of Sexual Behavior

Early interest *Sexual curiosity and feelings typically begin well before the teenage years. Children may first discover such feelings in unexpected places and may be confused and anxious about them for a while.*

Sexual dysfunctions are, by definition, different from the usual patterns of sexual functioning. But in the sexual realm, what is "the usual"? In the mid-1980s, clinicians found their efforts to prevent the spread of AIDS hindered by a lack of available data and began to conduct large surveys on sexual behavior. Collectively, studies conducted over the past two decades provide a wealth of useful, sometimes eye-opening information about sexual patterns in the "normal" populations of North America (Kelly, 2005; Brown & Ceniceros, 2001; Laumann et al., 1999, 1994; Seidman & Rieder, 1995; Janus & Janus, 1993).

TEENAGERS

More than 90 percent of boys masturbate by the end of adolescence, compared to 50 percent of girls. For the vast majority of them, masturbation began by age 14. Males report masturbating an average of one to two times a week, females once a month.

Around 20 percent of teenagers have heterosexual intercourse by the age of 15, and 80 percent by age 19. Today's teenagers are having intercourse younger than those of past generations. Most teens who are sexually experienced engage in only one sexual relationship at a time. Over the course of their teen years, however, most have at least two sex partners.

Extended periods without sex are still common, even for teenagers in a relationship. Half of sexually experienced adolescent girls have intercourse once a month or less. Sexually experienced teenage boys spend an average of six months of the year without intercourse.

Condom use by teenagers has increased somewhat during the past decade, partly because of warnings about AIDS. However, at most half of teenagers report having used a condom the last time they had sex. Less than a third of teenagers use condoms consistently and appropriately.

EARLY ADULTHOOD (AGES 18–24)

More than 80 percent of unmarried young adults have intercourse in a given year. Of those who are sexually active, around a third have intercourse two or three times a month and another third engage in it two or three times a week. Masturbation remains common in young adulthood: close to 60 percent of men masturbate, a third of them at least once a week, and 36 percent of women masturbate, a tenth of them at least once a week.

MID-ADULTHOOD (AGES 25–59)

From the ages of 25 to 59, sexual relationships last longer and are more monogamous. More than 90 percent of people in this age range have sexual intercourse in a given year. Half of the unmarried men have two or more partners in a given year, compared to a quarter of the unmarried women.

Among sexually active adults, close to 60 percent of men have intercourse up to three times a week and around 60 percent of women once or twice a week. Middle-aged adults are still masturbating. Half of all middle-aged men masturbate at least monthly. Half of all women between 25 and 50 masturbate at least monthly, but only a third of those between 51 and 64 do so.

OLD AGE (OVER AGE 60)

More and more people stop having intercourse as the years go by—a total of 10 percent in their 40s, 15 percent in their 50s, 30 percent in their 60s, and 45 percent in their 70s. The decline in men's sexual activity usually comes gradually as they advance in age and their health fails. Sexual activity is more likely to drop off sharply for elderly women, commonly because of the death or illness of a partner. Elderly women also seem to lose interest in sex before elderly men do. Half of the women in their 60s report limited sexual interest, compared to fewer than 10 percent of the men.

Among elderly persons who remain sexually active, those in their 60s have intercourse an average of four times a month, those in their 70s two or three times a month. Around 70 percent of elderly men and 50 percent of elderly women continue to have sexual fantasies. Around half of men and a fourth of women continue to masturbate into their 90s.

Clearly sexual interests and behaviors remain an important part of life for large numbers of people, even as they grow older and as their sexual responses change to some degree.

•**EXCITEMENT PHASE**•The phase of the sexual response cycle marked by changes in the pelvic region, general physical arousal, and increases in heart rate, muscle tension, blood pressure, and rate of breathing.

•**FEMALE SEXUAL AROUSAL DISORDER**• A female dysfunction marked by a persistent inability to attain sexual excitement, including adequate lubrication or genital swelling, during sexual activity.

•**MALE ERECTILE DISORDER**•A dysfunction in which a man repeatedly fails to attain or maintain an erection during sexual activity.

•**NOCTURNAL PENILE TUMESCENCE (NPT)**• Erection during sleep.

Cultural standards can also set the stage for hypoactive sexual desire and sexual aversion. Some men adopt our culture's double standard and thus cannot feel sexual desire for a woman they love and respect. More generally, because our society equates sexual attractiveness with youthfulness, many aging men and women lose interest in sex as their self-image or their attraction to their partner diminishes with age (LoPiccolo, 2004, 1995).

The trauma of sexual molestation or assault is especially likely to produce the fears, attitudes, and memories found in these sexual dysfunctions. Sexual aversion is very common in victims of sexual abuse and may persist for years, even decades (Heiman & Heard-Davison, 2004). In extreme cases, individuals may experience vivid flashbacks of the assault during adult sexual activity.

Disorders of Excitement

The **excitement phase** of the sexual response cycle is marked by changes in the pelvic region, general physical arousal, and increases in heart rate, muscle tension, blood pressure, and rate of breathing. In men, blood pools in the pelvis and leads to erection of the penis; in women, this phase produces swelling of the clitoris and labia, as well as lubrication of the vagina. Dysfunctions affecting the excitement phase are *female sexual arousal disorder* (once referred to as "frigidity") and *male erectile disorder* (once called "impotence").

FEMALE SEXUAL AROUSAL DISORDER Women with a **sexual arousal disorder** are persistently unable to attain or maintain proper lubrication or genital swelling during sexual activity (see Table 13-2). Understandably, many of them also experience an orgasmic disorder or other sexual dysfunction. In fact, this disorder is rarely diagnosed alone (Heard-Davison et al., 2004; Heiman, 2002). Studies vary widely in their estimates of its prevalence, but most agree that more than 10 percent of women experience it (Bancroft et al., 2003; Laumann et al., 1999, 1994; Rosen et al., 1993). Because lack of sexual arousal in women is so often tied to an orgasmic disorder, researchers usually study and explain the two problems together. Correspondingly, we shall consider the causes of these problems together when we look at female orgasmic disorder.

MALE ERECTILE DISORDER Men with **erectile disorder** persistently fail to attain or maintain an adequate erection during sexual activity. This problem occurs in about 10 percent of the general male population, including Robert, the man whose difficulties opened this chapter (Heiman, 2002; Laumann et al., 1999). Carlos Domera also has erectile disorder:

Table **13-2** DSM Checklist

FEMALE SEXUAL AROUSAL DISORDER

1. Persistent or recurrent inability to attain, or to maintain until completion of the sexual activity, adequate lubrication or swelling response of sexual excitement.
2. Significant distress or interpersonal difficulty.

MALE ERECTILE DISORDER

1. Persistent or recurrent inability to attain, or to maintain until completion of the sexual activity, an adequate erection.
2. Significant distress or interpersonal difficulty.

Based on APA, 2000, 1994.

Carlos Domera is a 30-year-old dress manufacturer who came to the United States from Argentina at age 22. He is married to an American woman, Phyllis, also age 30. They have no children. Mr. Domera's problem was that he had been unable to have sexual intercourse for over a year due to his inability to achieve or maintain an erection. He had avoided all sexual contact with his wife for the prior five months, except for two brief attempts at lovemaking which ended when he failed to maintain his erection.

The couple separated a month ago by mutual agreement due to the tension that surrounded their sexual problem and their inability to feel comfortable with each other. Both professed love and concern for the other, but had serious doubts regarding their ability to resolve the sexual problem. . . .

Mr. Domera conformed to the stereotype of the "macho Latin lover," believing that he "should always have erections easily and be able to make love at any time." Since he couldn't "perform" sexually, he felt humiliated and inadequate, and he dealt with this by avoiding not only sex, but any expression of affection for his wife.

Ms. Domera felt "he is not trying; perhaps he doesn't love me, and I can't live with no sex, no affection, and his bad moods." She had requested the separation temporarily, and he readily agreed. However, they had recently been seeing each other twice a week. . . .

During the evaluation he reported that the onset of his erectile difficulties was concurrent with a tense period in his business. After several "failures" to complete intercourse, he concluded he was "useless as a husband" and therefore a "total failure." The anxiety of attempting lovemaking was too much for him to deal with.

He reluctantly admitted that he was occasionally able to masturbate alone to a full, firm erection and reach a satisfying orgasm. However, he felt ashamed and guilty about this, from both childhood masturbatory guilt and a feeling that he was "cheating" his wife. It was also noted that he had occasional firm erections upon awakening in the morning. Other than the antidepressant, the patient was taking no drugs, and he was not using much alcohol. There was no evidence of physical illness.

(Spitzer et al., 1983, pp. 105–106)

Unlike Mr. Domera, most men with an erectile disorder are over the age of 50, largely because so many cases are associated with ailments or diseases of older adults (Cameron et al., 2005). The disorder is experienced by 5 to 9 percent of all men who are 40 years old and increases to at least 15 percent at age 60 (Laumann et al., 1999; Feldman et al., 1994). Moreover, according to surveys, half of all adult men experience erectile difficulty during intercourse at least some of the time.

Most cases of erectile disorder result from an interaction of biological, psychological, and sociocultural processes (Rosen, 2003). One study found that only 10 of 63 cases of this disorder were caused by purely psychosocial factors, and only 5 were the result of physical impairment alone (LoPiccolo, 1991).

BIOLOGICAL CAUSES The same hormonal imbalances that can cause hypoactive sexual desire can also produce erectile disorder (Hyde, 2005). More commonly, however, vascular problems—problems with the body's blood vessels—are involved (Rosen, 2003; Bach et al., 2001). An erection occurs when the chambers in the penis fill with blood, so any condition that reduces blood flow into the penis, such as heart disease or clogging of the arteries, may lead to the disorder (LoPiccolo, 2004, 1997). It can also be caused by damage to the nervous system as a result of diabetes, spinal cord injuries, multiple sclerosis, kidney failure, or treatment with an artificial kidney machine (Frohman, 2002; Leiblum & Segraves, 1995). In addition, as is the case with hypoactive sexual desire, the use of certain medications and various forms of substance abuse, from alcohol abuse to cigarette smoking, may interfere with erections (Westheimer & Lopater, 2005; Rosen & Marin, 2003).

Medical procedures, including ultrasound recordings and blood tests, have been developed for diagnosing biological causes of erectile disorder. Measuring **nocturnal penile tumescence (NPT),** or erections during sleep, is particularly useful in assessing whether physical factors are responsible (Westheimer & Lopater, 2005; Althof & Seftel, 1995). Men typically have erections during *rapid eye movement (REM) sleep,* the phase of sleep in which dreaming takes place. A healthy man is likely to have two to five REM periods each night, and perhaps two to three hours of penile erections (see Figure 13-3). Abnormal or absent nightly erections usually (but not always) indicate some physical basis for erectile failure. As a rough screening device, a patient may be instructed to fasten a simple "snap gauge" band around his penis before going to sleep and then check it the next morning. A broken band indicates that erection has occurred during the night. An unbroken band indicates a lack of nighttime erections

FIGURE **13-3** **Measurements of erections during sleep** *Subject A, a man without erectile problems, has normal erections during REM sleep. Subject B has erectile problems that seem to be at least partly psychogenic—otherwise he would not have any erections during REM sleep. Subject C's erectile disorder is related to organic problems, an interpretation supported by his lack of erections during REM sleep. (Adapted from Bancroft, 1989.)*

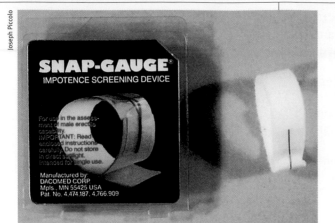

Joseph Piccolo

Psychological or organic? *The snap gauge, worn around the penis at night, is a fabric band with three plastic filaments. If the filaments are broken in the morning, the man knows that he has experienced normal erections during REM sleep and that erectile failures during intercourse are probably due to psychological factors.*

and suggests that the person's general erectile problem may have a physical basis (Mohr & Beutler, 1990).

PSYCHOLOGICAL CAUSES Any of the psychological causes of hypoactive sexual desire can also interfere with arousal and lead to erectile disorder (Rosen, 2003). As many as 90 percent of all men with severe depression, for example, experience some degree of erectile dysfunction (Seidman, 2002; Leiblum & Segraves, 1995).

One well-supported psychological explanation for erectile disorder is a cognitive theory developed by William Masters and Virginia Johnson (1970). The explanation emphasizes **performance anxiety** and the **spectator role.** Once a man begins to experience erectile problems, for whatever reason, he becomes fearful about failing to have an erection and worries during each sexual encounter. Instead of relaxing and enjoying the sensations of sexual pleasure, he remains distanced from the activity, watching himself and focusing on the goal of reaching erection. Instead of being an aroused participant, he becomes a judge and spectator. Whatever the initial reason for the erectile dysfunction, the resulting spectator role becomes the reason for the ongoing problem. In this vicious cycle, the original cause of the erectile failure becomes less important than fear of failure.

SOCIOCULTURAL CAUSES Each of the sociocultural factors that contribute to hypoactive sexual desire has also been tied to erectile disorder. Men who have lost their jobs and are under financial stress, for example, are more likely to develop erectile difficulties than other men (Morokoff & Gillilland, 1993). Marital stress, too, has been tied to this dysfunction (Metz & Epstein, 2002). Two relationship patterns in particular may contribute to it (LoPiccolo, 2004, 1991). In one, the wife provides too little physical stimulation for her aging husband, who, because of normal aging changes, now requires more intense, direct, and lengthy physical stimulation of the penis for erection to occur. In the second relationship pattern, a couple believes that only intercourse can give the wife an orgasm. This idea increases the pressure on the man to have an erection and makes him more vulnerable to erectile dysfunction. If the wife reaches orgasm manually or orally during their sexual encounter, his pressure to perform is reduced.

Disorders of Orgasm

During the **orgasm phase** of the sexual response cycle, an individual's sexual pleasure peaks and sexual tension is released as the muscles in the pelvic region contract, or draw together, rhythmically (see Figure 13-4). The man's semen is ejaculated, and the outer third of the woman's vaginal wall contracts. Dysfunctions of this phase of the sexual response cycle are *premature ejaculation, male orgasmic disorder,* and *female orgasmic disorder.*

FIGURE **13-4 Normal male sexual anatomy**
Changes in the male anatomy occur during the different phases of the sexual response cycle. (Adapted from Hyde, 1990, p. 199.)

Full erection

Partially stimulated state

Unstimulated state

Partial elevation of testes

Desire

Internal sphincter of bladder closes

Penile contractions

Urethral contractions

Contractions force the seminal fluid through the urethra

Seminal vesicles contract

Prostate gland contracts

Rectal sphincter contracts

Orgasm

PREMATURE EJACULATION Eddie is typical of many men in his experience of premature ejaculation:

> Eddie, a 20-year-old student, sought treatment after his girlfriend ended their relationship because his premature ejaculation left her sexually frustrated. Eddie had had only one previous sexual relationship, during his senior year in high school. With two friends he would drive to a neighboring town and find a certain prostitute. After picking her up, they would drive to a deserted area and take turns having sex with her, while the others waited outside the car. Both the prostitute and his friends urged him to hurry up because they feared discovery by the police, and besides, in the winter it was cold. When Eddie began his sexual relationship with his girlfriend, his entire sexual history consisted of this rapid intercourse, with virtually no foreplay. He found caressing his girlfriend's breasts and genitals and her touching of his penis to be so arousing that he sometimes ejaculated before complete entry of the penis, or after at most only a minute or so of intercourse.
>
> *(LoPiccolo, 1995, p. 495)*

A man suffering from **premature ejaculation** persistently reaches orgasm and ejaculates with very little sexual stimulation before, on, or shortly after penetration, and before he wishes to (see Table 13-3 on page 387). Around 29 percent of men in the United States experience premature ejaculation at some time (Heiman, 2002; Laumann et al., 1999, 1994). The typical duration of intercourse in our society has increased over the past several decades, in turn increasing the distress of men who suffer from premature ejaculation, typically men under the age of 30 (Bancroft, 1989).

Psychological, particularly behavioral, explanations of premature ejaculation have received more research support than other kinds of explanations. The dysfunction seems to be typical of young, sexually inexperienced men such as Eddie, who simply have not learned to slow down, control their arousal, and extend the pleasurable process of making love (Brown & Ceniceros, 2001; Metz & Pryor, 2000). In fact, premature ejaculation is very common when a young man has his first sexual encounter. With continued sexual experience, most men acquire greater control over their sexual responses. Men of any age who have sex only occasionally are also prone to ejaculate prematurely (LoPiccolo, 2004, 1985).

Clinicians have also suggested that premature ejaculation may be related to anxiety, hurried masturbation experiences during adolescence (in fear of being "caught" by parents), or poor recognition of one's own sexual arousal (Westheimer & Lopater, 2005; Dunn, Croft, & Hackette, 1999). However, these theories have only sometimes received clear research support.

MALE ORGASMIC DISORDER A man with **male orgasmic disorder** repeatedly can not reach orgasm or is very delayed in reaching orgasm after normal sexual excitement. The disorder occurs in 8 percent of the male population (Heiman, 2002; Laumann et al., 1999) and is typically a source of great frustration and upset, as in the case of John:

> John, a 38-year-old sales representative, had been married for 9 years. At the insistence of his 32-year-old wife, the couple sought counseling for their sexual problem—his inability to ejaculate during intercourse. During the early years of the marriage, his wife had experienced difficulty reaching orgasm until he learned to delay his ejaculation for a long period of time. To do this, he used mental distraction techniques and regularly smoked marijuana before making love. Initially, John felt very satisfied that he could make love for longer and longer periods of time without ejaculation and regarded his ability as a sign of masculinity.
>
> About 3 years prior to seeking counseling, after the birth of their only child, John found that he was losing his erection before he was able to ejaculate. His wife suggested different intercourse positions, but the harder he tried, the more

•**PERFORMANCE ANXIETY**•The fear of performing inadequately and a related tension experienced during sex.

•**SPECTATOR ROLE**•A state of mind that some people experience during sex, focusing on their sexual performance to such an extent that their performance and their enjoyment are reduced.

•**ORGASM PHASE**•The phase of the sexual response cycle during which an individual's sexual pleasure peaks and sexual tension is released as muscles in the pelvic region contract rhythmically.

•**PREMATURE EJACULATION**•A dysfunction in which a man reaches orgasm and ejaculates before, on, or shortly after penetration and before he wishes to.

•**MALE ORGASMIC DISORDER**•A male dysfunction characterized by repeated inability to reach orgasm or long delays in reaching orgasm after normal sexual excitement.

Grand Theft Auto: the sexual controversy *One of the most popular and controversial video game series on the market is* Grand Theft Auto. *The violence on display in these games has raised widespread concerns and led to several lawsuits. Just as controversial is the sexually explicit content in some of the games, particularly a recent version,* Grand Theft Auto: San Andreas. *Fearing that the sexual material in this game was much too graphic and suggestive for children, parents and politicians successfully pressured the video game industry to change the game's rating. Similarly, the producer of the game, Rockstar Games, eventually bowed to public pressure: it stopped manufacturing the initial version of the game and worked to develop enhanced security measures to prevent children's access to the game's sexual material.*

difficulty he had in reaching orgasm. Because of his frustration, the couple began to avoid sex altogether. John experienced increasing performance anxiety with each successive failure, and an increasing sense of helplessness in the face of his problem.

(Rosen & Rosen, 1981, pp. 317–318)

A low testosterone level, certain neurological diseases, and some head or spinal cord injuries can interfere with ejaculation (McKenna, 2005; LoPiccolo, 2004, 1995). Drugs that slow down the sympathetic nervous system (such as alcohol, some medications for high blood pressure, and certain psychotropic medications) can also affect ejaculation (Altman, 2001; Segraves, 1998, 1995, 1993). For example, *fluoxetine,* or Prozac, and other serotonin-enhancing antidepressants appear to interfere with ejaculation in as many as 40 percent of men who take them (Clayton et al., 2002; Pesce et al., 2002).

A leading psychological cause of male orgasmic disorder appears to be performance anxiety and the spectator role, the cognitive factors also involved in male erectile disorder. Once a man begins to focus on reaching orgasm, he may stop being an aroused participant in his sexual activity and instead become an unaroused, self-critical, and fearful observer (Wiederman, 2001). Finally, male orgasmic disorder may develop out of hypoactive sexual desire (Rosen & Leiblum, 1995). A man who engages in sex largely because of pressure from his partner, without any real desire for it, simply may not get aroused enough to reach orgasm.

FEMALE ORGASMIC DISORDER Stephanie and Bill, married for three years, came for sex therapy because of her lack of orgasm.

Stephanie had never had an orgasm in any way, but because of Bill's concern, she had been faking orgasm during intercourse until recently. Finally she told him the truth, and they sought therapy together. Stephanie had been raised by a strictly religious family. She could not recall ever seeing her parents kiss or show physical affection for each other. She was severely punished on one occasion when her mother found her looking at her own genitals, at about age 7. Stephanie received no sex education from her parents, and when she began to menstruate, her mother told her only that this meant that she could become pregnant, so she mustn't ever kiss a boy or let a boy touch her. Her mother restricted her dating severely, with repeated warnings that "boys only want one thing." While her parents were rather critical and demanding of her (asking her why she got one B among otherwise straight A's on her report card, for example), they were loving parents and their approval was very important to her.

(LoPiccolo, 1995, p. 496)

Women with **female orgasmic disorder** rarely reach orgasm or generally experience a very delayed one. Around 24 percent of women apparently have this problem—including more than a third of postmenopausal women (Heiman, 2002; Rosen & Leiblum, 1995). Studies indicate that 10 percent or more of women today have never had an orgasm, either alone or during intercourse, and at least another 9 percent rarely have orgasms (Bancroft et al., 2003; LoPiccolo, 1995). At the same time, half of all women experience orgasm in intercourse at least fairly regularly (LoPiccolo & Stock, 1987). Women who are more sexually assertive (Hurlbert, 1991) and more comfortable with masturbation (Kelly, Stressberg, & Kircher, 1990) tend to have orgasms more regularly. Female orgasmic disorder appears to be more common among single women than among women who are married or cohabiting (Laumann et al., 1999, 1994).

Most clinicians agree that orgasm during intercourse is not mandatory for normal sexual functioning. Many women instead reach orgasm with their partners by direct stimulation of the clitoris (LoPiccolo, 2002, 1995). Although early psychoanalytic theory considered a lack of orgasm during intercourse to be pathological, evidence suggests

>>LOOKING BACK
Nightly Visits
Orgasms can sometimes occur during sleep. Ancient Babylonians said that such nocturnal orgasms were caused by a "maid of the night" who visited men in their sleep and a "little night man" who visited women (Kahn & Fawcett, 1993). **<<**

Table 13-3 DSM Checklist

PREMATURE EJACULATION

1. Persistent or recurrent ejaculation with minimal sexual stimulation before, on, or shortly after penetration and before the person wishes it.
2. Significant distress or interpersonal difficulty.

MALE ORGASMIC DISORDER

1. Persistent or recurrent delay in, or absence of, orgasm following a normal sexual excitement phase during sexual activity.
2. Significant distress or interpersonal difficulty.

FEMALE ORGASMIC DISORDER

1. Persistent or recurrent delay in, or absence of, orgasm following a normal sexual excitement phase during sexual activity.
2. Significant distress or interpersonal difficulty.

Based on APA, 2000, 1994.

•**FEMALE ORGASMIC DISORDER**•A dysfunction in which a woman rarely has an orgasm or repeatedly experiences a very delayed one.

that women who rely on stimulation of the clitoris for orgasm are entirely normal and healthy (Stock, 1993).

As we observed earlier, female orgasmic disorder typically is linked to female sexual arousal disorder, and the two tend to be studied, explained, and treated together. Once again, biological, psychological, and sociocultural factors may combine to produce these disorders (Williams & Leiblum, 2002).

BIOLOGICAL CAUSES A variety of physiological conditions can affect a woman's arousal and orgasm. Diabetes can damage the nervous system in ways that interfere with arousal, lubrication of the vagina, and orgasm. Lack of orgasm has sometimes been linked to multiple sclerosis and other neurological diseases, to the same drugs and medications that may interfere with ejaculation in men, and to postmenopausal changes in skin sensitivity and in the structure of the clitoris and the vaginal walls (Clayton et al., 2002; Frohman, 2002; Stahl, 2001).

PSYCHOLOGICAL CAUSES The psychological causes of hypoactive sexual desire and sexual aversion may also lead to the female arousal and orgasmic disorders (Heard-Davison et al., 2004). In addition, as psychodynamic theorists might predict, memories of childhood traumas and relationships have sometimes been associated with these disorders. In one large study, memories of an unhappy childhood or loss of a parent during childhood were tied to lack of orgasm in adulthood (Raboch & Raboch, 1992). In another, childhood memories of a positive relationship with one's mother, affection between the parents, the mother's positive personality, and the mother's expression of positive emotions were all predictors of orgasm (Heiman et al., 1986).

SOCIOCULTURAL CAUSES For years many clinicians have believed that female arousal and orgasmic disorders may result from society's recurrent message to women that they should repress and deny their sexuality, a message that has often led to "less permissive" sexual attitudes and behavior among women than among men (see Figure 13-5). In fact, many women with female arousal and orgasmic disorders report that they had a strict religious upbringing, were punished for childhood masturbation, received no preparation for the onset of menstruation, were restricted in their dating as teenagers, and were told that "nice girls don't" (LoPiccolo & van Male, 2000; LoPiccolo, 1997; Masters & Johnson, 1970).

FIGURE 13-5 Is sex in a casual relationship acceptable? *Men and women around the globe have different opinions on this issue. On a scale ranging from "totally unacceptable" to "totally acceptable," college women from the United States, Russia, and Japan rated casual sex as "unacceptable" on average, whereas the ratings by men in those countries ranged from "fairly acceptable" to "quite acceptable" (Sprecher & Hatfield, 1996). Both men and women from the various countries typically considered sex among engaged or pre-engaged couples to be "quite acceptable."*

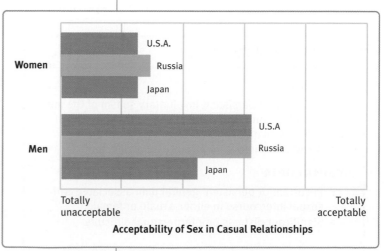

Women — U.S.A. / Russia / Japan

Men — U.S.A / Russia / Japan

Totally unacceptable — Totally acceptable

Acceptability of Sex in Casual Relationships

•**VAGINISMUS**•A condition marked by involuntary contractions of the muscles around the outer third of the vagina, preventing entry of the penis.

•**DYSPAREUNIA**•A disorder in which a person experiences severe pain in the genitals during sexual activity.

A sexually restrictive history, however, is just as common among women who function well in sexual encounters (LoPiccolo, 2002, 1997; LoPiccolo & Stock, 1987). In addition, cultural messages about female sexuality have been more positive in recent years, while the rate of female arousal and orgasmic disorders remains the same. Why, then, do some women and not others develop sexual arousal and orgasmic dysfunctions? Researchers suggest that unusually stressful events, traumas, or relationships may help produce the fears, memories, and attitudes that often characterize these dysfunctions (Westheimer & Lopater, 2005; Heiman & Heard-Davison, 2004). For example, more than half of women molested as children or raped as adults have arousal and orgasm dysfunctions (Browne & Finklehor, 1986).

Research has also related orgasmic behavior to certain qualities in a woman's intimate relationships (Metz & Epstein, 2002). One study found that the likelihood of reaching orgasm was tied to how much emotional involvement each subject had during her first experience of intercourse and how long that relationship lasted, the pleasure the woman obtained during the experience, her current attraction to her partner's body, and her marital happiness (Heiman et al., 1986). Interestingly, the same study found that erotic fantasies during sex with their current partner were much more common in orgasmic than in nonorgasmic women.

Disorders of Sexual Pain

Two sexual dysfunctions do not fit neatly into a specific phase of the sexual response cycle. These are the sexual pain disorders, *vaginismus* and *dyspareunia*, each marked by enormous physical discomfort when sexual activity is attempted.

VAGINISMUS In **vaginismus**, involuntary contractions of the muscles around the outer third of the vagina prevent entry of the penis (see Table 13-4). Severe cases can prevent a couple from ever having intercourse. Perhaps 20 percent of women occasionally experience pain during intercourse, but vaginismus probably occurs in less than 1 percent of all women (LoPiccolo & van Male, 2000; LoPiccolo, 1995).

Most clinicians agree with the cognitive-behavioral position that vaginismus is usually a learned fear response, set off by a woman's expectation that intercourse will be painful and damaging. A variety of factors apparently can set the stage for this fear, including anxiety and ignorance about intercourse, exaggerated stories about how painful and bloody the first occasion of intercourse is for women, trauma caused by an unskilled lover who forces his penis into the vagina before the woman is aroused and lubricated, and, of course, the trauma of childhood sexual abuse or adult rape (Westheimer & Lopater, 2005; Heiman & Heard-Davison, 2004; LoPiccolo, 1995).

Some women experience painful intercourse because of an infection of the vagina or urinary tract, a gynecological disease such as herpes simplex, or the physical effects of menopause. In such cases vaginismus can be overcome only if the women receive medical treatment for these conditions (LoPiccolo, 2002, 1995). Many women who have vaginismus also have other sexual dysfunctions (Heard-Davison et al., 2004; Reissing et al., 2003). Some, however, enjoy sex greatly, have a strong sex drive, and reach orgasm with stimulation of the clitoris. They just fear penetration of the vagina.

DYSPAREUNIA A person with **dyspareunia** (from Latin words meaning "painful mating") experiences severe pain in the genitals during sexual activity. Surveys suggest that as many as 14 percent of women and 3 percent of men suffer from this problem to some degree (Heiman, 2002; Laumann et al., 1999). Sufferers typically enjoy sex and get aroused but find their sex lives very limited by the pain that accompanies what used to be a positive event.

Dyspareunia in women usually has a physical cause (Bergeron et al., 2002; LoPiccolo, 1995). Among the most common are injury to the vagina, cervix, uterus, or pelvic ligaments during childbirth. Similarly, the scar left by an episiotomy (a cut often made to enlarge the vaginal entrance and ease delivery) can cause pain. Dyspareunia

Table 13-4 DSM Checklist

VAGINISMUS
1. Recurrent or persistent involuntary spasm of the muscles of the outer third of the vagina that interferes with sexual intercourse.
2. Significant distress or interpersonal difficulty.

DYSPAREUNIA
1. Recurrent or persistent genital pain associated with sexual intercourse in either a male or female.
2. Significant distress or interpersonal difficulty.

Based on APA, 2000, 1994.

has also been tied to collision of the penis with remaining parts of the hymen; infection of the vagina; wiry pubic hair that rubs against the labia during intercourse; pelvic diseases; tumors; cysts; and allergic reactions to the chemicals in vaginal douches and contraceptive creams, the rubber in condoms or diaphragms, or the protein in semen.

Although relationship problems or the psychological aftereffects of sexual abuse may contribute to this disorder, psychosocial factors alone are rarely responsible for it (Binik et al., 2002; Pukall et al., 2000). In cases that are truly psychogenic, the woman is in fact likely to be suffering from hypoactive sexual desire (Steege & Ling, 1993). That is, penetration into an unaroused, unlubricated vagina is painful.

Treatments for Sexual Dysfunctions

The last 35 years have brought major changes in the treatment of sexual dysfunctions. For the first half of the twentieth century, the leading approach was long-term psychodynamic therapy. Clinicians assumed that sexual dysfunctioning was caused by failure to progress properly through the psychosexual stages of development, and they used techniques of free association and therapist interpretations to help clients gain insight about themselves and their problems. Although it was expected that broad personality changes would lead to improvement in sexual functioning, psychodynamic therapy was typically unsuccessful (Bergler, 1951).

In the 1950s and 1960s, behavioral therapists offered new treatments for sexual dysfunctions. Usually they tried to reduce the fears that they believed were causing the dysfunctions by applying such procedures as relaxation training and systematic desensitization (Lazarus, 1965; Wolpe, 1958). These approaches had some success, but they failed to work in cases where the key problems included misinformation, negative attitudes, and lack of effective sexual technique (LoPiccolo, 2002, 1995).

A revolution in the treatment of sexual dysfunctions occurred with the publication of William Masters and Virginia Johnson's landmark book *Human Sexual Inadequacy* in 1970. The *sex therapy* program they introduced has evolved into a complex approach, which now includes techniques from the various models, particularly cognitive, behavioral, couple, and family systems therapies (Bach et al., 2001; Leiblum & Rosen, 2000). In recent years, biological interventions, particularly drug therapies, have often been added to the treatment arsenal (Segraves & Althof, 2002).

What Are the General Features of Sex Therapy?

Modern sex therapy is short-term and instructive, typically lasting 15 to 20 sessions. It centers on specific sexual problems rather than on broad personality issues (Westheimer & Lopater, 2005; LoPiccolo, 2002, 1995). Carlos Domera, the Argentine man with an erectile disorder whom we met earlier, responded successfully to the multiple techniques of modern sex therapy:

At the end of the evaluation session the psychiatrist reassured the couple that Mr. Domera had a "reversible psychological" sexual problem that was due to several factors, including his depression, but also more currently his anxiety and embarrassment, his high standards, and some cultural and relationship difficulties that made communication awkward and relaxation nearly impossible. The couple was advised that a brief trial of therapy, focused directly on the sexual problem, would very likely produce significant improvement within ten to fourteen sessions. They were assured that the problem was almost certainly not physical in origin, but rather psychogenic, and that therefore the prognosis was excellent.

Mr. Domera was shocked and skeptical, but the couple agreed to commence the therapy on a weekly basis, and they were given a typical first "assignment" to do at home: a caressing massage exercise to try together with specific instructions not to attempt genital stimulation or intercourse at all, even if an erection might occur.

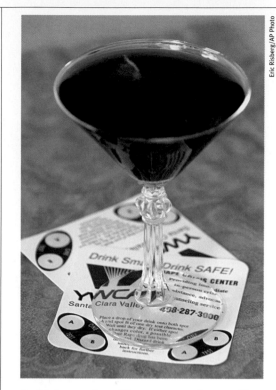

Eric Risberg/AP Photo

Do "date rape drugs" increase sexual arousal? *Many people mistakenly believe that so-called date rape drugs operate primarily by sexually arousing female victims. In fact, however, these tasteless, odorless, and colorless drugs (GHB, rohypnol, and ketamine) that sexual predators slip into the drinks or food of unsuspecting individuals, setting them up for sexual assault, operate largely by producing a near-unconscious yet responsive state in victims, eliminating clear thinking, reducing inhibitions, and impairing memory (HHS, 2004). In an effort to help women detect such drugs, special "detection coasters," such as the ones in this photo, are now being manufactured. Detection coasters are supposed to turn dark blue within 30 seconds if splashes of alcohol from the drinks sitting on them contain a date rape drug.*

>>**LOOKING AROUND**

Unusual State Sex Laws

Seven states in the United States have laws banning the cohabitation of unmarried persons. **«**

- -

Four states have laws against intercourse outside of marriage. **«**

- -

Most sex laws of this kind, which may date back centuries, are not enforced. **«**

- -

(Eisner, 2005)

>>LOOKING AROUND
Eye of the Beholder

In the movie *Annie Hall,* Annie's psycho-therapist asks her how often she and her boyfriend, Alvie Singer, sleep together. Simultaneously, across town, Alvie's therapist asks him the same question. Alvie answers, "Hardly ever, maybe three times a week," while Annie responds, "Constantly, I'd say three times a week." «

Not surprisingly, during the second session Mr. Domera reported with a cautious smile that they had "cheated" and had had intercourse "against the rules." This was their first successful intercourse in more than a year. Their success and happiness were acknowledged by the therapist, but they were cautioned strongly that rapid initial improvement often occurs, only to be followed by increased performance anxiety in subsequent weeks and a return of the initial problem. They were humorously chastised and encouraged to try again to have sexual contact involving caressing and non-demand light genital stimulation, without an expectation of erection or orgasm, and to avoid intercourse.

During the second and fourth weeks Mr. Domera did not achieve erections during the love play, and the therapy sessions dealt with helping him to accept himself with or without erections and to learn to enjoy sensual contact without intercourse. His wife helped him to believe genuinely that he could please her with manual or oral stimulation and that, although she enjoyed intercourse, she enjoyed these other stimulations as much, as long as he was relaxed.

Mr. Domera struggled with his cultural image of what a "man" does, but he had to admit that his wife seemed pleased and that he, too, was enjoying the nonintercourse caressing techniques. He was encouraged to view his new love-making skills as a "success" and to recognize that in many ways he was becoming a better lover than many husbands, because he was listening to his wife and responding to her requests.

By the fifth week the patient was attempting intercourse successfully with relaxed confidence, and by the ninth session he was responding regularly with erections. If they both agreed, they would either have intercourse or choose another sexual technique to achieve orgasm. Treatment was terminated after ten sessions.

(Spitzer et al., 1983, pp. 106–107)

As Mr. Domera's treatment indicates, modern sex therapy includes a variety of principles and techniques. The following ones are applied in almost all cases, regardless of the dysfunction:

1. **Assessment and conceptualization of the problem.** Patients are initially given a medical examination and are interviewed concerning their "sex history" (see Figure 13-6). The therapist's focus during the interview is on gathering information about past life events and, in particular, current factors that are contributing to the dysfunction (Bach et al., 2001). Sometimes proper assessment requires a team of specialists, perhaps including a psychologist, urologist, and neurologist.

2. **Mutual responsibility.** Therapists stress the principle of *mutual responsibility.* Both partners in the relationship share the sexual problem, regardless of who has the actual dysfunction, and treatment will be more successful when both are in therapy (Bach et al., 2001).

3. **Education about sexuality.** Many patients who suffer from sexual dysfunctions know very little about the physiology and techniques of sexual activity (Westheimer & Lopater, 2005). Thus sex therapists may discuss these topics and offer educational materials, including instructional books and videotapes.

4. **Attitude change.** Therapists help patients examine and change any beliefs about sexuality that are preventing sexual arousal and pleasure (Millner, 2005; Bach et al., 2001; Rosen, Leiblum, & Spector, 1994). Some of these mistaken beliefs are widely shared in our society (see Box 13-2 on page 392) and can result from past traumatic events, family attitudes, or cultural ideas.

5. **Elimination of performance anxiety and the spectator role.** Therapists often teach couples *sensate focus,* or *nondemand pleasuring,* a series of sensual tasks, sometimes called "petting" exercises, in which the partners focus on the sexual pleasure that can be achieved by exploring and caressing each other's

>>LOOKING AROUND
"Hooking Up"

In colleges around the country, "hooking up" has become an alternative to "dating" for many students. The people who used to be "boyfriends" or "girlfriends" are now "hookups." «

- -

"Hooking up" refers to a sexual encounter—anything from kissing to intercourse—between acquaintances who have no plans to repeat the experience or even necessarily to talk afterward. «

- -

Several college surveys reveal that 60 percent of students have "hooked up" at least once and that they usually did so after consuming alcohol. «

- -

(McGinn, 2004)

body at home, without demands to have intercourse or reach orgasm—demands that may be interfering with arousal. Couples are told at first to refrain from intercourse at home and to restrict their sexual activity to kissing, hugging, and sensual massage of various parts of the body, but not of the breasts or genitals. Over time, they learn how to give and receive greater sexual pleasure and they build back up to the activity of sexual intercourse.

6. **Increasing sexual and general communication skills.** Couples are told to use their sensate-focus sessions at home to try sexual positions in which the person being caressed can guide the other's hands and control the speed, pressure, and location of the caressing. Couples are also taught to give instructions in a nonthreatening, informative manner ("It feels better over here, with a little less pressure"), rather than a threatening uninformative manner ("The way you're touching me doesn't turn me on"). Moreover, couples are often given broader training in how best to communicate with each other (Bach et al., 2001).

7. **Changing destructive lifestyles and marital interactions.** A therapist may encourage a couple to change their lifestyle or take other steps to improve a situation that is having a destructive effect on their relationship—to distance themselves from interfering in-laws, for example, or to change a job that is too demanding. Similarly, if the couple's general relationship is marked by conflict, the therapist will try to help them improve it (Metz & Epstein, 2002).

8. **Addressing physical and medical factors.** When sexual dysfunctions are caused by a medical problem, such as disease, injury, medication, or substance abuse, therapists try to address that problem (Winton, 2000). If antidepressant medications are causing a man's erectile disorder, for example, the clinician may lower the dosage of the medication, change the time of day when the drug is taken, or prescribe a different antidepressant (Segraves, 1998, 1995).

CALLAHAN

"When I touch him he rolls into a ball."

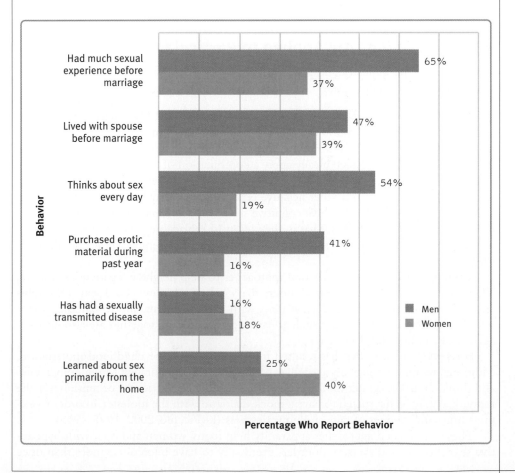

FIGURE 13-6 Sexual behavior and gender
According to questionnaires, men are much more likely than women to think about sex on a daily basis and to have purchased sexual material, such as erotic magazines, within the past year. Women are more likely to have learned about sex from the home. (Adapted from Michael et al., 1994; Janus & Janus, 1993.)

[BOX 13-2]

Sex-Role Myths

MYTHS OF MALE SEXUALITY

◆ A real man isn't into stuff like feelings and communicating.

◆ A man is always interested in and ready for sex.

◆ Sex is centered on a hard penis and what is done with it.

◆ A man should be able to make the earth move for his partner.

◆ Men don't have to listen to women in sex.

◆ Bigger is better.

◆ Men should be able to last all night during sex.

◆ Women typically dislike or disapprove of men who are unable to have an erection.

◆ If a man can't have an erection, he must not really love his partner.

◆ If a man knows that he might not be able to get an erection, it's unfair for him to start sexual activity with a partner.

◆ Focusing more intensely on one's erection—trying harder—is the best way to get an erection.

MYTHS OF FEMALE SEXUALITY

◆ Sex is only for women under 30.

◆ Normal women have an orgasm every time they have sex.

◆ All women can have multiple orgasms.

◆ Pregnancy and delivery reduce women's sexual responsiveness.

◆ A woman's sex life ends with menopause.

◆ A sexually responsive woman can always be aroused by her partner.

◆ Nice women aren't aroused by erotic books or films.

◆ Women are "frigid" if they don't like the more exotic forms of sex.

◆ If a woman can't have an orgasm quickly and easily, there's something wrong with her.

◆ Feminine women don't initiate sex or become unrestrained during sex.

◆ Contraception is a woman's responsibility, and she's just making up excuses if she says contraception issues are inhibiting her sexually.

MYTHS OF MALE AND FEMALE SEXUALITY

◆ All touching is sexual or should lead to sex.

◆ Sex equals intercourse.

◆ Good sex requires orgasm.

◆ It isn't romantic if a person asks the partner what he or she enjoys.

◆ Too much masturbation is bad.

◆ Someone with a sex partner does not masturbate.

◆ Fantasizing about someone else during sex means a person is not happy with the person he or she is in a relationship with.

(BACH ET AL., 2001, P. 585)

What Techniques Are Applied to Particular Dysfunctions?

In addition to the general components of sex therapy, specific techniques can help in each of the sexual dysfunctions.

HYPOACTIVE SEXUAL DESIRE AND SEXUAL AVERSION Hypoactive sexual desire and sexual aversion are among the most difficult dysfunctions to treat because of the many issues that may feed into them (Westheimer & Lopater, 2005; LoPiccolo, 2004, 2002, 1997). Thus therapists typically apply a combination of techniques. In a technique called *affectual awareness,* patients visualize sexual scenes in order to discover any feelings of anxiety, vulnerability, and other negative emotions they may have concerning sex. In another technique, patients receive cognitive *self-instruction training* to help them change their negative reactions to sex. That is, they learn to replace negative statements during sex with "coping statements," such as "I can allow myself to enjoy sex; it doesn't mean I'll lose control."

Therapists may also use behavioral approaches to help heighten a patient's sex drive. They may instruct clients to keep a "desire diary" in which they record sexual thoughts and feelings, to read books and view films with erotic content, and to fantasize about sex. Pleasurable shared activities such as dancing and walking together are also encouraged (LoPiccolo, 2002, 1997).

For sexual aversion that has resulted from sexual assault or childhood molestation, additional techniques may be needed. A patient may be encouraged to remember, talk, and think about the assault until the memories no longer arouse fear or tension. Or the individual may be instructed to have a mock dialogue with the molester, in order to express lingering feelings of rage and powerlessness (LoPiccolo, 2002, 1997, 1995).

These and related approaches apparently help many women and men with hypoactive sexual desire and aversion disorders eventually to have intercourse more than once a week (Heard-Davison et al., 2004; Hurlbert, 1993). However, only a few controlled studies have been conducted. Finally, biological interventions, such as hormone treatments, have been used, particularly among women whose problems arose after removal of their ovaries or later in life; these interventions have received some research support (Gale Group, 2005; Davis, 2000, 1998; Shifren et al., 2000).

ERECTILE DISORDER Treatments for erectile disorder focus on reducing a man's performance anxiety or increasing his stimulation or both (Segraves & Althof, 2002; Rosen, 2000). During sensate-focus exercises, the couple may be instructed to try the *tease technique:* the partner keeps caressing the man, but if the man gets an erection, the partner stops caressing him until he loses it. This exercise reduces pressure on the man to perform and at the same time teaches the couple that erections occur naturally in response to stimulation, as long as the partners do not keep focusing on performance. In another technique, the couple may be instructed to use manual or oral sex to try to achieve the woman's orgasm, again reducing pressure on the man to perform (LoPiccolo, 2004, 2002, 1995).

Biological approaches, applied particularly when erectile disorder has biological causes, gained great momentum with the development in 1998 of *sildenafil* (trade name Viagra) (Gross & Blundo, 2005; Perelman, 2002). This drug increases blood flow to the penis within one hour of ingestion; the increased blood flow enables the user to attain an erection during sexual activity (see Box 13-3 on the next page). Sildenafil appears to be relatively safe except for men with certain coronary heart diseases and cardiovascular diseases, particularly those who are taking nitroglycerin and other heart medications (Bach et al., 2001). In recent years, two other erectile dysfunction drugs have been approved—*tadalafil* (Cialis) and *vardenafil* (Levitra)—and are now actively competing with Viagra for a share of the lucrative marketplace. In addition, several other erectile dysfunction drugs are currently in development.

Most of the other biological approaches for erectile disorder have been around for years (Wylie et al., 2003; Frohman, 2002; Heiman, 2002). These include gel suppositories, injections of drugs into the penis, and a *vacuum erection device* (*VED*), a hollow cylinder that is placed over the penis. Here a man uses a hand pump to pump air out of the cylinder, drawing blood into his penis and producing an erection. In another biological approach, surgeons may implant a *penile prosthesis*—a semirigid rod made of rubber and wire—to produce an artificial erection. However, because the new drugs are easy to take and helpful to more than half of patients, drug therapy is the approach now receiving the most attention (Bach et al., 2001).

MALE ORGASMIC DISORDER Like treatment for male erectile disorder, therapies for male orgasmic disorder include techniques to reduce performance anxiety and increase stimulation (LoPiccolo, 2004; Segraves & Althof, 2002). In one technique, a man may be instructed to masturbate to orgasm in the presence of his partner or to masturbate just short of orgasm before inserting his penis for intercourse (Marshall, 1997). This increases the likelihood that he will ejaculate during intercourse. He then is instructed to insert his penis at ever earlier stages of masturbation.

When male orgasmic disorder is caused by physical factors such as neurological damage or injury, treatment may include a drug to increase arousal of the sympathetic nervous system (Murphy & Lipshultz, 1988). However, few studies have systematically tested the effectiveness of such treatments (Rosen & Leiblum, 1995).

PREMATURE EJACULATION Premature ejaculation has been treated successfully for years by behavioral procedures (Heiman, 2002; Masters & Johnson, 1970). In the *stop-start,* or *pause,* procedure, the penis is manually stimulated until the man is highly aroused. The couple then pauses until his arousal subsides, after which the stimulation is resumed. This sequence is repeated several times before stimulation is carried through to ejaculation, so the man ultimately experiences much more total time of stimulation than he has ever experienced before (LoPiccolo, 2004, 1995). Eventually the couple

Courtesy of the Everett Collection

Myth breakers *Few television shows have gone further to challenge old myths about female sexuality than the comedy series* Sex and the City. *Although most sex theorists acknowledge this show's role in helping to change women's (and men's) misconceptions about female sexuality, some worry that it has created a few myths of its own that may be difficult for today's women to identify with or live up to.*

>>**LOOKING AROUND**
The Next Sex Drug?

In 2005, a pharmaceutical company announced that it is currently developing a drug named **dapoxetine** for treatment of premature ejaculation. ‹‹

Early studies indicate that the new drug increases intercourse time from under one minute to, on average, more than three minutes. ‹‹

Several drugs are also currently being developed for treatment of female hyposexual desire, particularly among postmenopausal women. ‹‹

(Bunch, 2005; Tyre, 2004)

[BOX **13-3**]

Sociocultural Landscape: Sexism, Viagra, and the Pill

Many of us believe that we live in an enlightened world, where sexism is declining and where health care and benefits are available to men and women in equal measure. Periodically, however, such illusions are shattered. The responses of government agencies and insurance companies to the discovery and marketing of Viagra in 1998 may be a case in point.

Consider, first, the nation of Japan. In early 1999, just six months after Viagra's sensational introduction in the United States, the drug was approved for use among men in Japan (Martin, 2000). In contrast, low-dose contraceptives—"the pill"—were not approved for use among women in that country until June 1999—a full 40 years after their introduction elsewhere! Many observers believe that birth control pills would still be un-

available to women in Japan had Viagra not received its quick approval.

Has the United States been able to avoid such an apparent double standard in its health-care system? Not really. Before Viagra was introduced, insurance companies were not required to reimburse women for the cost of prescription contraceptives. As a result, women had to pay 68 percent more out-of-pocket expenses for health care than did men, largely because of uncovered reproductive health-care costs (Hayden, 1998). Some legislators had sought to correct this problem by requiring contraceptive coverage in health insurance plans, but their efforts failed in state after state for more than a decade.

In contrast, when Viagra was introduced in 1998, many insurance companies readily agreed to cover the new drug and many states included Viagra as part of Medicaid coverage. As the public outcry grew over the contrast between coverage of Viagra for men and lack of coverage of oral contraceptives for women, laws across the country finally began to change. In fact, by the

end of 1998, nine states required prescription contraceptive coverage (Hayden, 1998). Today 22 states require such coverage by private insurance companies and 35 states require it for state employees (CRR, 2005). Moreover, if the proposed Equity in Prescription Insurance and Contraceptive Coverage Act is passed by Congress, all insurers in the nation will be required to reimburse women for the cost of oral contraceptives.

In the meantime, wishful thinkers express hope that generous private donors will help foot the bill of oral contraceptives as some donors have done for Viagra. Immediately after Viagra's approval, one noted philanthropist donated $1 million to provide this drug to the needy. In explaining his action, he said, "I saw an article saying that at $10 apiece, a lot of impotent men wouldn't be able to afford it. So I said [to my wife], . . . 'let's help,' and by Tuesday we had it done" (Carlson, 1998).

progresses to putting the penis in the vagina, making sure to withdraw it and to pause whenever the man becomes too highly aroused. According to clinical reports, after two or three months many couples can enjoy prolonged intercourse without any need for pauses (LoPiccolo, 2004, 2002, 1995).

In a related procedure, the *squeeze technique,* a man with this dysfunction reaches near-ejaculation and then he or his partner applies a firm squeeze to the ridge of his penis below its head. If done correctly, the squeeze causes a partial or total loss of erection (Masters & Johnson, 1970). As in the stop–start procedure, this sequence is repeated several times.

Some clinicians treat premature ejaculation with *fluoxetine* (Prozac) and other serotonin-enhancing antidepressant drugs (Brown & Ceniceros, 2001). Because these drugs often reduce sexual arousal or orgasm, the reasoning goes, they may be helpful to men who experience premature ejaculation. Although some studies have reported positive results (Althof, 1995; Althof et al., 1994), researchers have yet to examine the long-term impact of these drugs on men with premature ejaculation. Nor have they determined whether such drugs may be combined effectively with psychological and interpersonal techniques (Rosen & Leiblum, 1995).

FEMALE AROUSAL AND ORGASMIC DISORDERS Specific treatments for female arousal and orgasmic dysfunctions include cognitive-behavioral techniques, self-exploration, enhancement of body awareness, and directed masturbation training (Millner, 2005; Heiman, 2002, 2000; LoPiccolo, 2002, 1997). These procedures are especially useful for women who have never had an orgasm under any circumstances. Hormone therapy is also being used increasingly (Davis, 2000, 1998; Warnock et al., 1999).

In **directed masturbation training,** a woman is taught step by step how to masturbate effectively and eventually to reach orgasm during sexual interactions. The training includes use of diagrams and reading material, private self-stimulation, erotic material and fantasies, "orgasm triggers" such as holding her breath or thrusting her pelvis, sensate focus with her partner, and sexual positioning that produces stimulation of the clitoris during intercourse. This training program appears to be highly effective: over 90 percent of women learn to have an orgasm during masturbation, about 80 percent during caressing by their partners, and about 30 percent during intercourse (LoPiccolo, 2002, 1997; Heiman & LoPiccolo, 1988).

As we observed earlier, a lack of orgasm during intercourse is not necessarily a sexual dysfunction, provided the woman enjoys intercourse and can reach orgasm through caressing, either by her partner or by herself. For this reason some therapists believe that the wisest course is simply to educate women whose only concern is lack of orgasm during intercourse, informing them that they are quite normal.

VAGINISMUS Specific treatment for vaginismus, involuntary contractions of the muscles around the vagina, takes two approaches (Kabakci & Batur, 2003; Heiman, 2002). First, a woman may practice tightening and relaxing her vaginal muscles until she gains more voluntary control over them. Second, she may receive gradual behavioral exposure treatment to help her overcome her fear of penetration, beginning by inserting increasingly large dilators in her vagina at home and at her own pace and eventually ending with the insertion of her partner's penis. Over 75 percent of the women treated for vaginismus eventually have pain-free intercourse (Heinman, 2002; Beck, 1993). Many women with this problem, however, report that they received ineffective or inaccurate forms of treatment when they first sought help from their physicians (Ogden & Ward, 1995).

DYSPAREUNIA We saw earlier that the most common cause of dyspareunia, genital pain during intercourse, is physical, such as pain-causing scars or lesions. When the cause is known, a couple can learn intercourse positions that avoid putting pressure on the injured area. A medical intervention may also be tried, but it must still be combined with other sex therapy techniques to overcome the years of sexual anxiety and lack of arousal (Heard-Davison et al., 2004; Bergeron et al., 2002, 2001; Binik et al., 2002, 2000). Because many cases of dyspareunia are in fact caused by undiagnosed physical problems, it is very important that clients receive expert gynecological exams (Reid & Lininger, 1993).

What Are the Current Trends in Sex Therapy?

Sex therapists have now moved well beyond the approach first developed by Masters and Johnson (Bach et al., 2001; Rosen & Leiblum, 1995). For example, today's sex therapists regularly treat partners who are living together but not married. They also treat sexual dysfunctions that arise from psychological disorders such as depression, mania, schizophrenia, and certain personality disorders (Rowlands, 1995). In addition, sex therapists no longer screen out clients with severe marital discord, the elderly, the medically ill, or the physically handicapped (Schover, 2000; Dupont, 1995) or clients with a homosexual

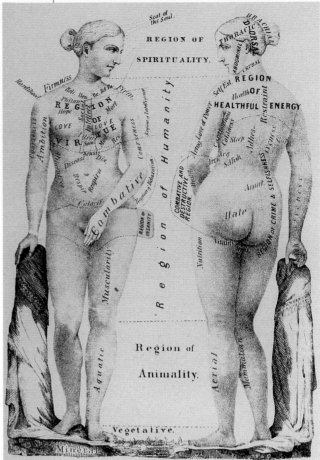

From Joseph R. Buchanan, *Outlines of Lectures on the Neurological System of Anthropology*, Cincinnati, 1854. The Oskar Diethelm Library, Department of Psychiatry, Cornell University Medical College and The New York Hospital, New York

"The region of insanity" *Medical authorities described "excessive passion" in Victorian women as dangerous and as a possible cause of insanity (Gamwell & Tomes, 1995). This illustration from a nineteenth-century medical textbook even labels a woman's reproductive organs as her "region of insanity."*

•**DIRECTED MASTURBATION TRAINING**•
A sex therapy approach that teaches women with female arousal or orgasmic disorders how to masturbate effectively and eventually to reach orgasm during sexual interactions.

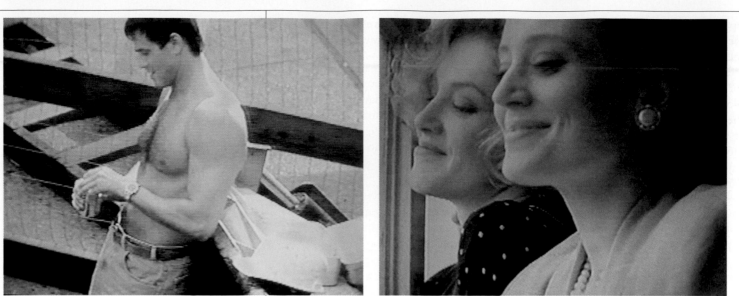

A new message *Over the past several decades, Western society has increasingly viewed female sexual arousal and expression as normal and healthful and has sent this message to women through novels, movies, television shows, and magazines. This Diet Coke ad in which two women openly ogle a sexy construction worker was one of the most discussed television commercials of the 1990s.*

orientation or those who have no long-term sex partner (Stravynski et al., 1997). Sex therapists are also paying more attention to excessive sexuality, sometimes called *sexual addiction* (Kafka, 2000).

Many sex therapists currently worry about the sharp increase in the use of drugs and other medical interventions for sexual dysfunctions, particularly for hypoactive sexual desire and male erectile disorder. Their concern is that therapists will increasingly choose the biological interventions rather than integrating biological, psychological, and sociocultural interventions (Heiman, 2002; Leiblum, 2002; Millner & Ullery, 2002). In fact, a narrow approach of any kind probably cannot fully address the complex factors that cause most sexual problems. It took sex therapists years to recognize the considerable advantages of an integrated approach to sexual dysfunctions. The development of new medical interventions should not lead to its abandonment.

Paraphilias

Paraphilias are disorders in which individuals repeatedly have intense sexual urges or fantasies or display sexual behaviors that involve nonhuman objects, children, nonconsenting adults, or the experience of suffering or humiliation. Many people with a paraphilia can become aroused only when a paraphilic stimulus is present, fantasized about, or acted out. Others need the stimulus only during times of stress or under other special circumstances.

According to DSM-IV-TR, a diagnosis of paraphilia should be applied only when the urges, fantasies, or behaviors last at least six months (see Table 13-5). For most paraphilias, the urges, fantasies, or behaviors must also cause great distress or interfere with one's social life or job performance in order for a diagnosis to be applied (APA, 2000). For certain paraphilias, however, DSM-IV-TR clarifies that performance of the sexual behavior indicates a disorder even if the individual experiences no distress or impairment (APA, 2000). People who initiate sexual contact with children, for example, warrant a diagnosis of pedophilia regardless of how troubled the individuals may or may not be over their behavior.

Some people with one kind of paraphilia display others as well (Langstrom & Zucker, 2005; McAnulty et al., 2001). Relatively few people receive a formal diagnosis of paraphilia, but the large market in paraphilic pornography leads clinicians to suspect that the patterns may be quite common (APA, 2000). People whose paraphilias involve children or nonconsenting adults often come to the attention of clinicians when they get into legal trouble (Maletzky & Steinhauser, 2004). Some experts argue that, with the exception of such nonconsensual paraphilias, paraphilic activities should be considered a disorder only when they are the exclusive or preferred means of achieving sexual excitement and orgasm (Moser, 2001).

•**PARAPHILIAS**•Disorders characterized by recurrent and intense sexual urges, fantasies, or behaviors involving nonhuman objects, children, nonconsenting adults, or experiences of suffering or humiliation.

•**FETISHISM**•A paraphilia consisting of recurrent and intense sexual urges, fantasies, or behaviors that involve the use of a nonliving object, often to the exclusion of all other stimuli.

Although theorists have proposed various explanations for paraphilias, there is little formal evidence to support them (McConaghy, 2005; Weiss, 2001). Moreover, none of the many treatments applied to paraphilias have received much research or proved clearly effective (McConaghy, 2005; Maletzky, 2002). Psychological and sociocultural treatments for paraphilias have been available the longest, but today's professionals are also using biological interventions. Some clinicians administer drugs called *antiandrogens* that lower the production of testosterone, the male sex hormone, and reduce the sex drive (Briken et al., 2003; Krueger & Kaplan, 2002; Raymond et al., 2001). Although such drugs do indeed reduce paraphilic patterns, several of them disrupt normal sexual feelings and behavior as well. Thus the drugs tend to be applied primarily when the paraphilias are of danger either to the individuals themselves or to other people. Clinicians have also become interested in the possible use of serotonin-enhancing antidepressant medications to treat persons with paraphilias, hoping that the drugs will reduce these compulsion-like sexual behaviors just as they help reduce other kinds of compulsions.

Fetishism

Key features of **fetishism** are recurrent intense sexual urges, sexually arousing fantasies, or behaviors that involve the use of a nonliving object, often to the exclusion of all other stimuli. Usually the disorder begins in adolescence. Almost anything can be a fetish; women's underwear, shoes, and boots are particularly common (APA, 2000, 1994). Some people with fetishism commit thievery in order to collect as many of the desired objects as possible. The objects may be touched, smelled, worn, or used in some other way while the person masturbates, or the individual may ask a partner to wear the object when they have sex. Several of these features are seen in the following case:

A 32-year-old, single male . . . related that although he was somewhat sexually attracted by women, he was far more attracted by "their panties."

To the best of the patient's memory, sexual excitement began at about age 7, when he came upon a pornographic magazine and felt stimulated by pictures of partially nude women wearing "panties." His first ejaculation occurred at 13 via masturbation to fantasies of women wearing panties. He masturbated into his older sister's panties, which he had stolen without her knowledge. Subsequently he stole panties from her friends and from other women he met socially. He found pretexts to "wander" into the bedrooms of women during social occasions, and would quickly rummage through their possessions until he found a pair of panties to his satisfaction. He later used these to masturbate into, and then "saved them" in a "private cache." The pattern of masturbating into women's underwear had been his preferred method of achieving sexual excitement and orgasm from adolescence until the present consultation.

(Spitzer et al., 1994, p. 247)

Researchers have not been able to pinpoint the causes of fetishism. Psychodynamic theorists view fetishes as defense mechanisms that help people avoid the anxiety produced by normal sexual contact. Psychodynamic treatment for this problem, however, has met with little success (LoPiccolo, 1992).

Behaviorists propose that fetishes are acquired through classical conditioning (Akins, 2004; Doctor & Neff, 2001). In one behavioral study, male subjects were shown a series of slides of nude women along with slides of boots (Rachman, 1966). After many trials, the subjects became aroused by the boot photos alone. If early sexual experiences similarly occur in the presence of particular objects, perhaps the stage is set for development of fetishes.

Behaviorists have sometimes treated fetishism with *aversion therapy* (Krueger & Kaplan, 2002). In one study, an electric shock was administered to the arms or legs of subjects with fetishes while they imagined their objects of desire (Marks & Gelder, 1967). After two weeks of therapy all subjects in the study showed at least some improvement. In another aversion technique, *covert sensitization,* people with fetishism are guided to

---

Table 13-5 DSM Checklist

PARAPHILIA

1. Over a period of at least six months, recurrent, intense sexually arousing fantasies, sexual urges, or behaviors involving certain inappropriate stimuli or situations (nonhuman objects; the suffering or humiliation of oneself or one's partner; or children or other nonconsenting persons).

2. Significant distress or impairment over the fantasies, urges, or behaviors. (In some paraphilias—pedophilia, exhibitionism, voyeurism, frotteurism, and sexual sadism—the performance of paraphilic behaviors indicates a disorder, even in the absence of distress or impairment.)

Based on APA, 2000.

>>PSYCH•LISTINGS

Some Brain Parts Involved in Sexual Responses

Sensory vagus nerves ‹‹

Midbrain reticular formation ‹‹

Basal ganglia ‹‹

Anterior insula cortex ‹‹

Amygdala ‹‹

Cerebellum ‹‹

Hypothalamus ‹‹

Pituitary gland ‹‹

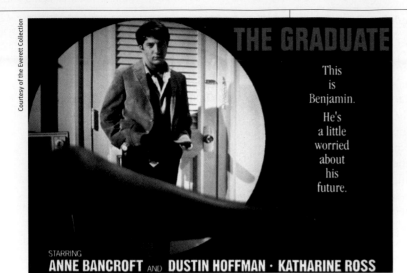

Mrs. Robinson's stockings *The 1967 film* The Graduate *helped define a generation by focusing on the personal confusion, apathy, and sexual adventures of a young man in search of meaning. Marketers decided to promote this film by using a fetishistic-like photo of Mrs. Robinson putting on her stockings under Benjamin's watchful eye, a scene forever identified with the movie.*

•**MASTURBATORY SATIATION**•A behavioral treatment in which a client masturbates for a very long period of time while fantasizing in detail about a paraphilic object. The procedure is expected to produce a feeling of boredom that in turn becomes linked to the object.

•**ORGASMIC REORIENTATION**•A procedure for treating certain paraphilias by teaching clients to respond to new, more appropriate sources of sexual stimulation.

•**TRANSVESTIC FETISHISM**•A paraphilia consisting of repeated and intense sexual urges, fantasies, or behaviors that involve dressing in clothes of the opposite sex. Also known as *transvestism* or *cross-dressing.*

•**EXHIBITIONISM**•A paraphilia in which persons have repeated sexually arousing urges or fantasies about exposing their genitals to another person, and may act upon those urges.

•**VOYEURISM**•A paraphilia in which a person has repeated and intense sexual desires to observe unsuspecting people in secret as they undress or to spy on couples having intercourse, and may act upon these desires.

imagine the pleasurable object and repeatedly to pair this image with an *imagined* aversive stimulus until the object of sexual pleasure is no longer desired.

Another behavioral treatment for fetishism is **masturbatory satiation** (Krueger & Kaplan, 2002; Quinsey & Earls, 1990). In this method, the client masturbates to orgasm while fantasizing about a sexually appropriate object, then switches to fantasizing in detail about fetishistic objects while masturbating again and continues the fetishistic fantasy for an hour. The procedure is meant to produce a feeling of boredom, which in turn becomes linked to the fetishistic object.

Yet another behavioral approach to fetishism, also used for other paraphilias, is **orgasmic reorientation,** which teaches individuals to respond to more appropriate sources of sexual stimulation. People are shown conventional stimuli while they are responding to unconventional objects. A person with a shoe fetish, for example, may be instructed to obtain an erection from pictures of shoes and then to begin masturbating to a picture of a nude woman. If he starts to lose the erection, he must return to the pictures of shoes until he is masturbating effectively, then change back to the picture of the nude woman. When orgasm approaches, he must direct all attention to the conventional stimulus.

Transvestic Fetishism

Transvestic fetishism, also known as **transvestism** or **cross-dressing,** is a recurrent need or desire to dress in clothes of the opposite sex in order to achieve sexual arousal. In the following passage, a 42-year-old married father describes his pattern:

I have been told that when I dress in drag, at times I look like Whistler's Mother [laughs], especially when I haven't shaved closely. I usually am good at detail, and I make sure when I dress as a woman that I have my nails done just so, and that my colors match. Honestly, it's hard to pin a date on when I began cross dressing. . . . If pressed, I would have to say it began when I was about 10 years of age, fooling around with and putting on my mom's clothes. . . . I was always careful to put everything back in its exact place, and in 18 years of doing this in her home, my mother never, I mean never, suspected, or questioned me about putting on her clothes. I belong to a transvestite support group . . . , a group for men who cross dress. Some of the group are homosexuals, but most are not. A true transvestite—and I am one, so I know—is not homosexual. We don't discriminate against them in the group at all; hey, we have enough trouble getting acceptance as normal people and not just a bunch of weirdos ourselves. They are a bunch of nice guys . . . , really. Most of them are like me.

Most of [the men in the group] have told their families about their dressing inclinations, but those that are married are a mixed lot; some wives know and some don't, they just suspect. I believe in honesty, and told my wife about this before we were married. We're separated now, but I don't think it's because of my cross dressing. . . . I have been asked many times why I cross dress, and it's hard to explain, other than it makes me feel good. There is something deep down that it gratifies. Some of my friends, when I was growing up, suggested psychotherapy, but I don't regard this as a problem. If it bothers someone else, then they have the problem. . . . I function perfectly well sexually with my wife, though it took her some time to be comfortable with me wearing feminine underwear; yes, sometimes I wear it while making love, it just makes it more exciting.

(Janus & Janus, 1993, p. 121)

Like this man, the typical person with transvestism, almost always a heterosexual male, begins cross-dressing in childhood or adolescence (Langstrom & Zucker, 2005; Doctor &

Neff, 2001). He is the picture of characteristic masculinity in everyday life and is usually alone when he cross-dresses. A small percentage of such men cross-dress to visit bars or social clubs. Some wear a single item of women's clothing, such as underwear or hosiery, under their masculine clothes. Others wear makeup and dress fully as women. Some married men with transvestism involve their wives in their cross-dressing behavior (Kolodny, Masters, & Johnson, 1979). The disorder is often confused with *gender identity disorder* (*transsexualism*), but, as we shall see, they are two separate patterns.

The development of transvestic fetishism sometimes seems to follow the behavioral principles of operant conditioning. In such cases, parents or other adults may openly encourage the individuals to cross-dress as children or even reward them for this behavior. In one case, a woman was delighted to discover that her young nephew enjoyed dressing in girls' clothes. She had always wanted a niece, and she proceeded to buy him dresses and jewelry and sometimes dressed him as a girl and took him out shopping.

A group approach *"Crossroads" is a self-help group for men with transvestic fetishism, a recurrent need to dress in women's clothing as a means to achieve sexual arousal.*

Exhibitionism

A person with **exhibitionism** has recurrent urges to expose his genitals to another person, almost always a member of the opposite sex, or has sexually arousing fantasies of doing so. He may also carry out those urges but rarely attempts to initiate sexual activity with the person to whom he exposes himself (APA, 2000, 1994; Maletzky, 2000). More often, he wants to provoke shock or surprise. Sometimes an exhibitionist will expose himself in a particular neighborhood at particular hours. Around half of all women report having seen or had direct contact with an exhibitionist, or so-called flasher (Doctor & Neff, 2001). The urge to exhibit typically becomes stronger when the person has free time or is under significant stress.

Generally the disorder begins before age 18 and is most common in males (APA, 2000, 1994). Persons with exhibitionism are typically immature in their dealings with the opposite sex and have difficulty in interpersonal relationships. Around 30 percent of them are married and another 30 percent divorced or separated; their sexual relations with their wives are not usually satisfactory (Doctor & Neff, 2001). Many have doubts or fears about their masculinity, and some seem to have a strong bond to a possessive mother.

As with other paraphilias, treatment generally includes aversion therapy and masturbatory satiation, possibly combined with orgasmic reorientation, social skills training, or insight therapy (Krueger & Kaplan, 2002; Maletzky 2002, 2000). Clinicians have also reported some success with hypnotherapy (Epstein, 1983; Polk, 1983).

Voyeurism

A person who engages in **voyeurism** has recurrent and intense urges to secretly observe unsuspecting people as they undress or to spy on couples having intercourse. The person may also masturbate during the act of observing or when thinking about it afterward but does not generally seek to have sex with the person being spied on. This disorder usually begins before the age of 15 and tends to persist (APA, 2000, 1994).

The vulnerability of the people being observed and the probability that they would feel humiliated if they knew they were under observation are often part of the individual's enjoyment. In addition, the risk of being discovered often adds to the excitement, as we see in the following statement by a man with this disorder:

> Looking at a nude girlfriend wouldn't be as exciting as seeing her the sneaky way. It's not just the nude body but the sneaking out and seeing what you're not supposed to see. The risk of getting caught makes it exciting. I don't want to get caught, but every time I go out I'm putting myself on the line.
>
> *(Yalom, 1960, p. 316)*

>>LOOKING AROUND

Cybersex Almost 19 percent of all Internet visits by Americans are to "adult" Web sites, where individuals talk in chat rooms, view erotica, or the like (CNN, 2004). Female visitors tend to join chat rooms, while male users tend to visit visual erotica sites (Cooper et al., 1999). Around 3 percent of all Internet users are considered sexually compulsive in their online behavior (Bailey, 2003). <<

Dangerous Interactions A study of Internet chat rooms for children and teens estimated that two-thirds of the visitors were actually adults pretending to be children and seeking to engage in sex talk or to acquire or trade pornographic material (Lamb, 1998). <<

Playful context *Dressing in clothes of the opposite sex does not necessarily convey a paraphilia. Back in 1966, for example, The Rolling Stones dressed as women to publicize the song "Have You Seen Your Mother, Baby, Standing in the Shadows," from their album* Between the Buttons. *In case you have trouble recognizing them, the Stones are (left to right) Brian Jones, Keith Richards, Mick Jagger, Charlie Watts, and Bill Wyman sitting in the front.*

•**FROTTEURISM**•A paraphilia consisting of repeated and intense sexual urges, fantasies, or behaviors that involve touching and rubbing against a nonconsenting person.

•**PEDOPHILIA**•A paraphilia in which a person has repeated and intense sexual urges or fantasies about watching, touching, or engaging in sexual acts with prepubescent children, and may carry out these urges or fantasies.

•**SEXUAL MASOCHISM**•A paraphilia characterized by repeated and intense sexual urges, fantasies, or behaviors that involve being humiliated, beaten, bound, or otherwise made to suffer.

Voyeurism, like exhibitionism, can play a role in normal sexuality, but in such cases it is engaged in with the consent or understanding of the partner. The clinical disorder of voyeurism is marked by the repeated invasion of other people's privacy. Some people with voyeurism are unable to have normal sexual relations; others, however, have a normal sex life apart from their voyeurism.

Many psychodynamic clinicians propose that people with voyeurism are seeking by their actions to gain power over others, possibly because they feel inadequate or are sexually or socially shy (Metzl, 2004). Others have explained voyeurism as an attempt to reduce fears of castration, originally produced by the sight of an adult's genitals. Theoretically, people with voyeurism are repeating the behavior that produced the original fright, to reassure themselves that there is nothing to fear (Fenichel, 1945). Behaviorists explain the disorder as a learned behavior that can be traced to a chance and secret observation of a sexually arousing scene. If such observations are repeated on several occasions while the onlooker masturbates, a voyeuristic pattern may develop.

Frotteurism

A person who develops **frotteurism** has repeated and intense sexual urges to touch and rub against a nonconsenting person or has sexually arousing fantasies of doing so. The person may also act on the urges. Frottage (from French *frotter,* "to rub") is usually committed in a crowded place, such as a subway or a busy sidewalk (Horley, 2001; Krueger & Kaplan, 2000). The person, almost always a male, may rub his genitals against the victim's thighs or buttocks or fondle her genital area or breasts with his hands. Typically he fantasizes during the act that he is having a caring relationship with the victim. This paraphilia usually begins in the teenage years or earlier, often after the person observes others committing an act of frottage. After the person reaches the age of about 25, the acts gradually decrease and often disappear (APA, 2000, 1994).

Pedophilia

A person with **pedophilia** gains sexual gratification by watching, touching, or engaging in sexual acts with prepubescent children, usually 13 years old or younger (see Box 13-4). Some people with this disorder are satisfied by child pornography (Linz & Imrich, 2001) or seemingly innocent material such as children's underwear ads; others are driven to actually watching, fondling, or engaging in sexual intercourse with children (Howitt, 1995). Some people with pedophilia are attracted only to children; others are attracted to adults as well (APA, 2000, 1994). Both boys and girls can be pedophilia victims, but there is evidence suggesting that two-thirds of them are girls (Doctor & Neff, 2001; Koss & Heslet, 1992).

People with pedophilia usually develop their disorder during adolescence. Some were themselves sexually abused as children, and many were neglected, excessively punished, or deprived of genuinely close relationships during their childhood (Sawle & Kear, 2001; Berlin, 2000; Howitt, 1995). It is not unusual for them to be married and to have sexual difficulties or other frustrations in life that lead them to seek an area in which they can be masters. Often these people are immature: their social and sexual skills may be underdeveloped, and thoughts of normal sexual relationships fill them with anxiety (Doctor & Neff, 2001). Some people with pedophilia also exhibit distorted thinking, such as "It's all right to have sex with children as long as they agree" (Abel et al., 2001, 1984). Studies have found that most men with this disorder also display at least one additional psychological disorder such as an anxiety or mood disorder, substance-related disorder, another paraphilia, or personality disorder (Cohen & Galynker, 2002; 2002; Raymond et al., 1999). In recent years, some theorists have proposed that pedophilia may be related to a biochemical or brain structure abnormality (Cantor et al., 2004; Maes et al., 2001), but a clear biological factor has yet to emerge in research.

[BOX 13-4]

Serving the Public Good

As clinical practitioners and researchers conduct their work, should they consider the potential impact of their decisions on society? Many people, including a large number of clinicians, believe that the answer to this question is a resounding yes. Two clashes between the clinical field and the public interest in the 1990s—each centering on the disorder of *pedophilia*—brought this issue to life.

In 1994, the newly published DSM-IV ruled that people should receive a diagnosis of pedophilia only if their recurrent fantasies, urges, or behaviors involving sexual activity with children cause them significant distress or impairment in social, occupational, or other spheres of functioning. Critics worried that this criterion seemed to suggest that pedophilic behavior is acceptable, even normal, as long as it causes no distress or impair-

ment. Even the U.S. Congress condemned the DSM-IV definition.

In response to these criticisms, the American Psychiatric Association clarified its position in 1997, stating, "An adult who engages in sexual activity with a child is performing a criminal and immoral act which never can be considered moral or socially acceptable behavior." In 2000 the Association went further still and changed the criteria for pedophilia in its newly published DSM-IV-TR, so that the disorder is now diagnosed if persons act on their sexual urges, regardless of whether they experience distress or impairment (APA, 2000). Similarly, acting on one's recurrent sexual urges or fantasies warrants a diagnosis in cases of exhibitionism, voyeurism, frotteurism, and sexual sadism.

Another clash between the clinical field and public sensibilities occurred in 1998 when a review article in the presti-

gious journal *Psychological Bulletin* concluded that the effects of child sexual abuse are not as long-lasting as usually believed. The study set off a firestorm, with critics arguing that the conclusion runs counter to evidence from a number of studies. Furthermore, many people worried that the article's conclusions could be used to legitimize pedophilia. After a groundswell of criticism, the American Psychological Association, publisher of the journal, acknowledged in 1999 that it should have given more thought to how the study would be received and should have either presented the article with an introduction outlining the Association's stance against child abuse or paired it with articles offering different viewpoints (Fowler, 1999). The Association also said that in the future it will more carefully weigh the potential consequences of research publications.

Most pedophilic offenders are imprisoned or forced into treatment if they are caught (Stone et al., 2000). After all, they are committing child sexual abuse when they take any steps toward sexual contact with a child. Treatments include those already mentioned for other paraphilias, such as aversion therapy, masturbatory satiation, orgasmic reorientation, and antiandrogen drugs (Krueger & Kaplan, 2002; LoPiccolo, 1992). There is also a cognitive-behavioral treatment for pedophilia: *relapse-prevention training,* modeled after the relapse-prevention programs used in the treatment of substance dependence (Marques et al., 2005; Witkiewitz & Marlatt, 2004; Laws et al., 2000) (see pages 367–368). In this approach, clients identify the kinds of situations that typically trigger their pedophilic fantasies and actions (such as depressed mood or distorted thinking). They then learn strategies for avoiding the situations or coping with them more effectively. Relapse-prevention training has sometimes been of help in pedophilia and in certain other paraphilias.

Sexual Masochism

A person with **sexual masochism** is intensely sexually aroused by the act or thought of being humiliated, beaten, bound, or otherwise made to suffer. Many people have fantasies of being forced into sexual acts against their will, but only those who are very distressed or impaired by the fantasies receive this diagnosis. Some people with the disorder act on the masochistic urges by themselves, perhaps tying, sticking pins into, or even cutting themselves. Others have their sexual partners restrain, tie up, blindfold, spank, paddle, whip, beat, electrically shock, "pin and pierce," or humiliate them (APA, 2000, 1994).

An industry of products and services has arisen to meet the desires of people with sexual masochism. Here a 34-year-old woman describes her work as the operator of a sadomasochism house:

≫PSYCH•NOTES

Linguistic Roots

Paraphilia	from Greek *para* ("faulty, abnormal") and *philos* ("dear, friendly") ≪
Pedophilia	from Greek *paido-* ("child, boy") and *philos* ("dear, friendly") ≪
Incest	from Latin *incestus* ("impure") ≪
Transvestism	from Latin *trans* ("across") and *vestire* ("to clothe") ≪

Does pornography lead to sexual misconduct?
In 1979, prior to the growth of the video sex industry, these women in New York City marched down 42nd Street to protest the proliferation of X-rated movie theaters in that area of the city. The concerns behind such rallies are that pornography offends many people's values, degrades women, and, in excess, may contribute to paraphilias and sexual misconduct. Today's clinicians acknowledge such concerns, but most are careful to further clarify that, in moderation, exposure to sexually explicit material can often play a constructive role in fulfilling sexual needs and fantasies.

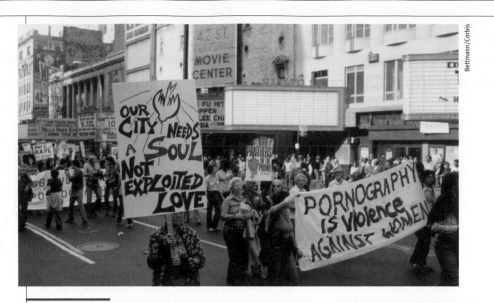

Bettmann/Corbis

I get people here who have been all over looking for the right kind of pain they feel they deserve. Don't ask me why they want pain, I'm not a psychologist; but when they have found us, they usually don't go elsewhere. It may take some of the other girls an hour or even two hours to make these guys feel like they've had their treatment—I can achieve that in about 20 minutes. . . . Remember, these are businessmen, and they are not only buying my time, but they have to get back to work, so time is important.

Among the things I do, that work really quickly and well, are: I put clothespins on their nipples, or pins in their [testicles]. Some of them need to see their own blood to be able to get off. . . .

. . . All the time that a torture scene is going on, there is constant dialogue. . . . I scream at the guy, and tell him what a no-good rotten bastard he is, how this is even too good for him, that he knows he deserves worse, and I begin to list his sins. It works every time. Hey, I'm not nuts, I know what I'm doing. I act very tough and hard, but I'm really a very sensitive woman. But you have to watch out for a guy's health . . . you must not kill him, or have him get a heart attack. . . . I know of other places that have had guys die there. I've never lost a customer to death, though they may have wished for it during my "treatment." Remember, these are repeat customers. I have a clientele and a reputation that I value.

(Janus & Janus, 1993, p. 115)

In one form of sexual masochism, *hypoxyphilia,* people strangle or smother themselves (or ask their partner to strangle them) in order to enhance their sexual pleasure. There have, in fact, been a disturbing number of clinical reports of *autoerotic asphyxia,* in which individuals, usually males and as young as 10 years old, may accidentally induce a fatal lack of oxygen by hanging, suffocating, or strangling themselves while masturbating. There is some debate as to whether the practice should be characterized as sexual masochism, but it is at least sometimes accompanied by other acts of bondage (Blanchard & Hucker, 1991).

Most masochistic sexual fantasies begin in childhood. However, the person does not act out the urges until later, usually by early adulthood. The disorder typically continues for many years. Some people practice more and more dangerous acts over time or during times of particular stress (Santtila et al., 2002; APA, 2000, 1994).

In many cases sexual masochism seems to have developed through the behavioral process of classical conditioning (Akins, 2004). One case study tells of a teenage boy with a broken arm who was caressed and held close by an attractive nurse as the physician set his fracture without anesthesia (Gebhard, 1965). The powerful combination of pain and sexual arousal he felt then may have been the cause of his later masochistic urges and acts.

•**SEXUAL SADISM**•A paraphilia characterized by repeated and intense sexual urges, fantasies, or behaviors that involve inflicting suffering on others.

Sexual Sadism

A person with **sexual sadism,** usually male, is intensely sexually aroused by the thought or act of inflicting suffering on others by dominating, restraining, blindfolding, cutting, strangling, mutilating, or even killing the victim (Marshall & Kennedy, 2003). The label is derived from the name of the famous Marquis de Sade (1740–1814), who tortured others in order to satisfy his sexual desires. People who fantasize about sadism typically imagine that they have total control over a sexual victim who is terrified by the sadistic act. Many carry out sadistic acts with a consenting partner, often a person with sexual masochism. Some, however, act out their urges on nonconsenting victims (Marshall & Yates, 2004). A number of rapists and sexual murderers, for example, exhibit sexual sadism (Lalumiere et al., 2005). In all cases, the real or fantasized victim's suffering is the key to arousal.

Fantasies of sexual sadism, like those of sexual masochism, may first appear in childhood (Johnson & Becker, 1997); the sadistic acts, when they occur, develop by early adulthood (APA, 2000, 1994). The pattern is long-term. Sadistic acts sometimes stay at the same level of cruelty, but often they become more and more severe over the years (Santtila et al., 2002). Obviously, people with severe forms of the disorder may be highly dangerous to others.

Some behaviorists believe that classical conditioning is at work in sexual sadism (Akins, 2004). While inflicting pain, perhaps unintentionally, on an animal or person, a teenager may feel intense emotions and sexual arousal. The association between inflicting pain and being aroused sexually sets the stage for a pattern of sexual sadism. Behaviorists also propose that the disorder may result from modeling, when adolescents observe others achieving sexual satisfaction by inflicting pain. The many sexual magazines, books, and videos in our society make such models readily available (Seto, Maric, & Barbaree, 2001; Lebegue, 1991).

Psychodynamic and cognitive theorists view people with sexual sadism as having underlying feelings of sexual inadequacy; they inflict pain in order to achieve a sense of power or control, which in turn increases their sexual arousal (Doctor, 2003; Rathbone, 2001). In contrast, certain biological studies have found signs of possible abnormalities in the endocrine systems of persons with sadism (Langevin et al., 1988). None of these explanations, however, has been thoroughly investigated.

Sexual sadism has been treated by aversion therapy. The public's view of and distaste for this procedure have been influenced by Anthony Burgess's novel (later a movie) *A Clockwork Orange,* which describes simultaneous presentations of sadistic images and drug-induced stomach spasms to a sadistic young man until he is conditioned to feel nausea at the sight of such images. It is not clear that aversion therapy is helpful in cases of sexual sadism. However, relapse-prevention training, used in some criminal cases, may be of value (Marques et al., 2005; Maletzky, 2003, 2002; Laws et al., 2000).

A Word of Caution

The definitions of the paraphilias, like those of sexual dysfunctions, are strongly influenced by the norms of the particular society in which they occur (McConaghy, 2005; APA, 2000). Some clinicians argue that except when people are hurt by them, many paraphilic behaviors should not be considered disorders at all. Especially in light of the stigma associated with sexual disorders and the self-revulsion that many people experience when they believe they have such a disorder, we need to be very careful about applying these labels to others or to ourselves. Keep in mind that for years clinicians considered homosexuality a paraphilia, and their judgment was used to justify laws and even police actions against homosexual persons (Kirby, 2000). Only when the gay rights movement helped change society's understanding of and attitudes toward homosexuality did clinicians stop considering it a disorder. In the meantime, the clinical field had unintentionally contributed to the persecution, anxiety, and humiliation of millions of people because of personal sexual behavior that differed from the conventional norms (see Box 13-5 on the next page).

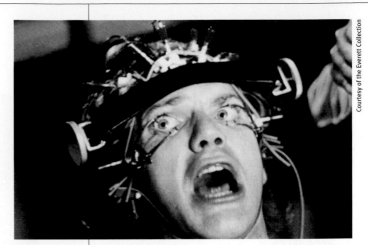

Courtesy of the Everett Collection

Cinematic introduction *In one of filmdom's most famous scenes, Alex, the sexually sadistic character in* A Clockwork Orange, *is forced to observe violent images while he experiences painful stomach spasms. Public attitudes toward aversion therapy were greatly influenced by this 1971 portrayal of the treatment approach.*

>>**LOOKING AROUND**
Sex and the Law

The majority of arrests for sexual offenses involve acts of exhibitionism, pedophilia, or voyeurism (APA, 2000). <<

In 1996 the California state legislature passed the first law in the United States allowing state judges to order **antiandrogen** drug treatments, often referred to as "chemical castration," for repeat sex crime offenders, such as men who repeatedly commit pedophiliac acts or rape. <<

According to a Supreme Court decision in the 1997 case of *Kansas v. Hendricks,* convicted sex offenders may be removed from prison prior to release and committed to a mental hospital if a court judges them likely to engage in further "predatory acts of sexual violence" as the result of a "mental abnormality" or "personality disorder." They must then remain institutionalized until their disorder and sexual dangerousness are rectified. <<

[BOX **13-5**]

Homosexuality and Society

Homosexuality is not new; it has always existed in all cultures, as has the controversy that surrounds it. While most cultures do not openly advocate homosexuality, over the course of history few have condemned it as fiercely as Western culture does today (Dalton, 2004; Minton, 2002; Nussbaum, 2002). Nevertheless, research shows that a society's acceptance or rejection of people who engage in homosexual behavior does not affect the rate of the behavior.

Before 1973, the DSM listed homosexuality as a sexual disorder. Protests by gay activist groups and many psychotherapists eventually led to its elimination from the diagnostic manual as a sexual disorder (Robertson, 2004). Most clinicians in the Western world now view homosexuality as a variant of normal sexual behavior, not a disorder (Robertson, 2004).

Despite the growing acceptance of homosexuality by the clinical field, many people in Western society continue to hold antihomosexual attitudes and to spread myths about the lifestyles of homosexual persons (Kirby, 2000; Parker & Bhugra, 2000). Contrary to these myths, research has shown that homosexual persons do not suffer from gender confusion, and there is not an identifiable "homosexual personality."

Psychologists do continue to debate one issue: whether homosexual people choose their lifestyle or whether it is a natural part of their physiological makeup. This debate has been fueled by findings— pro and con (Hyde, 2005; Minton, 2002; Pillard & Bailey, 1995; LeVay & Hamer, 1994). In the early 1990s, for example, two influential genetic linkage studies concluded that homosexuality may in some instances be passed on by the mother's genes (Hu et al., 1995; Hamer et al., 1993), although more recent research has failed to support this particular conclusion (Rice et al., 1999). In addition, two studies found that when one identical twin was homosexual, his twin was also homosexual in more than 50 percent of the cases sampled. The number dropped to less than 20 percent when the siblings were fraternal twins or

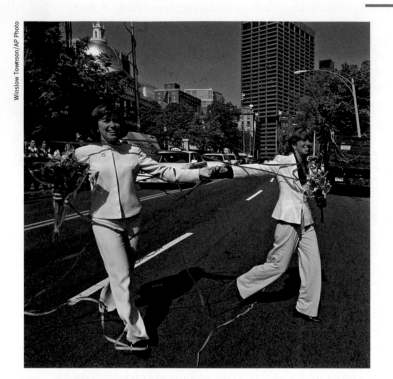

The great debate: gay marriage *Two women cross a Boston street after being married at a Unitarian church in 2004. The joy on their faces belies the intense social controversy swirling around the issue of gay marriage in the United States. While many people strongly believe that homosexual couples should have the right to a legal marriage, others propose that their rights should be limited to civil unions only, and still others are against any kind of formal union. Clearly, the agreement among most psychologists that homosexuality is not a disorder has not put the social issues surrounding homosexuality to rest.*

nontwins and to under 10 percent when the siblings were adopted and biologically unrelated (Bailey et al., 1999, 1993, 1991). Although environmental factors also have a major impact on homosexuality—otherwise all persons with a homosexual identical twin would be homosexual—genetics may well play a key role in it (Hyde, 2005).

Homosexual people are found in every socioeconomic group, every race, and every profession. It is impossible to identify a characteristic that consistently separates them from the rest of the population other than their sexual orientation. The homosexual community argues that since sexual orientation is the only variable that consistently separates homosexual from heterosexual couples, gay couples should have the same rights as heterosexual ones. Today, a number of marriages are performed for same-sex couples (Leiblum, 2004). Furthermore, homosexual couples

are increasingly asserting their rights to housing reserved for heterosexual couples only and to spousal health insurance coverage; recent court decisions have supported such rights.

Homosexuality continues to be a lifestyle that many people adopt, whether because of environmental or genetic factors. Now that most psychologists agree that homosexuality is not a disorder, a key issue remains: How will society react to a significant proportion of its population that typically differs from the rest in but one way— their sexual orientation? So far, Western society cannot claim to have dealt very effectively or fairly with this question, but at least a trend toward understanding and equality seems to be emerging. Research suggests that through education and exposure, people of different sexual orientations can indeed learn to accept and work with one another (Guth et al., 2004).

Gender Identity Disorder

One of the most fascinating disorders related to sexuality is **gender identity disorder,** or **transsexualism,** a disorder in which people persistently feel that a vast mistake has been made—they have been assigned to the wrong sex (see Table 13-6). Such persons would like to get rid of their primary and secondary sex characteristics—many of them find their own genitals repugnant—and acquire the characteristics of the other sex (APA, 2000, 1994). Men with gender identity disorder outnumber women by around 2 to 1. People with the problem often experience anxiety or depression and may have thoughts of suicide (Hepp et al., 2005; Doctor & Neff, 2001; Bradley, 1995). Reactions of this kind are likely related to the confusion and pain brought on by the disorder itself, but they may also be tied to the prejudice typically experienced by individuals who display this pattern (Whittle, 2002; Lombardi et al., 2001). Some studies also suggest that many people with gender identity disorder further manifest a personality disorder (Hepp et al., 2005).

People with gender identity disorder usually feel uncomfortable wearing the clothes of their own sex and dress instead in clothes of the opposite sex. Their condition is not, however, transvestic fetishism (transvestism). People with that paraphilia cross-dress in order to become sexually aroused; persons with transsexualism have much deeper reasons for cross-dressing, reasons of gender identity. In addition to engaging in cross-dressing, individuals with transsexualism often take up roles and activities that are traditionally associated with the other sex (Brown et al., 1996; Bradley, 1995).

Sometimes gender identity disorder emerges in children (Zucker, 2005). Like adults with this disorder, they feel uncomfortable about their assigned sex and yearn to be members of the opposite sex. This childhood pattern usually disappears by adolescence or adulthood, but in some cases it develops into adult gender identity disorder (Cohen-Kettenis, 2001). Thus adults with this disorder may have had a childhood gender identity disorder, but most children with the disorder do not become transsexual adults. Some adults with gender identity disorder do not develop any symptoms until mid-adulthood.

Various theories have been proposed to explain this disorder (Gehring & Knudson, 2005; Doctor & Neff, 2001), but research to test the ideas has been limited and generally weak. Many clinicians suspect that biological—perhaps genetic—factors play a key role in the disorder (Henningsson et al., 2005). There is indeed evidence that the disorder sometimes runs in families (Green, 2000). Moreover, one biological study has received considerable attention (Zhou et al., 1995). Dutch investigators autopsied the brains of six people who had changed their sex from male to female. They found that a cluster of cells in the hypothalamus called the *bed nucleus of stria terminalis* (*BST*) was only half as large in these subjects as it was in a control group of normal men. Normally, a woman's BST is much smaller than a man's, so in effect the subjects with gender identity disorder were found to have a female-sized BST. Recent studies tell a similar story (Swaab, 2005). Scientists do not know for certain what the BST does in humans, but they know that it helps regulate sexual behavior in male rats. Although other interpretations are possible, it may well be that men who develop gender identity disorder have a key biological difference that leaves them very uncomfortable with their assigned sex characteristics.

Although many persons with gender identity disorder receive psychotherapy (Affateti et al., 2004), a large number also address their concerns and conflicts through biological interventions. For example, many adults with this disorder change their sexual characteristics by means of *hormone treatments* (Hepp et al., 2002; Bradley, 1995). Physicians prescribe the female sex hormone *estrogen* for male patients, causing breast development, loss of body and facial hair, and change in body fat distribution. Similar treatments with the male sex hormone *testosterone* are given to women with gender identity disorder.

•**GENDER IDENTITY DISORDER**•A disorder in which a person persistently feels extremely uncomfortable about his or her assigned sex and strongly wishes to be a member of the opposite sex. Also known as *transsexualism*.

Table **13-6** DSM Checklist

GENDER IDENTITY DISORDER

1. Strong and persistent cross-gender identification (for example, a stated desire to be the other sex, frequent passing as the other sex, desire to live or be treated as the other sex, or the conviction that one has the typical feelings and reactions of the other sex).
2. Persistent discomfort with one's sex or a sense of inappropriateness in the gender role of that sex (for example, preoccupation with getting rid of primary and secondary sex characteristics or belief that one was born the wrong sex).
3. Significant distress or impairment.

Based on APA, 2000, 1994.

(l.) Bettmann Archives (r.) David Levenson/Rex USA Ltd.

James and Jan *Feeling like a woman trapped in a man's body, the British writer James Morris (left) underwent sex-change surgery, described in his 1974 autobiography,* Conundrum. *Today Jan Morris (right) is a successful author and seems comfortable with her change of gender.*

Hormone therapy and psychotherapy enable many persons with this disorder to lead a satisfactory existence in the gender role that they believe represents their true identity. For others, however, this is not enough, and their dissatisfaction leads them to undergo one of the most controversial practices in medicine: **sex-change,** or **sexual reassignment, surgery** (Hepp et al., 2002; Liedl, 1999). This surgery is preceded by one to two years of hormone therapy. The operation itself involves, for men, amputation of the penis, creation of an artificial vagina, and face-changing plastic surgery. For women, surgery may include bilateral mastectomy and hysterectomy. The procedure for creating a functioning penis, called *phalloplasty,* is performed in some cases, but it is not yet perfected (Doctor & Neff, 2001). Doctors have, however, developed a silicone prosthesis that gives the patient the appearance of having male genitals. Studies in Europe suggest that 1 of every 30,000 men and 1 of every 100,000 women seek sex-change surgery (APA, 2000). In the United States, more than 6,000 persons are estimated to have undergone this surgical procedure (Doctor & Neff, 2001).

Clinicians have heatedly debated whether sexual reassignment is an appropriate treatment for gender identity disorder. Some consider it a humane solution, perhaps the most satisfying one to people with the disorder (Denny, 2004; Cohen-Kettenis & Gooren,

Consumer discomfort *When producing this commercial for television play during the 1997 Super Bowl, Holiday Inn greatly underestimated the degree of discomfort many people have regarding the issue of transsexualism. In the commercial, an attractive woman shocks a classmate at a high school reunion by revealing that she has had a sex-change operation since they were in school together. Holiday Inn executives expected viewers to chuckle and, in turn, consider the significant changes made in recent times at the hotel chain. Far from amused, millions of viewers were offended and even outraged, and Holiday Inn had to scrap the ad within 48 hours of its debut.*

Holiday Inn, HO/AP Photo

1999; Cohen-Kettenis & van Goozen, 1997). Others argue that sexual reassignment is a "drastic nonsolution" for a largely psychological problem. Although sexual reassignment surgery appears to be on the increase (Olsson & Moller, 2003), the long-term psychological outcome of this procedure is not clear. Some people seem to function well for years after such treatments (Lewins, 2002; Michel et al., 2002), but others experience psychological difficulties. Without any form of treatment, gender identity disorder among adults is usually long-term, but some cases of recovery without intervention have reportedly occurred (Marks et al., 2000).

Our gender is so basic to our sense of identity that it is hard for most of us to imagine wanting to change it, much less to imagine the feelings of conflict and stress experienced by those who question their assigned gender. Whether the underlying cause is biological, psychological, or sociocultural, gender identity disorder is a dramatic dysfunction that shakes the foundations of the sufferer's existence.

>>LOOKING AROUND
Landmark Case

The first sex-change operation took place in 1931, but the procedure did not gain acceptance in the medical world until 1952, when an operation converted an ex-soldier named George Jorgensen into a woman, renamed Christine Jorgensen. This transformation made headlines around the world. <<

PUTTING IT together
A Private Topic Draws Public Attention

For all the public interest in sexual disorders, clinical theorists and practitioners have only recently begun to understand their nature and how to treat them. As a result of research done over the past few decades, people with sexual dysfunctions are no longer doomed to a lifetime of sexual frustration. At the same time, however, insights into the causes and treatment of other kinds of sexual disorders—paraphilias and gender identity disorder—remain limited.

Studies of sexual dysfunctions have pointed to many psychological, sociocultural, and biological causes. Often, as we have seen with so many disorders, the various causes may *interact* to produce a particular dysfunction, as in erectile disorder and female orgasmic disorder. For some dysfunctions, however, one cause alone is dominant, and integrated explanations may be inaccurate and unproductive. Premature ejaculation, for example, appears to have largely psychological causes, while dyspareunia usually has a physical cause.

Recent work has also yielded important progress in the treatment of sexual dysfunctions, and people with such problems are now often helped greatly by therapy. Sex therapy today is usually a complex program tailored to the particular problems of an individual or couple. Techniques from the various models may be combined, although in some instances the particular problem calls primarily for one approach (Bach et al., 2001).

One of the most important insights to emerge from all this work is that *education* about sexual dysfunctions can be as important as therapy. Sexual myths are still taken so seriously that they often lead to feelings of shame, self-hatred, isolation, and hopelessness—feelings that themselves contribute to sexual difficulty. Even a modest amount of education can help persons who are in treatment.

In fact, most people can benefit from a more accurate understanding of sexual functioning. Public education about sexual functioning—through books, television and radio, school programs, group presentations, and the like—has become a major clinical focus. It is important that these efforts continue and even increase in the coming years.

─[SUMMARY AND REVIEW]─

■ **Sexual dysfunctions** *Sexual dysfunctions* make it difficult or impossible for a person to have or enjoy sexual intercourse. *pp. 377–378*

■ **Disorders of desire** DSM-IV-TR lists two disorders of the *desire phase* of the *sexual response cycle: hypoactive sexual desire disorder,* marked by a lack of interest in sex, and *sexual aversion disorder,* marked by a persistent revulsion to sexual activity. Biological causes for these disorders include abnormal hormone levels, certain drugs, and some medical illnesses. Psychological and sociocultural causes include specific

•**SEX-CHANGE SURGERY**•A surgical procedure that changes a person's sex organs and features, and, in turn, sexual identity. Also known as *sexual reassignment surgery.*

>>LOOKING AROUND

Sexual Census The World Health Organization estimates that around 115 million acts of sexual intercourse occur each day. **<<**

- -

Unequal Distribution Sex is not distributed equally. Half of all sexual activity in the United States is engaged in by 15 percent of adults (General Social Survey, 1998). **<<**

- -

Sexual Duration In a survey of people in the United States, respondents estimated that their average sexual experience lasts 39 minutes, including foreplay (Kanner, 1995). **<<**

Pedophila and the arts *The growing public awareness of pedophilia has led to an increase in the number of books, plays, movies, and television shows about the subject. Indeed, a recent production of the much-loved 1893 opera* Hansel and Gretel *was presented as an adults-only "study of pedophilia." In this scene from the opera, the witch gestures in front of a picture of one of the young victims.*

fears, situational pressures, relationship problems, and the trauma of having been sexually molested or assaulted. *pp. 378–382*

■ **Disorders of excitement** Disorders of the *excitement phase* are *female sexual arousal disorder,* marked by a persistent inability to attain or maintain adequate lubrication or genital swelling during sexual activity, and *male erectile disorder,* a repeated inability to attain or maintain an erection during sexual activity. Biological causes of male erectile disorder include abnormal hormone levels, vascular problems, medical conditions, and certain medications. Psychological and sociocultural causes include the combination of *performance anxiety* and the *spectator role,* situational pressures such as job loss, and relationship problems. *pp. 382–384*

■ **Disorders of orgasm** *Premature ejaculation,* a persistent tendency to reach orgasm and ejaculate before or shortly after penetration, has been attributed to behavioral causes, such as inappropriate early learning and inexperience. *Male orgasmic disorder,* a repeated absence of or long delay in reaching orgasm, can have biological causes such as low testosterone levels, neurological diseases, and certain drugs, and psychological causes such as performance anxiety and the spectator role. The dysfunction may also develop from hypoactive sexual desire.

Female orgasmic disorder is a persistent absence of or long delay in orgasm in women. It, along with female sexual arousal disorder, has been tied to biological causes such as medical diseases and changes that occur after menopause, psychological causes such as memories of childhood traumas, and sociocultural causes such as relationship problems. Most clinicians agree that orgasm during intercourse is not critical to normal sexual functioning, provided a woman can reach orgasm with her partner during direct stimulation of the clitoris. *pp. 384–388*

■ **Sexual pain disorders** In *vaginismus,* involuntary contractions of the muscles around the outer third of the vagina prevent entry of the penis. In *dyspareunia,* the person experiences severe pain in the genitals during sexual activity. Dyspareunia usually occurs in women and typically has a physical cause such as injury resulting from childbirth. *pp. 388–389*

■ **Treatments for sexual dysfunctions** In the 1970s the work of William Masters and Virginia Johnson led to the development of *sex therapy.* Today sex therapy combines a variety of cognitive, behavioral, couple, and family systems therapies. It generally includes features such as careful assessment, education, acceptance of mutual responsibility, attitude changes, *sensate-focus* exercises, improvements in communication, and couple therapy. In addition, specific techniques have been developed for each of the sexual dysfunctions. The use of biological treatments for sexual dysfunctions is also increasing. *pp. 389–396*

■ **Paraphilias** Paraphilias are disorders characterized by recurrent and intense sexual urges, fantasies, or behaviors involving either nonhuman objects, children, nonconsenting adults, or experiences of suffering or humiliation. The disorders are found primarily in men. The paraphilias include *fetishism, transvestic fetishism (transvestism), exhibitionism, voyeurism, frotteurism, pedophilia, sexual masochism,* and *sexual sadism.* Although various explanations have been proposed for these disorders, research has revealed little about their causes. A range of treatments have been tried, including *aversion therapy, masturbatory satiation, orgasmic reorientation,* and *relapse-prevention training. pp. 396–403*

■ **Gender identity disorder** People with *gender identity disorder,* or *transsexualism,* persistently feel that they have been assigned to the wrong sex and are preoccupied with acquiring the physical characteristics of the other sex. Men apparently outnumber females with this disorder by around 2 to 1. Its causes are not well understood. *Hormone treatments* and *psychotherapy* have been used to help some people adopt the gender role they believe to be right for them. *Sex-change operations* have also been performed, but the appropriateness of surgery as a form of "treatment" has been hotly debated. *pp. 405–407*

>>> CRITICAL THOUGHTS <<<

1. Prevalence rates for sexual behavior are typically based on surveys of the general population. However, many people feel that sex is private and refuse to participate in such surveys, and those who do respond tend to be more liberal, sexually experienced, and unconventional than the norm. What problems might this cause for sex researchers? *pp. 377–389*

2. Some theorists suggest that recent increases in the number of men receiving treatment for hypoactive sexual desire disorder may be linked to the impact of the women's movement (LoPiccolo, 1995). If this is the case, what factors might account for it? *pp. 378–382*

3. Some theorists cite performance anxiety and the spectator role as contributing factors in certain sexual dysfunctions. Are there other areas of dysfunction in life that might also be explained by performance anxiety and the spectator role? *p. 384*

4. A key technique in sex therapy is to have a couple explore and caress each other's body (*sensate focus*) while resisting orgasm or intercourse. Why might people become more aroused during sexual caressing if they are prohibited from reaching orgasm or having intercourse? *pp. 390–391*

5. Although Viagra and "the pill" both relate to sexual behavior, they serve different purposes and have different religious implications. Could these differences, rather than sexism, explain the responses of insurance companies and government agencies when these products were first introduced? *p. 394*

6. Sex is one of the topics most commonly searched for on the Internet. Why might it be such a popular search topic? Is the availability of sex chat groups and other sexual material on the Internet psychologically healthy or damaging? *pp. 407, 377–407*

⊙—[CYBERSTUDY]————————————————»»

SEARCH THE *ABNORMAL PSYCHOLOGY* CD-ROM FOR

▲ Chapter 13 Video Cases and Discussions
   How does stress affect sexual functioning?
   Are sexual beliefs and practices really changing?
   How do people with gender identity disorder feel about themselves and their bodies?

▲ Chapter 13 Practical, Research, and Decision-Making Exercises
   Examining your own biases and myths about sex
   Uncovering sexual disorders in the media and the arts

▲ Chapter 13 Practice Test and Feedback

LOG ON TO THE COMER WEB PAGE FOR

▲ Suggested Web links, exercises, FAQ page, additional Chapter 13 practice test questions
   ‹www.worthpublishers.com/comer›

————————————————————————————————<<<

Schizophrenia

What . . . does schizophrenia mean to me? It means fatigue and confusion, it means trying to separate every experience into the real and the unreal and sometimes not being aware of where the edges overlap. It means trying to think straight when there is a maze of experiences getting in the way, and when thoughts are continually being sucked out of your head so that you become embarrassed to speak at meetings. It means feeling sometimes that you are inside your head and visualizing yourself walking over your brain, or watching another girl wearing your clothes and carrying out actions as you think them. It means knowing that you are continually "watched," that you can never succeed in life because the laws are all against you and knowing that your ultimate destruction is never far away.

(Rollin, 1980, p. 162)

Does it surprise you to see such a coherent firsthand description of how it feels to suffer from **schizophrenia?** People who have this disorder, though they previously functioned well or at least acceptably, deteriorate into an isolated wilderness of unusual perceptions, odd thoughts, disturbed emotions, and motor abnormalities. In Chapter 15 we shall see that schizophrenia is no longer the hopeless disorder of times past and that some sufferers, though certainly not all, now make remarkable recoveries. However, in this chapter let us first take a look at the symptoms of this disorder and at the theories that have been developed to explain them.

People with schizophrenia experience **psychosis,** a loss of contact with reality. Their ability to perceive and respond to the environment becomes so disturbed that they may not be able to function at home, with friends, in school, or at work. They may have hallucinations (false sensory perceptions) or delusions (false beliefs), or they may withdraw into a private world. As we observed in Chapter 12, taking LSD or abusing amphetamines or cocaine may produce psychosis. So may injuries or diseases of the brain. Most commonly, however, psychosis appears in the form of schizophrenia.

Schizophrenia appears to have been with us throughout history; it is one of the conditions commonly described as "madness" (Cutting, 1985). The Bible, for example, speaks of King Saul's mad rages and terrors and of David feigning madness in order to escape his enemies. In 1865 a Belgian psychiatrist named Benedict Morel (1809–1873) applied the label *démence précoce* ("early dementia") to a 14-year-old boy who showed the symptoms of this disorder, and in 1899 Emil Kraepelin introduced the use of the Latin form of Morel's label, "dementia praecox." In 1911, however, the Swiss psychiatrist Eugen Bleuler (1857–1939) coined a new term, "schizophrenia," by combining Greek words that mean "split mind." Bleuler meant this name to imply (1) a fragmentation of thought processes, (2) a split between thoughts and emotions, and (3) a withdrawal from reality.

Approximately 1 of every 100 people in the world suffers from schizophrenia during his or her lifetime (APA, 2000). An estimated 24 million people worldwide are afflicted with this disorder, 2.5 million in the United States (Lambert & Kinsley, 2005; Bichsel, 2001). Its financial cost is enormous—according to some estimates, more than $100 billion annually, including the costs of hospitalization,

•**SCHIZOPHRENIA**•A psychotic disorder in which personal, social, and occupational functioning deteriorate as a result of strange perceptions, disturbed thought processes, unusual emotions, and motor abnormalities.

•**PSYCHOSIS**•A state in which a person loses contact with reality in key ways.

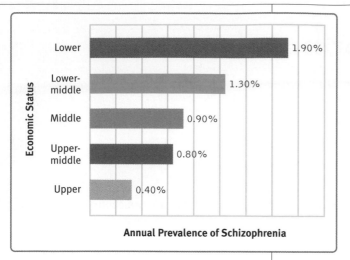

FIGURE 14-1 Socioeconomic class and schizophrenia *Poor people in the United States are more likely than wealthy people to experience schizophrenia. (Adapted from Keith et al., 1991.)*

FIGURE 14-2 Do the course and outcome of schizophrenia differ from country to country? *Yes, according to a World Health Organization study. In developing countries, patients with schizophrenia seem to recover more quickly, more often, and more completely; to receive less antipsychotic medication; to be hospitalized less often; and to become less impaired socially than patients in developed countries. (Adapted from Jablensky, 2000.)*

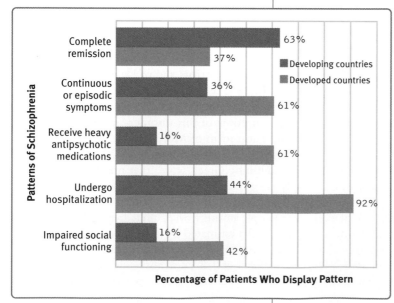

lost wages, and disability benefits (Keltner & Folks, 2001; Black & Andreasen, 1994). The emotional cost is even greater. In addition, sufferers have an increased risk of suicide and of physical—often fatal—illness (Kim et al., 2003). As we discussed in Chapter 10, it is estimated that around one-third of persons with the disorder attempt suicide and up to 15 percent of sufferers are successful (Hawton et al., 2005; Meltzer, 2005; Lambert & Kinsley, 2005).

Although schizophrenia appears in all socioeconomic groups, it is found more frequently in the lower levels (Lambert & Kinsley, 2005) (see Figure 14-1), leading some theorists to believe that the stress of poverty is itself a cause of the disorder. However, it could be that schizophrenia causes its victims to fall from a higher to a lower socioeconomic level or to remain poor because they are unable to function effectively (Munk & Mortensen, 1992). This is sometimes called the *downward drift* theory.

Equal numbers of men and women receive a diagnosis of schizophrenia. In men, however, the disorder often begins earlier and may be more severe (Folsom et al., 2006). The average age of onset for men is 21 years, compared to 27 years for women. Almost 3 percent of all those who are divorced or separated suffer from schizophrenia sometime during their lives, compared to 1 percent of married people and 2 percent of people who remain single (Keith et al., 1991). Again, however, it is not clear whether marital problems are a cause or a result.

Rates of schizophrenia appear to differ between racial and ethnic groups, particularly between African Americans and white Americans. As many as 2.1 percent of African Americans receive a diagnosis of schizophrenia, compared with 1.4 percent of white Americans (Folsom et al., 2006). Similarly, studies find that African American patients are more likely than white patients to be assessed as having symptoms of hallucinations, paranoia, and suspiciousness (Mark et al., 2003; Trierweiler et al., 2000). And still other studies suggest that African Americans with schizophrenia are overrepresented in state hospitals (Barnes, 2004). For example, in Tennessee's state hospitals 48 percent of those with a diagnosis of schizophrenia are African American, although only 16 percent of the state population is African American (Barnes, 2004; Lawson et al., 1994).

It is not clear why African Americans have a higher likelihood than white Americans of receiving this diagnosis. One possibility is that African Americans are indeed more prone to develop the disorder (Barnes, 2004). Another possibility is that clinicians from majority groups are unintentionally biased in their diagnoses of African Americans or misread cultural differences as symptoms of schizophrenia (Barnes, 2004).

Yet another explanation for the difference between African Americans and white Americans may lie in the economic sphere. On average, African Americans are more likely than white Americans to be poor and, indeed, when economic differences are controlled for, the prevalence rates of schizophrenia become closer for the two racial groups. On the other hand, economic factors do not fully explain the observed racial differences. After all, although similarly economically disadvantaged, Hispanic Americans have a lower lifetime rate of schizophrenia—0.8 percent—than either of the other two racial groups (Keith et al., 1991).

It also appears that schizophrenia differs from country to country in certain respects. Although the overall prevalence of this disorder is stable—around 1 percent—in countries across the world, the *course* and *outcome* of the disorder may vary considerably. According to a 10-country study conducted by the World Health Organization (WHO), schizophrenic patients in "Third World" countries have better recovery rates than those in Western countries (Jablensky, 2000). The WHO study followed the progress of 467 patients from *developing countries* (Colombia, India, and Nigeria) over a two-year period and compared it to that of 603 patients from *developed countries* (Czech Republic, Denmark, Ireland, Japan, Russia, the United Kingdom, and the United States). As we can see in Figure 14-2, during the course of a two-year observation period, the schizophrenic patients from the developing countries were more likely than those in the developed countries to recover from their disorder and less likely to experience continuous or episodic symptoms, display impaired social functioning, require heavy antipsychotic drugs, or require hospitalization.

Some clinical theorists believe that these differences partly reflect genetic differences from population to population (Jablensky, 2000). However, others argue that the psychosocial environments of developing countries tend to be more supportive and therapeutic than those of developed countries, leading to more favorable outcomes for people with schizophrenia (Jablensky, 2000; Karno & Jenkins, 1993; Warner, 1985). Developing countries, for example, seem to provide more family and social support to people with schizophrenia, make available more relatives and friends to help care for such individuals, and act less judgmental, critical, and hostile toward persons with schizophrenia.

People today, like those of the past, show great interest in schizophrenia, flocking to plays and movies (including the remarkably popular horror movies) that explore or exploit our fascination with the disorder (see Box 14-1 on page 415). Yet, as we shall see, all too many people with schizophrenia are neglected in our country, their needs almost entirely ignored. Although effective interventions have been developed, most sufferers live without adequate treatment and without nearly fulfilling their potential as human beings (Torrey, 2001).

The Clinical Picture of Schizophrenia

For years schizophrenia was a "wastebasket category" for diagnosticians, particularly for those in the United States, where the label might be assigned to anyone who acted unpredictably or strangely. Some clinicians were known to say that "even a trace of schizophrenia is schizophrenia" (Lewis & Piotrowski, 1954). The disorder is defined more precisely today, but still its symptoms vary greatly, and so do its triggers, course, and responsiveness to treatment (APA, 2000). In fact, a number of clinicians believe that schizophrenia is actually a group of distinct disorders that happen to have some features in common (Cohen & Docherty, 2005). To see the variety of forms schizophrenia may take, consider three people who were diagnosed as suffering from it. The cases are taken from the files of Silvano Arieti (1974), a famous theorist on the disorder.

ANN, 26 YEARS OLD

Ann graduated from high school and from a school for commercial art. . . . At the age of 18 she began going out with Henry. . . . They became engaged shortly thereafter and went out together frequently until their marriage . . . . Married life was considered a boring routine by both Ann and Henry. There was very little conversation between them. . . .

Ann's disappointment in Henry increased. They had nothing in common; she was artistically inclined, whereas he had only an ordinary, conventional outlook toward life. It was at this time that she started to go dancing and then met Charles. Her interest in him increased, but . . . a divorce was not compatible with the precepts of the Catholic church. Her conflict grew and put her in a state of great agitation. . . .

. . . One evening she came home from dancing and told her mother that she was going to give up her husband Henry, marry Charles, go to Brazil with him, and have twenty babies. She was talking very fast and saying many things, several of which were incomprehensible. At the same time she also told her mother that she was seeing the Virgin Mary in visions. She then went to her mother-in-law and told her to take back her son Henry, because he was too immature. The following day Ann went to work and tried to get the entire office down on their knees with her to recite the rosary. A few days later, her mother took her to a priest, whom she "told off" in no uncertain terms. She finally spit at him. A psychiatrist was consulted, and he recommended hospitalization.

(Arieti, 1974, pp. 173–177)

>>PSYCH•LISTINGS

Primary Causes of Premature Death among People with Schizophrenia

Suicide <<
- -
Accidents <<
- -
Inadequate medical care <<
- -
Infections, heart disease, diabetes <<
- -
Unhealthy lifestyles <<
- -
Homelessness <<
- -

(Torrey, 2001)

>>IN THEIR WORDS

"No great genius was ever without some tincture of madness." <<

Aristotle

- -

"I shouldn't precisely have chosen madness if there had been any choice, but once such a thing has taken hold of you, you can't very well get out of it." <<

Vincent van Gogh, 1889

RICHARD, 23 YEARS OLD

In high school, Richard was an average student. After graduation from high school, he was drafted into the army. . . . Richard remembered [the] period . . . after his discharge from the army . . . as one of the worst in his life. . . . Any, even remote, anticipation of disappointment was able to provoke attacks of anxiety in him. . . .

Approximately two years after his return to civilian life, Richard left his job because he became overwhelmed by these feelings of lack of confidence in himself, and he refused to go look for another one. He stayed home most of the day. His mother would nag him that he was too lazy and unwilling to do anything. He became slower and slower in dressing and undressing and taking care of himself. When he went out of the house, he felt compelled "to give interpretations" to everything he looked at. He did not know what to do outside the house, where to go, where to turn. If he saw a red light at a crossing, he would interpret it as a message that he should not go in that direction. If he saw an arrow, he would follow the arrow interpreting it as a sign sent by God that he should go in that direction. Feeling lost and horrified, he would go home and stay there, afraid to go out because going out meant making decisions or choices that he felt unable to make. He reached the point where he stayed home most of the time. But even at home, he was tortured by his symptoms. He could not act; any motion that he felt like making seemed to him an insurmountable obstacle, because he did not know whether he should make it or not. He was increasingly afraid of doing the wrong thing. Such fears prevented him from dressing, undressing, eating, and so forth. He felt paralyzed and lay motionless in bed. He gradually became worse, was completely motionless, and had to be hospitalized. . . .

Being undecided, he felt blocked, and often would remain mute and motionless, like a statue, even for days.

(Arieti, 1974, pp. 153–155)

LAURA, 40 YEARS OLD

Laura's desire was to become independent and leave home [in Austria] as soon as possible. . . . She became a professional dancer at the age of 20 . . . and was booked for vaudeville theaters in many European countries. . . .

It was during one of her tours in Germany that Laura met her husband. . . . They were married and went to live in a small provincial town in France where the husband's business was. . . . She spent a year in that town and was very unhappy. . . . [Finally] Laura and her husband decided to emigrate to the United States. . . .

They had no children, and Laura . . . showed interest in pets. She had a dog to whom she was very devoted. The dog became sick and partially paralyzed, and veterinarians felt that there was no hope of recovery. . . . Finally [her husband] broached the problem to his wife, asking her "Should the dog be destroyed or not?" From that time on Laura became restless, agitated, and depressed. . . .

. . . Later Laura started to complain about the neighbors. A woman who lived on the floor beneath them was knocking on the wall to irritate her. According to the husband, this woman had really knocked on the wall a few times; he had heard the noises. However, Laura became more and more concerned about it. She would wake up in the middle of the night under the impression that she was hearing noises from the apartment downstairs. She would become upset and angry at the neighbors. . . . Later she became more disturbed. She started to feel that the neighbors were now recording everything she said; maybe they had hidden wires in the apartment. She started to feel "funny" sensations. There were many strange things happening, which she did not know how to explain; people were looking at her in a funny way in the street; in the butcher shop, the butcher had purposely served her last, although she was in the middle of the line. During the next few days she felt that people were planning to harm either her or her

[BOX **14-1**]

A Beautiful Mind: Movies vs. Reality

As we have observed, mental disorders and the people who experience them are popular subjects throughout the arts, including, of course, the cinema. One of the most successful such movies in recent years was *A Beautiful Mind,* based on the true story of John Forbes Nash. As the movie reveals, Nash is a brilliant mathematician who developed schizophrenia early in his academic and research career and struggled with the disorder for 35 years, unable to hold an academic position or function independently for most of those years. Nevertheless, in 1994 he was awarded the Nobel Prize in Economics for his earlier doctoral work on *game theory,* a mathematical model of conflict resolution. For his doctoral thesis in 1951, Nash had altered this theory in key ways, and while he was later struggling with schizophrenia, his revised theory went on to greatly influence the field of economics—thus his Nobel Prize in that field.

The movie is true to the spirit of Nash's battle against and ultimate triumph over schizophrenia. Similarly, it does capture the essence of Nash's relationship with his wife, Alicia, whose loving devotion, support, and patience have, by everyone's account, been key to his improvement and later accomplishments. At the same time, the movie takes certain liberties with the facts of Nash's life and struggle. Because this film has been so popular and influential—it has provided millions of people with their primary education on schizophrenia—it may be useful to correct some of the movie's misrepresentations, each done in the spirit of artistic license.

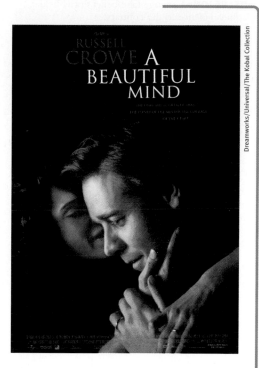

Dreamworks/Universal/The Kobal Collection

MOVIE	REALITY
◆ Nash's hallucinations and delusions begin in 1948, when he is a 20-year-old graduate student at Princeton University.	◆ His symptoms first appeared in 1958, when he was 30 years old, teaching and conducting research at MIT. In that same year, *Fortune* magazine had named him one of the country's leading mathematicians (Wallace, 2002).
◆ Nash regularly interacts with a high-spirited roommate at Princeton and with a secretive federal agent at MIT, each of whom is but a visual hallucination.	◆ In his battle with schizophrenia, Nash experienced only auditory hallucinations (voices), never visual ones.
◆ Nash is hospitalized on one occasion for his psychotic symptoms.	◆ He was committed to mental hospitals several times throughout the course of his disorder.
◆ Nash meets his wife at MIT in 1952, when Alicia, a physics major, takes his calculus course. They marry in 1957 and remain married to the present day.	◆ After Nash's disorder worsened and his accusations against her intensified, an exasperated and frightened Alicia divorced him in 1963. She remained devoted to him, however. After his mother died in 1970, Alicia agreed to reunite with him, and they have continued to be together since then. They remarried in 2001 (Nasar, 2002).
◆ Although Nash stops taking antipsychotic drugs for years, he returns to them by the movie's end, saying that he has been helped by new (atypical) antipsychotic drugs.	◆ Nash refused to take any more medications in 1970, and he reports that he has not taken any such drugs since then (Duncan, 2002).
◆ Nash has one child, a son named John Charles Nash, born to him and Alicia.	◆ Nash also has an older son named John David Stier, born to him and a woman with whom Nash had a relationship before his marriage to Alicia. Nash currently has close relationships with both sons.
◆ Nash's son, John Charles Nash, is depicted as a healthy child, free of psychological disorders.	◆ Like his father, John Charles Nash went on to develop schizophrenia. Despite this disorder, the son, too, has earned a Ph.D. in mathematics.

•**POSITIVE SYMPTOMS**•Symptoms of schizophrenia that seem to be excesses of or bizarre additions to normal thoughts, emotions, or behaviors.

•**DELUSION**•A strange false belief firmly held despite evidence to the contrary.

•**FORMAL THOUGHT DISORDER**•A disturbance in the production and organization of thought.

> husband. . . . In the evening when she looked at television, it became obvious to her that the programs referred to her life. Often the people on the programs were just repeating what she had thought. They were stealing her ideas. She wanted to go to the police and report them.
>
> *(Arieti, 1974, pp. 165–168)*

What Are the Symptoms of Schizophrenia?

Ann, Richard, and Laura all deteriorated from a normal level of functioning to become ineffective in dealing with the world. Each experienced some of the symptoms found in schizophrenia. The symptoms can be grouped into three categories: *positive symptoms* (excesses of thought, emotion, and behavior), *negative symptoms* (deficits of thought, emotion, and behavior), and *psychomotor symptoms.* It appears that some people with schizophrenia are more dominated by positive symptoms and others by negative symptoms, although both kinds of symptoms are typically displayed to some degree (Alves et al., 2005; Blanchard, Horan, & Collins, 2005). On average, men with schizophrenia seem more likely to display negative symptoms than women, but both sexes display positive symptoms to the same degree (Usall et al., 2002; Shtasel et al., 1992). In addition, around half of people with schizophrenia display significant difficulties with memory and other kinds of cognitive functioning (Julien, 2005; Heinrichs, 2005).

POSITIVE SYMPTOMS **Positive symptoms** are "patholological excesses," or bizarre additions, to a person's behavior. *Delusions, disorganized thinking and speech, heightened perceptions and hallucinations,* and *inappropriate affect* are the ones most often found in schizophrenia.

DELUSIONS Many people with schizophrenia develop **delusions,** ideas that they believe wholeheartedly but that have no basis in fact (see Box 14-2). The deluded person may consider the ideas enlightening or may feel confused by them. Some people hold a single delusion that dominates their lives and behavior, whereas others have many delusions. *Delusions of persecution* are the most common in schizophrenia (APA, 2000). People with such delusions believe they are being plotted or discriminated against, spied on, slandered, threatened, attacked, or deliberately victimized. Laura believed that her neighbors were trying to irritate her and that other people were trying to harm her and her husband. Another woman with schizophrenia vividly recalled her delusions of persecution:

> I felt as if I was being put on a heavenly trial for misdeeds that I had done and was being held accountable by God. Other times I felt as if I was being pursued by the government for acts of disloyalty. . . . I felt that the government agencies had planted transmitters and receivers in my apartment so that I could hear what they were saying and they could hear what I was saying. I also felt as if the government had bugged my clothing, so that whenever I went outside my apartment I felt like I was being pursued. I felt like I was being followed and watched 24 hours a day.
>
> I would like to point out that these were my feelings then, and in hindsight I hold nothing against these government agencies. I now know that this constant monitoring was either punishment at the hands of God's servants for deeds I committed earlier in my life (sort of like being punished in hell but while I was still alive) or alternatively, but less likely, that I just imagined these things.
>
> *(Anonymous, 1996, p. 183)*

People with schizophrenia may also experience *delusions of reference:* they attach special and personal meaning to the actions of others or to various objects or events. Richard, for example, interpreted arrows on street signs as indicators of the direction he should take. People who experience *delusions of grandeur* believe themselves to be great inventors, religious saviors, or other specially empowered persons. And those with *delusions of control* believe their feelings, thoughts, and actions are being controlled by other

Delusions of grandeur *In 1892, an artist who was a patient at a mental hospital claimed credit for this painting,* Self-Portrait as Christ. *Although few people with schizophrenia have his artistic skill, a number display similar delusions of grandeur.*

[BOX **14-2**]

Relationships of the Mind

hile playing in a professional tennis tournament in 1993, Monica Seles was stabbed by a 38-year-old man from Germany. The attacker was obsessed with another tennis star, Steffi Graf, and believed that it was his responsibility to help Graf's career by striking down her rival. Seles did not return to professional tennis for two years.

In 1989 the actress Rebecca Shaeffer of the television show *My Sister Sam* was shot and killed outside her West Hollywood apartment by a fan. He had closely followed Shaeffer's career for months, and eventually he journeyed to her apartment building. When she failed to greet him warmly, he took her rebuff as a sign of arrogance and shot her.

Stalking is a growing problem in today's world (Rosenfeld & Cling, 2004; Pathe, 2002). At least 200,000 people are victimized by stalkers in the United States each year (Corwin, 1993). As many as 1 in 12 women and 1 in 50 men are stalked during their lifetimes (Abrams & Robinson, 1998; Klein, 1998). The majority of victims experience substantial stress; indeed, many develop posttraumatic stress symptoms (Knox & Roberts, 2005; Kamphuis & Emmelkamp, 2001).

Stalking occurs in various forms and has a range of causes (Knox & Roberts, 2005; Kropp et al., 2002). However, many stalkers suffer from *erotomanic delusions,* beliefs without any basis whatsoever that they are loved by someone who may actually be a casual acquaintance or a complete stranger (Fouilhoux et al., 2004; Silva et al., 2000). Some people with such delusions, like Shaeffer's and Graf's pursuers, develop fantasies in which they feel driven to protect, harm, or even kill the object of their desire (Menzies et al., 1995).

Apple Corps/Camera Press/Retna Ltd., USA

The price of fame? *When the Beatles were enjoying worldwide success and fame, few could envision that John Lennon (second from left) would later be shot dead in 1980 and that George Harrison (far right) would nearly be stabbed to death in 1999, each by a fan with erotomanic delusions.*

people. This man hospitalized for schizophrenia imagined he was being controlled by telepathy:

> The inmates, here, hate me extremely because I am sane. . . . They talk to me telepathically, continuously and daily almost without cessation, day and night. . . . By the power of their imagination and daily and continuously, they create extreme pain in my head, brain, eyes, heart, stomach and in every part of my body. Also by their imagination and daily and continuously, they lift my heart and stomach and they pull my heart, and they stop it, move it, twist it and shake it and pull its muscles and tissues. . . . By telepathy and imagination, they force me to say orally whatever they desire, whenever they desire and as long as they desire. I never said a word of my own. I never created a thought or image of my own.
>
> *(Arieti, 1974, pp. 404–405)*

DISORGANIZED THINKING AND SPEECH People with schizophrenia may not be able to think logically and may speak in peculiar ways. These **formal thought disorders** can cause the sufferer great confusion and make communication extremely difficult. Often they take the form of positive symptoms (pathological excesses), as in *loose associations, neologisms, perseveration,* and *clang.*

>>**LOOKING AROUND**
Neologisms in Literature

In *Alice in Wonderland,* Lewis Carroll often combined two legitimate words to form a nonsensical word. Some such words are now part of the English language ("chortle," "galumph"). <<

People who have **loose associations,** or **derailment,** the most common formal thought disorder, rapidly shift from one topic to another, believing that their incoherent statements make sense. A single, perhaps unimportant word in one sentence becomes the focus of the next. One man with schizophrenia, asked about his itchy arms, responded:

> The problem is insects. My brother used to collect insects. He's now a man 5 foot 10 inches. You know, 10 is my favorite number. I also like to dance, draw, and watch television.

Some people with schizophrenia use *neologisms,* made-up words that typically have meaning only to the person using them. One individual stated, for example, "I am here from a foreign university . . . and you have to have a *'plausity'* of all acts of amendment to go through for the children's code . . . it is an *'amorition'* law . . . the children have to have this *'accentuative'* law so they don't go into the mortite law of the church" (Vetter, 1969, p. 189). Others may display the formal thought disorder of *perseveration,* in which they repeat their words and statements again and again. Finally, some use *clang,* or rhyme, to think or express themselves. When asked how he was feeling, one man replied, "Well, hell, it's well to tell." Another described the weather as "So hot, you know it runs on a cot."

Formal thought disorders are not unique to schizophrenia. Loose associations and perseverations are common in cases of severe mania, for example. Even people who function normally may organize statements loosely or may on occasion use words that others fail to understand, especially when they are fatigued or feeling ill; but the instances of formal thought disorder in schizophrenia are much more common and severe (Holzman, 1986). Research suggests that some disorganized speech or thinking may appear long before a full pattern of schizophrenia unfolds (Covington et al., 2005; Metsanen et al., 2005).

HEIGHTENED PERCEPTIONS AND HALLUCINATIONS A deranged character in Edgar Allan Poe's "The Tell-Tale Heart" asks, "Have I not told you that what you mistake for madness is but the overacuteness of the senses?" Similarly, the perceptions and attention of some people with schizophrenia seem to intensify. The persons may feel that their senses are being flooded by all the sights and sounds that surround them. This makes it almost impossible for them to attend to anything important:

Inner torment *Like this young woman, people with schizophrenia often appear to be trying to fight off the strange thoughts and perceptions that pervade their minds.*

> Everything seems to grip my attention. . . . I am speaking to you just now, but I can hear noises going on next door and in the corridor. I find it difficult to shut these out, and it makes it more difficult for me to concentrate on what I am saying to you.
>
> *(McGhie and Chapman, 1961)*

Laboratory studies have repeatedly found problems of perception and attention among people with schizophrenia (Gilmore et al., 2005; Silver & Feldman, 2005). In one study, subjects were instructed to listen for a particular syllable recorded against an ongoing background of speech (Harris et al., 1985). As long as the background speech was kept simple, subjects with and without schizophrenia were equally successful at picking out the syllable in question; but when the background speech was made more distracting, the subjects with schizophrenia became less able to identify the syllable. In many studies, subjects with this disorder have also demonstrated deficiencies in *smooth pursuit eye movement,* weaknesses that may be related again to attention problems. When asked to keep their head still and track a moving object back and forth with their eyes, subjects with schizophrenia tend to perform more poorly than those without schizophrenia (Boudet et al., 2005; Zanelli et al., 2005).

The various perception and attention problems in schizophrenia may develop years before the onset of the actual disorder (Moratori et al., 2005; Cornblatt & Keilp, 1994). It is possible that such problems further contribute to the memory impairments that are experienced by many individuals with the disorder (Silver & Feldman, 2005; Hartman et al., 2003).

Another kind of perceptual problem in schizophrenia consists of **hallucinations,** perceptions that occur in the absence of external stimuli. People who have *auditory* hallucinations, by far the most common kind in schizophrenia, hear sounds and voices that seem to come from outside their heads (Folsom et al., 2006). The voices may talk directly to the hallucinator, perhaps giving commands or warning of dangers, or they may be experienced as overheard:

> The voices . . . were mostly heard in my head, though I often heard them in the air, or in different parts of the room. Every voice was different, and each beautiful, and generally, speaking or singing in a different tone and measure, and resembling those of relations or friends. There appeared to be many in my head, I should say upwards of fourteen. I divide them, as they styled themselves, or one another, into voices of contrition and voices of joy and honour.
>
> *("Perceval's Narrative," in Bateson, 1974)*

Research suggests that people with auditory hallucinations actually produce the nerve signals of sound in their brains, "hear" them, and then believe that external sources are responsible (Keefe et al., 2002). One study measured blood flow in *Broca's area,* the region of the brain that helps people produce speech (McGuire et al., 1996, 1995, 1993). The researchers found more blood flow in Broca's area while patients were experiencing auditory hallucinations. A related study instructed six men with schizophrenia to press a button whenever they experienced an auditory hallucination (Silbersweig et al., 1995). PET scans revealed increased activity near the surfaces of their brains, in the tissues of the brain's hearing center, when they pressed the button.

Hallucinations can also involve any of the other senses. *Tactile* hallucinations may take the form of tingling, burning, or electric-shock sensations. *Somatic* hallucinations feel as if something is happening inside the body, such as a snake crawling inside one's stomach. *Visual* hallucinations may produce vague perceptions of colors or clouds or distinct visions of people or objects. People with *gustatory* hallucinations regularly find that their food or drink tastes strange, and people with *olfactory* hallucinations smell odors that no one else does, such as the smell of poison or smoke.

Hallucinations and delusional ideas often occur together. A woman who hears voices issuing commands, for example, may have the delusion that the commands are being placed in her head by someone else. A man with delusions of persecution may hallucinate

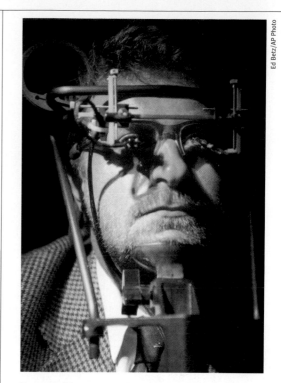

Ed Betz/AP Photo

Poor tracking *Clinical researcher Michael Obuchowski demonstrates a device that reveals how well a person's eyes track a moving laser dot. People with schizophrenia tend to perform poorly on this and other eye pursuit tasks.*

D. Silbersweig, M.D., and E. Stern, M.D., Functional Neuroimaging Laboratory, The New York Hospital-Cornell Medical Center, New York, NY

The human brain during hallucinations *This PET scan, taken at the moment a subject was experiencing auditory and visual hallucinations, shows heightened activity (yellow-orange) in hearing-related tissues at the brain's surface (Silbersweig et al., 1995). Conversely, the front of the brain, which is responsible for determining the source of sounds and other sensations, was quiet during the hallucinations. Thus a person who is hallucinating seems to hear sounds produced by his or her own brain, but the brain cannot recognize that the sounds are actually coming from within.*

•LOOSE ASSOCIATIONS•A common thinking disturbance in schizophrenia, characterized by rapid shifts from one topic of conversation to another. Also known as *derailment.*

•HALLUCINATION•The experiencing of sights, sounds, or other perceptions in the absence of external stimuli.

the smell of poison in his bedroom or the taste of poison in his coffee. Might one symptom cause the other? Whatever the cause and whichever comes first, the hallucination and delusion eventually feed into each other (see Box 14-3):

> I thought the voices I heard were being transmitted through the walls of my apartment and through the washer and dryer and that these machines were talking and telling me things. I felt that the government agencies had planted transmitters and receivers in my apartment so that I could hear what they were saying and they could hear what I was saying.
>
> *(Anonymous, 1996, p. 183)*

INAPPROPRIATE AFFECT Many people with schizophrenia display **inappropriate affect,** emotions that are unsuited to the situation. They may smile when making a somber statement or on being told terrible news, or they may become upset in situations that should make them happy. They may also undergo inappropriate shifts in mood. During a tender conversation with his wife, for example, a man with schizophrenia suddenly started yelling obscenities at her and complaining about her inadequacies.

In at least some cases, these emotions may be merely a response to other features of the disorder. Consider a woman with schizophrenia who smiles when told of her husband's serious illness. She may not actually be happy about the news; in fact, she may not be understanding or even hearing it. She could, for example, be responding instead to another of the many stimuli flooding her senses, perhaps a joke coming from an auditory hallucination.

NEGATIVE SYMPTOMS **Negative symptoms** are those that seem to be "pathological deficits," characteristics that are lacking in an individual. *Poverty of speech, blunted and flat affect, loss of volition,* and *social withdrawal* are commonly found in schizophrenia. Such deficits greatly affect one's life and activities.

POVERTY OF SPEECH People with schizophrenia often display **alogia,** or **poverty of speech,** a reduction in speech or speech content. Some people with this negative kind of formal thought disorder think and say very little. Others say quite a bit but still manage to convey little meaning. These speech problems do not necessarily carry over to the realm of writing (Salome et al., 2002). Nevertheless, they are revealed in the following diary entry written on February 27, 1919, by Vaslav Nijinsky, one of the twentieth century's great ballet dancers, as his schizophrenic disorder was unfolding:

> I do not wish people to think that I am a great writer or that I am a great artist nor even that I am a great man. I am a simple man who has suffered a lot. I believe I suffered more than Christ. I love life and want to live, to cry but cannot—I feel such a pain in my soul—a pain which frightens me. My soul is ill. My soul, not my mind. The doctors do not understand my illness. I know what I need to get well. My illness is too great to be cured quickly. I am incurable. Everyone who reads these lines will suffer—they will understand my feelings. I know what I need. I am strong, not weak. My body is not ill—it is my soul that is ill. I suffer, I suffer. Everyone will feel and understand. I am a man, not a beast. I love everyone, I have faults, I am a man—not God. I want to be God and therefore I try to improve myself. I want to dance, to draw, to play the piano, to write verses, I want to love everybody. That is the object of my life.
>
> *(Nijinsky, 1936)*

BLUNTED AND FLAT AFFECT Many people with schizophrenia have a *blunted affect*—they show less anger, sadness, joy, and other feelings than most people. And some show almost no emotions at all, a condition known as **flat affect.** Their faces are still, their eye contact is poor, and their voices are monotonous. In some cases, people with these problems

•**INAPPROPRIATE AFFECT**•Display of emotions that are unsuited to the situation; a symptom of schizophrenia.

•**NEGATIVE SYMPTOMS**•Symptoms of schizophrenia that seem to be deficits in normal thought, emotions, or behaviors.

•**ALOGIA**•A decrease in speech or speech content; a symptom of schizophrenia. Also known as *poverty of speech.*

•**FLAT AFFECT**•A marked lack of expressed emotions; a symptom of schizophrenia.

•**AVOLITION**•A symptom of schizophrenia marked by apathy and an inability to start or complete a course of action.

[BOX 14-3]

Howling for Attention

▌ *It's when I was bitten by a rabid dog. . . . When I'm emotionally upset, I feel as if I am turning into something else: my fingers go numb, as if I had pins and needles right in the middle of my hand; I can no longer control myself. . . . I get the feeling I'm becoming a wolf. I look at myself in the mirror and I witness my transformation. It's no longer my face; it changes completely. I stare, my pupils dilate, and I feel as if hairs are growing all over my body, as if my teeth are getting longer. . . . I feel as if my skin is no longer mine.* ▌

(BENEZECH, DEWITTE, & BOURGEOIS, 1989)

Lycanthropy, the delusion of being an animal, is a rare psychological syndrome. The word "lycanthropy" comes from the Greek *lykos,* "wolf," and *anthropos,* "man." Accounts have been found all over the world of people who take on the characteristics and behavior of wolves or other animals. Belief in these tales has persisted for centuries. In the Middle Ages, lycanthropy was thought to be the result of demonic possession (Lehmann, 1985). In some societies it occurred after special ointments, probably hallucinogenic drugs, were applied, often for religious purposes (Lévi-Strauss, 1977). In other societies, cases seem to have been closely linked to mental disorders, includ-ing schizophrenia, severe mood disorders, and certain forms of brain damage.

Mention of lycanthropy continues to produce an image of a werewolf baring its fangs at a terrified villager on a fog-shrouded moor. The legend was that the former had been bitten by another were-wolf in an unbroken chain that passes on the legacy. But there are now more rea-sonable explanations for this type of behavior. One explanation is that some people afflicted with lycanthropy actually suffer from *congenital generalized hyper-trichosis,* an extremely rare disease marked by excessive amounts of hair on the face and upper body (Maugh, 1995). Others may suffer from *porphyria,* an inherited blood disease whose victims sprout extra facial hair and are sensitive to sunlight. Still another current explana-tion ties lycanthropy to a disturbance in the activity of the *temporal lobe* of the brain, which is close to areas of the brain that may be responsible for visual hallucinations.

Despite these rational hypotheses, be-liefs in werewolves as supernatural beings are likely to continue for the foreseeable future. Tales of demonic possession are more alluring than histories of congenital disease or temporal lobe abnormalities. Nor are publishers or movie producers likely to say good-bye to such good friends. Old explanations of lycanthropy may be flawed scientifically, but the profits they produce are far from a delusion.

Polygram/Universal/The Kobal Collection

Crying wolf *In the film* An American Werewolf in London, *a possessed man cries out in terror as his body changes into that of a wolf.*

---

may have *anhedonia,* a general lack of pleasure or enjoyment. In other cases, however, blunted or flat affect may reflect an inability to express emotions as others do. One study had subjects view very emotional film clips. Subjects with schizophrenia showed less fa-cial expression than the others; however, they reported feeling just as much positive and negative emotion and in fact displayed greater skin arousal (Kring & Neale, 1996).

LOSS OF VOLITION Many people with schizophrenia experience **avolition,** or apathy, feeling drained of energy and of interest in normal goals and unable to start or follow through on a course of action (Lysaker & Bell, 1995). This problem is particularly com-mon in people who have had schizophrenia for many years, as if they have been worn down by it. Similarly, individuals with the disorder may display *ambivalence,* or conflict-ing feelings, about most things. The avolition and ambivalence of Richard, the young man whose case was presented earlier, made eating, dressing, and undressing impossible ordeals for him.

SOCIAL WITHDRAWAL People with schizophrenia may withdraw from their social environ-ment and attend only to their own ideas and fantasies. Because their ideas are illogical and confused, the withdrawal has the effect of distancing them still further from reality. In fact, studies have found that subjects with this disorder are typically less knowledge-able about everyday social issues than are other people (Venneri et al., 2002; Cutting &

>>PSYCH•NOTES

Social Impact

One study indicates that people with schizo-phrenia who maintain frequent social interac-tions live 25 percent longer on average than those with few such interactions (Christensen et al., 1999). ‹‹

A catatonic pose *These patients, photographed in the early 1900s, display features of catatonia, including catatonic posturing, in which they assume bizarre positions for long periods of time.*

Murphy, 1990, 1988). The social withdrawal seems also to lead to a breakdown of social skills, including the ability to recognize other people's needs and emotions accurately (Corrigan & Penn, 2001; Trumbetta & Mueser, 2001).

PSYCHOMOTOR SYMPTOMS People with schizophrenia sometimes experience *psychomotor symptoms,* for example, awkward movements or repeated grimaces and odd gestures. These unusual gestures often seem to have a private purpose—perhaps ritualistic or magical.

The psychomotor symptoms of schizophrenia may take certain extreme forms, collectively called **catatonia** (Caroff et al., 2004). People in a *catatonic stupor* stop responding to their environment, remaining motionless and silent for long stretches of time. Recall how Richard would lie motionless and mute in bed for days. People who display *catatonic rigidity* maintain a rigid, upright posture for hours and resist efforts to be moved. Others exhibit *catatonic posturing,* assuming awkward, bizarre positions for long periods of time. They may spend hours holding their arms out at a 90-degree angle or balancing in a squatting position. They may also display "waxy flexibility," indefinitely maintaining postures into which they have been placed by someone else. If a nurse raises a patient's arm or tilts the patient's head, for example, the individual will remain in that position until moved again. Finally, people who display *catatonic excitement,* a different form of catatonia, move excitedly, sometimes with wild waving of arms and legs.

What Is the Course of Schizophrenia?

Schizophrenia usually first appears between the person's late teens and mid-30s (APA, 2000). Although its course varies widely from case to case, many sufferers seem to go through three phases—prodromal, active, and residual. During the *prodromal phase,* symptoms are not yet obvious, but persons are beginning to deteriorate. They may withdraw socially, speak in vague or odd ways, develop strange ideas, or express little emotion. During the *active phase,* symptoms become apparent. Sometimes this phase is triggered by stress in the person's life. For Laura, the middle-aged woman described earlier, the immediate trigger was the loss of her cherished dog. Finally, many people with schizophrenia eventually enter a *residual phase,* in which they return to a prodromal-like level of functioning. The striking symptoms of the active phase lessen, but some negative symptoms, such as blunted emotions, may remain (Andreasen, 2001). Although one-quarter or more of patients recover completely from schizophrenia (Torrey, 2001; McGuire, 2000), the majority continue to have at least some residual problems for the rest of their lives.

Each of these phases may last for days or for years. A fuller recovery from schizophrenia is more likely in persons who functioned quite well before the disorder (had good *premorbid functioning*) or whose disorder was initially triggered by stress, came on abruptly, or developed during middle age (Mamounas et al., 2001; Lindström, 1996; Tolbert, 1996). Relapses are apparently more likely during times of stress (Norman & Malla, 2001).

Diagnosing Schizophrenia

DSM-IV-TR calls for a diagnosis of schizophrenia only after symptoms of the disorder continue for six months or more. In addition, people suspected of having this disorder must show a deterioration in their work, social relations, and ability to care for themselves (see Table 14-1). Emil Kraepelin, writing in 1896, distinguished three patterns of schizophrenia: *hebephrenic* (what we would today term "disorganized"), *catatonic,* and *paranoid* schizophrenia. To these categories DSM-IV-TR adds two other types of schizophrenia: *undifferentiated* and *residual.*

Table 14-1 DSM Checklist

SCHIZOPHRENIA

1. At least two of the following symptoms, each present for a significant portion of time during a one-month period:
   a. Delusions.
   b. Hallucinations.
   c. Disorganized speech.
   d. Grossly disorganized or catatonic behavior.
   e. Negative symptoms.
2. Functioning markedly below the level achieved prior to onset.
3. Continuous signs of the disturbance for at least six months, at least one month of which includes symptoms in full and active form (as opposed to attenuated form).

Based on APA, 2000, 1994.

The central symptoms of *disorganized type of schizophrenia* are confusion, incoherence, and flat or inappropriate affect. Attention and perception problems, extreme social withdrawal, and odd mannerisms or grimaces are common. So is flat or inappropriate affect. Silliness, in particular, is common; some patients giggle constantly without apparent reason. This is why the pattern was first called "hebephrenic," after Hebe, the goddess who, according to Greek mythology, often acted like a clown to make the other gods laugh. Not surprisingly, people with disorganized schizophrenia are typically unable to take good care of themselves, maintain social relationships, or hold a job.

The central feature of *catatonic type of schizophrenia* is a psychomotor disturbance of some sort. Some of the people in this category spend their time in a catatonic stupor, others in the throes of catatonic excitement. Richard, the unemployed young man who became mute and statuelike, might receive a diagnosis of this type of schizophrenia.

People with *paranoid type of schizophrenia* have an organized system of delusions and auditory hallucinations that may guide their lives. Laura would receive this diagnosis. She believed people were out to get her (delusions of persecution) and that people on television were stealing her ideas (delusions of reference). In addition, she heard noises from the apartment downstairs and felt "funny sensations" that confirmed her beliefs.

When people with this disorder do not fall neatly into one of the other categories, they are diagnosed with *undifferentiated type of schizophrenia*. Because this category is somewhat vague, it has been assigned to a wide assortment of unusual patterns over the years. Many clinicians believe that it is in fact overused.

When the symptoms of schizophrenia lessen in strength and number yet remain in a residual form, the patient's diagnosis is usually changed to *residual type of schizophrenia*. As we observed earlier, people with this pattern may continue to display blunted or inappropriate emotions, as well as social withdrawal, eccentric behavior, and some illogical thinking.

How Do Theorists Explain Schizophrenia?

As with many other kinds of disorders, biological, psychological, and sociocultural theorists have each proposed explanations for schizophrenia. So far, the biological explanations have received by far the most research support. This is not to say that psychological and sociocultural factors play no role in the disorder. Rather, a *diathesis-stress relationship* may be at work: people with a biological predisposition will develop schizophrenia only if certain kinds of events or stressors are also present (Gottesman & Reilly, 2003). Similarly, a diathesis-stress relationship often seems to be operating in the development of other kinds of psychotic disorders (see Box 14-4 on page 426).

Biological Views

What is arguably the most enlightening research on schizophrenia during the past several decades has come from genetic and biological investigations (Weyandt, 2006). These studies have revealed the key roles of inheritance and brain activity in the development of this disorder and have opened the door to important changes in its treatment.

GENETIC FACTORS Following the principles of the diathesis-stress perspective, genetic researchers believe that some people inherit a biological predisposition to schizophrenia and develop the disorder later when they face extreme stress, usually during late adolescence or early adulthood. The genetic view has been supported by studies of (1) relatives of people with schizophrenia, (2) twins with this disorder, (3) people with schizophrenia who are adopted, and (4) genetic linkage and molecular biology.

ARE RELATIVES VULNERABLE? Family pedigree studies have found repeatedly that schizophrenia is more common among relatives of people with the disorder (Stone et al., 2005; Andreasen, 2001; Kendler et al., 1994, 1993). And the more closely related the relatives

No, it's not "the King" *But surveys indicate that as many as one of every eight Americans believes that Elvis Presley is still alive—a belief that has led to numerous Elvis sightings at 7-Eleven stores around the country and encouraged an army of Elvis impersonators. Clinicians stop short of calling such beliefs delusions, however, noting that the Elvis loyalists do not hold on to their beliefs with a high degree of conviction. Most can be persuaded that Elvis has indeed "left the building."*

•**CATATONIA**•A pattern of extreme psychomotor symptoms found in some forms of schizophrenia, which may include catatonic stupor, rigidity, or posturing.

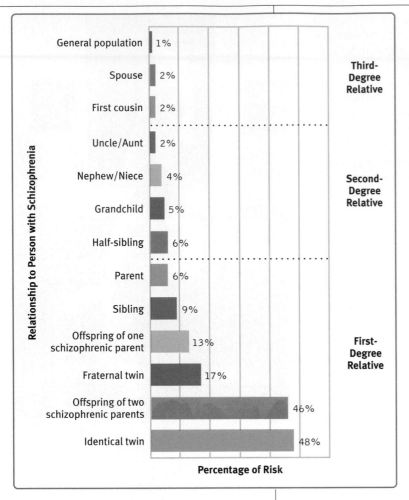

Third-
Degree
Relative

Second-
Degree
Relative

First-
Degree
Relative

Percentage of Risk

FIGURE **14-3** **Family links** *People who are biologically related to individuals with schizophrenia have a
heightened risk of developing the disorder during
their lifetimes. The closer the biological relationship
(that is, the more similar the genetic makeup), the
greater the risk of developing the disorder. (Adapted
from Gottesman, 1991, p. 96.)*

are to the person with schizophrenia, the greater their likelihood of developing the disorder (see Figure 14-3).

As we saw earlier, 1 percent of the general population develops schizophrenia. The prevalence rises to 3 percent among
second-degree relatives with this disorder—that is, half-siblings,
uncles, aunts, nephews, nieces, and grandchildren (Gottesman
& Reilly, 2003; Gottesman, 1991; Gottesman & Shields, 1982).
And it reaches an average of 10 percent among first-degree relatives (parents, siblings, and children). Of course, this trend by
itself does not establish a genetic basis for the disorder. The neuroscientist Solomon Snyder (1980) points out, "Attendance at
Harvard University also runs in families but would hardly be
considered a genetic trait." Close family members are exposed
to many of the same environmental influences as the person
with schizophrenia, and it may be these influences that lead to
the disorder.

**IS AN IDENTICAL TWIN MORE VULNERABLE THAN A FRATERNAL
TWIN?** Twins, who are among the closest of relatives, have received particular study by schizophrenia researchers. If both
members of a pair of twins have a particular trait, they are said
to be *concordant* for that trait. If genetic factors are at work in
schizophrenia, identical twins (who share all genes) should have
a higher concordance rate for this disorder than fraternal twins
(who share only some genes). This expectation has been supported consistently by research (Lambert & Kinsley, 2005; Folsom et al., 2006; Gottesman, 1991). Studies have found that if
one identical twin develops schizophrenia, there is a 48 percent
chance that the other twin will do so as well. If the twins are
fraternal, on the other hand, the second twin has approximately
a 17 percent chance of developing the disorder.

Once again, however, factors other than genetics may explain these concordance
rates. For example, if one twin is exposed to a particular danger during the prenatal period, such as an injury or virus, the other twin is likely to be exposed to it as well (Davis
& Phelps, 1995). This is especially true for identical twins, whose prenatal environment
is particularly similar. Thus a predisposition to schizophrenia could be the result of a prenatal problem, and twins, particularly identical twins, would still be expected to have a
higher concordance rate.

ARE THE BIOLOGICAL RELATIVES OF AN ADOPTEE VULNERABLE? Adoption studies look at
adults with schizophrenia who were adopted as infants and compare them with both their
biological and their adoptive relatives. Because they were reared apart from their biological relatives, similar symptoms in those relatives would indicate genetic influences. Conversely, similarities to their adoptive relatives would suggest environmental influences.

Seymour Kety and his colleagues (1988, 1978, 1975, 1974, 1968) conducted a pioneering study in Copenhagen, Denmark, where detailed records of adoptions and mental disorders are available. In a sample of nearly 5,500 adults who had been adopted early
in life, the researchers found 33 with schizophrenia. They then selected 33 matching
control subjects from the same large sample—normal adoptees similar in age, sex, and
schooling to the subjects with schizophrenia. Next the investigators located 365 biological and adoptive relatives of these 66 adoptees, including both parents and siblings, and
separated the relatives into four groups: (1) biological relatives of adoptees with schizophrenia; (2) adoptive relatives of adoptees with schizophrenia; (3) biological relatives of
normal adoptees; and (4) adoptive relatives of normal adoptees. Thirty-seven of the relatives were found to qualify for a diagnosis of either schizophrenia or a schizophrenia-
like disorder (see Table 14-2). Most of them turned out to be biological relatives of the
adoptees with schizophrenia, a result that strongly supports the genetic explanation. Altogether 14 percent of the biological relatives of the adoptees with the disorder were
themselves classified as schizophrenic, whereas only 2.7 percent of their adoptive rela-

tives received this classification. The biological and adoptive relatives of the normal adoptees had schizophrenia prevalence rates of 3.4 percent and 5.5 percent, respectively. More recent adoption studies in other countries have yielded similar findings (Janicak et al., 2001).

WHAT DO GENETIC LINKAGE AND MOLECULAR BIOLOGY STUDIES SUGGEST?

As with bipolar disorders (see Chapter 8), researchers have run studies of *genetic linkage* and *molecular biology* to pinpoint the possible genetic factors in schizophrenia (Stone et al., 2005; Owen & O'Donovan, 2003). In one approach, they select large families in which schizophrenia is very common, take blood and DNA samples from all members of the families, and then compare gene fragments from members with and without schizophrenia. Applying this procedure to families from around the world, various studies have identified possible gene defects on chromosomes 1, 6, 8, 10, 13, 15, 18, and 22, and the X chromosome, each of which may help predispose individuals to develop schizophrenia (Folsom et al., 2006; Harrison & Weinberger, 2005).

These varied findings may indicate that some of the suspected gene sites are cases of mistaken identity and do not actually contribute to schizophrenia. Alternatively, it may be that different kinds of schizophrenia are linked to different genes. It is most likely, however, that schizophrenia, like a number of other disorders, is a *polygenic disorder*, caused by a combination of gene defects (Harrison & Weinberger, 2005).

How might genetic factors lead to the development of schizophrenia? Research has pointed to two kinds of biological abnormalities that could conceivably be inherited— *biochemical abnormalities* and *abnormal brain structure* (Kendler, 2005).

BIOCHEMICAL ABNORMALITIES We have seen that the brain is made up of neurons whose impulses (or "messages") are carried from one to another by neurotransmitters. After an impulse arrives at a receiving neuron, it travels down the body of that neuron until it reaches the nerve ending. The nerve ending then releases neurotransmitters that

Natacha Pisarenko/AP Photo

A new genetic technique *A "transegenic" mouse looks around at the Argentine laboratory in which it lives. The laboratory has developed a technique for modifying the neurological genes of mice, enabling researchers to better study and develop treatments for schizophrenia and other disorders of the brain. Several research teams in the United States and England have purchased and conducted studies on such mice.*

Table **14-2**

An Array of Psychotic Disorders

Disorder	Key Features	Duration	Lifetime Prevalence
Schizophrenia	Various psychotic symptoms such as delusions, hallucinations, disorganized speech, flat or inappropriate affect, and catatonia	6 months or more	1.0%
Brief psychotic disorder	Various psychotic symptoms such as delusions, hallucinations, disorganized speech, flat or inappropriate affect, and catatonia	Less than 1 month	Unknown
Schizophreniform disorder	Various psychotic symptoms such as delusions, hallucinations, disorganized speech, flat or inappropriate affect, and catatonia	1 to 6 months	0.2%
Schizoaffective disorder	Marked symptoms of both schizophrenia and a mood disorder	6 months or more	Unknown
Delusional disorder	Persistent delusions that are not bizarre and not due to schizophrenia; persecutory, jealous, grandiose, and somatic delusions are common	1 month or more	0.1%
Shared psychotic disorder	Person adopts delusions that are held by another individual, such as a parent or sibling; Also known as *folie à deux*	No minimum length	Unknown
Psychotic disorder due to a general medical condition	Hallucinations or delusions caused by a medical illness or brain damage	No minimum length	Unknown
Substance-induced psychotic disorder	Hallucinations or delusions caused directly by a substance, such as an abused drug	No minimum length	Unknown

[BOX 14-4]

Postpartum Psychosis: The Case of Andrea Yates

On the morning of June 20, 2001, the nation's television viewers watched in horror as officials escorted 36-year-old Andrea Yates to a police car. Just minutes before, she had called police and explained that she had drowned her five children in the bathtub because "they weren't developing correctly" and because she "realized [she had not been] a good mother to them." Homicide sergeant Eric Mehl described how she looked him in the eye, nodded, answered with a polite "Yes, sir" to many of his questions, and twice recounted the order in which the children had died: first 3-year-old Paul, then 2-year-old Luke, followed by 5-year-old John and 6-month-old Mary. She then described how she had had to drag 7-year-old Noah to the bathroom and how he had come up twice as he fought for air. Signs of mental disturbance were present during this 17-minute conversation. Yates sat in silence if Mehl asked too many questions and could give only short answers to simple questions. Later she told doctors she wanted her hair shaved so she could see the number 666—the mark of the Antichrist—on her scalp (Roche, 2002).

In Chapter 9 we observed that as many as 80 percent of mothers experience "baby blues" soon after giving birth, while between 10 and 30 percent display the clinical syndrome of *postpartum depression*. Yet another postpartum disorder that has become all too familiar to the public in recent times, by way of cases such as that of Andrea Yates, is *postpartum psychosis*.

Courtesy of Yates Family/Getty Images

Family tragedy *In this undated photograph, Andrea Yates poses with her husband and four of the five children she later drowned.*

travel to and attach to receptors on yet another neuron, thus relaying the message to the next "station" by causing that neuron to fire.

Over the past three decades, researchers have developed a **dopamine hypothesis** to explain their findings on schizophrenia: certain neurons that use the neurotransmitter dopamine fire too often and transmit too many messages, thus producing the symptoms of the disorder (McGowan et al., 2004). This hypothesis has undergone challenges and adjustments in recent years, but it is still the foundation for present biochemical explanations of schizophrenia. The chain of events leading to this hypothesis began with the accidental discovery of **antipsychotic drugs,** medications that help remove the symptoms of schizophrenia. As we shall see in Chapter 15, the first group of antipsychotic medications, the **phenothiazines,** were discovered in the 1950s by researchers who were looking for better *antihistamine* drugs to combat allergies. Although phenothiazines failed as antihistamines, their effectiveness in reducing schizophrenic symptoms became obvious, and clinicians began to prescribe them widely.

Researchers soon learned that these early antipsychotic drugs often produce troublesome muscular tremors, symptoms that are identical to the central symptom of *Parkinson's disease,* a disabling neurological illness. This undesired reaction to antipsychotic drugs gave researchers their first important clue to the biology of schizophrenia. Scientists already knew that people who suffer from Parkinson's disease have abnormally low levels of the neurotransmitter dopamine in some areas of the brain and that lack of dopamine is the reason for their uncontrollable shaking. If antipsychotic drugs produce

•**DOPAMINE HYPOTHESIS**•The theory that schizophrenia results from excessive activity of the neurotransmitter dopamine.

•**ANTIPSYCHOTIC DRUGS**•Drugs that help correct grossly confused or distorted thinking.

•**PHENOTHIAZINES**•A group of antihistamine drugs that became the first group of effective antipsychotic medications.

Postpartum psychosis affects about 1 in 1,000 mothers who have recently given birth. Within days or at most a few months of childbirth, the woman develops signs of losing touch with reality, such as delusions (for example, she may become convinced that her baby is the devil); hallucinations (perhaps hearing voices); extreme anxiety, confusion, and disorientation; disturbed sleep; and illogical or chaotic thoughts (for example, thoughts about killing herself or her child) (Nonacs, 2002).

Women with a history of bipolar disorder, schizophrenia, or depression are particularly vulnerable to the disorder (Nonacs, 2002). In addition, women who have previously experienced postpartum depression or postpartum psychosis have an increased likelihood of developing this disorder after subsequent births (Ruta & Cohen, 1998). Andrea Yates, for example, had developed signs of postpartum depression (and perhaps postpartum psychosis) and attempted suicide after the birth of her fourth child. At that time, however, she appeared to respond well to a combination of medications, including antipsychotic drugs, and so she and her husband later decided to conceive a fifth child.

Although they were warned that she was at risk for serious postpartum symptoms once again, they believed that the same combination of medications would help if the symptoms were to recur (King, 2002).

After the birth of her fifth child, the symptoms did in fact recur, along with features of psychosis. Yates again attempted suicide. Although she was hospitalized twice and treated with various medications, her condition failed to improve as various medications were added and withdrawn. Six months after giving birth to Mary, her fifth child, she drowned all five of her children.

Most clinicians who are knowledgeable about this rare disorder agree that Yates was indeed a victim of postpartum psychosis. Although only a fraction of women with the disorder actually harm their children, the Yates case reminds us that such an outcome is indeed possible (Dobson & Sales, 2000). The case also reminds us that early detection and intervention are critical.

Could more have been done for this woman as her disorder was progressing? In retrospect, obviously. And, in fact, fingers have been pointed at her husband, her doctors, her insurers, and others who failed to

appreciate or respond properly to the severity of her disorder, failed to make long-term hospitalization available to her, offered her relatively little in the way of treatment options, allowed her to be alone at home with her children while her stress built up and her symptoms continued, and failed to dissuade her from having a fifth child.

On March 13, 2002, a Texas jury found Andrea Yates guilty of murdering her children and she was sentenced to life in prison. She had pleaded *not guilty by reason of insanity* during her trial, but the jury concluded that despite her profound disorder (which even the prosecutors had acknowledged), she did know right from wrong. The jury reached its verdict after 3 hours and 40 minutes of deliberation. The verdict itself stirred debate throughout the United States, but clinicians and the public alike were united in the belief that, at the very least, the mental health system had tragically failed this woman and her five children. A Texas appeals court reversed Yates's conviction in 2005, citing the inaccurate testimony of a prosecution witness. In turn, Yates was scheduled for a new trial in 2006 and was sent to a mental health facility for treatment while awaiting retrial.

Parkinsonian symptoms in persons with schizophrenia while removing their psychotic symptoms, perhaps the drugs reduce dopamine activity. And, scientists reasoned further, if lowering dopamine activity helps remove the symptoms of schizophrenia, perhaps schizophrenia is related to excessive dopamine activity in the first place.

HOW STRONG IS THE DOPAMINE-SCHIZOPHRENIA LINK? Since the 1960s, research has supported and helped clarify the dopamine hypothesis. It has been found, for example, that some people with Parkinson's disease develop schizophrenic symptoms if they take too much *L-dopa,* a medication that raises dopamine levels in patients with that disease (Grilly, 2002; Carey et al., 1995). The L-dopa apparently raises the dopamine activity so much that it produces psychosis.

Support for the dopamine hypothesis has also come from research on *amphetamines,* drugs that, as we saw in Chapter 12, stimulate the central nervous system. Investigators first noticed during the 1970s that people who take high doses of amphetamines may develop *amphetamine psychosis*—a syndrome very similar to schizophrenia. They also found that antipsychotic drugs can reduce the symptoms of amphetamine psychosis, just as they reduce the symptoms of schizophrenia (Janowsky et al., 1973). Eventually it was learned that amphetamines increase dopamine activity in the brain, thus producing schizophrenic symptoms.

Investigators have located areas of the brain that are rich in dopamine receptors and have found that phenothiazines and other antipsychotic drugs bind to many of these

>>PSYCH•NOTES

Rapid Growth At birth, neurons in the human brain form more than 50 trillion synapses or connections. That number increases twenty-fold to more than 1,000 trillion in the first months of life (Begley, 1997). «

Brain Size The human brain is approximately one-quarter its final size at birth; the rest of the body is one-twentieth (Swerdlow, 1995). «

receptors (Burt et al., 1977; Creese et al., 1977). Apparently the drugs are *dopamine antagonists*—drugs that bind to dopamine receptors, prevent dopamine from binding there, and so prevent the neurons from firing (Iversen, 1975). Researchers have identified five kinds of dopamine receptors in the brain—called the D-1, D-2, D-3, D-4, and D-5 receptors—and have found that phenothiazines bind most strongly to the *D-2 receptors* (Julien, 2005).

WHAT IS DOPAMINE'S PRECISE ROLE? These and related findings suggest that in schizophrenia, messages traveling from dopamine-sending neurons to dopamine receptors on other neurons, particularly to the D-2 receptors, may be transmitted too easily or too often. This theory is appealing because certain dopamine neurons are known to play a key role in guiding attention (Cohen et al., 1988). People whose attention is severely disturbed by excessive dopamine activity might well be expected to suffer from the problems of attention, perception, and thought found in schizophrenia.

Why might dopamine be overactive in people with schizophrenia? It may be that people with this disorder have a larger-than-usual number of dopamine receptors, particularly D-2 receptors (Sedvall, 1990; Seidman, 1990). Remember that when dopamine carries a message to a receiving neuron, it must bind to a receptor on the neuron. A greater number of receptors will ensure more dopamine binding and thus more neuron firing. Autopsies have in fact found an unusually large number of dopamine receptors in people with schizophrenia (Owen et al., 1987, 1978; Lee & Seeman, 1980).

Though enlightening, the dopamine hypothesis has certain problems. The greatest challenge to it has come with the recent discovery of a new group of antipsychotic drugs, referred to as **atypical antipsychotics,** which are often more effective than the traditional ones. The new drugs bind not only to D-2 dopamine receptors, like the traditional, or conventional, antipsychotic drugs, but also to many D-1 receptors and to receptors for other neurotransmitters such as *serotonin*. Thus, it may be that schizophrenia is related to abnormal activity or interactions of both dopamine and serotonin and perhaps other neurotransmitters (for example, *glutamate* and *GABA*) as well, rather than to abnormal dopamine activity alone (Folsom et al., 2006; Javitt & Coyle, 2004).

In yet another challenge to the dopamine hypothesis, some theorists claim that excessive dopamine activity contributes primarily to the positive symptoms of schizophrenia such as delusions and hallucinations. In support of that notion, it turns out that positive symptoms respond well to the conventional antipsychotic drugs, which bind so strongly to D-2 receptors, whereas negative symptoms (such as flat affect and loss of volition) respond best to the atypical antipsychotic drugs, which bind less strongly to D-2 receptors (Julien, 2005). Still other studies suggest that negative symptoms may be related primarily to abnormal brain structure, rather than to dopamine overactivity (Maruff et al., 2005).

ABNORMAL BRAIN STRUCTURE During the past decade, researchers also have linked schizophrenia, particularly cases dominated by negative symptoms, to abnormalities in brain structure (Weyandt, 2006). Using CAT and MRI scanning techniques, they have found, for example, that many people with schizophrenia have *enlarged ventricles*—the brain cavities that contain cerebrospinal fluid (Cahn et al., 2002; Lieberman et al., 2001). On average the ventricles of these individuals are 15 percent larger than those of other persons (Torrey, 2002, 2001). In addition to displaying more negative symptoms and fewer positive ones, patients who have enlarged ventricles tend to experience a poorer social adjustment prior to the disorder, greater cognitive disturbances, and poorer responses to conventional antipsychotic drugs (Bornstein et al., 1992).

It may be that enlarged ventricles are actually a sign that nearby parts of the brain have not developed properly or have been damaged, and perhaps these problems are the ones that help produce schizophrenia. In fact, studies suggest that some patients with schizophrenia also have smaller temporal lobes and frontal lobes than other people, smaller amounts of cortical gray matter, and, perhaps most important, abnormal blood flow—either reduced or heightened—in certain areas of the brain (Lambert & Kinsley, 2005; Montoya et al., 2005; Whitford et al., 2005). Still other studies have linked

Not-so-identical twins *The man on the left is normal, while his identical twin, on the right, has schizophrenia. Magnetic resonance imaging (MRI), shown in the background, clarifies that the brain of the twin with schizophrenia is smaller overall than his brother's and has larger ventricles, indicated by the dark butterfly-shaped spaces.*

schizophrenia to structural and cellular abnormalities of the hippocampus, amygdala, and thalamus, among other brain areas (Folsom et al., 2006; Spaniel et al., 2003).

VIRAL PROBLEMS What might cause the biochemical and structural abnormalities found in many cases of schizophrenia? Various studies have pointed to genetic factors, poor nutrition, fetal development, birth complications, immune reactions, and toxins (Andreasen, 2001; McNeil & Cantor-Graae, 2001). In addition, some investigators suggest that the brain abnormalities may result from exposure to *viruses* before birth. Perhaps the viruses enter the fetus's brain and interrupt proper brain development, or perhaps the viruses remain quiet until puberty or young adulthood, when, activated by changes in hormones or by another viral infection, they help to bring about schizophrenic symptoms (Lambert & Kinsley, 2005; Torrey, 2001, 1991).

Some of the evidence for the viral theory comes from animal model investigations, and some is circumstantial evidence, such as the finding that an unusually large number of people with schizophrenia are born during the winter (Meyer et al., 2005; Torrey, 2001, 1991). The winter birth rate among people with schizophrenia is 5 to 8 percent higher than among other persons. This finding could be due to an increase in fetal or infant exposure to viruses at that time of year. The viral theory has also received support from investigations of fingerprints. Normally, identical twins have almost identical numbers of fingerprint ridges. People with schizophrenia, however, often have significantly more or fewer ridges than their nonschizophrenic identical twins (Van Os et al., 1997; Torrey et al., 1994). Fingerprints form in the fetus during the second trimester of pregnancy, just when the fetus is most vulnerable to certain viruses. Thus the fingerprint irregularities of some people with schizophrenia could reflect a viral infection contracted during the prenatal period, an infection that also predisposed the individuals to schizophrenia.

More direct evidence for the viral theory of schizophrenia comes from studies showing that more mothers of persons with schizophrenia were exposed to the influenza virus during pregnancy than mothers of people without schizophrenia (Brown et al., 2004; Limosin et al., 2003). Other studies have found antibodies to particular viruses, including viruses usually found in animals, in the blood of 40 percent of subjects with schizophrenia (Leweke et al., 2004; Yolken et al., 2000; Torrey et al., 1994). The presence of such antibodies suggests that the subjects were at some time exposed to those particular viruses.

Together, the biochemical, brain structure, and viral findings are beginning to shed much light on the mysteries of schizophrenia. At the same time, it is important to recognize that many people who exhibit these biological abnormalities never develop schizophrenia. Why not? Possibly, as we noted earlier, because biological factors merely set the stage for schizophrenia, while key psychological and sociocultural factors must be present for the disorder to appear.

Psychological Views

When schizophrenia investigators began to identify genetic and biological factors during the 1950s and 1960s, many clinicians abandoned the psychological theories of the disorder. During the past decade, however, the tables have been turned and psychological factors are once again being considered important pieces of the schizophrenia puzzle. The leading psychological theories have come from the psychodynamic, behavioral, and cognitive perspectives.

THE PSYCHODYNAMIC EXPLANATION Freud (1924, 1915, 1914) believed that schizophrenia develops from two psychological processes: (1) *regression* to a pre-ego stage and (2) efforts to *reestablish* ego control. He proposed that when their world is extremely harsh or withholding—for example, when parents are cold or unnurturing—people who develop schizophrenia regress to the earliest point in their development, to the pre-ego state of *primary narcissism,* in which they recognize and meet only their own needs. Their near-total regression leads to self-centered symptoms such as neologisms, loose associations, and delusions of grandeur. Once people regress to such an infantile state, Freud continued, they then try to reestablish ego control and contact with reality. Their

Ballet artist Vaslav Nijinsky *The renowned dancer, performing here in* Schéhérazade, *developed severe schizophrenia and spent the last years of his life in a mental institution.*

•ATYPICAL ANTIPSYCHOTIC DRUGS• A relatively new group of antipsychotic drugs whose biological action is different from that of the traditional antipsychotic drugs.

•**SCHIZOPHRENOGENIC MOTHER**•A type of mother—supposedly cold, domineering, and uninterested in the needs of others—who was once thought to cause schizophrenia in her child.

efforts give rise to yet other schizophrenic symptoms. Auditory hallucinations, for example, may be an individual's attempt to substitute for a lost sense of reality.

Years later, the noted psychodynamic clinician Frieda Fromm-Reichmann (1948) elaborated on Freud's notion that cold or unnurturing parents may set schizophrenia in motion. She described the mothers of people who develop this disorder as cold, domineering, and uninterested in their children's needs. According to Fromm-Reichmann, these mothers may appear to be self-sacrificing but are actually using their children to meet their own needs. At once overprotective and rejecting, they confuse their children and set the stage for schizophrenic functioning. She called them **schizophrenogenic** (schizophrenia-causing) **mothers.**

Fromm-Reichmann's theory, like Freud's, has received little research support (Willick, 2001). The majority of people with schizophrenia do not appear to have mothers who fit the schizophrenogenic description. In fact, some studies have suggested that quite a different personality style may prevail among their mothers. In one study the mothers of subjects with this disorder were found to be shy, withdrawn, and anxious, among other qualities, while the mothers of normal control subjects seemed more likely to display what Fromm-Reichmann would have called a schizophrenogenic maternal style (Waring & Ricks, 1965).

Most of today's psychodynamic theorists have, in fact, rejected the views of Freud and Fromm-Reichmann. Although these theorists may retain some of the early notions (Spielrein, 1995), more and more of them believe that biological abnormalities leave certain persons particularly prone to extreme regression or other unconscious acts that may contribute to schizophrenia (Willick, Milrod, & Karush, 1998). For example, self theorists, who believe that schizophrenia reflects a struggling fragmented self, suggest that biological deficiencies explain the failure of people with this disorder to develop an integrated self (Pollack, 1989; Kohut & Wolf, 1978).

THE BEHAVIORAL VIEW Behaviorists usually cite *operant conditioning* and principles of reinforcement as the cause of schizophrenia (Liberman, 1982; Ullmann & Krasner, 1975). They propose that most people become quite proficient at reading and responding to social cues, that is, to other people's smiles, frowns, and comments. People who respond to such cues in a socially acceptable way are better able to satisfy their own emotional needs and achieve their goals. Some people, however, are not reinforced for their attention to social cues, either because of unusual circumstances or because important figures in their lives are socially inadequate. As a result, they stop attending to such cues and focus instead on irrelevant cues—the brightness of light in a room, a bird flying above, or the sound of a word rather than its meaning. As they attend more and more to irrelevant cues, their responses become increasingly bizarre. Because the bizarre responses are rewarded with attention or other types of reinforcement, they are likely to be repeated again and again.

Support for the behavioral position has been circumstantial. As we shall see in Chapter 15, researchers have found that patients with schizophrenia are capable of learning at least some appropriate verbal and social behaviors if hospital personnel consistently ignore their bizarre responses and reinforce normal responses with cigarettes, food, attention, or other rewards (Belcher, 1988; Braginsky, Braginsky, & Ring, 1969). If bizarre verbal and social responses can be eliminated by appropriate reinforcements, perhaps they were acquired through improper learning in the first place. Of course, an effective treatment does not necessarily indicate the cause of a disorder. Today the behavioral view is usually considered at best a partial explanation for schizophrenia. Although it may help explain why a given person displays more schizophrenic behavior in some situations than in others, it is too limited, in the opinion of many, to account for schizophrenia's origins and its many symptoms.

THE COGNITIVE VIEW A leading cognitive explanation of schizophrenia agrees with the biological view that during hallucinations and related perceptual difficulties the brains of people with schizophrenia are actually producing strange and unreal sensations—sensations triggered by biological factors. According to the cognitive explanation, however, further features of the disorder emerge when the individuals attempt to understand their unusual experiences. When first confronted by voices, visions, or other troubling sensations, these people turn to friends and relatives. Naturally, the friends and relatives deny the reality of the sensations, and eventually the sufferers conclude that the others are trying to hide the truth. They begin to reject all feedback and may develop beliefs (delusions) that they are being persecuted (Garety, 1991; Maher, 1974). In short, says this theory, people with schizophrenia take a "rational path to madness" (Zimbardo, 1976).

Researchers have established that people with schizophrenia do indeed experience sensory and perceptual problems. As we saw earlier, many of them have hallucinations, for example, and most have trouble keeping their attention focused (APA, 2000; Elkins & Cromwell, 1994). But researchers have yet to provide clear, direct support for the cognitive notion that misinterpretations of such sensory problems actually produce a syndrome of schizophrenia.

"And only *you* can hear this whistle?"

Sociocultural Views

Sociocultural theorists, believing that people with mental disorders are victims of social forces, claim that *social labeling* and *family dysfunctioning* contribute to the development of schizophrenia. Although societal and family forces are considered important in the development of this disorder, research has not yet clarified what the precise causal relationships might be.

SOCIAL LABELING Many sociocultural theorists believe that the features of schizophrenia are influenced by the diagnosis itself (Modrow, 1992). In their opinion, society assigns the label "schizophrenic" to people who fail to conform to certain norms of behavior. Once the label is assigned, justified or not, it becomes a self-fulfilling prophecy that promotes the development of many schizophrenic symptoms. Certainly sufferers of schizophrenia have attested to the power that labeling has had on their lives:

> Like any worthwhile endeavor, becoming a schizophrenic requires a long period of rigorous training. My training for this unique calling began in earnest when I was six years old. At that time my somewhat befuddled mother took me to the University of Washington to be examined by psychiatrists in order to find out what was wrong with me. These psychiatrists told my mother: "We don't know exactly what is wrong with your son, but whatever it is, it is very serious. We recommend that you have him committed immediately or else he will be completely psychotic within less than a year." My mother did not have me committed since she realized that such a course of action would be extremely damaging to me. But after that ominous prophecy my parents began to view and treat me as if I were either insane or at least in the process of becoming that way. Once, when my mother caught me playing with some vile muck I had mixed up—I was seven at the time—she gravely told me, "They have people put away in mental institutions for doing things like that." Fear was written all over my mother's face as she told me this. . . . The slightest odd behavior on my part was enough to send my parents into paroxysms of apprehension. My parents' apprehensions in turn made me fear that I was going insane. . . . My fate had been sealed not by my genes, but by the attitudes, beliefs, and expectations of my parents. . . . I find it extremely difficult to condemn my parents for behaving as if I were going insane when the psychiatric authorities told them that this was an absolute certainty.
>
> *(Modrow, 1992, pp. 1–2)*

Like this man, people who are called schizophrenic may be viewed and treated as "crazy." Perhaps the expectations of other people subtly encourage the individuals to display psychotic behaviors. In turn, they come to accept their assigned role and learn to play it convincingly.

>>LAB•NOTES

A Rose by Any Other Name?

One study asked subjects to evaluate an individual based strictly on his label—a "schizophrenic," "person with schizophrenia," "person with severe mental illness," or "consumer of mental health services." Subjects had less negative reactions to the individual labeled a "consumer" and believed that he had fewer symptoms, was likely to improve, and was less responsible for his disorder (Penn & Nowlin-Drummond, 2001). ‹‹

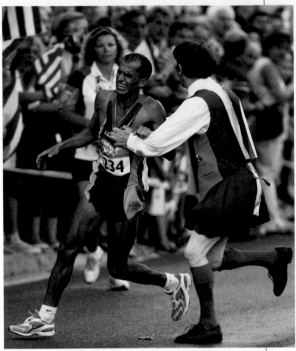

Koji Sasahara/AP Photo

Public misperception *According to surveys, many people believe that individuals with severe mental disorders are typically violent or dangerous, despite research findings to the contrary (Monahan, 2001, 1993, 1992). A key reason for this public perception is that dangerous or inappropriate acts by such individuals receive enormous attention from the media. For example, the world watched in confusion and horror as a defrocked priest—wearing a kilt and green beret—grabbed a Brazilian runner and knocked him into the crowd four miles from the finish line during the Marathon event at the 2004 Olympic games in Greece. The ex-priest, who claimed that he performed this act to highlight the "second coming of Jesus Christ," was called a "lunatic" and "crazy" by several on-the-scene athletes, spectators, and commentators, and many clinicians expressed the belief that his behavior was driven by religious delusions. Others argued that the attacker was merely a publicity-seeker who enjoyed the attention he received when disrupting major sporting events such as the Olympic race and, before that, the British Grand Prix, Wimbledon Championships, and cricket and rugby matches.*

>>IN THEIR WORDS

"Her face was a solemn mask, and she could neither give nor receive affection." <<

Mother, 1991, describing her
daughter who has schizophrenia

We have already seen the very real dangers of diagnostic labeling. In the famous Rosenhan (1973) study, discussed in Chapter 3, eight normal people presented themselves at various mental hospitals, complaining that they had been hearing voices utter the words "empty," "hollow," and "thud." They were quickly diagnosed as schizophrenic, and all eight were hospitalized. Although the pseudopatients then dropped all symptoms and behaved normally, they had great difficulty getting rid of the label and gaining release from the hospital.

The pseudopatients reported that staff members were authoritarian in their behavior toward patients, spent limited time interacting with them, and responded curtly and uncaringly to questions. In fact, they generally treated patients as though they were invisible. "A nurse unbuttoned her uniform to adjust her brassiere in the presence of an entire ward of viewing men. One did not have the sense that she was being seductive. Rather, she didn't notice us." In addition, the pseudopatients described feeling powerless, bored, tired, and uninterested. The deceptive design and possible implications of this study have aroused the emotions of clinicians and researchers, pro and con. The investigation does demonstrate, however, that the label "schizophrenic" can itself have a negative effect not just on how people are viewed but on how they themselves feel and behave.

FAMILY DYSFUNCTIONING Theorists have suggested for years that certain patterns of family interactions can promote—or at least sustain—schizophrenic symptoms. One leading theory has focused on *double-bind communications.*

DO DOUBLE-BIND COMMUNICATIONS CAUSE SCHIZOPHRENIA? One of the best-known family theories of schizophrenia is the **double-bind hypothesis** (Visser, 2003; Bateson, 1978; Bateson et al., 1956). It says that some parents repeatedly communicate pairs of mutually contradictory messages that place children in so-called double-bind situations: the children cannot avoid displeasing their parents because nothing they do is right. In theory, the symptoms of schizophrenia represent the child's attempt to deal with the double binds.

Double-bind messages typically consist of a verbal communication (the *primary communication*) and an accompanying—and contradictory—nonverbal communication (the *metacommunication*). If one person says to another, "I'm glad to see you," yet frowns and avoids eye contact, the two messages are incongruent. According to this theory, a child who is repeatedly exposed to double-bind communications will adopt a special life strategy for coping with them. One strategy, for example, is always to ignore primary communications and respond only to metacommunications: be suspicious of what anyone is saying, wonder about its true meaning, and focus on clues only in gestures or tones. People who increasingly respond to messages in this way may progress toward paranoid schizophrenia.

The double-bind hypothesis is closely related to the psychodynamic notion of a schizophrenogenic mother. When Fromm-Reichmann described schizophrenogenic mothers as overprotective and rejecting at the same time, she was in fact describing someone who is likely to send double-bind messages. Like the schizophrenogenic mother theory, the double-bind hypothesis has been popular in the clinical field over the years, but systematic investigations have not supported it (Chaika, 1990). In one study, clinicians analyzed letters written by parents to their children in the hospital (Ringuette & Kennedy, 1966). One group of parents had children with schizophrenia; the other had children with other disorders. On average, the letters of both groups of parents contained similar degrees of double-bind communication.

THE ROLE OF FAMILY STRESS Although the double-bind explanation and various other family theories of schizophrenia have not received much research support, studies do suggest that schizophrenia, like certain other mental disorders, is often linked to *family stress* (Boye et al., 2002; Schiffman et al., 2002, 2001; Miklowitz et al., 1995). Parents of people with this disorder often (1) display more conflict, (2) have greater difficulty communicating with one another, and (3) are more critical of and overinvolved with their children than other parents.

Family theorists have long recognized that some families are high in **expressed emotion**—that is, members frequently express criticism, disapproval, and hostility toward each other and intrude on one another's privacy. Individuals who are trying to recover from schizophrenia are almost four times more likely to relapse if they live with such a family than if they live with one low in expressed emotion (Nomura et al., 2005; Linszen et al., 1997; Brown et al., 1962). Do such findings mean that family dysfunctioning helps cause and maintain schizophrenia? Not necessarily. It is also the case that individuals with schizophrenia greatly disrupt family life. In so doing, they themselves may help produce the family problems that clinicians and researchers continue to observe (Lauber et al., 2005).

A SOCIOCULTURAL-EXISTENTIAL VIEW The final explanation of schizophrenia that we shall examine is also the most controversial. The famous clinical theorist R. D. Laing (1967, 1964, 1959) combined sociocultural principles with the existential philosophy that was his hallmark, arguing that schizophrenia is actually a *constructive* process in which people try to cure themselves of the confusion and unhappiness caused by their social environment. Laing believed that, left alone to complete this process, people with schizophrenia would indeed achieve a healthy outcome.

According to Laing's existential principles, human beings must be in touch with their *true* selves in order to give meaning to their lives. Unfortunately, said Laing, this is difficult to do in present-day society. Other people's expectations, demands, and standards require us to develop a *false* self rather than a true one. Some people—those who develop schizophrenia—have especially difficult obstacles to deal with, according to Laing. They experience a lifetime of confusing communications and demands from their families and community. Out of desperation they eventually undertake an inner search for strength and purpose. They withdraw from others and attend increasingly to their own inner cues in order to recover their wholeness as human beings. Laing argued that these people would emerge stronger and less confused if they were allowed to continue this inner search. Instead, as he saw it, society and its clinicians tell the individuals that they are sick, manipulate them into the role of patient, and subject them to treatments that actually serve to produce further psychotic symptoms. In attempting to cure these people, he said, society dooms them to suspension in an inner world.

Most of today's theorists reject Laing's controversial notion that schizophrenia is constructive. For the most part, research has simply not addressed the issue (Howells & Guirguis, 1985). Laing's ideas do not lend themselves to empirical research (Hirsch & Leff, 1975), and the existentialists who embrace his view typically have little confidence in traditional research approaches. It is worth noting, however, that many persons with schizophrenia have themselves rejected the theory.

> "Schizophrenia's a reasonable reaction to an unreasonable society." It's great on paper. Poetic, noble, etc. But if you happen to be a schizophrenic, it's got some not-so-cheery implications. . . . One of R.D.'s worst sins is how blithely and misleadingly he glides over the suffering involved. . . . Pulling off a revolution and ushering in a new era in which truth and beauty reign triumphant seems unlikely when you're having trouble brushing your teeth or even walking.
>
> *(Vonnegut, 1974, p. 91)*

PUTTING IT together
Psychological and Sociocultural Models Lag Behind

Schizophrenia—a bizarre and frightening disorder—was studied intensively throughout the twentieth century. Only since the discovery of antipsychotic drugs, however, have clinicians acquired any practical insight into its course and causes. Theories abounded before that time, but they typically failed to find empirical support, instead contributing

Hugh Scoggins/AP Photo

Lobbying against stigmatization *In order to bring public attention to the plight of people with schizophrenia and other severe mental disorders, members of the Florida Alliance for the Mentally Ill chained together figures without faces in 1997 and placed them outside the state capitol building. The members were also trying to alert the state's legislators to the treatment needs of the tens of thousands of faceless patients who are held captive by their disorders.*

•**DOUBLE-BIND HYPOTHESIS**•A theory that some parents repeatedly communicate pairs of messages that are mutually contradictory, helping to produce schizophrenia in their children.

•**EXPRESSED EMOTION**•The general level of criticism, disapproval, and hostility expressed in a family. People recovering from schizophrenia are considered more likely to relapse if their families rate high in expressed emotion.

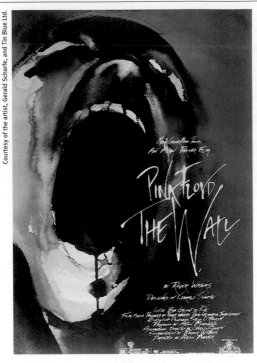

"Is there anybody out there?" *Schizophrenia is a popular subject throughout the arts, where it is often depicted in positive terms. Pink Floyd's hugely popular album and movie* The Wall, *for example, follows the lead of R. D. Laing and of certain sociocultural theorists and portrays the disorder as a constructive inward search undertaken by some persons in order to cure themselves of confusion and unhappiness caused by society.*

>>PSYCH•NOTES

Private Notions

Surveys suggest that as many as 22 percent of people in the United States believe the earth has been visited by aliens from outer space (Andrews, 1998). «

to inaccurate stereotyping of people with schizophrenia and their parents and resulting in ineffective forms of treatment.

Research conducted during the past three decades has changed the earlier view of schizophrenia as a single disorder with numerous faces. Many studies suggest that the different types of schizophrenia may actually represent different disorders (Grilly, 2002). In other words, each "type" may have a distinct course; distinct biological, genetic, and perhaps psychological and sociocultural origins; and a distinct response to treatment.

As with most other psychological disorders, clinical theorists now believe that schizophrenia, in any of its forms, is probably caused by a combination of factors. At the same time, researchers have been far more successful in identifying the biological influences than the psychological and sociocultural ones. While biological investigations have closed in on specific genes, abnormalities in brain biochemistry and structure, and even viral infections, most of the psychological and sociocultural research has been able to cite only general factors, such as the roles of family conflict and diagnostic labeling. Clearly, researchers must identify psychological and sociocultural factors with greater precision if we are to gain a full understanding of the disorder. The exciting, at times spectacular, progress now being made in the biological study of schizophrenia is indeed impressive, but it must not blind us to the significant gaps, uncertainties, and confusions that continue to obscure our view.

┤ SUMMARY AND REVIEW ├

- **The clinical picture of schizophrenia** *Schizophrenia* is a disorder in which personal, social, and occupational functioning deteriorate as a result of disturbed thought processes, distorted perceptions, unusual emotions, and motor abnormalities. Approximately 1 percent of the world's population suffers from this disorder. *pp. 411–416*

- **Symptoms of schizophrenia** The symptoms of schizophrenia fall into three groupings. *Positive symptoms* include *delusions,* certain *formal thought disorders, hallucinations* and other *disturbances in perception and attention,* and *inappropriate affect. Negative symptoms* include *poverty of speech, blunted and flat affect, loss of volition,* and *social withdrawal.* The disorder may also include *psychomotor symptoms,* collectively called *catatonia* in their extreme form. Schizophrenia usually emerges during late adolescence or early adulthood and tends to progress through three phases: *prodromal, active,* and *residual. pp. 416–422*

- **Diagnosing schizophrenia** DSM-IV-TR identifies five patterns of schizophrenia: *disorganized, catatonic, paranoid, undifferentiated,* and *residual.* Moreover, it is not uncommon for some patients to be dominated by positive symptoms and others to display more negative ones. *pp. 422–423*

- **Biological explanations** The biological explanations of schizophrenia point to genetic, biochemical, structural, and viral causes. The *genetic* view is supported by studies of relatives, twins, adoptees, and genetic linkage and by molecular biology. The leading *biochemical* explanation holds that the brains of people with schizophrenia, particularly those with largely positive symptoms, may contain an unusually large number of *dopamine* receptors, especially *D-2 receptors,* leading to excessive dopamine activity. Brain-imaging techniques have also detected *abnormal brain structures* in many people with schizophrenia, particularly those with a number of negative symptoms, including *enlarged ventricles* and *abnormal blood flow* in certain parts of the brain. Finally, some researchers believe that schizophrenia is related to a *virus* that settles in the fetus and perhaps lies quiet until adolescence or young adulthood. *pp. 423–429*

- **Psychological explanations** The leading psychological explanations for schizophrenia come from the psychodynamic, behavioral, and cognitive models. In influential *psychodynamic* explanations, Freud held that schizophrenia involves *regression* to a state of primary narcissism and efforts to *restore* ego control, and Fromm-Reichmann proposed that *schizophrenogenic mothers* help produce this disorder. Contemporary psychodynamic theorists, however, ascribe the disorder to a combination of biological and psychodynamic factors. *Behaviorists* suggest that people with schizophrenia fail to learn to attend to appropriate social cues. And *cognitive* theorists contend that when people with schizophrenia try to understand their strange biological sensations, they develop delusional thinking. None of these theories have received compelling research support. *pp. 429–431*

■ **Sociocultural explanations** One sociocultural explanation holds that society expects persons who are *labeled* as having schizophrenia to behave in certain ways and that these expectations actually lead to further symptoms. Other sociocultural views point to *family dysfunctioning* as a cause of schizophrenia, including such features as *double-bind communications.* Such specific family features have not been implicated by research, although general *family stress and conflict* have repeatedly been linked to schizophrenia. Finally, R. D. Laing has presented schizophrenia as a *constructive* process by which people try to cure themselves of the confusion and unhappiness caused by their society and family. *pp. 431–433*

■ **The diathesis-stress explanation** Most clinical theorists now agree that schizophrenia can probably be traced to a combination of biological, psychological, and sociocultural factors. However, the biological factors have been more precisely identified. *pp. 433–434*

>>> | **CRITICAL THOUGHTS** | <<<

1. The philosopher Friedrich Nietzsche said: "Insanity in individuals is something rare—but in groups, parties, nations and epochs, it is the rule." What behaviors committed by groups might be considered psychotic if an individual were to perform them? *pp. 416–422*

2. Some experts believe that *erotomanic delusions* are more common today than they were in the past. Why might this be? Do high-profile cases such as Monica Seles's and Rebecca Shaeffer's heighten or lower the probability that other cases of erotomanic delusions and stalking will emerge? *p. 417*

3. Was the voice heard by Ray Kinsella ("If you build it, they will come") in the movie *Field of Dreams* a form of spiritual inspiration or an auditory hallucination? *pp. 418–420*

4. The psychodynamic explanations of schizophrenia reflect a long-standing tradition in the clinical field and in society of pointing to parents as key causes of mental disorders, even in cases where evidence is lacking. Why are parents and family life so likely to be blamed, and why are these explanations so resistant to change? *pp. 429–430*

5. Rosenhan's pseudopatient study is one of the most controversial in the clinical field. What kinds of ethical, legal, and therapeutic concerns does it raise? *pp. 431–432*

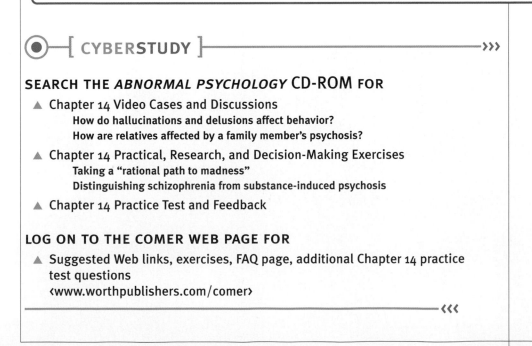

⊙—[CYBER**STUDY**]————————————————————>>>

SEARCH THE *ABNORMAL PSYCHOLOGY* CD-ROM FOR

▲ Chapter 14 Video Cases and Discussions
   How do hallucinations and delusions affect behavior?
   How are relatives affected by a family member's psychosis?

▲ Chapter 14 Practical, Research, and Decision-Making Exercises
   Taking a "rational path to madness"
   Distinguishing schizophrenia from substance-induced psychosis

▲ Chapter 14 Practice Test and Feedback

LOG ON TO THE COMER WEB PAGE FOR

▲ Suggested Web links, exercises, FAQ page, additional Chapter 14 practice test questions
   <www.worthpublishers.com/comer>

————————————————————————————<<<

Treatments for Schizophrenia and Other Severe Mental Disorders

They call us insane—and in reality they are as inconsistent as we are, as flighty and changeable. This one in particular. One day he derides and ridicules me unmercifully; the next he talks to me sadly and this morning his eyes misted over with tears as he told me of the fate ahead. Damn him and all of his wisdom!

He has dinned into my ears a monotonous dirge—"Too Egotistical—too Egotistical—too Egotistical. Learn to think differently."—And how can I do it? How—how—can I do it? How the hell can I do it? I have tried to follow his suggestions but have not learned to think a bit differently. It was all wasted effort. Where has it got me?

(Jefferson, 1948)

With these words, Lara Jefferson, a young woman with schizophrenia, described her treatment experience in the 1940s. Her pain and frustration were typical of those experienced by hundreds of thousands of similar patients during that period of time. In fact, for much of human history, persons with schizophrenia were considered beyond help. They and their therapists faced the daunting task of trying to communicate while speaking virtually different languages. The disorder is still extremely difficult to treat, but clinicians are much more successful today than they were in the past. Much of the credit goes to *antipsychotic drugs,* medications that help many people with schizophrenia think clearly and profit from therapies that previously would have had little effect on them.

As we shall see, each of the models offers treatments for schizophrenia, and all have been influential at one time or another. However, a mere description of the different approaches cannot convey the unhappiness and pain suffered by the victims of this disorder as the various methods of treatment evolved over the years. People with schizophrenia have been subjected to more mistreatment and indifference than perhaps any other group of patients. Even today the majority of them do not receive adequate care, largely for reasons of economics and political priorities (Torrey, 2001).

To better convey the plight of people with schizophrenia, this chapter will depart from the usual format and discuss the treatments from a historical perspective. Ultimately, a look at how treatment has changed over the years will help us understand the nature, problems, and promise of today's approaches. As we observed in Chapter 14, the label "schizophrenia" was assigned to most people with psychosis throughout much of the twentieth century. In particular, many people whose bipolar disorders or major depressive disorders included psychotic features were inaccurately given a diagnosis of schizophrenia. Thus, our discussions of past treatments for schizophrenia, particularly the failures of institutional care, are as applicable to these other severe mental disorders as they are to schizophrenia.

Today, of course, improvements in diagnostic procedures and in the DSM have helped disentangle schizophrenia from other disorders. Nevertheless, any disorder that includes psychotic features presents formidable obstacles to treatment, and so even some of our discussions about more recent approaches to schizophrenia, such as the community mental health movement, apply to other severe mental disorders as well.

•**STATE HOSPITALS**•Public mental hospitals in the United States, run by the individual states.

Institutional Care in the Past

For more than half of the twentieth century, most people diagnosed with schizophrenia were *institutionalized* in a public mental hospital. Because patients with this disorder failed to respond to traditional therapies, the primary goals of these establishments were to restrain them and give them food, shelter, and clothing. Patients rarely saw therapists and were generally neglected. Many were abused. Oddly enough, this state of affairs unfolded in an atmosphere of good intentions.

As we saw in Chapter 1, the move toward institutionalization in hospitals began in 1793, when the French physician Philippe Pinel "unchained the insane" at La Bicêtre asylum and began the practice of "moral treatment." For the first time in centuries, patients with severe disturbances were viewed as human beings who should be cared for with sympathy and kindness. As Pinel's ideas spread throughout Europe and the United States, they led to the creation of large mental hospitals rather than asylums to care for those with severe mental disorders (Goshen, 1967).

These new mental hospitals, typically located in isolated areas where land and labor were cheap, were meant to protect patients from the stresses of daily life and offer them a healthful psychological environment in which they could work closely with therapists (Grob, 1966). States throughout the United States were even required by law to establish public mental institutions, **state hospitals,** for patients who could not afford private ones.

Eventually, however, the state hospital system encountered serious problems. Between 1845 and 1955 nearly 300 state hospitals opened in the United States, and the number of hospitalized patients on any given day rose from 2,000 in 1845 to nearly 600,000 in 1955. During this expansion, wards became overcrowded, admissions kept rising, and state fund-

---

[BOX 15-1]

Lobotomy: How Could It Happen?

In 1949 a *New York Times* article reported on a medical procedure that appeared to offer hope to sufferers of severe mental disorders, people for whom no future had seemed possible outside of very overcrowded state mental institutions:

I *Hypochondriacs no longer thought they were going to die, would-be suicides found life acceptable, sufferers from persecution complex forgot the machinations of imaginary conspirators. Prefrontal lobotomy, as the operation is called, was made possible by the localization of fears, hates, and instincts [in the prefrontal cortex of the brain]. It is fitting, then, that the Nobel Prize in medicine should be shared by Hess and Moniz. Surgeons now think no more of operations on the brain than they do of removing an appendix.* I

We now know that the lobotomy was hardly a miracle treatment. Far from "curing" people with mental disorders, the procedure left thousands upon thousands extremely withdrawn, subdued, and even stuporous. The first lobotomy was performed by the Portuguese neuropsychiatrist Egas Moniz in 1935 (Tierney, 2000). His particular procedure, called a prefrontal leukotomy, consisted of drilling two holes in either side of the skull and inserting an instrument resembling an icepick into the brain tissue to cut or destroy nerve fibers. Moniz believed that severe abnormal thinking could be

Bettmann Archives

Lessons in psychosurgery
Neuropsychiatrist Walter Freeman performs a lobotomy in 1949 before a group of interested onlookers by inserting a needle through a patient's eye socket into the brain.

ing was unable to keep up. Too many aspects of treatment became the responsibility of nurses and attendants, whose knowledge and experience at that time were limited.

The priorities of the public mental hospitals, and the quality of care they provided, changed over those 110 years. In the face of overcrowding and understaffing, the emphasis shifted from giving humanitarian care to keeping order. In a throwback to the asylum period, difficult patients were restrained, isolated, and punished; individual attention disappeared. Patients were transferred to *back wards,* or chronic wards, if they failed to improve quickly (Bloom, 1984). Most of the patients on these wards suffered from schizophrenia (Hafner & an der Heiden, 1988). The back wards were in fact human warehouses filled with hopelessness. Staff members relied on straitjackets and handcuffs to deal with difficult patients. More "advanced" forms of treatment included medical approaches such as *lobotomy* (see Box 15-1).

Many patients not only failed to improve under these conditions but also developed additional symptoms, apparently as a result of institutionalization itself. The most common pattern of decline was called the *social breakdown syndrome:* extreme withdrawal, anger, physical aggressiveness, and loss of interest in personal appearance and functioning (Oshima et al., 2005; Gruenberg, 1980). Often more troublesome than patients' original symptoms, this new syndrome made it impossible for them to return to society even if they somehow recovered from the symptoms that had first brought them to the hospital.

Overcrowded conditions *A night nurse sits in the ward of a public mental hospital in 1956 darning socks while the patients sleep. The beds in the ward are crammed close together, leaving no personal space of any kind for the patients.*

changed by cutting the nerve pathways that carried such thoughts from one part of the brain to another. In the 1940s Walter Freeman and his surgical partner, James Watts, developed a second kind of psychosurgery called the transorbital lobotomy, in which the surgeon inserted a needle into the brain through the eye socket and rotated it in order to destroy the brain tissue.

Altogether, an estimated 50,000 people in the United States alone received lobotomies (Johnson, 2005). Why was the lobotomy so enthusiastically accepted by the medical community in the 1940s and 1950s? The neuroscientist Elliot Valenstein (1986) points first to the extreme overcrowding in mental hospitals at the time. This crowding was making it difficult to maintain decent standards in the hospitals. Valenstein also points to the personalities of the inventors of the procedure as important factors. Although

these individuals were gifted and dedicated physicians, Valenstein also believes that their professional ambitions led them to move too quickly and boldly in applying the procedure. Indeed, in 1949 Moniz was awarded the Nobel Prize for his work.

The prestige and diplomatic skills of Moniz and Freeman were so great and the field of neurology was so small that their procedures drew little criticism. Physicians may also have been misled by the seemingly positive findings of early studies of the lobotomy, which, as it turned out, were not based on sound methodology (Swayze, 1995; Valenstein, 1986).

By the 1950s, better studies revealed that in addition to having a fatality rate of 1.5 to 6 percent, lobotomies could cause serious problems such as brain seizures, huge weight gain, loss of motor coordination, partial paralysis, incontinence, endocrine malfunctions, and very poor

intellectual and emotional responsiveness. When the public became concerned that the procedure might be used to control violent criminals, the lobotomy became a civil rights issue as well. Finally, the discovery of effective antipsychotic drugs put an end to this inhumane treatment for mental disorders (Tierney, 2000).

Today's psychosurgical procedures are greatly refined and hardly resemble the lobotomies of 50 years back. Moreover, such procedures are considered experimental and used only as a last resort in the most severe cases of obsessive-compulsive disorder and depression (Weingarten & Cummings, 2001; Goodman et al., 1992). Even so, many professionals believe that any kind of surgery that destroys brain tissue is inappropriate and perhaps unethical, and that it keeps alive one of the clinical field's most shameful and ill-advised efforts at cure.

Institutional Care Takes a Turn for the Better

In the 1950s, clinicians developed two institutional approaches that finally brought some hope to patients who had lived in institutions for years: *milieu therapy,* based on humanistic principles, and the *token economy program,* based on behavioral principles. These approaches particularly helped improve the personal care and self-image of patients, problem areas that had been worsened by institutionalization. The approaches were soon adapted by many institutions and are now standard features of institutional care.

Milieu Therapy

In the opinion of humanistic theorists, institutionalized patients deteriorate because they are deprived of opportunities to exercise independence, responsibility, and positive self-regard and to engage in meaningful activities. Thus the premise of **milieu therapy** is that institutions cannot be of help to patients unless they can somehow create a social climate, or milieu, that promotes productive activity, self-respect, and individual responsibility.

The pioneer of this approach was Maxwell Jones, a London psychiatrist who in 1953 converted a ward of patients with various psychological disorders into a therapeutic community. The patients were referred to as "residents" and were regarded as capable of running their own lives and making their own decisions. They participated in community government, working with staff members to establish rules and determine sanctions. In fact, patients and staff members alike were valued as important therapeutic agents. The atmosphere was one of mutual respect, support, and openness. Patients could also take on special projects, jobs, and recreational activities. In short, their daily schedule was designed to resemble life outside the hospital.

Milieu-style programs have since been set up in institutions throughout the Western world. The programs vary from setting to setting, but at a minimum staff members try to encourage interactions (especially group interactions) between patients and staff, to keep patients active, and to raise patients' expectations of what they can accomplish.

Research over the years has shown that patients with schizophrenia and other severe mental disorders in milieu hospital programs often improve and that they leave the hospital at higher rates than patients in programs offering primarily custodial care (Paul & Lentz, 1977; Cumming & Cumming, 1962). Many of these persons remain impaired, however, and must live in sheltered settings after their release. Despite its limitations, milieu therapy continues to be practiced in many institutions, often combined with other hospital approaches (Dobson et al., 1995). Moreover, we shall see that many halfway houses and other community programs for individuals with severe mental disorders are run in accordance with the same principles of resident self-government and work schedules that have proved effective in hospital milieu programs.

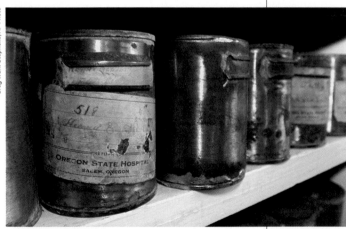

Greg Wahl-Stephens/AP Photo

A graphic reminder *During the rise of the state hospital system, tens of thousands of patients with schizophrenia and other severe mental disorders were abandoned by their families and condemned to live the rest of their lives in the back wards of the public mental institutions. We are reminded of their tragic plight by the numerous brass urns currently stored in one of the buildings at Oregon State Hospital. The urns contain the unclaimed ashes of deceased patients from decades past. Mental health advocates and government officials are working to find a proper burial place for the remains and to perhaps establish a memorial.*

The Token Economy

In the 1950s behaviorists had little status in mental institutions and were permitted to work only with patients whose problems seemed hopeless. Among the "hopeless" were patients diagnosed with schizophrenia. Through years of experimentation, behaviorists discovered that the systematic application of *operant conditioning* techniques on hospital wards could help change the behaviors of these individuals (Ayllon, 1963; Ayllon & Michael, 1959). Programs that apply these techniques are called **token economy programs.**

In token economies patients are rewarded when they behave acceptably and are not rewarded when they behave unacceptably. The immediate rewards for acceptable behavior are often tokens that can later be exchanged for food, cigarettes, hospital privileges, and other desirable items, thus creating a "token economy." Acceptable behaviors likely to be targeted include caring for oneself and for one's possessions (making the bed, getting dressed), going to a work program, speaking normally, following ward rules, and showing self-control.

HOW EFFECTIVE ARE TOKEN ECONOMY PROGRAMS?

Researchers have found that token economies do help reduce psychotic and related behaviors (Kopelowicz et al., 2002; Emmelkamp, 1994). In one very successful program, Gordon Paul and Robert Lentz (1977) set up a hospital token economy for 28 patients diagnosed with chronic schizophrenia, most of whom improved greatly. After four and a half years, 98 percent of the subjects had been released, mostly to sheltered-care facilities, compared with 71 percent of patients treated in a milieu program and 45 percent of patients who received custodial care only.

WHAT ARE THE LIMITATIONS OF TOKEN ECONOMIES?

Some clinicians have voiced reservations about the claims made for token economy programs (Kazdin, 1983). One problem is that many token economy studies, unlike Paul and Lentz's, are uncontrolled. When administrators set up a token economy, they usually bring all ward patients into the program rather than dividing the ward into a token economy group and a control group. As a result, patients' improvements can be compared only with their own past behaviors—a comparison that may be misleading. Changes in the physical setting, for example, or a general increase in staff attention could be causing patients' improvement, rather than the token economy per se.

Many clinicians have also raised ethical and legal concerns. If token economy programs are to be effective, administrators need to control the important rewards in a patient's life, perhaps including such basic ones as food and a comfortable bed. But aren't there some things in life to which all human beings are entitled? Court decisions have now ruled that patients do indeed have certain basic rights that clinicians cannot violate, regardless of the positive goals of a treatment program. They have a right to food, storage space, and furniture, as well as freedom of movement (Emmelkamp, 1994).

Still other clinicians have questioned the quality of the improvements made under token economy programs. Are behaviorists changing a patient's psychotic thoughts and perceptions or simply improving the patient's ability to imitate normal behavior? This issue is illustrated by the case of a middle-aged man named John, who had the delusion that he was the U.S. government (Comer, 1973). Whenever he spoke, he spoke as the government. "We are happy to see you. . . . We need people like you in our service. . . . We are carrying out our activities in John's body." When John's hospital ward was converted into a token economy, the staff members targeted his delusional statements and required him to identify himself properly to earn tokens. If he called himself John, he received tokens; if he insisted on describing himself as the government, he received nothing. After a few months on the token economy program, John stopped referring to himself as the government. When asked his name, he would say, "John." Although staff members were understandably pleased with his improvement, John himself had a different view of the situation. In a private discussion he said:

> We're tired of it. Every damn time we want a cigarette, we have to go through their bullshit. "What's your name? . . . Who wants the cigarette? . . . Where is the government?" Today, we were desperate for a smoke and went to Simpson, the damn nurse, and she made us do her bidding. "Tell me your name if you want a cigarette. What's your name?" Of course, we said, "John." We needed the cigarettes. If we told her the truth, no cigarettes. But we don't have time for this nonsense. We've got business to do, international business, laws to change, people to recruit. And these people keep playing their games.
>
> *(Comer, 1973)*

•**MILIEU THERAPY**•A humanistic approach to institutional treatment based on the belief that institutions can help patients recover by creating a climate that promotes self-respect, responsible behavior, and meaningful activity.

•**TOKEN ECONOMY PROGRAM**•A behavioral program in which a person's desirable behaviors are reinforced systematically throughout the day by the awarding of tokens that can be exchanged for goods or privileges.

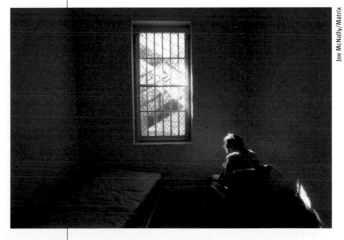

Joe McNally/Matrix

Environmental change *A mixture of clinical enlightenment and judicial decisions over the past several decades has led mental hospitals throughout the United States to establish minimum standards for mental health care and for treatment environments. Many older institutions have been closed or redesigned to meet such standards. Shortly after this photograph was taken, for example, this lonely, bland, and unsafe wing of a mental hospital was closed.*

Critics of the behavioral approach would argue that John was still delusional and therefore as psychotic as before. Behaviorists, however, would argue that at the very least, John's judgment about the consequences of his behavior had improved. Learning to keep his delusion to himself might even be a step toward changing his private thinking.

Last, it has often been difficult for patients to make a satisfactory transition from hospital token economy programs to community living. In an environment where rewards are contingent on proper conduct, proper conduct becomes contingent on continued rewards. Some patients who find that the real world doesn't reward them so concretely abandon their newly acquired behaviors.

Nevertheless, token economies have had a most important effect on the treatment of people with schizophrenia and other severe mental disorders. They were among the first hospital treatments that actually changed psychotic symptoms and got chronic patients moving again. These programs are no longer as popular as they once were, but they are still used in many mental hospitals, usually along with medication, and in some community residences as well. The approach has also been applied to other clinical problems, including mental retardation, delinquency, and hyperactivity, as well as in other fields, such as education and business (Spiegler & Guevremont, 2003).

Antipsychotic Drugs

Milieu therapy and token economy programs helped improve the gloomy outlook for patients diagnosed with schizophrenia, but it was the discovery of **antipsychotic drugs** in the 1950s that truly revolutionized treatment for this disorder. These drugs eliminate many of its symptoms and today are almost always a part of treatment (see Figure 15-1). What is more, as we saw in Chapter 14, they have influenced the way clinicians now view schizophrenia.

The discovery of antipsychotic medications dates back to the 1940s, when researchers developed the first *antihistamine drugs* to combat allergies. Although antihistamines also produced considerable tiredness and drowsiness, they quickly became popular, and many such drugs were developed. The French surgeon Henri Laborit soon discovered that one group of antihistamines, *phenothiazines,* could also be used to help calm patients about to undergo surgery. After experimenting with several phenothiazine antihistamines and becoming most impressed with one called *chlorpromazine,* Laborit reported, "It provokes not any loss of consciousness, not any change in the patient's mentality but a slight tendency to sleep and above all 'disinterest' for all that goes on around him."

Laborit suspected that chlorpromazine might also have a calming effect on persons with severe psychological disorders. The psychiatrists Jean Delay and Pierre Deniker (1952) therefore tested the drug on six patients with psychotic symptoms and did indeed observe a sharp reduction in their symptoms. In 1954, chlorpromazine was approved for sale in the United States as an antipsychotic drug under the trade name Thorazine.

Since the discovery of the phenothiazines, other kinds of antipsychotic drugs have been developed (see Table 15-1). The ones developed throughout the 1960s, 1970s, and 1980s are now referred to as *"conventional" antipsychotic drugs* in order to distinguish them from the *"atypical" antipsychotics* (also called *"second generation" antipsychotic drugs*) that have been developed in recent years. The conventional drugs are also known as **neuroleptic drugs** because they often produce undesired movement effects similar to the symptoms of neurological diseases. Among the best known conventional drugs are *thioridazine* (Mellaril), *fluphenazine* (Prolixin), *trifluoperazine* (Stelazine), and *haloperidol* (Haldol). As we saw in Chapter 14, antipsychotic drugs reduce psychotic symptoms at least in part by blocking excessive activity of the neurotransmitter *dopamine,* particularly at the brain's dopamine D-2 receptors (Julien, 2005).

Table 15-1

Antipsychotic Drugs

Class/Generic Name	Trade Name
Conventional antipsychotics	
Chlorpromazine	Thorazine
Triflupromazine	Vesprin
Thioridazine	Mellaril
Mesoridazine	Serentil
Trifluoperazine	Stelazine
Fluphenazine	Prolixin, Permitil
Perphenazine	Trilafon
Acetophenazine	Tindal
Chlorprothixene	Taractan
Thiothixene	Navane
Haloperidol	Haldol
Loxapine	Loxitane
Molindone hydrochloride	Moban, Lidone
Pimozide	Orap
Atypical antipsychotics	
Risperidone	Risperdal
Clozapine	Clozaril
Olanzapine	Zyprexa
Quetiapine	Seroquel
Ziprasidone	Geodon
Aripiprazole	Abilify

How Effective Are Antipsychotic Drugs?

Research has repeatedly shown that antipsychotic drugs reduce symptoms in the majority of patients diagnosed with schizophrenia (Julien, 2005). Moreover, in direct comparisons the drugs appear to be a more effective treatment for schizophrenia than any of the other approaches used alone, such as psychodynamic therapy, milieu therapy, or electroconvulsive therapy (May, Tuma, & Dixon, 1981; May & Tuma, 1964).

In most cases, the drugs produce the maximum level of improvement within the first six months of treatment (Szymanski et al., 1996); however, symptoms may return if patients stop taking the drugs too soon (Rzewuska, 2002). In one study, when the antipsychotic medications of people with chronic schizophrenia were changed to a placebo after five years, 75 percent of the patients relapsed within a year, compared to 33 percent of similar patients who continued to receive medication (Sampath et al., 1992).

As we observed in Chapter 14, antipsychotic drugs, particularly the conventional ones, reduce the positive symptoms of schizophrenia, such as hallucinations and delusions, more completely, or at least more quickly, than the negative symptoms, such as flat affect, poverty of speech, and loss of volition (Julien, 2005). Correspondingly, people who display largely positive symptoms generally have better rates of recovery from schizophrenia than those with predominantly negative symptoms (Lindström, 1996). Inasmuch as men with schizophrenia tend to have more negative symptoms than women, it is not surprising that they require higher doses and respond less readily to the antipsychotic drugs (Szymanski et al., 1996, 1995).

Although antipsychotic drugs are now widely accepted, patients often dislike the powerful effects of the drugs—both intended and unintended—and some refuse to take them (Olfson et al., 2000). But like Edward Snow, a writer who overcame schizophrenia, many are greatly helped by the medications.

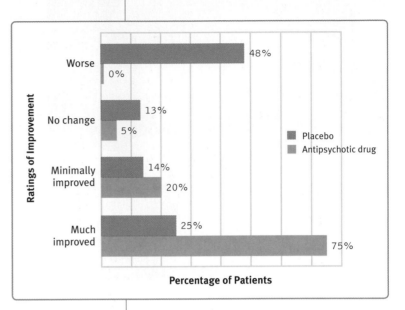

FIGURE 15-1 **The effectiveness of antipsychotic drugs** *An early influential study found that after six weeks of treatment, 75 percent of patients with schizophrenia who had been given antipsychotic drugs were much improved, compared to only 25 percent of patients given placebos. In fact, close to half of those on the placebos worsened. (Adapted from Cole et al., 1964.)*

> In my case it was necessary to come to terms with a specified drug program. I am a legalized addict. My dose: 100 milligrams of Thorazine and 60 milligrams of Stelazine daily. I don't feel this dope at all, but I have been told it is strong enough to flatten a normal person. It keeps me—as the doctors agree—sane and in good spirits. Without the brain candy, as I call it, I would go—zoom—right back into the bin. I've made the institution scene enough already to be familiar with what it's like and to know I don't want to go back.
>
> *(Snow, 1976)*

The Unwanted Effects of Conventional Antipsychotic Drugs

In addition to reducing psychotic symptoms, the conventional antipsychotic drugs sometimes produce disturbing movement problems (Julien, 2005). These effects are called **extrapyramidal effects** because they appear to be caused by the drugs' impact on the extrapyramidal areas of the brain, areas that help control motor activity. These undesired effects are so common that they are listed as a separate category of disorders—*medication-induced movement disorders*—in DSM-IV-TR (APA, 2000). They include *Parkinsonian and related symptoms, neuroleptic malignant syndrome,* and *tardive dyskinesia.*

PARKINSONIAN AND RELATED SYMPTOMS

The most common extrapyramidal effects are *Parkinsonian symptoms,* reactions that closely resemble the features of the neurological disorder Parkinson's disease. At least half of patients on conventional antipsychotic drugs experience muscle tremors and muscle rigidity at some point in their treatment; they may shake, move slowly, shuffle their feet, and show little facial expression (Janno

•**ANTIPSYCHOTIC DRUGS**•Drugs that help correct grossly confused or distorted thinking.

•**NEUROLEPTIC DRUGS**•Conventional antipsychotic drugs, so called because they often produce undesired effects similar to the symptoms of neurological disorders.

•**EXTRAPYRAMIDAL EFFECTS**•Unwanted movements, such as severe shaking, bizarre-looking grimaces, twisting of the body, and extreme restlessness, sometimes produced by conventional antipsychotic drugs.

Unwanted effects *This man has a severe case of Parkinson's disease, a disorder caused by low dopamine activity, and his muscle tremors prevent him from shaving himself. The conventional antipsychotic drugs often produce similar Parkinsonian symptoms.*

et al., 2004; Janicak et al., 2001; APA, 2000). Some also display related symptoms such as *dystonia,* involuntary muscle contractions that produce bizarre and uncontrollable movements of the face, neck, tongue, and back, and *akathisia,* great restlessness, agitation, and discomfort in the limbs, which causes individuals to move their arms and legs continually in search of relief.

The Parkinsonian and related symptoms seem to be the result of medication-induced reductions of dopamine activity in the *basal ganglia* and the *substantia nigra,* parts of the brain that coordinate movement and posture (Julien, 2005; Pickar et al., 1991). In most cases, the symptoms can be reversed if an anti-Parkinsonian drug is taken along with the antipsychotic drug. Alternatively, clinicians may have to reduce the dose of the antipsychotic drug or stop it altogether.

NEUROLEPTIC MALIGNANT SYNDROME In as many as 1 percent of patients, particularly elderly ones, conventional antipsychotic drugs produce *neuroleptic malignant syndrome,* a severe, potentially fatal reaction consisting of muscle rigidity, fever, altered consciousness, and improper functioning of the autonomic nervous system (Grilly, 2002; Keltner & Folks, 2001). As soon as the syndrome is recognized, drug use is discontinued and each neuroleptic symptom is treated medically. In addition individuals may be given dopamine-enhancing drugs.

TARDIVE DYSKINESIA Whereas most undesired drug effects appear within days or weeks, a reaction called **tardive dyskinesia** (meaning "late-appearing movement disorder") does not usually unfold until after a person has taken conventional antipsychotic drugs for more than a year. Sometimes it does not even appear until after the medications are stopped (Julien, 2005; Wyatt, 1995). This syndrome may include involuntary writhing or ticlike movements of the tongue, mouth, face, or whole body; involuntary chewing, sucking, and lip smacking; and jerky movements of the arms, legs, or entire body. It is sometimes accompanied by memory difficulties (Sorokin et al., 1988).

Most cases of tardive dyskinesia are mild and involve a single symptom, such as tongue flicking; however, some are severe and include such features as continual rocking back and forth, irregular breathing, and grotesque twisting of the face and body. It is believed that more than 10 percent of the people who take conventional drugs for an extended time develop tardive dyskinesia to some degree, and the longer the drugs are taken, the greater the risk becomes (Julien, 2005; APA, 2000). Patients over 50 years of age seem to be at greater risk.

Tardive dyskinesia can be difficult, sometimes impossible, to eliminate. If it is discovered early and the conventional drugs are stopped immediately, it eventually disappears in most cases (Grilly, 2002; APA, 2000). Early detection, however, is elusive because some of the symptoms are similar to psychotic symptoms. Clinicians may easily overlook them, continue to administer the drugs, and unintentionally create a more serious case of tardive dyskinesia. The longer patients are on the conventional antipsychotic drugs, the less likely it is that their tardive dyskinesia will disappear, even when the drugs are stopped. Researchers do not fully understand why conventional antipsychotic drugs cause tardive dyskinesia; however, they suspect that, once again, the problem is related to the drugs' effect on dopamine receptors in the basal ganglia and substantia nigra (Julien, 2005).

HOW SHOULD CONVENTIONAL ANTIPSYCHOTIC DRUGS BE PRESCRIBED? Today clinicians are more knowledgeable and more cautious about prescribing conventional antipsychotic drugs than they have been in the past. Previously, when patients did not improve with such a drug, their clinicians would keep increasing the dose (Kane, 1992); today a clinician will typically stop the drug (Coryell et al., 1998). Similarly, today's clinicians try to prescribe the lowest effective dose for each patient and to gradually reduce or stop medication weeks or months after the patient begins functioning normally (Torrey, 2001).

•**TARDIVE DYSKINESIA**•Extrapyramidal effects that appear in some patients after they have taken conventional antipsychotic drugs for an extended time.

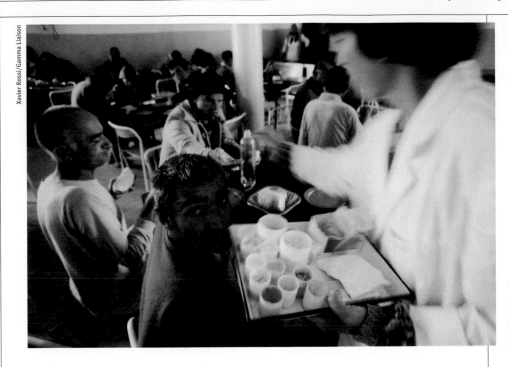

The drug revolution *Since the 1950s medications have become the center of treatment for patients hospitalized with schizophrenia and other severe mental disorders. The medications have resulted in shorter hospitalizations that last weeks rather than years.*

New Antipsychotic Drugs

Chapter 14 noted that "atypical" antipsychotic drugs have been developed in recent years. The most effective and widely used of these new drugs are *clozapine* (trade name Clozaril), *risperidone* (Risperdal), *olanzapine* (Zyprexa), *quetiapine* (Seroquel), *ziprasidone* (Geodon), and *aripiprazole* (Abilify). As we have observed, the drugs are called *atypical* because their biological operation differs from that of the conventional antipsychotic medications: the atypicals are received at fewer dopamine D-2 receptors and more D-1, D-4, and serotonin receptors than the others (Julien, 2005).

In fact, atypical antipsychotic drugs appear to be more effective than the conventional drugs, helping as many as 85 percent of persons with schizophrenia, compared with the 65 percent helped by most of the conventional drugs (Julien, 2005). Unlike the conventional drugs, the new drugs reduce not only the positive symptoms of schizophrenia, but also the negative ones (deLima et al, 2005). Another major benefit of the atypical antipsychotic drugs is that they cause fewer extrapyramidal symptoms and do not seem to produce tardive dyskinesia (Conley & Kelley, 2005) (see Figure 15-2). Given such advantages,

FIGURE 15-2 Conventional versus atypical antipsychotic drugs: the side effect advantage *Conventional antipsychotic drugs are much more likely than atypical antipsychotic drugs to produce undesired extrapyramidal symptoms. (A) The dose-response curve for conventional drugs shows that, beginning with low doses of the drugs, extrapyramidal side effects emerge and keep intensifying right along with increases in the drug doses. (B) In contrast, the dose-response curve for atypical antipsychotic drugs indicates that extrapyramidal side effects typically do not even appear until a patient is taking relatively high doses of the drugs. (Adapted from Casey, 1995, p. 107.)*

[BOX **15-2**]

Just Because You're Paranoid . . .

When *clozapine* (brand name Clozaril) was approved in 1990 for use as the first atypical antipsychotic drug in the United States, it opened the door to more effective and safer treatments for schizophrenia. However, the early use of this drug in the United States brought only frustration and heartache to hundreds of thousands of prospective users.

The problem with clozapine began with the discovery that a small percentage of people who take this drug develop *agranulocytosis,* a life-threatening drop in white blood cell count. The U.S. Food and Drug Administration (FDA) thus approved clozapine with the requirement that patients who take it must have their blood tested every week for signs of agranulocytosis.

Unfortunately, the drug's manufacturer decided to require all clozapine users in the United States to purchase an entire treatment package consisting of the med-

ication and weekly testing by the drug company's own subsidiaries. Most patients in the United States could not afford the company's fee for this combination— a whopping $9,000 a year. What's more,

their insurance companies refused to pay for it. Clearly patients were caught in the middle between big business and the health industry.

A flurry of lawsuits followed. So did federal investigations and hearings. After several years the drug's manufacturer finally agreed to sell clozapine separately, allowing patients to get blood tests elsewhere at a lower cost. Moreover, the FDA reduced its requirement for such tests to every two weeks, rather than every week, after patients have received clozapine treatment for six months (Bender, 1998). Sadly, however, many patients had already lost valuable time. Unable to fully appreciate or bring such injustices to the public's attention, persons with schizophrenia had been victimized by society once again— a tradition whose roots date back to past "treatments" such as asylums, the lobotomy, and deinstitutionalization.

it is not surprising that over half of all medicated patients with schizophrenia now take the atypical drugs (Edlinger et al., 2005; Torrey, 2001). Moreover, many patients with bipolar or other severe mental disorders also seem to be helped by several of the atypical antipsychotic drugs (Julien, 2005). Studies indicate, for example, that olanzapine, prescribed alone or in combination with mood-stabilizing drugs, is very effective in cases of acute mania (Dennehy et al., 2003; Gonzalez-Pinto et al., 2002).

Yet the atypical antipsychotic drugs have serious problems as well (Folsom et al., 2006). For example, people who use one of the atypical drugs, clozapine, have around a 1 percent risk of developing **agranulocytosis,** a life-threatening drop in white blood cells (other atypical antipsychotic drugs do not produce this undesired effect). Patients who take clozapine must therefore have frequent blood tests so that this effect can be spotted early and the drug stopped (Julien, 2005) (see Box 15-2). In addition, several of the atypical antipsychotic drugs tend to cause weight gain and are very expensive.

Psychotherapy

Before the discovery of antipsychotic drugs, psychotherapy was not really an option for people diagnosed with schizophrenia. Most were too far removed from reality to profit from it. Only a handful of therapists, apparently blessed with extraordinary patience and skill, specialized in the psychotherapeutic treatment of this disorder and reported a measure of success (Will, 1967, 1961; Sullivan, 1962, 1953; Fromm-Reichmann, 1950, 1948, 1943). These therapists believed that the first task of such therapy was to win the trust of patients with schizophrenia and build a close relationship with them.

The well-known clinical theorist and therapist Frieda Fromm-Reichmann, for example, would initially tell her patients that they could continue to exclude her from their private world and hold onto their disorder as long as they wished. She reported that eventually, after much testing and acting out, the patients would accept, trust, and

•AGRANULOCYTOSIS• A life-threatening reduction in white blood cells. This condition is sometimes produced by the atypical antipsychotic drug *clozapine.*

grow attached to her, and begin to talk to her about their problems. Case studies seemed to attest to the effectiveness of such approaches and to the importance of trust and emotional bonding in treatment. Here a recovered woman tells her therapist how she had felt during their early interactions:

> At the start, I didn't listen to what you said most of the time but I watched like a hawk for your expression and the sound of your voice. After the interview, I would add all this up to see if it seemed to show love. The words were nothing compared to the feelings you showed. I sense that you felt confident I could be helped and that there was hope for the future. . . .
>
> The problem with schizophrenics is that they can't trust anyone. They can't put their eggs in one basket. The doctor will usually have to fight to get in no matter how much the patient objects. . . .
>
> Loving is impossible at first because it turns you into a helpless little baby. The patient can't feel safe to do this until he is absolutely sure the doctor understands what is needed and will provide it.
>
> *(Hayward & Taylor, 1965)*

Today psychotherapy is successful in many more cases of schizophrenia (Julien, 2005). By helping to relieve thought and perceptual disturbances, antipsychotic drugs allow people with schizophrenia to learn about their disorder, participate actively in therapy, think more clearly about themselves and their relationships, and make changes in their behavior (Lublin, 2001; Svensson et al., 2000). The most helpful forms of psychotherapy include *insight therapy* and two broader sociocultural therapies—*family therapy* and *social therapy*. Often these approaches are combined and tailored to a patient's particular needs (Jeffries, 1995; Prendergast, 1995).

Insight Therapy

A variety of insight therapies, from cognitive to psychodynamic, may be used in cases of schizophrenia (Kingdon & Turkington, 2005; Tarrier, 2005; Zimmermann et al., 2005). Such approaches may be offered in individual or group formats. Studies suggest that the particular orientations of insight therapists are often less important than their levels of experience with schizophrenia (Karon & Vandenbos, 1996). In addition, the therapists who are most successful tend to be those who take an active role, setting limits, expressing opinions, challenging patients' statements, providing guidance, displaying empathy, and gaining trust (Fox, 2000; Whitehorn & Betz, 1975).

Family Therapy

Around 25 percent of persons who are recovering from schizophrenia live with family: parents, siblings, spouses, or children (Torrey, 2001). Such situations create special pressures, so that even if family stress was not a factor in the onset of the disorder, a patient's recovery may be greatly influenced by the behavior and reactions of the relatives at home.

Generally speaking, persons with schizophrenia who feel positively toward their relatives do better in treatment (Camacho et al., 2005; Lebell et al., 1993). As we observed in Chapter 14, recovered patients living with relatives who display high levels of *expressed emotion*—that is, relatives who are very critical, emotionally overinvolved, and hostile—often have a higher relapse rate than those living with more positive and supportive relatives (Janicak et al., 2001).

For their part, family members may be greatly affected by the social withdrawal and unusual behaviors of a relative with schizophrenia (Glanville & Dixon, 2005; Lauber et al., 2005; Creer & Wing, 1974). One individual complained, "In the evening you go into the sitting room and it's in darkness. You turn on the light and there he is just sitting there, staring in front of him."

"I'M GLAD YOU CAME TO ME. VISIONS OF GHOSTS OF CHRISTMAS PAST, PRESENT AND FUTURE ARE CLEARLY DELUSIONS BASED ON UNDERLYING PSYCHOLOGICAL CONFLICTS."

To address such issues, clinicians now commonly include family therapy in their treatment of schizophrenia, providing family members with guidance, training, practical advice, psychoeducation about the disorder, and emotional support and empathy (Hahlweg & Wiedemann, 2002). In family therapy, relatives develop more realistic expectations and become more tolerant, less guilt-ridden, and more willing to try new patterns of communication. Family therapy also helps the person with schizophrenia cope with the pressures of family life, make better use of family members, and avoid troublesome interactions.

Research has found that family therapy—particularly when it is combined with drug therapy—helps reduce tensions within the family and so helps relapse rates go down (Falloon, 2002; Hahlweg & Wiedemann, 2002; Pilling et al., 2002). The principles of this approach are evident in the following description:

Mark was a 32-year-old single man living with his parents. He had a long and stormy history of schizophrenia with many episodes of psychosis, interspersed with occasional brief periods of good functioning. Mark's father was a bright but neurotically tormented man gripped by obsessions and inhibitions in spite of many years of psychoanalysis. Mark's mother appeared weary, detached, and embittered. Both parents felt hopeless about Mark's chances of recovery and resentful that needing to care for him would always plague their lives. They acted as if they were being intentionally punished. It gradually emerged that the father, in fact, was riddled with guilt and self-doubt; he suspected that his wife had been cold and rejecting toward Mark as an infant and that he had failed to intervene, due to his unwillingness to confront his wife and the demands of graduate school that distanced him from home life. He entertained the fantasy that Mark's illness was a punishment for this. Every time Mark did begin to show improvement—both in reduced symptoms and in increased functioning—his parents responded as if it were just a cruel torment designed to raise their hopes and then to plunge them into deeper despair when Mark's condition deteriorated. This pattern was especially apparent when Mark got a job. As a result, at such times, the parents actually became more critical and hostile toward Mark. He would become increasingly defensive and insecure, finally developing paranoid delusions, and usually would be hospitalized in a panicky and agitated state.

All of this became apparent during the psychoeducational sessions. When the pattern was pointed out to the family, they were able to recognize their self-fulfilling prophecy and were motivated to deal with it. As a result, the therapist decided to see the family together. Concrete instances of the pattern and its consequences were explored, and alternative responses by the parents were developed. The therapist encouraged both the parents and Mark to discuss their anxieties and doubts about Mark's progress, rather than to stir up one another's expectations of failure. The therapist had regular individual sessions with Mark as well as the family sessions. As a result, Mark has successfully held a job for an unprecedented 12 months.

(Heinrichs & Carpenter, 1983, pp. 284–285)

The families of persons with schizophrenia may also turn to *family support groups* and *family psychoeducational programs* for assistance, encouragement, and advice (Chien et al., 2004; Powder, 2004; McFarlane, 2002). In such programs, family members meet with others in the same situation to share their thoughts and emotions, provide mutual support, and learn about schizophrenia. Although research has yet to determine the usefulness of these groups, the approach has become popular.

Social Therapy

Many clinicians believe that the treatment of people with schizophrenia should include techniques that address social and personal difficulties in the clients' lives. These clinicians offer practical advice; work with clients on problem solving, decision making, and social skills; make sure that the clients are taking their medications properly; and may even help them find work, financial assistance, and proper housing (Kersting, 2005; Bellack et al., 2004; Pratt & Mueser, 2002).

Research finds that this practical, active, and broad approach, called *social therapy* or *personal therapy,* does indeed help keep people out of the hospital (Hogarty, 2002). One study compared the progress of four groups of patients with chronic schizophrenia after their discharge from a state hospital (Hogarty et al., 1986, 1974). One group received both antipsychotic medications and social therapy in the community, while the other groups received medication only, social therapy only, or no treatment of any kind. The researchers' first finding was that chronic patients need to continue taking medication after being released in order to avoid rehospitalization. Over a two-year period, 80 percent of those who did not continue medication needed to be hospitalized again, compared to 48 percent of those who received medication. They also found that among the patients on medication, those who also received social therapy adjusted to the community and avoided rehospitalization most successfully. Clearly, social therapy played an important role in their recovery.

The Community Approach

The broadest approach for the treatment of schizophrenia and other severe mental disorders is the *community approach.* In 1963, partly in response to the terrible conditions in public mental institutions, the U.S. government ordered that patients be released and treated in the community. Congress passed the *Community Mental Health Act,* which stipulated that patients with psychological disorders were to receive a range of mental health services—outpatient therapy, inpatient treatment, emergency care, preventive care, and aftercare—in their communities rather than being transported to institutions far from home. The act was aimed at a variety of psychological disorders, but patients diagnosed with schizophrenia, especially those who had been institutionalized for years, were affected most. Other countries around the world put similar sociocultural treatment programs into action shortly thereafter (Hafner & an der Heiden, 1988).

Thus began four decades of **deinstitutionalization,** an exodus of hundreds of thousands of patients with schizophrenia and other long-term mental disorders from state institutions into the community. On a given day in 1955 close to 600,000 patients were living in state institutions; today only around 60,000 patients reside in those settings (Torrey, 2001). Clinicians have learned that patients recovering from schizophrenia and other severe disorders can profit greatly from community programs (Prince, 2005). As we shall see, however, the actual quality of community care for these people has been inadequate throughout the United States. The result is a "revolving door" syndrome: many patients have been released to the community, readmitted to an institution within months, released a second time, admitted yet again, and so on, over and over (Torrey, 2001).

What Are the Features of Effective Community Care?

People recovering from schizophrenia and other severe disorders need medication (see Box 15-3 on page 451), psychotherapy, help in handling daily pressures and responsibilities, guidance in making decisions, training in social skills, residential supervision, and vocational counseling—a combination of services sometimes called *assertive community treatment* (Julien, 2005). Those whose communities help them meet these needs make greater progress than people living in other communities (Prince, 2005; Zygmunt et al., 2002). Some of the key features of effective community care programs are (1) coordination of patient services, (2) short-term hospitalization, (3) partial hospitalization, (4) supervised residencies, and (5) occupational training.

•**DEINSTITUTIONALIZATION**•The discharge of large numbers of patients from long-term institutional care so that they might be treated in community programs.

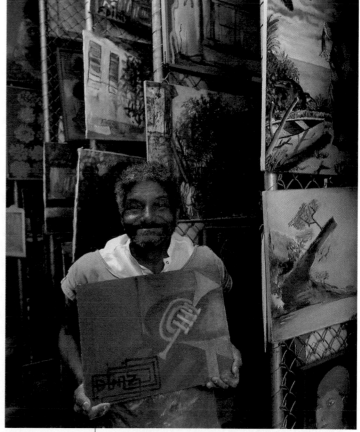

Art that heals *Art and other creative activities can be therapeutic for people with schizophrenia and other severe mental disorders. More than 250,000 pieces of patient-produced art are on display at the Museum of the Unconscious in Rio de Janeiro, Brazil, where supervisors work closely with patients every day. One of the museum's most famous and talented patients, Fernando Diniz, poses with some of his extraordinary artwork.*

Silvia Izquierdo/AP Photo

Music and movement can also help heal *Yet another creative activity that can often be therapeutic for people with mental disorders—from mild to severe—is dance therapy. Here people with various kinds of psychological disorders dance during the 2005 Carnival parade in front of the Psychiatric Institute in Rio de Janeiro, Brazil.*

COORDINATED SERVICES When the Community Mental Health Act was first passed, it was expected that community care would be provided by a **community mental health center,** a treatment facility that would supply medication, psychotherapy, and inpatient emergency care to people with severe disturbances, as well as coordinate the services offered by other community agencies. Each center was expected to serve a geographic area with a population of 50,000 to 200,000 people.

When community mental health centers are available and do in fact provide these services, patients with schizophrenia and other severe disorders often make significant progress (Kersting, 2005; Fenton et al., 2002; Scott & Dixon, 1995). They are better integrated into the community and function more effectively than patients who receive only standard outpatient care (Madianos & Madianou, 1992). Coordination of services is particularly important for the so-called *mentally ill chemical abusers (MICAs),* patients with psychotic disorders as well assubstance-related disorders (see Box 15-4 on page 453).

SHORT-TERM HOSPITALIZATION When people develop severe psychotic symptoms, today's clinicians first try to treat them on an outpatient basis, usually with a combination of antipsychotic medication and psychotherapy (Marder, 1996). If this approach fails, *short-term hospitalization*—in a mental hospital or a general hospital's psychiatric unit—that lasts a few weeks (rather than months or years) may be tried (Fenton et al., 2002). Soon after the patients improve, they are released for **aftercare,** a general term for follow-up care and treatment in the community (Sederer, 1992). Short-term hospitalization usually leads to greater improvement and a lower rehospitalization rate than extended institutionalization (Caton, 1982). Countries throughout the world now favor this policy (Hafner & an der Heiden, 1988).

PARTIAL HOSPITALIZATION People's needs may fall between full hospitalization and outpatient therapy, and so some communities offer **day centers** or **day hospitals,** all-day programs in which patients return to their homes for the night. Such programs actually originated in Moscow in 1933, when a shortage of hospital beds necessitated the premature release of many patients. Today's day centers provide patients with daily supervised activities, therapy, and programs to improve social skills. People recovering from schizophrenia and other severe disdorders in day centers often do better than those who spend extended periods in a hospital or in traditional outpatient therapy (Mayahara & Ito, 2002; Yoshimasu et al., 2002).

Another kind of institution that has become a popular setting for the treatment of people with schizophrenia and other severe disorders is the *semihospital,* or *residential crisis center.* Semihospitals are houses or other structures in the community that provide 24-hour nursing care for people with severe mental disorders (Torrey, 2001). Many individuals who would otherwise be cared for in state hospitals are now being transferred to these virtual hospitals (Fenton et al., 2002).

SUPERVISED RESIDENCES Many people do not require hospitalization but, at the same time, are unable to live alone or with their families. **Halfway houses,** also known as *crisis houses* or *group homes,* often serve individuals well (Levy et al., 2005). Such residences may shelter between one and two dozen people. The live-in staff usually are *paraprofessionals*—lay people who receive training and ongoing supervision from outside mental health professionals. The houses are usually run with a *milieu therapy* philosophy that emphasizes mutual support, resident responsibility, and self-government. Research indicates that halfway houses help many people recovering from schizophrenia and other severe disorders adjust to community life and avoid rehospitalization (Hansson et al., 2002; McGuire, 2000). Here is how one woman described living in a halfway house after 10 hospitalizations in 12 years:

•**COMMUNITY MENTAL HEALTH CENTER**• A treatment facility that provides medication, psychotherapy, and emergency care for psychological problems and coordinates treatment in the community.

•**AFTERCARE**•A program of posthospitalization care and treatment out in the community.

•**DAY CENTER**•A program that offers hospital-like treatment during the day only. Also known as a *day hospital.*

•**HALFWAY HOUSE**•A residence for people with schizophrenia or other severe problems, often staffed by paraprofessionals. Also known as a *group home* or *crisis house.*

[**BOX 15-3**]

Sociocultural Landscape: First Dibs on Atypical Antipsychotic Drugs

We observed in Chapter 9 that depressed African Americans in the United States are less likely than depressed white Americans to be prescribed second-generation antidepressant drugs, the newer drugs that have fewer side effects than tricyclics and MAO inhibitors (see p. 268). Thus many African Americans may be receiving less effective biological care than white Americans for their depressive disorders.

Unfortunately, a similar pattern appears to be at work in cases of schizophrenia when people are prescribed atypical antipsychotic medications, the newer drugs that are often more effective and have fewer undesired effects than conventional antipsychotic medications. The following prescription patterns have emerged in a number of recent studies:

◆ African Americans with schizophrenia and other psychotic disorders are significantly less likely than white Americans to be prescribed atypical antipsychotic drugs (49 percent compared to 66 percent, respectively) (Herbeck et al., 2004).

◆ In turn, African American patients are less likely to be helped by their antipsychotic medications and more likely to experience tardive dyskinesia and extrapyramidal effects in response to their medications for schizophrenia.

◆ It appears that one reason for this racial disparity may be economic. On average, African American patients are less likely than white Americans to have private health insurance or any health insurance at all (Kass et al., 1999). Schizophrenic patients without private insurance are more likely to be prescribed conventional antipsychotic medications, which are much cheaper, and less likely to receive atypical antipsychotics, which are much more expensive (Herbeck et al, 2004).

◆ Another reason for this racial disparity may be the agents of treatment. In general, African American patients are more likely to have a family physician rather than a psychiatrist prescribe their psychotropic drugs (Mark et al., 2002; Pingitore et al., 2001). It turns out that family physicians are more likely to prescribe *conventional* antipsychotic drugs than *atypical* antipsychotic drugs (Mark et al., 2003, 2002).

◆ African American patients appear to respond more readily and quickly than other racial groups to antipsychotic drugs, yet they are also more likely to be prescribed dosages in excess of recommended levels. This leaves African American patients with schizophrenia, once again, more vulnerable than white American patients to tardive dyskinesia and extrapyramidal effects (Mark et al., 2003).

Rick Gomez/Corbis

Corbis

The halfway house changed my life. First of all, I discovered that some of the staff members had once been clients in the program! That one single fact offered me hope. For the first time, I saw proof that a program could help someone, that it was possible to regain control over one's life and become independent. The house was democratically run; all residents had one vote and the staff members, outnumbered 5 to 22, could not make rules or even discharge a client from the program without majority sentiment. There was a house bill of rights that was strictly observed by all. We helped one another and gave support. When residents were in a crisis, no staff member hustled them off or increased their medication to calm them down. Residents could cry, be comforted and hugged until a solution could be found, or until they accepted that it was okay to feel bad. Even anger was an acceptable feeling that did not have to be feared, but could be expressed and turned into constructive energy. If you disliked some aspect of the program or the behavior of a staff member, you could change things rather than passively accept what was happening. Choices were real, and failure and success were accepted equally. . . . Bit by bit, my distrust faltered and the fears lessened. I slept better and made friends. . . . Other residents and staff members who had hallucinated for years and now were able to control their hallucinations shared with me some of the techniques that had worked for them. Things like diet . . . and interpersonal relationships became a few of my tools.

(Lovejoy, 1982, pp. 605–609)

OCCUPATIONAL TRAINING Paid employment provides income, independence, self-respect, and the stimulation of working with others. It also brings companionship and order to one's daily life. For these reasons, occupational training and placement are important services for people with schizophrenia and other severe mental disorders (Kersting, 2005; Twamley et al., 2005).

Many people recovering from such disorders receive occupational training in a **sheltered workshop**—a supervised workplace for employees who are not ready for competitive or complicated jobs. The workshop replicates a typical work environment: products such as toys or simple appliances are manufactured and sold, workers are paid according to performance, and all are expected to be at work regularly and on time. For some, the sheltered workshop becomes a permanent workplace. For others, it is an important step toward better-paying and more demanding employment or a return to a previous job (Chalamat et al., 2005; Bustillo et al., 2001; Bell et al., 1996). In the United States, occupational training is not consistently available to people with severe mental disorders (Torrey, 2001; Drake et al., 1996). Some studies find that fewer than 15 percent of such people are competitively employed (Honberg, 2005; Blyler, 2003).

How Has Community Treatment Failed?

There is no doubt that effective community programs can help people with schizophrenia and other severe mental disorders recover. However, fewer than half of all the people who need them receive appropriate community mental health services (McGuire, 2000; PORT, 1998). In fact, in any given year, 40 to 60 percent of all people with schizophrenia and other severe mental disorders receive no treatment at all (Wang et al., 2002; Torrey, 2001). Two factors are primarily responsible: *poor coordination* of services and *shortage* of services.

POOR COORDINATION OF SERVICES The various mental health agencies in a community often fail to communicate with one another (Leshner et al., 1992). There may be an opening at a nearby halfway house, for example, and the therapist at the community mental health center may not know about it. In addition, even within a community agency a patient may not have continuing contacts with the same staff members and may fail to receive consistent services. Still another problem is poor communication between state hospitals and community mental health centers (Torrey, 2001, 1997; Leshner et al., 1992). Sometimes community agencies are not even informed when patients are discharged from the hospital. This problem had its beginnings in the early days of deinstitutionalization, when hospitals were often forced to discharge patients before many community mental health centers were open and ready to serve them (Leshner et al., 1992).

It is not surprising, then, that a growing number of community therapists have become **case managers** for people with schizophrenia and other severe mental disorders (Kersting, 2005; Chan et al., 2000). Like the social therapists described earlier, they offer therapy and advice, teach problem-solving and social skills, and ensure that medications are being taken properly. In addition, they try to coordinate available community services, guide clients through the community system, and, perhaps most important, help protect clients' legal rights. Many professionals now believe that effective case management is the key to success for a community program.

SHORTAGE OF SERVICES The number of community programs available to people with severe mental disorders falls woefully short (Julien, 2005). The roughly 800 community mental health centers now operating in the United States are only one-third of the number projected in the early 1960s. Halfway houses and sheltered workshops are in similarly short supply.

•**SHELTERED WORKSHOP**•A supervised workplace for people who are not yet ready for competitive jobs.

•**CASE MANAGER**•A community therapist who offers a full range of services for people with schizophrenia or other severe disorders, including therapy, advice, medication, guidance, and protection of patients' rights.

[BOX 15-4]

Mentally Ill Chemical Abusers: A Challenge for Treatment

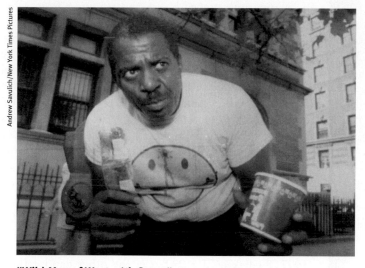

"Wild Man of West 96th Street" *The case of Larry Hogue, the so-called Wild Man of West 96th Street, helped bring the plight of MICAs to public attention.*

▌ *A state appeals court yesterday ordered Larry Hogue, who has for years frightened residents of Manhattan's Upper West Side with his bizarre behavior, to remain in a state mental hospital until a hearing next week. . . . Before he was arrested, Mr. Hogue had attacked passers-by and cars in the area around West 96th Street and Amsterdam Avenue. . . .*

. . . Mr. Hogue has been arrested 30 times and served at least six terms in prison, ranging from five days to a year, according to law-enforcement records. He now faces charges of criminal mischief for scraping the paint off a car last August. ▌

(*NEW YORK TIMES,* FEBRUARY 9, 1993)

uring the 1990s, Larry Hogue, nicknamed the "Wild Man of West 96th Street" by neighbors, became the best-known *mentally ill chemical abuser* (*MICA*) in the United States. MICAs are individuals who suffer from both a mental disorder (in his case schizophrenia) and a substance-related disorder. Between 20 and 50 percent of all people with chronic mental disorders may be MICAs (NSDUH, 2005; Torrey, 2001).

MICAs tend to be young and male. They often rate below average in social functioning and school achievement and above average in poverty, acting-out behavior,

emergency room visits, and encounters with the criminal justice system (Bartels et al., 1993; O'Hare, 1992). MICAs commonly report greater distress and have poorer treatment outcomes than people with mental disorders who do not abuse substances (Carey et al., 1991).

The relationship between substance abuse and mental dysfunctioning is complex. A mental disorder may precede substance abuse, and the drug may be taken as a form of self-medication or as a result of impaired judgment (Torrey, 2001; Ziedonis et al., 2000). Conversely, substance abuse may cause or exacerbate psychopathology. Cocaine and amphetamines, for example, exacerbate the symptoms of psychosis and can quickly intensify the symptoms of schizophrenia (Grilly, 2002; Laruelle & Abi-Dargham, 1999). Whichever begins first, substance abuse and mental disorders interact to create a unique problem that is greater than the sum of its parts (Meydan et al., 2005). The course and outcome of one problem can be significantly influenced by the other.

Treatment of MICAs has been undermined by the tendency of patients to hide their drug abuse problems and for clinicians to underdiagnose them (Lehman et al., 1996). Unrecognized substance abuse

may lead to misdiagnosis and misunderstanding of the disorders (Shaner et al., 1993). The treatment of MICAs is further complicated by the fact that many treatment facilities are designed and funded to treat *either* mental disorders *or* substance abuse; only some are equipped or willing to treat both. As a result, it is not uncommon for MICA patients to be rejected as inappropriate for treatment in both substance abuse and mental health programs (NSDUH, 2005; Torrey, 2001). Many such individuals fall through the cracks in this way and find themselves in jail, like Larry Hogue, or in homeless shelters for want of the treatment they sought in vain (Blanchard et al., 2000).

Experts describe the ideal MICA treatment program as a safe and supportive therapeutic environment that offers techniques for treating both mental disorders and substance abuse and takes into account the unique effects of both problems (Kersting, 2005; Akerele & Levin, 2002; Anderson, 2000). One particularly inspiring development is the establishment of self-help groups for MICAs living in the community.

The problem of falling through the cracks is perhaps most poignantly seen in the case of *homeless* MICAs (Blanchard et al., 2000). Researchers estimate that 10 to 20 percent of the homeless population may be MICAs (Drake et al., 1991). MICAs typically remain homeless longer than other homeless people and are more likely to experience extremely harsh conditions, such as living on the winter streets rather than in a homeless shelter. They are also more likely to be jailed, to trade sexual favors for food or money, to share needles, to engage in unprotected sex, and to be victimized in other ways (Susser et al., 1996). Homeless MICAs need programs committed to building trust and providing intensive case management and long-term practical assistance (Drake et al., 1991). In short, therapists must tailor treatment programs to MICAs' unique combination of problems rather than expecting the MICAs to adapt to traditional forms of care.

Christopher Morris/Black Star

Community care in action *Clinicians have learned that people with schizophrenia and other severe disorders often make great progress in well-coordinated community treatment programs. Here patients begin their day with breakfast at New York City's Fountain House, a day center that provides daily activities and therapy as well as extensive occupational training.*

Also disturbing, the community mental health centers that do exist generally fail to provide adequate services for people with severe disorders. They tend to devote their efforts and money to people with less disabling problems, such as anxiety disorders or problems in social adjustment. Only a fraction of the patients treated by community mental health centers suffer from schizophrenia or other disorders marked by psychosis (Torrey, 2001).

Why is there such a shortage of services for people with severe mental disorders? First, it appears that most mental health professionals simply prefer to work with people whose problems are less extreme and shorter-term (Torrey, 2001; Lee et al., 1993). Second, neighborhood residents often object to the presence of community programs for patients recovering from severe disorders, sometimes going so far as to picket, protest, and even vandalize community facilities (Cowan, 2002; Leshner et al., 1992). This has been referred to as the NIMBY syndrome—an acronym for "not in my backyard."

But perhaps the primary reason for the shortage of community care is economic. On the one hand, more public funds are available for people with psychological disorders now than in the past. In 1963 a total of $1 billion was spent in this area, whereas today more than $61 billion is spent on people with mental disorders (Torrey, 1997; Redick et al., 1992). On the other hand, rather little of this new money is going to community treatment programs for people with severe disorders. Much of it goes to monthly income payments such as *social security disability income,* to services for persons with mental disorders in nursing homes and general hospitals, and to community services for people who are less disturbed (Torrey, 2001; Stein, 1993). Moreover, a considerable amount still goes to state hospitals, even though the populations of these hospitals have decreased more than 80 percent since 1963. Today the financial burden of providing community treatment for persons with long-term severe disorders often falls on local governments and nonprofit organizations rather than the federal or state government, and local resources cannot always meet this challenge.

WHAT ARE THE CONSEQUENCES OF INADEQUATE COMMUNITY TREATMENT?

What happens to persons with schizophrenia and other severe disorders whose communities do not provide the services they need and whose families cannot afford private treatment (see Figure 15-3)? As we have observed, a large number receive no treatment at all; many others spend a short time in a state hospital or semihospital and are then discharged prematurely, often without adequate follow-up treatment (Torrey, 2001).

Many of the people with schizophrenia and other severe disorders return to their families and receive medication and perhaps emotional and financial support, but little else in the way of treatment. Around 8 percent enter an alternative institution such as a nursing home or rest home, where they receive only custodial care and medication (Torrey, 2001; Smyer, 1989). As many as 18 percent are placed in privately run residences where supervision is provided by untrained individuals—foster homes (small or large), boardinghouses, congregate care homes, and similar facilities (Torrey, 2001). These residences vary greatly in quality. Some of them are legitimate "bed and care" facilities, providing three meals a day, medication reminders, and at least a small degree of staff supervision. However, many fail to offer even these minimal services.

Another 31 percent of people with schizophrenia and other severe disorders live in totally unsupervised settings. Some of these individuals are equal to the challenge of living alone, support themselves effectively, and maintain nicely furnished apartments. But many cannot really function independently and wind up in rundown single-room-occupancy hotels (SROs) or rooming houses, often located in inner-city neighborhoods (Torrey, 2001). They may live in conditions that are substandard and unsafe. The following newspaper account from the mid-1980s describes the kinds of conditions that continue in many locations today (Torrey, 2001):

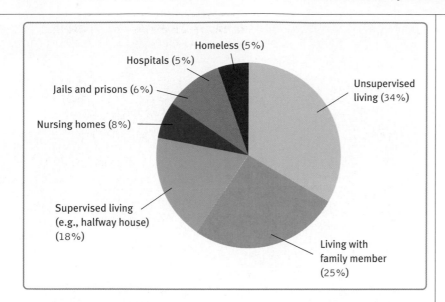

Homeless (5%)

Hospitals (5%)

Jails and prisons (6%)

Nursing homes (8%)

Unsupervised living (34%)

Supervised living (e.g., halfway house) (18%)

Living with family member (25%)

FIGURE 15-3 **Where do people with schizophrenia live?** *More than one-third live in unsupervised residences, 6 percent in jails, and 5 percent on the streets or in homeless shelters (Torrey, 2001).*

Hundreds of mentally ill patients throughout Dade County are being packed into aging hotels and homes that are little better than slums, according to health officials, who say the appalling living conditions virtually ensure patients will sink deeper into insanity.

Florida's policy of emptying its mental institutions, a paucity of appropriate "halfway houses," and lax inspections of existing homes have left many mentally ill without the care that might ease them back into normal life.

It also has left them without protection. Released from hospitals into overburdened halfway houses, the indigent patients eventually are shunted to landlords, some of whom jam them, perhaps three to a room, into decaying and dangerous buildings and then collect their welfare payments as rent.

The worst buildings, found scattered throughout Little Havana and the dying hotel district in South Miami Beach, contain the stuff of nightmares. Piles of trash and feces litter the floors. Half-naked men wander purposelessly through hallways, and doors swing open into hot and fetid rooms where others, gazing vacantly at the ceiling, lie neglected on dirty cots. . . .

In one instance, [the state Department of Health and Rehabilitative Services] released patients to a Little Havana house run by a landlord who three years earlier lost his state license to operate a group home because of its life-threatening conditions.

The landlord . . . didn't apply for a license for his latest home at 218 SW Eighth Ave. Instead, he used plywood sheets to divide the coral rock house into 12-foot by 14-foot boxes and then told HRS workers he would take in the mentally ill.

Each of the boxes, strung along trash-strewn passageways in the two-story house, contains a narrow bed, a fan and a chest of drawers. Hot meal containers and plastic forks fill waste bins. Most of the boxes also contained people like Vallant Garez, a timid 55-year-old whose bed sores attest to hours spent in bed, staring at a paint-chipped wall a foot from his pillow.

(Miami Herald, August 20, 1984*)*

Most of the residents in poorly supervised or unsupervised settings survive on government disability payments (Torrey, 2001; Barker et al., 1992), and many spend their days wandering through neighborhood streets. Thus it is sometimes said that people with severe mental disorders are now "dumped" in the community, just as they were once "warehoused" in institutions.

Finally, a great number of people with schizophrenia and other severe disorders have become homeless (Folsom et al., 2006; Gilligan, 2001). There are between 250,000 and

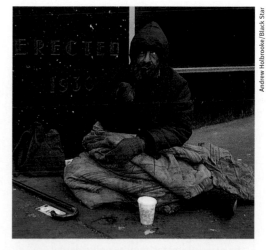

Andrew Holbrooke/Black Star

Society's forgotten people *Tens of thousands of homeless people in the United States suffer from schizophrenia or another severe mental disorder. The deinstitutionalization movement, failures in community treatment, and changing insurance priorities have left these individuals untreated and uncared for.*

David Duprey/AP Photo

Helping to meet the need *Because formal community services fall short for so many people with schizophrenia, the contributions of volunteers become especially important. Here a young man with schizophrenia tries a mountain bike while his volunteer friend of 12 years looks on. The volunteer was enlisted by Compeer Inc., an organization in Rochester, New York, dedicated to befriending community residents who have psychological disorders.*

550,000 homeless people in the United States, and approximately one-third have a severe mental disorder, commonly schizophrenia (Skelton, 2004; Torrey, 2001). Many such persons have been released from hospitals. Others are young adults who were never hospitalized in the first place. Another 135,000 or more people with severe mental disorders end up in prisons because their disorders have led them to break the law (Honberg, 2005; Perez et al., 2003). Certainly deinstitutionalization and the community mental health movement have failed these individuals, and many report actually feeling relieved if they are able to return to hospital life (Drake & Wallach, 1992).

The Promise of Community Treatment

Despite these very serious problems, proper community care has shown great potential for assisting in the recovery from schizophrenia and other severe disorders, and clinicians and many government officials continue to press to make it more available. Since the early 1990s, government and professional agencies have created task forces whose purpose is to find more effective ways for the federal government, states, and local organizations to meet the needs of people with such disorders (Knowlton, 1997; Leshner et al., 1992).

Another important development has been the formation of *national interest groups* in countries around the world that push for better community treatment (Johnson, 2002; Torrey, 2001). In the United States, for example, the *National Alliance for the Mentally Ill* began in 1979 with 300 members and has expanded to around 220,000 members in more than 1,100 chapters (NAMI, 2005, 2002). Made up largely of relatives of people with severe mental disorders (particularly schizophrenia, bipolar disorders, and major depressive disorder), this group has become a powerful lobbying force in state legislatures and has pressured community mental health centers to treat more persons with schizophrenia and other severe disorders.

Today community care is a major feature of treatment for people recovering from severe mental disorders in countries around the world (Dencker & Dencker, 1995; Fog, 1995). Some countries, learning from the mistakes of deinstitutionalization in the United States, have organized their own community programs better and as a result have had more success with them (Honkonen et al., 2003; Fakhoury & Priebe, 2002; Gaal et al.,

2002). Both in the United States and abroad, varied and well-coordinated community treatment is seen as an important part of the solution to the problem of schizophrenia and other severe disorders (Melle et al., 2000).

PUTTING IT together
An Important Lesson

After years of frustration and failure, clinicians now have an arsenal of weapons to use against schizophrenia and other disorders marked by psychosis—medication, institutional programs, psychotherapy, and community programs. It has become very clear that antipsychotic medications open the door for recovery from these disorders, but in most cases other kinds of treatment are also needed to help the recovery process along. The various approaches must be combined in a way that meets each individual's specific needs.

Working with schizophrenia and other severe disorders has taught therapists an important lesson: no matter how compelling the evidence for biological causation may be, a strictly biological approach to the treatment of psychological disorders is a mistake more often than not (McCabe et al., 1999). Largely on the basis of biological discoveries and pharmacological advances, hundreds of thousands of patients with schizophrenia and other severe mental disorders were released to their communities in the 1960s. Little attention was paid to the psychological and sociocultural needs of these individuals, and many of them have been trapped in their pathology ever since. Clinicians must remember this lesson, especially in today's climate, when managed care and government priorities often promote medication as the sole treatment for psychological problems.

When Kraepelin described schizophrenia at the turn of the twentieth century, he estimated that only 13 percent of its victims ever improved. Today, even with shortages in community care, many more such individuals show improvement (Torrey, 2001; McGuire, 2000). Twenty-five percent or more are believed to recover from schizophrenia completely, and an equal number return to relatively independent lives, although their occupational and social functioning may continue to fall short of earlier levels. These improvements notwithstanding, the clinical field still has far to go (Conley et al., 2005). Studies suggest that the recovery rates could be considerably higher (McGuire, 2000). It is unacceptable that the majority of people with this and other severe mental disorders receive few or none of the effective community interventions that have been developed, worse still that tens of thousands have become homeless. Although many factors have contributed to this state of affairs, neglect by clinical practitioners has certainly played a big role in it. It is now up to these professionals, along with public officials, to address the needs of all people with schizophrenia and other severe disorders.

John Stanmeyer/VII/AP Photo

Incarceration posing as treatment *Even as countries around the world move away from long-term institutional treatment and toward community mental health, the horrors of asylums and overcrowded public mental hospitals continue in parts of today's world. At the Panti Bina Laras Cipayung, a government-run center for mental patients in Jakarta, Indonesia, over 300 men and women live in dungeonlike conditions, chained to walls, mostly naked and without medications, due to lack of government funding. The center has a budget of less than one U.S. dollar per day to provide each patient with food and medicine.*

>>LOOKING BACK

Momentous Meeting

On February 9, 1962, the famed psychiatrist William Menninger, who had pioneered effective treatments for psychological casualties in World War II, met with President John F. Kennedy in the Oval Office, seeking the president's public support for the value of psychological treatment. It was the first time in American history that a well-known mental health expert had had the ear of a president (Moskowitz, 2001). One year later, almost to the day, Kennedy gave a famous speech calling for the "bold new approach" of community treatment, leading to Congress's passage of the Community Mental Health Act. <<

>>LOOKING AROUND

Lobotomies at All Socioeconomic Levels

A sister of President John Kennedy, Rosemary Kennedy, suffered from mild mental retardation. She received a lobotomy in the 1940s at age 23 (Weil, 2005). <<

[SUMMARY AND REVIEW]

■ **Overview of treatment** For years all efforts to treat schizophrenia brought only frustration. The disorder is still difficult to treat, but today's therapies are more successful than those of the past. *p. 437*

■ **Past institutional care** For more than half of the twentieth century, the main treatment for schizophrenia and other severe mental disorders was *institutionalization* and *custodial care*. Because patients failed to respond to traditional therapies, they were usually placed in overcrowded public institutions (*state hospitals* in the United States), typically in *back wards* where the primary goal was to maintain and restrain them. Between 1845 and 1955 the number of state hospitals and mental patients rose steadily, while the quality of care declined. *pp. 438–439*

■ **Improved institutional care** In the 1950s two in-hospital approaches were developed, *milieu therapy* and *token economy programs*. They often brought improvement and particularly helped patients to care for themselves and feel better about themselves. *pp. 440–442*

■ **Antipsychotic drugs** The discovery of *antipsychotic drugs* in the 1950s revolutionized the treatment of schizophrenia and other disorders marked by psychosis. Today they are almost always a part of treatment. Theorists believe that the first generation of antipsychotic drugs operate by reducing excessive dopamine activity in the brain. These "conventional" antipsychotic drugs reduce the positive symptoms of schizophrenia more completely, or more quickly, than the negative symptoms.

The conventional antipsychotic drugs can also produce dramatic unwanted effects, particularly movement abnormalities called extrapyramidal effects, which include Parkinsonian and related symptoms, neuroleptic malignant syndrome, and tardive dyskinesia. Tardive dyskinesia apparently occurs in more than 10 percent of the people who take conventional antipsychotic drugs for an extended time and can be difficult or impossible to eliminate, even when the drugs are stopped. Recently atypical antipsychotic drugs (such as clozapine, risperidone, and olanzapine) have been developed, which seem to be more effective than the conventional drugs and to cause fewer or no extrapyramidal effects. *pp. 442–446*

■ **Psychotherapy** Today *psychotherapy* is often employed successfully in combination with antipsychotic drugs. Helpful forms include *insight therapy, family therapy,* and *social therapy. Family support groups* and *family psychoeducational programs* are also growing in number. *pp. 446–449*

■ **The community approach** A *community approach* to the treatment of schizophrenia and other severe mental disorders began in the 1960s, when a policy of *deinstitutionalization* in the United States brought about a mass exodus of hundreds of thousands of patients from state institutions into the community. Among the key elements of effective community care programs are coordination of patient services by a *community mental health center, short-term hospitalization* (followed by *aftercare*), *day centers, halfway houses,* and *occupational training*.

Unfortunately, the quality and funding of community care for people with schizophrenia and other severe disorders have been inadequate throughout the United States, often resulting in a "revolving door" syndrome. One consequence is that many people with such disorders are now homeless or in jail. Still others live in *nursing homes* or *rest homes* where they do not receive effective treatment, and many live in *boardinghouses* or *single-room-occupancy hotels. pp. 449–456*

■ **The promise of community treatment** The potential of proper community care to help people recovering from schizophrenia and other severe disorders continues to capture the interest of clinicians and policy makers. One major development has been the formation of *national interest groups* that are successfully promoting community treatment for people with these disorders. *pp. 456–457*

>>> CRITICAL THOUGHTS <<<

1. Why have more people with schizophrenia than people with other disorders been the victims of mistreatment (lobotomy or deinstitutionalization, for example)? *pp. 437–457*

2. In the early years of antipsychotic drug use, patients who failed to respond to these drugs were likely to receive higher and higher dosages until many of them seemed to be walking zombies. Why might clinicians have used this medication strategy, even when the drugs failed to reduce symptoms? *pp. 442–444*

3. Should pharmaceutical companies have so much control over the cost and distribution of critical breakthrough drugs, such as antipsychotic drugs, that could improve millions of lives? *pp. 442–446*

4. The atypical antipsychotic drug *clozapine* was available in Europe 15 years before its approval in the United States. Might the FDA be too cautious in its approach to approving new drugs? *p. 446*

5. The public often perceives people with schizophrenia as dangerous and violent even though most persons with this disorder are far from dangerous. Why does the public hold such a perception, and how can it be changed? *p. 453*

6. As a result of deinstitutionalization, some of today's homeless shelters use buildings that were once state hospitals, and, in fact, some of the homeless mentally ill now find themselves back in the same place where they were confined years earlier, only under totally different circumstances. How might individuals react when they return to their former hospital residences under such circumstances? *pp. 454–457*

●─[CYBER**STUDY**]──────────────────>>>

SEARCH THE *ABNORMAL PSYCHOLOGY* CD-ROM FOR

▲ Chapter 15 Video Cases and Discussions
   Witness past hospital treatments for people with schizophrenia.
   Observe people before and after antipsychotic drug treatments.
   Is drug therapy sufficient?

▲ Chapter 15 Practical, Research, and Decision-Making Exercises
   Uncovering the attitudes of community residents
   Protecting the rights of people with severe mental disorders
   Diagnosing psychotic disorders

▲ Chapter 15 Practice Test and Feedback

LOG ON TO THE COMER WEB PAGE FOR

▲ Suggested Web links, exercises, FAQ page, additional Chapter 15 practice test questions
   <www.worthpublishers.com/comer>

──────────────────────────────<<<

CHAPTER **16**

Personality Disorders

TOPIC OVERVIEW section on left

While interviewing for the job of editor, Frederick said, "This may sound self-serving, but I am extraordinarily gifted. I am certain that I will do great things in this position, that I and the newspaper will soon set the standard for journalism in this city." The committee was impressed. Certainly, Frederick's credentials were strong, but even more important, his self-confidence and boldness had wowed them.

A year later, many of the same individuals were describing Frederick differently— arrogant, self-serving, cold, ego-maniacal, draining. He had performed well as editor (though not as spectacularly as he seemed to think), but that performance could not outweigh his impossible personality. Colleagues below and above him had grown weary of his manipulations, his emotional outbursts, his refusal ever to take the blame, his nonstop boasting, and his grandiose plans. Once again Frederick had outworn his welcome.

To be sure, Frederick had great charm, and he knew how to make others feel important, when it served his purpose. Thus he always had his share of friends and admirers. But in reality they were just passing through, until Frederick would tire of them or feel betrayed by their lack of enthusiasm for one of his self-serving interpretations or grand plans. Or until they simply could take Frederick no longer.

Bright and successful though he was, Frederick always felt entitled to more than he was receiving—to higher grades at school, greater compensation at work, more attention from girlfriends. If criticized even slightly, he reacted with fury, and was certain that the critic was jealous of his superior intelligence, skill, or looks. At first glance, Frederick seemed to have a lot going for him socially. Typically, he could be found in the midst of a deep, meaningful romantic relationship—one in which he might be tender, attentive, and seemingly devoted to his partner. But Frederick would always tire of his partner within a few weeks or months and would turn cold or even mean. Often he started affairs with other women while still involved with the current partner. The breakups—usually unpleasant and sometimes ugly— rarely brought sadness or remorse to him, and he would almost never think about his former partner again. He always had himself.

Each of us has a *personality*—a unique and enduring pattern of inner experience and outward behavior. We tend to react in our own predictable and consistent ways. These consistencies, often called *personality traits,* may be the result of inherited characteristics, learned responses, or a combination of the two. Yet our personalities are also flexible. We learn from experience. As we interact with our surroundings, we try out various responses to see which are more effective. This is a flexibility that people who suffer from a personality disorder usually do not have.

A **personality disorder** is an inflexible pattern of inner experience and outward behavior. The pattern is seen in most of the person's interactions, continues for years, and differs markedly from the experiences and behaviors usually expected of people (see Table 16-1 on the next page). Frederick seems to display such a disorder. For most of his life, his narcissism, grandiosity, outbursts, and insensitivity to others have been excessive and have dominated his functioning. The

•**PERSONALITY DISORDER**•A very rigid pattern of inner experience and outward behavior that differs from the expectations of one's culture and leads to dysfunctioning.

Table 16-1 DSM Checklist

PERSONALITY DISORDER

1. An enduring pattern of inner experience and behavior that deviates markedly from the expectations of the individual's culture, with at least two of the following areas affected: • cognition • affectivity • interpersonal functioning • impulse control.
2. Pattern is inflexible and pervasive across a broad range of personal and social situations.
3. Pattern is stable and long-lasting, and its onset can be traced back at least to adolescence or early adulthood.
4. Significant distress or impairment

Based on APA, 2000, 1994.

rigid traits of people with personality disorders often lead to psychological pain for the individual and social or occupational difficulties (Haslam et al., 2002) (see Box 16-1 on page 466). The disorders may also bring pain to others. Witness the upset and turmoil experienced by Frederick's co-workers and girlfriends.

Personality disorders typically become recognizable in adolescence or early adulthood, although some start during childhood (Kernberg & Wiener, 2004; APA, 2000). These are among the most difficult psychological disorders to treat. Many sufferers are not even aware of their personality problems and fail to trace their difficulties to their inflexible style of thinking and behaving. It has been estimated that between 9 and 13 percent of all adults may have a personality disorder (Phillips, Yen, & Gunderson, 2004).

As we saw in Chapter 4, DSM-IV-TR distinguishes Axis II disorders, disorders of long standing that usually begin well before adulthood and continue into adult life, from the Axis I disorders, more acute disorders that often begin as a noticeable change in a person's usual behavior and are, in many cases, of limited duration. The personality disorders are Axis II disorders; these patterns are not typically marked by changes in intensity or periods of clear improvement (Skodol et al., 2005).

It is common for a person with a personality disorder to also suffer from an acute (Axis I) disorder, a relationship called *comorbidity* (Brieger et al., 2003, 2002). Perhaps personality disorders predispose people to develop certain Axis I disorders. For example, people with avoidant personality disorder, who fearfully shy away from all relationships, may be prone to develop a social phobia. Or certain Axis I disorders may set the stage for a personality disorder. Or perhaps some biological factor creates a predisposition to both (Koenigsberg, Woo-Ming, & Siever, 2002, 1999). Whatever the reason for the relationship, research indicates that the presence of a personality disorder complicates a person's chances for a successful recovery from psychological problems (Skodol et al., 2005; Tyrer & Simmonds, 2003).

DSM-IV-TR identifies 10 personality disorders and separates them into three groups, called *clusters* (APA, 2000, 1994). One cluster, marked by odd or eccentric behavior, consists of the *paranoid, schizoid,* and *schizotypal* personality disorders. A second group features dramatic behavior and consists of the *antisocial, borderline, histrionic,* and *narcissistic* personality disorders. The final cluster features a high degree of anxiety and includes the *avoidant, dependent,* and *obsessive-compulsive* personality disorders.

The personality disorders listed in DSM IV-TR overlap so much that it can be difficult to distinguish one from the other (Gunderson & Ronningstam, 2001) (see Figure 16-1). In fact, diagnosticians sometimes determine that particular individuals have more than one such personality disorder (Grilo et al., 2002). In addition, clinicians often disagree as to the correct diagnosis for people with a DSM-IV-TR personality disorder. This lack of agreement has raised serious questions about the *validity* (accuracy) and *reliability* (consistency) of the present DSM categories. In fact, as we shall see later in the chapter, there is a growing movement in the clinical field to eliminate the current categories and adopt instead an alternative—"dimensional"—way of thinking about and classifying disorders of personality. Before considering this alternative approach, however, let us examine DSM-IV-TR's 10 current categories. Two of these categories—*antisocial* and *borderline* personality disorders—will receive particular attention inasmuch as they have received much more attention than the other personality disorders by clinicians, research, and the public.

Early notions of personality *Scientists have long suspected that biological factors help account for personality and personality disorders. In the theory of phrenology, Franz Joseph Gall (1758-1828) held that the brain consists of distinct portions, each responsible for some aspect of personality. Phrenologists tried to assess personality by feeling bumps and indentations on a person's head.*

FIGURE **16-1 Prominent and central features of DSM-IV-TR's 10 personality disorders** *The symptoms of the various disorders often overlap greatly, leading to frequent misdiagnosis or to multiple diagnoses for a given client.*

As we begin our examination of the DSM-IV-TR personality disorders, it is important to note that diagnoses of such disorders can easily be overdone. We may catch glimpses of ourselves or of people we know in the descriptions of these disorders, and we may be tempted to conclude that we or they have a personality disorder. In the vast majority of instances, such interpretations are incorrect. We all display personality traits. Only occasionally are they so inflexible, maladaptive, and distressful that they can be considered disorders.

"Odd" Personality Disorders

The cluster of *"odd" personality disorders* consists of the *paranoid, schizoid,* and *schizotypal* personality disorders. People with these disorders typically display odd or eccentric behaviors that are similar to but not as extensive as those seen in schizophrenia, including extreme suspiciousness, social withdrawal, and peculiar ways of thinking and perceiving things. Such behaviors often leave the person isolated. Some clinicians believe that these personality disorders are actually related to schizophrenia, and they call them *schizophrenia-spectrum disorders.* In support of this idea, people with these personality disorders often qualify for an additional diagnosis of schizophrenia or have close relatives with schizophrenia (Keown, Holloway, & Kuipers, 2002; APA, 2000).

•PARANOID PERSONALITY DISORDER•
A personality disorder marked by a pattern of distrust and suspiciousness of others.

"I like the way I look, but I hate my personality."

Clinicians have learned much about the symptoms of the odd personality disorders but have not been so successful in determining their causes or how to treat them. In fact, people with these disorders rarely seek treatment (Fabrega et al., 1991).

Paranoid Personality Disorder

People with **paranoid personality disorder** deeply distrust other people and are suspicious of their motives (APA, 2000, 1994). Because they believe that everyone intends them harm, they shun close relationships. Their trust in their own ideas and abilities can be excessive, though, as we see in the case of Charles:

Charles, an only child of poorly educated parents, had been recognized as a "child genius" in early school years. He received a Ph.D. degree at 24, and subsequently held several responsible positions as a research physicist in an industrial firm.

His haughty arrogance and narcissism often resulted in conflicts with his superiors; it was felt that he spent too much time working on his own "harebrained" schemes and not enough on company projects. Charles . . . began to feel that both his superiors and his subordinates were "making fun of him" and not taking him seriously. To remedy this attack upon his status, Charles began to work on a scheme that would "revolutionize the industry," a new thermodynamic principle which, when applied to his company's major product, would prove extremely efficient and economical. After several months . . . he presented his plans to the company president. Brilliant though it was, the plan overlooked certain obvious simple facts of logic and economy.

Upon learning of its rejection, Charles withdrew to his home where he became obsessed with "new ideas," proposing them in intricate schematics and formulas to a number of government officials and industrialists. These resulted in new rebuffs which led to further efforts at self inflation.

(Millon, 1969, pp. 329–330)

Ever on guard and cautious, and seeing threats everywhere, people like Charles continually expect to be the targets of some trickery (see Figure 16-2). They find "hidden" meanings in everything, which are usually belittling or threatening. In a study that required individuals to role-play, subjects with paranoia were more likely than control

>>LOOKING AROUND
Distrusting Souls

According to surveys, the people who tend to be the most distrustful in the United States are those who were repeatedly warned by their parents against trusting strangers. Other characteristics: they are under 30 years of age; are socially isolated; live in the city; live in poor or crime-ridden neighborhoods; and report having no religious affiliation (Pew Research Center, 1997). **<<**

subjects to read hostile intentions into the actions of others. In addition, they more often chose anger as the appropriate role-play response (Turkat et al., 1990).

Quick to challenge the loyalty or trustworthiness of acquaintances, people with paranoid personality disorder remain cold and distant. A woman might avoid confiding in anyone, for example, for fear of being hurt; or a husband might, without any justification, persist in questioning his wife's faithfulness. Although inaccurate and inappropriate, their suspicions are not usually *delusional;* the ideas are not so bizarre or so firmly held as to clearly remove the individuals from reality (Fenigstein, 1996).

People with this disorder are critical of weakness and fault in others, particularly at work. They are unable to recognize their own mistakes, however, and are extremely sensitive to criticism. They often blame others for the things that go wrong in their lives, and they repeatedly bear grudges (Agronin, 2006; Fenigstein, 1996). Between 0.5 and 3 percent of adults are believed to experience this disorder, apparently more men than women (Mattia & Zimmerman, 2001; APA, 2000, 1994).

How Do Theorists Explain Paranoid Personality Disorder?
The proposed explanations of paranoid personality disorder, like those of most other personality disorders, have received little systematic research. Psychodynamic theories, the oldest of the explanations for this disorder, trace the pattern to early interactions with demanding parents, particularly distant, rigid fathers and overcontrolling, rejecting mothers (Kernberg & Caligor, 2005; Sperry, 2003). (We shall see that psychodynamic explanations for almost all the personality disorders begin the same way—with repeated mistreatment during childhood and lack of love.) According to one psychodynamic view, some individuals come to view their environment as hostile as a result of their parents' persistently unreasonable demands. They must always be on the alert because they cannot trust others, and they are likely to develop feelings of extreme anger (Cameron, 1974). They also project these feelings onto others and, as a result, feel increasingly persecuted (Garfield & Havens, 1991). Similarly, some cognitive theorists suggest that people with paranoid personality disorder generally hold broad maladaptive assumptions such as "People are evil" and "People will attack you if given the chance" (Beck et al., 2004, 2001).

Biological theorists propose that paranoid personality disorder has genetic causes (Jang & Vernon, 2001). A study that looked at self-reports of suspiciousness in 3,810 Australian twin pairs found that if one twin was excessively suspicious, the other had an increased likelihood of also being suspicious (Kendler et al., 1987). Once again, however, it is important to note that such similarities between twins might also be the result of common environmental experiences.

Treatments for Paranoid Personality Disorder
People with paranoid personality disorder do not typically see themselves as needing help, and few come to treatment willingly (Millon, 1999). Furthermore, many who are in treatment view the role of patient as inferior and distrust and rebel against their therapists (Bender, 2005). Thus it is not surprising that therapy for this disorder, as for most other personality disorders, has limited effect and moves very slowly (Piper & Joyce, 2001).

Object relations therapists, the psychodynamic therapists who give center stage to relationships, try to see past the patient's anger and work on what they view as his or her deep wish for a satisfying relationship (Auchincloss & Weiss, 1992). Behavioral and cognitive therapists, for their part, try to help these individuals control their anxiety and improve their skills at solving interpersonal problems (Farmer & Nelson-Gray, 2005). Cognitive therapists also try to guide the clients to develop more realistic interpretations of other people's words and actions and to become more aware of other people's points of view (Leahy, Beck, & Beck, 2005; Beck et al., 2004). Drug therapy is of limited help (Agronin, 2006; Koenigsberg et al., 2002).

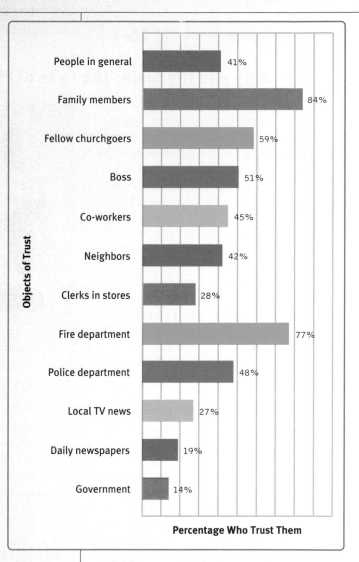

FIGURE 16-2 Whom do you trust? *Although distrust and suspiciousness are the hallmarks of paranoid personality disorder, even persons without this disorder are surprisingly untrusting. In a recent survey of a broad sample of society, only 41 percent of respondents said that they generally trust people. Most do trust their family members and local fire department; however, few trust clerks in stores, daily newspapers, or the government. (Adapted from Pew Research Center for the People and the Press, 1997.)*

[BOX 16-1]

Personality and the Brain: The Case of Phineas Gage

Most people are aware that damage to particular regions in the brain can cause motor dysfunction, memory or language problems, or even the loss of particular senses such as vision or hearing. However, clinical scientists have come to appreciate that damage to the brain from strokes, injury, or tumors can also bring about major changes in personality. The tragic story of Phineas Gage provided science with history's most memorable evidence of this fact.

In mid-September 1848, 25-year-old Gage was laying tracks for a railroad, a hazardous but common occupation in those years. The smart, careful, and friendly Gage was admired and liked by the men he supervised, and the company that wrote the paychecks called him "the most efficient and capable" employee they had. But that was all to change in a few seconds' time, when a rock-blasting mishap hurled a three-foot-long tamping iron under Gage's left cheek and straight through the top of his skull, piercing a one-and-a-half-inch hole through his brain's frontal lobes (Damasio, 1994).

Miraculously, Gage's body survived. But you could say that Gage himself, at least as others had known him, did not. From an even-tempered, responsible, and likable young man, Gage turned "fitful, irreverent, indulging at times in the grossest profanity which was not previously his custom, manifesting but little deference for his fellows, impatient of restraint or advice when it conflicts with his desires, at times pertinaciously obstinate, yet capricious and vacillating, devising many plans of future operation which are no sooner arranged than they are abandoned" (Harlow, 1868, as cited in Damasio, 1994). Beyond being blind in one eye, Gage suffered no lasting physical or mental defects. He remained nimble, alert, and able to speak and think. The wound in his head laid waste to his personality alone.

After the accident, Gage could not keep his job, as he no longer had the motivation to perform up to expectations. His newly unpleasant behavior drove friends away and destroyed the possibility of finding a

An 1850s artist offered these drawings of the injury suffered by Phineas Gage when a three-foot tamping iron penetrated his brain. Although the holes in Gage's head eventually healed, his previous personality did not survive.

AP Photo/Courtesy of Harvard Medical School

romantic partner with whom to share his life. Gage moved from job to job, including a stint in a circus sideshow in New York. This once-promising and ambitious young man eventually ended up a penniless ward of his mother and sister. He died of a brain seizure at the age of 38 (Damasio, 1994).

What, exactly, was the critical injury suffered by Gage? *Why* did his personality change so profoundly? In his book *Descartes' Error* (1994), the neuroscientist Antonio Damasio speculates that the destruction of Gage's temporal lobe resulted in his inability to experience appropriate emotion. Imagine being unable to experience shame at saying rude things to your host at a dinner, or anger at being duped by a con man who invests your money in a speculative venture, or fear at walking through a dangerous area of town at midnight. Imagine being unable to feel affection for a spouse or child or pleasure at engaging in one activity versus another. All of these failures of emotion would leave you socially helpless, indecisive, and unable to behave consistently in ways designed to further your own interests. You would be, in any sense of the word, perfectly unreasonable. In short, you might be much like Phineas Gage.

Gage was far from the last person to lose this critical faculty. Damasio (1994)

documents a number of such patients who display startling results in tests of their emotional capacities. When shown emotion-arousing pictures that raise the galvanic skin responses (GSR) of most people, frontally damaged patients register no GSR reaction at all. When performing "gambling" tasks in certain studies, control subjects adopt low-risk strategies, while frontally damaged patients engage in high-risk and bankrupting tactics. Most telling, when gamblers in such studies are hooked to a polygraph, the GSRs of control subjects increase (signaling increasing dread and nervousness) throughout the task, while those of patients remain constant.

If the ability to *feel* appropriately has such a profound impact on a person's personality and successes, then we shouldn't be surprised to hear that scientists in the relatively new and sometimes controversial field of *evolutionary psychology* have argued persuasively that emotions are adaptive, indeed critical, to an organism's survival. This goes even for those darker emotions we normally view as counterproductive, such as jealousy (Buss, 2000) and vengefulness (Cosmides & Tooby, 2000). Such emotions, although unpleasant, may help us to navigate dangers and respond to social threats that a completely dispassionate, cool-headed person might miss.

Schizoid Personality Disorder

People with **schizoid personality disorder** persistently avoid and are removed from social relationships and demonstrate little in the way of emotion (APA, 2000, 1994). Like people with paranoid personality disorder, these individuals do not have close ties with other people. The reason they avoid social contact, however, has nothing to do with paranoid feelings of distrust or suspicion—it is that they genuinely prefer to be alone. Take Roy:

> Roy was a successful sanitation engineer involved in the planning and maintenance of water resources for a large city; his job called for considerable foresight and independent judgment but little supervisory responsibility. In general, he was appraised as an undistinguished but competent and reliable employee. There were few demands of an interpersonal nature made of him, and he was viewed by most of his colleagues as reticent and shy and by others as cold and aloof.
>
> Difficulties centered about his relationship with his wife. At her urging they sought marital counseling for, as she put it, "he is unwilling to join in family activities, he fails to take an interest in the children, he lacks affection and is disinterested in sex."
>
> The pattern of social indifference, flatness of affect and personal isolation which characterized much of Roy's behavior was of little consequence to those with whom a deeper or more intimate relationship was not called for; with his immediate family, however, these traits took their toll.
>
> *(Millon, 1969, p. 224)*

People like Roy, often described as "loners," make no effort to start or keep friendships, take little interest in having sexual relationships, and even seem indifferent to their families. They seek out jobs that require little or no contact with others. When necessary, they can form work relations to a degree, but they prefer to keep to themselves. Many live by themselves as well. Not surprisingly, their social skills tend to be weak. If they marry, their lack of interest in intimacy may create marital or family problems, as it did for Roy.

People with schizoid personality disorder focus mainly on themselves and are generally unaffected by praise or criticism. They rarely show any feelings, expressing neither joy nor anger. They seem to have no need for attention or acceptance; are typically viewed as cold, humorless, or dull; and generally succeed in being ignored. This disorder is estimated to be present in fewer than 1 percent of the population (Mattia & Zimmerman, 2001). It is slightly more likely to occur in men than in women, and men may also be more impaired by it (APA, 2000).

How Do Theorists Explain Schizoid Personality Disorder? Many psychodynamic theorists, particularly object relations theorists, propose that schizoid personality disorder has its roots in an unsatisfied need for human contact (Kernberg & Caligor, 2005; Carstairs, 1992; Horner, 1991, 1975). The parents of people with this disorder, like those of people with paranoid personality disorder, are believed to have been unaccepting or even abusive of their children. Whereas individuals with paranoid symptoms react to such parenting chiefly with distrust, those with schizoid personality disorder are left unable to give or receive love. They cope by avoiding all relationships (Sperry, 2003).

Cognitive theorists propose, not surprisingly, that people with schizoid personality disorder suffer from deficiencies in their thinking. Their thoughts tend to be vague and empty, and they have trouble scanning the environment to arrive at accurate perceptions (Beck & Freeman, 1990). Unable to pick up emotional cues from others, they simply cannot respond to emotions. As this theory might predict, children with schizoid personality disorder develop language and motor skills very slowly, whatever their level of intelligence (Wolff, 1991).

Alone, either way *Different DSM-IV-TR personality disorders often yield similar behaviors. People with either schizoid or avoidant personality disorder spend much of their time alone. The former, however, truly want to be alone, whereas the latter yearn for but fear social relationships.*

•SCHIZOTYPAL PERSONALITY DISORDER•
A personality disorder characterized by extreme discomfort in close relationships, odd forms of thinking and perceiving, and behavioral eccentricities.

TREATMENTS FOR SCHIZOID PERSONALITY DISORDER Their social withdrawal prevents most people with schizoid personality disorder from entering therapy unless some other disorder, such as alcoholism, makes treatment necessary. These clients are likely to remain emotionally distant from the therapist, seem not to care about their treatment, and make limited progress at best (Millon, 1999; Quality Assurance Project, 1990).

Cognitive therapists have sometimes been able to help people with this disorder experience more positive emotions and more satisfying social interactions (Leahy et al., 2005; Beck et al., 2004). Their techniques include presenting clients with lists of emotions to think about or having them write down and remember pleasurable experiences. Behavioral therapists have sometimes had success teaching social skills to such clients, using role playing, exposure techniques, and homework assignments as tools (Farmer & Nelson-Gray, 2005; Piper & Joyce, 2001). Group therapy is apparently useful when it offers a safe setting for social contact, although people with this disorder may resist any pressure to take part (Piper & Joyce, 2001). As with paranoid personality disorder, drug therapy has offered limited help (Koenigsberg et al., 2002).

Schizotypal Personality Disorder

People with **schizotypal personality disorder** display a range of interpersonal problems marked by extreme discomfort in close relationships, very odd patterns of thinking and perceiving, and behavioral eccentricities (APA, 2000, 1994). Anxious around others, they seek isolation and have few close friends. Many feel intensely lonely. The disorder is more severe than the paranoid and schizoid personality disorders, as we see in the case of Harold:

Harold was the fourth of seven children. . . . "Duckie," as Harold was known, had always been a withdrawn, frightened and "stupid" youngster. The nickname "Duckie" represented a peculiar waddle in his walk; it was used by others as a term of derogation and ridicule. Harold rarely played with his sibs or neighborhood children; he was teased unmercifully because of his "walk" and his fear of pranksters. Harold was a favorite neighborhood scapegoat; he was intimidated even by the most innocuous glance in his direction. . . .

Harold's family was surprised when he performed well in the first few years of schooling. He began to falter, however, upon entrance to junior high school. At about the age of 14, his schoolwork became extremely poor, he refused to go to classes and he complained of a variety of vague, physical pains. By age 15 he had totally withdrawn from school, remaining home in the basement room that he shared with two younger brothers. Everyone in his family began to speak of him as "being touched." He thought about "funny religious things that didn't make sense"; he also began to draw "strange things" and talk to himself. When he was 16, he once ran out of the house screaming "I'm gone, I'm gone, I'm gone . . . ," saying that his "body went to heaven" and that he had to run outside to recover it; rather interestingly, this event occurred shortly after his father had been committed by the courts to a state mental hospital. By age 17, Harold was ruminating all day, often talking aloud in a meaningless jargon; he refused to come to the family table for meals.

(Millon, 1969, pp. 347–348)

As with Harold, the thoughts and behaviors of people with schizotypal personality disorder can be noticeably disturbed. These symptoms may include *ideas of reference*— beliefs that unrelated events pertain to them in some important way—and *bodily illusions,* such as sensing an external "force" or presence. A number of people with this disorder see themselves as having special extrasensory abilities, and some believe that they have magical control over others. Examples of schizotypal eccentricities include repeatedly arranging cans to align their labels, organizing closets extensively, or wearing an odd assortment of clothing. The emotions of these individuals may be inappropriate, flat, or humorless.

>>LOOKING AROUND
A Common Belief

People who think that they have extrasensory abilities are not necessarily suffering from schizotypal personality disorder. In fact, according to one large survey, half of all people believe in ESP (Kanner, 1995). **<<**

People with schizotypal personality disorder often have great difficulty keeping their attention focused (Lenzenwerger et al., 1991). Correspondingly, their conversation is typically digressive and vague, even sprinkled with loose associations (Caplan et al., 1990). They tend to drift aimlessly and lead an idle, unproductive life (Skodol et al., 2002). They are likely to choose undemanding jobs in which they can work below their capacity and are not required to interact with other people. It has been estimated that 2 to 4 percent of all people—slightly more males than females—may have a schizotypal personality disorder (Mattia & Zimmerman, 2001; APA, 2000).

HOW DO THEORISTS EXPLAIN SCHIZOTYPAL PERSONALITY DISORDER?
Because the symptoms of schizotypal personality disorder so often resemble those of schizophrenia, researchers have hypothesized that similar factors are at work in both disorders (Koenigsberg et al., 2005; Raine et al., 1997). They have in fact found that schizotypal symptoms, like schizophrenic patterns, are often linked to family conflicts and to psychological disorders in parents (Asarnow et al., 1991). They have also learned that defects in attention and short-term memory may contribute to schizotypal personality disorder, just as they apparently do to schizophrenia (Koenigsberg et al., 2005; Roitman et al., 2000, 1997). For example, subjects with either disorder perform poorly on *backward masking,* a laboratory test of attention that requires subjects to identify a visual stimulus immediately after a previous stimulus has flashed on and off the screen. People with these disorders have a hard time shutting out the first stimulus in order to focus on the second. Finally, researchers have begun to link schizotypal personality disorder to some of the same biological factors found in schizophrenia, such as high activity of the neurotransmitter dopamine, enlarged brain ventricles, smaller temporal lobes, and loss of gray matter (Cocarro, 2001; Downhill et al., 2001). As we saw in Chapter 14, there are indications that these biological factors may have a genetic base.

Although these findings do suggest a close relationship between schizotypal personality disorder and schizophrenia, the personality disorder has also been linked to mood disorders. Relatives of people with depression have a higher than usual rate of schizotypal personality disorder, and vice versa. Thus, at the very least, this personality disorder is not tied exclusively to schizophrenia (Schulz et al., 1986).

TREATMENTS FOR SCHIZOTYPAL PERSONALITY DISORDER
Therapy is as difficult in cases of schizotypal personality disorder as it is in cases of paranoid and schizoid personality disorders. Most therapists agree on the need to help these clients "reconnect" with the world and recognize the limits of their thinking and their powers. The therapists may thus try to set clear limits—for example, by requiring punctuality—and work on helping the clients recognize where their views end and those of the therapist begin (Stone, 1989). Other therapy goals are to increase positive social contacts, ease loneliness, reduce overstimulation, and help the individuals become more aware of their personal feelings (Sperry, 2003; Piper & Joyce, 2001).

Cognitive therapists further try to teach clients to evaluate their unusual thoughts or perceptions objectively and to ignore the inappropriate ones (Leahy et al., 2005; Beck et al., 2004). A therapist may keep track of a person's odd or magical predictions, for example, and later point out their inaccuracy. When a client is speaking and begins to digress, the therapist might ask the individual to sum up what he or she is trying to say. On occasion, specific behavioral methods, such as speech lessons, social skills training, and tips on appropriate dress and manners, have helped clients learn to blend in better and be more comfortable around others (Farmer & Nelson-Gray, 2005; Liebowitz et al., 1986).

Antipsychotic drugs have been given to people with schizotypal personality disorder, again because of the disorder's similarity to schizophrenia (Markovitz, 2001). In low doses the drugs appear to have helped some people, usually by reducing certain of their thought problems (Koenigsberg et al., 2002; Coccaro, 2001).

The Kobal Collection

Taxi Driver *Some of film's most memorable characters have displayed personality disorders. Travis Bickle, of* Taxi Driver *fame, seemed to manifest the symptoms of schizotypal personality disorder, including social discomfort and a reduced capacity for interpersonal relationships. He also displayed self-referential interpretations of various events, cognitive distortions, a highly suspicious nature, grandiosity, emotional flatness, and temporary psychotic episodes.*

"Dramatic" Personality Disorders

The cluster of *"dramatic" personality disorders* includes the *antisocial, borderline, histrionic,* and *narcissistic* personality disorders. The behaviors of people with these problems are so dramatic, emotional, or erratic that it is almost impossible for them to have relationships that are truly giving and satisfying.

These personality disorders are more commonly diagnosed than the others. However, only the antisocial and borderline personality disorders have received much study, partly because they create so many problems for other people. The causes of the disorders, like those of the odd personality disorders, are not well understood. Treatments range from ineffective to moderately effective.

Antisocial Personality Disorder

Sometimes described as "psychopaths" or "sociopaths," people with **antisocial personality disorder** persistently disregard and violate others' rights (APA, 2000, 1994). Aside from substance-related disorders, this is the disorder most closely linked to adult criminal behavior (see Box 16-2 on page 472). DSM-IV-TR stipulates that a person must be at least 18 years of age to receive this diagnosis; however, most people with antisocial personality disorder displayed some patterns of misbehavior before they were 15, including truancy, running away, cruelty to animals or people, and destroying property.

Robert Hare (1993), a leading researcher of antisocial personality disorder, recalls an early professional encounter with a prison inmate named Ray:

In the early 1960s, I found myself employed as the sole psychologist at the British Columbia Penitentiary. . . . I wasn't in my office for more than an hour when my first "client" arrived. He was a tall, slim, dark-haired man in his thirties. The air around him seemed to buzz, and the eye contact he made with me was so direct and intense that I wondered if I had ever really looked anybody in the eye before. That stare was unrelenting—he didn't indulge in the brief glances away that most people use to soften the force of their gaze.

Without waiting for an introduction, the inmate—I'll call him Ray—opened the conversation: "Hey, Doc, how's it going? Look, I've got a problem. I need your help. I'd really like to talk to you about this."

Eager to begin work as a genuine psychotherapist, I asked him to tell me about it. In response, he pulled out a knife and waved it in front of my nose, all the while smiling and maintaining that intense eye contact.

Once he determined that I wasn't going to push the button, he explained that he intended to use the knife not on me but on another inmate who had been making overtures to his "protégé," a prison term for the more passive member of a homosexual pairing. Just why he was telling me this was not immediately clear, but I soon suspected that he was checking me out, trying to determine what sort of a prison employee I was. Following our session, in which he described his "problem" not once or twice but many times, I kept quiet about the knife. To my relief, he didn't stab the other inmate, but it soon became evident that Ray had caught me in his trap: I had shown myself to be a soft touch who would overlook clear violations of fundamental prison rules in order to develop "professional" rapport with the inmates.

From that first meeting on, Ray managed to make my eight-month stint at the prison miserable. His constant demands on my time and his attempts to manipulate me into doing things for him were unending. On one occasion, he convinced me that he would make a good cook . . . and I supported his request for a transfer from the machine shop (where he had apparently made the knife). What I didn't consider was that the kitchen was a source of sugar, potatoes, fruit, and other ingredients that could be turned into alcohol. Several months after I had recommended the transfer, there was a mighty eruption below the floorboards directly under the warden's table. When the commotion died down, we found an elaborate system for distilling alcohol below the floor. Something had gone wrong and one of the pots had exploded. There was nothing unusual about the presence of a still in a maximum-security prison, but the audacity of placing one under the warden's seat shook up a lot of people. When it was discovered that Ray was the brains behind the bootleg operation, he spent some time in solitary confinement.

Once out of "the hole," Ray appeared in my office as if nothing had happened and asked for a transfer from the kitchen to the auto shop—he really felt he had a knack, he saw the need to prepare himself for the outside world, if he only had the time to practice he could have his own body shop on the outside. . . . I was still feeling the sting of having arranged the first transfer, but eventually he wore me down.

Soon afterward I decided to leave the prison to pursue a Ph.D. in psychology, and about a month before I left Ray almost persuaded me to ask my father, a roofing contractor, to offer him a job as part of an application for parole.

Ray had an incredible ability to con not just me but everybody. He could talk, and lie, with a smoothness and a directness that sometimes momentarily disarmed even the most experienced and cynical of the prison staff. When I met him he had a long criminal record behind him (and, as it turned out, ahead of him); about half his adult life had been spent in prison, and many of his crimes had been violent. . . . He lied endlessly, lazily, about everything, and it disturbed him not a whit whenever I pointed out something in his file that contradicted one of his lies. He would simply change the subject and spin off in a different direction. Finally convinced that he might not make the perfect job candidate in my father's firm, I turned down Ray's request—and was shaken by his nastiness at my refusal.

Before I left the prison for the university, I took advantage of the prison policy of letting staff have their cars repaired in the institution's auto shop—where Ray still worked, thanks (he would have said no thanks) to me. The car received a beautiful paint job and the motor and drivetrain were reconditioned.

With all our possessions on top of the car and our baby in a plywood bed in the backseat, my wife and I headed for Ontario. The first problems appeared soon after we left Vancouver, when the motor seemed a bit rough. Later, when we encountered some moderate inclines, the radiator boiled over. A garage mechanic discovered ball bearings in the carburetor's float chamber; he also pointed out where one of the hoses to the radiator had clearly been tampered with. These problems were repaired easily enough, but the next one, which arose while we were going down a long hill, was more serious. The brake pedal became very spongy and then simply dropped to the floor—no brakes, and it was a long hill. Fortunately, we made it to a service station, where we found that the brake line had been cut so that a slow leak would occur. Perhaps it was a coincidence that Ray was working in the auto shop when the car was being tuned up, but I had no doubt that the prison "telegraph" had informed him of the owner of the car.

(Hare, 1993)

Like Ray, people with antisocial personality disorder lie repeatedly (Seto et al., 1997). Many cannot work consistently at a job; they are absent frequently and are likely to quit their jobs altogether. Usually they are also careless with money and frequently fail to pay their debts. They are often impulsive, taking action without thinking of the consequences (Blair, Mitchell, & Blair, 2005). Correspondingly, they may be irritable, aggressive, and quick to start fights. Many travel from place to place.

Recklessness is another common trait: people with antisocial personality disorder have little regard for their own safety or for that of others, even their children. They are self-centered as well, and likely to have trouble maintaining close relationships (Birchnell, 1996). Usually they develop a knack for gaining personal profit at the expense of other people. Because the pain or damage they cause seldom concerns them, clinicians

[BOX **16-2**]

When Life Imitates Art

Oliver Stone's 1994 movie *Natural Born Killers* tells the tale of two sociopathic thrill seekers, Mickey and Mallory, who grow world-famous as they travel the countryside committing brutal murders. Stone meant to satirize our culture's appetite for violence, but the film itself inspired more copycat killings than any other movie ever made (Shnayerson, 1996). Numerous young people went on similar killing sprees, citing *Natural Born Killers* as their inspiration.

The copycat phenomenon is not new (Bushman & Anderson, 2001). When Stanley Kubrick's film *A Clockwork Orange* was released in 1971, critics praised its powerful social statement. But when some British youths copied the actions of the

W.B. Productions Ltd/Photofest

movie's gang leader and raped a woman to the tune of "Singin' in the Rain," Kubrick had the film banned in Britain (Shnayerson, 1996).

Must individuals already be antisocial in order to be influenced by films such as these, or do the films confuse people who are not antisocial by glorifying criminal and violent behavior? Should filmmakers and writers consider the possible psychological influence of their work on suggestible individuals before they undertake such projects? These are but a few of the important questions that are raised by the copycat phenomenon. Clinical, legal, and political figures have readily offered answers to such questions, but in fact the phenomenon is far from being understood.

commonly say that they lack a moral conscience. They think of their victims as weak and deserving of being conned or robbed.

Surveys indicate that up to 3.5 percent of people in the United States meet the criteria for antisocial personality disorder (Sperry, 2003; Mattia & Zimmerman, 2001). White Americans are somewhat more likely than African Americans to receive the diagnosis (Robins et al., 1991), and the disorder is as much as four times more common among men than women (Anderson et al., 2001; Kessler & Zhao, 1999).

Because people with this disorder are often arrested, researchers frequently look for people with antisocial patterns in prison populations (Blair et al., 2005; Fazel & Danesh, 2002). Among men in urban jails, the antisocial personality pattern has been strongly linked to past arrests for crimes of violence (Abram & Teplin, 1990). For many people with this disorder, criminal behavior declines after the age of 40; some, however, continue their criminal activities throughout their lives (Hurt & Oltmanns, 2002).

Studies and clinical observations also indicate higher rates of alcoholism and other substance-related disorders among people with antisocial personality disorder than in the rest of the population (Westermeyer & Thuras, 2005; Myers, Stewart, & Brown, 1998). Perhaps intoxication and substance abuse help trigger the development of antisocial personality disorder by loosening a person's inhibitions. Perhaps this personality disorder somehow makes a person more prone to abuse substances. Or perhaps antisocial personality disorder and substance abuse both have the same cause, such as a deepseated need to take risks. Interestingly, drug users with the personality disorder often cite the recreational aspects of drug use as their reason for starting and continuing it (Mirin & Weiss, 1991).

Finally, children with conduct disorder and an accompanying attention-deficit hyperactivity disorder may have a heightened risk of developing antisocial personality disorder (Lahey et al., 2005; Hill, 2003; APA, 2000, 1994). These two childhood disorders, which we shall examine in Chapter 17, often bear similarities to antisocial personality disorder. Like adults with antisocial personality disorder, children with a conduct disorder persistently lie and violate rules and other people's rights; and children with attention-deficit hyperactivity disorder lack foresight and judgment and fail to learn from experience.

≫LOOKING BACK
Previous Identity

Antisocial personality disorder was referred to as "moral insanity" during the nineteenth century. ≪

Intriguing as these observations may be, however, the precise connection between the childhood disorders and the personality disorder has been difficult to pinpoint.

HOW DO THEORISTS EXPLAIN ANTISOCIAL PERSONALITY DISORDER?

Explanations of antisocial personality disorder come from the psychodynamic, behavioral, cognitive, and biological models. As with many other personality disorders, psychodynamic theorists propose that this one, too, begins with an absence of parental love during infancy, leading to a lack of basic trust (Sperry, 2003). In this view, some children—the ones who develop antisocial personality disorder—respond to the early inadequacies by becoming emotionally distant, and they bond with others through the use of power and destructiveness. In support of the psychodynamic explanation, researchers have found that people with this disorder are more likely than others to have had significant stress in their childhoods, particularly in such forms as family poverty, family violence, and parental conflict or divorce (Martens, 2005; Paris, 2001).

Many behavioral theorists have suggested that antisocial symptoms may be learned through *modeling,* or imitation. As evidence, they point to the higher rate of antisocial personality disorder found among the parents of people with this disorder (Paris, 2001). Other behaviorists have suggested that some parents unintentionally teach antisocial behavior by regularly rewarding a child's aggressive behavior (Capaldi & Patterson, 1994; Patterson, 1986, 1982). When the child misbehaves or becomes violent in reaction to the parents' requests or orders, for example, the parents may give in to restore peace. Without meaning to, they may be teaching the child to be stubborn and perhaps even violent.

The cognitive view says that people with antisocial personality disorder hold attitudes that trivialize the importance of other people's needs (Levenson, 1992). Such a philosophy of life, some theorists suggest, may be far more common in our society than people recognize (see Figure 16-3). Cognitive theorists further propose that people with this disorder have genuine difficulty recognizing a point of view other than their own.

Finally, studies suggest that biological factors may play an important role in antisocial personality disorder. Research reveals that people with this disorder often experience less anxiety than other people, and so may lack a key ingredient for learning (Blair et al., 2005; Zuckerman, 1996). This would help explain why they have so much trouble learning from negative life experiences or tuning in to the emotional cues of others. Several studies have found that subjects with antisocial personality disorder are less

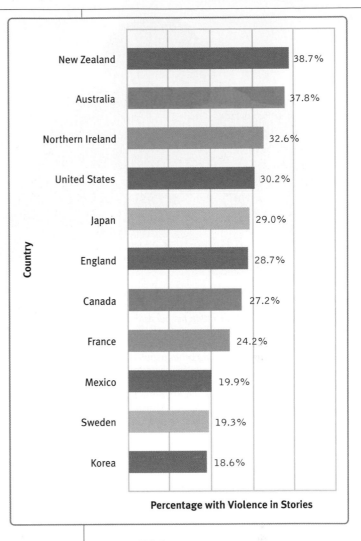

Percentage with Violence in Stories

FIGURE **16-3** **Are some cultures more antisocial than others?** *In a cross-cultural study, teenagers were asked to write stories describing how imaginary characters would respond to various conflicts. About one-third of the respondents from New Zealand, Australia, Northern Ireland, and the United States described violent responses, compared to less than one-fifth of the subjects from Korea, Sweden, and Mexico. (Adapted from Archer & McDaniel, 1995.)*

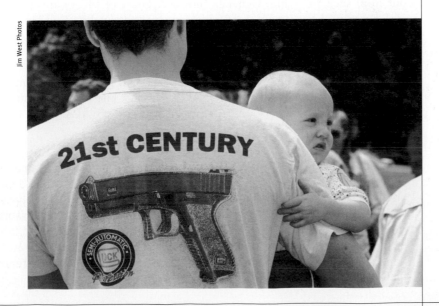

Negative models *Behavioral theorists claim that aggressive and other antisocial behaviors may be learned through modeling, or imitation—a learning process that can begin very early in life. The heightened rate of such behaviors found among the parents of people with antisocial personality disorder is consistent with this claim.*

Mixed verdict *Crime boss Tony Soprano of the popular television series* The Sopranos *displays many symptoms of sociopathy, including his persistent disregard for and violation of others' rights, incessant lying, self-centeredness, and lack of conscience after cheating, robbing, or even killing other people. Nevertheless, clinicians point out that this character also possesses several qualities uncharacteristic of the personality disorder, such as genuine concern for and close personal relationships with his children and friends, bouts of overwhelming anxiety, and a capacity to persevere in and profit from long-term therapy.*

•**BORDERLINE PERSONALITY DISORDER**•
A personality disorder characterized by repeated instability in interpersonal relationships, self-image, and mood and by impulsive behavior.

able than control subjects to learn laboratory tasks, such as finding their way out of a maze, when the key reinforcements are punishments such as shock or loss of money (Lykken, 1995, 1957; Newman et al., 1992, 1987). When experimenters make the punishments very apparent or force subjects to pay attention to them, learning improves; left to their own devices, however, subjects with this disorder are not influenced much by punishments. Perhaps they simply do not react as anxiously as other people to negative events.

Why should people with antisocial personality disorder experience less anxiety than other people? The answer may lie in the biological realm (Kumari et al., 2005; Retz et al., 2004). Subjects with the disorder often respond to warnings or expectations of stress with low brain and bodily arousal, such as slow autonomic arousal and slow EEG waves (Lindberg et al., 2005; Dinn & Harris, 2000; Patrick et al., 1993, 1990). Perhaps because of the low arousal, the individuals easily tune out threatening or emotional situations, and so are unaffected by them.

It could also be argued that because of their physical underarousal, people with antisocial personality disorder will be more likely than other people to take risks and seek thrills. That is, they may be drawn to antisocial activity precisely because it meets an underlying biological need for more excitement and arousal. In support of this idea, as we observed earlier, antisocial personality disorder often goes hand in hand with sensation-seeking behavior (Hesselbrock & Hesselbrock, 1992).

TREATMENTS FOR ANTISOCIAL PERSONALITY DISORDER Approximately one-quarter of all people with antisocial personality disorder receive treatment for it (Regier et al., 1993), yet treatment is typically ineffective (Reid & Gacono, 2000). A major obstacle to treatment is the individuals' lack of conscience or desire to change (Millon, 1999; Widiger et al., 1992). Most of those in therapy have been forced to participate by an employer, their school, or the law, or else they come to the attention of therapists when they also develop another psychological disorder (Agronin, 2006). Not surprisingly, one study found that 70 percent of these patients left treatment prematurely (Gabbard & Coyne, 1987).

Some cognitive therapists try to guide clients with antisocial personality disorder to think about moral issues and about the needs of other people (Leahy et al., 2005; Beck et al., 2004). In a similar vein, a number of hospitals and prisons have tried to create a therapeutic community for people with this disorder, a structured environment that teaches responsibility toward others (Piper & Joyce, 2001; Reid & Burke, 1989). Still another popular approach uses physically challenging wilderness programs to build self-confidence, self-esteem, and commitment to others in a group. Some patients seem to profit from such programs. Generally, however, most of today's treatment approaches have little or no impact on people with antisocial personality disorder.

Borderline Personality Disorder

People with **borderline personality disorder** display great instability, including major shifts in mood, an unstable self-image, and impulsivity. These characteristics combine to make their relationships very unstable as well (Paris, 2005; APA, 2000, 1994). Some of Ellen Farber's difficulties are typical:

Ellen Farber, a 35-year-old, single insurance company executive, came to a psychiatric emergency room of a university hospital with complaints of depression and the thought of driving her car off a cliff. An articulate, moderately overweight, sophisticated woman, Ms. Farber appeared to be in considerable distress. She reported a 6-month period of increasingly persistent dysphoria and lack of energy and pleasure. Feeling as if she were "made of lead," Ms. Farber had recently been spending 15–20 hours a day in her bed. She also reported daily episodes of binge eating, when she would consume "anything I can find," including entire chocolate cakes or boxes of cookies. She reported problems with intermittent binge eating since adolescence, but these had recently increased in frequency, resulting in a 20-pound weight gain over the last few months. In the past her weight had often varied greatly as she had gone on and off a variety of diets. . . .

She attributed her increasing symptoms to financial difficulties. Ms. Farber had been fired from her job two weeks before coming to the emergency room. She claimed it was because she "owed a small amount of money." When asked to be more specific, she reported owing $150,000 to her former employers and another $100,000 to various local banks. Further questions revealed that she had always had difficulty managing her money and had been forced to declare bankruptcy at age 27. From age 30 to age 33, she had used her employer's credit cards to finance weekly "buying binges," accumulating the $150,000 debt. She . . . reported that spending money alleviated her chronic feelings of loneliness, isolation, and sadness. Experiencing only temporary relief, every few days she would impulsively buy expensive jewelry, watches, or multiple pairs of the same shoes. . . .

In addition to lifelong feelings of emptiness, Ms. Farber described chronic uncertainty about what she wanted to do in life and with whom she wanted to be friends. She had many brief, intense relationships with both men and women, but her quick temper led to frequent arguments and even physical fights. Although she had always thought of her childhood as happy and carefree, when she became depressed, she began to recall [being abused verbally and physically by her mother].

(Spitzer et al., 1994, pp. 395–397)

>>**LOOKING AROUND**

Dealing with Anger

Women are 56 percent more likely than men to "yell a lot" when angry. ‹‹

Men are 35 percent more likely than women to "seethe quietly" when angry. ‹‹

According to surveys, men are three times more likely than women to use sex as a way to calm down when angry. ‹‹

Women are 2.5 times more likely than men to turn to food as a way to calm down when angry. ‹‹

(Zoellner, 2000)

Like Ellen Farber, people with borderline personality disorder swing in and out of very depressive, anxious, and irritable states that last anywhere from a few hours to a few days or more (see Table 16-2 on the next page). Their emotions seem to be always in conflict with the world around them. They are prone to bouts of anger, which sometimes result in physical aggression and violence. Just as often, however, they direct their impulsive anger inward and inflict bodily harm on themselves. Many seem troubled by deep feelings of emptiness (Koenigsberg et al., 2002, 1999).

Borderline personality disorder is a complex disorder, and is fast becoming one of the more common conditions seen in clinical practice. Research indicates that as many as 10 percent of outpatients and 20 percent of inpatients may meet the diagnostic criteria for the disorder (Widiger & Frances, 1989). Many of the patients who come to

Self-mutilation *This woman's self-inflicted knife wounds are evident as she interacts with an acquaintance. People who cut themselves repeatedly may do so out of frustration, to combat negative feelings, to cry out for help, or to document their psychological pain. Efforts at self-mutilation are a common symptom of borderline personality disorder.*

Table 16-2

Comparison of Personality Disorders

	DSM-IV Cluster	Similar Disorders On Axis I	Responsiveness to Treatment
Paranoid	Odd	Schizophrenia; delusional disorder	Modest
Schizoid	Odd	Schizophrenia; delusional disorder	Modest
Schizotypal	Odd	Schizophrenia; delusional disorder	Modest
Antisocial	Dramatic	Conduct disorder	Poor
Borderline	Dramatic	Mood disorders	Moderate
Histrionic	Dramatic	Somatoform disorders; mood disorders	Modest
Narcissistic	Dramatic	Cyclothymic disorder (mild bipolar disorder)	Poor
Avoidant	Anxious	Social phobia	Moderate
Dependent	Anxious	Separation anxiety disorder; dysthymic disorder (mild depressive disorder)	Moderate
Obsessive-compulsive	Anxious	Obsessive-compulsive anxiety disorder	Moderate

mental health emergency rooms are individuals with this disorder who have intentionally hurt themselves. Their impulsive, self-destructive activities may range from alcohol and substance abuse to delinquency, unsafe sex, and reckless driving (Trull et al., 2003, 2000) (see Box 16-3). Many engage in so-called self-injurious or self-mutilation behaviors, such as cutting or burning themselves or banging their heads (Conklin & Westen, 2005). Although these behaviors typically cause immense physical suffering, those with borderline personality disorder often feel as if the physical discomfort offers relief from their emotional suffering. It may serve as a distraction from their emotional or interpersonal upsets, "snapping" them out of an "emotional overload" (Stanley & Brodsky, 2005). Scars and bruises may also provide the individuals with a kind of documentation or concrete evidence of their emotional distress (Paris, 2005; Stanley & Brodsky, 2005). Finally, like Ellen Farber, many people with borderline personality disorder try to hurt themselves as a way of dealing with their chronic feelings of emptiness, boredom, and identity confusion.

Suicidal threats and actions are also common. Studies suggest that 70 percent of people with borderline personality disorder attempt suicide at least once in their lives; around 6 to 10 percent actually commit suicide (Soloff et al., 2005; Stanley & Brodsky, 2005). The rate of suicide among individuals with the disorder may be as much as 50 times higher than the rate found in the general population (Skodol, 2005; Work Group on Borderline Personality Disorder, 2001). Not surprisingly, it is also common for people with this disorder to enter clinical treatment by way of the emergency room after a suicide attempt (Lambert, 2003).

People with borderline personality disorder frequently form intense, conflict-ridden relationships in which their feelings are not necessarily shared by the other person (Modestin & Villiger, 1989). They may come to idealize another person's qualities and abilities after just a brief first encounter (Skodol, 2005). They also may violate the boundaries of relationships (Skodol et al., 2002). Thinking in dichotomous (black-and-white) terms, they quickly become furious when their expectations are not met; yet they remain very attached to the relationships (Bender et al., 2001). In fact, people with this disorder have recurrent fears of impending abandonment and frequently engage in

[BOX **16-3**]

Gambling and Other Impulse Problems

Impulsivity is a symptom of many psychological disorders, including the antisocial and borderline personality disorders (Looper & Paris, 2000). DSM-IV-TR also lists several disorders of which impulsivity, rather than personality, is the *main* feature. People with these *impulse-control disorders* fail to resist an impulse, drive, or temptation to perform acts that are harmful to themselves or others (APA, 2000, 1994). Usually they experience growing tension before the act and relief when they give in to the impulse. Some, but not all, feel regret or guilt afterward. Around 9 percent of adults display an impulse-control disorder in a given year (Kessler et al., 2005). The impulse-control disorders include pyromania, kleptomania, intermittent explosive disorder, trichotillomania, and pathological gambling.

◆ *Pyromania* is the deliberate and repeated setting of fires to achieve intense pleasure or relief from tension. It is different from *arson,* the setting of fires for revenge or financial gain.

◆ *Kleptomania* is a recurrent failure to resist the impulse to steal. People with this disorder often have more than enough money to pay for the articles they steal.

◆ Individuals with *intermittent explosive disorder* have periodic aggressive outbursts in which they may seriously attack people and destroy property. Their explosiveness far exceeds any provocation.

◆ People with *trichotillomania* repeatedly pluck hair from various parts of their bodies, particularly the scalp, eyebrows, and eyelashes (Pelissier & O'Connor, 2004).

◆ The most common of the impulse-control disorders is *pathological gambling,* persistent and repeated gambling behavior that disrupts one's life at home or at work (APA, 2000, 1994).

It is estimated that as many as 3.4 percent of adults and 3 to 8 percent of teenagers and college students suffer from pathological gambling (Sadock &

Sadock, 2003; APA, 2000). Clinicians are careful, however, to distinguish between pathological and social gambling (Kaminer et al., 2002). Pathological gambling is defined less by the amount of time or money spent in gambling than by the addictive and impulsive nature of the behavior (Petry, 2001). People with this disorder cannot walk away from a bet and are restless and irritable if gambling is denied them. Repeated losses of money lead to more gambling in an effort to win the money back, and the gambling continues even in the face of financial, social, and health problems. Many people go through four progressive phases during episodes of pathological gambling: winning, losing, desperation, and hopelessness (Rosenthal, 1992).

A great deal of attention has been directed in recent years toward the treatment of pathological gambling. Treatments that combine cognitive, behavioral, and other approaches and that help build coping skills tend to be the most effective (Szegedy-Maszak, 2005; Echeburúa et al., 1996). People who join self-help support groups, such as *Gamblers Anonymous,* a network patterned after Alcoholics Anonymous, seem to have a higher recovery rate, perhaps in part because they have admitted that they have a problem and are seeking to conquer it.

Recently journalists and others have asked whether the "medicalization" of gambling has the effect of somehow excusing a pattern of irresponsible, often illegal, behavior (Castellani, 2000; Vatz & Weinberg, 1993). However, several studies suggest that pathological gambling and other impulse-control disorders are complex problems that often involve a variety of causes, including biochemical factors (Szegedy-Maszak, 2005).

Michael Conroy/AP Photo

frantic efforts to avoid real or imagined separations from important people in their lives (Skodol, 2005). Sometimes they cut themselves or carry out other self-destructive acts to prevent partners from leaving.

Sufferers of borderline personality disorder typically experience dramatic shifts in their identity. An unstable sense of self may produce rapid shifts in goals, aspirations, friends, and even sexual orientation (Skodol, 2005). The individuals may also experience

Changing a personality *In 1974 the newspaper heiress Patty Hearst was kidnapped by a terrorist group called the Symbionese Liberation Army. After being locked in a closet for months and experiencing other tortures, the young woman participated with the group in various antisocial activities. Had Hearst's personality been changed? Would anyone subjected to such tortures have undergone a shift in values and behaviors? Did she have a personality disorder—dependent, antisocial, borderline—that left her vulnerable to the techniques of her captors? A jury ruled in 1976 that Hearst, shown here during a bank robbery, had acted with free will and in accordance with her own personality and sentenced her to seven years in prison for grand theft. She was released after two years when President Jimmy Carter commuted her sentence.*

an occasional sense of dissociation, or detachment, from their own thoughts or bodies. Indeed, at times they may experience no sense of themselves at all, leading to the feelings of emptiness described earlier (Linehan, Cochran, & Kehrer, 2001).

Between 1.5 and 2.5 percent of the general population are thought to suffer from borderline personality disorder (Arntz, 2005). Close to 75 percent of the patients who receive the diagnosis are women. The course of the disorder varies from person to person. In the most common pattern, the individual's instability and risk of suicide peak during young adulthood and then gradually wane with advancing age (Hurt & Oltmanns, 2002; APA, 2000). Males with borderline personality disorder may display more aggressive, disruptive, and antisocial behaviors than females (Bradley, Conklin, & Westen, 2005). Given the chaotic and unstable relationships characteristic of borderline personality disorder, it is not surprising that this disorder tends to interfere with job performance more than most other personality disorders do (Zanarini et al., 2005).

HOW DO THEORISTS EXPLAIN BORDERLINE PERSONALITY DISORDER? Because a fear of abandonment tortures so many people with borderline personality disorder, psychodynamic theorists have looked once again to early parental relationships to explain the disorder (Gunderson, 2001, 1996). Object relations theorists, for example, propose that an early lack of acceptance by parents may lead to a loss of self-esteem, increased dependence, and an inability to cope with separation (Kernberg & Caligor, 2005; Bartholomew et al., 2001).

Research has found that the early childhoods of people with the disorder are often consistent with this view. In many cases, the parents of such individuals neglected or rejected them, verbally abused them, or otherwise behaved inappropriately (Bradley, Jenei, & Westen, 2005; Guttman, 2002). Similarly, their childhoods were often marked by multiple parent substitutes, divorce, death, or traumas such as physical or sexual abuse (Sansone et al., 2005; Yen et al., 2002). Indeed, research suggests that early sexual abuse is a common contributor to the development of borderline personality disorder (Bradley et al., 2005); children who experience such abuse are four times more likely to develop the disorder than those who do not (Zelkowitz et al., 2001). At the same time, it is important to recognize that the vast majority of persons with histories of physical, sexual, or psychological abuse do not go on to develop this disorder (Skodol, 2005).

Some features of borderline personality disorder have also been linked to biological abnormalities. Sufferers who are particularly impulsive—those who attempt suicide or are very aggressive toward others—apparently have lower brain serotonin activity (Norra et al., 2003). People with the disorder also experience abnormalities in sleep that are similar to those of depressed persons (Siever & Davis, 1991). In accord with these biological findings, close relatives of those with borderline personality disorder are five times more likely than the general population to have the same personality disorder (Torgersen, 2000, 1984; Kendler et al., 1991).

A number of theorists currently use a *biosocial theory* to explain borderline personality disorder (Linehan et al., 2001; Linehan 1987, 1993). According to this view, the disorder results from a combination of internal forces (for example, difficulty identifying and controlling one's emotions, abnormal neurotransmitter reactions) and external forces (for example, environments in which a child's emotions are punished, ignored, trivialized, or disregarded). Parents may, for example, misinterpret their child's intense emotions as exaggerations or attempts at manipulation rather than as serious expressions of unsettled internal states. According to the biosocial theory, if children have intrinsic difficulties identifying and controlling their emotions and if their parents further teach them to ignore their intense feelings, the children may never learn how to properly recognize and control their emotional arousal, how to tolerate emotional distress, or when to trust their emotional responses. In turn, such children will be at risk for the development of borderline personality disorder (Linehan et al., 2001; Linehan, 1993). Note that this theory is similar to one of the leading explanations for eating disorders. As we observed in Chapter 11, the theorist Hilde Bruch proposed that children whose parents do not respond accurately to the children's internal cues may never learn to identify cues of hunger, thus increasing their risk of developing an eating disorder (see pages 322–324). Small wonder that a large number of people with borderline personality disorder also display an eating disorder (Sansone et al, 2005). Recall, for example, Ellen Farber's dysfunctional eating pattern.

Finally, some sociocultural theorists suggest that cases of borderline personality disorder are particularly likely to emerge in cultures that change rapidly. As a culture loses its stability, they argue, it inevitably leaves many of its members with problems of identity, a sense of emptiness, high anxiety, and fears of abandonment (Paris, 1991). Family units may come apart, leaving people with little sense of belonging. Changes of this kind in society today may explain growing reports of the disorder.

TREATMENTS FOR BORDERLINE PERSONALITY DISORDER It appears that psychotherapy can eventually lead to some degree of improvement for people with borderline personality disorder (Sperry, 2003; Gunderson, 2001). It is not easy, however, for a therapist to strike a balance between empathizing with the borderline client's dependency and anger and challenging his or her way of thinking (Goin, 2001). Given the emotionally draining demands of clients with borderline personality disorder, some therapists refuse to see such clients. The wildly fluctuating interpersonal attitudes of clients with the disorder can also make it difficult for therapists to establish collaborative and productive working relationships with them (Bender & Oldham, 2005). Moreover, such clients may violate the boundaries of the client-therapist relationship (for example, calling the therapist's emergency contact number to discuss matters of a less urgent nature) (Gutheil, 2005). Finally, when borderline clients do make progress in treatment, termination can be difficult because of the individuals' remaining difficulties with relationships and abandonment (Sansone et al., 1991).

Traditional Freudian psychoanalysis has not been effective with these individuals (Bender & Oldham, 2005). The clients often experience the psychoanalytic therapist's reserved style and encouragement of free association as suggesting disinterest and abandonment. The clients may also have difficulties tolerating interpretations made by psychoanalytic therapists, experiencing them as attacks.

Contemporary psychodynamic approaches, such as *relational psychoanalytic therapy* (see page 59), in which therapists take a more supportive and egalitarian posture, have proved to be more effective than traditional psychoanalytic approaches (Bender & Oldham, 2005). In such contemporary approaches, therapists work to provide an empathic setting within which borderline clients can explore their unconscious conflicts and pay particular attention to their central relationship disturbance, poor sense of self, and pervasive loneliness and emptiness (Gabbard, 2001; Piper & Joyce, 2001). Research has found that contemporary psychodynamic approaches often help reduce suicide attempts, self-harm behaviors, and the number of hospitalizations, and bring at least some improvement to individuals with the disorder (Roth & Fonagy, 2005; Clarkin et al., 2001).

Over the past two decades, an *integrative* treatment approach for borderline personality disorder, called *dialectical behavior therapy* (DBT), has received growing research support and is now considered the treatment of choice in many clinical circles (Heard & Linehan, 2005; Linehan, 1993, 1992; Linehan et al., 2001). In DBT, which grows largely from the cognitive and behavioral models, therapists actively and supportively try to help clients increase their ability to tolerate distress, learn new social skills, and respond more effectively to life situations. Similar to the contemporary psychodynamic approaches, the relationship between the client and therapist is emphasized in DBT: the DBT therapists regularly empathize with their clients and with the emotional turmoil they are experiencing, locate the kernals of truth in their inappropriate demands, and examine alternative ways for the clients to get valid needs met. The therapists may also model alternative ways of interpreting and reacting to situations. Frequently DBT is supplemented by the clients' participation in skills–building groups where they can practice new ways of relating to other persons in a safe environment and at the same time provide validation and support for other group members (Heard & Linehan, 2005).

DBT has received more research support than any other treatment for borderline personality disorder (Lieb et al., 2004). Persons treated with DBT display significantly fewer suicidal behaviors and require fewer hospitalizations than those who receive other forms of treatment (Linehan et al., 1999, 1993, 1991). DBT clients are also more likely

•HISTRIONIC PERSONALITY DISORDER•
A personality disorder characterized by a pattern of excessive emotionality and attention seeking. Once called *hysterical personality disorder*.

to remain in treatment and to report less anger, greater social adjustment, improved work performance, and a greater reduction in substance abuse.

Finally, antidepressant, antibipolar, antianxiety, and antipsychotic drugs have helped calm the emotional and aggressive storms of some people with borderline personality disorder (Agronin, 2006; Gruettert & Friege, 2005; Fava et al., 2002). However, given the numerous suicide attempts by individuals with this disorder, the use of drugs on an outpatient basis is controversial. Additionally, clients with the disorder have been known to adjust or discontinue their medication dosages without consulting their clinicians. Today, most professionals believe that psychotropic drug treatment for borderline personality disorder should be used largely as an adjunct to psychotherapy approaches, and indeed many individuals seem to benefit from a combination of psychotherapy and drug therapy (Soloff, 2005; Livesley, 2000; Stone, 2000).

Histrionic Personality Disorder

People with **histrionic personality disorder,** once called **hysterical personality disorder,** are extremely emotional—they are typically described as "emotionally charged"—and continually seek to be the center of attention (APA, 2000, 1994). Their exaggerated, rapidly changing moods can complicate life considerably, as we see in the case of Suzanne:

Suzanne, an attractive and vivacious woman, sought therapy in the hope that she might prevent the disintegration of her third marriage. The problem she faced was a recurrent one, her tendency to become "bored" with her husband and increasingly interested in going out with other men. She was on the brink of "another affair" and decided that before "giving way to her impulses again" she had "better stop and take a good look" at herself. . . .

Suzanne was quite popular during her adolescent years. . . . Rather than going on to college, Suzanne attended art school where she met and married a fellow student—a "handsome, wealthy ne'er-do-well." Both she and her husband began "sleeping around" by the end of the first year, and she "wasn't certain" that her husband was the father of her daughter. A divorce took place several months after the birth of this child.

Soon thereafter she met and married a man in his forties who gave both Suzanne and her daughter a "comfortable home, and scads of attention and love." It was a "good life" for the four years that the marriage lasted. . . . In the third year of this marriage she became attracted to a young man, a fellow dancing student. The affair was brief, but was followed by a quick succession of several others. Her husband learned of her exploits, but accepted her regrets and assurances that they would not continue. They did continue, and the marriage was terminated after a stormy court settlement.

Suzanne "knocked about" on her own for the next two years until she met her present husband, a talented writer who "knew the scoop" about her past. . . . She had no inclination to venture afield for the next three years. She enjoyed the titillation of "playing games" with other men, but she remained loyal to her husband, even though he was away on reportorial assignments for periods of one or two months. The last trip, however, brought forth the "old urge" to start an affair. It was at this point that she sought therapy.

(Millon, 1969, p. 251)

People with histrionic personality disorder are always "on stage," using theatrical gestures and mannerisms and the most grandiose language to describe ordinary everyday events. Like a chameleon, they keep changing themselves to attract and impress an audience, and in their pursuit they change not only their surface characteristics—according to the latest fads—but also their opinions and beliefs. In fact, their speech is actually scanty in detail and substance, and they seem to lack a sense of who they really are.

Approval and praise are the life's blood of these individuals; they must have others present to witness their exaggerated emotional states. Vain, self-centered, demanding,

>>LOOKING BACK
Portrait in Vanity

King Frederick V, ruler of Denmark from 1746 to 1766, had his portrait painted at least 70 times by the same artist, Carl Pilo (Shaw, 2004). <<

and unable to delay gratification for long, they overreact to any minor event that gets in the way of their quest for attention. Some make suicide attempts, often to manipulate others (Lambert, 2003; APA, 2000).

People with this disorder may draw attention to themselves by exaggerating their physical illnesses or fatigues. They may also behave very provocatively and try to achieve their goals through sexual seduction. Most obsess over how they look and how others will perceive them, often wearing bright, eye-catching clothes. They exaggerate the depth of their relationships, considering themselves to be the intimate friends of people who see them as no more than casual acquaintances. Often they become involved with romantic partners who may be exciting but who do not treat them well.

This disorder was once believed to be more common in women than in men, and clinicians long described the "hysterical wife" (Anderson et al., 2001; Char, 1985). Research, however, has revealed gender bias in past diagnoses. When evaluating case studies of people with a mixture of histrionic and antisocial traits, clinicians in several studies gave a diagnosis of histrionic personality disorder to women more than men (Ford & Widiger, 1989; Hamilton et al., 1986). The latest statistics suggest that around 2 percent of adults have this personality disorder, with males and females equally affected (Mattia & Zimmerman, 2001; APA, 2000).

Transient hysterical symptoms *These avid Harry Potter fans express themselves with exaggerated and theatrical emotionality and lack of restraint at the midnight launch of the latest book in the series by J. K. Rowling. Similar reactions, along with occasional fainting, tremors, and even convulsions, have been common at concerts by Frank Sinatra, Elvis Presley, the Beatles, and other musical idols dating back to the 1940s. Small wonder that expressive fans of this kind are regularly described as "hysterical" or "histrionic" by the press—the same labels applied to the personality disorders and somatoform disorders that are marked by such behaviors and symptoms.*

HOW DO THEORISTS EXPLAIN HISTRIONIC PERSONALITY DISORDER?

The psychodynamic perspective was originally developed to help explain cases of hysteria (see Chapter 7), so it is no surprise that these theorists continue to have a strong interest in histrionic personality disorder today. Most psychodynamic theorists believe that as children, people with this disorder experienced unhealthy relationships in which cold and controlling parents left them feeling unloved and afraid of abandonment (Bender et al., 2001; Gunderson, 1988). To defend against deep-seated fears of loss, the individuals learned to behave dramatically, inventing crises that would require other people to act protectively (Kuriansky, 1988).

Some psychodynamic theories focus exclusively on female patients. They suggest that an early lack of maternal nurturance causes some daughters to develop an intense need for their father's attention and to seek it through displays of affection and dependence that go far beyond the usual behavior of young girls toward their fathers. These highly flirtatious and dramatic displays of emotion establish a histrionic pattern that extends to later relationships in their lives (Phillips & Gunderson, 1994; Gabbard, 1990). Such individuals enter adulthood as "unhappy little girls," looking at men as idealized fathers and always trying to manipulate them (Char, 1985).

Cognitive explanations look instead at the lack of substance and extreme suggestibility found in people with histrionic personality disorder. These theories see the individuals as becoming less and less interested in knowing about the world at large because they are so self-focused and emotional. With no detailed memories of what they never learned, they must rely on hunches or on other people to provide them with direction in life (Hollander, 1988). Some cognitive theorists also propose that people with this disorder hold a general assumption that they are helpless to care for themselves, and so they constantly seek out others who will meet their needs (Beck et al., 2004).

Finally, sociocultural theorists believe that histrionic personality disorder is produced in part by society's norms and expectations. Until recently, our society encouraged girls to hold on to childhood and dependency as they grew up (Hollander, 1988). The vain, dramatic, and selfish behavior of the histrionic person may actually be an exaggeration of femininity as our culture once defined it (Beck et al., 2004; Sprock, 2000).

TREATMENTS FOR HISTRIONIC PERSONALITY DISORDER

Unlike people with most other personality disorders, those with histrionic personality disorder often seek out treatment on their own (Nestadt et al., 1990). Working with them can be very difficult, however, because of the demands, tantrums, and seductiveness they are likely to deploy

>>Q & A

What is the difference between an egoist and an egotist?

An **egoist** is a person concerned primarily with his or her own interests. An **egotist** has an inflated sense of self-worth. A boastful egotist is not necessarily a self-absorbed egoist. <<

•NARCISSISTIC PERSONALITY DISORDER•
A personality disorder marked by a broad pattern of grandiosity, need for admiration, and lack of empathy.

(Gutheil, 2005; Phillips & Gunderson, 1994). Another problem is that these individuals may pretend to have important insights or to experience change during treatment, merely to please the therapist. To head off such problems, therapists must remain objective and maintain strict professional boundaries (Sperry, 2003; Gabbard, 1990).

Cognitive therapists have tried to help people with this disorder to change their belief that they are helpless and also to develop better, more deliberate ways of thinking and solving problems. Psychodynamic therapy and group therapy have also been applied (Beck et al., 2004; Freeman, 2002). In all these approaches, therapists ultimately aim to help the clients recognize their excessive dependency, find inner satisfaction, and become more self-reliant (Chodoff, 1989). Clinical case reports suggest that each of the approaches can be useful. Drug therapy is less successful, however, except as a means of relieving the depressive symptoms experienced by some patients (Fava et al., 2002; Koenigsberg et al., 2002).

Narcissistic Personality Disorder

People with **narcissistic personality disorder** are generally grandiose, need much admiration, and feel no empathy with others (APA, 2000, 1994). Convinced of their own great success, power, or beauty, they expect constant attention and admiration from those around them. Frederick, the man whom we met at the beginning of this chapter, was one such person. So is Steven, a 30-year-old artist, married, with one child:

Steven came to the attention of a therapist when his wife insisted that they seek marital counseling. According to her, Steve was "selfish, ungiving and preoccupied with his work." Everything at home had to "revolve about him, his comfort, moods and desires, no one else's." She claimed that he contributed nothing to the marriage, except a rather meager income. He shirked all "normal" responsibilities and kept "throwing chores in her lap," and she was "getting fed up with being the chief cook and bottlewasher, tired of being his mother and sleep-in maid."

On the positive side, Steven's wife felt that he was basically a "gentle and good-natured guy with talent and intelligence." But this wasn't enough. She wanted a husband, someone with whom she could share things. In contrast, he wanted, according to her, "a mother, not a wife"; he didn't want "to grow up, he didn't know how to give affection, only to take it when he felt like it, nothing more, nothing less."

Steve presented a picture of an affable, self-satisfied and somewhat disdainful young man. He was employed as a commercial artist, but looked forward to his evenings and weekends when he could turn his attention to serious painting. He claimed that he had to devote all of his spare time and energies to "fulfill himself," to achieve expression in his creative work. . . .

His relationships with his present co-workers and social acquaintances were pleasant and satisfying, but he did admit that most people viewed him as a "bit self-centered, cold and snobbish." He recognized that he did not know how to share his thoughts and feelings with others, that he was much more interested in himself than in them and that perhaps he always had "preferred the pleasure" of his own company to that of others.

(Millon, 1969, pp. 261–262)

The Greek myth has it that Narcissus died enraptured by the beauty of his own reflection in a pool, pining away with longing to possess his own image. His name has come to be synonymous with extreme self-involvement, and indeed people with narcissistic personality disorder have a grandiose sense of self-importance. They exaggerate their achievements and talents, expecting others to recognize them as superior, and often appear arrogant. They are very choosy about their friends and associates, believing that their problems are unique and can be appreciated only by other "special," high-status people. Because of their charm, they often make favorable first impressions. Yet they can rarely maintain long-term relationships.

>>BY THE NUMBERS
Stolen Glances

22% Percentage of people who regularly check their reflections in store windows and the like «

69% Those who steal glances at least occasionally «

9% Those who never look at themselves in public mirrors or windows «

(Kanner, 1995)

Like Steven, people with narcissistic personality disorder are seldom interested in the feelings of others. Many take advantage of others to achieve their own ends, perhaps partly out of envy; at the same time they believe others envy them (Sperry, 2003; Wink, 1996). Though grandiose, some of these individuals react to criticism or frustration with bouts of rage or humiliation. Others may react with cold indifference. And still others become extremely pessimistic and filled with depression. Periods of zest may alternate with periods of disappointment (Wink, 1996).

Less than 1 percent of adults display narcissistic personality disorder, up to 75 percent of them men (Mattia & Zimmerman, 2001; APA, 2000). Narcissistic-type behaviors and thoughts are common and normal among teenagers and do not usually lead to adult narcissism (APA, 1994).

How Do Theorists Explain Narcissistic Personality Disorder?

Psychodynamic theorists more than others have theorized about narcissistic personality disorder, and, again, they propose that the problem begins with cold, rejecting parents. They argue that some people with this background spend their lives defending against feeling unsatisfied, rejected, unworthy, and wary of the world (Bornstein, 2005; Wink, 1996). They do so by repeatedly telling themselves that they are actually perfect and desirable, and also by seeking admiration from others. Object relations theorists, the psychodynamic theorists who emphasize relationships, interpret the grandiose self-image as a way for these people to convince themselves that they are totally self-sufficient and without need of warm relationships with their parents or anyone else (Kernberg & Caligor, 2005; Kernberg, 1989). In support of the psychodynamic theories, research has found that children who are abused or who lose parents through adoption, divorce, or death are at particular risk for the later development of narcissistic personality disorder (Kernberg, 1989). Studies also reveal that people with this disorder do indeed believe that other persons are basically unavailable to them (Bender et al., 2001).

A number of behavioral and cognitive theorists propose that narcissistic personality disorder may develop when people are treated *too positively* rather than too negatively in early life. They hold that certain individuals acquire a superior and grandiose attitude when their "admiring or doting parents" teach them to "overvalue their self worth" (Sperry, 2003; Millon, 1987). In support of this explanation, firstborn and only children, who are often viewed by their parents as having special talents or intelligence, score higher than other children on measures of narcissism (Curtis & Cowell, 1993).

Finally, many sociocultural theorists see a link between narcissistic personality disorder and "eras of narcissism" in society (Cooper & Ronningstam, 1992). They suggest that family values and social ideals in certain societies periodically break down, producing generations of youth who are self-centered and materialistic and have short attention spans. Western cultures in particular, which encourage self-expression, individualism, and competitiveness, are considered likely to produce such generations of narcissism.

Treatments for Narcissistic Personality Disorder

Narcissistic personality disorder is one of the most difficult personality patterns to treat (Lawrence, 1987). The clients who consult therapists usually do so because of a related disorder, most commonly depression (Piper & Joyce, 2001; Millon, 1999). Once in treatment, the individuals may try to manipulate the therapist into supporting their sense of superiority. Some also seem to project their grandiose attitudes onto their therapists and develop a love-hate stance toward them (Uchoa, 1985).

Psychodynamic therapists seek to help people with this disorder recognize and work through their basic insecurities and defenses (Adler, 2000). Cognitive therapists, focusing on the self-centered thinking of such clients, try to redirect the clients' focus onto the opinions of others, teach them to interpret criticism more rationally, increase their ability to empathize, and change their all-or-nothing notions (Leahy et al., 2005; Beck et al., 2004). None of the approaches have had much success, however.

"I'm attracted to you, but then I'm attracted to me, too."

Richard Cline/Cartoonbank.com

•**AVOIDANT PERSONALITY DISORDER**•
A personality disorder characterized by consistent discomfort and restraint in social situations, overwhelming feelings of inadequacy, and extreme sensitivity to negative evaluation.

•**DEPENDENT PERSONALITY DISORDER**•
A personality disorder characterized by a pattern of clinging and obedience, fear of separation, and an ongoing need to be taken care of.

"Anxious" Personality Disorders

The cluster of *"anxious" personality disorders* includes the *avoidant, dependent,* and *obsessive-compulsive personality disorders.* People with these patterns typically display anxious and fearful behavior. Although many of the symptoms of these disorders are similar to those of the anxiety and depressive disorders, researchers have not found direct links between this cluster and those Axis I patterns (Weston & Siever, 1993). As with most of the other personality disorders, research support for the various explanations is very limited. At the same time, treatments for these disorders appear to be modestly to moderately helpful—considerably better than for other personality disorders.

Avoidant Personality Disorder

People with **avoidant personality disorder** are very uncomfortable and inhibited in social situations, overwhelmed by feelings of inadequacy, and extremely sensitive to negative evaluation (APA, 2000, 1994). They are so fearful of being rejected that they give no one an opportunity to reject them—or to accept them either:

> James was a bookkeeper for nine years, having obtained his position upon graduation from high school. He spoke of himself as a shy, fearful and quiet boy ever since early childhood. . . .
>
> James was characterized by his supervisor as a loner, a peculiar young man who did his work quietly and efficiently. They noted that he ate alone in the company cafeteria and never joined in coffee breaks or in the "horsing around" at the office. . . .
>
> As far as his social life was concerned, James had neither dated nor gone to a party in five years. . . . He now spent most of his free time reading, watching TV, daydreaming and fixing things around the house.
>
> James experienced great distress when new employees were assigned to his office section. Some 40 people worked regularly in this office and job turnover resulted in replacement of four or five people a year. . . . In recent months, a clique formed in his office. Although James very much wanted to be a member of this "in-group," he feared attempting to join them because "he had nothing to offer them" and thought he would be rejected. In a short period of time, he, along with two or three others, became the object of jokes and taunting by the leaders of the clique. After a few weeks of "being kidded," he began to miss work, failed to complete his accounts on time, found himself unsure of what he was doing and made a disproportionate number of errors. . . .
>
> *(Millon, 1969, pp. 231–232)*

>>BY THE NUMBERS

Feelings of Shyness

48% Percentage of people in the United States who consider themselves to be shy to some degree **<<**

62% Percentage of shy people who experience their feelings of shyness daily **<<**

64% Percentage of shy people who believe that their shyness is the result of external factors beyond their control, such as early family experience **<<**

(Carducci, 2000)

People like James actively avoid occasions for social contact. At the center of this withdrawal lies not so much poor social skills as a dread of criticism, disapproval, or rejection. They are timid and hesitant in social situations, afraid of saying something foolish or of embarrassing themselves by blushing or acting nervous. Even in intimate relationships they express themselves very carefully, afraid of being shamed or ridiculed.

People with this disorder believe themselves to be unappealing or inferior to others. They exaggerate the potential difficulties of new situations, so they seldom take risks or try out new activities. They usually have few or no close friends, though they actually yearn for intimate relationships, and frequently feel depressed and lonely. As a substitute, some develop an inner world of fantasy and imagination (Millon, 1990).

Avoidant personality disorder is similar to a *social phobia* (see Chapter 5), and many people with one of these disorders also experience the other (Ralevsky et al., 2005). The similarities include a fear of humiliation and low confidence. A key difference between the two conditions is that people with a social phobia primarily fear social *circumstances,* while people with the personality disorder tend to fear close social *relationships* (Turner et al., 1986).

Between 1 and 2 percent of adults have avoidant personality disorder, men as frequently as women (Mattia & Zimmerman, 2001; APA, 2000). Many children and teenagers are also painfully shy and avoid other people, but this is usually just a normal part of their development.

How Do Theorists Explain Avoidant Personality Disorder?
Theorists often assume that avoidant personality disorder has the same causes as anxiety disorders—such as early traumas, conditioned fears, upsetting beliefs, or biochemical abnormalities. However, research has not yet tied the personality disorder directly to the anxiety disorders (Weston & Siever, 1993). In the meantime, psychodynamic and cognitive explanations are the most popular among clinicians.

Psychodynamic theorists focus mainly on the general sense of shame felt by people with avoidant personality disorder. Some trace the shame to childhood experiences such as early bowel and bladder accidents (Gabbard, 1990). If parents repeatedly punish or ridicule a child for having such accidents, the child may develop a negative self-image. This may lead to the individual's feeling unlovable throughout life and distrusting the love of others (Liebowitz et al., 1986). Similarly, cognitive theorists believe that harsh criticism and rejection in early childhood may lead certain people to assume that others in their environment will always judge them negatively. These individuals come to expect rejection, misinterpret the reactions of others to fit that expectation, discount positive feedback, and generally fear social involvements—setting the stage for avoidant personality disorder (Beck et al., 2004, 2001). In several studies, subjects with this disorder were asked to recall their childhood, and their descriptions supported both the psychodynamic and cognitive theories (Grilo & Masheb, 2002; Meyer & Carver, 2000). They remembered, for example, feeling rejected and isolated, receiving little encouragement from their parents, and experiencing few displays of parental love or pride.

Treatments for Avoidant Personality Disorder
People with avoidant personality disorder come to therapy in the hope of finding acceptance and affection. Keeping them in treatment can be a challenge, however, for many of them soon begin to avoid the sessions (Millon, 1999; Beck & Freeman, 1990). Often they distrust the therapist's sincerity and start to fear his or her rejection. Thus, as with several of the other personality disorders, a key task of the therapist is to gain the individual's trust (Millon, 1999; Gabbard, 1990).

Beyond building trust, therapists tend to treat people with avoidant personality disorder much as they treat people with social phobias and other anxiety disorders (Markovitz, 2001; Reich, 2000). Such approaches have had at least modest success (Crits-Christoph & Barber, 2002). Psychodynamic therapists try to help clients recognize and resolve the unconscious conflicts that may be operating (Sperry, 2003). Cognitive therapists help them change their distressing beliefs and thoughts, carry on in the face of painful emotions, and improve their self-image (Leahy et al., 2005; Beck et al., 2004). Behavioral therapists provide social skills training as well as exposure treatments that require people to gradually increase their social contacts (Farmer & Nelson-Gray, 2005; Stanley et al., 2003; Crits-Christoph & Barber, 2002). Group therapy may also be applied to provide practice in social interactions (Piper & Joyce, 2001; Azima, 1993). Antianxiety and antidepressant drugs are sometimes useful in reducing the social anxiety of people with the disorder, although the symptoms may return when medication is stopped (Fava et al., 2002; Koenigsberg et al., 2002).

Dependent Personality Disorder

People with **dependent personality disorder** have a pervasive, excessive need to be taken care of (APA, 2000, 1994). As a result, they are clinging and obedient, fearing separation from their parent, spouse, or other person with whom they are in a close relationship.

Peter Turnley/Corbis

A lonely life This woman paints a sad and lonely figure as she sits by the Paris grave of the late Jim Morrison, lead singer of the rock group The Doors. Legions of Morrison fans have visited the grave for a variety of reasons—from curiosity to admiration—since his 1971 death. Clinicians believe, however, that in some cases the overly devoted fans of Morrison and other long-gone celebrities—particularly fans who build their lives around the celebrities—manifest avoidant personality disorder. Uncomfortable and inhibited in real social situations, some people with this personality disorder develop an inner world of fantasy and imagined relationships.

>>IN THEIR WORDS

"The deepest principle of human nature is the craving to be appreciated." <<

William James

They rely on others so much that they cannot make the smallest decision for themselves. Mr. G. is a case in point.

Mr. G.['s] . . . place of employment for the past 15 years had recently closed and he had been without work for several weeks. He appeared less dejected about the loss of his job than about his wife's increasing displeasure with his decision to "stay at home until something came up." She thought he "must be sick" and insisted that he see a doctor. . . .

Mr. G. was born in Europe, the oldest child and only son of a family of six children. . . . His mother kept a careful watch over him, prevented him from engaging in undue exertions and limited his responsibilities; in effect, she precluded his developing many of the ordinary physical skills and competencies that most youngsters learn in the course of growth. . . .

A marriage was arranged by his parents. His wife was a sturdy woman who worked as a seamstress, took care of his home, and bore . . . four children. Mr. G. performed a variety of odds-and-ends jobs in his father's tailoring shop. His mother saw to it, however, that he did no "hard or dirty work," just helping about and "overlooking" the other employees. As a consequence, Mr. G. learned none of the skills of the tailoring trade.

Shortly before the outbreak of World War II, Mr. G. came to visit two of his sisters who previously had emigrated to the United States; when hostilities erupted

[BOX **16-4**]

Internet Dependence: A New Kind of Problem

The computer age has apparently brought with it a new psychological problem—an uncontrollable need to be on-line (Beard, 2005; Davis, 2001). Some clinicians consider it a kind of *substance-related disorder*. Others think it has the qualities of an *impulse-control disorder*.

And many note that the pattern resembles *dependent personality disorder*, except that in this new pattern the individual is excessively dependent on a cyberbeing and on numerous fellow users, ever seeking their company, guidance, and reassurance, and fearful of separation.

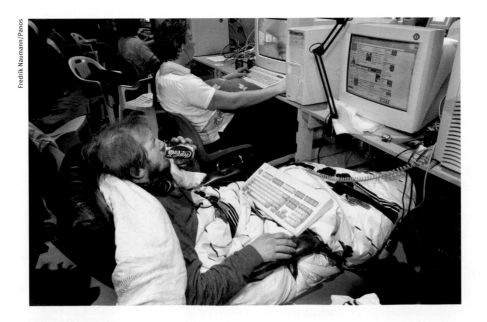

Fredrik Naumann/Panos

For some people, the Internet has become a black hole. Sufferers spend up to 60 hours a week surfing the Net, participating in chat groups, posting messages and receiving responses in news groups, e-mailing acquaintances, or playing complex computer games (Beard, 2005; Black, Belsare, & Schlosser, 1999). A number describe their need to be on-line as an obsession for which they have unintentionally sacrificed their jobs, education, friends, even spouses. University students seem especially prone to the problem:

I *I was first introduced while I was studying at the university in '91. . . . I discovered by accident one day that you could send little messages to people in other universities and even people in America and other exotic places like Mexico and Finland! Well, that was the point of no return for me and I began spending inordinately large periods of time on-line. That was at the beginning of my final year. . . . [My] attendance record got worse and worse [and] predictably enough I failed in spectacular fashion. But I didn't mind so much because I had the Net to catch me, I'd made many friends on and off-line* in Europe he was unable to return home. All members of his family, with the exception of a young son, perished in the war.

During the ensuing years, he obtained employment at a garment factory owned by his brothers-in-law. Again he served as a helper, not as a skilled workman. Although he bore the brunt of essentially good-humored teasing by his co-workers throughout these years, he maintained a friendly and helpful attitude, pleasing them by getting sandwiches, coffee and cigarettes at their beck and call.

He married again to a hard-working, motherly type woman who provided the greater portion of the family income. Shortly thereafter, the son of his first wife emigrated to this country. Although the son was only 19 at the time, he soon found himself guiding his father's affairs, rather than the other way around.

(Millon, 1969, p. 242)

It is normal and healthy to depend on others, but those with dependent personality disorder constantly need assistance with even the simplest matters and demonstrate extreme feelings of inadequacy and helplessness. Afraid that they cannot care for themselves, they cling desperately to friends or relatives (see Box 16-4).

We observed earlier that people with avoidant personality disorder have difficulty *initiating* relationships. In contrast, people with dependent personality disorder have difficulty with *separation*. The individuals feel completely helpless and devastated when a

through it, including my then girlfriend, so life wasn't that bad really, was it? . . .

I've [since] learned to censor out some things, and not to get entwined up to my arse in endless threads of chat. Okay, so this is bad in some ways, but I feel a little more in control of my life. I don't find myself involuntarily glued to my screen at 4 A.M. talking about something that isn't even interesting, begging myself to go to bed.

(ANONYMOUS, 1996)

Like the person quoted in this excerpt, growing numbers of users have become absorbed in the social world of the Internet. Chat rooms allow them to "talk" with other computer users around the world 24 hours a day, 365 days a year; news groups allow them to post messages and receive responses. These services have allowed people to create social worlds, replete with acquaintanceship, friendship, and romance.

One study of 18,000 Internet users found that as many as 16 percent of respondents were overly dependent on it (Greenfield, 1999). Another found that

one-quarter of employees spend more than 20 percent of their workday surfing on non–work-related Web sites (Hayday, 2002). In still other research, the investigator Kimberly S. Young (1999, 1998, 1996) classified subjects as dependent on the Internet if they met four or more of the following criteria over a 12-month period:

1. Felt preoccupied with the Internet
2. Needed to spend increasing amounts of time on the Internet to achieve satisfaction
3. Were unable to control their Internet use
4. Felt restless or irritable when they tried to cut down or stop Internet use
5. Used the Internet as a way of escaping from problems or of improving their mood
6. Lied to family members or friends to conceal the extent of their involvement with the Internet
7. Risked the loss of a significant relationship, job, or educational or career opportunity because of the Internet

8. Kept returning to the Internet even after spending an excessive amount of money on on-line fees
9. Went through withdrawal when off-line
10. Stayed on-line longer than they originally intended

Not surprisingly, the availability of counseling programs and workshops for Internet dependence is on the increase, particularly on college campuses. Among the most popular treatment approaches are support groups similar to Alcoholics Anonymous—some of them, ironically, operating on the Internet. Such groups have attracted many subscribers; the individuals who sign up admit to the problem, provide support for each other, and swap methods for reducing their use of the Internet (Murray, 1996). This sounds to some clinicians "like having an Alcoholics Anonymous meeting in a bar" (Orzack, 1996). Others point out, however, that many dependent Internet users cannot tear themselves away from their computers long enough to visit a traditional treatment center (Belluck, 1996).

Cell phone dependence *Oblivious to their immediate environment, including alluring billboard ads, these individuals, like millions of people throughout the world, talk nonstop on their cell phones. Many clinicians believe that the proliferation of cell phones has created a widespread dependence on these electronic devices and has heightened the risk of developing dependent personality disorder in today's world. Indeed, studies reveal that a growing number of cell phone users react with intense anxiety and worry, physical discomfort, feelings of separation, and a loss of self-esteem when forced to shut off their portable phones for more than a few minutes (Chaparro, 2004).*

close relationship ends, and they quickly seek out another relationship to fill the void. Many cling persistently to relationships with partners who physically or psychologically abuse them.

Lacking confidence in their own ability and judgment, people with this disorder seldom disagree with others and allow even important decisions to be made for them. They may depend on a parent or spouse to decide where to live, what job to have, and which neighbors to befriend (APA, 2000, 1994; Overholser, 1996). Because they so fear rejection, they are overly sensitive to disapproval and keep trying to meet other people's wishes and expectations, even if it means volunteering for unpleasant or demeaning tasks.

Many people with dependent personality disorder feel distressed, lonely, and sad; often they dislike themselves. Thus they are at risk for depressive, anxiety, and eating disorders (Godt, 2002; Skodol et al., 1999). Their fear of separation and their feelings of helplessness may leave them particularly prone to suicidal thoughts, especially when they believe that a relationship is about to end (Kiev, 1989).

Studies suggest that over 2 percent of the population experience dependent personality disorder (Mattia & Zimmerman, 2001). For years clinicians have believed that more women than men display this pattern (Anderson et al., 2001), but some research suggests that the disorder is just as common in men (APA, 2000; Reich, 1990).

HOW DO THEORISTS EXPLAIN DEPENDENT PERSONALITY DISORDER? Psychodynamic explanations for this personality disorder are very similar to those for depression. Freudian theorists argue, for example, that unresolved conflicts during the oral stage of development can give rise to a lifelong need for nurturance, thus heightening the likelihood of a dependent personality disorder (Bornstein, 2005). Similarly, object relations theorists say that early parental loss or rejection may prevent normal experiences of *attachment* and *separation,* leaving some children with fears of abandonment that persist throughout their lives. Still other psychodynamic theorists suggest that, to the contrary, many parents of people with this disorder were overinvolved and overprotective, thus increasing their children's dependency, insecurity, and separation anxiety (Sperry, 2003).

Behaviorists propose that parents of people with dependent personality disorder unintentionally rewarded their children's clinging and "loyal" behavior, while at the same time punishing acts of independence, perhaps through the withdrawal of love. Alternatively, some parents' own dependent behaviors may have served as models for their children.

Finally, cognitive theorists identify two maladaptive attitudes as helping to produce and maintain this disorder: (1) "I am inadequate and helpless to deal with the world," and (2) "I must find a person to provide protection so I can cope" (Beck et al., 2004, 2001). Dichotomous (black-and-white) thinking may also play a key role: "If I am to be dependent, I must be completely helpless," or "If I am to be independent, I must be alone." Such thinking prevents sufferers from making efforts to be autonomous.

TREATMENTS FOR DEPENDENT PERSONALITY DISORDER In therapy, people with this personality disorder usually place all responsibility for their treatment and well-being on the clinician (Gutheil, 2005; Perry, 1989). Thus a key task of therapy is to help patients accept responsibility for themselves. Because the domineering behaviors of a spouse or parent may help foster a patient's symptoms, some clinicians propose couple or family therapy as well, or even separate therapy for the partner or parent (Millon, 1999).

Treatment for dependent personality disorder can be at least modestly helpful. Psychodynamic therapy for this pattern focuses on many of the same issues as therapy for depressed people, including the *transference* of dependency needs onto the therapist (Sperry, 2003; Gabbard, 2001). Behavioral therapists often provide assertiveness training to help clients better express their own wishes in relationships (Farmer & Nelson-Gray, 2005). Cognitive therapists try to help clients challenge and change their assumptions of incompetence and helplessness (Beck et al., 2004; Freeman, 2002). Antidepressant drug therapy has been helpful for persons whose personality disorder is accompanied by depression (Fava et al., 2002).

Finally, as with avoidant personality disorder, a group therapy format can be helpful because it provides opportunities for the client to receive support from a number of peers rather than from a single dominant person (Sperry, 2003; Azima, 1993). In addition, group members may serve as models for one another as they practice better ways to express feelings and solve problems.

Obsessive-Compulsive Personality Disorder

People with **obsessive–compulsive personality disorder** are so preoccupied with order, perfection, and control that they lose all flexibility, openness, and efficiency. Their concern for doing everything "right" impairs their productivity, as in the case of Wayne:

Wayne was advised to seek assistance from a therapist following several months of relatively sleepless nights and a growing immobility and indecisiveness at his job. When first seen, he reported feelings of extreme self-doubt and guilt and prolonged periods of tension and diffuse anxiety. It was established early in therapy that he always had experienced these symptoms. They were now merely more pronounced than before.

The precipitant for this sudden increase in discomfort was a forthcoming change in his academic post. New administrative officers had assumed authority at the college, and he was asked to resign his deanship to return to regular departmental instruction. In the early sessions, Wayne spoke largely of his fear of facing classroom students again, wondered if he could organize his material well, and doubted that he could keep classes disciplined and interested in his lectures. It was his preoccupation with these matters that he believed was preventing him from concentrating and completing his present responsibilities.

At no time did Wayne express anger toward the new college officials for the "demotion" he was asked to accept. He repeatedly voiced his "complete confidence" in the "rationality of their decision." Yet, when face-to-face with them, he observed that he stuttered and was extremely tremulous.

Wayne was the second of two sons, younger than his brother by three years. His father was a successful engineer, and his mother a high school teacher. Both were "efficient, orderly and strict" parents. Life at home was "extremely well planned," with "daily and weekly schedules of responsibilities posted" and "vacations arranged a year or two in advance." Nothing apparently was left to chance. . . . Wayne adopted the "good boy" image. Unable to challenge his brother either physically, intellectually or socially, he became a "paragon of virtue." By being punctilious, scrupulous, methodical and orderly, he could avoid antagonizing his perfectionistic parents, and would, at times, obtain preferred treatment from them. He obeyed their advice, took their guidance as gospel and hesitated making any decision before gaining their approval. Although he recalled "fighting" with his brother before he was six or seven, he "restrained his anger from that time on and never upset his parents again."

(Millon, 1969, pp. 278–279)

In Wayne's concern with rules and order and doing things right, he has trouble seeing the larger picture. When faced with a task, he and others who have obsessive-compulsive personality disorder may become so focused on organization and details that they fail to grasp the point of the activity. As a result, their work is often behind schedule (some seem unable to finish any job), and they may neglect leisure activities and friendships.

People with this personality disorder set unreasonably high standards for themselves and others. They can never be satisfied with their performance, but they typically refuse to seek help or to work with a team, convinced that others are too careless or incompetent to do the job right. Because they are so afraid of making mistakes, they may be reluctant to make decisions.

These individuals also tend to be rigid and stubborn, particularly in their morals, ethics, and values. They live by a strict personal code and use it as a yardstick for measuring

•OBSESSIVE-COMPULSIVE PERSONALITY DISORDER•A personality disorder marked by such an intense focus on orderliness, perfectionism, and control that the individual loses flexibility, openness, and efficiency.

>>PSYCH•NOTES
A Critical Difference

People with obsessive-compulsive anxiety disorder typically do not want or like their symptoms; those with obsessive-compulsive personality disorder often embrace their symptoms and rarely wish to resist them (Zohar & Pato, 1991). <<

others. They may have trouble expressing much affection, and their relationships are sometimes stiff and superficial. In addition, they are often stingy with their time or money. Some cannot even throw away objects that are worn out or useless (Sperry, 2003; APA, 2000, 1994).

Between 2 and 5 percent of the population are believed to display obsessive-compulsive personality disorder, with white, educated, married, and employed individuals receiving the diagnosis most often (Mattia & Zimmerman, 2001; APA, 2000). Men are twice as likely as women to display the disorder.

Many clinicians believe that obsessive-compulsive personality disorder and obsessive-compulsive disorder (the anxiety disorder) are closely related. Certainly, the two disorders share a number of features. Moreover, many people who suffer from the anxiety disorder qualify for the personality disorder diagnosis as well (Albert et al., 2004). However, other personality disorders (avoidant, histrionic, schizotypal, and dependent) may be even more common among those with the anxiety disorder (Steketee, 1990). In fact, researchers have not found a specific link between obsessive-compulsive personality disorder and the obsessive-compulsive anxiety disorder (Albert et al., 2004).

HOW DO THEORISTS EXPLAIN OBSESSIVE-COMPULSIVE PERSONALITY DISORDER?

Most explanations of obsessive-compulsive personality disorder borrow heavily from those of obsessive-compulsive anxiety disorder, despite the doubts concerning a link between the two disorders. As with so many of the personality disorders, psychodynamic explanations dominate and research evidence is limited.

Freudian theorists suggest that people with obsessive-compulsive personality disorder are *anal regressive*. That is, because of overly harsh toilet training during the anal stage, they become filled with anger, and they remain *fixated* at this stage. To keep their anger under control, they persistently resist both their anger and their instincts to have bowel movements. In turn, they become extremely orderly and restrained; many become passionate collectors. Other psychodynamic theorists suggest that any early struggles with parents over control and independence may ignite the aggressive impulses at the root of this personality disorder (Kuriansky, 1988; Mollinger, 1980).

Cognitive theorists have little to say about the origins of obsessive-compulsive personality disorder, but they do propose that illogical thinking processes help keep it going (Beck et al., 2004, 2001). They point, for example, to dichotomous thinking, which may produce rigidity and perfectionism. Similarly, they note that people with this disorder tend to misread or exaggerate the potential outcomes of mistakes or errors.

TREATMENTS FOR OBSESSIVE-COMPULSIVE PERSONALITY DISORDER

People with obsessive-compulsive personality disorder do not usually believe there is anything wrong with them. They therefore are not likely to seek treatment unless they are also suffering from another disorder, most frequently anxiety or depression, or unless someone close to them insists that they get treatment (Beck & Freeman, 1990). Individuals with the obsessive-compulsive personality disorder often respond well to psychodynamic or cognitive therapy (Gabbard, 2001; Primac, 1993). Psychodynamic therapists typically try to help them recognize, experience, and accept their underlying feelings and insecurities, and perhaps to take risks and accept their personal limitations (Sperry, 2003; Salzman, 1989). Cognitive therapists focus on helping clients to change their dichotomous thinking, perfectionism, indecisiveness, procrastination, and chronic worrying (Leahy et al., 2005; Beck et al., 2004). In contrast to people with obsessive-compulsive anxiety disorder, those with the personality disorder do not respond exceptionally well to drug therapy or behavioral therapy.

Toilet rage *According to Freud, toilet training often produces rage in a child. If parents are too harsh in their approach, the child may become fixated at the anal stage and prone to obsessive-compulsive functioning later in life.*

What Problems Are Posed by the DSM-IV-TR Categories?

Most of today's clinicians believe that personality disorders are important and troubling patterns. Yet these disorders are particularly hard to diagnose and easy to misdiagnose, difficulties that indicate serious problems with the *validity* (accuracy) and *reliability* (consistency) of the DSM-IV-TR categories (Jablensky, 2002).

One problem is that some of the criteria used to diagnose personality disorders cannot be observed directly. To distinguish paranoid from schizoid personality disorder, for example, clinicians must ask not only whether people avoid forming close relationships, but also *why*. In other words, the diagnoses often rely heavily on the impressions of the individual clinician. A related problem is that clinicians differ widely in their judgments about when a normal personality style crosses the line and deserves to be called a disorder (Clark, 2002). Some even believe that it is wrong ever to think of personality styles as mental disorders, however troublesome they may be (Kendell, 2002).

The similarity of personality disorders within a cluster, or even between clusters, poses yet another problem (Grilo et al., 2002). Within DSM-IV-TR's "anxious" cluster, for example, there is considerable overlap between the symptoms of avoidant personality disorder and those of dependent personality disorder (Bornstein, 1998). When clinicians see similar feelings of inadequacy, fear of disapproval, and the like, is it reasonable to consider them separate disorders? Also, the many borderline traits ("dramatic" cluster) found among some people with dependent personality disorder ("anxious" cluster) may indicate that these two disorders are but different versions of one basic pattern (Dolan et al., 1995).

In fact, some research suggests that people with disorders of personality *typically* meet diagnostic criteria for several personality disorders (Langenbucher & Nathan, 2006; Widiger & Clark, 2000). Once again, when two or more personality disorders occur in the same person, it is not clear whether the various disorders actually represent multiple pathologies or a single underlying pathology.

Yet another problem with the DSM-IV-TR categories is that people with quite different personalities may qualify for the same personality disorder diagnosis (Costello, 1996). Individuals must meet a certain number of criteria from DSM-IV-TR to receive a given diagnosis, but no single feature is necessary for that diagnosis (Millon, 2002, 1999). A diagnosis of borderline personality disorder, for example, requires that 5 of 9 possible symptoms be present. This means that 126 distinct symptom combinations can characterize people with the disorder (Skodol, 2005).

Partly because of these problems, diagnosticians keep changing the criteria used to assess each of the personality disorders. In fact, the diagnostic categories themselves have changed more than once, and they will no doubt change again. For example, DSM-IV-TR dropped a past category, **passive-aggressive personality disorder,** a

Dysfunctional toons *As the messages and technology found in film animation have become more complex over time, so have the personality problems of animated characters. (Left) Troubled characters of the past were usually defined by a single undesirable personality trait, as demonstrated by Snow White's friend Grumpy, second from left. (Right) Today's characters have "clusters" of problematic traits. For example, some critics suggest that the* South Park *kids display enduring grumpiness (especially Cartman, second from left); disrespect for authority, irreverence, and self-absorption; disregard for the feelings of others; general lack of conscience; and a tendency to get into trouble.*

•PASSIVE-AGGRESSIVE PERSONALITY DISORDER• A category of personality disorder listed in past versions of the DSM, marked by a pattern of negative attitudes and resistance to the demands of others.

pattern of negative attitudes and passive resistance to the demands of others, because research failed to show that this was more than a single trait. The pattern is now being studied more carefully and may be included once again in future editions of the DSM.

Are There Better Ways to Classify Personality Disorders?

In light of these concerns, it is not surprising that today's leading criticism of DSM-IV-TR's approach to personality disorders is that the classification system uses multiple *categories*—categories that serve to *dichotomize* personality problems (Clark, 2005). Like a light switch that is either on or off, this categorical approach assumes that a personality disorder is either entirely present or absent. But what about a person who meets many, but not all, of the criteria for a particular personality disorder? Although this person may display a persistent, debilitating, and impairing personality pattern that requires clinical attention, his or her problems would remain undiagnosed. In addition, dichotomizing problems of personality does not allow one to distinguish between this troubled but undiagnosable person and other individuals who do not suffer from any problems of personality. In fact, it has been estimated that in clinical practice as many as 60 percent of clients with personality problems are not diagnosable according to the DSM criteria (Westen & Arkowitz-Westen, 1998).

Given such difficulties, many theorists now believe that the DSM-IV-TR personality disorders actually differ more in *degree* than in type of dysfunction, and they have proposed that the disorders should be organized by the severity of certain key traits, or personality dimensions, rather than by the presence or absence of specific traits. A growing number of these theorists suggest that a *dimensional* approach to classifying personality pathology would more accurately reflect the personality problems seen in people (Widiger, 2006; Trull & Durrett, 2005). In such an approach, each key trait (for example, agreeableness or honesty or self-absorption) is seen as varying along a continuum in which there is no clear boundary between normal and abnormal. People with a personality disorder are those who display extreme degrees of several of these key traits—degrees not commonly found in the general population.

We can all probably generate an extensive list of traits, or dimensions, on which our friends vary. For example, they might differ in the extent to which they dwell on their problems, socialize with others, spend frivolously, and enjoy soft music. Clearly some of these dimensions are more important than others to one's functioning. What personality dimensions should clinicians use to help identify and distinguish people with personality problems? Many theorists believe that they should rely upon the dimensions identified in the "Big Five" theory of personality—the dimensional theory that has been studied the most by personality theorists.

THE "BIG FIVE" THEORY OF PERSONALITY AND PERSONALITY DISORDERS

A large body of research conducted with diverse populations consistently suggests that the basic structure of personality may consist of five "supertraits," or factors—*neuroticism, extroversion, openness to experiences, agreeableness,* and *conscientiousness* (Costa & McCrae, 2005). Each of these factors, which are frequently referred to as the "Big Five," consists of a number of subfactors. Anxiety and hostility, for example, are subfactors of the neuroticism factor, while optimism and friendliness are subfactors of the extroversion factor. Theoretically, everyone's personality can be summarized by a combination of these supertraits. One person may display high levels of neuroticism and agreeableness, medium extroversion, and low conscientiousness and openness to experiences. In contrast, another person may display high levels of agreeableness and conscientiousness, medium neuroticism and extroversion, and low openness to experiences. And so on.

Many theorists have further considered how the "Big Five" model of personality might relate to the impairments seen across the DSM-IV-TR personality disorders (Clark, 2005; Costa & McCrae, 2005). Research suggests that the majority of these personality disorders are characterized by high levels of neuroticism and low levels of agreeableness (Saulsman & Page, 2004). In addition, persons suffering from the personality disorders that involve reclusiveness (schizoid, schizotypal, and avoidant personality disorders) display particularly low levels of extroversion; persons suffering from disorders marked by gregariousness (histrionic and narcissistic personality disorders) exhibit particularly high levels of extroversion; those with obsessive-compulsive personality disorder display elevated levels of conscientiousness; and people whose disorders are characterized by recklessness (antisocial and borderline personality disorders) display low levels of conscientiousness.

Many proponents of the five-factor model further argue that it would be best to describe all people with personality disorders as being high, low, or in between on the five supertraits, and to drop the DSM's current use of personality disorder categories altogether.

ALTERNATIVE DIMENSIONAL APPROACHES Although many clinical theorists now agree that a dimensional approach would reflect personality pathology more accurately than the categorical DSM-IV-TR approach, not all of them believe that the "Big Five" model is the most useful dimensional approach. Some worry that too few trait adjectives are included in the five-factor model and others suggest that ratings of simple adjective lists cannot adequately capture the complex patterns of pathology displayed by many people with personality disorders. Can, for example, ratings of simple adjectives fully depict persons who waver back and forth between exaggerated feelings of self-worth and profound feelings of inadequacy? Or individuals who demonstrate both intense anger and an inability to express emotion?

With these concerns in mind, a number of theorists have proposed alternative dimensional models (Bagby et al., 2005; Widiger & Simonsen, 2005). In one such effort, the researchers Jonathan Shedler and Drew Westen (2004) have developed a dimensional approach consisting of 12 broad factors rather than 5 factors—broad factors that collectively comprise 200 descriptive *statements* such as "The individual tends to elicit liking in others," "The individual tends to get into power struggles," "The individual's emotions tend to change rapidly and exaggeratedly," and "The individual fantasizes about finding ideal, perfect love." To describe a given person with a personality disorder, the clinician rates each of these 200 statements on a scale from 0 to 7. Research suggests that the resulting descriptions effectively capture the complexity of personality dysfunctioning and, at the same time, provide numerical scores that can be used in systematic studies of personality disorders (Westen & Muderrisoglu, 2006; Westen et al., 2005; Shedler & Westen, 2004).

It is not yet certain where these proposed dimensional models of personality pathology will lead, although a number of influential theorists predict that the next edition of the DSM (DSM-V) will use some such model rather than the categorical model currently in DSM-IV-TR (Widiger et al., 2005). At the very least, the current debate indicates once again that most clinicians believe personality dysfunctions represent important forms of abnormality that must be better understood and treated.

Personality au naturel *As suggested by the varied reactions of these polar bears to events at Canada's Hudson Bay, human beings are not the only creatures who demonstrate differences in personality, mood, and lifestyle. Natural data of this kind have led many theorists to suspect that inborn, biological factors contribute, at least in part, to personality differences and personality disorders.*

PUTTING IT together
Disorders of Personality Are Rediscovered

During the first half of the twentieth century, clinicians believed deeply in the unique, enduring patterns we call personality, and they tried to define important personality traits. They then discovered how readily people can be shaped by the situations in which they find themselves, and a backlash developed. The concept of personality seemed to lose legitimacy, and for a while it became almost an obscene word in some circles. The clinical category of personality disorders experienced a similar rejection. When psychodynamic and humanistic theorists dominated the clinical field, *neurotic character disorders,* a set of diagnoses similar to today's personality disorders, were considered useful clinical categories (Millon et al., 2000). But their popularity declined as other models grew in influence.

During the past two decades, serious interest in personality and personality disorders has rebounded (Lenzenweger & Clarkin, 2005). In case after case, clinicians have

> **>>IN THEIR WORDS**
>
> "In most of us, by the age of thirty, the character has set like plaster and will never soften again." **<<**
>
> William James, *Principles of Psychology,* 1890
>
> -
>
> "We continue to shape our personality all our life." **<<**
>
> Albert Camus

Michio Hoshino/Minden Pictures

>>BY THE NUMBERS

Personality Disorder Demographics

59% Percentage of people with severe personality disorders who are male <<

23% Individuals with severe personality disorders who have never married <<

19% Individuals with severe personality disorders who are racial or ethnic minority group members <<

6% Individuals with severe personality disorders who are unemployed <<

(Cloninger & Svrakic, 2005)

>>IN THEIR WORDS

Speaking of Personality

"We have to distrust each other. It's our only defense against betrayal." <<
Tennessee Williams, American playwright

"What loneliness is more lonely than distrust?" <<
George Eliot, British novelist

"Anger is a brief lunacy." <<
Horace, Roman poet

"The hysterical find too much significance in things. The depressed find too little." <<
Mason Cooley, American aphorist

"When you stop drinking, you have to deal with this marvelous personality that started you drinking in the first place." <<
Jimmy Breslin, American journalist

concluded that rigid personality traits do seem to pose special problems, and they have developed new objective tests and interview guides to assess these disorders, setting in motion a wave of systematic research (Widiger, 2005, 2002; Clark & Harrison, 2001). So far, only the antisocial and borderline personality disorders have received extensive study. As other patterns of personality pathology attract their fair share of research attention, clinicians should be better able to answer some pressing questions: How common are the various personality disorders? How useful are the present categories? And what treatments are most effective?

One of the most important questions is, Why do people develop troubled patterns of personality? As we have seen, psychological, as opposed to biological and sociocultural, theories have offered the most suggestions so far, but these proposed explanations are not very precise, and they do not have strong research support. Given the current enthusiasm for biological explanations, genetic and biological factors are likely to receive more study in the coming years, helping researchers determine their possible interaction with psychological causes. And one would hope that sociocultural factors will be studied as well. As we have seen, sociocultural theorists have only occasionally offered explanations for personality disorders. However, sociocultural factors may well play an important role in these disorders and should be examined more carefully, especially since, by definition, patterns diagnosed as a personality disorder differ markedly from the expectations of a person's culture.

The future is likely to bring major changes to the explanations and treatments for personality disorders, and the classification of personality disorders will probably undergo change as well. Such changes, however, are now more likely to be based on research than on clinical intuitions and impressions. For the many people caught in the web of rigid and maladaptive personality traits, these changes should make an important difference, and one long overdue.

[SUMMARY AND REVIEW]

■ **Personality disorders** A *personality disorder* is an inflexible pattern of inner experience and outward behavior. Such patterns are wide-ranging and enduring, differ markedly from social norms, and lead to distress or impairment. Explanations for most of the personality disorders have received only limited research support. DSM-IV-TR distinguishes 10 personality disorders and separates them into three *clusters*. *pp. 461–463*

■ **"Odd" personality disorders** Three of the personality disorders are marked by the kinds of odd or eccentric behavior often seen in the Axis I disorder schizophrenia. People with *paranoid personality disorder* display a broad pattern of distrust and suspiciousness. Those with *schizoid personality disorder* persistently avoid social relationships, have little or no social interests, and show little emotional expression. Individuals with *schizotypal personality disorder* display a range of interpersonal problems marked by extreme discomfort in close relationships, very odd forms of thinking and behavior, and behavioral eccentricities. People with these three kinds of disorders usually are resistant to treatment, and treatment gains tend to be modest at best. *pp. 463–469*

■ **"Dramatic" personality disorders** Four of the personality disorders are marked by highly dramatic, emotional, or erratic symptoms. People with *antisocial personality disorder* display a pattern of disregard for and violation of the rights of others. No known treatment is notably effective. People with *borderline personality disorder* display a pattern of instability in interpersonal relationships, self-image, and mood, along with extreme impulsivity. Treatment apparently can be helpful and lead to some improvement. People with *histrionic personality disorder* (once called *hysterical personality disorder*) display a pattern of extreme emotionality and attention seeking. Clinical case reports suggest that treatment is helpful on occasion. Finally, people with *narcissistic personality disorder* display a pattern of grandiosity, need for admiration, and lack of empathy. It is one of the most difficult disorders to treat. *pp. 470–483*

■ **"Anxious" personality disorders** Three of the personality disorders are marked by the kinds of symptoms found in the Axis I anxiety and depressive disorders. People with *avoidant personality disorder* are consistently uncomfortable and inhibited in social situations, overwhelmed by feelings of inadequacy, and extremely sensitive to negative evaluation. People with *dependent personality disorder* have a persistent need to be taken care of, are submissive and clinging, and fear separation. Individuals with *obsessive-compulsive personality disorder* are so preoccupied with order, perfection, and control that they lose their flexibility, openness, and efficiency. A variety of treatment strategies have been used for people with these disorders and apparently have been modestly to moderately helpful. *pp. 484–490*

■ **Problems posed by the DSM-IV-TR categories** It appears that the DSM-IV-TR personality disorders are commonly misdiagnosed, an indication of serious problems in the *validity* and *reliability* of the diagnostic categories. Given the significant problems posed by DSM-IV-TR's *categorical* approach, many of today's theorists believe that personality disorders should instead be described and classified by a *dimensional* approach. *pp. 491–493*

>>> **CRITICAL THOUGHTS** <<<

1. It is common for people outside the clinical field to mistakenly diagnose mental disorders in themselves, relatives, or acquaintances, and the personality disorders are among the most favored of their diagnoses. Why do you think these disorders are particularly subject to such efforts at amateur psychology? *pp. 461–494*

2. What might be the difference between "normal" lying and "pathological" lying? *pp. 470–473, 481*

3. How do various institutions in our society—business, government, academia, science, religion—view lying, and how might these views affect the prevalence and nature of individual lies? *pp. 470–473, 481*

4. Why do people often admire someone who deceives—a flatterer, an art forger, a jewel thief? *pp. 470–473, 481*

5. Some people believe that the past 15 years have witnessed an increase in narcissistic behavior and thinking in Western society. What features of Western society during this span of time (for example, child-rearing philosophies, advertising campaigns, sports heroes, book topics, television programming, and movies) may be contributing to a rise in narcissistic behavior? *p. 483*

6. Invent a way of organizing and defining personality disorders that improves upon the present diagnostic system. How would the DSM-IV-TR categories fit into your new scheme? *pp. 491–493*

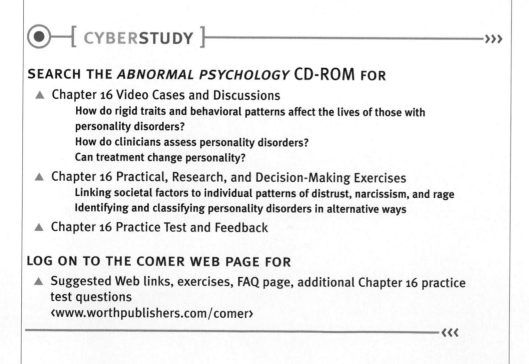

◉—[**CYBER**STUDY]————————————————>>>

SEARCH THE *ABNORMAL PSYCHOLOGY* CD-ROM FOR

▲ Chapter 16 Video Cases and Discussions
   How do rigid traits and behavioral patterns affect the lives of those with personality disorders?
   How do clinicians assess personality disorders?
   Can treatment change personality?

▲ Chapter 16 Practical, Research, and Decision-Making Exercises
   Linking societal factors to individual patterns of distrust, narcissism, and rage
   Identifying and classifying personality disorders in alternative ways

▲ Chapter 16 Practice Test and Feedback

LOG ON TO THE COMER WEB PAGE FOR

▲ Suggested Web links, exercises, FAQ page, additional Chapter 16 practice test questions
   <www.worthpublishers.com/comer>

<<<

Disorders of Childhood and Adolescence

Billy, a 7-year-old . . . child, was brought to a mental health clinic by his mother because "he is unhappy and always complaining about feeling sick." . . . His mother describes Billy as a child who has never been very happy and never wanted to play with other children. From the time he started nursery school, he has complained about stomachaches, headaches, and various other physical problems. . . .

Billy did well in first grade, but in second grade he is now having difficulty completing his work. He takes a lot of time to do his assignments and frequently feels he has to do them over again so that they will be "perfect." Because of Billy's frequent somatic complaints, it is hard to get him off to school in the morning. If he is allowed to stay home, he worries that he is falling behind in his schoolwork. When he does go to school, he often is unable to do the work, which makes him feel hopeless about his situation. . . .

His worries have expanded beyond school, and frequently he is clinging and demanding of his parents. He is fearful that if his parents come home late or leave and go somewhere without him that something may happen to them. . . .

Although Billy's mother acknowledges that he has never been really happy, in the last 6 months, she feels, he has become much more depressed. He frequently lies around the house, saying that he is too tired to do anything. He has no interest or enjoyment in playing. His appetite has diminished. He has trouble falling asleep at night and often wakes up in the middle of the night or early in the morning. Three weeks ago, he talked, for the first time, about wanting to die. . . .

(Spitzer et al., 1994)

In the past year, Eddie [age 9] had been suspended twice for hyperactive and impulsive behavior. Most recently, he had climbed onto the overhead lights of the classroom and caused an uproar when he could not get himself down. His teachers complain that other children cannot concentrate when Eddie is in the room because he walks around constantly. Even when he is seated, his rapid foot and hand movements are disruptive to the other children. Eddie has almost no friends and does not play games with his classmates due to his impulsivity and overly active behavior. After school, he likes to play with his dog or ride his bike alone.

Eddie's mother reports that he has been excessively active since he was a toddler. At the age of three, Eddie would awaken at 4:30 AM each day and go downstairs without any supervision. Sometimes he would "demolish" the kitchen or living room, and at other times he would leave the house by himself. Once when he was four years old, he was found walking alone on a busy street in the early morning. Luckily, a passerby rescued him before he got into traffic.

After being rejected by a preschool because of his hyperactivity and impulsivity, Eddie attended a kindergarten and had a very difficult year. For first and second grade, he attended a special behavioral program. For third grade, he was allowed to attend a regular education class, with pull-out services for help with his behavior.

(Spitzer et al., 1994)

Billy and Eddie are both displaying psychological disorders. Their disorders are disrupting the boys' family ties, school performances, and social relationships, but each disorder does so in a particular way and for particular reasons. Billy, who may qualify for a diagnosis of *major depressive disorder,* struggles constantly with sadness, worry, and perfectionism, along with stomachaches and other physical ailments. Eddie, on the other hand, cannot concentrate and is overly active and impulsive—difficulties that comprise attention-deficit/hyperactivity disorder (ADHD). Like Billy, Eddie and others with ADHD may experience bouts of unhappiness, but for them such feelings are brought about by the repeated criticisms and social rebukes that they receive; in contrast, Billy's unhappiness is at the center of his disorder—the primary cause of his suffering and impaired functioning.

Abnormal functioning can occur at any time in life. Some patterns of abnormality, however, are more likely to emerge during particular periods—during childhood, for example, or, at the other end of the spectrum, during old age. In this chapter we shall focus on disorders that have their onset during childhood or early adolescence. In the next chapter, we shall turn to problems that are more common among the elderly.

Childhood and Adolescence

Theorists often view life as a series of stages on the road from birth to death (see Box 17-1 on page 500). Most people pass through these stages in the same order, though at their own rates and in their own ways. As we observed in Chapter 3, Freud proposed that each child passes through the same five stages—the *oral, anal, phallic, latency,* and *genital stages.* The influential psychodynamic theorist Erik Erikson (1963) added old age as one of life's most meaningful stages. Although theorists may disagree with the details of these schemes, most agree that we confront key pressures during each stage in life and either grow or decline depending on how we meet those pressures. Each stage offers many opportunities for dysfunction, whether because of biological limitations, psychological struggles, or extraordinary environmental stress.

People often think of childhood as a carefree and happy time—yet it can also be frightening and upsetting. In fact, children of all cultures typically experience at least some emotional and behavioral problems as they encounter new people and situations. Surveys reveal that *worry* is a common experience: close to half of all children in the United States have multiple fears, particularly concerning school, health, and personal safety (Beidel & Turner, 2005; Szabo & Lovibond, 2004). Bed-wetting, nightmares, temper tantrums, and restlessness are other problems experienced by many children.

Adolescence can also be a difficult period. Physical and sexual changes, social and academic pressures, personal doubts, and temptations cause many teenagers to feel anxious, confused, and depressed (Weisz et al., 2006; King et al., 2005). Today's teens, although generally happy and optimistic and often spiritual, tend to feel less trusting, more sensitive, and more isolated from their families than adolescents of decades past (Begley, 2000).

Along with these common psychological difficulties, at least one-fifth of all children and adolescents in North America also experience a diagnosable psychological disorder (Jaffee et al., 2005; Phares, 2003). Boys with disorders outnumber girls, even though most of the adult psychological disorders are more common among women. Because certain disorders of children—childhood anxiety disorders and childhood depression—have adult counterparts, those patterns were examined in the chapters on anxiety and mood disorders (see pages 140 and 272–273). In contrast, other childhood disorders—conduct disorders, ADHD, and elimination disorders, for example—usually disappear or radically change form by adulthood, so those patterns will be examined in this chapter. There are also disorders that begin at birth or in childhood and persist in stable forms into

The burdens of childhood *As this young child sits alone on the steps of his school, carrying the weight of the world on his shoulders, we are reminded that childhood is often a burdensome period of life.*

Michael Prince/Corbis

adult life. These include mental retardation and autism, the former an extensive disturbance in intellect, the latter marked by a lack of responsiveness to the environment. Such lifespan disorders will also be examined in this chapter.

Oppositional Defiant Disorder and Conduct Disorder

Most children break rules or misbehave on occasion (see Figure 17-1 and Box 17-2 on page 502). If they consistently display extreme hostility and defiance, however, they may qualify for a diagnosis of oppositional defiant disorder or conduct disorder. Those with **oppositional defiant disorder** are often hostile (they argue repeatedly with adults, lose their temper, feel great anger and resentment) and disobedient (they ignore adult rules and requests), and display negative behaviors (they may try to annoy other people and blame others for their own mistakes and problems). Approximately 8 percent of children qualify for this diagnosis (Kessler et al., 2005; APA, 2000). The disorder is more common in boys than in girls before puberty but equal in both sexes after puberty.

Children with **conduct disorder,** a more severe problem, repeatedly violate the basic rights of others. They are often aggressive and may be physically cruel to people or animals, deliberately destroy other people's property, skip school, or run away from home (see Table 17-1 on page 502). Many steal from, threaten, or harm their victims, committing such crimes as shoplifting, forgery, breaking into buildings or cars, mugging, and armed robbery. As they get older, their acts of physical violence may include rape or, in rare cases, homicide (APA, 2000, 1994). The symptoms of conduct disorder are apparent in this summary of a clinical interview with a 15-year-old boy named Derek:

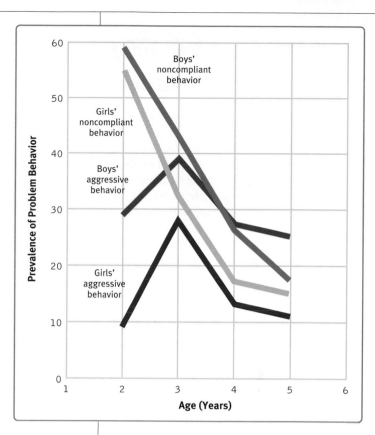

FIGURE **17-1** **Early misbehavior** *Teachers' evaluations of more than 700 preschoolers indicated that the rates of both noncompliant and aggressive behavior dropped as the children grew older. (Adapted from Crowther et al., 1981.)*

Questioning revealed that Derek was getting into . . . serious trouble of late, having been arrested for shoplifting 4 weeks before. Derek was caught with one other youth when he and a dozen friends swarmed a convenience store and took everything they could before leaving in cars. This event followed similar others at a compact disc store and a retail clothing store. Derek blamed his friends for getting caught because they apparently left him behind as he straggled out of the store. He was charged only with shoplifting, however, after police found him holding just three candy bars and a bag of potato chips. Derek expressed no remorse for the theft or any care for the store clerk who was injured when one of the teens pushed her into a glass case. When informed of the clerk's injury, for example, Derek replied, "I didn't do it, so what do I care?"

The psychologist decided to question Derek further about other legal violations in the past. He discovered a rather extended history of trouble. Ten months earlier, Derek had been arrested for vandalism—breaking windows and damaging cars—on school property. He was placed on probation for 6 months because this was his first offense. In addition, Derek boasted of other exploits for which he was not caught, including several shoplifting attempts, heavy marijuana use on the weekends, joyriding, and missing school. . . . Derek had missed 23 days (50 percent) of school since the beginning of the academic year. . . . In addition, Derek described break-in attempts of his neighbors' apartments and his precocious sexual activity. . . . Only rarely during the interview did Derek stray from his bravado.

(Kearney, 1999, pp. 104–105)

Conduct disorder usually begins between 7 and 15 years of age (APA, 2000). Around 10 percent of children, three-quarters of them boys, qualify for this diagnosis (Hibbs &

•**OPPOSITIONAL DEFIANT DISORDER**•A childhood disorder in which children argue repeatedly with adults, lose their temper, and swear, feeling intense anger and resentment.

•**CONDUCT DISORDER**•A childhood disorder in which the child repeatedly violates the basic rights of others, displaying aggression and sometimes destroying others' property, stealing, or running away from home.

[BOX **17-1**]

The Etiology and Treatment of Childhood   *Jordan W. Smoller*

Childhood is a syndrome that has only recently begun to receive serious attention from clinicians. The syndrome itself, however, is not at all recent. As early as the eighth century, the Persian historian Kidnom made reference to "short, noisy creatures," who may well have been what we now call "children." The treatment of children, however, was unknown until this century, when so-called child psychologists and child psychiatrists became common. Despite this history of clinical neglect, it has been estimated that well over half of all Americans alive today have experienced childhood directly (Seuss, 1983). In fact, the actual numbers are probably much higher, since these data are based on self-reports which may be subject to social desirability biases and retrospective distortion. Clinicians are still in disagreement about the significant clinical features of childhood, but the proposed DSM-IV will almost certainly include the following core features:

1. Congenital onset
2. Dwarfism
3. Emotional lability and immaturity
4. Knowledge deficits
5. Legume anorexia

Congenital Onset In one of the few existing literature reviews on childhood, Temple-Black (1982) has noted that childhood is almost always present at birth, although it may go undetected for years or even remain subclinical indefinitely. This observation has led some investigators to speculate on a biological contribution to childhood. As one psychologist has put it, "we may soon be in a position to distinguish organic childhood from functional childhood" (Rogers, 1979).

Dwarfism This is certainly the most familiar clinical marker of childhood. It is widely known that children are physi-

cally short relative to the population at large. Indeed, common clinical wisdom suggests that the treatment of the so-called small child (or "tot") is particularly difficult. These children are known to exhibit infantile behavior and display a startling lack of insight (Tom & Jerry, 1967).

Emotional Lability and Immaturity This aspect of childhood is often the only basis for a clinician's diagnosis. As a result, many otherwise normal adults are misdiagnosed as children and must suffer the unnecessary social stigma of being labeled a "child" by professionals and friends alike.

Knowledge Deficits While many children have IQs within or even above the norm, almost all will manifest knowledge deficits. Anyone who has known a real child has experienced the frustration of trying to discuss any topic that requires some general knowledge.

Legume Anorexia This last identifying feature is perhaps the most unexpected. Folk wisdom is supported by empirical observation—children will rarely eat their vegetables (see Popeye, 1957, for review).

CAUSES OF CHILDHOOD

Now that we know what it is, what can we say about the causes of childhood? Recent years have seen a flurry of theory and speculation from a number of perspectives. Some of the most prominent are reviewed below.

Sociological Model Emile Durkind was perhaps the first to speculate about sociological causes of childhood. He points out two key observations about children: (1) the vast majority of children are unemployed, and (2) children represent one of the least educated segments of our society. In fact, it has been estimated that less than 20 percent of children have had more than a fourth-grade education. . . . One promising rehabilitation program (Spanky & Alfalfa, 1978) has trained victims of severe childhood to sell lemonade.

Biological Model The observation that childhood is usually present from birth has led some to speculate on a biological contribution. An early investigation by Flintstone and Jetson (1939) indicated that childhood runs in families. Their survey of over 8,000 American families revealed that over half con-

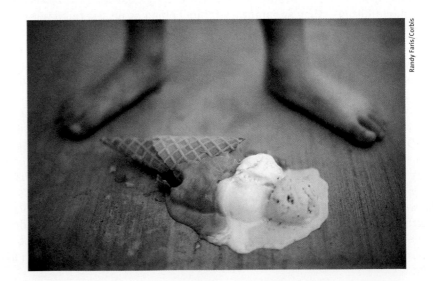

Randy Faris/Corbis

tained more than one child. Further investigation revealed that even most nonchild family members had experienced childhood at some point. . . .

Psychological Models A considerable number of psychologically based theories of the development of childhood exist. They are too numerous to review here. Among the more familiar models are Seligman's "learned childishness" model. According to this model, individuals who are treated like children eventually give up and become children. As a counterpoint to such theories, some experts have claimed that childhood does not really exist. Szasz (1980) has called "childhood" an expedient label. In seeking conformity, we handicap those whom we find unruly or too short to deal with by labeling them "children."

TREATMENT OF CHILDHOOD

Efforts to treat childhood are as old as the syndrome itself. Only in modern times, however, have humane and systematic treatment protocols been applied. The overwhelming number of children has made government intervention inevitable. The nineteenth century saw the institution of what remains the largest single program for the treatment of childhood—so-called public schools. Under this colossal program, individuals are placed into treatment groups on the basis of the severity of their condition. For example, those most severely afflicted may be placed in a "kindergarten" program. Patients at this level are typically short, unruly, emotionally immature, and intellectually deficient.

Unfortunately, the "school" system has been largely ineffective. Not only is the program a massive tax burden, but it has failed even to slow down the rising incidence of childhood. Faced with this failure and the growing epidemic of childhood,

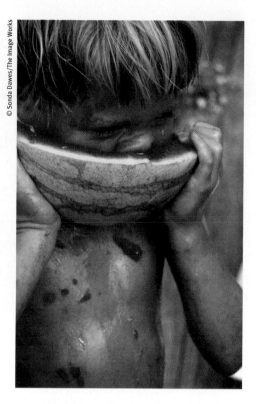

© Sonda Dawes/The Image Works

mental health professionals are devoting increasing attention to the treatment of childhood. . . . The following case (taken from Gumbie & Pokey, 1957) is typical.

Billy J., age 8, was brought to treatment by his parents. Billy's affliction was painfully obvious. He stood only 4′3″ high and weighed a scant 70 pounds, despite the fact that he ate voraciously. Billy presented a variety of troubling symptoms. His voice was noticeably high for a man. He displayed legume anorexia and, according to his parents, often refused to bathe. His intellectual functioning was also below normal—he had little general knowledge and could barely write a structured sentence. Social skills were also deficient. He often spoke inappropriately and exhibited "whining behavior." His sexual experience was nonexistent. Indeed, Billy considered women "icky." . . .

After years of this kind of frustration, startling new evidence has come to light which suggests that the prognosis in cases

of childhood may not be all gloom. . . . Moe, Larrie, and Kirly (1974) began a large-scale longitudinal study. These investigators studied two groups. The first group comprised 34 children currently engaged in a long-term conventional treatment program. The second was a group of 42 children receiving no treatment. . . .

The results . . . of a careful 10-year follow-up were startling. . . . Shemp (1984) found subjects improved. Indeed, in most cases, the subjects appeared to be symptom-free. Moe et al. report a spontaneous remission rate of 95 percent, a finding that is certain to revolutionize the clinical approach to childhood.

These recent results suggest that the prognosis for victims of childhood may not be so bad as we have feared. We must not, however, become too complacent. Despite its apparently high spontaneous remission rate, childhood remains one of the most serious and rapidly growing disorders facing mental health professionals today. And beyond the psychological pain it brings, childhood has recently been linked to a number of physical disorders. Twenty years ago, Howdi, Doodi, and Beauzeau (1965) demonstrated a sixfold increased risk of chickenpox, measles, and mumps among children as compared with normal controls. Later, Barbie and Kenn (1971) linked childhood to an elevated risk of accidents—compared with normal adults, victims of childhood were much more likely to scrape their knees, lose their teeth, and fall off their bikes.

Clearly, much more research is needed before we can give any real hope to the millions of victims wracked by this insidious disorder.

This "clinical review" of the "disorder" called childhood originally appeared in Glenn C. Ellenbogen (Ed.), *Oral Sadism and the Vegetarian Personality* (New York: Brunner/Mazel, 1986).

[BOX 17-2]

Bullying: A Growing Crisis?

*D*oes bullying qualify as a national crisis? Even to pose the question sounds a bit silly, conjuring up images of the schoolyard thug from the *Calvin and Hobbes* comic strip or Bart's nemesis on *The Simpsons*. But many sober voices say that bullying is no laughing matter and warn that if society continues to overlook this problem, it will place its citizens, particularly its children, at considerable risk (Rigby, 2002).

Recently the Secret Service released a report examining the dozens of school shootings that have taken place across the United States since 1997. It found that bullying was a factor in two-thirds of them (Crisp, 2001). In some cases, the shooters had been bullies; much more often, they had been the *victims* of bullying. A survey released by the Kaiser Family Foundation and Nickelodeon asked a national sample of children aged 8 to 15 what issues in school concerned them most, and all age groups pointed to teasing and bullying as

SW Productions/Photodisc

"big problems" that ranked higher than racism, AIDS, and peer pressure to try sex or alcohol (Cukan, 2001). Similarly, one recent study found that almost half of sixth

graders report being bullied at school and that victims typically reacted with feelings of humiliation, anxiety, or dislike for school (Nishina et al., 2005). Reports such

---

Table **17-1** DSM Checklist

CONDUCT DISORDER

1. A repetitive and persistent pattern of behavior in which the basic rights of others or major age-appropriate societal norms or rules are violated, with at least three of the following present in the past twelve months (and at least one in the past six months):
   a. Frequent bullying or threatening of others.
   b. Frequent provoking of physical fights.
   c. Using dangerous weapons.
   d. Physical cruelty to people.
   e. Physical cruelty to animals.
   f. Stealing while confronting a victim.
   g. Forcing someone into sexual activity.
   h. Fire-setting.
   i. Deliberately destroying others' property.
   j. Breaking into a house, building, or car.
   k. Frequent manipulation of others.
   l. Stealing items of nontrivial value without confronting a victim.
   m. Frequent staying out beyond curfews, beginning before the age of 13.
   n. Running away from home overnight at least twice.
   o. Frequent truancy from school, beginning before the age of 13.
2. Significant impairment.

Based on APA, 2000, 1994.

Jensen, 2005; Kessler et al., 2005). Children with a mild conduct disorder often improve over time, but severe cases may continue into adulthood and develop into antisocial personality disorder or other psychological problems (Phares, 2003). Usually, the earlier the onset of the conduct disorder, the poorer the eventual outcome. Research indicates that more than 80 percent of individuals who develop conduct disorder first display a pattern of oppositional defiant disorder (Lahey & Loeber, 1994).

Many clinical theorists believe that there are actually several kinds of conduct disorder. One team of researchers, for example, distinguishes four patterns: (1) the *overt-destructive* pattern, in which individuals display openly aggressive and confrontational behaviors; (2) the *overt-nondestructive* pattern, dominated by openly offensive but nonconfrontational behaviors such as lying; (3) the *covert-destructive* pattern, characterized by secretive destructive behaviors such as violating other people's property, breaking and entering, and setting fires; and (4) the *covert-nondestructive* pattern, in which individuals secretly commit nonaggressive behaviors, such as being truant from school (McMahon & Frick, 2005). Some individuals with conduct disorder display only one of these patterns, while others display a combination of them. It may be that the different patterns have different causes.

as these have elevated bullying from a narrow concern that is best dealt with by students themselves (or perhaps by the teachers and parents of those directly involved) to a widespread problem that requires the attention of school-level programs and statewide policies.

For instance, in the wake of shooting disasters such as those at Columbine High School in Littleton, Colorado (where 2 students murdered 12 of their peers and a teacher and injured dozens of others before committing suicide), and at Santana in California (where a 15-year-old killed 2 and injured 13 at his high school), many schools have put "zero tolerance" programs in place. These rules require immediate suspension of pupils who bring any weapon into the school—or indeed any object at all that could be used in a threatening way. A growing number of schools, too, have implemented programs—with names like "Taking the Bully by the Horns"—that teach children how to deal level-headedly with their tormenters and when to ask a teacher for help (Rahey & Craig, 2002).

While acknowledging the important impact and role of bullying in the recent wave of school shootings, some experts worry that the public, school officials, and policymakers are focusing on this issue so intensely that more subtle and perhaps more significant factors are being ignored by clinicians and researchers. Why has the public concentrated so much attention on bullying as it tries to sort out school shootings and other unthinkable acts by schoolchildren? Perhaps, some experts argue, because bullying offers a quick explanation and a ready focus for intervention and change. After all, teachers and administrators have been observing and dealing with bullies since the first little red schoolhouse appeared on the prairie. As Charles Ewing, a law professor, psychologist, and expert on homicides by children, puts it, "It's not rocket science to figure out who these unhappy kids are" (Cukan, 2001).

At the same time, the commonplace nature of bullying that makes it seem so familiar and treatable might actually render it an elusive problem to address. One study found that a full 30 percent of American students are involved in moderate or frequent bullying—11 percent have been victims, 13 percent have been bullies, and 6 percent have been both (Tanner, 2001). Other studies report even higher rates (Haynie et al., 2001). How easy can it be for clinicians to identify which children will turn dangerously violent if indeed one-third of all children have experienced bullying? How can we rid ourselves of a problem as pervasive as this? As one commentator said, "Short of raising kids in isolation chambers . . . bullying behaviors can never be eliminated entirely from the sustained hazing ritual known as growing up" (Angier, 2001).

Other researchers distinguish yet another pattern of aggression found in certain cases of conduct disorder, *relational aggression,* in which the individuals are socially isolated and primarily display social misdeeds such as slandering others, spreading rumors, and manipulating friendships (Underwood, 2003). Relational aggression is more common among girls than boys.

More than one-third of boys and one-half of girls with conduct disorder also display attention-deficit/hyperactivity disorder (ADHD), a disorder that we shall be looking at shortly (Waschbusch, 2002). In most such cases, ADHD is believed to precede and help cause the conduct disorder. Individuals with both of these disorders typically have more severe symptoms, commit a higher number of aggressive acts, and display more violence when they become adults (McMahon & Frick, 2005).

Many children with conduct disorder also experience depression. In such cases, the conduct disorder typically precedes the onset of depressive symptoms. This combination of symptoms places the individuals at higher risk for suicide (Loeber & Keenan, 1994). Anxiety may also accompany conduct problems, especially among girls.

Many children with conduct disorder are suspended from school, placed in foster homes, or incarcerated. When children between the ages of 8 and 18 break the law, the legal system often labels them *juvenile delinquents* (Heilbrun et al., 2005). More than half

Cris Bouroncle/AFP/Getty Images

Breeding ground for antisocial behavior? *Conduct disorders are more common among children who have been exposed regularly to community violence. Thus clinicians worry that life in war-torn areas may foster antisocial behaviors among the young residents who are raised there. Here an Iraqi girl "plays" with a plastic handgun, pointing it at the head of a young playmate, while a soldier looks on.*

Alternative intervention for antisocial behavior by the young *Many children with conduct disorder wind up incarcerated in* juvenile detention, *or* juvenile training, *centers when their antisocial behaviors place them in conflict with the law. Here inmates at a juvenile detention center in Alabama spend Christmas waiting in line to go outside for physical training. Institutionalization in such centers has not met with much success and has in fact often strengthened antisocial behaviors.*

> **>>LOOKING AROUND**
>
> **Narrowing the Gender Gap**
>
> The number of teenage girls arrested for aggravated assault has doubled over the past 20 years, compared to a rise of 13 percent among boys. **<<**
>
> -
>
> The number of girls arrested for weapons possession has increased 125 percent over the past 20 years, compared to a rise of 22 percent among boys. **<<**
>
> -
>
> Today, one of every three teens arrested for violent crimes is female. **<<**
>
> -
>
> (Scelfo, 2005)

of the juveniles who are arrested each year are *recidivists,* meaning they have records of previous arrests. Boys are much more involved in juvenile crime than girls, although rates for girls are on the increase. Girls are most likely to be arrested for drug use, sexual offenses, and running away, boys for drug use and crimes against property. Arrests of teenagers for serious crimes have at least tripled during the past 20 years (U.S. Department of Justice, 2000, 1994).

What Are the Causes of Conduct Disorder?

Many cases of conduct disorder have been linked to genetic and biological factors, particularly cases marked by destructive behaviors (Blair et al., 2006; Simonoff, 2001). In addition, a number of cases have been linked to drug abuse, poverty, traumatic events, and exposure to violent peers or community violence (Hibbs & Jensen, 2005; Hill & Maughan, 2001). Most often, however, conduct disorder has been tied to troubled parent-child relationships, inadequate parenting, family conflict, marital conflict, and family hostility (Phares, 2003; Biederman et al., 2001). Children whose parents reject, leave, coerce, or abuse them or fail to provide appropriate and consistent supervision are apparently more likely to develop conduct problems. Similarly, children seem more prone to this disorder when their parents are antisocial, display excessive anger, or have substance-related, mood, or schizophrenic disorders (Julien, 2005) (see Box 17-3).

How Do Clinicians Treat Conduct Disorder?

Because aggressive behaviors become more locked in with age, treatments for conduct disorder are generally most effective with children younger than 13 (Hibbs & Jensen, 2005). A number of interventions, from sociocultural to child-focused, have been developed in recent years to treat children with the disorder. As we shall see, several of these have had modest (and at times moderate) success, but clearly no one of them alone is the answer for this difficult problem. In fact, given that conduct disorder affects all spheres of the child's life—family, school, social, and community—today's clinicians are increasingly combining several approaches into a wide-ranging treatment program (Henggler & Lee, 2003).

SOCIOCULTURAL TREATMENTS Given the importance of family factors in conduct disorder, therapists often use family interventions. One such approach, used with preschoolers, is called *parent-child interaction therapy* (Querido & Eyberg, 2005). Here therapists teach parents to work with their child positively, to set appropriate limits, to act consistently, to be fair in their discipline decisions, and to establish more appropriate expectations regarding the child. The therapists also try to teach the child better social skills. Ideally, these efforts strengthen the relationship between the parents and child, improve the parents' attitudes, lead to greater parent control, and help bring about improvements in the child's behavior. A related family intervention for very young children, *video tape modeling,* works toward the same goals with the help of video tools (Webster-Stratton, 2005).

When children reach school age, therapists often use a family intervention called *parent management train*ing. In this approach (1) parents are again taught more effective ways to deal with their children and (2) parents and children meet together in behavior-oriented family therapy (Kazdin, 2005, 2003, 2002; Frick & McCoy, 2001). Typically, the family and therapist target particular behaviors for change; then, with the help of written manuals, therapy rehearsals and practice, and homework, the parents are taught how to better identify problem behaviors, to stop rewarding unwanted behaviors, and to reward proper behaviors with consistency (Kendall, 2000). Like the preschool family interventions, parent management training has often achieved a measure of success.

[BOX **17-3**]

Child Abuse

❚ *What I remember most about my mother was that she was always beating me. She'd beat me with her high-heeled shoes, with my father's belt, with a potato masher. When I was eight, she black and blued my legs so badly, I told her I'd go to the police. She said, "Go, they'll just put you into the darkest prison." So I stayed. When my breasts started growing at 13, she beat me across the chest until I fainted. Then she'd hug me and ask forgiveness. . . . Most kids have nightmares about being taken away from their parents. I would sit on our front porch crooning softly of going far, far away to find another mother.* ❚

(*TIME*, SEPTEMBER 5, 1983, P. 20)

A problem that affects all too many children and has an enormous impact on their psychological development is *child abuse,* the nonaccidental use of excessive physical or psychological force by an adult on a child, often with the intention of hurting or destroying the child. At least 5 percent, and perhaps as many as 26 percent, of children in the United States are physically abused each year (Phares, 2003). Surveys suggest that one of every 10 children is the victim of severe violence, such as being kicked, bitten, hit, beaten, or threatened with a knife or a gun. In fact, some observers believe that physical abuse and neglect are the leading causes of death among young children.

Overall, girls and boys are physically abused at approximately the same rate (Humphrey, 2006). However, boys are at greatest risk when they are under the age of 12, while the risk for girls is highest when they are older than 12 (Azar et al., 1998). Although child abuse occurs in all socioeconomic groups, it is apparently more common among the poor (Mammen et al., 2002). Children who are either physically or intellectually disabled are more likely to receive physical abuse than children without such problems (Westcott & Jones, 1999).

Abusers are usually the child's parents (Humphrey, 2006). Clinical investigators have learned that abusive parents often have poor impulse control, low self-esteem, and weak parenting skills (Tolan et al.,

Honoré Daumier's Fatherly Discipline

Honoré Daumier, *Fatherly Discipline*, 1851. The Art Institute of Chicago, Arthur Heun Fund, 1952.

2006; Mammen et al., 2002). Many have been abused themselves as children and have had poor role models (McCaghy et al., 2006). In some cases, they are experiencing the stress of marital discord or family unemployment.

Studies suggest that the victims of child abuse may suffer both immediate and long-term psychological effects. Research has revealed, for example, that abused children have more performance and behavior problems in school. Long-term negative effects include lack of social acceptance, more medical illnesses and psychological disorders, more abuse of alcohol and other substances, more arrests during adolescence and adulthood, a greater risk of becoming criminally violent, a higher unemployment rate, and a higher suicide rate (Safren et al., 2002; Molnar et al., 2001; Widom, 2001, 1991, 1989). Finally, as many as one-third of abuse victims grow up to be abusive, neglectful, or inadequate parents themselves (Heyman & Slep, 2002; Clarke et al., 1999).

Two forms of child abuse have received special attention of late: psychological and sexual abuse. *Psychological abuse* may include severe rejection, excessive discipline, scapegoating and ridicule, isolation, and refusal to provide help for a

child with psychological problems. It probably accompanies all forms of physical abuse and neglect, and often occurs by itself. *Child sexual abuse,* the use of a child for gratification of adult sexual desires, may occur outside of or within the home (McCaghy et al., 2006). In 25 percent of cases, the child is younger than 7 (Wurtele & Schmitt, 1992). Surveys suggest that at least 13 percent of women were forced into sexual contact with an adult male during their childhood, many of them with their father or stepfather (Phares, 2003; Hill, 2003). At least 4 percent of men were also sexually abused during childhood (Romano & DeLuca, 2001). Child sexual abuse appears to be equally common across all socioeconomic classes, races, and ethnic groups (McCaghy et al., 2006).

A variety of therapies have been used in cases of child abuse, including groups sponsored by *Parents Anonymous,* which help parents to develop insight into their behavior, provide training on alternatives to abuse, and teach parenting skills (Tolan et al., 2006; Wolfe et al., 1988). Still other treatments help parents deal more effectively with the stresses that often trigger the abuse, such as unemployment, marital conflict, and feelings of depression.

Research suggests that the psychological needs of the child victims should be addressed as early as possible (Gray et al., 2000; Roesler & McKenzie, 1994). Clinicians and educators have launched *early detection programs* that aim to (1) educate all children about child abuse; (2) teach them skills for avoiding or escaping from abusive situations; (3) encourage children to tell another adult if they are abused; and (4) assure them that abuse is never their own fault (Godenzi & DePuy, 2001; Finkelhor et al., 1995). These programs seem to increase the likelihood that children will report abuse, reduce their tendency to blame themselves for it, and increase their feelings of efficacy (MacIntyre & Carr, 1999; Finkelhor et al., 1995).

Photo by BWP Media via Getty Images

Unthinkable *A surveillance camera shows the 1993 abduction of 2-year-old James Bulger from a shopping mall in England. The child holds the hand of one of his abductors—two 10-year-old boys who were later convicted of his torture and murder. The legal case stirred the emotions of people around the world and clarified that some children are indeed capable of extreme antisocial behavior.*

FIGURE **17-2** **Teenage crime** *Although teenagers make up only 14 percent of the total population, they commit around 30 percent of all violent crimes and 34 percent of all murders. They are also the victims of 33 percent of all violent crimes. (Adapted from Levesque, 2002; Benson, 1996; FBI Uniform Crime Reports, 1996; National Crime Victimization Survey, 1996, 1993.)*

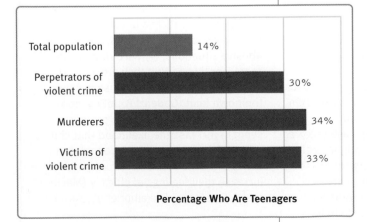

- Total population — 14%
- Perpetrators of violent crime — 30%
- Murderers — 34%
- Victims of violent crime — 33%

Percentage Who Are Teenagers

Other sociocultural approaches, such as residential treatment in the community and programs at school, have also helped some children improve (Chamberlain & Smith, 2005; Henggeler & Lee, 2003). In one such approach, *treatment foster care,* delinquent boys and girls with conduct disorder are assigned to a foster home in the community by the juvenile justice system. While there, the children, foster parents, and biological parents all receive training and treatment interventions, including family therapy with both sets of parents, individual treatment for the child, and meetings with school, parole, and probation officers. In addition, the children and their parents continue to receive treatment and support after they leave foster care. This program is apparently most beneficial when all the intervention components are applied simultaneously.

In contrast to these sociocultural interventions, institutionalization in so-called *juvenile training centers* has not met with much success (Heilbrun et al., 2005; Tate et al., 1995). In fact, such institutions frequently serve to strengthen delinquent behavior rather than resocialize young offenders (see Figure 17-2).

CHILD-FOCUSED TREATMENTS Treatments that focus primarily on the child with conduct disorder, particularly cognitive-behavioral interventions, have achieved some success in recent years (Kazdin, 2005, 2003, 2002; Lochman, Barry, & Pardini, 2003). In an approach called *problem-solving skills training,* therapists combine modeling, practice, role-playing, and systematic rewards to help teach children constructive thinking and positive social behaviors. During therapy sessions, the therapists may play games and solve tasks with the children and later help the children apply the lessons and skills derived from the games and tasks to real-life situations.

In another child-focused approach, the *Anger Coping and Coping Power Program,* children with conduct problems participate in group sessions that teach them to manage their anger more effectively, view situations in perspective, solve problems, become aware of their emotions, build social skills, set goals, and handle peer pressure. (While the children receive this group training, their parents participate in group sessions of their own.) Studies indicate that child-focused approaches such as these do indeed help reduce aggressive behaviors and prevent substance use in adolescence (Lochman et al., 2003).

Recently, drug therapy has also been used on children with conduct disorder. Studies suggest that *stimulant drugs,* such as *Ritalin,* may be particularly helpful in reducing their aggressive behaviors at home and at school (Connor et al., 2002; Gerardin et al., 2002).

PREVENTION It may be that the greatest hope for dealing with the problem of conduct disorder lies in *prevention* programs that begin in the earliest stages of childhood (Hill & Maughan, 2001; LeMarquand, Tremblay, & Vitaro, 2001). These programs try to change unfavorable social conditions before a conduct disorder is able to develop. The programs

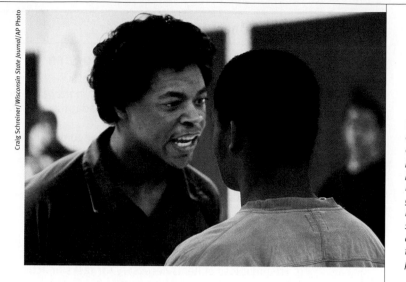

Prevention: Scared Straight *Rather than waiting for children or adolescents to develop oppositional defiant disorder, conduct disorder, or other antisocial patterns, many clinicians call for better prevention programs. In one such program, "at risk" children visit nearby prisons where inmates describe how drugs, gang life, and other antisocial behaviors led to their imprisonment. Here an inmate at a Wisconsin prison, serving life without parole for the killing of a friend, confronts a young visitor and "explains" in no uncertain terms how his lifestyle led to his crime and present predicament.*

may offer training opportunities for young people, recreational facilities, and health care, and may try to ease the stresses of poverty and improve parents' child-rearing skills. All such approaches work best when they educate and involve the family.

Attention-Deficit/Hyperactivity Disorder

Children who display **attention–deficit/hyperactivity disorder (ADHD)** have great difficulty attending to tasks or behave overactively and impulsively, or both (see Table 17-2 on the next page). The disorder often appears before the child starts school, as with Eddie, one of the boys we met at the beginning of this chapter. Steven is another child whose symptoms began very early in life:

Steven's mother cannot remember a time when her son was not into something or in trouble. As a baby he was incredibly active, so active in fact that he nearly rocked his crib apart. All the bolts and screws became loose and had to be tightened periodically. Steven was also always into forbidden places, going through the medicine cabinet or under the kitchen sink. He once swallowed some washing detergent and had to be taken to the emergency room. As a matter of fact, Steven had many more accidents and was more clumsy than his older brother and younger sister. . . . He always seemed to be moving fast. His mother recalls that Steven progressed from the crawling stage to a running stage with very little walking in between.

    Trouble really started to develop for Steven when he entered kindergarten. Since his entry into school, his life has been miserable and so has the teacher's. Steven does not seem capable of attending to assigned tasks and following instructions. He would rather be talking to a neighbor or wandering around the room without the teacher's permission. When he is seated and the teacher is keeping an eye on him to make sure that he works, Steven's body still seems to be in motion. He is either tapping his pencil, fidgeting, or staring out the window and daydreaming. Steven hates kindergarten and has few long-term friends; indeed, school rules and demands appear to be impossible challenges for him. The effects of this mismatch are now showing in Steven's schoolwork and attitude. He has fallen behind academically and has real difficulty mastering new concepts; he no longer follows directions from the teacher and has started to talk back.

(Gelfand, Jenson, & Drew, 1982, p. 256)

    The symptoms of ADHD often feed into one another (Stevens & Ward–Estes, 2006). Children who have trouble focusing attention may keep turning from task to task until

•ATTENTION-DEFICIT/HYPERACTIVITY DISORDER (ADHD)•A disorder marked by inability to focus attention or overactive and impulsive behavior, or both.

Table 17-2 DSM Checklist

ATTENTION-DEFICIT/HYPERACTIVITY DISORDER

1. Either of the following groups:
   A. At least six of the following symptoms of *inattention,* persisting for at least six months to a degree that is maladaptive and inconsistent with development level:
      a. Frequent failure to give close attention to details, or making careless mistakes.
      b. Frequent difficulty in sustaining attention.
      c. Frequent failure to listen when spoken to directly.
      d. Frequent failure to follow through on instructions and failure to finish work.
      e. Difficulty organizing tasks and activities.
      f. Avoidance of, dislike of, and reluctance to engage in tasks that require sustained mental effort.
      g. Frequent loss of items necessary for tasks or activities.
      h. Easy distraction by irrelevant stimuli.
      i. Forgetfulness in daily activities.
   B. At least six of the following symptoms of *hyperactivity-impulsivity,* persisting for at least six months to a degree that is maladaptive and inconsistent with developmental level:
      a. Fidgeting with hands or feet, or squirming in seat.
      b. Frequent wandering from seat in classroom or similar situation.
      c. Frequent running about or climbing excessively in situations in which it is inappropriate.
      d. Frequent difficulty playing or engaging in leisure activities quietly.
      e. Frequent "on the go" activity or acting as if "driven by a motor."
      f. Frequent excessive talking.
      g. Frequent blurting out of answers before questions have been completed.
      h. Frequent difficulty awaiting turn.
      i. Frequent interrupting of or intruding on others.
2. The presence of some symptoms before the age of 7.
3. Impairment from the symptoms in at least two settings.
4. Significant impairment.

Based on APA, 2000, 1994.

---

they end up trying to run in several directions at once. Similarly, constantly moving children may find it hard to attend to tasks or show good judgment. In many cases one of these symptoms stands out much more than the other. About half of the children with ADHD also have learning or communication problems, many perform poorly in school, a number have difficulty interacting with other children, and about 80 percent misbehave, often quite seriously (Stevens & Ward-Estes, 2006; Phares, 2003). It is also common for the children to have anxiety or mood problems (Julien, 2005).

Around 5 percent of schoolchildren display ADHD, as many as 90 percent of them boys. Those whose parents have had ADHD are more likely than others to develop it (APA, 2000, 1994). The disorder usually persists throughout childhood (APA, 2000, 1994). Many children show a marked lessening of symptoms as they move into mid-adolescence, but between 35 and 60 percent of affected children continue to have ADHD as adults (Julien, 2005; Kessler et al., 2005). The symptoms of restlessness and overactivity are not usually as pronounced in adult cases.

What Are the Causes of ADHD?

Today's clinicians generally consider ADHD to have several interacting causes. Biological factors have been identified in many cases, particularly abnormal activity of the

•**METHYLPHENIDATE**•A stimulant drug, known better by the trade name *Ritalin,* commonly used to treat ADHD.

neurotransmitter *dopamine* and abnormalities in the *frontal-striatal* regions of the brain (Brown, 2005; Julien, 2005). The disorder has also been linked to high levels of stress and to family dysfunctioning (Barkley, 2004, 2002, 1998). In addition, sociocultural theorists have noted that ADHD symptoms and a diagnosis of ADHD may themselves create interpersonal problems and produce additional symptoms in the child. That is, children who are hyperactive tend to be viewed particularly negatively by their peers and by their parents, and they often view themselves negatively as well (Busch et al., 2002; McCormick, 2000).

Three other explanations for attention-deficit/hyperactivity disorder have received considerable press coverage: (1) ADHD is caused by sugar or food additives, (2) ADHD results from environmental toxins such as lead, and (3) excessive exposure of children to television can contribute to ADHD. Only the third of these explanations has found any degree of research support. One study indicated, for example, a link between excessive TV watching during the first three years of life and weak attention at age 7 (Christakis et al., 2004).

How Do Clinicians Assess ADHD?

ADHD is a difficult disorder to assess. Ideally, the child's behavior should be observed in several environmental settings (school, home, with friends), because the symptoms of hyperactivity and inattentiveness must be present across multiple settings in order to fit DSM-IV-TR's criteria. Because children with this disorder often give poor descriptions of their symptoms and tend to underreport the severity and impairment of their behaviors, it is important to obtain reports of the child's symptoms from their parents and teachers. In addition to these reports and to clinical observations, clinicians commonly employ diagnostic interviews, ratings scales, and psychological tests to assess ADHD. Intelligence tests and neuropsychological tests may also be used (Nichols & Waschbusch, 2004).

How Is ADHD Treated?

There is heated disagreement about the most effective treatment for ADHD (Barkley, 2004; Hoagwood et al., 2000). The most common approach has been the use of stimulant drugs, such as **methylphenidate (Ritalin)** (see Box 17-4 on the next page). These drugs have a quieting effect on as many as 80 percent of children with ADHD and often increase their ability to solve problems, perform academically, and control aggression

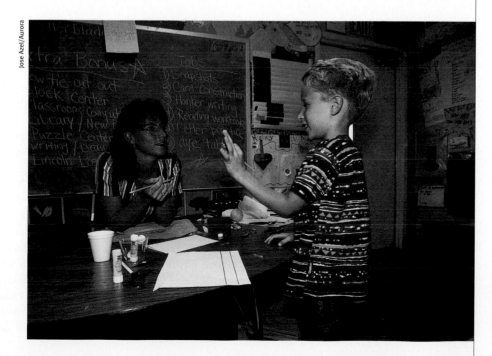

Jose Azel/Aurora

Behavioral intervention *Educational and treatment programs for children with ADHD use behavioral principles that clearly spell out target behaviors and program rewards and systematically reinforce appropriate behaviors by the children.*

[BOX 17-4]

Ritalin: Chemical Straightjacket or Miracle Drug?

▌ *When Tom was born, he acted like a "crack baby," his mother, Ann, says. "He responded violently to even the slightest touch, and he never slept." Shortly after Tom turned two, the local day care center asked Ann to withdraw him. They deemed his behavior "just too aberrant," she remembers. Tom's doctors ran a battery of tests to screen for brain damage, but they found no physical explanation for his lack of self-control. In fact, his IQ was high—even though he performed poorly in school. Eventually, Tom was diagnosed with attention-deficit/hyperactivity disorder (ADHD). . . . The psychiatrist told Ann that in terms of severity, Tom was 15 on a scale of one to 10. As therapy, this doctor prescribed methylphenidate, a drug better known by its brand name, Ritalin.* ▌

(LEUTWYLER, 1996, P. 13)

Like Tom, millions of children and adults with ADHD are treated with *methylphenidate,* a stimulant drug that has actually been available for decades, or with certain other stimulants. Although a variety of manufacturers now produce methylphenidate, the drug continues to be known to the public by its most famous trade name, *Ritalin.* As researchers have confirmed Ritalin's quieting effect on children and adults with ADHD and its ability

to help them focus and solve complex tasks, use of the drug has increased enormously—according to some estimates, at least a threefold increase since 1990 alone (DEA, 2000; Robison et al., 1999) (see Figure 17-3). This increase in use also extends to preschoolers (Zito et al., 2000). As many as 10 to 12 percent of all American boys may take Ritalin for ADHD, and the number of girls taking it is growing. Around 8.5 tons of Ritalin are produced each year, and 90 percent of it is used in the United

FIGURE 17-3 **The rise of Ritalin** *The use of Ritalin has been increasing since the early 1980s, when researchers discovered that it helped people with ADHD. (Adapted from Drug Enforcement Administration, 2000, 1996.)*

(Barkley, 2004, 2002; Wilens et al., 2003). However, some clinicians worry about the possible long-term effects of the drugs and others question whether the favorable findings of the drug studies (most of which have been done on white children) are applicable to children from minority groups (Biederman, Spencer, & Wilens, 2005, 2004).

Behavioral therapy is also applied widely. Here parents and teachers learn how to reward attentiveness or self-control in the children, often placing them on a token economy program. Such operant conditioning treatments have been helpful for a number of children, especially when combined with stimulant drug therapy (Barkley, 2004, 2002).

Because children with ADHD often display other (comorbid) psychological disorders as well, researchers have further tried to determine which treatments work best for different combinations of disorders. It appears that for children with ADHD alone, either medication or medication combined with behavioral therapy is more effective than behavioral therapy alone (MTA Cooperative Group, 2004, 1999). For children who display both ADHD and conduct disorder, medication appears to be the most effective approach. Children with ADHD and anxiety disorders seem to benefit from either medication, behavioral therapy, or both. Those with a combination of ADHD, conduct disorder, and anxiety symptoms respond best when treated with both medication and

States (DEA, 2000; Diller, 1999). In recent years, certain other stimulant drugs have also been found to be helpful in cases of ADHD, leading to corresponding increases in their use (Biederman et al., 2005).

Many clinicians and parents, however, have questioned the need for and safety of Ritalin. During the late 1980s, several lawsuits were filed against physicians, schools, and even the American Psychiatric Association, claiming misuse of Ritalin (Safer, 1994). Most of the suits were dismissed, yet the media blitz they engendered has affected public perceptions (Safer & Krager, 1992). At the same time, Ritalin has become a popular recreational drug among teenagers; some snort it to get high, and a number become dependent on it. This development has further raised public concerns about the drug (Biederman et al., 2005).

Extensive investigations conducted during the 1990s indicate that ADHD may in fact be overdiagnosed in the United States and that many children who receive Ritalin have been inaccurately diagnosed (DEA, 2000; UNINCB, 1996). ADHD can be reliably diagnosed only after a battery of observations, interviews, psychological tests, and physical exams (Nichols & Waschbusch, 2004). Yet studies have found that only one-third to one-half of children who receive this diagnosis from pediatricians or family physicians undergo psychological or educational testing to support the conclusion (Hoagwood et al., 2000; Miller, 1999; Leutwyler, 1996).

On the positive side, Ritalin is apparently very helpful to children and adults who do suffer from ADHD (Biederman et al., 2005). Parent training and behavioral programs are also effective in many cases, but not in all. Furthermore, the behavioral programs are often more likely to be effective in combination with Ritalin or similar drugs (MTA Cooperative Group, 2004, 1999; Pelham et al., 2000, 1998). When children with ADHD are taken off the drug—frequently because of the drug's negative publicity—many fare badly (Safer & Krager, 1992).

Studies to date suggest that Ritalin is safe for most people with ADHD (Biederman et al., 2005; Pennington, 2002). Its undesired effects are usually no worse than insomnia, stomachaches, headaches, or loss of appetite. However, a recent wave of research and case reports suggest that, in a small number of cases, Ritalin and related drugs may increase the risk of having a heart attack, particularly in adults with hypertension (Carey, 2006).

They may also cause psychotic symptoms or facial tics in a small number of cases. And Ritalin can affect the growth of some children, thus requiring "drug holidays" to prevent this effect.

In 2006, the FDA acknowledged the low risks of heart attacks and psychotic symptoms but, after some debate, decided against ordering "black box" warnings on the containers of Ritalin and other ADHD drugs. Clearly, however, more studies are needed to ascertain the long-term effects of these drugs (Biederman et al., 2005).

The question, then, is what to do about a drug that is helpful for many people but almost certainly overused and even abused in some cases. The solution recommended by growing numbers of clinicians is better control of its use. Clearly, researchers must continue to study Ritalin and related drugs, and pediatricians and others who work with children must be better trained in the assessment of ADHD, must be required to conduct broader testing before diagnosing ADHD, and must stay aware of helpful treatments other than Ritalin. Only under these circumstances will drugs such as Ritalin fulfill their potential as a useful treatment for a serious problem.

behavioral therapy (Stevens & Ward-Estes, 2006; Jensen et al., 2001). The treatments that are of help to children and adolescents tend to be effective also for adults with ADHD (Biederman et al., 2005; Faraone et al., 2004).

The Sociocultural Landscape: ADHD and Race

Throughout this book, we have seen that race often affects how persons are diagnosed and treated for various psychological disorders. Thus, we should not be totally surprised that race also seems to come into play with regard to ADHD.

A number of studies indicate that African American and Hispanic American children with significant attention and activity problems are less likely than white American children with similar symptoms to be assessed for ADHD, receive an ADHD diagnosis, or undergo treatment for this disorder (Bussing et al., 2005, 2003, 1998; Stevens et al., 2005). Moreover, among those who do receive an ADHD diagnosis and treatment, children from racial minorities are less likely than white American children to be treated with stimulant drugs or a combination of stimulants and behavioral therapy—the interventions that seem to be of most help to those with ADHD (Stevens et al.,

"You will like Mr. Woofard. He has an attention-deficit disorder."

2005; Cooper, 2004; Hoagwood et al., 2000; Samuel et al., 1997). And, finally, among children who do receive stimulant drug treatment for ADHD, children from racial minorities are less likely than white American children to receive the promising (but more expensive) *long-acting* stimulant drugs that have been developed in recent years (Cooper, 2004). It is important to note that these patterns are not due to racial differences in drug tolerance: research clarifies that children of all races respond similarly to the various stimulant drugs.

In part, these racial differences in diagnosis and treatment are tied to economic factors. Studies consistently reveal that poorer children are less likely than wealthier ones to be identified as having ADHD and less likely to receive effective treatment, and racial minority families have, on average, lower incomes and weaker insurance coverage than white American families. Consistent with this point, one study found that privately insured African American children with ADHD do in fact receive higher, more effective doses of stimulant drugs than do Medicaid-insured African American children with ADHD (Lipkin et al., 2005).

A growing number of clinical theorists further believe that social bias and stereotyping may contribute to the racial differences in diagnosis and treatment that have been observed. The theorists argue that our society often views the learning and behavioral symptoms of ADHD as medical problems when exhibited by white American children, but as indicators of poor parenting, lower IQ, substance use, or violence when displayed by African American and Hispanic American children (Kendall & Hatton, 2002). This notion has been supported by the finding that white American parents of ADHD children are more likely than African American parents to believe that ADHD is caused by genetic and biological problems, and less likely than African American parents to cite parenting issues or life stressors as causes of ADHD (Stief, 2004). Small wonder that, according to several studies, African American and Hispanic American parents are less inclined than white American parents to believe that their children may have ADHD or to seek ADHD evaluations and treatments for their children (Stevens et al., 2005; Kendall & Hatton, 2002). In a similar vein, some studies have found that, all symptoms being equal, teachers are more likely to conclude that overactive white American children have ADHD but that overactive African American or Hispanic American children have other kinds of difficulties (Raymond, 1997; Samuel et al., 1997).

Whatever the reason—economic disadvantage, social bias, racial stereotyping, or other factors—it appears that children from racial minority groups are less likely to receive a proper ADHD diagnosis and treatment. While many of today's clinical theorists correctly alert us to the possibility that ADHD may be generally overdiagnosed and overtreated, it is important that they also recognize that children from certain segments of society may, in fact, be underdiagnosed and undertreated.

Elimination Disorders

Children with elimination disorders repeatedly urinate or pass feces in their clothes, in bed, or on the floor. They already have reached an age at which they are expected to control these bodily functions, and their symptoms are not caused by physical illness.

Enuresis

Enuresis is repeated involuntary (or in some cases intentional) bed-wetting or wetting of one's clothes. It typically occurs at night during sleep but may also occur during the day. Children must be at least 5 years of age to receive this diagnosis. The problem may be triggered by stressful events, such as a hospitalization, entrance into school, or family problems, as we see in the case of Amber:

>>PSYCH•LISTINGS

Most Common Fears of Children

1. Not being able to breathe ‹‹
2. Being hit by a car or truck ‹‹
3. Falling from high places ‹‹
4. Contracting germs or getting a serious illness ‹‹
5. Being bombed or invaded ‹‹
6. Getting burned by fire ‹‹
7. Getting lost in a strange place ‹‹
8. Having their house burglarized ‹‹

(Neal et al., 1993)

Amber . . . was a 7-year-old . . . referred to an outpatient mental health clinic for children and families. At the time of her initial assessment, Amber was in second grade. She was referred to the clinic by her father, Mr. Dillon, who was quite upset about his daughter's problems. During the telephone screening interview, he reported that Amber was wetting her bed more at night and often needed to urinate during school. She was also experiencing minor academic problems. . . .

During [her] assessment session [with a psychologist] Amber said that she was getting into a lot of trouble at home and that her parents were mad at her. When asked why they were mad, Amber said she wasn't doing well in school and that she felt "nervous." . . . She said her grades had been getting worse over the course of the school year and that she was having trouble concentrating on her assigned work. She had apparently been a very good student the year before, especially in reading, but was now struggling with different subjects. . . .

[Amber acknowledged that] she wet her bed at night about once or twice a week. In addition, she often had to use the bathroom at school, going about three or four times a day. This was apparently a source of annoyance for her team teacher. . . . On one occasion, Amber said that she didn't make it to the bathroom in time and slightly wet her pants. Fortunately, this was not noticeable, but Amber was quite embarrassed about the incident. In fact, she now placed a wad of toilet tissue in her underwear to diminish the results of any possible mishaps in the future. . . .

[In a separate assessment interview, the psychologist asked Amber's parents] if any significant changes were going on at home. The question seemed to strike a nerve, as both parents paused and looked at each other nervously before answering. Finally, Mr. Dillon said that he and his wife had been having marital problems within the past year and that they were fighting more than usual. In fact, the possibility of divorce had been raised and both were now considering separation.

(Kearney, 1999, pp. 60–62)

•ENURESIS•A childhood disorder marked by repeated bed-wetting or wetting of one's clothes.

The prevalence of enuresis decreases with age. As many as 10 percent of children who are 5 years old suffer from this disorder, compared to 3 to 5 percent of 10-year-olds and 1 percent of 15-year-olds (APA, 2000). Those with enuresis typically have a close relative (parent, sibling) who has had or will have the same disorder (Christophersen & Purvis, 2001).

Research has not favored one explanation for enuresis over the others. Psychodynamic theorists explain it as a symptom of broader anxiety and underlying conflicts (Olmos de Paz, 1990). Family theorists point to disturbed family interactions (Fletcher, 2000). Behaviorists view the problem as the result of improper, unrealistic, or coercive toilet training (Christophersen & Purvis, 2001). And biological theorists suspect that children with this disorder often have a small bladder capacity or an inadequacy of the muscles that inhibit urination (Nield & Kamat, 2004).

Most cases of enuresis correct themselves even without treatment. However, therapy, particularly behavioral therapy, can speed up the process (Nield & Kamat, 2004). In a widely used classical conditioning approach, the *bell-and-battery technique,* a bell and a battery are wired to a pad consisting of two metallic foil sheets, and the entire apparatus is placed under the child at bedtime (Houts, 2003; Mowrer & Mowrer, 1938). A single drop of urine sets off the bell, awakening the child as soon as he or she starts to wet. Thus the bell (unconditioned stimulus) paired with the sensation of a full bladder (conditioned stimulus) produces the response of waking. Eventually, a full bladder alone awakens the child.

Another effective behavioral treatment method is *dry-bed training,* in which children receive training in cleanliness and retention control, are awakened periodically during the night, practice going to the bathroom, and are appropriately rewarded (Christophersen & Purvis, 2001; Azrin et al., 1979). Like the bell-and-battery technique, this behavioral approach is often effective, according to research.

Constructive play *Because young children typically have difficulty recognizing and expressing their feelings, many therapists, particularly psychodynamic ones, use play therapy as part of treatment. During therapy, children play with toys, draw, and make up stories, and in so doing reveal their feelings and thoughts.*

"I wish I'd started therapy at your age."

Early start *A number of theorists worry that in our therapy-oriented society, parents and clinicians are sometimes too quick to subject children to therapy, particularly when the children are merely experiencing the normal anxieties, mood changes, and other struggles that accompany childhood.*

Encopresis

Encopresis, repeatedly defecating into one's clothing, is less common than enuresis, and it is also less well researched. This problem seldom occurs at night during sleep (Walker, 2003). It is usually involuntary, starts after the age of 4, and affects about one percent of 5-year-olds (see Table 17-3). The disorder is more common in boys than in girls (APA, 2000).

Encopresis causes intense social problems, shame, and embarrassment (Cox et al., 2002). Children who suffer from it usually try to hide their condition and to avoid situations, such as camp or school, in which they might embarrass themselves (APA, 2000, 1994). Cases may stem from stress, constipation, improper toilet training, or a combination of these factors. In fact, most children with encopresis have a history of repeated constipation, a history that may contribute to improper intestinal functioning (Partin et al., 1992). Because physical problems are so often linked to this disorder, a medical examination is typically conducted first, followed by a psychological evaluation.

The most common and successful treatments for encopresis are behavioral and medical approaches or a combination of the two (Christophersen & Purvis, 2001; McGrath et al., 2000). Among other features of treatment, practitioners often try to eliminate the child's constipation and to stimulate regular bowel functioning with high-fiber diets, mineral oil, laxatives, and lubricants (McClung et al., 1993). Family therapy has also proved helpful (Wells & Hinkle, 1990).

Table 17-3

Comparison of Childhood Disorders

Disorder	Usual Age of Identification	Prevalence Among All Children	Gender with Greater Prevalence	Elevated Family History	Recovery by Adulthood
Conduct disorder	7–15 years	10%	Males	Yes	Often
ADHD	Before 12 years	5%	Males	Yes	Often
Enuresis	5–8 years	5%	Males	Yes	Usually
Encopresis	After 4 years	1%	Males	Unclear	Usually
Learning disorders	6–9 years	5%	Males	Yes	Often
Autism	0–3 years	0.25%	Males	Yes	Sometimes
Mental retardation	Before 10 years	1–3%	Males	Unclear	Sometimes

Long-Term Disorders That Begin in Childhood

As we discussed at the beginning of this chapter, many childhood disorders change or subside as the person ages. Two groups of disorders that emerge during childhood, however, are likely to continue unchanged throughout life: the *pervasive developmental disorders* and *mental retardation*. Researchers have investigated both of these categories extensively. In addition, although it was not always so, clinicians have developed a range of treatment approaches that can make a major difference in the lives of people with these problems.

Pervasive Developmental Disorders

Pervasive developmental disorders are a group of disorders marked by impaired social interactions, unusual communications, and inappropriate responses to stimuli in the environment. The group includes *autistic disorder, Asperger's disorder, Rett's disorder,* and *childhood disintegrative disorder.* Because autistic disorder initially received more attention than the others, these disorders are often referred to as *autistic-spectrum disorders.* Although the patterns are similar in many ways, they do differ significantly in the degree of social impairment sufferers experience and in the time of onset (Kabot et al., 2003). Given the low prevalence of Rett's disorder and childhood disintegrative disorder, we will examine only autistic disorder and Asperger's disorder in this chapter.

AUTISTIC DISORDERS A child named Mark presents a typical picture of autism:

In retrospect [Susan, Mark's mother] can recall some things that appeared odd to her. For example, she remembers that . . . Mark never seemed to anticipate being picked up when she approached. In addition, despite Mark's attachment to a pacifier (he would complain if it were mislaid), he showed little interest in toys. In fact, Mark seemed to lack interest in anything. He rarely pointed to things and seemed oblivious to sounds. . . . Mark spent much of his time repetitively tapping on tables, seeming to be lost in his own world.

After his second birthday, Mark's behavior began to trouble his parents. . . . Mark, they said, would "look through" people or past them, but rarely at them. He could say a few words but didn't seem to understand speech. In fact, he did not even respond to his own name. Mark's time was occupied examining familiar objects, which he would hold in front of his eyes while he twisted and turned them. Particularly troublesome were Mark's odd movements—he would jump, flap his arms, twist his hands and fingers, and perform all sorts of facial grimaces, particularly when he was excited—and what Robert [Mark's father] described as Mark's rigidity. Mark would line things up in rows and scream if they were disturbed. He insisted on keeping objects in their place and would become upset whenever Susan attempted to rearrange the living room furniture. . . .

Slowly, beginning at age five, Mark began to improve. . . . The pronoun in the sentence was inappropriate and the sentence took the form of a question he had been asked previously, but the meaning was clear.

(Wing, 1976)

Mark was displaying **autistic disorder,** or **autism,** a pattern first identified by the American psychiatrist Leo Kanner in 1943. Children with this disorder are extremely unresponsive to others, uncommunicative, repetitive, and rigid (see Table 17-4 on the next page). Their symptoms appear early in life, typically before 3 years of age. Just a decade ago, autism seemed to affect around one out of every 2,000 children (APA, 2000). However, in recent years there has been a steady increase in the number of children diagnosed with autism, and it now appears that at least one in 600 and perhaps as many as one in 200 children display the disorder (Fombonne, 2003; Wing & Potter, 2002).

Around 80 percent of all cases of autism occur in boys. As many as 90 percent of children with the disorder remain severely disabled into adulthood. They have enormous difficulty maintaining employment, performing household tasks, and leading

•**ENCOPRESIS**•A childhood disorder characterized by repeated defecating in inappropriate places, such as one's clothing.

•**AUTISTIC DISORDER**•A pervasive developmental disorder marked by extreme unresponsiveness to others, poor communication skills, and highly repetitive and rigid behavior. Also known as *autism.*

>>**IN THEIR WORDS**

"97X Bam. The Future of Rock and Roll . . .
97X Bam. The Future of Rock and Roll . . .
97X Bam. The Future of Rock and Roll . . .
97X Bam. The Future of Rock and Roll . . ." «
Raymond Babbit, *Rain Man,* 1988 (echolalic response to a radio advertisement)

Autistic acts *This autistic child is comforted by standing on her chair and watching television close up, and she often repeats this behavior. People with autism often interact with objects and people in unusual ways that seem to fascinate, stimulate, comfort, or reassure them.*

independent lives (Siegel & Ficcaglia, 2006). Moreover, even the highest-functioning adults with autism typically have problems displaying closeness, empathy, and support in their social interactions and communications and have restricted interests and activities (Baron-Cohen & Wheelwright, 2003).

WHAT ARE THE FEATURES OF AUTISM? The individual's lack of *responsiveness*—including extreme aloofness, lack of interest in other people, low empathy, and inability to share attention with others—has long been considered the central feature of autism (Siegel & Ficcaglia, 2006). Like Mark, children with this disorder typically do not reach for their parents during infancy. Instead they may arch their backs when they are held and appear not to recognize or care about those around them.

Language and communication problems take various forms in autism. Approximately half of all sufferers fail to speak or develop language skills (Dawson & Castelloe, 1992). Those who do talk may show peculiarities in their speech. One of the most common speech problems is *echolalia,* the exact echoing of phrases spoken by others. The individuals repeat the words with the same accent or inflection, but with no sign of understanding or intent of communicating. Some even repeat a sentence days after they have heard it (*delayed echolalia*).

Because they have difficulty empathizing and sharing a frame of reference with others, individuals with autism may also display other speech oddities, such as *pronominal reversal,* or confusion of pronouns—the use of "you" instead of "I." When Mark was hungry, he would say, "Do you want dinner?" In addition, individuals may have

---

Table 17-4 DSM Checklist

AUTISTIC DISORDER

1. A total of at least six items from the following groups of symptoms:
   A. Impairment in social interaction, as manifested by at least two of the following:
      a. Marked impairment in the use of multiple nonverbal behaviors such as eye-to-eye gaze, facial expression, body postures, and gestures to regulate social interaction.
      b. Failure to develop peer relationships appropriately.
      c. Lack of spontaneous seeking to share enjoyment, interests, or achievements with other people.
      d. Lack of social or emotional reciprocity.
   B. Impairment in communication, as manifested by at least one of the following:
      a. Delay in, or total lack of, the development of spoken language.
      b. In individuals with adequate speech, marked impairment in the ability to start or sustain a conversation with others.
      c. Stereotyped and repetitive use of language, or idiosyncratic language.
      d. Lack of varied, spontaneous make-believe play or social imitative play.
   C. Restricted repetitive and stereotyped patterns of behavior, interests, and activities, as manifested by at least one of the following:
      a. Abnormal preoccupation with one or more stereotyped and restricted patterns of interest.
      b. Inflexible adherence to specific nonfunctional routines or rituals.
      c. Stereotyped and repetitive motor mannerisms (e.g., hand or finger flapping or twisting).
      d. Persistent preoccupation with parts of objects.
2. Prior to 3 years of age, delay or abnormal functioning in either social interaction, language, or symbolic or imaginative play.

Based on APA, 2000, 1994.

problems naming objects, using abstract language, employing a proper tone when talking, speaking spontaneously, using language for conversational purposes, or understanding speech.

Autism is also marked by *limited imaginative or abstract play* and by *very repetitive and rigid behavior.* Children with the disorder may be unable to play in a varied, spontaneous way. Unlike other individuals of the same age, the children may fail to include others in their play or to represent social experiences when they are playing; in fact, they often fail to see themselves as others see them and have no desire to imitate or be like others (Siegel & Ficcaglia, 2006). Typically they become very upset at minor changes of objects, persons, or routines, and resist any efforts to change their own repetitive behaviors. Mark, for example, lined things up and screamed if they were disturbed. Similarly, children with autism may react with tantrums if a parent wears an unfamiliar pair of glasses, a chair is moved to a different part of the room, or a word in a song is changed. Leo Kanner (1943) labeled such reactions a *perseveration of sameness.* Furthermore, many sufferers become strongly attached to particular objects—plastic lids, rubber bands, buttons, water. They may collect these objects, carry them, or play with them constantly. Some are fascinated by movement and may watch spinning objects, such as fans, for hours.

The *motor movements* of people with autism may also be unusual. Mark would jump, flap his arms, twist his hands and fingers, rock, walk on his toes, spin, and make faces. These acts are called *self-stimulatory behaviors.* Some individuals also perform *self-injurious behaviors,* such as repeatedly lunging into or banging their head against a wall, pulling their hair, or biting themselves.

The symptoms of this disorder suggest a very disturbed and contradictory pattern of reactions to stimuli (see Box 17-5). Sometimes individuals with autism seem *overstimulated* by sights and sounds and to be trying to block them out, while at other times they seem *understimulated* and to be performing self-stimulatory actions. They may, for example, fail to react to loud noises, yet turn around when they hear soda being poured (Dawson, et al, 1998). Similarly, they may fail to recognize that they have reached the edge of a dangerous high place, yet immediately spot a small object that is out of position in their room.

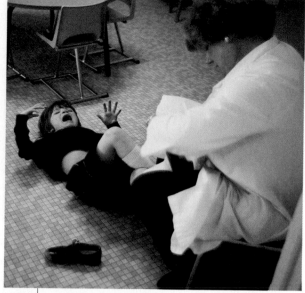

Autistic acts, take II *When upset, some children with autism, particularly those who cannot express themselves verbally, display physical outbursts. This 6-year-old child throws a tantrum and exhibits self-stimulatory hand shaking while under the care of a doctor at Bretonneau Hospital in Tours, France.*

[BOX **17-5**]

A Special Kind of Talent

Most people are familiar with the savant syndrome, thanks to Dustin Hoffman's portrayal of a man with autism in the movie *Rain Man* (right). The savant skills that Hoffman portrayed—counting 246 toothpicks in the instant after they fall to the floor, memorizing the phone book through the G's, and doing numerical calculations at lightning speed—were based on the astounding talents of certain real-life people who are otherwise limited by autism or mental retardation.

A *savant* (French for "learned" or "clever") is a person with a major mental disorder or intellectual handicap who has some spectacular ability, some area of exceptional brilliance. Often these abilities are remarkable only in light of the handi-

cap, but sometimes they are remarkable by any standard (Yewchuk, 1999).

A common savant skill is calendar calculating, the ability to calculate what day of the week a date will fall on, such as New Year's Day in 2050 (Heavey et al., 1999). A

common musical skill such individuals may possess is the ability to play a piece of classical music flawlessly from memory after hearing it only once. Other individuals can paint exact replicas of scenes they saw years ago (Hou et al., 2000).

Some theorists believe that savant skills do indeed represent special forms of cognitive functioning; others propose that the skills are merely a positive side to certain cognitive deficits (Scheuffgen et al., 2000; Miller, 1999). Special memorization skills, for example, may be facilitated by the very narrow and intense focus often found in cases of autism.

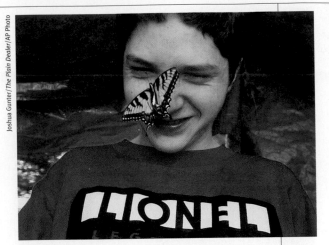

Asperger's disorder and personal achievement
Although significantly impaired by many autistic-spectrum deficits and limitations, individuals with Asperger's disorder maintain relatively high language, intellectual, and adaptive skills; indeed, some reach impressive heights. A butterfly perches on the nose of this 14-year-old boy with Asperger's disorder, a recent winner of a national achievement award for activities such as playing the piano at nursing homes and raising chickens, peacocks, strawberries, and more on his family's farm in Ohio.

ASPERGER'S DISORDER Around the time that Kanner first identified autism, a Viennese physician named Hans Asperger began to note a syndrome in which children display significant social impairments yet manage to maintain relatively high levels of cognitive function and language. Those with **Asperger's disorder,** or **Asperger's syndrome,** experience the kinds of social deficits, impairments in expressiveness, idiosyncratic interests, and restricted and repetitive behaviors that characterize individuals with autism, but at the same time they often have normal (or near normal) intellectual, adaptive, and language skills (Siegel & Ficcaglia, 2006; Ozonoff et al., 2002). Many individuals with this disorder want to fit in and interact with others, but their impaired social functioning makes it hard for them to do so. They wind up appearing awkward and unaware of conventional social rules (ASA, 2006).

Clinical research suggests that there may be several subtypes of Asperger's disorder, each having a particular set of symptoms. One team of researchers has distinguished three subtypes: rule boys, logic boys, and emotion boys (Sohn & Grayson, 2005). *Rule boys* are Asperger sufferers who need to have a set of rules that govern their lives. They are extremely stubborn about following these rules, and may become aggressive when the rules are not clearly laid out. At the same time, they are typically able to respect authority figures and structure. *Logic boys* are primarily interested in the *reasons* behind rules; rules alone are not sufficient. They want to know how the world works, often question the logic of others' reasoning, and may have their own reasons for why things are happening. In turn, they are typically unwilling to accept illogical events and often become overly analytical. *Emotion boys* tend to be run by their feelings. They have more tantrums than others with Asperger's disorder and seem less available to others. It is hard to sway them with rules or reason, and they often act out.

Asperger's disorder appears to be more prevalent than autism. Approximately one in 250 individuals displays this pattern, again 80 percent of them boys (CADDRE, 2004). It is important to diagnose and treat Asperger's disorder early in life so that the individual has a better chance of being successful at school and living independently. Although Asperger individuals must contend with deficits throughout their lives, many are able to complete a high level of education, such as college or trade school. Similarly, they may successfully hold jobs, particularly ones that require a focus on details and limited social interactions (ASA, 2005). Despite their social deficits, some people with Asperger's disorder further manage to have romantic—even marital—relationships, particularly with others who display the same disorder.

WHAT ARE THE CAUSES OF PERVASIVE DEVELOPMENTAL DISORDERS? Much more research has been conducted on autism than on Asperger's disorder or other pervasive developmental disorders. Currently, many clinicians and researchers believe that the other pervasive developmental disorders are caused by factors similar to those responsible for autism and that people with the other disorders can often be helped by interventions similar to ones that bring positive change in cases of autism. It is quite possible, however, that in the coming years, as Asperger's disorder and other pervasive developmental disorders receive more and more study, clear differences in the causes and treatments of the various disorders will emerge.

A variety of explanations have been offered for autism. This is one disorder for which sociocultural explanations have probably been overemphasized. In fact, such explanations initially led investigators in the wrong direction. More recent work in the psychological and biological spheres has persuaded clinical theorists that cognitive limitations and brain abnormalities are the primary causes of autism.

SOCIOCULTURAL CAUSES At first, theorists thought that family dysfunction and social stress were the primary causes of autism. When he first identified autism, for example, Leo Kanner (1954, 1943) argued that particular *personality characteristics of the parents* created an unfavorable climate for development and contributed to the child's disorder. He saw these parents as very intelligent yet cold—"refrigerator parents." These claims had enormous influence on the public and on the self-image of the parents themselves, but research has totally failed to support a picture of rigid, cold, rejecting, or disturbed parents (Roazen, 1992).

•**ASPERGER'S DISORDER**•A pervasive developmental disorder in which individuals display profound social impairment yet maintain a relatively high level of cognitive functioning and language skills. Also known as *Asperger's syndrome.*

•**THEORY OF MIND**•Awareness that other people base their behaviors on their own beliefs, intentions, and other mental states, not on information they have no way of knowing.

•**CEREBELLUM**•An area of the brain that coordinates movement in the body and perhaps helps control a person's ability to shift attention rapidly.

Similarly, some clinical theorists have proposed that a high degree of *social and environmental stress* is a factor in autism. Once again, however, research has not supported this notion. Investigators who have compared children with autism to children without the disorder have found no differences in the rate of parental death, divorce, separation, financial problems, or environmental stimulation (Cox et al., 1975).

PSYCHOLOGICAL CAUSES According to certain theorists, people with autism have a central perceptual or cognitive disturbance that makes normal communication and interactions impossible. One influential explanation holds that individuals with the disorder fail to develop a **theory of mind**—an awareness that other people base their behaviors on their own beliefs, intentions, and other mental states, not on information that they have no way of knowing (Hale & Tager-Flusberg, 2005; Frith, 2000).

By 3 to 5 years of age, most children can take the perspective of another person into account and use it to anticipate what the person will do. In a way, they learn to read others' minds. Let us say, for example, that we watch Jessica place a marble in a container and then we observe Frank move the marble to a nearby room while Jessica is taking a nap. We know that later Jessica will search first in the container for the marble, because she is not aware that Frank moved it. We know that because we take Jessica's perspective into account. A normal child would also anticipate Jessica's search correctly. A person with autism would not. He or she would expect Jessica to look in the nearby room, because that is where the marble actually is. Jessica's own mental processes would be unimportant to the person.

Studies show that people with autism do have this kind of "mindblindness," although they are not necessarily the only kinds of individuals with this limitation (Dahlgren et al., 2003). They thus have great difficulty taking part in make-believe play, using language in ways that include the perspectives of others, developing relationships, or participating in human interactions. Why do people with autism have this and other cognitive limitations? Some theorists believe that they suffered early biological problems that prevented proper cognitive development.

BIOLOGICAL CAUSES For years researchers have tried to determine what biological abnormalities might cause theory-of-mind deficits and the other features of autism. They have not yet developed a detailed biological explanation, but they have uncovered some promising leads (Volkmar, 2001; Rodier, 2000). First, examinations of the relatives of people with autism keep suggesting a *genetic factor* in this disorder. The prevalence of autism among their siblings, for example, is as high as 6 to 8 per 100 (Piven et al., 1997), a rate much higher than the general population's. Moreover, identical twins of people with autism display the highest risk of all (Treffert, 1999). In addition, chromosomal abnormalities have been discovered in 10 to 12 percent of people with the disorder (Sudhalter et al., 1990).

Some studies have also linked autism to *prenatal difficulties* or *birth complications* (Rodier, 2000; Simon, 2000). The chances of developing the disorder are higher when the mother had rubella (German measles) during pregnancy, was exposed to toxic chemicals before or during pregnancy, or had complications during labor or delivery. In 1998 one team of investigators proposed that a *postnatal event*—the vaccine for measles, mumps, and rubella—might produce autism in some children, alarming many parents of toddlers. However, to date, research has not confirmed a link between the vaccine and the disorder (Institute of Medicine, 2004; Taylor et al., 1999).

Finally, researchers have identified specific *biological abnormalities* that may contribute to autism. Some recent studies have pointed to the **cerebellum,** for example (DeLong, 2005; Pierce & Courchesne, 2002, 2001). Brain scans and autopsies reveal abnormal development in this brain area occurring early in the life of people with autism. Scientists have long known that the cerebellum coordinates movement in the body, but they now suspect that it also helps control a person's ability to shift attention rapidly. It may be that people whose cerebellum develops abnormally will have great difficulty adjusting their level of attention, following verbal and facial cues, and making sense of social information—all key features of autism.

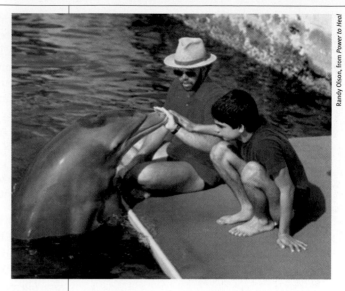

Animal connection *Children with autism are often unresponsive to other people. Yet many of them interact warmly with animals. Regular sessions of stroking and touching this dolphin have helped this young teenager overcome his autistic fear of touch and behave more spontaneously.*

>>IN THEIR WORDS

"Autism is . . . genetically lethal [for researchers]. That means people who have it don't usually have children. If it is not passed on, the genetics are difficult to study." <<

Marvin Schwalb, molecular geneticist, 1999

In a similar vein, neuroimaging studies indicate that many children with autism have increased brain volume and white matter (Filipek, 1999) and structural abnormalities in the brain's limbic system, brain stem nuclei, and amygdala (Newschaffer, Fallin, & Lee, 2002). Many individuals with the disorder also experience reduced activity in the brain's temporal and frontal lobes when they perform language and motor initiation tasks—tasks that normally require activity by the brain's left hemisphere (Escalante, Minshew, & Sweeney, 2003).

Many researchers believe that autism may in fact have multiple biological causes (Mueller & Courchesne, 2000). Perhaps all relevant biological factors (genetic, prenatal, birth, and postnatal) eventually lead to a common problem in the brain—a "final common pathway," such as neurotransmitter abnormalities, that produces the cognitive problems and other features of the disorder.

HOW DO CLINICIANS AND EDUCATORS TREAT PERVASIVE DEVELOPMENTAL DISORDERS? Treatment can help people with autism adapt better to their environment, although no treatment yet known totally reverses the autistic pattern. Treatments of particular help are *behavioral therapy, communication training, parent training,* and *community integration.* In addition, psychotropic drugs and certain vitamins have sometimes helped when combined with other approaches (Osterling, Dawson, & McPartland, 2001; Volkmar, 2001).

BEHAVIORAL THERAPY Behavioral approaches have been used in cases of autism for more than 30 years to teach new, appropriate behaviors, including speech, social skills, classroom skills, and self-help skills, while reducing negative, dysfunctional ones. Most often, the therapists use modeling and operant conditioning. In modeling, they demonstrate a desired behavior and guide people with the disorder to imitate it. In operant conditioning, they reinforce such behaviors, first by shaping them—breaking them down so they can be learned step by step—and then rewarding each step clearly and consistently (Lovaas, 2003, 1987; Erba, 2000). With careful planning and execution, these procedures often produce new, more functional behaviors.

A long-term study compared the progress of two groups of children with autism (McEachin et al., 1993; Lovaas, 1987). Nineteen received intensive behavioral treatments, and 19 served as a control group. The treatment began when the children were 3 years old and continued until they were 7. By the age of 7, the behavioral group was doing better in school and scoring higher on intelligence tests than the control group. Many were able to go to school in regular classrooms. The gains continued into the subjects' teenage years. In light of such findings, many clinicians now consider early behavioral programs to be the preferred treatment for autism.

A recent behavioral program that has achieved considerable success is the *Learning Experiences . . . An Alternative Program (LEAP)* for preschoolers with autism (Kohler, Strain, & Goldstein, 2005). In this program, four autistic children are integrated with 10 normal children in a classroom. The normal children learn how to use modeling and operant conditioning in order to help teach social, communication, play, and other skills to the autistic children. The program has been found to significantly improve the cognitive functioning of autistic children, as well as their social engagements, peer interactions, play behaviors, and other behaviors. Moreover, the normal children in the classroom experience no negative effects as a result of serving as intervention agents.

Learning to speak *Behaviorists have had success teaching many children with autism to speak. The therapist systematically models how to position the mouth and how to make appropriate sounds, and then rewards the child's accurate imitations.*

As such programs suggest, therapies for people with autism, particularly behavioral ones, tend to provide the most benefit when they are started early in the children's lives (Palmer, 2003; Rogers, 1998). Very young autistic children often begin with services at home, but ideally, by the age of 3 they attend special programs outside the home. The Individuals with Disabilities Education Act, a federal law, lists autism as one of 10 disorders for which school districts must provide a free education from birth to age 22, in the least restrictive or most appropriate setting possible. Typically, services are provided by education, health, or social service agencies until the children reach 3 years of age; then the department of education for each state determines what services will be offered (NRC, 2001).

Given the recent increases in the prevalence of autism, many school districts are now trying to provide education and training for autistic children in special classes that operate at the district's own facilities. However, most school districts remain ill equipped to meet the profound needs of students with autism. The most fortunate students are sent by their school districts to attend special schools, where education and therapy are combined. At such schools, specially trained teachers help the children improve their skills, behaviors, and interactions with the world. The higher-functioning students with autism may eventually spend at least part of their school day returning to normal classrooms in their own school district, where they can develop social and academic skills in the company of nonautistic students (Smith et al., 2002).

Although significantly impaired, children with Asperger's disorder have less profound educational and treatment needs than do those with autism. Once diagnosed, many such children are assigned to special programs (either within their own school system or at special schools) in which they receive a combination of education and cognitive-behavioral therapy tailored to their particular impairments. In one such program, *cognitive social integration therapy,* the children are taught to be more flexible with regard to social rules, problem solving, and behavioral choices (Sohn & Grayson, 2005). The teacher works with the Asperger students in groups, acknowledging their thoughts and feelings, teaching them how to prevent anxiety in the face of change, and helping them to develop new social skills and other kinds of abilities. The teacher also helps ensure that the newly learned skills generalize to the individual's life by using techniques such as rehearsal, role playing, and visual imaging throughout the group sessions.

COMMUNICATION TRAINING Even when given intensive behavioral treatment, half of the people with autism remain speechless. As a result, they are often taught other forms of communication, including *sign language* and *simultaneous communication,* a method combining sign language and speech. They may also learn to use **augmentative communication systems,** such as "communication boards" or computers that use pictures, symbols, or written words to represent objects or needs. A child may point to a picture of a fork to give the message "I am hungry," for example, or point to a radio for "I want music."

Some programs now use *child-initiated interactions* to help improve the communication skills of autistic children (Koegel, Koegel, & Brookman, 2005). In such programs, teachers try to identify *intrinsic* reinforcers rather than trivial ones like food or candy. The children are first encouraged to choose items that they are interested in, and they then learn to initiate questions ("What's that?"; "Where is it?"; "Whose is it?") in order to obtain the items. Studies find that child-directed interventions of this kind often increase self-initiated communications, improve language development, and heighten participation in interactions (Koegel et al., 2005).

PARENT TRAINING Today's treatment programs involve parents in a variety of ways. Behavioral programs, for example, often train parents so that they can apply behavioral techniques at home (Schreibman & Koegel, 2005; Erba, 2000). Instruction manuals for parents and home visits by teachers and other professionals are often included in such programs. Research has consistently demonstrated that the behavioral gains produced by trained parents are typically equal to or greater than those generated by teachers. Moreover, parent-run interventions tend to produce greater generalization of skills.

In addition to parent-training programs, individual therapy and support groups are becoming more available to help the parents of autistic children deal with their own emotions and needs. A number of parent associations and lobbies also offer emotional support and practical help.

COMMUNITY INTEGRATION Many of today's school-based and home-based programs for autism teach self-help, self-management, and living, social, and work skills as early as possible, to help the children function better in their communities (Koegel et al., 1992). In addition, greater numbers of carefully run *group homes* and *sheltered workshops* are now available for teenagers and young adults with autism (Van Bourgondien & Schopler, 1990). These and related programs help the individuals become a part of their community; they also reduce the concerns of aging parents whose children will always need supervision (Pfeiffer & Nelson, 1992).

•**AUGMENTATIVE COMMUNICATION SYSTEM**•A method for enhancing the communication skills of individuals with autism, mental retardation, or cerebral palsy by teaching them to point to pictures, symbols, letters, or words on a communication board or computer.

Mental Retardation

Ed Murphy, aged 26, can tell us what it's like to be diagnosed as retarded:

> What is retardation? It's hard to say. I guess it's having problems thinking. Some people think that you can tell if a person is retarded by looking at them. If you think that way you don't give people the benefit of the doubt. You judge a person by how they look or how they talk or what the tests show, but you can never really tell what is inside the person.
>
> *(Bogdan & Taylor, 1976, p. 51)*

For much of his life Ed was labeled mentally retarded and was educated and cared for in special institutions. During his adult years, clinicians discovered that Ed's intellectual ability was in fact higher than had been assumed. In the meantime, however, he had lived the childhood and adolescence of a person labeled retarded, and his statement reveals the kinds of difficulties often faced by people with this disorder.

The term "mental retardation" has been applied to a varied population, including children in institutional wards who rock back and forth, young people who work in special job programs, and men and women who raise and support their families by working at undemanding jobs. In recent years, the less stigmatizing term *developmental disability* has become synonymous with mental retardation in many clinical settings (Phares, 2003). Approximately three of every 100 persons meet the criteria for this diagnosis (Leonard & Wen, 2002; APA, 2000). Around three-fifths of them are male and the vast majority are considered *mildly* retarded.

According to DSM-IV-TR, people should receive a diagnosis of **mental retardation** when they display general *intellectual functioning* that is well below average, in combination with poor *adaptive behavior* (APA, 2000, 1994). That is, in addition to having a low IQ (a score of 70 or below), a person with mental retardation must have great difficulty in areas such as communication, home living, self-direction, work, or safety (APA, 2000, 1994). The symptoms must also appear before the age of 18 (see Table 17-5). Although these DSM-IV-TR criteria may seem straightforward, they are in fact hard to apply.

ASSESSING INTELLIGENCE Educators and clinicians administer intelligence tests to measure intellectual functioning (see Chapter 4). These tests consist of a variety of questions and tasks that rely on different aspects of intelligence, such as knowledge, reasoning, and judgment. Having difficulty in one or two of these subtests or areas of functioning does not necessarily reflect low intelligence (see Box 17-6 on page 524). It is an individual's overall test score, or **intelligence quotient (IQ),** that is thought to indicate general intellectual ability.

Many theorists have questioned whether IQ tests are indeed valid. Do they actually measure what they are supposed to measure? The correlation between IQ and school performance is rather high—around .50—indicating that many children with lower IQs do, as one might expect, perform poorly in school, while many of those with higher IQs perform better (Sternberg et al., 2001). At the same time, the correlation also suggests that the relationship is far from perfect. That is, a particular child's school performance is often higher or lower than his or her IQ might predict. Moreover, the accuracy of IQ tests at measuring extremely low intelligence has not been adequately evaluated, so it is difficult to properly assess people with severe mental retardation (Bebko & Weiss, 2006).

Intelligence tests also appear to be socioculturally biased, as we observed in Chapter 4 (Gopaul-McNicol & Armour-Thomas, 2002). Children reared in households at the middle and upper socioeconomic levels tend to have an advantage on the tests because they are regularly exposed to the kinds of language and thinking that the tests evaluate. The tests rarely measure the "street sense" needed for survival by people who live in poor, crime-ridden areas—a kind of know-how that certainly requires intellectual skills. Similarly, members of cultural minorities and people for whom English is a second language often appear to be at a disadvantage in taking these tests.

Table 17-5 DSM Checklist

MENTAL RETARDATION

1. Significantly subaverage intellectual functioning: an IQ of approximately 70 or below on an individually administered IQ test.
2. Concurrent deficits or impairments in present adaptive functioning in at least two of the following areas:
   a. Communication.
   b. Self-care.
   c. Home living.
   d. Social/interpersonal skills.
   e. Use of community resources.
   f. Self-direction.
   g. Functional academic skills.
   h. Work.
   i. Leisure.
   j. Health.
   k. Safety.
3. Onset before the age of 18.

Based on APA, 2000, 1994.

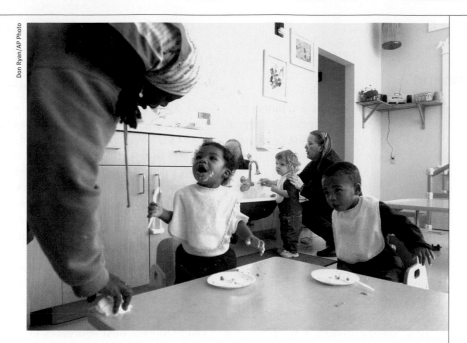

Don Ryan/AP Photo

Getting a head start *Studies suggest that IQ scores and school performances of children from poor neighborhoods can be improved by enriching their daily environments at a young age through programs such as Head Start, thus revealing the powerful effect of the environment on IQ scores and intellectual performance. The teachers in this classroom try to further stimulate and enrich the lives of preschool children in a Head Start program in Oregon.*

If IQ tests do not always measure intelligence accurately and objectively, then the diagnosis of mental retardation also may be biased. That is, some people may receive the diagnosis partly because of test inadequacies, cultural differences, discomfort with the testing situation, or the bias of a tester.

ASSESSING ADAPTIVE FUNCTIONING Diagnosticians cannot rely solely on a cutoff IQ score of 70 to determine whether a person suffers from mental retardation. Some people with a low IQ are quite capable of managing their lives and functioning independently, while others are not. The cases of Brian and Jeffrey show the range of adaptive abilities.

> Brian comes from a lower-income family. He always has functioned adequately at home and in his community. He dresses and feeds himself and even takes care of himself each day until his mother returns home from work. He also plays well with his friends. At school, however, Brian refuses to participate or do his homework. He seems ineffective, at times lost, in the classroom. Referred to a school psychologist by his teacher, he received an IQ score of 60.
>
> Jeffrey comes from an upper-middle-class home. He was always slow to develop, and sat up, stood, and talked late. During his infancy and toddler years, he was put in a special stimulation program and given special help and attention at home. Still Jeffrey has trouble dressing himself today and cannot be left alone in the backyard lest he hurt himself or wander off into the street. Schoolwork is very difficult for him. The teacher must work slowly and provide individual instruction for him. Tested at age 6, Jeffrey received an IQ score of 60.

Brian seems well adapted to his environment outside of school. However, Jeffrey's limitations are pervasive. In addition to his low IQ score, Jeffrey has difficulty meeting challenges at home and elsewhere. Thus a diagnosis of mental retardation may be more appropriate for Jeffrey than for Brian.

Several scales, such as the *Vineland* and *AAMR adaptive behavior scales and the Scales of Independent Behavior Revised,* have been developed to assess adaptive behavior (Bruininks et al., 1996; Lambert, Nihira, & Leland, 1993). Here again, however, some people function better in their lives than the scales predict, while others fall short. Moreover, several clinicians and educators argue that the adaptive scales do not include a sufficient number of indictors of social, communicative, academic, physical, and community competence (Jacobson & Mulick, 1996).

•**MENTAL RETARDATION**•A disorder marked by intellectual functioning and adaptive behavior that are well below average.

•**INTELLIGENCE QUOTIENT (IQ)**•A score derived from intelligence tests that theoretically represents a person's overall intellectual capacity.

[BOX **17-6**]

Reading and 'Riting and 'Rithmetic

Over 20 percent of children, boys more often than girls, develop slowly and function poorly compared to their peers in an area such as learning, communication, or coordination (APA, 2000). The children do not suffer from mental retardation, and in fact they are often very bright, yet their problems may interfere with school performance, daily living, and in some cases social interactions (Gorman, 2003; Geisthardt & Munsch, 1996). Similar difficulties may be seen in the children's close biological relatives. According to DSM-IV-TR, these children may be suffering from a learning disorder, a communication disorder, or a developmental coordination disorder.

The skill in arithmetic, written expression, or reading exhibited by children with *learning disorders* is well below their intellectual capacity and causes academic and personal dysfunctioning (APA, 2000, 1994). One learning disorder is called *mathematics disorder* and is diagnosed in children who have markedly impaired mathematical skills. Children with *disorder of written expression* make extreme and persistent errors in spelling, grammar, punctuation, and paragraph organization. And children with *reading disorder,* also known as *dyslexia,* have great difficulty recognizing words and comprehending as they read. They typically read slowly and haltingly and may omit, distort, or substitute words as they go.

The *communication disorders* take various forms as well (APA, 2000, 1994). Children with *phonological disorder* consistently fail to make correct speech sounds at an appropriate age, so that many of them seem to be talking baby talk. Those with *expressive language disorder* have trouble using language to express themselves. They may struggle at learning new words, confine their speech to short simple sentences, or show a general lag in language development. Children with *mixed receptive/expressive language disorder* have difficulty comprehending and expressing language. And those who suffer from *stuttering* display a disturbance in the fluency and timing of their speech. They may repeat, prolong, or interject sounds, pause before finishing a word, or experience excessive tension in the muscles used for speech.

Finally, children with *developmental coordination disorder* perform coordinated motor activities at a level well below that of others their age (APA, 2000, 1994). Younger children with this disorder are clumsy and are slow to master skills such as tying shoelaces, buttoning shirts, and zipping pants. Older children with the disorder may have great difficulty assembling puzzles, building models, playing ball, and printing or writing.

Studies have linked these various developmental disorders to genetic defects, birth injuries, lead poisoning, inappropriate diet, sensory or perceptual dysfunction, and poor teaching (Grigorenko, 2001; Lovett, 2000). Research implicating each of these factors has been limited, however, and the precise causes of the disorders remain unclear.

Some of the disorders respond to special treatment approaches (Pless & Carlson, 2000; Merzenich et al., 1996). Reading therapy, for example, is very helpful in mild cases of reading disorder, and speech therapy brings about complete recovery in most cases of phonological disorder (Merzenich et al., 1996). Furthermore, learning, communication, and developmental coordination disorders often disappear before adulthood, even without any treatment (APA, 2000).

The inclusion of learning, communication, and coordination problems in the DSM is controversial. Many clinicians view them as strictly educational or social problems, best addressed at school or at home. The framers of DSM-IV-TR have reasoned, however, that the additional problems created by these disorders and the frequent links to other psychological problems justify their clinical classifications (Mishna, 1996). Of special concern are studies that have found an increased risk of depression and even suicide in adolescents with certain of these problems, particularly the learning disorders (Huntington & Bender, 1993).

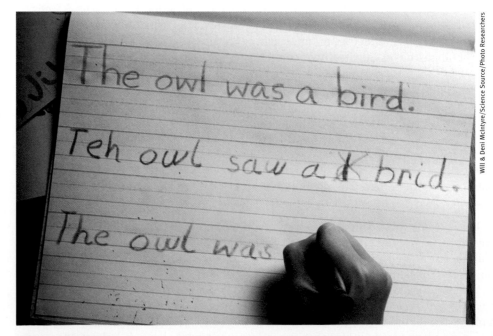

Dyslexic impairment *A student with dyslexia has trouble copying words. His mistakes reflect the difficulties he experiences when reading.*

Thus to properly diagnose mental retardation, clinicians should probably observe the functioning of each individual in his or her everyday environment, taking both the person's background and the community's standards into account. Even then, however, such judgments may be subjective, as clinicians may not be familiar with the standards of a particular culture or community.

WHAT ARE THE CHARACTERISTICS OF MENTAL RETARDATION? The most consistent feature of mental retardation is that the person learns very slowly (Hodapp & Dykens, 2003; Kail, 1992). Other areas of difficulty are attention, short-term memory, planning, and language. Those who are institutionalized with mental retardation are particularly likely to have these limitations. It may be that the unstimulating environment and minimal interactions with staff in many institutions contribute to such difficulties.

DSM-IV-TR describes four levels of mental retardation: *mild* (IQ 50–70), *moderate* (IQ 35–49), *severe* (IQ 20–34), and *profound* (IQ below 20). In contrast, the American Association of Mental Retardation (1992) prefers to distinguish different kinds of mental retardation according to the level of support the person needs in various aspects of his or her life—*intermittent, limited, extensive,* or *pervasive.*

MILD RETARDATION Some 80–85 percent of all people with mental retardation fall into the category of **mild retardation** (IQ 50–70) (Leonard & Wen, 2002; APA, 2000). They are sometimes called "educably retarded" because they can benefit from schooling and can support themselves as adults. Mild mental retardation is not usually recognized until children enter school and are assessed there. The individuals demonstrate rather typical language, social, and play skills, but they need assistance when under stress—a limitation that becomes increasingly apparent as academic and social demands increase. Interestingly, the intellectual performance of individuals with mild mental retardation often seems to improve with age; some even seem to leave the label behind when they leave school, and they go on to function well in the community (Bebko & Weiss, 2006). Their jobs tend to be unskilled or semiskilled.

Research has linked mild mental retardation mainly to sociocultural and psychological causes, particularly poor and unstimulating environments, inadequate parent-child interactions, and insufficient learning experiences during a child's early years (Bebko & Weiss, 2006; Stromme & Magnus, 2000). These relationships have been observed in studies comparing deprived and enriched environments (see Figure 17-4). In fact, some community programs have sent workers into the homes of young children with low IQ scores to help enrich the environment there, and their interventions have often improved the children's functioning. When continued, programs of this kind also help improve the individual's later performance in school and adulthood (Sparling et al., 2005; Ramey & Ramey, 2004, 1998, 1992).

Although sociocultural and psychological factors seem to be the leading causes of mild mental retardation, at least some biological factors also may be operating. Studies suggest, for example, that a mother's moderate drinking, drug use, or malnutrition during pregnancy may lower her child's intellectual potential (Neisser et al., 1996; Stein et al., 1972). Similarly, malnourishment during a child's early years may hurt his or her intellectual development, although this effect can usually be reversed at least partly if a child's diet is improved before too much time goes by.

MODERATE, SEVERE, AND PROFOUND RETARDATION Approximately 10 percent of persons with mental retardation function at a level of **moderate retardation** (IQ 35–49). They typically receive their diagnosis earlier in life than do individuals with mild retardation, as they demonstrate clear deficits in language development and play during their preschool years. By middle school they further display significant delays in their acquisition of reading and number skills and adaptive skills. By adulthood, however, many individuals with moderate mental retardation manage to acquire a fair degree of

•**MILD RETARDATION**•A level of mental retardation (IQ between 50 and 70) at which people can benefit from education and can support themselves as adults.

•**MODERATE RETARDATION**•A level of mental retardation (IQ between 35 and 49) at which people can learn to care for themselves and can benefit from vocational training.

FIGURE **17-4 Mental retardation and socioeconomic class** *The prevalence of mild mental retardation is much higher in the lower socioeconomic classes than in the upper classes. In contrast, the forms of mental retardation that result in greater impairment are evenly distributed. (Adapted from Popper, 1988; Birch et al., 1970.)*

•**SEVERE RETARDATION**•A level of mental retardation (IQ between 20 and 34) at which individuals require careful supervision and can learn to perform basic work in structured and sheltered settings.

•**PROFOUND RETARDATION**•A level of mental retardation (IQ below 20) at which individuals need a very structured environment with close supervision.

•**DOWN SYNDROME**•A form of mental retardation caused by an abnormality in the twenty-first chromosome.

•**FETAL ALCOHOL SYNDROME**•A group of problems in a child, including lower intellectual functioning, low birth weight, and irregularities in the hands and face, that result from excessive alcohol intake by the mother during pregnancy.

communication skill, learn to care for themselves, benefit from vocational training, and can work in unskilled or semiskilled jobs, usually under supervision. Most such persons also function well in the community if they have supervision (Bebko & Weiss, 2006; APA, 2000, 1994).

Approximately 3 to 4 percent of people with mental retardation display **severe retardation** (IQ 20–34). They typically demonstrate basic motor and communication deficits during infancy. Many also show signs of neurological dysfunction and have an increased risk for brain seizure disorder, or epilepsy. In school, they may be able to string together only two or three words when speaking. Individuals in this category usually require careful supervision, profit somewhat from vocational training, and can perform only basic work tasks in structured and sheltered settings. Their understanding of communication is usually better than their speech. Most are able to function well in the community if they live in group homes, in community nursing homes, or with their families (Bebko & Weiss, 2006; APA, 2000, 1994). They are rarely able to live independently.

Around 1 to 2 percent of all people with mental retardation fall into the category of **profound retardation** (IQ below 20). This level of retardation is very noticeable at birth or early infancy (Jacobson & Mulick, 1996). With training, people with profound mental retardation may learn or improve basic skills such as walking, some talking, and feeding themselves. They need a very structured environment, with close supervision and considerable help, including a one-to-one relationship with a caregiver, in order to develop to the fullest (Bebko & Weiss, 2006; APA, 2000, 1994).

Severe and profound levels of mental retardation often appear as part of larger syndromes that include severe physical handicaps. The physical problems are often even more limiting than the individual's low intellectual functioning and in some cases can be fatal.

WHAT ARE THE CAUSES OF MENTAL RETARDATION? The primary causes of moderate, severe, and profound retardation are biological, although people who function at these levels are also greatly affected by their family and social environment (Bebko & Weiss, 2006; Hodapp & Dykens, 2003). Sometimes genetic factors are at the root of these biological problems, in the form of chromosomal or metabolic disorders. In fact, researchers have identified 1,000 genetic causes of mental retardation, although few of them have undergone much study (Dykens & Hodapp, 2001; Azar, 1995). Other biological causes of these kinds of mental retardation come from unfavorable conditions that occur before, during, or after birth, such as birth injuries (Bebko & Weiss, 2006).

CHROMOSOMAL CAUSES The most common of the chromosomal disorders leading to mental retardation is **Down syndrome,** named after Langdon Down, the British physician who first identified it. Fewer than 1 of every 1,000 live births result in Down syn-

Reaching higher *Until the 1970s, clinicians were pessimistic about the potential of people with Down syndrome. Today these people are viewed as individuals who can learn and accomplish many things in their lives. Derek Finstad, a 16-year-old with this disorder, celebrates with his football teammates after the team's 56–0 season-opening victory.*

Brian Davies/The Appeal Democrat

drome, but this rate increases greatly when the mother's age is over 35. Many older expectant mothers are now encouraged to undergo *amniocentesis* (testing of the amniotic fluid that surrounds the fetus) during the fourth month of pregnancy to identify Down syndrome and other chromosomal abnormalities.

Individuals with Down syndrome may have a small head, flat face, slanted eyes, high cheekbones, and, in some cases, protruding tongue. The latter may affect their ability to pronounce words clearly. They are often very affectionate with family members but in general display the same range of personality characteristics as people in the general population (Carr, 1994).

Several types of chromosomal abnormalities may cause Down syndrome. The most common type (94 percent of cases) is *trisomy 21,* in which the individual has three free-floating twenty-first chromosomes instead of two (Pueschel & Thuline, 1991). In a second type, *translocation,* the person has two normal twenty-first chromosomes and a third twenty-first chromosome fused with another chromosome (the fifteenth or thirteenth). And in a third extremely rare type, *mosaicism,* cells with two and cells with three twenty-first chromosomes are found in the same person. Most people with Down syndrome range in IQ from 35 to 55 (AAMR, 2005). The individuals appear to age early, and many even show signs of dementia as they approach 40 (Bebko & Weiss, 2006; Lawlor et al., 2001). Studies suggest that Down syndrome and early dementia often occur together because the genes that produce them are located close to each other on chromosome 21 (Selkoe, 1991).

Fragile X syndrome is the second most common chromosomal cause of mental retardation. Children born with a fragile X chromosome (that is, an X chromosome with a genetic abnormality that leaves it prone to breakage and loss) generally display mild to moderate degrees of intellectual dysfunctioning, language impairments, and, in some cases, behavioral problems—difficulties that become particularly apparent as adolescence approaches (Eliez & Feinstein, 2001; Dykens et al., 1994). Typically, these individuals are shy and anxious, and males often display theory-of-mind deficits (AAMR, 2005).

METABOLIC CAUSES In metabolic disorders, the body's breakdown or production of chemicals is disturbed. The metabolic disorders that affect intelligence and development are typically caused by the pairing of two defective *recessive* genes, one from each parent. Although one such gene would have no influence if it were paired with a normal gene, its pairing with another defective gene leads to major problems for the child.

The most common metabolic disorder to cause mental retardation is *phenylketonuria (PKU),* which strikes 1 of every 17,000 children. Babies with PKU appear normal at birth but cannot break down the amino acid *phenylalanine.* The chemical builds up and is converted into substances that poison the system, causing severe retardation and several other symptoms. Today infants can be screened for PKU, and if started on a special diet before 3 months of age, they may develop normal intelligence.

Children with *Tay-Sachs disease,* another metabolic disorder resulting from a pairing of recessive genes, progressively lose their mental functioning, vision, and motor ability over the course of two to four years, and eventually die. One of every 30 persons of Eastern European Jewish ancestry carries the recessive gene responsible for this disorder, so that one of every 900 Jewish couples is at risk for having a child with Tay-Sachs disease.

PRENATAL AND BIRTH-RELATED CAUSES As a fetus develops, major physical problems in the pregnant mother can threaten the child's prospects for a normal life (Bebko & Weiss, 2006; Neisser et al., 1996). When a pregnant woman has too little iodine in her diet, for example, her child may develop *cretinism,* marked by an abnormal thyroid gland, slow development, mental retardation, and a dwarflike appearance. The disorder is rare today because the salt in most diets now contains extra iodine. Also, any infant born with this disorder may quickly be given thyroid extract to bring about a normal development.

Other prenatal problems may also cause mental retardation. As we observed in Chapter 12, children whose mothers drink too much alcohol during pregnancy may be born with **fetal alcohol syndrome,** a group of very serious problems that includes lower intellectual functioning. In fact, a generally safe level of alcohol consumption during pregnancy has not been established by research. In addition, certain maternal

PhotoTake/Robert Harding

A viral cause *This micrographic photograph shows cytomegalovirus (CMV), magnified 24,000 times—a common virus that infects most people worldwide. The virus (red) usually results in no harm and rarely causes illness. However, some babies born to women who have a first-time CMV infection during pregnancy may develop severe symptoms during their early years, including cognitive impairment, vision and hearing problems, and damage to their salivary glands, lungs, kidneys, and liver. CMV contracted during pregnancy is the primary viral cause of mental retardation. In contrast, infants and children who get a CMV infection after birth typically have few, if any, symptoms or complications.*

>>IN THEIR WORDS

"The IQ test was invented to predict academic performance, nothing else. If we wanted something that would predict life success, we'd have to invent another test completely." **<<**

Robert Zajonc, psychologist, 1984

infections during pregnancy—*rubella* (German measles) and *syphilis,* for example—may cause childhood problems that include mental retardation.

Birth complications can also lead to mental retardation. A prolonged period without oxygen (*anoxia*) during or after delivery can cause brain damage and retardation in a baby (Erickson, 1992). Similarly, although premature birth does not necessarily lead to long-term problems for children, researchers have found that a birth weight of less than 3.5 pounds may sometimes result in retardation (Neisser et al., 1996).

CHILDHOOD PROBLEMS After birth, particularly up to age 6, certain injuries and accidents can affect intellectual functioning and in some cases lead to mental retardation. Poisonings, serious head injuries caused by accident or abuse, excessive exposure to X rays, and excessive use of certain drugs pose special dangers (Evans, 2006). For example, a serious case of *lead poisoning,* from eating lead-based paints or inhaling high levels of automobile fumes, can cause retardation in children. Mercury, radiation, nitrite, and pesticide poisoning may do the same. In addition, certain infections, such as *meningitis* and *encephalitis,* can lead to mental retardation if they are not diagnosed and treated in time (Baroff & Olley, 1999; Berney, 1993).

INTERVENTIONS FOR PEOPLE WITH MENTAL RETARDATION The quality of life attained by people with mental retardation depends largely on sociocultural factors: where they live and with whom, how they are educated, and the growth opportunities available at home and in the community. Thus intervention programs for these individuals try to provide comfortable and stimulating residences, a proper education, and social and economic opportunities. At the same time, the programs seek to improve the self-image and increase the self-esteem of individuals with mental retardation. Once these needs are met, formal psychological or biological treatments are also of help in some cases.

WHAT IS THE PROPER RESIDENCE? Until recent decades, parents of children with mental retardation would send them to live in public institutions—**state schools**—as early as possible. These overcrowded institutions provided basic care, but residents were neglected, often abused, and isolated from society.

> They had me scheduled to go to P-8—a back ward—when just one man looked at me. I was a wreck. I had a beard and baggy State clothes on. I had just arrived at the place. I was trying to understand what was happening. I was confused. What I looked like was P-8 material. There was this supervisor, a woman. She came on the ward and looked right at me and said: "I have him scheduled for P-8." An older attendant was there. He looked over at me and said, "He's too bright for that ward. I think we'll keep him." . . .
>
> Of course I didn't know what P-8 was then, but I found out. I visited up there a few times on work detail. That man saved my life. Here was a woman that I had never known who they said was the building supervisor looking over me. At that point I'm pretty positive that if I went there I would have fitted in and I would still be there.
>
> *(Bogdan & Taylor, 1976, p. 49)*

During the 1960s and 1970s, the public became more aware of these sorry conditions, and, as part of the broader *deinstitutionalization* movement (see Chapter 15), demanded that many people with mental retardation be released from the state schools (Beyer, 1991). In many cases, the releases occurred without adequate preparation or supervision. Like deinstitutionalized people suffering from schizophrenia, the individuals were virtually dumped into the community. Often they failed to adjust and had to be institutionalized once again.

Since that time, reforms have led to the creation of *small institutions* and other *community residences* (group homes, halfway houses, local branches of larger institutions, and independent residences) that teach self-sufficiency, devote more staff time to patient care, and offer educational and medical services. Many of these settings follow the prin-

---

>>BY THE NUMBERS
Residential Shift

200,000 Number of people with mental retardation who lived in large state institutions in 1967 **<<**

- -

60,000 People with mental retardation currently living in state institutions **<<**

- -

(Lakin et al., 1999, 1996)

Elwyn Inc./AP Photo

Public institutions for mental retardation: the early years *Children with mental retardation sit in a classroom at the Elwyn School in Pennsylvania in 1900. This school, founded in 1852, was one of the country's first residential facilities for individuals with mental retardation.*

ciples of **normalization** first started in Denmark and Sweden—they attempt to provide living conditions similar to those enjoyed by the rest of society, flexible routines, and normal developmental experiences, including opportunities for self-determination, sexual fulfillment, and economic freedom (Hodapp & Dykens, 2003).

Today the vast majority of children with mental retardation live at home rather than in an institution. As they approach adulthood and as their parents age, however, the family may become less able to provide the kinds of assistance and experiences these individuals require (Krauss et al., 1992), and a community residence becomes an appropriate alternative for some. Most people with mental retardation, including almost all with mild mental retardation, now spend their adult lives either in the family home or in a community residence (Blacher & Baker, 1994, 1992; Jacobson & Schwartz, 1991).

WHICH EDUCATIONAL PROGRAMS WORK BEST? Because early intervention seems to offer such great promise, educational programs for individuals with mental retardation may begin during the earliest years. The appropriate education depends on the individual's degree of retardation (Bebko & Weiss, 2006; Patton et al., 2000). Educators hotly debate whether special classes or mainstreaming is most effective once the children enter school (Hardman, Drew, & Egan, 2002). In **special education,** children with mental retardation are grouped together in a separate, specially designed educational program. In contrast, **mainstreaming,** or **inclusion,** places them in regular classes with nonretarded students. Neither approach seems consistently superior (Bebko & Weiss, 2006). It may well be that mainstreaming is better for some areas of learning and for some children, special classes for others (Cummins & Lau, 2003).

Teacher preparedness is another factor that may play into decisions about mainstreaming and special education classes. Many teachers report feeling inadequately prepared to provide training and support for children with mental retardation, especially children who have additional disabilities or problems (Scheuermann et al., 2003). Brief training courses for teachers appear to address such concerns, build teacher confidence, and provide valuable information regarding children with special needs (Campbell, Gilmore, & Cuskelly, 2003).

Teachers who work with individuals with mental retardation often use operant conditioning principles to improve the self-help, communication, social, and academic skills of the individuals (Ardoin et al., 2004; Bennett-Gates & Zigler, 1999). They break learning tasks down into small steps, giving positive reinforcement as each increment is accomplished. In addition, many institutions, schools, and private homes have set up *token economy programs*—the operant conditioning programs that have also been used to treat institutionalized patients suffering from schizophrenia.

•**STATE SCHOOL**•A state-supported institution for people with mental retardation.

•**NORMALIZATION**•The principle that institutions and community residences should expose people with mental retardation to living conditions and opportunities similar to those found in the rest of society.

•**SPECIAL EDUCATION**•An approach to educating children with mental retardation in which they are grouped together and given a separate, specially designed education.

•**MAINSTREAMING**•The placement of children with mental retardation in regular school classes. Also known as *inclusion.*

Working for money, independence, and self-respect *Individuals with mental retardation need the personal and financial rewards that come with work. For many, this means employment in a sheltered workshop. Some countries and programs, however, are now thinking "outside the box" and trying to involve such individuals in more stimulating and everyday occupations. Here a 28-year-old waiter serves beverages in a café in Slovakia. He is one of five waiters with mental retardation who work at the café.*

WHEN IS THERAPY NEEDED? Like anyone else, people with mental retardation sometimes experience emotional and behavioral problems. As many as 25 percent of them have a psychological disorder other than mental retardation (McBrien, 2003; Dykens & Hodapp, 2001). Furthermore, some suffer from low self-esteem, interpersonal problems, and difficulties adjusting to community life. These problems are helped to some degree by either individual or group therapy (Rush & Frances, 2000). In addition, large numbers of people with mental retardation are given psychotropic medications (Matson et al., 2000). Many clinicians argue, however, that too often the medications are used simply for the purpose of making the individuals easier to manage.

HOW CAN OPPORTUNITIES FOR PERSONAL, SOCIAL, AND OCCUPATIONAL GROWTH BE INCREASED? People need to feel effective and competent in order to move forward in life. Those with mental retardation are most likely to achieve these feelings if their communities allow them to grow and to make many of their own choices (Harris, Kasari, & Sigman, 1996). Denmark and Sweden, where the normalization movement began, have again been leaders in this area, developing youth clubs that encourage those with mental retardation to take risks and function independently (Perske, 1972). The Special Olympics program has also encouraged those with mental retardation to be active in setting goals, participate in their environment, and interact socially with others (Weiss et al., 2003).

Socializing, sex, and marriage are difficult issues for people with mental retardation and their families, but with proper training and practice, the individuals can usually learn to use contraceptives and carry out responsible family planning (Lumley & Scotti, 2001; Bennett-Gates & Zigler, 1999). The National Association for Retarded Citizens offers guidance in these matters, and some clinicians have developed *dating skills programs* (Valenti-Hein et al., 1994).

Some states restrict marriage for people with mental retardation (Levesque, 1996). These laws are rarely enforced, however, and in fact between one-quarter and half of all people with mild mental retardation eventually marry (Grinspoon et al., 1986). Contrary to popular myths, the marriages can be very successful. Moreover, although some individuals may be incapable of raising children, many are quite able to do so, either on their own or with special help and community services (Levesque, 1996; Bakken et al., 1993).

Finally, adults with mental retardation—whatever the severity—need the personal and financial rewards that come with holding a job (Kiernan, 2000; Bennett-Gates & Zigler, 1999). Many work in **sheltered workshops,** protected and supervised workplaces that train them at a pace and level tailored to their abilities. After training in the workshops, many with mild or moderate retardation move on to hold regular jobs (Moore, Flowers, & Taylor, 2000).

•**SHELTERED WORKSHOP**•A protected and supervised workplace that offers job opportunities and training at a pace and level tailored to people with various psychological disabilities.

Normal needs *The interpersonal and sexual needs of people with mental retardation are normal, and many, such as this engaged couple, demonstrate considerable ability to express intimacy.*

Although training programs for people with mental retardation have improved greatly in quality over the past 30 years, there are too few of them. Consequently, most of these individuals fail to receive a complete range of educational and occupational training services. Additional programs are required so that more people with mental retardation may achieve their full potential, as workers and as human beings.

PUTTING IT together

Clinicians Discover Childhood and Adolescence

Early in the twentieth century, mental health professionals virtually ignored children (Phares, 2003). At best, they viewed them as small adults and treated their psychological disorders as they would adult problems (Peterson & Roberts, 1991). Today the problems and special needs of young people have caught the attention of researchers and clinicians. Although all of the leading models have been used to help explain and treat these problems, the sociocultural perspective—especially the family perspective—is considered to play a special role.

Because children and adolescents have limited control over their lives, they are particularly affected by the attitudes and reactions of family members. Clinicians must therefore deal with those attitudes and reactions as they try to address the problems of the young. Treatments for conduct disorder, ADHD, mental retardation, and other problems of childhood and adolescence typically fall short unless clinicians educate and work with the family as well.

At the same time, clinicians who work with children and adolescents have learned that a narrow focus on any one model can lead to problems. For years autism was explained exclusively by family factors, misleading theorists and therapists alike, and adding to the pain of parents already devastated by their child's disorder. Similarly, in the past, the sociocultural model often led professionals wrongly to accept anxiety among young children and depression among teenagers as inevitable, given the many new experiences confronted by the former and the latter group's preoccupation with peer approval.

The increased clinical focus on the young has also been accompanied by increased attention to their human and legal rights. More and more, clinicians have called on government agencies to protect the rights and safety of this often powerless group. In doing so, they hope to fuel the fights for greater educational resources and against child abuse and neglect, sexual abuse, malnourishment, and fetal alcohol syndrome.

>>**BY THE NUMBERS**

Teenage Concerns

59% Percentage of today's teens who worry about being victims of violence <<

58% Teens who worry about getting sexually transmitted diseases <<

54% Teens who worry about being able to afford college <<

43% Teens who worry about finding good jobs in the future <<

(Begley, 2000)

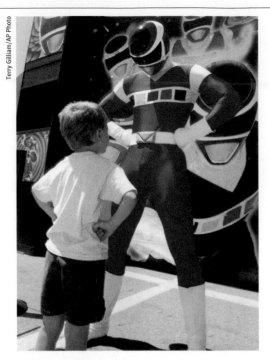

Terry Gilliam/AP Photo

Undesirable effects? *A 4-year-old flexes his muscles in front of the Red Ranger during a Power Rangers Rocket Tour. Some child theorists worry that the fantasy heroes or heroines to which children are regularly exposed in cartoons, toys, video games, or movies may predispose them to aggressive behavior, overactivity, or other problematic patterns. Research, however, has not consistently demonstrated that such heroes have a negative impact on development. In fact, other experts argue that superhero play is a healthy activity.*

As the problems and, at times, mistreatment of young people receive greater attention, the special needs of these individuals are becoming more visible. Thus the study and treatment of psychological disorders among children and adolescents are likely to continue at a rapid pace. Now that clinicians and public officials have "discovered" this population, they are not likely to underestimate their needs and importance again.

[SUMMARY AND REVIEW]

■ **Disorders of childhood and adolescence** Emotional and behavioral problems are common in childhood and adolescence, but in addition, at least one-fifth of all children and adolescents in the United States experience a diagnosable psychological disorder. *pp. 497–499*

Children with *oppositional defiant disorder* and *conduct disorder* exceed the normal breaking of rules and act very aggressively. Children with oppositional defiant disorder argue repeatedly with adults, lose their temper, and feel intense anger and resentment. Those with conduct disorder, a more severe pattern, repeatedly violate the basic rights of others. Children with this disorder often are violent and cruel, and may deliberately destroy property, steal, and run away. *pp. 499–507*

Children who display *attention-deficit/hyperactivity disorder (ADHD)* attend poorly to tasks or behave overactively and impulsively, or both. *Ritalin* and other *stimulant drugs* and *behavioral programs* are often effective treatments. Children with an *elimination disorder—enuresis* or *encopresis*—repeatedly urinate or pass feces in inappropriate places. Behavioral approaches, such as the *bell-and-battery technique,* are effective treatments for enuresis. *pp. 507–514*

■ **Long-term disorders that begin in childhood** *Pervasive developmental disorders* and mental retardation are problems that emerge early and typically continue throughout a person's life. People with *autism,* the most heavily researched pervasive developmental disorder, are extremely unresponsive to others, have poor communication skills (including *echolalia* and *pronominal reversal*), and behave in a very rigid and repetitive manner (displaying *perseveration of sameness, strong attachments to objects, self-stimulatory behaviors,* and *self-injurious behaviors*). Individuals with *Asperger's disorder,* another kind of pervasive developmental disorder, display profound social impairment, yet maintain relatively high levels of cognitive functioning and language skills.

The leading explanations of autism point to cognitive deficits, such as failure to develop a *theory of mind,* and biological abnormalities, such as abnormal development of the *cerebellum,* as causal factors. Although no treatment totally reverses the autistic pattern, significant help is available in the form of *behavioral treatments, communication training, treatment and training for parents,* and *community integration. pp. 515–521*

People with *mental retardation* are significantly below average in *intelligence* and *adaptive ability.* Approximately three of every 100 people qualify for this diagnosis. *Mild retardation,* by far the most common level of mental retardation, has been linked primarily to *environmental factors* such as understimulation, inadequate parent-child interactions, and insufficient early learning experiences. *Moderate, severe,* and *profound mental retardation* are caused primarily by *biological factors,* although individuals who function at these levels are also enormously affected by their family and social environment. The leading biological causes are *chromosomal abnormalities* (as in *Down syndrome*); *metabolic disorders* that typically are caused by the pairing of two defective *recessive genes* (for example, *phenylketonuria,* or *PKU,* and *Tay-Sachs disease*); disorders resulting from *prenatal problems* (cretinism and *fetal alcohol syndrome*); disorders resulting from *birth complications,* such as *anoxia* or *extreme prematurity;* and *childhood diseases* and *injuries.*

Today intervention programs for people with mental retardation emphasize the importance of a *comfortable and stimulating residence,* either the family home or a small institution or group home that follows the principles of *normalization.* Other important interventions include *proper education, therapy* for psychological problems, and programs offering *training in socializing, sex, marriage, parenting,* and *occupational skills.*

One of the most intense debates in the field of education centers on whether individuals with mental retardation profit more from *special classes* or from *mainstreaming*. Research has not consistently favored one approach over the other. *pp. 522–531*

>>> CRITICAL THOUGHTS <<<

1. Although boys with psychological disorders outnumber girls, adult women with such disorders outnumber adult men. How might this age-related shift in prevalence rates reflect the special pressures felt by women in Western society? What other explanations might there be for the shift? *pp. 497–514*

2. What psychological effects might bullying have on its victims? Why do many individuals seem able to overcome the trauma of being bullied, while others do not? *pp. 502–503*

3. The overall rate of repeated arrests of adolescents sent to juvenile training centers has been estimated to be as high as 80 percent (Erickson, 1992). How might the training centers themselves be contributing to this recidivism rate? *pp. 503–504*

4. Why are people so fascinated by the savant syndrome, and might their fascination lead them to glamorize it? What hidden reminders of human equality or messages of hope may be derived from observations of savant functioning? *p. 517*

5. Clinicians sometimes use punishment to help eliminate the self-injurious behaviors of children with autism. The children may be squirted in the face with water, pinched, or, in extreme cases, shocked whenever they act to hurt themselves. Who should make the decision about whether to use punishments in given cases? *pp. 520–521*

6. In past times, a child with a learning, communication, or coordination disorder might simply be called a "weak" reader, "clumsy," or the like. What are the advantages and disadvantages to the child of affixing clinical names to the patterns? Should these patterns be listed in DSM-IV-TR as psychological disorders? *p. 524*

7. What might be the merits and flaws of *special classes* versus *mainstreaming* for people with mental retardation? *p. 529*

8. Do violent action figures help produce oppositional defiant disorder, conduct disorder, or other childhood problems? *p. 532*

◉─[CYBER**STUDY**]──────────────>>>

SEARCH THE *ABNORMAL PSYCHOLOGY* CD-ROM FOR

▲ Chapter 17 Video Cases and Discussions
   How do children express anxiety and depression?
   Observe interventions for autism.
   Witness savant skills.

▲ Chapter 17 Practical, Research, and Decision-Making Exercises
   Appreciating the impact of childhood disorders on the family
   Distinguishing childhood disorders from normal variations in mood or behavior

▲ Chapter 17 Practice Test and Feedback

LOG ON TO THE COMER WEB PAGE FOR

▲ Suggested Web links, exercises, FAQ page, additional Chapter 17 practice test questions
   <www.worthpublishers.com/comer>

─────────────────────────────<<<

Disorders of Aging and Cognition

Harry appeared to be in perfect health at age 58. . . . He worked in the municipal water treatment plant of a small city, and it was at work that the first overt signs of Harry's mental illness appeared. While responding to a minor emergency, he became confused about the correct order in which to pull the levers that controlled the flow of fluids. As a result, several thousand gallons of raw sewage were discharged into a river. Harry had been an efficient and diligent worker, so after puzzled questioning, his error was attributed to the flu and overlooked.

Several weeks later, Harry came home with a baking dish his wife had asked him to buy, having forgotten that he had brought home the identical dish two nights before. Later that week, on two successive nights, he went to pick up his daughter at her job in a restaurant, apparently forgetting that she had changed shifts and was now working days. A month after that, he quite uncharacteristically argued with a clerk at the phone company; he was trying to pay a bill that he had already paid three days before. . . .

Months passed and Harry's wife was beside herself. She could see that his problem was worsening. Not only had she been unable to get effective help, but Harry himself was becoming resentful and sometimes suspicious of her attempts. He now insisted there was nothing wrong with him, and she would catch him narrowly watching her every movement. . . . Sometimes he became angry—sudden little storms without apparent cause. . . . More difficult for his wife was Harry's repetitiveness in conversation: He often repeated stories from the past and sometimes repeated isolated phrases and sentences from more recent exchanges. There was no context and little continuity to his choice of subjects. . . .

Two years after Harry had first allowed the sewage to escape, he was clearly a changed man. Most of the time he seemed preoccupied; he usually had a vacant smile on his face, and what little he said was so vague that it lacked meaning. . . . Gradually his wife took over getting him up, toileted, and dressed each morning. . . .

Harry's condition continued to worsen slowly. When his wife's school was in session, his daughter would stay with him some days, and neighbors were able to offer some help. But occasionally he would still manage to wander away. On those occasions he greeted everyone he met—old friends and strangers alike—with "Hi, it's so nice." That was the extent of his conversation, although he might repeat "nice, nice, nice" over and over again. . . . When Harry left a coffee pot on a unit of the electric stove until it melted, his wife, desperate for help, took him to see another doctor. Again Harry was found to be in good health. [However] the doctor ordered a CAT scan [and eventually concluded] that Harry had "Pick-Alzheimer disease" and that there was no known cause and no effective treatment. . . .

Because Harry was a veteran . . . [he qualified for] hospitalization in a regional veterans' hospital about 400 miles away from his home. . . . Desperate, five years after the accident at work, [his wife] accepted with gratitude [this] hospitalization. . . .

•GEROPSYCHOLOGY• The field of psychology concerned with the mental health of elderly people.

At the hospital the nursing staff sat Harry up in a chair each day and, aided by volunteers, made sure he ate enough. Still, he lost weight and became weaker. He would weep when his wife came to see him, but he did not talk, and he gave no other sign that he recognized her. After a year, even the weeping stopped. Harry's wife could no longer bear to visit. Harry lived on until just after his sixty-fifth birthday, when he choked on a piece of bread, developed pneumonia as a consequence, and soon died.

(Heston, 1992, pp. 87–90)

Harry suffered from a form of *Alzheimer's disease.* This term is familiar to almost everyone in our society. It seems as if each decade is marked by a disease that everyone dreads—a diagnosis no one wants to hear because it feels like a death sentence. Cancer used to be such a diagnosis, then AIDS. But medical science has made remarkable strides with those diseases, and patients who now develop them have reason for hope and expectations of improvement. Alzheimer's disease, on the other hand, remains incurable and almost untreatable, although, as we shall see later, researchers are currently making enormous progress toward understanding it and reversing, or at least slowing, its march.

What makes Alzheimer's disease particularly frightening is that it means not only eventual physical death but also, as in Harry's case, a slow psychological death—a progressive *dementia,* or deterioration of one's memory and related cognitive faculties. There are dozens of causes of dementia; however, Alzheimer's disease is the most common one.

Although dementia is currently the most publicized and feared psychological problem among the elderly, it is hardly the only one. Indeed, a variety of psychological disorders are tied closely to later life. As with childhood disorders, some of the disorders of old age are caused primarily by pressures that are particularly likely to appear at that time of life, others by unique traumatic experiences, and still others—like dementia—by biological abnormalities.

Old Age and Stress

Old age is usually defined in our society as the years past age 65. By this account, more than 35 million people in the United States are "old," representing around 13 percent of the total population; this is an 11-fold increase since 1900 (Webster, 2005; Dietch, 2001; Fisher, Zeiss, & Carstensen, 2001) (see Figure 18-1). Not only is the overall population of the elderly on the rise; the number of people over 80 will double in the next 10 years. Indeed, people over 80 represent the fastest-growing segment of the population in the United States and in most countries around the world. Older women outnumber older men by 3 to 2.

Like childhood, old age brings special pressures, unique upsets, and profound biological changes. People become more prone to illness and injury as they age, and they are likely to experience the stress of loss—the loss of spouses, friends, and adult children, and the loss of former activities and roles (Inselmann, 2004). Many lose their sense of purpose after they retire. Even favored pets and possessions are sometimes lost.

The stresses of elderly people need not necessarily result in psychological problems (Nordhus & Nielsen, 2005). In fact, some older persons use the changes that come with aging as opportunities for learning and growth. For others, however, the stresses of old age do lead to psychological difficulties (Aldwin, Spiro, & Park, 2006). Studies indicate that as many as 50 percent of elderly people would benefit from mental health services, yet fewer than 20 percent actually receive them. **Geropsychology,** the field of psychology dedicated to the mental health of elderly people, has developed almost entirely within the last 30 years, and at present fewer than

FIGURE 18-1 On the rise *The population of people aged 65 and older in the United States increased 11-fold during the twentieth century. The percentage of elderly people in the population increased from 4 percent in 1900 to 12.5 percent in 2000 and is expected to be 20 percent in 2030 (U.S. Census, 2000; Hobbs, 1997; AARP, 1990).*

4 percent of all clinicians work primarily with elderly persons (Birren & Schroots, 2001, 2000).

The psychological problems of elderly persons may be divided into two groups. One group consists of disorders that may be common among people in all age groups but are often connected to the process of aging when they occur in an elderly person. These include *depressive, anxiety,* and *substance-related disorders.* The other group consists of disorders of cognition, such as *delirium* and *dementia,* that result from brain abnormalities. As in Harry's case, these brain abnormalities are most often tied to aging, but they can sometimes occur in younger individuals as well. Elderly persons with one of these psychological problems often display others as well. For example, many who suffer from dementia also experience depression and anxiety (Biringer et al., 2005; Heun & Hein, 2005). And those who are depressed have an increased likelihood of displaying a pattern of alcohol abuse (Devanand, 2002).

Making a difference *Many people come to feel unimportant and lonely and develop low self-esteem as they become older—ingredients that may contribute to depression. To help prevent these feelings and at the same time make an important contribution to the community, some older individuals now offer their expertise and wisdom to young people who are trying to master new skills, start new careers, undertake business projects, and the like. This elderly man, who volunteers regularly at an elementary school, is teaching math to a first grader, using a math board game as one of his tools.*

Depression in Later Life

Depression is one of the most common mental health problems of older adults. The features of depression are the same for elderly people as for younger people, including feelings of profound sadness and emptiness; low self-esteem, guilt, and pessimism; and loss of appetite and sleep disturbances (Nelson et al., 2005) (see Box 18-1 on the next page). Depression is particularly common among those who have recently experienced a trauma, such as the loss of a spouse or close friend or the development of a serious physical illness (Alexopoulos, 2005; Freyne et al., 2005; Shear, 2005).

[Oscar] was an 83-year-old married man with an episode of major depressive disorder. . . . He said that about one and one-half years prior to beginning treatment, his brother had died. In the following months, two friends whom he had known since childhood died. Following these losses, he became increasingly anxious [and] grew more and more pessimistic. Reluctantly, he acknowledged, "I even thought about ending my life." Review of his symptoms indicated that while . . . anxiety was a prominent part of his clinical picture, so was depression. . . .

During . . . treatment, [Oscar] discussed his relationship with his brother. He discussed how distraught he was to watch his brother's physical deterioration from an extended illness. He described the scene at his brother's deathbed and the moment "when he took his final breath." He experienced guilt over the failure to carry out his brother's funeral services in a manner he felt his brother would have wanted. While initially characterizing his relationship with his brother as loving and amiable, he later acknowledged that he disapproved of many ways in which his brother acted. Later in therapy, he also reviewed different facets of his past relationships with his two deceased friends. He expressed sadness that the long years had ended. . . . [Oscar's] life had been organized around visits to his brother's home and outings with his friends. . . . [While] his wife had encouraged him to visit with other friends and family, it became harder and harder to do so as he became more depressed.

(Hinrichsen, 1999, p. 433)

Overall, as many as 20 percent of people experience depression at some point during old age (Knight et al., 2006; Blazer, 2002). The rate is highest in older women. This

>>IN THEIR WORDS

"I am an old man and have known many troubles, but most of them never happened." <<

Mark Twain

"What an amount of good nature and humor it takes to endure the gruesome business of growing old." <<

Sigmund Freud, 1937

[BOX **18-1**]

Sleep and Sleep Disorders among the Old and Not So Old

Sleep is affected by both physical and psychosocial factors. Sleep deprivation for 100 hours or more leads to hallucinations, paranoia, and bizarre behavior. When people remain awake for over 200 hours, they frequently experience periods of "microsleep," naps lasting two to three seconds. The body simply refuses to be entirely deprived of sleep for long.

To learn more about sleep, researchers bring people into the laboratory and record their activities as they sleep, using various types of recording devices. One important discovery has been that eyes move rapidly about 25 percent of the time a person is asleep (Aserinsky & Kleitman, 1953), a phenomenon known as *rapid eye movement,* or *REM*. REM sleep is often called "paradoxical sleep" because it resembles both deep sleep and wakefulness. Despite small movements and muscle twitches, the body is immobilized, almost paralyzed. At the same time, the eyes are darting back and forth, blood flow to the brain increases, and brainwave activity is almost identical to that of an awake and alert person. Eighty percent of subjects who are awakened from REM sleep report that they were dreaming.

DSM-IV-TR identifies a number of sleep disorders. The *dyssomnias* (insomnia, hypersomnia, breathing-related sleep disorder, narcolepsy, and circadian rhythm sleep disorder) involve disturbances in the amount, quality, or timing of sleep. The *parasomnias* (nightmare disorder, sleep terror disorder, and sleepwalking disorder) involve abnormal events that occur during sleep.

The most common of these disorders is *insomnia,* a dyssomnia in which people repeatedly have great difficulty falling asleep or maintaining sleep. More than 20 percent of the entire population experience this pattern each year (APA, 2000). People with insomnia feel as though they are almost constantly awake. Often they are very sleepy during the day and have difficulty functioning effectively. The problem may be caused by factors such as anxiety or depression, medical ailments, pain, or medication effects (Sadock & Sadock, 2003).

SLEEP DISORDERS AMONG THE ELDERLY

Insomnia is more common among older persons than younger ones (Knight et al., 2006). Al least 40 percent of the population over 65 years of age experience some measure of insomnia (Chong et al., 2005). Elderly people may be particularly prone to this problem because so many of them have medical ailments, experience pain, take medications, or grapple with depression and anxiety—each a known contributor to insomnia (Ancoli-Israel & Cooke, 2005; Asplund, 2005). In addition, some of the normal physical changes that occur as people age may heighten the chances of insomnia. As we age, for example, our body rhythms change, we naturally spend less time in deep sleep and REM sleep, our sleep is more readily interrupted, and we take longer to get back to sleep.

Another sleep disorder commonly found among the elderly is *breathing-related sleep disorder,* a respiratory problem in which persons are periodically deprived of oxygen to the brain while they sleep, so that they frequently wake up. *Sleep apnea,* the most common form of this disorder, may occur in more than 10 percent of the elderly population; it is less common in younger age groups (APA, 2000, 1994). Its victims, typically overweight persons who are heavy snorers, actually stop breathing for up to 30 seconds or more as they sleep. Hundreds of episodes may occur nightly, without the victim's awareness.

SLEEP DISORDERS THROUGHOUT THE LIFE SPAN

As we have observed, insomnia and breathing-related sleep disorder are particularly common among older persons, although they are found in younger persons as well. Other sleep disorders are just as common—in a few cases more common—among the other age groups.

In contrast to insomnia, *hypersomnia* is a sleep disorder characterized by a heightened need for sleep and excessive sleepi-

rate among the elderly is about the same as that among younger adults—even lower, according to some studies. However, it climbs much higher among aged persons who live in nursing homes, as opposed to those in the community (Fisher et al., 2001).

Several studies suggest that depression raises an elderly person's chances of developing significant medical problems (Aldwin et al., 2006; Alexopoulos, 2005). For example, older depressed people with high blood pressure are almost three times as likely to suffer a stroke as older nondepressed people with the same condition. Similarly, elderly people who are depressed recover more slowly and less completely from heart attacks, hip fractures, pneumonia, and other infections and illnesses. Small wonder that among the elderly in nursing homes, increases in clinical depression are tied to increases in the death rate (Fisher et al., 2001; Parmelee et al., 1991).

As we observed in Chapter 10, elderly persons are also more likely to commit suicide than younger ones, and often their suicides are related to depression (Preville et al., ness. Sufferers may need extra hours of sleep each night and may need to sleep during the daytime as well (APA, 2000, 1994).

Narcolepsy, a disorder marked by repeated sudden bouts of REM sleep during waking hours, afflicts more than 135,000 people in the United States (NINDS, 2006). Although narcolepsy is a biological disorder, the bouts of REM sleep are often triggered by strong emotions. Sufferers may suddenly fall into REM sleep in the midst of an argument or during an exciting part of a football game.

People with *circadian rhythm sleep disorder* experience excessive sleepiness or insomnia as a result of a mismatch between their own sleep-wake pattern and the sleep-wake schedule of most other people in their environment. Often the disorder takes the form of falling asleep late and awakening late. This dyssomnia can result from night-shift work, frequent changes in work shifts, or repeated episodes of jet lag (Ohayon et al., 2002).

Nightmare disorder is the most common of the parasomnias. Although most people experience nightmares from time to time, in this disorder nightmares become frequent and cause such great distress that the individual must receive treatment. Such nightmares often increase under stress.

Persons with *sleep terror disorder* awaken suddenly during the first third of their evening sleep, screaming in extreme fear and agitation. They are in a state of panic, are often incoherent, and have a heart rate to match. Sleep terrors most often appear in children and disappear during adolescence. Up to 6 percent of children experience them at some time (APA, 2000).

People with a *sleepwalking disorder*—usually children—repeatedly leave their beds and walk around, without being conscious of the episode or remembering it later. The episodes occur in the first third of the individuals' nightly sleep. Those who are awakened while sleepwalking are confused for several moments. If allowed to continue sleepwalking, they eventually return to bed. Sleepwalkers usually manage to avoid obstacles, climb stairs, and perform complex activities, in a seemingly emotionless state. Accidents do happen, however: tripping, bumping into furniture, and even falling out of windows have all been reported. Up to 5 percent of children experience this disorder for an extended period of time, and as many as 30 percent have occasional episodes. Sleepwalking usually disappears by age 15 (APA, 2000, 1994).

2005). The overall rate of suicide in the United States is 12 per 100,000 persons; among the elderly it is 19 per 100,000. Among 80- to-85-year-olds in particular, it is 27 per 100,000; and among white American men over the age of 85, it is 65 per 100,000 (CDC, 2001; Fisher et al., 2001).

Like younger adults, older individuals who are depressed may be helped by cognitive therapy, interpersonal therapy, antidepressant medications, or a combination of these approaches (Knight et al., 2006; Alexopoulos, 2005). Both individual and group therapy formats have been used. More than half of elderly patients with depression improve with these various treatments. At the same time, it is sometimes difficult to use antidepressant drugs effectively and safely with older persons because the body breaks the drugs down differently in later life (Rubin, 2005; Sadavoy, 2004). Electroconvulsive therapy, applied with certain modifications, has also been used for elderly people who are severely depressed and unhelped by other approaches (Blazer, 2002).

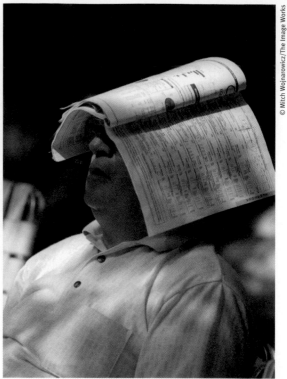

Racing to mental health *Gerontologists propose that elderly people need to pursue pleasurable and personally meaningful activities in order to thrive psychologically. With this in mind, the elderly men on the left compete in a race in the Senior Olympics. On the other hand, the elderly gentleman on the right, also interested in racing, watches a competition at the Saratoga Springs horse racing track with the daily post parade statistics program resting on his head. Which of these two activities might clinical theorists have more confidence in as a key to successful psychological functioning during old age?*

Anxiety Disorders in Later Life

Anxiety is also common among elderly people (Schuurmans et al., 2005; Wetherell & Gatz, 2001). At any given time, around 6 percent of elderly men and 11 percent of elderly women in the United States experience at least one of the anxiety disorders (Fisher et al., 2001). Surveys indicate that generalized anxiety disorder is particularly common, experienced by up to 7 percent of all elderly persons (Flint, 1994). The prevalence of anxiety also increases throughout old age. For example, individuals over 85 years of age report higher rates of anxiety than those between 65 and 84 years. In fact, all of these numbers may be low, as anxiety in the elderly tends to be underreported (Jeste, Blazer, & First, 2005). Both the elderly individual and the clinician may interpret physical symptoms of anxiety, such as heart palpitations and sweating, as symptoms of a medical condition.

There are many things about aging that may heighten the anxiety levels of certain individuals. Declining health, for example, has often been pointed to, and in fact, older persons who experience significant medical illnesses or injuries report more anxiety than those who are healthy or injury-free (Nordhus & Nielsen, 2005; Fisher et al., 2001). Researchers have not, however, been able to determine why certain individuals who experience such problems in old age become anxious while others who face similar circumstances remain relatively calm (see Box 18-2).

Older adults with anxiety disorders have been treated with psychotherapy of various kinds, particularly cognitive therapy (Knight et al., 2006; Mohlman et al., 2003). Many also receive benzodiazepines or other antianxiety medications; those with obsessive-compulsive disorder or panic disorder may be treated with serotonin-enhancing antidepressant drugs such as fluoxetine (Prozac), just as younger sufferers are. Again, however, all such drugs must be used cautiously with older people (Tamblyn et al., 2005).

Substance Abuse in Later Life

Although alcohol abuse and other forms of substance abuse are significant problems for many older persons, the prevalence of such patterns actually appears to decline after age 60, perhaps because of declining health or reduced financial status (Aldwin et al., 2006;

>>LOOKING AROUND
Aging and Religion

On average, the death rate of elderly people who regularly attend religious services is 46 percent lower than the rate of those who attend infrequently (Krause, 2006; Koenig et al., 1999). **<<**

Around 73 percent of elderly persons say religion is very important to them, compared to 48 percent of young adults (Aldwin et al., 2006; Gallup poll, 2004). **<<**

[BOX **18-2**]

The Oldest Old

Clinicians suggest that aging need not inevitably lead to psychological problems. Nor apparently does it always lead to physical problems.

When researchers studied people over 95 years of age—often called the "oldest old"—they were surprised to find that these individuals are on average more healthy, clear-headed, and agile than those in their 80s and early 90s (Corliss & Lemonick, 2004; Perls, 1995). Many of the oldest old are, in fact, still employed, sexually active, and able to enjoy the outdoors and the arts.

Ethan Hoffman/Picutre Project, New York, NY

Some scientists believe that individuals who live this long carry "longevity" genes that make them resistant to disabling or terminal infections (Corliss & Lemonick, 2004; Perls, 1995). The individuals themselves often credit a good frame of mind or regular behaviors that they have maintained for many years—for example, eating healthful food, pursuing regular exercise, and not smoking.

John Parrish, a 104-year-old medicine man living in Monument Valley, Arizona.

Oslin & Holden, 2002). The majority of older adults do not misuse alcohol or other substances despite the fact that aging can sometimes be a time of considerable stress and that in our society alcohol and drugs are widely turned to in times of stress. At the same time, accurate data about the rate of substance abuse among older adults are difficult to gather because many elderly persons do not suspect or admit that they have such a problem (Jeste et al., 2005). Some regard it as shameful, others fail to realize that their drinking has become a problem, and a number misuse their medications without being aware of it (Gallagher-Thompson & Thompson, 1995).

Surveys find that 4 to 7 percent of older people, particularly men, have alcohol-related disorders in a given year (Knight et al., 2006; Adams & Cox, 1997). Men under 30 are four times as likely as men over 60 to exhibit a behavioral problem associated with alcohol abuse, such as repeated falling, spells of dizziness or blacking out, secretive drinking, or social withdrawal. Older patients who are institutionalized, however, do display high rates of problem drinking. For example, alcohol problems among older persons admitted to general and mental hospitals range from 15 percent to 49 percent, and estimates of alcohol-related problems among patients in nursing homes range from 26 percent to 60 percent (Klein & Jess, 2002; Gallagher-Thompson & Thompson, 1995).

Researchers often distinguish between older problem drinkers who have had alcohol-related problems for many years, perhaps since their 20s, and those who do not start the pattern until their 50s or 60s. The latter group typically begins abusive drinking as a reaction to the negative events and pressures of growing older, such as the death of a spouse, living alone, or unwanted retirement (Onen et al., 2005). Alcohol abuse and dependence in elderly people are treated much as in younger adults (see Chapter 12), with such approaches as detoxification, Antabuse, Alcoholics Anonymous (AA), and cognitive-behavioral therapy (Knight et al., 2006; Gurnack et al., 2002).

A leading kind of substance problem in the elderly is the *misuse of prescription drugs* (Beckman, Parker, & Thorslund, 2005). Most often it is unintentional. Older people receive twice as many prescriptions on average as younger persons, and one-quarter or more take at least three drugs daily (Wilder-Smith, 2005; Blazer, 2002). Thus their risk of confusing medications or skipping doses is high. Physicians and pharmacists often try to simplify medications, educate older patients about their prescriptions, clarify directions, and teach them to watch for undesired effects (Rubin, 2005). On the other hand, physicians themselves are sometimes to blame in cases of prescription drug misuse, perhaps overprescribing medications for elderly patients or unwisely mixing certain

>>BY THE NUMBERS
Prescription Drugs and the Elderly

25% Percentage of all prescribed drugs that are taken by elderly people ‹‹

13% Percentage of the total population who are elderly ‹‹

(Blazer, 2002)

•**DELIRIUM**•A rapidly developing clouding of consciousness; the person has great difficulty concentrating, focusing attention, and following an orderly sequence of thought.

•**DEMENTIA**•A syndrome marked by severe problems in memory and in at least one other cognitive function.

•**ALZHEIMER'S DISEASE**•The most common form of dementia, usually occurring after the age of 65.

medicines (Spinewine et al., 2005; Wilder-Smith, 2005). In a poignant letter published in the magazine *Aging* in 1990, a 72-year-old woman revealed that because of problems earlier in her life, her physician prescribed first tranquilizers, then a stimulant, and then medication for severe headaches. Eventually she increased the dosage of these various medications, noting that the drugs no longer had the same effect and that she did not feel well. She said she felt no guilt about what had happened because "after all I was only following the doctor's orders at all times" (Reynolds, 1990, p. 27). Her functioning became so impaired, however, that she needed hospitalization and therapy to end her addiction.

Psychotic Disorders in Later Life

Elderly people have a higher rate of psychotic symptoms than younger persons (Fisher et al., 2001). Among aged people, these symptoms are usually due to underlying medical conditions such as delirium and dementia, the disorders of cognition that we shall be turning to in the next section. However, some elderly persons suffer from *schizophrenia* or *delusional disorder.*

Actually, schizophrenia is less common in older persons than in younger ones. In fact, many persons with schizophrenia find that their symptoms lessen in later life (Fisher et al., 2001). Improvement can occur in people who have displayed schizophrenia for 30 or more years, particularly in such areas as social skills and work capacity, as we are reminded by the remarkable late-life improvement of the Nobel Prize recipient John Nash (see page 415).

It is uncommon for *new* cases of schizophrenia to emerge in late life. Thus some of the elderly people with schizophrenia have been receiving antipsychotic drugs and related treatments for many years and are continuing to do so in old age (Sadavoy, 2004). In contrast, others have been untreated for years and continue to be untreated as elderly persons, winding up in nursing homes, in run-down apartments, homeless, or in jail.

Another kind of psychotic disorder found among the elderly is *delusional disorder,* in which individuals develop beliefs that are false but not bizarre. This disorder is rare in most age groups—around 3 of every 10,000 persons—but its prevalence appears to increase in the elderly population (Fisher et al., 2001; APA, 2000, 1994). Older persons with a delusional disorder may develop deeply held suspicions of persecution; they believe that other persons—often family members, doctors, or friends—are conspiring against, cheating, spying on, or maligning them. They may become irritable, angry, or depressed, or pursue legal action because of such ideas (APA, 2000). It is not clear why this disorder increases among elderly people, but some clinicians suggest that the rise is related to the deficiencies in hearing, social isolation, greater stress, or heightened poverty experienced by many elderly persons (Fisher et al., 2001; APA, 2000, 1994).

Disorders of Cognition

Most of us worry from time to time that we are losing our memory and other mental abilities. We rush out the door without our keys; we meet a familiar person and cannot remember her name; or in the middle of an important test our mind goes blank. Actually such mishaps are a common and quite normal feature of stress or of aging (Hoyer & Verhaeghen, 2006). As people move through middle age, these memory difficulties and lapses of attention increase, and they may occur regularly by the age of 60 or 70. Sometimes, however, people experience memory and other cognitive changes that are far more extensive and problematic.

In Chapter 7 we observed that problems in memory and related cognitive processes can occur without biological causes, in the form of *dissociative disorders.* More often, however, cognitive problems do have organic roots, particularly when they appear late in life. The leading cognitive disorders among elderly persons are *delirium* and *dementia.*

"My inner child just turned sixty-five."

Delirium

Delirium is a clouding of consciousness. As the person's awareness of the environment becomes less clear, he or she has great difficulty concentrating, focusing attention, and thinking sequentially, which leads to misinterpretations, illusions, and, on occasion, hallucinations (Kempler, 2005; APA, 2000, 1994). Sufferers may believe that it is morning in the middle of the night or that they are home when actually they are in a hospital room.

This state of massive confusion typically develops over a short period of time, usually hours or days. Delirium apparently affects more than 2 million people in the United States each year (Clary & Krishnan, 2001). It may occur in any age group, including children, but is most common in elderly persons. In fact, when elderly people enter a hospital to be treated for a general medical condition, one in 10 of them shows the symptoms of delirium (APA, 2000, 1994). At least another 10 percent develop delirium during their stay in the hospital (APA, 2000; Inouye et al., 1999; Inouye, 1998).

Fever, certain diseases and infections, poor nutrition, head injuries, strokes, and stress (including the trauma of surgery) may all cause delirium (Wetterling, 2005; Schneider et al., 2002). So may intoxication by certain substances, such as prescription drugs. Partly because older people face so many of these problems, they are more likely than younger ones to experience delirium. If a clinician accurately identifies delirium, it can often be easy to correct—by treating the underlying infection, for example, or changing the patient's drug prescription (Sadavoy, 2004). However, the syndrome is not always recognized for what it is (Monette et al., 2001; Inouye, 1999, 1998). One study on a medical ward found that admission doctors detected only one of 15 consecutive cases of delirium (Cameron et al., 1987). Incorrect diagnosis of this kind may contribute to a high death rate for older people with delirium (Gonzalez et al., 2005; Coulson & Almeida, 2002).

Dementia

People with **dementia** experience significant memory losses along with losses in other cognitive functions such as abstract thinking or language (APA, 2000, 1994). Those with certain forms of dementia may also undergo personality changes—they may begin to behave inappropriately, for example—and their symptoms may worsen steadily.

At any given time, around 3 to 9 percent of the world's adult population are suffering from dementia (Berr et al., 2005). Its occurrence is closely related to age (see Figure 18-2). Among people 65 years of age, the prevalence is around 1 to 2 percent, increasing to more than 33 percent for those over the age of 85 (Knight et al., 2006; Rubin, 2005).

Altogether, 5 million persons in the United States experience some form of dementia (Reuters, 2004; Katzman, 2001). More than 70 forms have been identified (Noll & Turkington, 1994). Like delirium, dementia is sometimes the result of nutritional or other problems that can be corrected. Most forms of dementia, however, are caused by brain diseases or injuries, such as Alzheimer's disease or stroke, which are currently difficult or impossible to correct.

ALZHEIMER'S DISEASE **Alzheimer's disease** is named after Alois Alzheimer, the German physician who formally identified it in 1907. Alzheimer first became aware of the syndrome in 1901 when a new patient, Auguste D., was placed under his care:

> On November 25, 1901, a . . . woman with no personal or family history of mental illness was admitted to a psychiatric hospital in Frankfurt, Germany, by her husband, who could no longer ignore or hide quirks and lapses that had overtaken her in recent months. First, there were unexplainable bursts of anger, and then a strange series of memory problems. She became increasingly unable to locate things in her own home and began to make surprising mistakes in the kitchen.

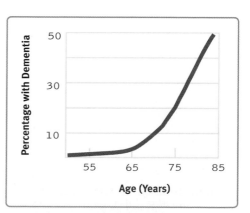

Environmental comfort *In addition to providing support, psychotropic medications, and other such measures to help calm and lift the spirits of elderly residents, some long-term care facilities have redesigned their buildings so that the settings themselves have soothing and uplifting effects. At this facility in Baltimore, an elderly resident feels one of the fiber-optic light curtains that decorate the rooms. The rooms are also made more peaceful by the use of soft changing colors and sounds of the ocean, woods, and streams.*

FIGURE **18-2** **Dementia and age** *The occurrence of dementia is closely related to age. Fewer than 1 percent of all 60-year-olds have dementia, compared to as many as 50 percent of those who are 85. After 60, the prevalence of dementia doubles every six years up to age 85 or so, then the increase tapers off. (Adapted from Cowley, 2000; Alzheimer's Association, 1997; Ritchie et al., 1992.)*

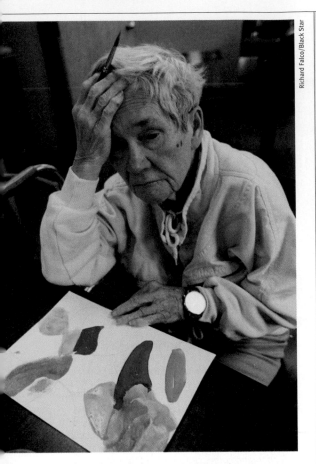

Losing one's mind *Because of their short-term memory problems, people with advanced cases of Alzheimer's disease, one source of dementia, are often unable to complete simple tasks such as painting a picture. In addition, their long-term memory deficits may prevent them from recognizing even close relatives or friends.*

By the time she arrived at Städtische Irrenanstalt, the Frankfurt Hospital for the Mentally Ill and Epileptics, her condition was as severe as it was curious. The attending doctor, senior physician Alois Alzheimer, began the new file with these notes. . . .

> She sits on the bed with a helpless expression.
> "What is your name?"
> *Auguste.*
> "Last name?"
> *Auguste.*
> "What is your husband's name?"
> *Auguste, I think.*
> "How long have you been here?"
> (She seems to be trying to remember.)
> *Three weeks.*

It was her second day in the hospital. Dr. Alzheimer, a thirty-seven-year-old neuropathologist and clinician, . . . observed in his new patient a remarkable cluster of symptoms: severe disorientation, reduced comprehension, aphasia (language impairment), paranoia, hallucinations, and a short-term memory so incapacitated that when he spoke her full-name, *Frau Auguste D_____*, and asked her to write it down, the patient got only as far as "Frau" before needing the doctor to repeat the rest.

He spoke her name again. She wrote "Augu" and again stopped.

When Alzheimer prompted her a third time, she was able to write her entire first name and the initial "D" before finally giving up, telling the doctor, "I have lost myself."

Her condition did not improve. It became apparent that there was nothing that anyone at this or any other hospital could do for Frau D. except to insure her safety and try to keep her as clean and comfortable as possible for the rest of her days. Over the next four and a half years, she became increasingly disoriented, delusional, and incoherent. She was often hostile.

"Her gestures showed a complete helplessness," Alzheimer later noted in a published report. "She was disoriented as to time and place. From time to time she would state that she did not understand anything, that she felt confused and totally lost. . . . Often she would scream for hours and hours in a horrible voice."

By November 1904, three and a half years into her illness, Auguste D. was bedridden, incontinent, and largely immobile. . . . Notes from October 1905 indicate that she had become permanently curled up in a fetal position with her knees drawn up to her chest, muttering but unable to speak, and requiring assistance to be fed.

(Shenk, 2001, pp. 12–14)

•**NEUROFIBRILLARY TANGLES**•Twisted protein fibers that form within certain brain cells as people age. People with Alzheimer's disease have an excessive number of such tangles.

•**SENILE PLAQUES**•Sphere-shaped deposits of beta-amyloid protein that form in the spaces between certain brain cells and in certain blood vessels as people age. People with Alzheimer's disease have an excessive number of such plaques.

Alzheimer's disease is the most common form of dementia, accounting for as many as two-thirds of all cases (Julien, 2005). This gradually progressive disease sometimes appears in middle age (*early onset*), but most often it occurs after the age of 65 (*late onset*), and its prevalence increases markedly among people in their late 70s and early 80s (see Table 18-1).

Although some people with Alzheimer's disease may survive for as many as 20 years, the time between onset and death is typically 8 to 10 years (Julien, 2005). It usually begins with mild memory problems, lapses of attention, and difficulties in language and communication (Shenk, 2001). As symptoms worsen, the person has trouble completing complicated tasks or remembering important appointments. Eventually sufferers also have difficulty with simple tasks, distant memories are forgotten, and changes in personality often become very noticeable. For example, a man may become uncharacteristically aggressive.

People with Alzheimer's disease may at first deny that they have a problem (Shenk, 2001), but they soon become anxious or depressed about their state of mind; many also become agitated (Janzing, 2003; Zal, 1999). A woman from Virginia describes her memory loss as the disease progresses:

> Very often I wander around looking for something which I know is very pertinent, but then after a while I forget about what it is I was looking for. . . . Once the idea is lost, everything is lost and I have nothing to do but wander around trying to figure out what it was that was so important earlier.
>
> *(Shenk, 2001, p. 43)*

As the symptoms of dementia intensify, people with Alzheimer's disease show less and less awareness of their limitations. They may withdraw from others during the late stages of the disorder, become more confused about time and place, wander, and show very poor judgment. Eventually they become fully dependent on other people (Brooks, 2005). They may lose almost all knowledge of the past and fail to recognize the faces of even close relatives. They also become increasingly uncomfortable at night and take frequent naps during the day (Tractenberg, Singer, & Kaye, 2005). The late phase of the disorder can last from two to five years, with the individuals requiring constant care (Mace & Rabins, 1991).

Alzheimer's victims usually remain in fairly good health until the later stages of the disease. As their mental functioning declines, however, they become less active and spend much of their time just sitting or lying in bed. As a result, they are prone to develop illnesses such as pneumonia, which can result in death. Alzheimer's disease is responsible for 45,000 deaths each year in the United States, which makes it the eighth leading cause of death in the country (Cowley, 2002).

In most cases, Alzheimer's disease can be diagnosed with certainty only after death (APA, 2000), when structural changes in the person's brain, such as excessive *neurofibrillary tangles* and *senile plaques,* can be fully examined. **Neurofibrillary tangles,** twisted protein fibers found *within* the cells of the hippocampus and certain other brain areas, occur in all people as they age, but people with Alzheimer's disease form an extraordinary number of them (Thompson, 2000; Selkoe, 1992).

Senile plaques are sphere-shaped deposits of a small molecule known as the *beta-amyloid protein* that form in the spaces *between* cells in the hippocampus, cerebral cortex,

---

Table 18-1 DSM Checklist

DEMENTIA OF THE ALZHEIMER'S TYPE

1. The development of multiple cognitive deficits manifested by both memory impairment and at least one of the following cognitive disturbances:
   a. Aphasia.
   b. Apraxia.
   c. Agnosia.
   d. Disturbance in executive functioning.
2. Significant impairment in social or occupational functioning, along with significant decline from a previous level of functioning.
3. Gradual onset and continuing cognitive decline.

Based on APA, 2000, 1994.

Cognitive fitness center *A number of senior living community programs now include cognitive fitness centers where elderly persons sit at computers and work on memory and cognitive software programs. Research on brain plasticity suggests that "cognitive calisthenics" of this kind may provide challenging workouts for the brain and help prevent or reverse certain symptoms of aging, including memory loss, declining vision and hearing, and reduced motor control.*

and certain other brain regions, as well as in some nearby blood vessels. The formation of plaques is also a normal part of aging, but again it is exceptionally high in people with Alzheimer's disease (Selkoe, 2002, 2000, 1992). For most people, the majority of their beta-amyloid proteins are composed of 40 amino acids (*AB40*) while a small percentage of their beta-amyloid proteins have 42 amino acids (*AB42*). Research suggests that people with Alzheimer's disease have a relatively high number of the AB42 kind of beta amyloids and these are the kind that form plaques (Graff-Radford, 2005). Plaques may interfere with communications between cells and so cause cell breakdown or cell death.

Scientists do not fully understand why some people develop these problems and Alzheimer's disease. Research has suggested several possible causes, however, including genetic factors and abnormalities in brain structure and brain chemistry.

WHAT ARE THE GENETIC CAUSES OF ALZHEIMER'S DISEASE? It appears that Alzheimer's disease often has a genetic basis (Williams, 2003). Because many cases seem to run in families, clinicians now distinguish between *familial* Alzheimer's disease and *sporadic* Alzheimer's disease, which is not associated with a family history of the brain disease. Studies have found that particular genes are responsible for the production of proteins called *beta-amyloid precursor protein* (*beta-APP*), *presenilin,* and *interleukin-1.* Many theorists now believe that some families transmit *mutations,* or abnormal forms, of these genes, increasing the likelihood of plaque and tangle formations and, in turn, of Alzheimer's disease (Farlow et al., 2001; St. George-Hyslop, 2000; Selkoe, 1999, 1998, 1996). Genetic studies have also linked certain kinds of Alzheimer's disease to defects on chromosomes 1, 14, 19, and 21 (Turkington & Harris, 2001; Higgins et al., 1997). All of these discoveries are promising; but since many people with Alzheimer's disease do not have a clear family history of the disorder, scientists cannot be certain about the influence of genetic mutations on the disease's development in the population as a whole.

WHAT ARE THE STRUCTURAL AND BIOCHEMICAL CAUSES OF ALZHEIMER'S DISEASE? Whether it is genetic factors or other kinds of factors that predispose individuals to Alzheimer's disease, we still need to know what brain abnormalities they set in motion. That is, what abnormalities in brain structure or brain chemistry lead to Alzheimer's disease and to the excessive numbers of tangles and plaques that are its hallmark? Researchers have identified a number of possibilities. To understand these possible explanations, we need first to understand some basic information about the operation and biology of memory.

The human brain has two memory systems that work together to help us learn and recall. **Short-term memory,** or **working memory,** gathers new information. **Long-term memory** is the accumulation of information that we have stored over the years, information that first made its way through the short-term memory system. The information held in short-term memory must be transformed, or *consolidated,* into long-term memory if we are to hold on to it. Remembering information that has been stored in long-term memory is called *retrieval* and is described as going into one's long-term memory to bring it out for use again in short-term, or working, memory. Information in long-term memory can be classified as either procedural or declarative. *Procedural memories* are learned skills we perform without needing to think about them, such as walking, cutting with scissors, or writing. *Declarative memory* consists of names, dates, and other facts that have been learned. Declarative memory is usually affected more profoundly than procedural memory in cases of dementia.

Certain *brain structures* seem to be especially important in memory. Among the most important structures in short-

Missing pieces *These self-portraits by the German artist Anton Räderscheidt, painted after a stroke temporarily damaged his right parietal lobe, show the importance of memory and attention. Shortly after his stroke, the artist omitted half of his face (upper left). Within nine months, he had recovered his cognitive skills and was able to complete all the details in his painting (lower right).*

term memory are the **prefrontal lobes,** located just behind the forehead (Anderson, 2000). When animals or humans acquire new information, their prefrontal lobes become more active (Haxby et al., 1996). Apparently this activity enables them to hold information temporarily and to continue working with the information as long as it is needed. Among the brain areas most important to long-term memory are the **temporal lobes** (including the *hippocampus* and *amygdala,* key structures under the temporal lobes) and the **diencephalon** (including the *mammillary bodies, thalamus,* and *hypothalamus*), which seem to help transform short-term into long-term memory. Cases of dementia involve damage to one or more of these areas (van der Flier et al., 2005; Caine et al., 2001) (see Box 18-3 on the next page and Figure 18-3).

Memory researchers have also identified *biochemical changes* that occur in cells as memories form. For example, when new information is acquired and stored, *proteins* are produced in key brain cells. Several chemicals are responsible for the production of proteins, including *acetylcholine, glutamate, RNA* (*ribonucleic acid*), and *calcium*. If the activity of any of these chemicals is disturbed, the proper production of proteins may be prevented and the formation of memories interrupted (Martinez & Derrick, 1996; Rosenzweig, 1996). For example, by blocking the activity of glutamate, animal researchers have prevented short-term memory. Similarly, by blocking the cellular production of RNA or of calcium, they have interrupted the formation of long-term memories.

With this background information in mind, let us return to the biological causes of Alzheimer's disease. One line of research suggests that some of the *proteins* involved in memory formation may take an abnormal form and essentially run amok in people with Alzheimer's disease (Graff-Radford, 2005; Hardy & Selkoe, 2002). Studies suggest, for example, that two key proteins—*beta-amyloid protein* and *tau protein*—operate abnormally in such individuals. As we observed earlier, abnormal stucture and activity by the beta-amyloid protein seem to be involved in the formation of plaques in the hippocampus and certain other brain areas. Similarly, abnormal activity of the tau protein apparently leads to the formation of tangles in those brain areas.

Another line of research points to abnormal activity by the neurotransmitters and related chemicals involved in the production of the memory proteins. Many studies have found that *acetylcholine* and *glutamate* are in low supply, or at least function differently, in

•**SHORT-TERM MEMORY**•The memory system that collects new information. Also known as *working memory*.

•**LONG-TERM MEMORY**•The memory system that contains all the information that we have stored over the years.

•**PREFRONTAL LOBES**•Regions of the brain that play a key role in short-term memory, among other functions.

•**TEMPORAL LOBES**•Regions of the brain that help transform short-term to long-term memory, among other functions.

•**DIENCEPHALON**•A brain area (consisting of the mammillary bodies, thalamus, and hypothalamus) that helps transform short-term to long-term memory, among other functions.

Thalamus
Selected neurons shrink or die

Cerebral cortex
Large neurons shrink
Amyloid deposits develop in spaces between cells

Mammillary bodies

Hypothalamus
Selected neurons die

Basal forebrain
Acetylcholine-secreting neurons shrink or die

Amygdala
Amyloid deposits develop in spaces between cells
Neurofibrillary tangles develop within neurons

Locus ceruleus
Neurons die

Hippocampus
Large neurons shrink or die
Amyloid deposits develop in spaces between cells
Neurofibrillary tangles develop within neurons

FIGURE **18-3** **The aging brain** *In old age, our brain undergoes changes that affect memory, learning, and reasoning to some degree. These same changes occur to an excessive degree in people with Alzheimer's disease. (Adapted from Selkoe, 1992, p. 136.)*

[BOX **18-3**]

Amnestic Disorders: Forgetting to Remember

People who suffer from dementia experience both severe memory problems and other cognitive impairments. In contrast, those with *amnestic disorders*, another group of disorders caused by brain diseases or injuries, have memory problems only. Amnestic disorders are just as likely to occur in younger people as among the elderly.

Retrograde amnesia is an inability to remember events from the past (Kempler, 2005). *Anterograde amnesia* is an ongoing inability to form new memories. People with amnestic disorders sometimes suffer from retrograde amnesia, depending on the particular disorder, but they almost always experience anterograde amnesia.

In anterograde amnesia, it is as though information from short-term memory can no longer cross over into long-term memory. Not surprisingly, it is often the result of damage to the brain's *temporal lobes* or *diencephalon,* the areas largely responsible for transforming short-term memory into long-term memory. In severe forms of anterograde amnesia, new acquaintances are forgotten almost immediately, and problems solved one day must be tackled again the next. The person may not remember anything that has happened since his or her problem first began. Nevertheless, sufferers may continue to possess

all of their earlier verbal skills and many problem-solving abilities, and their IQ is not changed. The best known of the amnestic disorders are *Korsakoff's syndrome* and disorders resulting from *head injuries* or *brain surgery.*

KORSAKOFF'S SYNDROME

Fred, a 69-year-old man, was admitted to a mental hospital in a state of confusion, the result of *Korsakoff's syndrome,* an amnestic disorder that causes its victims to keep forgetting newly learned information (anterograde amnesia):

I *Fred . . . had a history of many years of heavy drinking, although he denied drinking during the past several years. When seen in the admitting ward, the patient was neatly dressed, but there was some deterioration of his personal habits. Although pleasant and sociable with the interviewer and ward personnel, he was definitely confused. He wandered about the ward, investigating objects and trying on other people's clothing. He talked freely, though his speech tended to be rambling and at times incoherent. Most of his spontaneous conversation centered on himself, and there were a number of hypochondriacal complaints. Fred was disoriented for time and place, although he was able to give his name. He could not give his correct address, said his age*

was 91, and was unable to name the day, the month, or the year. He did not know where he was, although he said he was sent here by his landlord because he had been drinking. He admitted that he had been arrested for fighting and drinking, but he said that he had never had an attack of delirium tremens. [Fred] showed the characteristic symptom picture of Korsakoff's syndrome, with disorientation, confusion, and a strong tendency toward confabulation. When asked where he was, he said he was in a brewery. He gave the name of the brewery, but when asked the same question a few minutes later, he named another brewery. Similarly, he said that he knew the examiner, called him by an incorrect name, and a little later changed the name again. When leaving the examining room, he used still another name when he said politely, "Goodbye, Mr. Wolf!" I

(KISKER, 1977, P. 308)

As we observed in Chapter 12, approximately 5 percent of people with chronic alcoholism develop Korsakoff's syndrome. A combination of excessive drinking and improper diet produce a deficiency of *vitamin B* (*thiamine*), which leads to damage in portions of the *diencephalon* (Harding et al., 2000). Sufferers of this disorder primarily lose memories of factual knowledge

---

>>LAB•NOTES

Busy Mind, Healthier Brain

Researchers have found fewer plaques and tangles in the brains of lab mice that live in intellectually stimulating environments—chew toys, running wheels, and tunnels—than in those of mice that live in less stimulating settings (Lazarov et al., 2005). ‹‹

the brains of Alzheimer victims (Bissette et al., 1996; Lee et al., 1996). Other studies suggest that victims may display an imbalance in the metabolism of *calcium.*

A third explanation for Alzheimer's disease holds that certain substances found in nature may act as toxins and damage the brain. For example, researchers have detected high levels of *zinc* in the brains of some Alzheimer's victims. This finding has gained particular attention because in some animal studies zinc was observed to trigger a clumping of the beta–amyloid protein, similar to the plaques found in the brains of Alzheimer patients (Turkington & Harris, 2001).

Finally, two other explanations for Alzheimer's disease have been offered. One is the *autoimmune theory.* On the basis of certain irregularities found in the immune systems of people with Alzheimer's disease, several researchers have speculated that changes in aging brain cells may trigger an *autoimmune response* (that is, a mistaken attack by the immune system against itself) that leads to this disease (Hüll et al., 1996; McGeer & McGeer, 1996). The other explanation is a *viral theory.* Because Alzheimer's disease resembles *Creutzfeldt-Jacob disease,* another form of dementia that is known to be caused by a slow-acting virus, some researchers propose that a similar virus may cause Alzheimer's disease (Prusiner, 1991). However, no such virus has been isolated from the brains of Alzheimer's victims.

but still maintain their intellectual and language skills (Verfaellie et al., 1990). This may explain why Korsakoff's patients tend to *confabulate*. Like Fred, they use their general intellect to make up elaborate stories and lies in an effort to replace the memories they keep losing.

HEAD INJURIES AND BRAIN SURGERY

Both head injuries and brain surgery can cause amnestic disorders (Richardson, 2002; Zec et al., 2002, 2001). Either may destroy memory-related brain structures or cut the connections between memory-related areas of the brain. Television shows and movies often portray bumps on the head as a quick and easy way to lose one's memory. In fact, *mild* head injuries, such as a concussion that does not result in coma or a period of unconsciousness, rarely cause much memory loss, and what loss there is usually disappears within days or at most months. In contrast, almost half of all *severe* head injuries do cause some permanent learning and memory problems, both anterograde and retrograde. Altogether, 2 million people in the United States suffer traumatic brain injuries each year (Waxweiler et al., 1995). More than 20 percent of them ex-

perience lifelong aftereffects (NCIPC, 1999). The leading causes are car accidents and falls.

Brain surgery may create more specific memory problems. The most famous case of memory loss as a result of brain surgery is that of H.M., a man whose identity has been protected for decades (Kensinger, Ullman, & Corkin, 2001; Corkin, 1984, 1968; Milner, 1971). H.M. suffered from severe *brain seizure disorder,* or *epilepsy,* a disorder that produced seizures in his temporal lobes. To reduce his symptoms, doctors removed parts of both his temporal lobes in 1953, along with the amygdala and hippocampus. At that time, the involvement of these brain areas in the formation of memories was not known. (Today temporal lobe surgery is usually

limited to either the right or left side of the brain). H.M. has experienced severe anterograde amnesia ever since his surgery a half-century ago. He is unable to recognize anyone he has met since the day of his operation.

Part of the game? *Hard hits to the head are common in contact sports such as hockey, football, and boxing and often result in concussions and at least temporary losses of memory. Repeated hits may, in fact, lead to repeated concussions, further affecting memory and other cognitive functions and, in some cases, endangering the athlete's physical integrity or life.*

OTHER FORMS OF DEMENTIA A number of other disorders may also lead to dementia. **Vascular dementia,** also known as **multi-infarct dementia,** may follow a cerebrovascular accident, or *stroke,* during which blood flow to specific areas of the brain was cut off, thus damaging the areas (Ghika & Bogousslavsky, 2002). In many cases, the patient may not even be aware of the stroke. Like Alzheimer's disease, vascular dementia is progressive, but its symptoms begin suddenly rather than gradually. Moreover, cognitive functioning may continue to be normal in areas of the brain that have not been affected by the stroke, in contrast to the broad cognitive deficiencies usually displayed by Alzheimer patients. Vascular dementia is the second most common type of dementia among the elderly, accounting for 8 to 29 percent of cases (Selkoe, 1992; Katzman, 1981). Some people have both Alzheimer's disease and vascular dementia (Desmond et al., 2000).

Pick's disease, a rare disorder that affects the frontal and temporal lobes, offers a clinical picture similar to Alzheimer's disease, but the two diseases can be distinguished at autopsy (Hodges, 2001). *Creutzfeldt-Jakob disease,* another source of dementia, has symptoms that often include spasms of the body. As we observed earlier, this disease is caused by a slow-acting virus that may live in the body for years before the disease develops (APA, 2000) (see Box 18-4 on page 551). Once launched, however, the disease has a

•VASCULAR DEMENTIA•Dementia caused by a cerebrovascular accident, or stroke, which restricts blood flow to certain areas of the brain. Also known as *multi-infarct dementia*.

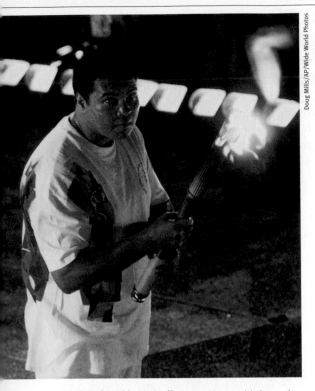

Doug Mills/AP/Wide World Photos

Victim of Parkinson's disease *The world cheered when Muhammad Ali, considered the most skilled and influential athlete of his generation, lit the Olympic flame in 1996. At the same time, Ali's slow gait, halting verbal responses, and shaking hands and limbs demonstrated the impairment that Parkinson's disease can bring.*

»»LOOKING AROUND

The Case of Ronald Reagan

Ronald Reagan's mother and older brother both suffered from dementia. **‹‹**

- -

Mildly forgetful during the late years of his presidency (1980-1988), Reagan experienced bouts of forgetfulness that began to interfere with his daily functioning by 1992. **‹‹**

- -

At the conclusion of a medical exam in 1992, Reagan looked up at his doctor of many years with an utterly blank face and said, "What am I supposed to do next?" **‹‹**

- -

In 1994 Reagan's doctors arrived at a formal diagnosis of Alzheimer's disease. **‹‹**

(Shenk, 2001)

---

rapid course. *Huntington's disease* is an inherited progressive disease in which memory problems worsen over time, along with personality changes and mood difficulties (Ranen, 2002). Huntington's victims have movement problems, too, such as severe twitching and spasms. Children of people with Huntington's disease have a 50 percent chance of developing it. *Parkinson's disease,* the slowly progressive neurological disorder marked by tremors, rigidity, and unsteadiness, causes dementia in 20 to 60 percent of cases, particularly in older people or individuals whose cases are advanced (APA, 2000). And, lastly, cases of dementia may also be caused by viral and bacterial *infectious disorders* such as HIV and AIDs, meningitis, and advanced syphilis; by *brain seizure disorder;* by *drug abuse;* or by *toxins* such as mercury, lead, or carbon monoxide.

THE ASSESSMENT AND TREATMENT OF DEMENTIA As we observed earlier, most cases of Alzheimer's disease can be *diagnosed* with certainty only after death, when an autopsy is performed. In addition, the *treatment* of this disease has been at best modestly helpful. However, growing research has raised hopes that Alzheimer's disease and other forms of dementia may be assessed and treated more effectively or even prevented in the near future (Kalb, 2000).

CAN ALZHEIMER'S DISEASE AND OTHER FORMS OF DEMENTIA BE PREDICTED OR ASSESSED BEFORE THE ONSET OF SYMPTOMS? Several research teams are currently trying to develop tools that can identify persons likely to develop dementia. One of the most promising lines of work comes from the laboratory of the brain researcher Lisa Mosconi (2005) and her colleagues at the New York University School of Medicine. Using a special kind of PET scan (*PET with fluoro-deoxyglucose*), Mosconi and her associates examined activity in certain parts of the *hippocampus* in 53 elderly subjects and then conducted follow-up studies of these subjects for 10 to 24 years. (Recall that the hippocampus plays a major role in long-term memory.) Eventually, 19 of the study's participants developed mild dementia (often an early stage of Alzheimer's disease) and another six developed Alzheimer's itself. The researchers found that those who developed these cognitive impairments had indeed displayed lower hippocampus activity on their initial PET scans than the subjects who remained healthy. Overall, the special PET scans, administered years before the onset of symptoms, predicted mild dementia with an accuracy rate of 71 percent and Alzheimer's disease with an accuracy rate of 83 percent.

In another line of work the researcher Neill Graff-Radford (2005) and his colleagues took repeated samples of blood from 563 normal elderly subjects over a period of two to 12 years and measured levels of the beta-amyloid protein in the blood samples. (Recall that clusters of the beta-amyloid protein, particularly the AB42 kind, form senile plaques.) Graff-Radford and his colleagues found that subjects whose blood contained an unusually high proportion of AB42 beta-amyloid proteins went on to develop mild dementia or Alzheimer's disease earlier than the other subjects, and, overall, they were three times more likely to develop these disorders.

Finally, the researcher Henry Brodaty (2005) has identified three simple memory tests, each of which can be administered in less than five minutes by family physicians, that can help reveal the earliest stages of memory impairment. Brodarty believes that family physicians should routinely administer one of these tests—*the General Practitioner Assessment of Cognition, the Mini-Cog,* and *the Memory Impairment Screen*—when patients are over 75 or when cognitive impairment is suspected. If the test indicates memory impairment, then the patient can be referred to a memory clinic for more specialized evaluation.

As we shall see shortly, the most effective interventions for Alzheimer's disease and other kinds of dementia are those that help prevent these problems, or at least ones that are applied early. Clearly, then, it is essential to have tools that identify the disorders as early as possible, preferably years before the onset of symptoms. That is what makes the research advances in assessment and diagnosis so exciting.

WHAT TREATMENTS ARE CURRENTLY AVAILABLE FOR DEMENTIA? A common approach to the treatment of dementia is the use of drugs that affect the neurotransmitters known to play important roles in memory (Sadavoy, 2004). Four such drugs, *tacrine* (trade name

[BOX **18-4**]

Mad Human Disease?

In the 1980s British farmers first became aware of *bovine spongiform encephalopathy,* or *mad cow disease.* Cows with this disease became disoriented, uncoordinated, and irritable, and eventually died. Autopsies revealed holes and tangles of protein in their brains. Researchers traced the disease to a particular feeding practice: sick cattle and parts of cattle that could not be sold for meat were ground up and fed to other cattle. British officials promptly banned the practice, but symptoms of the disease do not appear until years after the infection is contracted, so a continuing epidemic unfolded (Hileman, 2001). Some 200,000 cows have now died of the disease.

What does mad cow disease have to do with abnormal psychology in humans? Clinicians have come to appreciate that *Creutzfeldt-Jakob disease* (*CJD*), a form of human dementia, is somewhat similar, clinically and biologically, to mad cow disease. CJD is a rare progressive dementia— incurable and fatal—apparently caused by an infectious protein that stays in the body for decades before producing symptoms (APA, 2000; Prusiner, 1995).

Although scientists at first believed that it was impossible for mad cow disease to "jump species," many now believe that a new variant of CJD, called *vCJD,* may be contracted by people who eat the meat of cows infected with mad cow disease. To

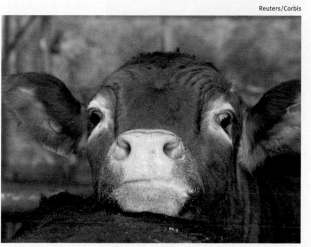

Reuters/Corbis

date, about 150 people in the world have died of vCJD, but nobody knows how many have been infected—like mad cow disease and conventional CJD, vCJD may take years to produce symptoms (Quaid, 2005). Although the absolute number of cases remains small, the rate of residents in the United Kingdom infected with vCJD has grown by 23 percent each year since 1994 (Hileman, 2001).

Once people became aware of the possible connection between mad cow disease and vCJD, panic swept across the United Kingdom and around the world. Most nations banned imports of British beef. Healthy cows could not be distinguished from infected ones, and so the United Kingdom agreed to destroy almost half of the nation's herd. By 2000, the number of slaughtered cows had reached 8 million.

The United States and Canada tried to avoid this health problem by taking measures to prevent the spread of mad cow disease and the emergence of vCJD. For example, government agencies in each country banned the feeding of meat made from cud-chewing animals to other cud-chewing animals (cows and sheep). Similarly, each country banned imports of live cattle and sheep from countries where mad cow disease had been identified. However, such measures had limitations. For example, banned meat could still be fed to poultry, fish, and pigs, whose remains, in turn, could be fed to cattle (Burros, 2001). Moreover, the efforts of the government agencies in each country to monitor farms and slaughterhouses for compliance with feed regulations and other safeguards were often unsystematic (Burros, 2001).

Thus it was not a total surprise when a cow in each country was found to have mad cow disease in 2003. By 2006, four such cows had been identified in Canada and two in the United States (CBC, 2006; CNN, 2006). In response to these revelations, each country quarantined certain herds, slaughtered suspect cows, and instituted extensive testing and tracking programs. Despite such measures, a number of countries have canceled imports of Canadian and U.S. beef, leading to billions of dollars in lost revenues.

Cognex), *donepezil* (Aricept), *rivastigmine* (Exelon), and *galantamine* (Reminyl), prevent the breakdown of acetylcholine, one of the neurotransmitters in low supply among people with Alzheimer's disease (Julien, 2005). Some Alzheimer patients who take these drugs improve slightly in short-term memory and reasoning ability, as well as in their use of language and their ability to cope under pressure (Olsen et al., 2005; Lyketsos et al., 1996). Although the benefits of the drugs are limited and the risk of harmful effects (particularly for tacrine) is sometimes high, these drugs have been approved by the Food and Drug Administration. Clinicians believe that they may be of most use to persons in the early stages of Alzheimer's disease or to those with a mild form of dementia (Keltner & Folks, 2001). Another drug, *memantine* (Namenda), was introduced in 2004 for the treatment of more advanced cases of Alzheimer's disease. This drug affects glutamate, another neurotransmitter linked to memory. It consistently improves cognition, even in severely impaired patients, although once again the improvement is modest (Julien, 2005).

Rick Falco/SIPA Press/Black Star

Day treatment *Two women go their separate ways in a New Jersey day-care facility for patients with Alzheimer's disease. Such facilities, which are growing in number, provide special programs and activities for patients. The individuals return to their families each night.*

Tacrine and related drugs are prescribed *after* a person has developed Alzheimer's disease. A number of studies seem to suggest, however, that certain substances may actually help prevent or delay the onset of the disease. For example, one team of researchers concluded that women who take *estrogen,* the female sex hormone, for years after menopause cut their risk of developing Alzheimer's disease in half (Kawas et al., 1997). Similarly, long-term use of *nonsteroid anti-inflammatory drugs* such as *ibuprofen* and *naprosyn* (drugs found in Advil, Motrin, Nuprin, and other pain relievers) seems to greatly reduce the risk of Alzheimer's disease.

Cognitive treatments have been applied in cases of Alzheimer's didease, with some temporary success (Knight et al., 2006; Fabre, 2004). In Japan, for example, a number of persons with the disease meet regularly in classes, performing simple calculations and reading aloud essays and novels. Proponents of this approach claim that it works like a mental exercise that helps rehabilitate those parts of the brain linked to memory, reasoning, and judgment.

Behavioral interventions have also been tried, with modest success. They typically focus on changing everyday patient behaviors that are stressful for the family, such as wandering at night, loss of bladder control, demands for attention, and inadequate personal care (Knight et al., 2006; Fisher & Carstensen, 1990). In these techniques therapists use a combination of role-playing exercises, modeling, and practice to teach family members how and when to apply reinforcement in order to shape more positive behaviors.

Caregiving can take a heavy toll on the close relatives of people with dementia (Cummings, 2005; Kiecolt-Glaser et al., 2002, 1996). It is hard to take care of someone who is becoming increasingly lost, helpless, and medically ill. And it is very painful to witness mental and physical decline in someone you love:

> I have really struggled with the honesty issue. What do you say to someone who sits on her bed and says that she has never stayed out overnight without letting her parents know where she is? What do you say to someone who thinks she is a teacher and if she doesn't get home and into her classroom there will be a whole class of children left unattended? What do you say to someone who thinks she has no money to pay bills and will lose everything she owns if she doesn't get home to a job that you know she has been retired from for years? I couldn't find any reason for telling her over and over that she has a horrible terrible degenerating disease that was making her feel the way she does.
>
> I found that she became less anxious if I just listened to what she was saying and feeling. Sometimes saying nothing was better than anything I could say. Telling her that I would take care of some of these things put her a bit more at ease. It may feel better for me to verbalize the facts, but what she needs is comfort and security—not the truth. The truth won't change anything.
>
> *(Shenk, 2001, p. 147)*

>>LOOKING AROUND

Home Care Around 70 percent of people with Alzheimer's disease live at home. Around three-fourths of their caregivers are women (McParland et al., 2002; Kalb, 2000). **<<**

- -

Caregiver Stress According to research, caring for a loved one with Alzheimer's disease takes an average of 69 to 100 hours per week. The major worries reported by caregivers are the cost of help (54%), the effects of Alzheimer's-related stress within the family (49%), and lack of time for caregivers to attend to their own needs (49%) (Thomas et al., 2002; Alzheimer's Association, 1997). **<<**

One of the most frequent reasons for the institutionalization of Alzheimer's victims is that overwhelmed caregivers can no longer cope with the difficulties of keeping them at home (Cummings, 2005; Kaplan, 1998). Many caregivers experience anger and depression, and their own physical and mental health often declines (Sherwood et al., 2005; Graesel, 2002). Clinicians now recognize that one of the most important aspects of treating Alzheimer's disease and other forms of dementia is to focus on the emotional needs of the caregivers: their need for regular time out, for education about the disease, and for psychotherapy when stress begins to build (Knight et al., 2006; Gaugler et al., 2003).

Some clinicians also provide caregiver support groups (Pillemer & Suitor, 2002; Gallagher-Thompson et al., 2000, 1991).

In recent years, sociocultural approaches have begun to play an important role in treatment (Brooks, 2005; Kalb, 2000) (see Box 18-5 on page 555). A number of *day-care facilities* for patients with dementia have been developed, providing treatment programs and activities for outpatients during the day and returning them to their homes and families at night. In addition, many *assisted-living facilities* have been built, in which individuals suffering from dementia live in cheerful apartments, receive needed supervision, and take part in various activities that bring more joy and stimulation to their lives. These apartments are typically designed to meet the special needs of the residents— providing more light, for example, or enclosing gardens with circular paths so the individuals can go for strolls alone without getting lost. Studies suggest that such facilities often help slow the cognitive decline of residents and enhance their enjoyment of life.

Overcoming strokes *Cerebrovascular accidents, or* strokes, *may cause severe damage, psychologically as well as physically. They may produce vascular dementia, for example, or leave victims markedly depressed and anxious. Thus, groups such as the "Handicapables" in Sun City, Arizona, a water-therapy and support club for stroke victims, are often critical to a successful physical and psychological recovery.*

Given the progress now unfolding in the understanding and treatment of Alzheimer's disease and other forms of dementia, researchers are looking forward to advances in the coming years. The brain changes responsible for dementia are tremendously complex, but given the amount of research under way, most investigators believe that exciting breakthroughs are just over the horizon.

Issues Affecting the Mental Health of the Elderly

As the study and treatment of elderly people have progressed, three issues have raised concern among clinicians: the problems faced by elderly members of racial and ethnic minority groups, the inadequacies of long-term care, and the need for a health-maintenance approach to medical care in an aging world (Gallagher-Thompson & Thompson, 1995).

Discrimination due to race and ethnicity has long been a problem in the United States (see Chapter 3), and many people suffer as a result, particularly those who are old (Utsey et al., 2002; Cavanaugh, 1990). To be both old and a member of a minority group is considered a kind of "double jeopardy" by many observers. For older women in minority groups, the difficulties are sometimes termed "triple jeopardy," as many more older women than older men live alone, are widowed, and are poor. Clinicians must take into account their older patients' race, ethnicity, and gender as they try to diagnose and treat their mental health problems (Knight et al., 2006; Ayalon et al., 2005; Sadavoy et al., 2004) (see Figure 18-4 on the next page).

Some elderly people in minority groups face language barriers that interfere with their medical and mental health care. Others may hold cultural beliefs that prevent them from seeking services. Moreover, many members of minority groups do not trust the majority establishment or do not know about medical and mental health services that are sensitive to their culture and their particular needs (Ayalon & Huyck, 2001; Ralston, 1991; Jackson, 1988). As a result, it is common for elderly members of racial and ethnic minority groups to rely largely on family members or friends for remedies and health care.

Many older people require *long-term care,* a general term that may refer variously to the services offered in a partially supervised apartment, in a senior housing complex for mildly impaired elderly persons, or in a nursing home where skilled medical and nursing care are available around the clock. The quality of care in such residences varies widely.

At any given time in the United States, only about 5 percent of the elderly population actually live in nursing homes, but 25 to 30 percent eventually wind up being placed in such facilities (Fisher et al., 2001). Thus many older adults live in fear of being "put away." They fear having to move, losing independence, and living in a medical

>>BY THE NUMBERS
Varied Life Spans

76 years Average human life span **<<**

200 years Life span of some marine clams **<<**

150 years Life span of some giant tortoises **<<**

90 years Life span of killer whales **<<**

50 years Life span of bats **<<**

13 years Life span of canaries **<<**

2 years Life span of mice **<<**

24 days Life span of worms **<<**

17 days Life span of male houseflies **<<**

(CDC, 2004; Ash, 1999)

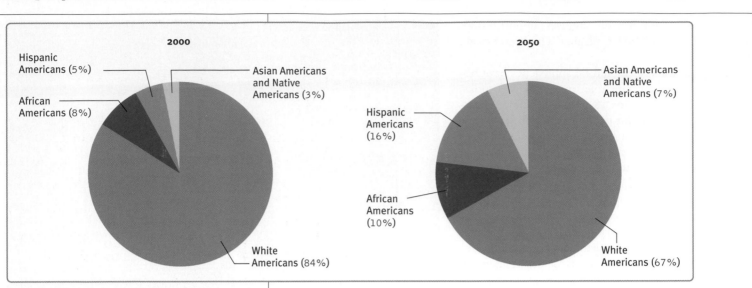

2000

Hispanic Americans (5%)

African Americans (8%)

Asian Americans and Native Americans (3%)

White Americans (84%)

2050

Asian Americans and Native Americans (7%)

Hispanic Americans (16%)

African Americans (10%)

White Americans (67%)

FIGURE **18-4** **Ethnicity and old age** *The elderly population is becoming racially and ethnically more diverse. In the United States today, 84 percent of all people over the age of 65 are white Americans. By 2050, only 67 percent of the elderly will be in this group. (Adapted from Cavanaugh & Blanchard-Fields, 2006; U.S. Census, 2000; Hobbs, 1997.)*

environment. Many elderly people know someone who died shortly after being admitted to a long-term care facility, and this increases their fears about the quality of life in such settings (Gallagher-Thompson & Thompson, 1995).

Many also worry about the cost of long-term care facilities. Families today are trying to keep elderly relatives at home longer, and so most older people enter nursing homes only in the last stages of a disease and in need of almost total care. Around-the-clock nursing care is expensive, and nursing home costs continue to rise. The health insurance plans available today do not adequately cover the costs of long-term or permanent placement. Worry over these issues can greatly harm the mental health of older adults, perhaps leading to depression and anxiety as well as family conflict (Banerjee & Macdonald, 1996).

Finally, medical scientists suggest that the current generation of young adults should take a *health-maintenance,* or *wellness,* approach to their own aging process (Aldwin et al., 2006; Aldwin & Gilmer, 2004). In other words, they should do things that promote physical and mental health—avoid smoking, eat well-balanced and healthful meals, exercise regularly, and take advantage of psychoeducational, stress management, and other mental health programs. There is a growing belief that older adults will adapt more readily to changes and negative events if their physical and psychological health is good (Gallagher-Thompson & Thompson, 1995).

Social connections *Recognizing that elderly people continue to need social companionship and stimulation, many retirement homes now offer student visitation programs. The elderly residents benefit emotionally and cognitively from such visits, while the students learn much about aging and about life. The engaged looks on the faces of these residents during their interactions with several students are a far cry from the lost and lonely faces often found in less stimulating nursing and retirement homes.*

Chuck Savage/Corbis

[BOX **18-5**]

"You Are the Music, while the Music Lasts"   *Clayton S. Collins*

Oliver Sacks [a well-known neurologist and writer] danced to the Dead. For three solid hours. At 60. And with "two broken knees." . . .

The power of music—. . . to "bring back" individuals rendered motionless and mute by neurological damage and disorders—is what's driving Sacks these days. The . . . author (*Migraine, A Leg to Stand On, The Man Who Mistook His Wife for a Hat, Seeing Voices* and *Awakenings*) . . . is working on another case-study book, one that deals in part with the role of music as a stimulus to minds that have thrown up stiff sensory barriers. . . .

"One sees how robust music is neurologically," Sacks says. "You can lose all sorts of particular powers but you don't tend to lose music and identity." . . .

Much of what he has encountered, particularly in working with patients at Beth Abraham Hospital, Bronx, N.Y., . . . relates to music.

"One saw patients who couldn't take a single step, who couldn't walk, but who could dance," he says. "There were patients who couldn't speak, but who could sing. The power of music in these patients was instantaneous . . . from a frozen Parkinsonian state to a freely flowing, moving, speaking state."

Sacks remembers a woman with Parkinson's who would sit perfectly still until "activated" by the music of Chopin, which she loved and knew by heart. She didn't have to hear a tune played. "It was sometimes sufficient to give her an opus number," Sacks says. "You would just say 'Opus 49,' and the F-minor 'Fantasy' would start playing in her mind. And she could move. . . ."

"Deeply demented people respond to music, babies respond to music, fetuses probably respond to music. Various animals respond to music," Sacks says. "There is something about the animal nervous system . . . which seems to respond to music all the way down . . . ," Sacks says, citing the case of a patient with damage to the frontal lobes of his brain.

"When he sings, one almost has the strange feeling that [music] has given him his frontal lobes back, given him back, temporally, some function that has been lost on an organic basis," Sacks says, adding a quote from T. S. Eliot: "You are the music, while the music lasts."

The effects of music therapy may not always last. Sacks will take what he can get. "To organize a disorganized person for a minute is miraculous. And for half an hour, more so." . . .

The key, says Sacks, is for patients to "learn to be well" again. Music can restore to them, he says, the identity that predates the illness. "There's a health to music, a life to music." . . . Music's been healing for thousands of years, Sacks says. "It's just being looked at now more systematically and with these special populations."

"Greg" was an amnesiac with a brain tumor and no coherent memories of life since about 1969—but an encyclopedic memory of the years that came before, and a real love of Grateful Dead tunes.

Sacks took Greg to that night's [Grateful Dead] performance. "In the first half of the concert they were doing early music, and Greg was enchanted by everything," Sacks recalls. "I mean, he was not an amnesiac. He was completely oriented and organized and with it." Between sets Sacks went backstage and introduced Greg to band member Micky Hart, who was impressed with Greg's knowledge of the group but quite surprised when Greg asked after Pigpen. When told the former band member had died 20 years before, "Greg was very upset," Sacks recalls. "And then 30 seconds later he asked 'How's Pigpen?'"

During the second half, the band played its newer songs. And Greg's world began to fall apart. "He was bewildered and enthralled and frightened. Because the music for him—and this is an extremely musical man, who understands the idiom of the Grateful Dead—was both familiar and unfamiliar. . . . He said, 'This is like the music of the future.'"

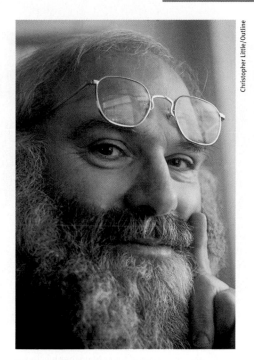

Musical awakenings *Over the years, Oliver Sacks has treated neurological disorders with techniques ranging from medication to the music of the Grateful Dead.*

Sacks tried to keep the new memories fresh. But the next day, Greg had no memory of the concert. It seemed as if all had been lost. "But—and this is strange—when one played some of the new music, which he had heard for the first time at the concert, he could sing along with it and remember it."

It is an encouraging development. . . . Children have been found to learn quickly lessons that are embedded in song. Sacks, the one-time quiet researcher, is invigorated by the possibilities. He wonders whether music could carry such information, to give his patient back a missing part of his life. To give Greg "some sense of what's been happening in the last 20 years, where he has no autobiography of his own."

That would have Sacks dancing in the aisles.

(Excerpted by permission from *Profiles*, the magazine of Continental Airlines, February 1994.)

PUTTING IT together
Clinicians Discover the Elderly

Early in the twentieth century, mental health professionals focused little on the elderly. But like the problems of children, those of aging persons have now caught the attention of researchers and clinicians. Current work is bringing important changes in how we understand and treat the psychological problems of the elderly. No longer do clinicians simply accept depression or anxiety in elderly people as inevitable. No longer do they overlook the dangers of prescription drug misuse by the elderly. And no longer do they underestimate the dangers of delirium or the prevalence of dementia. Similarly, geropsychologists have become more aware of the importance of addressing the health care and financial needs of the elderly as keys to their psychological well-being.

As the elderly population grows ever larger, the special needs of people in this age group are becoming more visible. Thus the study and treatment of their psychological problems, like those of children, will probably continue at a rapid pace. Clinicians and public officials are not likely to underestimate their needs and importance again.

Particularly urgent is dementia and its devastating impact on the elderly and their families. The complexity of the brain makes dementia difficult to understand, diagnose, and treat. However, researchers announce exciting new discoveries almost daily. To date, this research has been largely biological; but dementia has such a powerful impact on patients and their families that psychological and sociocultural investigations will not lag behind for long. In fact, society's special interest in and focus on Alzheimer's disease have reminded everyone about the importance of memory and related cognitive faculties. Memory is so central to our lives and to our self-concept that psychological and sociocultural research in this area is of potential value to every person's well-being. Thus, we can expect such work to grow and expand in the years to come.

Amy Rohl/The Hutchinson News/AP Photo

Social connections of a different kind *Clinicians and researchers have learned that elderly people, including those in nursing and retirement homes, often benefit greatly from the companionship of loving and nonjudgmental animals. Here, Duke, a "therapy dog," visits with residents at a retirement home in Kansas, clearly brightening their day. This retirement home is just one of many stops (nursing homes, schools, hospice organizations) that Duke makes over the course of a week.*

─[SUMMARY AND REVIEW]─

■ **Disorders of later life** The problems of elderly people are often linked to the losses and other stresses and changes that accompany advancing age. As many as 50 percent of the elderly would benefit from mental health services, yet fewer than 20 percent receive them. *Depression* is a common mental health problem among this age group. Older people may also suffer from *anxiety disorders.* Between 4 and 6 percent exhibit *alcohol-related problems* in any given year, and many others *misuse prescription drugs.* In addition, some elderly persons display psychotic disorders such as *schizophrenia* or *delusional disorder. pp. 535–542*

■ **Disorders of cognition** Older people are more likely than people of other age groups to experience *delirium,* a clouding of consciousness in which a person has great difficulty concentrating, focusing attention, and following an orderly sequence of thought.

Dementia, a syndrome characterized by severe memory loss and other cognitive disturbances, becomes increasingly common in older age groups. It can result from dozens of brain illnesses or injuries, most commonly *Alzheimer's disease* or *vascular dementia.* Alzheimer's disease has been linked to an unusually high number of *neurofibrillary tangles* and *senile plaques* in the brain. A number of causes have been proposed for this disease, including *genetic factors, abnormal neurotransmitter activity, slow-acting infections, immune system problems,* and high levels of *zinc* or *aluminum* in the brain.

Researchers are making significant strides at better assessing dementia and even at identifying persons who will eventually develop this problem. Drug, cognitive, and behavioral therapies have been applied to dementia, with limited success. Addressing the needs of *caregivers* is now also recognized as a key part of treatment. In addition, sociocultural approaches such as *day-care facilities* are on the rise. The coming years are expected to see major treatment breakthroughs. *pp. 542–553*

■ **Key issues** In studying and treating the problems of old age, clinicians have become concerned about three issues: *the problems of elderly members of racial and ethnic minority groups, inadequacies of long-term care,* and *the need for health maintenance by young adults. pp. 553–555*

>>> CRITICAL THOUGHTS <<<

1. Need aging lead to depression and other psychological problems? What kinds of attitudes, preparations, and activities might help an individual enter old age with peace of mind and even positive anticipation? *pp. 536–542*

2. What changes in medical practice, patient education, or family interactions might address the growing problem of misuse of prescription drugs among the elderly? *pp. 540–542*

3. The "oldest old" often seem particularly well adjusted. Does their positive frame of mind lead to longevity, or does outstanding health produce greater happiness? Why do many in this age group attribute their longevity to psychological factors, while scientists seem to prefer biological explanations? *p. 541*

4. Current research developments suggest that diagnosticians may eventually be able to identify victims of Alzheimer's disease years before their memory begins to fail noticeably. Would people be better off knowing or not knowing that they will eventually develop a disease that currently has no known cure? *pp. 543–553*

5. Initially, some scientists argued that mad cow disease could not be transmitted from one species to another, while others countered that it was indeed possible (Aldhous, 1996). When scientists disagree, how should the public proceed? *p. 551*

◉─[CYBER**STUDY**]──────────────>>>

SEARCH THE *ABNORMAL PSYCHOLOGY* CD-ROM FOR

▲ Chapter 18 Video Cases and Discussions
   How can people cope effectively with the challenges and pressures of aging?
   What problems are faced by sufferers of dementia and their caregivers?

▲ Chapter 18 Practical, Research, and Decision-Making Exercises
   Misinterpreting physical symptoms of aging
   Experiencing the effects of memory loss

▲ Chapter 18 Practice Test and Feedback

LOG ON TO THE COMER WEB PAGE FOR

▲ Suggested Web links, exercises, FAQ page, additional Chapter 18 practice test questions
   ‹www.worthpublishers.com/comer›

──────────────────────<<<

Law, Society, and the Mental Health Profession

Dear Jodie:

There is a definite possibility that I will be killed in my attempt to get Reagan. It is for this very reason that I am writing you this letter now. As you well know by now, I love you very much. The past seven months I have left you dozens of poems, letters and messages in the faint hope you would develop an interest in me. . . . Jodie, I would abandon this idea of getting Reagan in a second if I could only win your heart and live out the rest of my life with you, whether it be in total obscurity or whatever. I will admit to you that the reason I'm going ahead with this attempt now is because I just cannot wait any longer to impress you. I've got to do something now to make you understand in no uncertain terms that I am doing all of this for your sake. By sacrificing my freedom and possibly my life I hope to change your mind about me. This letter is being written an hour before I leave for the Hilton Hotel. Jodie, I'm asking you please to look into your heart and at least give me the chance with this historical deed to gain your respect and love. I love you forever.

JOHN HINCKLEY

John W. Hinckley Jr. wrote this letter to the actress Jodie Foster in March 1981. Soon after writing it, he stood waiting, pistol ready, outside the Washington Hilton Hotel. Moments later, President Ronald Reagan came out of the hotel, and the popping of pistol fire was heard. As Secret Service men pushed Reagan into the limousine, a policeman and the president's press secretary fell to the pavement. The president had been shot, and by nightfall most of America had seen the face and heard the name of the disturbed young man from Colorado.

We have observed throughout this book that the psychological dysfunctioning of an individual does not occur in isolation. It is influenced—sometimes caused—by societal and social pressures, and it affects the lives of relatives, friends, and acquaintances. The case of John Hinckley demonstrates in powerful terms that individual dysfunction may, in some cases, also affect the well-being and rights of people the person does not know.

By the same token, clinical scientists and practitioners do not conduct their work in isolation. As they study and treat people with psychological problems, they are affecting and being affected by other institutions of society. We have seen, for example, how the government regulates the use of psychotropic medications, how clinicians have helped carry out the government's policy of deinstitutionalization, and how clinicians have called the psychological ordeal of Vietnam veterans to the attention of society.

In short, like their clients, clinical professionals operate within a complex social system, and in fact, it is the system that defines and regulates their professional responsibilities. Just as we must understand the social context in which abnormal behavior occurs in order to understand the behavior, so must we understand the context in which this behavior is studied and treated.

Two social institutions have a particularly strong impact on the mental health profession—the legislative and judicial systems. These institutions—collectively, the *legal field*—have long been responsible for promoting and protecting both the public good and the rights of individuals. Sometimes the relationship between the legal field and the mental health field has been friendly, and they have worked together to protect the rights and meet the needs of troubled individuals and of society at large. At other times they have clashed, and one field has imposed its will on the other.

This relationship has two distinct aspects. On the one hand, mental health professionals often play a role in the criminal justice system, as when they are called upon to help the courts assess the mental stability of people accused of crimes. They responded to this call in the Hinckley case, as we shall see, and in thousands of other cases. This aspect of the relationship is sometimes termed *psychology in law;* that is, clinical practitioners and researchers operate within the legal system. On the other hand, there is another aspect to the relationship, called *law in psychology.* The legislative and judicial systems act upon the clinical field, regulating certain aspects of mental health care. The courts may, for example, force some individuals to enter treatment, even against their will. In addition, the law protects the rights of patients.

The intersections between the mental health field and the legal and judicial systems are collectively referred to as **forensic psychology** (Simon & Gold, 2004; Otto & Heibrun, 2002). Forensic psychologists or psychiatrists (or related mental health professionals) may perform such varied activities as testifying in criminal trials or civil suits, researching the reliability of eyewitness testimony, or helping police profile the personality of a serial killer on the loose.

Psychology in Law: How Do Clinicians Influence the Criminal Justice System?

To arrive at just and appropriate punishments, the courts need to know whether defendants are *responsible* for the crimes they commit and *capable* of defending themselves in court. If not, it would be inappropriate to find individuals guilty or punish them in the usual manner. The courts have decided that in some instances people who suffer from severe *mental instability* may not be responsible for their actions or may not be able to defend themselves in court, and so should not be punished in the usual way. Although the courts make the final judgment as to mental instability, their decisions are guided to a large degree by the opinions of mental health professionals.

When people accused of crimes are judged to be mentally unstable, they are usually sent to a mental institution for treatment, a process called **criminal commitment.** Actually there are several forms of criminal commitment. In one, individuals are judged mentally unstable *at the time of their crimes* and so innocent of wrongdoing. They may plead **not guilty by reason of insanity (NGRI)** and bring mental health professionals into court to support their claim. When people are found not guilty on this basis, they are committed for treatment until they improve enough to be released.

In a second form of criminal commitment, individuals are judged mentally unstable *at the time of their trial* and so are considered unable to understand the trial procedures and defend themselves in court. They are committed for treatment until they are competent to stand trial. Once again, the testimony of mental health professionals helps determine the defendant's psychological functioning.

These judgments of mental instability have generated many arguments. Some people consider the judgments to be loopholes in the legal system that allow criminals to escape proper punishment for wrongdoing. Others argue that a legal system simply cannot be just unless it allows for extenuating circumstances, such as mental instability. The practice of criminal commitment differs from country to country. In this chapter we shall observe primarily how it operates in the United States. Although the specific principles and procedures of each country may differ, most countries grapple with the same issues, concerns, and decisions that we shall be examining.

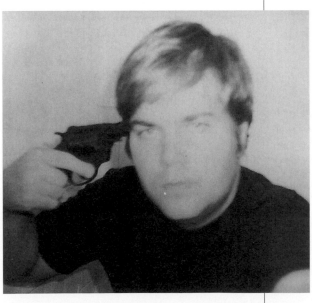

Would-be assassin *Few courtroom decisions have spurred as much debate or legislative action as the jury's verdict that John Hinckley, having been captured in the act of shooting President Ronald Reagan, was not guilty by reason of insanity.*

AP/Wide World Photos

Criminal Commitment and Insanity during Commission of a Crime

Consider once again the case of John Hinckley. Was he insane at the time he shot the president? If insane, should he be held responsible for his actions? On June 21, 1982, 15 months after he shot four men in the nation's capital, a jury pronounced Hinckley not guilty by reason of insanity. Hinckley thus joined Richard Lawrence, a house painter who shot at Andrew Jackson in 1835, and John Schrank, a saloonkeeper who shot former president Teddy Roosevelt in 1912, as a would-be assassin who was found not guilty by reason of insanity.

Although most Americans were shocked by the Hinckley verdict, those familiar with the insanity defense were not so surprised. In this case, as in other federal court cases at that time, the prosecution had the burden of proving that the defendant was sane beyond a reasonable doubt. Many state courts placed a similar responsibility on the prosecution. To present a clear-cut demonstration of sanity can be difficult, especially when the defendant has exhibited bizarre behavior in other areas of life. In fact, a few years later, Congress passed a law making it the defense's burden in federal cases to prove that defendants are insane, rather than the prosecution's burden to prove them sane. The majority of state legislatures have since followed suit (Steadman et al., 1993).

It is important to recognize that "insanity" is a *legal* term (Swallow, Yutzy, & Dinwiddie, 2005). That is, the definition of "insanity" used in criminal cases was written by legislators, not by clinicians. Defendants may have mental disorders but not necessarily qualify for a legal definition of insanity. Modern Western definitions of insanity can be traced to the murder case of Daniel M'Naghten in England in 1843. M'Naghten shot and killed Edward Drummond, the secretary to British Prime Minister Robert Peel, while trying to shoot Peel. Because of M'Naghten's apparent delusions of persecution, the jury found him to be not guilty by reason of insanity. The public was outraged by this decision, and their angry outcry forced the British law lords to define the insanity defense more clearly. This legal definition, known as the **M'Naghten test,** or **M'Naghten rule,** stated that experiencing a mental disorder at the time of a crime does not by itself mean that the person was insane; the defendant also had to be *unable to know right from wrong.* The state and federal courts in the United States adopted this test as well.

In the late nineteenth century some state and federal courts in the United States, dissatisfied with the M'Naghten rule, adopted a different test—the **irresistible impulse test.** This test, which had first been used in Ohio in 1834, emphasized the inability to control one's actions. A person who committed a crime during an uncontrollable "fit of passion" was considered insane and not guilty under this test.

For years state and federal courts chose between the M'Naghten test and the irresistible impulse test to determine the sanity of criminal defendants. For a while a third test, called the **Durham test,** also became popular, but it was soon replaced in most courts. This test, based on a decision handed down by the Supreme Court in 1954 in the case of *Durham v. United States,* stated simply that people are not criminally responsible if their "unlawful act was the product of mental disease or mental defect." This test was meant to offer more flexibility in court decisions, but it proved too flexible. Insanity defenses could point to such problems as alcoholism or other forms of substance dependence and conceivably even headaches or ulcers, which were listed as psychophysiological disorders in DSM-I.

In 1955 the American Law Institute (ALI) formulated a test that combined aspects of the M'Naghten, irresistible impulse, and Durham tests. The **American Law Institute test** held that people are not criminally responsible if at the time of a crime they had a mental disorder or defect that prevented them from knowing right from wrong *or* from being able to control themselves and to follow the law. For a time the new test became the most widely accepted legal test of insanity. After the Hinckley verdict, however, there was a public uproar over the "liberal" ALI guidelines, and people called for tougher standards.

Partly in response to this uproar, the American Psychiatric Association recommended in 1983 that people should be found not guilty by reason of insanity *only if*

•FORENSIC PSYCHOLOGY•The branch of psychology concerned with intersections between psychological practice and research and the judicial system. Also related to the field of *forensic psychiatry.*

•CRIMINAL COMMITMENT•A legal process by which people accused of a crime are instead judged mentally unstable and sent to a mental health facility for treatment.

•NOT GUILTY BY REASON OF INSANITY (NGRI)•A verdict stating that defendants are not guilty of committing a crime because they were insane at the time of the crime.

•M'NAGHTEN TEST•A widely used legal test for insanity that holds people to be insane at the time they committed a crime if, because of a mental disorder, they did not know the nature of the act or did not know right from wrong. Also known as *M'Naghten rule.*

•IRRESISTIBLE IMPULSE TEST•A legal test for insanity that holds people to be insane at the time they committed a crime if they were driven to do so by an uncontrollable "fit of passion."

•DURHAM TEST•A legal test for insanity that holds people to be insane at the time they committed a crime if their act was the result of a mental disorder or defect.

•AMERICAN LAW INSTITUTE TEST•A legal test for insanity that holds people to be insane at the time they committed a crime if, because of a mental disorder, they did not know right from wrong or could not resist an uncontrollable impulse to act.

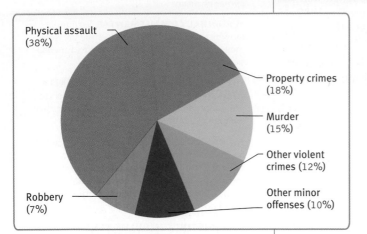

Physical assault (38%)

Property crimes (18%)

Murder (15%)

Other violent crimes (12%)

Robbery (7%)

Other minor offenses (10%)

FIGURE **19-1** **Crimes for which persons are found not guilty by reason of insanity (NGRI)** *A review of NGRI verdicts in eight states revealed that most people who were acquitted on this basis had been charged with a crime of violence. (Based on Steadman et al., 1993; Callahan et al., 1991.)*

they did not know right from wrong at the time of the crime; an inability to control themselves and to follow the law should no longer be sufficient grounds for a judgment of insanity. In short, the association was calling for a return to the M'Naghten test. This test now is used in all cases tried in federal courts and in about half of the state courts (Steadman et al., 1993). The more liberal ALI standard is still used in the remaining state courts, except in Idaho, Montana, and Utah, which have done away with the insanity plea altogether. Research has not found, however, that the stricter M'Naghten definition actually reduces the likelihood of verdicts of not guilty by reason of insanity (Ogloff et al., 1992).

People suffering from severe mental disorders in which confusion is a major feature may not be able to tell right from wrong or to control their behavior. It is therefore not surprising that approximately two-thirds of defendants who are acquitted of a crime by reason of insanity qualify for a diagnosis of schizophrenia (Steadman et al., 1993). The vast majority of these acquitted defendants have a history of past hospitalization, arrest, or both. About half who successfully plead insanity are white, and 86 percent are male. Their mean age is 32 years. The crimes for which defendants are found not guilty by reason of insanity vary greatly. However, approximately 65 percent are violent crimes of some sort (Steadman et al., 1993). Close to 15 percent of those acquitted are accused specifically of murder (see Figure 19-1 and Box 19-1).

WHAT CONCERNS ARE RAISED BY THE INSANITY DEFENSE? Despite the changes in the insanity tests, criticism of the insanity defense continues (Sales & Shuman, 2005; Slovenko, 2004, 2002, 1995). One concern is the fundamental difference between the law and the science of human behavior. The law assumes that individuals have free will and are generally responsible for their actions. Several models of human behavior, in contrast, assume that physical or psychological forces act to determine the individual's behavior. Inevitably, then, legal definitions of insanity and responsibility will differ from those suggested by clinical research.

A second criticism points to the uncertainty of scientific knowledge about abnormal behavior. During a typical insanity defense trial, the testimony of defense clinicians conflicts with that of clinicians hired by the prosecution, and so the jury must weigh the claims of "experts" who disagree in their assessments (Gutheil, 2004; Resnick & Noffsinger, 2004). Some people see this lack of professional agreement as evidence that clinical knowledge in some areas may be too incomplete to be allowed to influence important legal decisions. Others counter that the field has made great strides—for example, developing several psychological scales to help clinicians discriminate more consistently between the sane and insane as defined by the M'Naghten standard (Rogers & Shuman, 2005, 2000).

Even with helpful scales in hand, however, clinicians making judgments of legal insanity face a problem that is difficult to overcome: they must evaluate a defendant's state of mind during an event that occurred weeks, months, or years earlier. Because mental states can and do change over time and across situations, clinicians can never be entirely certain that their assessments of mental instability at the time of the crime are accurate.

Perhaps the most often heard criticism of the insanity defense is that it allows dangerous criminals to escape punishment. Granted, some people who successfully plead insanity are released from treatment facilities just months after their acquittal. Yet the number of such cases is quite small. According to surveys, the public dramatically overestimates the percentage of defendants who plead insanity, guessing it to be 30 to 40 percent, when in fact it is less than 1 percent (Steadman et al., 1993). Moreover, only a minority of these persons fake or exaggerate their psychological symptoms (Resnick & Harris, 2002; Perlin, 2000), and only one-quarter of defendants who plead insanity are actually found not guilty on this basis (Callahan et al., 1991). In the end, fewer than 1 of every 400 defendants in the United States is found not guilty by reason of insanity.

[BOX 19-1]

Famous Insanity Defense Cases

1977 In Michigan, Francine Hughes poured gasoline around the bed where her husband, Mickey, lay in a drunken stupor. Then she lit a match and set him on fire. At her trial she explained that he had beaten her repeatedly for 14 years, and he had threatened to kill her if she tried to leave him. The jury found her not guilty by reason of temporary insanity, making her into a symbol for many abused women across the nation. Some people saw the decision as confirmation of a woman's right to self-defense in her own home.

1978 David "Son of Sam" Berkowitz, a serial killer in New York City, explained that a barking dog had sent him demonic messages to kill. Although two psychiatrists assessed him as psychotic, he was found guilty of his crimes. Long after his trial, he said that he had actually made up the delusions.

1979 Kenneth Bianchi, one of the pair known as the Hillside Strangler, entered a plea of not guilty by reason of insanity but was found guilty along with his cousin of sexually assaulting and murdering women in the Los Angeles area in late 1977 and early 1978. He claimed that he had multiple personality disorder.

1980 In December, Mark David Chapman murdered John Lennon. Chapman later explained that he had killed the rock music legend because he believed Lennon to be a "sell-out." He also described hearing the voice of God, considered himself his generation's "catcher in the rye" (from the J. D. Salinger novel), and compared himself to Moses. Despite clinical testimony that supported Chapman's plea of not guilty by reason of insanity, he was ultimately convicted of murder.

1981 In an attempt to prove his love for the actress Jodie Foster, John Hinckley Jr. tried to assassinate President Ronald Reagan. Hinckley was found not guilty by reason of insanity and was committed to St. Elizabeths Hospital for the criminally insane in Washington, D.C., where he remains today.

1992 Jeffrey Dahmer, a 31-year-old mass murderer in Milwaukee, was tried for the killings of 15 young men. Dahmer apparently drugged some of his victims and performed crude lobotomies on them in an attempt to create zombielike companions for himself. He also dismembered his victims' bodies and stored their parts to be eaten. Although his defense attorney argued that Dahmer was not guilty by reason of insanity, the jury found him guilty as charged. He was beaten to death by another inmate in 1995.

1994 On June 23, 1993, 24-year-old Lorena Bobbitt cut off her husband's penis with a 12-inch kitchen knife while he slept. During her trial, defense attorneys argued that after years of abuse by John Bobbitt, his wife suffered a brief psychotic episode and was seized by an "irresistible impulse" to cut off his penis after he came home drunk and raped her. In 1994, the jury acquitted her of the charge of malicious wounding by reason of temporary insanity. She was committed to a state mental hospital for further assessment and treatment and released a few months later.

1997 John E. Du Pont, 57-year-old heir to his family's chemical fortune, shot and killed the Olympic wrestling champion Dave Schultz in January 1995. The murder took place on Du Pont's 800-acre estate, where he had built a sports center for amateur athletes. Schultz, his close friend, had coached wrestlers at the center. In 1997 Du Pont was found guilty of third-degree murder, but mentally ill. He was sentenced to prison for 13 to 30 years and assigned to receive treatment at the prison's mental health unit.

2003 For three weeks in October 2002, John Allen Muhammad and Lee Boyd Malvo went on a sniping spree in the Washington, D.C., area, shooting 10 people dead and wounding three others. Attorneys for Malvo, a teenager, argued that he had acted under the influence of the middle-aged Muhammad and that he should be found not guilty of the crimes by reason of insanity. The jury, however, found Malvo guilty of capital murder, and sentenced him to life in prison.

2006 On June 20, 2001, Andrea Yates, a 36-year-old woman, drowned each of her five children in the bathtub. Yates had a history of *postpartum depression* and *postpartum psychosis:* she believed that she was the devil, that she had failed to be a good mother, and that her children were not developing correctly. She had in fact been hospitalized twice for her disorder and was in treatment just prior to the killings. Given such problems and history, she pleaded not guilty by reason of insanity. The jury agreed that she had a profound disorder, but it concluded that she did know right from wrong at the time of the murders. In 2002 she was found guilty and sentenced to life in prison in Texas. This verdict was overturned in 2005 when a Texas appeals court decided that a prosecution witness at the trial had provided misinformation in his testimony. A retrial was set for 2006, and Yates was permitted to reside and receive treatment in a mental health facility while awaiting her new trial.

Pool photo by Getty Images

A verdict of guilty *Andrea Yates is led into a district court in Texas for arraignment on multiple counts of murder in the drowning of her five children.*

Neemah Aaron/AP Photo

Executing the mentally ill: the case of Charles Singleton *One of the most controversial executions in recent years was that of Charles Singleton, a man who killed a store clerk in Alabama and was sentenced to death in 1979 for this crime. Singleton developed schizophrenia after his sentencing, and it soon became clear that his psychosis would subside whenever he was taking psychotropic medications and reappear when he stopped the medications. Inasmuch as the United States does not allow executions if the persons involved cannot understand why they are being executed (Parry, 2005), the state wanted Singleton to take the medications. However, the inmate's lawyer argued that the state did not have the right to force him to take medications, especially since the drugs would open the door to his execution. After years of legal appeals, the U.S. Supreme Court ruled in 2003 that Singleton was, by then, taking medications voluntarily, and Singleton was executed by lethal injection in 2004.*

•GUILTY BUT MENTALLY ILL•A verdict stating that defendants are guilty of committing a crime but are also suffering from a mental illness that should be treated during their imprisonment.

During most of U.S. history, a successful insanity plea amounted to the equivalent of a long-term prison sentence. In fact, treatment in a mental hospital often resulted in a longer period of confinement than a verdict of guilty would have brought (Nwokike, 2005; Perlin, 2000). Because hospitalization resulted in little, if any, improvement, clinicians were reluctant to predict that the offenders would not repeat their crimes. Moreover, tragic cases would occasionally call into question clinicians' ability to make such judgments and to predict dangerousness (Hooper et al., 2005). In Idaho, for example, a young man raped two women and was found not guilty by reason of insanity. He was released after less than a year of treatment, shot a nurse, and this time was convicted of assault with intent to kill. The uproar over this 1981 case led the Idaho state legislature to abolish the insanity plea.

Today, however, offenders are being released from mental hospitals earlier and earlier. This trend is the result of the increasing effectiveness of drug therapy and other treatments in institutions, the growing reaction against extended institutionalization, and a greater emphasis on patients' rights (Slovenko, 2004; Salekin & Rogers, 2001). In 1992, in the case of *Foucha v. Louisiana,* the U.S. Supreme Court clarified that the *only* acceptable basis for determining the release of hospitalized offenders is whether or not they are still "insane"; they cannot be kept indefinitely in mental hospitals solely because they are dangerous. Some states are able to maintain control over offenders even after their release from hospitals (Hiday, 1999). The states may insist on community treatment, monitor the patients closely, and rehospitalize them if necessary.

WHAT OTHER VERDICTS ARE AVAILABLE? In recent years 13 states have added another verdict option—**guilty but mentally ill.** Defendants who receive this verdict are found to have had a mental illness at the time of their crime, but the illness was not fully related to or responsible for the crime. The guilty-but-mentally-ill option enables jurors to convict a person they view as dangerous while also suggesting that the individual receive needed treatment. Defendants found to be guilty but mentally ill are given a prison term with the added recommendation that they also undergo treatment if necessary.

In Georgia, juries given the option of finding a person guilty but mentally ill have delivered fewer insanity acquittals (Callahan et al., 1992). Studies with mock juries have found that many jurors prefer having this third option, seeing it as "moral, just and an adequate means of providing for the treatment needs of mentally ill offenders" (Boudouris, 2000; Roberts, Golding, & Fincham, 1987). However, those who criticize this option point out that appropriate mental health care is supposed to be available to all prisoners anyway, regardless of the verdict. They argue that the new option differs from a guilty verdict in name only (Slovenko, 2004, 2002, 1995; Melville &Naimark, 2002). Critics also believe that the option may confuse jurors.

Some states allow still another kind of defense, *guilty with diminished capacity.* Here a defendant's mental dysfunctioning is viewed as an extenuating circumstance that the court should take into consideration in determining the precise crime of which he or she is guilty (Leong, 2000). The defense lawyer argues that because of mental dysfunctioning, the defendant could not have *intended* to commit a particular crime. The person can then be found guilty of a lesser crime—of manslaughter (unlawful killing without intent), say, instead of murder in the first degree (planned murder). The case of Dan White, who shot and killed Mayor George Moscone and City Supervisor Harvey Milk of San Francisco in 1978, illustrates the use of this verdict.

On the morning of November 27, 1978, Dan White loaded his .38 caliber revolver. White had recently resigned his position as a San Francisco supervisor because of family and financial pressures. Now, after a change of heart, he wanted his job back. When he asked Mayor George Moscone to reappoint him, however, the mayor refused. Supervisor Harvey Milk was among those who had urged Moscone to keep White out, for Milk was America's first openly gay politician, and Dan White had been an outspoken opponent of measures supporting gay rights.

White avoided the metal detector at City Hall's main entrance by climbing through a basement window after telling construction workers who recognized him that he had forgotten his keys. After they unlocked the window for him, he went straight to the mayor's office. . . . White pulled out his gun and shot the mayor once in the arm and once in the chest. As Moscone lay bleeding on the floor, White walked over to him and, from only inches away, fired twice into Moscone's head.

White then reloaded his gun, ran down the hall, and spotted Harvey Milk. White asked to talk with him. Right after the two men went into White's former office, three more shots rang out. Milk crumpled to the floor. Once again White from point-blank range fired two more bullets into his victim's head. Shortly afterward he turned himself in to the police. Several months later the jury rendered its verdict: Dan White was not guilty of murder, only voluntary manslaughter.

Murder is the illegal killing of a human being with malice aforethought, that is, with the intent to kill. Manslaughter is the illegal killing of a human being without malice aforethought. The attacker may intend to harm the victim, but not to kill. If the victim nonetheless dies, the crime is voluntary manslaughter. Involuntary manslaughter is an illegal killing from negligence rather than intentional harm. . . .

. . . Defense attorney Douglas Schmidt argued that a patriotic, civic-minded man like Dan White—high school athlete, decorated war veteran, former fireman, policeman, and city supervisor—could not possibly have committed such an act unless something had snapped inside him. The brutal nature of the two final shots to each man's head only proved that White had lost his wits. White was not fully responsible for his actions because he suffered from "diminished capacity." Although White killed Mayor George Moscone and Supervisor Harvey Milk, he had not planned his actions. On the day of the shootings, White was mentally incapable of planning to kill, or even of wanting to do such a thing.

Well known in forensic psychiatry circles, Martin Blinder, professor of law and psychiatry at the University of California's Hastings Law School in San Francisco, brought a good measure of academic prestige to White's defense. White had been, Blinder explained to the jury, "gorging himself on junk food: Twinkies, Coca-Cola. . . . The more he consumed, the worse he'd feel and he'd respond to his ever-growing depression by consuming ever more junk food." Schmidt later asked Blinder if he could elaborate on this. "Perhaps if it were not for the ingestion of this junk food," Blinder responded, "I would suspect that these homicides would not have taken place." From that moment on, Blinder became known as the author of the Twinkie defense. . . .

Dan White was convicted only of voluntary manslaughter, and was sentenced to seven years, eight months. (He was released on parole January 6, 1984.) Psychiatric testimony convinced the jury that White did not wish to kill George Moscone or Harvey Milk.

The angry crowd that responded to the verdict by marching, shouting, trashing City Hall, and burning police cars was in good part homosexual. Gay supervisor Harvey Milk had worked well for their cause, and his loss was a serious setback for human rights in San Francisco. Yet it was not only members of the gay community who were appalled at the outcome. Most San Franciscans shared their feelings of outrage.

(Coleman, 1984, pp. 65–70)

Because of possible miscarriages of justice, many legal experts have argued against the "diminished capacity" defense (Slovenko, 2002, 1992; Coleman, 1984), and a number of states have eliminated it. Some studies find, however, that jurors are often capable of using the option in careful and appropriate ways (Finkel & Duff, 1989).

>>IN THEIR WORDS

"I feel the insanity defense should be retained. I bear no grudge against John Hinckley, but I sure don't hope he wins the Irish Sweepstakes." ‹‹

James Brady, presidential news secretary shot by John Hinckley

---

>>LOOKING AROUND
The Aftermath

Dan White Convicted of involuntary manslaughter in the killings of San Francisco Mayor George Moscone and City Supervisor Harvey Milk in 1978, Dan White was released from prison in 1984 and spent a year on parole. He committed suicide in 1985. ‹‹

- -

Daniel M'Naghten After being judged not guilty by reason of insanity, Daniel M'Naghten lived in a mental hospital until his death 22 years later (Slovenko, 2002, 1995). ‹‹

- -

John Hinckley In 2005 a U.S. federal judge ruled that John Hinckley may leave St. Elizabeths Hospital in Washington, D.C., where he is currently confined, for seven overnight visits to his parents' home in Virginia. Three of the visits can last three nights and the other four can last four nights. ‹‹

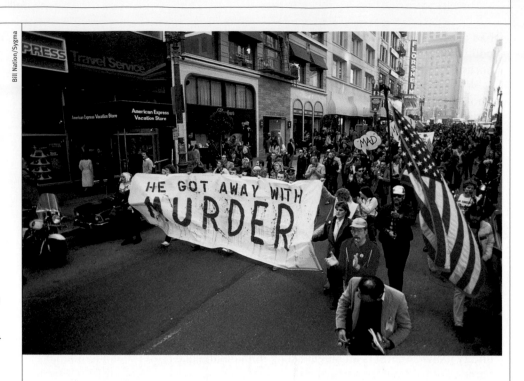

Justice served? *Mass protests took place in San Francisco after Dan White was convicted of voluntary manslaughter rather than premeditated murder in the killings of Mayor George Moscone and Supervisor Harvey Milk, one of the nation's leading gay activists. For many, the 1979 verdict highlighted the serious pitfalls of the "diminished capacity" defense.*

WHAT ARE SEX-OFFENDER STATUTES? Since 1937, when Michigan passed the first "sex psychopath" law, some states have placed sex offenders in a special legal category (Zonana et al., 2004; Winick & La Fond, 2003; Reid, 2002). These states believe that people who are repeatedly found guilty of certain sex crimes have a mental disorder, and so the states categorize them as *mentally disordered sex offenders*.

People classified in this way have been convicted of a criminal offense and are thus judged to be responsible for their actions. Nevertheless, like people found not guilty by reason of insanity, mentally disordered sex offenders are committed to a mental health facility. In part, such laws reflect a belief held by some legislators that such sex offenders are psychologically disturbed. On a practical level, the laws help protect sex offenders from the physical abuse that they often receive in prison society.

Over the last two decades, a growing number of states have been changing or abolishing these sex-offender laws. There are several reasons for this trend. First, certain states have found the laws difficult to apply. Some state laws, for example, require that the offender be found "sexually dangerous beyond a reasonable doubt"—a judgment that is often beyond the reach of the clinical field's expertise (Szasz, 1991). Furthermore, there is evidence that racial bias can affect the use of the sex-offender classification (Sturgeon & Taylor, 1980). White Americans are twice as likely to be granted sex-offender status as African Americans or Hispanic Americans who have been convicted of similar crimes. Finally, the courts have become less concerned about the rights and needs of sex offenders in recent years as the public has increasingly expressed outrage over the high number of sex crimes taking place across the country, particularly those in which children are victims. In fact, in the 1997 case of *Kansas v. Hendricks* the Supreme Court ruled (5 to 4) that individuals who have been convicted of sex crimes may be removed from prison before their release and subjected to involuntary civil commitment in a mental hospital if a court judges them likely to engage in further "predatory acts of sexual violence" as a result of "mental abnormality" or "personality disorder."

Criminal Commitment and Incompetence to Stand Trial

Regardless of their state of mind at the time of a crime, defendants may be judged to be **mentally incompetent** to stand trial. The competence requirement is meant to ensure that defendants understand the charges they are facing and can work with their lawyers to prepare and conduct an adequate defense (Swallow et al., 2005; Resnick &

•MENTAL INCOMPETENCE•A state of mental instability that leaves defendants unable to understand the legal charges and proceedings they are facing and unable to prepare an adequate defense with their attorney.

Noffsinger, 2004). This minimum standard of competence was specified by the Supreme Court in the case of *Dusky v. United States* (1960).

The issue of competence is most often raised by the defendant's attorney, although prosecutors, arresting police officers, and even the judge may raise it as well. They prefer to err on the side of caution, because some convictions have been reversed on appeal when a defendant's competence was not established at the beginning. When the issue of competence is raised, the judge orders a psychological evaluation, usually on an inpatient basis (see Table 19-1 on the next page). Approximately 20 percent of defendants who receive such an evaluation are in fact found to be incompetent to stand trial (Hiday, 1999). If the court decides that the defendant is incompetent, the person is assigned to a mental health facility until competent to stand trial (Perlin, 2003).

Many more cases of criminal commitment result from decisions of mental incompetence than from verdicts of not guilty by reason of insanity (Roesch et al., 1999). However, the majority of criminals currently institutionalized for psychological treatment in the United States are not from either of these two groups. Rather, they are convicted inmates whose psychological problems have led prison officials to decide they need treatment—either in mental health units within the prison or in mental hospitals (Way et al., 2005; Ogloff, 2002) (see Figure 19-2).

It is possible that an innocent defendant, ruled incompetent to stand trial, could spend years in a mental health facility with no opportunity to disprove the criminal accusations. Some defendants have, in fact, served longer "sentences" in mental health facilities awaiting a ruling of competence than they would have served in prison had they been convicted (Meyer, 1992). Such a possibility was reduced when the Supreme Court ruled, in the case of *Jackson v. Indiana* (1972), that an incompetent defendant cannot be indefinitely committed. After a reasonable amount of time, he or she should either be found competent and tried, set free, or transferred to a mental health facility under *civil* commitment procedures.

Until the early 1970s, most states required the commitment of mentally incompetent defendants to maximum-security institutions for the "criminally insane" (Winick, 1983). Under current law, the courts have greater flexibility. In some cases, particularly when the charge is a minor one, the defendant may even be treated on an outpatient basis.

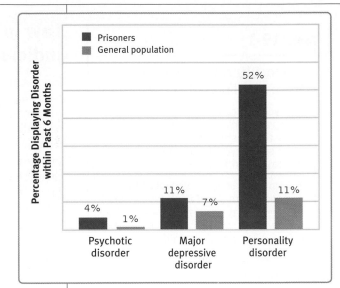

FIGURE 19-2 Prison and mental health
According to studies conducted in several Western countries, psychological disorders are much more prevalent in prison populations than in the general population. For example, schizophrenia is 4 times more common and personality disorders 5 times more common among prisoners than among non-prisoners. In fact, antisocial personality disorder is 10 times more common. (Based on Fazel & Danesh, 2002.)

Population unserved *The majority of people who receive treatment under criminal commitment procedures are inmates who develop psychological problems while they are in prison. Given the overcrowded and unsafe conditions in most prisons, the prevalence of psychological problems among prisoners is extraordinarily high, and only a fraction of those who need treatment are afforded mental health services.*

Table **19-1**

Sociocultural Landscape: Race and Forensic Psychology

- Psychologically disturbed people from racial minority groups are more likely than disturbed white Americans to be sent to prison, as opposed to mental health facilities.

- Among defendants evaluated for competence to stand trial, those from racial minority groups are more likely than white American defendants to be referred for *inpatient* evaluations.

- Among defendants evaluated for competence to stand trial, those from racial minority groups are more likely than white Americans to have the evaluation occur in a *strict-security inpatient* setting, rather than in the noncorrectional mental health system.

- When nonwhite and white defendants are evaluated for competence to stand trial, the defendants from racial minority groups are more likely to be found incompetent to stand trial.

Source: Pinals et al., 2004; Grekin et al., 1994; Arvanites, 1989

•**CIVIL COMMITMENT**•A legal process by which an individual can be forced to undergo mental health treatment.

Law in Psychology: How Do the Legislative and Judicial Systems Influence Mental Health Care?

Just as clinical science and practice have influenced the legal system, so the legal system has had a major impact on clinical practice. First, courts and legislatures have developed the process of **civil commitment,** which allows certain people to be forced into mental health treatment. Although many people who show signs of mental disturbance seek treatment voluntarily, a large number are not aware of their problems or are simply not interested in undergoing therapy. What are clinicians to do for these people? Should they force treatment upon them? Or do people have the right to feel miserable and function poorly? The law has answered this question by developing civil commitment guidelines under which certain people can be forced into treatment.

Second, the legal system, on behalf of the state, has taken on the responsibility for protecting patients' rights during treatment. This protection extends not only to patients who have been involuntarily committed but also to those who seek treatment voluntarily, even on an outpatient basis.

Civil Commitment

Every year in the United States large numbers of people with mental disorders are involuntarily committed to treatment. Typically they are committed to *mental institutions,* but 27 states also have *outpatient* civil commitment laws that allow patients to be forced into community treatment programs (Monahan et al., 2005; Perlin, 2003). Civil commitments have long caused controversy and debate. In some ways the law provides greater protection for suspected criminals than for people suspected of psychosis (Burton, 1990).

WHY COMMIT? Generally our legal system permits involuntary commitment of individuals when they are considered to be *in need of treatment* and *dangerous to themselves or others.* People may be dangerous to themselves if they are suicidal or if they act recklessly (for example, drinking a drain cleaner to prove that they are immune to its chemicals). They may be dangerous to others if they seek to harm them or if they unintentionally place others at risk. The state's authority to commit disturbed individuals rests on its duties to protect the interests of the individual and of society: the principles of *parens patriae* and *police power* (Swallow et al., 2005). Under *parens patriae* ("parent of the country"), the state can make decisions that promote the patient's best interests and provide protection from self-harm, including a decision of involuntary hospitalization. Conversely, *police power* allows the state to take steps to protect society from a person who is violent or otherwise dangerous.

WHAT ARE THE PROCEDURES FOR CIVIL COMMITMENT? Civil commitment laws vary from state to state (Swallow et al., 2005). Some basic procedures, however, are common to most of these laws. Often family members begin commitment proceedings. In response to a son's psychotic behavior and repeated assaults on other people, for example, his parents may try to persuade him to seek admission to a mental institution. If the son refuses, the parents may go to court and seek an involuntary commitment order. If the son is a minor, the process is simple. The Supreme Court, in the case of *Parham v. J. R.* (1979), has ruled that a hearing is not necessary in such cases, as long as a mental health professional considers commitment necessary. If the son is an adult, however, the process is more involved. The court will usually order a mental examination and allow the person to contest the commitment in court, often represented by a lawyer (Perlin, 2000; Holstein, 1993).

Although the Supreme Court has offered few guidelines concerning specific procedures of civil commitment, one important decision, in the case of *Addington v. Texas* (1979), outlined the *minimum standard of proof* needed for commitment. Here the Court ruled that before an individual can be committed, there must be "clear and convincing" proof that he or she is mentally ill and has met the state's criteria for involuntary commitment. The ruling does not suggest what criteria should be used. That matter is still left to each state. But, whatever the state's criteria, clinicians must offer clear and con-

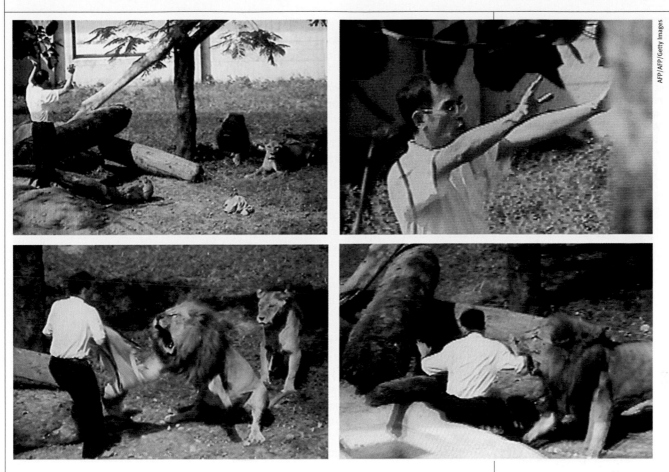

Dangerous to oneself *The public often thinks that the term "dangerous to oneself" refers exclusively to those who are suicidal. There are, however, other ways that people may pose a danger to themselves, be in need of treatment, and be subject to civil commitment. This sequence of photos shows a man being attacked by a lion at the zoo after he crossed a barbed wire fence to "preach" to two of the animals.*

vincing proof that the individual meets those criteria. When is proof clear and convincing, according to the Court? When it provides 75 percent certainty that the criteria of commitment have been met. This is far less than the near-total certainty ("beyond a reasonable doubt") required to convict people of committing a crime.

EMERGENCY COMMITMENT Many situations require immediate action; no one can wait for commitment proceedings when a life is at stake. Consider, for example, an emergency room patient who is suicidal or hearing voices demanding hostile actions against others. He or she may need immediate treatment and round-the-clock supervision. If treatment could not be given in such situations without the patient's full consent, the consequences could be tragic.

Therefore, many states give clinicians the right to certify that certain patients need temporary commitment and medication (Winick, 2001). In past years, these states required certification by two *physicians* (not necessarily psychiatrists in some of the states). Today states may allow certification by other mental health professionals as well. The clinicians must declare that the state of mind of the patients makes them dangerous to themselves or others. By tradition, the certifications are often referred to as *two-physician certificates,* or *2 PCs.* The length of such emergency commitments varies from state to state, but three days is often the limit (Holstein, 1993). Should clinicians come to believe that a longer stay is necessary, formal commitment proceedings may be initiated during the period of emergency commitment.

WHO IS DANGEROUS? In the past, people with mental disorders were actually less likely than others to commit violent or dangerous acts. This low rate of violence was apparently related to the fact that so many such individuals lived in institutions. As a result of deinstitutionalization, however, hundreds of thousands of people with severe disturbances now live in the community and receive little, if any, treatment. Some of these individuals are indeed dangerous to themselves or others (Cole & Glass, 2005; Corrigan & Watson, 2005).

>>LOOKING AROUND

Arresting the Homeless

Many homeless people with severe mental disorders currently wind up in jail rather than in treatment. Most of them are charged with such infractions as disorderly conduct, trespassing, not paying for a meal, menacing, panhandling, loitering, or "lewd and lascivious behavior" (for example, urinating on a street corner) (Mulhern, 1990; Valdiserri, Carroll, & Harti, 1986). **<<**

>>**LOOKING AROUND**

At Special Risk

People with severe mental disorders are more likely to be victims than perpetrators of violence. In any given year at least 16 percent of those with severe disorders report being violently victimized (Walsh et al., 2005). Those who are homeless are at particular risk. «

Although approximately 90 percent of people with mental disorders are in no way violent or dangerous (Swanson et al., 1990), studies now suggest at least a small relationship between severe mental disorders and violent behavior (Walsh et al., 2002; Monahan, 2001). After reviewing a number of studies, John Monahan (2001, 1993, 1992), a law and psychology professor, concluded that the rate of violent behavior among persons with severe mental disorders, particularly psychotic disorders, is at least somewhat higher than that of people without such disorders:

◆ Approximately 15 percent of patients in mental hospitals have assaulted another person prior to admission.

◆ Around 25 percent of patients in mental hospitals assault another person during hospitalization.

◆ Approximately 12 percent of all people with schizophrenia, major depression, or bipolar disorder have assaulted other people, compared with 2 percent of persons without a mental disorder. Between 25 and 35 percent of people who display a substance-related disorder have assaulted others.

◆ Approximately 4 percent of people who report having been violent during the past year suffer from schizophrenia, whereas 1 percent of nonviolent persons suffer from schizophrenia.

Monahan cautions that the findings do not suggest that people with mental disorders are generally dangerous. Nor do they justify the "caricature of the mentally disordered" that is often portrayed by the media, the "shunning of former patients by employers and neighbors," or the "lock 'em up" laws proposed by some politicians. But they do indicate that a severe mental disorder may be more of a risk factor for violence than mental health experts used to believe.

A judgment of *dangerousness* is often required for involuntary civil commitment. But can mental health professionals accurately predict who will commit violent acts? Research suggests that psychiatrists and psychologists are wrong more often than right when they make *long-term* predictions of violence (Eccleston & Ward, 2004; West, 2001). Most often they overestimate the likelihood that a patient will eventually be violent. On the other hand, studies suggest that *short-term* predictions—that is, predictions of imminent violence—can be more accurate (Binder, 1999). Researchers are now working, with some success, to develop new assessment techniques that use statistical approaches and are more objective in their predictions of dangerousness than the subjective judgments of clinicians (Monahan et al., 2005; Banks et al., 2004).

Failure to predict *The 1990s witnessed the growth of a new form of dangerousness—children and adolescents who shoot family members, schoolmates, and teachers. A school-cafeteria surveillance camera captures Dylan Klebold and Eric Harris in the midst of their killing rampage at Columbine High School in Littleton, Colorado, on April 20, 1999. Earlier videos made by the two boys suggest that they had planned their attack for more than a year. Despite building a violent Web site, threatening other students, having problems with the law, and, in the case of one boy, receiving treatment for mental health problems, professionals were not able to predict or prevent their violent behavior.*

Reuters Newmedia Inc./Corbis

WHAT ARE THE PROBLEMS WITH CIVIL COMMITMENT? Civil commitment has been criticized on several grounds. First is the difficulty of assessing a person's dangerousness. If judgments of dangerousness are often inaccurate, how can one justify their being used to deprive people of liberty (Ennis & Emory, 1978)? Second, the legal definitions of "mental illness" and "dangerousness" are vague. The terms may be defined so broadly that they could be applied to almost anyone an evaluator views as undesirable (see Box 19-2). Indeed, many civil libertarians worry about the use of involuntary commitment to control people, as occurred in the former Soviet Union and certain other countries where mental hospitals routinely housed people with unpopular political views (Morse, 1982; Ennis & Emory, 1978). A third problem is the sometimes questionable therapeutic value of civil commitment. Research suggests that many people committed involuntarily do not typically respond well to therapy (Winick, 2002; Wanck, 1984). It may be that people often need a sense of choice or control in order to succeed in treatment (Langer, 1983).

On the basis of these and other arguments, some clinicians suggest that involuntary commitment should be abolished (Szasz, 1977, 1963). Others, however, advocate finding a more systematic way to evaluate dangerousness when decisions are to be made about commitment. They suggest instituting a process of *risk assessment* that would arrive at statements such as "The patient is believed to have *X* likelihood of being violent

> **>>LAB•NOTES**
> **Substance Abuse May Be the Key**
>
> Research indicates that among people who experience severe mental disorders, those who abuse substances are the ones most likely to be violent and to be convicted of violent criminal offenses (Wallace et al., 2004). **<<**

[BOX **19-2**]

The Separation of Mind and State

During the presidential campaigns of 1992 and 1996, the independent candidate Ross Perot was branded "emotionally unbalanced" by some of his detractors. Perot reacted with good humor and even adopted Willie Nelson's "Crazy" as his theme song. The strategy of questioning the psychological stability of political opponents was taken to the extreme in the former Soviet Union, particularly under the rule of Joseph Stalin, when many political dissidents were placed in mental hospitals to get them out of the way.

Politically motivated labeling was at work during the mid-nineteenth-century debate over slavery in the United States, when those who favored slavery attacked Abraham Lincoln in the press as "insane" for his antislavery stance (Gamwell & Tomes, 1995). Many people, even among those who were against slavery, feared radical abolitionists and called them mentally unbalanced, blaming them for the nation's turmoil.

The trial of the abolitionist John Brown brought the issue out front for all to see. Brown, a white opponent of slavery, organized a small force of African Americans and white Americans to attack the federal armory at Harpers Ferry in Virginia. He was

"Last Moments of John Brown" *The abolitionist John Brown's journey to execution is portrayed in Thomas Hovenden's painting* The Last Moments of John Brown, *1884.*

captured after two days and tried for murder and treason. Many of Brown's supporters, including his own defense attorneys, urged him to plead not guilty by reason of insanity to avoid the death penalty (Gamwell & Tomes, 1995). Some fellow abolitionists, however, were offended by

the suggestion that Brown's actions represented insanity, and Brown himself proudly maintained that he was mentally stable. In the end, Brown was convicted and executed.

As the historians Lynn Gamwell and Nancy Tomes (1995) point out, it was in the interests of both sides of the case to have Brown declared legally insane. Many people who opposed slavery believed that an insanity verdict would distance Brown's radical behavior from their own efforts in the public's mind and would calm public fears of violence by abolitionists. Many of those who defended slavery believed that a judgment of insanity would hurt Brown's reputation and prevent him from becoming a martyr for the abolitionist cause—as in fact he did become. Obviously, the verdict pleased neither side.

Clinical labels have been used for political gain throughout the ages. We may not always be able to stop the practice, but we should at least be aware of it. As we read about historical events, we must be careful to weigh the available evidence and separate mental health labels that are used correctly from those that seek merely to further a political cause.

Save the brain? *In order to understand criminal behavior and to predict dangerousness more accurately, clinical researchers often interview and study individuals who have committed crimes, particularly brutal crimes. In a celebrated case, authorities temporarily had the brain of serial murderer Jeffrey Dahmer stored in formaldehyde after he died in 1995, hoping that investigators could dissect and study it. However, in response to a petition from Dahmer's father, a judge ordered that the brain be cremated.*

>>**LOOKING AROUND**
No Right to Vote

Forty-two states deny voting privileges to people judged variously as "incompetent," "insane," "incapacitated," "idiot," "lunatic," and of "unsound mind" (Moore, 1997). <<

to the following people or under the following conditions over *Y* period of time." Proponents argue that this would be a more useful and appropriate way of deciding where and how people with psychological disorders should be treated (Banks et al., 2004; Eccleston & Ward, 2004).

TRENDS IN CIVIL COMMITMENT The flexibility of the involuntary commitment laws probably reached a peak in 1962. That year, in the case of *Robinson v. California,* the Supreme Court ruled that imprisoning people who suffered from drug addictions might violate the Constitution's ban on cruel and unusual punishment, and it recommended involuntary civil commitment to a mental hospital as a more reasonable action. This ruling encouraged the civil commitment of many kinds of "social deviants." In the years immediately following, civil commitment procedures granted far fewer rights to "defendants" than the criminal courts did (Holstein, 1993). In addition, involuntarily committed patients found it particularly difficult to obtain release.

During the late 1960s and early 1970s, reporters, novelists, civil libertarians, and others spoke out against the ease with which so many people were being unjustifiably committed to mental hospitals. As the public became more aware of these issues, state legislatures started to pass stricter standards for involuntary commitment (Benditt, 2002; Perlin, 2000). Some states, for example, spelled out specific types of behavior that had to be observed before an assessment of dangerousness could be made. Rates of involuntary commitment then declined and release rates rose.

Fewer people are institutionalized through civil commitment procedures today than in the past. The lower commitment rate has not led to more criminal behavior or more arrests of people who would have been committed under more flexible criteria (Teplin, Abram, & McClelland, 1994; Hiday, 1992). Nevertheless, some clinicians and states are concerned that commitment criteria are now too strict, and they are moving toward broadening the criteria once again (Bloom, 2004; Taxman & Messina, 2002). It is not yet clear whether this broadening will lead to a return to the vague commitment procedures of the past.

Protecting Patients' Rights

Over the past two decades, court decisions and state and federal laws have significantly expanded the rights of patients with mental disorders, in particular the *right to treatment* and the *right to refuse treatment* (Slovenko, 2004).

HOW IS THE RIGHT TO TREATMENT PROTECTED? When people are committed to mental institutions and do not receive treatment, the institutions become, in effect, prisons for the unconvicted. To many patients in the late 1960s and the 1970s, large state mental institutions were just that. Thus some patients and their attorneys began to demand that the state honor their **right to treatment.** In the landmark case of *Wyatt v. Stickney,* a suit on behalf of institutionalized patients in Alabama in 1972, a federal court ruled that the state was constitutionally obligated to provide "adequate treatment" to all people who had been committed involuntarily. Because conditions in the state's hospitals were so terrible, the judge laid out goals that state officials had to meet, including more therapists, better living conditions, more privacy, more social interactions and physical exercise, and a more proper use of physical restraint and medication. Other states have since adopted many of these standards.

Another important decision was handed down in 1975 by the Supreme Court in the case of *O'Connor v. Donaldson.* After being held in a Florida mental institution for more than 14 years, Kenneth Donaldson sued for release. Donaldson had repeatedly sought release and had been overruled by the institution's psychiatrists. He argued that he and his fellow patients were receiving poor treatment, were being largely ignored by the staff, and were allowed little personal freedom. The Supreme Court ruled in his favor, fined the hospital's superintendent, and said that such institutions must review patients' cases periodically. The justices also ruled that the state cannot continue to institutionalize against their will people who are not dangerous and who are capable of surviving on their own or with the willing help of responsible family members or friends. In a later case of importance, *Youngberg v. Romeo* (1982), the Supreme Court further ruled that people committed involuntarily have a right to "reasonably nonrestrictive confinement conditions" as well as "reasonable care and safety."

To help protect the rights of patients, Congress passed the Protection and Advocacy for Mentally Ill Individuals Act in 1986 (Woodside & Legg, 1990). This law set up *protection and advocacy systems* in all states and U.S. territories and gave public advocates who worked for patients the power to investigate possible abuse and neglect and to correct those problems legally.

In recent years public advocates have argued that the right to treatment should also be extended to the tens of thousands of people with severe mental disorders who are repeatedly released from hospitals into ill-equipped communities. Many such people have no place to go and are unable to care for themselves, often winding up homeless or in prisons (Torrey, 2001). A number of advocates are now suing federal and state agencies throughout the country, demanding that they fulfill the promises of the community mental health movement (see Chapter 15).

HOW IS THE RIGHT TO REFUSE TREATMENT PROTECTED? During the past two decades the courts have also decided that patients, particularly those in institutions, have the **right to refuse treatment** (Huss & Zeiss, 2005; Perlin, 2004, 2000). The courts have been reluctant to make a single general ruling on this right because there are so many different kinds of treatment, and a general ruling based on one of them might have unintended effects. Therefore, rulings usually target one specific treatment at a time.

Most of the right-to-refuse-treatment rulings center on *biological treatments* (Wettstein, 1999). These treatments are easier to impose on patients without their cooperation than psychotherapy, and they often seem more hazardous. For example, state rulings have consistently granted patients the right to refuse *psychosurgery,* the most irreversible form of physical treatment—and therefore the most dangerous.

Some states have also acknowledged a patient's right to refuse *electroconvulsive therapy* (*ECT*), the treatment used in many cases of severe depression (see Chapter 9). However, the right-to-refuse issue is more complex with regard to ECT than to psychosurgery. ECT is very effective for many people with severe depression; yet it can cause great upset and can also be misused. Today many states grant patients—particularly voluntary patients—the right to refuse ECT. Usually a patient must be informed fully about the nature of the treatment and must give written consent to it. A number of states continue to permit ECT to be forced on committed patients (Baldwin & Oxlad, 2000), whereas others require the consent of a close relative or other third party in such cases.

•**RIGHT TO TREATMENT**•The legal right of patients, particularly those who are involuntarily committed, to receive adequate treatment.

•**RIGHT TO REFUSE TREATMENT**•The legal right of patients to refuse certain forms of treatment.

Dewey Fladd, Canandaigua, NY

Hospital neglect *While some countries have increasingly attended to the rights of patients in recent decades, including their rights to treatment and to humane treatment conditions, many countries have lagged behind. This heartwrenching scene inside a mental hospital in the southern Philippines underscores this point.*

In the past, patients did not have the right to refuse *psychotropic medications.* As we have seen, however, many psychotropic drugs are very powerful, and some produce effects that are unwanted and dangerous. As these harmful effects have become more apparent, some states have granted patients the right to refuse medication. Typically, these states require physicians to explain the purpose of the medication to patients and obtain their written consent. If a patient's refusal is considered incompetent, dangerous, or irrational, the state may allow it to be overturned by an independent psychiatrist, medical committee, or local court (Wettstein, 1999, 1988). However, the refusing patient is supported in this process by a lawyer or other patient advocate.

WHAT OTHER RIGHTS DO PATIENTS HAVE? Court decisions have protected still other patient rights over the past several decades. Patients who perform work in mental institutions, particularly private institutions, are now guaranteed at least a *minimum wage.* In addition, a district court ruled in 1974 that patients released from state mental hospitals have a right to *aftercare* and to an *appropriate community residence,* such as a group home. And in the 1975 case of *Dixon v. Weinberger,* another district court ruled that people with psychological disorders should receive treatment in the *least restrictive facility* available. If an inpatient program at a community mental health center is available, for example, then that is the facility to which they should be assigned, not a mental hospital. In the 1999 case of *Olmstead v. L.C. et al.,* the Supreme Court again confirmed that patients have a right to community treatment.

THE "RIGHTS" DEBATE Certainly, people with psychological disorders have civil rights that must be protected at all times. However, many clinicians express concern that the patients' rights rulings and laws may unintentionally deprive these patients of opportunities for recovery. Consider the right to refuse medication. If medications can help a patient with schizophrenia to recover, doesn't the patient have the right to that recovery? If confusion causes the patient to refuse medication, can clinicians in good conscience delay medication while legal channels are cleared? The psychologist Marilyn Whiteside raised similar concerns in her description of a 25-year-old patient with mental retardation:

He was 25 and severely retarded. And after his favorite attendant left, he became self-abusive. He beat his fists against the side of his head until a football helmet had to be ordered for his protection. Then he clawed at his face and gouged out one of his eyes.

The institution psychologists began a behavior program that had mildly aversive consequences: they squirted warm water in his face each time he engaged in self-abuse. When that didn't work, they requested permission to use an electric prod. The Human Rights Committee vetoed this "excessive and inhumane form of correction" because, after all, the young man was retarded, not criminal.

Since nothing effective could be done that abridged the rights and negated the dignity of the developmentally disabled patient, he was verbally reprimanded for his behavior—and allowed to push his thumb through his remaining eye. He is now blind, of course, but he has his rights and presumably his dignity.

(Whiteside, 1983, p. 13)

Despite such legitimate concerns, we should keep in mind that the clinical field has not always done an effective job of protecting patients' rights. Over the years, many patients have been overmedicated and received improper treatments (Crane, 1973). Similarly, some institutions have misused patients' labor. Furthermore, one must ask whether the field's present state of knowledge justifies clinicians' overriding of patients' rights. Can clinicians confidently say that a given treatment will help a patient? Can they predict when a treatment will have harmful effects? Since clinicians themselves often disagree, it seems appropriate for patients, their advocates, and outside evaluators to play key roles in decision making.

In What Other Ways Do the Clinical and Legal Fields Interact?

Mental health and legal professionals may influence each other's work in other ways as well. During the past two decades, their paths have crossed in four key areas: *malpractice suits, professional boundaries, jury selection,* and *psychological research of legal topics.*

Law in Psychology: Malpractice Suits

The number of **malpractice suits** against therapists has risen so sharply in recent years that clinicians have coined terms for the fear of being sued—"litigaphobia" and "litiga-stress." Claims have been made against clinicians in response to a patient's attempted suicide, sexual activity with a patient, failure to obtain informed consent for a treatment, negligent drug therapy, omission of drug therapy that would speed improvement, improper termination of treatment, and wrongful commitment (Feldman, Moritz, & Benjamin, 2005; Meyer & Simon, 2004; Ash, 2002).

Improper termination of treatment was at issue in one highly publicized case in 1985. A man being treated for alcohol-related depression was released from a state hospital in Alabama. Two and a half months later, he shot and killed a new acquaintance in a motel lounge. He was convicted of murder and sentenced to life in prison. The victim's father, claiming negligence, filed a civil suit against a psychologist, physician, and social worker at the state hospital, and after two years of legal action a jury awarded him a total of almost $7 million. The state supreme court later overturned the verdict, saying that a state hospital is entitled to a certain degree of immunity in such cases.

Two investigators who studied the effects of this case found that the hospital had released 11 percent of its patients during the six months before the lawsuit was filed, 10 percent during the two years it was being litigated, but only 7 percent during the six months after the verdict (Brodsky & Poythress, 1990). Although judgments about a patient's improvement are supposed to be made on their own merits, they were apparently being affected by a heightened fear of litigation at this hospital. Clearly a malpractice suit, or the fear of one, can have significant effects on clinical decisions and practice, for better or for worse (Feldman et al., 2005; Switzer, 2000).

Law in Psychology: Professional Boundaries

During the past several years the legislative and judicial systems have helped to change the *boundaries* that distinguish one clinical profession from another. In particular, they have given more authority to psychologists and blurred the lines that once separated psychiatry from psychology. A growing number of states, for example, are ruling that psychologists can admit patients to the state's hospitals, a power previously held only by psychiatrists (Halloway, 2004).

In 1991, with the blessings of Congress, the Department of Defense (DOD) started to reconsider the biggest difference of all between the practices of psychiatrists and psychologists—the authority to prescribe drugs, a role heretofore denied to psychologists. The DOD set up a trial training program for Army psychologists. Given the apparent success of this trial program, the American Psychological Association recommended in 1996 that all psychologists be allowed to attend a special educational program in prescription services and receive certification to prescribe medications if they pass. In turn, several states introduced legislation regarding the expansion of prescription privileges. In 2002 New Mexico became the first one to grant prescription privileges to psychologists who receive special pharmacological training and Louisiana granted such privileges in 2004 (Bradshaw, 2005; Stambor, 2005).

As the action by the American Psychological Association in the prescription matter suggests, the legislative and judicial systems do not simply take it upon themselves to interfere in the affairs of clinical professionals. In fact, professional associations of psychologists, psychiatrists, and social workers lobby in state legislatures across the country for laws and decisions that may increase the authority of their members. In each instance,

•MALPRACTICE SUIT• A lawsuit charging a therapist with improper conduct in the course of treatment.

>>LAB•NOTES
Faulty Lie Detectors

Studies have found that supposed experts on lying are not very effective at detecting falsehoods (Stroemwall & Granhag, 2003). When viewing videotaped statements and evaluating their truth or falsehood in one study, police identified only 51 percent of the lies and clinical psychologists and federal judges identified only 62 percent of them (Ekman et al., 1999). <<

clinicians seek the involvement of other institutions as well, a further demonstration of the way the mental health system interacts with other sectors of our society.

Psychology in Law: Jury Selection

During the past 25 years, more and more lawyers have turned to clinicians for psychological advice in conducting trials (Davis & Follette, 2004; Kressel & Kressel, 2002). A new breed of clinical specialists, known as "jury specialists," has evolved. They advise lawyers about which jury candidates are likely to favor their side and which strategies are likely to win jurors' support during trials. The jury specialists make their suggestions on the basis of surveys, interviews, analyses of jurors' backgrounds and attitudes, and laboratory simulations of upcoming trials. However, it is not clear that a clinician's advice is more valid than a lawyer's instincts or that the judgments of either are particularly accurate (Van Wallendael & Cutler, 2004).

Psychology in Law: Psychological Research of Legal Topics

Psychologists have sometimes conducted studies and developed expertise on topics of great importance to the criminal justice system. In turn, these studies influence how the system carries out its work. Psychological investigations of two topics, *eyewitness testimony* and *patterns of criminality,* have gained particular attention.

EYEWITNESS TESTIMONY In criminal cases testimony by eyewitnesses is extremely influential. It often determines whether a defendant will be found guilty or not guilty. But how accurate is eyewitness testimony? This question has become urgent, as a troubling number of prisoners (many on death row) have recently had their convictions overturned after DNA evidence revealed that they could not have committed the crimes of which they had been convicted. To date, at least 123 prisoners have been freed after new DNA evidence indicated their innocence.

While some witnesses may have reason to lie (for example, prosecutors may reduce an eyewitness's own punishment in exchange for testimony), most eyewitnesses undoubtedly try to tell the truth about what or who they saw. Yet research indicates that eyewitness testimony can be highly unreliable (Pansky et al., 2005; Loftus, 2003), partly because crimes are typically unexpected and fleeting and therefore are not the sort of events most reliably remembered. During the event, for example, lighting may be poor or other distractions may be present. Witnesses may have had other things on their minds, such as concern for their own safety or that of bystanders. Psychological studies indicate that such concerns may greatly impair later memory (Yarmey, 2004).

Moreover, in laboratory studies researchers have found it easy to fool subjects who are trying to recall the details of an observed event simply by introducing misinformation. After a suggestive description by the researcher, stop signs can be transformed into yield signs, white cars into blue ones, and Mickey Mouse into Minnie Mouse (Pickel, 2004; Loftus, 2003). In addition, laboratory studies indicate that persons who are highly suggestible have the poorest recall of observed events (Liebman et al., 2002).

As for identifying actual perpetrators, research has found that accuracy is greatly influenced by the method used in identification (Wells & Olsen, 2003). The traditional police lineup, for example, is not always a highly reliable technique, and witnesses' errors committed during lineups tend to stick (Koehnken et al., 1996). Researchers have also

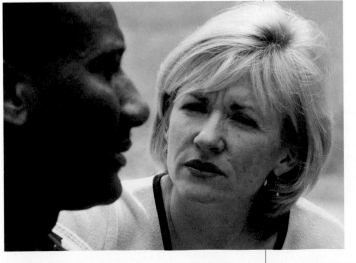

A failure of eyewitness testimony *Psychological research has indicated that eyewitness testimony is often invalid. Here a woman talks to the man whom she had identified as her rapist back in 1984. DNA testing eventually proved that a different person had, in fact, raped her, and the incorrectly identified man was released. In the meantime, however, he had served 11 years of a life sentence in prison.*

learned that witnesses' confidence is not necessarily related to accuracy (Ghetti et al., 2004). Witnesses who are "absolutely certain" are no more likely to be correct in their recollections than those who are only "fairly sure." Yet the degree of a witness's confidence often influences whether jurors will believe the testimony (Smith et al., 1989).

Psychological investigations into eyewitnesses' memory have not yet undone the judicial system's reliance on or respect for those witnesses' testimony. Nor should it. The distance between laboratory studies and real-life events is often great, and the implications of such research must be carefully considered and applied (Wagstaff et al., 2003). Still, eyewitness research has begun to make an impact. Studies of hypnosis and of its ability to create false memories, for example, have led most states to prohibit eyewitnesses from testifying about events or details if their recall of the events was initially helped by hypnosis.

PATTERNS OF CRIMINALITY A growing number of television shows, movies, and books suggest that clinicians often play a major role in criminal investigations by providing police with *psychological profiles* of perpetrators—"He's probably white, in his 30s, has a history of animal torture, has few friends, and is subject to emotional outbursts." The study of criminal behavior patterns and the practice of profiling has increased in recent years; however, it is not nearly as revealing or influential as the media and the arts would have us believe (Norris, 2006; Petherick, 2006).

On the positive side, researchers have gathered information about the psychological features of various criminals, and they have indeed found that perpetrators of particular kinds of crimes—serial murder or serial sexual assault, for example—frequently share a number of traits and background features (Palermo et al., 2005; Winerman, 2004) (see Box 19-3 on the next page). But while such traits are *often* present, they are not *always* present, and so applying profile information to a particular crime can be wrong and misleading. Increasingly police are consulting psychological profilers, and this practice appears to be helpful as long as the limitations of profiling are recognized and the contributions of profilers are combined with other, often more compelling clues to help the police pursue leads and narrow their investigations (Palermo et al., 2005).

A reminder of the limitations of profiling information comes from the case of the snipers who terrorized the Washington, D.C., area for three weeks in October 2002, shooting 10 people dead and seriously wounding 3 others (Turvey & McGrath, 2006). Most of the profiling done by FBI psychologists had suggested that the sniper was acting alone; it turned out that the attacks were conducted by a pair: a middle-aged man, John Allen Muhammad, and a teenaged boy, Lee Boyd Malvo. Although profiles had suggested a young thrill-seeker, Muhammad was 41. Profilers had believed the attacker to be white, but neither Muhammad nor Malvo is white. The prediction of a *male* attacker was correct, but then again female serial killers are rare (Davison, 2004).

Failure of profiling *Massive numbers of police search for clues outside a Home Depot in Virginia in 2002, hoping to identify and capture the serial sniper who killed 10 people and terrorized residents throughout Washington, D.C., Maryland, and Virginia. As it turned out, psychological profiling in this case offered limited help and, in fact, misled the police in certain respects.*

[BOX **19-3**]

Serial Murderers: Madness or Badness?

A shy, brilliant boy, he skipped two grades in school and entered Harvard at age 16. He went on to receive a Ph.D. in mathematics from the University of Michigan in 1967. Securing a highly prestigious position at the University of California, Berkeley, he seemed destined for fame and success. But . . . two years into his stint at Berkeley, he decided to drop out of society—opting instead for a grubby . . . existence in rural Montana.

It was here, alone in a 10-foot-by-12-foot shack, that this reclusive eccentric produced his most renowned works: sixteen bombs, three deaths, twenty-three maimings, several taunting letters to The New York Times, *and a 35,000-word anti-technology manifesto. By the end of his eighteen-year rampage, "Unabomber"—his FBI code name—had become a household word. On April 3, 1996, federal agents raided Theodore Kaczynski's Montana cabin, and his reign of mail bomb terror, which had captured the attention of a nation, was finally put to an end.*

(DUFFY, 1996; THOMAS, 1996)

Murder by mail *A hazardous-material worker sprays his colleagues as they depart the Senate Office Building after searching the building for traces of anthrax, an acute infectious disease caused by a spore-forming bacterium. In late 2001, a number of anthrax-tainted letters were mailed to people throughout eastern parts of the United States, leading to 5 deaths and to severe illness in 13 other people. As of 2006, the serial killer responsible for these acts had continued to elude criminal investigators.*

Theodore Kaczynski is one of a growing list of serial killers who have fascinated and horrified Americans over the years: Ted Bundy, David Berkowitz ("Son of Sam"), Albert DeSalvo, John Wayne Gacy, Jeffrey Dahmer, John Allen Muhammad, John Lee Malvo. Serial murderers often seem to kill for the sheer thrill of the experience. Clinical theorists do not yet understand these individuals, but they are beginning to use the information that has been gathered about them to speculate on the psychology behind their violence.

Although each follows his own pattern (Homant & Kennedy, 2006; Fox & Levin, 2005), many serial killers appear to have certain characteristics in common. Most are white males between 25 and 34 years old, of average to high intelligence, generally clean-cut, smooth-talking, attractive, and skillful manipulators. For the most part, these men have no permanent ties to any community and move from place to place in pursuit of the kill. They typically select their victims carefully. Many are fascinated by police work and the popular media and follow their crimes closely in the news (Ressler & Schactman, 1992; Holmes & De-Burger, 1985). Only 8 percent of the serial killers in the United States are women, al-

though this represents a much higher percentage than that found in any other country (Davison, 2004; Hickey, 2002).

Many serial killers have mental disorders, but they do not typically fit the legal criteria of insanity (Kelleher & Van Nuys, 2002; Ferreira, 2000). Park Dietz, a psychiatrist and highly regarded expert on the subject, offers this explanation:

None of the serial killers I've had the occasion to study or examine has been legally insane, but none has been normal, either. They've all been people who've got mental disorders. But despite their mental disorders, which have to do with their sexual interests and their character, they've been people who knew what they were doing, knew what they were doing was wrong, but chose to do it anyway.

(DOUGLAS, 1996, PP. 344–345)

As a result, the plea of not guilty by reason of insanity is generally unsuccessful for serial killers. This outcome may also be influenced by the concern of communities that a defendant found not guilty by reason of insanity may be released too quickly (Gresham, 1993).

A number of serial killers seem to display severe personality disorders (Homant & Kennedy, 2006; Whitman & Akutagawa, 2004). Lack of conscience and an utter dis-

regard for people and the rules of society—key features of antisocial personality disorder—are typical. Narcissistic thinking is quite common as well. The feeling of being special may even give the killer an unrealistic belief that he will not get caught (Beasley, 2004; Scarf, 1996). Often it is this sense of invincibility that leads to his capture.

Sexual dysfunction and fantasy also seem to play a part (Arndt et al., 2004; Whitman & Akutagawa, 2004). Studies have found that vivid fantasies, often sexual and sadistic, may help drive the killer's behavior (Homant & Kennedy, 2006; Lachmann & Lachmann, 1995). Some clinicians also believe that the killers may be trying to overcome general feelings of powerlessness by controlling, hurting, or eliminating those who are momentarily weaker (Fox & Levin, 2005, 1999). Studies show that many serial killers were abused as children—physically, sexually, and emotionally (Beasley, 2004; Pincus, 2001).

Despite such profiles and suspicions, clinical theorists do not yet understand why serial killers behave as they do. Thus most agree with Dietz when he asserts, "It's hard to imagine any circumstance under which they should be released to the public again" (Douglas, 1996, p. 349).

What Ethical Principles Guide Mental Health Professionals?

Discussions of the legal and mental health systems may sometimes give the impression that clinicians as a group are uncaring and are considerate of patients' rights and needs only when they are forced to be. This, of course, is not true. Most clinicians care greatly about their clients and strive to help them while at the same time respecting their rights and dignity. In fact, clinicians do not rely exclusively on the legislative and court systems to ensure proper and effective clinical practice. They also regulate themselves by continually developing and revising ethical guidelines for members of the clinical field. Many legal decisions do nothing more than place the power of the law behind these already existing professional guidelines.

Each profession within the mental health field has its own **code of ethics** (Pipes, Holstein, & Aguirre, 2005). The code of the American Psychological Association (2002, 1992) is typical. This code, highly respected by other mental health professionals and public officials, includes specific guidelines:

1. **Psychologists are permitted to offer advice** in self-help books, on television and radio programs, in newspaper and magazine articles, through mailed material, and in other places, provided they do so responsibly and professionally and base their advice on appropriate psychological literature and practices.

2. **Psychologists may not conduct fraudulent research, plagiarize the work of others, or publish false data.** During the past 25 years cases of scientific fraud or misconduct have been discovered in all of the sciences, including psychology. These acts have led to misunderstandings of important issues, taken scientific research in the wrong direction, and damaged public trust. Unfortunately, the impressions created by false findings may continue to influence the thinking of both the public and other scientists for years (Pfeifer & Snodgrass, 1990).

3. **Psychologists must acknowledge their limitations** with regard to patients who are disabled or whose gender, ethnicity, language, socioeconomic status, or sexual orientation differs from that of the therapist. This guideline often requires psychotherapists to obtain additional training or supervision, consult with more knowledgeable colleagues, or refer clients to more appropriate professionals.

4. **Psychologists who make evaluations and testify in legal cases must base their assessments on sufficient information and substantiate their findings appropriately** (Faigman & Monahan, 2005). If an adequate examination of the individual in question is not possible, psychologists must make clear the limited nature of their testimony.

5. **Psychologists may not take advantage of clients and students, sexually or otherwise.** This guideline relates to the widespread social problem of sexual harassment, as well as the problem of therapists who take sexual advantage of clients in therapy. The code specifically forbids a sexual relationship with a present or former therapy client for at least two years after the end of treatment; and even then such a relationship is permitted only in "the most unusual circumstances." Furthermore, psychologists may not accept as clients people with whom they have previously had a sexual relationship.

   Clients may suffer great emotional damage from sexual involvement with their therapists (Garrett, 2002; Malley & Reilly, 1999). A number of therapists are now treating clients whose primary problem is that they previously experienced some form of sexual misconduct by a therapist (Bloom et al., 1999; Luepker, 1999; Wincze et al., 1996). Many such clients experience the symptoms of posttraumatic stress disorder or major depressive disorder.

   How many therapists actually have a sexual relationship with a client? On the basis of various surveys, reviewers have estimated that some form of

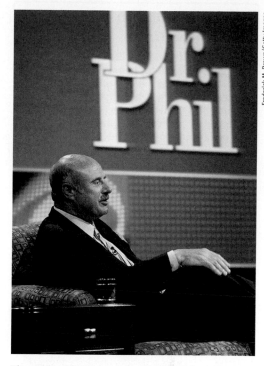

Frederick M. Brown/Getty Images

The ethics of giving professional advice *Like the enormously popular psychologist Phil McGraw ("Dr. Phil"), many of today's clinicians offer advice to millions of people in books, at workshops, on television and radio programs, and in tape packages. Their presentations often affect people greatly, and so they, too, are bound by the field's ethics code to act responsibly and to base their advice on appropriate psychological theories and findings.*

•**CODE OF ETHICS**•A body of principles and rules for ethical behavior, designed to guide decisions and actions by members of a profession.

sexual misconduct with patients may be engaged in by around 8 percent of today's male therapists and 2 percent of female therapists (Celenza, 2005; Malley & Reilly, 1999; Hankins et al., 1994). Although the vast majority of therapists keep their sexual behavior within appropriate professional bounds, their ability to control private feelings is apparently another matter. In surveys, close to 90 percent of therapists reported having been sexually attracted to a client, at least on occasion (Garrett, 2002; Pope, 2000; Pope & Tabachnick, 1993). Although few of these therapists acted on their feelings, most of them felt guilty, anxious, or concerned about the attraction (Pope et al., 1986).

Given such sexual issues, it is not surprising that sexual ethics training is given high priority in many clinical training programs (Garrett, 2002; Housman & Stake, 1999). In addition, consumer-oriented brochures on sexual misconduct in psychotherapy have been developed to help clients evaluate the appropriateness of their therapists' behavior (Thorn, Shealy, & Briggs, 1993).

6. **Psychologists must adhere to the principle of confidentiality.** All of the state courts uphold laws protecting therapist **confidentiality,** and in the 1996 case of *Jaffee v. Redmond,* the Supreme Court applied this principle to federal courts as well. For peace of mind and to ensure effective therapy, clients must be able to trust that their private exchanges with a therapist will not be repeated to others (Knapp & VandeCreek, 2006). There are times, however, when the principle of confidentiality must be compromised (Caudill & Kaplan, 2005; Nagy, 2005). A therapist in training, for example, must discuss cases on a regular basis with a supervisor. Clients, in turn, must be informed when such discussions are occurring.

A second exception arises in cases of outpatients who are clearly dangerous. The 1976 case of *Tarasoff v. Regents of the University of California,* one of the most important cases to affect client-therapist relationships, concerned an outpatient at a University of California hospital. He had confided to his therapist that he wanted to harm his former girlfriend, Tanya Tarasoff. Several days after ending therapy, the former patient fulfilled his promise. He stabbed Tanya Tarasoff to death.

Should confidentiality have been broken in this case? The therapist, in fact, felt that it should. Campus police were notified, but the patient was released after some questioning. In their suit against the hospital and therapist, the victim's parents argued that the therapist should have also warned them and their daughter that the patient intended to harm Ms. Tarasoff. The California Supreme Court agreed: "The protective privilege ends where the public peril begins."

The current code of ethics for psychologists thus declares that therapists have a **duty to protect**—a responsibility to break confidentiality, even without the client's consent, when it is necessary "to protect the client or others from harm." Since the *Tarasoff* ruling, California's courts have further held that therapists must also protect people who are close to a client's intended victim and thus in danger. A child, for example, is likely to be at risk when a client plans to assault the child's mother. In addition, a California Court of Appeals ruled that therapists must act to protect people even when information about the dangerousness of a client is received from the client's family, rather than from the client (Thomas, 2005). At the same time, the California courts have limited certain features of the Tarasoff ruling, clarifying, for example, that the duty to protect applies only when the intended victim is readily identifiable, as opposed to the public at large, and only when the intended object of violence is a person, as opposed to property. Many, but not all, states have adopted the California court rulings or similar ones (Bloom, 1990; Pietrofesa et al., 1990), and a number have passed "duty to protect" bills that clarify the rules of confidentiality for therapists and protect them from certain civil suits (Simon, 2001; Bersoff, 1999).

•**CONFIDENTIALITY**•The principle that certain professionals will not divulge the information they obtain from a client.

•**DUTY TO PROTECT**•The principle that therapists must break confidentiality in order to protect a person who may be the intended victim of a client.

•**EMPLOYEE ASSISTANCE PROGRAM**• A mental health program offered by a business to its employees.

•**STRESS-REDUCTION AND PROBLEM-SOLVING SEMINAR**•A workshop or series of group sessions offered by a business in which mental health professionals teach employees how to cope with and solve problems and reduce stress.

Mental Health, Business, and Economics

The legislative and judicial systems are not the only social institutions with which mental health professionals interact. The *business* and *economic* fields are two other sectors that influence and are influenced by clinical practice and study. To be sure, health care in all its varieties is itself a business, and many decisions in the clinical field are based on economic considerations (see Box 19-4 on the next page), but the mental health field in turn influences the conduct of business and economic programs.

Bringing Mental Health Services to the Workplace

Collectively, psychological disorders are among 10 leading categories of work-related disorders and injuries in the United States. In fact, almost 12 percent of all employees are said to experience psychological problems that are serious enough to affect their work. Psychological problems contribute to 60 percent of all absenteeism from work, up to 90 percent of industrial accidents, and 65 percent of work terminations (Kemp, 1994). Alcohol abuse and other substance-related disorders are particularly damaging, increasing absences by as much as six times, accidents by four times, and workers' compensation claims by five times (Martin, Kraft, & Roman, 1994; Wright, 1984). The business world has often turned to clinical professionals to help prevent and correct such problems (Scott & Geller, 2005; Thomas & Hersen, 2004). Two common means of providing mental health care in the workplace are *employee assistance programs* and *problem-solving seminars.*

Employee assistance programs, mental health services made available by a place of business, are run either by mental health professionals who work directly for a company or by outside mental health agencies (Jacobson, 2005; Masi, 2005). Companies publicize such programs at the work site, educate workers about psychological dysfunctioning, and teach supervisors how to identify workers who are having psychological problems. Businesses believe that employee assistance programs save them money in the long run by preventing psychological problems from interfering with work performance and by reducing employee insurance claims, although these beliefs have not undergone extensive testing (Attridge, 2004).

Stress-reduction and problem-solving seminars are workshops or group sessions in which mental health professionals teach employees techniques for coping, solving problems, and handling and reducing stress (Daw, 2001; Kagan et al., 1995). Programs of this kind are just as likely to be aimed at high-level executives as at assembly-line workers. Often employees are required to attend such workshops, which may run for several days, and are given time off from their jobs to do so. Again, the businesses expect these programs to save money by helping workers to achieve a healthier state of mind, suffer less dysfunction on the job, and improve their performance.

The Economics of Mental Health

We have already seen how economic decisions by the government may influence the clinical field's treatment of people with severe mental disorders. For example, the desire of the state and federal governments to reduce costs was an important consideration in the country's deinstitutionalization movement, which contributed to the premature release of hospital patients into the community. Economic decisions by government agencies may affect other kinds of clients and treatment programs as well.

On the one hand, government funding for services to people with psychological disorders has risen sharply over the past three decades, from $3 billion in 1969 to around $61 billion today (Torrey, 2001, 1997; Redick et al., 1992). On the other hand, much of that money is spent on income support, housing subsidies, and other such expenses, rather than directly on mental health services (Sperling, 2005). Government funding for services actually appears to be decreasing. It currently covers less than half the cost of all mental health services, leaving most of the expense to individual patients and their private insurance companies (Taube, 1990).

Joseph Cultice/AP Photo

Mental health and the arts *The mental health field also interacts with segments of society beyond the legislative, judicial, business, and economic fields. As we have seen throughout this book, for example, mental health themes often play a major role in the arts, greatly influencing the public's view of mental dysfunctioning. Here the popular duo Insane Clown Posse pose in their stage makeup prior to performing at a musical concert. Many patient advocates worry that the unflattering terms used in the names of this and other musical groups (for example, Bad Brains, 10,000 Maniacs, The Dissociatives, and Disturbed) may contribute to the stigmatization of people with psychological disorders.*

>>LOOKING AROUND

Declining Costs Mental health expenditures by insurance companies fell 54 percent during the 1990s. Total health care spending fell just 7 percent during the same decade (*Wall Street Journal*, 1998). <<

Without Coverage The number of people in the United States who do not have health insurance is 44 million. <<

Mental Health Parity To date 35 states have passed laws requiring insurance companies to provide clients with equal coverage (parity) for medical and mental disorders. However, several of these states exclude certain mental disorders from the insurance parity laws (NMHA, 2005; Roberts & Brennan, 2005). <<

The Itemized Statement in Clinical Psychiatry: A New Concept in Billing

❚ (In this article, by Robert S. Hoffman, M.D., which originally appeared in *The Journal of Irreproducible Results,* 1980, the psychiatrist's biting wit is equaled only by his sense of outrage over the growing demands made by insurance companies.) ❚

Due to the rapidly escalating costs of health care delivery, there has been increasing pressure on physicians to document and justify their charges for professional services. This has created a number of serious problems, particularly in the field of psychiatry. Chief among these is the breach of confidentiality that arises when sensitive clinical information is provided to third-party insurance carriers, e.g. the patient's diagnosis or related details about his/her psychiatric disorder. Even when full disclosure of such information is made, insurance carriers frequently deny benefits because the description of the treatment appears imprecise or inadequate. There also has been some criticism of the standard hourly fee-for-service, the argument being that psychiatrists, like other medical specialists, should be required to adjust their fees depending upon the particular treatment offered.

In view of these considerations, a method is required which will bring psychiatric billing in line with accepted medical practice. The procedure illustrated below, which we have successfully employed in our clinic for the past two years, achieves this goal. It requires only a modest investment in time and effort: the tape-recording of all psychotherapy sessions, transcription of tapes, tabulation of therapeutic interventions, and establishment of a relative value scale for the commonly used maneuvers. This can easily be managed by two full-time medical billing personnel per psychiatrist. The method, in our hands, has been found to increase collections from third-party carriers by 65% and to raise a typical psychiatrist's annual net income almost to the level of a municipal street sweeper or plumber's assistant.

Below is a specimen monthly statement illustrating these principles:

CALVIN L. SKOLNIK, M.D., INC.
A Psychiatry Corporation

Jan. 5, 1978

Mr. Sheldon Rosenberg
492 West Maple Dr.
East Orange, N.J.

Dear Mr. Rosenberg:

In response to the request by your insurer, Great Lakes Casualty and Surety Co., for more precise documentation of professional services rendered, I have prepared the enclosed itemization for the month of December. I trust that this will clarify the situation sufficiently for your benefit payments to be resumed.

Until next Tuesday at 11:00, I remain

Cordially,

Calvin L. Skolnik, M.D.

The growing economic role of private insurance companies has had a significant effect on the way clinicians go about their work. As we observed in Chapter 1, to reduce their expenses and keep track of their payments, most of these companies have developed **managed care programs,** in which the insurance company decides such questions as which therapists clients may choose, the cost of sessions, and the number of sessions for which a client may be reimbursed (Corcoran et al., 2005). These and other insurance plans may also control expenses through the use of **peer review systems,** in which clinicians who work for the insurance company periodically review a client's treatment program and recommend that insurance benefits be either continued or

•**MANAGED CARE PROGRAM**•An insurance program in which the insurance company decides the cost, method, provider, and length of treatment.

Charges

140	clarifications	@ .25	35.00
157	restatements	@ .25	39.25
17	broad-focus questions	@ .35	5.95
42	narrow-focus questions	@ .30	12.60
86	reflections of dominant emotional theme	@ .35	30.10
38	resolutions of inconsistencies	@ .45	17.10
22	pointings out of nonverbal communications	@ .40	8.80
187	encouragements to say more	@ .15	28.05
371	sympathetic nods with furrowed brow	@ .10	37.10
517	acknowledgments of information reception (Uh-huhs, Umhmmm, etc.)	@ .08	41.36
24	interpretations of unconscious defense configurations	@ .30	7.20
16	absolutions for evil deeds	@ .50	8.00
2	pieces of advice	@ .75	1.50
6	expressions of personal feelings	@ .50	3.00
2	personal reminiscences	@ .65	1.30
35	misc. responses (sighs, grunts, belches, etc.)	@ .20	7.00
7	listening to remarks disparaging therapist's appearance, personal habits, or technique	@ 1.75	12.25
12	listening to sarcastic remarks about psychiatry	@ 1.00	12.00
3	listening to psychiatrist jokes	@ .80	2.40
3	telephone calls to therapist	@ .15	.45
1	telephone call to therapist at especially inopportune moment	@ 10.50	10.50
22	Kleenex tissues	@ .005	.11
1	ashtray	@ 3.50	3.50
1	filling and repainting of 1 ashtray-size dent in wall	@ 27.50	27.50
1	shampooing of soft drink stain on carpet	@ 15.00	15.00
1	letter of excuse from work	@ 2.50	2.50
2	surcharges for unusually boring or difficult sessions	@ 35.00	70.00
	Subtotal: charges		$438.52

Credits

4	unusually interesting anecdotes	@ .45	1.80
3	good jokes	@ .50	1.50
1	item of gossip about another patient which was found useful in her therapy	@ 3.50	3.50
1	apology for sarcastic remark	@ 1.00	1.00
1	use of case history at American Psychiatric Association convention		10.00
1/2	chicken salad sandwich on whole wheat w/mayo	@ 1.75	.88
7	bummed cigarettes (65¢/pack)		.23
1	damaged Librium tablet, returned unused		.10
	Subtotal: credits		$18.99

Total: PLEASE REMIT— $419.53

stopped. Typically, insurers require detailed reports or session notes from the therapist, often including intimate personal information about the patient.

As we also observed in Chapter 1, many therapists and clients dislike managed care programs and peer reviews (Mechanic, 2004). They believe that the reports required of therapists breach confidentiality, even when efforts are made to protect anonymity, and that the value of therapy in a given case is sometimes difficult to convey in a brief report. They also argue that the priorities of managed care programs inevitably shorten therapy, even if longer-term treatment would be advisable in particular cases. The priorities may also favor treatments that offer short-term results (for example, drug therapy)

•**PEER REVIEW SYSTEM**•A system by which clinicians paid by an insurance company may periodically review a patient's progress and recommend the continuation or termination of insurance benefits.

"*I wish I could help you. The problem is that you're too sick for managed care.*"

over more costly approaches that might achieve a more promising long-term improvement. As in the medical field, disturbing stories are often heard about patients who are prematurely cut off from mental health services by their managed care programs. In short, many clinicians fear that the current system amounts to regulation of therapy by insurance companies rather than by therapists.

The Person within the Profession

The actions of clinical researchers and practitioners not only influence and are influenced by other institutions but are closely tied to their personal needs and goals (see Box 19-5). We have seen that the human strengths, imperfections, wisdom, and clumsiness of clinical professionals may affect their theoretical orientations, their interactions with clients, and the kinds of clients with whom they choose to work. We have also looked at how personal leanings may sometimes override professional standards and scruples and, in extreme cases, lead clinical scientists to commit research fraud and clinical practitioners to engage in sexual misconduct with clients.

A national survey of the mental health of therapists found that 84 percent reported being in therapy at least once (Pope & Brown, 1996; Pope & Tabachnick, 1994). Their reasons were largely the same as those of other clients, with emotional problems, depression, and anxiety topping the list. In fact, 61 percent of the therapists reported having experienced depression, 29 percent reported having had suicidal feelings, and 4 percent said they had attempted suicide (Pope & Tabachnick, 1994). It is not clear why so many therapists report having psychological problems. Perhaps their jobs are highly stressful; indeed, research suggests that therapists often experience some degree of job burnout (Rosenberg & Pace, 2006). Or perhaps therapists are simply more aware of their own negative feelings or are more likely to pursue treatment for their problems. Alternatively, individuals with personal concerns may be more inclined to choose clinical work as a profession. Whatever the reason, clinicians bring to their work a set of psychological concerns and emotions that may, along with other important factors, affect how they listen and respond to clients.

The science and profession of abnormal psychology seek to understand, predict, and change abnormal functioning. But we must not lose sight of the broader context in which its activities are conducted. Mental health researchers and clinicians are human

>>BY THE NUMBERS
Countertransference

87% Percentage of therapists who report having been angry at a client on at least one occasion ◄◄

78% Therapists who report having told a client that they were angry with him or her ◄◄

57% Therapists who report having raised their voice at a client ◄◄

(Pope & Tabachnick, 1993)

[BOX **19-5**]

Therapists under Attack

According to surveys, more than 80 percent of therapists have on at least one occasion feared that a client might physically attack them (Pope & Tabachnick, 1993). Are such concerns exaggerated? Not always. In fact, a number of therapists have found out that their rights—including the right to a safe practice—may be violated (Freed & Geller, 2005; Fry et al., 2002). More than 10 percent of therapists have been attacked by a patient at least once in private therapy, and an even larger percentage have been assaulted in mental hospitals (Tryon, 1987; Bernstein, 1981). Similarly,

Corbis

a number of therapists have been stalked or harassed by patients (Dinkelmeyer & Johnson, 2002).

Patients have used a variety of weapons in their attacks, including such common objects as shoes, lamps, fire extinguishers, and canes. Some have used guns or knives and have severely wounded or even killed a therapist.

Many therapists who have been attacked continue to feel anxious and insecure in their work for a long time afterward. Some try to be more selective in accepting patients and look for cues that signal impending violence. It is possible that such concerns represent a significant distraction from the task at hand when they are in session with clients.

beings, living within a society of human beings, working to serve human beings. The mixture of discovery, misdirection, promise, and frustration that we have encountered throughout this book is thus to be expected. When one thinks about it, could the study and treatment of human behavior really proceed in any other way?

PUTTING IT together
Operating within a Larger System

At one time clinical researchers and professionals conducted their work largely in isolation. Today, however, their activities have numerous ties to the legislative, judicial, economic, and other established systems. One reason for this growing interconnectedness is that the clinical field has achieved a high level of respect and acceptance in our society. Clinicians now serve millions of people in many ways. They have much to say about almost every aspect of society, from education to ecology, and are widely looked to as sources of expertise. When a field achieves such prominence, it inevitably affects how other institutions are run. It also attracts public scrutiny, and various institutions begin to keep an eye on its activities.

Today, when people with psychological problems seek help from a therapist, they are entering a complex system consisting of numerous interconnected parts. Just as their personal problems have grown within a social structure, so will their treatment be affected by the various parts of a larger system—the therapist's values and needs, legal and economic forces, societal attitudes, and yet other forces. These many forces influence clinical research as well.

The effects of this larger system on an individual's psychological needs can be positive or negative, like a family's impact on each of its members. When the system protects a client's rights and confidentiality, for example, it is serving the client well. When economic, legal, or other societal forces limit treatment options, cut off treatment prematurely, or stigmatize a person, the system is adding to the person's problems.

Because of the enormous growth and impact of the mental health profession in our society, it is important that we understand its strengths and weaknesses. As we have seen throughout this book, the field has gathered much knowledge, especially during the past several decades. What mental health professionals do not know and cannot do, however, still outweigh what they do know and can do. Everyone who turns to the clinical field—

>>BY THE NUMBERS
Business and Mental Health

$13 million Amount of money that the American Psychiatric Association receives annually from advertising by pharmaceutical companies «

$10 million Amount that the American Psychiatric Association receives annually from membership dues «

$20 million Amount that the American Medical Association receives annually from selling its membership list to pharmaceutical companies «

(Thomas, 2004)

directly or indirectly—must recognize that it is young and imperfect. Society is vastly curious about behavior and often in need of information and help. What we as a society must remember, however, is that the field is still *putting it all together.*

[SUMMARY AND REVIEW]

■ **The legal system and the mental health field** The mental health profession interacts with the *legislative and judicial systems* in two key ways. First, clinicians help assess the mental stability of people accused of crimes. Second, the legislative and judicial systems help regulate mental health care. *pp. 559–560*

■ **Criminal commitment** The punishment of persons convicted of crimes depends on the assumption that individuals are *responsible for their acts* and are *capable of defending themselves in court.* Evaluations by clinicians may help judges and juries decide the culpability of defendants and sometimes result in criminal commitment.

If defendants are judged to have been *mentally unstable at the time they committed a crime,* they may be found *not guilty by reason of insanity* and placed in a treatment facility rather than a prison. "Insanity" is a legal term, defined by legislators, not by clinicians. In federal courts and about half the state courts, insanity is judged in accordance with the *M'Naghten test,* which holds that defendants were insane at the time of a criminal act if they did not know the nature or quality of the act or did not know right from wrong at the time they committed it. Other states use the broader *American Law Institute test.*

The insanity defense has been criticized on several grounds, and some states have added an additional option, *guilty but mentally ill.* Defendants who receive this verdict are sentenced to prison with the proviso that they will also receive psychological treatment. Still another verdict option is *guilty with diminished capacity.* A related category consists of convicted *sex offenders,* who are considered in some states to have a mental disorder and are therefore assigned to treatment in a mental health facility.

Regardless of their state of mind at the time of the crime, defendants may be found *mentally incompetent to stand trial,* that is, incapable of fully understanding the charges or legal proceedings that confront them. If so, they are typically sent to a mental hospital until they are competent to stand trial. *pp. 560–567*

■ **Civil commitment** The legal system also influences the clinical profession. First, courts may be called upon to commit noncriminals to mental hospitals for treatment, a process called *civil commitment.* Society allows involuntary commitment of people considered to be *in need of treatment* and *dangerous to themselves or others.* Laws governing civil commitment procedures vary from state to state, but a *minimum standard of proof*—clear and convincing evidence of the necessity of commitment—has been defined by the Supreme Court. *pp. 568–572*

■ **Protecting patients' rights** The courts and legislatures significantly affect the mental health profession by specifying legal rights to which patients are entitled. The rights that have received the most attention are the *right to treatment* and the *right to refuse treatment. pp. 572–574*

■ **Other clinical-legal interactions** Mental health and legal professionals also cross paths in four other areas. First, *malpractice suits* against therapists have increased in recent years. Second, the legislative and judicial systems help define *professional boundaries.* Third, lawyers may solicit the advice of mental health professionals regarding the *selection of jurors* and case strategies. Fourth, psychologists may *investigate legal phenomena* such as *eyewitness testimony* and *patterns of criminality. pp. 575–578*

■ **Ethical principles** Each clinical profession has a *code of ethics.* The psychologists' code includes prohibitions against *engaging in fraudulent research* and against *taking advantage of clients and students, sexually or otherwise.* It also establishes guidelines for respecting patient *confidentiality.* The case of *Tarasoff v. Regents of the University of California* helped to determine the circumstances in which therapists have a *duty to protect* the client or others from harm and must break confidentiality. *pp. 579–580*

■ **Mental health, business, and economics** Clinical practice and study also intersect with the business and economic worlds. Clinicians often help to address psychological problems in the workplace, for example, through *employee assistance programs* and *stress-reduction and problem-solving seminars.*

Reductions in government funding of clinical services have left much of the expense for these services to be paid by insurance companies. Private insurance companies are setting up *managed care programs* whose structure and reimbursement procedures influence and often reduce the duration and focus of therapy. Their procedures, which include *peer review systems,* may also compromise patient confidentiality and the quality of therapy services. *pp. 581–584*

■ **The person within the profession** Mental health activities are affected by the personal needs, values, and goals of the human beings who provide the clinical services. These factors inevitably affect the choice, direction, and even quality of their work. *pp. 584–585*

>>> CRITICAL THOUGHTS <<<

1. In some states, the defense must prove that a defendant was not guilty by reason of insanity, while in other states the prosecution must prove that a defendant making this plea was not insane. Which burden of proof is more appropriate? *pp. 560–562*

2. After a patient has been criminally committed to an institution, why might a clinician be reluctant to declare that the person is mentally stable and unlikely to commit the same crime again, even if the patient shows significant improvement? *pp. 562–564*

3. Today how are people who have been institutionalized viewed and treated by others? Is the stigma of hospitalization a legitimate argument against civil commitment? *pp. 568–572*

4. Most psychiatrists do not want psychologists to be granted the authority to prescribe psychotropic medications. Surprisingly, many psychologists oppose the idea as well (Heiby, 2002). Why might they take this position? *pp. 575–576*

5. Although more than two-thirds of therapists have felt sexually attracted to a client on at least one occasion, only around one-third of clients have ever felt sexually attracted to their therapist (Pope & Brown, 1996). How might these different reactions be explained? *pp. 579–580*

6. How might lingering anxiety affect the behavior and effectiveness of clinicians who have been attacked? What do patient attacks on therapists suggest about therapists' ability to predict dangerousness? *p. 585*

⊙—[CYBERSTUDY]————————————————— >>>

SEARCH THE *ABNORMAL PSYCHOLOGY* CD-ROM FOR

▲ Chapter 19 Video Cases and Discussions
   Can clinicians predict dangerousness and violence?
   When are people not responsible for criminal acts?
   Did the hospital treatments of past times violate patients' rights?

▲ Chapter 19 Practical, Research, and Decision-Making Exercises
   Resolving ethical dilemmas in clinical practice
   Predicting dangerousness

▲ Chapter 19 Practice Test and Feedback

LOG ON TO THE COMER WEB PAGE FOR

▲ Suggested Web links, exercises, FAQ page, additional Chapter 19 practice test questions
   <www.worthpublishers.com/comer>

————————————————————————————————— <<<

[glossary]

ABAB design A single-subject experimental design in which behavior is measured during a baseline period, after a treatment has been applied, after baseline conditions have been reintroduced, and after the treatment has been reintroduced. Also called a *reversal design*.

Abnormal psychology The scientific study of abnormal behavior in order to describe, predict, explain, and change abnormal patterns of functioning.

Acetylcholine A neurotransmitter that has been linked to depression and dementia.

Acute stress disorder An anxiety disorder in which fear and related symptoms are experienced soon after a traumatic event and last less than a month.

Addiction Physical dependence on a substance, marked by such features as tolerance, withdrawal symptoms during abstinence, or both.

Affect An experience of emotion or mood.

Aftercare A program of posthospitalization care and treatment in the community.

Agoraphobia An anxiety disorder in which a person is afraid to be in places or situations from which escape might be difficult (or embarrassing) or help unavailable if paniclike symptoms were to occur.

Agranulocytosis A life-threatening reduction in white blood cells. This condition is sometimes produced by clozapine, one of the atypical antipsychotic drugs.

Alcohol Any beverage containing ethyl alcohol, including beer, wine, and liquor.

Alcohol dehydrogenase An enzyme that breaks down alcohol in the stomach before it enters the blood.

Alcoholics Anonymous (AA) A self-help organization that provides support and guidance for persons with patterns of alcohol abuse or dependence.

Alcoholism A pattern of behavior in which a person repeatedly abuses or develops a dependence on alcohol.

Alogia A decrease in speech or speech content; a symptom of schizophrenia. Also known as *poverty of speech*.

Alprazolam A benzodiazepine drug shown to be effective in the treatment of anxiety disorders. Marketed as *Xanax*.

Altruistic suicide Suicide committed by people who intentionally sacrifice their lives for the well-being of society.

Alzheimer's disease The most common form of dementia, usually occurring after the age of 65.

Amenorrhea The absence of menstrual cycles.

American Law Institute (ALI) test A legal test for insanity that holds people to be insane at the time of committing a crime if, because of a mental disorder, they did not know right from wrong or they could not resist an uncontrollable impulse to act.

Amnesia Loss of memory.

Amnestic disorders Organic disorders in which the primary symptom is memory loss.

Amniocentesis A prenatal procedure used to test the amniotic fluid that surrounds the fetus for the possibility of birth defects.

Amphetamine A stimulant drug that is manufactured in the laboratory.

Amygdala A structure in the brain that plays a key role in emotion and memory.

Anaclitic depression A pattern of depressed behavior found among very young children that is caused by separation from the mother.

Analog observation A method for observing behavior in which people are observed in artificial settings such as clinicians' offices or laboratories.

Analogue experiment A research method in which the experimenter produces abnormal-like behavior in laboratory subjects and then conducts experiments on the subjects.

Anal stage In psychoanalytic theory, the second 18 months of life, during which the child's focus of pleasure shifts to the anus.

Anesthesia A lessening or loss of sensation of touch or for pain.

Anomic suicide Suicide committed by individuals whose social environment fails to provide stability, thus leaving them without a sense of belonging.

Anorexia nervosa A disorder marked by the pursuit of extreme thinness and by an extreme loss of weight.

Anoxia A complication of birth in which the baby is deprived of oxygen.

Antabuse (disulfiram) A drug that causes intense nausea, vomiting, increased heart rate, and dizziness when taken with alcohol. It is often taken by people who are trying to refrain from drinking alcohol.

Antagonist drugs Drugs that block or change the effects of an addictive drug.

Anterograde amnesia The inability to remember new information acquired after the event that triggered amnesia.

Antianxiety drugs Psychotropic drugs that help reduce tension and anxiety. Also called *minor tranquilizers* or *anxiolytics*.

Antibipolar drugs Psychotropic drugs that help stabilize the moods of people suffering from a bipolar mood disorder.

Antibodies Bodily chemicals that seek out and destroy foreign invaders such as bacteria or viruses.

Antidepressant drugs Psychotropic drugs that improve the mood of people with depression.

Antigen A foreign invader of the body, such as a bacterium or virus.

Antipsychotic drugs Drugs that help correct grossly confused or distorted thinking, such as that found in psychotic disorders.

Antisocial personality disorder A personality disorder marked by a general pattern of disregard for and violation of other people's rights.

Anxiety The central nervous system's physiological and emotional response to a vague sense of threat or danger.

Anxiety disorder A disorder in which anxiety is a central symptom.

Anxiety sensitivity A tendency of certain persons to focus on their bodily sensations, assess them illogically, and interpret them as harmful.

Anxiolytics Drugs that reduce anxiety.

Arbitrary inference An error in logic in which a person draws negative conclusions on the basis of little or even contrary evidence.

Asperger's disorder A pervasive developmental disorder in which individuals display profound social impairment yet maintain a relatively high level of cognitive functioning and language skills. Also known as *Asperger's syndrome*.

Assertiveness training A cognitive-behavioral approach to increasing assertive behavior that is socially desirable.

Assessment The process of collecting and interpreting relevant information about a client or subject.

Asthma A medical problem marked by narrowing of the trachea and bronchi, which results in shortness of breath, wheezing, coughing, and a choking sensation.

Asylum A type of institution first established in the sixteenth century to provide care for persons with mental disorders. Most became virtual prisons.

Attention-deficit/hyperactivity disorder (ADHD) A disorder in which persons are unable to focus their attention or behave overactively and impulsively, or both.

Attribution An explanation of things we see going on around us which points to particular causes.

Atypical antipsychotic drugs A new group of antipsychotic drugs that operate in a biological manner that is different from the way traditional antipsychotic drugs operate.

Auditory hallucination A hallucination in which a person hears sounds or voices that are not actually present.

Augmentative communication system A method for teaching communication skills to individuals with autism, mental retardation, or cerebral palsy by pointing to pictures, symbols, letters, or words on a communication board or computer.

Aura A warning sensation that may precede a migraine headache.

Autistic disorder A pervasive developmental disorder marked by extreme unresponsiveness to others, poor communication skills, and highly repetitive and rigid behavior. Also known as *autism*.

Autoerotic asphyxia A fatal lack of oxygen that persons may unintentionally produce while hanging, suffocating, or strangling themselves during masturbation.

Automatic thoughts Numerous unpleasant thoughts that come into the mind, helping to cause or maintain depression, anxiety, or other forms of psychological dysfunction.

Autonomic nervous system (ANS) The network of nerve fibers that connect the central nervous system to all the other organs of the body.

Aversion therapy A treatment based on the principles of classical conditioning in which people are repeatedly presented with shocks or another unpleasant stimulus while they are performing undesirable behaviors such as taking a drug.

Avoidant personality disorder A personality disorder in which an individual is consistently uncomfortable and restrained in social situations, overwhelmed by feelings of inadequacy, and extremely sensitive to negative evaluation.

Avolition A symptom of schizophrenia marked by apathy and an inability to start or complete a course of action.

Axon A long fiber extending from the body of a neuron.

Barbiturates A group of addictive sedative-hypnotic drugs used to reduce anxiety or to help persons fall asleep.

Baroreceptors Sensitive nerves in the blood vessels that are responsible for signaling the brain that blood pressure is becoming too high.

Baseline data An individual's initial response level on a test or scale.

Basic irrational assumptions According to Albert Ellis, the inaccurate and inappropriate beliefs held by people with various psychological problems.

Battery A series of tests, each of which measures a specific skill area.

B-cell A lymphocyte that produces antibodies.

Behavioral medicine A field of treatment that combines psychological and physical interventions to treat or prevent medical problems.

Behavioral model A theoretical perspective that emphasizes behavior and the ways in which it is learned.

Behavioral self-control training (BSCT) A cognitive-behavioral approach to treating alcohol abuse and dependence in which people are taught to keep track of their drinking behavior and to apply coping strategies in situations that typically trigger excessive drinking.

Behavioral therapy A therapeutic approach that seeks to identify problem-causing behaviors and change them. Also known as *behavior modification*.

Behaviors The responses an organism makes to its environment.

Bender Visual–Motor Gestalt Test A neuropsychological test in which a subject is asked to copy a set of nine simple designs and later reproduce the designs from memory.

Benzodiazepines The most common group of antianxiety drugs, including Valium and Xanax.

Bereavement The process of working through the grief that one feels when a loved one dies.

Beta-amyloid protein A small molecule that forms sphere-shaped deposits called senile plaques, linked to aging and to Alzheimer's disease.

Bilateral electroconvulsive therapy (ECT) A form of electroconvulsive therapy in which one electrode is applied to each side of the forehead and electrical current is passed through the brain.

Binge An episode of uncontrollable eating during which a person eats a very large quantity of food.

Binge-eating disorder A type of eating disorder in which a person displays a pattern of binge eating without accompanying compensatory behaviors.

Binge-eating/purging-type anorexia nervosa A type of anorexia nervosa in which people have eating binges but still lose excessive weight by forcing themselves to vomit after meals or by abusing laxatives or diuretics.

Biofeedback training A treatment technique in which a person is given information about physiological reactions as they occur and learns to control the responses voluntarily.

Biological challenge test A procedure used to produce panic in subjects or clients by having them exercise vigorously or perform other tasks in the presence of a researcher or therapist.

Biological model The theoretical perspective that points to biological processes as the key to human behavior.

Biological therapy The use of physical and chemical procedures to help people overcome psychological problems.

Biopsychosocial theories Explanations that attribute the cause of abnormality to an interaction of genetic, biological, developmental, emotional, behavioral, cognitive, social, and societal influences.

Bipolar disorder A disorder marked by alternating or intermixed periods of mania and depression.

Bipolar I disorder A type of bipolar disorder in which a person experiences full manic and major depressive episodes.

Bipolar II disorder A type of bipolar disorder in which a person experiences mildly manic (hypomanic) episodes and major depressive episodes.

Birth complications Problematic biological conditions during birth that can affect the physical and psychological well-being of the child.

Blind design An experiment in which subjects do not know whether they are in the experimental or the control condition.

Blunted affect A symptom of schizophrenia in which a person shows less emotion than most people.

Body dysmorphic disorder A somatoform disorder marked by excessive worry that some aspect of one's physical appearance is defective. Also known as *dysmorphophobia*.

Borderline personality disorder A personality disorder in which an individual displays repeated instability in interpersonal relationships, self-image, and mood, as well as extremely impulsive behavior.

Brain region A distinct area of the brain formed by a large group of neurons.

Brain wave The fluctuations of electrical potential that are produced by neurons in the brain.

Breathing-related sleep disorder A sleep disorder in which sleep is frequently disrupted by a breathing problem, causing excessive sleepiness or insomnia.

Brief psychotic disorder Psychotic symptoms that appear suddenly after a very stressful event or a period of emotional turmoil and last anywhere from a few hours to a month.

Bulimia nervosa A disorder marked by frequent eating binges that are followed by forced vomiting or other extreme compensatory behaviors. Also known as *binge-purge syndrome*.

Caffeine A stimulant drug that is commonly consumed in the form of coffee, tea, cola, and chocolate.

Cannabis drugs Drugs produced from the different varieties of the hemp plant, *Cannabis sativa*. They cause a mixture of hallucinogenic, depressant, and stimulant effects.

Case manager A community therapist who offers a full range of services for persons with schizophrenia or other severe disorders, including therapy, advice, medication, guidance, and protection of patients' rights.

Case study A detailed account of a person's life and psychological problems.

Catatonia A pattern of extreme psychomotor symptoms, found in some forms of schizophrenia, that may include catatonic stupor, rigidity, or posturing.

Catatonic excitement A form of catatonia in which a person moves excitedly, sometimes with wild waving of the arms and legs.

Catatonic stupor A symptom associated with schizophrenia in which a person becomes almost totally unresponsive to the environment, remaining motionless and silent for long stretches of time.

Catatonic type of schizophrenia A type of schizophrenia dominated by severe psychomotor disturbances.

Catharsis The reliving of past repressed feelings in order to settle internal conflicts and overcome problems.

Caudate nuclei Structures in the brain, within the region known as the basal ganglia, that help convert sensory information into thoughts and actions.

Central nervous system The brain and spinal cord.

Cerebellum An area of the brain that coordinates movement in the body and perhaps helps control a person's rapid attention to things.

Checking compulsion A compulsion in which people feel compelled to check the same things over and over.

Child abuse The nonaccidental use of excessive physical or psychological force by an adult on a child, often aimed at hurting or destroying the child.

Chlorpromazine A phenothiazine drug commonly used for treating schizophrenia. Marketed as *Thorazine.*

Chromosomes The structures located within a cell that contain genes.

Chronic headaches Frequent intense aches in the head or neck that are not caused by another medical disorder.

Circadian rhythms Internal "clocks" consisting of repeated biological fluctuations.

Circadian rhythm sleep disorder A sleep disorder caused by a mismatch between the sleep-wake cycle in a person's environment and the person's own circadian sleep-wake cycle.

Cirrhosis An irreversible condition, often caused by excessive drinking, in which the liver becomes scarred and begins to change in anatomy and functioning.

Civil commitment A legal process by which certain individuals can be forced to undergo mental health treatment.

Clang A rhyme used by some persons with schizophrenia as a guide to forming thoughts and statements.

Classical conditioning A process of learning by temporal association in which two events that repeatedly occur close together in time become fused in a person's mind and so produce the same response.

Classification system A list of disorders, along with descriptions of symptoms and guidelines for making appropriate diagnoses.

Cleaning compulsion A common compulsion in which people feel compelled to keep cleaning themselves, their clothing, and their homes.

Client-centered therapy The humanistic therapy developed by Carl Rogers in which clinicians try to help clients by being accepting, empathizing accurately, and conveying genuineness.

Clinical interview A face-to-face encounter in which clinicians ask questions of clients, weigh their responses and reactions, and learn about them and their psychological problems.

Clinical psychologist A mental health professional who has earned a doctorate in clinical psychology.

Clinical psychology The study, assessment, treatment, and prevention of abnormal behavior.

Clitoris The female sex organ located in front of the urinary and vaginal openings. It becomes enlarged during sexual arousal.

Clozapine A commonly prescribed atypical antipsychotic drug.

Cocaine An addictive stimulant taken from the coca plant; the most powerful natural stimulant known.

Code of ethics A body of principles and rules for ethical behavior, designed to guide decisions and actions by members of a profession.

Cognition The capacity to think, remember, and anticipate.

Cognitive behavior Thoughts and beliefs, many of which remain private.

Cognitive-behavioral model A theoretical perspective that views cognitions as learned behaviors.

Cognitive model A theoretical perspective that emphasizes the process and content of thinking as causes of psychological problems.

Cognitive therapy A therapy developed by Aaron Beck that helps people identify and change the maladaptive assumptions and ways of thinking that help cause their psychological disorders.

Cognitive triad The three forms of negative thinking that theorist Aaron Beck says lead people to feel depressed. The triad consists of a negative view of one's experiences, oneself, and the future.

Coitus Sexual intercourse.

Community mental health treatment A treatment approach that emphasizes community care.

Community mental health center A community treatment facility that provides medication, psychotherapy, and, ideally, emergency care to patients and coordinates their treatment in the community.

Comorbidity The occurrence of two or more disorders in the same person.

Compulsion A repetitive and rigid behavior or mental act that persons feel they must perform in order to prevent or reduce anxiety.

Compulsive ritual A detailed, often elaborate, set of actions that a person often feels compelled to perform, always in an identical manner.

Computerized axial tomography (CAT scan) A composite image of the brain created by compiling X-ray images taken from many angles.

Concordance A statistical measure of the frequency with which family members (often both members of a pair of twins) have the same particular characteristic.

Conditioned response (CR) A response previously associated with an unconditioned stimulus that comes to be produced by a conditioned stimulus.

Conditioned stimulus (CS) A previously neutral stimulus that comes to be associated with a nonneutral stimulus, and can then produce responses similar to those produced by the nonneutral stimulus.

Conditioning A simple form of learning in which a given stimulus comes to produce a given response.

Conditions of worth According to client-centered theorists, the internal standards by which a person judges his or her own lovability and acceptability, determined by the standards to which the person was held as a child.

Conduct disorder A childhood disorder in which the child repeatedly violates the basic rights of others, displaying aggression and sometimes destroying others' property, lying, or running away from home.

Confabulation A made-up description of one's experience to fill in a gap in one's memory.

Confederate An experimenter's accomplice, who helps create a particular impression in a study while pretending to be just another subject.

Confidentiality The principle that certain professionals will not divulge the information they obtain from a client.

Confound In an experiment, a variable other than the independent variable that may also be acting on the dependent variable.

Continuous amnesia An inability to recall newly occurring events as well as certain past events.

Control group In an experiment, a group of subjects who are not exposed to the independent variable.

Conversion disorder A somatoform disorder in which a psychosocial need or conflict is converted into dramatic physical symptoms that affect voluntary motor or sensory function.

Convulsion A brain seizure.

Coronary arteries Blood vessels that surround the heart and are responsible for carrying oxygen to the heart muscle.

Coronary heart disease Illness of the heart caused by a blocking of the coronary arteries.

Correlation The degree to which events or characteristics vary along with each other.

Correlation coefficient (r) A statistical term that indicates the direction and the magnitude of a correlation, ranging from −1.00 to +1.00.

Correlational method A research procedure used to determine how much events or characteristics vary along with each other.

Corticosteroids A group of hormones released by the adrenal glands at times of stress.

Cortisol A hormone released by the adrenal glands when a person is under stress.

Counseling psychology A mental health specialty similar to clinical psychology that requires completion of its own graduate training program.

Countertransference A phenomenon of psychotherapy in which therapists' own feelings, history, and values subtly influence the way they interpret a patient's problems.

Couple therapy A therapy format in which the therapist works with two people who share a long-term relationship. Also called *marital therapy*.

Covert desensitization Desensitization that focuses on imagining confrontations with the frightening objects or situations while in a state of relaxation.

Covert sensitization A behavioral treatment for eliminating unwanted behavior by pairing the behavior with unpleasant mental images.

Crack A powerful, ready-to-smoke freebase cocaine.

Cretinism A disorder marked by mental retardation and physical abnormalities; caused by low levels of iodine in the mother's diet during pregnancy.

Creutzfeldt-Jakob disease A form of dementia caused by a slow-acting virus that may live in the body for years before the disease unfolds.

Criminal commitment A legal process by which persons accused of a crime are instead judged mentally unstable and sent to a mental health facility for treatment.

Crisis intervention A treatment approach that tries to help people in a psychological crisis view their situation more accurately, make better decisions, act more constructively, and overcome the crisis.

Critical incident stress debriefing Training in how to help victims of disasters or other horrifying events talk about their feelings and reactions to the traumatic incidents.

Cross-tolerance Tolerance that a person develops for a substance as a result of regularly using another substance similar to it.

Culture A people's common history, values, institutions, habits, skills, technology, and arts.

Culture-sensitive therapies Treatment approaches that seek to address the unique issues faced by members of various cultural and ethnic groups.

Cyclothymic disorder A disorder marked by numerous periods of hypomanic symptoms and mild depressive symptoms.

D-2 receptors The subgroup of dopamine receptors that have been linked to schizophrenia.

Day center A program that offers hospital-like treatment during the day only. Also called *day hospital*.

Death darer A person who is ambivalent about the wish to die even as he or she attempts suicide.

Death ignorer A person who attempts suicide without recognizing the finality of death.

Death initiator A person who attempts suicide believing that the process of death is already under way and that he or she is simply quickening the process.

Death seeker A person who clearly intends to end his or her life at the time of a suicide attempt.

Declarative memory Memory of learned information such as names, dates, and other facts.

Deinstitutionalization The discharge of large numbers of patients from long-term institutional care so that they might be treated in community programs.

Déjà vu The haunting sense of having previously seen or experienced a new scene or situation.

Delirium A rapidly developing clouded state of consciousness in which a person has great difficulty concentrating, focusing attention, and keeping a straightforward stream of thought.

Delirium tremens (DT's) A dramatic withdrawal reaction experienced by some people who are alcohol-dependent; consists of mental confusion, clouded consciousness, and terrifying visual hallucinations. Also called *alcohol withdrawal delirium*.

Delusion A strange false belief firmly held despite evidence to the contrary.

Delusional disorder A disorder consisting of persistent, nonbizarre delusions that are not part of a schizophrenic disorder.

Delusion of control The belief that one's impulses, feelings, thoughts, or actions are being controlled by other people.

Delusion of grandeur The belief that one is a great inventor, historical figure, or other specially empowered person.

Delusion of persecution The belief that one is being plotted or discriminated against, spied on, slandered, threatened, attacked, or deliberately victimized.

Delusion of reference A belief that attaches special and personal meaning to the actions of others or to various objects or events.

Dementia A syndrome marked by severe problems in memory and at least one other cognitive function.

Demonology The belief that abnormal behavior results from supernatural causes such as evil spirits.

Dendrite An extension located at one end of a neuron that receives impulses from other neurons.

Denial An ego defense mechanism in which a person fails to acknowledge unacceptable thoughts, feelings, or actions.

Dependent personality disorder A personality disorder characterized by a pattern of clinging and obedience, fear of separation, and a persistent, excessive need to be taken care of.

Dependent variable The variable in an experiment that is expected to change as the independent variable is manipulated.

Depersonalization disorder A disorder marked by a persistent and recurrent feeling of being detached from one's own mental processes or body; that is, one feels unreal and alien.

Depressant A substance that slows the activity of the central nervous system and in sufficient dosages causes a reduction of tension and inhibitions.

Depression A low state marked by significant levels of sadness, lack of energy, low self-worth, guilt, or related symptoms.

Derailment A common thinking disturbance in schizophrenia, involving rapid shifts from one topic of conversation to another. Also called *loose associations*.

Desensitization *See* Systematic desensitization.

Desire phase The phase of the sexual response cycle consisting of an urge to have sex, sexual fantasies, and sexual attraction to others.

Detoxification Systematic and medically supervised withdrawal from a drug.

Deviance Variance from common patterns of behavior.

Diagnosis A determination that a person's problems reflect a particular disorder.

***Diagnostic and Statistical Manual of Mental Disorders* (DSM)** The classification system for mental disorders developed by the American Psychiatric Association.

Diathesis–stress view The view that a person must first have a predisposition to a disorder and then be subjected to immediate psychosocial stress in order to develop the disorder.

Diazepam A benzodiazepine drug, marketed as *Valium*.

Dichotomous thinking Viewing problems and solutions in rigid "either/or" terms.

Diencephalon A brain area (consisting of the mammillary bodies, thalamus, and hypothalamus) that plays a key role in transforming short-term to long-term memory, among other functions.

Directed masturbation training A sex therapy approach that teaches women with female arousal or orgasmic disorders how to masturbate effectively and eventually to reach orgasm during sexual interactions.

Disaster Response Network (DRN) A network of thousands of volunteer mental health professionals who mobilize to provide free emergency psychological services at disaster sites throughout North America.

Disorganized type of schizophrenia A type of schizophrenia marked primarily by confusion, incoherence, and flat or inappropriate affect.

Displacement An ego defense mechanism that channels unacceptable id impulses toward another, safer substitute.

Dissociative amnesia A dissociative disorder marked by an inability to recall important personal events and information.

Dissociative disorders Disorders marked by major changes in memory that are not due to clear physical causes.

Dissociative fugue A dissociative disorder in which a person travels to a new location and may assume a new identity, simultaneously forgetting his or her past.

Dissociative identity disorder A disorder in which a person develops two or more distinct personalities. Also called *multiple personality disorder*.

Disulfiram (Antabuse) An antagonist drug used in treating alcohol abuse or dependence.

Dopamine The neurotransmitter whose high activity has been shown to be related to schizophrenia.

Dopamine hypothesis The theory that schizophrenia results from excessive activity of the neurotransmitter dopamine.

Double-bind hypothesis A theory that some parents repeatedly communicate pairs of messages that are mutually contradictory, helping to produce schizophrenia in their children.

Double-blind design Experimental procedure in which neither the subject nor the experimenter knows whether the subject has received the experimental treatment or a placebo.

Double depression A sequence in which dysthymic disorder leads to a major depressive disorder.

Down syndrome A form of mental retardation related to an abnormality in the twenty-first chromosome.

Drapetomania According to a nineteenth-century diagnostic category, an obsessive desire for freedom that drove some slaves to try to flee from captivity.

Dream A series of ideas and images that form during sleep and are interpreted by psychodynamic theorists as clues to the unconscious.

Drug Any substance other than food that affects the body or mind.

Drug maintenance therapy An approach to treating substance dependence in which clients are given legally and medically supervised doses of the drug on which they are dependent or a substitute drug.

Drug therapy The use of psychotropic drugs to reduce the symptoms of psychological disorders.

DSM-IV-TR The text revision of DSM-IV, the current edition of the *Diagnostic and Statistical Manual of Mental Disorders*.

Durham test A legal test for insanity that holds people to be insane at the time of committing a crime if the act was the result of a mental disorder or defect.

Duty to protect The principle that therapists must break confidentiality in order to protect a person who may be the intended victim of a client.

Dyslexia A disorder in which persons show a marked impairment in the ability to recognize words and to comprehend what they read. Also known as *reading disorder*.

Dyspareunia A disorder in which a person experiences severe pain in the genitals during sexual activity.

Dyssomnias Sleep disorders in which the amount, quality, or timing of sleep is disturbed.

Dysthymic disorder A mood disorder that is similar to but longer-lasting and less disabling than a major depressive disorder.

Eccentric A person who deviates from an established behavioral pattern or exhibits odd or whimsical behavior.

Echolalia A symptom of autism or schizophrenia in which a person responds to statements by repeating the other person's words.

Ego According to Freud, the psychological force that employs reason and operates in accordance with the reality principle.

Ego defense mechanisms According to psychoanalytic theory, strategies developed by the ego to control unacceptable id impulses and to avoid or reduce the anxiety they arouse.

Egoistic suicide Suicide committed by people over whom society has little or no control, people who are not concerned with the norms or rules of society.

Ego theory The psychodynamic theory that emphasizes the ego and considers it an independent force.

Eidetic imagery A strong visual image of an object or scene that persists in some persons long after the object or scene is removed.

Ejaculation Contractions of the muscles at the base of the penis that cause sperm to be ejected.

Electra complex According to Freud, the pattern of desires all girls experience during the phallic stage, in which they develop a sexual attraction to their father.

Electroconvulsive therapy (ECT) A form of treatment, used primarily in cases of unipolar depression, in which electrodes attached to a person's head send an electric current through the brain, causing a brain seizure.

Electroencephalograph (EEG) A device that records electrical impulses in the brain.

Electromyograph (EMG) A device that provides feedback about the level of muscular tension in the body.

Electrooculograph A device that records the movement of the eyes.

Emergency commitment Temporary commitment to a mental hospital of a patient who is behaving in a bizarre or violent way.

Employee assistance program A mental health program that some businesses offer to their employees.

Encopresis A childhood disorder characterized by repeated defecation in inappropriate places, such as into one's clothing.

Endocrine system The system of glands located throughout the body that helps control important activities such as growth and sexual activity.

Endogenous depression A depression that appears to develop without external reasons and is assumed to be caused by internal factors.

Endorphins Neurotransmitters that help relieve pain and reduce emotional tension; sometimes referred to as the body's own opioids.

Enmeshed family pattern A family system in which members are overinvolved with each other's affairs and overconcerned about each other's welfare.

Enuresis A childhood disorder marked by repeated bed-wetting or wetting of one's clothes.

Epidemiological study A study that measures the incidence and prevalence of a disorder in a given population.

Ergot alkaloid A naturally occurring compound from which LSD is derived.

Essential hypertension High blood pressure caused by a combination of psychosocial and physiological factors.

Estrogen The primary female sex hormone.

Ethyl alcohol The chemical compound in all alcoholic beverages that is rapidly absorbed into the blood and immediately begins to affect the person's functioning.

Evoked potentials The brain response patterns recorded on an electroencephalograph while a person performs a task such as observing a flashing light.

Excitement phase The phase of the sexual response cycle marked by changes in the pelvic region, general physical arousal, and increases in heart rate, muscle tension, blood pressure, and rate of breathing.

Exhibitionism A paraphilia in which persons have repeated sexually arousing urges or fantasies about exposing their genitals to another person and may act upon those urges.

Existential anxiety According to existential theorists, a universal fear of the limits and responsibilities of one's existence.

Existential model The theoretical perspective that human beings are born with the total freedom to either face up to one's existence and give meaning to one's life or to shrink from that responsibility.

Existential therapy A therapy that encourages people to accept responsibility for their lives and to live with greater meaning and values.

Exorcism The practice in early societies of treating abnormality by coaxing evil spirits to leave the person's body.

Experiment A research procedure in which a variable is manipulated and the effect of the manipulation is observed.

Experimental group In an experiment, the subjects who are exposed to the independent variable under investigation.

Exposure and response prevention A behavioral treatment for obsessive-compulsive disorder in which individuals are exposed to anxiety-arousing thoughts or situations and then prevented from performing their compulsive acts.

Exposure treatments Behavioral treatments in which persons with fears are exposed to their dreaded objects or situations.

Expressed emotion The general level of criticism, disapproval, hostility, and intrusiveness expressed in a family.

External validity The degree to which the results of a study may be generalized beyond that study.

Extrapyramidal effects Unwanted movements, such as severe shaking, bizarre-looking twisting of the face and body, and extreme restlessness, sometimes produced by traditional antipsychotic drugs.

Eye movement desensitization and reprocessing A behavioral exposure treatment in which clients move their eyes in a saccadic (rhythmic) manner from side to side while flooding their minds with images of objects and situations they ordinarily avoid.

Facilitated communication A controversial method for teaching individuals with autism to communicate. The therapist, or "facilitator," provides physical assistance as the individual types or points to letters on a keyboard or communication board.

Factitious disorder An illness with no identifiable physical cause in which the patient is believed to be intentionally producing or faking symptoms in order to assume a sick role.

Family pedigree study A research design in which investigators determine how many and which relatives of a person with a disorder have the same disorder.

Family systems theory A theory that views the family as a system of interacting parts and proposes that members interact in consistent ways and operate by unstated rules.

Family therapy A therapy format in which the therapist meets with all members of a family and helps them change in therapeutic ways.

Fantasy An ego defense mechanism in which a person uses imaginary events to satisfy unacceptable impulses.

Fear The central nervous system's physiological and emotional response to a serious threat to one's well-being.

Fear hierarchy A list of objects or situations that frighten a person, starting with those that are slightly feared and ending with those that are feared greatly; used in systematic desensitization.

Female orgasmic disorder A dysfunction in which a woman rarely has an orgasm or repeatedly experiences a very delayed one following a normal sexual excitement phase.

Female sexual arousal disorder A female dysfunction marked by a persistent inability to attain or maintain adequate lubrication or genital swelling during sexual activity.

Fetal alcohol syndrome A group of problems in a child, including lower intellectual functioning, low birth weight, and irregularities in the hands and face, that result from excessive alcohol intake by the mother during pregnancy.

Fetishism A paraphilia consisting of recurrent and intense sexual urges, fantasies, or behaviors that involve the use of a nonliving object, often to the exclusion of all other stimuli.

Fixation According to Freud, a condition in which the id, ego, and superego do not mature properly, causing the person to become entrapped at an early stage of development.

Flashback The recurrence of LSD-induced sensory and emotional changes long after the drug has left the body. Or, in posttraumatic stress disorder, the reexperiencing of past traumatic events.

Flat affect A symptom of schizophrenia in which the person shows almost no emotion at all.

Flooding A treatment for phobias in which a person is exposed repeatedly and intensively to a feared object and made to see that it is actually harmless.

Forensic psychology The branch of psychology concerned with intersections between psychological practice and research and the judicial system. Also related to the field of *forensic psychiatry*.

Formal thought disorder A disturbance in the production and organization of thought.

Free association A psychodynamic technique in which a person describes any thought, feeling, or image that comes to mind, even if it seems unimportant.

Free-base A technique for ingesting cocaine in which the pure-cocaine basic alkaloid is chemically separated from processed cocaine, vaporized by heat from a flame, and inhaled through a pipe.

Free-floating anxiety Chronic and persistent feelings of anxiety that are not clearly attached to a specific, identifiable threat.

Frotteurism A paraphilia consisting of repeated and intense sexual urges, fantasies, or behaviors that involve touching and rubbing against a nonconsenting person.

Fusion The final merging of two or more subpersonalities in multiple personality disorder.

Galvanic skin response (GSR) Changes in the electrical resistance of the skin.

Gamma aminobutyric acid (GABA) A neurotransmitter whose low activity has been linked to generalized anxiety disorder.

Gender identity disorder A disorder in which a person persistently feels extremely uncomfortable about his or her assigned sex and strongly wishes to be a member of the opposite sex. Also called *transsexualism*.

Gender-sensitive therapies Treatment approaches geared to the special pressures of being a woman in Western society. Also called *feminist therapies*.

Generalized amnesia A loss of memory for events that occurred over a limited period of time as well as for certain events that occurred prior to that period.

Generalized anxiety disorder A disorder marked by persistent and excessive feelings of anxiety and worry about numerous events and activities.

General paresis An irreversible medical disorder whose symptoms include psychological abnormalities, such as delusions of grandeur; caused by syphilis.

Genes Chromosome segments that control the characteristics and traits we inherit.

Genetic linkage study A research approach in which extended families with high rates of a disorder over several generations are observed in order to determine whether the disorder closely follows the distribution pattern of other family traits.

Genital stage In Freud's theory, the stage beginning at approximately 12 years old, when the child begins to find sexual pleasure in heterosexual relationships.

Geropsychology The field of psychology concerned with the mental health of elderly people.

Gestalt therapy The humanistic therapy developed by Fritz Perls in which clinicians actively move individuals toward self-recognition and self-acceptance by using techniques such as role playing and skillful frustration.

Glia Brain cells that support the neurons.

Glutamate A common neurotransmitter that has been linked to memory and to dementia.

Grief The reaction one experiences when a loved one is lost.

Group home A special home where people with disorders or disabilities live and are taught self-help, living, and working skills.

Group therapy A therapy format in which a group of people with similar problems meet together with a therapist to work on their problems.

Guided participation A modeling technique in which a client systematically observes and imitates the therapist while the therapist confronts feared items.

Guilty but mentally ill A verdict stating that defendants are guilty of committing a crime but are also suffering from a mental illness that should be treated during their imprisonment.

Habituation training A therapeutic technique in which a therapist tries to call forth a client's obsessive thoughts again and again, with the expectation that the thoughts will eventually lose their threatening meaning and cause less anxiety.

Halfway house A residence for people with severe psychological problems who cannot yet live alone or with their families; often staffed by paraprofessionals. Also known as *group home.*

Hallucination The experiencing of imagined sights, sounds, or other sensory experiences as if they were real.

Hallucinogens Substances that primarily cause powerful changes in sensory perception, including strengthening a person's perceptions and producing illusions and hallucinations. Also called *psychedelic drugs.*

Hallucinosis A form of intoxication caused by hallucinogens, consisting of perceptual distortions and hallucinations.

Hardiness A set of positive attitudes and reactions in response to stress.

Health maintenance The principle that young adults should act to promote their physical and mental health to best prepare for the aging process. Also called *wellness.*

Helper T-cell A lymphocyte that identifies foreign invaders and then both multiplies and triggers the production of other kinds of immune cells.

Heroin A highly addictive substance derived from morphine; illegal in the United States under all circumstances.

High The pleasant feeling of relaxation and euphoria that follows the rush from certain recreational drugs.

Hippocampus A brain area located below the cerebral cortex that is involved in memory.

Histrionic personality disorder A personality disorder in which an individual displays a pattern of excessive emotionality and attention seeking. Once called *hysterical personality disorder.*

Homosexuality Sexual preference for a person of one's own gender.

Hopelessness A pessimistic belief that one's present circumstances, problems, or mood will not change.

Hormones The chemicals released by glands into the bloodstream.

Humanistic model The theoretical perspective that human beings are born with a natural inclination to be friendly, cooperative, and constructive and are driven to self-actualize.

Humanistic therapy A system of therapy that tries to help clients look at themselves accurately and acceptingly so that they can fulfill their positive inborn potential.

Humors According to Greek and Roman physicians, bodily chemicals that influence mental and physical functioning.

Huntington's disease An inherited disease, characterized by progressive problems in cognition, emotion, and movement, which results in dementia.

Hypertension Chronic high blood pressure.

Hypnosis A sleeplike suggestible state during which a person can be directed to act in unusual ways, to experience unusual sensations, to remember seemingly forgotten events, or to forget remembered events.

Hypnotic amnesia Loss of memory produced by hypnotic suggestion.

Hypnotic therapy A treatment in which a person undergoes hypnosis and is then guided to recall forgotten events or perform other therapeutic activities. Also called *hypnotherapy.*

Hypnotism A procedure that places persons in a trancelike mental state during which they become extremely suggestible.

Hypoactive sexual desire disorder A disorder marked by a lack of interest in sex.

Hypochondriasis A somatoform disorder in which people mistakenly fear that minor changes in their physical functioning indicate a serious disease.

Hypomanic pattern A pattern in which a person displays symptoms of mania, but the symptoms are less severe and cause less impairment than a manic episode.

Hypothalamic-pituitary-adrenal (HPA) pathway One route by which the brain and body produce arousal and fear. At times of stress, the hypothalamus signals the pituitary gland, which in turn signals the adrenal glands. Stress hormones are then released to various body organs.

Hypothalamus A part of the brain that helps maintain various bodily functions, including eating and hunger.

Hypothesis A hunch or prediction that certain variables are related in certain ways.

Hypoxyphilia A pattern in which people strangle or smother themselves, or ask their partners to strangle or smother them, to increase their sexual pleasure.

Hysteria A term once used to describe what are now known as conversion disorder, somatization disorder, and pain disorder associated with psychological factors.

Hysterical disorder A disorder in which physical functioning is changed or lost, without an apparent physical cause.

Hysterical somatoform disorders Somatoform disorders in which people experience actual changes in their physical functioning.

Iatrogenic disorder A disorder that is unintentionally produced by a practitioner.

Id According to Freud, the psychological force that produces instinctual needs, drives, and impulses.

Ideas of reference Beliefs that unrelated events pertain to oneself in some important way.

Identification Unconsciously incorporating the values and feelings of one's parents and fusing them with one's identity. Also, an ego defense mechanism in which persons take on the values and feelings of a person who is causing them anxiety.

Idiographic understanding An understanding of the behavior of a particular individual.

Illogical thinking According to cognitive theories, illogical ways of thinking that may lead to self-defeating conclusions and psychological problems.

Immune system The body's network of activities and cells that identify and destroy antigens and cancer cells.

Impulse-control disorders Disorders in which people repeatedly fail to resist an impulse, drive, or temptation to perform an act that is harmful to themselves or to others.

Inappropriate affect A symptom of schizophrenia in which a person displays emotions that are unsuited to the situation.

Incest Sexual relations between close relatives.

Incidence The number of new cases of a disorder occurring in a population over a specific period of time.

Independent variable The variable in an experiment that is manipulated to determine whether it has an effect on another variable.

Individual therapy A therapeutic approach in which a therapist sees a client alone for sessions that may last from fifteen minutes to two hours.

Insanity defense A legal defense in which persons charged with a criminal offense claim to be not guilty by reason of insanity at the time of the crime.

Insomnia The most common dyssomnia, characterized by difficulties initiating and maintaining sleep.

Integrity test A test that seeks to measure whether the test taker is generally honest or dishonest.

Intelligence quotient (IQ) A general score derived from an intelligence test that theoretically represents a person's overall intellectual capacity.

Intelligence test A test designed to measure a person's intellectual ability.

Intermittent explosive disorder An impulse-control disorder in which people periodically fail to resist aggressive impulses and commit serious assaults on other people or destroy property.

Internal validity The accuracy with which a study can pinpoint one of various possible factors as the cause of a phenomenon.

International Classification of Diseases (ICD) The classification system for medical and mental disorders that is used by the World Health Organization.

Interpersonal psychotherapy (IPT) A treatment for unipolar depression that is based on the belief that clarifying and changing one's interpersonal problems will help lead to recovery.

Intoxication A temporary drug-induced state in which people display symptoms such as impaired judgment, mood changes, irritability, slurred speech, and loss of coordination.

In vivo desensitization Desensitization that makes use of actual objects or situations, as opposed to imagined ones.

Irresistible impulse test A legal test for insanity that holds people to be insane at the time of committing a crime if they were driven to do so by an uncontrollable "fit of passion."

Isolation An ego defense mechanism in which people unconsciously isolate and disown undesirable and unwanted thoughts, experiencing them as foreign intrusions.

Jamais vu The experience of not recognizing a scene or situation that one has previously experienced.

Killer T-cell A lymphocyte that seeks out and destroys body cells that have been infected by viruses.

Kleptomania An impulse-control disorder characterized by the recurrent failure to resist impulses to steal objects not needed for personal use or monetary value.

Korsakoff's syndrome An amnestic disorder marked by extreme confusion, memory impairment, and other neurological symptoms; caused by long-term alcoholism, an accompanying poor diet, and, in turn, a deficiency of vitamin B (thiamine).

Latency stage In psychoanalytic theory, the stage children enter at 6 years of age in which their sexual desires apparently subside.

Latent content The symbolic meaning behind a dream's content.

Lateral hypothalamus (LH) The region of the hypothalamus that, when activated, produces hunger.

L-dopa A drug used in the treatment of Parkinson's disease, a disease in which dopamine is low.

Learned helplessness The perception, based on past experiences, that one has no control over one's reinforcements.

Learning disorder A developmental disorder marked by impairments in cognitive skills such as reading, mathematics, or language.

Libido The sexual energy that fuels the id.

Life change units (LCUs) A system for measuring the stress associated with various life events.

Light therapy A treatment for seasonal affective disorder in which patients are exposed to extra light for several hours. Also called *phototherapy*.

Lithium A metallic element that occurs in nature as a mineral salt and is a highly effective treatment for bipolar disorders.

Lobotomy Psychosurgery in which a surgeon cuts the connections between the brain's frontal lobes and the lower centers of the brain.

Localized amnesia An inability to recall any of the events that occurred over a limited period of time.

Locus ceruleus A small area of the brain that seems to be active in the regulation of emotions. Many of its neurons use norepinephrine.

Longitudinal study A study that observes the same subjects on many occasions over a long period of time.

Long-term care Extended personal and medical support provided to elderly and other persons who may be impaired. It may range from partial support in a supervised apartment to intensive care at a nursing home.

Long-term memory The memory system that contains all the information that a person has stored over the years.

Loose associations A common thinking disturbance in schizophrenia, involving rapid shifts from one topic of conversation to another. Also known as *derailment*.

Lycanthropy A condition in which persons believe themselves to be possessed by wolves or other animals.

Lymphocytes White blood cells that circulate through the lymph system and bloodstream, helping the body identify and destroy antigens and cancer cells.

Lysergic acid diethylamide (LSD) A hallucinogenic drug derived from ergot alkaloids.

Magnetic resonance imaging (MRI) The use of the magnetic property of certain atoms in the brain to create a detailed picture of the brain's structure.

Mainstreaming An approach to educating children with mental retardation in which they are placed in regular classes with children who are not mentally retarded. Also called *inclusion*.

Major depressive disorder A severe pattern of depression that is disabling and is not caused by such factors as drugs or a general medical condition.

Male erectile disorder A dysfunction in which a man persistently fails to attain or maintain an erection during sexual activity.

Male orgasmic disorder A male dysfunction characterized by a repeated inability to reach orgasm or by long delays in reaching orgasm after normal sexual excitement.

Malingering Intentionally faking illness to achieve some external gains, such as financial compensation or military deferment.

Malpractice suit A lawsuit charging a therapist with improper conduct or decision-making in the course of treatment.

Managed care program A system of health-care coverage in which the insurance company largely controls the cost, method, provider, and length of treatment.

Mania A state or episode of euphoria or frenzied activity in which people may have an exaggerated belief that the world is theirs for the taking.

Manifest content The consciously remembered content of a dream.

Mantra A sound, uttered or thought, used to focus one's attention and to turn away from ordinary thoughts and concerns during meditation.

MAO inhibitor An antidepressant drug that prevents the action of the enzyme monoamine oxidase.

Marijuana One of the cannabis drugs, derived from the leaves and flowering tops of the hemp plant, *Cannabis sativa*.

Marital therapy A therapy approach in which the therapist works with two people who share a long-term relationship. Also known as *couple therapy.*

Masturbation Self-stimulation of the genitals to achieve sexual arousal.

Masturbatory satiation A behavioral treatment in which a client masturbates for a very long period of time while fantasizing in detail about a paraphilic object. The procedure is expected to produce a feeling of boredom that in turn becomes linked to the object.

Mean The average of a group of scores.

Meditation A technique of turning one's concentration inward and achieving a slightly changed state of consciousness.

Melancholia A condition described by early Greek and Roman philosophers and physicians as consisting of unshakable sadness. Today it is known as *depression.*

Melatonin A hormone released by the pineal gland when a person's surroundings are dark.

Memory The faculty for recalling past events and past learning.

Mental incompetence A state of mental instability that leaves defendants unable to understand the legal charges and proceedings they are facing and unable to adequately prepare a defense with their attorneys.

Mentally ill chemical abusers (MICAs) Persons suffering from both schizophrenia (or another severe psychological disorder) and a substance-related disorder.

Mental retardation A disorder in which people display general intellectual functioning and adaptive behavior that are well below average.

Mental status exam A set of interview questions and observations designed to reveal the degree and nature of a person's abnormal functioning.

Mesmerism The method employed by Austrian physician F. A. Mesmer to treat hysterical disorders; a precursor of *hypnotism.*

Metabolism An organism's chemical and physical breakdown of food and the process of converting it into energy. Also, an organism's biochemical transformation of various substances, as when the liver breaks down alcohol into acetylaldehyde.

Methadone A laboratory-made opioidlike drug.

Methadone maintenance program An approach to treating heroin dependence in which people are given legally and medically supervised doses of methadone, a laboratory-produced opioid, as a substitute for heroin.

Methylphenidate A stimulant drug, known better by the trade name Ritalin, commonly used to treat ADHD.

Migraine headache An extremely severe headache that occurs on one side of the head, often preceded by a warning sensation and sometimes accompanied by dizziness, nausea, or vomiting.

Mild retardation A level of mental retardation (IQ between 50 and 70) at which persons can benefit from education and support themselves as adults.

Milieu therapy A humanistic approach to institutional treatment based on the belief that institutions can help patients recover by creating a climate that builds self-respect, individual responsibility, and meaningful activity.

Mind-body dualism René Descartes's position that the mind is separate from the body.

Minnesota Multiphasic Personality Inventory (MMPI) A widely used personality inventory consisting of a large number of statements that subjects mark as being true or false for them.

Mixed design A research design in which a correlational method is mixed with an experimental method. Also known as *quasi-experiment.*

M'Naghten test A widely used legal test for insanity that holds people to be insane at the time of committing a crime if, because of a mental disorder, they did not know the nature of the act or did not know right from wrong.

Model A set of assumptions and concepts that helps scientists explain and interpret observations. Also called *paradigm.*

Modeling A process of learning in which an individual acquires responses by observing and imitating others. Also, a therapy approach based on the same principle.

Moderate retardation A level of mental retardation (IQ between 35 and 49) in which persons can learn to care for themselves and benefit from vocational training.

Monoamine oxidase (MAO) A body chemical that destroys the neurotransmitter norepinephrine.

Monoamine oxidase (MAO) inhibitors Antidepressant drugs that lower MAO activity and thus increase the level of norepinephrine activity in the brain.

Mood disorder A disorder affecting one's emotional state, including major depressive disorder and bipolar disorders.

Moral treatment A nineteenth-century approach to treating people with mental dysfunction which emphasized moral guidance and humane and respectful treatment.

Morphine A highly addictive substance derived from opium that is particularly effective in relieving pain.

Multiaxial system A classification system in which different "axes," or branches of information, are required from the diagnostician. DSM-IV-TR is a multiaxial system.

Multicultural perspective The view that each culture within a larger society has a particular set of values and beliefs, as well as special external factors, that help account for the behavior and functioning of its members.

Multicultural psychology The field of psychology that examines the impact of culture, race, ethnicity, gender, and similar factors on our behaviors and thoughts, and also focuses on how such factors may influence the origin, nature, and treatment of abnormal behavior.

Multidimensional risk perspective A theory that identifies several different kinds of risk factors that may combine to help cause a disorder. The more such factors present, the greater the risk of developing the disorder.

Multiple personality disorder A dissociative disorder in which a person develops two or more distinct personalities. Also called *dissociative identity disorder.*

Munchausen syndrome An extreme and long-term form of factitious disorder in which a person produces symptoms, gains admission to a hospital, and receives treatment.

Munchausen syndrome by proxy A factitious disorder in which parents make up or produce physical illnesses in their children.

Muscle contraction headache A headache caused by the narrowing of muscles surrounding the skull. Also called *tension headache.*

Narcissistic personality disorder A personality disorder marked by a broad pattern of grandiosity, need for admiration, and lack of empathy.

Narcolepsy A dyssomnia characterized by sudden onsets of REM sleep during waking hours, generally brought on by strong emotion.

Narcotic Any natural or synthetic opioidlike drug.

Narcotic antagonist A substance that attaches to opioid receptors in the brain and, in turn, blocks the effects of opioids.

Natural experiment An experiment in which nature, rather than an experimenter, manipulates an independent variable.

Naturalistic observation A method of observing behavior in which clinicians or researchers observe people in their everyday environments.

Negative correlation A statistical relationship in which the value of one variable increases while the other variable decreases.

Negative symptoms Symptoms of schizophrenia that seem to be deficits of normal thought, emotion, or behavior.

Neologism A made-up word that has meaning only to the person using it.

Nerve ending The region at the end of a neuron from which an impulse is sent to a neighboring neuron.

Neurofibrillary tangles Twisted protein fibers that form within certain brain cells as people age.

Neuroimaging techniques Neurological tests that provide images of brain structure or brain activity, including CT scans, PET scans, and MRIs.

Neuroleptic drugs A term used for the traditional antipsychotic drugs because they often produce undesired effects similar to the symptoms of neurological disorders.

Neuroleptic malignant syndrome A severe, potentially fatal reaction to antipsychotic drugs, marked by muscle rigidity, fever, altered consciousness, and autonomic dysfunction.

Neurological Relating to the structure or activity of the brain.

Neurological test A test that directly measures brain structure or activity.

Neuromodulator A neurotransmitter that helps modify or regulate the effect of other neurotransmitters.

Neuron A nerve cell. The brain contains billions of neurons.

Neuropsychological test A test that detects brain impairment by measuring a person's cognitive, perceptual, and motor performances.

Neurosis Freud's term for disorders characterized by intense anxiety, attributed to failure of a person's ego defense mechanisms to cope with unconscious conflicts.

Neurotransmitter A chemical that, released by one neuron, crosses the synaptic space to be received at receptors on the dendrites of neighboring neurons.

Neutralizing Attempting to eliminate thoughts that one finds unaccetable by thinking or behaving in ways that make up for those thoughts and so put matters right internally.

Nicotine patch A patch attached to the skin like a Band-Aid, with nicotine content that is absorbed through the skin, that supposedly eases the withdrawal reaction brought on by quitting cigarette smoking.

Nightmare disorder A parasomnia characterized by chronic distressful, frightening dreams.

Nocturnal penile tumescence (NPT) The occurrence of erections during sleep.

Nomothetic understanding A general understanding of the nature, causes, and treatments of abnormal psychological functioning in the form of laws or principles.

Norepinephrine A neurotransmitter whose abnormal activity is linked to depression and panic disorder.

Normalization The principle that institutions and community residences should expose persons with mental retardation to living conditions and opportunities similar to those found in the rest of society.

Norms A society's stated and unstated rules for proper conduct.

Not guilty by reason of insanity (NGRI) A verdict stating that defendants are not guilty of committing a crime because they were insane at the time of the crime.

Object relations theory The psychodynamic theory that views the desire for relationships as the key motivating force in human behavior.

Observer drift The tendency of an observer who is rating subjects in an experiment to gradually and involuntarily change criteria, thus making the data unreliable.

Obsession A persistent thought, idea, impulse, or image that is experienced repeatedly, feels intrusive, and causes anxiety.

Obsessive-compulsive disorder A disorder characterized by recurrent and unwanted thoughts and/or a need to perform rigidly repetitive physical or mental actions.

Obsessive-compulsive personality disorder A personality disorder in which an individual is so focused on orderliness, perfectionism, and control that he or she loses flexibility, openness, and efficiency.

Oedipus complex In Freudian theory, the pattern of desires emerging during the phallic stage in which boys become attracted to their mother as a sexual object and see their father as a rival they would like to push aside.

Operant conditioning A process of learning in which behavior that leads to satisfying consequences, or rewards, is likely to be repeated.

Opioid Opium or any of the drugs derived from opium, including morphine, heroin, and codeine.

Opium A highly addictive substance made from the sap of the opium poppy seed.

Oppositional defiant disorder A childhood disorder in which children argue repeatedly with adults, lose their temper, and feel great anger and resentment.

Oral stage The earliest developmental stage in Freud's conceptualization of psychosexual development during which the infant's main gratification comes from feeding and from the body parts involved in it.

Orbitofrontal cortex A region of the brain in which impulses involving excretion, sexuality, violence, and other primitive activities normally arise.

Orgasm A peaking of sexual pleasure, consisting of rhythmic muscular contractions in the pelvic region, during which a man's semen is ejaculated and the outer third of a woman's vaginal wall contracts.

Orgasmic reorientation A procedure for treating certain paraphilias by teaching clients to respond to new, more appropriate sources of sexual stimulation.

Orgasm phase The phase of the sexual response cycle during which an individual's sexual pleasure peaks and sexual tension is released as muscles in the pelvic region contract rhythmically.

Outpatient A person who receives diagnosis or treatment in a clinic, hospital, or therapist's office but is not hospitalized overnight.

Pain disorder associated with psychological factors A somatoform disorder marked by pain, with psychosocial factors playing a central role in the onset, severity, or continuation of the pain.

Panic attack A short bout of panic that occurs suddenly, reaches a peak within minutes, and gradually passes.

Panic disorder An anxiety disorder marked by recurrent and unpredictable panic attacks.

Panic disorder with agoraphobia A panic disorder in which panic attacks lead to agoraphobic patterns of behavior.

Paranoid personality disorder A personality disorder marked by a pattern of extreme distrust and suspiciousness of others.

Paranoid type of schizophrenia A type of schizophrenia in which the person has an organized system of delusions and hallucinations.

Paraphilias Disorders characterized by recurrent and intense sexual urges, fantasies, or behaviors involving nonhuman objects, children, nonconsenting adults, or experiences of suffering or humiliation.

Paraprofessional A person without previous professional training who provides services under the supervision of a mental health professional.

Parasomnias Sleep disorders characterized by the occurrence of abnormal events during sleep.

Parasuicide A suicide attempt that does not result in death.

Parasympathetic nervous system The group of nerve fibers of the autonomic nervous system that help maintain normal organ functioning. They slow organ functioning after stimulation and help return other bodily processes to normal.

Parens patriae The principle by which the state can make decisions to promote the individual's best interests and protect him or her from self-harm or neglect.

Parkinsonian symptoms Symptoms similar to those found in Parkinson's disease. Patients with schizophrenia who take conventional antipsychotic medications may display one or more of these symptoms.

Parkinson's disease A slowly progressive neurological disease, marked by tremors and rigidity, that may also cause dementia.

Participant modeling A behavioral treatment in which people with fears observe a therapist (model) interacting with a feared object and then interact with the object themselves.

Passive-aggressive personality disorder A category of personality disorder, listed in past versions of DSM, marked by a pattern of negative attitudes and resistance to the demands of others.

Pathological gambling An impulse-control disorder characterized by recurrent and persistent maladaptive gambling behavior that disrupts personal, family, or vocational pursuits.

Pedophilia A paraphilia in which a person has repeated and intense sexual urges or fantasies about watching, touching, or engaging in sexual acts with prepubescent children, and may carry out these urges or fantasies.

Peer review system A system by which clinicians paid by an insurance company may periodically review a patient's progress and recommend the continuation or termination of insurance benefits.

Penile prosthesis A surgical implant consisting of a semirigid rod made of rubber and wire that produces an artificial erection.

Performance anxiety The fear of performing inadequately and a related tension experienced during sex.

Perseveration The persistent repetition of words and statements.

Personality A unique and long-term pattern of inner experience and outward behavior that leads to consistent reactions across various situations.

Personality disorder A very rigid pattern of inner experience and outward behavior that differs from the expectations of one's culture and leads to dysfunctioning.

Personality inventory A test designed to measure broad personality characteristics that consists of statements about behaviors, beliefs, and feelings. People evaluate the statements as either characteristic or uncharacteristic of themselves.

Pervasive developmental disorders A broad category of disorders beginning in early childhood, characterized by severe and pervasive impairments in social interaction and communication or the presence of rigid and repetitive behaviors, interests, and activities.

Phallic stage In psychoanalytic theory, the period between the third and fourth years when the focus of sexual pleasure shifts to the genitals.

Phalloplasty A surgical procedure designed to create a functional penis.

Phenothiazines A group of antihistamine drugs that became the first group of effective antipsychotic medications.

Phenylketonuria (PKU) A metabolic disorder caused by the body's inability to break down the amino acid phenylalanine, resulting in mental retardation and other symptoms.

Phobia A persistent and unreasonable fear of a particular object, activity, or situation.

Pick's disease A neurological disease that affects the frontal and temporal lobes, causing dementia.

Placebo A sham treatment that a subject believes to be genuine.

Placebo therapy A sham treatment that the subject in an experiment believes to be genuine.

Play therapy An approach to treating childhood disorders that helps children express their conflicts and feelings indirectly by drawing, playing with toys, and making up stories.

Pleasure principle The pursuit of gratification that characterizes id functioning.

Plethysmograph A device used to measure sexual arousal.

Polygraph A test that seeks to determine whether or not the test taker is telling the truth by measuring physiological responses such as respiration level, perspiration level, and heart rate. Also known as a *lie-detector test*.

Polysubstance use The use of two or more substances at the same time.

Polysubstance-related disorder A long-term pattern of maladaptive behavior centered on the abuse of or dependence on a combination of drugs.

Positive correlation A statistical relationship in which the values of two variables increase together or decrease together.

Positive psychology The study and enhancement of positive feelings, traits, and abilities.

Positive symptoms Symptoms of schizophrenia that seem to be excesses, that is, bizarre additions to normal thoughts, emotions, or behaviors.

Positron emission tomography (PET scan) A computer-produced motion picture showing rates of metabolism throughout the brain.

Postpartum depression An episode of depression experienced by some new mothers that begins within four weeks after giving birth.

Postpartum psychosis An episode of psychosis experienced by a small percentage of new mothers that begins within days or weeks after giving birth.

Posttraumatic stress disorder An anxiety disorder in which fear and related symptoms continue to be experienced long after a traumatic event.

Poverty of content A lack of meaning in spite of high emotion that is found in the speech of some people with schizophrenia.

Predisposition An inborn or acquired vulnerability for developing certain symptoms or disorders.

Prefrontal lobes Regions of the brain that play a key role in short-term memory, among other functions.

Premature ejaculation A dysfunction in which a man reaches orgasm and ejaculates before, on, or shortly after penetration and before he wishes it.

Premorbid The period prior to the onset of a disorder.

Preoccupation somatoform disorders Somatoform disorders in which people misinterpret and overreact to minor, even normal, bodily symptoms or features.

Preparedness A predisposition to develop certain fears.

Prevalence The total number of cases of a disorder occurring in a population over a specific period of time.

Prevention A key feature of community mental health programs that seek to prevent or minimize psychological disorders.

Primary gain In psychodynamic theory, the gain achieved when hysterical symptoms keep internal conflicts out of awareness.

Primary hypersomnia A sleep disorder in which the main problem is excessive sleepiness for at least a month.

Primary insomnia A sleep disorder in which the main problem is an inability to initiate or maintain sleep.

Primary personality The subpersonality that appears more often than the others in individuals with multiple personality disorder.

Private psychotherapy An arrangement in which a person directly pays a therapist for counseling services.

Proband The person who is the focus of a genetic study.

Procedural memory Memory of learned skills that a person performs without needing to think about them.

Prodromal phase The period during which the symptoms of schizophrenia are not yet prominent, but the person has begun to deteriorate from previous levels of functioning.

Profound retardation A level of mental retardation (IQ below 20) at which individuals need a very structured environment with constant aid and supervision.

Projection An ego defense mechanism whereby individuals attribute to other people characteristics or impulses they do not wish to acknowledge in themselves.

Projective test A test that consists of vague material that people interpret or respond to.

Protection and advocacy system The system by which lawyers and advocates who work for patients may investigate the patients' treatment and protect their rights.

Prozac Trade name for fluoxetine, a second-generation antidepressant.

Psychedelic drugs Substances such as LSD that cause profound perceptual changes. Also called *hallucinogenic drugs.*

Psychiatric social worker A mental health specialist who is qualified to conduct psychotherapy upon earning a master's degree or doctorate in social work.

Psychiatrist A physician who in addition to medical school has completed three to four years of residency training in the treatment of abnormal mental functioning.

Psychoanalysis Either the theory or the treatment of abnormal psychological functioning that emphasizes unconscious psychological forces as the cause of psychopathology.

Psychodynamic model The theoretical perspective that sees all human functioning as being shaped by dynamic (interacting) psychological forces and explains people's behavior by reference to unconscious internal conflicts.

Psychodynamic therapy A system of therapy whose goals are to help clients uncover past traumatic events and the inner conflicts that have resulted from them, settle those conflicts, and resume personal development.

Psychogenic perspective The view that the chief causes of abnormal functioning are psychological.

Psychological autopsy A procedure used to analyze information about a deceased person, for example, in order to determine whether the person's death was a suicide.

Psychological debriefing A form of crisis intervention in which victims of traumatic incidents are helped to talk about their feelings and reactions to the incidents. Also called *critical incident stress debriefing.*

Psychomotor symptoms Disturbances in movement sometimes found in certain disorders such as schizophrenia.

Psychoneuroimmunology The study of the connections among stress, the body's immune system, and illness.

Psychopathology An abnormal pattern of functioning that may be described as deviant, distressful, dysfunctional, and/or dangerous.

Psychopathy *See* Antisocial personality disorder.

Psychopharmacologist A psychiatrist who primarily prescribes medications. Also called *pharmacotherapist.*

Psychophysiological disorders Illnesses that result from an interaction of both psychosocial and physical factors. DSM-IV-TR labels these illnesses *psychological factors affecting medical condition.* Also called *psychosomatic disorders.*

Psychophysiological test A test that measures physical responses (such as heart rate and muscle tension) as possible indicators of psychological problems.

Psychosexual stages The developmental stages defined by Freud in which the id, ego, and superego interact.

Psychosis A state in which a person loses contact with reality in key ways.

Psychosomatic illnesses Illnesses that result from an interaction of both physical and psychosocial causes. DSM-IV-TR labels these illnesses *psychological factors affecting medical condition.* Also called *psychophysiological illnesses.*

Psychosurgery Brain surgery for mental disorders.

Psychotherapy A treatment system in which words and acts are used by a client (patient) and therapist in order to help the client overcome psychological difficulties.

Psychotropic medications Drugs that primarily affect the brain and reduce various symptoms of mental dysfunctioning.

Pyromania An impulse-control disorder characterized by a pattern of fire setting for pleasure, gratification, or relief from tension.

Quasi-experiment An experiment in which investigators do not randomly assign the subjects to control and experimental groups but instead make use of groups that already exist in the world at large. Also called a *mixed design.*

Random assignment A selection procedure that ensures that subjects are randomly placed either in the control group or in the experimental group.

Rap group A group that meets to help members talk about and explore problems in an atmosphere of mutual support.

Rape Forced sexual intercourse or another sexual act upon a nonconsenting person or intercourse with an underage person.

Rapid eye movement (REM) sleep The period of the sleep cycle during which the eyes move quickly back and forth, indicating that the person is dreaming.

Rapprochement movement An effort to identify a set of common strategies that characterize the work of all effective therapists.

Rational-emotive therapy A cognitive therapy developed by Albert Ellis that helps people identify and change the irrational assumptions and thinking that help cause their psychological disorders.

Rationalization An ego defense mechanism in which one creates acceptable reasons for unwanted or undesirable behavior.

Reaction formation An ego defense mechanism whereby one counters an unacceptable desire by taking on a lifestyle that directly opposes the unwanted impulse.

Reactive depression A depression that appears to be triggered by clear events. Also known as *exogenous depression.*

Reactivity The extent to which the very presence of an observer affects a person's behavior.

Reality principle The recognition, characterizing ego functioning, that we cannot always express or satisfy our id impulses.

Receptor A site on a neuron that receives a neurotransmitter.

Regression An ego defense mechanism in which a person returns to a more primitive mode of interacting with the world.

Reinforcement The desirable or undesirable stimuli that result from an organism's behavior.

Relapse-prevention training An approach to treating alcohol abuse that is similar to behavioral self-control training but also has people plan ahead for risky situations and reactions.

Relational psychoanalytic therapy A form of psychodynamic therapy that considers therapists to be active participants in the formation of patients' feelings and reactions and therefore calls for therapists to disclose their own experiences and feelings in discussions with patients.

Relaxation training A treatment procedure that teaches people to relax at will.

Reliability A measure of the consistency of test or research results.

Repression A defense mechanism whereby the ego prevents unacceptable impulses from reaching consciousness.

Residential treatment center A place where people formerly dependent on drugs live, work, and socialize in a drug-free environment. Also called a *therapeutic community.*

Residual type of schizophrenia A type of schizophrenia in which the acute symptoms of the disorder have lessened in strength and number yet remain in residual form.

Resistance A defense mechanism that blocks a person's free associations or causes the person to change the subject to avoid a painful discussion.

Resolution phase The fourth phase in the sexual response cycle, characterized by relaxation and a decline in arousal following orgasm.

Response inventories Tests designed to measure a person's responses in one specific area of functioning, such as affect, social skills, or cognitive processes.

Response prevention *See* Exposure and response prevention.

Response set A particular way of responding to questions or statements on a test, such as always selecting "true," regardless of the actual questions.

Restricting-type anorexia nervosa A type of anorexia nervosa in which people reduce their weight by severely restricting their food intake.

Reticular formation The brain's arousal center, which helps people to be awake, alert, and attentive.

Retrograde amnesia A lack of memory about events that occurred before the event that triggered amnesia.

Retrospective analysis A psychological autopsy in which clinicians and researchers piece together information about a person's suicide from the person's past.

Reversal design A single-subject experimental design in which behavior is measured to provide a baseline (A), then again after the treatment has been applied (B), then again after the conditions during baseline have been reintroduced (A), and then once again after the treatment is reintroduced (B). Also known as *ABAB design*.

Reward A pleasurable stimulus given to an organism which encourages a specific behavior.

Reward center A dopamine-rich pathway in the brain that produces feelings of pleasure when activated.

Reward-deficiency syndrome A condition, suspected to be present in some individuals, in which the brain's reward center is not readily activated by the usual events in their lives.

Right to refuse treatment The legal right of patients to refuse certain forms of treatment.

Right to treatment The legal right of patients, particularly those who are involuntarily committed, to receive adequate treatment.

Risperidone A commonly prescribed atypical antipsychotic drug.

Ritalin Trade name of methylphenidate, a stimulant drug that is helpful in many cases of attention-deficit/hyperactivity disorder (ADHD).

Role play A therapy technique in which clients are instructed to act out roles assigned to them by the therapist.

Rorschach test A projective test, in which a person reacts to inkblots, designed to help reveal psychological features of the person.

Rosenthal effect The general finding that the results of any experiment often conform to the expectations of the experimenter.

Rush A spasm of warmth and ecstasy that occurs when certain drugs, such as heroin, are ingested.

Sample A group of subjects that is representative of the larger population about which a researcher wishes to make a statement.

Savant A person with a mental disorder or significant intellectual deficits who has some extraordinary ability despite the disorder or deficits.

Schizoaffective disorder A disorder in which symptoms of both schizophrenia and a mood disorder are prominent.

Schizoid personality disorder A personality disorder in which a person persistently avoids social relationships and shows little emotional expression.

Schizophrenia A psychotic disorder in which personal, social, and occupational functioning deteriorate as a result of strange perceptions, disturbed thought processes, unusual emotions, and motor abnormalities.

Schizophreniform disorder A disorder in which all of the key features of schizophrenia are present but last only between one and six months.

Schizophrenogenic mother A type of mother—supposedly cold, domineering, and uninterested in the needs of others—who was once thought to cause schizophrenia in the child.

Schizotypal personality disorder A personality disorder in which a person displays a pattern of interpersonal problems marked by extreme discomfort in close relationships, odd forms of thinking and perceiving, and behavioral eccentricities.

School phobia A childhood pattern in which children fear going to school and often stay home for a long period of time. Also called *school refusal*.

Scientific method The process of systematically gathering and evaluating information through careful observations to gain an understanding of a phenomenon.

Seasonal affective disorder (SAD) A mood disorder in which mood episodes are related to changes in season.

Second-generation antidepressants New antidepressant drugs that differ structurally from tricyclics and MAO inhibitors.

Second messengers Chemical changes within a neuron just after the neuron receives a neurotransmitter message and just before it responds.

Secondary gain In psychodynamic theory, the gain achieved when hysterical symptoms elicit kindness from others or provide an excuse for avoiding unpleasant activities.

Sedative-hypnotic drug A drug used in low doses to reduce anxiety and in higher doses to help people sleep. Also called *anxiolytic drug*.

Selective amnesia An inability to recall some of the events that occurred over a limited period of time.

Selective serotonin reuptake inhibitors (SSRIs) A group of second-generation antidepressant drugs that increase serotonin activity specifically without affecting other neurotransmitters.

Self-actualization The humanistic process by which people fulfill their potential for goodness and growth.

Self-efficacy The judgment that one can master and perform needed behaviors whenever necessary.

Self-help group A group made up of people with similar problems who help and support one another without the direct leadership of a clinician. Also called *mutual help group*.

Self-hypnosis The process of hypnotizing oneself—for example, to forget unpleasant events.

Self-instruction training A cognitive treatment developed by Donald Meichenbaum that teaches people to use coping self-statements at times of stress or discomfort. Also called *stress inoculation training*.

Self-monitoring Client's obeservation of their own behavior.

Self-statements According to some cognitive theorists, statements about oneself, sometimes counterproductive, that come to mind during stressful situations.

Self theory The psychodynamic theory that emphasizes the role of the self—a person's unified personality.

Senile Characteristic of or associated with old age.

Senile plaques Sphere-shaped deposits of beta-amyloid protein that form in the spaces between certain brain cells and in certain blood vessels as people age.

Sensate focus A treatment for sexual disorders that instructs couples to take the focus away from orgasm or intercourse and instead spend time concentrating on the pleasure achieved by such acts as kissing, hugging, and mutual massage. Also known as *nondemand pleasuring*.

Separation anxiety disorder A childhood disorder marked by excessive anxiety, even panic, whenever the child is separated from home or a parent.

Serotonin A neurotransmitter whose abnormal activity is linked to depression, obsessive-compulsive disorder, and eating disorders.

Severe retardation A level of mental retardation (IQ between 20 and 34) in which individuals require careful supervision and can learn to perform basic work in structured and sheltered settings.

Sex-change surgery A surgical procedure that changes a person's sex organs and features and thus sexual identity.

Sex offender statute The presumption by some state legislatures that people who are repeatedly found guilty of certain sex crimes have a mental disorder and should be categorized as "mentally disordered sex offenders."

Sexual aversion disorder A disorder characterized by an aversion to and avoidance of genital sexual interplay.

Sexual dysfunction A disorder marked by a persistent inability to function normally in some area of the human sexual response cycle.

Sexual masochism A paraphilia characterized by repeated and intense sexual urges, fantasies, or behaviors that involve being humiliated, beaten, bound, or otherwise made to suffer.

Sexual pain disorder A dysfunction in which a person experiences pain during sexual arousal or intercourse. See also Dyspareunia *and* Vaginismus.

Sexual response cycle The general sequence of behavior and feelings that occurs during sexual activity, consisting of desire, excitement, orgasm, and resolution.

Sexual sadism A paraphilia characterized by repeated and intense sexual urges, fantasies, or behaviors that involve inflicting suffering on others.

Shaping A learning procedure in which successive approximations of the desired behavior are rewarded until finally the exact and complete behavior is learned.

Shared psychotic disorder A disorder in which a person embraces delusions held by another individual. Also known as *folie à deux*.

Sheltered workshop A protected and supervised workplace that offers job opportunities and training at a pace and level tailored to people with various disabilities.

Short-term memory The memory system that collects new information. Also known as *working memory*.

Shuttle box A box separated in the middle by a barrier that an animal can jump over in order to escape or avoid shock.

Sildenafil A drug used to treat erectile disorder that helps increase blood flow to the penis during sexual activity. Marketed as *Viagra*.

Single-subject experiment A research method in which a single subject is observed and measured both before and after the manipulation of an independent variable.

Situation anxiety The various levels of anxiety produced in a person by different situations. Also called *state anxiety*.

Sleep apnea A disorder in which a person frequently stops breathing for up to 30 or more seconds while asleep.

Sleep terror disorder A parasomnia in which persons awaken suddenly during the first third of sleep, screaming out in extreme fear and agitation.

Sleepwalking disorder A parasomnia in which people repeatedly leave their beds and walk around without being conscious of the episode or remembering it later.

Social phobia A severe and persistent fear of social or performance situations in which embarrassment may occur.

Social skills training A therapy approach that helps people learn or improve social skills and assertiveness through the use of role playing and rehearsing of desirable behaviors.

Social therapy An approach to therapy in which the therapist makes practical advice and life adjustment a central focus of treatment for schizophrenia. Therapy also focuses on problem solving, decision making, development of social skills, and management of medications. Also known as *personal therapy.*

Sociocultural model The theoretical perspective that emphasizes the effect of society, culture, and social and family groups on individual behavior.

Sociopathy *See* Antisocial personality disorder.

Sodium amobarbital (Amytal) A drug used to put people into a near-sleep state during which some can better recall forgotten events.

Sodium pentobarbital (Pentothal) *See* Sodium amobarbital.

Somatization disorder A somatoform disorder marked by numerous recurring physical ailments without an organic basis. Also called *Briquet's syndrome.*

Somatoform disorder A physical illness or ailment that is largely explained by psychosocial causes, in which the patient experiences no sense of wanting or guiding his or her symptoms.

Somatogenic perspective The view that abnormal psychological functioning has physical causes.

Special education An approach to educating children with mental retardation in which they are grouped together and given a separate, specially designed education.

Specific phobia A severe and persistent fear of a specific object or situation (other than agoraphobia and social phobia).

Spectator role A state of mind that some people experience during sex in which they focus on their sexual performance to such an extent that their performance and their enjoyment are reduced.

Standardization The process of administering a test to a large group of persons whose performance then serves as a common standard or norm against which any individual's score can be measured.

State-dependent learning Learning that becomes associated with the conditions under which it occurred so that what is learned is best remembered under the same conditions.

State hospitals State-run public mental institutions in the United States.

State school A state-supported institution for individuals with mental retardation.

Statistical analysis The application of principles of probability to the findings of a study in order to learn how likely it is that the findings have occurred by chance.

Statistical significance A measure of the probability that a study's findings occurred by chance rather than because of the experimental manipulation.

Stimulant drug A substance that increases the activity of the central nervous system.

Stimulus generalization A phenomenon in which responses to one stimulus are also produced by similar stimuli.

Stress management program An approach to treating generalized and other anxiety disorders that teaches people techniques for reducing and controlling stress.

Stress response A person's particular reactions to stress.

Stressor An event that creates a sense of threat by confronting a person with a demand or opportunity for change of some kind.

Stress-reduction seminar A workshop or series of group sessions offered by a business in which mental health professionals teach employees how to cope with and solve problems and reduce stress. Also known as *problem-solving seminar.*

Structured interview An interview format in which the clinician asks prepared questions.

Stutter A disturbance in the normal fluency and timing of speech.

Subintentional death A death in which the victim plays an indirect, hidden, partial, or unconscious role.

Subject An individual chosen to participate in a study. Also called a *participant*.

Sublimation In psychoanalytic theory, the rechanneling of id impulses into endeavors that are both socially acceptable and personally gratifying. It can also be used as an ego defense mechanism.

Subpersonalities The distinct personalities found in individuals suffering from multiple personality disorder. Also known as *alternate personalities.*

Substance abuse Such excessive and repeated reliance on a drug that the behavior disrupts the person's life.

Substance dependence Such excessive reliance on a drug that one makes it the center of one's life and perhaps builds a tolerance to it or experiences withdrawal symptoms when one stops taking it, or both. Also known as *addiction.*

Substance-related disorder A pattern of maladaptive behavior centered on the use of, abuse of, or dependence on certain substances.

Suicide A self-inflicted death in which the person acts intentionally, directly, and consciously.

Suicide prevention program A program that tries to identify people who are at risk of killing themselves and to offer them crisis intervention.

Superego According to Freud, the psychological force that emphasizes one's conscience, values, and ideals.

Supportive nursing care A treatment, applied to anorexia nervosa in particular, in which trained nurses conduct a day-to-day hospital program.

Symbolic loss According to Freudian theory, the loss of a valued object (for example, a loss of employment) which is unconsciously interpreted as the loss of a loved one. Also called *imagined loss.*

Sympathetic nervous system The nerve fibers of the autonomic nervous system that quicken the heartbeat and produce other changes experienced as fear or anxiety.

Symptom A physical or psychological sign of a disorder.

Synapse The tiny space between the nerve ending of one neuron and the dendrite of another.

Syndrome A cluster of symptoms that usually occur together.

Synergistic effect In pharmacology, an increase of effects that occurs when more than one drug is acting on the body at the same time.

Synesthesia A crossing over of sensory perceptions caused by LSD and other hallucinogenic drugs. For example, a loud sound may be seen or a color may be felt.

Systematic desensitization A behavioral treatment that uses relaxation training and a fear hierarchy to help people with phobias react calmly to the objects or situations they dread.

Tacrine A drug used in the treatment of Alzheimer's disease that helps prevent the breakdown of acetycholine.

Tarantism A disorder occurring throughout Europe between A.D. 900 and 1800 in which people would suddenly start to jump around, dance, and go into convulsions. Also known as *St. Vitus's dance.*

Tardive dyskinesia A condition characterized by extrapyramidal effects that appear in some patients after they have taken traditional antipsychotic drugs for an extended time.

Tay-Sachs disease A metabolic disorder that causes progressive loss of intellectual functioning, vision, and motor functioning, resulting in death.

Temporal lobes Regions of the brain that play a key role in transforming short-term memory to long-term memory, among other functions.

Tension headache *See* Muscle contraction headache.

Test A device for gathering information about a few aspects of a person's psychological functioning from which broader information about the person can be inferred.

Testosterone The principal male sex hormone.

Tetrahydrocannabinol (THC) The main active ingredient of cannabis substances.

Thanatos According to the Freudian view, the basic death instinct that functions in opposition to the life instinct.

Thematic Apperception Test (TAT) A projective test consisting of pictures that show people in ambiguous situations that the client is asked to interpret.

Theory of mind Awareness that other people base their behaviors on their own beliefs, intentions, and mental states, not on information they have no way of knowing.

Therapist A professional clinician who applies a system of therapy to help a person overcome psychological difficulties.

Therapy A systematic process for helping persons overcome their psychological problems. It consists of a patient, a trained therapist, and a series of contacts between them.

Token economy program A behavioral program in which a person's desirable behaviors are reinforced systematically throughout the day by the awarding of tokens that can be exchanged for goods or privileges.

Tolerance Upon regular use of a drug, the need of the brain and the body for ever-larger doses in order to achieve the drug's earlier effects.

Trait anxiety The general level of anxiety that a person brings to the various events in his or her life.

Tranquilizer A drug that reduces anxiety.

Transference According to psychodynamic theorists, a process in which a therapist's patients respond to the therapist as they did or do to important figures in their lives.

Transvestic fetishism A paraphilia consisting of repeated and intense sexual urges, fantasies, or behaviors that involve dressing in clothes of the opposite sex. Also known as *transvestism* or *cross-dressing.*

Treatment A procedure designed to help change abnormal behavior into more normal behavior. Also called *therapy.*

Trephination An ancient operation in which a stone instrument was used to cut away a circular section of the skull, perhaps to treat abnormal behavior.

Trichotillomania An impulse-control disorder (or compulsion) in which people repeatedly pull at and even yank out their hair, eyelashes, and eyebrows.

Tricyclic An antidepressant drug, such as imipramine, that has three rings in its molecular structure.

Trisomy A chromosomal abnormality in which an individual has three chromosomes of one kind rather than the usual two.

Tube and intravenous feeding Forced nourishment sometimes provided to sufferers of anorexia nervosa when their condition becomes life-threatening.

Type A personality style A personality pattern characterized by hostility, cynicism, drivenness, impatience, competitiveness, and ambition.

Type B personality style A personality pattern in which persons are more relaxed, less aggressive, and less concerned about time.

Tyramine A chemical that, if allowed to accumulate, can raise blood pressure dangerously. It is found in many common foods and is broken down by MAO.

Ulcer A lesion that forms in the wall of the stomach or of the duodenum.

Unconditional positive regard Full, warm acceptance of a person regardless of what he or she says, thinks, or feels; a critical component of client-centered therapy.

Unconditioned response (UCR) The natural, automatic response produced by an unconditioned stimulus.

Unconditioned stimulus (UCS) A stimulus that produces an automatic, natural response.

Unconscious The deeply hidden mass of memories, experiences, and impulses that is viewed in Freudian theory as the source of much behavior.

Undifferentiated type of schizophrenia A type of schizophrenia in which no single set of psychotic symptoms (incoherence, psychomotor disturbances, delusions, or hallucinations) dominates.

Undoing An ego defense mechanism in which a person unconsciously cancels out an unacceptable desire or act by performing another act.

Unilateral electroconvulsive therapy (ECT) A form of electroconvulsive therapy in which electrodes are attached to the head so that electrical current passes through only one side of the brain.

Unipolar depression Depression without a history of mania.

Unstructured interview An interview format in which the clinician asks spontaneous questions that are based on issues that arise during the interview.

Vacuum erection device (VED) A non-surgical device that can be used to produce an erection. It consists of a hollow cylinder that is placed over the penis and connected to a hand pump.

Vaginismus A condition marked by involuntary contractions of the muscles around the outer third of the vagina during sexual activity, preventing entry of the penis.

Validity The accuracy of a test's or study's results; that is, the extent to which the test or study actually measures or shows what it claims to.

Valium The trade name of diazepam, an antianxiety drug.

Variable Any characteristic or event that can vary across time, locations, or persons.

Vascular dementia Dementia caused by a cerebrovascular accident, or stroke, that restricts blood flow to certain areas of the brain. Also called *multi-infarct dementia*.

Ventromedial hypothalamus (VMH) The region of the hypothalamus that, when activated, depresses hunger.

Visual hallucinations Hallucinations in which a person may either experience vague visual perceptions, perhaps of colors or clouds, or have distinct visions of people, objects, or scenes that are not there.

Voyeurism A paraphilia in which a person has repeated and intense sexual desires or urges to secretly observe unsuspecting people as they undress or have intercourse. The person may also act on these desires.

Waxy flexibility A type of catatonia in which a person maintains a posture into which he or she has been placed by someone else.

Weight set point The weight level that a person is predisposed to maintain, controlled, in part, by the hypothalamus.

Windigo An intense fear of being turned into a cannibal by a flesh-eating monster. The disorder was once found among Algonquin Indian hunters.

Withdrawal Unpleasant, sometimes dangerous reactions that may occur when people who use a drug regularly stop taking or reduce their dosage of the drug.

Working through The psychodynamic treatment process of repeatedly facing conflicts, reinterpreting feelings, and overcoming one's problems. ◄◄◄

[references]

Journal Abbreviations

Academ. Med. *Academic Medicine*
Accid. Anal. Prev. *Accident Analysis and Prevention*
Acta Genet. Med. Gemelol. *Acta Geneticae Medicae et Gemoliologiae*
Acta Paediatr. *Acta Paediatrica*
Acta Psychiatr. Belg. *Acta Psychiatrica Belgica*
Acta Psychiatr. Scandin. *Acta Psychiatrica Scandinavica*
Adap. Phys. Activ. Q. *Adapted Physical Activity Quarterly*
Addic. Behav. *Addictive Behaviors*
Addic. Disord. Treat. *Addictive Disorders and Their Treatment*
Addiction *Addiction*
Admin. Pol. Ment. Hlth. *Administration and Policy in Mental Health*
Admin. Policy Ment. Hlth. *Administration and Policy in Mental Health*
Adol. Psychiat. *Adolescent Psychiatry*
Adolescence *Adolescence*
Adv. Behav. Res. Ther. *Advances in Behavior Research and Therapy*
Adv. Drug React. Toxicol. Rev. *Advanced Drug Reaction and Toxicology Review*
Adv. Biochem. Psychopharm. *Advances in Biochemical Psychopharmacology*
Adv. Mind-Body Med. *Advances in Mind-Body Medicine*
Aggress. Viol. Behav. *Aggression and Violent Behavior*
Aging *Aging*
Aging Ment. Hlth. *Aging and Mental Health*
Aging Neuropsychol. Cog. *Aging, Neuropsychology, and Cognition*
Alc. Res. Hlth. *Alcohol Research and Health*
Alcohol Alcoholism *Alcohol and Alcoholism*
Alcohol.: Clin. Exp. Res. *Alcoholism: Clinical and Experimental Research*
Alcohol.: Treat. Q. *Alcoholism: Treatment Quarterly*
Alz. Disease Assoc. Disord. *Alzheimer's Disease and Associated Disorders*
Am. Demogr. *American Demographics*
Am. Heart J. *American Heart Journal*
Amer. Behav. Sci. *American Behavioral Scientist*
Amer. Educ. Res. J *American Educational Research Journal*
Amer. Fam. Physician. *American Family Physician*
Amer. Hlth. *American Health*
Amer. J. Addict. *American Journal on Addictions*
Amer. J. Cardiol. *American Journal of Cardiology*
Amer. J. Clin. Hyp. *American Journal of Clinical Hypnosis*
Amer. J. Clin. Hypnother. *American Journal of Clinical Hypnotherapy*
Amer. J. Clin. Nutr. *American Journal of Clinical Nutrition*
Amer. J. Comm. Psychol. *American Journal of Community Psychology*
Amer. J. Criminal Justice *American Journal of Criminal Justice*
Amer. J. Digestive Dis. *American Journal of Digestive Diseases*
Amer. J. Drug Alc. Abuse *American Journal of Drug and Alcohol Abuse*
Amer. J. Epidemiol. *American Journal of Epidemiology*
Amer. J. Fam. Ther. *American Journal of Family Therapy*

Amer. J. Forens. Psychol. *American Journal of Forensic Psychology*
Amer. J. Ger. Pharmacother. *American Journal of Geriatric Pharmacotherapy*
Amer. J. Ger. Psychiat. *American Journal of Geriatric Psychiatry*
Amer. J. Hlth. Sys. Pharmacol. *American Journal of Health Systems and Pharmacology*
Amer. J. Hospice Pall. Care *American Journal of Hospice and Palliative Care*
Amer. J. Med. Genet. *American Journal of Medical Genetics*
Amer. J. Ment. Def. *American Journal of Mental Deficiency*
Amer. J. Ment. Retard. *American Journal on Mental Retardation*
Amer. J. Obstet. Gynecol. *American Journal of Obstetrics and Gynecology*
Amer. J. Orthopsychiat. *American Journal of Orthopsychiatry*
Amer. J. Psychiat. *American Journal of Psychiatry*
Amer. J. Psychoanal. *American Journal of Psychoanalysis*
Amer. J. Psychother. *American Journal of Psychotherapy*
Amer. J. Pub. Hlth. *American Journal of Public Health*
Amer. Psychiat. Assoc. Res. Rep.
Amer. Psychologist *American Psychologist*
Amer. Sci. *American Scientist*
Amer. Sociol. Rev. *American Sociological Review*
Análi. Modif. Cond. *Análisis y Modificación de Conducta*
Animal Welfare *Animal Welfare*
Ann. Amer. Psychother. Assn. *Annals of the American Psychotherapy Association*
Ann. Behav. Med. *Annals of Behavioral Medicine*
Ann. Clin. Psychiat. *Annals of Clinical Psychiatry*
Ann. Internal Med. *Annals of Internal Medicine*
Ann. Med. *Annals of Medicine*
Ann. N.Y. Acad. Sci. *Annals of the New York Academy of Sciences*
Ann. Neurol. *Annals of Neurology*
Ann. Pharmacother. *Annals of Pharmacotherapy*
Annales Medico Psychologiques *Annales Medico Psychologiques*
Annu. Rev. Clin. Psychol. *Annual Review of Clinical Psychology*
Annu. Rev. Med. *Annual Review of Medicine*
Annu. Rev. Neurosci. *Annual Review of Neuroscience*
Annu. Rev. Psychol. *Annual Review of Psychology*
Anthropol. Med. *Anthropology and Medicine*
Anx. Disorders *Anxiety Disorders*
Anx., Stress, Coping: Inter. J. *Anxiety, Stress, and Coping: An International Journal*
Aphasiology *Aphasiology*
Appl. Cog. Psychol. *Applied Cognitive Psychology*
Appl. Dev. Sci. *Applied Developmental Science*
Appl. Neuropsychol. *Applied Neuropsychology*
Appl. Prev. Psychol. *Applied and Preventive Psychology*
Appl. Psychol. Measure. *Applied Psychological Measurement*
Appl. Psychophysiol. Biofeedback *Applied Psychophysiology and Biofeedback*
Arch. Fam. Med. *Archives of Family Medicine*
Arch. Gen. Psychiat. *Archives of General Psychiatry*
Arch. Geront. Geriat. *Archives of Gerontology and Geriatrics*

Arch. Internal Med. *Archives of Internal Medicine*
Arch. Neurol. *Archives of Neurology*
Arch. Neurol. Psychiat. *Archives of Neurology and Psychiatry Chicago*
Arch. Pediatr. Adoles. *Archives of Pediatric and Adolescent Medicine*
Arch. Psychiat. Psychother. *Archives of Psychiatry and Psychotherapy*
Arch. Psychiatr. Nursing *Archives of Psychiatric Nursing*
Arch. Sex. Behav. *Archives of Sexual Behavior*
Arch. Suic. Res. *Archives of Suicide Research*
Arch. Women's Ment. Hlth. *Archives of Women's Mental Health*
Assessment *Assessment*
Assoc. Res. Nerv. Ment. Dis.
Austral. Fam. Physician. *Australian Family Physician*
Austral. J. Clin. Exp. Hyp. *Australian Journal of Clinical and Experimental Hypnosis*
Austral. J. Psychol. *Australian Journal of Psychology*
Austral. New Zeal. J. Ment. Hlth. Nurs. *Australian and New Zealand Journal of Mental Health Nursing*
Austral. New Zeal. J. Psychiat. *Australian and New Zealand Journal of Psychiatry*
Austral. Psychologist *Australian Psychologist*
Autism *Autism*
Aviat. Space, Envir. Med. *Aviation, Space, and Environmental Medicine*

Bagimlik Dergisi *Bagimlik Dergisi*
Basic Appl. Soc. Psychol. *Basic and Applied Social Psychology*
Behav. Brain Res. *Behavioral Brain Research*
Behav. Change *Behaviour Change*
Behav. Cog. Psychother. *Behavioural and Cognitive Psychotherapy*
Behav. Genet. *Behavioral Genetics*
Behav. Hlth. Manage. *Behavioral Health Management*
Behav. Intervent. *Behavioral Interventions*
Behav. Med. *Behavioral Medicine*
Behav. Mod. *Behavior Modification*
Behav. Neurosci. *Behavioral Neuroscience*
Behav. Pharmacol. *Behavioural Pharmacology*
Behav. Psychother. *Behavioural Psychotherapy*
Behav. Res. Meth. Instru. Computers *Behavioral Research Methods, Instruments, and Computers*
Behav. Res. Ther. *Behaviour Research and Therapy*
Behav. Sci. *Behavioral Science*
Behav. Sci. Law *Behavioral Sciences and the Law*
Behav. Ther. *Behavior Therapy*
Behav. Ther. Exp. Psychiat. *Behaviour Therapy and Experimental Psychiatry*
Behav. Therapist *Behavior Therapist*
Bioethics *Bioethics*
Biofeed. Self-Reg. *Biofeedback and Self-Regulation*
Biol. Psychiat. *Biological Psychiatry*
Biol. Psychol. *Biological Psychology*
Biol. Rhythm Res. *Biological Rhythm Research*
Biol. Signals Recept. *Biological Signals and Receptors*
Bipolar Disord. *Bipolar Disorders*
Br. J. Clin. Psychol. *British Journal of Clinical Psychology*
Brain Behav. Immun. *Brain, Behavior, and Immunity*
Brain Cognit. *Brain and Cognition*
Brain Inj. *Brain Injury*
Brain Res. *Brain Research Reviews*
Brief Treat. Crisis Intervent. *Brief Treatment and Crisis Intervention*

Brit. J. Prev. Soc. Med. *British Journal of Preventive and Social Medicine*

Brit. J. Addic. *British Journal of Addiction*

Brit. J. Clin. Psychol. *British Journal of Clinical Psychology*

Brit. J. Cog. Psychother. *British Journal of Cognitive Psychotherapy*

Brit. J. Criminol. *British Journal of Criminology*

Brit. J. Dev. Psychol. *British Journal of Developmental Psychology*

Brit. J. Forensic Prac. *British Journal of Forensic Practice*

Brit. J. Guid. Couns. *British Journal of Guidance and Counselling*

Brit. J. Med. Psychol. *British Journal of Medical Psychology*

Brit. J. Psychiat. *British Journal of Psychiatry*

Brit. J. Psychol. *British Journal of Psychology*

Brit. J. Psychother. *British Journal of Psychotherapy*

Brit. J. Urol. *British Journal of Urology*

Brit. Med. J. *British Medical Journal*

Bull. Amer. Acad. Psychiat. Law *Bulletin of the American Academy of Psychiatry and the Law*

Bull. Assoc. Amer. Med. Colleges *Bulletin of the Association of American Medical Colleges*

Bull. Menninger Clin. *Bulletin of the Menninger Clinic*

Bull. Psychol. *Bulletin de Psychologie*

Bull. Psychon. Soc. *Bulletin of the Psychonomic Society*

Bull. Psychosom. Soc. *Bulletin of the Psychosomatic Society*

Bull. Suicidol. *Bulletin of Suicidology*

Calif. Law Rev. *California Law Review*

Can. J. Behav. Sci. *Canadian Journal of Behavioural Science*

Canad. J. Couns. *Canadian Journal of Counselling*

Canad. J. Neurol. Sci. *Canadian Journal of Neurological Science*

Canad. J. Psychiat. *Canadian Journal of Psychiatry*

Canad. J. Psychoanal. *Canadian Journal of Psychoanalysis*

Canad. Med. Assoc. J. *Canadian Medical Association Journal*

Canad. Psychol. *Canadian Psychology*

Cell *Cell*

Cephalalgia *Cephalalgia*

Cesko. Psychol. *Ceskoslovenska Psychologie*

Chem. Eng. News *Chemical and Engineering News*

Child Abuse Negl. *Child Abuse and Neglect*

Child Adol. Ment. Hlth. *Child and Adolescent Mental Health*

Child Adol. Psychiat. Clin. N. Amer. *Child and Adolescent Psychiatric Clinics of North America*

Child Dev. *Child Development*

Child Maltreat.: J. Amer. Profess. Soc. Abuse Child. *Child Maltreatment: Journal of the American Professional Society on the Abuse of Children*

Child Psychiat. Human Dev. *Child Psychiatry and Human Development*

Child Psychol. Psychiat. Rev. *Child Psychology and Psychiatry Review*

Chin. J. Clin. Psychol. *Chinese Journal of Clinical Psychology*

Chin. Ment. Hlth. J. *Chinese Mental Health Journal*

Chinese Ment. Hlth. J. *Chinese Mental Health Journal*

Chron. Higher Educ. *Chronicle of Higher Education*

Circulation *Circulation*

Clin. Case Stud. *Clinical Case Studies*

Clin. Child Fam. Psychol. Rev. *Clinical Child and Family Psychology Review*

Clin. Child Psychol. Psychiat. *Clinical Child Psychology and Psychiatry*

Clin. Electroencephalogr. *Clinical Electroencephalography*

Clin. Geront. *Clinical Gerontologist*

Clin. J. Pain *Clinical Journal of Pain*

Clin. Neuropharmacol. *Clinical Neuropharmacology*

Clin. Neuropsychiat.: J. Treat. Eval. *Clinical Neuropsychiatrics: Journal of Treatment and Evaluation*

Clin. Pediatr. *Clinical Pediatrics*

Clin. Pharmacol. Ther. *Clinical and Pharmacological Therapy*

Clin. Psychol. Psychother. *Clinical Psychology and Psychotherapy*

Clin. Psychol. Rev. *Clinical Psychology Review*

Clin. Psychol.: Sci. Prac. *Clinical Psychology: Science and Practice*

Clin. Psychologist *Clinical Psychologist*

Clin. Rehab. *Clinical Rehabilitation*

Clin. Soc. Work J. *Clinical Social Work Journal*

Clin. Ther.: Inter. J. Drug Ther. *Clinical Therapeutics: The International Journal of Drug Therapy*

Clinica-y-Salud *Clinica-y-Salud*

Clinician's Res. Dig. *Clinician's Research Digest*

CNS Drug Rev. *CNS Drug Reviews*

CNS Drugs *CNS Drugs*

CNS Spectrums *CNS Spectrums*

Cog. Behav. Pract. *Cognitive and Behavioral Practice*

Cog. Brain Res. *Cognitive Brain Research*

Cog. Emot. *Cognition & Emotion*

Cog. Neuropsychiat. *Cognitive Neuropsychiatry*

Cog. Ther. Res. *Cognitive Therapy and Research*

Coll. Student J. *College Student Journal*

Comm. Ment. Hlth. J. *Community Mental Health Journal*

Communic. Res. *Communication Research*

Community Dent. Oral Epidemiol. *Community Dentistry and Oral Epidemiology*

Comp. Hum. Behav. *Computers in Human Behavior*

Comprehen. Psychiat. *Comprehensive Psychiatry*

Comprehen. Ther. *Comprehensive Therapy*

Consciousness Cog.: Inter. J. *Consciousness and Cognition: An International Journal*

Contemp. Fam. Therap: Internat. J. *Contemporary Family Therapy: An International Journal*

Contemp. Hyp. *Contemporary Hypnosis*

Contemp. Psychol. *Contemporary Psychology*

Couns. Psychologist *Counseling Psychologist*

Couns. Psychology Q. *Counselling Psychology Quarterly*

Criminal Behav. Ment. Hlth. *Criminal Behaviour and Mental Health*

Criminal Justice Behav. *Criminal Justice and Behavior*

Crisis *Crisis*

Cult. Div. Ethnic Minority Psychol. *Cultural Diversity and Ethnic Minority Psychology*

Cult. Med. Psychiat. *Culture, Medicine, and Psychiatry*

Cult. Psychiat. *Cultural Psychiatry*

Curr. Direct. Psychol. Sci. *Current Directions in Psychological Science*

Curr. Opin. Neurobiol. *Current Opinion in Neurobiology*

Curr. Opin. Psychiat. *Current Opinion in Psychiatry*

Curr. Probl. Pediatr. *Current Problems in Pediatrics*

Curr. Psychol.: Dev. Learn. Personal. Soc. *Current Psychology: Developmental, Learning, Personality, Social*

CyberPsychol. Behav. *CyberPsychology and Behavior*

Death Stud. *Death Studies*

Dement. Ger. Cogn. Disord. *Dementia and Geriatric Cognitive Disorders*

Depress. Anx. *Depression and Anxiety*

Deviant Behav.: Interdiscip. J. *Deviant Behaviour: An Interdisciplinary Journal*

Dev. Disabil. Bull. *Developmental Disabilities Bulletin*

Dev. Med. Child Neurol. *Developmental Medicine and Child Neurology*

Dev. Neuropsychol. *Developmental Neuropsychology*

Dev. Psychol. *Developmental Psychology*

Dev. Psychopathol. *Development and Psychopathology*

Direct. Psychiat. *Directions in Psychiatry*

Dis. Nerv. Syst. *Diseases of the Nervous System*

Diss. Abstr. Inter. *Dissertation Abstracts International*

Diss. Abstr. Inter.: Sect. A: Human Soc. Sci. *Dissertation Abstracts International: Section A: Humanities and Social Sciences*

Diss. Abstr. Inter.: Sect. B: Sci. Eng. *Dissertation Abstracts International: Section B: The Sciences and Engineering*

Dissociat.: Prog. Dissociat. Disorders *Dissociation: Progress in the Dissociative Disorders*

Dreaming *Dreaming*

Drug Alc. Dep. *Drug and Alcohol Dependence*

Drug Alc. Rev. *Drug and Alcohol Review*

Drug Benef. Trends *Drug Benefit Trends*

Drugs *Drugs*

Early Ed. Dev. *Early Education and Development*

Eat. Behav. *Eating Behaviors*

Eat. Disord.: J. Treat. Prev. *Eating Disorders: The Journal of Treatment and Prevention*

Eat. Weight Disord. *Eating and Weight Disorders*

Educ. Psychol. Meas. *Educational and Psychological Measurement*

Educ. Train. Dev. Disabil. *Education and Training in Developmental Disabilities*

eMed. J. *eMedicine Journal*

Emotion *Emotion*

Empir. Stud. Arts *Empirical Studies of the Arts*

Encephale *Encephale*

Endocrine Res. *Endocrine Research*

Eta Evolutiva *Eta Evolutiva*

Ethical Human Psychol. Psychiat. *Ethical Human Psychology and Psychiatry*

Ethics Behav. *Ethics & Behavior*

Eur. Arch. Psychiat. Clin. Neurosci. *European Archives of Psychiatry and Clinical Neuroscience*

Eur. Arch. Psychiat. Neurol. Sci. *European Archives of Psychiatry and Neurological Science*

Eur. Child Adol. Psychiat. *European Child and Adolescent Psychiatry*

Eur. Eat. Disord. Rev. *European Eating Disorders Review*

Eur. J. Cog. Psychol. *European Journal of Cognitive Psychology*

Eur. J. Med. Res. *European Journal of Medical Research*

Eur. J. Pers. *European Journal of Personality*

Eur. J. Psychiat. *European Journal of Psychiatry*

Eur. J. Psychoanal. Ther. Res. *European Journal for Psychoanalytic Therapy and Research*

Eur. J. Psychol. Assess. *European Journal of Psychological Assessment*

Eur. Neurol. *European Neurology*

Eur. Neuropsychopharmacology *European Neuropsychopharmacology*

Eur. Psychiat. *European Psychiatry*

Eur. Psycholog. *European Psychologist*

Eur. Urol. *European Urology*

Evol. Psychiat. *Evolution Psychiatrique*

Evolution Psychiatr. *Evolution Psychiatrique*
Exp. Clin. Psychopharmacol. *Experimental and Clinical Psychopharmacology*

Fam. Hlth. *Family Health*
Fam. J.: Counsel. Ther. Couples Fam. *The Family Journal: Counseling and Therapy for Couples and Families*
Fam. Pract. News *Family Practice News*
Fam. Pract. Res. J. *Family Practice Research Journal*
Fam. Process *Family Process*
Fam. Rel.: Interdiscip. J. Appl. Fam. Stud. *Family Relations: Interdisciplinary Journal of Applied Family Studies*
Fam. Ther. *Family Therapy*
Fed. Probation *Federal Probation*
Focus Autism Other Dev. Disabil. *Focus on Autism and Other Developmental Disabilities*
Focus Autistic Behav. *Focus on Autistic Behavior*

G. Ital. Suic. *Giornale Italiano di Suicidologia*
Gedragstherapie *Gedragstherapie*
Gen. Hosp. Psychiat. *General Hospital Psychiatry*
Gender Soc. *Gender and Society*
German J. Psychiat. *German Journal of Psychiatry*
Gerontol. Geriat. Educ. *Gerontology and Geriatrics Education*
Gerontologist *Gerontologist*

Harvard Educ. Rev. *Harvard Educational Review*
Harvard Rev. Psychiat. *Harvard Review of Psychiatry*
Headache *Headache*
Hippocampus *Hippocampus*
Hist. Psychiat. *History of Psychiatry*
Hlth. Affairs *Health Affairs*
Hlth. Care Women Inter. *Health Care for Women International*
Hlth. Psychol. *Health Psychology*
Hlth. Soc. Work *Health and Social Work*
Homeostasis: Hlth. Dis. *Homeostasis: Health and Disease*
Hong Kong J. Psychiat. *Hong Kong Journal of Psychiatry*
Hosp. Comm. Psychiat. *Hospital and Community Psychiatry*
Hosp. Practitioner *Hospital Practitioner*
Howard J. Criminal Justice *Howard Journal of Criminal Justice*
Human Mutat. *Human Mutation*
Human Psychopharmacol. Clin. Exp. *Human Psychopharmacology Clinical and Experimental*
Humanist. Psycholog. *Humanistic Psychologist*

Imag. Cog. Pers. *Imagination, Cognition and Personality*
Indian J. Clin. Psychol. *Indian Journal of Clinical Psychology*
Indian Med. J. *Indian Medical Journal*
Indiv. Psychol.: J. Adlerian Theory Res. Prac. *Individual Psychology: A Journal of Adlerian Theory, Research, and Practice*
Infancy *Infancy*
Infant Ment. Hlth. J. *Infant Mental Health Journal*
Injury Prev. *Injury Prevention*
Inquiry *Inquiry*
Int. For. Logotherapy *International Forum for Logotherapy*
Integ. Physiol. Behav. Sci. *Integrative Physiological and Behavioral Science*
Integ. Psychiat. *Integrated Psychiatry*
Inter. Clin. Psychopharmacology *International Clinical Psychopharmacology*

Inter. Forum Psychoanal. *International Forum of Psychoanalysis*
Inter. J. Addic. *International Journal of Addiction*
Inter. J. Aging Human Dev. *International Journal of Aging and Human Development*
Inter. J. Behav. Dev. *International Journal of Behavioral Development*
Inter. J. Behav. Med. *International Journal of Behavioral Medicine*
Inter. J. Clin. Exp. Hyp. *International Journal of Clinical and Experimental Hypnosis*
Inter. J. Compar. Psychol. *International Journal of Comparative Psychology*
Inter. J. Eat. Disorders *International Journal of Eating Disorders*
Inter. J. Emerg. Mental Hlth. *International Journal of Emergency Mental Health*
Inter. J. Epidemiol. *International Journal of Epidemiology*
Inter. J. Forens. Ment. Hlth. *International Journal of Forensic Mental Health*
Inter. J. Ger. Psychiat. *International Journal of Geriatric Psychiatry*
Inter. J. Group Psychother. *International Journal of Group Psychotherapy*
Inter. J. Law Psychiat. *International Journal of Law and Psychiatry*
Inter. J. Men's Hlth. *International Journal of Men's Health*
Inter. J. Ment. Hlth. *International Journal of Mental Health*
Inter. J. Ment. Hlth. Nurs. *International Journal of Mental Health Nursing*
Inter. J. Ment. Hlth. Promot. *International Journal of Mental Health Promotion*
Inter. J. Methods Psychiatr. Res. *International Journal of Methods in Psychiatric Research*
Inter. J. Neuropsychopharmacol. *International Journal of Neuropsychopharmacology*
Inter. J. Neurosci. *International Journal of Neuroscience*
Inter. J. Nurs. Stud. *International Journal of Nursing Studies*
Inter. J. Obesity *International Journal of Obesity*
Inter. J. Offend. Ther. Compar. Crimin. *International Journal of Offender Therapy and Comparative Criminology*
Inter. J. Psychiat. Clin. Prac. *International Journal of Psychiatry in Clinical Practice*
Inter. J. Psychiat. Med. *International Journal of Psychiatry in Medicine*
Inter. J. Psychoanal. *International Journal of Psychoanalysis*
Inter. J. Psychoanal. Psychother. *International Journal of Psychoanalytic Psychotherapy*
Inter. J. Psychol. Religion *International Journal for the Psychology of Religion*
Inter. J. Psychopharmacol. *International Journal of Psychopharmacology*
Inter. J. Psychophysiol. *International Journal of Psychophysiology*
Inter. J. Psychosoc. Rehab. *International Journal of Psychosocial Rehabilitation*
Inter. J. Psychosom. *International Journal of Psychosomatics*
Inter. J. Soc. Psychiat. *International Journal of Social Psychiatry*
Inter. J. Sport Psychol. *International Journal of Sport Psychology*
Inter. J. STD AIDS *International Journal of STD and AIDS*
Inter. J. Stress Manag. *International Journal of Stress Management*

Inter. J. Transgenderism *International Journal of Transgenderism*
Inter. Med. J. *International Medical Journal*
Inter. Psychoger. *International Psychogeriatrics*
Inter. Rev. Psychiat. *International Review of Psychiatry*
Inter. Rev. Psychoanal. *International Review of Psychoanalysis*
Irish J. Psychol. Med. *Irish Journal of Psychological Medicine*
Israel J. Psychiat. Rel. Sci. *Israel Journal of Psychiatry and Related Sciences*
Issues Ment. Hlth. Nurs. *Issues in Mental Health Nursing*
Ital. J. Neurol. Sci. *Italian Journal of Neurological Sciences*

J. Abnorm. Behav. *Journal of Abnormal Behavior*
J. Abnorm. Child Psychol. *Journal of Abnormal Child Psychology*
J. Abnorm. Psychol. *Journal of Abnormal Psychology*
J. Abnorm. Soc. Psychol. *Journal of Abnormal and Social Psychology*
J. Addic. Diseases *Journal of Addictive Diseases*
J. Adol. Hlth. *Journal of Adolescent Health*
J. Adol. *Journal of Adolescence*
J. Adol. Res. *Journal of Adolescent Research*
J. Adv. Nurs. *Journal of Advanced Nursing*
J. Affect. Disorders *Journal of Affective Disorders*
J. Aggress. Maltreat. Trauma *Journal of Aggression, Maltreatment, and Trauma*
J. Aging Hlth. *Journal of Aging and Health*
J. Alcohol Drug Educ. *Journal of Alcohol and Drug Education*
J. Alcohol Stud. *Journal of Alcohol Studies*
J. Amer. Acad. Child Adol. Psychiat. *Journal of the American Academy of Child and Adolescent Psychiatry*
J. Amer. Acad. Child Psychiat. *Journal of the American Academy of Child Psychiatry*
J. Amer. Acad. Psychiat. Law *Journal of the American Academy of Psychiatry and the Law*
J. Amer. Acad. Psychoanal. Dynamic Psychiat. *Journal of the American Academy of Psychoanalysis and Dynamic Psychiatry*
J. Amer. Acad. Psychoanal. *Journal of the American Academy of Psychoanalysis*
J. Amer. Board Fam. Pract. *Journal of American Board of Family Practitioners*
J. Amer. Coll. Hlth. *Journal of American College Health*
J. Amer. Coll. Nutr. *Journal of the American College of Nutrition*
J. Amer. Ger. Soc. *Journal of the American Geriatrics Society*
J. Amer. Med. Women's Assoc. *Journal of the American Medical Women's Association*
J. Amer. Osteopath Assoc. *Journal of American Osteopath Associates*
J. Amer. Psychiat. Nurs. Assoc. *Journal of the American Psychiatric Nurses Association*
J. Amer. Psychoanal. Assoc. *Journal of the American Psychoanalytical Association*
J. Anx. Dis. *Journal of Anxiety Disorders*
J. App. Cog. Psychol. *Journal of Applied Cognitive Psychology*
J. App. Psychol. *Journal of Applied Psychology*
J. Appl. Behav. Anal. *Journal of Applied Behavior Analysis*
J. Appl. Behav. Sci. *Journal of Applied Behavioral Sciences*
J. Appl. Physiol. *Journal of Applied Physiology*

J. Appl. Psychoanal. Stud. *Journal of Applied Psychoanalytic Studies*
J. Appl. Psychol. *Journal of Applied Psychology*
J. Appl. Rehabil. Counsel. *Journal of Applied Rehabilitation Counseling*
J. Appl. School Psychol. *Journal of Applied School Psychology*
J. Appl. Soc. Psychol. *Journal of Applied Social Psychology*
J. Appl. Soc. Sci. *Journal of Applied Social Sciences*
J. Asthma *Journal of Asthma*
J. Attent. Disorders *Journal of Attention Disorders*
J. Autism Child. Schizo. *Journal of Autism and Childhood Schizopherenia*
J. Autism Dev. Disorders *Journal of Autism and Developmental Disorders*
J. Behav. Decis. Making *Journal of Behavioral Decision Making*
J. Behav. Educ. *Journal of Behavioral Education*
J. Behav. Hlth. Serv. Res. *Journal of Behavioral Health Services and Research*
J. Behav. Ther. Exp. Psychiat. *Journal of Behavior Therapy and Experimental Psychiatry*
J. Biol. Rhythms *Journal of Biological Rhythms*
J. Black Psychol. *Journal of Black Psychology*
J. Cardiovasc. Pharmacol. Ther. *Journal of Cardiovascular Pharmacology and Therapy*
J. Child Adol. Psychopharmacol. *Journal of Child and Adolescent Psychopharmacology*
J. Child Adoles. Group Ther. *Journal of Child and Adolescence Group Therapy*
J. Child Psychol. Psychiat. Allied Disc. *Journal of Child Psychology, Psychiatry, and Allied Disciplines*
J. Child Psychol. Psychiat. *Journal of Child Psychology and Psychiatry*
J. Child Sex. Abuse *Journal of Child Sexual Abuse*
J. Clin. Child Adol. Psychol. *Journal of Clinical Child and Adolescent Psychology*
J. Clin. Child Psychol. *Journal of Clinical Child Psychology*
J. Clin. Exp. Neuropsychol. *Journal of Clinical and Experimental Neuropsychology*
J. Clin. Exp. Psychopathol. *Journal of Clinical and Experimental Psychopathology*
J. Clin. Geropsychol. *Journal of Clinical Geropsychology*
J. Clin. Psychiat. *Journal of Clinical Psychiatry*
J. Clin. Psychoanal. *Journal of Clinical Psychoanalysis*
J. Clin. Psychol. *Journal of Clinical Psychology*
J. Clin. Psychol. Med. Settings *Journal of Clinical Psychology in Medical Settings*
J. Clin. Psychopharmacol. *Journal of Clinical Psychopharmacology*
J. Cog. Psychother. *Journal of Cognitive Psychotherapy*
J. Coll. Student Dev. *Journal of College Student Development*
J. Comm. Psychol. *Journal of Community Psychology*
J. Compar. Physiol. Psychol. *Journal of Comparative and Physiological Psychology*
J. Cons. Clin. Psychol. *Journal of Consulting and Clinical Psychology*
J. Cons. Stud. *Journal of Consciousness Studies*
J. Contemp. Psychother. *Journal of Contemporary Psychotherapy*
J. Contemp. Health Law and Policy *The Journal of Contemporary Health Law and Policy*
J. Couns. Dev. *Journal of Counseling & Development*
J. Couns. Psychol. *Journal of Counseling Psychology*
J. Cross-Cult. Geront. *Journal of Cross-Cultural Gerontology*
J. Cross-Cult. Psychol. *Journal of Cross-Cultural Psychology*

J. Dev. Behav. Pediatr. *Journal of Development and Behavioral Pediatrics*
J. Dev. Phys. Disabil. *Journal of Developmental and Physical Disabilities*
J. Drug Educ. *Journal of Drug Education*
J. Drug Issues *Journal of Drug Issues*
J. Early Adolescence *Journal of Early Adolescence*
J. ECT *Journal of ECT*
J. Emerg. Med. Serv. *Journal of Emergency Medical Services*
J. Epidemiol. Comm. Hlth. *Journal of Epidemiology and Community Health*
J. Exp. Anal. Behav. *Journal of Experimental Analysis of Behavior*
J. Exp. Child Psychol. *Journal of Experimental Child Psychology*
J. Exp. Psychol. Gen. *Journal of Experimental Psychology General*
J. Exp. Psychol. *Journal of Experimental Psychology*
J. Exp. Soc. Psychol. *Journal of Experimental Social Psychology*
J. Fam. Issues *Journal of Family Issues*
J. Fam. Prac. *Journal of Family Practice*
J. Fam. Psychother. *Journal of Family Psychotherapy*
J. Forens. Psychol. Pract. *Journal of Forensic Psychology Practice*
J. Forensic Sci. *Journal of Forensic Sciences*
J. Gamb. Stud. *Journal of Gambling Studies*
J. Gay Lesbian Psychother. *Journal of Gay and Lesbian Psychotherapy*
J. Gen. Internal Med. *Journal of General Internal Medicine*
J. Gen. Psychol. *Journal of Genetic Psychology*
J. Gend.-Specif. Med. *Journal of Gender-Specific Medicine*
J. Ger. A: Biol. Sci. Med. Sci. *Journal of Gerontology, A: Biological Science and Medical Science*
J. Ger. B: Psychol. Sci. Soc. Sci. *Journal of Gerontology, B.: Psychological Science and Social Science*
J. Ger. *Journal of Gerontology*
J. Ger. Psychiat. *Journal of Geriatric Pschiatry*
J. Geriat. Psychiat. Neurol. *Journal of Geriatric Psychiatry and Neurology*
J. Hellenic Psychol. Soc. *Journal of the Hellenic Psychological Society*
J. Hist. Behav. Sci. *Journal of the History of the Behavioral Sciences*
J. Hist. Neurosci. *Journal of the History of the Neurosciences*
J. Hlth. Care Poor Underserved *Journal of Health Care for the Poor and Underserved*
J. Hlth. Soc. Behav. *Journal of Health and Social Behavior*
J. Homosex. *Journal of Homosexuality*
J. Human. Psychol. *Journal of Humanistic Psychology*
J. Individ. Psychol. *Journal of Individual Psychology*
J. Intell. Disab. Res. *Journal of Intellectual Disability Research*
J. Inter. Neuropsychol. *Journal of the International Neuropsychological Society*
J. Inter. Soc. Life Info. Sci. *Journal of the International Society of Life Information Science*
J. Interpers. Violence *Journal of Interpersonal Violence*
J. Law Health *Journal of Law and Health*
J. Learn. Dis. *Journal of Learning Disorders*
J. Loss Trauma *Journal of Loss and Trauma*
J. Manage. *Journal of Management*
J. Marital Fam. Ther. *Journal of Marital and Family Therapy*
J. Marr. Fam. *Journal of Marriage and Family*
J. Med. Ethics *Journal of Medical Ethics*

J. Med. Genet. *Journal of Medical Genetics*
J. Med. Internet Res. *Journal of Medical Internet Research*
J. Ment. Hlth. Admin. *Journal of Mental Health Administration*
J. Ment. Hlth. Couns. *Journal of Mental Health Counseling*
J. Ment. Hlth. UK *Journal of Mental Health UK*
J. Ment. Imagery *Journal of Mental Imagery*
J. Mind Behav. *Journal of Mind and Behavior*
J. Music Ther. *Journal of Music Therapy*
J. Nerv. Ment. Dis. *Journal of Nervous and Mental Diseases*
J. Neurochem. *Journal of Neurochemistry*
J. Neuroimmun. *Journal of Neuroimmunology*
J. Neurol. Neurosurg. Psychiat. *Journal of Neurology and Neurosurgical Psychiatry*
J. Neuropsych. Clin. Neurosci. *Journal of Neuropsychiatry and Clinical Neurosciences*
J. Neuropsychiat. Clin. Neurosci. *Journal of Neuropsychiatry and Clinical Neurosciences*
J. Neurosci. *Journal of Neuroscience*
J. Neurotrauma *Journal of Neurotrauma*
J. Nurs. Scholarship *Journal of Nursing Scholarship*
J. Occup. Hlth. Psychol. *Journal of Occupational Health Psychology*
J. Occup. Med. *Journal of Occupational Medicine*
J. Pain Sympt. Manag. *Journal of Pain and Symptom Management*
J. Pediatr. Psychol. *Journal of Pediatric Psychology*
J. Perinat. Med. *Journal of Perinatal Medicine*
J. Pers. *Journal of Personality*
J. Pers. Assess. *Journal of Personality Assessment*
J. Pers. Disorders *Journal of Personality Disorders*
J. Pers. Soc. Psychol. *Journal of Personality and Social Psychology*
J. Pharmacol. Exp. Ther. *Journal of Pharmacology and Experimental Therapeutics*
J. Pineal Res. *Journal of Pineal Research*
J. Positive Behav. Interventions *Journal of Positive Behavior Interventions*
J. Prev. Psychiat. *Journal of Preventive Psychiatry*
J. Primary Prev. *Journal of Primary Prevention*
J. Psychiat. Law *Journal of Psychiatry and Law*
J. Psychiat. Neurosci. *Journal of Psychiatry & Neuroscience*
J. Psychiatr. Ment. Hlth. Nurs. *Journal of Psychiatric and Mental Health Nursing*
J. Psychiatr. Prac. *Journal of Psychiatric Practice*
J. Psychiatr. Res. *Journal of Psychiatric Research*
J. Psychoact. Drugs. *Journal of Psychoactive Drugs*
J. Psychol. Christianity *Journal of Psychology and Christianity*
J. Psychol. Human Sex. *Journal of Psychology and Human Sexuality*
J. Psychol. *Journal of Psychology*
J. Psychol. Pract. *Journal of Psychological Practice*
J. Psychol. Theol. *Journal of Psychology and Theology*
J. Psychol.: Interdiscip. Appl. *Journal of Psychology: Interdisciplinary and Applied*
J. Psychopath. Behav. Ass. *Journal of Psychopathology and Behavioral Assessment*
J. Psychopharmacol. *Journal of Psychopharmacology*
J. Psychosom. Med. *Journal of Psychosomatic Medicine*
J. Psychosom. Res. *Journal of Psychosomatic Research*
J. Psychother. Prac. Res. *Journal of Psychotherapy Practice and Research*
J. Rat.-Emot. & Cog.-Behav. Ther. *Journal of Rational-Emotive & Cognitive-Behavior Therapy*
J. Rehab. *Journal of Rehabilitation*
J. Reprod. Infant Psychol. *Journal of Reproductive and Infant Psychology*

J. Res. Adol. *Journal of Research on Adolescence*
J. Res. Pers. *Journal of Research in Personality*
J. Rural Commun. Psychol. *Journal of Rural Community Psychology*
J. Sci. Study Religion *Journal for the Scientific Study of Religion*
J. Sex Educ. Ther. *Journal of Sex Education and Therapy*
J. Sex Marital Ther. *Journal of Sex and Marital Therapy*
J. Sex Res. *Journal of Sex Research*
J. Sex. Aggress. *Journal of Sexual Aggression*
J. Sleep Res. *Journal of Sleep Research*
J. Soc. Behav. Pers. *Journal of Social Behavior and Personality*
J. Soc. Clin. Psychol. *Journal of Social and Clinical Psychology*
J. Soc. Distress Homeless *Journal of Social Distress and the Homeless*
J. Soc. Issues *Journal of Social Issues*
J. Soc. Pers. Relationships *Journal of Social and Personal Relationships*
J. Soc. Psychol. *Journal of Social Psychology*
J. Sociol. *Journal of Sociology*
J. Sociol. Soc. Welfare *Journal of Sociology and Social Welfare*
J. Spec. Group Work *Journal of Specialists in Group Work*
J. Sport Behav. *Journal of Sport Behavior*
J. Sport Exercise Psychol. *Journal of Sport and Exercise Psychology*
J. Sport. Psychol. *Journal of Sport Psychology*
J. Stud. Alc. *Journal of Studies on Alcohol*
J. Subst. Abuse Treatm. *Journal of Substance Abuse Treatments*
J. Substance Abuse. *Journal of Substance Abuse*
J. Toxicol.: Clin. Toxicol. *Journal of Toxicology: Clinical Toxicology*
J. Traum. Stress *Journal of Traumatic Stress*
J. Trauma Dissoc. *Journal of Trauma and Dissociation*
J. Urology *Journal of Urology*
J. Women's Hlth. *Journal of Women's Health*
J. Workplace Behav. Hlth. *Journal of Workplace Behavioral Health*
J. Youth Adolescence *Journal of Youth and Adolescence*
JAMA *Journal of the American Medical Association*
Jap. J. Hyp. *Japanese Journal of Hypnosis*
Jpn. J. Psychiatry. *Japanese Journal of Psychiatry*

Kindheit Entwicklung *Kindheit und Entwicklung*

Lancet *Lancet*
Law Human Behav. *Law and Human Behavior*
Law Med. Health Care *Law, Medicine and Health Care*
Law Psychol. Rev. *Law and Psychology Review*
Learn. Memory *Learning and Memory*

Marriage Fam. Rev. *Marriage and Family Review*
Med. Anthropol. *Medical Anthropology*
Med. Aspects Human Sex. *Medical Aspects of Human Sexuality*
Med. J. Austral. *Medical Journal of Australia*
Med. Sci. Law *Medicine, Science and the Law*
Med. Sci. Sports Exercise *Medicine and Science in Sports and Exercise*
Medica Psicosomatica *Medica Psicosomatica*
Mem. Cog. *Memory and Cognition*
Memory *Memory*
Ment. Hlth. Aspects Dev. Disabil. *Mental Health Aspects of Developmental Disabilities*

Ment. Hlth. Religion Cult. *Mental Health, Religion and Culture*
Ment. Hlth. Serv. Res. *Mental Health Services Research*
Ment. Physi. Disabil. Law. *Mental and Physical Disability Law*
Ment. Retard. Disabil. Res. Rev. *Mental Retardation and Developmental Disabilities Research Reviews*
Ment. Retard. *Mental Retardation*
Merrill-Palmer Quart. *Merrill-Palmer Quarterly*
Michigan Sociol. Rev. *Michigan Sociological Review*
Military Med. *Military Medicine*
MMW Fortschr. Med. *MMW Fortschritte der Medizin*
MMWR CDC *Morbidity and Mortality Weekly Report by the Centers for Disease Control and Prevention*
Mol. Psychiat. *Molecular Psychiatry*
Monit. Psychol. *Monitor on Psychology*
Mortality *Mortality*
Mt. Sinai J. Med. *Mt. Sinai Journal of Medicine*

N. Engl. J. Med. *New England Journal of Medicine*
Nat. Genet. *Nature Genetics*
Natl. Geogr. *National Geographic Magazine*
Natl. Psychol. *National Psychology*
Natl. Vital Statistics Rep. *National Vital Statistics Reports*
Nature *Nature*
Ned. Tidjschr. Geneeskd. *Nederlands Tidjschrift voor Geneeskunde*
Nerv. Child. *Nervous Child*
Neurochem. Inter. *Neurochemistry International*
Neurol. Clin. *Neurologic Clinics*
Neurology *Neurology*
Neuropsychiat. Basal Ganglia *Neuropsychiatry of the Basal Ganglia*
Neuropsychiat., Neuropsychol., Behav. Neurol. *Neuropsychiatry, Neuropsychology, and Behavioral Neurology*
Neuropsychobiology *Neuropsychobiology*
Neuropsychol. *Neuropsychology*
Neuropsychopharmacology *Neuropsychopharmacology*
Neurorep.: Rapid Communic. Neurosci. Res. *Neuroreport: For Rapid Communication of Neuroscience Research*
Neurosci. Biobehav. Rev. *Neuroscience and Biobehavioral Reviews*
Neurotoxicol. Teratol. *Neurotoxicology and Teratology*
New Zeal. Med. J. *New Zealand Medical Journal*
Nicotine Tobacco Res. *Nicotine Tobacco Research*
NORC *National Opinion Research Center*
Nord. Sex. *Nordisk Sexologi*
Nordisk Psykologi *Nordisk Psykologi*
NY St. J. Med. *New York State Journal of Medicine*

Obesity Hlth. *Obesity and Health*
Obstet. Gynecol. Clin. North Am. *Obstetrics and Gynecology Clinics of North America*
Omega: J. Death Dying *Omega: Journal of Death and Dying*

Pain Med. *Pain Medicine*
Pain *Pain*
Patient Educ. Counsel. *Patient Education and Counseling*
Pediatr. Clin. N. Amer. *Pediatric Clinics of North America*
Percept. Motor Skills *Perceptual and Motor Skills*
Pers. Individ. Diff. *Personality and Individual Differences*

Pers. Relationships *Personal Relationships*
Pers. Soc. Psychol. Bull. *Personality and Social Psychology Bulletin*
Pharma Marketletter *Pharma Marketletter*
Pharmacol. Biochem. Behav. *Pharmacological Biochemical Behavior*
Pharmacol. Biochem. Behav. *Pharmacology, Biochemistry and Behavior*
Pharmacol. Rev. *Pharmacological Reviews*
Pharmacopsychiatry *Pharmacopsychiatry*
Philos. Psychiat. Psychol. *Philosophy, Psychiatry, and Psychology*
Physician Sports Med. *The Physician and Sports Medicine*
Physiol. Behav. *Physiology and Behavior*
Police J. *Police Journal*
Postgrad. Med. J. *Postgraduate Medical Journal*
Praxis Kinderpsychol. Kinderpsych. *Praxis der Kinderpsychologie und Kinderpsychiatrie*
Prev. Treat. *Prevention and Treatment*
Prevent. Sci. *Prevention Science*
Prim. Care Psychiat. *Primary Care Psychiatry*
Primary Psychiat. *Primary Psychiatry*
Proc. Annu. Meet. Am. Psychopathol. Assoc. *Proceedings of the Annual Meeting of the American Psychopathology Association*
Proc. Natl. Acad. Sci. USA *Proceedings of the National Academy of Science USA*
Proc. R. Soc. Med. *Proceedings of the Royal Society of Medicine*
Profess. Psychol.: Res. Pract. *Professional Psychology: Research and Practice*
Profess. Psychologist *Professional Psychologist*
Profess. School Couns. *Professional School Counseling*
Prog. Neuropsychopharmacol. Biol. Psychiat. *Progressive Neuropsychopharmacological Biological Psychiatry*
Prog. Neuropsychopharmacol. *Progressive Neuropsychopharmacology*
Psichiatria-e-Psicoterapia *Psichiatria-e-Psicoterapia*
Psiquiatria *Psiquiatria*
PsycCRITIQUES *PsycCRITIQUES*
Psychiat. Psychoanal. *Psychiatry and Psychoanalysis*
Psychiat. Clin. Neurosci. *Psychiatry and Clinical Neurosciences*
Psychiat. Genet. *Psychiatric Genetics*
Psychiat. Quart. *Psychiatric Quarterly*
Psychiat. Res. *Psychiatry Research*
Psychiat. Res.: Neuroimaging *Psychiatry Research: Neuroimaging*
Psychiatr. Ann. *Psychiatric Annals*
Psychiatr. Bull. *Psychiatric Bulletin*
Psychiatr. Clin. N. Amer. *Psychiatric Clinics of North America*
Psychiatr. Hosp. *Psychiatric Hospital*
Psychiatr. J. Univ. Ottawa *Psychiatric Journal of the University of Ottawa*
Psychiatr. News *Psychiatric News*
Psychiatr. Quart. *Psychiatric Quarterly*
Psychiatr. Rehab. J. *Psychiatric Rehabilitation Journal*
Psychiatr. Serv. *Psychiatric Services*
Psychiatr. Times *Psychiatric Times*
Psychiatria Fennica *Psychiatria Fennica*
Psychiatria Hungarica *Psychiatria Hungarica*
Psychiatriki *Psychiatriki*
Psychiatry, Psychol. Law *Psychiatry, Psychology and Law*
Psychiatry: Interpers. Biol. Process. *Psychiatry: Interpersonal and Biological Processes*
Psychoanal. Inq. *Psychoanalytic Inquiry*
Psychoanal. Psychol. *Psychoanalytic Psychology*
Psychoanal. Q. *Psychoanalytic Quarterly*

Psychoanal. Rev. *Psychoanalytic Review*
Psychoanalytic Psychother. *Psychoanalytic Psychotherapy*
Psychodyn. Pract.: Indiv. Groups Org. *Psychodynamic Practice: Individuals, Groups and Organisations*
Psychohist. Rev. *Psychohistory Review*
Psychol. Addict. Behav. *Psychology of Addictive Behavior*
Psychol. Aging *Psychology and Aging*
Psychol. Assess. *Psychological Assessment*
Psychol. Bull. *Psychological Bulletin*
Psychol. Crime Law *Psychology, Crime, and Law*
Psychol. Hlth. *Psychology and Health*
Psychol. Hlth. Med. *Psychology, Health and Medicine*
Psychol. Med. *Psychological Medicine*
Psychol. Psychother.: Theory Res. Prac. *Psychology and Psychotherapy: Theory, Research and Practice*
Psychol. Pub. Pol. Law *Psychology, Public Policy and Law*
Psychol. Rec. *Psychological Record*
Psychol. Rep. *Psychological Reports*
Psychol. Rev. *Psychological Review*
Psychol. Schools *Psychology in the Schools*
Psychol. Sci. *Psychological Science*
Psychol. Sci. Pub. Interest *Psychological Science in the Public Interest*
Psychol. Serv. *Psychological Services*
Psychol. Today *Psychology Today*
Psychol. Women Quart. *Psychology of Women Quarterly*
Psychol.: J. Hellen. Psychol. Soc. *Psychology: The Journal of the Hellenic Psychological Society*
The Psychologist *The Psychologist*
Psychol: J. Human Behav. *Psychology: A Journal of Human Behavior*
Psycholoog *Psycholoog*
Psychoneuroendocrinology *Psychoneuroendocrinology*
Psycho-Oncology *Psycho-Oncology*
Psychopathology *Psychopathology*
Psychopharmacol. Bull. *Psychopharmacology Bulletin*
Psychopharmacology (Berl.) *Psychopharmacology (Berlin)*
Psychopharmacology *Psychopharmacology*
Psychophysiology *Psychophysiology*
Psychosom.: J. Cons. Liaison Psychiat. *Psychosomatics: Journal of Consultation Liaison Psychiatry*
Psychosom. Med. *Psychosomatic Medicine*
Psychosomatics *Psychosomatics*
Psychother. Forum *Psychotherapie Forum*
Psychother. Priv. Prac. *Psychotherapy in Private Practice*
Psychother. Psychosom. *Psychotherapy and Psychosomatics*
Psychother. Res. *Psychotherapy Research*
Psychother.: Theory Res. Prac. *Psychotherapy: Theory, Research, and Practice*
Psychotherapy *Psychotherapy*
Pub. Hlth. Rep. *Public Health Reports*
Public Pers. Manag. *Public Personnel Management*

Q. Rev. Biol. *The Quarterly Review of Biology*
Quart. J. Stud. Alcohol. *Quarterly Journal on the Studies of Alcoholism*

Rehab. Couns. Bull. *Rehabilitation Counseling Bulletin*
Rehab. Nursing *Rehabilitation Nursing*
Rehab. Psychol. *Rehabilitation Psychology*
Remed. Spec. Educ. *Remedial and Special Education*

Reprod. Nutr. Dev. *Reproductive and Nutritional Development*
Res. Aging *Research on Aging*
Res. Nursing Hlth. *Research in Nursing and Health*
Res. Soc. Work Prac. *Research on Social Work Practice*
Res. Dev. Disabil. *Research in Developmental Disabilities*
Rev. Bras. Psicanal *Revista Brasileira De Psicanalise*
Rev. Gen. Psychol. *Review of General Psychology*
Revista Argentina de Clinica Psicologica *Revista Argentina de Clinica Psicologica*
Revista Brasileira de Psiquiatria *Revista Brasileira de Psiquiatria*
Ricerche di Psicologia *Ricerche di Psicologia*
Roper Rev. *Roper Review*

S. Afr. J. Psychol. *South African Journal of Psychology*
S. Afr. Psychiat. Rev. *South African Psychiatry Review*
Salud Mental *Salud Mental*
Scand. J. Psychol. *Scandinavian Journal of Psychology*
Scand. J. Work Envir. Hlth. *Scandinavian Journal of Work, Environment and Health*
Schizo. Bull. *Schizophrenic Bulletin*
Schizo. Res. *Schizophrenia Research*
Sci. News *Science News*
Science *Science*
Scientif. Amer. *Scientific American*
Sem. in Neuro. *Seminars in Neurology*
Sex. Abuse: J. Res. Treat. *Sexual Abuse: Journal of Research and Treatment*
Sex. Disability *Sexual Disability*
Sex. Marital Ther. *Sexual and Marital Therapy*
Sex. Relat. Ther. *Sexual and Relationship Therapy*
Sex. Relationship Ther. *Sexual Relationship Therapy*
Sexualities, Evol. Gender *Sexualities, Evolution and Gender*
Sleep Hyp. *Sleep and Hypnosis*
Soc. Behav. Pers. *Social Behavior and Personality*
Soc. Forces *Social Forces*
Soc. Indicators Res. *Social Indicators Research*
Soc. Psychiat. *Social Psychiatry*
Soc. Psychiat. Psychiatr. Epidemiol. *Social Psychiatry and Psychiatric Epidemiology*
Soc. Sci. Inter. *Social Science International*
Soc. Sci. Med. *Social Science and Medicine*
Soc. Sci. Res. *Social Science Research*
Soc. Study Addict. *Society for the Study of Addiction*
Soc. Work *Social Work*
Soc. Work Hlth. Care *Social Work Health Care*
Sport Psychol. *Sport Psychologist*
Sports Med. *Sports Medicine*
Steroids *Steroids*
Stress Hlth.: J. Inter. Soc. Invest. Stress *Stress and Health: Journal of the International Society for the Investigation of Stress*
Stress, Trauma, Crisis *Stress, Trauma, Crisis*
Stress, Trauma, Crisis: Inter. J. *Stress, Trauma, Crisis: International Journal*
Stress: Inter. J. Biol. Stress *Stress: The International Journal of the Biology of Stress*
Subs. Abuse *Substance Abuse*
Substance Use Misuse *Substance Use and Misuse*
Suic. Life-Threat. Behav. *Suicide and Life-Threatening Behavior*

Tex. Mon. Mag. *Texas Monthly Magazine*
Topics Early Childhood Spec. Ed. *Topics in Early Childhood Special Education*
Transcult. Psychiatr. Res. Rev. *Transcultural Psychiatric Research Review*
Transplant Proc. *Transplant Proceedings*
Trauma, Violence, Abuse *Trauma, Violence, Abuse*

Trends Cog. Sci. *Trends in Cognitive Sciences*
Trends Cell Biol. *Trends in Cell Biology*
Trends Neurosci. *Trends in Neuroscience*
Trends Pharmacol. Sci. *Trends in Pharmacological Sciences*

Verhaltenstherapie *Verhaltenstherapie*
Vet. Hum. Toxicol. *Veterinary and Human Toxicology*
Violence Against Women *Violence Against Women*
Visual Cog. *Visual Cognition*

Western J. Nurs. Res. *Western Journal of Nursing Research*
Women Hlth. *Women & Health*
Women Ther. *Women and Therapy*

Zeitschr. Klin. Psychol. Psychother.: Forsch. Prax. *Zeitschrift Fuer Klinische Psychologie und Psychotherapie Forschung und Praxis*
Zeitschrift Gerontopsychol. Psychiat. *Zeitschrift fur Gerontopsychologie und Psychiatrie*

References

AA World Services (2005). AA fact file. New York: AA World Services.

AAAAI (American Academy of Allergy Asthma & Immunology). (2005, June). Topic of the Month: Enjoy summer vacation with allergies and asthma. Milwaukee, WI: Author.

Aalto-Setala, T., & Marttunen, M. (2003). Substance use disorders (SUD) among youth: Prevalence, course and comorbidity. *Psychiatria Fennica, 34,* 107–117.

AAMR (American Association on Mental Retardation). (2005). *AAMR fact sheets.* From AAMR.

Aanstoos, C. M. (2003). The relevance of humanistic psychology. *J. Human. Psychol., 43*(3), 121–132.

AAP (American Academy of Pediatrics). (1999). Media education, policy statement. *Pediatrics, 104*(2), 341–343.

AARP (American Association of Retired Persons). (1990). *A profile of older Americans.* Washington, DC: Author.

Abbey, S. E. (2005). Somatization and somatoform disorders. In J. L. Levenson (Ed.), *The Amerian Psychiatric Publishing textbook of psychosomatic medicine* (pp. 271–296). Washington, DC: American Psychiatric Publishing.

Abdulhamid, I. (2002). Munchausen by proxy. *eMed. J., 3*(1).

Abel, G. G., Becker, J. V., & Cunningham-Rathner, J. (1984). Complications, consent, and cognitions in sex between children and adults. *Inter. J. Law Psychiat., 7,* 89–103.

Abel, G. G., Jordan, A., Hand, C. G., Holland, L. A., & Phipps, A. (2001). Classification models of child molesters utilizing the Abel Assessment for child sexual abuse interest. *Child Abuse Negl., 25*(5), 703–718.

Abela, J. R. Z., Brozina, K., & Seligman, M. E. P. (2004). A test of integration of the activation hypothesis and the diathesis-stress component of the hopelessness theory of depression. *Brit. J. Clin. Psychol., 32*(2), 111–128.

Abou-Saleh, M. T. (1992). Lithium. In E. S. Paykel (Ed.), Handbook of affective disorders. New York: Guilford Press.

Abou-Saleh, M. T., Ghubash, R., Karim, L., Krymski, M., & Anderson, D. N. (1999). The role of pterins and related factors in the biology of early postpartum depression. *Eur. Neuropsychopharmacology, 9*(4), 295–300.

Abraham, K. (1911). Notes on the psychoanalytic investigation and treatment of manic-depressive insanity and allied conditions. In *Selected papers on psychoanalysis* (pp. 137–156). New York: Basic Books. (Work republished 1960)

Abraham, K. (1916). The first pregenital stage of the libido. In *Selected papers on psychoanalysis* (pp. 248–279). New York: Basic Books. (Work republished 1960)

Abraham, S., & Llewellyn-Jones, D. (1984). *Eating disorders: The facts.* New York: Oxford University Press.

Abram, K. M., & Teplin, L. A. (1990). Drug disorder, mental illness, and violence. *Nat. Inst. Drug Abuse Res. Monogr. Ser., 103,* 222–238.

Abrams, K. M., & Robinson, G. E. (1998). Stalking: Part I. An overview of the problem. *Canad. J. Psychiat., 43*(5), 473–476.

Abramson, L. Y., Alloy, L. B., Hankin, B. L., Haeffel, G. J., MacCoon, D. G., & Gibb, B. E. (2002). Cognitive vulnerability—Stress models of depression in a self-regulatory and psychobiological context. In I. H. Gotlib & C. L. Hammen (Eds.), *Handbook of depression* (pp. 268–294). New York: Guilford Press.

Abramson, L. Y., Metalsky, G. I., & Alloy, L. B. (1989). Hopelessness depression: A theory-based subtype of depression. *Psychol. Rev., 96*(2), 358–372.

Abramson, L. Y., Seligman, M. E., & Teasdale, J. D. (1978). Learned helplessness in humans: Critique and reformulation. *J. Abnorm. Psychol., 87*(1), 49–74.

Achenbach, T. M., Krukowski, R. A., Dumenci, L., & Ivanova, M. Y. (2005). Assessment of adult psychopathology: Meta-analyses and implications of cross-informant correlations. *Psychol. Bull., 131*(3), 361–382.

Acocella, J. (1999). *Creating hysteria: Women and multiple personality disorder.* San Francisco: Jossey-Bass.

Acosta, M. C., Haller, D. L., & Schnoll, S. H. (2005). Cocaine and stimulants. In R. J. Frances, A. H. Mack, & S. I. Miller (Eds.), *Clinical textbook of addictive disorders* (3rd ed., pp. 184–218). New York: Guilford Press.

Adam, K. S., Bouckoms, A., & Streiner, D. (1982). Parental loss and family stability in attempted suicide. *Arch. Gen. Psychiat., 39* (9), 1081–1085.

Adams, L., Gouvousis, A., VanLue, M., & Waldron, C. (2004). Social story intervention: Improving communication skills in a child with an autism spectrum disorder. *Focus Autism Other Dev. Disabil., 19*(2), 87–94.

Adams, P. R., & Adams, G. R. (1984). Mount Saint Helen's ashfall: Evidence for a disaster stress reaction. *Amer. Psychologist, 39,* 252–260.

Adams, R. E., & Boscarino, J. A. (2005). Stress and well-being in the aftermath of the World Trade Center attack: The continuing effects of a communitywide disaster. *J. Comm. Psychol., 33*(2), 175–190.

Adams, W. L., & Cox, N. S. (1997). Epidemiology of problem drinking among elderly people. In A. Gurnack (Ed.), *Older adults' misuse of alcohol, medicines, and other drugs.* New York: Springer.

Adelson, R. (2005). Limit violations just spur more drinking. *Monitor Psychol., 36*(9), 20–21.

Ader, R., Felten, D. L., & Cohen, N. (Eds.). (2001). *Psychoneuroimmunology* (3rd ed., Vols. 1 & 2). San Diego, CA: Academic Press.

Adler, G. (2000). The alliance and the more disturbed patient. In S. T. Levy (Ed.), *The therapeutic alliance. Workshop series of the American Psychoanalytic Association, Monograph 9.* Madison, CT: International Universities Press.

Adler, T. (1992). Prenatal cocaine exposure has subtle, serious effects. *APA Monitor, 23*(11), 17.

Affatati, V., de Nicola, V., Santoro, M., Bellomo, A., Todarello, G., & Todarello, O. (2004). Psychotherapy of gender identity disorder: Problems and perspectives. *Medica Psicosomatica, 49*(1–2), 57–64.

Agran, M., Sinclair, T., Alper, S., Cavin, M., Wehmeyer, M., & Hughes, C. (2005). Using self-monitoring to increase following-direction skills of students with moderate to severe disabilities in general education. *Educ. Train. Dev. Disabil., 40*(1), 3–13.

Agras, W. S. (1995). Treatment of eating disorders. In A. F. Schatzberg & C. B. Nemeroff (Eds.), *The American Psychiatric Press textbook of psychopharmacology.* Washington, DC: American Psychiatric Press.

Agras, W. S., Sylvester, D., & Oliveau, D. (1969). The epidemiology of common fears and phobias. *Comprehen. Psychiat., 10*(2), 151–156.

Agronin, M. E. (2006). Personality disorders. In D. V. Jeste & J. H. Friedman (Eds.), *Psychiatry for neurologists.* Totowa, NJ: Humana Press.

AHA (American Heart Association). (2005). Coronary heart disease and angina pectoris. Dallas, TX: Author.

AHA (American Heart Association). (2005). Risk factors and coronary heart disease. Dallas, TX: Author.

Aiken, L. R. (1985). *Psychological testing and assessment* (5th ed.). Boston: Allyn & Bacon.

Aiken, L. R., & Groth-Marnat, G. (2006). *Psychological testing and assessment* (12th ed.). New York: Pearson/Allyn & Bacon.

Akechi, T., Okamura, H., Yamawaki, S., & Uchitomi, Y. (2001). Why do some cancer patients with depression desire an early death and others do not? *Psychosomatics, 42*(2), 141–145.

Akerele, E. O., & Levin, F. R. (2002). Substance abuse among patients with schizophrenia. *J. Psychiat. Prac., 8*(2), 70–80.

Akhtar, S., Wig, N. H., Verma, V. K., Pershod, D., & Verma, S. K. (1975). A phenomenological analysis of symptoms in obsessive-compulsive neuroses. *Brit. J. Psychiat., 127,* 342–348.

Akins, C. K. (2004). The role of Pavlovian conditioning in sexual behavior: A comparative analysis of human and nonhuman animals. *Inter. J. Compat. Psychol., 17*(2–3), 241–262.

Akins, C. K., Panicker, S., & Cunningham, C. L. (Eds.). (2005). *Laboratory animals in research and teaching: Ethics, care, and methods.* Washington, DC: American Psychological Association.

Akiskal, H. S. (2005). Searching for behavioral indicators of bipolar II in patients presenting with major depressive episodes: The "red sign," the "rule of three" and other biographic signs of temperamental extravagance, activation and hypomania. *J. Affect. Disorders, 84*(2–3), 279–290.

Akiskal, H. S. (2005). The dark side of bipolarity: Detecting bipolar depression in its pleomorphic expressions. *J. Affect. Disorders, 84*(2–3), 107–115.

Akyuz, G., Sar, V., Kugu, N., & Dogan, O. (2005). Reported childhood trauma, attempted suicide and self-mutilative behavior among women in the general population. *Eur. Psychiat., 20*(3), 268–273.

Albert, U., Maina, G., Forner, F., & Bogetto, F. (2004). DSM-IV obsessive-compulsive personality disorder: Prevalence in patients with anxiety disorders and in healthy comparison subjects. *Comprehen. Psychiat., 45*(5), 325–332.

Aldhous, P. (1996, April 27). Matching proteins raise CJD fears. *New Scientist,* p. 21.

Aldwin, C. M., & Gilmer, D. F. (2004). *Health, illness, and optimal aging. Biological and psychosocial perspectives.* Thousand Oaks, CA: Sage.

Aldwin, C. M., Spiro, A. III, & Park, C. L. (2006). Health, behavior, and optimal aging: A life span developmental perspective. In J. E. Birren & K. W. Schaie (Eds.), *Handbook of the psychology of aging* (6th ed., pp. 85–104). San Diego, CA: Elsevier Academic Press.

Alegria, M., Kessler, R. C., Bijl, R., Lin, E., Heeringa, S. G., Takeuchi, D. T., et al. (2000). Comparing data on mental health service use between countries. In G. Andrews & S. Henderson (Eds.), *Unmet need in psychiatry: Problems, resources, responses* (pp. 97–118). New York: Cambridge University Press.

Alegria, M., Takeuchi, D., Canino, G., Duan, N., Shrout, P., Meng, X. L., et al. (2004). Considering context, place and culture: The National Latino and Asian American Study. *Inter. J. Methods Psychiatr. Res., 13*(4), 208–220.

Alexander, J. F., Sexton, T. L., & Robbins, M. S. (2002). The developmental status of family therapy in family psychology intervention science. In H. A. Liddle, D. A. Santiseban, R. F. Levant, & J. H. Bray (Eds.), *Family psychology: Science-based interventions* (pp. 17–40) Washington, DC: American Psychological Association.

Alexopoulos, G. S. (2005). Depression in the elderly. *Lancet, 365*(9475), 1961–1970.

Ali, L., & Miller, L. (2004, August 9). The new infidelity: Overworked and underappreciated, more American wives are seeking comfort in the arms of other men. *Newsweek* (Internet ed.), p. 51.

Allan, C. A., Smith, I., & Mellin, M. (2000). Detoxification from alcohol: A comparison of home detoxification and hospital-based day patient care. *Alcohol Alcoholism, 35*(1), 66–69.

Allard, R., Marshall, M., & Plante, M. C. (1992). Intensive follow-up does not decrease the risk of repeat suicide attempts. *Suic. Life-Threat. Behav., 22,* 303–314.

Allderidge, P. (1979). Hospitals, madhouses and asylums: Cycles in the care of the insane. *Brit. J. Psychiat., 134,* 321–334.

Allen, C. (2005). The links between heroin, crack cocaine and crime: Where does street crime fit in? *Brit. J. Criminol., 45*(3), 355–372.

Allen, J. G. (1993). Dissociative processes: Theoretical underpinnings of a working model for clinician and patient. *Bull. Menninger Clin., 57*(3), 287–308.

Allen, J. J. B. (2002). The role of psychophysiology in clinical assessment: ERPs in the evaluation of memory. *Psychophysiology, 39*(3), 261–280.

Allen, N. B., Gilbert, P., & Semedar, A. (2004). Depressed mood as an interpersonal strategy: The importance of relational models. In N. Haslem (Ed.), *Relational models theory: A contemporary overview* (pp. 309–334). Mahwah, NJ: Lawrence Erlbaum Associates.

Allgood-Merten, B., Lewinsohn, P. M., & Hops, H. (1990). Sex differences and adolescent depression. *J. Abnorm. Psychol., 99*(1), 55–63.

Allison, K. C., & Friedman, L. S. (2004, September 27). Soothing a sensitive gut. *Newsweek, 144*(13), 71.

Allsop, S., Saunders, B., & Phillips, M. (2000). The process of relapse in severely dependent male problem drinkers. *Addiction, 95*(1), 95–106.

Althof, S. E. (1995). Pharmacologic treatment of rapid ejaculation. Special issue: Clinical sexuality. *Psychiatr. Clin. N. Amer., 18*(1), 85–94.

Althof, S. E., Levine, S. B., Corty, E., Risen, C., & Stern, E. (1994, March). *The role of clomipramine in the treatment of premature ejaculation.* Paper presented at the 16th annual meeting of the Society for Sex Therapy and Research.

Althof, S. E., & Seftel, A. D. (1995). The evaluation and management of erectile dysfunction. *Psychiatr. Clin. N. Amer., 18*(1), 171–191.

Altman, C. A. (2001). Effects of selective-serotonin reuptake inhibitors on sexual function. *J. Clin. Psychopharmacol., 21*(2), 241–242.

Alves, T. M., Pereira, J. C. R., & Elkis, H. (2005). The psychopathological factors of refractory schizophrenia. *Revista Brasilieira de Psiquiatria, 27*(2), 108–112.

Alzheimer's Association. (1997, February 17). Survey: Stress on Alzheimer caregivers. Cited in *USA Today*, p. 1D.

Amass, L., Kamien, J. B., & Mikulich, S. K. (2000). Efficacy of daily and alternate-day dosing regimens with the combination buprenorphine-naloxone tablet. *Drug Alc. Dep., 58*(1–2), 143–152.

American Society for Aesthetic Plastic Surgery. (2004). 11.9 million cosmetic procedures in 2004: American society for aesthetic plastic surgery reports 44 percent increase. Press release from ASAPS.

Amsterdam, J. D. (2003). A double-blind, placebo-controlled trial of the safety and efficacy of Selegiline Transdermal System without dietary restrictions in patients with major depressive disorder. *J. Clin. Psychiat., 64,* 208–214.

Ancoli-Israel, S., & Cooke, J. R. (2005). Prevalence and comorbidity of insomnia and effect on functioning in elderly populations. *J. Amer. Ger. Soc., 53*(Suppl. 7), S264–S271.

Andersen, A. E. (1985). *Practical comprehensive treatment of anorexia nervosa and bulimia.* Baltimore: Johns Hopkins University Press.

Anderson, A. J. (2000). Therapeutic program models for mentally ill chemical abusers. *Inter. J. Psychosoc. Rehab., 4,* 93–105.

Anderson, D. (1994). *Breaking the tradition on college campuses: Reducing drug and alcohol misuse.* Fairfax, VA: George Mason University Press.

Anderson, K. E., Taber, K. H., & Hurley, R. A. (2005). Functional imaging. In T. W. McAllister, S. C. Yudofsky, & J. M. Silver (Eds.), *Textbook of traumatic brain injury* (pp. 107–133). Washington, DC: American Psychiatric Publishing.

Anderson, K. G., Sankis, L. M., & Widiger, T. A. (2001). Pathology versus statistical infrequency: Potential sources of gender bias in personality disorder criteria. *J. Nerv. Ment. Dis., 189*(10), 661–668.

Anderson, R. N. (2002). Deaths: Leading causes for 2000. *Natl. Vital Statistics Rep., 50*(16), [np].

Anderson-Fye, E. P. (2004). A "Coca-Cola" shape: Cultural change, body image, and eating disorders in San Andres, Belize. *Cult. Med. Psychiat., 28*(4), 561–595.

Andrade, V. M. (1996). Superego, narcissism and culture. *Revista Brasilieira de Psicanalise, 30*(2), 385–405.

Andrasik, F., & Walch, S. E. (2003). Headaches. In A. M. Nezu, C. J. Nezu, P. A. Geller, & I. B. Weiner (Eds.), *Handbook of psychology: Health psychology* (Vol. 9, pp. 245–266). New York: Wiley.

Andreasen, N. C. (2001). *Brave new brain: Conquering mental illness in the era of the genome.* New York: Oxford University Press.

Andreasen, N. C. (Ed.) (2005). *Research advances in genetics and genomics: Implications for psychiatry.* Washington, DC: American Psychiatric Publishing.

Andresen, J. (2000). Meditation meets behavioral medicine: The story of experimental research on meditation. *J. Consciousness. Stud., 7*(11–12), 17–73.

Andrews, B., & Wilding, J. M. (2004). The relation of depression and anxiety to life-stress and achievement in students. *Brit. J. Psychol., 95*(4), 509–521.

Andrews, V. (1998, December 14). Abducted by aliens? Or just a little schizoid? *HealthScout.*

Angier, N. (2001, May 20). Bully for you: Why push comes to shove. *New York Times,* Sect. 4, p. 1.

Angst, J., Gamma, A., Endrass, J., Goodwin, R., Ajdacic, V., Eich, D., et al. (2004). Obsessive-compulsive severity spectrum in the community: Prevalence, comorbidity, and course. *Eur. Arch. Psychiat. Clin. Neurosci., 254*(3), 156–164.

Angst, J., Gamma, A., Endrass, J., Hantouche, E., Goodwin, R., Ajdacic, V., et al. (2005). Obsessive-compulsive syndromes and disorders: Significance of comorbidity with bipolar and anxiety syndromes. *Eur. Arch. Psychiat. Clin. Neurosci., 255*(1), 65–71.

Angst, J., Sellaro, R., Stassen, H. H., & Gamma, A. (2005). Diagnostic conversion from depression to bipolar disorders: Results of a long-term prospective study of hospital admissions. *J. Affect. Disorders, 84*(2–3), 149–157.

Anonymous. (1996). First person account: Social, economic, and medical effects of schizophrenia. *Schizo. Bull., 22*(1), 183.

Anooshian, J., Streltzer, J., & Goebert, D. (1999). Effectiveness of a psychiatric pain clinic. *Psychosomatics, 40*(3), 226–232.

Anthony, J. C., Arria, A. M., & Johnson, E. O. (1995). Epidemiological and public health issues for tobacco, alcohol, and other drugs. In J. M. Oldham & M. B. Riba (Eds.), *American Psychiatric Press review of psychiatry* (Vol. 14). Washington, DC: American Psychiatric Press.

Antoni, M. H. (2005). Behavioural interventions and psychoneuroimmunology. In K. Vedhara & M. Irwin (Eds.), *Human psychoneuroimmunology.* Oxford, England: Oxford University Press.

Antony, M. M., & Barlow, D. H. (2002). Specific phobias. In D. H. Barlow (Ed.), *Anxiety and its disorders: The nature and treatment of anxiety and panic* (2nd ed., pp. 380–417). New York: Guilford Press.

Antony, M. M., & Swinson, R. P. (2000). *Phobic disorders and panic in adults: A guide to assessment and treatment.* Washington, DC: American Psychological Association.

APA (American Psychiatric Association). (1993). *Practice guideline for major depressive disorder in adults.* Washington, DC: Author.

APA (American Psychiatric Association). (1994). *Diagnostic and statistical manual of mental disorders* (4th ed.). Washington, DC: Author.

APA (American Psychiatric Association). (2000). *DSM-IV text revision.* Washington, DC: Author.

APA (American Psychological Association). (1992). Ethical principles of psychologists and code of conduct. Washington: DC: Author.

APA (American Psychological Association). (2002). Ethical principles of psychologists and code of conduct. Washington: DC: Author.

APA (American Psychological Association). (2005). Executive summary: Risk factors for meeting the public's need for health service psychologists. Washington, DC: Author.

APA (American Psychological Association). (2005, March 3). American Psychological Association announces plans for next phase of tsunami relief efforts. Press release.

Appel, J. B., West, W. B., and Buggy, J. (2004). LSD, Serotonin (5 HT) and the evolution of a behavioral assay. *Neurosci. Biobehav. Rev., 27* 693–701.

Apter, A., Kronenberg, S., & Brent, D. (2005). Turning darkness into light: A new landmark study on the treatment of adolescent depression. Comments on the TADS study. *Eur. Child Adol. Psychiat., 14*(3), 113–116.

Archer, D., & McDaniel, P. (1995). Violence and gender: Differences and similarities across societies. In R. B. Ruback & N. A. Weiner (Eds.), *Interpersonal violent behaviors: Social and cultural aspects.* New York: Springer.

Ardoin, S. P., Martens, B. K., Wolfe, L. A., Hilt, A. M., & Rosenthal, B. D. (2004). A method for conditioning reinforcer preferences in students with moderate mental retardation. *J. Dev. Phys. Disabil., 16*(1), 33–51.

Arieti, S. (1974). *Interpretation of schizophrenia.* New York: Basic Books.

Arieti, S., & Bemporad, J. (1978). *Severe and mild depression: The psychotherapeutic approach.* New York: Basic Books.

Aring, C. D. (1974). The Gheel experience: Eternal spirit of the chainless mind! *JAMA, 230*(7), 998–1001.

Aring, C. D. (1975). Gheel: The town that cares. *Fam. Hlth., 7*(4), 54–55, 58, 60.

Armour, D., & Paton, C. (2004). Melatonin in the treatment of insomnia in children and adolescents. *Psychiatr. Bull., 28*(6), 222–224.

Arndt, W. B., Hietpas, T., & Kim, J. (2004). Critical characteristics of male serial murderers. *Amer. J. Criminal Justice, 29*(1), 117–131.

Arnette, J. J. (1996). Physiological effects of chronic grief: A biofeedback treatment approach. *Death Stud., 20,* 59–72.

Arntz, A. (2005). Introduction to special issue: Cognition and emotion in borderline personality disorder. *J. Behav. Ther. Exp. Psychiat., 36*(3), 167–172.

Arvanites, T. M. (1989). The differential impact of deinstitutionalization on white and nonwhite defendants found incompetent to stand trial. *Bull. Amer. Acad. Psychiat. Law, 17,* 311–320.

ASA (Autism Society of America). (2005). Asperger's syndrome.

ASA (Autism Society of America). (2006). Asperger's syndrome.

Asarnow, J. R., Asarnow, R. F., Hornstein, N., & Russell, A. (1991). Childhood-onset schizophrenia: Developmental perspectives on schizophrenic disorders. In E. F. Walker (Ed.), *Schizophrenia: A life-course developmental perspective.* San Diego: Academic Press.

Asberg, M., Traskman, L., & Thoren, P. (1976). 5 HIAA in the cerebrospinal fluid: A biochemical suicide predictor? *Arch. Gen. Psychiat., 33*(10), 1193–1197.

Aserinsky, E., & Kleitman, N. (1953). Eye movements during sleep. *Fed. Process, 13,* 6–7.

Ash, P. (2002). Malpractice in child and adolescent psychiatry. *Child Adol. Psychiat. Clin. N. Amer., 11*(4), 869–885

Ash, R. (1998). *The top 10 of everything 1999.* New York: DK Publishing.

Ash, R. (1999). *Fantastic book of 1001 facts.* New York: DK Publishing.

Ash, R. (2001). *The top 10 of everything 2002* (American ed.). New York: DK Publishing.

Ashton, C. H. (2001). Pharmacology and effects of cannabis: A brief review. *Brit. J. Psychiat., 178,* 101–106.

Ashton, J. R., & Donnan, S. (1981). Suicide by burning as an epidemic phenomenon: An analysis of 82 deaths and inquests in England and Wales in 1978–9. *Psychol. Med., 11*(4), 735–739.

Asimov, I. (1997). *Isaac Asimov's book of facts.* New York: Random House (Wings Books).

Asmundson, G. J. G., & Taylor, S. (2005). *It's not all in your head. How worrying about your health could be making you sick — and what you can do about it.* New York: Guilford Press.

Asmundson, G. J. G., Stapleton, J. A., & Taylor, S. (2004). Are avoidance and numbing distinct PTSD symptom clusters? *J. Traum. Stress, 17*(6), 467–475.

Asplund, R. (2005). Sleep and sensory organ functions in the elderly. *Sleep Hyp., 7*(2), 68–76.

Associated Press. (2005, March 8). Dominican man dies after drinking contest. *Associated Press (Santo Domingo)/Netscape News with CNN.*

Astin, J. A. (2004). Mind-body therapies for the management of pain. *Clin. J. Pain, 20*(1), 27–32.

Ator, N. A. (2005). Contributions of GABA-sub(A) receptor subtype selectivity to abuse liability and dependence potential of pharmacological treatments for anxiety and sleep disorders. *CNS Spectrums, 10*(1), 31–39.

Attridge, M. (2004). The business case for the integration of employee assistance, work-life and wellness services: A literature review. *J. Workplace Behav. Hlth., 20*(1–2), 31–55.

Auchincloss, E. L., & Weiss, R. W. (1992). Paranoid character and the intolerance of indifference. *J. Amer. Psychoanal. Assoc., 40*(4), 1013–1037.

Avery, D., & Lubrano, A. (1979). Depression treated with imipramine and ECT: The De-Carolis study reconsidered. *Amer. J. Psychiat., 136,* 559–569.

Awata, S., Seki, T., Koizumi, Y., Sato, S., Hozawa, A., Omori, K., et al. (2005). Factors associated with suicidal ideation in an elderly urban Japanese population: A community-based,

cross-sectional study. *Psychiat. Clin. Neurosci., 59*(3), 327–336.

Ayalon, L., Arean, P. A., & Alvidrez, J. (2005). Adherence to antidepressant medications in black and Latino elderly patients. *Amer. J. Ger. Psychiat., 13*(7), 572–580.

Ayalon, L., & Huyck, M. H. (2001). Latino caregivers of relatives with Alzheimer's disease. *Clin. Geront., 24*(3–4), 93–106.

Ayalon, L., & Young, M. A. (2003). A comparison of depressive symptoms in African Americans and Caucasian Americans. *J. Cross-Cult. Psychol. 34*(1), 111–124.

Ayd, F. J., & Palma, J. M. (1999, May). Suicide: Risk recognition and prevention. *Psychiat. Times, XVI*(5).

Ayd, F. J., Jr. (1956). A clinical evaluation of Frenquel. *J. Nerv. Ment. Dis., 124,* 507–509.

Ayllon, T. (1963). Intensive treatment of psychotic behavior by stimulus satiation and food reinforcement. *Behav. Res. Ther., 1,* 53–62.

Ayllon, T., & Michael, J. (1959). The psychiatric nurse as a behavioural engineer. *J. Exp. Anal. Behav., 2,* 323–334.

Ayoub, C. C., Deutsch, R. M., & Kinscherff, R. (2000). Munchausen by proxy: Definitions, identification, and evaluation. In R. M. Reece (Ed.), *Treatment of child abuse: Common ground for mental health, medical, and legal practitioners* (pp. 213–226). Baltimore: Johns Hopkins University Press.

Ayoub, C. C., Deutsch, R. M., & Kinscherff, R. (2000). Psychosocial management issues in Munchausen by proxy. In R. M. Reese (Ed.), *Treatment of child abuse: Common ground for mental health, medical, and legal practitioners* (pp. 226–235). Baltimore: Johns Hopkins University Press.

Azar, B. (1995). Mental disabilities and the brain-gene link. *APA Monitor, 26*(12), 18.

Azar, S. T., Ferraro, M. H., & Breton, S. J. (1998). Intrafamilial child maltreatment. In T. H. Ollendick & M. Hersen (Eds.), *Handbook of child psychopathology* (3rd ed.). New York: Plenum.

Azima, F. J. C. (1993). Group psychotherapy with personality disorders. In H. I. Kaplan & B. J. Sadock (Eds.), *Comprehensive group psychotherapy* (3rd ed.). Baltimore: Williams & Wilkins.

Azrin, N. H., Thienes-Hontos, P., & Bensalel-Azrin, V. (1979). Elimination of enuresis without a conditioning apparatus: An extension by office instruction of the child and parents. *Behav. Ther., 10,* 14–19.

Babor, T. F., Steinberg, K., Anton, R., & Del Bocca, F. (2000). Talk is cheap: Measuring drinking outcomes in clinical trials. *J. Stud. Alc., 61*(1), 55–63.

Bach, A. K., Wincze, J. P., & Barlow, D. H. (2001). Sexual dysfunction. In D. H. Barlow (Ed.), *Clinical handbook of psychological disorders: A step-by-step treatment manual* (3rd ed., pp. 562–608). New York: Guilford Press.

Bachmann, A. W., Sedgley, T. L., Jackson, R. V., Gibson, J. N., Young, R. McD., & Torpy, D. J. (2005). Glucocorticoid receptor polymorphisms and post-traumatic stress disorder. *Psychoneuroendocrinology, 30*(3), 297–306.

Backmund, M., Meyer, K., Eichenlaub, D., & Schuetz, C. G. (2001). Predictors for completing an inpatient detoxification program among

intravenous heroin users, methadone substituted and codeine substituted patients. *Drug Alc. Dep., 64*(2), 173–180.

Baer, L. (2001). *The imp of the mind: Exploring the silent epidemic of obsessive bad thoughts.* New York: Dutton/Penguin Books.

Baer, L., Platman, S. R., Kassir, S., & Fieve, R. R. (1971). Mechanisms of renal lithium handling and their relationship to mineral corticoids: A dissociation between sodium and lithium ions. *J. Psychiatr. Res., 8*(2), 91–105.

Bagby, E. (1922). The etiology of phobias. *J. Abnorm. Psychol., 17,* 16–18.

Bagby, R. M., Costa, P. T. Jr., Widiger, T. A., Ryder, A. G., & Marshall, M. (2005). DSM-IV personality disorders and the five-factor model of personality: A multi-method examination of domain—and facet-level predictions. *Eur. J. Pers., 19*(4), 307–324.

Baggot, M., & Mendelson, J. (2001). Does MDMA cause brain damage? In J. Holland (Ed.), *Ecstasy: The complete guide: A comprehensive look at the risks and benefits of MDMA* (pp. 110–145). Rochester, VT: Park Street Press.

Bagley, C. (1991). Poverty and suicide among Native Canadians: A replication. *Psychol. Rep., 69*(1), 149–150.

Bahrick, H. (1996, January). Cited in G. Neimeyer, Anecdotes for education. *Newsletter for Abnormal Psychology.*

Bailey, D. S. (2003). Compulsive cybersex can jeopardize marriage, rest of life. *Monitor Psychol., 34*(9), 20.

Bailey, D. S. (2003). Help the media prevent copycat suicides. *Monitor Psychol., 34*(9), 14.

Bailey, J. E., Argyropoulos, S. V., Lightman, S. L., & Nutt, D. J. (2003). Does the brain noradrenaline network mediate the effects of the CO-sub-2 challenge? *J. Psychopharmacol., 17*(3), 252–259.

Bailey, J. M., & Pillard, R. C. (1991). A genetic study of male sexual orientation. *Arch. Gen. Psychiat., 48*(12),1089–1096.

Bailey, J. M., Pillard, R. C., Dawood, K., Miller, M. B., Farrer, L. A., Trivedi, S., et al. (1999). A family history study of male sexual orientation using three independent samples. *Behav. Genet. 29*(2), 79–86.

Bailey, J. M., Pillard, R. C., Neale, M. C., et al. (1993). Heritable factors influence sexual orientation in women. *Arch. Gen. Psychiat., 50*(3), 217–223.

Bakken, J., Miltenberger, R. G., & Schauss, S. (1993). Teaching parents with mental retardation: Knowledge versus skills. *Amer. J. Ment. Retard., 97*(4), 405–417.

Baldwin, D., Broich, K., Fritze, J., Kasper, S., Westenberg, H., & Moller, H. J. (2003). Placebo-controlled studies in depression: Necessary, ethical and feasible. *Eur. Arch. Psychiat. Clin. Neurosci., 253*(1), 22–28.

Baldwin, S., & Oxlad, M. (2000). *Electroshock and minors: A fifty-year review.* Westport, CT: Greenwood.

Ball, S. G., Kuhn, A., Wall, D., Shekhar, A., & Goddard, A. W. (2005). Selective serotonin reuptake inhibitor treatment for generalized anxiety disorder: A double-blind, prospective comparison between paroxetine and sertraline. *J. Clin. Psychiat., 66*(1), 94–99.

Bancroft, J. (1989). *Human sexuality and its problems.* New York: Churchill-Livingstone.

Bancroft, J., Loftus, J., & Long, J. S. (2003). Distress about sex: A national survey of women in heterosexual relationships. *Arch. Sex. Behav., 32*(3), 193–208.

Bandura, A. (1971). Psychotherapy based upon modeling principles. In A. E. Bergin & S. L. Garfield (Eds.), *Handbook of psychotherapy and behavior change.* New York: Wiley.

Bandura, A. (1977). Self-efficacy: Toward a unifying theory of behavioral change. *Psychol. Rev., 84*(2), 191–215.

Bandura, A. (2004). Swimming against the mainstream: The early years from chilly tributary to transformative mainstream. *Behav. Res. Ther., 42*(6), 613–630.

Bandura, A., Adams, N. E., & Beyer, J. (1977). Cognitive processes mediating behavioral change. *J. Pers. Soc. Psychol., 35*(3), 125–139.

Bandura, A., & Rosenthal, T. (1966). Vicarious classical conditioning as a function of arousal level. *J. Pers. Soc. Psychol., 3,* 54–62.

Bandura, A., Roth, D., & Ross, S. (1963). Imitation of film-mediated aggressive models. *J. Abnorm. Soc. Psychol., 66,* 3–11.

Banerjee, S., & Macdonald, A. (1996). Mental disorder in an elderly home care population: Associations with health and social service use. *Brit. J. Psychiat., 168,* 750–756.

Banks, S., Robbins, P. C., Silver, E., Vesselinov, R., Steadman, H. J., Monahan, J., et al. (2004). A multiple-models approach to violence risk assessment among people with mental disorder. *Criminal Justice Behav., 31*(3), 324–340.

Barber, A. (1999, March). HerZines. Some yet-to-be exploited niches in the women's magazine market. *Am. Demogr.*

Bareggi, S. R., Bianchi, L., Cavallaro, R., Gervasoni, M., Siliprandi, F., & Bellodi, L. (2004). Citalopram concentrations and response in obsessive-compulsive disorder: Preliminary results. *CNS Drugs, 18*(5), 329–335.

Barker, P. R., Manderscheid, R. W., Hendershot, G. E., Jack, S. S., Schoenborn, C. A., & Goldstrom, I. (1992). Serious mental illness and disability in the adult household population: United States, 1989. In R. W. Manderscheid & M. A. Sonnenschein (Eds.), *Mental health, United States, 1992.* Washington, DC: U.S. Department of Health and Human Services.

Barkley, R. A. (1998). *Attention-deficit hyperactivity disorder: A handbook for diagnosis and treatment* (2nd ed.). New York: Guilford Press.

Barkley, R. A. (Ed.). (2002). Taking charge of ADHD: The complete authoritative guide for parents, revised edition. *J. Amer. Acad. Child Adol. Psychiat., 41*(1), 101–102.

Barkley, R. A. (2004). Adolescents with attention-deficit/hyperactivity disorder: An overview of empirically based treatments. *J. Psychiatr. Pract., 10*(1), 39–56.

Barlow, D. H. (Ed.). (2002). *Anxiety and its disorders: The nature and treatment of anxiety and panic* (2nd ed.). New York: Guilford Press.

Barnes, A. (2004). Race, schizophrenia, and admission to state psychiatric hospitals. *Admin. Policy Ment. Hlth, 31*(3), 241–252.

Barnes, G. E., & Prosen, H. (1985). Parental death and depression. *J. Abnorm. Psychol., 94*(1), 64–69.

Baroff, G. S., & Olley, J. G. (1999). *Mental retardation: Nature, cause, and management* (3rd ed.). Philadelphia: Brunner/Mazel.

Baron, M. (2002). Manic-depression genes and the new millennium: Poised for discovery. *Mol. Psychiat., 7*(4), 342–358.

Baron-Cohen, S., & Wheelwright, S. (2003). The Friendship Questionnaire: An investigation of adults with Asperger syndrome or high-functioning autism, and normal sex differences. *J. Autism Dev. Disorders, 33,* 509–517.

Barrett, P. M., Rapee, R. M., Dadds, M. M., & Ryan, S. M. (1996). Family enhancement of cognitive style in anxious and aggressive children. *J. Abnorm. Child Psychol., 24*(2), 187–203.

Barrett, P. M., & Shortt, A. L. (2003). Parental involvement in the treatment of anxious children. In A. E. Kazdin & J. R. Weisz (Eds.), *Evidence-based psychotherapies for children and adolescents.* New York: Guilford Press.

Barrington, M. R. (1980). Apologia for suicide. In M. P. Battin & D. J. Mayo (Eds.), *Suicide: The philosophical issues.* New York: St. Martin's Press.

Barsky, A. J. (2005). The patient with hypochondriasis. *N. Engl. J. Med., 345*(19), 1395–1399.

Barsky, A. J., & Ahern, D. K. (2004). Cognitive behavior therapy for hypochondriasis: A randomized controlled trial. *JAMA, 291*(12), 1464–1470.

Bartels, S., Teague, G., Drake, R., Clark, R., Bush, P., & Noordsy, D. (1993). Substance abuse in schizophrenia: Service utilization and costs. *J. Nerv. Ment. Dis., 181*(4), 227–232.

Bartholomew, K. (2000). Clinical protocol. *Psychoanal. Inq., 20*(2), 227–248.

Bartholomew, K., Kwong, M. J., & Hart, S. D. (2001). Attachment. In W. J. Livesley (Ed.), *Handbook of personality disorders: Theory, research, and treatment* (pp. 196–230). New York: Guilford Press.

Barton, A. (2004). Women and community punishment: The probation hostel as a semi-penal institution for female offenders. *Howard J. Criminal Justice, 43*(2), 149–163.

Bartrop, R. W., Lockhurst, E., Lazarus, L., Kiloh, L. G., & Penny, R. (1977). Depressed lymphocyte function after bereavement. *Lancet, 1,* 834–836.

Basson, R., Berman, J., Burnett, A., Derogatis, L., Ferguson, D., Fourcroy, J., et al. (2001). Report of the International Consensus Development Conference on Female Dysfunction: Definitions and classifications. *J. Sex Marital Ther., 27*(2), 83–94.

Bates, G. W., Thompson, J. C., & Flanagan, C. (1999). The effectiveness of individual versus group induction of depressed mood. *J. Psychol., 133*(3), 245–252.

Bateson, G. (1974) *Perceval's narrative: A patient's account of his psychosis.* New York: William Morrow.

Bateson, G. (1978, April 21). The double-bind theory—Misunderstood? *Psychiatr. News,* p. 40.

Bateson, G., Jackson, D., Haley, J., & Weakland, J. (1956). Toward a theory of schizophrenia. *Behav. Sci., 1,* 251–264.

Batres, A. R. (2003). Lessons from combat veterans. In J. K. Doka & M. Lattanzi-Licht (Eds.), *Living with grief: Coping with public tragedy.* New York: Brunner-Routledge.

Baucom, D. H., Epstein, N., & Gordon, K. C. (2000). Marital therapy: Theory, practice, and empirical status. In C. R. Snyder & R. E. Ingram (Eds.), *Handbook of psychological change: Psychotherapy processes & practices for the 21st century* (pp. 280–308). New York: Wiley.

Baucom, D. H., Gordon, K. C., & Snyder, D. K. (2005). Treating affair couples: An integrative approach. In J. Lebow (Ed.), *Handbook of clinical family therapy* (pp. 431–463). New York: Wiley.

Bauer, M. E. (2005). Stress, glucocorticoids and ageing of the immune system. *Stress: Inter. J. Biol. Stress, 8*(1), 69–83.

Baum, A., Gatchel, R. J., & Schaeffer, M. (1983). Emotional, behavioural and physiological effects of chronic stress at Three Mile Island. *J. Cons. Clin. Psychol., 51,* 565–572.

Baumann, B., & Bogerts, B. (2001). Neuroanatomical studies on bipolar disorder. *Brit. J. Psychiat., 178,* 142–147.

Baxter, L. R. Jr., Ackermann, R. F., Swerdlow, N. R., Brody, A., Saxena, S., Schwartz, J. M., et al. (2000). Specific brain system mediation of obsessive-compulsive disorder responsive to either medication or behavior therapy. In W. K. Goodman, M. V. Rudorfer, & J. D. Maser (Eds.), *Obsessive-compulsive disorder: Contemporary issues in treatment* (pp. 573–609). Mahwah, NJ: Lawrence Erlbaum Associates.

Baxter, L. R., Jr., Clark, E. C., Iqbal, M., & Ackermann, R. F. (2001). Cortical-subcortical systems in the mediation of obsessive-compulsive disorder: Modeling the brain's mediation of a classic "neurosis." In D. G. Lichter & J. L. Cummings (Eds.), *Frontal-subcortical circuits in psychiatric and neurological disorders* (pp. 207–230). New York: Guilford Press.

Baxter, L. R., Schwartz, J. M., Bergman, K. S., Szuba, M. P., Guze, B. H., Mazziotta, J. C., et al. (1992). Caudate glucose metabolic rate changes with both drug and behavior therapy for obsessive-compulsive disorder. *Arch. Gen. Psychiat., 49,* 681–689.

Baxter, L. R., Schwartz, J. M., Guze, B. H., Bergman, K., et al. (1990). PET imaging in obsessive compulsive disorder with and without depression. Symposium: Serotonin and its effects on human behavior (1989, Atlanta, GA). *J. Clin. Psychiat., 51*(Suppl.), 61–69.

Bazargan, M., Bazargan-Hejazi, S., & Baker, R. S. (2005). Treatment of self-reported depression among Hispanics and African Americans. *J. Hlth Care Poor Underserved, 16,* 328–344.

Beach, S. R. H., & Jones, D. J. (2002). Marital and family therapy for depression in adults. In I. H. Gotlib & C. L. Hammen (Eds.), *Handbook of depression* (pp. 422–440). New York: Guilford Press.

Beals, J., Manson, S. M., Whitesell, N. R., Spicer, P., Novins, D. K., & Mitchell, C. M. (2005). Prevalence of DSM-IV disorders and attendant help-seeking in 2 American Indian reservation populations. *Arch. Gen. Psychiat., 62*(1), 99–108.

Beard, K. W. (2005). Internet addiction: A review of current assessment techniques and potential assessment questions. *CyberPsychol. Behav., 8*(1), 7–14.

Beasley, J. O. II (2004). Serial murder in America: Case studies of seven offenders. *Behav. Sci. Law, 22*(3), 395–414.

Beauchamp, T. L., & Childress, J. F. (1979). *Principles of biomedical ethics.* New York: Oxford University Press.

Beautrais, A., Joyce, P., & Mulder, R. (2000). Unmet need following serious suicide attempt: Follow-up of 302 individuals for 30 months. In

G. Andrews & S. Henderson (Eds.), *Unmet need in psychiatry: Problems, resources, responses.* New York: Cambridge University Press.

Bebko, J. M., & Weiss, J. A. (2006). Mental retardation. In M. Hersen & J. C. Thomas (Series Eds.) & R. T. Ammerman (Vol. Ed.), *Comprehensive handbook of personality and psychopathology: Vol. 3 Child psychopathology* (pp. 233–253). Hoboken, NJ: Wiley.

Beck, A. T. (1967). *Depression: Clinical, experimental and theoretical aspects.* New York: Harper & Row.

Beck, A. T. (1976). *Cognitive therapy and the emotional disorders.* New York: International University Press.

Beck, A. T. (1985). Theoretical perspectives on clinical anxiety. In A. H. Tuma & J. D. Maser (Eds.), *Anxiety and the anxiety disorders.* Hillsdale, NJ: Erlbaum.

Beck, A. T. (1991). Cognitive therapy: A 30-year retrospective. *Amer. Psychologist, 46*(4), 368–375.

Beck, A. T. (1993). Cognitive approaches to stress. In P. M. Lehrer & R. L. Woolfolk (Eds.), *Principles and practice of stress management* (2nd ed.). New York: Guilford Press.

Beck, A. T. (2002). Cognitive models of depression. In R. L. Leahy & E. T. Dowd (Eds.), *Clinical advances in cognitive psychotherapy: Theory and application* (pp. 29–61). New York: Springer.

Beck, A. T. (2004). A cognitive model of schizophrenia. *J. Cog. Psychother., 18*(3), 281–288.

Beck, A. T. (2004). Cognitive therapy, behavior therapy, psychoanalysis, and pharmacotherapy: A cognitive continuum. In M. J. Mahoney, P. DeVito, D. Martin, & A. Freeman (Eds.), *Cognition and psychotherapy* (2nd ed., pp. 197–220). New York: Springer Publishing.

Beck, A. T., Butler, A. C., Brown, G. K., Dahlsgaard, K. K., Newman, C. F., & Beck, J. S. (2001). Dysfunctional beliefs discriminate personality disorders. *Behav. Res. Ther., 39*(10), 1213–1225.

Beck, A. T., & Emery, G., with Greenberg, R. L. (1985). Differentiating anxiety and depression: A test of the cognitive content-specificity hypothesis. *J. Abnorm. Psychol., 96,* 179–183.

Beck, A. T., & Freeman, A. (1990). *Cognitive therapy of personality disorders.* New York: Guilford Press.

Beck, A. T., Freeman, A., Davis, D. D., et al. (2004). *Cognitive therapy of personality disorders* (2nd ed.). New York: Guilford Press.

Beck, A. T., Resnik, H., & Lettieri, D. (Eds.). (1974). The prediction of suicide. Philadelphia: Charles Press.

Beck, A. T., Rush, A. J., Shaw, B. F., & Emery, G. (1979). *Cognitive therapy of depression.* New York: Guilford Press.

Beck, A. T., Ward, C. H., Mendelson, M., Mock, J. E., & Erbaugh, J. (1962). Reliability of psychiatric diagnosis: 2. A study of consistency of clinical judgments and ratings. *Amer. J. Psychiat., 119,* 351–357.

Beck, A. T., & Weishaar, M. E. (2005). Cognitive therapy. In D. Wedding & R. J. Corsini (Eds.), *Current psychotherapies* (6th ed., pp. 241–272). Ithaca, IL: F. E. Peacock.

Beck, J. G. (1993). Vaginismus. In W. O'Donohue & J. H. Geer (Eds.), *Handbook of sexual dysfunctions: Assessment and treatment* (pp. 381–397). Needham Heights, MA: Allyn & Bacon.

Beck, J. G., & Bozman, A. (1996). Gender differences in sexual desire: The effects of anger and anxiety. *Arch. Sex. Behav., 24*(6), 595–612.

Becker-Blease, K. A., & Freyd, J. J. (2005). Beyond PTSD: An evolving relationship between trauma theory and family violence research. *J. Interpers. Viol., 20*(4), 403–411.

Beckerman, N. L. (2004). The impact of post-traumatic stress disorder on couples: A theoretical framework for assessment and intervention. *Fam. Ther., 31*(3), 129–144.

Beckman, A. G. K., Parker, M. G., & Thorslund, M. (2005). Can elderly people take their medicine? *Patient Educ. Couns., 59*(2), 186–191.

Becvar, D. S. (2001). *In the presence of grief: Helping family members resolve death, dying, and bereavement issues.* New York: Guilford Press.

Becvar, D. S. (2003). Introduction to the special section: Death, dying and bereavement. *J. Marital Fam. Ther., 29*(4), 437–438.

Beebe, D. K. (1991). Emergency management of the adult female rape victim. *Amer. Fam. Physician, 43,* 2041–2046.

Begley, S. (2000, May 8). A world of their own. *Newsweek,* pp. 52–63.

Beidel, D. C., & Turner, S. M. (2005). *Childhood anxiety disorders: A guide to research and treatment.* New York: Routledge/Taylor & Francis.

Beidel, D. C., Turner, S. M., & Morris, T. L. (1995). A new inventory to assess childhood social anxiety and phobia: The social phobia and anxiety inventory for children. *Psychol. Assess., 7*(1), 73–79.

Beidel, D. C., Turner, S. M., & Morris, T. L. (2000). Behavioral treatment of childhood social phobia. *J. Cons. Clin. Psychol., 68*(6), 1072–1080.

Belcher, J. R. (1988). The future role of state hospitals. *Psychiatr. Hosp., 19*(2), 79–83.

Belkin, L. (1990, June 6). Doctor tells of first death using his suicide device. *New York Times,* A1, p. 3.

Bell, M. D., Lysaker, P. H., & Milstein, R. M. (1996). Clinical benefits of paid work activity in schizophrenia. *Schizo. Bull., 22*(1), 51–67.

Bellack, A. S., Mueser, K. T., Gingerich, S., & Agresta, J. (2004). *Social skills training for schizophrenia.* New York: Guilford Press.

Bellinger, D. L., Madden, K. S., Felten, S. Y., & Felten, D. L. (1994). Neural and endocrine links between the brain and the immune system. In C. S. Lewis, C. O'Sullivan, & J. Barraclough (Eds.), *The psychoimmunology of cancer: Mind and body in the fight for survival.* Oxford, England: Oxford University Press.

Bellodi, L., Caldirola, D., & Bertani, A. (2003). Does the brain noradrenaline network mediate the effects of the CO-sub-2 challenge? *J. Psychopharmacol., 17*(3), 263–264.

Belluck, P. (1996, December 1). The symptoms of Internet addiction. *New York Times,* p. 5.

Bemporad, J. R. (1992). Psychoanalytically orientated psychotherapy. In E. S. Paykel (Ed.), *Handbook of affective disorders.* New York: Guilford Press.

Bemporad, J. R. (1997). Cultural and historical aspects of eating disorders. *Theor. Med., 18*(4), 401–420.

Benazzi, F., Koukopoulos, A., & Akiskal, H. S. (2004). Toward a validation of a new definition of agitated depression as a bipolar mixed state (mixed depression). *Eur. Psychiat., 19*(2), 85–90.

Bender, D. S. (2005). The therapeutic alliance in the treatment of personality disorders. *J. Psychiat. Pract., 11*(2), 73–87.

Bender, D. S., Farber, B. A., & Geller, J. D. (2001). Cluster B personality traits and attachment. *J. Amer. Acad. Psychoanal., 29*(4), 551–563.

Bender, D. S., & Oldham, J. M. (2005). Psychotherapies for borderline personality disorder. In J. G. Gunderson & P. D. Hoffman (Eds.), *Understanding and treating borderline personality disorder* (pp. 21–41). Washington, DC: American Psychiatric Publishing.

Bender, K. J. (1998). FDA approves reduced clozapine monitoring; increased patient access versus increased risk. *Psychiatr. Times, XV*(5).

Bender, L. (1938). *A visual motor gestalt test and its clinical use.* New York: American Orthopsychiatric Assoc.

Bender, R., Jockel, K. H., Trautner, C., Spraul, M., & Berger, M. (1999). Effect of age on excess mortality in obesity. *JAMA, 281*(16), 1498–1504.

Benditt, T. (2002). Mental illness and commitment. In J. M. Humber & R. F. Almeder (Eds.), *Mental illness and public health care: Biomedical ethics reviews. Contemporary issues in biomedicine, ethics, and society* (pp. 1–24). Totowa, NJ: Humana.

Benezech, M., DeWitte, J. J. E., & Bourgeois, M. (1989). A lycanthropic murderer [Letter to the editor]. *Amer. J. Psychiat., 146*(7), 942.

Bengtsson, H. (2005). Children's cognitive appraisal of others' distressful and positive experiences. *Inter. J. Behav. Dev., 29,* 457–466.

Benight, C. C., Harper, M. L., Zimmer, D. L., Lowery, M., Sanger, J., & Laudenslager, M. L. (2004). Repression following a series of natural disasters: Immune and neuroendocrine correlates. *Psychol. Hlth., 19*(3), 337–352.

Bennett, M. P. (1998). The effect of mirthful laughter on stress and natural killer cell cytotoxicity. *Diss. Abstr. Inter.: Sect. B: Sci. Eng., 58*(7–B), 3553.

Bennett-Gates, D., & Zigler, E. (1999). Effectance motivation and the performance of individuals with mental retardation. In E. Zigler & D. Bennett-Gates (Eds.), *Personality development in individuals with mental retardation* (pp. 145–164). New York: Cambridge University Press.

Benowitz, N. (1990). Clinical pharmacology of caffeine. *Annu. Rev. Med., 41,* 277–288.

Benson, J. (1996, January 15). Crime: Law and order. *Newsweek,* pp. 48–54.

Bergeron, S., Binik, Y. M., Khalife, S., Pagidas, K., Glazer, H. I., Meana, M., et al. (2001). A randomized comparison of group cognitive-behavioral therapy, surface electromyographic biofeedback, and vestibulectomy in the treatment of dyspareunia resulting from vulvar vestibulitis. *Pain, 91,* 297–306.

Bergeron, S., Brown, C., Lord, M., Oala, M., Binik, Y. M., & Khalife, S. (2002). Physical therapy for vulvar vestibulitis syndrome: A retrospective study. *J. Sex Marital Ther., 28,* 183–192.

Bergin, A. E., & Richards, P. S. (2001). Religious values and mental health. In A. E. Kazdin (Ed.), *Encyclopedia of psychology.* New York: American Psychological Association & Oxford University Press.

Bergler, E. (1951). *Neurotic counterfeit sex.* New York: Grune & Stratton.

Berk, M., Dodd, S., & Malhi, G. S. (2005). "Bipolar missed states": The diagnosis and clinical salience of bipolar mixed states. *Austral. New Zeal. J. Psychiat., 39*(4), 215–221.

Berk, S. N., & Efran, J. S. (1983). Some recent developments in the treatment of neurosis. In C. E. Walker (Ed.), *The handbook of clinical psychology: Theory, research, and practice* (Vol. 2). Homewood, IL: Dow Jones-Irwin.

Berlin, F. S. (2000). The etiology and treatment of sexual offending. In D. H. Fishbein (Ed.), *The science, treatment, and prevention of antisocial behaviors: Application to the criminal justice system* (pp. 21-1–21-15). Kingston, NJ: Civic Research Institute.

Berman, A. L. (1986). Helping suicidal adolescents: Needs and responses. In C. A. Corr & J. N. McNeil (Eds.), *Adolescence and death*. New York: Springer.

Berman, A. L., & Jobes, D. A. (1991). *Adolescent suicide: Assessment and intervention*. Washington, DC: American Psychological Association.

Berman, A. L., & Jobes, D. A. (1995). Suicide prevention in adolescents (age 12–18). [Special issue: Suicide prevention: Toward the year 2000.] *Suic. Life-Threat. Behav., 25*(1), 143–154.

Berman, B. (2004). Complementary and alternative medicine: Is it just a case of more tools for the medical bag? *Clin. J. Pain, 20*(1), 1–2.

Berney, B. (1993). Round and round it goes: The epidemiology of childhood lead poisoning, 1950–1990. *Milbank Quarterly, 71*(1), 3–39.

Bernstein, H. A. (1981). Survey of threats and assaults directed toward psychotherapists. *Amer. J. Psychother., 35*, 542–549.

Berr, C., Wancata, J., & Ritchie, K. (2005). Prevalence of dementia in the elderly in Europe. *Eur. Neuropsychopharmacology, 15*(4), 463–471.

Bersoff, D. M. (Ed.). (1999). *Ethical conflicts in psychology* (2nd ed.). Washington, DC: American Psychological Association.

Berthier, M. L., Kulisevsky, J., Gironell, A., & Lopez, O. L. (2001). Obsessive-compulsive disorder and traumatic brain injury: Behavioral, cognitive, and neuroimaging findings. *Neuropsychiat., Neuropsychol., Behav. Neurol., 14*(1), 23–31.

Beutler, L. E. (1991). Have all won and must all have prizes? Revisiting Luborsky et al.'s verdict. *J. Cons. Clin. Psychol., 59*, 226–232.

Beutler, L. E. (2000). David and Goliath: When empirical and clinical standards of practice meet. *Amer. Psychologist, 55*(9), 997–1007.

Beutler, L. E. (2002). The dodo bird is extinct. *Clin. Psychol.: Sci. Prac., 9*(1), 30–34.

Beutler, L. E., Clarkin, J. F., & Bongar, B. (2000). *Guidelines for the systematic treatment of the depressed patient*. New York: Oxford University Press.

Beutler, L. E., & Malik, M. L. (Eds.). (2002). *Rethinking the DSM: A psychological perspective. Decade of behavior*. Washington, DC: American Psychological Association.

Beutler, L. E., Malik, M., Talebi, H., Fleming, J., & Moleiro, C. (2004). Use of psychological tests/instruments for treatment planning. In M. E. Maruish (Ed.), *The use of psychological testing for treatment planning and outcomes assessment: Volume 1: General considerations* (3rd ed., pp. 111–145). Mahwah, NJ: Lawrence Erlbaum Associates.

Beutler, L. E., Williams, R. E., Wakefield, P. J., & Entwistle, S. R. (1995). Bridging scientist and practitioner perspectives in clinical psychology. *Amer. Psychologist, 50*(12), 984–994.

Beyer, H. A. (1991). Litigation involving people with mental retardation. In J. L. Matson & J. A. Mulick (Eds.), *Handbook of mental retardation* (2nd ed.). New York: Pergamon Press.

Bhattacharjee, C., Bradley, P., et al. (2000). Do animals bite more during a full moon? Retrospective observational analysis. *Brit. Med. J., 321*(7276), 1559–1561.

Bichsel, S. (2001). Schizophrenia and severe mental illness: Guidelines for assessment, treatment, and referral. In E. R. Welfel & R. E. Ingersoll (Eds.), *The mental health desk reference* (pp. 142–154). New York: Wiley.

Bickman, L. (2005). A common factors approach to improving mental health services. *Ment. Hlth Serv. Res., 7*(1), 1–4.

Biederman, J., Mick, E., Faraone, S. V., & Burback, M. (2001). Patterns of remission and symptom decline in conduct disorder: A four-year prospective study of an ADHD sample. *J. Amer. Acad. Child Adol. Psychiat., 40*(3), 290–298.

Biederman, J., Spencer, T., & Wilens, T. (2004). Evidence-based pharmacotherapy for attention-deficit hyperactivity disorder. *Inter. J. Neuropsychopharmacol., 7*, 77–97.

Biederman, J., Spencer, T., & Wilens, T. (2005). Evidence-based pharmacotherapy of attention-deficit hyperactivity disorder. In D. J. Stein, B. Lerer, & S. Stahl, *Evidence-based psychopharmacology* (pp. 255–289). New York: Cambridge University Press.

Bigler, E. D. (2005). Structural imaging. In T. W. McAllister, S. C. Yudofsky, & J. M. Silver (Eds.), *Textbook of traumatic brain injury* (pp. 79–105). Washington, DC: American Psychiatric Publishing.

Bill W. (1957). *Alcoholics Anonymous comes of age: A brief history of AA*. New York: Alcoholics Anonymous World Services.

Binder, R. L. (1999). Are the mentally ill dangerous? *J. Amer. Acad. Psychiat. Law, 27*(2), 189–201.

Binet, A., & Simon, T. (1916). *The development of intelligence in children (The Binet-Simon Scale)*. Baltimore: Williams & Wilkins.

Binik, Y. M., Bergeron, S., & Khalife, S. (2000). Dyspareunia. In S. R. Leiblum & R. C. Rosen (Eds.), *Principles and practice of sex therapy* (3rd ed., pp. 154–180). New York: Guilford Press.

Binik, Y. M., Reissing, E., Pukall, C., Flory, N., Payne, K. A., & Khalife, S. (2002). The female sexual pain disorders: Genital pain or sexual dysfunction? *Arch. Sex. Behav., 31*(5), 425–429.

Biondi, M., & Picardi, A. (2003). Increased probability of remaining in remission from panic disorder with agoraphobia after drug treatment in patients who received concurrent cognitive-behavioural therapy: A follow-up study. *Psychother. Psychosom., 72*(1), 34–42.

Birch, H. G., Richardson, S. A., Baird, D., et al. (1970). *Mental subnormality in the community—A clinical and epidemiological study*. Baltimore: Williams & Wilkins.

Biringer, E., Mykletun, A., Dahl, A. A., Smith, A. D., Engedal, K., Nygaard, H. A., & Lund, A. (2005). The association between depression, anxiety, and cognitive function in the elderly general population: The Hordaland Health Study. *Inter. J. Ger. Psychiat., 20*(10), 989–997.

Birmingham, C. L., & Beumont, P. (2004). *Medical management of eating disorders: A practical handbook for health care professionals*. New York: Cambridge University Press.

Birmingham, C. L., Jones, P., & Hoffer, L. J. (2003). The management of adult obesity. *Eat. Weight Disord., 8*(2), 157–163.

Birren, J. E., & Schroots, J. F. (Eds.). (2000). *A history of geropsychology in autobiography*. Washington, DC: American Psychological Association.

Birren, J. E., & Schroots, J. J. F. (2001). History of geropsychology. In J. E. Birren & K. W. Schaie (Eds.), *Handbook of the psychology of aging* (5th ed., pp. 3–28). San Diego, CA: Academic.

Birtchnell, J. (1996). Detachment. In C. G. Costello (Ed.), *Personality characteristics of the personality disordered*. New York: Wiley.

Bissette, G., Seidler, F. J., Nemeroff, C. B., & Slotkin, T. A. (1996). High affinity choline transporter status in Alzheimer's disease tissue from rapid autopsy. In R. J. Wurtman, S. Corkin, J. H. Growdon, & R. M. Nitsch (Eds.), *The neurobiology of Alzheimer's disease*. New York: New York Academy of Sciences.

Bisson, J. I., & Deahl, M. P. (1994). Psychological debriefing and prevention of post-traumatic stress: More research is needed. *Brit. J. Psychiat., 165*(6), 717–720.

Bisson, J. I., Jenkins, P. L., Alexander, J., & Bannister, C. (1997). Randomised controlled trial of psychological debriefing for victims of acute burn trauma. *Brit. J. Psychiat., 171*, 78–81.

Blacher, J., & Baker, B. L. (1992). Toward meaningful involvement in out-of-home placement settings. *Ment. Retard., 30*(1), 35–43.

Blacher, J., & Baker, B. L. (1994). Family involvement in residential treatment of children with retardation: Is there evidence of detachment? *J. Child Psychol. Psychiat. Allied Disc., 35*(3), 505–520.

Black, D. W., & Andreasen, N. C. (1994). Schizophrenia, schizophreniform disorder, and delusional (paranoid) disorder. In R. E. Hales, S. C. Yudofsky, & J. A. Talbott (Eds.), *The American Psychiatric Press textbook of psychiatry* (2nd ed.). Washington, DC: American Psychiatric Press.

Black, D. W., Belsare, G., & Schlosser, S. (1999). Clinical features, psychiatric comorbidity, and health-related quality of life in persons reporting compulsive computer use behavior. *J. Clin. Psychiat., 60*(12), 839–844.

Black, D. W., Blum, N., Pfohl, B., & Hale, N. (2004). Suicidal behavior in borderline personality disorder: Prevalence, risk factors, prediction, and prevention. *J. Pers. Disorders, 18*(3), 226–239.

Black, K. J. (2005). Diagnosis. In E. H. Rubin & C. F. Zorumski (Eds.), *Adult psychiatry* (2nd ed.). Oxford, England: Blackwell Publishing Ltd.

Black, S. T. (1993). Comparing genuine and simulated suicide notes: A new perspective. *J. Cons. Clin. Psychol., 61*(4), 699–702.

Black, S. T. (1995). Comparing genuine and simulated suicide notes: Response to Diamond et al. (1995). *J. Cons. Clin. Psychol., 63*(1), 49–51.

Black, S. T., & Lester, D. (2003). The content of suicide notes: Does it vary by method of suicide, sex, or age? *Omega: J. Death Dying, 46*(3), 241–249.

Blair, J., Mitchell, D., & Blair, K. (2005). *The psychopath: Emotion and the brain*. Malden, MA: Blackwell Publishing.

Blair, R. J. R., Peschardt, K. S., Budhani, S., & Pine, D. S. (2006). Neurobiology of aggression in children. In R. J. Nelson (Ed.), *Biology of aggression* (pp. 351–370). New York: Oxford University Press.

Blanchard, E. B., Rowell, D., Kuhn, E., Rogers, R., & Wittrock, D. (2005). Posttraumatic stress and depression symptoms in a college population one year after the September 11 attacks: The effect of proximity. *Behav. Res. Ther., 43*(1), 143–150.

Blanchard, J. J., Brown, S. A., Horan, W. P., & Sherwood, A. R. (2000). Substance use disorders in schizophrenia: Review, integration, and a proposed model. *Clin. Psychol. Rev., 20*(2), 207–234.

Blanchard, J. J., Horan, W. P., & Collins, L. M. (2005). Examining the latent structure of negative symptoms: Is there a distinct subtype of negative symptom schizophrenia? *Schizo. Res., 77*(2–3), 151–165.

Blanchard, J. J., Sayers, S. L., Collins, L. M., & Bellack, A. S. (2004). Affectivity in the problem-solving interactions of schizophrenia patients and their family members. *Schizo. Res., 69*(1), 105–117.

Blanchard, R., & Hucker, S. J. (1991). Age, transvestism, bondage, and concurrent paraphilic activities in 117 fatal cases of autoerotic asphyxia. *Brit. J. Psychiat., 159,* 371–377.

Blatt, S. J. (1995). The destructiveness of perfectionism. Implications for the treatment of depression. *Amer. Psychologist., 50*(12), 1003–1020.

Blatt, S. J. (1999). Personality factors in brief treatment of depression: Further analyses of the NIMH-sponsored Treatment for Depression Collaborative Research Program. In D. S. Janowsky (Ed.), *Psychotherapy indications and outcomes.* Washington, DC: American Psychiatric Press.

Blatt, S. J. (2004). Developmental origins (distal antecedents). In S. J. Blatt, *Experiences of depression: Theoretical, clinical, and research perspectives* (pp. 187–229). Washington, DC: American Psychological Association.

Blazer, D. (2002). *Depression in late life* (3rd ed.). New York: Springer.

Blazer, D. G., Hughes, D., George, L. K., Swartz, M., & Boyer, R. (1991). Generalized anxiety disorder. In L. N. Robins & D. A. Regier (Eds.), *Psychiatric disorders in America: The Epidemiologic Catchment Area Study.* New York: Maxwell Macmillan International.

Blier, P., & de Montigny, C. (1994, July). Current advances and trends in the treatment of depression. *TIPS, 15,* 220–226.

Bliss, E. L. (1980). Multiple personalities: A report of 14 cases with implications for schizophrenia and hysteria. *Arch. Gen. Psychiat., 37*(12), 1388–1397.

Bliss, E. L. (1980). *Multiple personality, allied disorders and hypnosis.* New York: Oxford University Press.

Bliss, E. L. (1985). "How prevalent is multiple personality?": Dr. Bliss replies. *Amer. J. Psychiat., 142*(12), 1527.

Bloom, B. L. (1984). *Community mental health: A general introduction* (2nd ed.). Monterey, CA: Brooks/Cole.

Bloom, F., Lazerson, A., & Hofstadter, L. (1985). *Brain, mind, and behavior.* New York: W. H. Freeman.

Bloom, J. D. (1990). The Tarasoff decision & gun control legislation. *Inter. J. Offend. Ther. Compar. Criminol., 34*(1), v–viii.

Bloom, J. D. (2004). Thirty-five years of working with civil commitment statutes. *J. Amer. Acad. Psychiat. Law, 32*(4), 430–439.

Bloom, J. D., Nadelson, C. C., & Notman, M. T. (Eds.). (1999). *Physician sexual misconduct.* Washington, DC: American Psychiatric Press.

Bluglass, K. (2001). Treatment of perpetrators. In G. Adshead & D. Brooke (Eds.), *Munchausen's syndrome by proxy: Current issues in assessment, treatment and research* (pp. 175–184). London: Imperial College Press.

Blum, K., Braverman, E. R., Holder, J. M., Lubar, J. F., Monastra, V. J., Miller, D., et al. (2000). Reward deficiency syndrome: A biogenetic model for the diagnosis and treatment of impulsive, addictive, and compulsive behaviors. *J. Psychoact. Drugs, 32*(Suppl.), 1–68.

Blum, K., Cull, J. G., Braverman, E. R., & Comings, D. E. (1996). Reward deficiency syndrome. *Amer. Sci., 84*(2), 132–144.

Blum, K., Noble, E. P., Sheridan, P. J., Montgomery, A., Ritchie, T., Jagadeeswaran, P., et al. (1990). Allelic association of human dopamine D2 receptor gene in alcoholism. *JAMA, 263*(15), 2055–2060.

Blume, S. B., & Zilberman, M. L. (2005). Addictive disorders in women. In R. J. Frances, A. H. Mack, & S. I. Miller (Eds.), *Clinical textbook of addictive disorders* (3rd ed., pp. 437–453). New York: Guilford Press.

Blumer, D. (2002). The illness of Vincent van Gogh. *Amer. J. Psychiat., 159*(4), 519–526.

Blyler, C. R. (2003). Understanding the employment rate of people with schizophrenia: Different approaches lead to different implications for policy. In M. F. Lenzenweger & J. M. Hooley (Eds.), *Principles of experimental psychopathology: Essays in honor of Brendan A. Maher* (pp. 107–115). Washington, DC: American Psychological Association.

Bockoven, J. S. (1963). *Moral treatment in American psychiatry.* New York: Springer.

Boergers, J., Spirito, A., & Donaldson, D. (1998). Reasons for adolescent suicide attempts: Associations with psychological functioning. *J. Amer. Acad. Child Adol. Psychiat., 37*(12), 1287–1293.

Bogdan, R., & Taylor, S. (1976, January). The judged, not the judges: An insider's view of mental retardation. *Amer. Psychologist., 31*(1), 47–52.

Bohne, A., Keuthen, N., Wilheim, S., Deckersback, T., & Jenike, M. (2002). Prevalence of symptoms of body dysmorphic disorder and its correlates: A cross-cultural comparison. *Psychosom. J. Cons. Liaison Psychiat., 43*(6), 486–490.

Boland, R. J., & Keller, M. B. (2002). Course and outcome of depression. In I. H. Gotlib & C. L. Hammen (Eds.), *Handbook of depression* (pp. 43–60). New York: Guilford Press.

Boldrini, M., Underwood, M. D., Mann, J. J., & Arango, V. (2005). More tryptophan hydroxylase in the brainstem dorsal raphe nucleus in depressed suicides. *Brain Res., 1041*(1), 19–28.

Bolgar, H. (1965). The case study method. In B. B. Wolman (Ed.), *Handbook of clinical psychology.* New York: McGraw-Hill.

Bolwig, T. G. (2005). Letters to the Editor: First-line use of ECT. *J. ECT, 21*(1), 51.

Bonanno, G. A. (2004). Loss, trauma, and human resilience. *Amer. Psychologist, 59*(1), 20–28.

Bongar, B., Lomax, J. W., & Marmatz, M. (1992). Training and supervisory issues in the assessment and management of the suicidal patient. In B. Bongar (Ed.), *Suicide: Guidelines for assessment, management and treatment* (pp. 253–267). New York: Oxford University Press.

Bonner, R. L. (1992). Isolation, seclusion, and psychosocial vulnerability as risk factors for suicide behind bars. In R. W. Maris, A. L. Berman, J. T. Maltsberger, & R. I. Yufit (Eds.), *Assessment and prediction of suicide.* New York: Guilford Press.

Borger, S. C., Cox, B. J., & Asmundson, G. J. G. (2005). PTSD and other mental health problems in adults who report histories of severe physical abuse and neglect. In T. A. Corales (Ed.), *Trends in posttraumatic stress disorder research* (pp. 249–261). Hauppauge, NY: Nova Science Publishers.

Borkovec, T. D., & Roemer, L. (1995). Perceived functions of worry among generalised anxiety subjects: Distraction from more emotionally distressing topics? *Behav. Ther. Exp. Psychiat., 26,* 25–30.

Borkovec, T. D., & Sharpless, B. (2004). Generalized anxiety disorder: Bringing cognitive-behavioral therapy into the valued present. In V. M. Follette, M. M. Linehan, & S. C. Hayes (Eds.), *Mindfulness and acceptance: Expanding the cognitive-behavioral tradition* (pp. 209–242). New York: Guilford Press.

Bornstein, R. A., Schwarzkopf, S. B., Olson, S. C., & Nasrallah, H. A. (1992). Third-ventricle enlargement and neuropsychological deficit in schizophrenia. *Biol. Psychiat., 31*(9), 954–961.

Bornstein, R. F. (2005). Psychodynamic theory and personality disorders. In S. Strack (Ed.), *Handbook of personality and psychopathology* (pp. 164–180). Hoboken, NJ: Wiley.

Boros, S., Ophoven, J., Anderson, R., & Brubaker, L. (1995). Munchausen syndrome by proxy: A profile for medical child abuse. *Austral. Fam. Physician, 24*(5), 768–773.

Borthwick, A., Holman, C., Kennard, D., McFetridge, M., Messruther, K., & Wilkes, J. (2001). The relevance of moral treatment to contemporary mental health care. *J. Ment. Hlth UK., 10*(4), 427–439.

Boscarino, J. A., Adams, R. E., & Figley, C. R. (2004). Mental health service use 1 year after the World Trade Center disaster: Implications for mental health care. *Gen. Hosp. Psychiat., 26*(5), 346–358.

Bossolo, L., & Lichtenstein, B. (2002). Many Americans still feeling effects of September 11th; Are reexamining their priorities in life. *APA Online.*

Bott, E. (1928). Teaching of psychology in the medical course. *Bull. Assoc. Amer. Med. Colleges, 3,* 289–304.

Boudet, C., Bocca, M. L., Chabot, B., Delamillieure, P., Brazo, P. Denise, P., & Dollfus, S. (2005). Are eye movement abnormalities indicators of genetic vulnerability to schizophrenia? *Eur. Psychiat., 20*(4), 339–345.

Boudouris, J. (2000). The insanity defense in Polk County, Iowa. *Amer. J. Forens. Psychol., 18*(1), 41–79.

Bourgeois, M. (1991). Serotonin, impulsivity and suicide. *Human Psychopharmacol. Clin. Exp., 6*(Suppl.), 31–36.

Bourin, M., Malinge, M., & Guitton, B. (1995). [Provocative agents in panic disorder.] *Therapie 50*(4), 301–306. [French]

Bourne, E. J., Brownstein, A., & Garano, L. (2004). *Natural relief for anxiety: Complementary strategies for easing fear, panic & worry.* Oakland, CA: New Harbinger Publications.

Bowden, C. L. (2005). A different depression: Clinical distinctions between bipolar and unipolar depression. *J. Affect. Disorders, 84*(2–3), 117–125.

Bowden, C. L. (2005). Atypical antipsychotic augmentation of mood stabilizer therapy in bipolar disorder. *J. Clin. Psychiat., 66*(Suppl. 3), 12–19.

Bowden, C. L., & Singh, V. (2005). Valproate in bipolar disorder: 2000 onwards. *Acta Psychiatr. Scandin., 111*(Suppl. 426), 13–20.

Bowen, M. A. (1960). A family concept of schizophrenia. In D. D. Jackson (Ed.), *The etiology of schizophrenia.* New York: Basic Books.

Bower, G. H. (1981). Mood and memory. *Amer. Psychologist, 36*(2), 129–148.

Boyce, W. T., Chesney, M., Alkon, A., Tschann, J. M., et al. (1995). Psychobiologic reactivity to stress and childhood respiratory illnesses: Results of two prospective studies. *Psychosom. Med., 57,* 411–422.

Boye, B., Bentsen, H., & Malt, U. F. (2002). Does guilt proneness predict acute and long-term distress in relatives of patients with schizophrenia? *Acta Pyschiatr. Scandin., 106*(5), 351–357.

Boyle, S. H., Williams, R. B., Mark, D. B., Brummett, B. H., Siegler, I. C., Helms, M. J., et al. (2004). Hostility as a predictor of survival in patients with coronary artery disease. *Psychosom. Med., 66*(5), 629–632.

Boyles, S. (2002, January 8). More people seeking treatment for depression. *WebMDHealth.* Retrieved January 9, 2002, from www.webcenter.health.web

Braback, L., & Humble, M. (2001). Young woman dies of water intoxication after taking one tablet of ecstasy. Today's drug panorama calls for increased vigilance in health care. *Lakartidningen, 98*(9), 817–819.

Bradley, B. P., Mogg, K., Falla, S. J., & Hamilton, L. R. (1998). Attentional bias for threatening facial expressions in anxiety: Manipulation of stimulus duration. *Cog. Emot., 12*(6), 737–753.

Bradley, R., Conklin, C. Z., & Westen, D. (2005). The borderline personality diagnosis in adolescents: Gender differences and subtypes. *J. Child Psychol. Psychiat., 46,* 1006–1019.

Bradley, R., Greene, J., Russ, E., Dutra, L., & Westen, D. (2005). A multidimensional meta-analysis of psychotherapy for PTSD. *Amer. J. Psychiat., 162*(2), 214–227.

Bradley, R., Jenei, J., & Westen, D. (2005). Etiology of borderline personality disorder: Disentangling the contributions of intercorrelated antecedents. *J. Nerv. Ment. Dis., 193,* 24–31.

Bradley, S. J. (1995). Psychosexual disorders in adolescence. In J. M. Oldham & M. B. Riba (Eds.), *American Psychiatric Press review of psychiatry,* (Vol. 14). Washington, DC: American Psychiatric Press.

Bradshaw, J. (2005). RxP training issue still boiling. *The National Psychologist, 14*(5), pp. 1, 3.

Braginsky, B. M., Braginsky, D. D., & Ring, K. (1969). *Methods of madness: The mental hospital as a last resort.* New York: Holt.

Bram, T. and Björgvinsson, T. (2004). A psychodynamic clinician's foray into cognitive-behavioral therapy utilizing exposure-response prevention for obsessive-compulsive disorder. *Am. J. Psychother., 58,* 304–320.

Brambrink, D. K. (2004). A comparative study for the treatment of anxiety in women using electromyographic biofeedback and progressive relaxation and coping with stress: A manual for women. *Diss. Abstr. Inter.: Sect. B: Sci. Eng., 65*(6-B), 3146.

Brandon, S. (1981). *The history of shock treatment. In Electroconvulsive therapy: An appraisal.* Oxford: Oxford University Press.

Brauer, A. (1999). Biofeedback and anxiety. *Psychiatr. Times, XVI*(2).

Braun, D. L. (1996, July 28). Interview. In S. Gilbert, More men may seek eating-disorder help. *New York Times.*

Breier, A. (2001). A new era in the pharmacotherapy of psychotic disorders. *J. Clin. Psychiat., 62*(Suppl. 2), 3–5.

Bremner, J. D. (2002). *Does stress damage the brain? Understanding trauma-related disorders from a mind-body perspective.* New York: Norton.

Bremner, J. D., & Brett, E. (1997). Trauma-related dissociative states and long-term psychopathology in posttraumatic stress disorder. *J. Traum. Stress, 10,* 37–50.

Bremner, J. D., & Vermetten, E. (2004). Neuroanatomical changes associated with pharmacotherapy in posttraumatic stress disorder. In R. Yehuda & B. McEwen (Eds.), *Biobehavioral stress response: Protective and damaging effects* (pp. 154–157). New York: New York Academy of Sciences.

Bremner, J. D., Vythilingam, M., Vermetten, E., Vaccarino, V., & Charney, D. S. (2004). Deficits in hippocampal and anterior cingulate functioning during verbal declarative memory encoding in midlife major depression. *Amer. J. Psychiat., 161*(4), 637–645.

Brems, C. (1995). Women and depression: A comprehensive analysis. In W. Beckham & W. Leber (Eds.), *Handbook of depression* (2nd ed.). New York: Guilford Press.

Brende, J. O., & Parson, E. R. (1985). *Vietnam veterans.* New York: Plenum.

Brenner, I. (1999). Deconstructing DID. *Amer. J. Psychother., 53*(3), 344–360.

Brent, D. A. (2001). Assessment and treatment of the youthful suicidal patient. In H. Hendin & J. J. Mann (Eds.), *The clinical science of suicide prevention* (Vol. 932, pp. 106–131). New York: Annals of the New York Academy of Sciences.

Brent, D. A., Kupfer, D. J., Bromet, E. J., & Dew, M. A. (1988). The assessment and treatment of patients at risk for suicide. In A. J. Frances & R. E. Hales (Eds.), *American Psychiatric Press review of psychiatry* (Vol. 7). Washington, DC: American Psychiatric Press.

Brent, D. A., & Mann, J. J. (2003). Familial factors in adolescent suicidal behavior. In A. Apter & R. A King (Eds.), *Suicide in children and adolescents* (pp. 86–117). New York: Cambridge University Press.

Breslau, N., Roth, T., Burduvali, E., Kapke, A., Schults, L., & Roehrs, T. (2005). Sleep in lifetime posttraumatic stress disorder: A community-based polysomnographic study: Correction. *Arch. Gen. Psychiat., 62*(2), 172.

Brewerton, T. D., Lydiard, R. B., Herzog, D. B., Brotman, A. W., et al. (1995). Comorbidity of Axis I psychiatric disorders in bulimia nervosa. *J. Clin. Psychiat., 56*(2), 77–80.

Brick, J. (2004). Medical consequences of alcohol abuse. In J. Brick (Ed.), *Handbook of the medical consequences of alcohol and drug abuse* (pp. 7–47). New York: Haworth Press.

Brieger, P., Ehrt, U., Bloeink, R., & Marneros, A. (2002). Consequences of comorbid personality disorders in major depression. *J. Nerv. Ment Dis., 190*(5), 304–309.

Brieger, P., Ehrt, U., & Marneros, A. (2003). Frequency of comorbid personality disorders in bipolar and unipolar affective disorders. *Comprehen. Psychiat., 44*(1), 28–34.

Briken, P., Hill, A., & Berner, W. (2003). Pharmacotherapy of paraphilias with long-acting agonists of luteinizing hormone-releasing hormone: A systematic review. *J. Clin. Psychiat., 64*(8), 890–897.

Britt, R. R. (2005). The odds of dying. *LiveScience.com.* Rape and sexual assault: Reporting to police and medical attention, 1992–2000. Retrieved January 12, 2005, from www.ojp.usdoj.gov/bjs/abstract/rsarp00.htm

Brock, D. W. (2001). Physician-assisted suicide—The worry about abuse. In L. M. Kopelman & K. A. De Ville (Eds.), *Physician-assisted suicide: What are the issues?* (pp. 59–74). Dordrecht, Netherlands: Kluwer Academic.

Brodaty, H. (2005). What is the best dementia screening instrument for general practitioners to use? *Alzheimer's Association International Conference on Prevention of Dementia,* June 18, 2005, Washington, DC.

Brodsky, S., & Poythress, N. (1990). Presentation. American Psychological Association Convention, Boston.

Brody, C. L., Hamer, D. H., & Haaga, D. A. F. (2005). Depression vulnerability, cigarette smoking, and the serotonin transporter gene. *Addict. Behav., 30*(3), 557–566.

Brody, H. (2000). Better health from your inner pharmacy. *Psychol. Today, 32*(4), 60–67.

Bromet, E. J., Hough, L., & Connell, M. (1984). Mental health of children near the Three Mile Island reactor. *J. Prev. Psychiat., 2,* 275–301.

Bromet, E. J., & Litcher, L. (2002). Psychological response of mothers of young children to the Three Mile Island and Chernobyl nuclear plant accidents one decade later. In J. H. Havenaar, J. G. Cwikel, & E. J. Bromet (Eds.), *Toxic turmoil: Psychological and societal consequences of ecological disasters* (pp. 69–84). New York: Kluwer Academic/Plenum Publishers.

Bromet, E. J., Schulberg, H. C., & Dunn, L. (1982). Reactions of psychiatric patients to the Three Mile Island nuclear accident. *Arch. Gen. Psychiat., 39*(6), 725–730.

Brommelhoff, J. A., Conway, K., Merikangas, K., & Levy, B. R. (2004). Higher rates of depression in women: Role of gender bias within the family. *J. Women's Hlth., 13*(1), 69–76.

Brooks, G. R., & Richardson, F. C. (1980). Emotional skills training: A treatment program for duodenal ulcer. *Behav. Ther., 11*(2), 198–207.

Brooks, M. K. (2005). Dementia and wandering behavior: Concern for the lost elder. *Soc. Work Hlth. Care, 41*(2), 95–97.

Brown, A. S. (2003). A review of the déjà vu experience. *Psychol. Bull., 129*(3), 394–413.

Brown, A. S. (2004). The déjà vu illusion. *Curr. Dir. Psychol. Sci., 13*(6), 256–259.

Brown, A. S., Begg, M. D., Gravenstein, S., Schaefer, C. A., Wyatt, R. J., Bresnahan, M., Babulas, V. P., & Susser, E. S. (2004). Serologic evidence of prenatal influenza in the etiology of schizophrenia. *Arch. Gen. Psychiat., 61*(8), 774–780.

Brown, G. P., & Beck, A. T. (2002). Dysfunctional attitudes, perfectionism, and models of vulnerability to depression. In G. L. Flett & P. L. Hewitt (Eds.), *Perfectionism: Theory, research, and treatment* (pp. 231–251). Washington, DC: American Psychological Association.

Brown, G. R., & Ceniceros, S. (2001). Human sexuality in health and disease. In D. Wedding (Ed.), *Behavior and medicine* (3rd ed., pp. 171–184). Seattle: Hogrefe & Huber.

Brown, G. R., Wise, T. N., Costa, P. T., Herbst, J. H., & Fagan, P. J. (1996). Personality characteristics and sexual functioning of 188 cross-dressing men. *J. Nerv. Ment. Dis., 184*(5), 265–273.

Brown, G. W., & Harris, T. O. (1978). *Social origins of depression: A study of psychiatric disorder in women.* London: Tavistock.

Brown, G. W., Harris, T. O., & Hepworth, C. (1995). Loss, humiliation and entrapment among women developing depression: A patient and non-patient comparison. *Psychol. Med., 25,* 7–21.

Brown, G. W., Monck, E. M., Carstairs, G. M., & Wing, J. K. (1962). Influence on family life on the course of schizophrenic illness. *Brit. J. Prev. Soc. Med., 16,* 55–68.

Brown, J. H., Henteleff, P., Barakat, S., & Rowe, C. J. (1986). Is it normal for terminally ill patients to desire death? *Amer. J. Psychiat., 143*(2), 208–211.

Brown, L. (1993). Enrollment of drug abusers in HIV clinical trials: A public health imperative for communities of color. *J. Psychoactive Drugs, 25*(1), 45–48.

Brown, P. J., Read, J. P., & Kahler, C. W. (2003). Comorbid posttraumatic stress disorder and substance use disorders: Treatment outcomes and the role of coping. In P. Ouimette & P. J. Brown (Eds.), *Trauma and substance abuse: Causes, consequences, and treatment of comorbid disorders.* Washington, DC: American Psychological Association.

Brown, R. J. (2002). The cognitive psychology of dissociative states. *Cog. Neuropsychiat., 7*(3), 221–235.

Brown, R. J., Schrag, A., & Trimble, M. R. (2005). Dissociation, childhood interpersonal trauma, and family functioning in patients with somatization disorder. *Amer. J. Psychiat., 162*(5), 899–905.

Brown, R. P., Gerbarg, P., & Bottiglieri, T. (2002). S-adenosylmethionine (SAMe) for depression. *Psychiatr. Ann., 32*(1), 29–44.

Brown, T. A., Hertz, R. M., & Barlow, D. H. (1992). New developments in cognitive-behavioral treatment of anxiety disorders. In A. Tasman & M. B. Riba (Eds.), *Review of psychiatry* (Vol. 11). Washington, DC: American Psychiatric Press.

Brown, T. A., O'Leary, T. A., & Barlow, D. A. (2001). Generalized anxiety disorder. In D. H. Barlow (Ed.), *Clinical handbook of psychological disorders: A step-by-step treatment manual* (3rd ed. pp. 154–208). New York: Guilford Press.

Brown, T. E. (2005). *Attention deficit disorder: The unfocused mind in children and adults.* New Haven: Yale University Press.

Browne, A., & Finklehor, D. (1986). Impact of child sexual abuse: A review of the research. *Psychol. Bull., 99*(1), 66–77.

Brownell, K. D., & Napolitano, M. A. (1995). Distorting reality for children: Body size proportions of Barbie and Ken dolls. *Inter. J. Eat. Disorders, 18*(3), 295–298.

Brownell, K. D., & O'Neil, P. M. (1993). Obesity. In D. H. Barlow (Ed.), *Clinical handbook of psychological disorders: A step-by-step treatment manual* (2nd ed.). New York: Guilford Press.

Brownell, K. D., & Wadden, T. A. (1992). Etiology and treatment of obesity: Understanding a serious, prevalent, and refractory disorder. *J. Cons. Clin. Psychol., 60*(4), 505–517.

Bruce, M. L., & Kim, K. M. (1992). Differences in the effects of divorce on major depression in men and women. *Amer. J. Psychiat., 149*(7), 914–917.

Bruch, H. (1962). Perceptual and conceptual disturbances in anorexia nervosa. *Psychosom. Med., 24,* 187–194.

Bruch, H. (1973). *Eating disorders: Obesity, anorexia nervosa and the person within.* New York: Basic Books.

Bruch, H. (1978). *The golden cage: The enigma of anorexia nervosa.* Cambridge, MA: Harvard University Press.

Bruch, H. (1982). Anorexia nervosa: Therapy and theory. *Amer. J. Psychiat., 139,* 1531–1538.

Bruch, H. (1991). The sleeping beauty: Escape from change. In S. I. Greenspan & G. H. Pollock (Eds.), *The course of life: Vol. 4. Adolescence.* Madison, CT: International Universities Press.

Bruch, H. (2001). *The golden cage: The enigma of anorexia nervosa.* Cambridge, MA: Harvard University Press.

Bruininks, R. H., Woodcock, R. W., Weatherman, R. F., & Hill, B. K. (1996). *Scales of Independent Behavior—Revised: Comprehensive manual.* Itasca, IL: Riverside.

Brumberg, J. J. (1988). *Fasting girls: The history of anorexia nervosa.* New York: Penguin Books.

Bruni, F. (1998, November 22). Behind the jokes, a life of pain and delusion; For Letterman stalker, mental illness was family curse and scarring legacy. *New York Times,* Sect. 1, p. 45.

Bryant, R. A., Guthrie, R. M., & Moulds, M. L. (2001). Hypnotizability in acute stress disorder. *Amer. J. Psychiat., 158*(4), 600–604.

Bryant, R. A., & Harvey, A. G. (1995). Posttraumatic stress in volunteer firefighters: Predictors of stress. *J. Nerv. Ment. Dis., 183*(4), 267–271.

Bryant, R. A., Moulds, M. L., Guthrie, R. M., & Nixon, R. D. V. (2005). The additive benefit of hypnosis and cognitive-behavioral therapy in treating acute stress disorder. *J. Cons. Clin. Psychol., 73*(2), 334–340.

Bulik, C. M., Sullivan, P. F., Carter, F. A., McIntosh, V. V., & Joyce, P. R. (1998). The role of exposure with response prevention in the cognitive-behavioural therapy for bulimia nervosa. *Psychol. Med., 28*(3), 611–623.

Bunch, W. (2005, June 8). Viagra giving rise to new breed of bedroom pills. *Philadelphia Inquirer.*

Bunney, W. E., & Bunney, B. G. (2000). Molecular clock genes in man and lower animals: Possible implications for circadian abnormalities in depression. *Neuropsychopharmacology, 22*(4), 335–345.

Bureau of Justice Statistics. (1999). *Report on U.S. prison population.* Washington, DC.

Burnam, M. A., Stein, J. A., Golding, J. M., & Siegel, J. M. (1988). Sexual assault and mental disorders in a community population. *J. Cons. Clin. Psychol., 56,* 843–850.

Burns, L. H. (1995). An overview of sexual dysfunction in the infertile couple. *J. Fam. Psychother., 6*(1), 25–46.

Burr, J. A., Hartman, J. T., & Matteson, D. W. (1999). Black suicide in U.S. metropolitan areas: An examination of the racial inequality and social integration-regulation hypotheses. *Soc. Forces, 77*(3), 1049–1080.

Burros, M. (2001, May 8). Experts see flaws in U.S. mad cow safeguards. *New York Times.*

Burt, D. R., Creese, I., & Snyder, S. H. (1977). Anti-schizophrenic drugs: Chronic treatment elevates dopamine receptor binding in brain. *Science, 196*(4287), 326–328.

Burton, V. S. (1990). The consequences of official labels: A research note on rights lost by the mentally ill, mentally incompetent, and convicted felons. *Comm. Ment. Hlth. J., 26*(3), 267–276.

Burvill, P. W. (1998). Migrant suicide rates in Australia and in country of birth. *Psychol. Med., 28*(1), 201–208.

Busch, B., Biederman, J., Cohen, L. G., Sayer, J. M., Monuteaux, M. C., Mick, E., Zallen, B., & Faraone, S. V. (2002). Correlates of ADHD among children in pediatric and psychiatric clinics. *Psychiatr. Serv., 53*(9), 1103–1111.

Busch, F. N., Rudden, M. G., & Shapiro, T. (2004). *Psychodynamic treatment of depression.* Washington, DC: American Psychiatric Publishing.

Bushman, B. J., & Anderson, C. A. (2001). Media violence and the American public: Scientific facts versus media misinformation. *Amer. Psychologist, 56*(6/7), 477–489.

Bushman, B. J., Baumeister, R. F., & Stack, A. D. (1999). Catharsis, aggression, and persuasive influence: Self-fulfilling or self-defeating prophecies? *J. Pers. Soc. Psychol., 76*(3), 367–376.

Buss, D. M. (2000). *The dangerous passion: Why jealousy is as necessary as love and sex.* New York: Free Press.

Bussing, R., Koro-Ljungberg, M. E., Gary, F., Mason, D. M., & Garvan, C. W. (2005). Exploring help-seeking for ADHD symptoms: A mixed-methods approach. *Harvard Rev. Psychiat., 13*(2), 85–101.

Bussing, R., Zima, B. T., & Belin, T. R. (1998). Differential access to care for children with ADHD in special education programs. *Psychiatr. Serv., 19*(9), 1226–1229.

Bussing, R., Zima, B. T., Gary, F. A., & Garvan, C. W. (2003). Barriers to detection, help-seeking, and service use for children with ADHD symptoms. *J. Behav. Hlth. Serv. Res., 30*(2), 176–189.

Bustillo, J. R., Lauriello, J., Horan, W. P., & Keith, S. J. (2001). The psychosocial treatment of schizophrenia: An update. *Amer. J. Psychiat., 158*(2), 163–175.

Butcher, J. N. (Ed.). (2000). *Basic sources on the MMPI-2.* Minneapolis, MN: University of Minnesota Press.

Butler, G., Fennel, M., Robson, P., & Gelder, M. (1991). A comparison of behavior therapy and cognitive behavior therapy in the treatment of generalized anxiety disorder. *J. Cons. Clin. Psychol., 59*(1), 167–175.

Butler, R. N. (1975). Psychiatry and the elderly: An overview. *Amer. J. Psychiat., 132,* 893–900.

Butryn, M. L., & Wadden, T. A. (2005). Treatment of overweight in children and adolescents: Does dieting increase the risk of eating disorders? *Inter. J. Eat. Disorders, 37*(4), 285–293.

Button, E. (1993). *Eating disorders: Personal construct therapy and change.* Chichester, England: Wiley.

Button, E. J., & Warren, R. L. (2001). Living with anorexia nervosa: The experience of a cohort of sufferers from anorexia nervosa 7.5 years after initial presentation to a specialized eating disorders service. *Eur. Eating Disord. Rev., 9*(2), 74–96.

Bydlowski, S., Corcos, M., Jeammet, P., Paterniti, S., Berthoz, S., Laurier, C., et al. (2005). Emotion-processing deficits in eating disorders. *Inter. J. Eat. Disorders, 37*(4), 321–329.

Byrne, M., Carr, A., & Clark, M. (2004). The efficacy of behavioral couples therapy and emotionally focused therapy for couple distress. *Contemp. Fam. Ther.: Inter. J., 26*(4), 361–387.

CADDRE (Center for Autism and Developmental Disabilities Research and Epidemiology). (2004). *The epidemiology and etiology of autistic spectrum disorder: A prospective study.* Children's Hospital of Pennsylvania. Retrieved October 7, 2005, from www.aboard.org/aboard/presentations/Levy/CADDRE_files/Default.htm

Cadoret, R. J., Yates, W. R., Troughton, E., Woodworth, G., & Stewart, M. A. (1995). Adoption study demonstrating two genetic pathways to drug abuse. *Arch. Gen. Psychiatry, 52,* 42–52.

Cahn, W., Pol, H. E. H., Bongers, M., Schnack, H. G., Mandi, R. C. W., Van Haren, N. E. M., et al. (2002). Brain morphology in antipsychotic-naïve schizophrenia: A study of multiple brain structures. *Brit. J. Psychiat., 181*(Suppl 43), s66–s72.

Cain, D. J. (2002). Defining characteristics, history, and evolution of humanistic psychotherapies. In D. J. Cain & J. Seeman (Eds.), Humanistic psychotherapies: Handbook of research and practice. Washington, DC: American Psychological Association.

Cain, D. J. (2003). Advancing humanistic psychology and psychotherapy: Some challenges and proposed solutions. *J. Human. Psychol., 43*(3), 10–41.

Caine, D., Patterson, K., Hodges, J. R., Heard, R., & Haliday, G. (2001). Severe anterograde amnesia with extensive hippocampal degeneration in a case of rapidly progressive frontotemporal dementia. *Neurocase, 7*(1), 57–64.

Caldwell, L. D., & White, J. L. (2005). African-centered therapeutic and counseling interventions for African American males. In G. R. Brooks & G. E. Good (Eds.), *The new handbook of psychotherapy and counseling with men: A comprehensive guide to settings, problems, and treatment approaches* (Rev. & abridged ed., pp. 323–336). San Francisco: Jossey-Bass.

Calev, A., Gaudino, E. A., Squires, N. K., Zervas, I. M., & Fink, M. (1995). ECT and non-memory cognition: A review. *Br. J. Clin. Psychol., 34,* 505–515.

Calev, A., Nigal, D., Shapira, B., Tubi, N., et al. (1991). Early and long-term effects of electroconvulsive therapy and depression on memory and other cognitive functions. *J. Nerv. Ment. Dis., 179*(9), *526–533.*

Callahan, C. M., Wolinsky, F. D., Stump, T. E., Nienaber, N. A., Hui, S. L., & Tierney, W. M. (1998). Mortality, symptoms, and functional impairment in late-life depression. *J. Gen. Intern. Med., 13*(11), 746–752.

Callahan, K. L., Hilsenroth, M. J., Yonai, T., & Waehler, C. A. (2005). Longitudinal stress responses to the 9/11 terrorist attacks in a New York metropolitan college sample. *Stress, Trauma, Crisis: Inter. J., 8*(1), 45–60.

Callahan, L. A., McGreevy, M. A., Cirincione, C., & Steadman, H. J. (1992). Measuring the effects of the GBMI verdict: Georgia's 1982 GBMI reform. *Law Human Behav., 16*(4), 447–461.

Callahan, L. A., Steadman, H. J., McGreevy, M. A., & Robbins, P. C. (1991). The volume and characteristics of insanity defense pleas: An eight-state study. *Bull. Amer. Acad. Psychiat. Law, 19*(4), 331–338.

Camacho, E. B., Leon, E. C., & Uribe, M. P. O. (2005). Nature and schizophrenia. *Salud Mental., 28*(2), 59–72.

Cameron, A., Rosen, R. C., & Swindle, R. W. (2005). Sexual and relationship characateristics among an internet-based sample of U.S. men with and without erectile dysfunction. *J. Sex Marital Ther., 31*(3), 229–242.

Cameron, D. J., Thomas, R. I., Mulvhill, M., & Bronheim, H. (1987). Delirium: A test of the Diagnostic and Statistical Manual III criteria on medical inpatients. *J. Amer. Ger. Soc., 35,* 1007–1010.

Cameron, N. (1974). Paranoid conditions and paranoia. In S. Arieti & E. Brody (Eds.), *American handbook of psychiatry.* New York: Basic Books.

Cameron, P. M., Leszcz, M., Bebchuk, W., Swinson, R. P., Antony, M. M., Azim, H. F., et al. (1999). The practice and roles of the psychotherapies: A discussion paper. *Canad. J. Psychiat., 44*(Suppl 1), 18S-31S.

Campbell, J., Gilmore, L., & Cuskelly, M. (2003). Changing student teachers' attitudes towards disability and inclusion. *J. Intell. Dev. Disab., 28,* 369–379.

Canals, J., Blade, J., Carbvajo, G., & Domenech-Llaberia, E. (2001). The Beck Depression Inventory: Psychometric characteristics and usefulness in nonclinical adolescents. *Eur. J. Psychol. Assess., 17*(1), 63–68.

Canetto, S. S. (1995). Elderly women and suicidal behavior. In S. S. Canetto & D. Lester (Eds.), *Women and suicidal behavior.* New York: Springer.

Canetto, S. S. (1995). Suicidal women: Prevention and intervention strategies. In S. S. Canetto & D. Lester (Eds.), *Women and suicidal behavior.* New York: Springer.

Canetto, S. S., & Lester, D. (1995). Gender and the primary prevention of suicide mortality. [Special issue]. *Suic. Life-Threat. Behav., 25*(1), 58–69.

Cantor, J. M., Blanchard, R., Christensen, B. K., Dickey, R., Klassen, P. E., Beckstead, A. L., et al. (2004). Intelligence, memory, and handedness in pedophilia. *Neuropsychol., 18*(1), 3–14.

Capaldi, D. M., & Patterson, G. R. (1994). Interrelated influences of contextual factors on antisocial behavior in childhood and adolescence for males. In D. C. Fowles, P. Sutker, & S. H. Goodman (Eds.), *Progress in experimental personality and psychopathology research.* New York: Springer.

Caplan, P. J. (2004). Review of rethinking mental health and disorder. *Contemporary Psychology 49*(6), 794–797.

Caplan, P. J., & Cosgrove, L. (Eds.). (2004). *Bias in psychiatric diagnosis.* Northvale, NJ: Jason Aronson.

Caplan, R., Perdue, S., Tanguay, P. E., & Fish, B. (1990). Formal thought disorder in childhood onset schizophrenia and schizotypal personality disorder. *J. Child Psychol. Psychiat. Allied Disc., 31*(7), 1103–1114.

Carducci, B. (2000). Shyness: The new solution. *Psychol. Today, 33*(1), 38–45.

Carek, P. J., & Dickerson, L. M. (1999). Current concepts in the pharmacological management of obesity. *Drugs, 57*(6), 883–904.

Carey, B. (2006). Heart risks with stimulant use? Maybe. Worry? For some. *New York Times,* Feb. 21, section F., p. 1.

Carey, M., Carey, K., & Meisler, A. (1991). Psychiatric symptoms in mentally ill chemical abusers. *J. Nerv. Ment. Dis., 179*(3), 136–138.

Carey, R. J., Pinheiro-Carrerra, M., Dai, H., Tomaz, C., et al. (1995). L-DOPA and psychosis: Evidence for L-DOPA-induced increases in prefrontal cortex dopamine and in serium corticosterone. *Biol. Psychiat., 38*(10), 669–676.

Carlson, G. A., Asarnow, J. R., & Orbach, I. (1994). Developmental aspects of suicidal behavior in children and developmentally delayed adolescents. In G. Noam & S. Borst (Eds.), *Children, youth, and suicide: Developmental perspectives. New directions for child development* (pp. 93–107). San Francisco: Jossey-Bass/Pfieffer.

Carlson, G. A., Rich, C. L., Grayson, P., & Fowler, R. C. (1991). Secular trends in psychiatric diagnosis of suicide victims. *J. Affect. Disorders, 21*(2), 127–132.

Carlson, M. (1998, June 22). The best things in life aren't free. *Time, 151,* pp. 21.

Carmichael, M. (2004, September 27). Cut stress–cut sugar. *Newsweek, 144*(13), p. 56.

Carney, S. M., & Goodwin, G. M. (2005). Lithium—A continuing story in the treatment of bipolar disorder. *Acta Psychiatr. Scandin., 111*(Suppl. 426), 7–12.

Caroff, S. N., Mann, S. C., Francis, A., & Fricchione, G. L. (Eds.). (2004). *Catatonia: From psychopathology to neurobiology.* Washington, DC: American Psychiatric Publishing.

Carr, D., House, J. S., Kessler, R. C., Nesse, R. M., Sonnega, J., & Wortman, C. (2000). Marital quality and psychological adjustment to widowhood among older adults: A longitudinal analysis. *J. Ger. B Psychol. Sci. Soc. Sci., 55B*(4), S197-S207.

Carr, D., House, J. S., Wortman, C., Neese, R., & Kessler, R. C. (2001). Psychological adjustment to sudden and anticipated spousal loss among older widowed persons. *J. Ger. B Psychol. Sci. Soc. Sci., 56B*(4), S237-S248.

Carr, J. E. (1994). Annotation: Long term outcome for people with Down syndrome. *J. Child Psychol. Psychiat. Allied Disc, 35*(3), 425–439.

Carr, J. E. (2001). Stress and illness. In D. Wedding (Ed.), *Behavior and medicine* (3rd ed., pp. 231–246). Seattle: Hogrefe & Huber.

Carrasco, J. L., Diaz-Marsa, M., Hollander, E., Cesar, J., & Saiz-Ruiz, J. (2000). Decreased platelet monoamine oxidase activity in female bulimia nervosa. *Eur. Neuropsychopharmacology, 10*(2), 113–117.

Carrasco, M. J. (2005). Cultural competence in mental health. *NAMI Advocate, 3*(1), 13–14.

Carrier, J. W. (2004). Assessing suicidal risk. In D. Capuzzi (Ed.), *Suicide across the life span: Implications for counselors* (pp. 139–162). Alexandria, VA: American Counseling Association.

Carrier, J. W., & Ennis, K. (2004). Depression and suicide. In D. Capuzzi (Ed.), *Suicide across the life span: Implications for counselors* (pp. 39–62). Alexandria, VA: American Counseling Association.

Carroll, K. M. (2005). Matching and differential therapies: Providing substance abusers with appropriate treatment. In R. J. Frances, A. H. Mack, & S. I. Miller (Eds.), *Clinical textbook of addictive disorders* (3rd ed., pp. 637–662). New York: Guilford Press.

Carroll, K. M., & Rounsaville, B. J. (1995). Psychosocial treatments. In J. M. Oldham & M. B. Riba (Eds.), *American Psychiatric Press review of psychiatry* (Vol. 14). Washington, DC: American Psychiatric Press.

Carstairs K. (1992). Paranoid-schizoid or symbiotic? *Inter. J. Psychoanal., 73*(1), 71–85.

Casey, D. E. (1995). Motor and mental aspects of EPS. *Inter. J. Psychopharmacology, 10,* [np].

Casey, L. M., Oei, T. P. S., & Newcombe, P. A. (2004). An integrated cognitive model of panic disorder: The role of positive and negative cognitions. *Clin. Psychol. Rev., 24*(5), 529–555.

Casey, P. (2001). Multiple personality disorder. *Prim. Care Psychiat., 7*(1), 7–11.

Cash, T. F., & Henry, P. E. (1995). Women's body images: The results of a national survey in the U. S. A. *Sex Roles, 33*(1/2), 19–28.

Caskey, J. D., & Rosenthal, S. L. (2005). Conducting research on sensitive topics with adolescents: Ethical and developmental considerations. *J. Dev. Behav. Pediatr., 26*(1), 61–67.

Casper, R. C. (1995). Biology of eating disorders. In A. F. Schatzberg & C. B. Nemeroff (Eds.), *The American Psychiatric Press textbook of psychopharmacology.* Washington, DC: American Psychiatric Press.

Caspi, A., Sugden, K., Moffitt, T. E., Taylor, A., Craig, I. W., Harrington, H. L., et al. (2003). Influence of life stress on depression: Moderation by a polymorphism in the 5-HTT gene. *Science, 301*(5631), 386–389.

Cassells, C., Paterson, B., Dowding, D., & Morrison, R. (2005). Long- and short-term risk factors in the prediction of inpatient suicide: A review of the literature. *Crisis, 26*(2), 53–63.

Castellani, B. (2000). *Pathological gambling: The making of a medical problem.* Albany: State University of New York Press.

Castrogiovanni, P., Pieraccini, F., & Di Muro, A. (1998). Suicidality and aggressive behavior. *Acta Psychiatr. Scandin., 97*(2), 144–148.

Caton, C. L. (1982). Effect of length of inpatient treatment for chronic schizophrenia. *Amer. J. Psychiat., 139*(7), 856–861.

Cauchon, D. (1999, February). Patients often aren't informed of danger. *USA Today.*

Cauchon, D. (2004, November 16). Pennies pay off when Ohio collector cashes in. *USA Today,* p. 3A.

Caudill, O. B., & Kaplan, A. I. (2005). Protecting privacy and confidentiality. *J. Aggress. Maltreat. Trauma, 11*(1–2), 117–134.

Cauli, O., & Morelli, M. (2005). Caffeine and the dopaminergic system. *Behav. Pharmacol., 16*(2), 63–77.

Cautela, J. R. (2000). Rationale and procedures for covert conditioning. *Psicoterapia Cognitiva e Comportamentale, 6*(2), 194–205.

Cauwels, J. M. (1983). *Bulimia: The binge-purge compulsion.* New York: Doubleday.

Cavanaugh, J. C. (1990). *Adult development and aging.* Belmont, CA: Wadsworth.

Cavanaugh, J. C., & Blanchard-Fields, F. (2006). *Adult development and aging* (5th ed.). Belmont, CA: Wadsworth/Thomson Learning.

CBC News. (2006, January 23). Indepth: Mad cow. Timeline of BSE in Canada and the U.S. *CBC News Online*

CDC (Centers for Disease Control and Prevention). (1997). Cited in NCIPC (National Center for Injury Prevention and Control), *Impaired driving fact sheet.* Atlanta, GA: Author.

CDC (Centers for Disease Control and Prevention). (2001). Report. Atlanta, Georgia: Author.

CDC (Centers for Disease Control and Prevention). (2002). Alcohol use. NCHS fast stats. Atlanta, GA: Author.

CDC (Centers for Disease Control and Prevention). (2004). Alcohol and public health. Atlanta, GA: Author.

Celenza, A. (2005). Sexual boundary violations: How do they happen? *Direct. Psychiat., 25*(2), 141–149.

Cerletti, U., & Bini, L. (1938). L'elettroshock. *Arch. Gen. Neurol. Psychiat. & Psychoanal., 19,* 266–268.

Chaika, E. O. (1990). *Understanding psychotic speech: Beyond Freud and Chomsky.* Springfield, IL: Thomas.

Chait, L. D., Fishman, M. W., & Schuster, C. R. (1985). "Hangover" effects the morning after marijuana smoking. *Drug Alc. Dep., 15*(3), 229–238.

Chalamat, M., Mihalopoulos, C., Carter, R., & Vos, T. (2005). Assessing cost-effectiveness in mental health: Vocational rehabilitation for schizophrenia and related conditions. *Austral. New Zeal. J. Psychiat., 39*(8), 693–700.

Chamberlain, S. R., Blackwell, A. D., Fineberg, N. A., Robbins, T. W., & Sahakian, B. J. (2005). The neuropsychology of obsessive compulsive disorder: The importance of failures in cognitive and behavioural inhibition as candidate endopyhenotypic markers. *Neurosci. Biobehav. Rev., 29*(3), 399–419.

Chamberlain, P., & Smith, D. K. (2005). Multidimensional treatment foster care: A community solution for boys and girls referred from juvenile justice. In E. D. Hibbs & P. S. Jensen (Eds.), *Psychosocial treatments for child and adolescent disorders: Empirically based strategies for clinical practice* (2nd ed., pp. 557–574). Washington, DC: American Psychological Association.

Chambless, D. L. (2002). Identification of empirically supported counseling psychology interventions: Commentary. *Counseling Psychologist, 30*(2), 302–308.

Chambless, D. C., Cherney, J., Caputo, G. C., & Reinstein, B. J. (1987). Anxiety disorders and alcoholism: A study with inpatient alcoholics. *J. Anx. Dis., 1,* 29–40.

Chambless, D. L., & Ollendick, T. H. (2001). Empirically supported psychological interventions: Controversies and evidence. *Annu. Rev. Psychol., 52,* 685–716.

Chan, S., MacKenzie, A., Ng, D. T., & Leung, J. K. (2000). An evaluation of the implementation of case management in the community psychiatric nursing service. *J. Adv. Nurs., 31*(1), 144–156.

Chaparro, S. (2004). Cited in T. Sauthoff, Professor assigns 48 hours without using cell phone. *The Daily Targum,* April 5, 2004, p. 1.

Chapman, S., & Morrell, S. (2000). Barking mad? Another lunatic hypothesis bites the dust. *Brit. Med. J., 321*(7276), 1561–1563.

Char, W. F. (1985). The hysterical spouse. *Med. Aspects Human Sex., 19*(9), 123–133.

Charman, D. P. (Ed.). (2004). *Core processes in brief psychodynamic psychotherapy: Advancing effective practice.* Mahwah, NJ: Lawrence Erlbaum Associates.

Charney, D. S., Woods, S. W., Goodman, W. K., & Heninger, G. R. (1987). Neurobiological mechanisms of panic anxiety: Biochemical and behavioral correlates of yohimbine-induced anxiety. *Amer. J. Psychiat., 144*(8), 1030–1036.

Charney, D. S., Woods, S. W., Price, L. H., Goodman, W. K., Glazer, W. M., & Heninger, G. R. (1990). Noradrenergic dyssregulation in panic disorder. In J. C. Ballenger (Ed.), *Neurobiology of panic disorder.* New York: Wiley-Liss.

Chase, M. (1993, May 28). Psychiatrists declare severe PMS a depressive disorder. *Wall Street Journal,* pp. B1, B6.

Chassin, L., Collins, R. L., Ritter, J., & Shirley, M. C. (2001). Vulnerability to substance use disorders across the life span. In R. E. Ingram & J. M. Price (Eds.), *Vulnerability to psychopathology: Risk across the lifespan* (pp. 165–172). New York: Guilford Press.

Chatlos, C. (1987). *Crack: What you should know about the cocaine epidemic.* New York: Perigee Books.

Chavez, M. L., & Spitzer, M. F. (2002). Herbals and other dietary supplements for premenstrual syndrome and menopause. *Psychiatr. Ann., 32*(1), 61–71.

Chen, T.-J., Yu, Y. W.-Y., Chen, M.-C., Wang, S.-Y., Tsai, S.-J., & Lee, T.-W. (2005). Serotonin dysfunction and suicide attempts in major depressives: An auditory event-related potential study. *Neuropsychobiology, 52*(1), 287–36.

Chen, Y. R., Swann, A. C., & Burt, D. B. (1996). Stability of diagnosis in schizophrenia. *Amer. J. Psychiat., 153*(5), 682–686.

Chien, W. T., Norman, I., & Thompson, D. R. (2004). A randomized controlled trial of a mutual support group for family caregivers of patients with schizophrenia. *Inter. J. Nurs. Stud., 41*(6), 637–649.

Chiu, L. H. (1971). Manifested anxiety in Chinese and American children. *J. Psychol., 79,* 273–284.

Choca, J. P. (2004). Case reports. In J. P. Choca, *Interpretive guide to the Millon Clinical Multiaxial Inventory* (3rd ed., pp. 289–326). Washington, DC: American Psychological Association.

Chochinov, H. M., & Schwartz, L. (2002). Depression and the will to live in the psychological landscape of terminally ill patients. In K. Foley & H. Hendin (Eds.), *The case against assisted suicide: For the right to end-of-life care* (pp. 261–278). Baltimore, MD: The John Hopkins University Press.

Chodoff, P. (1989). Histrionic personality disorder. In American Psychiatric Association (Ed.), *Treatments of psychiatric disorders: A task force report of the American Psychiatric Association*. Washington, DC: American Psychiatric Press.

Chong, L., Zhen-Ying, W., & Chang-Jun, Z. (2005). Sleep problems and related factors of elderly in Xinxiang. *Chinese Ment. Hlth. J., 19*(11), 755–757.

Chou, T. (1992). Wake up and smell the coffee: Caffeine, coffee and the medical consequences. *Western Journal of Medicine, 157,* 544–553.

Christakis, D. A., Zimmerman, F. J., DiGiuseppe, D. L., & McCarty, C. A. (2004). Early television exposure and subsequent attentional problems in children. *Pediatrics, 113,* 708–713.

Christensen, A. J., Dornick, R., Ehlers, S. L., & Schultz, S. K. (1999). Social environment and longevity in schizophrenia. *Psychosom. Med., 61*(2), 141–145.

Christensen, A., Sevier, M., Simpson, L. E., & Gattis, K. S. (2004). Acceptance, mindfulness, and change in couple therapy. In V. M. Follette, M. M. Linehan, & S. C. Hayes (Eds.), *Mindfulness and acceptance: Expanding the cognitive-behavioral tradition* (pp. 288–309). New York: Guilford Press.

Christophersen, E. R., & Purvis, P. C. (2001). Toileting problems in children. In C. E. Walker & M. C. Roberts (Eds.), *Handbook of clinical child psychopathology* (3rd ed., pp. 453–469). New York: Wiley.

Chu, J. A. (2000). "Memories of childhood abuse: Dissociation, amnesia, and corroboration": Reply. *Amer. J. Psychiat., 157*(8), 1348–1349.

Chung, M. C., Dennis, I., Easthope, Y., Werrett, J., & Farmer, S. (2005). A multiple-indicator multiple-case model for posttraumatic stress reactions: Personality, coping, and maladjustment. *Psychosom. Med., 67*(2), 251–259.

Ciano-Federoff, L. M., & Sperry, J. A. (2005). On "converting" hand pain into psychological pain: Treating hand pain vicariously through exposure-based therapy for PTSD. *Clin. Case Stud., 4*(1), 57–71.

Cichewicz, D. L. (2004). Synergistic interactions between cannabinoid and opioid analgesics. *Life Sci., 74*(11), 1317–1324.

Claes, L., Vandereycken, W., & Vertommen, H. (2002). Impulsive and compulsive traits in eating disordered patients compared with controls. *Pers. Individ. Diff., 32*(4), 707–714.

Clark, D. A. (2004). Cognitive-behavioral theory and treatment of obsessive-compulsive disorder: Past contributions and current developments. In R. L. Leahy (Ed.), *Contemporary cognitive therapy: Theory, research, and practice* (pp. 161–183). New York: Guilford Press.

Clark, D. A. (2004). *Cognitive-behavioral therapy for OCD.* New York: Guilford Press.

Clark, D. C. (1999). The puzzle of suicide in later life. In M. T. Stimming & M. Stimming (Eds.), *Before their time: Adult children's experiences of parental suicide.* Philadephia: Temple University Press.

Clark, H. W. (2001). Residential substance abuse treatment for pregnant and postpartum women and their children: Treatment and policy implications. *Child Welfare, 80*(2), 179–198.

Clark, K. (1936). Quoted in: Murders due to "Killer" drug. Reported by Universal News Service (syndicate).

Clark, L. A. (2002). Evaluation and devaluation in personality assessment. In J. Z. Sadler (Ed.), *Descriptions and prescriptions: Values, mental disorders, and the DSMs* (pp. 131–147). Baltimore, MD: Johns Hopkins University Press.

Clark, L. A. (2005, November). Dimensional bases of diagnosis. *Clinician's Res. Digest, Suppl. Bull. 33,* 1–2.

Clark, L. A., & Harrison, J. A. (2001). Assessment instruments. In W. J. Livesley (Ed.), *Handbook of personality disorders: Theory, research, and treatment* (pp. 277–306). New York: Guilford Press.

Clark, S. E., & Goldney, R. D. (2000). The impact of suicide on relatives and friends. In K. Hawton & K. van Heeringen (Eds.), *The international handbook of suicide and attempted suicide.* Chichester, England: Wiley.

Clarke, D., & Singh, R. (2005). The influence of pessimistic explanatory style on the relation between stressful life events and hospital doctors' psychological distress. *Soc. Behav. Pers., 33*(3), 259–271.

Clarke, G. N., Rohde, P., Lewinsohn, P. M., Hops, H., & Seeley, J. R. (1999). Cognitive-behavioral treatment of adolescent depression: Efficacy of acute group treatment and booster sessions. *J. Amer. Acad. Child Adol. Psychiat., 38*(3), 272–279.

Clarke, J., Stein, M. D., Sobota, M., Marisi, M., & Hanna, L. (1999). Victims as victimizers: Physical aggression by persons with a history of childhood abuse. *Arch. Internal Med., 159*(16), 1920–1924.

Clarke, J. C., & Saunders, J. B. (1988). *Alcoholism and problem drinking: Theories and treatment.* Sydney: Pergamon Press.

Clarkin, J. F., Foelsch, P. A., Levy, K. N., Hull, J. W., Delaney, J. C., & Kernberg, O. F. (2001). The development of a psychodynamic treatment for patients with borderline personality disorder: A preliminary study of behavioral change. *J. Per. Disorders, 15,* 487–495.

Clary, G. L., & Krishnan, K. R. (2001). Delirium: Diagnosis, neuropathogenesis and treatment. *J. Psychiatr. Prac., 7*(5), 310–323.

Clay, R. A. (1996). Psychologists' faith in religion begins to grow. *APA Monitor, 27*(8), 1, 48.

Clayton, A. H., Pradko, J. F., Croft, H. A., Montano, C. B., Leadbetter, R. A., Bolden-Watson, C., et al. (2002). Prevalence of sexual dysfunction among newer antidepressants. *J. Clin. Psychiat., 63*(4), 357–366.

Clayton, P. J. (2004). Bereavement and depression. In H. A. Sackeim & S. P. Roose (Eds.), *Late-life depression* (pp. 107–114). New York: Oxford University Press.

Clay-Warner, J., & Burt, C. H. (2005). Rape reporting after reforms: Have times really changed? *Violence Against Women, 11*(2), 150–176.

Clifford, J. S., Norcross, J. C., & Sommer, R. (1998). *Autobiographies of mental patients: Psychologists' uses and recommendations.* Paper presented at the 69th annual meeting of the Eastern Psychological Association, Boston.

Cling, B. J. (2004). Rape and rape trauma syndrome. In B. J. Cling (Ed.), *Sexualized violence against women and children: A psychology and law perspective* (pp. 13–47). New York: Guilford Press.

Cloninger, C. F., & Svrakic, D. M. (2005). Personality disorders. In E. H. Rubin & C. F. Zorumski (Eds.), *Adult psychiatry* (2nd ed., pp. 290–306). Oxford, England: Blackwell Publishing Ltd.

Clum, G. A., & Febbraro, G. A. R. (2001). Phobias. In H. S. Friedman (Ed.), *Specialty articles from the encyclopedia of mental health.* San Diego: Academic Press.

Clum, G., & Yang, B. (1995). Additional support for the reliability and validity of the Modified Scale for Suicide Ideation. *Psychol. Assess., 7*(1), 122–125.

CNN. (2004, June 4). Porn 3X more popular than searches. *CNNmoney.*

CNN. (2006, January 23). Mad cow case rocks Canada's beef industry. *Netscape News with CNN/AFP (Ottawa).*

Coambs, R. B., & McAndrews, M. P. (1994). The effects of psychoactive substances on workplace performance. In S. Macdonald & P. Roman (Eds.), *Research advances in alcohol and drug problems: Vol. 11. Drug testing in the workplace.* New York: Plenum Press.

Coccaro, E. F. (2001). Biological and treatment correlates. In W. J. Livesley (Ed.), *Handbook of personality disorders: Theory, research, and treatment* (pp. 124–135). New York: Guilford Press.

Coetzer, B. R. (2004). Obsessive-compulsive disorder following brain injury: A review. *Inter. J. Psychiat. Med., 34*(4), 363–377.

Coffey, C., Carlin, J. B., Lynskey, M., Li, N., & Patton, G. C. (2003). Adolescent precursors of cannabis dependence: Findings from the Victorian Adolescent Health Cohort Study. *Brit. J. Psychiat., 182*(4), 330–336.

Coffey, S. F., Gudleski, G. D., Saladin, M. E., & Brady, K. T. (2003). Impulsivity and rapid discounting of delayed hypothetical rewards in cocaine-dependent individuals. *Exp. Clin. Psychopharmacol., 11*(1), 18–25.

Cohen, A. S., & Docherty, N. M. (2005). Symptom-oriented versus syndrome approaches to resolving heterogeneity of neuropsychological functioning in schizophrenia. *J. Neuropsychiat. Clin. Neurosci., 17*(3), 384–390.

Cohen, C. I., & Cohen, S. I. (2002). Potential savings from splitting newer antidepressant medications. *CNS Drugs, 16*(5), 353–358.

Cohen, J., Goodman, R. F., Brown, E. J., & Mannarino, A. (2004). *Harvard Rev. Psychiatry, 12*(4), 213–216.

Cohen, L., Ardjoen, R. C., & Sewpersad, K. S. M. (1997). Type A behaviour pattern as a risk factor after myocardial infarction: A review. *Psychology and Health, 12,* 619–632.

Cohen, L. J., & Galynker, I. I. (2002). Clinical features of pedophilia and implications for treatment. *J. Psychiatr. Prac., 8*(5), 276–289.

Cohen, M. B., Baker, G., Cohen, R. A., Fromm-Reichmann, F., & Weigert, E. V. (1954). An intensive study of twelve cases of manic-depressive psychosis. *Psychiatry, 17,* 103–137.

Cohen, R. M., Semple, W. E., Gross, M., & Nordahl, T. E. (1988). From syndrome to illness: Delineating the pathophysiology of schizophrenia with PET. *Schizo. Bull., 14*(2), 169–176.

Cohen, S. (2002). Psychosocial stress, social networks, and susceptibility to infection. In H. G. Koenig & H. J. Cohen (Eds.), *The link between religion and health: Psychoneuroimmunology and the faith factor* (pp. 101–123). New York: Oxford University Press.

Cohen, S. (2005). Psychological stress, immunity and upper respiratory infections. In G. Miller & E. Chen (Eds.), *Current directions in health psychology.* Upper Saddle River, NJ: Pearson.

Cohen-Kettenis, P. T. (2001). Gender identity disorder in DSM? *J. Amer. Acad. Child Adol. Psychiat., 40*(4), 391.

Cohen-Kettenis, P. T., & Gooren, L. J. (1999). Transsexualism: A review of etiology, diagnosis and treatment. *J. Psychosom. Res., 46*(4), 315–333.

Cohen-Kettenis, P. T., & van Goozen, S. H. M. (1997). Sex reassignment of adolescent transsexuals: A follow-up study. *J. Amer. Acad. Child Adol. Psychiat., 36*(2), 263–271.

Cohen-Sandler, R., Berman, A. L., & King, R. A. (1982). A follow-up study of hospitalized suicidal children. *J. Amer. Acad. Child Psychiat., 214,* 398–403.

Colburn, D. (1996, November 19). Singer's suicide doesn't lead to "copycat" deaths. *Washington Post Health,* p. 5.

Cole, D. A., & Turner, J. E., Jr. (1993). Models of cognitive mediation and moderation in child depression. *J. Abnorm. Psychol., 102*(2), 271–281.

Cole, E., Daniel, J. H. (Eds.). (2005). *Featuring females: Feminist analyses of media.* Washington, DC: American Psychological Association.

Cole, J. O., Klerman, G. L., Goldberg, S. C., et al. (1964). Phenothiazine treatment in acute schizophrenia. *Arch. Gen. Psychiatry, 10,* 246–261.

Cole, M. (2005). Psychology and culture: Top down versus bottom up? *PsycCRITIQUES, 50*(19), [np].

Cole, T. B., & Glass, R. M. (Eds.). (2005). Mental illness and violent death: Major issues for public health. *JAMA, 294*(5), 623–624.

Coleman, L. (1984). *The reign of error: Psychiatry, authority, and law.* Boston: Beacon.

Coles, M. E., & Heimberg, R. G. (2005). Thought control strategies in generalized anxiety disorder. *Cog. Ther. Res., 229*(1), 47–56.

Coles, M. E., Heimberg, R. G., Frost, R. O., & Steketee, G. (2005). Not just right experiences and obsessive-compulsive features: experimental and self-monitoring perspectives. *Behav. Res. Ther., 43,* 153–167.

Colom, F., Vieta, E., Martinez, A. A., Reinares, M., Goikolea, J. M., Benabarre, A., et al. (2003). A randomized trial on the efficacy of group psychoeducation in the prophylaxis of recurrences in bipolar patients whose disease is in remission. *Arch. Gen. Psychiat., 60*(4), 402–407.

Colom, F., Vieta, E., Reinares, M., Martinez, A. A., Torrent, C., Goikolea, J. M., et al. (2003). Psychoeducation efficacy in bipolar disorders: Beyond compliance enhancement. *J. Clin. Psychiat., 64*(9), 1101–1105.

Comer, R. (1973). *Therapy interviews with a schizophrenic patient.* Unpublished manuscript.

Compas, B. E., & Gotlib, I. H. (2002). *Introduction to clinical psychology: Science and practice.* Boston: McGraw-Hill.

Conklin, C. Z., & Westen, D. (2005). Borderline personality disorder in clinical practice. *Amer. J. Psychiat., 162,* 867–875.

Conley, R. R., Kelly, D. L., Nelson, M. W., Richardson, C. M., Feldman, S., Benham, R., et al. (2005). Risperidone, quetiapine, and fluphenazine in the treatment of patients with therapy-refractory schizophrenia. *Clin. Neuropharmacol., 28*(4), 163–168.

Connelly, M., & Dutton, S. (2002). Bearing the brunt: New Yorkers react to 9/11. *The Roper Center for Public Opinion Research, 13*(5), 25.

Connor, J. P., Young, R. McD., Lawford, B. R., Ritchie, T. L., & Noble, E. P. (2002). D₂ dopamine receptor (DRD2) polymorphism is associated with severity of alcohol dependence. *Eur. Psychiat., 17*(1), 17–23.

Connor, J. P., Young, R. McD., Lawford, B. R., Ritchie, T. L., & Noble, E. P. (2002). D₂ dopamine receptor (DRD2) polymorphism is associated with severity of alcohol dependence. *Eur. Psychiat., 17*(1), 17–23.

Conrad, N. (1992). Stress and knowledge of suicidal others as factors in suicidal behavior of high school adolescents. *Issues Ment. Hlth. Nurs., 13*(2), 95–104.

Conwell, Y., Caine, E. D., & Olsen, K. (1990). Suicide and cancer in late life. *Hosp. Comm. Psychiat., 43,* 1334–1338.

Conwell, Y., & Duberstein, P. (2001). Suicide in elders. In H. Hendin & J. J. Mann (Eds.), *The clinical science of suicide prevention* (Vol. 932, pp. 132–148). New York: Annals of the New York Academy of Sciences.

Cook, C. E., Jeffcoat, A. R., & Perez-Reyes, M. (1985). Pharmacokinetic studies of cocaine and phencyclidine in man. In G. Barnett & C. N. Chiang (Eds.), *Pharmacokinetics and pharmacodynamics of psychoactive drugs.* Foster City, CA: Biomedical Publications.

Coons, P. M., & Bowman, E. S. (2001). Ten-year follow-up study of patients with dissociative identity disorder. *J. Trauma Dissoc., 2*(1), 73–89.

Coons, P. M., Bowman, E. S., & Milstein, V. (1988). Multiple personality disorder: A clinical investigation of 50 cases. *J. Nerv. Ment. Dis., 176*(9), 519–527.

Cooper, A. M., & Ronningstam, E. (1992). Narcissistic personality disorder. In A. Tasman & M. B. Riba (Eds.), *American Psychiatric Press review of psychiatry* (Vol. 11). Washington, DC: American Psychiatric Press.

Cooper, A. M., Scherer, C. R., Boies, S. C., & Gordon, B. L. (1999). Sexuality on the Internet: From sexual exploration to pathological expression. *Profess. Psychol.: Res. Pract., 30*(2), 154–164.

Cooper, J. L. (2004). Treatment for children with attention-deficit/hyperactivity disorder. *Diss. Abstr. Inter.: Sect. B: Sci. Eng., 65*(5-B), 2338.

Cooper, M. (2001). Eating disorders, culture, and cognition. In J. F. Schumaker & T. Ward (Eds.), *Cultural cognition and psychopathology.* Westport, CT: Praeger.

Cooper, M. L. (1994). Motivations for alcohol use among adolescents: Development and validation of a four-factor model. *Psychol. Assess., 6*(2), 117–128.

Corales, T. A. (Ed.). (2005). *Trends in posttraumatic stress disorder research.* Hauppauge, NY: Nova Science Publishers.

Corcoran, K., Gorin, S., & Moniz, C. (2005). Managed care and mental health. In S. A. Kirk (Ed.), *Mental disorders in the social environment: Critical perspectives* (pp. 430–442). New York: Columbia University Press.

Corey, G. (2001). *Theory and practice of counseling and psychotherapy* (6th ed.). Belmont, CA: Brooks/Cole.

Corey, G. (2004). *Theory and practice of counseling and psychotherapy (with web site, chapter quiz booklet, and InfoTrac.* Stanford, CT: Wadsworth Publishing.

Corkin, S. (1968). Acquisition of motor skill after bilateral medial temporal-lobe excision. *Neuropsychologia, 6,* 255–264.

Corkin, S. (1984). Lasting consequences of bilateral medial temporal lobectomy: Clinical course and experimental findings in H. M. *Sem. in Neuro., 4,* 249–259.

Corliss, R., & Lemonick, M. D. (2004, August 30). How to live to be 100. *Time, 164*(9), 40–46.

Cornblatt, B. A., & Keilp, J. G. (1994). Impaired attention, genetics, and the pathophysiology of schizophrenia. *Schizo. Bull., 20*(1), 31–46.

Cornish, J. W., McNicholas, L. F., & O'Brien, C. P. (1995). Treatment of substance-related disorders. In A. F. Schatzberg & C. B. Nemeroff (Eds.), *The American Psychiatric Press textbook of psychopharmacology.* Washington, DC: American Psychiatric Press.

Corrie, S., & Callanan, M. M. (2001). Therapists' beliefs about research and the scientist-practitioner model in an evidence-based health care climate? A qualitative study. *Brit. J. Med. Psychol., 74*(2), 135–149.

Corrigan, P. (2004). How stigma interferes with mental health care. *Amer. Psychologist, 59*(7), 614–625.

Corrigan, P. W. (Ed.). (2005). *On the stigma of mental illness: Practical strategies for research and social change.* Washington, DC: American Psychological Association.

Corrigan, P. W., & Penn, D. L. (Eds.). (2001). *Social cognition and schizophrenia.* Washington, DC: American Psychological Association.

Corrigan, P. W., & Watson, A. C. (2005). Mental illness and dangerousness: Fact or misperception, and implications for stigma. In P. W. Corrigan (Ed.), *On the stigma of mental illness: Practical strategies for research and social change* (pp. 165–179). Washington, DC: American Psychological Association.

Corwin, M. (1993, May 8). When the law can't protect. *Los Angeles Times,* p. A1.

Coryell, W., Miller, D. D., & Perry, P. J. (1998). Haloperidol plasma levels and dose optimization. *Amer. J. Psychiat., 155,* 48–53.

Cosgrove, L., & Riddle, B. (2004). Gender bias and sex distribution of mental disorders in the DSM-IV-TR. In L. Cosgrove & P. J. Caplan (Eds.), *Bias in psychiatric diagnosis* (pp. 127–140). Northvale, NJ: Jason Aronson.

Cosimides, L., & Tooby, J. (2000). Psychology and the emotions. In M. Lewis & J. M. Haviland (Eds.), *Handbook of emotions* (2nd ed.). New York: Guilford Press.

Costa, E. (1983). Are benzodiazepine recognition sites functional entities for the action of endogenous effectors or merely drug receptors? *Adv. in Biochem. & Psychopharm., 38,* 249–259.

Costa, E. (1985). Benzodiazepine-GABA interactions: A model to investigate the neurobiology of anxiety. In A. H. Tuma & J. Maser (Eds.), *Anxiety and the anxiety disorders*. Hillsdale, NJ: Erlbaum.

Costa, J. L., Brennen, M. B., & Hochgeschwender, U. (2002). The human genetics of eating disorders: Lessons from the leptin/melanocortin system. *Child Adol. Psychiat. Clin. N. Amer., 11*(2), 387–397.

Costa, P. T. Jr., & McCrae, R. R. (2005). A five-factor model perspective on personality disorders. In S. Strack (Ed.), *Handbook of personality and psychopathology* (pp. 442–461). Hoboken, NJ: Wiley.

Costantino, G., Flanagan, R., & Malgady, R. G. (2001). Narrative assessments: TAT, CAT, and TEMAS. In L. A. Suzuki, J. G. Ponterotto, & P. J. Meller (Eds.), *Handbook of multicultural assessment: Clinical, psychological, and educational applications* (2nd ed., pp. 217–236). San Francisco: Jossey-Bass.

Costello, C. G. (1996). The advantages of focusing on the personality characteristics of the personality disordered. In C. G. Costello (Ed.), *Personality characteristics of the personality disordered*. New York: Wiley.

Cottler, L. B., Campbell, W., Krishna, V. A. S., Cunningham-Williams, R. M., & Abdullah, A.-B. (2005). Predictors of high rates of suicidal ideation among drug users. *J. Nerv. Ment. Dis., 193*(7), 431–437.

Cottraux, J. (2005). Recent developments in research and treatment for social phobia (social anxiety disorder). *Curr. Opin. Psychiat., 18*(1), 51–54.

Coulson, B. S., & Almeida, O. P. (2002). Delirium: Moving behind the clinical diagnosis. *Revista Brasileora de Psiquiatria, 24*(Suppl. 1), 28–33.

Covington, M. A., He, C., Brown, C., Naci, L., McClain, J. T., Fjordbak, B. S., et al. (2005). Schizophrenia and the structure of language: The linguist's view. *Schizo. Res., 77*(1), 85–98.

Cowan, D., & Brunero, S. (1997). Group therapy for anxiety disorders using rationale emotive behaviour therapy. *Austral. New Zeal. J. Ment. Hlth. Nurs., 6*(4), 164–168.

Cowan, S. (2002). Public arguments for and against the establishment of community mental health facilities: Implications for mental health practice. *J. Ment. Hlth. UK, 11*(1), 5–15.

Cowley, G. (2000, January 31). Alzheimer's: Unlocking the mystery. *Newsweek,* pp. 46–51.

Cowley, G. (2002, June 24). Alzheimer's: The race to control a terrifying illness. *Newsweek, 139*(25), 42–50.

Cox, A., Rutter, M., Newman, S., & Bartak, L. (1975). A comparative study of infantile autism and specific developmental receptive language disorder: II. Parental characteristics. *Brit. J. Psychiat., 126,* 146–159.

Cox, D. J., Morris, J. B. Jr., Borowitz, S. M., & Sutphen, J. L. (2002). Psychological differences between children with and without chronic encopresis. *J. Pediatr. Psychol., 27*(7), 585–591.

Cox, W. M., Yeates, G. N., Gilligan, P. A. T., & Hosier, S. G. (2001). Individual differences. In N. Heather, T. J. Peters, & T. Stockwell (Eds.), *International handbook of alcohol dependence and problems.* New York: Wiley.

Coy, T. V. (1998). The effect of repressive coping style on cardiovascular reactivity and speech disturbances during stress. *Diss. Abstr. Inter.: Sect. B: Sci. Eng., 58*(8–B), 4512.

Coyne, J. C. (2001). Depression and the response of others. In W. G. Parrott (Ed.), *Emotions in social psychology: Essential readings* (pp. 231–238). Philadelphia: Psychology Press/Taylor & Francis.

Coyne, J. C., Schwenk, T. L., & Fechner-Bates, S. (1995). Nondetection of depression by primary care physicians reconsidered. *Gen. Hosp. Psychiat., 17*(1), 3–12.

Cozier-D'Amico, Y. C. (2004). Social factors, genetics, and hypertension in United States Black women. *Diss. Abstr. Inter.: Sect. B: Sci. Eng., 65*(3-B), 1275.

Crandall, C. S., Preisler, J. J., & Aussprung, J. (1992). Measuring life events stress in the lives of college students: The Undergraduate Stress Questionnaire (USQ). *Journal of Behavioral Medicine, 15*(6), 627–662.

Crane, G. E. (1973). Persistent dyskinesia. *Brit. J. Psychiat., 22,* 395–405.

Creamer, T. L., & Liddle, B. J. (2005). Secondary traumatic stress among disaster mental health workers responding to the September 11 attacks. *J. Traum. Stress, 18*(1), 89–96.

Creer, C., & Wing, J. K. (1974). *Schizophrenia at home.* London: National Schizophrenia Fellowship.

Creese, I., Burt, D. R., & Snyder, S. H. (1977). Dopamine receptor binding enhancement accompanies lesion-induced behavioral supersensitivity. *Science, 197,* 596–598.

CRI (Coffee Research Institute). (2001). [Coffee] consumption in the United States. Retrieved November 24, 2002, from www.coffeesearch.org

Crisp, A. H. (1981). Anorexia nervosa at a normal weight?: The abnormal-normal weight control syndrome. *Inter. J. Psychiat. Med., 11,* 203–233.

Crisp, M. (2001, April 8). Sticks & stones: 'New Kid' puts comic spin on a serious situation. *Sunday News* (Lancaster, PA), p. H–1.

Crits-Christoph, P. (2002). Psychodynamic-interpersonal treatment of generalized anxiety disorder. *Clin. Psycol. Sci. Prac., 9*(1), 81–84.

Crits-Christoph, P., & Barber, J. P. (2002). Psychological treatments for personality disorders. In P. E. Nathan & J. M. Gorman (Eds.), *A guide to treatments that work* (2nd ed., pp. 611–623). London: Oxford University Press.

Crits-Christoph, P., Gibbons, M. B. C., Losardo, D., Narducci, J., Schamberger, M., & Gallop, R. (2004). Who benefits from brief psychodynamic therapy for generalized anxiety disorder? *Canad. J. Psychoanal., 12*(2), 301–324.

Crompton, M. R. (1985). Alcohol and violent accidental and suicidal death. *Med. Sci. Law, 25,* 59–62.

Crow, S. J., Thuras, P., Keel, P. K., & Mitchell, J. E. (2002). Long-term menstrual and reproductive function in patients with bulimia nervosa. *Amer. J. Psychiat., 159*(6), 1048–1050.

Crowley, T. J., Macdonald, M. J., Whitmore, E. A., & Mikulich, S. K. (1998). Cannabis dependence, withdrawal, and reinforcing effects among adolescents with conduct symptoms and substance use disorder. *Drug Alc. Dep., 50*(1), 27–37.

Crowther, J. H., Bond, L. A., & Rolf, J. E. (1981). The incidence, prevalence, and severity of behavior disorder among preschool-age children in day care. *J. Abnorm. Child Psychol., 9,* 23–42.

Crowther, J. H., Snaftner, J., Bonifazi, D. Z., & Shepherd, K. L. (2001). The role of daily hassles in binge eating. *Inter. J. Eat. Disorders, 29*(4), 449–454.

CRR (Center for Reproductive Rights). (2005, August 1). Contraceptive coverage for all: EPICC Act is prescription for women's equality. (Item: F013). Retrieved October 16, 2005, from www.crlp.org/pub_fac_epicc.html

Cukan, A. (2001, March 8). Confronting a culture of cruelty. General feature release. *United Press International.*

Culp, A. M., Clyman, M. M., & Culp, R. E. (1995). Adolescent depressed mood, reports of suicide attempts, and asking for help. *Adolescence, 30*(120), 827–837.

Cumming, J., & Cumming, E. (1962). *Ego and milieu: Theory and practice of environmental therapy.* New York: Atherton.

Cummings, J. L. (2005). The neuropsychiatric burden of neurological diseases in the elderly. *Inter. Psychogeriatrics, 17*(3), 341–351.

Cummins, R. A., & Lau, A. L. (2003). Community integration or community exposure? A review and discussion in relation to people with an intellectual disability. *Journal of Applied Research in Intellectual Disabilities, 16,* 145–157.

Cuneo, M. W. (2000, November 28). Interviewed for article by J. W. Fountain. Exorcists and exorcisms proliferate across U.S. *New York Times, A* 16.

Cunningham-Owens, D. G. (2000). The challenges of diagnosis and continuing patient assessment. *Inter. J. Psychiat. Clin. Pract., 4*(Suppl. 1), S13–S18.

Curtis, G. C., Magee, W. J., Eaton, W. W., Wittchen, H.-U., & Kessler, R. C. (1998). Specific fears and phobias: Epidemiology and classification. *Brit. J. Psychiat., 173,* 212–217.

Curtis, J. M., & Cowell, D. R. (1993). Relation of birth order and scores on measures of pathological narcissism. *Psychol. Rep., 72*(1), 311–315.

Curtis, R., Groarke, A. M., Coughlan, R., & Gsel, A. (2004). The influence of disease severity, perceived stress, social support and coping in patients with chronic ilness: A 1-year follow-up. *Psychol. Hlth. Med., 9*(4), 456–475.

Curtis, V. (2005). Women are not the same as men: Specific clinical issues for female patients with bipolar disorder. *Bipolar Disord., 7*(Suppl. 1), 16–24.

Curtiss, L. M. (April, 2002). *The marketing of psychotropic drugs: Mind games with mind drugs or meeting the demand for information?* Unpublished thesis, Princeton University.

Cusack, J. R. (2002). Challenges in the diagnosis and treatment of bipolar disorder. *Drug Benef. Trends, 14*(10), 34–38.

Cuticchia, A. J. (2000). Future vision of the GDB human genome database. *Human Mutat., 15*(1), 62–67.

Cutler, D. L., Bigelow, D., Collins, V., Jackson, C., & Field, G. (2002). Why are severely mentally ill persons in jail and prison? In D. Cutler & P. Backlar (Eds.), *Ethics in community mental health care: Commonplace concerns* (pp. 137–154). New York: Kluwer Academic/Plenum Publishers.

Cutler, D. M., Glaeser, E. L., & Norberg, K. E. (2001). Explaining the rise in youth suicide. In J. Gruber (Ed.), *Risky behavior among*

youths: An economic analysis (pp. 219–269). Chicago: University of Chicago Press.

Cutright, P., & Fernquist, R. M. (2001). The relative gender gap in suicide: Societal integration, the culture of suicide and period effects in 20 developed countries, 1955–1994. *Soc. Sci. Res., 30*(1), 76–99.

Cutting, J. (1985). *The psychology of schizophrenia.* Edinburgh, Scotland: Churchill-Livingstone.

Cutting, J., & Murphy, D. (1988). Schizophrenic thought disorder: A psychological and organic interpretation. *Brit. J. Psychiat., 152,* 310–319.

Cutting, J., & Murphy, D. (1990). Impaired ability of schizophrenics, relative to manics or depressives, to appreciate social knowledge about their culture. *Brit. J. Psychiat., 157,* 355–358.

Cuvelier, M. (2002). Victim, not villain. The mentally ill are six to seven times more likely to be murdered. *Psychol. Today, 35*(3), 23.

Cytryn, L., & McKnew, D. H., Jr. (1996). *Growing up sad: Childhood depression and its treatment.* New York: Norton.

Dahle, K. P., Lohner, J. C., & Konrad, N. (2005). Suicide prevention in penal institutions: Validation and optimization of a screening tool for early identification of high-risk inmates in pretrial detention. *Inter. J. Forens. Ment. Hlth., 4*(1), 53–62.

Dahlgren, S., Sandberg, A. D., & Hjelmquist, E. (2003). The non-specificity of theory of mind deficits: Evidence from children with communicative disabilities. *Eur. J. Cog. Psychol., 15*(1), 129–155.

Daigle, M. S. (2005). Suicide prevention through means restriction: Assessing the risk of substitution: A critical review and synthesis. *Accid. Anal. Prev., 37*(4), 625–632.

Dalby, J. T. (1997). Elizabethan madness: On London's stage. *Psychol Rep., 81,* 1331–1343.

Dale, R. C., Heyman, I., Surtees, R. A., Church, A. J., Giovannoni, G., Goodman, R., et al. (2004). Dyskinesias and associated psychiatric disorders following streptococcal infections. *Arch. Dis. Child., 89*(7), 604–610.

Dalton, A. (2004). How to do the history of homosexuality. *Sexualities, Evol. Gender, 6*(2–3), 217–224.

Damasio, A. R. (1994). *Descartes' error: Emotion, reason, and the human brain.* New York: Avon Books.

Dana, R. H. (2000). Culture and methodology in personality assessment. In I. Cuellar & F. A. Paniagua (Eds.), Handbook of multicultural mental health (pp. 97–120). San Diego, CA: Academic.

Dana, R. H. (2005). *Multicultural assessment: Principles, applications, and examples.* Mahwah, NJ: Lawrence Erlbaum Associates.

Daniels, C. W. (2002). Legal aspects of polygraph admissibility in the United States. In M. Klener (Ed.), *The handbook of polygraph testing.* San Diego, CA: Academic.

Danilenko, K. V., & Putilov, A. A. (2005). Melatonin treatment of winter depression following total sleep deprivation: Waking EEC and mood correlates. *Neuropsychopharmacology, 30*(7), 1345–1352.

Dare, C., & Crowther, C. (1995). Psychodynamic models of eating disorders. In G. Szmukler, C. Dare, & J. Treasure (Eds.), *Handbook of eating disorders: Theory, treatment and research.* Chichester, England: Wiley.

Darke, S., Williamson, A., Ross, J., & Teesson, M. (2005). Attempted suicide among heroin users: 12-month outcomes from the Australian Treatment Outcome Study (ATOS). *Drug Alc. Depend., 78*(2), 177–186.

Daruna, J. H. (2004). *Introduction to psychoneuroimmunology.* San Diego, CA: Elsevier Academic Press.

Darvres-Bornoz, J., Lemperiere, T., Degiovanni, A., & Gaillard, P. (1995). Sexual victimization in women with schizophrenia and bipolar disorder. *Soc. Psychiat. Psychiatr. Epidemiol., 30*(2), 78–84.

Darwin, C. A. (1872). *The expression of the emotions in man and animals.* London: John Murray, Albemarle Street.

Dass, R., & Levine, S. (2002). Guided meditation. In A. A. Sheikh (Ed.), *Handbook of therapeutic imagery techniques. Imagery and human development series* (pp. 351–353). Amityville, NY: Baywood Publishing Co., Inc.

Dattilio, F. M. (2001). Variations in cognitive responses to fear in anxiety disorder subtypes. *Arch. Psychiat. Psychother., 3*(1), 17–30.

Davidson, J. R. T. (2004). Use of benzodiazepines in social anxiety disorder, generalized anxiety disorder, and posttraumatic stress disorder. *J. Clin. Psychiat., 65*(Suppl. 5), 29–33.

Davidson, J. R. T., Connor, K. M., Hertzberg, M. A., Weisler, R. H., Wilson, W. H., & Payne, V. M. (2005). Maintenance therapy with fluoxetine in posttraumatic stress disorder: A placebo-controlled discontinuation study. *J. Clin. Psychopharmacol., 25*(2), 166–169.

Davidson, K. W., Trudeau, K. J., Ockene, J. K., Orleans, C. T., & Kaplan, R. M. (2004). A primer on current evidence-based review systems and their implications for behavioral medicine. *Ann. Behav. Med., 28,* 226–238.

Davis, D., & Follette, W. C. (2004). Jurors can be selected: Noninformation, misinformation, and their strategic uses for jury selection. In W. T. O'Donohue & E. R. Levensky (Eds.), *Handbook of forensic psychology: Resource for mental health and legal professionals* (pp. 781–805). New York: Elsevier Science.

Davis, E. P., Snidman, N., Wadhwa, P. D., Glynn, L. M., Schetter, C. D., & Sandman, C. A. (2004). Prenatal maternal anxiety and depression predict negative behavioral reactivity in infancy. *Infancy, 6*(3), 319–331.

Davis, J. O., & Phelps, J. A. (1995). Twins with schizophrenia: Genes or germs? *Schizo. Bull., 21*(1), 13–18.

Davis, M. (1992). Analysis of aversive memories using the fear potentiated startle paradigm. In N. Butters & L. R. Squire (Eds.), *The neuropsychology of memory* (2nd ed.). New York: Guilford Press.

Davis, R. A. (2001). A cognitive-behavioral model of pathological Internet use. *Computers Hum. Behav., 17*(2), 187–195.

Davis, R. C., Brickman, E., & Baker, T. (1991). Supportive and unsupportive responses of others to rape victims: Effects on concurrent victim adjustment. *Amer. J. Comm. Psychol., 19,* 443–451.

Davis, R., Olmsted, M., Rockert, W., Marques, T., & Dolhanty, J. (1997). Group psychoeducation for bulimia nervosa with and without additional psychotherapy process sessions. *Inter. J. Eat. Disorders, 22,* 25–34.

Davis, S. (2000). Testosterone and sexual desire in women. *J. Sex Educ. Ther., 25*(1), 25–32.

Davis, S. R. (1998). The clinical use of androgens in female sexual disorders. *J. Sex Marital Ther., 24*(3), 153–163.

Davison, K. P., Pennebaker, J. W., & Dickerson, S. S. (2000). Who talks? The social psychology of illness support groups. *Amer. Psychologist, 55*(2), 205–217.

Davison, S. (2004). Murder most rare: The female serial killer. *Criminal Behav. Ment. Hlth., 14*(1), 59–60.

Daw, J. (2001). APA's disaster response network: Help on the scene. *Monit. Psychol., 32*(10), 14–15.

Daw, J. (2002). What have we learned since 9/11? *Monit. Psychol., 33*(8), 32–34.

DAWN (Drug Abuse Warning Network). (1998). Highlights from 1998 Report. *Drug Abuse Warning Network.*

DAWN (Drug Abuse Warning Network). (2002). Publications and tables from DAWN Emergency Department Data. Retrieved November 24, 2002, from www.dawninfo.net

Dawson, G., & Castelloe, P. (1992). Autism. In C. E. Walker (Ed.), *Clinical psychology: Historical and research foundations.* New York: Plenum Press.

Dawson, G., Meltzoff, A. N., Osterling, J., & Brown, E. (1998). Children with autism fail to orient to social stimuli. *J. Autism Dev. Disorders, 28,* 479–485.

Dawson, G. R., Collinson, N., & Atack, J. R. (2005). Development of subtype selective GABA-sub(A) modulators. *CNS Spectrums, 10*(1), 21–27.

de l'Etoile, S. K. (2002). The effect of musical mood induction procedure on mood state-dependent word retrieval. *J. Music Ther., 39*(2), 145–160.

De Leo, D., & Evans, R. (2004). *International suicide rates and prevention strategies.* Cambridge, MA: Hogrefe & Huber.

De Leo, D., Padoani, W., Scocco, P., Lie, D., Bille-Brahe, U., Arensman, E., et al. (2001). Attempted and completed suicide in older subjects: Results from the WHO/EURO Multicentre Study of Suicidal Behavior. *Inter. J. Ger. Psychiat., 16*(3), 300–310.

de Leon, F. C. P., Santillan-Doherty, A. M., Camacho, F. P., Lanzagorta, N., De Ovando, I. C., Campos, G., et al. (2003). Lunar and seasonal rhythms and childhood mortality. *Biol. Rhythm Res., 34*(5), 475–484.

de Lima, M. S., de Jesus Mari, J., Breier, A., Costa, A. M., de Sena, E. P., & Hotopf, M. (2005). Quality of life in schizophrenia: A multicenter, randomized, naturalistic, controlled trial comparing olanzapine to first-generation antipsychotics. *J. Clin. Psychiat., 66*(7), 831–838.

De Vries, R., DeBruin, D. A., & Goodgame, A. (2004). Ethics review of social, behavioral, and economic research: Where should we go from here? *Ethics Behav., 14*(4), 351–368.

de Waal, M. W. M., Arnold, I. A., Eekhof, J. A. H., & van Hemert, A. M. (2004). Somatoform disorders in general practice: Prevalence, functional impairment and comorbidity with anxiety and depressive disorders. *Brit. J. Psychiat., 184*(6), 470–476.

DEA (Drug Enforcement Administration). (1996). *Consumption of ritalin.* Washington, DC: Author.

DEA (Drug Enforcement Administration). (2000, May 16). DEA congressional testimony before the committee on education and the workforce: Subcommittee on early childhood and families.

DeCarlis, L., De Gasperi, A., Slim, A. O., Giacomoni, A., Corti, A., Mazza, E., et al. (2001). Liver transplantation for ecstasy-induced fulminant hepatic failure. *Transplant Proc., 33*(5), 2743–2744.

Decker, H. S. (2004). The psychiatric works of Emil Kraepelin: A many-faceted story of modern medicine. *J. Hist. Neurosci., 13*(3), 248–276.

Degun-Mather, M. (2002). Hypnosis in the treatment of a case of dissociative amnesia for a 12-year period. *Contemp. Hyp., 19*(1), 34–31.

Deitz, S. M. (1977). An analysis of programming DRL schedules in educational settings. *Behav. Res. Ther., 15*(1), 103–111.

Dekel, R., Goldblatt, H., Keidar, M., Solomon, Z., & Polliack, M. (2005). Being a wife of a veteran with posttraumatic stress disorder. *Fam. Rel.: Interdiscip. J. Appl. Fam. Stud., 54*(1), 24–36.

Delahanty, D. L., Nugent, N. R., Christopher, N. C., & Walsh, M. (2005). Initial urinary epinephrine and cortisol levels predict acute PTSD symptoms in child trauma victims. *Psychoneuroendocrinology, 30*(2), 121–128.

Delaney-Black, V., Covington, C., Nordstrom, B., Ager, J., Janisse, J., Hannigan, J. H., et al. (2004). Prenatal cocaine: Quantity of exposure and gender moderation. *J. Dev. Behav. Pediatr., 25*(4), 254–263.

DeLaune, K. A., & Schmitz, J. M. (2004). Treatment of nicotine addiction: A current perspective. *Addic. Disord. Treat., 3*(3), 97–109.

Delay, J., & Deniker, P. (1952). Le traitement des psychoses par une méthode neurolytique dérivée d'hibernothérapie: Le 4560 RP utilisé seul en cure prolongée et continuée. *Congrès des médicins aliénistes et neurologistes de France et des pays du langue francaise, 50,* 503–513.

Delgado, P. L. (2004). The neurotransmitter depiction challenge paradigm: Overview and historical context. *Primary Psychiat., 11*(6), 28–30.

Delisle, J. R. (1986). Death with honors: Suicide among gifted adolescents [Special issue]. *J. Couns. Dev., 64*(9), 558–560.

DeLong, G. R. (2005). The cerebellum in autism. In M. Coleman (Ed.), *The neurology of autism* (pp. 75–90). New York: Oxford University Press.

Delorme, R., Krebs, M. O., Chabane, N., Roy, I., Millet, B., Mouren-Simeoni, M. C., et al. (2004). Frequency and transmission of glutamate receptors GRIK2 and GRIK3 polymorphisms in patients with obsessive compulsive disorder. *Neurorep. Rapid Commun. Neurosci. Res., 15*(4), 699–702.

Dencker, S. J., & Dencker, K. (1995). The need for quality assurance for a better compliance and increased quality of life in chronic schizophrenic patients. XIIth AEP Congress: Improvement of compliance: Quality assurance: Increased quality of life in community care in schizophrenia. *Inter. Clin. Psychopharmacology, 9*(Suppl 5), 35–40.

Deniz, M. E., Hamarta, E., & Ari, R. (2005). An investigation of social skills and loneliness levels of university students with respect to their attachment styles in a sample of Turkish students. *Soc. Behav. Pers., 33*(1), 19–32.

Dennehy, E. B., Doyle, K., Suppes, T. (2003). The efficacy of olanzapine monotherapy for acute hypomania or mania in an outpatient setting. *Inter. Clin. Psychopharmacology, 18,* 143–145.

Denny, D. (2004). Changing models of transsexualism. *J. Gay Lesbian Psychother., 8*(1–2), 25–40.

Dentali, S. (2002). The uses of black cohosh in menopause and chaste tree fruit in premenstrual syndrome. In J. F. Rosenbaum & D. Mischoulon (Eds.), *Natural medications for psychiatric disorders: Considering the alternatives* (pp. 175–184). Philadelphia: Lippincott Williams & Wilkins.

Denton, W. H. (2003). Depression, marital discord and couple therapy. *Curr. Opin. Psychiat., 16*(1), 29–34.

DePlanque, D. (2005). Recreational cannabis use: not so harmless! *J Neurol Neurosurg Psychiat., 76*(3), 306.

DeRubeis, R. J., Hollon, S. D., Amsterdam, J. D., Shelton, R. C., Young, P. R., Salomon, R. M., et al. (2005). Cognitive therapy vs. medications in the treatment of moderate to severe depression. *Arch. Gen. Psychiat., 62,* 409–416.

Desmond, D. W., Morony, J. T., Paik, M. C., Sano, M., Mohr, J. P., Aboumatar, S., et al. (2000). Frequency and clinical determinants of dementia after ischemic stroke. *Neurology, 54*(5), 1124–1131.

Devanand, D. P. (2002). Comorbid psychiatric disorders in late life depression. *Biol. Psychiat., 52*(3), 236–242.

DeVeaugh-Geiss, J., Moroz, G., Biederman, J., Cantwell, D. P., et al. (1992). Clomipramine hydrochloride in childhood and adolescent obsessive compulsive disorder. A multicenter trial. *J. Amer. Acad. Child Adol. Psychiat., 31*(1), 45–49.

Deveny, K. (2003, June 30). We're not in the mood. *Newsweek, 141*(26), pp. 40–46.

Devineni, T., & Blanchard, E. B. (2005). A randomized controlled trial of an internet-based treatment for chronic headache. *Behav. Res. Ther., 43,* 277–292.

Dew, M. A., Bromet, E. J., Brent, D., & Greenhouse, J. B. (1987). A quantitative literature review of the effectiveness of suicide prevention centers. *J. Cons. Clin. Psychol., 55,* 239–244.

Dhossche, D., van-der-Steen, F., Ferdinand, R. (2002). Somatoform disorders in children and adolescents: A comparison with other internalizing disorders. *Ann. Clin. Psychiat., 14*(1), 23–31.

di Tomaso, E., Beltramo, M., & Piomelli, D. (1996, August 22). Brain cannabinoids in chocolate. *Nature* (London), *382,* 677–678.

Diamond, G. S., & Diamond, G. M. (2002). Studying a matrix of change mechanisms: An agenda for family-based process research. In H. A. Liddle, D. A. Santisteban, R. F. Levant, & J. H. Bray (Eds.), *Family psychology: Science-based interventions* (pp. 41–66). Washington, DC: American Psychological Association.

Diekstra, R. F. W. (1989). Suicide and attempted suicide: An international perspective. *Acta Psychiatr. Scandin., 80*(Suppl. 354), 1–24.

Diekstra, R. F. W., Kienhorst, C. W. M., & de Wilde, E. J. (1995). Suicide and suicidal behaviour among adolescents. In M. Rutter & D. J. Smith, *Psychosocial disorders in young people.* Chichester, England: Wiley.

Diener, E. (2000, January). Subjective well-being: The science of happiness and a proposal for a national index. *Amer. Psychologist, 55*(1), 34–43.

Diener, E., & Diener, C. (1996). Most people are happy. *Psychol. Sci., 7*(3), 181–185.

Diener, E., Sandvik, E., Pavot, W., & Fujita, F. (1992). Extraversion and subjective well-being in a U.S. national probability sample. *J. Res. Pers., 26*(3), 205–215.

Diener, E., Sandvik, E., Seidlitz, L., & Diener, M. (1993). The relationship between income and subjective well-being: Relative or absolute? *Soc. Indicators Res., 28*(3), 195–223.

Diener, E., & Seligman, M. E. P. (2002). Very happy people. *Psychol. Sci., 13*(1), 81–84.

Diener, E., & Seligman, M. E. P. (2004). Beyond money: Toward an economy of well-being. *Psychol. Sci. Publ. Interest, 5*(1), 1–31.

Dies, R. R. (2003). Group psychotherapies. In A. S. Gurman & S. B. Messer (Eds.), *Essential psychotherapies: Theory and practice* (2nd ed.). New York: Guilford Press.

Dietch, J. T. (2001). Old age. In D. Wedding (Ed.), *Behavior and medicine* (3rd ed., pp. 185–194). Seattle: Hogrefe & Huber.

Dikel, T. N., Engdahl, B., & Eberly, R. (2005). PTSD in former prisoners of war: Prewar, wartime, and postwar factors. *J. Traum. Stress, 18*(1), 69–77.

Diller, L. (2005). Antidepressants and children's depression. *Amer. J. Psychiat., 162*(6), 1226–1227.

Diller, L. H. (1999). Attention-deficit/hyperactivity disorder. *N. Engl. J. Med., 340,* 1766.

Dilts, S. L. Jr., & Dilts, S. L. (2005). Opioids. In R. J. Frances, A. H. Mack, & S. I. Miller (Eds.), *Clinical textbook of addictive disorders* (3rd ed., pp. 138–156). New York: Guilford Presss.

Dinkelmeyer, A., & Johnson, M. B. (2002). Stalking and harassment of psychotherapists. *Amer. J. Forens. Psychol., 20*(4), 5–20.

Dinn, W. M., & Harris, C. L. (2000). Neurocognitive function in antisocial personality disorder. *Psychiat. Res., 97*(2–3), 173–190.

Dinwiddie, S. H., Heath, A. C., Dunne, M. P., Bucholz, K. K., Madden, P. A. F., Slutske, W. F., et al. (2000). Early sexual abuse and lifetime psychopathology: A co-twin-control study. *Psychol. Med., 30*(1), 41–52.

Dirkzwager, A. J. E., Bramsen, I., & van der Ploeg, H. M. (2005). Factors associated with posttraumantic stress among peacekeeping soldiers. *Anx., Stress, Coping: Inter. J., 18*(1), 37–51.

Dobkin, P. L., & Da Costa, D. (2000). Group psychotherapy for medical patients. *Psychol., Health Med., 5*(1), 87–96.

Dobson, D. J. G., McDougall, G., Busheikin, J., & Aldous, J. (1995). Effects of social skills training and social milieu treatment on symptoms of schizophrenia. *Psychiatr. Serv., 46*(4), 376–380.

Dobson, V., & Sales, B. (2000). The science of infanticide and mental illness. *Psychol. Pub. Pol. Law, 6*(4), 19–25.

Doctor, R. (2003). The role of violence in perverse psychopathology. In R. Doctor (Ed.), *Dangerous patients: A psychodynamic approach to risk assessment and management* (pp. 107–114). London: Karnac Books.

Doctor, R. M., & Neff, B. (2001). Sexual disorders. In H. S. Friedman (Ed.), *Specialty articles from the encyclopedia of mental health.* San Diego: Academic Press.

Dodes, L. M., & Khantzian, E. J. (2005). Individual psychodynamic psychotherapy. In R. J. Frances, A. H. Mack, & S. I. Miller (Eds.), *Clini-

cal textbook of addictive disorders (3rd ed., pp. 457–473). New York: Guilford Press.

Dodgen, C. E. (2005). Cravings and relapse prevention. In C. E. Dodgen (Ed.), *Nicotine dependence: Understanding and applying the most effective treatment interventions* (pp. 175–195). Washington, DC: American Psychological Association.

Dohrmann, R. J., & Laskin, D. M. (1978). An evaluation of electromyographic feedback in the treatment of myofascial pain-dysfunction syndrome. *JAMA, 96,* 656–662.

Doka, K. (2002). How could God? Loss and the spiritual assumptive world. In J. Kauffman (Ed.), *Loss of the assumptive world: A theory of traumatic loss.* New York: Brunner-Routledge.

Doka, K. A., & Martin, T. (2001). Take it like a man: Masculine response to loss. In D. A. Lund (Ed.), *Men coping with grief* (pp. 37–47). Amityville, NY: Baywood Publishing.

Doka, K. J. (1999). A primer on loss and grief. In J. D. Davidson & K. J. Doka (Eds.), *Living with grief at work, at school, at worship.* Philadelphia: Brunner/Mazel.

Dolan, B., Evans, C., & Norton, K. (1995). Multiple Axis-II diagnoses of personality disorder. *Brit. J. Psychiat., 166,* 107–112.

Dole, V. P., & Nyswander, M. (1965). A medical treatment for heroin addiction. *JAMA, 193,* 646–650.

Dole, V. P., & Nyswander, M. (1967). Heroin addiction, a metabolic disease. *Arch. Internal Med., 120,* 19–24.

Domhoff, G. W. (2005). Refocusing the neurocognitive approach to dreams: A critique of the Hobson versus Solms debate. *Dreaming, 15*(1), 3–20.

Domino, G., & Swain, B. J. (1986). Recognition of suicide lethality and attitudes toward suicide in mental health professions. *Omega: J. Death Dying, 16*(4), 301–308.

Domino, G., & Takahashi, Y. (1991). Attitudes toward suicide in Japanese and American medical students. *Suic. Life-Threat. Behav., 21*(4), 345–359.

Dorwart, R. A., & Ostacher, M. J. (1999). A community psychiatry approach to preventing suicide. In D. G. Jacobs (Ed.), *The Harvard Medical School guide to suicide assessment and intervention.* San Francisco: Jossey-Bass.

Dosen, A. (2005). Applying the development perspective in the psychiatric assessment and diagnosis of persons with intellectual disability: Part II—Diagnosis. *J. Intell. Disab. Res., 49*(1), 9–15.

Dougall, A. L., & Baum, A. (2004). Psychoneuroimmuology and trauma. In B. L. Green & P. P. Schnurr (Eds.), *Trauma and health: Physical health consequences of exposure to extreme stress* (pp. 129–155). Washington, DC: American Psychological Association.

Douglas, J. (1996). *Mind hunter: Inside the FBI's elite serial crime unit.* New York: Pocket Star.

Doweiko, H. E. (1999). *Concepts of chemical dependency* (4th ed.). Pacific Grove, CA: Brooks/Cole.

Doweiko, H. E. (2002). *Concepts of chemical dependency.* Australia: Brooks/Cole.

Doweiko, H. E. (2006). *Concepts of chemical dependency* (6th ed.). Belmont, CA: Thomson Brooks/Cole.

Downey, A. M. (1991). The impact of drug abuse upon adolescent suicide. *Omega: J. Death Dying, 22*(4), 261–275.

Downey, R. G., Sinnett, E. R., & Seeberger, W. (1998). The changing face of MMPI practice. *Psychol. Rep., 83*(3, Pt. 2), 1267–1272.

Downhill, J. E., Jr., Buchsbaum, M. S., Hazlett, E. A., Barth, S., Roitman, S. L., Nunn, M., et al. (2001). Temporal lobe volume determined by magnetic resonance imaging in schizotypal personality disorder and schizophrenia. *Schizo. Res., 48*(2–3), 187–199.

Doyle, A. C. (1938). The sign of the four. In *The complete Sherlock Holmes.* Garden City, NY: Doubleday.

Doyle, A. C. (1938). The valley of fear. In *The complete Sherlock Holmes.* Garden City, NY: Doubleday.

Doyle, K. O., & Youn, S. (2000). Exploring the traits of happy people. *Soc. Indicators Res., 52*(2), 195–209.

Dozois, D. J. A., & Westra, H. A. (2004). The nature of anxiety and depression: Implications for prevention. In K. S. Dobson & D. J. A. Dozois (Eds.), *The prevention of anxiety and depression: Theory, research, and practice* (pp. 9–41). Washington, DC: American Psychological Association.

Draine, J., Salzer, M. S., Culhane, D. P., & Hadley, T. R. (2002). Role of social disadvantage in crime, joblessness, and homelessness among persons with serious mental illness. *Psychiatr. Serv., 53*(5), 565–573.

Drake, R. E., McHugo, G. J., Becker, D. R., Anthony, W. A., & Clark, R. E. (1996). The New Hampshire study of supported employment for people with severe mental illness. *J. Cons. Clin. Psychol., 64*(2), 391–399.

Drake, R. E., Osher, F., & Wallach, M. (1991). Homelessness and dual diagnosis. *Amer. Psychologist, 46*(11), 1149–1158.

Drake, R. E., & Wallach, M. A. (1992). Mental patients' attraction to the hospital: Correlates of living preference. *Comm. Ment. Hlth. J., 28*(1), 5–12.

Dratcu, L. (2000). Panic, hyperventilation and perpetuation of anxiety. *Prog. Neuropsychopharmacol. Biol. Psychiat., 24*(7), 1069–1089.

Drevets, W. C., & Todd, R. D. (2005). Depression, mania, and related disorders. In E. H. Rubin & C. F. Zorumski (Eds.), *Adult psychiatry* (2nd ed., pp. 91–129). Oxford, England: Blackwell Publishing Ltd.

Drobes, D. J., Saladin, M. E., & Tiffany, S. T. (2001). Classical conditioning mechanisms in alcohol dependence. In N. Heather, T. J. Peters, & T. Stockwell (Eds.), *International handbook of alcohol dependence and problems* (pp. 281–297). New York: Wiley.

Drummond, M. J. N. (2002). Men, body image, and eating disorders. *Inter. J. Men's Hlth., 1*(1), 89–103.

Druss, B. G., & Rosenheck, R. A. (1998). Mental disorders and access to medical care in the United States. *Amer. J. Psychiat., 155*(12), 1775–1777.

Duberstein, P. R., Conwell, Y., & Cox, C. (1998). Suicide in widowed persons: A psychological autopsy comparison of recently and remotely bereaved older subjects. *Amer. J. Ger. Psychiat., 6*(4), 328–334.

Duffy, B. (1996, April 15). The mad bomber? *U. S. News & World Report,* pp. 29–36.

Dugas, M. J., Buhr, K., & Ladouceur, R. (2002). The role of intolerance of uncertainty in

the etiology and maintenance of generalized anxiety disorder. In R. G. Heimberg, C. L. Turk, & D. S. Mennin (Eds.), *Generalized anxiety disorder: Advances in research and practice.* New York: Guilford Press.

Dugas, M. J., Marchand, A., & Ladouceur, R. (2005). Further validation of a cognitive-behavioral model o generalized anxiety disorder: Diagnostic and symptom specificity. *J. Anx. Disorders, 19*(3), 329–343.

Duggan, J. P., & Booth, D. A. (1986). Obesity, overeating, and rapid gastric emptying in rats with ventromedial hypothalamic lesions. *Science, 231*(4738), 609–611.

Duman, R. S. (2004). Depression: A case of neuronal life and death? *Biol. Psychiat., 56*(3), 141–145.

Dunbar, F. (1948). *Synopsis of psychosomatic diagnosis and treatment.* St. Louis: Mosby.

Duncan, A. E., Neuman, R. J., Kramer, J., Kuperman, S., Hesselbrock, V., Reich, T., et al. (2005). Are there subgroups of bulimia nervosa based on comorbid psychiatric disorders? *Inter. J. Eat. Disord., 37*(1), 19–25.

Duncan, B. L. (2002). Does drug company marketing now include product placement in the movies? *Ethical Human Sciences and Services, 4*(2), 147–150.

Dunn, A. L., Trivedi, M. H., Kampert, J. B., Clark, C. G., & Chambliss, H. O. (2005). Exercise treatment for depression: Efficacy and dose response. *Amer. J. Prev. Med., 28*(1), 1–8.

Dunn, E. F., & Steiner, M. (2000). The functional neurochemistry of mood disorders in women. In M. Steiner, K. A. Yonkers, & E. Erikson (Eds.), *Mood disorders in women* (pp. 71–82). London: Martin Dunitz.

Dunn, K. M., Croft, P. R., & Hackett, G. I. (1999). Association of sexual problems with social, psychological, and physical problems in men and women: A cross sectional population survey. *J. Epidemiol. Comm. Hlth., 53*(3), 144–148.

Dunner, D. L. (2005). Atypical antipsychotics: Efficacy across bipolar disorder subpopulations. *J. Clin. Psychiat., 66*(Suppl. 3), 20–27.

Dupont, R. L., & Dupont, C. M. (2005). Sedatives/hypnotics and benzodiazepines. In R. J. Frances, A. H. Mack, & S. I. Miller (Eds.), *Clinical textbook of addictive disorders* (3rd ed., pp. 219–242). New York: Guilford Press.

Dupont, S. (1995). Multiple sclerosis and sexual functioning: A review. *Clin. Rehab.* 9(2), 135–141.

Durkheim, E. (1897). Suicide. New York: Free Press. (Work republished 1951.)

Duval, F., Crocq, M.-A., Guillon, M.-S., Mokrani, M.-C., Monreal, J., Bailey, P., et al. (2004). Increased adrenocorticotropin suppression after dexamethasone administration in sexually abused adolescents with post-traumatic stress disorder. In R. Yehuda & B. McEwen (Eds.), *Biobehavioral stress response: Protective and damaging effects.* New York: New York Academy of Sciences.

Dykens, E. M., & Hodapp, R. M. (2001). Research in mental retardation: Toward an etiologic approach. *J. Child Psychol. Psychiat. Allied Discl., 42*(1), 49–71.

Dykens, E. M., Hodapp, R. M., & Leckman, J. F. (1994). *Behavior and development in Fragile X Syndrome.* Thousand Oaks, CA: Sage.

Easterbrook, G. (2005). The real truth about money. *Time, 165*(3), January 17, 2005, A32–A34.

Eaton, W. W., Dryman, A., & Weissman, M. M. (1991). Panic and phobia. In L. N. Robins & D. A. Regier (Eds.), *Psychiatric disorders in America: The Epidemiologic Catchment Area Study.* New York: Maxwell Macmillan International.

Ebstein, R. P., & Kotler, M. (2002). Personality, substance abuse, and genes. In J. Benjamin, R. P. Ebstein, & R. H. Belmaker (Eds.), *Molecular genetics and the human personality* (pp. 151–163). Washington, DC: American Psychological Association.

Eccleston, L., & Ward, T. (2004). Assessment of dangerous and criminal responsibility. In W. T. O'Donohue & E. R. Levensky (Eds.), *Handbook of forensic psychology: Resource for mental health and legal professionals* (pp. 85–101). New York: Elsevier Science.

Echeburúa, E., Báez, C., & Fernández-Montalvo, J. (1996). Comparative effectiveness of three therapeutic modalities in the psychological treatment of pathological gambling: Long-term outcome. *Behav. Cog. Psychother., 24,* 51–72.

Eddy, K. T., Dutra, L., Bradley, R., & Westen, D. (2004). A multidimensional meta-analysis of psychotherapy and pharmacotherapy for obsessive-compulsive disorder. *Clin. Psychol. Rev., 24,* 1011–1030.

Edlinger, M., Hausmann, A., Kemmler, G., Kurz, M., Kurzthaler, I., Walch, T., et al. (2005). Trends in the pharmacological treatment of patients with schizophrenia over a 12-year observation period. *Schizo. Res., 77*(1), 25–34.

Efron, S. (1997, October 21). Eating disorders in Asia. *Los Angeles Times.*

Ehlers, A., Clark, D. M., Hackman, A., McManus, F., & Fennell, M. (2005). Cognitive therapy for post-traumatic stress disorder: Development and evaluation. *Behav. Res. Ther., 43*(4), 413–431.

Ehrenfeld, T. (2005, June 13). An epilepsy drug may help alcoholics stop drinking. *Newsweek, 145,* 68.

Ehrman, M. (1995, June 25). Reaching out for virtual therapy. *Los Angeles Times,* pp. E1, E4.

Eifert, G. H., & Zvolensky, M. J. (2005). Somatoform disorders. In B. A. Winstead & J. E. Maddux (Eds.), *Psychopathology: Foundations for a contemporary understanding* (pp. 281–300). Mahwah, NJ: Lawrence Erlbaum Associates.

Eisenberg, L. (1958). School phobia: A study in the communication of anxiety. *Amer. J. Psychiat., 114,* 712–718.

Eisenthal, S., Koopman, C., & Lazare, A. (1983). Process analysis of two dimensions of the negotiated approach in relation to satisfaction in the initial interview. *J. Nerv. Ment. Dis., 171,* 49–54.

Eisner, A. (2005). Odd U.S. state laws ban owning skunks, swearing. *Reuters,* May 25, 2005.

Ekman, P., O'Sullivan, M., & Frank, M. G. (1999). A few can catch a liar. *Psychol. Sci., 10*(3), 263–266.

Eliez, S., & Feinstein, C. (2001). The fragile X syndrome: Bridging the gap from gene to behavior. *Curr. Opin. Psychiat., 14*(5), 443–449.

Elkin, I. (1994). The NIMH Treatment of Depression Collaborative Research Program: Where we began and where we are. In A. E. Bergin & S. L. Garfield (Eds.), *Handbook of psychotherapy and behavior change* (4th ed.). New York: Wiley.

Elkin, I., Parloff, M. B., Hadley, S. W., & Autry, J. H. (1985). National Institute of Mental Health Treatment of Depression Collaborative Research Program: Background and research plan. *Arch. Gen. Psychiat., 42,* 305–316.

Elkin, I., Shea, M. T., Watkins, J. T., Imber, S. D., et al. (1989). National Institute of Mental Health Treatment of Depression Collaborative Research Program: General effectiveness of treatments. *Arch. Gen. Psychiat., 46*(11), 971–982.

Elkins, I. J., & Cromwell, R. L. (1994). Priming effects in schizophrenia: Associative interference and facilitation as a function of visual context. *J. Abnorm. Psychol., 103*(4), 791–800.

Ellenberger, H. F. (1970). *The discovery of the unconscious.* New York: Basic Books.

Ellenberger, H. F. (1972). The story of "Anna O.": A critical review with new data. *J. History Behav. Sci., 8,* 267–279.

Elliott, R. (2002). The effectiveness of humanistic therapies. In D. J. Cain & J. Seeman (Eds.), *Humanistic psychotherapies: Handbook of research and practice* (pp. 57–82). Washington, DC: American Psychological Association.

Ellis, A. (1962). *Reason and emotion in psychotherapy.* Secaucus, NJ: Lyle Stuart.

Ellis, A. (1977). The basic clinical theory of rational-emotive therapy. In A. Ellis & R. Grieger (Eds.), *Handbook of rational-emotive therapy.* New York: Springer.

Ellis, A. (2001). *Overcoming destructive beliefs, feelings, and behaviors: New directions for rational emotive behavior therapy.* Amherst, NY: Prometheus.

Ellis, A. (2002). The role of irrational beliefs in perfectionism. In G. L. Flett & P. L. Hewitt (Eds.) *Perfectionism: Theory, research, and treatment* (pp. 217–229). Washington, DC: American Psychological Association.

Ellis, A. (2004). Expanding the ABCs of rational emotive behavior therapy. In M. J. Mahoney, P. DeVito, D. Martin, & A. Freeman (Eds.), *Cognition and psychotherapy* (2nd ed., pp. 185–196). New York: Springer.

Ellis, A. (2005). Rational-emotive therapy. In R. Corsini & D. Wedding (Eds.), *Current psychotherapies* (7th ed., pp. 166–201). Boston: Thomson/Brooks-Cole.

El-Mallakh, R. S., & Huff, M. O. (2001). Mood stabilizers and ion regulation. *Harvard Rev. Psychiat., 9*(1), 23–32.

Emanuel, E. J., Crouch, R. A., Arras, J. D., Moreno, J. D., & Grady, C. (Eds.). (2003). *Ethical and regulatory aspects of clinical research: Readings and commentary.* Baltimore: Johns Hopkins University Press.

Emery, G. (2004, June 30). Stress disorders hit U.S. troops in Iraq—Study. *Reuters (Boston).*

Emmelkamp, P. M. (1982). Exposure in vivo treatments. In A. Goldstein & D. Chambless (Eds.), *Agoraphobia: Multiple perspectives on theory and treatment.* New York: Wiley.

Emmelkamp, P. M. (1994). Behavior therapy with adults. In A. E. Bergin & S. L. Garfiel (Eds.), *Handbook of psychotherapy and behavior change* (4th ed.). New York: Wiley.

Engel, G. L. (1968). A life setting conducive to illness: The giving-up-given-up complex. *Ann. Internal Med., 69,* 293.

Engel, J. M., Jensen, M. P., & Schwartz, L. (2004). Outcome of biofeedback-assisted relaxation for pain in adults with cerebral palsy: Preliminary findings. *Appl. Psychophysiol. Biofeedback, 29*(2), 135–140.

Engelhard, I. M., & Arntz, A. (2005). The fallacy of ex-consequentia reasoning and the persistence of PTSD. *J. Behav. Ther. Exp. Psychiat., 36*(1), 35–42.

Ennis, B. J., & Emery, R. D. (1978). *The rights of patients* (ACLU Handbook Series). New York: Avon.

Enoch, M. A., Kaye, W. H., Rotondo, A., et al. (1998). 5-HT2A promoter polymorphism-1438G/A, anorexia nervosa, and obsessive-compulsive disorder [Letter]. *Lancet, 351,* 1785–1786.

Epstein, R. (2001). In her own words. *Psychol. Today, 34*(6), 36–37, 87.

Epstein, S. (1983). Hypnotherapeutic control of exhibitionism: A brief communication. *Inter. J. Clin. Exp. Hyp., 31*(2), 63–66.

Erba, H. W. (2000). Early intervention programs for children with autism: Conceptual frameworks for implementation. *Amer. J. Orthopsychiat., 70*(1), 82–94.

Erickson, M. T. (1992). *Behavior disorders of children and adolescents.* Englewood Cliffs, NJ: Prentice Hall.

Erikson, E. (1963). *Childhood and society.* New York: Norton.

Erlangsen, A., Vach, W., & Jeune, B. (2005). The effect of hospitalization with medical illnesses on the suicide risk in the oldest old: A population-based register study. *J. Amer. Ger. Soc., 53*(5), 771–776.

Ernst, N. D., & Harlan, W. R. (1991). Obesity and cardiovascular disease in minority populations: Executive summary. Conference highlights, conclusions, and recommendations. *Amer. J. Clin. Nutr., 53*(Suppl.), 1507–1511.

Erwin, E. (2000). Is a science of psychotherapy possibile: Subjectivity problems. *Amer. Psychologist, 55*(10), 1133–1138.

Escalante, P. R., Minshew, N. J., & Sweeney, J. A. (2003). Abnormal brain lateralization in high-functioning autism. *J. Autism Dev. Disorders, 33,* 539–543.

Escobar, J. I. (1995). Transcultural aspects of dissociative and somatoform disorders. *Psychiatr. Clin. N. Amer., 18*(3), 555–569.

Escobar, J. I. (2004, April 15). Transcultural aspects of dissociative and somatoform disorders. *Psychiatr. Times, XXI*(5), p. 10.

Escobar, J. I., Canino, G., Rubio-Stipec, M., & Bravo, M. (1992). Somatic symptoms after a natural disaster: A prospective study. *Amer. J. Psychiat., 149*(7), 965–967.

Escobar, J. I., Gara, M., Silver, R. C., Waitzkin, H., Holman, A., & Compton, W. (1998). Somatisation disorder in primary care. *Brit. J Psychiat., 173,* 262–266.

Escobar, J. I., Randolph, E. T., Puente, G., Spiwak, F., Asamen, J. K., Hill, M., et al. (1983). Posttraumatic stress disorder in Hispanic Vietnam veterans clinical phenomenology and sociocultural characteristics. *J. Nerv. Ment. Dis., 171,* 585–596.

Eser, A. (1981). "Sanctity" and "quality" of life in a historical comparative view. In S. E. Wallace & A. Eser (Eds.), *Suicide and euthanasia: The rights of personhood.* Knoxville: University of Tennessee Press.

European Monitoring Center for Drugs and Drug Addictions (2004). *Annual report: The state of the drugs problem in Europe.* Lisbon: EMCDDA.

Evans, G. W. (2006). Child development and the physical environment. *Annu. Rev. Psychol., 57,* 423–451.

Evans, J., Heron, J., Lewis, G., Araya, R., & Wolke, D. (2005). Negative self-schemas and the onset of depression in women: Longitudinal study. *Brit. J. Psychiat., 186*(4), 302–307.

Everson, S. A., Goldberg, D. E., Kaplan, G. A., Cohen, R. D., et al. (1996). Hopelessness and risk of mortality and incidence of myocardial infarction and cancer. *Psychosom. Med., 58,* 113–121.

Ewalt, D. M. (2002, February 25). "Web rage" in real world. *InformationWeek, 877,* 13.

Exner, J. E., Jr. (2003). *The Rorschach: A comprehensive system* (4th ed.). New York: Wiley.

Fabre, O. (2004). Therapy offers Alzheimer's hope to Japan's elderly. *Reuters (Sendai, Japan).*

Fábrega, H., Jr. (1990). The concept of somatization as a cultural and historical product of Western medicine. *Psychosom. Med., 52*(6), 653–672.

Fábrega, H., Jr. (2002). *Origins of psychopathology: The phylogenetic and cultural basis of mental illness.* New Brunswick, NJ: Rutgers University Press.

Fábrega, H., Jr. (2004). Psychiatric conditions in an evolutionary context. *Psychopath., 37*(6), 290–298.

Fábrega, H., Ulrich, R., Pilkonis, P., & Mezzich, J. (1991). On the homogeneity of personality disorder clusters. *Comprehen. Psychiat., 32*(5), 373–386.

Faedda, G. L., Tondo, L., Teichner, M. H., Baldessarini, R. J., Gelbard, H. A., & Floris, G. F. (1993). Seasonal mood disorders: Patterns of seasonal recurrence in mania and depression. *Arch. Gen. Psychiat., 50*(1), 17–23.

Fahrenberg, J., Foerster, F., & Wilmers, F. (1995). Is elevated blood pressure level associated with higher cardiovascular responsiveness in laboratory tasks and with response specificity? *Psychophysiology, 32*(1), 81–91.

Faigman, D. L., & Monahan, J. (2005) Psychological evidence at the dawn of the law's scientific age. *Annu. Rev. Psychol., 56,* 631–659.

Fairbank, J. A., & Keane, T. M. (1982). Flooding for combat-related stress disorders: Assessment of anxiety reduction across traumatic memories. *Behav. Ther., 13,* 499–510.

Fairburn, C. G. (1985). Cognitive-behavioural treatment for bulimia. In D. M. Garner & P. E. Garfinkel (Eds.), *Handbook of psychotherapy for anorexia nervosa and bulimia.* New York: Guilford Press.

Fairburn, C. G. (2005). Evidence-based treatment of anorexia nervosa. *Inter. J. Eat. Disorders, 37*(Suppl.), S26–S30.

Fairburn, C. G., Agras, W. S., Walsh, B. T., Wilson, G. T., & Stice, E. (2004). Prediction of outcome in bulimia nervosa by early change in treatment. *Amer. J. Psychiat., 161*(12), 2322–2324.

Fairburn, C. G., Cooper, Z., & Shafran, R. (2003). Cognitive behaviour therapy for eating disorders: A "transdiagnostic" theory and treatment. *Behav. Res. Ther., 41*(5), 509–528.

Fakhoury, W., & Priebe, S. (2002). The process of deinstitutionalization: An international overview. *Curr. Opin. Psychiat., 15*(2), 187–192.

Fallon, B. A. (2004). Pharmacotherapy of somatoform disorders. *J. Psychosom. Res., 56,* 455–460.

Fallon, I. R. H. (2002). Cognitive-behavioral family and educational interventions for schizophrenic disorders. In S. G. Hofmann & M. C. Tompson (Eds.), *Treating chronic and severe mental disorders: A handbook of empirically supported interventions.* New York: Guilford Press.

Faraone, S. V., Spencer, T., Aleardi, M., Pagano, C., & Biederman, J. (2004). Meta-analysis of the efficacy of methylphenidate for treating adult attention-deficit/hyperactivity disorder. *J. Clin. Psychopharmacol., 24,* 24–29.

Faravelli, C., Ravaldi, C., & Truglia, E. (2005). Unipolar depression. In C. Faravelli, D. J. Nutt, J. Zohar, & E. J. L. Griez (Eds.), *Mood disorders: Clinical management and research issues* (pp. 79–101). New York: Wiley

Farberow, N. L., & Litman, R. E. (1970). *A comprehensive suicide prevention program.* Unpublished final report, Suicide Prevention Center of Los Angeles, Los Angeles.

Farlow, M. R., Murrell, J. R., Unverzagt F. W., Phillips, M., Takao, M., Hulette, C., et al. (2001). Familial Alzheimer's disease with spastic paraparesis associated with a mutation at codon 261 of the presenilin 1 gene. In I. Khalid, S. S. Sisodia, & B. Winblad (Eds.), *Alzheimer's disease: Advances in etiology, pathogenesis and therapeutics.* Chichester, England: Wiley.

Farmer, R. F., & Nelson-Gray, R. O. (2005). Behavioral treatment of personality disorders. In R. F. Farmer & R. O. Nelson-Gray (Eds.), *Personality-guided behavior therapy* (pp. 203–243). Washington, DC: American Psychological Association.

Fasko, S. N., & Fasko, D. (1991). Suicidal behavior in children. *Psychol.: J. Human Behav., 27*(4)–*28*(1), 10–16.

Fava, M. (2000). New approaches to the treatment of refractory depression. *J. Clin. Psychiat., 61*(Suppl.), 26–32.

Fava, M., Farabaugh, A. H., Sickinger, A. H., Wright, E., Alpert, J. E., Sonawalla, S., et al. (2002). Personality disorders and depression. *Psychol. Med., 32*(6), 1049–1057.

Favaro, A., Ferrara, S., & Santonastaso, P. (2003). The spectrum of eating disorders in young women: A prevalence study in a general population sample. *Psychosom. Med., 65*(4), 701–708.

Fawcett, J. (1988). Predictors of early suicide: Identification and appropriate intervention. *J. Clin. Psychiat., 49*(Suppl.), 7–8.

Fawcett, J. (2004). Is suicide preventable? There is no room for complacency in patient treatment or clinician attitude when recognizing suicidal risk. *Psychiatr. Ann., 34*(5), 338–339.

Fawcett, J., Scheftner, W., Clark, D., Hedeker, D., et al. (1987). Clinical predictors of suicide in patients with major affective disorders: A controlled prospective study. *Am. J. Psychiatry, 144*(1), 35–40.

Fay, B. P. (1995). The individual versus society: The cultural dynamics of criminalizing suicide. *Hastings International and Comparative Law Review, 18,* 591–615.

Fayek, A. (2002). Analysis of a case of psychogenic amnesia: The issue of termination. *J. Clin. Psychoanal., 11*(4), 586–612.

Fazel, S., & Danesh, J. (2002). Serious mental disorder in 23,000 prisoners: A systematic review of 62 surveys. *Lancet, 359*(9306), 545–550.

FBI Uniform Crime Reports. (1996). *Crime in the United States: 1996 Uniform Crime Reports.* Washington, DC: FBI.

Feldman, H. A., Goldstein, I., Hatzichristou, D. G., Krane, R. J., & McKinlay, J. B. (1994). Impotence and its medical and psychosocial correlates: Results of the Massachusetts Male Aging Study. *J. Urology, 151,* 54–61.

Feldman, M. D. (2004). *Playing sick? Untangling the web of Munchausen syndrome, Munchausen by proxy, malingering and factitious disorder.* New York: Routledge.

Feldman, M. D., Ford, C. V., & Reinhold, T. (1994). *Patient or pretender: Inside the strange world of factitious disorders.* New York: Wiley.

Feldman, S., Bachman, J., & Bayer, J. (2002). Mental health parity: A review of research and a bibliography. *Admin. Pol. Ment. Hlth., 29*(3), 215–228.

Feldman, S. R., Moritz, S. H., & Bejamin, G. A. H. (2005). Suicide and the law: A practical overview for mental health professionals. *Women Ther., 28*(1), 95–103.

Felner, R. D., Felner, T. Y., & Silverman, M. M. (2000). Prevention in mental health and social intervention: Conceptual and methodological issues in the evolution of the science and practice of prevention. In J. Rappaport & E. Seidman (Eds.), *Handbook of community psychology* (pp. 9–42). New York: Kluwer Academic/Plenum Publishers.

Fenichel, O. (1945). *The psychoanalytic theory of neurosis.* New York: Norton.

Fenigstein, A. (1996). Paranoia. In C. G. Costello (Ed.), *Personality characteristics of the personality disordered.* New York: Wiley.

Fennig, S., Fennig, S., & Roe, D. (2002). Cognitive-behavioral therapy for bulimia nervosa: Time course and mechanisms of change. *Gen. Hosp. Psychiat., 24*(2), 87–92.

Fenton, W. S., Hoch, J. S., Herrell, J. M., Mosher, L., & Dixon, L. (2002). Cost and cost-effectiveness of hospital vs. residential crisis care for patients who have serious mental illness. *Arch. Gen. Psychiat., 59*(4), 357–364.

Fergusson, D. M., Woodward, L. J., & Horwood, L. J. (2000). Risk factors and life processes associated with the onset of suicidal behavior during adolescence and early adulthood. *Psychol. Med., 30*(1), 23–39.

Ferrada, N. M., Asberg, M., Ormstad, K., & Nordstrom, P. (1995). Definite and undetermined forensic diagnoses of suicide among immigrants in Sweden. *Acta Psychiatr. Scandin., 91*(2), 130–135.

Ferrando, S. J. (2001). Substance abuse and HIV infection. *Psychiatr. Ann., 31*(1), 57–62.

Ferreira, C. (2000). Serial killers—Victims of compulsion or masters of control? In D. H. Fishbein (Ed.), *The science, treatment, and prevention of antisocial behaviors: Application to the criminal justice system* (pp. 15-1–15-8). Kingston, NJ: Civic Research Institute.

Fetto, J. (2001, October 1). Pencil me in. *Amer. Demog.*

Fetto, J. (2002, Apr. 1). What seems to be the problem? *Amer. Demog.*

Fetto, J. (2002, May 1). Drugged out. *Amer. Demog.*

Fetto, J. (2002, May 1). You never call. *Amer. Demog. 4*(1), 8–9.

Feuer, C. A., Nishith, P., & Resick, P. (2005). Prediction of numbing and effortful avoidance in female rape survive with chronic PTSD. *J. Traum. Stress, 18*(2), 165–170.

Fichter, M. M., & Pirke, K. M. (1995). Starvation models and eating disorders. In G. Szmukler, C. Dare, & J. Treasure (Eds.), *Handbook of eating disorders: Theory, treatment and research.* Chichester, England: Wiley.

Fichtner, C. G., Kuhlman, D. T., Gruenfeld, M. J., & Hughes, J. R. (1990). Decreased episodic violence and increased control of dissociation in a carbamazepine-treated case of multiple personality. *Biol. Psychiat., 27*(9), 1045–1052.

Field, A., & Davey, G. (2005). Experimental methods in clinical and health research. In J. Miles & P. Gilbert (Eds.), *A handbook of research methods for clinical and health psychology* (pp. 175–184). New York: Oxford University Press.

Fieve, R. R. (1975). *Moodswing.* New York: Morrow.

Figley, C. R. (1978). Symptoms of delayed combat stress among a college sample of Vietnam veterans. *Military Med., 143*(2), 107–110.

Figley, C. R., & Leventman, S. (1990). Introduction: Estrangement and victimization. In C. R. Figley & S. Leventman (Eds.), *Strangers at home: Vietnam veterans since the war.* New York: Praeger.

Filipek, P. A. (1999). Neuroimaging in the developmental disorders: The state of the science. *J. Child Psychol. Psychiat., 40*(1), 113–128.

Finckh, U. (2001). The dopamine D2 receptor gene and alcoholism: Association studies. In D. P. Agarwal & H. K. Seitz (Eds.), *Alcohol in health and disease* (pp. 151–176). New York: Marcel Dekker.

Fine, C. G., & Madden, N. E. (2000). Group psychotherapy in the treatment of dissociative identity disorder and allied dissociative disorders. In R. H. Klein & V. L. Schermer (Eds.), *Group psychotherapy for psychological trauma* (pp. 298–325). New York: Guilford Press.

Finfgeld, D. L. (2002). Anorexia nervosa: Analysis of long-term outcomes and clinical implications. *Arch. Psychiatr. Nursing, 16*(4), 176–186.

Fink, M. (1992). Electroconvulsive therapy. In E. S. Paykel (Ed.), *Handbook of affective disorders.* New York: Guilford Press.

Fink, M. (2001). Convulsive therapy: A review of the first 55 years. *J. Affect. Disorders, 63*(1–3), 1–15.

Fink, P., Hansen, M. S., & Oxhoj, M. L. (2004). The prevalence of somatoform disorders among internal medical inpatients. *J. Psychosom. Res., 56*(4), 413–418.

Fink, P., Ørnbøl, E., Toft, T. T., Sparle, K. C., Frostholm, L., & Olesen, F. (2004). A new, empirically established hypochondriasis diagnosis. *Amer. J. Psychiat., 161*(9), 1680–1691.

Finkel, N. J., & Duff, K. (1989). The insanity defense: Giving jurors a third option. *Forensic Reports, 1,* 65–70.

Finkelhor, D., Asdigian, N., & Dziuba-Leatherman, J. (1995). Victimization prevention programs for children: A follow-up. *Amer. J. Pub. Hlth., 85*(12), 1684–1689.

Fishbain, D. A. (2000). Re: The meeting of pain and depression. Comorbidity in women. *Canad. J. Psychiat., 45*(1), 88.

Fisher, J. E., & Carstensen, L. L. (1990). Behavior management of the dementias. *Clin. Psychol. Rev., 10,* 611–629.

Fisher, J. E., Zeiss, A. M., & Carstensen, L. L. (2001). Psychopathology in the aged. In P. B. Sutker & H. E. Adams (Eds.), *Comprehensive handbook of psychopathology* (3rd ed., pp. 921–952). New York: Kluwer Academic/Plenum.

Fisher, P. H., Masia-Warner, C., & Klein, R. G. (2004). Skills for social and academic success: A school-based intervention for social anxiety disorder in adolescents. *Clin. Child Fam. Psychol. Rev., 7*(4), 241–249.

Fisher, S., Allan, A., & Allan, M. M. (2004). Exploratory study to examine the impact of television reports of prison escapes on fear of crime, operationalised as state anxiety. *Austral. J. Psychol., 56*(3), 181–190.

Fitz, A. (1990). Religious and familial factors in the etiology of obsessive-compulsive disorder: A review. *J. Psychol. Theol., 18*(2), 141–147.

Fitzgibbon, M. L., Spring, B., Avellone, M. E., Blackman, L. R., Pingitore, R., & Stolley, M. R. (1998). Correlates of binge eating among Hispanic, Black and White women. *Inter. J. Eat. Disorders, 24,* 43–52.

Flavin, D. K., Franklin, J. E., & Frances, R. J. (1990). Substance abuse and suicidal behavior. In S. J. Blumenthal & D. J. Kupfer (Eds.), *Suicide over the life cycle: Risk factors, assessment, and treatment of suicidal patients.* Washington, DC: American Psychiatry Press.

Fleck, D. E., Keck, P. E., Corey, K. B., & Strakowski, S. M. (2005). Factors associated with medication adherence in African American and white patients with bipolar disorder. *J. Clin. Psychiat., 66*(5), 646–652.

Fletcher, T. B. (2000). Primary nocturnal enuresis: A structural and strategic family systems approach. *J. Ment. Hlth Couns., 22*(1), 32–44.

Flint, A. J. (1994). Epidemiology and comorbidity of anxiety disorders in the elderly. *Amer. J. Psychiat., 151*(5), 640–649.

Foa, E. B., & Franklin, M. E. (2001). Obsessive-compulsive disorder. In D. H. Barlow (Ed.), *Clinical handbook of psychological disorders: A step-by-step treatment manual* (3rd ed.). New York: Guilford Press.

Foa, E. B., & Franklin, M. E. (2004). Psychotherapies for obsessive-compulsive disorder: A review. In M. Maj, N. Sartorius, A. Okasha, & J. Zohar (Eds.), *Obsessive-compulsive disorder* (pp. 93–115). New York: Wiley.

Foa, E. B., Hearst-Ikeda, D., & Perry, K. L. (1995). Evaluation of a brief cognitive-behavioral program for the prevention of chronic PTSD in recent assault victims. *J. Cons. Clin. Psychol., 63,* 948–955.

Foa, E. B., Liebowitz, M. R., Kozak, M. J., Davies, S., Campeas, R., Franklin, M. E., et al. (2005). Randomized placebo-controlled trial of exposure and ritual prevention, Clomipramine, and their combination in the treatment of obsessive-compulsive disorder. *Amer. J. Psychiat., 162*(1), 151–161.

Foa, E. B., Rothbaum, B. O., & Furr, J. M. (2003). Augmenting exposure therapy with other CBT procedures. *Psychiatr. Ann., 33*(1), 47–53.

Foderaro, L. (1995, June 16). The mentally ill debate what to call themselves. *New York Times,* p. B1.

Fog, R. (1995). New diagnostic vistas. XIIth AEP Congress: Improvement of compliance: Quality assurance: Increased quality of life in community care in schizophrenia. *Inter. Clin. Psychopharmacology, 9*(Suppl. 5), 71–73.

Fogel, B. S. (1986). ECT versus tricyclic antidepressants. *Amer. J. Psychiatry, 143*(1), 121.

Foley, K., & Hendin, H. (2002). Introduction: A medical, ethical, legal, and psychosocial perspective. In K. Foley & H. Hendin (Eds.), *The case against assisted suicide: For the right to end-of-life care* (pp. 1–16). Baltimore, MD: The John Hopkins University Press.

Foley, K., & Hendin, H. (Eds.). (2003). The case against assisted suicide: For the right to-end-life care. *J. Nerv. Ment. Dis., 191*(1), 62–64.

Folkman, S., & Moskowitz, J. T. (2004). Coping: Pitfalls and promise. *Annu. Rev. Psychol., 55,* 745–774.

Folsom, D. P., Fleisher, A. S., & Depp, C. A. (2006). Schizophrenia. In D. V. Jeste & J. H. Friedman (Eds.), *Psychiatry for neurologists* (pp. 59–66). Totowa, NJ: Humana Press.

Fombonne, E. (1995). Eating disorders: Time trends and possible explanatory mehanisms. In M. Rutter & D. J. Smith, *Psychosocial disorders in young people.* Chichester, England: Wiley.

Fombonne, E. (2003). Epidemiological surveys of autism and other pervasive developmental disorders: An update. *J. Autism Dev. Disorders, 33,* 365–382.

Ford, C. V. (2005). Deception syndromes: Factitious disorders and malingering. In J. L. Levenson (Ed.), *The American Psychiatric Publishing textbook of psychosomatic medicine* (pp. 297–309). Washington, DC: American Psychiatric Publishing.

Ford, J. D., & Stewart, J. (1999). Group psychotherapy for war-related PTSD with military veterans. In B. H. Young & D. D. Blake (Eds.), *Group treatments for post-traumatic stress disorder.* Philadelphia: Brunner/Mazel.

Ford, M. R., & Widiger, T. A. (1989). Sex bias in the diagnosis of histrionic and antisocial personality disorders. *J. Cons. Clin. Psychol., 57*(2), 301–305.

Ford, T. (2000). The influence of womanist identity on the development of eating disorders and depression in African American female college students. *Diss. Abstr. Inter., Sect. A: Human. Soc. Sci., 61,* 2194.

Foreman, W. (2005, June 26). Ghost fears keep visitors from Thailand. *Boston.com News.*

Foreyt, J. P., Poston, W. S. C., & Goodrick, G. K. (1996). Future directions in obesity and eating disorders. *Addic. Behav., 21*(6), 767–778.

Fountain, J. W. (2000, November 28). Exorcists and exorcisms proliferate across U.S. *New York Times,* A-16.

Fowler, J. S., Volkow, N. D., & Wolf, A. P. (1995). PET studies of cocaine in human brain. In A. Biegon & N. D. Volkow (Eds.), *Sites of drug action in the human brain.* Boca Raton, FL: CRC Press.

Fowler, R. (1999, June 10). Cited in Associated Press release (Philadelphia), Outrage over sex abuse study.

Fox, J., & Davis, C. (2005). Functional behavior assessment in schools: Current research findings and future directions. *J. Behav. Educ., 14*(1), 1–4.

Fox, J. A., & Levin, J. (1999). Serial murder: Popular myths and empirical realities. In M. D. Smith, M. A. Zahn, et al. (Eds.), *Homicide: A sourcebook of social research.* Thousand Oaks, CA: Sage.

Fox, J. A., & Levin, J. (2005). *Extreme killing: Understanding serial and mass murder.* Thousand Oaks, CA: Sage.

Fox, V. (2000). Empathy: The wonder quality of mental health treatment. *Psychiatr. Rehab. J., 23*(3), 292–293.

Foxhall, K. (2001). Preventing relapse: Looking at data differently led to today's influential relapse prevention therapy. *APA Monitor, 32*(6), 46–47.

Frances, R. J., & Franklin, J. E. (1988). Alcohol and other psychoactive substance use disorders. In J. A. Talbott, R. E. Hales, & S. C. Yudofsky (Eds.), *Textbook of psychiatry.* Washington, DC: American Psychiatric Press.

Frances, R. J., Mack, A., & Miller, S. I. (Eds.). (2005). *Clinical textbook of addictive disorders* (3rd ed.). New York: Guilford Press.

Franchi, S. (2004). Depression and marital discord. *Revista Argentina de Clinica Psicologica, 13*(3), 197–203.

Frangakis, C. E., & Petridou, E. (2001). On lunar phases and dog bites: Analyzing differential exposure. *Brit. Med. J. Rapid Responses,* March 12, 2001.

Frank, J. D. (1973). *Persuasion and healing* (Rev. ed.). Baltimore: Johns Hopkins University Press.

Frankel, F. H. (1993). Adult reconstruction of childhood events in the multiple personality literature. *Amer. J. Psychiat., 150*(6), 954–958.

Frankish, C. J. (1994). Crisis centers and their role in treatment: Suicide prevention versus health promotion. In A. A. Leenaars, J. T. Maltsberger, & R. A. Neimeyer (Eds.), *Treatment of suicidal people.* Washington, DC: Taylor & Francis.

Franklin, J., & Markarian, M. (2005). Substance abuse in minority populations. In R. J. Frances, A. H. Mack, & S. I. Miller (Eds.), *Clinical textbook of addictive disorders* (3rd ed., pp. 321–339). New York: Guilford Press.

Franklin, M. E., Abramowitz, J. S., Bux, D. A. Jr., Zoellner, L. A., & Feeny, N. C. (2002). Cognitive-behavioral therapy with and without medication in the treatment of obsessive-compulsive disorder. *Profess. Psychol.: Res. Pract., 33*(2), 162–168.

Franklin, M. E., Riggs, D. S., & Pai, A. (2005). Obsessive-compulsive disorder. In M. M. Antony, D. R. Ledley, & R. G. Heimberg (Eds.), *Improving outcomes and preventing relapse in cognitive-behavioral therapy* (pp. 128–173). New York: Guilford Press.

Franz, M., Dlabal, H., Kunz, S., Ulferts, J., Gruppe, H., & Gallhofer, B. (2001). Treatment of alcohol withdrawal: Tiapride and carbamazepine versus clomethiazole: A pilot study. *Eur. Arch. Psychiat. Clin. Neurosci., 251*(4), 185–195.

Fraser, G. A. (1993). Special treatment techniques to access the inner personality system of multiple personality disorder patients. *Dissociat.: Prog. Dissociat. Disorders, 6*(2–3), 193–198.

Frederick, C. J. (1969). Suicide notes: A survey and evaluation. *Bull. Suicidol., 8,* 17–26.

Fredericks, L. E. (2001). *The use of hypnosis in surgery and anesthesiology: Psychological preparation of the surgical patient.* Springfield, IL: Thomas.

Fredrickson, B. L., Tugade, M. M., Waugh, C. E., & Larkin, G. R. (2003). What good are positive emotions in crisis? A prospective study of resilience and emotion following the terrorist attacks on the United States on September 11th, 2001. *J. Pers. Soc. Psychol., 84,* 365–376.

Freed, A. O., & Geller, J. L. (2005). Client violence in social work practice: Prevention, intervention, and research. *Psychiat. Serv., 56*(3), 366.

Freeman, A. (2002). Cognitive-behavioral therapy for severe personality disorders. In S. G. Hofmann & M. C. Tompson (Eds.), *Treating chronic and severe mental disorders: A handbook of empirically supported interventions* (pp. 382–402). New York: Guilford Press.

Freeman, A. C. (2005). Eating disorders in males: A review. *S. Afr. Psychiat. Rev., 8*(2), 58–64.

Freeman, C. (1995). Cognitive therapy. In G. Szmukler, C. Dare, & J. Treasure (Eds.), *Handbook of eating disorders: Theory, treatment and research.* Chichester, England: Wiley.

Freeman, L. J., Templer, D. I., & Hill, C. (1999). The relationship between adult happiness and self-appraised childhood happiness and events. *J. Gen. Psychol., 160*(1), 46–54.

Freud, S. (1885). On the general effects of cocaine. *Med. Chir. Centralb., 20,* 373–375.

Freud, S. (1894). The neuropsychoses of defense. In J. Strachey (Ed.), *The standard edition of the complete psychological works of Sigmund Freud* (Vol. 3). London: Hogarth Press. (Work republished 1962)

Freud, S. (1909). Analysis of a phobia in a five-year-old boy. In *Sigmund Freud: Collected papers* (Vol. 3). New York: Basic Books.

Freud, S. (1914). On narcissism. In *Complete psychological works* (Vol. 14). London: Hogarth Press. (Work republished 1957)

Freud, S. (1915). A case of paranoia counter to psychoanalytic theory. In *Complete psychological works* (Vol. 14). London: Hogarth Press. (Work republished 1957)

Freud, S. (1917). *A general introduction to psychoanalysis* (J. Riviere, Trans.). New York: Liveright. (Work republished 1963)

Freud, S. (1917). Mourning and melancholia. In *Collected Papers* (Vol. 4, pp. 152–172). London: Hogarth Press and the Institute of Psychoanalysis. (Work republished 1950)

Freud, S. (1920). Beyond the pleasure principle. *S.E., 18,* 7–64.

Freud, S. (1924). The loss of reality in neurosis and psychosis. In *Sigmund Freud's collected papers* (Vol. 2, pp. 272–282). London: Hogarth Press.

Freud, S. (1933). *New introductory lectures on psychoanalysis.* New York: Norton.

Freud, S. (1961). *The future of an illusion.* New York: W. W. Norton.

Freyne, A., Keogh, F., Kelly, M., & Wrigley, M. (2005). A longitudinal study of depression in old age II: Depression and physical disability. *Irish J. Psychol. Med., 22*(3), 94–100.

Frick, P. J., & McCoy, M. G. (2001). Conduct disorder. In H. Orvaschel, J. Faust, et al. (Eds.), *Handbook of conceptualization and treatment of child psychopathology* (pp. 57–76). Amsterdam: Pergamon/Elsevier Science.

Friedman, H., & Eisenstein, T. K. (2004). Neurological basis of drug dependence and its effects on the immune system. *J. Neuroimmun., 147*(1–2), 106–108.

Friedman, M., & Rosenman, R. (1959). Association of specific overt behavior pattern with blood and cardiovascular findings. *JAMA, 169,* 1286.

Friedman, M., & Rosenman, R. (1974). *Type A behavior and your heart.* New York: Knopf.

Friedman, M., Thoresen, C., Gill, J., et al. (1984). Alteration of type A behavior and reduction in cardiac recurrences in postmyocardial infarction patients. *Am. Heart J., 108*(2), 653–665.

Friedman, S. (Ed.). (1994). *Anxiety disorders in African Americans.* New York: Springer.

Frith, U. (2000). Cognitive explanations of autism. In K. Lee (Ed.), *Childhood cognitive development: The essential readings. Essential readings in development psychology.* Malden, MA: Blackwell.

Frohman, E. M. (2002). Sexual dysfunction in neurological disease. *Clin. Neuropharmacol., 25*(3), 126–132.

Fromm-Reichmann, F. (1943). Psychotherapy of schizophrenia. *Amer. J. Psychiat., 111,* 410–419.

Fromm-Reichmann, F. (1948). Notes on the development of treatment of schizophrenia by psychoanalytic psychotherapy. *Psychiatry, 11,* 263–273.

Fromm-Reichmann, F. (1950). *Principles of intensive psychotherapy.* Chicago: University of Chicago.

Frosch, W. A., Robbins, E. S., & Stern, M. (1965). Untoward reactions to lysergic acid diethylamide (LSD) resulting in hospitalization. *N. Engl. J. Med., 273,* 1235–1239.

Frost, R. O., & Steketee, G. (2001). Obsessive-compulsive disorder. In H. S. Friedman (Ed.), *Specialty articles from the encyclopedia of mental health.* San Diego: Academic Press.

Frost, R. O., & Steketee, G. (Eds.). (2002). *Cognitive approaches to obsessions and compulsions: Theory, assessment, and treatment.* Amsterdam: Pergamon/Elsevier Science.

Fry, A. J., O'Riordan, D., Turner, M., & Mills, K. L. (2002). Survey of aggressive incidents experienced by community mental health staff. *Inter. J. Ment. Hlth. Nurs., 11*(2), 112–120.

Fry, R. (1993). Adult physical illness and childhood sexual abuse. *J. Psychosom. Res., 37*(2), 89–103.

Fu, A. Z., Krishnan, A. A., Harris, S. D., & Thompson, T. R. (2004). The economic burden of bipolar-related phases of depression versus mania. *Drug Benef. Trends, 16*(11), 569–575.

Fujita, F., & Diener, E. (2005). Life satisfaction set point: Stability and change. *J. Pers. Soc. Psychol., 88*(1), 158–164.

Furukawa, T. A., Ogura, A., Hirai, T., Fujihara, S., Kitamura, T., & Takahashi, K. (1999). Early parental separation experiences among patients with bipolar disorder and major depression: A case-control study. *J. Affect. Disorders, 52*(1–3), 85–91.

Fushimi, M., Sugawara, J., & Shimizu, T. (2005). Suicide patterns and characteristics in Akita, Japan. *Psychiat. Clin. Neurosci., 59*(3), 296–302.

Fyer, A. J., Mannuzza, S., Chapman, T. F., Martin, L. Y., et al. (1995). Specificity in familial aggregation of phobic disorders. *Arch. Gen. Psychiat., 52*(7), 564–573.

Fyer, A. J., Mannuzza, S., Gallops, M. S., Martin, L. Y., Aaronson, C., Gorman, J. M., et al. (1990). Familial transmission of simple phobias and fears: A preliminary report. *Arch. Gen. Psychiat., 47,* 252–256.

Fylan, F. (2005). Semi-structured interviewing. In J. Miles & P. Gilbert (Eds.), *A handbook of research methods for clinical and health psychology* (pp. 65–77). New York: Oxford University Press.

Gaal, E., VanWeeghel, J., VanCampen, M., & Linszen, D. (2002). The trainee project: Family-aided vocational rehabilitation of young people with schizophrenia. *Psychiatr. Rehab. J., 26*(1), 101–105.

Gabbard, G. O. (1990). *Psychodynamic psychiatry in clinical practice.* Washington, DC: American Psychiatric Press.

Gabbard, G. O. (2001). Psychoanalysis and psychoanalytic psychotherapy. In W. J. Livesley (Ed.), *Handbook of personality disorders: Theory, research, and treatment* (pp. 359–376). New York: Guilford Press.

Gabbard, G. O., & Coyne, L. (1987). Predictors of response of antisocial patients to hospital treatment. *Hosp. Comm. Psychiat., 38*(11), 1181–1185.

Galambos, N. L., Leadbeater, B. J., & Barker, E. T. (2004). Gender differences in and risk factors for depression in adolescence: A 4-year longitudinal study. *Inter. J. Behav. Dev., 28*(1), 16–25.

Galanter, M., & Brooks, D. (2001). Network therapy for addiction: Bringing family and peer support into office practice. *Inter. J. Group Psychother., 51*(1), 101–122.

Galanter, M., Hayden, F., Castaneda, R., & Franco, H. (2005). Group therapy, self-help groups, and network therapy. In R. J. Frances, A. H. Mack, & S. I. Miller (Eds.), *Clinical textbook of addictive disorders* (3rd ed., pp. 502–527). New York: Guilford Press.

Galanter, M., Talbott, D., Gallegos, K., & Rubenstone, E. (1990). Combined Alcoholics Anonymous and professional care for addicted physicians. *Amer. J. Psychiat., 147*(1), 64–68.

Gale Group. (2005). Vivus' testosterone spray for women with sexual desire disorder. *Pharma Marketletter, 2,* 1.

Galea, S., Ahern, J., Resnick, H., Kilpatrick, D., Bucuvalas, M., Gold, J., & Vlahov, D. (2002). Psychological sequelae of the September 11 terrorist attacks in New York City. *New Engl. J. Med., 13,* 982–987.

Galea, S., & Resnick, H. (2005). Posttraumatic stress disorder in the general population after mass terrorist incidents: Considerations about the nature of exposure. *CNS Spectrums, 10*(2), 107–115.

Gallagher, R. (1998, December 17). Interviewed in R. Vigoda, More college students showing signs of stress. *The Seattle Times.*

Gallagher-Thompson, D., Lovett, S., & Rose, J. (1991). Psychotherapeutic interventions for stressed family caregivers. In W. A. Myers (Ed.), *New techniques in the psychotherapy of older patients.* Washington, DC: American Psychiatric Press.

Gallagher-Thompson, D., Lovett, S., Rose, J., McKibbin, C., Coon, D., Futterman, A., & Thompson, L. W. (2000). Impact of psychoeducational interventions on distressed family caregivers. *J. Clin. Geropsychol., 6*(2), 91–110.

Gallagher-Thompson, D., & Thompson, L. W. (1995). Problems of aging. In R. J. Comer (Ed.), *Abnormal psychology.* New York: W. H. Freeman.

Gallup Poll. (1994). Religion is "very important" to 6 in 10 Americans. Poll conducted June 1994.

Gamwell, L., & Tomes, N. (1995). *Madness in America: Cultural and medical perceptions of mental illness before 1914.* Ithaca, NY: Cornell University Press.

Gao, L., & Greenfield, L. J. (2005). Activation of protein kinase C reduces benzodiazepine potency at GABA-sub(A) receptors in NT2-N neurons. *Neuropharmacology, 48*(3), 333–342.

Garber, J., & Horowitz, J. L. (2002). Depression in children. In I. H. Gotlib & C. L. Hammen (Eds.), *Handbook of depression* (pp. 510–540). New York: Guilford Press.

Garbino, J., Henry, J. A., Mentah, G., & Romand, J. A. (2001). Ecstasy ingestion and fulminant hepatic failure: Liver transplantation to be considered as a last therapeutic option. *Vet. Hum. Toxicol., 43*(2), 99–102.

Gardner, R. (1984, July 12). Full moon lunacy: Fact or fiction. *Trenton Times,* p. B1.

Gardner, R. A. (2004). The psychodynamics of patients with False Memory Syndrome (FMS). *J. Amer. Acad. Psychoanal. Dynamic Psychiat., 32*(1), 77–90.

Gardyn, R. (2002). Family matters. *Am. Demogr., 24*(8), 34.

Garety, P. (1991). Reasoning and delusions. *Brit. J. Psychiat., 159*(Suppl. 14), 14–18.

Garfield, D. A., & Havens, L. (1991). Paranoid phenomena and pathological narcissism. *Amer. J. Psychother., 45*(2), 160–172.

Garlow, S. J. (2002). Age, gender, and ethnicity differences in patterns of cocaine and ethanol use preceding suicide. *Amer. J. Psychiat., 159*(4), 615–619.

Garner, D. M. (2005). *Eating Disorder Inventory™-3 (EDI™-3).* Lutz, Florida: Psychological Assessment Resources, Inc. (PAR).

Garner, D. M., & Fairburn, C. G. (1988). Relationship between anorexia nervosa and bulimia nervosa: Diagnostic implications. In D. M. Garner & P. E. Garfinkel (Eds.), *Diagnostic issues in anorexia nervosa and bulimia nervosa.* Brunner/Mazel eating disorders monograph series, No. 2. New York: Brunner/Mazel.

Garner, D. M., Garfinkel, P. E., & O'Shaughnessy, M. (1985). The validity of the distinction between bulimia with and without anorexia nervosa. *Amer. J. Psychiat., 142,* 581–587.

Garner, D. M., Garfinkel, P. E., Schwartz, D., & Thompson, M. (1980). Cultural expectations of thinness in women. *Psychol. Rep., 47,* 483–491.

Garner, D. M., & Kearney-Cooke, A. (1997). The 1997 body image survey results. *Psychol. Today, 30*–44, 75–76, 78, 80, 84.

Garner, D. M., Olmsted, M. P., & Polivy, J. (1984). *The EDI.* Odessa, FL: Psychological Assessment Resources.

Garralda, M. E. (1996). Somatisation in children. *J. Child Psychol. Psychiat., 37*(1), 13–33.

Garrett, T. (2002). Inappropriate therapist-patient "relationships." In R. Goodwin & D. Cramer (Eds.), *Inappropriate relationships: The unconventional, the disapproved, and the forbidden* (pp. 147–170). Mahwah, NJ: Lawrence Erlbaum Associates.

Garroutte, E. M., Goldberg, J., Beals, J., Herrell, R., & Manson, S. M. (2003). Spirituality and attempted suicide among American Indians. *Soc. Sci. Med., 56*(7), 1571–1579.

Garroutte, E. M., Kunovich, R. M., Jacobsen, C., & Goldberg, J. (2004). Patient satisfaction and ethnic identity among American Indian older adults. *Soc. Sci. Med., 59*(11), 2233–2244.

Garssen, B., & Goodkin, K. (1999). On the role of immunological factors as mediators between psychosocial factors and cancer progression. *Psychiat. Res., 85*(1), 51–61.

Gatchel, R. J. (2001). Biofeedback and self-regulation of physiological activity: A major adjunctive treatment modality in health psychology. In A. Baum, T. A. Revenson, & J. E. Singer (Eds.), *Handbook of health psychology* (pp. 95–104). Mahwah, NJ: Erlbaum.

Gatchel, R. J. (2005). The biopsychosocial approach to pain assessment and management. In R. J. Gatchel (Ed.), *Clinical essentials of pain management* (pp. 23–46). Washington, DC: American Psychological Association.

Gatchel, R. J., & Maddrey, A. M. (2004). The biopsychosocial perspective of pain. In L. C. Leviton & J. M. Raczynski (Eds.), *Handbook of clinical health psychology: Volume 2. Disorders of behavior and health* (pp. 357–378). Washington, DC: American Psychological Association.

Gaugler, J. E., Jarrott, S. E., Zarit, S. H., Stephens, M. A. P., Townsend, A., & Greene, R. (2003). Adult day service use and reductions in caregiving hours: Effects on stress and psychological well-being for dementia caregivers. *Inter. J. Ger. Psychiat., 18*(1), 55–62.

Gaw, A. C. (2001). *Concise guide to cross-cultural psychiatry.* Washington, DC: American Psychiatric Publishing.

Gay, P. (1999, March 29). Psychoanalyst Sigmund Freud. *Time,* pp. 66–69.

Gebhard, P. H. (1965). Situational factors affecting human sexual behavior. In F. Beach (Ed.), *Sex and behavior.* New York: Wiley.

Gehring, D., & Knudson, G. (2005). Prevalence of childhood trauma in a clinical population of transsexual people. *Inter. J. Transgenderism, 8*(1), 23–30.

Geisthardt, C., & Munsch, J. (1996). Coping with school stress: A comparison of adolescents with and without learning disabilities. *J. Learn. Dis., 29*(3), 287–296.

Gelfand, D. M., Jenson, W. R., & Drew, C. J. (1982). *Understanding child behavior disorders.* New York: Holt, Rinehart & Winston.

Genchi, A. J., Alvarado, R. I. N., & Portocarrero, A. N. (2004). Sleep characteristics in subjects with major depression. *Psiquiatria, 20*(3), 1–3.

General Social Survey, University of Chicago (GSS). (1998, February). Cited in *J. Student,* Am. Demogr.

Gerardin, P., Cohen, D., Mazet, P., & Flament, M. F. (2002). Drug treatment of conduct disorder in young people. *Eur. Neuropsychopharmacology, 12*(5), 361–370.

Gerbasi, J. B., & Simon, R. I. (2003). Patients' rights and psychiatrists' duties: Discharging patients against medicine advice. *Harvard Rev. Psychiat., 11*(6), 333–343.

Geremia, G. M., & Neziroglu, F. (2001). Cognitive therapy in the treatment of body dysmorphic disorder. *Clin. Psychol. Psychother., 8,* 243–251.

Germer, J. (2005). The relationship between acculturation and eating disorders among Mexican American college females: An investigation. *Diss. Abstr. Inter.: Sect. B: Sci. Eng., 65*(7-B), 3706.

Gernsbacher, L. M. (1985). *The suicide syndrome.* New York: Human Sciences Press.

Gershon, E. S., & Nurnberger, J. I. (1995). Bipolar illness. In J. M. Oldham & M. B. Riba (Eds.), *American Psychiatric Press review of psychiatry* (Vol. 14). Washington, DC: American Psychiatric Press.

Gesch, C. B., Hammond, S. M., Hampson, S. E., Eves, A., & Crowder, M. J. (2002). Influence of supplementary vitamins, minerals and essential fatty acids on the antisocial behaviour of young adult prisoners: Randomised, placebo-controlled trial. *Brit. J. Psychiat., 181*(1), 22–28.

Gheorghiu, V. A., & Orleanu, P. (1982). Dental implant under hypnosis. *Amer. J. Clin. Hyp., 25*(1), 68–70.

Ghetti, S., Schaaf, J. M., Qin, J., & Goodman, G. S. (2004). Issues in eyewitness testimony. In W. T. O'Donohue & E. R. Levensky (Eds.), *Handbook of forensic psychology: Resource for mental health and legal professionals* (pp. 513–554). New York: Elsevier Science.

Ghika, J., & Bogousslavsky, J. (2002). Vascular dementia after stroke. In J. Bogousslavsky (Ed.), *Long-term effects of stroke* (pp. 235–262). New York: Marcel Dekker.

Gianaros, P. J., May, J. C., Siegle, G. J., & Jennings, J. R. (2005). Is there a functional neural correlate of individual differences in cardiovascular reactivity? *Psychosom. Med., 67*(1), 31–39.

Gianoulakis, C. (2001). Influence of the endogenous opioid system on high alcohol consumption and genetic predisposition to alcoholism. |*J. Psychiat. Neurosci., 26*(4), 304–318.

Gil, E., & Drewes, A. A. (Eds.). (2005). *Cultural issues in play therapy.* New York: Guilford Press.

Gilbert, P., Bailey, K. G., & McGuire, M. T. (2000). Evolutionary psychotherapy: Principles and outline. In P. Gilbert & K. G. Bailey (Eds.), *Genes on the couch: Explorations in evolutionary psychotherapy.* Philadelphia: Taylor & Francis.

Gilbert, S. C., Keery, H., & Thompson, J. K. (2005). The media's role in body image and eating disorders. In J. H. Daniel & E. Cole (Eds.), *Featuring females: Feminist analyses of media* (pp. 41–56). Washington, DC: American Psychological Association.

Gill, A. D. (1982). Vulnerability to suicide. In E. L. Bassuk, S. C. Schoonover, & A. D. Gill (Eds.), *Lifelines: Clinical perspectives on suicide.* New York: Plenum Press.

Gill, R. E. (2006). Psychology enrollment still booming. *Natl. Psychologist, 15*(1), 1–2.

Gillham, J. E., Reivich, K. J., Jaycox, L. H., & Seligman, M. E. (1995). Prevention of depressive symptoms in schoolchildren: Two-year follow-up. *Psychol. Sci., 6*(6), 343–351.

Gillham, J. E., Shatte, A. J., & Freres, D. R. (2000). Preventing depression: A review of cognitive-behavioral and family interventions. *Appl. Prev. Psychol., 9,* 63–88.

Gilligan, J. (2001). The last mental hospital. *Psychiatr. Quart., 72*(1), 45–61.

Gilmore, C. S., Clementz, B. A., & Buckley, P. F. (2005). Stimulus sequence affects schizophrenia–normal differences in event processing during an auditory oddball task. *Cog. Brain Res., 24*(2), 215–227.

Girdhar, S., Leenaars, A. A., Dogra, T. D., Leenaars, L., & Kumar, G. (2004). Suicide notes in India: What do they tell us? *Arch. Suic. Res., 8*(2), 179–185.

Gitlin, M. J. (2002). Pharmacological treatment of depression. In I. H. Gotlib & C. L. Hammen (Eds.), *Handbook of depression* (pp. 360–382). New York: Guilford Press.

Gjerdingen, D. K., & Center, B. A. (2005). First-time parents' postpartum changes in employment, childcare, and housework responsibilities. *Soc. Sci. Res., 34*(1), 103–116.

Glanville, D. N., & Dixon, L. (2005). Caregiver burden, family treatment approaches and service use in families of patients with schizophrenia. *Israel J. Psychiat. Rel. Sci., 42*(1), 15–22.

Glass, C. R., & Merluzzi, T. V. (2000). Cognitive and behavioral assessment. In C. E. Watkins, Jr., & V. L. Campbell (Eds.), *Testing and assessment in counseling practice* (2nd ed.). Mahwah, NJ: Erlbaum.

Glazer, M., Baer, R. D., Weller, S. C., de-Alba, J. E. G., & Liebowitz, S. W. (2004). Susto and soul loss in Mexicans and Mexican Americans. *J. Comp. Soc. Sci., 38*(3), 270–288.

Gleick, E. (1995, July 10). Sobering times for A. A. *Time,* pp. 49–50.

Gleser, G. C., Green, B. L., & Winget, C. N. (1981). *Prolonged psychological effects of disaster: A study of Buffalo Creek.* New York: Academic Press.

Glisky, E. L., Ryan, L., Reminger, S., Hardt, O., Hayes, S. M., & Hupbach, A. (2004). A case of psychogenic fugue: I understand, aber ich verstehe nichts. *Neuropsychologia, 42*(8), 1132–1147.

Gluck, J. P., & Bell, J. (2003). Ethical issues in the use of animals in biomedical and psychopharmacological research. *Psychopharmacology, 171*(1), 6–12.

Godenzi, A., & De Puy, J. (2001). Overcoming boundaries: A cross cultural inventory of primary prevention programs against wife abuse and child abuse. *J. Primary Prev., 21*(4), 455–475.

Godt, K. (2002). Personality disorders and eating disorders: The prevalence of personality disorders in 176 female outpatients with eating disorders. *Eur. Eat. Disord. Rev., 10*(2), 102–109.

Goin, M. K. (2001). Borderline personality disorder: The importance of establishing a treatment framework. *Psychiatr. Serv., 52*(2), 167–168.

Goisman, R. M., Warshaw, M. G., & Keller, M. B. (1999). Psychosocial treatment prescriptions for generalized anxiety disorder, panic disorder, and social phobia, 1991–1996. *Amer. J. Psychiat., 156*(11), 1819–1821.

Gold, E. R., (1986). Long-term effects of sexual victimization in childhood: An attributional approach. *J. Cons. Clin. Psychol., 54,* 471–475.

Gold, J. H. (1998). Gender differences in psychiatric illness and treatments: A critical review. *J. Nerv. Ment. Dis., 186*(12), 769–775.

Gold, S. D., Marx, B. P., Soler-Baillo, J. M., & Sloan, D. M. (2005). Is life stress more traumatic than traumatic stress? *J. Anx. Dis., 19,* 687–698.

Golden, R. N., Gaynes, B. N., Ekstrom, R. D., Damer, R. M., Jacobsen, F. M., Suppes, T., et al. (2005). The efficacy of light therapy in the treatment of mood disorders: A review and meta-analysis of the evidence. *Amer. J. Psychiat., 162*(4), 656–662.

Goldenberg, I., & Goldenberg, H. (2005). Family therapy. In R. Corsini & D. Wedding (Eds.), *Current psychotherapies* (7th ed., pp. 372–404). Boston: Thomson/Brooks-Cole.

Goldfried, M. R., & Wolfe, B. E. (1996). Psychotherapy practice and research. Repairing a strained alliance. *Amer. Psychologist, 51*(10), 1007–1016.

Goldiamond, I. (1965). Self-control procedures in personal behavior problems. *Psychol. Rep., 17,* 851–868.

Goldman, J. G. (1995). A mutual story-telling technique as an aid to integration after abreaction in the treatment of MPD. *Dissociat. Prog. Dissociat. Disorders 8*(1), 53–60.

Goldman, S., & Beardslee, W. R. (1999). Suicide in children and adolescents. In D. G. Jacobs (Ed.), *The Harvard Medical School guide to suicide assessment and intervention.* San Francisco: Jossey-Bass.

Goldney, R. D. (1998). Suicide prevention is possible: A review of recent studies. *Arch. Suic. Res., 4*(4): 329–339.

Goldney, R. D. (2003). Deinstitutionalization and suicide. *Crisis, 24*(1), 39–40.

Goldstein, A. (1994). *Addiction: From biology to drug policy.* New York: W. H. Freeman.

Goldstein, E. G. (2002). *Object relations theory and self psychology in social work practice.* New York: Free Press.

Gollan J. K., & Jacobson N. S. (2002). Developments in couple therapy research. In H. A. Liddle, D. A. Santiseban, R. F. Levant, & J. H. Bray (Eds.), *Family psychology: Science-based interventions.* Washington, DC: American Psychological Association.

Golub, D. (1995). Cultural variations in multiple personality disorder, In L. M. Cohen, J. N. Berzoff, M. R. Elin (Eds.), *Dissociative identity disorder.* Northvale, NJ: Jason Aronson.

Gonzalez, M., de Pablo, J., Valdes, M., Matrai, S., Peri, J. M., & Fuente, E. (2005). Delirium: A predictor of mortality in the elderly. *Eur. J. Psychiat., 19*(3), 165–171.

Gonzalez-Brignardello, M. P., & Vazquez, A. M. M. (2004). Intervention in a case of post-traumatic stress disorder with EMDR within a cognitive behavioral setting. *Clinica y Salud, 15*(3), 337–354.

Gonzalez-Pinto, A., Tohen, M., Lalaguna, B., Pérez-Heredia, J. L., Fernandez-Corres, B., Gutierrez, M., et al. (2002). Treatment of bipolar I rapid cycling patients during dysphoric mania with olanzapine. *J. Clin. Psychopharmacol., 22,* 450–454.

Goodman, S. H. (2002). Depression and early adverse experiences. In I. H. Gotlib & C. L. Hammen (Eds.), *Handbook of depression* (pp. 245–267). New York: Guilford Press.

Goodman, W. K., McDougle, C., & Price, L. H. (1992). Pharmacotherapy of obsessive compulsive disorder. *J. Clin. Psychiat., 53*(Suppl. 4), 29–37.

Goodwin, C. J. (2002). *Research in psychology: Methods and design* (3rd ed.). New York: Wiley.

Goodwin, F. K., & Jamison, K. R. (1984). The natural course of manic depressive illness. In R. M. Post & J. C. Ballenger (Eds.), *Neurobiology of mood disorders.* Baltimore: Williams & Wilkins.

Gopaul-McNicol, S., & Armour-Thomas, E. (2002). *Assessment and culture: Psychological tests with minority populations.* San Diego, CA: Academic.

Gorman, C. (2003, July 28). The new science of dyslexia. *Time, 162*(4), 53–59.

Gorman, J. M. (2003). Does the brain noradrena-line network mediate the effects of the CO-sub-2 challenge? *J. Psychopharmacol., 17*(3), 265–266.

Gorman, J. M. (2005). Benzodiazepines: Taking the good with the bad and the ugly. *CNS Spectrums, 10*(1), 14–15.

Gorman, J. M. (2005). In the wake of trauma. *CNS Spectrums, 10*(2), 81–85.

Gorwood, P., Bouvard, M., Mouren-Simeoni, et al. (1998). Genetics and anorexia nervosa: A review of candidate genes. *Psychiat. Genet., 8,* 1–12.

Goshen, C. E. (1967). *Documentary history of psychiatry: A source book on historical principles.* New York: Philosophy Library.

Gossop, M., Marsden, J., Stewart, D., & Treacy, S. (2001). Outcomes after methadone maintenance and methadone reduction treatments: Two-year follow-up results from the National Treatment Outcome Research Study. *Drug Alc. Dep., 62*(3), 255–264.

Gottesman, I. I. (1991). *Schizophrenia genesis.* New York: Freeman.

Gottesman, I. I., & Reilly, J. L. (2003). Strengthening the evidence for genetic factors in schizophrenia (without abetting genetic discrimination). In M. F. Lenzenweger & J. M. Hooley (Eds.), *Principles of experimental psychopathology: Essays in honor of Brendan A. Maher* (pp. 31–44). Washington, DC: American Psychological Association.

Gottesman, I. I., & Shields, J. (1984). Genetic theorizing and schizophrenia. In T. Millon (Ed.), *Theories of personality and psychopathology* (3rd ed.). New York: Holt, Rinehart and Winston.

Gottfredson, D. C., & Wilson, D. B. (2003). Characteristics of effective school-based substance abuse prevention. *Prevent. Sci., 4*(1), 27–38.

Gottfredson, L. S. (2005). Suppressing intelligence research: Hurting those we intend to help. In N. A. Cummings, & R. H. Wright (Eds.), *Destructive trends in mental health: The well-intentioned path to harm* (pp. 155–186). New York: Routledge.

Gotts, E. E., & Knudsen, T. E. (2005). *The clinical interpretation of the MMPI-2: A content cluster approach.* Mahwah, NJ: Lawrence Erlbaum Associates.

Gould, M. S. (2001). Suicide and the media. In H. Hendin & J. J. Mann (Eds.), *The clinical science of suicide prevention* (Vol. 932, pp. 200–224). New York: Annals of the New York Academy of Sciences.

Gould, M. S., Shaffer, D., & Davies, M. (1990). Truncated pathways from childhood to adulthood: Attrition in follow-up studies due to death. In L. Robins & M. Rutter (Eds.), *Straight and devious pathways from childhood to adulthood.* Cambridge, England: Cambridge University Press.

Gourion, D., Gourevitch, R., Le Provost, J. B., Olie, J. P., Loo, H., & Krebs, M. O. (2004). Neurodevelopmental hypothesis in schizophrenia. *Encephale, 30*(2), 109–118.

Gowers, S. G., North, C. D., & Byram, V. (1996). Life event precipitants of adolescent anorexia nervosa. *J. Child Psychol. Psychiat., 37*(4), 469–477.

Grace, S. L., Evindar, A., & Stewart, D. E. (2003). The effect of postpartum depression on child cognitive development and behavior: A review and critical analysis of the literature. *Arch. Women's Ment. Hlth., 6*(4), 263–274.

Graesel, E. (2002). When home care ends—Changes in the physical health of informal caregivers caring for dementia patients: A longitudinal study. *J. Amer. Ger. Soc. 50*(5), 843–849.

Graff-Radford, N. (2005). Plasma Aβ Levels as a premorbid biomarker for cognitive decline, mild cognitive impairment (MCI) and Alzheimer disease (AD). *Alzheimer's Association International Conference on Prevention of Dementia,* June 18, 2005, Washington, DC.

Graham, J. R. (1977). *The MMPI: A practical guide.* New York: Oxford University Press.

Graham, J. R. (2006). *MMPI-2: Assessing personality and psychopathology* (4th ed.). New York: Oxford University Press.

Granillo, T., Jones-Rodriguez, G., & Carvajal, S. C. (2005). Prevalence of eating disorders in Latina adolescents: Associations with substance use and other correlates. *J. Adol. Hlth., 36*(3), 214–220.

Grant, B. F., & Dawson, D. A. (1997). Age at onset of alcohol use and its association with DSM-IV alcohol abuse and dependence: Results from the National Longitudinal Alcohol Epidemiologic Survey. *J. Substance Abuse, 9,* 103–110.

Grant, B. F., Stinson, F. S., Dawson, D. A., Chou, P., Dufour, M. C., Compton, W., et al. (2004). Prevalence and co-occurrence of substance use disorders and independent mood and anxiety disorders: Results from the National Epidemiologic Survey on Alcohol and Related Conditions. *Arch. Gen. Psychiat., 61*(8), 807–816.

Grawe, K., Donate, R., & Bernauer, F. (1998). *Psychotherapy in transition.* Seattle: Hogrefe & Huber.

Gray, H. (1959). *Anatomy of the human body* (27th ed.). Philadelphia: Lea & Febiger.

Gray, J., Nielsen, D. R., Wood, L. E., Andresen, M., & Dolce, K. (2000). Academic progress of children who attended a preschool for abused children: A follow-up of the Keepsafe Project. *Child Abuse Negl.* 24(1), 25–32.

Gray, J. A., & McNaughton, N. (1996). The neuropsychology of anxiety: Reprise. In D. A. Hope (Ed.), *The Nebraska symposium on motivation* (Vol. 43). Lincoln: University of Nebraska Press.

Gray, M., & Gibson, S. (2004). Relapse prevention. In S. L. A. Straussner (Ed.), *Clinical work with substance-abusing clients* (2nd ed., pp. 146–168). New York: Guilford Press.

Gray, N. A., Zhou, R., Du, J., Moore, G. J., & Manji, H. K. (2003). The use of mood stabilizers as plasticity enhancers in the treatment of neuropsychiatric disorders. *J. Clin. Psychiat., 64*(Suppl. 5), 3–17.

Green, R. (2000). Family cooccurrence of "gender dysphoria": Ten siblings or parent-child pairs. *Arch. Sex. Behav., 29*(5), 499–507.

Green, S. A. (1985). *Mind and body: The psychology of physical illness.* Washington, DC: American Psychiatric Press.

Greenberg, L. S., Elliott, R., & Lietaer, G. (1994). Research on experiential psychotherapies. In A. E. Bergin & S. L. Garfield (Eds.), *Handbook of psychotherapy and behavior change.* New York: Wiley.

Greenberg, L. S., Watson, J. C., & Lietaer, G. (Eds.). (1998). *Handbook of experiential psychotherapy.* New York: Guilford Press.

Greenberg, P. E., Kessler, R. C., Birnbaum, H. G., Leong, S. A., Lowe, S. W., Berglund, P. A., et al. (2003). The economic burden of depression in the United States: How did it change between 1990 and 2000? *J. Clin. Psychiat., 64*(12), 1465–1475.

Greenberg, P. E., Sisitsky, T., Kessler, R. C., Finkelstein, S. N., Berndt, E. R., Davidson, J. R., et al. (1999). The economic burden of anxiety disorders in the 1990s. *J. Clin. Psychiat., 60*(7), 427–435.

Greene, R. L., & Clopton, J. R. (2004). Minnesota Multiphasic Personality Inventory-2 (MMPO-2). In M. E. Maruish (Ed.), *The use of psychological testing for treatment planning and outcomes assessment: Volume 3: Instruments for adults* (3rd ed., pp. 449–477). Mahwah, NJ: Lawrence Erlbaum Associates.

Greenfield, D. N. (1999). Psychological characteristics of compulsive internet use: A preliminary analysis. *CyberPsych. Behav., 2*(5), 403–412.

Greer, S. (1999). Mind-body research in psychooncology. *Adv. Mind-Body Med., 15*(4), 236–244.

Gregory, R. J. (2004). *Psychological testing: History, principles, and applications.* Needham Heights, MA: Allyn and Bacon.

Grekin, P. M., Jemelka, R., & Trupin, E. W. (1994). Racial differences in the criminalization of the mentally ill. *Bull. Amer. Acad. Psychiat. Law, 22,* 411–420.

Gresham, A. C. (1993). The insanity plea: A futile defense for serial killers. *Law Psychol. Rev., 17,* 193–208.

Grierson, B. (2003, July 27). A bad trip down memory lane. *New York Times.*

Griffiths, K. M., & Christensen, H. (2006). Review of randomised controlled trials of Internet interventions for mental disorders and related conditions. *Austral. Psychol. Soc., 10*(1), 16–29.

Griffiths, R., Gross, G., Russell, J., Thornton, C., Beumont, P. J. V., Schotte, D., & Touyz, S. W. (1998). Perceptions of bed rest of anorexic patients. *Inter. J. Eat. Disorders, 23,* 443–447.

Grigg, J. R. (1988). Imitative suicides in an active duty military population. *Military Med., 153*(2), 79–81.

Grigorenko, E. L. (2001). Developmental dyslexia: An update on genes, brains, and environments. *J. Child Psychol. Psychiat. Allied Disc., 42*(1), 91–125.

Grilly, D. M. (2002). *Drugs and human behavior* (4th ed.). Boston: Allyn and Bacon.

Grilly, D. M. (2006). *Drugs and human behavior* (5th ed.). Boston: Pearson.

Grilo, C. M., & Masheb, R. M. (2002). Childhood maltreatment and personality disorders in adult patients with binge eating disorder. *Acta Psychiatr. Scandin., 106*(3), 183–188.

Grilo, C. M., Sanislow, C. A., & McGlashan, T. H. (2002). Co-occurrence of DSM-IV personality disorders with borderline personality disorder. *J. Nerv. Ment. Dis., 190*(8), 552–553.

Grimm, W. (2001, February 1). Java straight up: Younger consumers want their caffeine fix. *Amer. Demogr.*

Grinfield, M. J. (1993, July). Report focuses on jailed mentally ill. *Psychiatr. Times,* pp. 1–3.

Grinfield, M. J. (1998, February). "Patient dumping"—Mentally ill get shortchanged. *Psychiatr. Times, XV* (2).

Grinspoon, L., et al. (Eds.). (1986). Paraphilias. *Harvard Med. Sch. Ment. Health Newsl., 3*(6), 1–5.

Grippo, A. J., Francis, J., Beltz, T. G., Felder, R. B., & Johnson, A. K. (2005). Neuroendocrine and cytokine profile of chronic mild stress-induced anhedonia. *Physiol. Behav., 84*(5), 697–706.

Grob, G. N. (1966). *State and the mentally ill: A history of Worcester State Hospital in Massachusetts, 1830–1920.* Chapel Hill: University of North Carolina Press.

Grof, P. (2005). Lithium in bipolar disorder. In S. Kasper & R. M. A. Hirschfeld (Eds.), *Handbook of bipolar disorder: Diagnosis and therapeutic approaches* (pp. 267–284). New York: Taylor & Francis.

Gross, B. (2004). Theft by deception. *Ann. Amer. Psychother. Assn., 7*(1), 36–37.

Gross, D. (2005, June 21). Marijuana-flavored candy blasted. *Associated Press (Atlanta)/Netscape News.*

Gross, G., & Blundo, R. (2005). Viagra: Medical technology constructing aging masculinity. *J. Sociol. Soc. Welfare, 32*(1), 85–97.

Grossman, J. A., & Kruesi, M. J. P. (2000). Innovative approaches to youth suicide prevention: An update of issues and research findings. In R. W. Maris, S. S. Canetto, J. L. McIntosh, & M. M. Silverman (Eds.), *Review of suicidology, 2000* (pp. 170–201). New York: Guilford Press.

Grove, W. M., Zald, D. H., Lebow, B. S., Snitz, B. E., & Nelson, C. (2000). Clinical versus mechanical prediction: A meta-analysis. *Psychol. Assess., 12,* 19–30.

Gruenberg, E. M. (1980). Mental disorders. In J. M. Last (Ed.), *Maxcy-Rosenau public health and preventive medicine* (11th ed.). New York: Appleton-Century-Crofts.

Gruettert, T., & Friege, L. (2005). Quetiapine in patients with borderline personality disorder and psychosis: A case series. *Inter. J. Psychiat. Clin. Pract., 9*(3), 180–186.

Grunbaum, J. A., Kann, L., Kinchen, S. A., Williams, B., Ross, J. G., Lowry, R., et al. (2002). Youth risk behavior surveillance: United States, 2001. In Surveillance Summary, *MMWR CDC, 51*(SS-4), 6–64.

Grunze, H. (2005). Reevaluating therapies for bipolar depression. *J. Clin Psychiat., 66*(Suppl. 5), 17–25.

Gruttadaro, D. (2005). Federal leaders call on schools to help. *NAMI Advocate, 3*(1), 7.

Guertin, T. L. (1999). Eating behavior of bulimics, self-identified binge eaters, and non-eating-disordered individuals: What differentiates these populations? *Clin. Psychol. Rev., 19*(1), 1–23.

Gunderson, J. G. (1988). Personality disorders. In A. M. Nicholi, Jr. (Ed.), *The new Harvard guide to psychiatry.* Cambridge, MA: Belknap Press.

Gunderson, J. G. (1996). The borderline patient's intolerance of aloneness: Insecure attachments and therapist availability. *Amer. J. Psychiat., 153*(6), 752–758.

Gunderson, J. G. (2001). *Borderline personality disorder: A clinical guide.* Washington, DC: American Psychiatric Publishing.

Gunderson, J. G., & Ronningstam, E. (2001). Differentiating narcissistic and antisocial personality disorders. *J. Pers. Disorders, 15*(2), 103–109.

Gupta, S. C., Basu, S., & Sinha, V. K. (2004). Prodrome in childhood and adolescent mania. *Hong Kong J. Psychiat., 14*(3), 26–30.

Gureje, O., Simon, G. E., Ustun, T. B., & Goldberg, D. P. (1997). Somatization in cross-cultural perspective: A World Health Organization study in primary care. *Amer. J. Psychiat., 154*(7), 989–995.

Gurman, A. S. (2003). Marital therapies. In A. S. Gurman & S. B. Messer (Eds.), *Essential psychotherapies: Theory and practice* (2nd ed.). New York: Guilford Press.

Gurman, A. S., & Messer, S. B. (2003). Contemporary issues in the theory and practice of psychotherapy: A framework for comparative study. In A. S. Gurman & S. B. Messer (Eds.), *Essential psychotherapies: Theory and practice* (2nd ed.). New York: Guilford Press.

Gurnack, A. M., Atkinson, R., & Osgood, N. J. (Eds.) (2002). *Treating alcohol and drug abuse in the elderly.* New York: Springer.

Guth, L. J., Lopez, D. F., Rojas, J., Clements, K. D., & Tyler, J. M. (2004). Experiential versus rational training: A comparison of student attitudes toward homosexuality. *J. Homosexuality, 48*(2), 83–102.

Gutheil, T. G. (2004). The expert witness. In R. J. Simon & L. H. Gold, *The American Psychiatric Publishing textbook of forensic psychiatry* (pp. 75–90). Washington, DC: American Psychiatric Publishing.

Gutheil, T. G. (2005). Boundary issues and personality disorders. *J. Psychiat. Pract., 11*(2), 88–96.

Guttman, H. A. (2002). The epigenesis of the family system as a context for individual development. *Fam. Process, 41*(3), 533–545.

Hadley, S. W., & Strupp, H. H. (1976). Contemporary views of negative effects in psychotherapy: An integrated account. *Arch. Gen. Psychiat., 33*(1), 1291–1302.

Hafner, H., & an der Heiden, W. (1988). The mental health care system in transition: A study in organization, effectiveness, and costs of complementary care for schizophrenic patients. In C. N. Stefanis & A. D. Rabavilis (Eds.), *Schizophrenia: Recent biosocial developments.* New York: Human Sciences Press.

Hafner, H., Maurer, K., Ruhrmann, S., Bechdolf, A., Klosterkotter, J., Wagner, M., et al. (2004). Early detection and secondary prevention of psychosis: Facts and visions. *Eur. Arch. Psychiat. Clin. Neurosci., 254*(2), 117–128.

Hahlweg, K., & Wiedemann, G. (2002). Principles and results of family therapy in schizophrenia. In A. Schaub (Ed.), *New family interventions and associated research in psychiatric disorders* (pp. 155–173). New York: Springer-Verlag.

Hakuhodo Institute of Life and Living. (2001). What price beauty? *From the HILL, 7*(4).

Halaas, J. L., Gajiwala, K. F., Maffei, M., Cohen, S. L., et al. (1995). Weight-reducing effects of the plasma protein encoded by the obese gene. *Science, 269,* 543–546.

Hale, C. M., & Tager-Flusberg, H. (2005). Social communication in children with autism: The relationship between theory of mind and discourse development. *Autism, 9*(2), 157–178.

Hale, E. (1983, April 17). Inside the divided mind. *New York Times Magazine,* pp. 100–106.

Haliburn, J. (2005). Australian and New Zealand clinical practice guidelines for the treatment of anorexia nervosa. *Austral. New Zeal. J. Psychiat., 39*(7), 639–640.

Hall, C. (1997, March 17). It's not only the string section that's highly strung. *Electronic Telegraph.*

Hall, C. W., & Webster, R. E. (2002). Traumatic symptomatology characteristics of adult children of alcoholics. *J. Drug Educ., 32*(3), 195–211.

Hall, F. S., Sora, I., Drgonova, J., Li, X. F., Goeb, M., & Uhl, G. R. (2004). Molecular mechanisms underlying the rewarding effects of cocaine. In T. Nabeshima, T. Yanagita, & S. Ali (Eds.), *Current status of drug dependence/abuse studies: Cellular and molecular mechanisms of drugs of abuse and neurotoxicity* (pp. 47–66). New York: New York Academy of Sciences.

Hall, L., with Cohn, L. (1980). *Eat without fear.* Santa Barbara, CA: Gurze.

Hall, N. W., & Zigler, E. (1997). Drug-abuse prevention efforts for young children: A review and critique of existing programs. *Amer. J. Orthopsychiat., 67*(1), 134–143.

Halloway, J. D. (2004). California psychologists prepare for hospital privileges battle. *APA Monitor on Psychology, 35*(1), 28–29.

Halls, S. B., & Hanson, J. (2003). Women's average weight chart and percent distribution. Retrieved January 2006 from www.halls.md/chart/height-weight.htm

Hallschmid, M., Benedict, C., Born, J., Fehm, H. L., & Kern, W. (2004). Manipulating central nervous mechanisms of food intake and body weight regulation by intranasal administration of neuropeptides in man. *Physiol. Behav., 83*(1), 55–64.

Halmi, K. A. (1995). Current concepts and definitions. In G. Szmukler, C. Dare, & J. Treasure (Eds.), *Handbook of eating disorders: Theory, treatment and research.* Chichester, England: Wiley.

Halmi, K. A., Agras, W. S., Kaye, W. H., & Walsh, B. T. (1994). Evaluation of pharmacologic treatments in eating disorders. In R. F. Prien & D. S. Robinson (Eds.), *Clinical evaluation of psychotropic drugs: Principles and guidelines.* New York: Raven Press, Ltd.

Ham, L. S., Hope, D. A., White, C. S., & Rivers, P. C. (2002). Alcohol expectancies and drinking behavior in adults with social anxiety disorder and dysthymia. *Cog. Ther. Res., 26*(2), 275–288.

Hamer, D. H., Hu, S., Magnuson, V. L., Hu, N., et al. (1993). A linkage between DNA markers on the X chromosome and male sexual orientation. *Science, 261,* 321–327.

Hamilton, S., Rothbart, M., & Dawes, R. N. (1986). Sex Roles, 15(5–6), 269–274.

Hammen, C. L., & Glass, D. R. (1975). Expression, activity, and evaluation of reinforcement. *J. Abnorm. Psychol., 84*(6), 718–721.

Hammen, C. L., & Krantz, S. (1976). Effect of success and failure on depressive cognitions. *J. Abnorm. Psychol., 85*(8), 577–588.

Hankin, B. L., & Abramson, L. Y. (1999). Development of gender differences in depression: Description and possible explanations. *Ann. Med., 31*(6), 372–379.

Hankin, B. L., & Abramson, L. Y. (2001). Development of gender differences in depression: An elaborated cognitive vulnerability-transactional stress theory. *Psychol. Bull., 127,* 773–796.

Hankin, J. R. (2002). Fetal alcohol syndrome prevention research. *Alc. Res. Hlth., 26*(1), 58–65.

Hankins, G. C., Vera, M. I., Barnard, G. W., & Herkov, M. J. (1994). Patient-therapist sexual involvement: A review of clinical and research data. *Bull. Amer. Acad. Psychiat. Law., 22*(1), 109–126.

Hanson, M., Tiberius, R., Hodges, B., MacKay, S., McNaughton, N., Dickens, S., et al. (2002). Implications of suicide contagion for the selection of adolescent standardized patients. *Academ. Med., 77*(Suppl. 10), S100–S102.

Hardin, S. B., Weinrich, S., Weinrich, M., Garrison, C., Addy, C., & Hardin, T. L. (2002). Effects of a long-term psychosocial nursing intervention on adolescents exposed to catastrophic stress. *Issues Ment. Hlth. Nurs., 23*(6), 537–551.

Harding, A., Halliday, G., Caine, D., & Kril, J. (2000). Degeneration of anterior thalamic nuclei differentiates alcoholics with amnesia. *Brain, 123*(1), 141–154.

Hardman, M. L., Drew, C. J., & Egan, M. W. (2002). *Human exceptionality: Society, school and family.* Boston: Allyn & Bacon.

Hardy, J., & Selkoe, D. J. (2002). The amyloid hypothesis of Alzheimer's disease: Progress and problems on the road to therapeutics. *Science, 297*(5580), 353–356.

Hare, R. D. (1993). *Without conscience: The disturbing world of the psychopaths among us.* New York: Pocket Books.

Harish, T., Grover, S., & Basu, D. (2005). Recurrent unipolar mania: Does it warrant a separate nosological status? *German J. Psychiat., 8*(1), 8–15.

Harkavy, J. M., & Asnis, G. (1985). Suicide attempts in adolescence: Prevalence and implications. *N. Engl. J. Med., 313,* 1290–1291.

Harlow, H. F., & Harlow, M. K. (1965). The affectional systems. In A. Schrier, H. Harlow, & F. Stollnitz (Eds.), *Behavior of nonhuman primates* (Vol. 2). New York: Academic Press.

Harlow, H. F., & Zimmermann, R. R. (1996). Affectional responses in the infant monkey. In L. C. Drickamer & L. D. Houck (Eds.), *Foundations of animal behavior: Classic papers with commentaries* (pp. 376–387). Chicago, IL: University of Chicago Press.

Harper, P. B., & Dwivedi, K. N. (Eds.). (2004). *Promoting the emotional well-being of children and adolescents and preventing their mental ill health: A handbook.* Philadelphia: Jessica Kingsley.

Harrington, R. C., Fudge, H., Rutter, M. L., Bredenkamp, D., Groothues, C., & Pridham, J. (1993). Child and adult depression: A test of continuities with data from a family study. *Brit. J. Psychiat., 162,* 627–633.

Harris Interactive. (2001). Dietary supplement barometer survey, for the Dietary Supplement Education Alliance. Retrieved August 16, 2002, from www.supplementinfo.org

Harris, A., Ayers, T., & Leek, M. R. (1985). Auditory span of apprehension deficits in schizophrenia. *J. Nerv. Ment. Dis., 173*(11), 650–657.

Harris, E. C., & Barraclough, B. (1998). Excess mortality of mental disorder. *Brit. J. Psychiat., 173,* 11–53.

Harris, R. J. (2003). Traditional nomothetic approaches. In S. F. Davis (Ed.), *Handbook of research methods in experimental psychology* (pp. 42–65). Malden, MA: Blackwell Publishers.

Harris, S., Kasari, C., & Sigman, M. D. (1996). Joint attention and language gains in children with Down syndrome. *Amer. J. Ment. Retard., 100,* 608–619.

Harrison, P. J., & Weinberger, D. R. (2005). Schizophrenia genes, gene expression, and neuropathology: On the matter of their convergence. *Mol. Psychiat., 10*(8), 804.

Harriss, L., & Hawton, K. (2005). Suicidal intent in deliberate self-harm and the risk of suicide: The predictive power of the Suicide Intent Scale. *J. Affect. Disorders, 86*(2–3), 225–233.

Hartman, M., Steketee, M. C., Silva, S., Lanning, K., & McCann, H. (2003). Working memory and schizophrenia: Evidence for slowed encoding. *Schizo. Res., 59*(2–3), 99–113.

Harvard School of Public Health. (1995). *Binge drinking on American college campuses: A new look at an old problem.* Boston: Author.

Harway, M. (Ed.). (2005). *Handbook of couples therapy.* New York: Wiley.

Hasin, D., Endicott, J., & Lewis, C. (1985). Alcohol and drug abuse in patients with affective syndromes. *Comprehen. Psychiat., 26,* 283–295.

Haslam, N., Reichert, T., & Fiske, A. P. (2002). Aberrant social relations in the personality disorders. *Psychol. Psychother.: Theory, Res. Prac., 75*(1), 19–31.

Hasman, A., & Holm, S. (2004). Nicotine conjugate vaccine: Is there a right to a smoking future? *J. Med. Ethics, 30*(4), 344–345.

Hassan, R. (1998). One hundred years of Emile Durkheim's *Suicide: A Study in Sociology. Austral. New Zeal. J. Psychiat., 32*(2), 168–171.

Hastings, J. F. (2001). Mental health and substance dependence among America's poor and non-poor populations. *Diss. Abstr. Inter.: Sect. A: Human Soc. Sci., 61*(8-A), 3351.

Hätönen, T., Alila, A., & Laakso, M. L. (1996). Exogenous melatonin fails to counteract the light-induced phase delay of human melatonin rhythm. *Brain Res., 710*(1–2), 125–130.

Hawkins, J. R. (2004). The role of emotional repression in chronic back pain: A study of chronic back pain patients undergoing psychodynamically oriented group psychotherapy as treatment for their pain. *Diss. Abstr. Inter.: Sect. B: Sci. Eng., 64*(8-B), 4038.

Hawkrigg, J. J. (1975). Agoraphobia. *Nursing Times, 71,* 1280–1282.

Hawton, K. (2001). The treatment of suicidal behavior in the context of the suicidal process. In K. van Heeringen (Ed.), *Understanding suicidal behavior: The suicidal process approach to research, treatment and prevention* (pp. 212–229). Chichester, England: Wiley.

Hawton, K., Sutton, L., Haw, C., Sinclair, J., & Deeks, J. J. (2005). Schizophrenia and suicide: Systematic review of risk factors. *Brit. J. Psychiat., 187*(1), 9–20.

Haxby, J. V., Ungerleider, L. G., Horwitz, B., Maisog, J. M., Rapoport, S. I., & Grady, C. L. (1996). Face encoding and recognition in the human brain. *Proc. Nat. Acad. Sci. USA, 93*(2), 922–927.

Hayaki, J., Friedman, M. A., & Brownell, K. D. (2002). Shame and severity of bulimic symptoms. *Eat. Behav., 3*(1), 73–83.

Hayday, G. (2002, August 26). Internet addicts surf on work time. *ZDNet.*

Hayden, L. A. (1998). Gender discrimination within the reproductive health care system: Viagra v. birth control. *J. Law Health, 13,* 171–198.

Hayes, L. M., & Rowan, J. R. (1988). *National study of jail suicides: Seven years later.* Alexandria, VA: National Center for Institutions and Alternatives.

Haynes, S. G., Feinleib, M., & Kannel, W. B. (1980). The relationship of psychosocial factors to coronary heart disease in the Framingham study: III. Eight-year incidence of coronary heart disease. *Amer. J. Epidemiol., 111,* 37–58.

Haynes, S. N. (2001). Clinical applications of analog behavioral observations: Dimensions of psychometric evaluations. *Psychol. Assess., 13*(1), 73–85.

Haynes, S. N. (2001). Introduction to the special section on clinical applications of analogue behavioral observation. *Psychol. Assess., 13*(1), 3–4.

Haynes, S. N., & Heiby, E. M. (Eds.). (2004). *Comprehensive handbook of psychological assessment: Vol. 3. Behavioral assessment.* Hoboken, NJ: Wiley.

Haynie, D. L., Nansel, T., Eitel, P., Crump, A. D., Saylor, K., Yu, K., & Simons, M. B. (2001). Bullies, victims, and bully/victims: Distinct groups of at-risk youth. *J. Early Adolescence, 21*(1), 29–49.

Hayward, M. D., & Taylor, J. E. (1965). A schizophrenic patient describes the action of intensive psychotherapy. *Psychiat. Quart., 30.*

Hazell, P., & Lewin, T. (1993). Friends of adolescent suicide attempters and completers. *J. Amer. Acad. Child Adol. Psychiat., 32*(1), 76–81.

Head, J, Stansfeld, S. A., & Siegrist, J. (2004). The psychosocial work environment and alcohol dependence: A prospective study. *Occupational Environmental Medicine, 61*(3), 219–224.

Heap, L. C., Pratt, O. E., Ward, R. J. Waller, S., Thomson, A. D., & Shaw, G. K. (2002). Individual susceptibility to Wernicke-Korsakoff syndrome and alcoholism-induced cognitive deficit impaired thiamine utilization found in alcoholics and alcohol abusers. *Psychiat. Genet., 12*(4), 217–224.

Heard, H. L., & Linehan, M. M. (2005). Integrative therapy for borderline personality disorder. In J. C. Norcross & M. R. Goldfried (Eds.), *Handbook of psychotherapy integration* (2nd ed., pp. 299–320). New York: Oxford University Press.

Heard-Davison, A., Heiman, J. R., & Briggs, B. (2004). Sexual disorders affecting women. In L. J. Haas (Ed.), *Handbook of primary care psychology* (pp. 495–509). New York: Oxford University Press.

Heather, N., Winton, M., & Rollnick, S. (1982). An empirical test of "a cultural delusion of alcoholics." *Psychol. Rep., 50*(2), 379–382.

Heavey, L., Pring, L., & Hermelin, B. (1999). A date to remember: The nature of memory in savant calendrical calculators. *Psychol. Med., 29*(1), 145–160.

Hechler, T., Beumont, P., Marks, P., & Touyz, S. (2005). How do clinical specialists understand the role of physical activity in eating disorders? *Eur. Eat. Disord. Rev., 13*(2), 125–132.

Hecimovic, H., & Gilliam, F. G. (2006). Neurobiology of depression and new opportunities for treatment. In F. G. Gilliam, A. M. Kanner, & Y. I. Sheline (Eds.), *Depression and brain dysfunction* (pp. 51–84). New York: Taylor & Francis.

Heffernan, T. M., Jarvis, H., Rodgers, J., Scholey, A. B., & Ling, J. (2001). Prospective memory, everyday cognitive failure and central executive function in recreational users of Ecstasy. *Human Psychopharmacol. Clin. Exp., 16*(8), 607–612.

Heiby, E. M. (2002). Concluding remarks on the debate about prescription privileges for psychologists. *J. Clin. Psychol., 58*(6), 709–722.

Heilbrun, K., Goldstein, N. E. S, & Redding, R. E. (Eds.). (2005). *Juvenile delinquency: Prevention, assessment, and intervention* (pp. 85–110). New York: Oxford University Press.

Heiman, J. R. (2000). Organic disorders in women. In S. R. Leiblum & R. C. Rosen (Eds.), *Principles and practice of sex therapy* (3rd ed., pp. 118–153). New York: Guilford Press.

Heiman, J. R. (2002). Psychologic treatments for female sexual dysfunction: Are they effective and do we need them? *Arch. Sex. Behav., 31,* 445–450.

Heiman, J. R. (2002). Sexual dysfunction: Overview of prevalence, etiological factors, and treatments. *J. Sex Res., 39*(1), 73–78.

Heiman, J. R., Gladue, B. A., Roberts, C. W., & LoPiccolo, J. (1986). Historical and current factors discriminating sexually functional from sexually dysfunctional married couples. *J. Marital Fam. Ther., 12*(2), 163–174.

Heiman, J. R., & Heard-Davison, A. R. (2004). Child sexual abuse and adult sexual relationships: Review and perspective. In L. K. Koenig, L. Doll, A. O'Leary, & W. Pequegnat (Eds.), *From child sexual abuse to adult sexual risk: Trauma, revictimization, and intervention* (pp. 13–47). Washington, DC: American Psychological Association.

Heiman, J. R., & LoPiccolo, J. (1988) *Becoming orgasmic: A personal and sexual growth program for women.* New York: Prentice Hall.

Heimberg, R. G. (2003). Cognitive-behavioral and psychotherapeutic strategies for social anxiety disorder. In M. R. Liebowitz (Ed.), *Beyond shyness: Recognition, diagnosis, and treatment of social anxiety disorder at the annual meeting of the Anxiety Disorders Association of America, Toronto, Ontario, Canada.*

Heimberg, R. G., Turk, C. L., Mennin, D. S. (Eds.). (2004). *Generalized anxiety disorder: Advances in research and practice.* New York: Guilford Press.

Heinlen, K. T., Welfel, E. R., Richmond, E. N., & O'Donnell, M. S. (2003). The nature, scope, and ethics of psychologists' e-therapy Web sites: What consumers find when surfing the Web. *Psychotherapy, Theory, Research, Practice, Training, 40*(1–2), 112–124.

Heinrichs, D. W., & Carpenter, W. T., Jr. (1983). The coordination of family therapy with other treatment modalities for schizophrenia. In W. McFarlane (Ed.), *Family therapy in schizophrenia.* New York: Guilford Press.

Heinrichs, R. W. (2005). The primacy of cognition in schizophrenia. *Amer. Psychologist, 60*(3), 229–242.

Helgeson, V. S. (2002). *The psychology of gender.* Upper Saddle River, NJ: Prentice Hall.

Helzer, J. E., Burnam, A., & McEvoy, L. T. (1991). Alcohol abuse and dependence. In L. N. Robins & D. S. Regier (Eds.), *Psychiatric disorders in America: The Epidemiological Catchment Area Study.* New York: Free Press.

Hempel, S. (2005). Reliability. In J. Miles & P. Gilbert (Eds.), *A handbook of research methods for clinical and health psychology* (pp. 193–204). New York: Oxford University Press.

Henderson, D. (2004, October 16). FDA orders strong antidepressant warnings. *Associated Press.*

Henderson, S. (2005, June 7). Court loss for medical marijuana. *Philadephia Inquirer.*

Hendin, H. (1999). Suicide, assisted suicide, and medical illness. *J. Clin. Psychiat., 60*(Suppl. 2), 46–50.

Hendin, H. (2002). The Dutch experience. In K. Foley & H. Hendin (Eds.), *The case against assisted suicide: For the right to end-of-life care* (pp. 97–121). Baltimore, MD: The John Hopkins University Press.

Hendin, H., Maltsberger, J. T., Lipschitz, A., Haas, A. P., & Kyle, J. (2001). Recognizing and responding to a suicide crisis. In H. Hendin & J. J. Mann (Eds.), *The clinical science of suicide prevention* (Vol. 932, pp. 169–187). New York: Annals of the New York Academy of Sciences.

Hendren, J. (1999, April 15). Prescription errors blamed on pharmaceutical name game. *Nando Times.*

Henggeler, S. W., & Lee, T. (2003). Multisystemic treatment of serious clinical problems. In A. E. Kazdin & J. R. Weisz (Eds.), *Evidence-based psychotherapies for children and adolescents.* New York: Guilford Press.

Henley, T. C., & Thorne, B. M. (2005). The lost millennium: Psychology during the Middle Ages. *Psychol. Rec., 55*(1), 103–113.

Henn, F. A., & Vollmayr, B. (2005). Stress models of depression: Forming genetically vulnerable strains. *Neurosci. Biobehav. Rev., 29*(4–5), 799–804.

Hennig, J. (2004). Personality, serotonin, and noradrenaline. In R. M. Stelmack (Ed.), *On the psychobiology of personality: Essays in honor of Marvin Zuckerman* (pp. 379–408). New York: Elsevier Science.

Henning, C. W., Crabtree, C. R., & Baum, D. (1998). Mental health CPR: Peer contracting as a response to potential suicide in adolescents. *Arch. Suic. Res., 4*(2), 169–187.

Henningsson, S., Westberg, L., Nilsson, S., Lundstrom, B., Ekselius, L., Bodlund, O., et al. (2005). Sex steroid-related genes and male-to-female transsexualism. *Psychoneuroendocrinology, 30*(7), 657–664.

Henry, R. G., & Miller, R. B. (2004). Marital problems occurring in midlife: Implications for couples therapists. *Amer. J. Fam. Ther., 32*(5), 405–417.

Hepp, U., Klaghofer, R., Burkhard, K., & Buddeberg, C. (2002). Treatment history of transsexual patients: A retrospective follow-up study., *Nervenarzt, 73*(3), 283–288.

Hepp, U., Kraemer, B., Schnyder, U., Miller, N., & Delsignore, A. (2005). Psychiatric comorbidity in gender identity disorder. *J. Psychosom. Res., 58*(3), 259–261.

Herbeck, D. M., West, J. C., Ruditis, I., Duffy, F. F., Fitek, D. J., Bell, C. C., et al. (2004). Variations in use of second-generation antipsychotic medication by race among adult psychiatric patients. *Psychiatr. Serv., 55*(6), 677–684.

Herman, N. J. (1999). Road rage: An exploratory analysis." *Michigan Sociol. Rev., 13,* 65–79.

Herning, R. I., Better, W. E., Tate, K., & Cadet, J. L. (2005). Cerebrovascular perfusion in marijuana users during a month of monitored abstinence. *Neurology, 64,* 488–493.

Hersen, M. (Ed.). (2004). *Psychological assessment in clinical practice: A pragmatic guide.* New York: Brunner-Routledge.

Hersen, M., Bellack, A. S., Himmelhoch, J. M., & Thase, M. E. (1984). Effects of social skill training, amitriptyline, and psychotherapy in unipolar depressed women. *Behav. Ther., 15,* 21–40.

Herzog, D. B., Dorer, D. J., Keel, P. K., Selwin, S. E., Ekeblad, E. R., Flores, A. T., et al. (1999). Recovery and relapse in anorexia and bulimia nervosa: A 7.5–year follow-up study. *J. Amer. Acad. Child Adol. Psychiat., 38*(7), 829–837.

Herzog, T., Zeeck, A., Hartmann, A., & Nickel, T. (2004). Lower targets for weekly weight gain lead to better results in inpatient treatment of anorexia nervosa: A pilot study. *Eur. Eat. Disord. Rev., 12*(3), 164–168.

Hess, N. (1995). Cancer as a defence against depressive pain. University College Hospital/ Middlesex Hospital Psychotherapy Department. *Psychoanalytic Psychother., 9*(2), 175–184.

Hesselbrock, M., & Hesselbrock, V. (1992). Relationship of family history, antisocial personality disorder and personality traits in young men at risk for alcoholism. *J. Stud. Alcohol, 53*(6), 1992, 619–625.

Hester, R. K. (1995). Behavioral self-control training. In R. K. Hester & W. R. Miller (Eds.), *Handbook of alcoholism treatment approaches: Effective alternatives* (2nd ed.). Boston: Allyn & Bacon.

Heston, L. L. (1992). *Mending minds: A guide to the new psychiatry of depression, anxiety, and other serious mental disorders.* New York: W. H. Freeman.

Hettema, J. M., Neale, M. C., & Kendler, K. S. (2001). A review and meta-analysis of genetic epidemiology off anxiety disorders. *Amer. J. Psychiat., 158*(10), 1568–1578.

Hettema, J. M., Prescott, C. A., & Kendler, K. S. (2001). A population-based twin study of generalized anxiety disorder in men and women. *J. Nerv. Ment. Dis., 189*(7), 413–420.

Heun, R., & Hein, S. (2005). Risk factors of major depression in the elderly. *Eur. Psychiat. 20*(3), 199–204.

HEW (Health Education and Welfare). (1976). Even my kids didn't know I was an alcoholic: An interview with Dick Van Dyke (ADM 76–348). Washington, DC: U.S. Government Printing Office.

Heydebrand, G., & Wetzel, R. D. (2005). Psychological testing. In E. H. Rubin & C. F. Zorumski (Eds.), *Adult psychiatry* (2nd ed.). Oxford, England: Blackwell Publishing Ltd.

Heyman, R. E., & Slep, A. M. S. (2002). Do child abuse and interparental violence lead to adulthood family violence? *J. Marr. Fam., 64*(4), 864–870.

HHS (Department of Health and Human Services). (2004). NIDA info facts: Rohypnol and GBH. Washington, DC: NIH-HHS-NIDA.

Hibbs, E. D., & Jensen, P. S. (Eds.). *Psychosocial treatments for child and adolescent disorders: Empirically based strategies for clinical practice* (2nd ed., pp. 3–8). Washington, DC: American Psychological Association.

Hickey, E. (2002). *Serial murderers and their victims* (3rd ed.). Belmont: Wadsworth.

Hiday, V. A. (1999). Mental illness and the criminal justice system. In A. V. Horwitz & T. L. Scheid (Eds.), *A handbook for the study of mental health: Social contexts, theories, and systems.* Cambridge, England: Cambridge University Press.

Higgins, G. A., Large, C. H., Rupniak, H. T., & Barnes, J. C. (1997). Apolipoprotein E and

Alzheimer's disease: A review of recent studies. *Pharmacol. Biochem. Behav., 56*(4), 675–685.

Higgins, S. T., Budney, A. J., Bickel, W. K., Hughes, J., Foerg, F., & Badger, G. (1993). Achieving cocaine abstinence with a behavioral approach. *Amer. J. Psychiat., 150*(5), 763–769.

Higgins, S. T., Heil, S. H., & Lussier, J. P. (2004). Clinical implications of reinforcement as a determinant of substance use disorders. *Annu. Rev. Psychol., 55,* 401–430.

Highet, N., Thompson, M., & McNair, B. (2005). Identifying depression in a family member: The carers' experience. *J. Affect. Disorders, 87*(1), 25–33.

Hilbert, A., Schnur, A. B., & Wilfley, D. E. (2005). Obesity and binge eating disorder. In E. H. Rubin & C. F. Zorumski (Eds.), *Adult psychiatry* (2nd ed., pp. 247–260). Oxford, England: Blackwell Publishing Ltd.

Hildebrand, K. M., Johnson, D. J., Dewayne, J., & Bogle, K. (2001). Comparison of patterns of alcohol use between high school and college athletes and non-athletes. *Coll. Student J., 35,* 358–365.

Hileman, B. (2001, April 9). The "mad" disease has many forms: Has the U.S. government taken sufficient measures to keep it from infecting humans? *Chem. Eng. News.*

Hilgard, E. R. (1977). Controversies over consciousness and the rise of cognitive psychology. *Austral. Psychologist, 12*(1), 7–26.

Hilgard, E. R. (1987). Research advances in hypnosis: Issues and methods. *Inter. J. Clin. Exp. Hyp., 35,* 248–264.

Hilgard, E. R. (1992). Dissociation and theories of hypnosis. In E. Fromm & M. R. Nash (Eds.), *Contemporary hypnosis research.* New York: Guilford Press.

Hill, A. J., & Robinson, A. (1991). Dieting concerns have a functional effect on the behaviour of nine-year-old girls. *Brit. J. Clin. Psychol., 30*(3), 265–267.

Hill, J. (2003). Childhood trauma and depression. *Curr. Opin. Psychiat., 16*(1), 3–6.

Hill, J., & Maughan, B. (Eds.). (2001). *Conduct disorders in childhood and adolescence.* New York: Cambridge University Press.

Hingson, R., Heeren, T., Zakocs, R., Kopstein, A., & Wechsler, H. (2002). Magnitude of alcohol-related morbidity, mortality, and alcohol dependence among U.S. college students age 18–24. *J. Stud. Alc., 63*(2), 136–144.

Hinrichsen, G. A. (1999). Interpersonal psychotherapy for late-life depression In M. Duffy (Ed.), *Handbook of counseling and psychotherapy with older adults.* New York: Wiley.

Hiroeh, U., Appleby, L., Mortensen, P.-B., & Dunn, G. (2001). Death by homicide, suicide, and other unnatural causes in people with mental illness: A population-based study. *Lancet, 358*(9299), 2110–2112.

Hirsch, A. T., Gervino, E. V., Nakao, S., Come, P. C., Silverman, K. J., & Grossman, W. (1989). The effect of caffeine on exercise tolerance and left ventricular function in patients with coronary artery disease. *Ann. Intern. Med., 110*(8), 593–598.

Hirsch, S., Adams, J. K., Frank, L. R., Hudson, W., Keene, R., Krawitz-Keene, G., et al. (Eds.). (1974). *Madness: Network news reader.* San Francisco: Glide Publications.

Hirsch, S., & Leff, J. (1975). *Abnormalities in parents of schizophrenics.* Oxford: Oxford University Press.

Hirschfeld, R. M. (1999). Efficacy of SSRIs and newer antidepressants in severe depression: Comparison with TCAs. *J. Clin. Psychiat., 60*(5), 326–335.

Hirschfeld, R. M., & Russell, J. M. (1997). Assessment and treatment of suicidal patients. *N. Engl. J. Med., 337,* 910–915.

Hitti, M. (2004). Brain chemicals suggest marijuana's effects. *WebMD.* Retrieved September 24, 2004, from my.webmd.com/content/Article/94/102660.htm

Hjerl, K., Andersen, E. W., Keiding, N., Mouridsen, H. T., Mortensen, P. B., & Jorgensen, T. (2003). Depression as a prognostic for breast cancer mortality. *Psychosom. J. Cons. Liaison Psychiat., 44*(1), 24–30.

Hlastala, S. A., Frank, E., Mallinger, A. G., Thase, M. E., Ritenour, A. M., & Kupfer, D. J. (1997). Bipolar depression: An underestimated treatment challenge. *Depress. Anx., 5,* 73–83.

Ho, T. P., Hung, S. F., Lee, C. C., Chung, K. F., et al. (1995). Characteristics of youth suicide in Hong Kong. *Soc. Psychiat. Psychiatr. Epidemiol., 30*(3), 107–112.

Hoagwood, K., Kelleher, K. J., Feil, M., & Comer, D. M. (2000). Treatment services for children with ADHD: A national perspective. *J. Amer. Acad. Child Adol. Psychiat., 39*(2), 198–206.

Hobbs, F. B. (1997). The elderly population. *U.S. Census Bureau: The official statistics.* Washington, DC: U.S. Census Bureau.

Hobson, A. (2004). A model for madness? Dream consciousness: Our understanding of the neurobiology of sleep offers insight into abnormalities in the waking brain. *Nature, 430*(6995), 21.

Hobson, C. J., Kamen, J., Szostek, J., Nethercut, C. M., Tiedmann, J. W., & Wojnarowicz, S. (1998). Stressful life events: A revision and update of the Social Readjustment Rating Scale. *Inter. J. Stress Manag., 5*(1), 1–23.

Hochman, G. (2000, Oct. 22). Portrait of madness. *The Philadelphia Inquirer (Inquirer Magazine).*

Hodapp, R. M., & Dykens, E. M. (2003). Mental retardation (intellectual disabilities). In E. J. Mash & R. A. Barkley (Eds.), *Child psychopathology* (2nd ed.). New York: Guilford Press.

Hodges, J. R. (2001). Frontotemporal dementia (Pick's disease): Clinical features and assessment. *Neurol., 56*(Suppl. 4), S6–S10.

Hodgson, R. J., & Rachman, S. (1972). The effects of contamination and washing in obsessional patients. *Behav. Res. Ther., 10,* 111–117.

Hoek, H. W., & van Koeken, D. (2003). Review of the prevalence and incidence of eating disorders. *Inter. J. Eat. Disorders, 34*(4), 383–396.

Hofmann, S. G., & Barlow, D. H. (2002). Social phobia (social anxiety disorder). In D. H. Barlow (Ed.), *Anxiety and its disorders: The nature and treatment of anxiety and panic* (2nd ed., pp. 454–476). New York: Guilford Press.

Hogan, R. A. (1968). The implosive technique. *Behav. Res. Ther., 6,* 423–431.

Hogarty, G. E. (2002). Personal therapy for schizophrenia and related disorders: A guide to individualized treatment. New York: Guilford Press.

Hogarty, G. E., Anderson, C. M., Reiss, D. J., Kornblith, S. J., Greenwald, D. P., Javna, C. D., et al. (1986). Family psychoeducation, social skills training, and maintenance chemotherapy in the aftercare treatment of schizophrenia: I. One-year effects of a controlled study on relapse and expressed emotion. *Arch. Gen. Psychiat., 43*(7), 633–642.

Hogarty, G. E., Schooler, N. R., & Ulrich, R. F. (1974). Drug and sociotherapy in the aftercare of schizophrenic patients: III. Two-year relapse rates. *Arch. Gen. Psychiat., 31*(5), 609–618.

Holaway, R. M., Rodebaugh, T. L., & Heimberg, R. G. (2006). The epidemiology of worry and generalized anxiety disorder. In G. C. L. Davey & A. Wells (Eds.), *Worry and psychological disorders: Theory, assessment and treatment.* Chichester, England: Wiley.

Holden, C. (2004, February 6). FDA weighs suicide risk in children on antidepressants. *Science, 303,* p. 745.

Holder, H., Longabaugh, R., Miller, W., et al. (1991). The cost effectiveness of treatment for alcoholism: A first approximation. *J. Stud. Alc., 52,* 517–540.

Holinger, P. C., & Offer, D. (1982). Prediction of adolescent suicide: A population model. *Amer. J. Psychiat., 139,* 302–307.

Holinger, P. C., & Offer, D. (1991). Sociodemographic, epidemiologic, and individual attributes. In L. Davidson & M. Linnoila (Eds.), *Risk factors for youth suicide.* New York: Hemisphere.

Holinger, P. C., & Offer, D. (1993). *Adolescent suicide.* New York: Guilford Press.

Holland, J. (2001). The history of MDMA. In J. Holland (Ed.), *Ecstasy: The complete guide: A comprehensive look at the risks and benefits of MDMA* (pp. 11–20). Rochester, VT: Park Street Press.

Hollander, M. H. (1988). Hysteria and memory. In H. M. Pettinati (Ed.), *Hypnosis and memory.* New York: Guilford Press.

Hollon, S. D., DeRubeis, R. J., Shelton, R. C., Amsterdam, J. D., Salomon, R. M., O'Reardon, J. P., et al. (2005). Prevention of relapse following cognitive therapy v. medications in moderate to severe depression. *Arch. Gen. Psychiat., 62,* 417–422.

Hollon, S. D., Haman, K. L., & Brown, L. L. (2002). Cognitive behavioral treatment of depression. In I. H. Gotlib & C. L. Hammen (Eds.), *Handbook of depression* (pp. 383–403). New York: Guilford Press.

Hollon, S. D., Stewart, M. O., & Strunk D. (2006). Enduring effects for cognitive behavior therapy in the treatment of depression and anxiety. *Annu. Rev. Psychol., 57,* 285–315.

Holmes, R. M., & DeBurger, J. E. (1985). Profiles in terror: The serial murderer. *Fed. Probation, 49,* 29–34.

Holmes, S. B., Banerjee, A. K., & Alexander, W. D. (1999). Hyponatreaemia and seizures after ecstasy use. *Postgrad. Med. J., 75*(879), 32–33.

Holmes, T. H., & Rahe, R. H. (1967). The Social Readjustment Rating Scale. *J. Psychosom. Res., 11,* 213–218.

Holmes, T. H., & Rahe, R. H. (1989). The Social Readjustment Rating Scale. In T. H. Holmes & E. M. David (Eds.), *Life change, life events, and illness: Selected papers.* New York: Praeger.

Holsboer, F. (2001). Stress, hypercortisolism and corticosteroid receptors in depression: Implications for therapy. *J. Affect. Disorders, 62*(1–2), 77–91.

Holstein, J. A. (1993). *Court-ordered insanity: Interpretive practice and involuntary commitment.* New York: Aldine de Gruyter.

Holtzheimer, P. E. III, Russo, J., Zatzick, D., Bundy, C., & Roy-Byrne, P. R. (2005). The impact of comorbid posttraumatic stress disorder on short-term clinical outcome in hospitalized patients with depression. *Amer. J. Psychiat., 162*(5), 970–976.

Holzman, P. S. (1986). Quality of thought disorder in differential diagnosis. *Schizo. Bull., 12,* 360–372.

Homant, R. J., & Kennedy, D. B. (2006). Serial murder: A biopsychosocial approach. In W. Petherick (Ed.), *Serial crime: Theoretical and practical issues in behavioral profiling* (pp. 189–228). San Diego, CA: Elsevier.

Honberg, R. (2005). Decriminalizing mental illness. *NAMI Advocate, 3*(1), 4–5.

Hong, J. P., Samuels, J., Bienvenu, O. J. III, Cannistraro, P., Grados, M., Riddle, M. A., et al. (2004). Clinical correlates of recurrent major depression in obsessive-compulsive disorder. *Depress. Anx., 20*(2), 86–91.

Honikman, J. I. (1999). Role of self-help techniques for postpartum mood disorders. In L. J. Miller (Ed.), *Postpartum mood disorders.* Washington, DC: American Psychiatric Press.

Honkonen, T., Karlsson, H., Koivisto, A. M., Stengard, E., Salokangas, R. K. R. (2003). Schizophrenic patients in different treatment settings during the era of deinstitutionalization: Three-year follow-up of three discharge cohorts in Finland. *Austral. New Zeal. J. Psychiat., 37*(2), 160–168.

Hooper, J. F., McLearen, A. M., & Barnett, M. E. (2005). The Alabama structured assessment of treatment completion for insanity acquittees (The AlaSATcom). *Inter. J. Law Psychiat., 28*(6), 604–612.

Horley, J. (2001). Frotteurism: A term in search of an underlying disorder? *J. Sex. Aggress., 7*(1), 51–55.

Horner, A. J. (1975). Stages and processes in the development of early object relations and their associated pathologies. *Inter. Rev. Psychoanal., 2,* 95–105.

Horner, A. J. (1991). *Psychoanalytic object relations therapy.* Northvale, NJ: Jason Aronson.

Horney, K. (1937). *The neurotic personality of our time.* New York: Norton.

Hornyak, L. M., & Green, J. P. (2000). *Healing from within: The use of hypnosis in women's health care. Dissociation, trauma, memory, and hypnosis book series.* Washington, DC: American Psychological Association.

Horowitz, J., Damato, E., Solon, L., Metzsch, G., & Gill, V. (1995). Postpartum depression: Issues in clinical assessment. *J. Perinat. Med., 15*(4), 268–278.

Horowitz, J. A., Damato, E. G., Duffy, M. E., & Solon, L. (2005). The relationship of maternal attributes, resources, and perceptions of postpartum experiences to depression. *Res. Nursing Hlth., 28*(2), 159–171.

Hou, C., Miller, B. L., Cummings, J. L., Goldberg, M., Mychack, P., Bottino, V., et al. (2000). Artistic savants. *Neuropsychiat., Neuropsychol., Behav. Neurol., 13*(1), 29–38.

Housman, L. M., & Stake, J. E. (1999). The current state of sexual ethics training in clinical psychology: Issues of quantity, quality and effectiveness. *Profess. Psychol.: Res. Pract., 30*(3), 302–311.

Houston, K., Hawton, K., & Sheppard, R. (2001). Suicide in young people aged 15–24: A psychological autopsy study. *J. Affect. Disorders, 63*(1–3), 159–170.

Houts, A. C. (2003). Behavioral treatment for enuresis. In A. E. Kazdin & J. R. Weisz (Eds.), *Evidence-based psychotherapies for children and adolescents.* New York: Guilford Press.

Hoven, C. W., Duarte, C. S., Lucas, C. P., Wu, P., Mandell, D. J., Goodwin, R. D., et al. (2005). Psychopathology among New York City public school children 6 months after September 11. *Arch. Gen. Psychiat., 62*(5), 545–551.

Howe, R., & Nugent, T. (1996, April 22). The gory details. *People,* pp. 91–92.

Howells, J. G., & Guirguis, W. R. (1985). *The family and schizophrenia.* New York: International Universities Press.

Howitt, D. (1995). *Paedophiles and sexual offences against children.* Chichester, England: Wiley.

Hoyer, W. J., & Verhaeghen, P. (2006). Memory aging. In J. E. Birren & K. W. Schaie (Eds.), *Handbook of the psychology of aging* (6th ed., pp. 209–232). San Diego, CA: Elsevier Academic Press.

Hoyert, D. L., Arias, E., Smith, B. L., Murphy, S. L., & Kochanek, K. D. (2001). Deaths: Final data for 1999. In *National Vital Statistics Report, 49*(8). Hyattsville, MD: National Center for Health Statistics.

Hoyt, M. F. (2003). Brief psychotherapies. In A. S. Gurman & S. B. Messer (Eds.), *Essential psychotherapies: Theory and practice* (2nd ed.). New York: Guilford Press.

Hrobjartsson, A., & Gotzsche, P. C. (2001). Is the placebo powerless? An analysis of clinical trials comparing placebo with no treatment. *N. Engl. J. Med., 344*(21), 1594–1602.

Hsu, L. K. G., & Holder, D. (1986). Bulimia nervosa: Treatment and short-term outcome. *Psychol. Med., 16,* 65.

Hu, S., Pattatucci, A. M. L., Patterson, C., Li, L., et al. (1995, November). Linkage between sexual orientation and chromosome Xq28 in males but not in females. *Nat. Genet., 11,* 248–256.

Hudson, J. L., & Rapee, R. M. (2004). From anxious temperament to disorder: An etiological model of generalized anxiety disorder. In R. G. Heimberg, C. L. Turk, & D. S. Mennin (Eds.), *Generalized anxiety disorder: Advances in research and practice* (pp. 51–74). New York: Guilford Press.

Hugdahl, K. (1995). *Psychophysiology: The mind-body perspective.* Cambridge, MA: Harvard University Press.

Hüll, M., Berger, M., Volk, B., & Bauer, J. (1996). Occurrence of interleukin-6 in cortical plaques of Alzheimer's disease patients may precede transformation of diffuse into neuritic plaques. In R. J. Wurtman, S. Corkin, J. H. Growdon, & R. M. Nitsch (Eds.), *The neurobiology of Alzheimer's disease.* New York: New York Academy of Sciences.

Hullett, C. R. (2005). Grieving families: Social support after the death of a loved one. In E. B. Ray (Ed.), *Health communication in practice: A case study approach* (pp. 211–221). Mahwah, NJ: Lawrence Erlbaum Associates.

Humphrey, J. A. (2006). *Deviant behavior.* Upper Saddle River, NJ: Pearson/Prentice Hall.

Humphreys, K. (1996). Clinical psychologists as psychotherapists. History, future, and alternatives. *Amer. Psychologist, 51*(3), 190–197.

Humphry, D., & Wickett, A. (1986). *The right to die: Understanding euthanasia.* New York: Harper & Row.

Hunnicutt, C. P., & Newman, I. A. (1993). Adolescent dieting practices and nutrition knowledge. Health values. *Journal of Health Behavior, Education and Promotion, 17*(4), 35–40.

Hunt, C., & Andrews, G. (1995). Comorbidity in the anxiety disorders: The use of a life-chart approach. *J. Psychiatr. Res., 29*(6), 467–480.

Huntington, D. D., & Bender, W. N. (1993). Adolescents with learning disabilities at risk: Emotional well-being, depression, suicide. *J. Learn. Dis., 26*(3), 159–166.

Huntjens, R. J. C., Peters, M. L., Postma, A., Woertman, L., Effting, M., & van der Hart, O. (2005). Transfer of newly acquired stimulus valence between identities in dissociative identity disorder (DID). *Behav. Res. Ther., 43*(2), 243–255.

Hurlbert, D. F. (1991). The role of assertiveness in female sexuality: A comparative study between sexually assertive and sexually nonassertive women. *J. Sex Marital Ther., 17*(3), 183–190.

Hurlbert, D. F. (1993). A comparative study using orgasm consistency training in the treatment of women reporting hypoactive sexual desire. *J. Sex Marital Ther., 19,* 41–55.

Hurt, S., & Oltmanns, T. F. (2002). Personality traits and pathology in older and younger incarcerated women. *J. Clin. Psychol., 58*(4), 457–464.

Huss, M. T., & Zeiss, R. A. (2005). You have the right not to have a hearing: An evaluation of the impact of fully advising civilly committed patients on their rights. *Inter. J. Law Psychiat., 28*(4), 334–341.

Hyams, H. (2003). Trauma post traumatic stress disorder (PTSD) and the case of Vincent Van Gogh. *Inter. J. Psychother., 8*(2), 95–107.

Hyde, J. S. (1990). *Understanding human sexuality* (4th ed.). New York: McGraw-Hill.

Hyde, J. S. (2005). The genetics of sexual orientation. In J. S. Hyde (Ed.), *Biological substrates of human sexuality.* Washington, DC: American Psychological Association.

Hyler, S. E., & Spitzer, R. T. (1978). Hysteria split asunder. *Amer. J. Psychiat., 135,* 1500–1504.

Hyman, Jr, I. E., & Loftus, E. F. (2002). False childhood memories and eyewitness memory errors. In M. L. Eisen (Ed.), *Memory and suggestibility in the forensic interview. Personality and clinical psychology series* (pp. 63–84). Mahwah, NJ: Lawrence Erlbaum Associates.

Hymowitz, N. (2005). Tobacco. In R. J. Frances, A. H. Mack, & S. I. Miller (Eds.), *Clinical textbook of addictive disorders* (3rd ed., pp. 105–137). New York: Guilford Press.

Ibanez, G. E., Buck, C. A., Khatchikian, N., & Norris, F. H. (2004). Qualitative analysis of coping strategies among Mexican disaster survivors. *Anx., Stress, Coping: Inter. J., 17*(1), 69–85.

Iga, M. (1993). Japanese suicide. In A. A. Leenaars (Ed.), *Suicidology.* Northvale, NJ: Jason Aronson.

Iga, M. (2001). The thorn in the chrysanthemum: Suicide and economic success in modern Japan. In E. S. Shneidman (Ed.), *Comprehending suicide: Landmarks in 20th-century suicidology* (pp. 59–68). Washington, DC: American Psychological Association.

Ihle, W., Jahnke, D., Heerwagen, A., & Neuperdt, C. (2005). Depression, anxiety, and eating disorders and recalled parental rearing behavior. *Kindheit Entwicklung, 14*(1), 30–38.

Iketani, T., Kiriike, N., Nakanishi, S., & Nakasuji, T. (1995). Effects of weight gain and resumption of menses on reduced bone density in patients with anorexia nervosa. *Biol. Psychiat., 37*(80), 521–527.

Innes, M. (2002). Satir's therapeutically oriented educational process: A critical appreciation. *Contemp. Fam. Therap: Internat. J., 24*(1), 35–56.

Inouye, S. K. (1998). Delirium in hospitalized older patients: Recognition and risk factors. *J. Geriat. Psychiat. Neurol., 11*(3), 118–125.

Inouye, S. K. (1999). Predisposing and precipitating factors for delirium in hospitalized older patients. *Dement. Ger. Cogn. Disord., 10*(5), 393–400.

Inouye, S. K., Bogardus, S. T., Jr., Charpentier, P. A., Leo-Summers, L., Acampora, D., Holford, T. R., et al. (1999). A multicomponent intervention to prevent delirium in hospitalized older patients. *N. Engl. J. Med., 340*(9), 669–676.

Inselmann, U. (2004). Bio-psycho-social burdens at old age: Theoretical and psychotherapeutic implications of the experience of loss. *Psychother. Forum, 12*(3), 140–146.

Institute of Medicine (of the National Academies). (2004). *Immunization safety review: Autism and vaccines.* Washington, DC: National Academies Press.

Irvine, M. (2005, May 30). Cult-like lure of "Ana" attracts anorexics. *Associated Press (Chicago)/Netscape News with CNN.*

Irwin, M. R., & Cole, J. C. (2005). Depression and psychonueroimmunology. In K. Vedhara & M. Irwin (Eds.), *Human psychoneuroimmunology.* Oxford, England: Oxford University Press.

Isacson, D., Bingefors, K., & von Knorring, L. (2005). The impact of depression is unevenly distributed in the population. *Eur. Psychiat., 20*(3), 205–212.

Isenberg, D. H., Loomis, C., Humphreys, K., & Maton, K. I. (2004). Self-help research: Issues of power sharing. In L. A. Jason, C. B. Keys, Y. Suarez-Balcazar, R. R. Taylor, & M. L. Davis (Eds.), *Participatory community research: Theories and methods in action.* Washington, DC: American Psychological Association.

Isometsae, E. T., & Loennqvist, J. K. (1998). Suicide attempts preceding completed suicide. *Brit. J. Psychiat., 173,* 531–535.

Ito, A., Ichihara, M., Hisanaga, N., Ono, Y., et al. (1992). Prevalence of seasonal mood changes in low latitude area: Seasonal Pattern Assessment Questionnaire score of Quezon City workers. *Jpn. J. Psychiatry, 46,* 249.

Iversen, L. L. (1975). Dopamine receptors in the brain. *Science, 188,* 1084–1089.

Jablensky, A. (2000). Epidemiology of schizophrenia: The global burden of disease and disability. *Eur. Arch. Psychiat. Clin. Neurosci., 250,* 274–285.

Jablensky, A. (2002). The classification of personality disorders: Critical review and need for rethinking. *Psychopathology, 35*(2–3), 112–116.

Jackson, J. S. (Ed.). (1988). *The black American elderly: Research on physical and psychosocial health.* New York: Springer.

Jackson, J. S., Torres, M., Caldwell, C. H., Neighbors, H. W., Nesse, R. M., Taylor, R. J., et al. (2004). The National Survey of American Life: A study of racial, ethnic and cultural influences on mental disorders and mental health. *Inter. J. Methods Psychiatr. Res., 13*(4), 196–207.

Jacobs, B. L. (Ed.). (1984). *Hallucinogens: Neurochemical, behavioral, and clinical perspectives.* New York: Raven Press.

Jacobs, B. L. (1994). Serotonin, motor activity and depression-related disorders. *Amer. Sci., 82,* 456–463.

Jacobs, D. G., Brewer, M., & Klein-Benheim, M. (1999). Suicide assessment: An overview and recommended protocol. In D. G. Jacobs (Ed.), *The Harvard Medical School guide to suicide assessment and intervention.* San Francisco: Jossey-Bass.

Jacobs, M. (2003). *Sigmund Freud.* London: Sage.

Jacobs, M. K., Christensen, A., Snibbe, J. R., Dolezal-Wood, S., Huber, A., & Polterok, A. (2001). A comparison of computer-based versus traditional individual psychotherapy. *Profess. Psychol.: Res. Pract., 32*(1), 92–96.

Jacobsen, L. K., Rabinowitz, I., Popper, M. S., Solomon, R. J., Sokol, M. S., & Pfeffer, C. R. (1994). Interviewing prepubertal children about suicidal ideation and behavior. *J. Amer. Acad. Child Adol. Psychiat., 33*(4), 439–452.

Jacobson, G. (1999). The inpatient management of suicidality. In D. G. Jacobs (Ed.), *The Harvard Medical School guide to suicide assessment and intervention.* San Francisco: Jossey-Bass.

Jacobson, J. M. (2005). Guest editorial: Workplace crisis intervention and employee assistance programs (EAPs). *Inter. J. Emerg. Ment. Hlth., 7*(3), 155–156.

Jacobson, J. W., & Mulick, J. A. (1996). Definition of mental retardation. In J. W. Jacobson & J. A. Mulick (Eds.), *Manual of diagnosis and professional practice in mental retardation* (pp. 13–53). Washington, DC: American Psychological Association.

Jacobson, J. W., & Schwartz, A. A. (1991). Evaluating living situations of people with development disabilities. In J. L. Matson & J. A. Mulick (Eds.), *Handbook of mental retardation.* New York: Pergamon Press.

Jacobson, N. S., Dobson, K. S., Truax, P. A., Addis, M. E., et al. (1996). A component analysis of cognitive-behavioral treatment for depression. *J. Consult. Clin. Psychol., 64*(2), 295–304.

Jaffe, J. H. (1985). Drug addiction and drug abuse. In Goodman & Gilman (Eds.), *The pharmacological basis of therapeutic behavior.* New York: Macmillan.

Jaffee, S. R., Harrington, H. L., Cohen, P., & Moffitt, T. E. (2005). Cumulative prevalence of psychiatric disorder in youths. *J. Amer. Acad. Child Adol. Psychiat., 44*(5), 406–407.

Jahangir, F., ur-Rehman, H., & Jan, T. (1998). Degree of religiosity and vulnerability to suicidal attempt/plans in depressive patients among Afghan refugees. *Inter. J. Psychol. Religion, 8*(4), 265–269.

Jambor, E. (2001). Media involvement and the idea of beauty. In R. McComb & J. Jacalyn (Eds.), *Eating disorders in women and children: Prevention, stress management, and treatment* (pp. 179–183). Boca Raton, FL: CRC Press.

James, W. (1890). *Principles of psychology* (Vol. 1). New York: Holt, Rinehart & Winston.

Jamison, K. R. (1995, February). Manic-depressive illness and creativity. *Scientif. Amer.,* pp. 63–67.

Jamison, K. R. (1995). *An unquiet mind.* New York: Vintage Books.

Jang, K. L., & Vernon, P. A. (2001). Genetics. In W. J. Livesley (Ed.), *Handbook of personality disorders: Theory, research, and treatment* (pp. 177–195). New York: Guilford Press.

Janicak, P. G., Davis, J. M., Preskorn, S. H., & Ayd, F. J. (2001). *Principles and practice of psychopharmacotherapy* (3rd ed.). Philadelphia: Lippincott Williams & Wilkin.

Janno, S., Holi, M., Tuisku, K., & Wahlbeck, K. (2004). Prevalence of neuroleptic-induced movement disorders in chronic schizophrenia inpatients. *Amer. J. Psychiat., 161*(1), 160–163.

Janowsky, D. S., El-Yousef, M. K., Davis, J. M., & Sekerke, H. J. (1973). Provocation of schizophrenic symptoms by intravenous administration of methylphenidate. *Arch. Gen. Psychiat., 28,* 185–191.

Jansen, K. L. R. (2001). Mental health problems associated with MDMA use. In J. Holland (Ed.), *Ecstasy: The complete guide: A comprehensive look at the risks and benefits of MDMA* (pp. 87–109). Rochester, VT: Park Street Press.

Janus, S. S., & Janus, C. L. (1993). *The Janus report on sexual behavior.* New York: Wiley.

Janzing, J. G. E. (2003). Depression and dementia: Missing the link. *Curr. Opin. Psychiat., 16*(1), 13–16.

Javitt, D. C., & Coyle, J. T. (2004). Decoding schizophrenia: A fuller understanding for signaling in the brain of people with this disorder offers a new hope for improved therapy. *Scientif. Amer., 290,* 48–56.

Jaycox, L. H., & Foa, E. B. (2001). Posttraumatic stress. In H. S. Friedman (Ed.), *Specialty articles from the encyclopedia of mental health.* San Diego: Academic Press.

Jefferson, D. J. (2005, August 8). America's most dangerous drug. *Newsweek, 146*(6), 40–48.

Jefferson, J. W., & Greist, J. H. (1994). Mood disorders. In R. E. Hales, S. C. Yudofsky, & J. A. Talbott (Eds.), *The American Psychiatric Press textbook of psychiatry* (2nd ed.). Washington, DC: American Psychiatric Press.

Jefferson, L. (1948). *These are my sisters.* Tulsa, OK: Vickers.

Jeffries, J. J. (1995). Working with schizophrenia: A clinician's personal experience. *Canad. J. Psychiat., 40*(3, Suppl. 1), S22–S25.

Jenike, M. A. (1992). New developments in treatment of obsessive-compulsive disorder. In A. Tasman & M. B. Riba (Eds.), *Review of psychiatry* (Vol. 11). Washington, DC: American Psychiatric Press.

Jenkins, R. L. (1968). The varieties of children's behavioral problems and family dynamics. *Amer. J. Psychiat., 124*(10), 1440–1445.

Jensen, G. M. (1998). The experience of injustice: Health consequences of the Japanese American internment. *Diss. Abstr. Inter.: Sect. A: Human Soc. Sci., 58*(7–A), 2718.

Jensen, P. S., Hinshaw, S. P., Kraemer, H. C., Lenora, N., Newcorn, J. H., Abikoff, H. B., et al. (2001). ADHD comorbidity findings from the MTA study: Comparing comorbid subgroups. *J. Amer. Acad. Child Adol. Psychiat., 40*(2), 147–158.

Jeste, D. V., Blazer, D. G., & First, M. (2005). Aging-related diagnostic variations: Need for diagnostic criteria appropriate for elderly psychiatric patients. *Biol. Psychiat., 58*(4), 265–271.

Joffe, C., Brodaty, H., Luscombe, G., & Ehrlich, F. (2003). The Sydney Holocaust study: Posttraumatic stress disorder and other psychosocial morbidity in an aged community sample. *J. Traum. Stress., 16*(1), 39–47.

Joffe, R. T., Singer, W., Levitt, A. J., & MacDonald, C. (1993). A placebo-controlled comparison of lithium and triiodothyronine augmentation of tricyclic antidepressants in unipolar refractory depression. *Arch. Gen. Psychiat., 50*, 387–393.

Johns, A. (2001). Psychiatric effects of cannabis. *Brit. J. Psychiat., 178*, 116–122.

Johnson, B. R., & Becker, J. V. (1997). Natural born killers?: The development of the sexually sadistic serial killer. *J. Amer. Acad. Psychiat. Law., 25*(3), 335–348.

Johnson, C. (1995, February 8). National Collegiate Athletic Association study. In *The Hartford Courant.*

Johnson, D. L. (2002). A brief history of the international movement of family organization for persons with mental illness. In H. P. Lefley & D. L. Johnson (Eds.), *Family intervention in mental illness: International perspectives.* Westport, CT: Praeger.

Johnson, L. A. (2005, July 21). Lobotomy back in spotlight after 30 years. *Netscape News.*

Johnson, M. E., Jones, G., & Brems, C. (1996). Concurrent validity of the MMPI-2 feminine gender role (GF) and masculine gender role (GM) scales. *J. Pers. Assess., 66*(1), 153–168.

Johnson, W. D. (1991). Predisposition to emotional distress and psychiatric illness amongst doctors: The role of unconscious and experiential factors. *Brit. J. Med. Psychol., 64*(4), 317–329.

Johnston, J. M. (2004). Eating disorders and childhood obesity: Who are the real gluttons? *Canad. Med. Assoc. J., 171*(12), 1459–1460.

Johnston, L. D., O'Malley, P. M., & Bachman, J. G. (1993). *National survey results on drug use from the Monitoring the Future Study, 1975–1992.* Rockville, MD: National Institute on Drug Abuse.

Johnston, L. D., O'Malley, P. M., & Bachman, J. G. (2002). *Monitoring the future: National results on adolescent drug use. Overview of key findings, 2001.* Bethesda, MD: National Institute on Drug Abuse.

Johnston, L. D., O'Malley, P. M., Bachman, J. G., & Schulenberg, J. E. (2005). *Monitoring the future national results on adolescent drug use: Overview of key findings, 2004.* (NIH Publication No. 05-5726). Bethesda, MD: National Institute on Drug Abuse.

Joiner, T. E. (1995). The price of soliciting and receiving negative feedback: Self-verification theory as a vulnerability to depression theory. *J. Abnorm. Psychol., 104*(2), 364–372.

Joiner, T. E., Jr. (2002). Depression in its interpersonal context. In I. H. Gotlib & C. L. Hammen (Eds.), *Handbook of depression* (pp. 295–313). New York: Guilford Press.

Jones, M. C. (1968). Personality correlates and antecedents of drinking patterns in males. *J. Cons. Clin. Psychol., 32*, 2–12.

Jones, M. C. (1971). Personality antecedents and correlates of drinking patterns in women. *J. Cons. Clin. Psychol., 36*, 61–69.

Jordan, D. (1997). *1,001 more facts somebody screwed up.* Atlanta, GA: Longstreet Press.

Joy, M. (2005). Humanistic psychology and animal rights: Reconsidering the boundaries of the humanistic ethic. *J. Human. Psychol., 45*(1), 106–130.

Judd, L. L., Akiskal, H. S., & Paulus, M. P. (1997). The role and clinical significance of subsyndromal depressive symptoms (SSD) in unipolar major depressive disorder. *J. Affect. Disorders, 45*(1–2), 5–17.

Judd, L. L., Rapaport, M. H., Yonkers, K. A., Rush, A. J., Frank, E., Thase, M. E., et al. (2004). Randomized, placebo-controlled trial of fluoxetine for acute treatment of minor depressive disorder. *Amer. J. Psychiat., 161*(10), 1864–1871.

Judd, L. L., Schettler, P. J., & Akiskal, H. S. (2002). The prevalence, clinical relevance, and public health significance of subthreshold depressions. *Psychiatr. Clin. N. Amer., 25*(4), 685–698.

Judd, L. L., Schettler, P. J., Akiskal, H. S., Maser, J., Coryell, W., Solomon, D., et al. (2003). Long-term symptomatic status of bipolar I vs. bipolar II disorders. *Inter. J. Neuropsychopharmacol., 6*(2), 127–137.

Judelson, D. A., Armstrong, L. E., Sokmen, B., Roti, M. W., Casa, D. J., & Kellogg, M. D. (2005). Effect of chronic caffeine intake on choice reaction time, mood, and visual vigilance. *Physiol. Behav., 85*(5), 629–634.

Juel-Nielsen, N., & Videbech, T. (1970). A twin study of suicide. *Acta Genet. Med. Gemellol., 19*, 307–310.

Julien, R. M. (2005). *A primer of drug action* (10th ed.). New York: Worth Publishers.

Jung, C. J. (1971). *Psychological types: The relations between the ego and the unconscious.* From *The Collected Works* (Vol. 6). Princeton, NJ: Princeton University Press (Original work published 1921.).

Kabakci, E., & Batur, S. (2003). Who benefits from cognitive behavioral therapy for vaginismus? *J. Sex Marital Ther., 29*, 277–288.

Kabat-Zinn, J., Massion, A. O., Kristeller, J., Peterson, L. G., et al. (1992). Effectiveness of a meditation-based stress reduction program in the treatment of anxiety disorders. *Amer. J. Psychiat., 149*(7), 936–943.

Kabot, S., Masi, W., & Segal, M. (2003). Advances in the diagnosis and treatment of autism spectrum disorders. *Profess. Psychol.: Res. Pract., 34*(1), 26–33.

Kafka, M. P. (2000). The paraphilia-related disorders: Nonparaphilic hypersexuality and sexual compulsivity/addiction. In S. R. Leiblum & R. C. Raymond (Eds.), *Principles and practice of sex therapy* (3rd ed., pp. 471–503). New York: Guilford Press.

Kagan, J. (2003). Biology, context and developmental inquiry. *Ann. Rev. Psychol., 54*, 1–23.

Kagan, J., & Snidman, N. (1991). Infant predictors of inhibited and uninhibited profiles. *Psychol. Sci., 2*, 40–44.

Kagan, J., & Snidman, N. (1999). Early childhood predictors of adult anxiety disorders. *Biol. Psychiat., 46*(11), 1536–1541.

Kagan, N. I., Kagan, H., & Watson, M. G. (1995). Stress reduction in the workplace: The effectiveness of psychoeducational programs. *J. Couns. Psychol., 42*(1), 71–78.

Kahn, A. P., & Fawcett, J. (1993). *The encyclopedia of mental health.* New York: Facts on File.

Kaij, L. (1960). *Alcoholism in twins: Studies on the etiology and sequels of abuse of alcohol.* Stockholm: Almquist & Wiksell.

Kail, R. (1992). General slowing of information-processing by persons with mental retardation. *Amer. J. Ment. Retard., 97*(3), 333–341.

Kaiser Family Foundation. (2001, November). *Understanding the effects of direct-to-consumer prescription drug advertising.* The Health Care Marketplace Project Publications: Menlo Park, CA.

Kalafat, J., & Ryerson, D. M. (1999). The implementation and institutionalization of a school-based youth suicide prevention program. *J. Primary Prev., 19*(3), 157–175.

Kalayjian, L. A., & Morrell, M. J. (2000). Female sexuality and neurological disease. *J. Sex Educ. Ther., 25*(1), 89–95.

Kalb, C. (2000, January 31). Coping with the darkness: Revolutionary new approaches in providing care for helping people with Alzheimer's stay active and feel productive. *Newsweek,* pp. 52–54.

Kalb, C. (2004, September 6). Know the numbers. *Newsweek, 144*(10), 72–73.

Kalidindi, S., & McGuffin, P. (2003). The genetics of affective disorders: Present and future. In R. Plomin, J. C. DeFries, I. W. Craig, & P. McGuffin (Eds.), *Behavioral genetics in the postgenomic era* (pp. 481–501). Washington, DC: American Psychological Association.

Kalin, N. H. (1993, May). The neurobiology of fear. *Scientif. Amer.,* pp. 94–101.

Kalodner, C. R., & Coughlin, J. W. (2004). Psychoeducational and counseling groups to prevent and treat eating disorders and disturbances. In J. L. DeLucia-Waack, D. A. Gerrity, C. R. Kalodner, & M. T. Riva (Eds.), *Handbook of group counseling and psychotherapy* (pp. 481–496). Thousand Oaks, CA: Sage.

Kaminer, Y., Burleson, J. A., & Jadamec, A. (2002). Gambling behavior in adolescent substance abuse. *Subs. Abuse, 23*(3), 191–198.

Kamphaus, R. W., & Frick, P. J. (2002). *Clinical assessment of child and adolescent personality and behavior* (2nd ed.). Boston: Allyn and Bacon.

Kamphuis, J. H., & Emmelkamp, P. M. G. (2001). Traumatic distress among support-seeking female victims of stalking. *Amer. J. Psychiat., 158*(5), 795–798.

Kane, J. M. (1992). Clinical efficacy of clozapine in treatment-refractory schizophrenia: An overview. *Brit. J. Psychiat., 160*(Suppl. 17), 41–45.

Kanner, B. (1995). *Are you normal?: Do you behave like everyone else?* New York: St. Martin's Press.

Kanner, B. (1998, February). Are you normal? Turning the other cheek. *American Demog.*

Kanner, B. (1998, May). Are you normal? Creatures of habit. *Am. Demogr.*

Kanner, L. (1943). Autistic disturbances of affective contact. *Nerv. Child. 2*, 217.

Kanner, L. (1954). To what extent is early infantile autism determined by constitutional inadequacies? *Proceedings of the Assoc. Res. Nerv. Ment. Dis., 33*, 378–385.

Kantrowitz, B., & Springen, K. (2004). What dreams are made of. *Newsweek, 144*(6), August 9, 2004, 40–47.

Kaplan, A. (1998, September). Caring for the caregivers: Family interventions and Alzheimer's disease. *Psychiatr. Times, XV*(9).

Kaplan, A. (1999). China's suicide patterns challenge depression theory. *Psychiatr. Times., XVI*(1).

Kaplan, A. S. (2005). From genes to treatment response: New research into the psychobiology of anorexia nervosa. *Inter. J. Eat. Disord., 37*(Suppl.), S87–S89.

Kaplan, A. S., & Garfinkel, P. E. (1999). Difficulties in treating patients with eating disorders: A review of patient and clinician variables. *Canad. J. Psychiat., 44*(7), 665–670.

Kaplan, H. S. (1974). *The new sex therapy: Active treatment of sexual dysfunction.* New York: Brunner/Mazel.

Kaplan, R. M. (2000). Two pathways to prevention. *Amer. Psychologist, 55*(4), 382–396.

Kapp, M. B. (2002). Regulating research for the decisionally impaired: Implications for mental health professionals. *J. Clin. Geropsychol., 8*(1), 35–51.

Kardiner, A. (1977). *My analysis with Freud: Reminiscences.* New York: Norton.

Karel, R. (1992, May 1). Hopes of many long-term sufferers dashed as FDA ends medical marijuana program. *Psychiatr. News.*

Karno, M., & Golding, J. M. (1991). Obsessive compulsive disorder. In L. N. Robins & D. A. Regier (Eds.), *Psychiatric disorders in America.* New York: The Free Press.

Karno, M., & Jenkins, J. H. (1993). Cross-cultural issues in the course and treatment of schizophrenia. *Psychiat. Clin. N. Amer., 16,* 339–350.

Karon, B. P. (1985). Omission in review of treatment interactions. *Schizo. Bull., 11*(1), 16–17.

Karon, B. P. (2005). Recurrent psychotic depression is treatable by psychoanalytic therapy without medication. *Ethical Human Psychol. Psychiat., 7*(1), 45–56.

Karon, B. P., & Vandenbos, G. R. (1996). *Psychotherapy of schizophrenia: The treatment of choice.* Northvale, NJ: Jason Aronson.

Karp, D. A. (1996). *Speaking of sadness: Depression, disconnection, and the meanings of illness.* New York: Oxford University Press.

Kaslow, N. J., McClure, E. B., & Connell, A. M. (2002). Treatment of depression in children and adolescents. In I. H. Gotlib & C. L. Hammen (Eds.), *Handbook of depression* (pp. 441–464). New York: Guilford Press.

Kaslow, N. J., Reviere, S. L., Chance, S. E., Rogers, J. H., Hatcher, C. A., Wasserman, F., et al. (1998). An empirical study of the psychodynamics of suicide. *J. Amer. Psychoanal. Assoc., 46*(3), 777–796.

Kasper, S. (2005). Atypical antipsychotics in bipolar disorder. In S. Kasper & R. M. A. Hirschfeld (Eds.), *Handbook of bipolar disorder: Diagnosis and therapeutic approaches* (pp. 315–330). New York: Taylor & Francis.

Kass, B., Weinick, R., & Monheit, A. (1999). *Racial and ethnic differences in health: Medical Expenditure Panel Survey Chartbook No. 2.* Rockville, MD: US Dept. of Health and Human Services, Agency for Health Care Policy and Research.

Kassel, J. D., Wagner, E. F., & Unrod, M. (1999). Alcoholism-behavior therapy. In M. Hersen & A. S. Bellack (Eds.), *Handbook of comparative interventions for adult disorders* (2nd ed.). New York: Wiley.

Kate, N. T. (1998, May). Freshmen get wholesome. *Am. Demogr.*

Katel, P., & Beck, M. (1996, March 29). Sick kid or sick Mom? *Newsweek,* p. 73.

Katon, W. J., & Walker, E. A. (1998). Medically unexplained symptoms in primary care. *J. Clin. Psychiat., 59*(Suppl. 20), 15–21.

Katz, E. C., Gruber, K., Chutuape, M. A., & Stitzer, M. L. (2001). Reinforcement-based outpatient treatment for opiate and cocaine abusers. *J. Subst. Abuse Treatm., 20*(1), 93–98.

Katzman, R. (1981, June). Early detection of senile dementia. *Hosp. Practitioner,* pp. 61–76.

Katzman, R. (2001). Epidemiology of Alzheimer's disease and dementia: Advances and challenges. In K. Iqbal, S. S. Sisodia, & B. Winblad (Eds.), *Alzheimer's disease: Advances in etiology, pathogenesis and therapeutics* (pp. 11–22). New York: Wiley.

Kauert, G., & Stefanie Iwersen-Bergmann, S. (2004). Illicit drugs as cause of traffic crashes, focus on cannabis. *Sucht (German Journal of Addiction Research and Practice), 50*(5), 327–333.

Kawas, C., Resnick, S., Morrison, A., Brookmeyer, R., Corrada, M., Zonderman, A., et al. (1997). A prospective study of estrogen replacement therapy and the risk of developing Alzheimer's disease: The Baltimore Longitudinal Study of Aging. *Neurology, 48*(6), 1517–1521.

Kaye, W. H., Frank, G. K., Bailer, U. F., Henry, S. E., Meltzer, C. C., Price, J. C., et al. (2005). Serotonin alterations in anorexia and bulimia nervosa: New insights from imaging studies. *Physiolog. Behav., 85*(1), 73–81.

Kaye, W. H., Gendall, H., & Strober, M. (1998). Serotonin neuronal function and selective serotonin reuptake inhibitor treatment in anorexia and bulimia nervosa. *Biol. Psychiat., 44*(9), 825–838.

Kaye, W. H., Gendall, K. A., Fernstrom, M. H., Fernstrom, J. D., McConaha, C. W., & Weltzin, T. E. (2000). Effects of acute tryptophan depletion on mood in bulimia nervosa. *Biol. Psychiat., 47*(2), 151–157.

Kaye, W. H., Strober, M., & Rhodes, L. (2002). Body image disturbance and other core symptoms in anorexia and bulimia nervosa. In D. J. Castle & K. A. Phillips (Eds.), *Disorders of body image* (pp. 67–82). Petersfield, England: Wrightson Biomedical.

Kazdin, A. E. (1983). Failure of persons to respond to the token economy. In E. B. Foa & P. M. G. Emmelkamp (Eds.), *Failures in behavior therapy.* New York: Wiley.

Kazdin, A. E. (1994). Methodology, design, and evaluation in psychotherapy research. In A. E. Bergin & S. L. Garfield (Eds.), *Handbook of psychotherapy and behavior change* (4th ed.). New York: Wiley.

Kazdin, A. E. (2000). *Psychotherapy for children and adolescents: Directions for research and practice.* New York: Oxford University Press.

Kazdin, A. E. (2002). Psychosocial treatments for conduct disorder in children and adolescents. In P. E. Nathan & J. M. Gorman (Eds.), *A guide to treatments that work* (2nd ed., pp. 57–85). London: Oxford University Press.

Kazdin, A. E. (2003). Problem-solving skills training and parent management training for conduct disorder. In A. E. Kazdin & J. R. Weisz (Eds.), *Evidence-based psychotherapies for children and adolescents.* New York: Guilford Press.

Kazdin, A. E. (Ed.). (2003). *Methodological issues & strategies in clinical research* (3rd ed.). Washington, DC: American Psychological Association.

Kazdin, A. E. (2004). Evidence-based treatments: Challenges and priorities for practice and research. *Child Adol. Psychiat. Clinics N. Amer., 13*(4), 923–940.

Kazdin, A. E. (2005). Child, parent, and family-based treatment of aggressive and anti-social behavior. In E. D. Hibbs & P. S. Jensen (Eds.), *Psychosocial treatments for child and adolescent disorders: Empirically based strategies for clinical practice* (2nd ed., pp. 445–476). Washington, DC: American Psychological Association.

Kearney, C. A. (2005). *Social anxiety and social phobia in youth: Characteristics, assessment, and psychological treatment.* New York: Springer Publishing.

Kearney-Cooke, A., & Steichen-Asch, P. (1990). Men, body image, and eating disorders. In A. E. Andersen (Ed.), *Males with eating disorders.* New York: Brunner/Mazel.

Keefe, R. S. E., Arnold, M. C., Bayen, U. J., McEvoy, J. P., & Wilson, W. H. (2002). Source-monitoring deficits for self-generated stimuli in schizophrenia: Multinomial modeling of data from three sources. *Schizo. Res., 57*(1), 51–68.

Keefe, R. S. E., Seidman, L. J., Christensen, B. K., Hamer, R. M., Sharma, T., Sitskoorn, M. M., et al. (2004). Comparative effect of atypical and conventional antipsychotic drugs on neurocognition in first-episode psychosis: A randomized, double-blind trial of olanzapine versus low doses of haloperidol. *Amer. J. Psychiat., 161*(6), 985–995.

Keel, P. K., & Mitchell, J. E. (1997). Outcome in bulimia nervosa. *Amer. J. Psychiat., 154,* 313–321.

Keel, P. K., Mitchell, J. E., Davis, T. L., & Crow, S. J. (2002). Long-term impact of treatment in women diagnosed with bulimia nervosa. *Inter. J. Eat. Disorders, 31*(2), 151–158.

Keel, P. K., Mitchell, J. E., Miller, K. B., Davis, T. L., & Crow, S. J. (1999). Long-term outcome of bulimia nervosa. *Arch. Gen. Psychiat., 56*(1), 63–69.

Keel, P. K., Mitchell, J. E., Miller, K. B., Davis, T. L., & Crow, S. J. (2000). Social adjustment over 10 years following diagnosis with bulimia nervosa. *Inter. J. Eat. Disorders, 27*(1), 21–28.

Keen, E. (1970). *Three faces of being: Toward an existential clinical psychology.* By the Meredith Corp. Reprinted by permission of Irvington Publishers.

Keesey, R. E., & Corbett, S. W. (1983). Metabolic defense of the body weight set-point. In A. J. Stunkard & E. Stellar (Eds.), *Eating and its disorders.* New York: Raven Press.

Keith, S. J., Regier, D. A., & Rae, D. S. (1991). Schizophrenic disorders. In L. N. Robins & D. S. Regier (Eds.), *Psychiatric disorders in America: The Epidemiological Catchment Area Study.* New York: Free Press.

Kelleher, M. D., & Van Nuys, D. (2002). *This is the Zodiac speaking: Into the mind of a serial killer.* Westport, CT: Praeger/Greenwood.

Keller, M. C., & Nesse, R. M. (2005). Is low mood an adaptation? Evidence for subtypes with symptoms that match precipitants. *J. Affect. Disorders, 86*(1), 27–35.

Kelley, T. M. (2004). Positive psychology and adolescent mental health: False promise or true breakthrough? *Adolescence, 39*(154), 257–278.

Kelly, K. (2005). Just don't do it! *U. S. News & World Report, 139*(14), 44–49.

Kelly, K. A. (1993). Multiple personality disorders: Treatment coordination in a partial hospital setting. *Bull. Menninger Clin., 57*(3), 390–398.

Kelly, M. P., Strassberg, D. S., & Kircher, J. R. (1990). Attitudinal and experiental correlates of anorgasmia. *Arch. Sex. Behav., 19,* 165–172.

Keltner, N. L., & Folks, D. G. (2001). *Psychotropic drugs* (3rd ed.). St. Louis, MO: Mosby.

Kemp, D. R. (1994). *Mental health in the workplace: An employer's and manager's guide.* Westport, CT: Quorum Books.

Kempler, D. (2005). *Neurocognitive disorders in aging.* Thousand Oaks, CA: Sage.

Kendall, J., & Hatton, D. (2002). Racism as a source of health disparity in families with children with attention deficit hyperactivity disorder. *Adv. Nurs. Sci., 25*(2), 22–39.

Kendall, P. C. (2000). *Childhood disorders.* Hove, England: Psychology Press/Taylor & Francis.

Kendall, P. C., & Pimentel, S. S. (2003). On the physiological constellation in youth with generalized anxiety disorder (GAD). *J. Anx. Disorders, 17,* 211–221.

Kendell, R. E. (2002). Personality disorder: Author's reply. *Brit. J. Psychiat., 181*(1), 77–78.

Kendler, K. S. (2005). Psychiatric genetics: A methodologic critique. *Amer. J. Psychiat., 162*(1), 3–11.

Kendler, K. S., Heath, A., & Martin, N. G. (1987). A genetic epidemiologic study of self-report suspiciousness. *Comprehen. Psychiat., 28*(3), 187–196.

Kendler, K. S., Heath, A., Neale, M., Kessler, R., & Eaves, L. (1992). A population-based twin study of alcoholism in women. *JAMA, 268*(14), 1877–1882.

Kendler, K. S., Karkowski, L. M., & Prescott, C. A. (1998). Stressful life events and major depression: Risk period, long-term contextual threat and diagnostic specificity. *J. Nerv. Ment. Dis., 186*(11), 661–669.

Kendler, K. S., Karkowski, L. M., & Prescott, C. A. (1999). Causal relationship between stressful life events and the onset of major depression. *Amer. J. Psychiat., 156*(6), 837–848.

Kendler, K. S., Kuhn, J. W., & Prescott, C. A. (2004). Childhood sexual abuse, stressful life events and risk for major depression in women. *Psychol. Med., 34*(8), 1475–1482.

Kendler, K. S., Myers, J., & Prescott, C. A. (2005). Sex differences in the relationship between social support and risk for major depression: A longitudinal study of opposite-sex twin pairs. *Amer. J. Psychiat., 162*(2), 250–256.

Kendler, K. S., Neale, M. C., Heath, A. C., Kessler, R. C., & Eaves, L. J. (1994). A twin-family study of alcoholism in women. *Amer. J. Psychiat., 151*(5), 707–715.

Kendler, K. S., Neale, M. C., Kessler, R. C., Heath, A. C., & Eaves, L. J. (1993). Panic disorder in women: A population-based twin study. *Psychol. Med., 23, 397–406.*

Kendler, K. S., Ochs, A. L., Gorman, A. M., Hewitt, J. K., Ross, D. E., & Mirsky, A. F. (1991). The structure of schizotypy: A pilot multitrait twin study. *Psychiat. Res., 36*(1), 19–36.

Kendler, K. S., Walters, E. E., & Kessler, R. C. (1997). The prediction of length of major depressive episodes: Results from an epidemiological sample of female twins. *Psychol. Med., 27*(1), 107–117.

Kendler, K. S., Walters, E. E., Neale, M. C., Kessler, R. C., et al. (1995). The structure of the genetic and environmental risk factors for six major psychiatric disorders in women: Phobia, generalized anxiety disorder, panic disorder, bulimia, major depression, and alcoholism. *Arch. Gen. Psychiat., 52*(5), 374–383.

Kennedy, C. A., Hill, J. M., & Schleifer, S. J. (2005). HIV/AIDS and substance use disorders. In R. J. Frances, A. H. Mack, & S. I. Miller (Eds.), *Clinical textbook of addictive disorders* (3rd ed., pp. 411–436). New York: Guilford Press.

Kennedy, P. (2004, June 13). One room, 3,000 brains. *The Boston Globe,* 3rd ed..

Kensinger, E. A., Ullman, M. T., & Corkin, S. (2001). Bilateral medial temporal lobe damage does not affect lexical or grammatical processing: Evidence from amnesic patient H. M. *Hippocampus, 11*(4), 347–360.

Keown, P., Holloway, F., & Kuipers, E. (2002). The prevalence of personality disorders, psychotic disorders and affective disorders amongst the patients seen by a community mental health team in London. *Soc. Psychiat. Psychiatr. Epidemiol., 37*(5), 225–229.

Kerkhof, A. J. F. M. (2005). Suicide prevention discussed at the WHO European Ministerial Conference on Mental Health. *Crisis, 26*(2), 51–52.

Kernberg, O. F. (1989). Narcissistic personality disorder in childhood. *Psychiatr. Clin. N. Amer., 12*(3), 671–694.

Kernberg, O. F. (1997). Convergences and divergences in contemporary psychoanalytic technique and psychoanalytic psychotherapy. In J. K. Zeig (Ed.), *The evolution of psychotherapy: The third conference.* New York: Brunner/Mazel.

Kernberg, O. F. (2001). The concept of libido in the light of contemporary psychoanalytic theorizing. In P. Hartocollis (Ed.), *Mankind's Oedipal destiny: Libidinal and aggressive aspects of sexuality* (pp. 95–111). Madison, CT: International Universities Press.

Kernberg, O. F. (2005). Object relations theories and technique. In E. S. Person, A. M. Cooper, & G. O. Gabbard (Eds.), *The American Psychiatric Publishing textbook of psychoanalysis* (pp. 57–75). Washington, DC: American Psychiatric Publishing.

Kernberg, O. F., & Caligor, E. (2005). A psychoanalytic theory of personality disorders. In M. F. Lenzenweger & J. F. Clarkin (Eds.), *Major theories of personality disorder* (2nd ed., pp. 114–156). New York: Guilford Press.

Kernberg, P. F., & Wiener, J. M. (2004). Personality disorders. In J. M. Wiener & M. K. Dulcan (Eds.), *The American Psychiatric Publishing textbook of child and adolescent psychiatry* (3rd ed., pp. 775–793). Washington, DC: American Psychiatric Publishing.

Kersting, K. (2005). Serious rehabilitation. *Monitor Psychol., 36*(1), 38–41.

Kessing, L. V. (2004). Endogenous: Reactive and neurotic depression—Diagnostic stability and long-term outcome. *Psychopathology, 37*(3), 124–130.

Kessler, D. A., & Pines, W. L. (1990). The federal regulation of prescription drug advertising and promotion. *JAMA, 264*(18), 2409–2415.

Kessler, R. C. (2002). Epidemiology of depression. In I. H. Gotlib & C. L. Hammen (Eds.), *Handbook of depression* (pp. 23–42). New York: Guilford Press.

Kessler, R. C., Adler, L. A., Barkley, R., Biederman, J., Connors, C. K., Faraone, S. V., et al. (2005). Patterns and predictors of attention-deficit/hyperactivity disorder persistence into adulthood: Results from the National Comorbidity Survey Replication. *Biol. Psychiat., 57*(11), 1442–1451.

Kessler, R. C., Berglund, P., Demler, O., Jim, R., Koretz, D., Merikangas, K. R., et al. (2003). The epidemiology of major depressive disorder: Results from the National Comorbidity Survey Replication (NCS-R). *JAMA, 289*(23), 3095–3105.

Kessler, R. C., Berglund, P., Demler, O., Jin, R., & Walters, E. E. (2005). Lifetime prevalence and age-of-onset distributions of DSM-IV disorders in the National Comorbidity Survey Replication. *Arch. Gen. Psychiat., 62,* 593–602.

Kessler, R. C., Berglund, P. A., DeWitt, D. J., Üstün, T. B., Wang, P. S., & Wittchen, H.-U. (2002). Distinguishing generalized anxiety disorder from major depression: Prevalence and impairment from current pure and comorbid disorders in the U.S. and Ontario. *Inter. J. Methods Psychiatr. Res., 11*(3), 99–111.

Kessler, R. C., Chiu, W. T., Demler, O., & Walters, E. E. (2005). Prevalence, severity, and comorbidity of 12-month DSM-IV disorders in the National Comorbidity Survey Replication. *Arch. Gen. Psychiat., 62,* 617–627.

Kessler, R. C., DuPont, R. L., Berglund, P., & Wittchen, H. U. (1999). Impairment in pure and comorbid generalized anxiety disorder and major depression at 12 months in two national surveys. *Amer. J. Psychiat., 156(12), 1915–1923.*

Kessler, R. C., Keller, M. B., & Wittchen, H. U. (2001). The epidemiology of generalized anxiety disorder. *Psychiatr. Clin. N. Amer., 24*(1), 19–39.

Kessler, R. C., McGonagle, K. A., Zhao, S., Nelson, C. B., Hughes, M., Eshleman, S., et al. (1994). Lifetime and 12-month prevalence of DSM-III-R psychiatric disorders among persons aged 15–54 in the United States: Results from the National Comorbidity Survey. *Arch. Gen. Psychiat., 51*(1), 8–19.

Kessler, R. C., Olfson, M., & Berglund, P. A. (1998). Patterns and predictors of treatment contact after first onset of psychiatric disorders. *Amer. J. Psychiat., 155*(1), 62–69.

Kessler, R. C., Sonnega, A., Bromet, E., Hughes, M., & Nelson, C. B. (1995). Posttraumatic stress disorder in the National Comorbidity Survey. *Arch. Gen. Psychiat., 52,* 1048–1060.

Kessler, R. C., Walters, E. E., & Wittchen, H. U. (2004). Epidemiology. In R. G. Heimberg, C. L. Turk., & D. S. Mennin (Eds.), *Generalized anxiety disorder: Advances in research and practice* (pp. 29–50). New York: Guilford Press.

Kessler, R. C., & Zhao, S. (1999). The prevalence of mental illness. In A. V. Horwitz & T. L. Scheid (Eds.), *A handbook for the study of mental health: Social contexts, theories, and systems.* Cambridge, England: Cambridge University Press.

Kettl, P. (1998). Alaska native suicide: Lessons for elder suicide. *Inter. Psychoger., 110*(2), 205–211.

Kety, S. S. (1974). From rationalization to reason. *Amer. J. Psychiat., 131*(9), 957–963.

Kety, S. S. (1988). Schizophrenic illness in the families of schizophrenic adoptees: findings from the Danish national sample. *Schizophr. Bull.,* 14(2), 217–222.

Kety, S. S., Rosenthal, D., Wender, P. H., et al. (1968). The types and prevalence of mental illness in the biological and adoptive families of schizophrenics. *J. Psychiatr. Res., 6,* 345–362.

Kety, S. S., Rosenthal, D., Wender, P. H., et al. (1975). Mental illness in the biological and adoptive families of adopted individuals who became schizophrenic: A preliminary report based on psychiatric interviews. In R. R. Fieve, D. Rosenthal, & H. Brill (Eds.), *Genetic research in psychiatry.* Baltimore, MD: Johns Hopkins University Press.

Kety, S. S., Rosenthal, D., Wender, P. H., Schulsinger, F., & Jacobsen, B. (1978). The biologic and adoptive families of adopted individuals who become schizophrenic: Prevalence of mental illness and other characteristics. In L. C. Wynne, R. L. Cromwell, & S. Matthysse (Eds.), *The nature of schizophrenia: New approaches to research and treatment.* New York: Wiley.

Keys, A., Brozek, J., Henschel, A., Mickelson, O., & Taylor, H. L. (1950). *The biology of human starvation.* Minneapolis: University of Minnesota Press.

Khan, S., Murray, R. P., & Barnes, G. E. (2002). A structural equation model of the effect of poverty and unemployment on alcohol abuse. *Addic. Behav., 27*(3), 405–423.

Khandker R. K., & Simoni-Wastila, L. J. (1998). Differences in prescription drug utilization and expenditures between blacks and whites in the Georgia Medicaid population. *Inquiry, 35,* 78–87.

Khouzam, H. R., Ghafoori, B., & Hierholzer, R. (2005). Progress in the identification, diagnosis and treatment of posttraumatic stress disorder. In T. A. Corales (Ed.), *Trends in posttraumatic stress disorder research* (pp. 1–28). Hauppauge, NY: Nova Science Publishers.

Kiecolt-Glaser, J. K., Dura, J. R., Speicher, C. E., Trask, O. J., & Glaser, R. (1991). Spousal caregivers of dementia victims: Longitudinal changes in immunity and health. *Psychosom. Med., 53,* 345–362.

Kiecolt-Glaser, J. K., & Glaser, R. (1999). Psychoneuroimmunology and immunotoxicology: Implications for carcinogenesis. *Psychosom. Med., 61*(3), 271–272.

Kiecolt-Glaser, J. K., & Glaser, R. (2002). Depression and immune function: Central pathways to morbidity and mortality. *J. Psychosom. Res., 53,* 873–876.

Kiecolt-Glaser, J. K., Glaser, R., Gravenstein, S., Malarkey, W. B., & Sheridan, J. (1996). Chronic stress alters the immune response to influenza virus vaccine in older adults. *Proc. Natl. Acad. Sci. USA, 93,* 3043–3047.

Kiecolt-Glaser, J. K., Glaser, R., Shuttleworth, E. C., Dyer, C. S., Ogrocki, P., & Speicher, C. E. (1987). Chronic stress and immunity in family caregivers of Alzheimer's disease victims. *Psychosom. Med., 49,* 523–535.

Kiecolt-Glaser, J. K., McGuire, L., Robles, T. F., & Glaser, R. (2002). Psychoneuroimmunology: Psychological influences on immune function and health. *J. Cons. Clin. Psychol., 70*(3), 537–547.

Kiecolt-Glaser, J. K., Page, G. G., Marucha, P. T., MacCallum, R. C., & Glaser, R. (1998). Psychological influences on surgical recovery. Perspectives from psychoneuroimmunology. *Amer. Psychologist, 53*(11), 1209–1218.

Kiernan, W. (2000). Where we are now: Perspectives on employment of persons with mental retardation. *Focus Autism Other Dev. Disabil., 15*(2), 90–96.

Kiesler, C. A. (2000). The next wave of change for psychology and mental health services in the health care revolution. *Amer. Psychologist, 55*(5), 481–487.

Kiesler, D. J. (1966). Some myths of psychotherapy research and the search for a paradigm. *Psychol. Bull., 65,* 110–136.

Kiesler, D. J. (1995). Research classic: "Some myths of psychotherapy research and the search for a paradigm": Revisited. *Psychother. Res., 5*(2), 91–101.

Kiev, A. (1989). Suicide in adults. In J. G. Howells (Ed.), *Modern perspectives in the psychiatry of the affective disorders.* New York: Brunner/Mazel.

Kihlström, J. F. (2001). *Dissociative disorders.* New York: Kluwer Academic/Plenum.

Kihlström, J. F. (2002). To honor Kraepelin . . .: From symptoms to pathology in the diagnosis of mental illness. In L. E. Beutler & M. L. Malik (Eds.), *Rethinking the DSM: A psychological perspective. Decade of behavior.* Washington, DC: American Psychological Association.

Kihlström, J. F. (2005). Is hypnosis an altered state of consciousness or what? *Contemp. Hyp., 22,* 34–38.

Killaspy, H., Ritchie, C. W., Greer, E., & Robertson, M. (2004). Treating the homeless mentally ill: Does a designated inpatient facility improve outcome? *J. Ment. Hlth. UK, 13*(6), 593–599.

Killen, J. D. (1996). Development and evaluation of a school-based eating disorder symptoms prevention program. In L. Smolak, M. P. Levine, & R. Striegel-Moore (Eds.), *The developmental psychopathology of eating disorders: Implications for research, prevention, and treatment.* Mahwah, NJ: Erlbaum.

Killen, J. D., Taylor, C. B., Hayward, C., Wilson, D. M., Hammer, L. D., Robinson, T. N., et al. (1994). The pursuit of thinness and onset of eating disorder symptoms in a community sample of adolescent girls: A three-year prospective analysis. *Inter. J. Eat. Disorders, 16,* 227–238.

Kim, C. H., Jayathilake, K., & Meltzer, H. Y. (2003). Hopelessness, neurocognitive function, and insight in schizophrenia: Relationship to suicidal behavior. *Schizo. Res., 60*(1), 71–80.

Kim, S. W., Grant, J. E., Kim, S. I., Swanson, T. A., Bernstein, G. A., Jaszcz, W. B., et al. (2004). A possible association of recurrent streptococcal infections and acute onset of obsessive-compulsive disorder. *J. Neuropsychiat. Clin Neurosci., 16*(3), 252–260.

Kimball, A. (1993). Nipping and tucking. In Skin deep: Our national obsession with looks. *Psychol. Today, 26*(3), 96.

Kinard, E. M. (1982). Child abuse and depression: Cause or consequence? *Child Welfare, 61,* 403–413.

Kinderman, P., & Bentall, R. P. (1997). Causal attributions in paranoia and depression: Internal, personal, and situational attributions for negative events. *J. Abnorm. Psychol., 106*(2), 341–345.

King, L. (2002, March 19). Interview with Russell Yates. *Larry King Live, CNN.*

King, M. B., & Mezey, G. (1987). Eating behaviour of male racing jockeys. *Psychol. Med., 17,* 249–253.

King, N. J., Heyne, D., & Ollendick, T. H. (2005). Cognitive-behavioral treatments for anxiety and phobic disorders in children and adolescents: A review. *Behav. Disorders, 30*(3), 241–257.

King, N. J., Muris, P., & Ollendick, T. H. (2004). Specific phobia. In J. S. March & T. L. Morris (Eds.), *Anxiety disorders in children and adolescents* (2nd ed., pp. 263–279). New York: Guilford Press.

King, R. A. (2003). Psychodynamic approaches to youth suicide. In R. A. King & A. Apter (Eds.), *Suicide in children and adolescents* (pp. 150–169). New York: Cambridge University Press.

King, R. A., & Apter, A. (Eds.). (2003). *Suicide in children and adolescents.* New York: Cambridge University Press.

Kingdon, D. G., & Turkington, D. (2005). *Cognitive therapy of schizophrenia.* New York: Guilford Press.

Kinzie, J., Leung, P., Boehnlein, J., & Matsunaga, D. (1992). Psychiatric epidemiology of an Indian village: A 19-year replication study. *J. Nerv. Ment. Dis., 180*(1), 33–39.

Kirby, M. (2000). Psychiatry, psychology, law and homosexuality—Uncomfortable bedfellows. *Psychiatry, Psychol. Law, 7*(2), 139–149.

Kirchmayer, U., Davoli, M., Verster, A. D., Amato, L., Ferri, M., & Perucci, C. A. (2002). A systematic review on the efficacy of naltrexone maintenance treatment in opioid dependence. *Addiction, 97*(10), 1241–1249.

Kirk, S. A., & Kutchins, H. (1992). *The selling of DSM: The rhetoric of science in psychiatry.* New York: Aldine de Gruyter.

Kirmayer, L. J. (2001). Cultural variations in the clinical presentation of depression and anxiety: Implications for diagnosis and treatment. *J. Clin. Psychiat., 62*(Suppl. 13), 22–28.

Kirmayer, L. J. (2002). The refugee's predicament. *Evol. Psychiat., 67*(4), 724–742.

Kirmayer, L. J. (2003). Failures of imagination: The refugee's narrative in psychiatry. *Anthropol. Med., 10*(2), 167–185.

Kirmayer, L. J., Groleau, D., Looper, K. J., & Dominice, M. (2004). Explaining medically unexplained symptoms. *Canad. J. Psychiat., 49*(10), 663–672.

Kirmayer, L. J., Robbins, J. M., & Paris, J. (1994). Somatoform disorders: Personality and the social matrix of somatic distress. *J. Abnorm. Psychol., 103*(1), 125–136.

Kirschenbaum, H. (2004). Carl Rogers's life and work: An assessment on the 100th anniversary of his birth. *J. Couns. Dev., 82*(1), 116–124.

Kisker, G. W. (1977). *The disorganized personality.* New York: McGraw-Hill.

Kjelsas, E., Bjornstrom, C., & Gotestam, K. G., (2004). Prevalence of eating disorders in female and male adolescents (14–15 years). *Eat. Behav., 5*(1), 13–25.

Kleber, H. D. (1981). Detoxification from narcotics. In J. H. Lowinson & P. Ruiz (Eds.), *Substance abuse: Clinical problems and perspectives.* Baltimore: William & Wilkins.

Klein, D. F. (1964). Delineation of two drug-responsive anxiety syndromes. *Psychopharmacologia, 5,* 397–408.

Klein, D. F., & Fink, M. (1962). Psychiatric reaction patterns to imipramine. *Amer. J. Psychiat., 119,* 432–438.

Klein, M. (1998, March). Looking out for Fido. *Am. Demogr.*

Klein, M. (1998, March). Stalking situations. *Am. Demogr.*

Klein, W. C., & Jess, C. (2002). One last pleasure? Alcohol use among elderly people in nursing homes. *Hlth. Soc. Work., 27*(3), 193–203.

Kleiner, M. (Ed.). (2002). *Handbook of polygraph testing.* San Diego, CA: Academic.

Kleinman, A. (1987). Anthropology and psychiatry: The role of culture in cross-cultural research on illness. *Brit. J. Psychiat., 151,* 447–454.

Klerman, G. L., & Weissman, M. M. (1992). Interpersonal psychotherapy. In E. S. Paykel (Ed.), *Handbook of affective disorders.* New York: Guilford Press.

Klerman, G. L., Weissman, M. M., Markowitz, J., Glick, I., Wilner, P. J., Mason, B., et al. (1994). Medication and psychotherapy. In A. E. Bergin & S. L. Garfield (Eds.), *Handbook of psychotherapy and behavior change* (4th ed.). New York: Wiley.

Kline, N. S. (1958). Clinical experience with iproniazid (Marsilid). *J. Clin. Exp. Psychopathol., 19*(1, Suppl.), 72–78.

Kling, K. C., Hyde, J. S., Showers, C. J., & Buswell, B. N. (1999). Gender differences in self-esteem: A meta-analysis. *Psychol. Bull., 125*(4), 470–500.

Klocek, J. W., Oliver, J. M., & Ross, M. J. (1997). The role of dysfunctional attitudes, negative life events, and social support in the prediction of depressive dysphoria: A prospective longitudinal study. *Soc. Behav. Pers., 25*(2), 123–136.

Klopfer, B., & Davidson, H. (1962). *The Rorschach technique.* New York: Harcourt, Brace.

Kluft, R. P. (1985). Hypnotherapy of childhood multiple personality disorder. *Amer. J. Clin. Hyp., 27*(4), 201–210.

Kluft, R. P. (1987). The simulation and dissimulation of multiple personality disorder. *Amer. J. Clin. Hyp., 30*(2), 104–118.

Kluft, R. P. (1988). The dissociative disorders. In J. Talbott, R. Hales, & S. Yudofsky (Eds.), *Textbook of psychiatry.* Washington, DC: American Psychiatric Press.

Kluft, R. P. (1991). Multiple personality disorder. In A. Tasman & S. M. Goldfinger (Eds.), *American Psychiatric Press review of psychiatry* (Vol. 10). Washington, DC: American Psychiatric Press.

Kluft, R. P. (1992). Discussion: A specialist's perspective on multiple personality disorder. *Psychoanal. Inq., 12*(1), 139–171.

Kluft, R. P. (1993). Basic principles in conducting the psychotherapy of multiple personality disorder. In R. P. Kluft & C. G. Fine (Eds.), *Clinical perspectives on multiple personality disorder.* Washington, DC: American Psychiatric Press.

Kluft, R. P. (1999). An overview of the psychotherapy of dissociative identity disorder. *Amer. J. Psychother., 53*(3), 289–319.

Kluft, R. P. (2000). The psychoanalytic psychotherapy of dissociative identity disorder in the context of trauma therapy. *Psychoanal. Inq., 20*(2), 259–286.

Kluft, R. P. (2001). Dissociative disorders. In H. S. Friedman (Ed.), *Specialty articles from the encyclopedia of mental health.* San Diego: Academic Press.

Kluger, J. (2004). Blowing a gasket. *Time, 164*(23), December 6, 2004, 72–80.

Knapp, M., Barrett, B., Byford, S., Hallam, A., Davis, H., Tsiantis, J., et al. (2005). Primary prevention of child mental health problems using primary health care professionals: Cost comparisons. *Inter. J. Ment. Hlth. Promot., 7*(1), 95–102.

Knapp, S. L., & VandeCreek, L. (2000). Recovered memories of childhood abuse: Is there an underlying professional consensus? *Profess. Psychol. Res. Pract., 31*(4), 365–371.

Knapp, S. L., & VandeCreek, L. D. (2006). Confidentiality, privileged communications, and record keeping. In S. J. Knapp & L. D. VandeCreek, *Practical ethics for psychologists: A positive approach* (pp. 111–128). Washington, DC: American Psychological Association.

Knezevic, G., Opacic, G., Savic, D., & Priebe, S. (2005). Do personality traits predict post-traumatic stress? A prospective study in civilians experiencing air attacks. *Psychol. Med., 356*(5), 659–663.

Knight, B. G., Kaskie, B., Shurgot, G. R., & Dave, J. (2006). Improving the mental health of older adults. In J. E. Birren & K. W. Schaie (Eds.), *Handbook of the psychology of aging* (6th ed., pp. 408–425). San Diego, CA: Elsevier Academic Press.

Knowlton, L. (1997, May). Outreach Program aids homeless mentally ill. *Psychiatr. Times, XIV*(5).

Knox, K., & Roberts, A. R. (2005). Crisis intervention with stalking victims. In A. R. Roberts (Ed.), *Crisis intervention handbook: Assessment, treatment, and research* (3rd ed., pp. 483–498). New York: Oxford University Press.

Knutson, B., Wolkowitz, O. M., Cole, S. W., Chan, T., Moore, E. A., Johnson, R. C., et al. (1998). Selective alteration of personality and social behavior by serotonergic intervention. *Amer. J. Psychiat., 155,* 373–379.

Koegel, L. K., Koegel, R. L., & Brookman, L. I. (2005). Child-initiated interactions that are pivotal in intervention for children with autism. In E. D. Hibbs & P. S. Jensen (Eds.), *Psychosocial treatments for child and adolescent disorders: Empirically based strategies for clinical practice* (2nd ed., pp. 633–657). Washington, DC: American Psychological Association.

Koegel, L. K., Koegel, R. L., Hurley, C., & Frea, W. D. (1992). Improving social skills and disruptive behavior in children with autism through self-management. *J. Appl. Behav. Anal., 25*(2), 341–353.

Koehnken, G., Malpass, R. S., & Wogalter, M. S. (1996). Forensic applications of line-up research. In S. L. Sporer, R. S. Malpass, & G. Koehnken (Eds.), *Psychological issues in eyewitness identification* (pp. 205–231). Hillsdale, NJ: Erlbaum.

Koenig, H. G. (2002). The connection between psychoneuroimmunology and religion. In H. G. Koenig & H. J. Cohen (Eds.), *The link between religion and health: Psychoneuroimmunology and the faith factor.* New York: Oxford University Press.

Koenig, H. G., Hays, J. C., Larson, D. B., George, L. K., Cohen, H. J., McCullough, M. E., et al. (1999). Does religious attendance prolong survival? A six-year-follow-up study of 3,968 older adults. *J. Ger. A Biol. Sci. Med. Sci., 54*(7), M370–M376.

Koenigsberg, H. W., Anwunah, I., New, A. S., Mitropoulou, V., Schopick, F., & Siever, L. J. (1999). Relationship between depression and borderline personality disorder. *Depress. Anx., 10*(4), 158–167.

Koenigsberg, H. W., Buchsbaum, M. S., Buchsbaum, B. R., Schneiderman, J. S., Tang, C. Y., New, A., et al. (2005). Functional MRI of visuospatial working memory in schizotypal personality disorder: A region-of-interest analysis. *Psychol. Med., 35*(7), 1019–1030.

Koenigsberg, H. W., Harvey, P. D., Mitropoulou, V., Schmeidler, J., New, A. S., Goodman, M., et al. (2002). Characterizing affective instability in borderline personality disorder. *Amer. J. Psychiat., 159*(5), 784–788.

Koenigsberg, H. W., Woo-Ming, A. M., & Siever, L. J. (2002). Pharmacological treatments for personality disorders. In P. E. Nathan & J. M. Gorman (Eds.), *A guide to treatments that work* (2nd ed., pp. 625–641). London: Oxford University Press.

Koh, K. B., Kim, D. K., Kim, S. Y., & Park, J. K. (2005). The relation between anger expression, depression, and somatic symptoms in depressive disorders and somatoform disorders. *J. Clin. Psychiat., 66*(4), 485–491.

Koh, M., Nishimatsu, Y., & Endo, S. (2000). Dissociative disorder. *J. Inter. Soc. Life Info. Sci., 18*(2), 495–498.

Kohler, F. W., Strain, P. S., & Goldstein, H. (2005). Learning experiences . . . An alternative program for preschoolers and parents: Peer-mediated interventions for young children with autism. In E. D. Hibbs & P. S. Jensen (Eds.), *Psychosocial treatments for child and adolescent disorders: Empirically based strategies for clinical practice* (2nd ed., pp. 659–687). Washington, DC: American Psychological Association.

Kohut, H. (1977). *The restoration of the self.* New York: International Universities Press.

Kohut, H. (1984). *How does analysis cure?* Chicago: University of Chicago Press.

Kohut, H. (2001). On empathy. *Eur. J. Psychoanal. Ther. Res., 2*(2), 139–146.

Kohut, H., & Wolf, E. S. (1978). The disorders of the self and their treatment: An outline. *Inter. J. Psychoanal., 59*(4), 413–425.

Kokish, R., Levenson, J. S., & Blasingame, G. D. (2005). Post-conviction sex offender polygraph examination: Client-reported perceptions of utility and accuracy. *Sex. Abuse: J. Res. Treat., 17*(2), 211–221.

Kolff, C. A., & Doan, R. N. (1985). Victims of torture: Two testimonies. In E. Stover & E. O. Nightingale (Eds.), *The breaking of bodies and minds: Torture, psychiatric abuse, and the health professions.* New York: W. H. Freeman.

Kolodny, R., Masters, W. H., & Johnson, J. (1979). *Textbook of sexual medicine.* Boston: Little, Brown.

Komaroff, A. L., Masuda, M., & Holmes, T. H. (1986). The Social Readjustment Rating Scale: A comparative study of Negro, white, and Mexican Americans. *J. Psychosom. Res., 12,* 121–128.

Komaroff, A. L., Masuda, M., & Holmes, T. H. (1989). The Social Readjustment Rating Scale: A comparative study of Black, white, and Mexican Americans. In T. H. Holmes and E. M. David (Eds.), *Life change, life events, and illness.* New York: Praeger.

Kong, D. (1998, November 18). Still no solution in the struggle on safeguards—Doing harm: Research on the mentally ill. *Boston Globe,* p. A1.

Koopman, C., Palesh, O., Marten, B., Thompson, B., Ismailji, T., Holmes, D., et al. D. (2004). Child abuse and adult interpersonal trauma as predictors of posttraumatic stress disorder symptoms among women seeking treatment for intimate partner violence. In T. A. Corales (Ed.), *Focus on posttraumatic stress disorder research* (pp. 1–16). Hauppauge, NY: Nova Science.

Koorengevel, K. M., Beersma, D. G. M., den Boer, J. A., & van den Hoofdakker, R. H. (2002). A forced desynchrony study of circadian pacemaker characteristics in seasonal affective disorder. *J. Biol. Rhythms, 17*(5), 463–475.

Koorengevel, K. M., Beersma, D. G. M., de Boer, J. A., & van den Hoofdakker, R. H. (2003). Mood regulation in seasonal affective disorder patients and healthy controls studied in forced desynchrony. *Psychiatr. Res., 117*(1), 57–74.

Kopelowicz, A., Liberman, R. P., & Zarate, R. (2002). Psychosocial treatments for schizophrenia. In P. E. Nathan & J. M. Gorman (Eds.), *A guide to treatments that work* (2nd ed., pp. 201–228). London: Oxford University Press.

Koponen, H., Rantakallio, P., Veijola, J., Jones, P., Jokelainen, J., & Isohanni, M. (2004). Childhood central nervous system infections and risk for schizophrenia. *Eur. Arch. Psychiat. Clin. Neurosci., 254*(1), 9–13.

Korchin, S. J., & Sands, S. H. (1983). Principles common to all psychotherapies. In C. E. Walker (Ed.), *The handbook of clinical psychology.* Homewood, IL: Dow Jones-Irwin.

Kordon, A., Kahl, K. G., Broocks, A., Voderholzer, U., Rasche-Rauchle, H., & Hohagen, F. (2005). Clinical outcome in patients with obsessive-compulsive disorder after discontinuation of SRI treatment: Results from a two-year follow-up. *Eur. Arch. Psychiat. Clin. Neurosci., 255*(1), 48–50.

Koren, D., Norman, D., Cohen, A., Berman, J., & Klein, E. M. (2005). Increased PTSD risk with combat-related injury: A matched comparison study of injured and uninjured soldiers experiencing the same combat events. *Amer. J. Psychiat., 162*(2), 276–282.

Koss, M. P. (1993). Rape: Scope, impact, interventions, and public policy responses. *Amer. Psychologist, 48*(10), 1062–1069.

Koss, M. P. (2005). Empirically enhanced reflections on 20 years of rape research. *J. Interpers. Violence, 20*(1), 100–107.

Koss, M. P., & Heslet, L. (1992). Somatic consequences of violence against women. *Arch. Fam. Med., 1*(1), 53–59.

Koss, M. P., & Kilpatrick, D. G. (2001). Rape and sexual assault. In E. Gerrity, T. M. Keane, & F. Tuma (Eds.), *The mental health consequences of torture* (pp. 177–193). New York: Kluwer Academic/Plenum.

Koss, M. P., Woodruff, W. J., & Koss, P. (1991). Criminal victimization among primary care medical patients: Prevalence, incidence, and physician usage. *Behav. Sci. Law, 9,* 85–96.

Kosslyn, S. M., & Rosenberg, R. S. (2004). *Psychology: The brain, the person, the world* (2nd ed.). Essex, England: Pearson Education Limited.

Kosten, T. R., George, T. P., & Kleber, H. D. (2005). The neurobiology of substance dependence: Implications for treatment. In R. J. Frances, A. H. Mack, & S. I. Miller (Eds.), *Clinical textbook of addictive disorders* (3rd ed., pp. 3–15). New York: Guilford Press.

Kouri, E. M., & Pope, H. G., Jr. (2000). Abstinence symptoms during withdrawal from chronic marijuana use. *Exp. Clin. Psychopharmacol., 8*(4), 483–492.

Kovacs, M., Goldston, D., & Gatsonis, C. (1993). Suicidal behaviors and childhood-onset depressive disorders: A longitudinal investigation. *J. Amer. Acad. Child Adol. Psychiat., 32,* 8–20.

Kraines, S. H., & Thetford, E. S. (1972). *Help for the depressed.* Springfield, IL: Thomas.

Krakauer, S. Y. (2001). *Treating dissociative identity disorder: The power of the collective heart.* Philadelphia: Brunner-Routledge.

Krantz, L. (1992). *What the odds are.* New York: Harper Perennial.

Krapohl, D. J. (2002). The polygraph in personnel screening. In M. Kleiner (Ed.), *The handbook of polygraph testing.* San Diego, CA: Academic.

Kratochwill, T. R. (1992). Single-case research design and analysis: An overview. In T. R. Kratochwill & J. R. Levin (Eds.), *Single-case research design and analysis: New directions for psychology and education.* Hillsdale, NJ: Erlbaum.

Krause, N. (2006). Religion and health in late life. In J. E. Birren & K. W. Schaie (Eds.), *Handbook of the Psychology of Aging* (6th ed., pp. 500–518). San Diego, CA: Elsevier Academic Press.

Krauss, M. W., Seltzer, M. M., & Goodman, S. J. (1992). Social support networks of adults with mental retardation who live at home. *Amer. J. Ment. Retard., 96*(4), 432–441.

Kress, V. E. W., Eriksen, K. P., Rayle, A. D., & Ford, S. J. W. (2005). The DSM-IV-TR and culture: Considerations for counselors. *J. Couns. Dev., 83*(1), 97–104.

Kressel, N. J., & Kressel, D. F. (2002). *Stack and sway: The new science of jury consulting.* Boulder, CO: Westview.

Kring, A. M., & Neale, J. M. (1996). Do schizophrenic patients show a disjunctive relationship among expressive, experiential, and psychophysiological components of emotion? *J. Abnorm. Psychol., 105*(2), 249–257.

Krishnan, K. R. R., Swartz, M. S., Larson, M. J., & Santo-Liquido, G. (1984). Funeral mania in recurrent bipolar affective disorders: Reports of three cases. *J. Clin. Psychiat., 45,* 310–311.

Kropp, P. R., Hart, S. D., & Lyon, D. R. (2002). Risk assessment of stalkers: Some problems and possible solutions. *Criminal Justice Behav., 29*(5), 590–616.

Krueger, R. G., & Kaplan, M. S. (2000). Evaluation and treatment of sexual disorders: Frottage. In L. Vandecreed & T. L. Jackson (Eds.), *Innovations in clinical practice: A source book* (Vol. 18, pp. 185–197). Sarasota, FL: Professional Resource Press.

Krueger, R. G., & Kaplan, M. S. (2002). Behavioral and psychopharmacological treatment of the paraphilic and hypersexual disorders. *J. Psychiatr. Prac., 8*(1), 21–32.

Kruger, S., Young, L. T., & Braunig, P. (2005). Pharmacotherapy of bipolar mixed states. *Bipolar Disord. 7*(3), 205–215.

Kubler, A., Murphy, K., & Garavan, H. (2005). Cocaine dependence and attention switching within and between verbal and visuospatial working memory. *Eur. J. Neurosci., 21*(7), 1984–1992.

Kuehner, C. (2005). An evaluation of the "Coping with Depression Course" for relapse prevention with unipolar depressed patients. *Psychother. Psychosomat., 74*(4), 254–259.

Kuhn, K. U., Joe, A. Y., Meyer, K., Reichmann, K., Maier, W., Rao, M. L., Reinhardt, M. J., Biersack, H. J., & Quednow, B. B. (2004). Neuroimaging and 5-HT-sub(2C) receptor polymorphism: A HMPAO-SPECT study in healthy male probands using mCPP-challenge of the 5-HT-sub(2C) receptor. *Pharmacopsychiatry, 37*(6), 286–293.

Kuhn, R. (1958). The treatment of depressive states with G-22355 (imipramine hydrochloride). *Amer. J. Psychiat., 115,* 459–464.

Kuhn, T. S. (1962). *The structure of scientific revolutions.* Chicago: University of Chicago Press.

Kulic, K. R. (2005). The crisis intervention semistructured interview. *Brief Treat. Crisis Intervent., 5*(2), 143–157.

Kulka, R. A., Schlesenger, W. E., Fairbank, J. A., Hough. R. L., Jordan, B. K., Marmar, C. R., et al. (1990). *Trauma and the Vietnam War generation: Report of findings from the National Vietnam Veterans Readjustment Study.* New York: Brunner/Mazel.

Kumari, V., Das, M., Hodgins, S., Zachariah, E., Barkataki, I., Howlett, M., et al. (2005). Association between violent behaviour and impaired prepulse inhibition of the startle response in antisocial personality disorder and schizophrenia. *Behav. Brain Res., 158,* 159–166.

Kung, S., & Mrazek, D. A. (2005). Psychiatric emergency department visits on full-moon nights. *Psychiatr. Serv., 56*(2), 221–222.

Kung, W. V. (2004). Cultural and practical barriers to seeking mental health treatment for Chinese Americans. *J. Comm. Psychol., 32*(1), 27–43.

Kupfer, D. J. (2005). The increasing medical burden in bipolar disorder. *JAMA, 293*(20), 2528–2530.

Kuriansky, J. B. (1988). Personality style and sexuality. In R. A. Brown & J. R. Field (Eds.), *Treatment of sexual problems in individual and couples therapy.* Costa Mesa, CA: PMA Publishing.

Kurtz, D. L., Stewart, R. B., Zweifel, M., Li, T.-K., & Froehlich, J. C. (1996). Genetic differences in tolerance and sensitization to the sedative/hypnotic effects of alcohol. *Pharmacol. Biochem. Behav., 53*(3), 585–591.

La Vaque, T. J., & Rossiter, T. (2001). The ethical use of placebo controls in clinical research: the Declaration of Helsinki. *Appl Psychophysiol Biofeedback, 26,* 23–37.

Lachmann, A., & Lachmann, F. M. (1995). The personification of evil: Motivations and fantasies of the serial killer. *Inter. Forum Psychoanal., 4*(1), 17–23.

Lacks, P. (1984). *Bender Gestalt screening for brain dysfunction.* New York: Wiley.

Lahey, B. B., & Loeber, R. (1994). Framework for a developmental model of oppositional defiant disorder and conduct disorder. In D. K. Routh (Ed.), *Disruptive behavior disorders in childhood* (pp. 139–180). New York: Plenum.

Lahey, B. B., Loeber, R., Burke, J. D., & Applegate, B. (2005). Predicting future antisocial personality disorder in males from a clinical assessment in childhood. *J. Cons. Clin. Psychol., 73*(3), 389–399.

Laing, R. D. (1959). *The divided self: An existential study in sanity and madness.* London: Tavistock.

Laing, R. D. (1964). *The divided self* (2nd ed.). London: Pelican.

Laing, R. D. (1967). *The politics of experience.* New York: Pantheon.

Lakin, K. C., Anderson, L., Prouty, R., & Polister, B. (1999). State institution populations less than one third of 1977, residents older with more impairments. *Ment. Retard., 37,* 85–86.

Lakin, K. C., Prouty, B., Smith, G., & Braddock, D. (1996). Nixon goal surpassed: Two-fold. *Ment. Retard., 34,* 67.

Lalonde, J. K., Hudson, J. I., Gigante, R. A., & Pope, H. G. Jr. (2001). Canadian and American psychiatrists' attitudes toward dissociative disorders diagnoses. *Canad. J. Psychiat., 46*(5), 407–412.

Lalonde, J. K., Hudson, J. I., & Pope, H. G. Jr. (2002). Canadian and American psychiatrists' attitudes toward dissociative disorder diagnoses: The authors reply. *Canad. J. Psychiat., 47*(3), 1.

Lalumiere, M. L., Harris, G. T., Quinsey, V. L., & Rice, M. E. (2005). Sexual interest in rape. In G. T Harris, V. L. Quinsey, M. E. Rice, & M. L. Lalumiere (Eds.), *The causes of rape: Understanding individual differences in male propensity for sexual aggression* (pp. 105–128). Washington, DC: American Psychological Association.

Lamb, M. (1998). Cybersex: Research notes on the characteristics of the visitors to online chat rooms. *Deviant Behav.: Interdiscip. J., 19,* 121–135.

Lambert, K., & Kinsley, C. H. (2005). *Clinical neuroscience: The neurobiological foundations of mental health.* New York: Worth Publishers.

Lambert, M. J., & Bergin, A. E. (1994). The effectiveness of psychotherapy. In A. E. Bergin & S. L. Garfield (Eds.), *Handbook of psychotherapy and behavioral change* (4th ed.). New York: Wiley.

Lambert, M. J., Harman, C., Slade, K., Whipple, J. L., & Hawkins, E. J. (2005). Providing feedback to psychotherapists on their patients' progress: Clinical results and practice suggestions. *J. Clin. Psychol., 61,* 165–174.

Lambert, M. J., Shapiro, D. A., & Bergin, A. E. (1986). The effectiveness of psychotherapy. In S. L. Garfield & A. E. Bergin (Eds.), *Handbook of psychotherapy and behavioral change* (3rd ed.). New York: Wiley.

Lambert, M. J., Weber, F. D., & Sykes, J. D. (1993, April). Psychotherapy versus placebo. Poster presented at the annual meeting of the Western Psychological Association, Phoenix, AZ.

Lambert, M. T. (2003). Suicide risk assessment and management: Focus on personality disorders. *Curr. Opin. Psychiat., 16*(1), 71–76.

Lambert, N., Nihira, K., & Leland, H. (1993). *AAMR Adaptive Behavior Scale: School* (2nd ed.). Austin, TX: Pro-Ed.

Landau, B. M. (2001). Psychotherapy online in 2001: For psychotherapists new to the Internet. *J. Ment. Imagery, 25*(1–2), 65–82.

Landon, T. M., & Barlow, D. H. (2004). Cognitive-behavioral treatment for panic disorder: Current status. *J. Psychiatr. Pract., 10*(4), 211–226.

Landry, M. J. (1994). *Understanding drugs of abuse: The processes of addiction, treatment, and recovery.* Washington, DC: American Psychiatric Press.

Landsbergis, P. A., Schnall, P. L., Belkic, K. L., Baker, D., Schwartz, J. E., & Pickering T. G. (2003). The workplace and cardiovascular disease: Relevance and potential role for occupational health psychology. In L. E. Tetrick & J. C. Quick (Eds.), *Handbook of occupational health psychology.* Washington, DC: American Psychological Association.

Landsbergis, P. A., Schnall, P. L., Warren, K., Pickering, T. G., & Schwartz, J. E. (1994). Association between ambulatory blood pressure and alternative formulations of job strain. *Scand. J. Work Envir. Hlth., 20,* 349–363.

Lane, J. (1999). Habitual moderate caffeine consumption elevates blood pressure and levels of stress hormones. Paper presented at 1999 meeting of the Society of Behavioral Medicine, San Diego, CA.

Lang, A. J. (2004). Treating generalized anxiety disorder with cognitive-behavioral therapy. *J. Clin. Psychiat., 65*(Suppl. 13), 14–19.

Lang, J. (1999, April 16). Local jails dumping grounds for mentally ill. *Detroit News.*

Lange, A., van de Ven, J. P., Schrieken, B., & Smit, M. (2004). "Interapy" burnout: Prevention and therapy of burnout via the Internet. *Verhaltenstherapie, 14*(3), 190–199.

Langenbucher, J., & Nathan, P. E. (2006). Diagnosis and classification. In F. Andrasik (Ed.), *Comprehensive handbook of personality and psychopathology, Volume II: Adult psychopathology* (pp. 3–20). Hoboken, NJ: Wiley.

Langer, E. J. (1983). *The psychology of control.* Beverly Hills, CA: Sage.

Langevin, R., Bain, J., Wortzman, G., Hucker, S., et al. (1988). Sexual sadism: Brain, blood, and behavior. *Ann. N.Y. Acad. Sci., 528,* 163–171.

Langstrom, N., & Zucker, K. J. (2005). Transvestic fetishism in the general population: Prevalence and correlates. *J. Sex Marital Ther., 31*(2), 87–95.

Lara, M. E., & Klein, D. N. (1999). Psychosocial processes underlying the maintenance and persistence of depression: Implications for understanding chronic depression. *Clin. Psychol. Rev., 19*(5), 553–570.

Larsson, B., & Ivarsson, T. (1998). Clinical characteristics of adolescent psychiatric inpatients who have attempted suicide. *Eur. Child Adol. Psychiat., 7*(4), 201–208.

Laruelle, M., & Abi-Dargham, A. (1999). Dopamine as the wind of the psychotic fire: New evidence from brain imaging studies. *J. Psychopharmacol., 13*(4), 358–371.

Lask, B., & Bryant-Waugh, R. (Eds.). (2000). *Anorexia nervosa and related eating disorders in childhood and adolescence* (2nd ed.). Hove, England: Psychology Press/Taylor & Francis.

Latner, J. D., & Wilson, G. T. (2002). Self-monitoring and the assessment of binge eating. *Behav. Ther., 33*(3), 465–477.

Lauber, C., Keller, C., Eichenberger, A., & Rossler, W. (2005). Family burden during exacerbation of schizophrenia: Quantification and determinants of additional costs. *Inter. J. Soc. Psychiat., 51*(3), 259–264.

Laumann, E. O., Gagnon, J. H., Michael, R. T., & Michaels, S. (1994). *The social organization of sexuality.* Chicago: University of Chicago Press.

Laumann, E. O., Paik, A., & Rosen, R. C. (1999). Sexual dysfunction in the United States: Prevalence and predictors. *JAMA, 281*(13), 1174.

Lauronen, E., Veijola, J., Isohanni, I., Jones, P. B., Nieminen, P., & Isohanni, M. (2004). Link between creativity and mental disorder. *Psychiatry: Interpers. Biol. Process., 67*(1), 81–98.

Laverty, W. H., & Kelly, I. W. (1998). Cyclical calendar and lunar patterns in automobile property accidents and injury accidents. *Percept. Motor Skills, 86,* 299–302.

Lawford, B. R., Young, R. McD., Rowell, J. A., Gibson, J. N., et al. (1997). Association of the D2 dopamine receptor A1 allele with alcoholism: Medical severity of alcoholism and type of controls. *Biol. Psychiat., 41,* 386–393.

Lawlor, B. A., McCarron, M., Wilson, G., & McLoughlin, M. (2001). Temporal lobe-oriented CT scanning and dementia in Down's syndrome. *Inter. J. Ger. Psychiat., 16*(4), 427–429.

Lawrence, C. (1987). An integrated spiritual and psychological growth model in the treatment of narcissism. *J. Psychol. Theol., 15*(3), 205–213.

Laws, D., Hudson, S., & Ward, T. (2000). *Remaking relapse prevention with sex offenders: A sourcebook.* Thousand Oaks, CA: Sage.

Lawson, W. B. (1986). Racial and ethnic factors in psychiatric research. *Hosp. Comm. Psychiat., 37,* 50–54.

Lawson, W. B. (1996). Clinical issues in the pharmacotherapy of African-Americans. *Psychopharmacol. Bull., 32,* 275–281.

Lawson, W. B., Hepler, N., Holladay, J., & Cuffel, B. (1994). Race as a factor in inpatient and outpatient admissions and diagnosis. *Hosp. Comm. Psychiat., 45*(1), 72–74.

Lay, B., Jennen-Steinmetz, C., Reinhard I., & Schmidt, M. H. (2002). Characteristics of inpatient weight gain in adolescent anorexia nervosa: Relation to speed of relapse and re-admission. *Eur. Eat. Disord. Rev., 10*(1), 22–40.

Lazarov, O., Robinson, J., Tang, Y. P., Hairston, I. S., Korade-Mirnics, Z., Lee, V. M., et al. (2005). Environmental enrichment reduces Abeta levels and amyloid deposition in transgenic mice. *Cell, 120*(5), 572–574.

Lazarus, A. A. (1965). The treatment of a sexually inadequate man. In L. P. Ullman & L. Krasner (Eds.), *Case studies in behavior modification.* New York: Holt, Rinehart & Winston.

Lazarus, R. S., & Folkman, S. (1984). *Stress, appraisal, and coping.* New York: Springer.

Le Unes, A. D., Nation, J. R., & Turley, N. M. (1980). Male-female performance in learned helplessness. *J. Psychol., 104,* 255–258.

Leahy, R. L. (2004). Cognitive-behavioral therapy. In R. G. Heimberg, C. J. Turk, & D. S. Mennin (Eds.), *Generalized anxiety disorder: Advances in research and practice.* New York: Guilford Press.

Leahy, R. L. (2005). Special series: Cognitive therapy of bipolar disorder: Introduction. *Cog. Behav. Pract., 12*(1), 64–65.

Leahy, R. L., Beck, J., & Beck, A. T. (2005). Cognitive therapy for the personality disorders. In S. Strack (Ed.), *Handbook of personality and psychopathology* (pp. 442–461). Hoboken, NJ: Wiley.

Lean, M. E., Han, T. S., & Seidell, J. C. (1999). Impairment of health and quality of life using new U.S. federal guidelines for the identification of obesity. *Arch. Internal Med., 159*(8), 837–843.

Leane, W., & Shute, R. (1998). Youth suicide: The knowledge and attitudes of Australian teachers and clergy. *Suic. Life-Threat. Behav., 28*(2), 165–173.

Leavitt, F. (2001). Iatrogenic recovered memories: Examining the empirical evidence. *Amer. J. Forens. Psychol., 19*(2), 21–32.

Leavitt, F. (2002). "The reality of repressed memories" revisited and principles of science. *J. Trauma. Dissoc., 3*(1), 19–35.

Lebegue, B. (1991). Paraphilias in U.S. pornography titles: "Pornography made me do it" (Ted Bundy). *Bull. Amer. Acad. Psychiat. Law, 19*(1), 43–48.

Lebell, M. B., Marder, S. R., Mintz, J., Mintz, L. I., Tompson, M., Wirshing, W., et al. (1993). Patients' perceptions of family emotional climate and outcome in schizophrenia. *Brit. J. Psychiat., 162,* 751–754.

LeCroy, C. W. (2005). Building an effective primary prevention program for adolescent girls: Empirically based design and evaluation. *Brief Treat. Crisis Intervent., 5*(1), 75–84.

Ledley, D. R., & Heimberg, R. G. (2005). Social anxiety disorder. In M. M. Antony, D. R. Ledley, & R. G. Heimberg (Eds.), *Improving outcomes and preventing relapse in cognitive-behavioral therapy* (pp. 38–76). New York: Guilford Press.

Ledoux, S., Miller, P., Choquet, M., & Plant, M. (2002). Family structure, parent-child relationships, and alcohol and other drug use among teenagers in France and the United Kingdom. *Alcohol Alcoholism, 37*(1), 52–60.

Lee, D. E. (1985). Alternative self-destruction. *Percept. Motor Skills, 61*(3, Part 2), 1065–1066.

Lee, E. H., Chung, B. Y., Park, H. B., & Chun, K. H. (2004). Relationships of mood disturbance and social support to symptom experience in Korean women with breast cancer. *J. Pain Sympt. Manag., 27*(5), 425–433.

Lee, J., & Sue, S. (2001). Clinical psychology and culture. In D. Matsumoto (Ed.), *The handbook of culture and psychology.* New York: Oxford University Press.

Lee, P. W. H., Lieh-Mak, F., Yu, K. K., & Spinks, J. A. (1993). Coping strategies of schizophrenic patients and their relationship to outcome. *Brit. J. Psychiat., 163,* 177–182.

Lee, R. K. K., Jimenez, J., Cox, A. J., & Wurtman, R. J. (1996). Metabotropic glutamate receptors regulate APP processing in hippocampal neurons and cortical astrocytes derived from fetal rats. In R. J. Wurtman, S. Corkin, J. H. Growdon, & R. M. Nitsch (Eds.), *The neurobiology of Alzheimer's disease.* New York: New York Academy of Sciences.

Lee, T., & Seeman, P. (1980). Elevation of brain neuroleptic/dopamine receptors in schizophrenia. *Amer. J. Psychiat., 137,* 191–197.

Leenaars, A. A. (1989). *Suicide notes: Predictive clues and patterns.* New York: Human Sciences Press.

Leenaars, A. A. (1991). Suicide in the young adult. In A. A. Leenaars (Ed.), *Life span perspectives of suicide: Time-lines in the suicide process.* New York: Plenum Press.

Leenaars, A. A. (2002). In defense of the idiographic approach: Studies of suicide notes and personal documents. *Arch. Suic. Res., 6*(1), 19–30.

Leenaars, A. A. (2004). Altruistic suicide: A few reflections. *Arch. Suic. Res., 8*(1), 1–7.

Leenaars, A. A., Connolly, J., Cantor, C., EchoHawk, M., He, Z.-X., Kokorina, N., et al. (2001). Suicide, assisted suicide and euthanasia: International perspectives. *Irish J. Psychol. Med., 18*(1), 33–37.

Leenaars, A. A., & Lester, D. (1992). Facts and myths of suicide in Canada and the United States. *J. Soc. Psychol., 132*(6), 787–789.

Leenaars, A. A., & Lester, D. (2004). The impact of suicide prevention centers on the suicide rate in the Canadian provinces. *Crisis, 25*(2), 65–68.

Leenaars, A. A., Lester, D., & Wenckstern, S. (2005). Coping with suicide in the schools: The art and the research. In D. Lester & R. I. Yufit (Eds.), *Assessment, treatment, and prevention of suicidal behavior* (pp. 347–377). New York: Wiley.

Leenaars, A. A., Moksony, F., Lester, D., & Wenckstern, S. (2003). The impact of gun control (Bill C-51) on suicide in Canada. *Death Stud., 27*(2), 103–124.

Leenstra, A. S., Ormel, J., & Giel, R. (1995). Positive life change and recovery from depression and anxiety: A three-stage longitudinal study of primary care attenders. *Brit. J. Psychiat., 166*(3), 333–343.

Legrand, L. N., Iacono, W. G., & McGue, M. (2005). Predicting addiction: Behavioral genetics uses twins and time to decipher the origins of addiction and learn who is most vulnerable. *Amer. Sci., 93*(2), March–April 2005, 140–147.

LeGrange, D., & Lock, J. (2002). Bulimia nervosa in adolescents: Treatment, eating pathology and comorbidity. *S. Afr. Psychiat. Rev., 5*(3), 19–22, 24–25.

Lehman, A. F., Myers, C. P., Dixon, L. B., & Johnson, J. L. (1996). Detection of substance use disorders among psychiatric inpatients. *J. Nerv. Ment. Dis., 184*(4), 228–233.

Lehmann, H. E. (1985). Current perspectives on the biology of schizophrenia. In M. N. Menuck & M. V. Seeman. *New perspectives in schizophrenia.* New York: Macmillan.

Leiblum, S. R. (2002). After sildenafil: Bridging the gap between pharmacologic treatment and satisfying sexual relationships. *J. Clin. Psychiat., 63*(Suppl. 5), 17–33.

Leiblum, S. R. (2004). Gay marriage: Notes from North America. *Sex. Relation. Ther., 19*(4), 361–362.

Leiblum, S. R., & Rosen, R. C. (Eds.). (2000). *Principles and practice of sex therapy* (3rd ed.). New York: Guilford Press.

Leiblum, S. R., & Segraves, R. T. (1995). Sex and aging. In J. M. Oldham & M. B. Riba (Eds.), *American Psychiatric Press review of psychiatry* (Vol. 14). Washington, DC: American Psychiatric Press.

Leibowitz, S. F., & Hoebel, B. G. (1998). Behavioral neuroscience of obesity. In G. A. Bray, C. Bouchard, & P. T. James (Eds.), *The handbook of obesity.* New York: Dekker.

Leichsenring, F. (2001). Comparative effects of short-term psychodynamic psychotherapy and cognitive-behavioral therapy in depression. A meta-analytic approach. *Clin. Psychol. Rev., 21*(3), 401–419.

Leichsenring, F., Rabung, S., & Leibing, E. (2004). The efficacy of short-term psychodynamic psychotherapy in specific psychiatric disorders: A meta-analysis. *Arch. Gen. Psychiat., 61*(12), 1208–1216.

Lekander, M. (2002). Ecological immunology: The role of the immune system in psychology and neuroscience. *Eur. Psychiat., 7*(2), 98–115.

LeMarquand, D., Tremblay, R. E., & Vitaro, F. (2001). The prevention of conduct disorder: A review of successful and unsuccessful experiments. In J. Hill & B. Maughan (Eds.), *Conduct disorders in childhood and adolescence* (pp. 449–477). New York: Cambridge University Press.

Lemonick, M. D., & Goldstein, A. (2002, April 14). At your own risk. *Time,* 46–57.

Lengua, L. J., Long, A. C., Smith, K. I., & Meltzoff, A. N. (2005). Pre-attack symptomatology and temperament as predictors of children's responses to the September 11 terrorist attacks. *J. Child Psychol. Psychiat., 46*(6), 631–645.

Lenox, R. H., McNamara, R. F., Papke, R. L., & Manji, H. K. (1998). Neurobiology of lithium: An update. *J. Clin. Psychiat., 59*(Suppl. 6), 37–47.

Lenzenweger, M. F., & Clarkin, J. F. (2005). The personality disorders: History, classification, and research issues. In J. F. Lenzenweger & J. F. Clarkin (Eds.), *Major theories of personality disorder* (2nd ed., pp. 1–42). New York: Guilford Press.

Leon, G. R. (1984). *Case histories of deviant behavior* (3rd ed.). Boston: Allyn & Bacon.

Leonard, H., & Wen, X. (2002). The epidemiology of mental retardation: Challenges and opportunities in the new millennium. *Ment. Retard. Disabil. Res. Rev., 8,* 117–134.

Leonardo, E. D., & Hen, R. (2006). Genetics of affective and anxiety disorders. *Annu. Rev. Psychol., 57,* 117–137.

Leong, G. B. (2000). Diminished capacity and insanity in Washington State: The battle shifts to admissibility. *J. Amer. Acad. Psychiat. Law, 28*(1), 77–81.

Leppamaki, S., Partonen, T., Vakkun, O., Lonnqvist, J., Partinen, M., & Laudon, M. (2003). Effect of controlled-release melatonin on sleep quality, mood, and quality of life in subjects with seasonal or weather-associated changes in mood and behaviour. *Eur. Neuropsychopharmacology, 13*(3), 137–145.

Leroux, J. A. (1986). Suicidal behavior and gifted adolescents. *Roper Rev., 9*(2), 77–79.

Leserman, J., Drossman, D. A., Li, Z., Toomey, T. C., et al. (1996). Sexual and physical abuse history in gastroenterology practice: How types of abuse impact health status. *Psychosom. Med., 58*(1), 4–15.

Leshner, A. I., et al. (1992). *Outcasts on the main street: Report of the Federal Task Force on Homelessness and Severe Mental Illness.* Washington, DC: Interagency Council on the Homeless.

Lester, D. (1972). Myth of suicide prevention. *Comprehen. Psychiat., 13*(6), 555–560.

Lester, D. (1974). The effects of suicide prevention centers on suicide rates in the United States. *Pub. Hlth. Rep., 89,* 37–39.

Lester, D. (1985). The quality of life in modern America and suicide and homicide rates. *J. Soc. Psychol., 125*(6), 779–780.

Lester, D. (1989). *Can we prevent suicide?* New York: AMS Press

Lester, D. (1991). The etiology of suicide and homicide in urban and rural America. *J. Rural Commun. Psychol., 12*(1), 15–27.

Lester, D. (1998). Differences in content of suicide notes by age and method. *Percept. Motor Skills, 87*(2), 530.

Lester, D. (2000). *Why people kill themselves: A 2000 summary of research on suicide.* Springfield, IL: Charles C. Thomas

Lester, D., & Saito, Y. (1999). The reasons for suicide in Japan. *Omega: J. Death Dying, 38*(1), 65–68.

Lester, D., Wood, P., Williams, C., & Haines, J. (2004). Motives for suicide: A study of Australian suicide notes. *Crisis, 25*(1), 33–34.

Letourneau, E., & O'Donohue, W. (1993). Sexual desire disorders. In W. O'Donohue & J. Geer (Eds.), *Handbook of sexual dysfunctions.* Boston: Allyn & Bacon.

Leutwyler, K. (1996). Paying attention: The controversy over ADHD and the drug Ritalin is obscuring a real look at the disorder and its underpinnings. *Scientif. Amer., 272*(2), 12–13.

Levant, R. F. (2000, February). Interviewed in P. A. McGuire. New hope for people with schizophrenia. *Monitor Psychol., 31*(2), 24–28.

LeVay, S., & Hamer, D. H. (1994). Evidence for a biological influence in male homosexuality. [Review]. *Scientif. Amer., 270*(5), pp. 44–49.

Levenson, E. (1987). Language and healing. In S. Slipp (Ed.), *Curative factors in dynamic psychotherapy* (pp. 91–103). New York: McGraw-Hill.

Levenson, M. R. (1992). Rethinking psychopathy. *Theory Psychol., 2*(1), 51–71.

Levesque, R. J. R. (1996). Regulating the private relations of adults with mental disabilities: Old laws, new policies, hollow hopes. *Behav. Sci. Law, 14,* 83–106.

Levesque, R. J. R. (2002). *Dangerous adolescents, model adolescents: Shaping the role and promise of education.* New York: Kluwer Academic/Plenum Publishers.

Levine, M. D. (1987). *How schools can help combat student eating disorders: Anorexia nervosa and bulimia.* Washington, DC: National Education Assoc.

Lévi-Strauss, C. (1977). *L'identité.* Paris: Presses Universitaires de France.

Levitt, J. L., Sansone, R. A., & Cohn, L. (Eds.). (2004). *Self-harm and eating disorders: Dynamics, assessment, and treatment.* New York: Brunner-Routledge.

Levitt, R. (1975). Psychopharmacology: A biological approach. New York: Wiley.

Levy, E., Shefler, G., Loewenthal, U., Umansky, R., Bar, G., & Heresco-Levy, U. (2005). Characteristics of schizophrenia residents and staff rejection in community mental health hostels. *Israel J. Psychiat. Rel. Sci., 42*(1), 23–32.

Levy, S. (2004, December 13). What your college kid is really up to. *Newsweek, 144*(24), 12.

Leweke, F. M., Gerth, C. W., Koethe, D., Klosterkotter, J., Ruslanova, I., Krivogorsky, B., et al. (2004). Antibodies to infectious agents in individuals with recent onset schizophrenia. *Eur. Arch. Psychiat. Clin. Neurosci., 254*(1), 4–8.

Lewin, B. D. (1950). *The psychoanalysis of elation.* New York: Norton.

Lewin, E. (2004). Does marriage have a future? *J. Marr. Fam., 66*(4), 1000–1006.

Lewins, F. (2002). Explaining stable partnerships among FTMs and MTFs: A significant difference? *J. Sociol., 38*(1), 76–88.

Lewinsohn, P. M., Antonuccio, D. O., Steinmetz, J. L., & Teri, L. (1984). *The coping with depression course.* Eugene, OR: Castalia.

Lewinsohn, P. M., & Clarke, G. N. (1999). Psychosocial treatment for adolescent depression. *Clin. Psychol. Rev., 19*(3), 329–342.

Lewinsohn, P. M., Clarke, G. N., Hops, H., & Andrews, J. (1990). Cognitive-behavioral treatment for depressed adolescents. *Behav. Ther., 21,* 385–401.

Lewinsohn, P. M., Hoberman, H. M., Rosenbaum, M. (1988). A prospective study of risk factors for unipolar depression. *J Abnorm Psychol., 97*(3), 251–264.

Lewinsohn, P. M., Rohde, P., Teri, L., & Tilson, M. (1990, April). Presentation. Western Psychological Association.

Lewinsohn, P. M., Sullivan, J. M., & Grosscup, S. J. (1982). Behavioral therapy: Clinical applications. In A. T. Rush (Ed.), *Short-term psychotherapies for the depressed patient.* New York: Guilford Press.

Lewinsohn, P. M., Youngren, M. A., & Grosscup, S. J. (1979). Reinforcement and depression. In R. A. Depue (Ed.), *The psychobiology of the depressive disorders.* New York: Academic Press.

Lewis, L. (2005). Patient perspectives on the diagnosis, treatment, and management of bipolar disorder. *Bipolar Disord., 7*(Suppl. 1), 33–37.

Lewis, L., & Hoofnagle, L. (2005). Patient perspectives on provider competence: A view from the Depression and Bipolar Support Alliance. *Admin. Policy Ment. Hlth., 32*(5–6), 497–503.

Lewis, N. D., & Piotrowski, Z. A. (1954) Clinical diagnosis of manic-depressive psychosis. *Proc. Annu. Meet. Am. Psychopathol. Assoc., 12* (42d Meeting), 25–28.

Lewis, O., & Chatoor, I. (1994). Eating disorders. In J. M. Oldham & M. B. Riba (Eds.), *Review of psychiatry* (Vol. 13). Washington, DC: American Psychiatric Press.

Lewis-Harter, S. (2000). Psychosocial adjustment of adult children of alcoholics: A review of the recent empirical literature. *Clin. Psychol. Rev., 20*(3), 311–337.

Lewy, A. J., Emens, J. S., Bernert, R. A., & Lefler, B. J. (2004). Eventual entrainment of the human circadian pacemaker by melatonin is independent of the circadian phase of treatment initiation: Clinical implications. *J. Biol. Rhythms, 19*(1), 68–75.

Ley, R. (2004). The CEO theory of catastrophic misinterpretations and panic: A cognitive executive-control economic-organizational model. *Behav. Therapist, 27*(1), 21.

Li, R., & El Mallakh, R. S. (2004). Differential response of bipolar and normal control lymphoblastoid cell sodium pump to ethacrynic acid. *J. Affect. Disorders, 80*(1), 11–17.

Li, T. K. (2000). Pharmacogenetics of responses to alcohol and genes that influence alcohol drinking. *J. Stud. Alc., 61*(1), 5–12.

Liberman, R. P. (1982). Assessment of social skills. *Schizo. Bull., 8*(1), 82–84.

Liberman, R. P., & Raskin, D. E. (1971). Depression: A behavioral formulation. *Arch. Gen. Psychiat., 24,* 515–523.

Libow, J. A. (1995). Munchausen by proxy victims in adulthood: A first look. *Child Abuse Negl., 19*(9), 1131–1142.

Libow, J. A., & Schreirer, H. A. (1998) Factitious disorder by proxy. In R. T. Ammerman & J. V. Campo (Eds.), *Handbook of pediatric psychology and psychiatry: Vol. 1. Psychological and psychiatric issues in the pediatric setting.* Boston: Allyn & Bacon.

Lickey, M. E., & Gordon, B. (1991). *Medicine and mental illness: The use of drugs in psychiatry.* New York: W. H. Freeman.

Lieb, K., Zanarini, C., Schmal, C., Linehan, M. M., & Bohus, M. (2004). Borderline personality disorder. *Lancet, 364,* 453–461.

Lieb, R., Merikangas, K. R., Hoefler, M., Pfister, H., Isensee, B., & Wittchen, H. U. (2002). Parental alcohol use disorders and alcohol use and disorders in offspring: A community study. *Psychol. Med., 32*(1), 63–78.

Lieber, A. L. (1978). Human aggression and the lunar synodic cycle. *J. Clin. Psychiat., 39*(5), 385–392.

Lieberman, J. A., Chakos, M., Wu, H., Alvir, J., Hoffman, E., Robinson, D., et al. (2001). Longitudinal study of brain morphology in first episode schizophrenia. *Biol. Psychiat., 49*(6), 487–499.

Liebman, J. I., McKinley-Pace, M. J., Leonard, A. M., Sheesley, L. A., Gallant, C. L., Renkey, M. E., & Lehman, E. B. (2002). Cognitive and psychosocial correlates of adults' eyewitness accuracy and suggestibility. *Pers. Individ. Diff., 33*(1), 49–66.

Liebowitz, M. R., Mangano, R. M., Bradwejn, J., & Asnis, G. (2005). A randomized controlled trial of venlafaxine extended release in generalized social anxiety disorder. *J. Clin. Psychiat., 66*(2), 238–247.

Liebowitz, M. R., Stone, M., & Turkat, I. D. (1986). Treatment of personality disorders. In A. Frances & R. Hales (Eds.), *American Psychiatric Association annual review* (Vol. 5). Washington, DC: American Psychiatric Press.

Liedl, B. (1999). Sex-adjusting surgery in transsexualism (in German). *MMW Fortschr. Med., 141*(23), 41–45.

Lifton, R. J. (2005). *Home from the war: Learning from Vietnam veterans: With a new preface by the author on the war in Iraq.* New York: Other Press.

Lilienfeld, S. O., & Lynn, S. J. (2003). Dissociative identity disorder: Multiple personalities, multiple controversies. In S. O. Lilienfeld, S. J. Lynn, et al. (Eds.), *Science and pseudoscience in clinical psychology.* New York: Guilford Press.

Limosin, F., Rouillon, F., Payan, C., Cohen, J. M., & Strub, N. (2003). Prenatal exposure to influenza as a risk factor for adult schizophrenia. *Acta Psychiatr. Scandin., 107,* 331–335.

Lindahl, V., Pearson, J. L., & Colpe, L. (2005). Prevalence of suicidality during pregnancy and the postpartum. *Arch. Women's Ment. Hlth., 8*(2), 77–87.

Lindberg, N., Tani, P., Virkkunen, M., Porkka-Heiskanen, T., Appelberg, B., Naukkarinen, H., et al. (2005). Quantitative electroencephalographic measures in homicidal men with antisocial personality disorder. *Psychiatr. Res., 136*(1), 7–15.

Linde, K., Berner, M., Egger, M., & Mulrow, C. (2005). St John's wort for depression: Meta-analysis of randomised controlled trials. *Brit. J. Psychiat., 186*(2), 99–107.

Lindholm, C., & Lindholm C. (1981). World's strangest mental illnesses. *Sci. Digest,* 52–58.

Lindner, M. (1968). *Hereditary and environmental influences upon resistance to stress.* Unpublished doctoral dissertation, University of Pennsylvania, Philadelphia.

Lindsay, D. S. (1994). Contextualizing and clarifying criticisms of memory work in psychotherapy. *Consciousness Cog., 3,* 426–437.

Lindsay, D. S. (1996). Contextualizing and clarifying criticisms of memory work in psychotherapy. In K. Pezdek & W. P. Banks (Eds.), *The recovered memory/false memory debate.* San Diego: Academic Press.

Lindsay, J., Sykes, E., McDowell, I., Verreault, R., & Laurin, D. (2004). More than the epidemiology of Alzheimer's disease: Contributions of the Canadian Study of Health and Aging. *Canad. J. Psychiat., 49*(2), 83–91.

Lindström, L. H. (1996). Clinical and biological markers for outcome in schizophrenia: A review of a longitudinal follow-up study in Uppsala schizophrenia research project. *Neuropsychopharmacology, 14,* 23S–26S.

Linehan, M. M. (1987). Dialectical behavior therapy for borderline personality disorder: Theory and method. *Bull. Menninger Clin., 51,* 261–276.

Linehan, M. M. (1992). Behavior therapy, dialectics, and the treatment of borderline personality disorder. In D. Silver & M. Rosenbluth (Eds.),

Handbook of borderline disorders. Madison, CT: International Universities Press.

Linehan, M. M. (1993). *Cognitive-behavioral treatment of borderline personality disorder.* New York: Guilford Press.

Linehan, M. M. (1993). *Skills training manual for treating borderline personality disorder.* New York: Guilford Press.

Linehan, M. M., Armstrong, H. E., Suarez, A., Allmon, D., & Heard, H. L. (1991). Cognitive-behavioral treatment of chronically parasuicidal borderline patients. *Arch. Gen. Psychiat., 48,* 1060–1064.

Linehan, M. M., Cochran, B. N., & Kehrer, C. A. (2001). Dialectical behavior therapy for borderline personality disorder. In D. H. Barlow (Ed.), *Clinical handbook of psychological disorders* (3rd ed., pp. 470–522). New York: Guilford Press.

Linehan, M. M., Heard, H. L., & Armstrong, H. E. (1993). Naturalistic follow-up of a behavioral treatment for chronically parasuicidal borderline patients. *Arch. Gen. Psychiat., 50,* 971–974.

Linehan, M. M., Schmidt, H. I., Dimeff, L. A., Craft, J. C., Kanter, J., & Comtois, K. A. (1999). Dialectical behavior therapy for patients with borderline personality disorder and drug dependence. *Amer. J. Addic., 8,* 279–292.

Ling, W., Huber, A., & Rawson, R. A. (2001). New trends in opiate pharmacotherapy. *Drug Alc. Rev., 20*(1), 79–94.

Link, B. G., Struening, E. L., Neese-Todd, S., Asmussen, S., & Phelan, J. C. (2001). Stigma as a barrier to recovery: The consequences of stigma for the self-esteem of people with mental illness. *Psychiatr. Serv., 52*(12), 1621–1626.

Link, B. G., Yang, L. H., Phelan, J. C., & Collins, P. Y. (2004). Measuring mental illness stigma. *Schizo. Bull., 30*(3), 511–541.

Linszen, D. H., Dingemans, P. M., Nugter, M. A., Willem, A. J., et al. (1997). Patient attributes and expressed emotion as risk factors for psychotic relapse. *Schizo. Bull., 23*(1), 119–130.

Linz, D., & Imrich, D. (2001). Child pornography. In S. O. White (Ed.), *Handbook of youth and justice* (pp. 79–111). New York: Kluwer Academic/ Plenum Press.

Lipkin, P. H., Cozen, M. A., Thompson, R. E., & Mostofsky, S. H. (2005). Stimulant dosage and age, race, and insurance type in a sample of children with attention-deficit/hyperactivity disorder. *J. Child Adol. Psychopharmacol., 15*(2), 240–248.

Lipton, A. A., & Simon, F. S. (1985). Psychiatric diagnosis in a state hospital: Manhattan State revisited. *Hosp. Comm. Psychiat., 36*(4), 368–373.

Liu, T., Hau, W., Wang, X., He, J., Li, H., Xiong, P., Fan, C., Tang, W., & Chen, S. (2002). Negative consequences of recreational use of amphetamine-type stimulants. *Chin. Ment. Hlth. J., 16*(5), 293–295.

Livesley, W. J. (2000). A practical approach to the treatment of patients with borderline personality disorder. *Psychiatr. Clin. N. Amer., 23*(1), 211–232.

Lochman, J. E., Barry, T. D., & Pardini, D. A. (2003). Anger control training for aggressive youth. In A. E. Kazdin & J. R. Weisz (Eds.), *Evidence-based psychotherapies for children and adolescents* (pp. 263–281). New York: Guilford Press.

Lock, J., & le Grange, D. (2005). Family-based treatment of eating disorders. *Inter. J. Eat. Disorders, 37*(Suppl.), S64–S67.

Loebel, J. P., Loebel, J. S., Dager, S. R., Centerwall, B. S., et al. (1991). Anticipation of nursing home placement may be a precipitant of suicide among the elderly. *J. Amer. Ger. Soc., 39*(4), 407–408.

Loeber, R., & Keenan, K. (1994). Interaction between conduct disorder and its comorbid conditions: Effects of age and gender. *Clinical Psychology Review, 14,* 497–523.

Loewenstein, R. J. (1991). Psychogenic amnesia and psychogenic fugue: A comprehensive review. In A. Tasman & S. M. Goldfinger (Eds.), *American Psychiatric Press review of psychiatry* (Vol. 10). Washington, DC: American Psychiatric Press.

Loftus, E. F. (1993). The reality of repressed memories. *Amer. Psychologist, 48,* 518–537.

Loftus, E. F. (1997). Repressed memory accusations: Devastated families and devastated patients. *Appl. Cog. Psychol., 11,* 25–30.

Loftus, E. F. (2000). Remembering what never happened. In E. Tulving, et al. (Eds.), *Memory, consciousness, and the brain: The Tallinn Conference.* Philadelphia: Psychology Press/Taylor & Francis.

Loftus, E. F. (2001). Imagining the past. *Psychologist, 14*(11), 584–587.

Loftus, E. F. (2003). Make-believe memories. *Amer. Psychologist, 58*(11), 867–873.

Loftus, E. F. (2003). Our changeable memories: Legal and practical implications. *Nature Reviews: Neuroscience, 4,* 231–234.

Logan, T. K., Walker, R., Jordan, C. E., & Leukefeld, C. G. (2006). *Women and victimization: Contributing factors, interventions, and implications.* Washington, DC: American Psychological Association.

Logue, A. W. (1991). *The psychology of eating and drinking.* New York: W. H. Freeman.

Lombardi, E. L., Wilchins, R. A., Priesing, D., & Malouf, D. (2001). Gender violence: Transgender experiences with violence and discrimination. *J. Homosex., 42*(1), 89–101.

Lombardo, T. W., & Gray, M. J. (2005). Beyond exposure for posttraumatic stress disorder (PTSD) symptoms: Broad-spectrum PTSD treatment strategies. *Behav. Mod., 29*(1), 3–9.

Lonigan, C. J., Shannon, M. P., Taylor, C. M., et al. (1994). Children exposed to disaster: II. Risk factors for the development of post-traumatic symptomatology. *J. Amer. Acad. Child Adol. Psychiat., 33,* 94–105.

Lonigan, C. J., Vasey, M. W., Phillips, B. M., & Hazen, R. A. (2004). Temperament, anxiety, and the processing of threat-relevant stimuli. *J. Clin. Child Adol. Psychol., 33*(1), 8–20.

Loomer, H. P., Saunders, J. C., & Kline, N. S. (1957). A clinical and phamacodynamic evaluation of iproniazid as a psychic energizer. *Amer. Psychiat. Assoc. Res. Rep., 8,* 129.

Looper, K. J., & Kirmayer, L. J. (2002). Behavioral medicine approaches to somatoform disorders. *J. Cons. Clin. Psychol., 70*(3), 810–827.

Looper, K. J., & Paris, J. (2000). What dimensions underlie Cluster B personality disorders? *Comprehen. Psychiat., 41*(6), 432–437.

López, S. R., & Guarnaccia, P. J. (2000). Cultural psychopathology: Uncovering the social world of mental illness. *Annu. Rev. Psychol., 51,* 571–598.

López, S. R., & Guarnaccia, P. J. (2005). Cultural dimensions of psychopathology: The social world's impact on mental illness. In B. A. Winstead & J. E. Maddux, *Psychopathology: Foundations for a contemporary understanding* (pp. 19–37). Mahwah, NJ: Lawrence Erlbaum Associates.

LoPiccolo, J. (1985). Advances in diagnosis and treatment of male sexual dysfunction. *J. Sex Marital Ther., 11*(4), 215–232.

LoPiccolo, J. (1991). Post-modern sex therapy for erectile failure. In R. C. Rosen & S. R. Leiblum (Eds.), *Erectile failure: Diagnosis and treatment.* New York: Guilford Press.

LoPiccolo, J. (1992). Paraphilias. *Nord. Sex., 10*(1), 1–14.

LoPiccolo, J. (1995). Sexual disorders and gender identity disorders. In R. J. Comer, *Abnormal psychology* (2nd ed.). New York: W. H. Freeman.

LoPiccolo, J. (1997). Sex therapy: A post-modern model. In S. J. Lynn & J. P. Garske (Eds.), *Contemporary psychotherapies: Models and methods* (2nd ed.). Columbus, OH: Merrill.

LoPiccolo, J. (2002). Postmodern sex therapy. In F. W. Kaslow (Ed.), *Comprehensive handbook of psychotherapy: Integrative/eclectic* (Vol. 4, pp. 411–435). New York: Wiley.

LoPiccolo, J. (2004). Sexual disorders affecting men. In L. J. Haas (Ed.), *Handbook of primary care psychology* (pp. 485–494). New York: Oxford University Press.

LoPiccolo, J., & Stock, W. E. (1987). Sexual function, dysfunction, and counseling in gynecological practice. In Z. Rosenwaks, F. Benjamin, & M. L. Stone (Eds.), *Gynecology.* New York: Macmillan.

LoPiccolo, J., & Van Male, L. M. (2000). Sexual dysfunction. In A. E. Kazdin (Ed.), *Encyclopedia of psychology* (Vol. 7, pp. 246–251). Washington, DC: Oxford University Press/American Psychological Association.

Lorand, S. (1968). Dynamics and therapy of depressive states. In W. Gaylin (Ed.), *The meaning of despair.* New York: Jason Aronson.

Lord, M. (2002). One year after 9/11—A nation changed. *U. S. News World Rep., 133*(7), 33.

Loros, J. J., Woodland-Hastings, J., & Schibler, U. (2004). Adapting to life on a rotating world at the gene expression level. In J. C. Dunlap, J. J. Loros, & P. J. Decoursey (Eds.), *Chronobiology: Biological timekeeping* (pp. 255–290). Sunderland, MA: Sinauer Associates.

Lovaas, O. I. (1987). Behavioral treatment and normal educational/intellectual functioning in young autistic children. *J. Cons. Clin. Psychol., 55*, 3–9.

Lovaas, O. I. (2003). *Teaching individuals with developmental delays: Basic intervention techniques.* Austin, TX: Pro-Ed.

Lovejoy, M. (1982). Expectations and the recovery process. *Schizo. Bull., 8*(4), 605–609.

Lovejoy, M. (2001). Disturbances in the social body: Differences in body image and eating problems among African-American and white women. *Gender Soc., 15*(2), 239–261.

Lovett, M. W. (2000). Developmental reading disorders. In M. J. Farah & T. E. Feinberg (Eds.), *Patient-based approaches to cognitive neuroscience: Issues in clinical and cognitive neuropsychology* (pp. 247–261). Cambridge, MA: MIT Press.

Lu, L. (1999). Personal or environmental causes of happiness: A longitudinal analysis. *J. Soc. Psychol., 139*(1), 79–90.

Lublin, H. (2001). Cognitive dysfunction in schizophrenia. *Acta Psychiatr. Scandin., 104*(Suppl. 508), 5–9.

Luborsky, L. (1973). Forgetting and remembering (momentary forgetting) during psychotherapy. In M. Mayman (Ed.), *Psychoanalytic research and psychological issues* (Monograph 30). New York: International Universities Press.

Luborsky, L. (2004). Helen Sargent's 1961 paper: Both a classic and still current. *Psychiat.: Interpers. Biol. Process., 67*(1), 23–25.

Luborsky, L., Diguer, L., Luborsky, E., & Schmidt, K. A. (1999). The efficacy of dynamic versus other psychotherapies: Is it true that "everyone has won and all must have prizes"?—An update. In D. S. Janowsky (Ed.), *Psychotherapy indications and outcomes.* Washington, DC: American Psychiatric Press.

Luborsky, L., Rosenthal, R., Diguer, L., Andrusyna, T. P., Berman, J. S., Levitt, J. T., Seligman, D. A., & Krause, E. D. (2002). The dodo bird verdict is alive and well—mostly. *Clin. Psychol.: Sci. Prac., 9*(1), 2–12.

Luborsky, L., Rosenthal, R., Diguer, L., Andrusyna. T. P., Levitt, J. T., Seligman, D. A., Berman, J. S., & Krause, E. D. (2003). Are some psychotherapies much more effective than others? *J. Appl. Psychoanal. Stud., 5*(4), 455–460.

Luborsky, L., Singer, B., & Luborsky, L. (1975). Comparative studies of psychotherapies. *Arch. Gen. Psychiat., 32*, 995–1008.

Lucas, R. E., Clark, A. E., Georgellis, Y., & Diener, E. (2003). Reexamining adaptation and the set point model of happiness: Reactions to changes in marital status. *J. Pers. Soc. Psychol., 84*(3), 527–539.

Lucas, R. E., Clark, A. E., Georgellis, Y., & Diener, E. (2004). Unemployment alters the set point for life satisfaction. *Psychol. Sci., 15*(1), 8–13.

Ludwig, A. M. (1994). Creative activity and mental illness in female writers. *Amer. J. Psychiat., 151*, 1650–1656.

Ludwig, A. M. (1995). *The price of greatness: Resolving the creativity and madness controversy.* New York: Guilford Press.

Luepker, E. T. (1999). Effects of practitioners' sexual misconduct: A follow-up study. *J. Amer. Acad. Psychiat. Law, 27*(1), 51–63.

Lumley, V. A., & Scotti, J. R. (2001). Supporting the sexuality of adults with mental retardation: Current status and future directions. *J. Positive Behav. Interventions, 3*(2), 109–119.

Lundqvist, D., & Ohman, A. (2005). Emotion regulates attention: The relation between facial configurations, facial emotion, and visual attention. *Visual Cog., 12*(1), 51–84.

Lundqvist T. (2005). Cognitive consequences of cannabis use: Comparison with abuse of stimulants and heroin with regard to attention, memory and executive functions. *Pharmacol Biochem Behav., 81*, 391–330.

Lutgendorf, S. K., Russell, D., Ullrich, P., Harris, T. B., & Wallace, R. (2004). Religious participation, interleukin-6, and mortality in older adults. *Hlth. Psychol., 23*(5), 465–475.

Lyketsos, C. G., Hoover, D. R., Guccione, M., Dew, M. A., et al. (1996). Changes in depressive symptoms as AIDS develops. *Amer. J. Psychiat., 153*(11), 1430–1437.

Lykken, D. T. (1957). A study of anxiety in the sociopathic personality. *J. Abnorm. Soc. Psychol., 55*, 6–10.

Lykken, D. T. (1995). *The antisocial personalities.* Hillsdale, NJ: Erlbaum.

Lykken, D. T., & Tellegen, A. (1996). Happiness is a stochastic phenomenon. *Psychol. Sci., 7*(3), 186–189.

Lyman, B. (1982). The nutritional values and food group characteristics of foods preferred during various emotions. *J. Psychol., 112*, 121–127.

Lyon, K. A. (1992). Shattered mirror: A fragment of the treatment of a patient with multiple personality disorder. *Psychoanal. Quarter., 12*(1), 71–94.

Lyon, M., Chatoor, I., Atkins, D., Silber, T., et al. (1997, Spring). Testing the hypothesis of the multidimensional model of anorexia nervosa in adolescents. *Adolescence, 32*(125), 101–111.

Lysaker, P., & Bell, M. (1995). Work and meaning: Disturbance of volition and vocational dysfunction in schizophrenia. *Psychiatry, 58*(4), 392–400.

MacDonald, W. L. (1998). The difference between blacks' and whites' attitudes toward voluntary euthanasia. *J. Sci. Study Religion, 37*(3), 411–426.

Mace, N., & Rabins, P. (1991). *The 36-hour day* (2nd ed.). Baltimore: Johns Hopkins University Press.

Maciejewski, P. K., Prigerson, H. G., & Mazure, C. M. (2001). Sex differences in event-related risk for major depression. *Psychol. Med., 31*, 593–604.

MacIntyre, D., & Carr, A. (1999). Helping children to the other side of silence: A study of the impact of the stay safe program on Irish children's disclosures of sexual victimization. *Child Abuse Negl., 23*(12), 1327–1340.

Mack, A., & Joy, J. (2001). *Marijuana as medicine? The science beyond the controversy.* Washington, DC: National Academy Press.

MacLaren, V. V. (2001). A qualitative review of the Guilty Knowledge Test. *J. Appl. Psychol., 86*(4), 674–683.

Maddux, J. E., & Winstead, B. A. (Eds.) (2005). *Psychopathology: Foundations for a contemporary understanding.* Mahwah, NJ: Lawrence Erlbaum Associates.

Madianos, M., Economou, M., Dafni, O., Koukia, E., Palli, A., & Rogakou, E. (2004). Family disruption, economic hardship and psychological distress in schizophrenia: Can they be measured? *Eur. Psychiat., 19*(7), 408–414.

Madianos, M. G., & Madianou, D. (1992). The effects of long-term community care on relapse and adjustment of persons with chronic schizophrenia. *Inter. J. Ment. Hlth., 21*(1), 37–49.

Madill, A., & Holch, P. (2004). A range of memory possibilities: The challenge of the false memory debate for clinicians and researchers. *Clin. Psychol. Psychother., 11*(5), 299–310.

Maes, M., DeVos, N., VanHunsel, F., VanWest, D., Westenberg, H., Cosyns, P., et al. (2001). Pedophilia is accompanied by increased plasma concentrations of catecholamines, in particular, epinephrine. *Psychiat. Res., 103*(1), 43–49.

Magherini, G., & Biotti, V. (1998). Madness in Florence in the 14th–18th centuries: Judicial inquiry and medical diagnosis, care, and custody. *Inter. J. Law and Psychiat., 21*(4), 355–368.

Maher, B. A. (1974). Delusional thinking and perceptual disorder. *J. Individ. Psychol., 30*(1), 98–113.

Maher, B. F. G., Stough, C., Shelmerdine, A., Wesnes, K., & Nathan, P. J. (2002). The acute effects of combined administration of Ginkgo biloba and Bacopa monniera on cognitive function in humans. *Human Psychopharmacol. Clin. Exp., 17*(3), 163–164.

Maher, W. B., & Maher, B. A. (1985). Psychopathology: I. From ancient times to the eighteenth century. In G. A. Kimble & K. Schlesinger (Eds.), *Topics in the history of psychology* (Vol. 2). Hillsdale, NJ: Erlbaum.

Maher, W. B., & Maher, B. A. (2003). Abnormal psychology. In D. K. Freedheim (Ed.), *Handbook of psychology: History of psychology* (Vol. 1, pp. 303–336). New York: Wiley.

Mahlberg, R., Kunz, D., Sutej, I., Kuhl, K. P., & Hellweg, R. (2004). Melatonin treatment of day-night rhythm disturbances and sundowning in Alzheimer disease: An open-label pilot study using actigraphy. *J. Clin. Psychopharmacol., 24*(4), 456–459.

Mahrer, A. R. (2000). Philosophy of science and the foundations of psychotherapy. *APA, 55*(10), 1117–1125.

Mahrer, A. R. (2003). What are the foundational beliefs in the field of psychotherapy? *Psychol.: J. Hellen. Psychol. Soc., 10*(1), 1–19.

Mahrer, A. R. (2005). What is psychotherapy for? A plausible alternative to empirically supported therapies, therapy relationships, and practice guidelines. *J. Contemp. Psychother., 35*(1), 99–115.

Maier, W., Hofgen, B., Zobel, A., & Rietschel, M. (2005). Genetic models of schizophrenia and bipolar disorder: Overlapping inheritance or discrete genotypes? *Eur. Arch. Psychiat. Clin. Neurosci., 255*(3), 159–166.

Majumdar, B., Browne, G., Roberts, J., & Carpio, B. (2004). Effects of cultural sensitivity training on health care attitudes and patient outcomes. *J. Nurs. Scholar., 36*(2), 161–166.

Malberg, J. E., & Bonson, K. R. (2001). How MDMA works in the brain. In J. Holland (Ed.), *Ecstasy: The complete guide: A comprehension look at the risks and benefits of MDMA* (pp. 29–38). Rochester, VT: Park Street Press.

Malcolm, A. H. (1990, June 9). Giving death a hand. *New York Times,* p. A6.

Maldonado, J. R., & Spiegel, D. (2003). Dissociative disorders. In S. C. Yudofsky & R. E. Hales (Eds.), *The American Psychiatric Publishing textbook of clinical psychiatry* (4th ed., pp. 709–742). Washington, DC: American Psychiatric Publishing.

Maletzky, B. M. (2000). Exhibitionism. In M. Hersen & M. Biaggio (Eds.), *Effective brief therapies: A clinician's guide.* San Diego, CA: Academic.

Maletzky, B. M. (2002). The paraphilias: Research and treatment. In P. E. Nathan & J. M. Gorman (Eds.), *A guide to treatments that work* (2nd ed., pp. 525–557). London: Oxford University Press.

Maletzky, B. M. (2003). A serial rapist treated with behavioral and cognitive techniques and followed for 12 years. *Clin. Case Stud., 2*(2), 127–153

Maletzky, B. M., & Steinhauser, C. (2004). Sexual deviations. In M. Hersen (Ed.), *Psychological assessment in clinical practice: A pragmatic guide* (pp. 197–241). New York: Brunner-Routledge.

Malik, M. L., & Beutler, L. E. (2002). The emergence of dissatisfaction with the DSM. In L. E. Beutler & M. L. Malik (Eds.), *Rethinking the DSM: A psychological perspective. Decade of behavior.* Washington, DC: American Psychological Association.

Maller, R. G., & Reiss, S. (1992). Anxiety sensitivity in 1984 and panic attacks in 1987. *J. Anx. Dis., 6*(3), 241–247.

Malley, P. B., & Reilly, E. P. (1999). *Legal and ethical dimensions for mental health professionals.* Philadelphia: Taylor & Francis.

Malone, K. M., Corbitt, E. M., Li, S., & Mann, J. J. (1996). Prolactin response to fenfluramine and suicide attempt lethality in major depression. *Brit. J. Psychiat., 168,* 324–329.

Maltsberger, J. T. (1999). The psychodynamic understanding of suicide. In D. G. Jacobs (Ed.), *The Harvard Medical School guide to suicide assessment and intervention.* San Francisco: Jossey-Bass.

Mammen, O. K., Kolk, D. J., & Pilkonis, P. A. (2002). Negative affect and parental aggression in child physical abuse. *Child Abuse Negl., 26,* 407–424.

Mamounas, J., Lykouras, E., Oulis, P., & Christodoulou, G. N. (2001). Premorbid adjustment in schizophrenia: Associations with clinical variables. *Psychiatriki, 12*(2), 134–141.

Manji, H. K., Bebchuk, J. M., Moore, G. J., Glitz, D., Hasanat, K. A., & Chen, G. (1999). Modulation of CNS signal transduction pathways and gene expression by mood-stabilizing agents: Therapeutic implications. *J. Clin. Psychiat., 60*(Suppl. 2), 27–39.

Mann, B. J. (1995). The North Carolina Dissociation Index: A measure of dissociation using items from the MMPI-2. *J. Pers. Assess., 64*(2), 349–359.

Mann, J. J., & Arango, V. (1999). The neurobiology of suicidal behavior. In D. G. Jacobs (Ed.), *The Harvard Medical School guide to suicide assessment and intervention.* San Francisco: Jossey-Bass.

Mann, J. J., Brent, D. A., & Arango, V. (2001). The neurobiology and genetics of suicide and attempted suicide: A focus on the serotonergic system. *Neurosychopharmacology, 24*(5), 467–477.

Mann, J. J., Oquendo, M., Underwood, M. D., & Arango, V. (1999). The neurobiology of suicide risk: A review for the clinician. *J. Clin. Psychiat., 60*(Suppl. 2), 7–11.

Manson, J. E., Willett, W. C., Stampfer, M. J., Colditz, G. A., et al. (1995). Body weight and mortality among women. *N. Engl. J. Med., 333*(11), 677–685.

Manson, S. M., & Good, B. J. (1993). *Cultural considerations in the diagnosis of DSM-IV mood disorders. Cultural proposals and supporting papers for DSM-IV.* Submitted to the DSM-IV Task Force by the Steering Committee, NIMH-Sponsored Group on Culture and Diagnosis.

Manuck, S. B., Cohen, S., Rabin, B. S., Muldoon, M. F., & Bachen, E. A. (1991). Individual differences in cellular immune responses to stress. *Psychol. Sci., 2,* 1–5.

Maranon, I., Icheburua, E., & Grijalvo, J. (2004). Prevalence of personality disorders in patients with eating disorders: A pilot study using the IPDE. *Eur. Eat. Disord. Rev., 12*(4), 217–222.

Marazitti, D., Akiskal, H. S., Rossi, A., & Cassano, G. B. (1999). Alteration of the plate-

let serotonin transporter in romantic love. *Psychol. Med., 29*(3), 741–745.

March, J. S., Franklin, M., & Foa, E. (2005). Cognitive-behavioral psychotherapy for pediatric obsessive-compulsive disorder. In P. S. Jensen & E. D. Hibbs (Eds.), *Psychosocial treatments for child and adolescent disorders: Empirically based strategies for clinical practice* (2nd ed., pp. 121–142). Washington, DC: American Psychological Association.

Marchione, M. (2005, March 8). Experimental diet pill keeping pounds off. *Associated Press (Orlando)/Netscape News with CNN.* .

Marder, S. L., & Kane, J. M. (Eds.). (2005). Optimizing pharmacotherapy to maximize outcome in schizophrenia: Optimizing the long-term effectiveness of antipsychotic therapy. *J. Clin. Psychiat., 66*(1), 122–125.

Marder, S. R. (1996). Management of schizophrenia. *J. Clin. Psychiat., 57*(Suppl. 3), 9–13.

Margo, J. L. (1985). Anorexia nervosa in adolescents. *Brit. J. Med. Psychol., 58*(2), 193–195.

Margraf, J., Ehlers, A., Roth, W. T., Clark, D. B., et al. (1991). How "blind" are double-blind studies? *J. Cons. Clin. Psychol., 59*(1), 184–187.

Maris, R. W. (1992). Overview of the study of suicide assessment and prediction. In R. W. Maris, A. L. Berman, J. T. Maltsberger, & R. I. Yufit (Eds.), *Assessment and prediction of suicide.* New York: Guilford Press.

Maris, R. W. (2001). Suicide. In H. S. Friedman (Ed.), *Specialty articles from the encyclopedia of mental health.* San Diego: Academic Press.

Mark, T. L., Dirani, R., Slade, E., & Russo, P. A. (2002). Access to new medications to treat schizophrenia. *J. Behav. Hlth. Serv. Res., 29*(1), 15–29.

Mark, T. L., Palmer, L. A., Russo, P. A., & Vasey, J. (2003). Examination of treatment pattern differences by race. *Ment. Hlth. Serv. Res., 5*(4), 241–250.

Markovitz, P. (2001). Pharmacotherapy. In W. J. Livesley (Ed.), *Handbook of personality disorders: Theory, research, and treatment* (pp. 475–494). New York: Guilford Press.

Marks, I. M. (1977). Phobias and obsessions: Clinical phenomena in search of a laboratory model. In J. Maser and M. Seligman (Eds.), *Psychopathology: Experimental models.* San Francisco: Freeman.

Marks, I. M. (1987). *Fears, phobias and rituals: Panic, anxiety and their disorders.* New York: Oxford University Press.

Marks, I. M., & Gelder, M. G. (1967). Transvestism and fetishism: Clinical and psychological changes during faradic aversion. *Brit. J. Psychiat., 113,* 711–730.

Marks, I. M., Green, R., & Mataix-Cols, D. (2000). Adult gender identity disorder can remit. *Comprehen. Psychiat., 41*(4), 273–275.

Marks, J. (1998, October 12). Mayor vs. drug czar. *U. S. News & World Report.*

Marlatt, G. A. (1985). Controlled drinking: The controversy rages on. *Amer. Psychologist, 40*(3), 374–375.

Marlatt, G. A., Blume, A. W., & Parks, G. A. (2001). Integrating harm reduction therapy and traditional substance abuse treatment. *J. Psychoact. Drugs, 33*(1), 13–21.

Marlatt, G. A., Kosturn, C. F., & Lang, A. R. (1975). Provocation to anger and opportunity for retaliation as determinants of alcohol consumption in social drinkers. *J. Abnorm. Psychol., 84*(6), 652–659.

Maron, E., Kuikka, J. T., Shlik, J., Vasar, V., Vanninen, E., & Tiihonen, J. (2004). Reduced brain serotonin transporter binding in patients with panic disorder. *Psychiat. Res Neuroimaging, 132*(2), 173–181.

Maron, E., Nikopensius, T., Koks, S., Altmae, S., Heinaste, E., Vabrit, K., et al. (2005). Association study of 909 candidate gene polymorphisms in panic disorder. *Psychiat. Genet., 15*(1), 17–24.

Marques, J. K., Wiederanders, M., Day, D. M., Nelson, C., & van Ommeren, A. (2005). Effects of a relapse prevention program on sexual recidivism: Final results from California's Sex Offender Treatment and Evaluation Project (SOTEP). *Sex. Abuse: J. Res. Treat., 17*(1), 79–107.

Marquis, J. N., & Morgan, W. G. (1969). *A guidebook for systematic desensitization.* Palo Alto, CA: Veterans Administration Hospital.

Marsh, E. J., & Bower, G. H. (2004). The role of rehearsal and generation in false memory creation. *Memory, 12*96), 748–761.

Marshall, J. J. (1997). Personal communication.

Marshall, W. L., & Kennedy, P. (2003). Sexual sadism in sexual offenders. An elusive diagnosis. *Aggress. Viol. Behav.,* 8 (1), 1–22.

Marshall, W. L., & Yates, P. (2004). Diagnostic issues in sexual sadism among sexual offenders. *J. Sex. Aggress., 10*(1), 21–27.

Marston, W. M. (1917). Systolic blood pressure changes in deception. *J. Exp. Physiol., 2,* 117–163.

Mart, E. G. (2004). Factitious disorder by proxy: A call for the abandonment of an outmoded diagnosis. *J. Psychiat. Law, 32*(3), 297–314.

Martens, W. H. J. (2005). Multidimensional model of trauma and correlated antisocial personality disorder. *J. Loss Trauma, 10*(2), 115–129.

Martin, G., Bergen, H. A., Roeger, L., & Allison, S. (2004). Depression in young adolescents: Investigations using 2 and 3 factor versions of the Parental Bonding Instrument. *J. Nerv. Ment. Dis., 192*(10), 650–657.

Martin, J. K., Kraft, J. M., & Roman, P. M. (1994). Extent and impact of alcohol and drug use problems in the workplace: A review of the empirical evidence. In S. Macdonald & P. Roman (Eds.), *Research advances in alcohol and drug problems: Vol. 11. Drug testing in the workplace.* New York: Plenum Press.

Martin, P. L. (2000). Potency and pregnancy in Japan: Did Viagra push the pill? *Tulsa Law. J.,* 35, 651–677.

Martin, S. (2002). Easing migraine pain. *Monit. Psychol., 33*(4), 71.

Martineau, C. (2004, March 18). Life: Telling a tale with too many words: Chantal Martineau explores hypergraphia, a rare compulsion to keep writing. *The Guardian* (London).

Martinez, J. L., Jr., & Derrick, B. E. (1996). Long-term potentiation and learning. In J. T. Spence, J. M. Darley, & D. J. Foss (Eds.), *Annual review of psychology* (Vol. 47). Palo Alto, CA: Annual Reviews.

Maruff, P., Wood, S. J., Velakoulis, D., Smith, D. J., Soulsby, B., Suckling, J., et al. (2005). Reduced volume of parietal and frontal association areas in patients with schizophrenia characterized by passivity delusions. *Psychol. Med., 35*(6), 783–789.

Marx, B. P., & Sloan, D. M. (2005). Peritraumatic dissociation and experimental avoidance as predictors of posttraumatic stress symptomatology. *Behav. Res. Ther., 43*(5), 569–583.

Marzuk, P. M., Tardiff, K., Leon, A. C., Stajic, M., Morgan, E. B., & Mann, J. J. (1992). Prevalence of cocaine use among residents of New York City who committed suicide during a one-year period. *Amer. J. Psychiat., 149*(3), 371–375.

Masdrakis, V. G., & Papakstas, I. G. (2004). The role of challenges in the research for the etiology of panic disorder. *Psychiatriki, 15*(2), 129–142.

Masi, D. A. (2005). Employee assistance programs in the new millennium. *Inter. J. Emerg. Ment. Hlth., 7*(3), 157–168.

Masling, J. (2004). A storied test. *PsycCRITIQUES,* [np].

Masling, J. M., & Bornstein, R. F. (2005). Scoring the Rorschach: Retrospect and prospect. In R. F. Bornstein & J. M. Masling (Eds.), *Scoring the Rorschach: Seven validated systems* (pp. 1–24). Mahwah, NJ: Erlbaum.

Maslow, A. H. (1970). *Motivation and personality* (2nd ed.). New York: Harper & Row.

Masters, W. H., & Johnson, V. E. (1966). *Human sexual response.* Boston: Little, Brown.

Masters, W. H., & Johnson, V. E. (1970). *Human sexual inadequacy.* Boston: Little, Brown.

Mathew, V. M., Lindesay, J., et al. (1991). Attempted suicide and the lunar cycle. *Psychol. Rep. 68*(3, Pt. 1), 927–930.

Matson, J. L., Bamburg, J. W., Mayville, E. A., Pinkston, J., Bielecki, J., Kuhn, D., et al. (2000). Psychopharmacology and mental retardation: A 10-year review (1990–1999). *Res. Dev. Disabil., 21*(4), 263–296.

Matsumoto, D. (1994). *Cultural influence on research methods and statistics.* Pacific Grove, CA: Brooks/Cole.

Matthews, L. R., (2005). Work potential of road accident survivors with post-traumatic stress disorder. *Behav. Res. Ther., 43*(4), 475–483.

Mattia, J. I., & Zimmerman, M. (2001). Epidemiology. In W. J. Livesley (Ed.), *Handbook of personality disorders: Theory, research, and treatment* (pp. 107–123). New York: Guilford Press.

Maugh, T. H., II. (1995, May 31). Researchers hone in on gene that may cause "werewolf" disorder. *Los Angeles Times,* p. A3.

May, P. A., & Gossage, J. P. (2001). Estimating the prevalence of fetal alcohol syndrome: A summary. *Alc. Res. Hlth., 25*(3), 159–167.

May, P. R. A., & Tuma, A. H. (1964). Choice of criteria for the assessment of treatment outcome. *J. Psychiatr. Res., 2*(3), 16–527.

May, P. R. A., Tuma, A. H., & Dixon, W. J. (1981). Schizophrenia: A follow-up study of the results of five forms of treatment. *Arch. Gen. Psychiat., 38,* 776–784.

May, R., Angel, E., & Ellenberger, H. F. (1958). *Existence: A new dimension in psychiatry and psychology.* New York: Basic Books.

May, R., & Yalom, I. (1995). Existential psychotherapy. In R. J. Corsini & D. Wedding (Eds.), *Current psychotherapies* (5th ed.). Itasca, IL: Peacock.

May, R., & Yalom, I. (2005). Existential therapy. In R. Corsini & D. Wedding (Eds.), *Current psychotherapies* (7th ed., pp. 269–298). Boston: Thomson/Brooks-Cole.

Mayahara, K., & Ito, H. (2002). Readmission of discharged schizophrenic patients with and without day care in Japan. *Inter. Med. J., 9*(2), 121–123.

Mayou, R., Kirmayer, L. J., Simon, G., Kroenke, K., & Sharpe, M. (2005). Somatoform disorders: Time for a new approach in DSM-V. *Amer. J. Psychiat., 162*(5), 847–855.

Mazarakis, N. K., & Nestoros, I. N. (2001). The neurophysiological substrate of anxiety: The role of the GABAergic system. *Psychol.: J. Hellenic Psychol. Soc., 8*(1), 40–59.

McAnulty, R. D., Adams, H. E., & Dillon, J. (2001). Sexual disorders: The paraphilias. In P. B. Sutker & H. E. Adams (Eds.), *Comprehensive handbook of psychopathology* (3rd ed.). New York: Kluwer Academic/Plenum.

McBrien, J. A. (2003). Assessment and diagnosis of depression in people with intellectual disability. *J. Intell. Disab. Res., 47*(1), 1–13.

McCabe, R. E., & Antony, M. M. (2005). Panic disorder and agoraphobia. In M. M. Antony, D. R. Ledley, & R. G. Heimberg (Eds.), *Improving outcomes and preventing relapse in cognitive-behavioral therapy* (pp. 1–37). New York: Guilford Press.

McCabe, R., Roder-Wanner, U. U., Hoffmann, K., & Priebe, S. (1999). Therapeutic relationships and quality of life: Association of two subjective constructs in schizophrenia patients. *Inter. J. Soc. Psychiat., 45*(4), 276–283.

McCaghy, C. H., Capron, T. A., Jamieson, J. D., & Carey, S. H. (2006). *Deviant behavior: Crime, conflict, and interest groups* (7th ed.). New York: Pearson/Allyn & Bacon.

McCance-Katz, E. F., & Kosten, T. R. (2005). Psychopharmacological treatments. In R. J. Frances, A. H. Mack, & S. I. Miller (Eds.), *Clinical textbook of addictive disorders* (3rd ed., pp. 688–614). New York: Guilford Press.

McCarroll, J. E., Fullerton, C. S., Ursano, R. J., & Hermsen, J. M. (1996). Posttraumatic stress symptoms following forensic dental identification: Mt. Carmel, Waco, Texas. *Amer. J. Psychiat., 153,* 778–782.

McClelland, S. (1998, September 21). Grief crisis counsellors under fire: Trauma teams were quick to descend on Peggy's Cove. Susan McClelland asks whether they do more harm than good. *Ottawa Citizen,* p. A4.

McCloud, A., Barnaby, B., Omu, N., Drummond, C., & Aboud, A. (2004). Relationship between alcohol use disorders and suicidality in a psychiatric population: In-patient prevalence study. *Brit. J. Psychiat., 184*(5), 439–445.

McClung, H. J., Boyne, L. J., Linsheid, T., Heitlinger, L. A., Murray, R. D., Fyda, J., et al. (1993). Is combination therapy for encopresis nutritionally safe? *Pediatrics, 91,* 591–594.

McConaghy, N. (2005). Sexual dysfunctions and disorders. In B. A. Winstead & J. E. Maddux (Eds.), *Psychopathology: Foundations for a contemporary understanding* (pp. 255–280). Mahwah, NJ: Lawrence Erlbaum Associates.

McCormick, L. H. (2000). Improving social adjustment in children with attention-deficit/hyperactivity disorder. *Arch. Fam. Med., 9*(2), 191–194.

McCoy, S. A. (1976). Clinical judgments of normal childhood behavior. *J. Cons. Clin. Psychol., 44*(5), 710–714.

McCready, W. C. (2006). Applying sampling procedures. In F. T. Leong & J. T. Austin, *The psychology research handbook, a guide for graduate students and research assistants* (2nd ed., pp. 147–160). Thousand Oaks, CA: Sage.

McDermott, B. M., & Jaffa, T. (2005). Eating disorders in children and adolescents: An update. *Curr. Opin. Psychiat., 18*(4), 407–410.

McDermut, W., Miller, I. W., & Brown, R. A. (2001). The efficacy of group psychotherapy for depression: A meta-analysis and review of the empirical research. *Clin. Psychol.: Sci. Prac., 8*(1), 98–116.

McDowell, D. (2005). Marijuana, hallucinogens, and club drugs. In R. J. Frances, A. H. Mack, & S. I. Miller (Eds.), *Clinical textbook of addictive disorders* (3rd ed., pp. 157–183). New York: Guilford Press.

McDowell, D. M., & Clodfelter, R. C., Jr. (2001). Depression and substance abuse: Considerations of etiology, comorbidity, evaluation, and treatment. *Psychiatr. Ann., 31*(4), 244–251.

McEachin, J. J., Smith, T., & Lovaas, O. I. (1993). Long-term outcome for children with autism who received early intensive behavioral treatment. *Amer. J. Ment. Retard., 97*(4), 359–372.

McElroy, S. L., Phillips, K. A., & Keck, P. E. Jr. (1994). Obsessive compulsive spectrum disorder. *J. Clin. Psychiat., 55*(Suppl), 33–51.

McEwen, B. S. (2002). Protective and damaging effects of stress mediators: The good and bad sides of the response to stress. *Metabolism, 51*(Suppl 1), 2–4.

McFarland, L. A., Ryan, A. M., Sacco, J. M., & Kriska, D. (2004). Examination of structured interview ratings across time: The effects of applicant race, rater race, and panel composition. *J. Manag., 30*(4), 435–452.

McFarlane, T., Carter, J., & Olmsted, M. (2005). Eating disorders. In M. M. Antony, D. R. Ledley, & R. G. Heimberg (Eds.), *Improving outcomes and preventing relapse in cognitive-behavioral therapy* (pp. 268–305). New York: Guilford Press.

McFarlane, W. R. (2002). *Multifamily groups in the treatment of severe psychiatric disorders.* New York: Guilford Press.

McGeer, P. L., & McGeer, E. G. (1996). Anti-inflammatory drugs in the fight against Alzheimer's disease. In R. J. Wurtman, S. Corkin, J. H. Growdon, & R. M. Nitsch (Eds.), *The neurobiology of Alzheimer's disease.* New York: New York Academy of Sciences.

McGehee, D. S., Heath, M. J. S., Gelber, S., Devay, P., & Role, L. W. (1995). Nicotine enhancement of fast excitatory synaptic transmission in CNS by presynaptic receptors. *Science, 269,* 1692–1696.

McGhie, A., & Chapman, J. S. (1961). Disorders of attention and perception in early schizophrenia. *Brit. J. Med. Psychol., 34,* 103–116.

McGinn, D. (2004, October 4). Mating behavior 101. *Newsweek, 144*(14), pp. 44–45.

McGinn, D., & DePasquale, R. (2004, August 23). Taking depression on. *Newsweek,* pp. 59–60.

McGowan, S., Lawrence, A. D., Sales, T., Quested, D., & Grasby P. (2004). Presynaptic dopaminergic dysfunction in schizophrenia: A positron emission tomography [¹⁸F] fluorodopa study. *Arch. Gen. Psychiat., 61,* 134–142.

McGowen, K. R. (2001). Clinical assessment of children and adolescents: A place to begin. In H. B. Vance & A. Pumariega (Eds.), *Clinical assessment of child and adolescent behavior* (pp. 19–31). Hoboken, NJ: Wiley.

McGrath, M. L., Mellon, M. W., & Murphy, L. (2000). Empirically supported treatments in pediatric psychology: Constipation and encopresis. *J. Pediatr. Psychol., 25*(4), 225–254.

McGrath, P. A., & Hillier, L. M. (2001). Recurrent headache: Triggers, causes, and contributing factors. In P. A. McGrath & L. M. Hiller (Eds.), *The child with headache: Diagnosis and treatment* (pp. 77–107). Seattle, WA: IASP Press.

McGuffin, P., Katz, R., Watkins, S., & Rutherford, J. (1996). A hospital-based twin register of the heritability of DSM-IV unipolar depression. *Arch. Gen. Psychiat., 53,* 129–136.

McGuire, D. (1982). The problem of children's suicide: Ages 5–14. *Inter. J. Offend. Ther. Compar. Crimin., 26*(1), 10–17.

McGuire, P. A. (2000, February). New hope for people with schizophrenia. *Monit. Psychol., 31*(2), 24–28.

McGuire, P. K., Shah, G. M. S., & Murray, R. M. (1993). Increased blood flow in Broca's area during auditory hallucinations in schizophrenia. *Lancet, 342,* 703–706.

McGuire, P. K., Silbersweig, D. A., Wright, I., Murray, R. M., et al. (1995). Abnormal monitoring of inner speech: A physiological basis for auditory hallucinations. *Lancet, 346,* 596–600.

McGuire, P. K., Silbersweig, D. A., Wright, I., Murray, R. M., Frackowiak, R. S., & Frith, C. D. (1996). The neural correlates of inner speech and auditory verbal imagery in schizophrenia: Relationship to auditory verbal hallucinations. *Brit. J. Psychiat., 169*(2), 148–159.

McIntosh, J. L. (1991). Epidemiology of suicide in the U.S. In A. A. Leenaars (Ed.), *Life span perspectives of suicide.* New York: Plenum Press.

McIntosh, J. L. (1992). Epidemiology of suicide in the elderly. *Suic. Life-Threat. Behav., 22*(1), 15–35.

McIntosh, J. L. (1995). Suicide prevention in the elderly (age 65–99) [Special issue: Suicide prevention: Toward the year 2000]. *Suic. Life-Threat. Behav., 25*(1), 180–192.

McIntosh, J. L., & Santos, J. F. (1982). Changing patterns in methods of suicide by race and sex. *Suic. Life-Threat. Behav., 12,* 221–233

McIntosh, J. L., Hubbard, R. W., & Santos, J. F. (1985). Suicide facts and myths: A study of prevalence. *Death Stud., 9,* 267–281.

McKenna, K. E. (2005). The central control and pharmacological modulation of sexual function. In J. S. Hyde (Ed.), *Biological substrates of human sexuality.* Washington, DC: American Psychological Association.

McKisack, C., & Waller, G. (1997). Factors influencing the outcome of group psychotherapy for bulimia nervosa. *Inter. J. Eat. Disorders, 22,* 1–13.

McLean, P. D., & Hakstian, A. R. (1979). Clinical depression: Comparative efficacy of outpatient treatments. *J. Cons. Clin. Psychol., 47*(5), 818–836.

McLeod, H. J., Byrne, M. K., & Aitken, R. (2004). Automatism and dissociation: disturbances of consciousness and volition from a psychological perspective. *Inter. J. Law Psychiat., 27*(5), 471–487.

McMahon, R. J., & Frick, P. J. (2005). Evidence-based assessment of conduct problems in children and adolescents. *J. Clin. Child Adol. Psychol., 34,* 477–505.

McNally, R. J. (2001). The cognitive psychology of repressed and recovered memories of childhood sexual abuse: Clinical implications. *Psychiatr. Ann., 31*(8), 509–514.

McNally, R. J. (2001). Vulnerability to anxiety disorders in adulthood. In R. E. Ingram & J. M. Price (Eds.), *Vulnerability to psychopathology: Risk across the lifespan* (pp. 304–321). New York: Guilford Press.

McNally, R. J. (2003). *Remembering trauma.* Cambridge: Belknap Press/Harvard University Press.

McNally, R. J. (2004, April 1). Psychological debriefing does not prevent posttraumatic stress disorder. *Psychiatr. Times,* p. 71.

McNally, R. J., Bryant, R. A., Ehlers, A. (2003). Does early psychological intervention promote recovery from posttraumatic stress? *Psychol. Sci. Publ. Interest, 4*(2), 45–79.

McNally, R. J., Clancy, S. A., & Barrett, H. M. (2004). Forgetting trauma? In P. Hertel, & D. Reisberg (Eds.), *Memory and emotion* (pp. 129–154). London: Oxford University Press.

McNally, R. J., Clancy, S. A., Barrett, H. M., & Parker, H. A. (2005). Reality monitoring in adults reporting repressed, recovered, or continuous memories of childhood sexual abuse. *J. Abnorm. Psychol., 114*(1), 147–152.

McNamara, D. (2004). Focus on rehab for patients with chronic PTSD: Pharmacotherapy useful. *Fam. Pract. News, 34*(12), 37–38.

McNeal, E. T., & Cimbolic, P. (1986). Antidepressants and biochemical theories of depression. *Psychol. Bull., 99*(3), 361–374.

McNeil, E. B. (1967). *The quiet furies.* Englewood Cliffs, NJ: Prentice Hall.

McNeil, T. F., & Cantor-Graae, E. (2001). Obstetric complications as risk factors for schizophrenia. *Inter. J. Ment. Hlth, 29*(4), 73–83.

McParland, E., Neugroschl, J., & Marin, D. (2002). Women as caregivers for patients with Alzheimer's disease. In F. Lewis-Hall, T. S. Williams, J. Panetta, & J. M. Herrera. (Eds.), *Psychiatric illness in women: Emerging treatments and research* (pp. 427–444). Washington, DC: American Psychiatric Publishing.

McSweeney, S. (2004). Depression in women. In L. Cosgrove & P. J. Caplan (Eds.), *Bias in psychiatric diagnosis* (pp. 183–188). Northvale, NJ: Jason Aronson.

Mechanic, D. (2004). The rise and fall of managed care. *J. Hlth. Soc. Behav., 45*(Suppl.), 76–86.

Mednick, S. A. (1971). Birth defects and schizophrenia. *Psychol. Today, 4,* 48–50.

Meehl, P. E. (1960). The cognitive activity of the clinician. *Amer. Psychologist, 15,* 19–27.

Meehl, P. E. (1996). *Clinical versus statistical prediction: A theoretical analysis and a review of the evidence.* Northvale, NJ: Jason Aronson.

Meichenbaum, D. H. (1975). A self-instructional approach to stress management: A proposal for stress inoculation training. In I. Sarason & C. D. Spielberger (Eds.), *Stress and anxiety* (Vol. 2). New York: Wiley.

Meichenbaum, D. H. (1977). *Cognitive-behavior modification: An integrative approach.* New York: Plenum Press.

Meichenbaum, D. H. (1993). Stress inoculation training: A 20-year update. In P. M. Lehrer & R. L. Woolfolk (Eds.), *Principles and practice of stress management* (2nd ed.). New York: Guilford Press.

Meichenbaum, D. H. (1997). The evolution of a cognitive-behavior therapist. In J. K. Zeig (Ed.), *The evolution of psychotherapy: The third conference.* New York: Brunner/Mazel.

Meissner, W. W. (2005). The dynamic unconscious: Psychic determinism, intrapsychic conflict, unconscious fantasy, dreams, and symptom formation. In E. S. Person, A. M. Cooper, & G. O. Gabbard (Eds.), *The American Psychiatric Publishing textbook of psychoanalysis* (pp. 21–37). Washington, DC: American Psychiatric Publishing.

Melamed, B. G., Kaplan, B., & Fogel, J. (2001). Childhood health issues across the life span. In A. Baum, T. A. Revenson, & J. E. Singer (Eds.), *Handbook of health psychology* (pp. 449–458). Mahwah, NJ.: Lawrence Erlbaum Associates.

Melfi, C. A., Croghan, T. W., Hanna, M. P., & Robinson, R. L. (2000). Racial variation in antidepressant treatment in a Medicaid population. *J. Clin. Psychiat., 61*(1), 16–21.

Melle, I., Friis, S., Hauff, E., & Vaglum, P. (2000). Social functioning of patients with schizophrenia in high-income welfare societies. *Psychiatr. Serv., 51*(2), 223–228.

Melo, J. A., Shendure, J., Pociask, K., & Silver, L. M. (1996, June). Identification of sex-specific quantiative trait loci controlling alcohol preference in C57BL/6 mice. *Nature Genetics, 13,* 147–153.

Meltzer, H. Y. (1991). The mechanism of action of novel antipsychotic drugs. *Schizo. Bull., 17*(2), 263–287.

Meltzer, H. Y. (2005). Suicidality in schizophrenia: Pharmacologic treatment. *Clin. Neuropsychiat.: J. Treat. Eval., 2*(1), 76–83.

Melville, J. (1978). *Phobias and obsessions.* New York: Penguin.

Melville, J. D., & Naimark, D. (2002). Punishing the insane: The verdict of guilty but mentally ill. *J. Amer. Acad. Psychiat. Law, 30*(4), 553–555.

Mendels, J. (1970). *Concepts of depression.* New York: Wiley.

Mendlewicz, J., Linkowski, P., & Wilmotte, J. (1980). Linkage between glucose-6–phosphate dehydrogenase deficiency in manic depressive psychosis. *Brit. J. Psychiat., 137,* 337–342.

Mendlewicz, J., Simon, P., Sevy, S., Charon, F., Brocas, H., Legros, S., et al. (1987). Polymorphic DNA marker on X chromosome and manic depression. *Lancet, 1,* 1230–1232.

Mennin, D. S. (2004). Emotion regulation therapy for generalized anxiety disorder. *Clin. Psychol. Psychother., 11*(1), 17–29.

Mennin, D. S., Heimberg, R. G., Turk, C. L., & Fresco, D. M. (2002). Applying an emotion regulation framework to integrative approaches to generalized anxiety disorder. *Clin. Psycol.: Sci. Pract., 9,* 85–90.

Mennin, D. S., Heimberg, R. G., Turk, C. L., & Fresco, D. M. (2005). Preliminary evidence for an emotion dysregulation model of generalized anxiety disorder. *Behav. Res. Ther., 43*(10), 1281–1310. .

Mennin, D. S., Turk, C. L., Heimberg, R. G., & Carmin, C. (2004). Regulation of emotion in generalized anxiety disorder. In M. A. Reinecke & D. A. Clark (Eds.), *Cognitive therapy over the lifespan: Theory, research, and practice* (pp. 60–89). New York: Wiley.

Menninger, K. (1938). *Man against himself.* New York: Harcourt.

Menzies, R. P. D., Federoff, J. P., Green, C. M., & Isaacson, K. (1995). Prediction of dangerous behaviour in male erotomania. *Brit. J. Psychiat., 116*(4), 529–536.

Merskey, H. (1986). Classification of chronic pain: Descriptions of chronic pain syndromes and definitions of pain terms. *Pain, 3,* 226.

Merskey, H. (2004). Somatization, hysteria, or incompletely explained symptoms? *Canad. J. Psychiat., 49*(10), 649–651.

Merzenich, M. M., Jenkins, W. M., Johnston, P., Schreiner, C., et al. (1996). Temporal processing deficits of language-learning impaired children ameliorated by training. *Science, 271,* 77–84.

Messas, G., Meira-Lima, I., Turchi, M., Franco, O., Guindalini, C., Castelo, A., et al. (2005). Association study of dopamine D2 and D3 receptor gene polymorphisms with cocaine dependence. *Psychiat. Genet., 15*(3), 171–174.

Metsänen, M., Wahlberg, K. -E., Saarento, O., Hakko, H., Tarvainen, T., Koistinen, P., et al. (2005). Stability of thought disorder index among high-risk and low-risk adoptees in the Finnish adoptive family study of schizophrenia. *European Psychiatry, 20*(1), 35–40.

Metz, M. E., & Epstein, N. (2002). Assessing the role of relationship conflict in sexual dysfunction. *J. Sex Marital Ther., 28*(2), 139–164.

Metz, M. E., & Pryor, J. L. (2000). Premature ejaculation: A psychophysiological approach for assessment and management. *J. Sex Marital Ther., 26*(4), 293–320.

Metzl, J. M. (2004). Voyeur nation? Changing definitions of voyeurism, 1950–2004. *Harvard Rev. Psychiat., 12*(q), 127–131.

Meuret, A. E., Ritz, T., Wilhelm, F. H., & Roth, W. T. (2005). Voluntary hyperventilation in the treatment of panic disorder—functions of hyperventilation, their implications for breathing training, and recommendations for standardization. *Clin. Psychol. Rev., 25*(3), 285–306.

Meydan, J., Liu, X., & Hasin, D. (2005). Letter to the Editors: Alcohol and drug use in schizophrenia as predictors of functional impairment. *Schizo. Res., 77*(1), 105–106.

Meyer, B., & Carver, C. S. (2000). Negative childhood accounts, sensitivity and pessimism: A study of avoidant personality disorder features in college students. *J. Pers. Disorders, 14*(3), 233–248.

Meyer, D. J., & Simon, R. I. (2004). Psychiatric malpractice and the standard of care. In R. I. Simon & L. H. Gold (Eds.), *The American Psychiatric Publishing textbook of forensic psychiatry* (pp. 185–204). Washington, DC: American Psychiatric Publishing.

Meyer, G. J., Finn, S. E., Eyde, L. D., Kay, G. G., Moreland, K. L., Dies, R. R., et al. (2001). Psychological testing and psychological assessment: A review of evidence and issues. *Amer. Psychologist, 56*(2), 128–165.

Meyer, G. J., Finn, S. E., Eyde, L. D., Kay, G. G., Moreland, K. L., Dies, R. R., et al. (2003). Psychological testing and psychological assessment: A review of evidence and issues. In A. E. Kazdin (Ed.), *Methodological issues and strategies in clinical research* (3rd ed., pp. 265–345). Washington, DC: American Psychological Association.

Meyer, G. J., Mihura, J. L., & Smith, B. L. (2005). The inter-clinician reliability of Rorschach interpretation in four data sets. *J. Pers. Assess., 84,* 296–314.

Meyer, J. S., & Quenzer, L. F. (2005). *Psychopharmacology: Drugs, the brain, and behavior.* Sunderland, MA: Sinauer Associates.

Meyer, R. G. (1992). *Abnormal behavior and the criminal justice system.* New York: Lexington Books.

Meyer, U., Feldon, J., Schedlowski, M., Yee, B. K. (2005) Towards an immuno-precipitated neurodevelopmental animal model of schizophrenia. *Neurosci. Biobehav. Rev., 29*(6), 913–947.

Meyer, V. (1966). Modification of expectations in cases with obsessional rituals. *Behav. Res. Ther., 4,* 273–280.

Meyerhoff, D. J., Blumenfeld, R., Truran, D., Lindgren, J., Flenniken, D., Cardenas, V., et al. (2004, April). Effects of heavy drinking, binge drinking, and family history of alcoholism on regional brain metabolites. *Alcohol.: Clin. Exp. Res.,* 650–661.

Mezulis, A. H., Abramson, L. Y., Hyde, J. S., & Hankin, B. L. (2004). Is there a universal positivity bias in attributes? A meta-analytic review of individual, developmental, and cultural differences in the self-serving attributional bias. *Psychol. Bull., 130*(5), 711–747.

Mezzasalma, M. A., Valenca, A. M., Lopes, F. L., Nascimento, I., Zin, W. A., & Nardi, A. E. (2004). Neuroanatomy of panic disorder. *Revista Brasileira de Psiquiatria, 26*(3), 202–206.

Miami Herald. (1984, August 20). For the mentally ill, warehouses are home. p. 1A.

Michael, R. T., Gagnon, J. H., Laumann, E. O., & Kolata, G. (1994). *Sex in America: A definitive survey.* Boston: Little, Brown.

Michael, T., Ehlers, A., Halligan, S. L., & Clark, D. M. (2005). Unwanted memories of assault: What intrusion characteristics are associated with PTSD? *Behav. Res. Ther., 43*(5), 613–628.

Michel, A., Ansseau, M., Legros, J.-J., Pitchot, W., & Mormont, C. (2002). The transsexual: What about the future. *Eur. Psychiat., 17*(6), 353–362.

Mickalide, A. D. (1990). Sociocultural factors influencing weight among males. In A. E. Andersen (Ed.), *Males with eating disorders.* New York: Brunner/Mazel.

Mickley, D. W. (2001). Medical aspects of anorexia and bulimia. In B. Kinoy (Ed.), *Eating disorders: New directions in treatment and recovery* (2nd ed., pp. 7–16). New York: Columbia University Press.

Miguel, E. C., Leckman, J. F., Rauch, S., do Rosario-Campos, M. C., Hounie, A. G., Mercadante, M. T., et al. (2005). Obsessive-compulsive disorder phenotypes: Implications for genetic studies. *Mol. Psychiat., 10*(3), 258–275.

Miguel, E. C., Rauch, S. L., & Jenike, M. A. (1997). Obsessive-compulsive disorder. *Neuropsychiat. Basal Ganglia, 20*(4), 863–883.

Miklowitz, D. J., Goldstein, M. J., & Nuechterlein, K. H. (1995). Verbal interactions in the families of schizophrenic and bipolar affective patients. *J. Abnorm. Psychol., 104*(2), 268–276.

Miller, A. (1999). Appropriateness of psychostimulant prescription to children: Theoretical and empirical perspectives. *Canad. J. Psychiat., 44*(10), 1017–1024.

Miller, F. G., Emanuel, E. J., Rosenstein, D. L., & Straus, S. E. (2004). Ethical issues concerning research in complementary and alternative medicine. *JAMA, 291*(5), 599–604.

Miller, G. E., & Cohen, S. (2005). Infectious disease and psychoneuroimmunology. In K. Vedhara & M. Irwin (Eds.), *Human Psychoneuroimmunology.* Oxford, England: Oxford University Press.

Miller, M. A., & Rahe, R. H. (1997). Life changes scaling for the 1990s. *J. Psychosom. Res., 43*(3), 279–292.

Miller, M. C. (2004). Hypochondria. *Harvard Mental Health Letter,* July 1, 2004.

Miller, M. C. (2005). Falling apart: Dissociation and its disorders. *Harvard Mental Health Letter,* January 1, 2005.

Miller, M. C. (2005). What is body dysmorphic disorder? *Harvard Mental Health Letter,* July 1, 2005.

Miller, M. C., Jacobs, D. G., & Gutheil, T. G. (1998). Talisman or taboo: The controversy of the suicide-prevention contract. *Harvard Rev. Psychiat., 6*(2), 78–87.

Miller, M., & Kantrowitz, B. (1999, January 25). Unmasking Sybil: A re-examination of the most famous psychiatric patient in history. *Newsweek,* pp. 66–68.

Miller, M. N., & Pumariega, A. (1999). Culture and eating disorders. *Psychiatr. Times, XVI*(2).

Miller, N. E. (1948). Studies of fear as an acquirable drive: I. Fear as motivation and fear-reduction as reinforcement in the learning of new responses. *J. Exp. Psychol., 38,* 89–101.

Miller, N. S., & Gold, M. S. (1990). Benzodiazepines: Tolerance, dependence, abuse, and addiction. *J. Psychoactive Drugs, 22*(1), 23–33.

Miller, P. M., Ingham, J. G., & Davidson, S. (1976). Life events, symptoms, and social support. *J. Psychiatr. Res., 20*(6), 514–522.

Miller, W. R. (1983). Controlled drinking. *Quart. J. Stud. Alcohol., 44,* 68–83.

Miller, W. R. (2000). Rediscovering fire: Small interventions, large effects. *Psychol. Addict. Behav., 14*(1), 6–18.

Miller, W. R., & Seligman, M. E. (1975). Depression and learned helplessness in man. *J. Abnorm. Psychol., 84*(3), 228–238.

Miller, W. R., Leckman, A. L., Delaney, H. D., & Tinchom, M. (1992). Long-term follow-up of behavioral self-control training. *J. Stud. Alc., 51,* 108–115.

Miller, W. R., Walters, S. T., & Bennett, M. E. (2001). How effective is alcoholism treatment in the United States? *J. Stud. Alcohol, 62*(2), 211–220.

Millner, V. (2005). Female sexual arousal disorder and counseling deliberations. *Fam. J.: Couns. Ther. Couples Fam., 13*(1), 95–100.

Millner, V., & Ullery, E. K. (2002). A holistic treatment approach to male erectile disorder. *Fam. J.: Couns. Ther. Couples Fam., 10*(4), 443–447.

Millon, T. (1969). *Modern psychopathology: A biosocial approach to maladaptive learning and functioning.* Philadelphia: Saunders.

Millon, T. (1987). *Millon Clinical Multiaxial Inventory-II: Manual for the MCMI-II* (2nd ed.). Minneapolis, MN: National Computer Systems.

Millon, T. (1990). The disorders of personality. In L. A. Pervin (Ed.), *Handbook of personality theory and practice.* New York: Guilford Press.

Millon, T. (1990). *Toward a new personology.* New York: Wiley.

Millon, T. (1999). *Personality-guided therapy.* New York: Wiley.

Millon, T. (2002). Assessment is not enough: The SPA should participate in constructing a comprehensive clinical science of personality. *J. Pers. Assess., 78*(2), 209–218.

Millon, T., Davis, R., Millon, C., Escovar, L., & Meagher, S. (2000). *Personality disorders in modern life.* New York: Wiley.

Milner, B. (1971). Interhemispheric difference in the localization of psychological processes in man. *Brit. Med. Bull., 27,* 272–277.

Milosevic, A., Agrawal, N., Redfearn, P., & Mair, L. (1999). The occurrence of toothwear in users of Ecstasy (3,4-methylenedioxymethamphetamine). *Community Dent. Oral Epidemiol., 27*(4), 283–287.

Milrod, B. (2002). A 9-year-old with conversion disorder, successfully treated with psychoanalysis. *Inter. J. Psychoanal., 83*(3), 623–631.

Mineka, S., & Ohman, A. (2002). Phobias and preparedness: The selective, automatic, and encapsulated nature of fear. *Biol. Psychiat., 51*(9), 927–937.

Mineka, S., & Zinbarg, R. (2006). A contemporary learning theory perspective on the etiology of anxiety disorders: It's not what you thought it was. *Amer. Psychologist, 61,* 10–26.

Minton, H. L. (2002). *Departing from deviance: A history of homosexual rights and emancipatory science in America.* Chicago: University of Chicago Press.

Minuchin, S. (1974). *Families and family therapy.* Cambridge, MA: Harvard University Press.

Minuchin, S. (1987). My many voices. In J. K. Zeig (Ed.), *The evolution of psychotherapy.* New York: Brunner/Mazel.

Minuchin, S. (1997). The leap to complexity: Supervision in family therapy. In J. K. Zeig (Ed.), *The evolution of psychotherapy: The third conference.* New York: Brunner/Mazel.

Minuchin, S., Rosman, B. L., & Baker, L. (1978). *Psychosomatic families: Anorexia nervosa in context.* Cambridge, MA: Harvard University Press.

Mio, J. S., Barker-Hackett, L., & Tumambing, J. (2006). *Multicultural psychology, Understanding our diverse communities.* New York: McGraw-Hill.

Miranda, J., Siddique, J., Belin, T. R., & Kohn-Wood, L. P. (2005). Depression prevalence in disadvantaged young black women: African and Caribbean immigrants compared to US-born African Americans. *Soc. Psychiat. Psychiatr. Epidemiol. 40*(4), 253–258.

Mirin, S. M., & Weiss, R. D. (1991). Substance abuse and mental illness. In R. J. Frances, A. H. Mack, & S. I. Miller (Eds.), *Clinical textbook of addictive disorders.* New York: Guilford Press.

Mirsky, I. A. (1958). Physiologic, psychologic, and social determinants of the etiology of duodenal ulcer. *Amer. J. Digestional Dis., 3,* 285–314.

Mirzaei, S., Gelpi, E., Roddrigues, M., Knoll, P., & Gutierrez-Lobos, K. (2005). Progress in post-traumatic stress disorder research. In T. A. Corales (Ed.), *Focus on posttraumatic stress disorder research* (pp. 157–177). Hauppauge, NY: Nova Science Publishers.

Mishara, B. L. (1999). Conceptions of death and suicide in children ages 6–12 and their implications for suicide prevention. *Suic. Life-Threat. Behav., 29*(2), 105–118.

Mishna, F. (1996). Clinical report. In their own words: Therapeutic factors for adolescents who have learning disabilities. *Inter. J. Group Psychother., 46*(2), 265–273.

Mitchell, I. (2001). Treatment and outcome for victims. In G. Adshead & D. Brooke (Eds.), *Munchausen's syndrome by proxy: Current issues in assessment, treatment and research* (pp. 185–196). London: Imperial College Press.

Mitchell, J. E. (2001). Psychopharmacology of eating disorders: Current knowledge and future directions. In R. H. Striegel-Moore & L. Smolak (Eds.), *Eating disorders: Innovative directions in research and practice* (pp. 197–212). Washington, DC: American Psychological Association.

Mitchell, J. E., Halmi, K., Wilson, G. T., Agras, W. S., Kraemer, H., & Crow, S. (2002). A randomized secondary treatment study of women with bulimia nervosa who fail to respond to CBT. *Inter. J. Eat. Disorders, 32*(3), 271–281.

Mitchell, J. E., Pyle, R. L., & Miner, R. A. (1982). Gastric dilation as a complication of bulimia. *Psychosomatics, 23,* 96–97.

Mitchell, J. T. (1983). When disaster strikes...the critical incident stress debriefing process. *J. Emerg. Med. Serv., 8,* 36–39.

Mitchell, J. T. (2003). Crisis intervention & CISM: A research summary. Retrieved from www.icisf.org/articles/cism_research_summary.pdf

Mitchell, J. T., & Everly, G. S. Jr. (2000). Critical incident stress management and critical incident stress debriefing: Evolutions, effects, and outcomes. In B. Raphael & J. P. Wilson (Eds.), *Psychological debriefing: Theory, practice, and evidence* (pp. 71–90). Cambridge, England: Cambridge University Press.

Mitchell, L. (2004). The great pretenders. *The Age.com.au.* Retrieved July 4, 2005, from global.factiva.com/en/arch/print_results.asp

Mitchell, S. A. (1997). *Influence and autonomy in psychoanalysis.* Hillsdale, NJ: Analytic Press.

Mittleman, M. A., Mintzer, D., Maclure, M., Tofler, G. H., Sherwood, J. B., & Muller, J. E. (1999). Triggering of myocardial infarction by cocaine. *Circulation, 99*(21), 2737–2741.

Mizes, J. S. (1993). Bulimia nervosa. In A. S. Bellack & M. Hersen (Eds.), *Handbook of behavior therapy in the psychiatric setting. Critical issues in psychiatry* (pp. 311–327). New York: Plenum Press.

Mizes, J. S. (1995). Eating disorders. In M. Hersen & R. T. Ammerman (Eds.), *Advanced abnormal child psychology.* Hillsdale, NJ: Erlbaum.

Mizes, J. S., & Bonifazi, D. Z. (2002). Bulimia nervosa. In M. Hersen (Ed.), *Clinical behavior therapy: Adults and children* (pp. 144–159). New York: Wiley.

Modestin, J., & Villiger, C. (1989). Follow-up study on borderline versus nonborderline personality disorders. *Comprehen. Psychiat., 30*(3), 236–244.

Modlin, T. (2002). Sleep disorders and hypnosis: To cope or cure? *Sleep Hyp., 4*(1), 39–46.

Modrow, J. (1992). *How to become a schizophrenic: The case against biological psychiatry.* Everett, WA: Apollyon Press.

Moene, F. C., Spinhoven, P., Hoogduin, K. A. L., & van Dyck, R. (2002). A randomised controlled clinical trial on the additional effect of hypnosis in a comprehensive treatment programme for in-patients with conversion disorder of the motor type. *Psychother. Psychosom., 71*(2), 66–76.

Mogg, K., & Bradley, B. P. (2005). Attentional bias in generalized anxiety disorder versus depressive disorder. *Cog. Ther. Res., 29*(1), 29–45.

Mohler, H., & Okada, T. (1977). Benzodiazepine receptor: Demonstration in the central nervous system. *Science, 198*(4319), 849–851.

Mohler, H., Richards, J. G., & Wu, J.-Y. (1981). Autoradiographic localization of benzodiazepine receptors in immunocytochemically identified Y-aminobutyric synapses. *Proc. Natl. Acad. Sci., USA, 78,* 1935–1938.

Mohlman, J., Gorenstein, E. E., Kleber, M., de Jesus, M., Gorman, J. M., & Papp, L. A. (2003). Standard and enhanced cognitive-behavior therapy for late-life generalized anxiety disorder: Two pilot investigations. *Amer. J. Ger. Psychiat., 11*(1), 24–32.

Mohr, D. C., & Beutler, L. E. (1990). Erectile dysfunction: A review of diagnostic and treatment procedures. *Clin. Psychol. Rev., 10*(1), 123–150.

Moldavsky, D. (2004, June 1). Transcultural psychiatry for clinical practice. *Psychiatr. Times, XXI*(7), p. 36.

Molina, I. A., Dulmus, C. N., & Sowers, K. M. (2005). Secondary prevention for youth violence: A review of selected school-based programs. *Brief Treat. Crisis Intervent., 5*(1), 1–3.

Mollinger, R. N. (1980). Antithesis and the obsessive-compulsive. *Psychoanal. Rev., 67*(4), 465–477.

Mollon, P. (2003). Releasing the self: The healing legacy of Heinz Kohut. *Psychodyn. Pract.: Indiv. Groups Org., 9*(1): 89–94.

Molnar, B. E., Buka, S. L., & Kessler, R. C. (2001). Child sexual abuse and subsequent psychopathology: Results from the National Comorbidity Survey. *Amer. J. Pub. Hlth., 91*(5), 753–760.

Monahan, J. (1992). Mental disorder and violent behavior: Perceptions and evidence. *Amer. Psychologist, 47*(4), 511–521.

Monahan, J. (1993). Limiting therapist exposure to *Tarasoff* liability: Guidelines for risk containment. *Amer. Psychologist, 48*(3), 242–250.

Monahan, J. (1993). Mental disorder and violence: Another look. In S. Hodgins (Ed.), *Mental disorder and crime.* Newbury Park, CA: Sage.

Monahan, J. (2001). Major mental disorder and violence: Epidemiology and risk assessment. In G. F. Pinard & L. Pagani (Eds.), *Clinical assessment of dangerousness: Empirical contributions* (pp. 89–102). New York: Cambridge University Press.

Monahan, J., Redlich, A. D., Swanson, J., Robbins, P. C., Appelbaum, P. S., Petrila, J., et al. (2005). Use of leverage to improve adherence to psychiatric treatment in the community. *Psychiat. Serv., 56*(1), 37–44.

Monette, J., du Fort, G. G., Fung, S. H., Massoud, F., Moride, Y., Arsenault, L., & Afilalo, M. (2001). Evaluation of the Confusion Assessment Method (CAM) as a screening tool for delirium in the emergency room. *Gen. Hosp. Psychiat., 23*(1), 20–25.

Monkul, E. S., Malhi, G. S., & Soares, J. C. (2005). Anatomical MRI abnormalities in bipolar disorder: Do they exist and do they progress? *Austral. New Zeal. J. Psychiat., 39*(4), 222–226.

Monroe, S. M., & Hadjiyannakis, K. (2002). The social environment and depression: Focusing on severe life stress. In I. H. Gotlib & C. L. Hammen (Eds.), *Handbook of depression: Research and treatment* (pp. 314–340). New York: Guilford Press.

Monson, C. M., Stevens, S. P., & Schnurr, P. P. (2005). Cognitive-behavioral couple's treatment for posttraumatic stress disorder. In T. A. Corales (Ed.), *Focus on posttraumatic stress disorder research* (pp. 245–274). Hauppauge, NY: Nova Science Publishers.

Montgomery, S. A., Bebbington, P., Cowen, P., Deakin, W., et al. (1993). Guidelines for treating depressive illness with antidepressants. *J. Psychopharmacol., 7*(1), 19–23.

Monti, F., Agostini, F., & Martini, A. (2004). Postpartum depression and mother-infant interaction. *Eta Evolutiva, 78,* 77–84.

Montoya, A., Lepage, M., & Malla, A. (2005). Temporal lobe dysfunction in patients with first-episode schizophrenia. *Salud Mental, 28*(2), 33–39.

Moore, C. L., Flowers, C. R., & Taylor, D. (2000). Vocational rehabilitation services: Indicators of successful rehabilitation for persons with mental retardation. *J. Appl. Rehabil. Counsel., 31*(2), 36–40.

Moore, M. T. (1997, October 30). Maine initiative would give the vote to all mentally ill. *USA Today,* p. 12A.

Moorhead, D. J., Stashwick, C. K., Reinherz, H. Z., Giaconia, R. M., Streigel-Moore, R. M., & Paradis, A. D. (2003). Child and adolescent predictors for eating disorders in a community population of young adult women. *Inter. J. Eat. Disorders, 33*(1), 1–9.

Moos, R. H., & Cronkite, R. C. (1999). Symptom-based predictors of a 10-year chronic course of treated depression. *J. Nerv. Ment. Dis., 187*(6), 360–368.

Morgan, A. H., & Hilgard, E. R. (1973). Age differences in susceptibility to hypnosis. *Inter. J. Clin. Exp. Hyp., 21,* 78–85.

Morgan, C. D., & Murray, H. A. (1935). A method of investigating fantasies: The Thematic Apperception Test. *Arch. Neurol. Psychiat., 34,* 289–306.

Morgan, J., & Laungani, P. (Eds.). (2002) *Death and bereavement around the world* (Vol. 1–4). Amityville, NY: Baywood.

MORI (Market Opinion Research International). (1999, May 22). Poll on animal experimentation. New Scientist.

Morokoff, P. J., & Gillilland, R. (1993). Stress, sexual functioning, and marital satisfaction. *J. Sex Res., 30*(1), 43–53.

Morse, S. J. (1982). A preference for liberty: The case against involuntary commitment of the mentally disordered. *Calif. Law Rev., 70,* 55–106.

Mortley, J., Wade, J., & Enderby, P. (2004). Superhighway to promoting a client-therapist partnership? Using the Internet to deliver word-retrieval computer therapy, monitored remotely with minimal speech and language therapy input. *Aphasiology, 18*(3), 193–211.

Mosconi, L. (2005). Hippocampal metabolism in the longitudinal prediction of decline from normal cognition to MCI and AD. *Alzheimer's Association International Conference on Prevention of Dementia,* June 18, 2005, Washington, DC.

Moser, C. (2001). Paraphilia: A critique of a confused concept. In P. J. Kleinplatz (Ed.), *New directions in sex therapy: Innovations and alternatives* (pp. 91–108). New York: Brunner-Routledge.

Moskowitz, E. S. (2001). *In therapy we trust: America's obsession with self-fulfillment.* Baltimore: Johns Hopkins University Press.

Moss, D. (2002). Biofeedback. In S. Shannon (Ed.), *Handbook of complementary and alternative therapies in mental health* (pp. 135–158). San Diego, Ca: Academic Press.

Mowbray, C. T., Grazier, K. L., & Holter, M. (2002). Managed behavioral health care in the public sector: Will it become the third shame of the States? *Psychiatr. Serv., 53*(2), 157–170.

Mowrer, O. H. (1939). A stimulus-response analysis of anxiety and its role as a reinforcing agent. *Psychol. Rev., 46,* 553–566.

Mowrer, O. H. (1947). On the dual nature of learning: A reinterpretation of "conditioning" and "problem-solving." *Harvard Educ. Rev., 17,* 102–148.

Mowrer, O. H., & Mowrer, W. M. (1938). Enuresis: A method for its study and treatment. *Amer. J. Orthopsychiat., 8,* 436–459.

Moynihan, R. (2004). Controversial disease dropped from Prozac product information. *Brit. Med. J., 328*(7436), 328, 365.

MRI (Matrix Research Institute). (1998). *The facts about mental illness and work.* Philadelphia, PA: Author.

MTA Cooperative Group. (1999). A 14-month randomized clinical trial of treatment strategies for attention-deficit/hyperactivity disorder. *Arch. Gen. Psychiat., 56,* 1073–1086.

MTA Cooperative Group. (2004). National Institute of Mental Health multimodal treatment study of ADHD follow-up: Changes in effectiveness and growth after the end of treatment. *Pediatrics, 113,* 762–769.

Mueller, R. A., & Courchesne, E. (2000). Autism's home in the brain: Reply. *Neurology, 54*(1), 270.

Mufson, L., Nomura, Y., & Warner, V. (2002). The relationship between parental diagnosis, offspring temperament and offspring psychopathology: A longitudinal analysis. *J. Affect. Disorders, 71*(1–3), 61–69.

Mulhern, B. (1990, December 15–18). Everyone's problem, no one's priority. *Capital Times.*

Mulholland, A. M., & Mintz, L. B. (2001). Prevalence of eating disorders among African American women. *J. Couns. Psychol., 48*(1), 111–116.

Munk, J. P., & Mortensen, P. B. (1992). Social outcome in schizophrenia: A 13–year follow-up. *Soc. Psychiat. Psychiatr. Epidemiol., 27*(3), 129–134.

Munn-Giddings, C., & Borkman, T. (2005). Self-help/mutual aid as a psychosocial phenomenon. In S. Ramon & J. E. Williams (Eds.), *Mental health at the crossroads: The promise of the psychosocial approach* (pp. 137–154). Burlington, VT: Ashgate Publishing.

Muñoz, R. F., Le, H.-N., Clarke, G., & Jaycox, L. (2002). Preventing the onset of major depression. In I. H. Gotlib & C. L. Hammen (Eds.), *Handbook of depression* (pp. 343–359). New York: Guilford Press.

Muratori, F., Picchi, L., Apicella, F., Salvadori, F., Espasa, F. P., Ferretti, D., et al. (2005). Psychodynamic psychotherapy for separation anxiety disorders in children. *Depress. Anx., 21,* 45–46.

Murdock, S. G., O'Neill, R. E., & Cunningham, E. (2005). A comparison of results and acceptability of functional behavioral assessment procedures with a group of middle school students with emotional/behavioral disorders (E/BD). *J. Behav. Educ., 14*(1), 5–18.

Murphy, G. M. Jr., Hollander, S. B., Rodrigues, H. E., Kremer, C., & Schatzberg, A. F. (2004). Effects of the serotonin transporter gene promoter polymorphism on mirtazapie and paroxetine efficacy and adverse events in geriatric major depression. *Arch. Gen. Psychiat., 61*(11), 1163–1169.

Murphy, J. B., & Lipshultz, L. I. (1988). Infertility in the paraplegic male. In E. A. Tanagho, T. F. Lue, & R. D. McClure (Eds.), *Contemporary management of impotence and infertility.* Baltimore: Williams & Wilkins.

Murphy, J. G., McDevitt-Murphy, M. E., & Barnett, N. P. (2005). Drink and be merry? Gender, life satisfaction, and alcohol consumption among college students. *Psychol. Addict. Behav., 19,* 184–191.

Murphy, S. M. (1990). Rape, sexually transmitted diseases and human immunodeficiency virus infection. *Inter. J. STD AIDS, 1,* 79–82.

Murphy, W. J. (2001). The Victim Advocacy and Research Group: Serving a growing need to provide rape victims with personal legal representation to protect privacy rights and to fight gender bias in the criminal justice system. *J. Soc. Distress Homeless, 10*(1), 123–138.

Murray, B. (1996). Computer addictions entangle students. *APA Monitor, 27*(6), 38–39.

Murray, J. B. (2001). Ecstasy is a dangerous drug. *Psychol. Rep., 88*(3, Pt. 1), 895–902.

Murray, K. (1993, May 9). When the therapist is a computer. *New York Times,* Section 3, p. 25.

Mydans, S. (1996, October 19). New Thai tourist sight: Burmese "giraffe women." *New York Times,* p. C1.

Myers, D. G. (2000). The funds, friends, and faith of happy people. *Amer. Psychologist, 55*(1), 56–67.

Myers, D. G., & Diener, E. (1996, May). The pursuit of happiness. *Scientif. Amer.,* pp. 70–72.

Myers, M. G., Stewart, D. G., & Brown, S. A. (1998). Progression from conduct disorder to antisocial personality disorder following treatment for adolescent substance abuse. *Amer. J. Psychiat., 155*(4), 479–485.

Mylant, M. L., Ide, B., Guevas, E., & Meehan, M. (2002). Adolescent children of alcoholics: Vulnerable or resilient? *J. Amer. Psychiat. Nurs. Assoc., 8*(2), 57–64.

Nace, E. P. (2005). Alcohol. In R. J. Frances, A. H. Mack, & S. I. Miller (Eds.), *Clinical textbook of addictive disorders* (3rd ed., pp. 75–104). New York: Guilford Press.

Nagle, D. L., McGrail, S. H., Vitale, J., Woolf, E. A., Dussault, B. J., Jr., DiRocco, L., et al. (1999). The mahogany protein is a receptor involved in suppression of obesity. *Nature, 398*(6723), 148–152.

Nagy, T. F. (2005). Privacy and confidentiality. In T. F. Nagy, *Ethics in plain English: An illustrative casebook for psychologists* (2nd ed., pp. 107–130). Washington, DC: American Psychological Association.

Nahas, G. G., Sutin, K. M., Harvey, D., Agurell, S., Pace, N., & Cancro, R. (Eds.). (1999). *Marihuana and medicine.* Clifton, NJ: Humana Press.

Naimi, T. S., Brewer, R. D., Mokdad, A., Denny, C., Serdula, M. K., & Marks, J. S. (2003). Binge drinking among US adults. *JAMA, 289*(1), 70–75.

Najman, J. M., Andersen, M. J., Bor, W., O'Callaghan, M. J., & Williams, G. M. (2000). Postnatal depression—Myth and reality: Maternal depression before and after the birth of a child. *Soc. Psychiat. Psychiatr. Epidemiol., 35*(1), 19–27.

Najman, J. M., Hallam, D., Bor, W., O'Callaghan, M., Williams, G. M., & Shuttlewood, G. (2005). Predictors of depression in very young children: A prospective study. *Soc. Psychiat. Psychiatr. Epidemiol., 40*(5), 367–374.

NAMI (National Alliance for the Mentally Ill). (1996, February 7). Survey on mental health insurance. Cited in *USA Today,* p. 4D.

NAMI (National Alliance for the Mentally Ill). (2002). Retrieved from www.nami.org

NAMI (National Alliance for the Mentally Ill). (2005). Retrieved from www.nami.org

NAPHS (National Association of Psychiatric Health Systems). (1999). *The NAPHS 1998 annual survey report—trends in psychiatric health systems: A benchmarking report.* Washington, DC: Author.

Narash-Eisikovits, O., Dierberger, A., & Westen, D. (2002). A multidimensional meta-analysis of pharmacotherapy for bulimia nervosa: Summarizing the range of outcomes in controlled clinical trials. *Harvard Rev. Psychiat., 10*(4), 193–211.

Nardi, A. E., Valenca, A. M., Nascimento, I., & Zin, W. A. (2001). Hyperventilation challenge test in panic disorder and depression with panic attacks. *Psychiat. Res., 105,* 57–65.

Narita, T., Sato, T., Hirano, S., Gota, M., Sakado, K., & Uehara, T. (2000). Parental child-rearing behavior as measured by the Parental Bonding Instrument in a Japanese population: Factor structure and relationship to a lifetime history of depression. *J. Affect. Disorders, 57*(1–3), 229–234.

Narrow, W. E., Rae, D. S., Robins, L. N., & Regier, D. A. (2002). Revised prevalence based estimates of mental disorders in the United States: Using a clinical significance criterion to reconcile 2 surveys' estimates. *Arch. Gen. Psychiat., 59*(2), 115–123.

Nasar, S. (2002, March 18). A majestic person, despite flaws: Some recent reports about mathematician John Nash distort the truth. *Los Angeles Times,* p. B3.

Nash, J. M. (1997, May 5). Addicted. *Time,* pp. 68–76.

Nash, J. M. (1997). Special report: Fertile minds. *Newsweek, 149*(5), 48–56.

Nash, M. R. (2001, July). The truth and the hype of hypnosis. *Scientif. Amer.,* pp. 47–55.

Nathan, P. E., & Lagenbucher, J. W. (1999). Psychopathology: Description and classification. *Annu. Rev. Psychol., 50,* 79–107.

National Crime Victimization Survey (NCVS). (1993). Highlights from 20 years of surveying crime victims: The National Crime Victimization Survey, 1973–1992. Washington, DC: Bureau of Justice Statistics.

National Crime Victimization Survey (NCVS). (1996). Washington, DC: Bureau of Justice Statistics.

National Mental Health Association (NMHA). (1999, June 5). Poll. *U.S. Newswire.*

NBJ (Nutrition Business Journal, Natural Foods Merchandiser). (2001). Annual review of the industry. New Hope Natural Media/Penton Media, Inc. (newhope.com)

NCCAM (National Center for Complementary and Alternative Medicine). (2002). NCCAM Home Page.

NCHS (National Center for Health Statistics). (1998). *Fastats A to Z. Divorce.* Washington, DC: Centers for Disease Control and Prevention.

NCHS (National Center for Health Statistics). (1999). *Fastats A to Z. Divorce.* Washington, DC: Centers for Disease Control and Prevention.

NCHS (National Center for Health Statistics). (2000). *Births, marriages, divorces, and deaths: Provisional data for January 1999.* Centers for Disease Control and Prevention (National Vital Statistics Reports, Vol. 48, No. 1).

NCHS (National Center for Health Statistics). (2002). *Health, United States, 2002. With chartbook on trends in the health of Americans.* Hyattsville, MD: Author.

NCHS (National Center for Health Statistics). (2002). *Illegal drug use.* Hyattsville, MD: Author.

NCHS (National Center for Health Statistics). (2005). Asthma prevalence, health care use and mortality, 2002. Hyattsville, MD: Author.

NCIPC (National Center for Injury Prevention and Control). (1999, October 25). *Epidemiology of traumatic brain injury in the United States.* Centers for Disease Control and Prevention.

Neal, A. M., Lilly, R. S., & Zakis, S. (1993). What are African American children afraid of? *J. Anx. Disorders, 7,* 129–139.

Neeleman, J., Wessely, S., & Lewis, G. (1998). Suicide acceptability in African- and white Americans: The role of religion. *J. Nerv. Ment. Dis., 186*(1), 12–16.

Nehlig, A. (2004). Dependence upon coffee and caffeine: An update. In A. Nehlig (Ed.), *Coffee, tea, chocolate, and the brain* (pp. 133–146). Boca Raton, FL: CRC Press.

Neimeyer, R. A., & Bonnelle, K. (1997). The suicide intervention response inventory: A revision and validation. *Death Stud., 21,* 59–81.

Neisser, U. (2004, September 14). Cited in S. Friess, Historical events can be 'misremembered', *USA Today,* D09.

Neisser, U., Boodoo, G., Bouchard, T. J., Jr., Boykin, A. W., et al. (1996). Intelligence: Knowns and unknowns. *Amer. Psychologist, 51*(2), 77–101.

Nelson, J. C., Clary, C. M., Leon, A. C., & Schneider, L. S. (2005). Symptoms of late-life depression: Frequency and change during treatment. *Amer. J. Ger. Psychiat., 13*(6), 520–526.

Nelson, T. D. (2006). *The psychology of prejudice* (2nd ed.). New York: Pearson/Allyn & Bacon.

Nelson, T. F., & Wechsler, H. (2001). Alcohol and college athletes. *Med. Sci. Sports Exercise, 33*(1), 43–47.

Nemecek, S. (1996, September). Mysterious maladies. *Sci. Amer.*, 24–26.

Ness, R. B., Grisso, J. A., Herschinger, N., Markovic, N., Shaw, L. M., Day, N. L., & Kline, J. (1999). Cocaine and tobacco use and the risk of spontaneous abortion. *N. Engl. J. Med., 340*(5), 333–339.

Nestadt, G., Romanoski, A. J., Chahal, R., Merchant, A., Folstein, M. F., Gruenberg, E. M., & McHugh, P. R. (1990). An epidemiological study of histrionic personality disorder. *Psychol. Med., 29,* 413–422.

Neto, J. A. de S., & Araujo, L. M. (2004). Melatonin and psychiatric disorders. *J. Brasileiro de Psiquiatria, 53*(1), 38–45.

Neugebauer, R. (1978). Treatment of the mentally ill in medieval and early modern England: A reappraisal. *J. Hist. Behav. Sci., 14,* 158–169.

Neugebauer, R. (1979). Medieval and early modern theories of mental illness. *Arch. Gen. Psychiat., 36,* 477–483.

Neuman, P. A., & Halvorson, P. A. (1983). *Anorexia nervosa and bulimia: A handbook for counselors and therapists.* New York: Van Nostrand-Reinhold.

Neumarker, K. J. (1997). Mortality and sudden death in anorexia nervosa. *Inter. J. Eat. Disorders, 21*(3), 205–212.

Neumeister, A., Charney, D. S., & Drevets, W. C. (2005). Hippocampus, VI: Depression and the hippocampus. *Amer. J. Psychiat., 162*(6), 1057.

New York Times. (1993, February 9). West Side man to stay in hospital until hearing. (By Mary B. Tabor). February 9.

Newman, C. F. (2005). Reducing the risk of suicide in patients with bipolar disorder: Interventions and safeguards. *Cog. Behav. Pract., 12*(1), 76–88.

Newman, F. L., & Wong, S. E. (2004). Progress and outcomes assessment of individual patient data: Selecting single-subject design and statistical procedures. In M. E. Maruish (Ed.), *The use of psychological testing for treatment planning and outcomes assessment: Volume 1: General considerations* (3rd ed., pp. 273–289). Mahwah, NJ: Lawrence Erlbaum Associates.

Newman, J. P., Kosson, D. S., & Patterson, C. M. (1987). Response perseveration in psychopaths. *J. Abnorm. Psychol., 96,* 145–149.

Newman, J. P., Kosson, D. S., & Patterson, C. M. (1992). Delay of gratification in psychopathic and nonpsychopathic offenders. *J. Abnorm. Psychol., 101*(4), 630–636.

Newschaffer, C., Fallin, D., & Lee, N. L. (2002). Heritable and non-heritable risk factors for autistic spectrum disorders. *Epidemiology Review, 24,* 137–153.

Neylan, T. C., Brunet, A., Pole, N., Best, S. R., Metzler, T. J., Yehuda, R., & Marmar, C. R. (2005). PTSD symptoms predict waking salivary cortisol levels in police officers. *Psychoneuroendocrinology, 30*(4), 373–381.

Neziroglu, F., McKay, D., Todaro, J., & Yaryura-Tobias, J. A. (1996). Effect of cognitive behavior therapy on persons with body dysmorphic disorder and comorbid Axis II diagnoses. *Behav. Ther., 27,* 67–77.

Nezlek, J. B., Hampton, C. P., & Shean, G. D. (2000). Clinical depression and day-to-day social interaction in a community sample. *J. Abnorm. Psychol., 109*(1), 11–19.

NHSDA (National Household Survey on Drug Abuse). (2002). *The NHSDA Report: Substance abuse or dependence.* Washington, DC: Author.

NIA (National Institute on Aging). (1996). *Aging America poses unprecendented challenge. 65+.* Washington, DC: Office of the Demography of Aging.

Nichols, S. L., & Waschbusch, D. A. (2004). A review of the validity of laboratory cognitive tasks used to assess symptoms of ADHD. *Child Psychiat. Human Dev., 34,* 297–315.

Nicolson, P. (1999). Loss, happiness and postpartum depression: The ultimate paradox. *Canad. Psychol., 40*(2), 162–178.

NIDA (National Institute on Drug Abuse). (1995). *Facts about teenagers and drug abuse. NIDA Capsule.* Bethesda, MD: Author.

NIDA (National Institute on Drug Abuse). (1998). *Economic costs of alcohol and drug abuse.* Bethesda, MD: Author.

NIDA (National Institute on Drug Abuse). (2000). *Economic costs of alcohol and drug abuse.* Bethesda, MD: Author.

NIDA (National Institute on Drug Abuse). (2002). *Marijuana abuse.* Bethesda, MD: Author.

Nield, L. S., & Kamat, D. (2004). Enuresis: How to evaluate and treat. *Clin. Pediatr., 43*(5), 409–415.

Nietzel, M. T., Bernstein, D. A., Milich, R. S., & Kramer, G. (2003). *Introduction to clinical psychology* (6th ed.). Upper Saddle River, NJ: Pearson Education.

NIH (National Institutes of Health). (1999, February 19). *American Indian: Facts-at-a-glance for women's health.* Bethesda, MD: Author.

Nijinsky, V. (1936). *The diary of Vaslav Nijinsky.* New York: Simon & Schuster.

Nilsson, L. G., Soderlung, H., Berger, K., Breteler, M., de Ridder, M., Dufouil, C., et al. (2005). Cognitive test battery of CASCADE: Tasks and data. *Aging Neuropsychol. Cog., 12*(1), 32–56.

Ninan, P. T., & Dunlop, B. W. (2005). Neurobiology and ethiology of panic disorder. *J. Clin. Psychiat., 66*(Suppl. 4), 3–7.

NINDS (National Institute of Neurological Disorders and Stroke). (2006). Narcolepsy fact sheet. Bethesda, MD: Author..

Nishina, A., Juvonen, J., & Witkow, M. R. (2005). Sticks and stones may break my bones, but names will make me feel sick: The psychosocial, somatic, and scholastic consequences of peer harassment. *J. Clin. Child Adol. Psychol., 34*(1), 37–48.

Nishino, S., Mignot, E., & Dement, W. C. (1995). Sedative hypnotics. In A. F. Schatzberg & C. B. Nemeroff (Eds.), *The American Psychiatric Press textbook of psychopharmacology.* Washington, DC: American Psychiatric Press.

NMHA (National Mental Health Association). (1999, June 5), Poll. *U.S. Newswire.*

NMHA (National Mental Health Association). (2005). It is time to pass comprehensive health insurance disorder parity. Alexandria, VA: NMHA.

Noeker, M. (2004). Facatitious disorder and factitious disorder by proxy. *Praxis der Kinderpsychol. Kinderpsych., 53*(7), 449–467.

Nolan, P. (2002). Object relations as a context for an integrative approach to psychotherapy. In P. Nolan & I. S. Nolan (Eds.), *Object relations and integrative psychotherapy: Tradition and innovation in theory and practice* (pp. 8–27). London: Whurr Publishers.

Nolan, S. A., Strassle, C. G., Roback, H. B., & Binder, J. L. (2004). Negative treatment effects in dyadic psychotherapy: A focus on prevention and intervention strategies. *J. Contemp. Psychother., 34*(4), 311–330.

Nolen-Hoeksema, S. (1987). Sex differences in unipolar depression: Evidence and theory. *Psychol. Bull., 101*(2), 259–282.

Nolen-Hoeksema, S. (1990). *Sex differences in depression.* Stanford, CA: Stanford University Press.

Nolen-Hoeksema, S. (1995). Gender differences in coping with depression across the lifespan. *Depression, 3,* 81–90.

Nolen-Hoeksema, S. (1998). The other end of the continuum: The costs of rumination: *Psychological Inquiry, 9*(3), 216–219.

Nolen-Hoeksema, S. (2000). The role of rumination in depressive disorders and mixed anxiety/depressive symptoms. *J. Abnorm. Psychol., 109,* 504–511.

Nolen-Hoeksema, S. (2002). Gender differences in depression. In I. H. Gotlib & C. L. Hammen (Eds.), *Handbook of depression* (pp. 492–509). New York: Guilford Press.

Nolen-Hoeksema, S. (2004). Gender differences in risk factors and consequences for alcohol use and problems. *Clin. Psychol. Rev., 24*(8), 981–1010.

Nolen-Hoeksema, S., & Corte, C. (2004). Gender and self-regulation. In K. D. Vohs & R. F. Baumeister (Eds.), *Handbook of self-regulation: Research, theory, and applications* (pp. 411–421). New York: Guilford Press.

Nolen-Hoeksema, S., & Girgus, J. (1995). Explanatory style and achievement, depression, and gender differences in childhood and early adolescence. In G. Buchanan & M. Seligman (Eds.), *Explanatory style.* Hillsdale, NJ: Erlbaum.

Noll, R., & Turkington, C. (1994). *The encyclopedia of memory and memory disorders.* New York: Facts on File.

Nomura, H., Inoue, S., Kamimura, N., Shimodera, S., Mino, Y., Gregg, L., & Tarrier, N. (2005). A cross-cultural study on expressed emotion in carers of people with dementia and schizophrenia: Japan and England. *Soc. Psychiat. Psychiatr. Epidemiol., 40*(7), 564–570.

Nonacs, R. (2002, March 12). Postpartum psychiatric illness. *eMed. J., 3*(3).

Noonan, D. (2003, June 16). A healthy heart. *Newsweek, 141*(24), 48–52.

Norcross, J. C., & Prochaska, J. O. (1984). Where do behavior (and other) therapists take their troubles? II. *Behav. Therapist, 7*(2), 26–27.

Norcross, J. C., Prochaska, J. O., & Farber, J. A. (1993). Psychologists conducting psychotherapy: New findings and historical comparisons on the psychotherapy division membership. *Psychotherapy, 30*(4), 692–697.

Nordhus, I. H., & Nielsen, G. H. (2005). Mental disorders in old age: Clinical syndromes, prevalence and benefits of psychological treatment. *Nordisk Psykologi, 57*(1), 86–103.

Nordstrom, P., Samuelsson, M., & Asberg, M. (1995). Survival analysis of suicide risk after attempted suicide. *Acta Psychiatr. Scandin., 91*(5), 336–340.

Norman, R. M. G., & Malla, A. K. (2001). Family history of schizophrenia and the relationship of stress to symptoms: Preliminary findings. *Austral. New Zeal. J. Psychiat.*, *35*(2), 217–223.

Norra, C., Mrazek, M., Tuchtenhagen, F., Gobbele, R., Buchner, H., Sass, H., & Herpertz, S. C. (2003). Enhanced intensity dependence as a marker of low serotonergic neurotransmission in borderline personality disorder. *J. Psychiatr. Res.*, *37*(1), 23–33.

Norris, G. (2006). Criminal profiling: A continuing history. In W. Petherick (Ed.), *Serial crime: Theoretical and practical issues in behavioral profiling*. San Diego, CA: Elsevier.

North, C. S. (2005). Somatoform disorders. In E. H. Rubin & C. F. Zorumski (Eds.), *Adult psychiatry* (2nd ed., pp. 261–274). Oxford, England: Blackwell Publishing Ltd.

North, C. S., Nixon, S. J., Shariat, S., Mallonee, S., McMillen, J. C., Spitznagel, E. L., et al. (1999). Psychiatric disorders among survivors of the Oklahoma City bombing. *JAMA*, *282*(8), 755–762.

North, C. S., & Yutzy, S. H. (2005). Dissociative disorders, factitious disorders, and malingering. In E. H. Rubin & C. F. Zorumski (Eds.), *Adult psychiatry* (2nd ed., pp. 275–289). Oxford, England: Blackwell Publishing Ltd.

Noyes, R. Jr., Stuart, S., Langbehn, D. R., Happel, R. L., Longley, S. L., & Yagla, S. J. (2002). Childhood antecedents of hypochondriasis. *Psychosomatics: J. Consult. Liaison Psychiat.*, *43*(4), 282–289.

Noyes, R., Jr. (1999). The relationship of hypochondriasis to anxiety disorders. *Gen. Hosp. Psychiat.*, *21*(1), 8–17.

Noyes, R., Jr. (2001). Comorbidity in generalized anxiety disorder. *Psychiatr. Clin. N. Amer.*, *24*(1), 41–55.

Noyes, R., Jr., Stuart, S., Langbehn, D. R., Happel, R. L., Longley, S. L., Muller, B. A., et al. (2003). Test of an interpersonal model of hypochondriasis. *Psychosom. Med.*, *65*(2), 292–300.

NRC (National Research Council). (2001). *Educating children with autism*. Washington, DC: National Academy Press.

NSDUH. (2005). *National survey on drug use*. Washington, DC: Department of Health and Human Services, Substance Abuse and Mental Health Services Administration, Office of Applied Studies.

Nussbaum, M. C. (2002). Other times, other places: Homosexuality in ancient Greece. In J. A. Winer, J. W. Anderson, B. J. Cohler, & R. D. Shelby (Eds.), *The annual of psychoanalysis, Volume 30: Rethinking psychoanalysis and the homosexualities* (pp. 9–22). Hillsdale, NJ: Analytic Press.

Nwokike, J. (2005). Federal insanity acquittees. *J. Amer. Acad. Psychiat. Law*, *33*(1), 126–128.

O'Brien, C. P., & Lyons, F. (2000). Alcohol and the athlete. *Sports Med.*, *29*, 295–300.

O'Brien, C. P., & McKay, J. (2002). Pharmacological treatments for substance use disorders. In P. E. Nathan & J. M. Gorman (Eds.), *A guide to treatments that work* (2nd ed). London: Oxford University Press.

O'Brien, C. P., O'Brien, T. J., Mintz, J., & Brady, J. P. (1975). Conditioning of narcotic abstinence symptoms in human subjects. *Drug. Alc. Dep.*, *1*, 115–123.

O'Connor, R. C., & Leenaars, A. A. (2004). A thematic comparison of suicide notes drawn

from Northern Ireland and the United States. *Curr. Psychol.: Dev., Learn., Personal., Soc.*, *22*(4), 339–347.

O'Hara, M. W. (2003). Postpartum depression. *Clinician's Research Digest, Supplemental Bulletin 29*.

O'Hare, T. (1992). The substance-abusing chronically mentally ill client: Prevalence, assessment, treatment and policy concerns. *Soc. Work*, *37*(2), 185–187.

O'Malley, S. S., Jaffe, A. J., Chang, G., Schottenfeld, R., Meyer, R., & Rounsaville, B. (1992). Naltrexone and coping skills therapy for alcohol dependence. *Arch. Gen. Psychiat.*, *49*, 881–888.

O'Malley, S. S., Jaffe, A. J., Rode, S., & Rounsaville, B. J. (1996). Experience of a "slip" among alcoholics treated with naltrexone or placebo. *Amer. J. Psychiat.*, *153*, 281–283.

O'Malley, S. S., Krishnan-Sarin, S., Farren, C., & O'Connor, P. G. (2000). Naltrexone-induced nausea in patients treated for alcohol dependence: Clinical predictors and evidence for opioid-mediated effects. *J. Clin. Psychopharmacol.*, *20*(1), 69–76.

Oderda, G. M., & Klein-Schwartz, W. (1983). Lunar cycle and poison center calls. *J. Toxicol. Clin. Toxicol.*, *20*(5), 487–495.

Oesterle, S., Hill, K. G., Hawkins, J. D., Guo, J., Catalano, R. F., & Abbott, R. D. (2004). Adolescent heavy episodic drinking trajectories and health in young adulthood. *J. Stud. Alc.*, *65*, 204–212.

Offman, A., & Kleinplatz, P. J. (2004). Does PMDD belong in the DSM? Challenging the medicalization of women's bodies. *Canad. J. Human Sexuality*, *13*, 17–27.

OFWW. (2004, December 25). Drivers admit to experiencing road rage. *Obesity, Fitness & Wellness Week*, 1209.

Ogden, J., & Ward, E. (1995). Help-seeking behavior in sufferers of vaginismus. *Sex. Marit. Ther.*, *10*(1), 23–30.

Ogloff, J. R. P. (2002). Identifying and accommodating the needs of mentally ill people in gaols and prisons. *Psychiatr. Psychol. Law.*, *9*(1), 1–33.

Ogloff, J. R. P., Schweighofer, A., Turnbull, S. D., & Whittemore, K. (1992). Empirical research regarding the insanity defense: How much do we really know? In J. R. P. Ogloff (Ed.), *Law and psychology: The broadening of the discipline* (pp. 171–210). Durham, NC: Carolina Academic Press.

Ohayon, M. M., & Roth, T. (2003). Place of chronic insomnia in the course of depressive and anxiety disorders. *J. Psychiatr. Res.*, *37*(1), 9–15.

Ohman, A., Erixon, G., & Lofberg, I. (1975). Phobias and preparedness: Phobic versus neutral pictures as continued stimuli for human autonomic responses. *J. Abnorm. Psychol.*, *84*, 41–45.

Ohman, A., & Mineka, S. (2003). The malicious serpent: Snakes as a prototypical stimulus for an evolved module of fear. *Curr. Direct. Psychol. Sci.*, *12*(1), 5–9.

Ohman, A., & Soares, J. J. F. (1993). On the automatic nature of phobic fear: Conditioned electrodermal responses to masked fear-relevant stimuli. *J. Abnorm. Psychol.*, *102*(1), 121–132.

Oldenburg, B., & Burton, N. W. (2004). Primary prevention. In J. Weinman & A. Kaptein

(Eds.), *Health psychology* (pp. 305–336). Malden, MA: Blackwell Publishers.

Olfson, M., & Klerman, G. L. (1993). Trends in the prescription of antidepressants by office based psychiatrists. *Amer. J. Psychiat.*, *150*(4), 571–577.

Olfson, M., Mechanic, D., Hansell, S., Boyer, C. A., Walkup, J., & Weiden, P. J. (2000). Predicting medication noncompliance after hospital discharge among patients with schizophrenia. *Psychiatr. Serv.*, *51*(2), 216–222.

Olivardia, R., Pope, H. G., Jr., & Phillips, K. A. (2000). *The Adonis complex: The secret crisis of male body*. New York: Free Press.

Olmos de Paz, T. (1990). Working-through and insight in child psychoanalysis. *Melanie Klein & Object Relations*, *8*(1), 99–112.

Olmsted, M. P., Kaplan, A. S., & Rockert, W. (1994). Rate and prediction of relapse in bulimia nervosa. *Amer. J. Psychiat.*, *151*(5), 738–743.

Olmsted, M. P., Kaplan, A. S., & Rockert, W. (2005). Defining remission and relapse in bulimia nervosa. *Inter. J. Eat. Disorders*, *38*(1), 1–6.

Olsen, C. E., Poulsen, H. D., & Lublin, H. K. F. (2005). Drug therapy of dementia in elderly patients: A review. *Nordic J. Psychiat.*, *59*(2), 71–77.

Olsson, S. E., & Moller, A. R. (2003). On the incidence and sex ratio of transsexualism in Sweden. *Arch. Sex. Behav.*, *32*(4), 381–386.

ONDCP (Office of National Drug Control Policy). (2000). Methadone. *ONDCP Drug Policy Information Clearinghouse Fact Sheet*.

Onen, S. H., Onen, F., Mangeon, J. P., Abidi, H., Courpron, P., & Schmidt, J. (2005). Alcohol abuse and dependence in elderly emergency department patients. *Arch. Geront. Geriat.*, *41*(2), 191–200.

Opinion Research Corporation. (2004). National Survey Press Release. May 17, 2004.

Oquendo, M. A., Brent, D. A., Birmaher, B., Greenhill, L., Kolko, D., Stanley, B., et al. (2005). Posttraumatic stress disorder comorbid with major depression: Factors mediating the association with suicidal behavior. *Amer. J. Psychiat.*, *162*(3), 580–586.

Oquendo, M. A., Dragatsi, D., Harkavy-Friedman, J., Dervic, K., Currier, D., Burke, A. K., et al. (2005). Protective factors against suicidal behavior in Latinos. *J. Nerv. Ment. Dis.*, *193*(7), 438–443.

Oquendo, M. A., Lizardi, D., Greenwald. S., Weissman, M. M., & Mann, J. J. (2004). Rates of lifetime suicide attempt and rates of lifetime major depression in different ethnic groups in the United States. *Acta Psychiatr. Scandin.*, *110*(6), 446–451.

Oquendo, M. A., Placidi, G. P. A., Malone, K. M., Campbell, C., Keilp, J., Brodsky, B., et al. (2003). Positron emission tomography of regional brain metabolic responses to a serotonergic challenge and lethality of suicide attempts in major depression. *Arch. Gen. Psychiat.*, *60*(1), 14–22.

Orsillo, S. M., Weathers, F. W., Litz, B. T., Steinberg, H. R., et al. (1996). Current and lifetime psychiatric disorders among veterans with war zone-related posttraumatic stress disorder. *J. Nerv. Ment. Dis.*, *184*, 307–313.

Orzack, M. H. (1996, December 1). Interview in P. Belluck, The symptoms of Internet addiction. *New York Times*, p. 5.

Oshima, I., Mino, Y., & Inomata, Y. (2005). Effects of environmental deprivation on negative symptoms of schizophrenia: A nationwide survey in Japan's psychiatric hospitals. *Psychiat. Res., 136*(2–3), 163–171.

Oslin, D. W. (2006). Addictions. In D. V. Jeste & J. H. Friedman (Eds.), *Psychiatry for neurologists* (pp. 93–104). Totowa, NJ: Humana Press.

Oslin, D. W., & Holden, R. (2002). Recognition and assessment of alcohol and drug dependence in the elderly. In A. M. Gurnack, R. Atkinson, & N. J. Osgood (Eds.), *Treating alcohol and drug abuse in the elderly.* New York: Springer.

Osterling, J., Dawson, G., & McPartland, J. (2001). Autism. In C. E. Walker & M. C. Roberts (Eds.), *Handbook of clinical child psychopathology* (3rd ed., pp. 432–452). New York: Wiley.

Osterweis, M., & Townsend, J. (1988). *Understanding bereavement reactions in adults and children: A booklet for lay people.* Rockville, MD: U.S. Department of Health and Human Services.

Ostrove, N. M. (2001, July 24). Statement before the subcommittee on consumer affairs, foreign commerce, and tourism, Senate committee on commerce, science, and transportation. Retrieved from www.fda.gov

Otten, K. L. (2004). An analysis of a classwide self-monitoring approach to improve the behavior of elementary students with severe emotional and behavioral disorders. *Diss. Abstr. Inter.: Sect. A: Human. Soc. Sci., 65*(3-A), 893.

Otto, M. W., & Deveney, C. (2005). Cognitive-behavioral therapy and the treatment of panic disorder: Efficacy and strategies. *J. Clin. Psychiat., 66*(Suppl. 4), 28–32.

Otto, R. K., & Heilbrun, K. (2002). The practice of forensic psychology: A look toward the future in light of the past. *Amer. Psychologist, 57*(1), 5–18.

Ouellette, S. C. (1993). Inquiries into hardiness. In L. Goldberger & S. Beznitz (Eds.), *Handbook of stress: Theoretical and clinical aspects* (2nd ed.). New York: Free Press.

Ouellette, S. C., & DiPlacido, J. (2001). Personality's role in the protection and enhancement of health: Where the research has been, where it is stuck, how it might move. In A. Baum, T. A. Revenson, & J. E. Singer (Eds.), *Handbook of health psychology.* Mahwah, NJ: Erlbaum.

Overholser, J. C. (1996). The dependent personality and interpersonal problems. *J. Nerv. Ment. Dis., 184*(1), 8–16.

Overton, D. (1964). State-dependent or "dissociated" learning produced with pentobarbital. *J. Compar. Physiol. Psychol., 57,* 3–12.

Overton, D. (1966). State-dependent learning produced by depressant and atropine-like drugs. *Psychopharmacologia, 10,* 6–31.

Ovsiew, F. (2006). Hysteria in neurological practice: The somatoform and dissociative disorders. In D. V. Jeste & J. H. Friedman (Eds.), *Psychiatry for neurologists* (pp. 67–80). Totowa, NJ: Humana Press.

Owen, C. C., et al. (1998). Lunar cycles and violent behaviour. *Austral. New Zeal. J. Psychiat., 32*(4), 496–499.

Owen, F., Crow, T. J., & Poulter, M. (1987). Central dopaminergic mechanisms in schizophrenia. *Acta Psychiatr. Belg., 87*(5), 552–565.

Owen, F., Crow, T. J., Poulter, M., et al. (1978). Increased dopamine receptor sensitivity in schizophrenia. *Lancet, 2,* 223–226.

Owen, M. J., & O'Donovan, M. C. (2003). Schizophrenia and genetics. In R. Plomin, J. C. DeFries, et al. (Eds.), *Behavioral genetics in the postgenomic era* (pp. 463–480). Washington, DC: American Psychological Association.

Owen-Howard, M. (2001). Pharmacological aversion treatment of alcohol dependence. I. Production and prediction of conditioned alcohol aversion. *Amer. J. Drug Alc. Abuse, 27*(3), 561–585.

Oxley, D. (2000). The school reform movement: Opportunities for community psychology. In J. Rappaport & E. Seidman (Eds.), *Handbook of community psychology.* New York: Kluwer Academic/Plenum Publishers.

Oyama, H., Watanabe, N., Ono, Y., Sakashita, T., Takenoshita, Y., Taguchi, M., et al. (2005). Community-based suicide prevention through group activity for the elderly successfully reduced the high suicide rate for females. *Psychiat. Clin. Neurosci., 59*(3), 337–344.

Ozer, E. J. (2005). The impact of violence on urban adolescents: Longitudinal effects of perceived school connection and family support. *J. Adol. Res., 20*(2), 167–192.

Ozer, E. J., Best, S. R., Lipsey, T. L., & Weiss, D. S. (2003). Predictors of posttraumatic stress disorder and symptoms in adults: A meta-analysis. *Psychol. Bull., 129*(1), 52–73.

Ozonoff, S., Dawson, G., & McPartland, J. (2002). *A parent's guide to Asperger syndrome and high-functioning autism: How to meet the challenges and help your child thrive.* New York: Guilford Press.

Padwa, L. (1996). *Everything you pretend to know and are afraid someone will ask.* New York: Penguin.

Pagnin, D., de Queirox, V., Pini, S., & Cassano, G.-B. (2004). Efficacy of ECT in depression: A meta-analytic review. *J. ECT, 20*(1), 13–20.

Painot, D., Jotterand, S., Kammer, A., Fossati, M., & Golay, A. (2001). Simultaneous nutritional cognitive-behavioral therapy in obese patients. *Patient Educ. Counsel., 42*(1), 47–52.

Pajer, K. (1995). New strategies in the treatment of depression in women. *J. Clin. Psychiat., 56*(Suppl. 2), 30–37.

Palermo, G. B., Kocsis, R. N., & Slovenko, R. (Eds.). (2005). *Offender profiling: An introduction to the sociopsychological analysis of violent crime.* Springfield, IL: Charles C. Thomas.

Palmer, A. (2003). Behavioral program helps autistic children make progress. *Monit. Psychol., 34*(9), 15.

Palmer, R. L., Birchall, H., McGrain, L., & Sullivan, V. (2002). Self-help for bulimic disorders: A randomised controlled trial comparing minimal guidance with face-to-face or telephone guidance. *Brit. J. Psychiat., 181*(3), 230–235.

Palmore, E. B. (2001). The Ageism Survey: First findings. *Gerontologist, 41*(5), 572–575.

Palmore, E. B. (2004). Research note: Ageism in Canada and the United States. *J. Cross-Cult. Ger., 19*(1), 41–46.

Palmore, E. B., Branch, L., & Harris, D. K. (Eds.) (2005). *Encyclopedia of ageism.* Binghamton, NY: Haworth Pastoral Press.

Panati, C. (1987). *Panati's extraordinary origin of everyday things.* New York: Harper & Row.

Pansky, A., Koriat, A., & Goldsmith, M. (2005). Eyewitness recall and testimony. In N. Brewer & K. D. Kipling (Eds.), *Psychology and law: An empirical perspective* (pp. 93–150). New York: Guilford Press.

Papadimitriou, G. N., Calabrese, J. R., Dikeos, D. G., Christodoulou, G. N. (2005). Rapid cycling bipolar disorder: Biology and pathogenesis. *Inter. J. Neuropsychopharmacol., 89*(2), 281–292.

Papolos, D., Hennen, J., Cockerham, M. S. (2005). Factors associated with parent-reported suicide threats by children and adolescents with community-diagnosed bipolar disorder. *J. Affect. Disorders, 86*(2–3), 267–275.

Paris, J. (1991). Personality disorders, parasuicide, and culture. *Transcult. Psychiatr. Res. Rev., 28*(1), 25–39.

Paris, J. (2001). Cultural risk factors in personality disorders. In J. F. Schumaker & T. Ward (Eds.), *Cultural cognition and psychopathology.* Westport, CT: Praeger.

Paris, J. (2001). Psychosocial adversity. In W. J. Livesley (Ed.), *Handbook of personality disorders: Theory, research, and treatment* (pp. 231–241). New York: Guilford Press.

Paris, J. (2005). Borderline personality disorder. *Canad. Med. Assoc. J., 172*(12), 1579–1583.

Paris, J. (2005). Understanding self-mutilation in borderline personality disorder. *Harvard Rev. Psychiat., 13*(3), 179–185.

Parker, A., & Bhugra, D. (2000). Attitudes of British medical students towards male homosexuality. *Sex. Relat. Ther., 15*(2), 141–149.

Parker, G. (1992). Early environment. In E. S. Paykel (Ed.), *Handbook of affective disorders.* New York: Guilford Press.

Parker, G., Hadzi-Pavlovic, D., Greenwald, S., & Weissman, M. (1995). Low parental care as a risk factor to lifetime depression in a community sample. *J. Affect. Disorders, 33*(3), 173–180.

Parker, G., Roy, K., Wilhelm, K., & Mitchell, P. (2001). Assessing the comparative effectiveness of antidepressant therapies: A prospective clinical practice study. *J. Clin. Psychiat., 62*(2), 117–125.

Parker, G. B., & Brotchie, H. L. (2004). From diathesis to dimorphism: The biology of gender differences in depression. *J. Nerv. Ment. Dis., 192*(3), 210–216.

Parker, S., Nichter, M., Vuckovic, N., Sims, C., & Ritenbaugh, C. (1995). Body image and weight concerns among African American and white adolescent females: Differences that make a difference. *Human Organization, 54*(2), 103–114.

Parmelee, P. A., Katz, I. R., & Lawton, M. P. (1991). The relations of pain to depression among institutionalized aged. *J. Ger., 46,* P15–P21.

Parrott, A. C. (1999). Does cigarette smoking cause stress? *Amer. Psychologist, 54*(10), 817–820.

Parrott, A. C. (2000). Cigarette smoking does cause distress. *Amer. Psychologist, 55*(10), 1159–1160.

Parry, B. L. (1999). Postpartum depression in relation to other reproductive cycle mood changes. In L. J. Miller (Ed.), *Postpartum mood disorders.* Washington, DC: American Psychiatric Press.

Parry, J. W. (2005). The death penalty and persons with mental disabilities: A lethal dose of stigma, sanism, fear of violence, and faulty predictions of dangerousness. *Ment. Phys. Disability Law Reporter, 29*(5), 667–669.

Partin, J. C., Hamill, S. K., Fischel, J. E., & Partin, J. S. (1992). Painful defecation and fecal soiling in children. *Pediatrics, 89*, 1007–1009.

Pathe, M. (2002). *Surviving stalking.* New York: Cambridge University Press.

Paton, C., & Beer, D. (2001). Caffeine: The forgotten variable. *Inter. J. Psychiat. Clin. Prac., 5*(4), 231–236.

Patrick, C. J., Bradley, M. M., & Lang, P. J. (1993). Emotion in the criminal psychopath: Startle reflex modulation. *J. Abnorm. Psychol., 102*(1), 82–92.

Patrick, C. J., Cuthbert, B. N., & Lang, P. J. (1990). Emotion in the criminal psychopath: Fear imagery. *Psychophysiology, 27*(Suppl.), 55.

Patterson, C. H. (2000). *Person-centered approach and client-centered therapy: Essential readers.* Ross-on-Wye, England: PCCS Books.

Patterson, G. R. (1982). *Coercive family process.* Eugene, OR: Castalia.

Patterson, G. R. (1986). Performance models for antisocial boys. *Amer. Psychologist, 41*, 432–444.

Patton, G. C., Selzer, R., Coffee, C., Carlin, J. B., & Wolfe, R. (1999). Onset of adolescent eating disorders: Population based cohort study over 3 years. *Brit. Med. J., 318*(7186), 765–768.

Patton, J. R., Polloway, E. A., & Smith, T. E. C. (2000). Educating students with mild mental retardation. *Focus Autism Other Dev. Disabil., 15*(2), 80–89.

Paul, G. L. (1967). The strategy of outcome research in psychotherapy. *J. Couns. Psychol., 31*, 109–118.

Paul, G. L., & Lentz, R. (1977). *Psychosocial treatment of the chronic mental patient.* Cambridge, MA: Harvard University Press.

Pauls, C. A., & Stemmler, G. (2003). Repressive and defensive coping during fear and anger. *Emotion, 3*(3), 284–302.

Paurohit, N., Dowd, E. T., & Cottingham, H. F. (1982). The role of verbal and nonverbal cues in the formation of first impressions of black and white counselors. *J. Couns. Psychol., 4*, 371–378.

Paxton, S. J., & Diggens, J. (1997). Avoidance coping, binge eating, and depression: An examination of the escape theory of binge eating. *Inter. J. Eat. Disorders, 22*, 83–87.

Paykel, E. S. (Ed.). (1982). *Handbook of affective disorders.* New York: Guilford Press.

Paykel, E. (2003). Life events: Effects and genesis. *Psychol. Med., 33*(7), 1145–1148.

Paykel, E. S. (2003). Life events and affective disorders. *Acta Psychiatr. Scandin., 108*(Suppl. 418), 61–66.

Paykel, E., Abbott, R., Jenkins, R., Brugha, T., & Meltzer, H. (2003). Urban-rural mental health differences in Great Britain: Findings from the National Morbidity Survey. *Inter. Rev. Psychiat., 15*(1–2), 97–107.

Paykel, E. S., & Cooper, Z. (1992). Life events and social stress. In E. S. Paykel (Ed.), *Handbook of affective disorders.* New York: Guilford Press.

Paykel, E. S., Rao, B. M., & Taylor, C. N. (1984). Life stress and symptom pattern in outpatient depression. *Psychol. Med., 14*(3), 559–568.

Payne, A. F. (1928). *Sentence completion.* New York: New York Guidance Clinics.

Payne, J. L., Potash, J. B., & DePaulo, J. R. Jr. (2005). Recent findings on the genetic basis of bipolar disorder. *Psychiatr. Clin. N. Amer., 28*(2), 481–498.

Payte, T. J. (1989). Combined treatment modalities: The need for innovative approaches. Third National Forum on AIDS and Chemical Dependency of the American Society of Addiction Medicine. *J. Psychoactive Drugs, 21*(4), 431–434.

Pearlman, E. (2005). Terror of desire: The etiology of eating disorders from an attachment theory perspective. *Psychoanal. Rev. 92*(2), 223–235.

Pearson, J. L. (2000). Suicidal behavior in later life: Research update. In R. W. Maris, S. S. Canetto, J. L. McIntosh, & M. M. Silverman (Eds.), *Review of suicidology, 2000.* New York: Guilford Press.

Peck, M. S. (2005). *Glimpses of the devil? A psychiatrist's personal accounts of possession, exorcism, and redemption.* New York: Free Press.

Pedersen, N. P., & Blessing, W. W. (2001). Cutaneous vasoconstriction contributes to hyperthermia induced by 3,4-methylenedioxymethamphetamine (ecstasy) in conscious rabbits. *J. Neurosci., 21*(21), 8648–8654.

Peele, S. (1989). *Diseasing of America: Addiction treatment out of control.* Lexington, MA: Lexington Books/D.C. Heath.

Peele, S. (1992). Alcoholism, politics, and bureaucracy: The consensus against controlled-drinking therapy in America. *Addic. Behav., 17*, 49–62.

Pelham, M. F., & Loell, M. R. (2005). Issues in neuropsychological assessment. In T. W. McAllister, S. C. Yudofsky, & J. M. Silver (Eds.), *Textbook of traumatic brain injury* (pp. 159–172). Washington, DC: American Psychiatric Publishing.

Pelham, W. E., Gnagy, E. M., Greiner, A. R., Hoza, B., Hinshaw, S. P., Swanson, J. M., et al. (2000). Behavioral versus behavioral and pharmacological treatment in ADHD children attending a summer treatment program. *J. Abnorm. Child Psychol., 28*, 507–525.

Pelham, W. E., Wheeler, T., & Chronis, A. (1998). Empirically supported psychosocial treatments for attention deficit hyperactivity disorder. *J. Clin. Child Psychol., 27*, 190–205.

Pelissier, M. C., & O'Connor, K. (2004). Cognitive-behavioral treatment of trichotillomania, targeting perfectionism. *Clin. Case Stud., 3*(1), 57–69.

Pendery, M. L., Maltzman, I. M., & West, L. J. (1982). Controlled drinking by alcoholics? New findings and a reevaluation of a major affirmative study. *Science, 217*(4555), 169–175.

Penn, D. L., & Nowlin-Drummond, A. (2001). Politically correct labels and schizophrenia: A rose by any other name? *Schizo. Bull., 27*(2), 197–203.

Pennington, B. F. (2002). *The development of psychopathology: Nature and nurture.* New York: Guilford Press.

Penninx, B. W., Guralnik, J. M., Ferrucci, L., Simonsick, E. M., Deeg, D. J., & Wallace, R. B. (1998). Depressive symptoms and physical decline in community-dwelling older persons. *JAMA, 279*(21), 1720–1726.

Pepe, M. (2002). Cited in Getting past the trauma. *Psychol. Today, 35*(1), 54.

Perelman, M. A. (2002). FSD partner issues: Expanding sex therapy with sildenafil. *J. Sex Marital Ther., 28*(Suppl. 1), 195–204.

Perez, A., Leifman, S., & Estrada, A. (2003). Reversing the criminalization of mental illness. *Crime and Delinquency, 49*(1), 62–78.

Perilla, J. L., Norris, F. H., & Lavizzo, E. A. (2002). Ethnicity, culture, and disaster response: Identifying and explaining ethnic differences in PTSD six months after Hurricane Andrew. *J. Soc. Clin. Psychol., 21*, 20–45.

Perkins, H. W. (2002). Surveying the damage: A review of research on consequences of alcohol misuse in college populations. *J. Alcohol Stud.,* Suppl. 14, 91–100.

Perkins, K., Grobe, J., DiAmico, D., Fonte, C., Wilson, A., & Stiller, R. (1996). Low-dose nicotine nasal spray use and effects during initial smoking cessation. *Exp. Clin. Psychopharmacol., 4*(2), 191–197.

Perlin, M. L. (2000). *The hidden prejudice: Mental disability on trial.* Washington, DC: American Psychological Association.

Perlin, M. L. (2003). Beyond Dusky and Godinez: Competency before and after trial. *Behav. Sci. Law., 21*(3), 297–310.

Perlin, M. L. (2003). Therapeutic jurisprudence and outpatient commitment law: Kendra's Law as case study. *Psychol. Publ. Policy Law, 9*(1–2), 183–208.

Perlin, M. L. (2004). "Salvation" or a "lethal dose"? Attitudes and advocacy in right to refuse treatment cases. *J. Forens. Psychol. Pract., 4*(4), 51–69.

Perls, T. T. (1995, January). The oldest old. *Scientif. Amer.,* pp. 70–75.

Perry, J. C. (1989). Dependent personality disorder. In American Psychiatric Association (Eds.), *Treatments of psychiatric disorders: A task force report of the American Psychiatric Association.* Washington, DC: American Psychiatric Press.

Perske, R. (1972). The dignity of risk and the mentally retarded. *Ment. Retard., 10*, 24–27.

Pesce, V., Seidman, S. N., & Roose, S. P. (2002). Depression, antidepressants and sexual functioning in men. *Sex. Relation. Ther., 17*(3), 281–287.

Pet Food Institute. www.petfoodinstitute.org

Peter, O., Attila, K., Viktor, V., & Sandor, F. (2004). Risk factors of attempted suicide in elderly: The role of cognitive impairment. *Psychiatria Hungarica, 19*(6), 524–530.

Peters, R. M. (2004). Racism and hypertension among African Americans. *Western J. Nurs. Res., 26*(6), 612–631.

Peterson, C. (1993). Helpless behavior. *Behav. Res. Ther., 31*(3), 289–295.

Peterson, L., & Roberts, M. C. (1991). Treatment of children's problems. In C. E. Walker (Ed.), *Clinical psychology: Historical and research foundations.* New York: Plenum Press.

Petherick, W. (Ed.). (2006). *Serial crime: Theoretical and practical issues in behavioral profiling.* San Diego, CA: Elsevier.

Petrie, K. J., Fontanilla, I., Thomas, M. G., Booth, R. J., & Pennebaker, J. W. (2004). Effect of written emotional expression on immune function in patients with human immunodeficiency virus infection: A randomized trial. *Psychosom. Med., 66*(2), 272–275.

Petrocelli, J. V. (2002). Effectiveness of group cognitive-behavioral therapy for general symptomatology: A meta-analysis. *J. Spec. Group Work, 27*(1), 92–115.

Petry, N. M. (2000). A comprehensive guide to the application of contingency management procedures in clinical settings. *Drug Alc. Dep., 58*(1–2), 9–25.

Petry, N. M. (2001). Substance abuse, pathological gambling, and impulsiveness. *Drug Alc. Dep., 63*(1), 29–38.

Pew Research Center for the People and the Press. (1997). *Trust and citizen engagement in metropolitan Philadelphia: A case study.* Washington, DC: Author.

Pfeffer, C. R. (1986). *The suicidal child.* New York: Guilford Press.

Pfeffer, C. R. (1993). Suicidal children. In A. A. Leenaars (Ed.), *Suicidology.* Northvale, NJ: Jason Aronson.

Pfeffer, C. R. (2000). Suicidal behavior in prepubertal children: From the 1980s to the new millennium. In R. W. Maris, S. S. Canetto, J. L. McIntosh, & M. M. Silverman (Eds.), *Review of suicidology, 2000.* New York: Guilford Press.

Pfeffer, C. R., Zuckerman, S., Plutchik, R., & Mizruchi, M. S. (1984). Suicidal behavior in normal school children: A comparison with child psychiatric inpatients. *J. Amer. Acad. Child Adol. Psychiat., 23,* 416–423.

Pfeifer, M. P., & Snodgrass, G. L. (1990). The continued use of retractable invalid scientific literature. *JAMA, 263*(10), 1420–1427.

Pfeiffer, S. I., & Nelson, D. D. (1992). The cutting edge in services for people with autism. *J. Autism Dev. Disorders, 22*(1), 95–105.

Phares, V. (2003). *Understanding abnormal child psychology.* Hoboken, NJ: Wiley.

Phillips, E. L., Greydanus, D. E., Pratt, H. D., & Patel, D. R. (2003). Treatment of bulimia nervosa: Psychological and psychopharmacologic considerations. *J. Adol. Res., 18*(3), 261–279.

Phillips, K. A. (Ed.). (2001). *Somatoform and factitious disorders: Review of psychiatry,* Vol. 20. Washington, DC: American Psychiatric Association.

Phillips, K. A. (2005). Olanzapine augmentation of fluoxetine in body dysmorphic disorder. *Amer. J. Psychiat., 162*(5), 1022.

Phillips, K. A. (2005). Placebo-controlled study of pimozide augmentation of fluoxetine in body dysmorphic disorder. *Amer. J. Psychiat., 162*(2), 377–379.

Phillips, K. A., & Castle, D. J. (2002). Body dysmorphic disorder. In D. J. Castle & K. A. Phillips (Eds.), *Disorders of body image.* Petersfield, England: Wrightson Biomedical Publishing, Ltd.

Phillips, K. A., & Gunderson, J. G. (1994). Personality disorders. In R. E. Hales, S. C. Yudofsky, & J. A. Talbott (Eds.), *The American Psychiatric Press textbook of psychiatry* (2nd ed.). Washington, DC: American Psychiatric Press.

Phillips, K. A., McElroy, S. L., Keck, P. E., Pope, H. G., et al. (1993). Body dysmorphic disorder: 30 cases of imagined ugliness. *Amer. J. Psychiat., 150*(2), 302–308.

Phillips, K. A., Yen, S., & Gunderson, J. G. (2004). Personality disorders. In R. E. Hales & S. C. Yudofsky (Eds.), *Essentials of clinical psychiatry* (2nd ed., pp. 567–589). Washington, DC: American Psychiatric Publishing.

Phillips, M. L., Medford, N., Senior, C., Bullmore, E. T., Suckling, J., Brammer, M. J., Andrew, C., Sierra, M., Williams, S. C. R., & David, A. S. (2001). Depersonalization disorder: Thinking without feeling. *Psychiat. Res.: Neuroimaging, 108*(3), 145–160.

Phillips, M. R., Liu, H., & Zhang, Y. (1999). Suicide and social change in China. *Cult. Med. Psychiat., 23*(1), 25–50.

Piacentini, J., Rotheram-Bors, M. J., Gillis, J. R., Graae, F., et al. (1995). Demographic predictors of treatment attendance among adolescent suicide attempters. *J. Cons.. Clin. Psychiat., 63*(3), 469–473.

Piaget, J., & Inhelder, B. (1969). *L' image mentale chez l' enfant: Étude sur le développement des représentations imagées (The psychology of the child).* Paris: Presses Universitaires de France.

Pickar, D., Owen, R. R., & Litman, R. E. (1991). New developments in pharmacotherapy of schizophrenia. In A. Tasman & S. M. Goldfinger (Eds.), *American Psychiatric Press review of psychiatry* (Vol. 10). Washington, DC: American Psychiatric Press.

Pickel, K. L. (2004). When a lie becomes the truth: The effects of self-generated misinformation on eyewitness memory. *Memory, 12*(1), 14–26.

Pickover, C. A. (1999). *Strange brains and genius: The secret lives of eccentric scientists and madmen.* New York: HarperCollins/Quill.

Pierce, K., & Courchesne, E. (2001). Evidence for a cerebellar role in reduced exploration and stereotyped behavior in autism. *Biol. Psychiat., 49*(8), 655–664.

Pierce, K., & Courchesne, E. (2002). "A further support to the hypothesis of a link between serotonin, autism and the cerebellum": Reply. *Biol. Psychiat., 52*(2), 143.

Pietrofesa, J. J., Pietrofesa, C. J., & Pietrofesa, J. D. (1990). The mental health counselor and "duty to warn." *J. Ment. Hlth. Couns., 12*(2), 129–137.

Pike, K. M., & Borovoy, A. (2004). The rise of eating disorders in Japan: Issues of culture and limitations of the model of "westernization." *Cult. Med. Psychiat., 28*(4): 493–531.

Pike, K. M., & Rodin, J. (1991). Mothers, daughters, and disordered eating. *J. Abnorm. Psychol., 100*(2), 198–204.

Pillard, R. C., & Bailey, J. M. (1995). A biologic perspective on sexual orientation. Special issue: Clinical sexuality. *Psychiatr. Clin. N. Amer., 18*(1), 71–84.

Pillemer, K., & Suitor, J. J. (2002). Peer support for Alzheimer's caregivers: Is it enough to make a difference? *Res. Aging, 24*(2), 171–192.

Pilling, S., Bebbington, P., Kuipers, E., Garety, P., Geddes, J., Orbach, G., & Morgan, C. (2002). Psychological treatments in schizophrenia: I. Meta-analysis of family intervention and cognitive behaviour therapy. *Psychol. Med., 32*(5), 763–782.

Pinals, D. A., Packer, I., Fisher, B., & Roy, K. (2004). Relationship between race and ethnicity and forensic clinical triage dispositions. *Psychiatric Services 55,* 873–878.

Pincus, J. H. (2001). *Base instincts: What makes killers kill?* New York: Norton.

Pine, D. S. (2005). Editorial: Where have all the clinical trials gone? *J. Child Psychol Psychiat., 46*(5), 449–450.

Pinel, J. P. J., Assanand, S., & Lehman, D. R. (2000). Hunger, eating, and ill health. *Amer. Psychologist, 55*(10), 1105–1116.

Pines, W. L. (1999). A history and perspective on direct-to-consumer promotion. *Food Drug Law J., 54,* 489–518.

Pingitore, D., Snowden, L. R., Sansome, R., & Klikman, M. (2001). Persons with depressive symptoms and the treatments they receive: A comparison of primary care physicians and psychiatrists. *Inter. J. Psychiat. Med., 31,* 41–60.

Pinhas, L., Toner, B. B., Ali, A., Garfinkel, P. E., & Stuckless, N. (1999). The effects of the ideal of female beauty on mood and body satisfaction. *Inter. J. Eat. Disorders, 25*(2), 223–226.

Piotrowski, C., Belter, R. W., & Keller, J. W. (1998). The impact of "managed care" on the practice of psychological testing: Preliminary findings. *J. Pers. Assess., 70*(3), 441–447.

Piper, A., & Merskey, H. (2004). The persistence of folly: A critical examination of dissociative identity disorder. Part I. The excesses of an improbable concept. *Canad. J. Psychiat., 49*(9), 592–600.

Piper, A., & Merskey, H. (2004). The persistence of folly: Critical examination of dissociative identity disorder. Part II. The defence and decline of multiple personality or dissociative identity disorder. *Canad. J. Psychiat., 49*(10), 678–683.

Piper, W. E., & Joyce, A. S. (2001). Psychosocial treatment outcome. In W. J. Livesley (Ed.), *Handbook of personality disorders: Theory, research, and treatment* (pp. 323–343). New York: Guilford Press.

Pipes, R. B., Holstein, J. E., & Aguirre, M. G. (2005). Examining the personal–professional distinction. *Amer. Psychologist, 60*(4), 325–334.

Pirkis, J., & Burgess, P. (1998). Suicide and recency of health care contacts: A systematic review. *Brit. J. Psychiat., 173,* 462–474.

Piven, J., Palmer, P., Jacobi, D., Childress, D., & Arndt, S. (1997). Broader autism phenotype: Evidence from a family history study of multiple-incidence autism families. *Amer. J. Psychiat., 154*(2), 185–190.

Plante, T. G. (1999). *Contemporary clinical psychology.* New York: Wiley.

Pleh, C. (2004). The tradition of positive psychology in Europe. *Ricerche di Psicologia, 27*(1), 13–22.

Pless, M., & Carlsson, M. (2000). Effects of motor skill intervention on developmental coordination disorder: A meta-analysis. *Adap. Phys. Activ. Q., 17*(4), 381–401.

Plunkett, M. C. B., & Southall, D. P. (2001). The presentation and natural history of Munchausen syndrome by proxy. In G. Adshead & D. Brooke (Eds.), *Munchausen's syndrome by proxy: Current issues in assessment, treatment and research* (pp. 77–88). London: Imperial College Press.

Pole, N., Best, S. R., Metzler, T., & Marmar, C. R. (2005). Why are Hispanics at greater risk for PTSD? *Cult. Div. Ethnic Minority Psychol., 11*(2), 144–161.

Polk, W. M. (1983). Treatment of exhibitionism in a 38-year-old male by hypnotically assisted covert sensitization. *Inter. J. Clin. Exp. Hyp., 31,* 132–138.

Pollack, M. H. (2005). The pharmacotherapy of panic disorder. *J. Clin. Psychiat., 66*(Suppl. 4), 23–27.

Pollack, W. (1989). Schizophrenia and the self: Contributions of psychoanalytic self-psychology. *Schizo. Bull., 15*(2), 311–322.

Pomerantz, J. M. (2003). No place to go: The mentally ill in jails and prisons. *Drug Benef. Trends, 15*(5), 29–30.

Pompili, M., Ruberto, A., Girardi, P., & Tatarelli, R. (2004). Understanding suicide in schizophrenia: A national imperative for prevention. *Psichiatria e Psicoterapia, 23*(4), 275–281.

Pope, H. G. Jr., Olivardia, R., Gruber A., & Borowiecki, J. (1999). Evolving ideals of male body image as seen through action toys. *Inter. J. Eat. Disorders, 26*(1), 65–72.

Pope, K. S. (2000). Therapists' sexual feelings and behaviors: Research, trends, and quandaries. In L. T. Szuchman & F. Muscarella (Eds.), *Psychological perspectives on human sexuality* (pp. 603–658). New York: Wiley.

Pope, K. S., & Brown, L. S. (1996). *Recovered memories of abuse: Assessment, therapy, forensics.* Washington, DC: American Psychological Association.

Pope, K. S., & Tabachnick, B. G. (1993). Therapists' anger, hate, fear, and sexual feelings: National survey of therapist responses, client characteristics, critical events, formal complaints, and training. *Profess. Psychol.: Res. Pract., 24*(2), 142–152.

Pope, K. S., & Tabachnick, B. G. (1994). Therapists as patients: A national survey of pscyhologists' experiences, problems, and beliefs. *Profess. Psychol.: Res. Pract., 25*(3), 247–258.

Pope, K. S., Tabachnick, B. G., & Keith-Spiegel, P. (1986). Sexual attraction to clients: The human therapist and the (sometimes) inhuman training system. *Amer. Psychologist, 41*(2), 147–158.

Popenhagen, M. P., & Qualley, R. M. (1998). Adolescent suicide: Detection, intervention, and prevention. *Profess. School Couns., 1*(4), 30–36.

Popper, C. W. (1988). Disorders usually first evident in infancy, childhood, or adolescence. In J. Talbott, R. S. Hales, & S. C. Yudofsky (Eds.), *Textbook of psychiatry.* Washington, DC: American Psychiatric Press.

Poretz, M., & Sinrod, B. (1991). *Do you do it with the lights on?* New York: Ballantine Books.

PORT (Patient Outcomes Research Team) (1998). Cited in S. Barlas, Patient outcome research team study on schizophrenia offers grim indictment. *Psychiatr. Times, XV*(6).

Post, R. M. (2005). The impact of bipolar depression. *J. Clin. Psychiat., 66*(Suppl. 5), 5–10.

Post, R. M., Ballenger, J. C., & Goodwin, F. K. (1980). Cerebrospinal fluid studies of neurotransmitter function in manic and depressive illness. In J. H. Wood (Ed.), *The neurobiology of cerebrospinal fluid* (Vol. 1). New York: Plenum Press.

Post, R. M., Lake, C. R., Jimerson, D. C., Bunney, J. H., Ziegler, M. G., & Goodwin, F. K. (1978). Cerebrospinal fluid norepinephrine in affective illness. *Amer. J. Psychiat., 135*(8), 907–912.

Poulos, C. X., Le, A. D., & Parker, J. L. (1995). Impulsivity predicts individual susceptibility to high levels of alcohol self-administration. *Behav. Pharmacol., 6*(8), 810–814.

Powder, J. (2004, February 4). Course to help relatives cope with mental illness; class seeking to promote understanding of ailments. *Baltimore Sun* [Howard ed..], Local Section, p. 4B.

Powsner, S., & Powsner, D. (2005). Cognition, copyright, and the classroom. *Amer. J. Psychiat., 56*(1), 37–44.

Pratt, S., & Mueser, K. T. (2002). Social skills training for schizophrenia. In S. G. Hofmann & M. C. Tompson (Eds.), *Treating chronic and severe mental disorders: A handbook of empirically supported interventions.* New York: Guilford Press.

Prendergast, M., Hall, E., & Wellisch, J. (2002). An outcome evaluation of the Forever free substance abuse treatment program: One-year post-release outcomes. Final Report, National Institute of Justice Grant 99-RT-VX-K003. Los Angeles: UCLA Drug Abuse Research Center.

Prendergast, P. J. (1995). Integration of psychiatric rehabilitation in the long-term management of schizophrenia. *Canad. J. Psychiat., 40*(3, Suppl. 1), S18–S21.

Preuss, U. W., Schuckit, M. A., Smith, T. L., Danko, G. P., Bucholz, K. K., Hesselbrock, M. N., et al. (2003). Predictors and correlates of suicide attempts over 5 years in 1,237 alcohol-dependent men and women. *Amer. J. Psychiat., 160*(1), 56–63.

Preville, M., Hebert, R., Boyer, R., Bravo, G., & Seguin, M. (2005). Physical health and mental disorder in elderly suicide: A case-control study. *Aging Ment. Hlth., 9*(6), 576–584.

Prien, R. F., Caffey, E. M., Jr., & Klett, C. J. (1974). Factors associated with treatment success in lithium carbonate prophylaxis. *Arch. Gen. Psychiat., 31*, 189–192.

Primac, D. W. (1993). Measuring change in a brief therapy of a compulsive personality. *Psychol. Rep., 72*(1), 309–310.

Prince, J. D. (2005). Predicting outpatient mental health program withdrawal among recently discharged inpatients with schizophrenia. *Psychol. Serv., 2*(2), 142–150.

Princeton Survey Research Associates. (1996). *Healthy steps for young children: Survey of parents.* Princeton: Author.

Prochaska, J. O. (1984). *Systems of psychotherapy.* Chicago: Dorsey.

Prochaska, J. O., & Norcross, J. C. (1994). *Systems of psychotherapy: A transtheoretical analysis* (3rd ed.). Pacific Grove, CA: Brooks/Cole.

Prochaska, J. O., & Norcross, J. C. (1999). *Systems of psychotherapy: A transtheoretical analysis* (4th ed.). Pacific Grove, CA: Brooks/Cole.

Prochaska, J. O., & Norcross, J. C. (2003). *Systems of psychotherapy: A transtheoretical analysis* (5th ed.). Pacific Grove, CA: Brooks/Cole.

Protopopescu, X., Pan, H., Tuesher, O., Cloitre, M., Goldstein, M., Engelien, W., et al. (2005). Differential time courses and specificity of amygdala activity in posttraumatic stress disorder subjects and normal control subjects. *Biol. Psychiat., 57*(5), 464–473.

Provini, C., Everett, J. R., & Pfeffer, C. R. (2000). Adults mourning suicide: Self-reported concerns about bereavement, needs for assistance, and help-seeking behavior. *Death Stud., 24*(1), 1–19.

Prowthrow-Stith, D., & Spivak, H. (1999) America's tragedy. *Psychiatr. Times, 16*(6).

Prudic, J., & Sackeim, H. A. (1999). Electroconvulsive therapy and suicide risk. *J. Clin. Psychiat., 60*(Suppl. 2), 104–110.

Prusiner, S. B. (1991). Molecular biology of prion diseases. *Science, 252*, 1515–1522.

Pryce, C. R., Ruedi-Bettschen, D., Dettling, A. C., Weston, A., Russig, H., Ferger, B., et al. (2005). Long-term effects of early-life environmental manipulations in rodents and primates: Potential animal models in depression research. *Neurosci. Biobehav. Rev., 29*(4–5), 649–674.

Pueschel, S. M., & Thuline, H. C. (1991). Chromosome disorders. In J. L. Matson & J. A. Mulick (Eds.), *Handbook of mental retardation.* New York: Pergamon.

Pugh, L. A. (2003). *The psychological effects of the September 11th terrorist attacks on individuals with prior exposure to traumatic events.* Princeton Thesis #15387, Mudd Lib.

Pukall, C. F., Reissing, E. D., Binik, Y. M., Khalife, S., & Abbott, F. V. (2000). New clinical and research perspectives on the sexual pain disorders. *J. Sex Educ. Ther., 25*(1), 36–44.

Pull, C. B. (2005). Current status of virtual reality exposure therapy in anxiety disorders. *Curr. Opin. Psychiat., 18*(1), 7–14.

Pumariega, A., Gustavson, C. R., Gustavson, J. C., Stone Mkotes, P., & Ayers, S. (1994). Eating attitudes in African-American women: The *Essence* eating disorders survey. *Eat. Disord.: J. Treat. Prev., 2*(1), 5–16.

Putnam, F. W. (1984). The psychophysiologic investigation of multiple personality disorder. *Psychiatr. Clin. N. Amer., 7*, 31–40.

Putnam, F. W. (1985). Multiple personality disorder. *Med. Aspects Human Sex., 19*(6), 59–74.

Putnam, F. W. (1988). The switch process in multiple personality disorder and other state-change disorders.

Putnam, F. W. (1992). Are alter personalities fragments of figments? *Psychoanal. Inq., 12*(1), 95–111.

Putnam, F. W. (2000). Dissociative disorders. In A. J. Sameroff, M. Lewis et al. (Eds.), *Handbook of developmental psychopathology* (2nd ed., pp. 739–754). New York: Kluwer Academic/Plenum Press.

Putnam, F. W., Zahn, T. P., & Post, R. M. (1990). Differential autonomic nervous system activity in multiple personality disorder. *J. Psychiatr. Res., 31*(3), 251–260.

Pyle, R. L. (1999). Dynamic psychotherapy. In M. Hersen & A. S. Bellack (Eds.), *Handbook of comparative interventions for adult disorders* (2nd ed.). New York: Wiley.

Quaid, L. (2005, July 27). Possible case of mad cow investigated. *Associated Press (Washington)/Netscape News with CNN.*

Quality Assurance Project. (1990) The treatment of paranoid, schizotypal and schizoid personality disorders. *Austral. New Zeal. J. Psychiat., 24*, 339–350.

Querido, J. G., & Eyberg, S. M. (2005). Parent-child interaction therapy: Maintaining treatment gains of preschoolers with disruptive behavior disorders. In E. D. Hibbs & P. S. Jensen (Eds.), *Psychosocial treatments for child and adolescent disorders: Empirically based strategies for clinical practice* (2nd ed., pp. 575–97). Washington, DC: American Psychological Association.

Quinn, M. M., & Poirier, J. M. (2004). Linking prevention research with policy: Examining the costs and outcomes of the failure to prevent emotional and behavioral disorders. In M. M. Quinn, S. R. Mathur, & R. B. Rutherford (Eds.), *Handbook of research in emotional and be-*

havioral disorders (pp. 78–97). New York: Guilford Press.

Quiñones-Jenab, V. (Ed.) (2001). *The biological basis of cocaine addiction.* New York: New York Academy of Sciences, Vol. 937.

Quinsey, V. L., & Earls, G. M. (1990). The modificator of sexual preferences. In W. L. Marshall, D. R. Laws, & H. E. Barbaree (Eds.), *Handbook of sexual assault.* New York: Plenum.

Raboch, J., & Raboch, J. (1992). Infrequent orgasm in women. *J. Sex Marital Ther., 18*(2), 114–120.

Rachman, S. (1966). Sexual fetishism: An experimental analog. *Psychol. Rec., 18,* 25–27.

Rachman, S. (1993). Obsessions, responsibility and guilt. *Behav. Res. Ther., 31*(2), 149–154.

Rahey, L., & Craig, W. M. (2002). Evaluation of an ecological program to reduce bullying in schools. *Canad. J. Couns., 36*(4), 281–296.

Raine, A., Benishay, D., Lencz, T., & Scarpa, A. (1997). Abnormal orienting in schizotypal personality disorder. *Schizo. Bull., 23*(1), 75–82.

Ralevski, E., Sanislow, C. A., Grilo, C. M., Skodol, A. E., Gunderson, J. G., Shea, M. T., et al. (2005). Avoidant personality disorder and social phobia: Distinct enough to be separate disorders? *Acta Psychiatr. Scandin., 112*(3), 208–214.

Ralston, P. A. (1991). Senior centers and minority elders: A critical review. *Gerontologist, 31,* 325–331.

Ramchandani, P., Stein, A., Evans, J., O'Connor, T. G., & ALSPAC Study Team. (2005). Paternal depression in the postnatal period and child development: A prospective population study. *Lancet, 365*(9478), 2201–2205.

Ramey, C. T., & Ramey, S. L. (1992). Effective early intervention. *Ment. Retard., 30*(6), 337–345.

Ramey, C. T., & Ramey, S. L. (1998). Early intervention and early experience. *Amer. Psychologist, 53,* 109–120.

Ramey, C. T., & Ramey, S. L. (2004). Early learning and school readiness: Can early intervention make a difference? *Merrill-Palmer Quart., 50*(4), 471–491.

Rand, C. S., & Kuldau, J. M. (1991). Restrained eating (weight concerns) in the general population and among students. *Inter. J. Eat. Disorders, 10*(6), 699–708.

Ranen, N. G. (2002). Psychiatric management of Huntington's disease. *Psychiatr. Ann., 32*(2), 105–110.

Rapee, R. M., & Spence, S. H. (2004). The etiology of social phobia: Empirical evidence and an initial model. *Clin. Psychol. Rev., 24,* 737–767.

Raphael, B., & Wilson, J. P. (Eds.) (2000). *Psychological debriefing: Theory, practice and evidence.* Cambridge, England: Cambridge University Press.

Rapoport, J. L. (1989, March). The biology of obsessions and compulsions. *Scientif. Amer.,* pp. 82–89.

Raskin, D. C., & Honts, C. R. (2002). The comparison question test. In M. Kleiner (Ed.), *The handbook of polygraph testing.* San Diego, CA: Academic.

Raskin, M., Peeke, H. V. S., Dickman, W., & Pinkster, H. (1982). Panic and generalized

anxiety disorders: Developmental antecedents and precipitants. *Arch. Gen. Psychiat., 39,* 687–689.

Raskin, N., & Rogers, C. (2005). Person-centered therapy. In R. Corsini & D. Wedding (Eds.), *Current psychotherapies* (7th ed., pp. 130–165). Boston: Thomson/Brooks-Cole.

Rathbone, J. (2001). *Anatomy of masochism.* New York: Kluwer Academic/Plenum.

Ray, O., & Ksir, C. (1993). *Drugs, society, and human behavior.* St. Louis: Mosby.

Raymond, K. B. (1997). The effect of race and gender on the identification of children with attention deficit hyperactivity disorder. *Diss. Abstr. Inter.: Sect. A: Human Soc. Sci., 57*(12-A), 5052.

Raymond, N. C., Coleman, E., Ohlerking, F., Christenson, G. A., & Miner, M. (1999). Psychiatric comorbidity in pedophilic sex offenders. *Amer. J. Psychiat., 156*(5), 786–788.

Raymond, N., Robinson, B., Kraft, C., Rittberg, B., & Coleman, E. (2001). Treatment of pedophilia with leuprolide acetate: A case study. *J. Psychol. Human Sex., 13*(3–4), 79–88.

Read, J., et al. (2001). Assessing suicidality in adults: Integrating childhood trauma as a major risk factor. *Profess. Psychol.: Res. Pract., 32,* 367–372.

Redfearn, P. J., Agrawakm N., & Mair, L. H. (1998). An association between the regular use of 3,4-methylenedioxy-methamphetamine (ecstasy) and excessive wear of the teeth. *Addiction, 93*(5), 745–748.

Redick, R. W., Witkin, M. J., Atay, J. E., & Manderscheid, R. W. (1992). Specialty mental health system characteristics. In R. W. Manderscheid & M. A. Sonnenschein (Eds.), *Mental health, United States, 1992.* Washington, DC: U.S. Department of Health and Human Services.

Redmond, D. E. (1977). Alterations in the function of the nucleus locus coeruleus: A possible model for studies of anxiety. In I. Hanin & E. Usdin (Eds.), *Animal models in psychiatry and neurology.* New York: Pergamon Press.

Redmond, D. E. (1979). New and old evidence for the involvement of a brain norepinephrine system in anxiety. In W. E. Fann, I. Karacan, A. D. Pokorny, & R. L. Williams (Eds.), *Phenomenology and treatment of anxiety.* New York: Spectrum.

Redmond, D. E. (1981). Clonidine and the primate locus coeruleus: Evidence suggesting anxiolytic and anti-withdrawal effects. In H. Lal & S. Fielding (Eds.), *Psychopharmacology of clonidine.* New York: Alan R. Liss.

Redmond, D. E. (1985). Neurochemical basis for anxiety and anxiety disorders: Evidence from drugs which decrease human fear or anxiety. In A. H. Tuma & J. Maser (Eds.), *Anxiety and the anxiety disorders.* Hillsdale, NJ: Erlbaum.

Redwine, L., Mills, P. J., Sada, M., Dimsdale, J., Patterson, T., & Grant, I. (2004). Differential immune cell chemotaxis responses to acute psychological stress in Alzheimer caregivers compared to non-caregiver controls. *Psychosom. Med., 66*(5), 770–775.

Reeb, R. N. (2000). Classification and diagnosis of psychopathology: Conceptual foundations. *J. Psychol. Pract., 6*(1), 3–18.

Rees, W. D., & Lutkin, S. G. (1967). Mortality of bereavement. *Brit. Med. J., 4,* 13–16.

Reese, S. (1998, January). Get it together, do-gooders. *Am. Demogr.*

Regehr, C., Cadell, S., & Jansen, K. (1999). Perceptions of control and long-term recovery from rape. *Amer. J. Orthopsychiat., 69*(1), 110–115.

Regier, D. A., Narrow, W. E., Rae, D. S., Manderscheid, R. W., Locke, B. Z., & Goodwin, F. K. (1993). The de facto U.S. Mental and Addictive Disorders Service System: Epidemiologic Catchment Area prospective 1-year prevalence rates of disorders in services. *Arch. Gen. Psychiat., 50,* 85–94.

Reich, G. (2005). Family relationships and family therapy of eating disorders. *Praxis Kinderpsychol. Kinderpsych. 54*(4), 318–336.

Reich, J. H. (1990). Comparisons of males and females with DSM-III dependent personality disorder. *Psychiat. Res., 33*(2), 207–214.

Reich, J. H. (2000). The relationship of social phobia to avoidant personality disorder: A proposal to reclassify avoidant personality disorder based on clinical empirical findings. *Eur. Psychiat., 15*(3), 151–159.

Reid, R., & Lininger, T. (1993). Sexual pain disorders in the female. In W. O'Donohue & J. Geer (Eds.), *Handbook of sexual dysfunctions.* Boston: Allyn & Bacon.

Reid, W. H. (2002). Sexual predator evaluations and commitments. *J. Psychiatr. Prac., 8*(5), 320–324.

Reid, W. H., & Burke, W. J. (1989). Antisocial personality disorder. In American Psychiatric Association (Eds.), *Treatments of psychiatric disorders: A task force report of the American Psychiatric Association.* Washington, DC: American Psychiatric Press.

Reid, W. H., & Gacono, C. (2000). Treatment of antisocial personality, psychopathy, and other characterologic antisocial syndromes. *Behav. Sci. Law, 18,* 647–662.

Reis, B. (2005). The self is alive and well and living in relational psychoanalysis. *Psychoanal. Psychol., 22*(1), 86–95.

Reis, B. E. (1993). Toward a psychoanalytic understanding of multiple personality disorder. *Bull. Menninger Clin., 57*(3), 309–318.

Reissing, E. D., Binik, Y. M., Khalife, S., Cohen, D., & Amsel, R. (2003). Etiological correlates of vaginismus: Sexual and physical abuse, sexual knowledge, sexual self-schema and relationship adjustment. *J. Sex Marital Ther., 29*(1), 47–59.

Reitan, R. M., & Wolfson, D. (1996). Theoretical, methodological, and validational bases of the Halstead-Reitan neuropsychological test battery. In I. Grant & K. M. Adams (Eds.), *Neuropsychological assessment of neuropsychiatric disorders* (2nd ed., pp. 3–42). New York: Oxford University Press.

Reitan, R. M., & Wolfson, D. (2001). The Halstad-Reitan Neuropsychological Test Battery: Research findings and clinical application. In A. S. Kaufman & N. L. Kaufman (Eds.), *Specific learning disabilities and difficulties in children and adolescents: Psychological assessment and evaluation* (pp. 309–346). New York: Cambridge University Press.

Ren, M., Senatorov, V. V., Chen, R.-W., & Chuang, D.-M. (2003). Postinsult treatment with lithium reduces brain damage and facilitates neurological recovery in a rat ischemia/reperfusion model. *Proc. Natl. Acad. Sci., 100,* 6210–6215.

Rende, R., Slomkowski, C., McCaffery, J., Lloyd-Richardson, E. E., & Niaura, R. (2005). A twin-sibling study of tobacco use in adolescence: Etiology of individual differences and extreme scores. *Nicotine and Tobacco Res., 7*(3), 413–419.

Reneman, L., Booij, J., Schmand, B., van den Brink, W., & Gunning, B. (2000). Memory disturbances in "ecstasy" users are correlated with an altered brain serotonin neurotransmission. *Psychopharmacology, 148*(3), 322–324.

Rennison, C. M. (2002, August). Rape and sexual assault: Reporting to police and medical attention, 1992–2000 (NCJ 194530). Washington, DC: U.S. Department of Justice Statistics Selected Findings.

Resick, P. A., & Calhoun, K. S. (2001). Posttraumatic stress disorder. In D. H. Barlow (Ed.), *Clinical handbook of psychological disorders: A step-by-step treatment manual* (3rd ed.). New York: Guilford Press.

Resnick, P. H. J., & Harris, M. R. (2002). Retrospective assessment of malingering in insanity defense cases. In R. I. Simon & D. W. Schuman (Eds.), *Retrospective assessment of mental states in litigation: Predicting the past* (pp. 101–134). Washington, DC: American Psychiatric Publishing.

Resnick, P. J., & Noffsinger, S. (2004). Competency to stand trial and the insanity defense. In R. I. Simon & L. H. Gold (Eds.), *The American Psychiatric Publishing textbook of forensic psychiatry* (pp. 329–347). Washington, DC: American Psychiatric Publishing.

Ressler, K., & Davis, M. (2003). Genetics of childhood disorders: L. Learning and memory, part 3: Fear conditioning. *J. Amer. Acad. Child Adol. Psychiat., 42*(5), 612–615.

Ressler, R. K., & Schactman, T. (1992). *Whoever fights monsters.* New York: St. Martin's Press.

Retz, W., Retz-Junginger, P., Supprian, T., Thome, J., & Rosier, M. (2004). Association of serotonin transporter promoter gene polymorphism with violence: Relation with personality disorders, impulsivity, and childhood ADHD psychopathology. *Behav. Sci. Law., 22*(3), 415–425.

Reuters. (2004, September 7). It's a bumper-to-bumper life. *Reuters (Washington)/Yahoo!News).*

Reuters. (2004). News release: Mars, Snickers to be downsized in obesity battle. September 27, 2004.

Reuters. (2004, June 5). Alzheimer's a growing and deadly problem. *Reuters (Washington)/Netscape News with CNN.*

Reynolds, C. F., III, Frank, E., Perel, J. M., Imber, S. D., Cornes, C., Miller, M. D., et al. (1999). Nortriptyline and interpersonal psychotherapy as maintenance therapies for recurrent major depression: A randomized controlled trial in patients older than 59 years. *JAMA, 281*(1), 39–45.

Reynolds, L. (1990). Drug-free after 30 years of dependence. *Aging, 361,* 26–27.

Rice, D. P., & Miller, L. S. (1998). Health economics and cost implications of anxiety and other mental disorders in the United States. *Brit. J. Psychiat., 173*(Suppl. 34), 4–9.

Rice, G., Anderson, C., Risch, N., & Ebers, G. (1999). Male homosexuality: Absence of linkage to microsatellite markers at Xq28. *Science, 284* (5414), 665–667.

Richard, I. H., & Lyness, J. M. (2006). An overview of depression. In D. V. Jeste & J. H. Friedman (Eds.), *Psychiatry for neurologists* (pp. 33–42). Totowa, NJ: Humana Press.

Richard, M. (2005). Effective treatment of eating disorders in Europe: Treatment outcome and its predictors. *Eur. Eat. Disord. Rev., 13*(3), 169–179.

Richard, M., Bauer, S., & Kordy, H. (2005). Relapse in anorexia and bulimia nervosa—A 2.5-year follow-up study. *Eur. Eat. Disord. Rev., 13*(3), 180–190.

Richards, P. S., & Bergin, A. E. (Eds.). (2000). Toward religious and spiritual competency for mental health professionals. In P. S. Richards & A. E. Bergin, *Handbook of psychotherapy and religious diversity.* Washington, DC: American Psychological Association.

Richards, P. S., & Bergin, A. E. (Eds.). (2004). *Casebook for a spiritual strategy in counseling and psychotherapy.* Washington, DC: American Psychological Association.

Richardson, J. T. E. (2002). The aetiology, assessment, and rehabilitation of memory impairment following mild head injury. *Tidsskrift for Norsk Psykologforening, 39*(8), 700–706.

Ridout, N., Astell, A. J., Reid, I. C., Glen, T., & O'Carroll, R. E. (2003). Memory bias for emotional facial expressions in major depression. *Cog. Emot., 17*(1), 101–122.

Rieber, R. W. (2002). The duality of the brain and the multiplicity of minds: Can you have it both ways? *Hist. Psychiat. 13*(49, pt1), 3–18.

Riess, H. (2002). Integrative time-limited group therapy for bulimia nervosa. *Inter. J. Group Psychother., 52*(1), 1–26.

Rigby, K. (2002). Bullying in childhood. In P. K. Smith & C. H. Hart (Eds.), *Blackwell handbook of childhood social development* (pp. 549–568). Malden, MA: Blackwell.

Rihmer, Z., & Angst, J. (2005). Epidemiology of bipolar disorder. In S. Kasper & R. M. A. Hirschfeld (Eds.), *Handbook of bipolar disorder: Diagnosis and therapeutic approaches* (pp. 21–45). New York: Taylor & Francis.

Rihmer, Z., Rutz, W., & Pihlgren, H. (1995). Depression and suicide on Gotland. An intensive study of all suicides before and after a depression-training programme for general practitioners. *J. Affect. Disorders, 35,* 147–152.

Ringuette, E., & Kennedy, T. (1966). An experimental study of the double bind hypothesis. *J. Abnorm. Psychol., 71,* 136–141.

Riskind, J. H. (2005). Cognitive mechanisms in generalized anxiety disorder: A second generation of theoretical perspectives. *Cog. Ther. Res., 29*(1), 1–5.

Riskind, J. H., & Williams, N. L. (2005). The looming cognitive style and generalized anxiety disorder: Distinctive danger schemas and cognitive phenomenology. *Cog. Ther. Res., 29*(1), 7–27.

Ritchie, K., Kildea, D., & Robine, J. M. (1992). The relationship between age and the prevalence of senile dementia: A meta-analysis of recent data. *Inter. J. Epidemiol., 21,* 763–769.

Ritter, A. (2001). Buprenorphine for the treatment of heroin dependence. *Drug Alc. Rev., 20*(1), 5–7.

Rivas-Vazquez, R. A. (2001). Antidepressants as first-line agents in the current pharmacotherapy of anxiety disorders. *Profess. Psychol.: Res. Pract., 32*(1), 101–104.

Ro, O., Martinsen, E. W., Hoffart, A., Sexton, H., & Rosenvinge, J. H. (2005). Adults with chronic eating disorders: Two-year follow-up after inpatient treatment. *Eur. Eat. Disord. Rev., 13*(4), 255–263.

Roan, S. (1995, September 19) A poor state of mind. *Los Angeles Times,* pp. E1, E7.

Roazen, P. (1992). The rise and fall of Bruno Bettelheim. *Psychohist. Rev., 20*(3), 221–250.

Robb, A. S., & Dadson, M. J. (2002). Eating disorders in males. *Child Adol. Psychiat. Clin. N. Amer., 11*(2), 399–418.

Robb, A. S., Silber, T. J., Orrell-Valente, J. K., Valadez-Meltzer, A., Ellis, N., Dadson, M., et al. (2002). Supplemental nocturnal nasogastric refeeding for better short-term outcome in hospitalized adolescent girls with anorexia nervosa. *Amer. J. Psychiat., 159*(8), 1347–1353.

Roberts, C. F., Golding, S. L., & Fincham, F. D. (1987). Implicit theories of criminal responsibility. *Law Human Behav., 11*(3), 297–232.

Roberts, E., & Brennan, W. (2005). Making the business case for comprehensive mental health benefits: Advice for advocates. *NAMI Advocate, 3*(3), 15–16.

Robertson, P. K. (2004). The historical effects of depathologizing homosexuality on the practice of counseling. *Fam. J.: Couns. Ther. Couples Fam., 12*(2), 163–169.

Robin, A. L. (2003). Behavioral family systems: Therapy for adolescents with anorexia nervosa. In A. E. Kazdin & J. R. Weisz (Eds.), *Evidence-based psychotherapies for children and adolescents.* New York: Guilford Press.

Robin, A. L., Siegel, P. T., & Moye, A. (1995). Family versus individual therapy for anorexia: Impact on family conflict. Topical Section: Treatment and therapeutic processes. *Inter. J. Eat. Disorders, 17*(4), 313–322.

Robins, L. N., Locke, B. Z., & Regier, D. A. (1991). An overview of psychiatric disorders in America. In L. N. Robins & D. A. Regier (Eds.), *Psychiatric disorders in America: The Epidemiological Catchment Area Study.* New York: Free Press.

Robinson, M. S., & Alloy, L. B. (2003). Negative cognitive styles and stress-reactive rumination interact to predict depression: A prospective study. *Cog. Ther. Res., 27*(3), 275–292.

Robison, L. M., Sclar, D. A., Skaer, T. L., & Galin, R. S. (1999). National trends in the prevalence of attention-deficit/hyperactivity disorder and the prescribing of methylphenidate among school children: 1990–1995. *Clin. Pediatr., 38*(4), 209–217.

Roche, T. (2002, January 20). The Yates odyssey. *TIME.com: Nation.*

Rochlen, A. B., Zack, J. S., & Speyer, C. (2004). Online therapy: Review of relevant definitions, debates, and current empirical support. *J. Clin. Psychol., 60*(3), 269–283.

Rodebaugh, T. L., Holaway, R. M., & Heimberg, R. G. (2004). The treatment of social anxiety disorder. *Clin. Psychol. Rev., 24,* 883–908.

Rodgers, C. S., Norman, S. B., Thorp, S. R., Lang, A. J., & Lebeck, M. M. (2005). Trauma exposure, posttraumatic stress disorder and health behaviors: Impact on special populations. In T. A. Corales (Ed.), *Focus on posttraumatic stress disorder research* (pp. 203–224). Hauppauge, NY: Nova Science Publishers.

Rodgers, J. (2000). Cognitive performance amongst recreational users of "ecstasy". *Psychopharmacology (Berl), 151*(1), 19–24.

Rodier, P. M. (2000, February). The early origins of autism. *Scientif. Amer.*, pp. 56–63.

Rodriguez, B. F., Weisberg, R. B., Pagano, M. E., Machan, J. T., Culpepper, L., & Keller, M. B. (2004). Frequency and patterns of psychiatric comorbidity in a sample of primary care patients with anxiety disorders. *Comprehen. Psychiat., 45*(2), 129–137.

Roehrich, L., & Kinder, B. N. (1991). Alcohol expectancies and male sexuality: Review and implications for sex therapy. *J. Sex Marital Ther., 17*(1), 45–54.

Roelofs, K., Hoogduin, K. A. L., Keijsers, G. P. J., Naering, G. W. B., Moene, F. C., & Sandijck, P. (2002). Hypnotic susceptibility in patients with conversion disorder. *J. Abnorm. Psychol., 111*(2), 390–395.

Roemer, L., Orsillo, S. M., & Barlow, D. H. (2002). Generalized anxiety disorder. In D. H. Barlow (Ed.), *Anxiety and its disorders: The nature and treatment of anxiety and panic* (2nd ed., pp. 477–515). New York: Guilford Press.

Roemer, L., Salters, K., Raffa, S. D., & Orsillo, S. M. (2005). Fear and avoidance of internal experiences in GAD: Preliminary tests of a conceptual model. *Cog. Ther. Res., 29*(1), 71–88.

Roesch, R. (1991). *The encyclopedia of depression.* New York: Facts on File.

Roesch, R., Zapf, P. A., Golding, S. L., & Skeem, J. L. (1999). Defining and assessing competence to stand trial. In A. K. Hess, I. B. Weiner, et al. (Eds.), *The handbook of forensic psychology* (2nd ed.). New York: Wiley.

Roesler, T. A., & McKenzie, N. (1994). Effects of childhood trauma on psychological functioning of adults sexually abused as children. *J. Nerv. Ment. Dis., 182*(3), 145–150.

Rogers, C. R. (1951). *Client-centered therapy.* Boston: Houghton Mifflin.

Rogers, C. R. (1954). The case of Mrs. Oak: A research analysis. In C. R. Rogers & R. F. Dymond (Eds.), *Psychotherapy and personality change* (pp. 259–269). Chicago: University of Chicago Press.

Rogers, C. R. (1957). The necessary and sufficient conditions of therapeutic personality change. *J. Cons. Clin. Psychol., 121*, 95–203.

Rogers, C. R. (1987). Rogers, Kohut, and Erickson: A personal perspective on some similarities and differences. In J. K. Zeig (Ed.), *The evolution of psychotherapy.* New York: Brunner/Mazel.

Rogers, C. R. (1992). The necessary and sufficient conditions of therapeutic personality change. *J. Cons. Clin. Psychol., 60*(6), 827–832.

Rogers, C. R. (2000). Interview with Carl Rogers on the use of the self in therapy. In M. Baldwin (Ed.), *The use of self in therapy* (2nd ed., pp. 29–38). Binghamton, NY: Haworth.

Rogers, P. (2005). Caffeine and health. *Psychologist, 18*(1), 9.

Rogers, R. (2004). Diagnostic, explanatory, and detection models of Munchausen by proxy: Extrapolations from malingering and deception. *Child Abuse Negl., 28*(2), 225–238.

Rogers, R., & Shuman, D. W. (2000). *Conducting insanity evaluations* (2nd ed.). New York: Guilford Press.

Rogers, R., & Shuman, D. W. (2005). *Fundamentals of forensic practice: Mental health and criminal law.* New York: Springer Science + Business-Media.

Rogers, S. J. (1998). Empirically supported comprehensive treatments for young children with autism. *J. Clin. Child Psychol., 27*, 168–179.

Roggla, H., & Uhl, A. (1995). Depression and relapses in treated chronic alcoholics. *Inter. J. Addic., 30*(3), 337–349.

Rogler, L. H., Malgady, R. G., & Rodriguea, O. (1989). *Hispanics and mental health: A framework for research.* Malabar, FL: Krieger Publishing.

Rohrer, G. E. (2005). The problem of assessment and diagnosis. In G. Rohrer, *Mental health and literature: Literary lunacy and lucidity* (pp. 1–23). Chicago, IL: Lyceum Books.

Roitman, S. E. L., Cornblatt, B. A., Bergman, A., Obuchowski, M., et al. (1997). Attention functioning in schizotypal personality disorder. *Amer. J. Psychiat., 154*(5), 655–660.

Roitman, S. E. L., Mitropoulou, V., Keefe, R. S. E., Silverman, J. M., Serby, M., Harvey, P. D., et al. (2000). Visuospatial working memory in schizotypal personality disorder patients. *Schizo. Res., 41*(3), 447–455.

Rollin, H. R. (1980). *Coping with schizophrenia.* London: Burnett.

Roloff, P. (2001). The nurse's role in a pilot program using a modified cognitive-behavioral approach. In B. Kinoy (Ed.), *Eating disorders: New directions in treatment and recovery* (2nd ed., pp. 127–132). New York: Columbia University Press.

Romano, E., & De Luca, R. V. (2001). Male sexual abuse: A review of effects, abuse characteristics, and links with later psychological functioning. *Aggress. Viol. Behav., 6*(1), 55–78.

Roozen, H. D., deKan, R., van den Brink, W., Kerkhof, A. J. F. M., & Geerlings, P. J. (2002). Dangers involved in rapid opioid detoxification while using opioid antagonists: Dehydration and renal failure. *Addiction, 97*(8), 1071–1073.

Roper Reports. (1998, February). Marriage: The art of compromise. *Am. Demogr.*

Rose, S., Bisson, J. I., & Wessely, S. (2001). Psychological debriefing for preventing post traumatic stress disorder (PTSD) (Cochrane Review). In The Cochrane Library, issue 4. Oxford, England: Update Software.

Rosen, E. F., Anthony, D. L., Booker, K. M., Brown, T. L., et al. (1991). A comparison of eating disorder scores among African American and white college females. *Bull. Psychon. Soc., 29*(1), 65–66.

Rosen, J. C., & Leitenberg, H. (1982). Bulimia nervosa: Treatment with exposure and response prevention. *Behav. Ther., 13*(1), 117–124.

Rosen, J. C., & Leitenberg, H. (1985). Exposure plus response prevention treatment of bulimia. In D. M. Garner & P. E. Garfinkel (Eds.), *Handbook of psychotherapy for anorexia nervosa and bulimia.* New York: Guilford Press.

Rosen, J. C., Orosan, P., & Reiter, J. (1995). Cognitive behavior therapy for negative body image in obese women. *Behav. Ther., 26*, 25–42.

Rosen, L. (2005). "Online therapy" is excellent e-primer. *Natl. Psychologist, 14*(6), 16.

Rosen, L. W., & Hough, D. O. (1988). Pathogenic weight-control behaviors of female college gymnasts. *Physician Sports Med., 16*(9), 141–144.

Rosen, L. W., McKeag, D. B., Hough, D. O., & Curley, V. (1986). Pathogenic weight-control behavior in female athletes. *Physician Sports Med., 14*(1), 79–86.

Rosen, R. C. (2000). Medical and psychological interventions for erectile dysfunction: Toward a combined treatment approach. In S. R. Leiblum & R. C. Rosen (Eds.), *Principles and practice of sex therapy* (3rd ed., pp. 276–304). New York: Guilford Press.

Rosen, R. C. (2003). Erectile dysfunction in middle-aged and older men. In S. B. Levine, S. E. Althof, & C. B. Risen (Eds.), *Handbook of clinical sexuality for mental health professionals* (pp. 237–256). New York: Brunner-Routledge.

Rosen, R. C., & Leiblum, S. R. (1995). Hypoactive sexual desire (Special issue: Clinical sexuality). *Psychiatr. Clin. N. Amer., 18*(1), 107–121.

Rosen, R. C., Leiblum, S. R., & Spector, I. (1994). Psychologically based treatment for male erectile disorder: A cognitive-interpersonal model. *J. Sex Marital Ther., 20*, 78–85.

Rosen, R. C., & Marin, H. (2003). Prevalence of antidepressant-associated erectile dysfunction. *J. Clin. Psychiat., 64*(Suppl. 10), 5–10.

Rosen, R. C., & Rosen, L. R. (1981). *Human sexuality.* New York: Knopf.

Rosen, R. C., Taylor, J. F., Leiblum, S. R., & Bachmann, G. A. (1993). Prevalence of sexual dysfunction in women: Results of a survey study of 329 women in an outpatient gynecological clinic. *J. Sex Marital Ther., 19*, 171–188.

Rosenberg, D. R., Russell, A., & Fougere, A. (2005). Neuropsychiatric models of OCD. In J. S. Abramowitz & A. C. Houts (Eds.), *Concepts and controversies in obsessive-compulsive disorder.* New York: Springer Science + Business Media, Inc.

Rosenberg, H. (1993). Prediction of controlled drinking by alcoholics and problem drinkers. *Psychol. Bull., 113*(1), 129–139.

Rosenberg, T., & Pace, M. (2006). Burnout among mental health professionals: Special considerations for the marriage and family therapist. *J. Marital Fam. Ther., 32*(1), 87–99.

Rosenfeld, B. (2004). Influence of depression and psychosocial factors on physician-assisted suicide. In B. Rosenfeld, *Assisted suicide and the right to die: The interface of social science, public policy, and medical ethics* (pp. 77–93). Washington, DC: American Psychological Association.

Rosenfeld, B., & Cling, B. J. (2004). Stalking. In B. J. Cling (Ed.), *Sexualized violence against women and children: A psychology and law perspective.* New York: Guilford Press.

Rosenhan, D. L. (1973). On being sane in insane places. *Science, 179*(4070), 250–258.

Rosenheck, R, & Fontana, A. (1996). Race and outcome of treatment for veterans suffering from PTSD. *J. Traum. Stress, 9*, 343–351.

Rosenthal, M. B., Berndt, E. R., Donohue, J. M., Frank, R. G., & Epstein, A. M. (2002). Promotion of prescription drugs to consumers. *N. Engl. J. Med., 346*(7), 498–505.

Rosenthal, N. E., & Blehar, M. C. (Eds.). (1989). *Seasonal affective disorders and phototherapy.* New York: Guilford Press.

Rosenthal, R. (1966). *Experimenter effects in behavioral research.* New York: Appleton-Century-Crofts.

Rosenthal, R. J. (1992). Pathological gambling. *Psychiatr. Ann., 22*(2), 72–78.

Rosenthal, R. N., & Levounis, P. (2005). Polysubstance use, abuse, and dependence. In R. J. Frances, A. H. Mack, & S. I. Miller (Eds.), *Clinical textbook of addictive disorders* (3rd ed., pp. 245–270). New York: Guilford Press.

Rosenzweig, M. R. (1996). Aspects of the search for neural mechanisms of memory. In J. T. Spence, J. M. Darley, & D. J. Foss (Eds.), *Annual review of psychology* (Vol. 47). Palo Alto, CA: Annual Reviews.

Rosik, C. H. (2003). Critical issues in the dissociative disorders field: Six perspectives from religiously sensitive practitioners. *J. Psychol. Theol., 31*(2), 113–128.

Rosmarin, P. C. (1989). Coffee and coronary heart disease: A review. *Prog Cardiovasc Dis., 32*(3), 239–245.

Ross, C. A., & Gahan, P. (1988). Techniques in the treatment of multiple personality disorder. *Amer. J. Psychother., 42*(1), 40–52.

Ross, C. A., Miller, S. D., Bjornson, L., Reagor, P., Fraser, G. A., & Anderson, G. (1991). Abuse histories in 102 cases of multiple personality disorder. *Canad. J. Psychiat., 36*, 97–101.

Ross, C. A., Norton, G. R., & Wozney, K. (1989). Multiple personality disorder: An analysis of 236 cases. *Canad. J. Psychiat., 34*(5), 413–418.

Roth, A., & Fonagy, P. (2005). *What works for whom? A critical review of psychotherapy research* (2nd ed.). New York: Guilford Press.

Rothbaum, B. O., Foa, E. B., Riggs, D. S., Murdock, T., & Walsh, W. (1992). A prospective examination of posttraumatic stress disorder in rape victims. *J. Traum. Stress, 5*(3), 455–475.

Rothblum, E. D. (1992). The stigma of women's weight: Social and economic realities. *Feminism Psychol., 2*(1), 61–73.

Rothenberg, A. (1990). *Creativity and madness: New findings and old stereotypes.* Baltimore: Johns Hopkins University Press.

Rousett, I., Kipman, A., Ades, P., & Gorwood, P. (2004). Personality, temperament and anorexia nervosa. *Annales Medico Psychologiques, 162*(3), 180–188.

Rowa, K., Kerig, P. K., & Geller, J. (2001). The family and anorexia nervosa: Examining parent-child boundary problems. *Eur. Eat. Disord. Rev., 9*(2), 97–114.

Rowlands, P. (1995). Schizophrenia and sexuality. *J. Sex Marital Ther., 10*(1), 47–61.

Roy-Byrne, P. P. (2005). The GABA-benzodiazepine receptor complex: Structure, function, and role in anxiety. *J. Clin. Psychiat., 66* (Suppl. 2), 14–20.

Roy-Byrne, P., Arguelles, L., Vitek, M. E., Goldberg, J., Keane, T. M., True, W. R., et al. (2004). Persistence and change of PTSD symptomatology: A longitudinal co-twin control analysis of the Vietnam Era Twin Registry. *Soc. Psychiat. Psychiatr. Epidemiol., 39*(9), 681–685.

Rozee, P. D. (2005). Resistance: Successes and challenges. In A. Barnes (Ed.), *The handbook of women, psychology, and the law* (pp. 265–279). New York: Wiley.

Rozin, P., & Stoess, C. (1993). Is there a general tendency to become addicted? *Addic. Behav., 18*, 81–87.

Rubertsson, C., Waldenstrom, U., Wickberg, B., Radestad, I., & Hildingsson, I. (2005). Depressive mood in early pregnancy and postpartum: Prevalence and women at risk in a national Swedish sample. *J. Reprod. Infant Psychol., 23*(2), 155–166.

Rubin, E. H. (2005). Psychiatry and old age. In E. H. Rubin & C. F. Zorumski (Eds.), *Adult psychiatry* (2nd ed.). Oxford, England: Blackwell Publishing Ltd.

Rubinstein, S., & Caballero, B. (2000). Is Miss America an undernourished role model? *JAMA, 283*(12), 1569.

Rudd, M. D. (2000). Integrating science into the practice of clinical suicidology: A review of the psychotherapy literature and a research agenda for the future. In R. W. Maris, S. S. Canetto, J. L. McIntosh, & M. M. Silverman (Eds.), *Review of suicidology, 2000.* New York: Guilford Press.

Rudd, M. D., Joiner, T., & Rajah, M. H. (2001). *Treating suicidal behavior: An effective time-limited approach.* New York: Guilford Press.

Ruedrich, S. L., Rossvanes, C. F., Dunn, J. E., & Delano, M. K. (2003). Cigarette smoking, and the use of tobacco products, by persons with developmental disabilities. *Ment. Hlth. Aspects Dev. Disabil., 6*(3), 99–106.

Rufer, M., Hand, I., Alsleben, H., Braatz, A., Ortmann, J., Katenkamp, B., Fricke, S., & Peter, H. (2005). Long-term course and outcome of obsessive-compulsive patients after cognitive-behavioral therapy in combination with either fluvoxamine or placebo: A 7-year follow-up of a randomized double-blind trial. *Eur. Arch. Psychiat. Clin. Neurosci., 255*(2), 121–128.

Rurup, M. L., Onwuteaka-Philipsen, B. D., Van Der Wal., G., Van Der Heide, A., & Van Der Mass, P. J. (2005). A "suicide pill" for older people: Attitudes of physicians, the general population, and relatives of patients who died after euthanasia or physician-assisted suicide in The Netherlands. *Death Stud., 29*(6), 519–534.

Rush, A. J., & Frances, A. (2000). Expert consensus guideline series: Treatment of psychiatric and behavioral problems in mental retardation. *Amer. J. Ment. Retard., 105*(3), 159–228.

Russell, G. (1979). Bulimia nervosa: An ominous variant of anorexia nervosa. *Psychol. Med., 9*(3), 429–448.

Ruta, N., & Cohen, L. S. (1998). Postpartum mood disorders: Diagnosis and treatment guidelines. *J. Clin. Psychiat., 59*(Suppl 2), 34–40.

Rutledge, P. C., & Sher, K. J. (2001). Heavy drinking from the freshman year into early young adulthood: The roles of stress, tension-reduction drinking motives, gender and personality. *J. Stud. Alc., 62*(4), 457–466.

Ruuska, J., Kaltiala-Heino, R., Rantanen, P., & Koivisto, A. M. (2005). Psychopathological distress predicts suicidal ideation and self-harm in adolescent eating disorder outpatients. *Eur. Child Adol. Psychiat., 14*(5), 276–281.

RWJF (The Robert Wood Johnson Foundation). (2001). Substance abuse fact sheet: The human cost of substance abuse. Retrieved November 24, 2002, from www.SALeaders.org

Ryan, C. (2004). Differences in the appraisal of intrusive thoughts and contamination fears in obsessive-compulsive disorder. *Behav. Cog. Psychother., 32*(2), 235–238.

Rzewuska, M. (2002). Drug maintenance treatment compliance and its correlation with the clinical picture and course of schizophrenia. *Prog. Neuropsychopharmacol. Biol. Psychiat., 26*(4), 811–814.

Sacks, O. (2000, May). *An anthropologist on Mars: Some personal perspectives on autism.* Keynote address. Eden Institute Foundation's Sixth Annual Princeton Lecture Series on Autism. Princeton, NJ.

Sadavoy, J. (2004). *Psychotropic drugs and the elderly: Fast facts.* New York: W. W. Norton.

Sadavoy, J., Meier, R., & Ong, A. Y. M. (2004). Barriers to access to mental health services for ethnic seniors: The Toronto Study. *Canad. J. Psychiat., 49*(3), 192–199.

Sadock, B. J., & Sadock, V. A. (2003). *Kaplan & Sadock's synopsis of psychiatry: Behavioral sciences/Clinical psychiatry* (9th ed.). Philadelphia: Lippincott Williams & Wilkins.

Safer, D. (1994). The impact of recent lawsuits on methylphenidates sales. *Clin. Pediatr., 33*(3), 166–168.

Safer, D., & Krager, J. (1992). Effect of a media blitz and a threatened lawsuit on stimulant treatment. *JAMA, 268*(8), 1004–1007.

Safren, S. A., Gershuny, B. S., Marzol, P., Otto, M. W., & Pollack, M. H. (2002). History of childhood abuse in panic disorder, social phobia, and generalized anxiety disorder. *J. Nerv. Ment. Dis., 190*(7), 453–456.

Sahoo, F. M., Sahoo, K., & Harichandan, S. (2005). Five big factors of personality and human happiness. *Soc. Sci. Inter., 21*(1), 20–28.

Sakheim, D. K., Hess, E. P., & Chivas, A. (1988). General principles for short-term inpatient work with multiple personality-disorder patients. *Psychotherapy, 24*, 117–124.

Saks, E. R., Jeste, D. V., Granholm, E., Palmer, B. W., & Schneiderman, L. (2002). Ethical issues in psychosocial interventions research involving controls. *Ethics Behav., 12*(1), 87–101.

Salekin, R. T., & Rogers, R. (2001). Treating patients found not guilty by reason of insanity. In J. B. Ashford, B. D. Sales, & W. H. Reid (Eds.) *Treating adult and juvenile offenders with special needs* (pp. 171–195). Washington, DC: American Psychological Association.

Sales, B. D., & Shuman, D. W. (2005). *Experts in court: Reconciling law, science, and professional knowledge.* Washington, DC: American Psychological Association.

Sales, E., Baum, M., & Shore, B. (1984). Victim readjustment following assault. *J. Soc. Issues, 40*(1), 117–136.

Salkovskis, P. (Ed.). (2004). Editorial. *Behav. Cog. Psychother., 32*(2), 129–130.

Salkovskis, P. M. (1985). Obsessional-compulsive problems: A cognitive-behavioural analysis. *Behav. Res. Ther., 23*, 571–584.

Salkovskis, P. M. (1989). Cognitive-behavioural factors and the persistence of intrusive thoughts in obsessional problems. *Behav. Res. Ther., 27*, 677–682.

Salkovskis, P. M. (1999). Understanding and treating obsessive-compulsive disorder. *Behav. Res. Ther., 37*(Suppl. 1), S29–S52.

Salkovskis, P. M., Thorpe, S. J., Wahl, K., Wroe, A. L., & Forrester, E. (2003). Neutralizing increases discomfort associated with obsessional thoughts: An experimental study with obsessional patients. *J. Abnorm. Psychol., 112*(4), 709–715.

Salkovskis, P. M., & Westbrook, D. (1989). Behaviour therapy and obsessional ruminations: Can failure be turned into success? *Behav. Res. Ther., 27,* 149–160.

Salloway, S., Harrington, C., & Jacobson, S. (2006). Psychiatric evaluation of the neurological patient. In D.V. Jeste & J. H. Friedman (Eds.), *Psychiatry for neurologists* (pp. 19–32). Totowa, NJ: Humana Press.

Salome, F., Boyer, P., & Fayol, M. (2002). Written but not oral verbal production is preserved in young schizophrenic patients. *Psychiat. Res., 111*(2–3), 137–145.

Salzman, L. (1989). *Compulsive personality disorder.* In *Treatments of psychiatric disorders.* Washington, DC: American Psychiatric Press.

Sampath, G., Shah, A., Kraska, J., & Soni, S. D. (1992). Neuroleptic discontinuation in the very stable schizophrenic patient: Relapse rates and serum neuroleptic levels. *Human Psychopharmacol. Clin. Exp., 7*(4), 255–264.

Samuel, V. J., Curtis, S., Thornell, A., George, P., Taylor, A., Brome, D. R., et al. (1997). The unexplored void of ADHD and African-American research: A review of the literature. *J. Attent. Disorders, 1*(4), 197–207.

Sanderson, R. E., Campbell, D., & Laverty, S. G. (1963). An investigation of a new aversive conditioning treatment for alcoholism. *Quart. J. Stud. Alcohol., 24,* 261–275.

Sandler, M. (1990). Monoamine oxidase inhibitors in depression: History and mythology. *J. Psychopharmacol., 4*(3), 136–139.

Sands, J. M., & Miller, L. E. (1991). Effects of moon phase and other temporal variable on absenteeism. *Psychol. Rep., 69*(3, Pt. 1), 959–962.

Sansone, R. A., Fine, M. A., & Dennis, A. B. (1991). Treatment impressions and termination experiences with borderline patients. *Amer. J. Psychother., 45*(2), 173–180.

Sansone, R. A., Levitt, J. L., & Sansone, L. A. (2005). The prevalence of personality disorders among those with eating disorders. *Eat. Disord.: J. Treat. Prev., 13*(1), 7–21.

Sansone, R. A., Songer, D. A., & Miller, K. A. (2005). Childhood abuse, mental healthcare utilization, self-harm behavior, and multiple psychiatric diagnoses among inpatients with and without a borderline diagnosis. *Comprehen. Psychiat., 46,* 117–120.

Santiseban, D. A., Muir-Malcolm, J. A., Mitrani, V. B., & Szapocznik, J. (2001). Chapter 16: Integrating the study of ethnic culture and family psychology intervention science. In H. A. Liddle, D. A. Santiseban, R. F. Levant, & J. H. Bray (Eds.), *Family psychology: Science-based interventions* (pp. 331–352). Washington, DC: American Psychological Association.

Santtila, P., Sandnabba, N. K., Alison, L., & Nordling, N. (2002). Investigating the underlying structure in sadomasochistically oriented behavior. *Arch. Sex. Behav., 31*(2), 185–196.

Sar, V., Akyuz, G., Kundakci, T., Kiziltan, E., Dogan, O. (2004). Childhood trauma, dissociation, and psychiatric comorbidity in patients with conversion disorder. *Amer. J. Psychiat., 161*(12), 2271–2276.

Sarbin, T. R. (2002). Dialogical components in theory-building: Contributions of Hilgard, Orne and Spanos. *Contemp. Hyp., 19*(4), 190–197.

Sareen, J., Houlahan, T., Cox, B. J., Asmundson, G. J. G. (2005). Anxiety disorders associated with suicidal ideation and suicide attempts in the National Comorbidity Survey. *J. Nerv. Ment. Dis., 193*(7), 450–454.

Sarid, O., Anson, O., Yaari, A., & Margalith, M. (2004). Coping styles and changes in humoural reaction during academic stress. *Psychol. Health Med. 9*(1), 85–98.

Sarro, S., & Sarro, V. (2004). Koro syndrome: A case report. *Transcult. Psychiatry, 41,* 558–560.

Sassi, R. B., & Soares, J. C. (2002). Neural circuitry and signaling in bipolar disorder. In G. B. Kaplan & Hammer, R. P. (Eds.), *Brain circuitry and signaling in psychiatry: Basic science and clinical implications.* Washington, DC: American Psychiatric Publishing, Inc.

Satir, V. (1964). *Conjoint family therapy: A guide to therapy and technique.* Palo Alto, CA: Science & Behavior Books.

Satir, V. (1967). *Conjoint family therapy* (Rev. ed.). Palo Alto, CA: Science & Behavior Books.

Satir, V. (1987). Going behind the obvious: The psychotherapeutic journey. In J. K. Zeig (Ed.), *The evolution of psychotherapy.* New York: Brunner/Mazel.

Saudino, K. J., Pedersen, N. L., Lichenstein, P., McClearn, G. E., & Plomin, R. (1997). Can personality explain genetic influence on life events? *J. Pers. Soc. Psychol., 72*(1), 196–206.

Saudino, K. J., Wertz, A. E., Gagne, J. R., & Chawla, S. (2004). Night and day: Are siblings as different in temperament as parents say they are? *J. Pers. Soc. Psychol., 87*(5), 698–706.

Saulsman, L. M., & Page, A. C. (2004). The five-factor model and personality disorder empirical literature: A meta-analytic review. *Clin. Psychol. Rev., 23,* 1055–1085.

Sauro, M. D., & Greenberg, R. P. (2005). Endogenous opiates and the placebo effect: A meta-analytic review. *J. Psychosom. Res., 58*(2), 115–120.

Saville, B. K., & Buskist, W. (2003). Traditional idiographic approaches: Small-N research designs. In S. F. Davis (Ed.), *Handbook of research methods in experimental psychology* (pp. 66–82). Malden, MA: Blackwell Publishers.

Sawle, G. A., & Kear, C. J. (2001). Adult attachment style and pedophilia: A developmental perspective. *Inter. J. Offend. Ther. Compar. Crimin., 45*(1), 32–50.

Scarf, M. (1996, June 10). The mind of the Unabomber. *New Republic,* pp. 20–23.

Scelfo, J. (2005, June 13). Bad girls go wild. *Newsweek,* 66–67.

Scharff, J. S. (2001). Freud and object relations theory. In D. E. Scharff (Ed.), *The psychoanalytic century: Freud's legacy for the future* (pp. 103–122). New York: Other Press.

Scharff, J. S., & Scharff, D. E. (2005). *The primer of object relations* (2nd ed.). New York: Jason Aronson.

Schechter, D., Singer, T. M., Kuperman, J., & Endicott, J. (1998). Selection of "normal" control subjects for psychiatric research: Update on a model for centralized recruitment. *Psychiat. Res., 79*(2), 175–185.

Scheff, T. J. (1999). *Being mentally ill: A sociological theory.* Hawthorne, NY: Aldine de Gruyter.

Schernhammer, E. (2005). Taking their own lives: The high rate of physician suicide. *N. Engl. J. Med., 352*(24), 2473–2476.

Scheuermann, B., Webber, J., Boutot, E. A., & Goodwin, M. (2003). Problems with personnel preparation in autism spectrum disorders. *Focus Autism Other Dev. Disabil., 18,* 197–206.

Scheuffgen, K., Happe, F., Anderson, M., & Frith, U. (2000). High "intelligence," low "IQ"? Speed of processing and measured IQ in children with autism. *Dev. Psychopathol., 12*(1), 83–90.

Schiffman, J., Abrahamson, A., Cannon, T., LaBrie, J., Parnas, J. Schulsinger, F., et al. (2001). Early rearing factors in schizophrenia. *Inter. J. Ment. Hlth., 30*(1), 3–16.

Schiffman, J., LaBrie, J., Carter, J., Cannon, T., Schulsinger, F., Parnas, J., et al. (2002). Perception of parent-child relationships in high-risk families, and adult schizophrenia outcome of offspring. *J. Psychiatr. Res., 36*(1), 41–47.

Schiffman, J., Pestle, S., Mednick, S., Ekstrom, M., Sorensen, H., & Mednick S. (2005). Childhood laterally and adult schizophrenia spectrum disorders: A prospective investigation. *Schizo. Res., 72*(2–3), 151–160.

Schiffman, J., Wawlker, E., Ekstrom, M., Schulsinger, F., Sorensen, H., & Mednick S. (2004). Childhood videotaped social and neuromotor precursors of schizophrenia: A prospective investigation. *Amer. J. Psychiat., 161*(11), 2021–2027.

Schildkraut, J. J. (1965). The catecholamine hypothesis of affective disorders: A review of supporting evidence. *Amer. J. Psychiat., 122*(5), 509–522.

Schimmack, U., & Diener, E. (2003). Experience sampling methodology in happiness research. *Journal of Happiness Studies, 4*(1), 1–4.

Schleifer, S. J., Keller, S. E., & Bartlett, J. A. (1999). Depression and immunity: Clinical factors and therapeutic course. *Psychiat. Res., 85*(1), 63–69.

Schleifer, S. J., Keller, S. E., Bartlett, J. A., Eckholdt, H. M., & Delaney, B. R. (1996). Immunity in young adults with major depressive disorder. *Amer. J. Psychiat., 153,* 477–482.

Schlenger, W. E., Caddell, J. M., Ebert, L., Jordan, B. K., Rourke, K. M., Wilson, D., et al. (2002). Psychological reactions to terrorist attacks. *JAMA, 288*(5), 581–588.

Schlesinger, J., & Ismail, H. (Eds.) (2004). Heroic, not disordered: Creativity and mental illness revisited: Comment. *Brit. J. Psychiat., 184*(4), 363–364.

Schlesinger, M., Dorwart, R., Hoover, C., & Epstein, S. (1997). Competition, ownership, and access to hospital services: Evidence from psychiatric hospitals. *Medical Care, 35*(9), 974–992.

Schmidtke, A., & Häfner, H. (1988). The Werther effect after television films: New evidence for an old hypothesis. *Psychol. Med., 18,* 665–676.

Schmidtke, A., Weinacker, B., Apter, A., Batt, A., Berman, A., Bille-Brahe, U., et al. (1999). Suicide rates in the world: Update. *Arch. Suic. Res., 5,* 81–89.

Schneider, F., Boehner, H., Habel, U., Salloum, J. B., Stierstorfer, A., Hummel, T. C., et al. (2002). Risk factors for postoperative delirium in vascular surgery. *Gen. Hosp. Psychiat., 24*(1), 28–34.

Schneider, K. J. (2003). Existential-humanistic psychotherapies. In A. S. Gurman & S. B. Messer (Eds.), *Essential psychotherapies: Theory and practice* (2nd ed.). New York: Guilford Press.

Schneiderman, N. (1999). Behavioral medicine and the management of HIV/AIDS. *Inter. J. Behav. Med., 6*(1), 3–12.

Schover, L. R. (2000). Sexual problems in chronic illness. In S. R. Leiblum & R. C. Rosen (Eds.), *Principles and practice of sex therapy* (3rd ed., pp. 398–422). New York: Guilford Press.

Schreiber, F. R. (1973). *Sybil.* Chicago: Regnery.

Schreiber, G. B., Robins, M., Striegel-Moore, R., Obarzanek, E., Morrison, J. A., & Wright, D. J. (1996). Weight medication efforts reported by Black and White preadolescent girls: National heart, lung, and blood institute growth and health study, *Pediatrics, 98,* 63–70.

Schreibman, L., & Koegel, R. L. (2005). Training for parents of children with autism: Pivotal responses, generalization, and individualization of interventions. In E. D. Hibbs & P. S. Jensen (Eds.), *Psychosocial treatments for child and adolescent disorders: Empirically based strategies for clinical practice* (2nd ed., pp. 605–631). Washington, DC: American Psychological Association.

Schuckit, M. (1999). Cited in C. Ginther, Schuckit addresses state-of-the-art addiction treatments. *Psychiatr. Times, XVI*(4).

Schuckit, M. A., Danko, G. P., Raimo, E. B., Smith, T. L., Eng, M. Y., Carpenter, K. K. T., et al. (2001). A preliminary evaluation of the potential usefulness of the diagnoses of polysubstance dependence. *J. Stud. Alc., 62*(1), 54–61.

Schultz, W. (2006). Behavioral theories and the neurophysiology of reward. *Annu. Rev. Psychol., 57,* 87–115.

Schulz, P. M., Schulz, S. C., Goldberg, S. C., Ettigi, P., Resnick, R. J., & Friedel, R. O. (1986). Diagnoses of the relatives of schizotypal outpatients. *J. Nerv. Ment. Dis., 174*(8), 457–463.

Schumaker, J. F. (2001). *The age of insanity: Modernity and mental health.* Westport, CT: Praeger.

Schuster, M. A., Stein, B. D., Jaycox, L. H., Collins, R. L., Marshall, G. N., Elliot, M. N., et al. (2001). A national survey of stress reactions after the September 11, 2001, terrorist attacks. *N. Engl. J. Med., 20,* 1507–1512.

Schuurmans, J., Comijs, H. C., Beekman, A. T. F., de Beurs, E., Deeg, D. J. H., Emmelkamp, P. M. G., et al. (2005). The outcome of anxiety disorders in older people at 6-year follow-up: Results from the Longitudinal Aging Study Amsterdam. *Acta Psychiatr. Scandin., 111*(6), 420–428.

Schwalb, M. (1999). Interviewed in M. S. Baum, Autism: Locked in a solitary world. *HealthState, 17*(2), 18–22.

Schwartz, J. B. (2000). Nutraceuticals: Sorting out fact, fiction, and uncertainty. *J. Gend. Specif. Med., 3*(4), 30–32, 37.

Schwartz, J. M., & Begley, S. (2002). *The mind and the brain: Neuroplasticity and the power of mental force.* New York: Regan Books/Harper Collins.

Schwartz, S. (1993). *Classic studies in abnormal psychology.* Mountain View, CA: Mayfield Publishing.

Schwartz, S., & Johnson, J. J. (1985). *Psychopathology of childhood.* New York: Pergamon Press.

Scott, A. (1995). "Reclaimed once more by the realities of life": Hysteria and the location of memory. *Brit. J. Psychother., 11*(3), 398–405.

Scott, J. (1990, Jul. 25). Vertigo, not madness, may have tormented Van Gogh. *Los Angeles Times,* p. A14.

Scott, J., & Colom, F. (2005). Psychosocial treatments for bipolar disorders. *Psychiatr. Clin. N. Amer., 28*(2), 371–384.

Scott, J. E., & Dixon, L. B. (1995). Assertive community treatment and case management for schizophrenia. *Schizo. Bull., 21*(4), 657–668.

Scott, M., & Geller, J. L. (Eds.). (2005). Mental health and productivity in the workplace: A handbook for organizations and clinicians. *Psychiatr. Serv., 56*(1), 110–111.

Sederer, L. I. (1992). Brief hospitalization. In A. Tasman & M. B. Riba (Eds.), *Review of psychiatry* (Vol. 11). Washington, DC: American Psychiatric Press.

Sedvall, G. (1990). Monoamines and schizophrenia. International Symposium: Development of a new antipsychotic: Remoxipride. *Acta Psychiatr. Scandin., 82*(Suppl. 358), 7–13.

Seeman, J. (2002). Looking back, looking ahead: A synthesis. In D. J. Cain & J. Seeman (Eds.), *Humanistic psychotherapies: Handbook of research and practice.* Washington, DC: American Psychological Association.

Segraves, R. T. (1993). Treatment-emergent sexual dysfunction in affective disorder: A review and management strategies. *J. Clin. Psychiat., Monogr. Ser., 11,* 7–63.

Segraves, R. T. (1995). Psychopharmacological influences on human sexual behavior. In J. M. Oldham & M. B. Riba (Eds.), *American Psychiatric Press review of psychiatry* (Vol. 14). Washington, DC: American Psychiatric Press.

Segraves, R. T. (1998). Antidepressant-induced sexual dysfunction. *J. Clin. Psychiat., 59*(Suppl. 4), 48–54.

Segraves, T., & Althof, S. (2002). Psychotherapy and pharmacotherapy for sexual dysfunctions. In P. E. Nathan & J. M. Gorman (Eds.), *A guide to treatments that work* (2nd ed., pp. 497–524). London: Oxford University Press.

Segrin, C. (2000). Social skills deficits associated with depression. *Clin. Psychol. Rev., 20*(3), 379–403.

Segrin, C. (2001). *Interpersonal processes in psychological problems.* New York: Guilford Press.

Segrin, C., Powell, H. L., Givertz, M., & Brackin, A. (2003). Symptoms of depression, relational quality, and loneliness in dating relationships. *Pers. Relationships, 10*(1), 25–36.

Seiden, R. H. (1981). Mellowing with age: Factors influencing the nonwhite suicide rate. *Inter. J. Aging Human Dev., 13,* 265–284.

Seidman, L. J. (1990). The neuropsychology of schizophrenia: A neurodevelopmental and case study approach. *J. Neuropsych. Clin. Neurosci., 2*(3), 301–312.

Seidman, S. N. (2002). Exploring the relationship between depression and erectile dysfunction in aging men. *J. Clin. Psychiat., 63* (Suppl. 5), 5–12.

Seidman, S. N., & Rieder, R. O. (1995). Sexual behavior through the life cycle: An empirical approach. In J. M. Oldham & M. B. Riba (Eds.), *American Psychiatric Press review of psychiatry* (Vol. 14). Washington, DC: American Psychiatric Press.

Seligman, M. E. P. (1971). Phobias and preparedness. *Behav. Ther., 2,* 307–320.

Seligman, M. E. P., Castellon, C., Cacciola, J., Schulman, P., et al. (1988). Explanatory style change during cognitive therapy for unipolar depression. *J. Abnorm. Psychol., 97*(1), 13–18.

Seligman, M. E. P., & Steen, T. A. (2005). Positive psychology progress: Empirical validation of interventions. *Amer. Psychologist, 60*(5), 410–421.

Selkoe, D. J. (1991). Amyloid protein and Alzheimer's disease. *Scientif. Amer., 265,* 68–78.

Selkoe, D. J. (1992). Alzheimer's disease: New insights into an emerging epidemic. *J. Geriat. Psychiat., 25*(2), 211–227.

Selkoe, D. J. (1996). Amyloid beta-protein and the genetics of Alzheimer's disease. *J. Biol. Chem., 271*(31):18295–18298.

Selkoe, D. J. (1998). The cell biology of beta-amyloid precursor protein and presenilin in Alzheimer's disease. *Trends Cell Biol., 8*(11), 447–453.

Selkoe, D. J. (1999). Translating cell biology into therapeutic advances in Alzheimer's disease. *Nature, 399*(Suppl. 6738), A23–31.

Selkoe, D. J. (2000). The origins of Alzheimer's disease: A is for amyloid. *JAMA, 283*(12), 1615–1617.

Selkoe, D. J. (2002). Alzheimer's disease is a synaptic failure. *Science, 298*(5594), 789–791.

Sellbom, M., Ben-Porath, Y. S., Graham, J. R., Arbisi, P. A., & Bagby, R. M. (2005). Susceptibility of the MMPI-2 clinical, Restructured Clinical (RC), and content scales to overreporting and underreporting. *Assessment, 12*(1), 79–85.

Selling, L. S. (1940). *Men against madness.* New York: Greenberg.

Selman, R. (1980). *The growth of interpersonal understanding.* New York: Academic Press.

Selye, H. (1974). *Stress without distress.* Philadelphia: Lippincott.

Selye, H. (1976). *Stress in health and disease.* Woburn, MA: Butterworth.

Serlin, I. (2005). Spiritual diversity and clinical practice. In J. L. Chin (Ed.), *The psychology of prejudice and discrimination: Disability, religion, physique, and other traits* (Vol. 4, pp. 27–49). Westport, CT: Praeger Publishers/Greenwood Publishing Group.

Serpell, L., & Treasure, J. (2002). Bulimia nervosa: Friend or foe? The pros and cons of bulimia nervosa. *Inter. J. Eat. Disorders, 32*(2), 164–170.

Seto, M. C., Khattar, N. A., Lalumiere, M. L., & Quinsey, V. L. (1997). Deception and sexual strategy in psychopathy. *Pers. Individ. Diff., 22*(3), 301–307.

Seto, M. C., Maric, A., & Barbaree, H. E. (2001). The role of pornography in the etiology of sexual aggression. *Aggress. Viol. Behav., 6*(1), 35–53.

Sexton, T. L., & Alexander, J. F. (2002). Family-based empirically supported interventions. *J. Couns. Psychol., 30*(2), 238–261.

Shadish, W. R., & Baldwin, S. A. (2005). Effects of behavioral marital therapy: A meta-analysis of randomized controlled trials. *J. Cons. Clin. Psychol., 73*(1), 6–14.

Shafran, R. (2005). Cognitive-behavioral models of OCD. In J. S. Abramowitz & A. C. Houts (Eds.), *Concepts and controversies in obsessive-compulsive disorder.* New York: Springer Science + Business Media, Inc.

Shafranske, E. P., & Sperry, L. (2005). Addressing the spiritual dimension in psychotherapy: Introduction and overview. In L. Sperry & E. P. Shafranske (Eds.). *Spiritually oriented psychotherapy.* Washington, DC: American Psychological Association.

Shah, A. A., & Treit, D. (2004). Infusions of midazolam into the medial prefrontal cortex produce anxiolytic effects in the elevated plusmaze and shock-probe burying tests. *Brain Res., 996*(1), 31–40.

Shamoo, A. E. (2002). Moral and compliance issues in clinical Research, Part 1: Where we are today, RAPS RA interactive (pp. 1–2).

Shaner, A., Khalsa, M., Roberts, L., Wilkins, J., Anglin, D., & Hsieh, S. (1993). Unrecognized cocaine use among schizophrenic patients. *Amer. J. Psychiat., 150*(5), 758–762.

Sharf, R. S. (2000). *Theories of psychotherapy & counseling: Concepts and cases* (2nd ed.). Pacific Grove, CA: Brooks/Cole.

Sharf, R. S. (2004). *Theories of psychotherapy & counseling: Concepts and cases* (3rd ed.). Australia: Thomson-Brooks/Cole.

Sharma, M. (Ed.). (2005). Editorial: Improving interventions for prevention and control of alcohol use in college students. *J. Alcohol Drug Educ., 49*(2), 3–6.

Sharma, V., Khan, M., & Smith, A. (2005). A closer look at treatment resistant depression: Is it due to a bipolar diathesis? *J. Affect. Disorders, 84*(2–3), 251–257.

Shastry, B. S. (2005). Bipolar disorder: An update. *Neurochem. Inter., 46*(4), 273–279.

Shaw, B. F. (1976). A systematic investigation of two psychological treatments of depression. *Diss. Abstr. Inter., 36*(8–B), 4179–4180.

Shaw, B. F. (1977). Comparison of cognitive therapy and behavior therapy in the treatment of depression. *J. Clin. Psychol., 45*, 543–551.

Shaw, K. (2004). *Oddballs and eccentrics.* Edison, NJ: Castle Books

Shea, S. C. (1998). The chronological assessment of suicide events: A practical interviewing strategy for the elicitation of suicidal ideation. *J. Clin. Psychiat., 59*(Suppl. 20), 58–72.

Shea, S. C. (1999). *The practical art of suicide assessment: A guide for mental health professionals and substance abuse counselors.* New York: Wiley.

Shea, S. C. (2004). Suicidal ideation: Clear understanding and use of an interviewing strategy such as the Chronological Assessment of Suicide Events (CASE Approach) can help clarify intent and immediate danger to the patient. *Psychiatr. Ann., 34*(5), 385–400.

Shea, T., Elkin, I., Imber, S., Sotsky, S., Watkins, J., Collins, J., et al. (1992). Course of depressive symptoms over follow-up: Findings from the National Institute of Mental Health treatment of depression collaborative research program. *Arch. Gen. Psychiat., 49*, 782–787.

Shear, K. (2005). Symposium Monograph Supplement: Bereavement-related depression in the elderly. *CNS Spectrums, 10*(8), 3–5.

Shear, M. K., Vander Bilt, J., Rucci, P., Endicott, J., Lydiard, B., Otto, M. W., et al. (2001). Reliability and validity of a structured interview guide for the Hamilton Anxiety Rating Scale (SIGH-A). *Depress. Anx., 13*(4), 166–178.

Shedler, J., & Block, J. (1990). Adolescent drug use and psychological health: A longitudinal inquiry. *Amer. Psychologist, 45*(5), 612–630.

Shedler, J., & Westen, D. (2004). Dimensions of personality pathology: An alternative to the five-factor model. *Amer. J. Psychiat., 161*, 1743–1754.

Sheler, J. L. (2004). The power of prayer. *U. S. News & World Report, 137*(22), December 20, 2004, 52–54

Shenefelt, P. D. (2003). Hypnosis-facilitated relaxation using self-guided imagery during dermatologic procedures. *Amer. J. Clin. Hyp., 45*(3), 225–232.

Shenk, D. (2001). *The forgetting: Alzheimer's: Portrait of an epidemic.* New York: Doubleday.

Shephard, B. (2004). Risk factors and PTSD: A historian's perspective. In G. M. Rosen (Ed.), *Posttraumatic stress disorder: Issues and controversies* (pp. 39–61). New York: Wiley.

Sher, L., Oquendo, M. A., Falgalvy, H. C., Grunebaum, M. F., Burke, A. K., Zalsman, G., et al. (2005). The relationship of aggression to suicidal behavior in depressed patients with a history of alcoholism. *Addic. Behav., 30*(6), 1144–1153.

Sheras, P. L. (2001). Problems of adolescence. In C. E. Walker & M. C. Roberts (Eds.), *Handbook of clinical child psychology* (3rd ed., pp. 619–803). New York: Wiley.

Sheras, P., & Worchel, S. (1979). *Clinical psychology: A social psychological approach.* New York: Van Nostrand.

Sherlock, R. (1983). Suicide and public policy: A critique of the "new consensus." *Bioethics, 4,* 58–70.

Sherwood, P. R., Given, C. W., Given, B. A., & Von Eye, A. (2005). Caregiver burden and depressive symptoms: Analysis of common outcomes in caregivers of elderly patients. *J. Aging Hlth., 17*(2), 125–147.

Shiffman, S., Gorsline, J., & Gorodetzky, C. W. (2002). Efficacy of over-the-counter nicotine patch. *Nicotine Tobacco Res., 4*(4), 477–483.

Shifren, J. L., Braunstein, G. D., Simon, J. A., Casson, P. R., Buster, J. E., Redmond, G. P., et al. (2000). Transdermal testosterone treatment in woman with impaired sexual function after oophorectomy. *N. Engl. J. Med., 343,* 682–731.

Shiho, Y., Tohru, T., Shinji, S., Manabu, T., Yuka, T., Eriko, T., et al. (2005). Suicide in Japan: Present condition and prevention measures. *Crisis, 26*(1), 12–19.

Shin, L. M., Wright, C. I., Cannistraro, P. A., Wedig, M. M., McMullin, K. Martis, B., et al. (2005). A functional magnetic resonance imaging study of amygdala and medial prefrontal cortex responses to overtly presented fearful faces in posttraumatic stress disorder. *Arch. Gen. Psychiat., 62*(3), 273–281.

Shisslak, C. M., Crago, M., McKnight, K. M., Estes, L. S., Gray, G., & Parnaby, O. G. (1998). Potential risk factors associated with weight control behaviors in elementary and middle school girls. *J. Psychosom. Res., 44*(3/4), 301–313.

Shnayerson, M. (1996, July). Natural opponents. *Vanity Fair,* pp. 98–105.

Shneidman, E. S. (1963). Orientations toward death: Subintentioned death and indirect suicide. In R. W. White (Ed.), *The study of lives.* New York: Atherton.

Shneidman, E. S. (1973). Suicide notes reconsidered. *Psychiatry, 36,* 379–394.

Shneidman, E. S. (1979). An overview: Personality, motivation, and behavior theories. In L. D. Hankoff & B. Einsidler (Eds.), *Suicide: Theory and clinical aspects.* Littleton, MA: PSG Publishing.

Shneidman, E. S. (1981). Suicide. *Suic. Life-Threat. Behav., 11*(4), 198–220.

Shneidman, E. S. (1985). *Definition of suicide.* New York: Wiley.

Shneidman, E. S. (1987, March). At the point of no return. *Psychol. Today.*

Shneidman, E. S. (1993). *Suicide as psychache: A clinical approach to self-destructive behavior.* Northvale, NJ: Jason Aronson.

Shneidman, E. S. (1999). Perturbation and lethality: A psychological approach to assessment and intervention. In D. G. Jacobs (Ed.). *The Harvard Medical School guide to suicide assessment and intervention.* San Francisco: Jossey-Bass.

Shneidman, E. S. (2001). *Comprehending suicide: Landmarks in 20th-century suicidology.* Washington, DC: American Psychological Association.

Shneidman, E. (2005). How I read. *Suic. Life-Threat. Behav., 35*(2), 117–120.

Shneidman, E. (2005). Prediction of suicide revisited: A brief methodological note. *Suic. Life-Threat. Behav., 35*(1), 1–2.

Shneidman, E. S., & Farberow, N. (1968). The Suicide Prevention Center of Los Angeles. In H. L. P. Resnick (Ed.), *Suicidal behaviors: Diagnosis and management.* Boston: Little, Brown.

Shorter, E. (1994). *From the mind into the body: The cultural origins of psychosomatic symptoms.* New York: Free Press.

Shtasel, D. L., Gur, R. E., Gallacher, F., Heimburg, C., et al. (1992). Gender differences in the clinical expression of schizophrenia. *Schizophr. Res., 7*(3), 225–231.

Shuttleworth-Edwards, A. B., Kemp, R. D., Rust, A. L., Muirhead, J. G. L., Hartman, N. P., & Radloff, S. E. (2004). Cross-cultural effects on IQ test performance: A review and preliminary normative indicators on WAIS-III test performance. *J. Clin. Exp. Neuropsychol., 26*(7), 903–920.

Sibinga, E. M. S., Ottolini, M. C., Duggan, A. K., & Wilson, M. H. (2004). Parent-pediatrician communication about complementary and alternative medicine use for children. *Clin. Pediatr., 43*(45), 367–373.

Siegel, B., & Ficcaglia, M. (2006). Pervasive developmental disorders. In M. Hersen & J. C. Thomas (Series Eds.) & R. T. Ammerman (Vol. Ed.), *Comprehensive handbook of personality and psychopathology: Vol. 3 Child psychopathology* (pp. 254–71). Hoboken, NJ: Wiley.

Siegel, R. K. (1990). In J. Sherlock, Getting high—Animals do it, too. *USA Today,* p. 1A.

Sierra, M., Phillips, M. L., Lambert, M. V., Senior, C., David, A. S., & Krystal, J. H. (2001). Lamotrigine in the treatment of depersonalization disorder. *J. Clin. Psychiat., 62*(10), 826–827.

Siever, L. J., & Davis, K. L. (1991). A psychobiological perspective on the personality disorders. *Amer. J. Psychiat., 148*(12), 1647–1658.

Sigerist, H. E. (1943). *Civilization and disease.* Ithaca, NY: Cornell University Press.

Silbersweig, D. A., Stern, E., Frith, C., Cahill, C., et al. (1995). A functional neuroanatomy of hallucinations in schizophrenia. *Nature, 378,* 176–179.

Silver, H., & Feldman, P. (2005). Evidence for sustained attention and working memory in schizophrenia sharing a common mechanism. *J. Neuropsychiat. Clin. Neurosci., 17*(3), 391–398.

Silverman, K., Evans, S. M., Strain, E. C., & Griffiths, R. R. (1992). Withdrawal syndrome after the double-blind cessation of caffeine consumption. *N. Engl. J. Med., 327*(16), 1109–1114.

Silverman, W. K., & Dick-Niederhauser, A. (2004). Separation anxiety disorder. In J. S. March & T. L. Morris (Eds.), *Anxiety disorders in children and adolescents* (2nd ed., pp. 164–188). New York: Guilford Press.

Simeon, D., Greenberg, J., Nelson, D., Schmeidler, J., & Hollander, E. (2005). Dissociation and posttraumatic stress 1 year after the World Trade Center disaster: Follow-up of a longitudinal survey. *J. Clin. Psychiat., 66*92), 231–237.

Simeon, D., Guralnik, O., Hazlett, E. A., Spiegel-Cohen, J., Hollander, E., & Buchsbaum, M. S. (2000). Feeling unreal: A PET study of depersonalization disorder. *Amer. J. Psychiat., 157*(11), 1782–1788.

Simeon, D., Knutelska, M., Nelson, D., & Guralnik, O. (2003). Feeling unreal: A depersonalization disorder update of 117 cases. *J. Clin. Psychiat., 64*(9), 990–997.

Simmon, J. (1990). Media and market study. In skin deep: Our national obsession with looks. *Psychol. Today, 26*(3), 96.

Simon, G. E., & Katzelnick, D. J. (1997). Depression, use of medical services and cost-offset effects. *J. Psychosom. Res., 42*(4), 333–344.

Simon, N. (2000). Autism's home in the brain. *Neurology, 54*(1), 269.

Simon, R. I. (2001). Duty to foresee, forewarn, and protect against violent behavior: A psychiatric perspective. In M. Shafi & S. L. Shafi (Eds.), *School violence: Assessment, management, prevention* (pp. 201–215). Washington, DC: American Psychiatric Press.

Simon, R. I., & Gold, L. H. (Eds.). (2004). *The American Psychiatric Publishing textbook of forensic psychiatry.* Washington, DC: American Psychiatric Publishing.

Simonoff, E. (2001). Genetic influences on conduct disorder. In J. Hill & B. Maughan (Eds.), *Conduct disorders in childhood and adolescence. Cambridge child and adolescent psychiatry* (pp. 202–234). New York: Cambridge University Press.

Simons, J. S., Gaher, R. M., Jacobs, G. A., Meyer, D., & Johnson-Jimenez, E. (2005). Associations between alcohol use and PTSD symptoms among American Red Cross disaster relief workers responding to the 9/11/2001 attacks. *Amer. J. Drug Alc. Abuse, 31*(2), 285–304.

Simpson, S. G. (1996, January 17). Cited in W. Leary, As fellow traveler of other illness, depression often goes in disguise. *New York Times,* p. C9.

Singh, V., Muzina, D. J., & Calabrese, J. R. (2005). Anticonvulsants in bipolar disorder. *Psychiatr. Clin. N. Amer., 28*(2), 301–323.

Sizemore, C. C. (1991). *A mind of my own: The woman who was known as "Eve" tells the story of her triumph over multiple personality disorder.* William Morrow.

Sizemore, C., & Pittillo, E. S. (1977). *I'm Eve.* Garden City, NY: Doubleday.

Sjolie, I. I. (2002). A logotherapist's view of somatization disorder and a protocol. *Int. For. Logotherapy, 25*(1), 24–29.

Skau, K., & Mouridsen, S. (1995). Munchausen syndrome by proxy: A review. *Acta Paediatr., 84,* 977–982.

Skelton, G. (2004, May 6). The State; George Skelton/CAPITOL JOURNAL; For mentally ill, ballot box budgeting might be the answer. *Los Angeles Times* [Home ed.], part B, p. 8.

Skodol, A. E. (2005). The borderline diagnosis: Concepts, criteria, and controversies. In J. G. Gunderson & P. D. Hoffman (Eds.), *Understanding and treating borderline personality disorder* (pp. 3–19). Washington, DC: American Psychiatric Publishing.

Skodol, A. E., Grilo, C. M., Pagano, M. E., Bender, D. S., Gunderson, J. G., Shea, M. T., et al. (2005). Effects of personality disorders on functioning and well-being in major depressive disorder. *J. Psychiat. Pract., 11*(6), 363–368.

Skodol, A. E., Gunderson, J. G., McGlashan, T. H., Dyck, I. R., Stout, R. L., Bender, D. S., et al. (2002). Functional impairment in patients with schizotypal, borderline, avoidant, or obsessive-compulsive personality disorder. *Amer. J. Psychiat., 159*(2), 276–283.

Skodol, A. E., Pagano, M. E., Bender, D. S., Shea, M. T., Gunderson, J. G., Yen, S., et al. (2005). Stability of functional impairment in patients with schizotypal, borderline, avoidant, or obsessive-compulsive personality disorder over two years. *Psychol. Med., 35*(3), 443–451.

Skodol, A. E., Stout, R. L., McGlashan, T. H., Grilo, C. M., Gunderson, J. G., Shea, M. T., et al. (1999). Co-occurrence of mood and personality disorders: A report from the Collaborative Longitudinal Personality Disorders Study (CLPS). *Depress. Anx., 10*(4), 175–182.

Sloan, D. M., Mizes, J. C., Helbok, C., & Muck, R. (2004). Efficacy of sertraline for bulimia nervosa. *Inter. J. Eat. Disorders, 36*(1), 48–54.

Slovenko, R. (1992). Is diminished capacity really dead? *Psychiatr. Ann., 22*(11), 566–570.

Slovenko, R. (1995). *Psychiatry and criminal culpability.* New York: Wiley-Interscience.

Slovenko, R. (2002). *Psychiatry in law/Law in psychiatry.* New York: Brunner-Routledge.

Slovenko, R. (2002). The role of psychiatric diagnosis in the law. *J. Psychiat. Law, 30*(3), 421–444.

Slovenko, R. (2004). A history of the intermix of psychiatry and law. *J. Psychiat. Law, 32*(4), 561–592.

Smedley, A., & Smedley, B. D. (2005). Race as biology is fiction, racism as a social problem is real. *Amer. Psychologist, 60*(1), 16–26.

Smith, A. L., & Weissman, M. M. (1992). Epidemiology. In E. S. Paykel (Ed.), *Handbook of affective disorders.* New York: Guilford Press.

Smith, D. (2001). Prevention: Still a young field. *APA Monitor, 32*(6), 70–72.

Smith, G. R., Rost, K., & Kashner, T. M. (1995). A trial of the effect of a standardized psychiatric consultation on health outcomes and costs in somatizing patients. *Arch. Gen. Psychiat., 52*(3), 238–243.

Smith, M. L., & Glass, G. V. (1977). Meta-analysis of psychotherapy outcome studies. *Amer. Psychologist, 32*(9), 752–760.

Smith, M. L., Glass, G. V., & Miller, T. I. (1980). *The benefits of psychotherapy.* Baltimore: Johns Hopkins University Press.

Smith, T. W., & Rasinski, K. A. (2002). Assassination and terror; Two American tragedies compared. *NORC, 13*(5), 34.

Smith, T., Lovaas, N. W., & Lovaas, O. I. (2002). Behaviors of children with high-functioning autism when paired with typically developing versus delayed peers: A preliminary study. *Behav. Intervent., 17*(3), 129–143.

Smith, V. L., Kassin, S. M., Ellsworth, P. C., Whitley, B. E., Greenberg, M. S., Wells, G. L., et al. (1989). Eyewitness accuracy and confidence: Within- versus between-subjects correlations. The role of eyewitness confidence in juror perceptions of credibility: Accuracy, confidence, and juror perceptions in eyewitness identification. *J. Appl. Psychol., 74*(2), 356–359.

Smoller, J. W., Rosenbaum, J. F., Biederman, J., Kennedy, J., Dai, D., Racette, S. R., et al. (2003). Association of a genetic marker at the corticotropin-releasing hormone locus with behavioral inhibition. *Biol Psychiat., 54*(12), 1376–1381.

Smyer, M. A. (1989). Nursing homes as a setting for psychological practice: Public policy perspectives. *Amer. Psychologist, 44*(10), 1307–1314.

Smyth, J. M., & Pennebaker, J. W. (2001). What are the health effects of disclosure? In A. Baum, T. A. Revenson, & J. E. Singer (Eds.), *Handbook of health psychology* (pp. 339–348). Mahwah, NJ: Erlbaum.

Snow, E. (1976, December). In the snow. *Tex. Mon. Mag.*

Snyder, D. K., & Castellani, A. M. (2006). Current status and future directions in couple therapy. *Annu. Rev. Psychol., 57,* 317–344.

Snyder, S. (1980). *Biological aspects of mental disorder.* New York: Oxford University Press.

Snyder, S. (1986). *Drugs and the brain.* New York: Scientific American Library.

Snyder, S. (1991). Drugs, neurotransmitters, and the brain. In P. Corsi (Ed.), *The enchanted loom: Chapters in the history of neuroscience.* New York: Oxford University Press.

Snyder, W. V. (1947). *Casebook of non-directive counseling.* Boston: Houghton Mifflin.

Soares, J. C., Mallinger, A. G., Dippold, C. S., Frank, E., & Kupfer, D. J. (1999). Platelet membrane phospholipids in euthymic bipolar disorder patients: Are they affected by lithium treatment? *Biol. Psychiat., 45*(4), 453–457.

Sobczak, S., Honig, A., van Duinen, M. A., & Riedel, W. J. (2002). Serotonergic dysregulation in bipolar disorders: A literature review of serotonergic challenge studies. *Bipolar Disord., 4*(6), 347–356.

Sobell, M. B., & Sobell, L. C. (1973). Individualized behavior therapy for alcoholics. *Behav. Ther., 4*(1), 49–72.

Sobell, M. B., & Sobell, L. C. (1984). The aftermath of heresy: A response to Pendery et al.'s (1982) critique of "Individualized Behavior Therapy for Alcoholics." *Behav. Res. Ther., 22*(4), 413–440.

Sobell, M. B., & Sobell, L. C. (1984). Under the microscope yet again: A commentary on Walker and Roach's critique of the Dickens Committee's enquiry into our research. *Brit. J. Addic., 79*(2), 157–168.

Sohn, A., & Grayson, C. (2005). *Parenting your Asperger child.* New York: Perigree

Solms, M. (2005). Neuroscience. In E. S. Person, A. M. Cooper, & G. O. Gabbard (Eds.), *The American Psychiatric Publishing textbook of psychoanalysis* (pp. 535–546). Washington, DC: American Psychiatric Publishing.

Soloff, P. H., Fabio, A., Kelly, T. M., Malone, K. M., & Mann, J. J. (2005). High-lethality status in patients with borderline personality disorder. *J. Pers. Disorders, 19*(4), 386–399.

Solomon, R. L. (1980). The opponent-process theory of acquired motivation: The costs of pleasure and the benefits of pain. *Amer. Psychologist, 35*, 691–712.

Somasundaram, D. J., & Rajadurai, S. (1995). War and suicide in northern Sri Lanka. *Acta Psychiatr. Scandin., 91*(1), 1–4.

Somer, E., & Dell, P. F. (2005). Development of the Hebrew-Multidimensional Inventory of Dissociation (H-MID): A valid and reliable measure of pathological dissociation. *J. Trauma Dissociat., 6*(1), 31–35.

Somers, J. M., Goldner, E. M., Waraich, P., & Hsu, L. (2004). Prevalence studies of substance-related disorders: A systematic review of the literature. *Canad. J. Psychiat., 49*(6), [np].

Sommer, B. R., & Schatzberg, A. F. (2002). Ginkgo biloba and related compounds in Alzheimer's disease. *Psychiat. Ann., 32*(1), 13–18.

Sommers-Flanagan, J., & Sommers-Flanagan, R. (2003). *Clinical interviewing* (3rd ed.). New York: Wiley.

Sorensen, J. L., & Copeland, A. L. (2000). Drug abuse treatment as an HIV prevention strategy: A review. *Drug Alc. Rev., 59*(1) 17–31.

Sorokin, J. E., Giordani, B., Mohs, R. C., Losonczy, M. F., et al. (1988). Memory impairment in schizophrenic patients with tardive dyskinesia. *Biol. Psychiatry, 23*(2), 129–135.

Sorrentino, D., Mucca, A., Merlotti, E., Galderisi, S., & Maj, M. (2005). Modified nutritional counseling to increase motivation to treatment in anorexia nervosa. *Eur. Psychiat., 20*(2), 186–187.

Sourander, A., Helstelae, L., Haavisto, A., & Bergroth, L. (2001). Suicidal thoughts and attempts among adolescents: A longitudinal 8-year follow-up study. *J. Affect. Disorders, 63*(1–3), 59–66.

Spalter, A. R., Gwirtsman, H. E., Demitrack, M. A., & Gold, P. W. (1993). Thyroid function in bulimia nervosa. *Biol. Psychiat., 33*, 408–414.

Spaniel, F., Hajek, T., Tintera, J., Harantova, P., Dezortova, M., & Hajek, M. (2003). Differences in fMRI and MRS in a monozygotic twin pair discordant for schizophrenia (case report). *Acta Psychiatr. Scandin.* 107(2), 155–157.

Spanier, C., Shiffman, S., Maurer, A., Reynolds, W., & Quick, D. (1996). Rebound following failure to quit smoking: The effects of attributions and self-efficacy. *Exp. Clin. Psychopharmacol., 4*(2), 191–197.

Spanos, N. P., & Coe, W. C. (1992). A social-psychological approach to hypnosis. In E. Fromm & M. R. Nash (Eds.), *Contemporary hypnosis research.* New York: Guilford Press.

Sparling, J., Dragomir, C., Ramey, S. L., & Florescu, L. (2005). An educational intervention improves developmental progress of young children in a Romanian orphanage. *Infant Ment. Hlth. J., 26*(2), 127–142.

Speranza, M., Corcos, M., Loas, G., Stephan, P., Guilbaud, O., Perez-Diaz, F., Venisse, J-L., Bizouard, P., Halfon, O., Flament, M., & Jeammet, P. (2005). Depressive personality dimensions and alexithymia in eating disorders. *Psychiat. Res., 135*(2), 153–163.

Sperling, A. (2005). Housing update: Threats continue to Section 8 program. *NAMI Advocate, 3*(1), 6.

Sperry, L. (2003). *Handbook of diagnosis and treatment of DSM-IV-TR personality disorders* (2nd ed.). New York: Brunner-Routledge.

Spiegel, A. (2005). The dictionary of disorder. *The New Yorker,* January 3, 2005, 56–63.

Spiegel, D. (1994). Dissociative disorders. In R. E. Hales, S. C. Yudofsky, & J. A. Talbott (Eds.), *The American Psychiatric Press textbook of psychiatry* (2nd ed.). Washington, DC: American Psychiatric Press.

Spiegel, D. (2002). Mesmer minus magic: Hypnosis and modern medicine. *Inter. J. Clin. Exp. Hyp., 50*(4), 397–406.

Spiegel, D., & Fawzy, F. I. (2002). Psychosocial interventions and prognosis in cancer. In H. G. Koenig & H. J. Cohen (Eds.), *The link between religion and health: Psychoneuroimmunology and the faith factor* (pp. 84–100). New York: Oxford University Press.

Spiegler, M. D., & Guevremont, D. C. (2003). *Contemporary behavior therapy.* Belmont, CA: Thomson/Wadsworth.

Spielberger, C. D. (1966). Theory and research on anxiety. In C. D. Spielberger (Ed.), *Anxiety and behavior.* New York: Academic Press.

Spielberger, C. D. (1972). Anxiety as an emotional state. In C. D. Spielberger (Ed.), *Anxiety: Current trends in theory and research* (Vol. 1). New York: Academic Press.

Spielberger, C. D. (1985). Anxiety, cognition, and affect: A state-trait perspective. In A. H. Tuma & J. Maser (Eds.), *Anxiety and the anxiety disorders.* Hillsdale, NJ: Erlbaum.

Spielrein, S. (1995). On the psychological content of a case of schizophrenia (dementia praecox). *Evolution Psychiatr., 60*(1), 69–95. [French.]

Spinewine, A., Swine, C., Dhillon, S., Franklin, B. D., Tulkens, P. M., Wilmotte, L., et al. (2005). Appropriateness of use of medicines in elderly inpatients: Qualitative study. *Brit. Med. J., 331*(7522), October, [np].

Spitz, R. A. (1945). Hospitalization: An inquiry into the genesis of psychiatric conditions of early childhood. In R. S. Eissler, A. Freud, H. Hartman, & E. Kris (Eds.), *The psychoanalytic study of the child* (Vol. 1). New York: International Universities Press.

Spitz, R. A. (1946). Anaclitic depression. *The psychoanalytic study of the child* (Vol. 2). New York: International Universities Press.

Spitzer, R. L., Gibbon, M., Skodol, A. E., Williams, J. B. W., & First, M. B. (Eds.). (1994). *DSM-IV casebook: A learning companion to the diagnostic and statistical manual of mental disorders* (4th ed.). Washington, DC: American Psychiatric Press.

Spitzer, R. L., Skodol, A., Gibbon, M., & Williams, J. B. W. (1981). *DSM-III case book* (1st ed.). Washington, DC: American Psychiatric Press.

Spitzer, R. L., Skodol, A., Gibbon, M., & Williams, J. B. W. (1983). *Psychopathology: A case book.* New York: McGraw-Hill.

Sprecher, S., & Hatfield, E. (1996). Premarital sexual standards among U. S. college students: Comparison with Russian and Japanese students. *Arch. Sex. Behav., 25*(3), 261–288.

Sprock, J. (2000). Gender-typed behavioral examples of histrionic personality disorder. *J. Psychopath. Behav. Ass., 22*(2), 107–122.

Squire, L. R. (1977). ECT and memory loss. *Amer. J. Psychiat., 134*, 997–1001.

Squire, L. R., & Slater, P. C. (1983). Electroconvulsive therapy and complaints of memory dysfunction: A prospective three-year follow-up study. *Brit. J. Psychiat., 142*, 1–8.

Sramek, J. J., & Pi, E. H. (1996). Ethnicity and antidepressant response. *Mt. Sinai J. Med., 63*, 320–325.

St. George-Hyslop, P. H. (2000). Molecular genetics of Alzheimer's disease. *Biol. Psychiat., 47*(3), 183–199.

St. George-Hyslop, P. H. (2000). Piecing together Alzheimer's. *Scientif. Amer., 76*–83.

Stack, S. (1987). Celebrities and suicide: A taxonomy and analysis, 1948–1983. *Amer. Sociol. Rev., 52*, 401–412.

Stack, S. (1998). The relationship of female labor force participation to suicide: A comparative analysis. *Arch. Suic. Res., 4*(3), 249–261.

Stack, S. (2003). Media coverage as a risk factor in suicide. *J. Epidemiol. Comm. Hlth., 57*(4), 238–240.

Stack, S. (2004). Emile Durkheim and altruistic suicide. *Arch. Suic. Res., 8*(1), 9–22.

Stack, S. (2005). Suicide in the media: A quantitative review of studies based on nonfictional stories. *Suic. Life-Threat. Behav., 35*(2), 121–133.

Stahl, S. M. (2001). The psychopharmacology of sex. Part 2: Effects of drugs and disease on the 3 phases of human sexual response. *J. Clin. Psychiat., 62*(3), 147–148.

Staley, J. K., Gottschalk, C., Petrakis, I. L., Gueorguieva, R., O'Malley, S., Baldwin, R., et al. (2005). Cortical gamma-aminobutyric acid type A-benzodiazepine receptors in recovery from alcohol dependence: Relationship to features of alcohol dependence and cigarette smoking. *Arch. Gen. Psychiat., 62*(8), 877–888.

Stambor, Z. (2005). Pursuing prescription privileges. *Monitor Psychol., 36*(7), 84–85.

Stanley, B., & Brodsky, B. S. (2005). Suicidal and self-injurious behavior in borderline personality disorder: A self-regulation model. In J. G. Gunderson & P. D. Hoffman (Eds.), *Understanding and treating borderline personality disorder: A guide for professionals and families* (pp. 43–63). Washington, DC: American Psychiatric Publishing.

Stanley, B., Molcho, A., Stanley, M., Winchel, R., Gameroff, M. J., Parsons, B., et al. (2000). Association of aggressive behavior with altered serotonergic function in patients who are not suicidal. *Amer. J. Psychiat., 157*(4), 609–614.

Stanley, M. A., Hopko, D. R., Diefenbach, G. J., Bourland, S. L., Rodriguez, H., & Wagener, P. (2003). Cognitive-behavior therapy for late-life generalized anxiety disorder in primary care: Preliminary findings. *Amer. J. Ger. Psychiat.*, *11*(1), 92–96.

Stanley, M., Stanley, B., Traskman-Bendz, L., Mann, J. J., & Meyendorff, E. (1986). Neurochemical findings in suicide completers and suicide attempters. In R. W. Maris (Ed.), *Biology of suicide*. New York: Guilford Press.

Stanley, M., Virgilio, J., & Gershon, S. (1982). Tritiated imipramine binding sites are decreased in the frontal cortex of suicides. *Science, 216,* 1337–1339.

Steadman, H. J., Monahan, J., Robbins, P. C., Appelbaum, P., Grisso, T., Klassen, D., et al. (1993). From dangerousness to risk assessment: Implications for appropriate research strategies. In S. Hodgins (Ed.), *Mental disorder and crime.* New York: Sage.

Steege, J. F., & Ling, F. W. (1993). Dyspareunia: A special type of chronic pelvic pain. *Obstet. Gynecol. Clin. North Am., 20,* 779–793.

Steen, S. N., Oppliger, R. A., & Brownell, K. D. (1988). Metabolic effects of repeated weight loss and regain in adolescent wrestlers. *JAMA, 260,* 47–50.

Steiger, H., Joober, R., Israel, M., Young, S. N., Kin, N. M. K. N. Y., Gauvin, L., et al. (2005). The 5HTTLPR polymorphism, psychopathologic symptoms, and platelet [subscript 3H-] paroxetine binding in bulimic syndromes. *Inter. J. Eat. Disord., 37*(1), 57–60.

Stein, D., Kaye, W. H., Matsunaga, H., Orbach, I., Har-Evan, D., Frank, G., et al. (2002). Eating-related concerns, mood, and personality traits in recovered bulimia nervosa subjects: A replication study. *Inter. J. Eat. Disorders, 32*(2), 225–229.

Stein, J. (2003). Just say Om. *Time, 162*(5), August 4, 2003, 48–56.

Stein, L. I. (1993). A system approach to reducing relapse in schizophrenia. *J. Clin. Psychiat., 54*(3 Suppl.), 7–12.

Stein, M. B., Jang, K. L., & Livesley, W. J. (1999). Heritability of anxiety sensitivity: A twin study. *Amer. J. Psychiat., 156*(2), 246–251.

Stein, Z., Susser, M., Saenger, G., & Marolla, F. (1972). Nutrition and mental performance. *Science, 178,* 708–713.

Steiner, H., Smith, C., Rosenkranz, R. T., & Litt, I. (1991). The early care and feeding of anorexics. *Child Psychiat. Human Dev., 21*(3), 163–167.

Steiner, M., & Tam, W. Y. K. (1999). Postpartum depression in relation to other psychiatric disorders. In L. J. Miller (Ed.), *Postpartum mood disorders.* Washington, DC: American Psychiatric Press.

Steinhausen, H. C. (2002). The outcome of anorexia nervosa in the 20th century. *Amer. J. Psychiat., 159*(8), 1284–1293.

Steinhausen, H. C., Boyadjieva, S., Grigoroiu-Serbanescu, M., Seidel, R., & Winkler-Metzke, C. (2000). A transcultural outcome study of adolescent eating disorders. *Acta Psychiatr. Scandin., 101*(1), 60–66.

Steketee, G. (1990). Personality traits and disorders in obsessive-compulsives. *J. Anx. Dis., 4*(4), 351–364.

Steketee, G., & Barlow, D. H. (2002). Obsessive-compulsive disorder. In D. H. Barlow (Ed.), *Anxiety and its disorders: The nature and treatment of anxiety and panic* (2nd ed., pp. 516–550). New York: Guilford Press.

Steketee, G., Frost, R., Bhar, S., Bouvard, M., Clamari, J., Carmin, C., et al. (2003). Psychometric validation of the obsessive beliefs questionnaire and the interpretation of intrusions inventory. Part I. *Behav. Res. Ther., 41*(8), 863–878.

Steptoe, A. (2001). Negative emotions in music making: The problem of performance anxiety. In P. N. Juslin & J. A. Sloboda (Eds.), *Music and emotion: Theory and research. Series in affective science* (pp. 291–307). London: Oxford University Press.

Stern Magazine. (2004). Survey. *Stern Magazine,* July 23, 2004.

Sternberg, R. J. (Ed.). (2004). *International handbook of intelligence.* Cambridge, England: Cambridge University Press.

Sternberg, R. J., Grigorenko, E. L., & Bundy, D. A. (2001). The predictive value of IQ. *Merrill-Palmer Q., 47*(1), 1–41.

Stetter, F. (2000). Psychotherapy. In G. Zernig, A. Saria, et al. (Eds.), *Handbook of alcoholism. Pharmacology and toxicology.* Boca Raton, FL: CRC Press.

Stetter, F., & Kupper, S. (2002). Autogenic training: A meta-analysis of clinical outcome studies. *Appl. Psychophysiol. Biofeedback, 27*(1), 45–98.

Stevens, J., Harman, J. S., & Kelleher, K. J. (2005). Race/ethnicity and insurance status as factors associated with ADHD treatment patterns. *J. Child Adol. Psychopharmacol., 15*(1), 88–96.

Stevens, J., & Ward-Estes, J. (2006). Attention-deficit/hyperactivity disorder. In M. Hersen & J. C. Thomas (Series Eds.) & R. T. Ammerman (Vol. Ed.), *Comprehensive handbook of personality and psychopathology: Vol. 3 Child psychopathology* (pp. 316–329). Hoboken, NJ: Wiley.

Stevens, K. R., & Munoz, L. R. (2004). Focus on research methods: Cigarette smoking: Evidence to guide measurement. *Res. Nursing Hlth., 27*(4), 281–292.

Stevens, L. M., Lynm, C., & Glass, R. M. (2002). Postpartum depression. *JAMA, 287*(6), 802.

Stewart, A. (2004). Prevention of eating disorders. In P. B. Harper & K. N. Dwivedi (Eds.), *Promoting the emotional well-being of children and adolescents and preventing their mental ill health: A handbook* (pp. 173–197). Philadelphia: Jessica Kingsley Publishers.

Stewart, M. E., Ebmeier, K. P., & Deary, I. J. (2005). Personality correlates of happiness and sadness: EPQ-R and TPQ compared. *Pers. Individ. Diff., 38*(5), 1085–1096.

Stewart, S. H., Taylor, S., Jang, K. L., Cox, B. J., Watt, M. C., Fedoroff, I. C., & Borger, S. C. (2001). Causal modeling of relations among learning history, anxiety sensitivity, and panic attacks. *Behav. Res. Ther., 39*(4), 443–456.

Stice, E., & Bearman, S. K. (2001). Body-image and eating disturbances prospectively predict increases in depressive symptoms in adolescent girls: A growth curve analysis. *Dev. Psychol., 37,* 597–607.

Stief, E. A. (2004). Parental perceptions of attention-deficit/hyperactivity disorder: Etiology, diagnosis, and treatment. *Diss. Abstr. Inter.: Sect. B: Sci. Eng., 64*(10-B), 5236.

Stillion, J. M. (1995). Through a glass darkly: Women and attitudes toward suicidal behavior. In S. S. Canetto & D. Lester (Eds.), *Women and suicidal behavior.* New York: Springer.

Stillion, J. M., & McDowell, E. E. (1996). *Suicide across the life span: Premature exits* (2nd ed.). Washington, DC: Taylor & Francis.

Stirman, S. W., & Pennebaker, J. W. (2001). Word use in the poetry of suicidal and non-suicidal poets. *Psychosom. Med., 63,* 517–522.

Stock, W. (1993). Inhibited female orgasm. In W. O'Donohue & J. Geer (Eds.), *Handbook of sexual dysfunctions.* Boston: Allyn & Bacon.

Stoil, M. (2001). Behavioral health's "finest hour." *Behav. Hlth. Manage., 21*(5), 8–10.

Stolberg, R. A., Clark, D. C., & Bongar, B. (2002). Epidemiology, assessment, and management of suicide in depressed patients. In I. H. Gotlib & C. L. Hammen (Eds.), *Handbook of depression* (pp. 581–601). New York: Guilford Press.

Stoll, A. L., Renshaw, P. F., Yurgelun-Todd, D. A., & Cohen, B. M. (2000). Neuroimaging in bipolar disorder. *Bipolar Disord., 2,* 148–164.

Stone, M. H. (1989). Schizoid personality disorder. In American Psychiatric Association (Eds.), *Treatments of psychiatric disorders: A task force report of the American Psychiatric Association.* Washington, DC: American Psychiatric Press.

Stone, M. H. (2000). Clinical guidelines for psychotherapy for patients with borderline personality disorder. *Psychiatr. Clin. N. Amer., 23*(1), 193–210.

Stone, T. H., Winslade, W. J., & Klugman, C. M. (2000). Sex offenders, sentencing laws and pharmacological treatment: A prescription for failure. *Behav. Sci. Law, 18*(1), 83–110.

Stone, W. S., Faraone, S. V., Seidman, L. J., Olson, E. A., & Tsuang, M. T. (2005). Searching for the liability to schizophrenia: Concepts and methods underlying genetic high-risk studies of adolescents. *J. Child Adol. Psychopharmacol., 1593*), 403–417.

Stowe, Z., Casarella, J., Landry, J., & Nemeroff, C. (1995). Sertraline in the treatment of women with postpartum major depression. *Depression, 3,* 49–55.

Strate, J. M., Zalman, M., & Hunter, D. J. (2005). Physician-assisted suicide and the politics of problem definition. *Mortality, 10*(1), 23–41.

Stratton, V. N., & Zalanowski, A. H. (1994). Affective impact of music vs. lyrics. *Empir. Stud. Arts, 12*(2), 173–184.

Stratton, V., & Zalanowski, A. (1999). *Study on music and emotion.* Paper presented at annual meeting of Eastern Psychological Association, Providence, RI.

Strauch, I. (2004). Cited in *Newsweek, 144*(6), August 9, 2004, 46.

Stravynski, A., Gaudette, G., Lesage, A., Arbel, N., et al. (1997). The treatment of sexually dysfunctional men without partners: A controlled study of three behavioural group approaches. *Brit. J. Psychiat., 170,* 338–344.

Stricker, G., & Trierweiler, S. J. (1995). The local clinical scientist. A bridge between science and practice. *Amer. Psychologist, 50*(12), 995–1002.

Strickland, B. R., Hale, W. D., & Anderson, L. K. (1975). Effect of induced mood states on activity and self-reported affect. *J. Cons. Clin. Psychol., 43*(4), 587.

Strickland, C. J. (1997). Suicide among American Indian, Alaskan Native, and Canadian Aboriginal youth: Advancing the research agenda. *Inter. J. Ment. Hlth., 25*(4), 11–32.

Strickland, T. L., Ranganath, V., Lin, K. M., et al. (1991). Psychopharmacologic considerations in the treatment of black American populations. *Psychopharmacol. Bull., 27,* 441–448.

Striegel-Moore, R. H., Fairburn, C. G., Wilfley, D. E., Pike, K. M., Dohm, F-A., & Kraemer, H. C. (2005). Toward an understanding of risk factors for binge-eating disorder in black and white women: A community-based case-control study. *Psychol. Med., 35*(6), 907–917.

Striegel-Moore, R. H., Silberstein, L. R., & Rodin, J. (1993). The social self in bulimia nervosa: Public self-consciousness, social anxiety, and perceived fraudulence. *J. Abnorm. Psychol., 102*(2), 297–303.

Striegel-Moore, R. H., & Smolak, L. (1997). The role of race in the development of eating disorders. In L. Smolak, M. P. Levine, & R. Striegel-Moore (Eds.), *Developmental psychopathology of eating disorders* (pp. 259–284). Mahwah, NJ: Erlbaum.

Striegel-Moore, R. H., Wilfley, D. E., Pike, L. M., Dohn, F. A., & Fairburn, C. G. (2000). Recurrent binge eating in Black American women. *Arch. Fam. Med., 9,* 83–87.

Strober, M., Freeman, R., Lampert, C., Diamond, J., & Kaye, W. (2000). Controlled family study of anorexia nervosa and bulimia nervosa: Evidence of shared liability and transmission of partial syndromes. *Amer. J. Psychiat., 157*(3), 393–401.

Strober, M., Freeman, R., Lampert, C., Diamond, J., & Kaye, W. (2001). Males with anorexia nervosa: A controlled study of eating disorders in first-degree relatives. *Inter. J. Eat. Disorders, 29*(3), 264–269.

Strober, M., & Yager, J. (1985). A developmental perspective on the treatment of anorexia nervosa in adolescents. In D. M. Garner & P. E. Garfinkel (Eds.), *Handbook of psychotherapy for anorexia nervosa and bulimia.* New York: Guilford Press.

Stroebe, M., Gergen, M. M., Gergen, K. J., & Stroebe, W. (1992). Broken hearts or broken bonds: Love and death in historical perspectives. *Amer. Psychologist, 47*(10), 1205–1212.

Stroebe, M., & Schut, H. (2005). To continue or relinquish bonds: A review of consequences for the bereaved. *Death Stud., 29*(6), 477–494.

Stroebe, M., Schut, H., & Stroebe, W. (2005). Attachment in coping with bereavement: A theoretical integration. *Rev. Gen. Psychol., 9*(1), 48–66.

Stroebe, M., van Son, M., Stroebe, W., Kleber, R., Schut, H., & van den Bout, J. (2000). On the classification and diagnosis of pathological grief. *Clin. Psychol. Rev., 20*(1), 57–75.

Stromme, P., & Magnus, P. (2000). Correlations between socioeconomic status, IQ and aetiology in mental retardation: A population-based study of Norwegian children. *Soc. Psychiat. Psychiatr. Epidemiol., 35*(1), 12–18.

Strümpfel, U., & Goldman, R. (2002). Contacting Gestalt therapy. In D. J. Cain & J. Seeman (Eds.), *Humanistic psychotherapies: Handbook of research and practice* (pp. 189–220). Washington, DC: American Psychologist Association.

Strupp, H. H. (1989). Psychotherapy: Can the practitioner learn from the researcher? *Amer. Psychologist, 44,* 717–724.

Strupp, H. H. (1996). The tripartite model and the Consumer Reports study. *Amer. Psychologist, 51*(10), 1017–1024.

Stuart, S., & Noyes, R., Jr. (1999). Attachment and interpersonal communication in somatization. *Psychosomatics, 40*(1), 34–43.

Stuart, S., O'Hara, M. W., & Gorman, L. L. (2003). The prevention and psychotherapeutic treatment of postpartum depression. *Arch. Women's Ment. Hlth., 6*(Suppl. 2), s57–s69.

Stunkard, A. J. (1975). From explanation to action in psychosomatic medicine: The case of obesity. *Psychosom. Med., 37,* 195–236.

Stunkard, A. J., Sorenson, T. I. A., Hanis, C., Teasdale, T. W., et al. (1986). An adoption study of human obesity. *N. Engl. J. Med., 314,* 193–198.

Sturgeon, V., & Taylor, J. (1980). Report of a five-year follow-up study of mentally disordered sex offenders released from Atascadero State Hospital in 1973. *Criminal Justice J. Western S. Univ., San Diego, 4, 31–64.*

Styron, W. (1990). *Darkness visible: A memoir of madness.* New York: Random House.

Su, J. C., & Birmingham, C. L. (2002). Zinc supplementation in the treatment of anorexia nervosa. *Eat. Weight Disord., 7*(1), 20–22.

Suarez, E. C. (2004). C-reactive protein is associated with psychological risk factors of cardiovascular disease in apparently healthy adults. *Psychosom. Med., 66*(5), 684–691.

Sudhalter, V., Cohen, I. L., Silverman, W., & Wolf-Schein, E. G. (1990). Conversational analyses of males with fragile X, Down syndrome, and autism: Comparison of the emergence of deviant language. *Amer. J. Ment. Retard., 94,* 431–441.

Sue, D. W. (2001). Multidimensional facets of cultural competence. *Couns. Psychologist, 29*(6), 790–821.

Sue, D. W. (2001). The superordinate nature of cultural competence. *Couns. Psychologist, 29*(6), 850–857.

Sue, D. W. (2002). Cultural competence in behavioral health care. In J. C. Chunn (Ed.), *The health behavioral change imperative: Theory, education, and practice in diverse populations* (pp. 41–50). New York: Kluwer Academic/Plenum Publishers.

Sue, D. W., Carter, R. T., Casas, J. M., Fouad, N. A., Ivey, A. E., Jensen, M., et al. (1998). *Multicultural aspects of counseling* (Vol. 11). Thousand Oaks, CA: Sage Publications.

Sue, D. W., & Sue, D. (2003) *Counseling the culturally diverse: Theory and practice* (4th ed.). New York: Wiley.

Sue, S. (2003). In defense of cultural competency in psychotherapy and treatment. *Amer. Psychologist, 58*(11), 964–970.

Suinn, R. M. (2001). The terrible twos—anger and anxiety. *Amer. Psychologist, 56*(1), 27–36.

Sullivan, H. S. (1953). *The interpersonal theory of psychiatry.* New York: Norton.

Sullivan, H. S. (1962). *Schizophrenia as a human process.* New York: Norton.

Sullivan, P. W., Valuck, R., Saseen, J., & MacFall, H. M. (2004). A comparison of the direct costs and cost effectiveness of serotonin reuptake inhibitors and associated adverse drug reactions. *CNS Drugs, 18*(13), 911–932.

Suls, J., & Rothman, A. (2004). Evolution of the biopsychosocial model: Prospects and challenges for health psychology. *Hlth. Psychol., 23*(2), 119–125.

Summers, M. (1996, December 9). Mister clean. *People,* pp. 139–140.

Sunstein, C. R., & Nussbaum, M. C. (Eds.). (2004). *Animal rights: Current debates and new directions.* PsychINFO Weekly 2005/03 Week 2.

Suppes, T., Baldessarini, R. J., Faedda, G. L., & Tohen, M. (1991). Risk of recurrence following discontinuation of lithium treatment in bipolar disorder. *Arch. Gen. Psychiat., 48*(12), 1082–1088.

Suppes, T., Kelly, D. I., & Perla, J. M. (2005). Challenges in the management of bipolar depression. *J. Clin. Psychiat., 66*(Suppl. 5), 11–16.

Susser, E., Neugebauer, R., Hoek, H. W., Brown, A. S., Lin, S., Labovitz, D., et al. (1996). Schizophrenia after prenatal famine. *Arch. Gen. Psychiat., 53*(1), 25–31.

Svartberg, M., & Stiles, T. C. (1991). Comparative effects of short-term psychodynamic psychotherapy: A meta-analysis. *J. Cons. Clin. Psychol., 59,* 704–714.

Svensson, B., Hansson, L., & Nyman, K. (2000). Stability of outcome in a comprehensive, cognitive therapy based treatment programme for long-term mentally ill patients. A 2-year follow-up study. *J. Ment. Hlth. UK, 9*(1), 51–61.

Swaab, D. F. (2005). The role of hypothalamus and endocrine system in sexuality. In J. S. Hyde (Ed.), *Biological substrates of human sexuality.* Washington, DC: American Psychological Association.

Swallow, M., Yutzy, S. H., & Dinwiddie, S. H. (2005). Forensic issues. In E. H. Rubin & C. F. Zorumski (Eds.), *Adult psychiatry* (2nd ed., pp. 420–428). Oxford, England: Blackwell Publishing.

Swann, A. C. (2005). Long-term treatment in bipolar disorder. *J. Clin. Psychiat., 66*(Suppl. 1), 7–12.

Swanson, J., Holzer, C., Ganju, V., & Jono, R. (1990). Violence and psychiatric disorder in the community: Evidence from the Epidemiological Catchment Area Surveys. *Hosp. Comm. Psychiat., 41,* 761–770.

Swartz, H. A. (1999). Interpersonal psychotherapy. In M. Hersen & A. S. Bellack (Eds.), *Handbook of comparative interventions for adult disorders* (2nd ed.). New York: Wiley.

Swayze, V. W. (1995). Frontal leukotomy and related psychosurgical procedures in the era before antipsychotics (1935–1954): A historical overview. *Amer. J. Psychiat., 152*(4), 505–515.

Sweeney, M. C. (2003). Gender- and culture-sensitive therapies. In J. O. Prochaska & J. C. Norcross, (Eds.), *Systems of psychotherapy: A transtheoretical analysis* (5th cd.). Pacific Grove, CA: Brooks/Cole.

Swendsen, J. D., & Mazure, C. M. (2000). Life stress as a risk factor for postpartum depression: Current research and methodology. *Clin. Psychol.: Sci. Prac., 7*(1), 17–31.

Swerdlow, J. L. (1995). Quiet miracles of the brain. *Natl. Geogr., 187*(6), 12–13.

Switzer, P. K. (2000). The effects that medical malpractice concerns have on the practice of psychiatry in South Carolina. *Diss. Abstr. Inter.: Sect. B: Sci. Eng., 61*(2-B), 764.

Swonger, A. K., & Constantine, L. L. (1983). *Drugs and therapy: A handbook of psychotropic drugs* (2nd ed.). Boston: Little, Brown.

Swora, M. G. (2001). Personhood and disease in Alcoholics Anonymous: A perspective from the anthropology of religious healing. *Ment. Health, Religion Cult., 4*(1), 1–21.

Szabo, M., & Lovibond, P. F. (2004). The cognitive content of thought-listed worry episodes in clinic-referred anxious and nonreferred children. *J. Clin. Child Adol. Psychol., 33*(3), 613–622.

Szasz, T. S. (1960). The myth of mental illness. *Amer. Psychologist, 15,* 113–118.

Szasz, T. S. (1963). *The manufacture of madness.* New York: Harper & Row.

Szasz, T. S. (1970). *The manufacture of madness: A comparative study of the Inquisition and the Mental Health Movement.* Syracuse, NY: Syracuse University Press.

Szasz, T. S. (1973). *The second sin.* Garden City, NY: Anchor Press.

Szasz, T. S. (1977). *Psychiatric slavery.* New York: Free Press.

Szasz, T. S. (1991). *The medicalization of sex. J. Human. Psychol., 31*(3), 34–42.

Szasz, T. S. (1997). *The manufacture of madness: A comprehensive study of the Inquisition and the mental health movement.* Syracuse, NY: Syracuse University Press.

Szasz, T. S. (2000). Second commentary on "Aristotle's function argument." *Philos. Psychiat. Psychol., 7*(1), 3–16.

Szasz, T. S. (2004). "Knowing what ain't so": R. D. Laing and Thomas Szasz. *Psychoanal. Rev., 91*(3), 331–346.

Szegedy-Maszak, M. (2004, November 20). Conquering our phobias. *U. S. News & World Report, 137*(20), 66–74.

Szegedy-Maszak, M. (2005). The worst of all bets. *U. S. News & World Report, 138*(19), 53–54.

Szymanski, S., Cannon, T. D., Gallacher, F., Erwin, R. J., & Gur, R. E. (1996). Course of treatment response in first-episode and chronic schizophrenia. *Amer. J. Psychiat., 153*(4), 519–525.

Szymanski, S., Lieberman, J., Alvir, J. M., Mayerhoff, D., et al. (1995). Gender differences in onset of illness, treatment response, course, and biologic indexes in first-episode schizophrenic patients. *Am. J. Psychiatry, 152*(5), 698–703.

Szymanski, S., Lieberman, J., Pollack, S., Kane, J. M., Safferman, A., Munne, R., et al. (1996). Gender differences in neuroleptic nonresponsive clozapine-treated schizophrenics. *Biol. Psychiat., 39,* 249–254.

Tacon, A., & Caldera, Y. (2001). Behavior modification. In R. McComb & J. Jacalyn (Eds.), *Eating disorders in women and children: Prevention, stress management, and treatment* (pp. 263–272). Boca Raton, FL: CRC Press.

TADS (Treatment for Adolescents with Depression Study Team, U.S.). (2004). Fluoxetine, cognitive behavioral therapy, and their combination for adolescents with depression: Treatment for Adolescents with Depression Study (TADS) randomized controlled trial. *JAMA, 292*(7), 807–820.

TADS (Treatment for Adolescents with Depression Study Team, U.S.). (2005). The Treatment for Adolescents with Depression Study (TADS): Demographic and clinical characteristics. *J. Amer. Acad. Child Adol. Psychiat., 44*(1), 28–40.

Tafet, G. E., Feder, D. J., Abulafia, D. P., & Roffman, S. S. (2005). Regulation of hypothalamic-pituitary-adrenal activity in response to cognitive therapy in patients with generalized anxiety disorder. *Cog. Affect. Behav. Neurosci., 5*(1), 37–40.

Talbott, J. A. (2004). Deinstitutionalization: Avoiding the disasters of the past. *Psychiatr. Serv., 55*(10), 1112–1115.

Tallis, F., Davey, G., & Capuzzo, N. (1994). The phenomenology of non-pathological worry: A preliminary investigation. In G. Davey & F. Tallis (Eds.), *Worrying: Perspectives on theory, assessment and treatment* (pp. 61–89). Chichester, England: John Wiley.

Tamblyn, R., Abrahamowicz, M., du Berger, R., McLeon, P., & Bartlett, G. (2005). A 5-year prospective assessment of the risk associated with individual benzodiazepines and doses in new elderly users. *J. Amer. Ger. Soc., 53*(2), 233–241.

Tanner, L. (2001, April 25). Study: 30% of kids deal with bullying: "Serious problem" shouldn't be accepted as normal, author says. *The Dallas Morning News,* p. 1A.

Tarrier, N. (2005). Schizophrenia. In M. M. Antony, D. R. Ledley, & R. G. Heimberg (Eds.), *Improving outcomes and preventing relapse in cognitive-behavioral therapy* (pp. 306–347). New York: Guilford Press.

Tartaglia, L. A., Dembski, M., Weng, X., Deng, N., et al. (1995). Identification and expression cloning of a leptin receptor, OB-R. *Cell, 83,* 1263–1271.

Tartaro, C., & Lester, D. (2005). An application of Durkheim's theory of suicide to prison suicide rates in the United States. *Death Stud., 29*(5), 413–422.

Tate, D. C., Reppucci, N. D., & Mulvey, E. P. (1995). Violent juvenile delinquents. *Amer. Psychologist, 50*(9), 777–781.

Taube, C. A. (1990). Funding and expenditures for mental illness. In R. W. Manderscheid & M. A. Sonnenschein (Eds.), *Mental health, United States, 1990.* (DHHS Publication No. ADM 90–1708). Washington, DC: U.S. Department of Health and Human Services.

Tavris, C. (1993). Beware the incest-survivor machine. *New York Times Book Review.*

Taxman, F. S., & Messina, N. P. (2002). Civil commitment: A coerced treatment model. In C. G. Leukefeld, F. Tims, & D. Farabee (Eds.), *Treatment of drug offenders: Policies and issues* (pp. 283–298). New York: Springer.

Taylor, B., Miller, E., Farrington, C. P., Petropoulos, M. C., Favot-Mayaud, I., Li, J., et al. (1999). Autism and measles, mumps, and rubella vaccine: No epidemiological evidence for a causal association. *Lancet, 353,* 2026–2029.

Taylor, C. B., Farquhar, J. W., Nelson, E., & Agras, S. (1977). Relaxation therapy and high blood pressure. *Arch. Gen. Psychiat., 34,* 339–342.

Taylor, E. A., & Stansfeld, S. A. (1984). Children who poison themselves. *Brit. J. Psychiat., 145,* 127–135.

Taylor, G. M., & Ste. Marie, D. M. (2001). Eating disorders symptoms in Canadian female pair and dance figure skaters. *Int. J. Sport Psychol., 32*(1), 21–28.

Taylor, J. R., & Carroll, J. L. (1987). Current issues in electroconvulsive therapy. *Psychol. Rep., 60*(3, Pt. 1).

Taylor, R. (1975). *Electroconvulsive treatment (ECT): The control of therapeutic power.* Exchange.

Taylor, S. E. (2004). The accidental neuroscientist: Positive resources, stress responses, and course of illness. In G. G. Berntson & J. T. Cacioppo (Eds.), *Essays in social neuroscience* (pp. 133–141). Cambridge, MA: MIT Press.

Taylor, S. E. (2006). *Health psychology* (6th ed.). New York: McGraw Hill.

Taylor, S., Wald, J., & Asmundson, G. J. G. (2005). Current status and future directions in the cognitive-behavioral treatment of PTSD. In T. A. Corales (Ed.), *Trends in posttraumatic stress disorder research* (pp. 263–284). Hauppauge, NY: Nova Science Publishers.

Telch, C. F., & Agras, W. S. (1993). The effects of a very low calorie diet on binge eating. *Behav. Ther., 24,* 177–193.

Telner, J. I., Lapierre, Y. D., Horn, E., & Browne, M. (1986). Rapid reduction of mania by means of reserpine therapy. *Amer. J. Psychiat., 143*(8), 1058.

Teng, C. T., Akerman, D., Cordas, T. A., Kasper, S., et al. (1995). Seasonal affective disorder in a tropical country: A case report. *Psychiatr. Res., 56*(1), 11–15.

Teplin, L. A., Abram, K. M., & McClelland, G. M. (1994). Does psychiatric disorder predict violent behavior among released jail detainees? *Amer. Psychologist, 49*(4), 335–342.

Teri, L., & Lewinsohn, P. M. (1986). Individual and group treatment of unipolar depression: Comparison of treatment outcome and identification of predictors of successful treatment outcome. *Behav. Ther., 17*(3), 215–228.

Terry, D., Mayocchi, L., & Hynes, G. (1996). Depressive symptomatology in new mothers: A stress and coping perspective. *J. Abnorm. Psychol., 105*(2), 220–231.

Thakker, J., & Ward, T. (1998). Culture and classification: The cross-cultural application of the DSM-IV. *Clin. Psych. Rev., 18,* 501–529.

Thakur, C. P., & Sharma, D. (1984). Full moon and crime. *Brit. Med. J. (Clin. Res. Ed.), 289*(6460), 1789–1791.

Thase, M. E. (2005). Correlates and consequences of chronic insomnia. *Gen. Hosp. Psychiat., 27*(2), 100–112.

Thase, M. E., Buysse, D. J., Frank, E., Cherry, C. R., et al. (1997). Which depressed patients will respond to interpersonal psychotherapy? The role of abnormal EEG sleep profiles. *Amer. J. Psychiatry, 154*(4), 502–509.

Thase, M. E., Frank, E., Kornstein, S., & Yonkers, K. A. (2000). Gender differences in response to treatments of depression. In E. Frank (Ed.), *Gender and its effects on psychopathology* (pp. 103–129). Washington, DC: American Psychiatric Press.

Thase, M. E., Jindal, R., & Howland, R. H. (2002). Biological aspects of depression. In I. H. Gotlib & C. L. Hammen (Eds.), *Handbook of depression* (pp. 192–218). New York: Guilford Press.

Thase, M. E., Trivedi, M. H., & Rush, A. J. (1995). MAOIs in the contemporary treatment of depression. *Neuropsychopharmacology, 12*(3), 185–219.

Theander, S. (1970). Anorexia nervosa. *Acta Psychiatr. Scandin.,* [Suppl.], pp. 1–194.

Theodorou, S., & Haber, P. S. (2005). The medical complications of heroin use. *Curr. Opin. Psychiat., 18*(3), 257–263.

Thienemann, M. (2004). Introducing a structured interview into a clinical setting. *J. Amer. Acad. Child Adol. Psychiat., 43*(8), 1057–1060.

Thigpen, C. H., & Cleckley, H. M. (1957). *The three faces of Eve.* New York: McGraw-Hill.

Thio, A. (2006). *Deviant behavior* (8th ed.). New York: Pearson/Allyn & Bacon.

Thomas, A. K., & Loftus, E. F. (2002). Creating bizarre false memories through imagination. *Mem. Cog., 30*(3), 423–431.

Thomas, E. (1995). *The very best men.* New York: Simon & Schuster.

Thomas, E. (1996, April 15). What the unabomber did to me. *Newsweek,* pp. 40–41.

Thomas, J. (2004). Firewall needed between marketing and science. *The National Psychologist, 13*(5), pp. 1, 5.

Thomas, J. (2005). Expansion of Tarasoff "duty to warn" headed to trial in California. *The National Psychologist, 14*(1), pp. 1, 3.

Thomas, J. C., & Hersen, M. (Eds.) (2004). *Psychopathology in the workplace: Recognition and adaptation.* New York: Brunner-Routledge.

Thomas, P., Chantoin-Merlet, S., Hazif-Thomas, C., Belmin, J., Montagne, B., Clement, J. P., et al. (2002). Complaints of informal caregivers providing home care for dementia patients: The Pixel study. *Inter. J. Ger. Psychiat., 17*(11), 1034–1044.

Thompson, A. H., Stuart, H., Bland, R. C., Arboleda-Florez, J., Warner, R., & Dickson, R. A. (2002). Attitudes about schizophrenia from the pilot site of the WPA worldwide campaign against the stigma of schizophrenia. *Soc. Psychiat. Psychiatr. Epidemiol., 37*(10), 475–482.

Thompson, R., & Keene, K. (2004). The pros and cons of caffeine. *The Psychologist, 17*(12), [np].

Thompson, R. A., & Sherman, R. T. (1993). *Helping athletes with eating disorders.* Champaign, IL: Human Kinetics.

Thompson, R. A., & Sherman, R. T. (1999). "Good athlete" traits and characteristics of anorexia nervosa: Are they similar? *Eat. Disord.: J. Treat. Prev., 7*(3), 181–190.

Thompson, R. A., & Sherman, R. T. (2005). The last word: Athletes, eating disorders, and the four-minute mile. *Eat. Disord.: J. Treat. Prev., 13*(3), 321–324.

Thompson, R. F. (2000). *The brain: A neuroscience primer.* New York: Worth.

Thompson-Brenner, H., & Westen, D. (2005). Personality subtypes in eating disorders: Validation of a classification in a naturalistic sample. *Brit. J. Psychiat., 186*(6), 516–524.

Thoresen, C. E., & Plante, T. G. (2005). Spirituality, religion, and health: What we know and what should you know? *Clinician's Res. Dig., Suppl. Bull. 32,* 1–2.

Thorn, B. E., Shealy, R. C., & Briggs, S. D. (1993). Sexual misconduct in psychotherapy: Reactions to a consumer-oriented brochure. *Profess. Psychol.: Res. Pract., 24*(1), 75–82.

Tierney, A. J. (2000). Egas Moniz and the origins of psychosurgery: A review commemorating the 50th anniversary of Moniz's Nobel Prize. *J. Hist. Neurosci., 9*(1), 22–36.

Tiggeman, M., & Wilson-Barrett, E. (1998). Children's figure ratings: Relationship to self-esteem and negative stereotyping. *Inter. J. Eat. Disorders, 23,* 83–88.

Time Poll. (2002). Kid poll: Young people's views on 9/11 anniversary conducted by *Nickelodeon* and *Time.*

Time. (1983, September 5). Child abuse: The ultimate betrayal (written by Ed Magnuson). *Time.*

Time. (1998, October 12). Numbers. *Time.*

Time/CNN Poll. (1998). From what sources do teenagers today mainly learn about sex? In R. Stodghill, II. (1999, March 12). Where'd you learn that? *Time, 151*(23).

Timko, C., Moos, R. H., Finney, J. W., & Lesar, M. D. (2000). Long-term outcomes of alcohol use disorders: Comparing untreated individuals with those in Alcoholics Anonymous and formal treatment. *J. Stud. Alc., 61*(4), 529–540.

Tobin, D. L. (2000). *Coping strategies therapy for bulimia nervosa.* Washington, DC: American Psychological Association.

Tolan, P., Gorman-Smith, D., & Henry, D. (2006). Family violence. *Annu. Rev. Psychol., 57,* 557–583.

Tolbert, H. A. (1996). Psychoses in children and adolescents: A review. *J. Clin. Psychiat., 57*(Suppl. 3), 4–8.

Tonigan, J. S. (2001). Benefits of Alcoholics Anonymous attendance: Replication of findings between clinical research sites in project MATCH. *Alcohol. Treat Q., 19*(1), 67–77.

Torgersen, S. (1983). Genetic factors in anxiety disorders. *Arch. Gen. Psychiat., 40,* 1085–1089.

Torgersen, S. (1983). Genetics of neurosis: The effects of sampling variation upon the twin concordance ratio. *Brit. J. Psychiat., 142,* 126–132.

Torgersen, S. (1984). Genetic and nosological aspects of schizotypal and borderline personality disorders: A twin study. *Arch. Gen. Psychiat., 41,* 546–554.

Torgersen, S. (1990). Comorbidity of major depression and anxiety disorders in twin pairs. *Amer. J. Psychiat., 147,* 1199–1202.

Torgersen, S. (2000). Genetics of patients with borderline personality disorder. *Psychiatr. Clin. N. Amer., 23*(1), 1–9.

Toro, J., Cervera, M., Feliu, M. H., Garriga, N., Jou, M., Martinez, E., & Toro, E. (2003). Cue exposure in the treatment of resistant bulimia nervosa. *Inter. J. Eat. Disorders, 34*(2), 227–234.

Toro, J., Gila, A., Castro, J., Pombo, C., & Guete, O. (2005). Body image, risk factors for eating disorders and sociocultural influences in Spanish adolescents. *Eat. Weight Disord., 10*(2), 91–97.

Torrey, E. F. (1991). A viral-anatomical explanation of schizophrenia. *Schizo. Bull., 17*(1), 15–18.

Torrey, E. F. (1997). *Out of the shadows: Confronting America's mental illness crisis.* New York: Wiley.

Torrey, E. F. (1999, April 16). Interviewed in J. Lang, Local jails dumping grounds for mentally ill: 700,000 acutely ill held yearly. *Detroit News.*

Torrey, E. F. (2001). *Surviving schizophrenia: A manual for families, consumers, and providers* (4th ed.). New York: HarperCollins.

Torrey, E. F. (2002). Studies of individuals with schizophrenia never treated with antipsychotic medications: A review. *Schizo. Res., 58*(2–3), 101–115.

Torrey, E. F. (2004). PORT updated treatment recommendations. *Schizo. Bull., 30*(3), 617–618.

Torrey, E. F., Bowler, A. E., Taylor, E. H., & Gottesman, I. I. (1994). *Schizophrenia and manic-depressive disorder.* New York: Basic Books.

Tousignant, M., Mishara, B. L., Caillaud, A., Fortin, V., & St. Laurent, D. (2005). The impact of media coverage of the suicide of a well-known Quebec reporter: The case of Gaetan Girouard. *Soc. Sci. Med., 60*(9), 1919–1926.

Tractenberg, R. E., Singer, C. M., & Kaye, J. A. (2005). Symptoms of sleep disturbance in persons with Alzheimer's disease and normal elderly. *J. Sleep Res., 14*(2), 177–185.

Treaster, J. B. (1992, September 20). After hurricane, Floridians show symptoms seen in war. *New York Times.*

Treasure, J., & Szmukler, G. I. (1995). Medical complications of chronic anorexia nervosa. In G. I. Szmukler, C. Dare, & J. Treasure (Eds.), *Handbook on eating disorders: Theory, treatment and research.* Chichester, England: Wiley.

Treasure, J., Todd, G., & Szmukler, G. (1995). The inpatient treatment of anorexia nervosa. In G. Szmukler, C. Dare, & J. Treasure (Eds.), *Handbook of eating disorders: Theory, treatment and research.* Chichester, England: Wiley.

Treffert, D. A. (1999). Pervasive developmental disorders. In S. D. Netherton, D. Holmes, & C. E. Walker (Eds.), *Child and adolescent psychological disorders: A comprehensive textbook.* New York: Oxford University Press.

Trierweiler, S. J., Neighbors, H. W., Munday, C., Thompson, S. E., Binion, V. J., & Gomez, J. P. (2000). Clinician attribution associated with diagnosis of schizophrenia in African American and non-African American patients. *J. Cons. Clin. Psychol., 68,* 171–175.

Troiano, R. P., Frongillo, E. A., Sobal, J., & Levitsky, D. A. (1996). The relationship between body weight and mortality: A quantitative analysis of combined information from existing studies. *Inter. J. Obesity, 20,* 63–75.

Trotter, R. J. (1985, November). Geschwind's syndrome: Van Gogh's malady. *Psychol. Today,* p. 46.

True, W. R., & Lyons, M. J. (1999). Genetic risk factors for PTSD: A twin study. In R. Yehuda (Ed.), *Risk factors for posttraumatic stress disorder.* Washington, DC: American Psychiatric Press.

True, W., Rice, L., Eisen, S. A., et al. (1993). A twin study of genetic and environmental contributions to the liability for posttraumatic stress symptoms. *Arch. Gen. Psychiatry, 50,* 257–264.

Trull, T. J., & Durrett, C. A. (2005). Categorical and dimensional models of personality disorder. *Annu. Rev. Clin. Psychol., 1*(1), 355–380.

Trull, T. J., Stepp, S. D., & Durrett, C. A. (2003). Research on borderline personality disorder: An update. *Curr. Opin. Psychiat., 16*(1), 77–82.

Trumbetta, S. L., & Mueser, K. T. (2001). Social functioning and its relationship to cognitive deficits over the course of schizophrenia. In R. S. E. Keefe & J. P. McEvoy (Eds.), *Negative symptom and cognitive deficit treatment response in schizophrenia* (pp. 33–67). Washington, DC: American Psychiatric Press.

Tryon, G. (1987). Abuse of therapist by patient. *Profess. Psychologist, 17, 357–363.*

Tryon, W. W. (2005). Possible mechanisms for why desensitization and exposure therapy work. *Clin. Psychol. Rev., 25*(1), 67–95.

Tsai, J. L., & Chentsova-Dutton, Y. (2002). Understanding depression across cultures. In I. H. Gotlib & C. L. Hammen (Eds.), *Handbook of depression* (pp. 467–491). New York: Guilford Press.

Tsai, J. L., Ying, Y. W., & Lee, P. A. (2001). Cultural predictors of self-esteem: A study of Chinese American female and male young adults. *Cult. Div. Ethnic Minority Psychol., 7,* 284–297.

Tsuang, M. T., Bar, J. L., Harley, R. M., & Lyons, M. J. (2001). The Harvard twin study of substance abuse: What we have learned. *Harv. Rev. Psychiat., 9*(6), 267–279.

Tsuchiya, K. J., Agerbo, E., & Mortensen, P. B. (2005). Parental death and bipolar disorder: A robust association was found in early maternal suicide. *J. Affect. Disorders, 86*(2–3), 151–159.

Turk, C. L., Heimberg, R. G., & Hope, D. A. (2001). Social anxiety disorder. In D. H. Barlow (Ed.), *Clinical handbook of psychological disorders: A step-by-step treatment manual* (3rd ed.). New York: Guilford Press.

Turk, C. L., Heimberg, R. G., Luterek, J. A., Mennin, D. S., & Fresco, D. M. (2005). Emotion dysregulation in generalized anxiety disorder: A comparison with social anxiety disorder. *Cog. Ther. Res., 29*(1), 89–106.

Turkat, I. D., Keane, S. P., & Thompson-Pope, S. K. (1990). Social processing errors among paranoid personalities. *J. Psychopathol. Behav. Assess., 12*(3), 263–269.

Turkington, C., & Harris, J. R. (2001). *The encyclopedia of memory and memory disorders* (2nd ed.). New York: Facts on File.

Turkington, D., Grant, J. B. F., Ferrier, I. N., Rao, N. S. K., Linsley, K. R., & Young, A. H. (2002). A randomized controlled trial of fluvoxamine in prostatodynia, a male somatoform pain disorder. *J. Clin. Psychiat., 63*(9), 778–781.

Turner, J., Batik, M., Palmer, L. J., Forbes, D., & McDermott, B. M. (2000). Detection and importance of laxative use in adolescents with anorexia nervosa. *J. Amer. Acad. Child Adol. Psychiat., 39*(3), 378–385.

Turner, S. M., Beidel, D. C., Dancu, C. V., & Keys, D. J. (1986). Psychopathology of social phobia and comparison to avoidant personality disorder. *J. Abnorm. Psychol., 95*(4), 389–394.

Turner, S. M., Beidel, D. C., & Frueh, B. C. (2005). Multicomponent behavioral treatment of chronic combat-related posttraumatic stress disorder: Trauma management therapy. *Behav. Mod., 29*(1), 39–69.

Turton, M. D., O'Shea, D., Gunn, I., Beak, S. A., et al. (1996, January 4). A role for glucagon-like peptide-1 in the central regulation of feeding. *Nature, 379,* 69–72.

Turvey, B. E., & McGrath, M. (2006). Criminal profilers and the media: Profiling the Beltway snipers. In W. Petherick (Ed.), *Serial crime: Theoretical and practical issues in behavioral profiling.* San Diego, CA: Elsevier.

Twain, M. (1884). *The adventures of Huckleberry Finn.*

Twamley, E. W., Padin, D. S., Damaris, S., Bayne, K. S., Narvaez, J. M., Williams, R. E., et al. (2005). Work rehabilitation for middle-aged and older people with schizophrenia: A compari-

son of three approaches. *J. Nerv. Ment. Dis., 193*(9), 596–602.

Tyre, P. (2004, November 8). Viagra for women? *Newsweek, 144*(19), p. 12.

Tyre, P. (2005, December 5). Fighting anorexia: No one to blame. *Newsweek, 146*(23), 50–59.

Tyrer, P., & Simmons, S. (2003). Treatment models for those with severe mental illness and comorbid personality disorder. *Brit. J. Psychiat., 182*(Suppl. 44), s15–s18.

Tyrer, P., & Steinberg, D. (2005). *Models for mental disorder: Conceptual models in psychiatry.* Chichester, England: John Wiley.

U.S. Census Bureau. (1990). *Statistical abstract of the United States.* Washington, DC: U.S. Government Printing Office.

U.S. Census Bureau. (2000). *Statistical abstract of the United States.* Washington, DC: U.S. Government Printing Office.

U.S. Department of Justice. (1994). *Violence between inmates: Domestic violence.* Annapolis Junction, MD: Bureau of Justice Statistics Clearinghouse.

U.S. Department of Justice. (2000). Report. Washington, DC: Author.

U.S. Department of Labor. (2002). Counselors. In Bureau of Labor Statistics, *Occupational outlook handbook* (2004–05 ed.). Washington, DC: Author.

U.S. Department of Labor. (2002). Social workers. In Bureau of Labor Statistics, *Occupational outlook handbook* (2004–05 ed.). Washington, DC: Author.

Uchoa, D. D. (1985). Narcissistic transference? *Rev. Bras. Psicanal., 19*(1), 87–96.

Ueda, K., & Matsumoto, Y. (2003). National strategy for suicide prevention in Japan. *Lancet, 361*(9360), 882.

Uher, R., & Treasure, J. (2005). Brain lesions and eating disorders. *J. Neurol, Neurosurg, Psychiat., 76*(6), 852–857.

Ullmann, L. P., & Krasner, L. (1975). *A psychological approach to abnormal behavior* (2nd ed.). Englewood Cliffs, NJ: Prentice Hall.

Ulrich, R. S. (1984). View from a window may influence recovery from surgery. *Science, 224,* 420–421.

Underwood, M. K. (2003). *Social aggression among girls.* New York: Guilford Press.

UNINCB (United Nations International Narcotics Control Board) Report. (1996). Cited in J. Roberts, Behavioral disorders are overdiagnosed in U.S. *Brit. Med. J., 312,* 657.

Urcuyo, K. R., Boyers, A. E., Carver, C. S., & Antoni, M. H. (2005). Finding benefit in breast cancer: Relations with personality, coping, and concurrent well-being. *Psychol. Hlth., 20*(2), 175–192.

Uretsky, S. (1999, June 28). Mate in two: Ideas of perfection vary. *HealthScout.*

Ursano, R. J., Boydstun, J. A., & Wheatley, R. D. (1981). Psychiatric illness in U.S. Air Force Vietnam prisoners of war: A five-year follow-up. *Amer. J. Psychiat., 138*(3), 310–314.

Ursano, R. J., Fullerton, C. S., Epstein, R. S., Crowley, B., Kao, T. C., Vance, K., et al. (1999). Acute and chronic posttraumatic stress disorder in motor vehicle accident victims. *Amer. J. Psychiat., 156*(4), 589–595.

Ursano, R. J., McCarroll, J. E., & Fullerton, C. S. (2003). Traumatic death in terrorism and

disasters: The effects of posttraumatic stress and behavior. In R. J. Ursano, C. S. Fullerton, & A. E. Norwood (Eds.), *Terrorism and disaster: Individual and community mental health interventions* (pp. 308–332). New York: Cambridge University Press.

Usall, J., Haro, J. M., Ochoa, S., Marquez, M., & Araya, S. (2002). Influence of gender on social outcome in schizophrenia. *Acta Psychiatr. Scandin., 106*(5), 337–342.

UTMB (University of Texas Medical Branch at Galveston). (1999, May 14). Mania drugs cut hospitalization costs. Study presented at meeting of American Psychiatric Association, May 17, 1999.

Utsey, S. O., Payne, Y. A., Jackson, E. S., & Jones, A. M. (2002). Race-related stress, quality of life indicators, and life satisfaction among elderly African Americans. *Cult. Div. Ethnic Minority Psychol., 8*(3), 224–233.

Vaillant, G. E. (1993). *The wisdom of the ego.* Cambridge, MA: Harvard University Press.

Vaillant, G. E., & Milofsky, E. S. (1982). Natural history of male alcoholism: IV. Paths to recovery. *Arch. Gen. Psychiat., 39,* 127–133.

Vakili, A., Tayebi, K., Jafari, M. R., Zarrindast, M. R., & Djahanguiri, B. (2004). Effect of ethanol on morphine state-dependent learning in the mouse: Involvement of GABAergic, opioidergic and cholinergic systems. *Alcohol Alcoholism, 39*(5), 427–432.

Valbak, K. (2001). Good outcome for bulimic patients in long-term group analysis: A single-group study. *Eur. Eat. Disord. Rev., 9*(1), 19–32.

Valdisseri, E. V., Carroll, K. R., & Hartl, A. J. (1986). A study of offenses committed by psychotic inmates in a county jail. *Hosp. Comm. Psychiat., 37,* 163–165.

Valenstein, E. S. (1986). *Great and desperate cures.* New York: Basic Books.

Valenti-Hein, D. C., Yarnold, P. R., & Mueser, K. T. (1994). Evaluation of the dating skills program for improving heterosocial interactions in people with mental retardation. *Behav. Mod., 18*(1), 32–46.

Van Bourgondien, M. E., & Schopler, E. (1990). Critical issues in the residential care of people with autism. *J. Autism Dev. Disorders, 20*(3), 391–399.

Van de Castle, R. (1993). Content of dreams. In M. A. Carskadon (Ed.), *Encyclopedia of sleep and dreams.* New York: Macmillan.

van der Flier, W. M., van der Vlies, A. E., Weverling-Rijnsburger, A. W. E., de Boer, N. L., Admiraal-Behloul, F., Bollen, E. L. E. M., et al. (2005). MRI measures and progression of cognitive decline in nondemented elderly attending a memory clinic. *Inter. J. Ger. Psychiat., 20*(11), 1060–1066.

van der Hart, O., Bolt, H., & van der Kolk B. A. (2005). Memory fragmentation in dissociative identity disorder. *J. Trauma Dissoc., 6*(1), 55–70.

van Egmond, J. J. (2003). The multiple meanings of secondary gain. *Amer. J. Psychoanal., 63*(2), 137–147.

van Emmerik, A. A., Kamphuis, J. H., Hulsbosch, A. M., & Emmelkamp, P. M. (2002). Single session debriefing after psychological trauma: A meta-analysis. *Lancet, 360* (9335), 766–771.

van Hout, W. J. P. J., & Emmelkamp, P. M. G. (2002). Exposure in vivo therapy in anxiety disorders: Procedure and efficacy. *Gedragstherapie, 35*(1), 7–23.

van Os, J., Fañanas, L., Cannon, M., Macdonald, A., & Murray, R. (1997). Dermatoglyphic abnormalities in psychosis: A twin study. *Biol. Psychiat., 41,* 624–626.

Van Praag, H. M. (1983). CSF 5–HIAA and suicide in non-depressed schizophrenics. *Lancet, 2,* 977–978.

Van Rossen & Associates (2002). Modeling advice. Retrieved January 2006 from www.modelingadvice.com

Van Wallendael, L., & Cutler, B. (2004). Limitations to empirical approaches to jury selection. *J. Forens. Psychol. Pract., 4*(2), 79–86.

van Walsum, K. L. (2004). Nos Malades: Three examples of Christian influences in care for the insane in pre-revolutionary France and Belgium. *J. Psychol. Christianity 23*(3), 219–233.

VandeCreek, L. (Ed.). *Innovations in clinical practice: Focus on adults.* Sarasota, FL: Professional Resource Press.

Vasey, M. W. (1993). Development and cognition in childhood anxiety: The example of worry. In T. H. Ollendick & R. J. Prinz (Eds.), *Advances in clinical child psychology* (vol. 15, pp. 1–39). New York: Plenum Press.

Vatz, R., & Weinberg, L. (1993, January 10). Keno krazy? *Washington Post,* p. C5.

Veale, D. (2004). Body dysmorphic disorder. *Postgrad. Med. J., 80,* 67–71.

Venditti, E., Wing, R., Jakicic, J., Butler, B., & Marcus, M. (1996). Weight cycling, psychological health, and binge eating in obese women. *J. Cons. Clin. Psychol., 64*(2), 400–405.

Venneri, A., Bartolo, A., McCrimmon, S., & St. Clair, D. (2002). Memory and dating of past events in schizophrenia. *J. Inter. Neuropsychol. Soc., 8*(6), 861–866.

Verfaellie, M., Cermak, L. S., Blackford, S. P., et al. (1990). Strategic and automatic priming of semantic memory in alcoholic Korsakoff patients. *Brain Cognit., 13*(2), 178–192.

Vernberg, E. M., La Greca, A. M., Silverman, W. K., & Prinstein, M. J. (1996). Prediction of posttraumatic stress symptoms in children after Hurricane Andrew. *J. Abnorm. Psychol., 105*(2), 237–248.

Vicary, J. R., & Karshin, C. M. (2002). College alcohol abuse: A review of the problems, issues, and prevention approaches. *J. Primary Prev., 22*(3), 299–331.

Vidovic, V., Juresa, V., Begovac, I., Mahnik, M., & Tocilj, G. (2005). Perceived family cohesion, adaptability and communication in eating disorders. *Eur. Eat. Disord. Rev., 13*(1), 19–28.

Vieta, E. (2005). The package of care for patients with bipolar depression. *J. Clin. Psychiat., 66*(Suppl. 5), 34–39.

Viney, W. (2000). Dix, Dorothea Lynde. In A. E. Kazdin (Ed.), *Encyclopedia of psychology* (Vol. 3, pp. 65–66). Washington, DC: Oxford University Press/American Psychological Association.

Vink, T., Hinney, A., van Elburg, A. A., van Goozen, S. H. M., Sandkuijl, L. A., Sinke, R. J., et al. (2001). Association between an agouti-related protein gene polymorphism and anorexia nervosa. *Mol. Psychiat., 6*(3), 325–328.

Vinogradov, S., Cox, P. D., & Yalom, I. D. (2003). Group therapy. In S. C. Yudofsky & R. E. Hales (Eds.), *The American Psychiatric Publishing textbook of clinical psychiatry.* New York: Wiley.

Visser, M. (2003). Gregory Bateson on deuterolearning and double bind: A brief conceptual history. *J. Hist. Behav. Sci., 39*(3), 269–278.

Vitaliano, P. P., Persson, R., Kiyak, A., Saini, H., & Echeverria, D. (2005). Caregiving and gingival symptom reports: Psychophysiologic mediators. *Psychosom. Med., 67*(6), 930–938.

Volkmar, F. R. (2001). Pharmacological interventions in autism: Theoretical and practical issues. *J. Clin. Child Psychol., 30*(1), 80–87.

Volkow, N. D., Fowler, J. S., & Wang, G. J. (2004). The addicted human brain viewed in the light of imaging studies: Brain circuits and treatment strategies. *Neuropharmacology, 47*(Suppl. 1), 3–13.

Volkow, N. D., Fowler, J. S., Wang., G. J., & Swanson, J. M. (2004). Dopamine in drug abuse and addiction: Results from imaging studies and treatment implications. *Mol. Psychiat., 9*(6), 557–569.

Volkow, N. D., Gillespie, H., Tancredi, L., & Hollister, L. (1995). The effects of marijuana in the human brain measured with regional brain glucose metabolism. In A. Biegon & N. D. Volkow (Eds.), *Sites of drug action in the human brain.* Boca Raton, FL: CRC Press.

Volkow, N. D., Wang, G. J., Fowler, J. S., Logan, J., Gatley, S. J., Wong, C., et al. (1999). Reinforcing effects of psychostimulants in humans are associated with increases in brain dopamine and occupancy of D$_2$ receptors. *J. Pharmacol. Exp. Ther., 291*(1), 409–415.

Von Burg, M., & Hibbard, R. (1995). Munchausen syndrome by proxy: A different kind of child abuse. *Indiana Med., 88*(5), 378–382.

Vonnegut, M. (1974, April). Why I want to bite R. D. Laing. *Harper's, 248*(1478), 80–92.

Vrij, A. (2004). The polygraph and lie detection. *Howard J. Criminal Justice, 43*(1), 108–110.

Wagenaar, A. C., Murray, D. M., & Toomey, T. L. (2000). Communities mobilizing for change on alcohol (CMCA): Effects of a randomized trial on arrests and traffic crashes. *Addiction, 95*(2), 209–217.

Wagstaff, G. F., MacVeigh, J., Boston, R., Scott, L., Brunas-Wagstaff, J., & Cole, J. (2003). Can laboratory findings on eyewitness testimony be generalized to the real world? An archival analysis of the influence of violence, weapon presence, and age on eyewitness accuracy. *J. Psychol.: Interdisc. Appl., 137*(1), 17–28.

Walcott, D. D., Pratt, H. D., & Patel, D. R. (2003). Adolescents and eating disorders: Gender, racial, ethnic, sociocultural and socioeconomic issues. *J. Adol. Res., 18*(3), 223–243.

Walji, M., Sagaram, S., Sagaram, D., Meric-Bernstam, F., Johnson, C., Mirza, N. Q., & Bernstam, E. V. (2004). Efficacy of quality criteria to identify potentially harmful information: A cross-sectional survey of complementary and alternative medicine Web sites. *J. Med. Internet Res., 6*(2), [np].

Walker, C. E. (2003). Elimination disorders: Enuresis and encopresis. In M. C. Roberts (Ed.), *Handbook of pediatric psychology* (3rd ed., pp. 544–560). New York: Guilford Press.

Wall, T. L., Shea, S. H., Chan, K. K., & Carr, L. G. (2001). A genetic association with the development of alcohol and other substance use behavior in Asian Americans. *J. Abnorm. Psychol., 110*(1), 173–178.

Wallace, C., Mullen, P. E., & Burgess, P. (2004). Criminal offending in schizophrenia over a 25-year period marked by disinstitutionalization and increasing prevalence of comorbid substance use disorders. *Amer. J. Psychiat., 161*(4), 716–727.

Wallace, M. (2002). Nash: Film no whitewash. *60 Minutes* interview, March 17, 2002.

Wallace, M., & Rabin, A. I. (1960). Temporal experience. *Psychol. Bull., 57*(3), 213–236.

Wallace, S. E. (1981). The right to live and the right to die. In S. E. Wallace & A. Eser (Eds.), *Suicide and euthanasia: The rights of personhood.* Knoxville: University of Tennessee Press.

Wallace, T. L., Stellitano, K. E., Neve, R. L., & Duman, R. S. (2004). Effects of cyclic adenosine monophosphate response element binding protein overexpression in the basolateral amygdala on behavioral models of depression and anxiety. *Biol. Psychiat., 56*(3), 151–160.

Wallis, C. (2005). The new science of happiness. *Time, 165*(3), January 17, 2005, A2–A9.

Wallis, C. (2005, February 28). The right (and wrong) way to treat pain. *Time, 165*(9), 46–57.

Walsh, E., Buckanan, A., & Fahy, T. (2002). Violence and schizophrenia: Examining the evidence. *Brit. J. Psychiat., 180*(6), 490–495.

Walsh, E., Moran, P., Scott, C., McKenzie, K., Burns, T., Creed, F., Tyrer, P., Murray, R. M., & Fahy, T. (2003). Prevalence of violent victimisation in severe mental illness. *Brit. J. Psychiat., 183*(3), 233–238.

Walsh, R. A., & McElwain, B. (2002). Existential psychotherapies. In D. J. Cain & J. Seeman (Eds.), *Humanistic psychotherapies: Handbook of research and practice* (pp. 253–278). Washington, DC: American Psychological Association.

Walters, E. E., & Kendler, K. S. (1995). Anorexia nervosa and anorexia-like syndromes in a population based female twin sample. *Amer. J. Psychiat., 152,* 64–71.

Walters, G. D. (2000). Behavioral self-control training for problem drinkers: A metal-analysis of randomized control studies. *Behav. Ther., 31*(1), 135–149.

Walters, G. D. (2002). The heritability of alcohol abuse and dependence: A meta-analysis of behavior genetic research. *Amer. J. Drug Alc. Abuse, 28*(3), 557–584.

Wampold, B. E. (2006). Designing a research study. In F. T. Leong & J. T. Austin, *The psychology research handbook, a guide for graduate students and research assistants* (2nd ed., pp. 93–103). Thousand Oaks, CA: Sage.

Wanck, B. (1984). Two decades of involuntary hospitalization legislation. *Amer. J. Psychiat., 41,* 33–38.

Wang Ping. (2000). *Aching for beauty: Footbinding in China.* Minneapolis, MN: University of Minnesota Press.

Wang, H. Y., Markowitz, P., Levinson, D., Undie, A. S., & Friedman, E. (1999). Increased membrane-associated protein kinase C activity and translocation in blood platelets from bipolar affective disorder patients. *J. Psychiatr. Res., 33*(2), 171–179.

Wang, P. S., Berglund, P., Olfson, M., Pincus, H. A., Wells, K. B., & Kessler, R. C. (2005). Failure and delay in initial treatment contact after first onset of mental disorders in the National Comorbidity Survey Replication. *Arch. Gen. Psychiat., 62,* 603–613.

Wang, P. S., Demler, O., & Kessler, R. C. (2002). Adequacy of treatment for serious mental illness in the United States. *Amer. J. Pub. Hlth., 92*(1), 92–98.

Wang, P. S., Lane, M., Olfson, M., Pincus, H. A., Wells, K. B., & Kessler, R. C. (2005). Twelve-month use of mental health services in the United States. *Arch. Gen. Psychiat., 62,* 629–640.

Waraich, P., Goldner, E. M., Somers, J. M., & Hsu, L. (2004). Prevalence and incidence studies of mood disorders: A systematic review of the literature. *Canad. J. Psychiat., 49*(2), 124–138.

Waring, M., & Ricks, D. (1965). Family patterns of children who become adult schizophrenics. *J. Nerv. Ment. Dis., 140*(5), 351–364.

Warner, J. (2004, June 25). Alien abduction tales offer clues on memory: Study: Distress doesn't necessarily validate traumatic memories. *WebMD Health,* June 25, 2004.

Warner, R. (1985). *Recovery from schizophrenia: Psychiatry and political economy.* London: Routledge & Kegan Paul.

Warnock, J. K., Bundren, J. C., & Morris, D. W. (1999). Female hypoactive sexual disorder: Case studies of physiologic androgen replacement. *J. Sex Marital Ther., 25*(3), 175–182.

Warren, R. (1997). REBT and generalized anxiety disorder. In J. Yankura, & W. Dryden (Eds.), *Using REBT with common psychological problems: A therapist's casebook.* New York: Springer.

Waschbusch, D. A. (2002). A meta-analytic examination of comorbid hyperactive-impulsive-attention problems and conduct problems. *Psychol. Bull., 128,* 118–150.

Washington, G., & Teague, K. (2005). Young African-American male suicide prevention and spirituality. *Stress, Trauma, & Crisis, 8*(2–3), 93–105.

Wasserman, I. M., & Stack, S. (2000). The relationship between occupation and suicide among African American males: Ohio, 1989–1991. In R. W. Maris, S. S. Canetto, J. L. McIntosh, & M. M. Silverman (Eds.), *Review of suicidology, 2000.* New York: Guilford Press.

Waterhouse, J. M., & DeCoursey, P. J. (2004). The relevance of circadian rhythms for human welfare. In J. C. Dunlap, J. L. Loros, & P. J. Decoursey (Eds.), *Chronobiology: Biological timekeeping* (pp. 325–356). Sunderland, MA: Sinauer Associates.

Waters, A. M., & Craske, M. G. (2005). Generalized anxiety disorder. In M. M. Antony, D. R. Ledley, & R. G. Heimberg (Eds.), *Improving outcomes and preventing relapse in cognitive-behavioral therapy* (pp. 77–126). New York: Guilford Press

Watson, J. B. (1930). *Behaviorism* (Rev. ed.). Chicago: University of Chicago Press.

Watson, J. B., & Rayner, R. (1920). Conditioned emotional reaction. *J. Exp. Psychol., 3,* 1–14.

Watson, P. J., & Shalev, A. Y. (2005). Assessment and treatment of adult acute responses to traumatic stress following mass traumatic events. *CNS Spectrums, 10*(2), 123–131.

Watson, S. J., Benson, J. A., Jr., & Joy, J. E. (2000). Marijuana and medicine: Assessing the science base: A summary of the 1999 Institute of Medicine Report. *Arch. Gen. Psychiat., 57*(6), 547–552.

Watt, T. T. (2002). Marital and cohabiting relationships of adult children of alcoholics: Evidence from the National Survey of Family and Households. *J. Fam. Issues, 23*(2), 246–265.

Watts, S., Noble, S., Smith, P., & Disco, M. (2002). First-line pharmacotherapy for tobacco use and dependence. *J. Amer. Board Fam. Pract., 15,* 489–497.

Waxweiler, R. J., Thurman, D., Sniezek, J., Sosin, D., & O'Neil, J. (1995). Monitoring the impact of traumatic brain injury: A review and update. *J. Neurotrauma, 12*(4), 509–516.

Way, B. B., Miraglia, R., Sawyer, D. A. Beer, R., & Eddy, J. (2005). Factors related to suicide in New York state prisons. *Inter. J. Law Psychiat., 28*(3), 207–221.

Way, B. M., Miraglia, R., Sawyer, D. A., Beer, R., & Eddy, J. (2005). Factors related to suicide in New York State prisons. *Inter. J. Law Psychiat., 28*(3), 207–221.

Webster, T. L. (2005). Adaptation processes for elderly care recipients and their caregivers in the context of a medicalized home environment. *Diss. Abstr. Inter. Sect. A: Human Soc. Sci., 65*(8-A), 3116.

Webster-Stratton, C. (2005). Early intervention with videotype modeling: Programs for families of children with oppositional defiant disorder or conduct disorder. In E. D. Hibbs & P. S. Jensen (Eds.), *Psychosocial treatments for child and adolescent disorders: Empirically based strategies for clinical practice* (2nd ed., pp. 507–55). Washington, DC: American Psychological Association.

Wechsler, H., Davenport, A., Dowdall, G., Moeykens, B., & Castillo, S. (1994). Health and behavioral consequences of binge drinking in college. *JAMA, 272*(21), 1672–1677.

Wechsler, H., Dowdell, G. W., Davenport, A., & Castillo, S. (1995). Correlates of college student binge drinking. *Amer. J. Pub. Hlth., 85*(7), 921–926.

Wechsler, H., et al. (1997). *Survey on college binge drinking.* Reported by Harvard University School of Public Health, Cambridge, MA.

Wechsler, H., Lee, J. E., Kuo, M., & Lee, H. (2000). College binge drinking in the 1990s: A continuing problem: Results of the Harvard School of Public Health 1999 College Alcohol Study. *J. Amer. Coll. Hlth., 48*(5), 199–210.

Wechsler, H., Lee, J. E., Kuo, M., Seibring, M., Nelson, T. F., & Lee, H. (2002). Trends in alcohol use, related problems and experience of prevention efforts among US college students 1993 to 2001: Results from the 2001 Harvard School of Public Health college alcohol study. *J. Amer. Coll. Hlth., 50,* 203–217.

Wechsler, H., Seibring, M., Liu, I. C., & Ahl, M. (2004). Colleges respond to student binge drinking: Reducing student demand or limiting access. *J. Amer. Coll. Hlth., 52*(4), 159–168.

Wechsler, H., & Wuethrich, B. (2002). *Dying to drink: Confronting binge drinking on college campuses.* Emmaus, PA: Rodale Press.

Weeks, D., & James, J. (1995). *Eccentrics: A study of sanity and strangeness.* New York: Villard.

Wegner, J. T., & Wegner, A. Z. (2001). Cognitive-behavioral therapy and other short-term approaches in the treatment of eating disorders. In B. P. Kinoy (Ed.), *Eating disorders: New directions in treatment and recovery* (2nd ed., pp. 112–126). New York: Columbia University Press.

Weiden, P. J., & Kane, J. M. (Eds.). (2005). Optimizing pharmacotherapy to maximize outcome in schizophrenia: What is effectiveness with antipsychotic medications? *J. Clin. Psychiat., 66*(1), 122–128.

Weil, M. (2005, January 8). Rosemary Kennedy, 86: President's disabled sister. *Washington Post,* p. B06.

Weinberg, M. K., Tronick, E. Z., Beeghly, M., Olson, K. L., Kernan, H., & Riley, J. M. (2001). Subsyndromal depressive symptoms and major depression in postpartum women. *Amer. J. Orthopsychiat., 71*(1), 87–97.

Weiner, H. (1977). *Psychobiology and human disease.* New York: Elsevier.

Weiner, I. B. (2000). Making Rorschach interpretation as good as it can be. *J. Pers. Assess., 74*(2), 164–174.

Weiner, I. B. (2004). Rorschach Inkblot Method. In M. E. Maruish (Ed.), *The use of psychological testing for treatment planning and outcomes assessment: Volume 3: Instruments for adults* (3rd ed., pp. 553–587). Mahwah, NJ: Lawrence Erlbaum Associates.

Weingarten, S. M., & Cummings, J. L. (2001). Psychosurgery of frontal-subcortical circuits. In D. G. Lichter & J. L. Cummings (Eds.), *Frontal-subcortical circuits in psychiatric and neurological disorders* (pp. 421–435). New York: Guilford Press.

Weishaar, M. E. (2000). Cognitive risk factors in suicide. In R. W. Maris, S. S. Canetto, J. L. McIntosh, & M. M. Silverman (Eds.), *Review of suicidology, 2000.* New York: Guilford Press.

Weisman, R. L. (Ed.) (2004). Introduction to the special section on integrating community mental health and the criminal justice systems for adults with severe mental illness: Bridges and barriers. *Psychiatr. Quart., 75*(2), 105–106.

Weisner, C. (2005). Substance misuse: What place for women-only treatment programs? *Soc. Study Addict., 100,* 7–8.

Weiss, B., & Garber, J. (2003). Developmental differences in the phenomenology of depression. *Dev. Psychopathol., 15,* 403–430.

Weiss, D. E. (1991). *The great divide.* New York: Poseidon Press/Simon & Schuster.

Weiss, D. S., Marmar, C. R., Schlenger, W. E., Fairbank, J. A., Jordan, B. K., Hough, R. L., et al. (1992). The prevalence of lifetime and partial posttraumatic stress disorder in Vietnam theater veterans. *J. Traum. Stress, 5*(3), 365–376.

Weiss, J., Diamond, T., Demark, J., & Lovald, B. (2003). Involvement in Special Olympics and its relations to self-concept and actual competency in participants with developmental disabilities. *Res. Dev. Disabil., 24,* 281–305.

Weiss, P. (2001). Psychological models of etiology of paraphilias. *Cesko. Psychol., 45*(3), 216–225.

Weiss, R. D., Griffin, M. L., Gallop, R. J., Najavits, L. M., Frank, A., Crits-Christoph, P., et al. (2005). The effect of 12-step self-help group attendance and participation on drug use outcomes among cocaine-dependent patients. *Drug Alc. Dep., 77*(2), 177–184.

Weissberg, R. P. (2000). Improving the lives of millions of school children. *Amer. Psychologist, 55,* 1360–1372.

Weissman, M. M. (2000). Social functioning and the treatment of depression. *J. Clin. Psychiat., 61*(Suppl.), 33–38.

Weissman, M. M., et al. (1992). The changing rate of major depression: Cross-national comparisons. Cross-national collaborative group. *JAMA, 268*(21), 3098–3105.

Weissman, M. M., Livingston Bruce, M., Leaf, P. J., Florio, L. P., & Holzer, C., III. (1991). Affective disorders. In L. N. Robins & D. A. Regier (Eds.), *Psychiatric disorders in America: The Epidemiologic Catchment Area Study.* New York: Free Press.

Weissman, M. M., & Markowitz, J. C. (2002). Interpersonal psychotherapy for depression. In I. H. Gotlib & C. L. Hammen (Eds.), *Handbook of depression* (pp. 404–421). New York: Guilford Press.

Weissman, S. W. (2000). America's psychiatric work force. *Psychiatr. Times, 17*(11).

Weisz, J. R., McCarty, C. A., & Valeri, S. M. (2006). Effects of psychotherapy for depression in children and adolescents: A meta-analysis. *Psychol. Bull., 132*(1), 132–149.

Weizhen, C., Panmin, Z., & Dongming, W. (2005). A comparative study of paroxetine and lorazepam in the treatment of generalized anxiety disorder. *Chinese Ment. Hlth. J., 18*(10), 740–741.

Welburn, K. R., Fraser, G. A., Jordan, S. A., Cameron, C., Webb, L. M., & Raine, D. (2003). Discriminating dissociative identity disorder from schizophrenia and feigned dissociation on psychological tests and structured interview. *J. Traum. Dissoc., 4*(2), 109–130.

Welch, S. S. (2001). A review of the literature on the epidemiology of parasuicide in the general population. *Psychiatr. Serv., 52*(3), 368–375.

Wells, A. (2005). The metacognitive model of GAD: Assessment of meta-worry and relationship with DSM-IV generalized anxiety disorder. *Cog. Ther. Res., 29*(1), 107–121.

Wells, A., & Carter, K. (1999). Preliminary tests of a cognitive model of generalised anxiety disorder. *Behav. Res. Ther., 37,* 585–594.

Wells, A., & Papageorgiou, C. (1998). Relationships between worry, obsessive-compulsive symptoms and meta-cognitive beliefs. *Behav Res Ther., 36,* 899–913.

Wells, D. L., Graham, L., & Hepper, P. G. (2002). The influence of auditory stimulation on the behaviour of dogs housed in a rescue shelter. *Animal Welfare, 11*(4), 385–393.

Wells, G. L., Small, M., Penrod, S., Malpass, R. S., Fulero, S. M., & Brimacombe, C. A. E. (1998). Eyewitness identification procedures: Recommendations for lineups and photospreads. *Law Human Behav., 22,* 603–647.

Wells, K. (2004). *Travels with barley,* New York: Free Press.

Wells, M. E., & Hinkle, J. S. (1990). Elimination of childhood encopresis: A family systems approach. *J. Ment. Hlth. Couns., 12*(4), 520–526.

Welsh, C. J., & Liberto, J. (2001). The use of medication for relapse prevention in substance dependence disorders. *J. Psychiatr. Prac., 7*(1), 15–31.

Wender, P. H., Kety, S. S., Rosenthal, D., Schulsinger, F., Ortmann, J., & Lunde, I. (1986). Psychiatric disorders in the biological and adoptive families of adopted individuals with affective disorders. *Arch. Gen. Psychiat., 43,* 923–929.

Wen-Hung, K., Gallo, J. J., & Eaton, W. W. (2004). Hopelessness, depression, substance disorder and suicidality: A 13-year community-based study. *Soc. Psychiat. Psychiatr. Epidemiol., 39*(6), 497–501.

Werth, J. (1995). Rational suicide reconsidered: AIDS as an impetus for change. Annual Conference of the Association for Death Education & Counseling. *Death Stud., 19*(1), 65–80.

Werth, J. (1996). *Rational suicide? Implications for mental health professionals.* Washington, DC: Taylor & Francis.

Werth, J. L. Jr. (Ed.). (1999). *Contemporary perspectives on rational suicide.* Philadelphia, PA: Brunner/Mazel.

Werth, J. L. Jr. (2000). Recent developments in the debate over physician-assisted death. In R. W. Maris, S. S. Canetto, J. L. McIntosh, & M. M. Silverman (Eds.), *Review of suicidology, 2000.* New York: Guilford Press.

Werth, J. L. Jr. (2004). The relationships among clinical depression, suicide, and other actions that may hasten death. *Behav. Sci. Law, 22*(5), 627–649.

Wertheimer, A. (2001). *A special scar: The experiences of people bereaved by suicide* (2nd ed.). East Sussex, England: Brunner-Routledge.

West, A. G. (2001). Current approaches to sex-offender risk assessment: A critical review. *Brit. J. Forensic Prac., 3*(3), 31–41.

Westcott, H. L., & Jones, D. P. H. (1999). Annotation: The abuse of disabled children. *J. Child Psychol. Psychiat., 40,* 497–506.

Westen, D., & Arkowitz-Westen, L. (1998). Limitations of axis II in diagnosing personality pathology in clinical practice. *Amer. J. Psychiatry, 155*(12), 1767–1771.

Westen, D., Dutra, L., & Shedler, J. (2005). Assessing adolescent personality pathology: Quantifying clinical judgment. *Brit. J. Psychiat., 186*(3), 227–238.

Westen, D., Feit, A., & Zittel, C. (1999). Focus chapter: Methodological issues in research using projective methods. In P. C. Kendall, J. N. Butcher, & G. N. Holmbeck (Eds.), *Handbook of research methods in clinical psychology* (2nd ed.). New York: Wiley.

Westen, D., & Muderrisoglu, S. (2006). Clinical assessment of pathological personality traits. *Amer. J. Psychiat.*

Westermeyer J. (1993). Substance use disorders among young minority refugees: Common themes in a clinical sample. *NIDA Res. Monogr. 130,* 308–320.

Westermeyer J. (2001). Alcoholism and co-morbid psychiatric disorders among American Indians. *Amer. Indian Alsk. Native Ment. Health Res. 10,* 27–51.

Westermeyer, J. (2004). Acculturation: Advances in theory, measurement, and applied research. *J. Nerv. Ment. Dis., 192*(5), 391–392.

Westermeyer, J., & Thuras, P. (2005). Association of antisocial personality disorder and substance disorder morbidity in a clinical sample. *Amer. J. Drug Alc. Abuse, 31*(1), 93–110.

Westheimer, R. K., & Lopater, S. (2002). *Human sexuality: A psychosocial perspective.* Baltimore: Lippincott Williams & Wilkins.

Westheimer, R. K., & Lopater, S. (2005). *Human sexuality: A psychosocial perspective* (2nd ed.). Baltimore, MD: Lippincott Williams & Wilkins.

Weston, S. C., & Siever, L. J. (1993, Spring). Biological correlates of personality disorders. *J. Pers. Disorders,* (Suppl.), pp. 129–148.

Wetchler, J. L. (2003). Structural family therapy. In J. L. Wetchler & L. L. Hecker (Eds.), *An introduction to marriage and family therapy.* Binghamton, NY: Haworth Clinical Practice Press.

Wetherell, J. L., & Gatz, M. (2001). Recruiting anxious older adults for a psychotherapy outcome study. *J. Clin. Geropsychol., 7*(1), 29–38.

Wetherell, J. L., Lang, A. J., & Stein, M. B. (2006). Anxiety disorders. In D. V. Jeste & J. H. Friedman (Eds.), *Psychiatry for neurologists* (pp. 43–58). Totowa, NJ: Humana Press.

Wetterberg, L. (1999). Melatonin and clinical application. *Reprod. Nutr. Dev., 39*(3), 367–382.

Wetterling, T. (2005). Somatic diseases in elderly patients with delirium. *Zeitschrift Gerontopsychol. Psychiat., 18*(1), 3–7.

Wettstein, R. M. (1988). Psychiatry and the law. In J. A. Talbott, R. E. Hales, & A. J. Frances (Eds.), *American Psychiatric Press textbook of psychiatry.* Washington, DC: American Psychiatric Press.

Wettstein, R. M. (1999). The right to refuse psychiatric treatment. *Psychiatr. Clin. N. Amer., 22*(1), 173–182.

Wetzel, R. D., & Murphy, G. E. (2005). Suicide. In E. H. Rubin & C. F. Zorumski (Eds.), *Adult psychiatry* (2nd ed., pp. 409–419). Oxford, England: Blackwell Publishing Ltd.

Weyandt, L. L. (2006). *The physiological basis of cognitive and behavioral disorders.* Mahwah, NJ: Lawrence Erlbaum Associates.

Whaley, A. L. (1998, January). Racism in the provision of mental health services: A social-cognitive analysis. *Amer. J. Orthopsychiat., 68*(1), 48–59.

Wheatley, D. (2004). Triple-blind, placebo-controlled trial of ginkgo biloba in sexual dysfunction due to antidepressant drugs. *Human Psychopharmacol. Clin. Exp., 19*(8), 545–548.

Whiffen, V. E., & Demidenko, N. (2006). Mood disturbance across the life span. In J. Worell & C. D. Goodheart (Eds.), *Handbook of girls' and women's psychological health* (pp. 51–59). New York: Oxford University Press.

Whisman, M. A. (2001). The association between depression and marital dissatisfaction. In S. R. H. Beach (Ed.), *Marital and family processes in depression: A scientific foundation for clinical practice* (pp. 3–24). Washington, DC: American Psychological Association.

Whisman, M. A., & McGarvey, A. L. (1995). Attachment, depressotypic cognitions, and dysphoria. *Cog. Ther. Res., 19*(6), 633–650.

Whitaker, R. (2002). *Mad in America: Bad science, bad medicine, and the enduring mistreatment of the mentally ill.* Cambridge, MA: Perseus.

Whitehead, W. E., Crowell, M. D., Heller, B. R., Robinson, J. C., et al. (1994). Modeling and reinforcement of the sick role during childhood predicts adult illness behavior. *Psychosom. Med., 56,* 541–550.

Whitehorn, J. C., & Betz, B. J. (1975). *Effective psychotherapy with the schizophrenic patient.* New York: Jason Aronson.

Whiteside, M. (1983, September 12). A bedeviling new hysteria. *Newsweek.*

Whitford, T. J., Farrow, T. F. D., Gomes, L., Brennan, J., Harris, A. W. F., & Williams, L. M. (2005). Grey matter deficits and symptom profile in first episode schizophrenia. *Psychiat. Res.: Neuroimaging, 139*(3), 229–238.

Whiting, J. W., et al. (1966). *I. Field guide for a study of socialization. Six cultures series.* New York: Wiley.

Whitman, T. A., & Akutagawa, D. (2004). Riddles in serial murder: A synthesis. *Aggress. Viol. Behav., 9*(6), 693–703.

Whittle, S. (2002). *Respect and equality: Transsexual and transgender rights.* London: Cavendish Publishing.

WHO (World Health Organization). (2004). Prevalence, severity, and unmet need for treatment of mental disorders in the World Health Organization World Mental Health Surveys. *JAMA, 291*(21), 2581–2590.

Wichniak, A., Riemann, D., Kiemen, A., Voderholzer, U., & Jernajczyk, W. (2000). Comparison between eye movement latency and REM sleep parameters in major depression. *Eur. Arch. Psychiat. Clin. Neurosci., 250*(1), 48–52.

Widiger, T. A. (2002). Personality disorders. In M. M. Antony & D. H. Barlow (Eds.), *Handbook of assessment and treatment planning for psychological disorders* (pp. 453–480). New York: Guilford Press.

Widiger, T. A. (2005). Personality disorders. In R. J. Craig (Ed.), *Clinical and diagnostic interviewing* (2nd ed., pp. 251–277). Lanham, MD: Jason Aronson.

Widiger, T. A. (2006). Understanding personality disorders. In S. K. Huprich, (Ed.), *Rorschach assessment of the personality disorders.* Mahwah, NJ: Lawrence Erlbaum Associates.

Widiger, T. A., & Clark, L. A. (2000). Toward DSM-V and the classification of psychopathology. *Psychol Bull., 126*(6), 946–963.

Widiger, T. A., & Frances, A. J. (1989). Epidemiology, diagnosis, and comorbidity of borderline personality disorder. In A. Tasman, R. E. Hales, & A. J. Frances (Eds.), *American Psychiatric Press review of psychiatry,* Vol. 8. Washington, DC: American Psychiatric Press.

Widiger, T. A., & Simonsen, E. (2005). Alternative dimensional models of personality disorder: Finding a common ground. *J. Pers. Disorders., 19*(2), 110–130.

Widiger, T. A., & Simonsen, E. (2005). Introduction to the special section: The American Psychiatric Association's research agenda for the DSM-V. *J. Pers. Disorders., 19*(2), 103–109.

Widiger, T. A., Corbitt, E. M., & Millon, T. (1992). Antisocial personality disorder. In A. Tasman & M. B. Riba (Eds.), *American Psychiatric Press review of psychiatry* (Vol. 11). Washington, DC: American Psychiatric Press.

Widiger, T. A., Simonsen, E., Krueger, R., Livesley, W. J., & Verheul, R. (2005). Personality disorder research agenda for the DSM-V. *J. Pers. Disorders, 19*(3), 315–338.

Widloecher, D. (2001). The treatment of affects: An interdisciplinary issue. *Psychoanal. Q., 70*(1), 243–264.

Widom, C. S. (1989). The cycle of violence. *Science, 244,* 160–166.

Widom, C. S. (1991, February). Presentation. Washington, DC: American Association for the Advancement of Science.

Widom, C. S. (2001). Child abuse and neglect. In S. O. White (Ed.), *Handbook of youth and justice* (pp. 31–47). New York: Kluwer Academic/Plenum Press.

Wiederhold, B. K., & Wiederhold, M. D. (2005). Posttraumatic stress disorder. In M. D.

Wiederhold & B. K. Wiederhold (Eds.), *Virtual reality therapy for anxiety disorders: Advances in evaluation and treatment* (pp. 117–124). Washington, DC: American Psychological Association.

Wiederhold, B. K., & Wiederhold, M. D. (2005). Specific phobias and social phobia. In M. D. Wiederhold & B. K. Weiderhold, *Virtual reality therapy for anxiety disorders: Advances in evaluation and treatment* (pp. 125–138). Washington, DC: American Psychological Association.

Wiederman, M. W. (2001). "Don't look now": The role of self-focus in sexual dysfunction. *Fam. J. Counsel. Ther. Couples Fam., 9*(2), 210–214.

Wiens, A. N., Mueller, E. A., & Bryan, J. E. (2001). Assessment strategies. In M. Hersen & V. B. Van Hasselt (Eds.), *Advanced abnormal psychology* (2nd ed., pp. 23–41). New York: Kluwer Academic/Plenum Press.

Wikan, U. (1991). *Managing turbulent hearts.* Chicago: University of Chicago Press.

Wikipedia (2005). List of wars and disasters by death toll. *Wikipedia, the free encyclopedia.* Retrieved from en.wikipedia.org/wiki/List_of_wars_and_disasters_by_death_toll

Wilder-Smith, O. H. G. (2005). Opioid use in the elderly. *Eur. J. Pain, 9*(2), 137–140.

Wilens, T., Pelham, W., Stein, M., Conners, C. K., Abikoff, H., Atkins, M., et al. (2003). ADHD treatment with once-daily OROS methylphenidate: Interim 12-month results from a long-term open-label study. *J. Amer. Acad. Child Adol. Psychiat., 42,* 424–433.

Wilkes, M. S., Bell, R. A., & Kravitz, R. L. (2000). Direct-to-consumer prescription drug advertising: Trends, impact, and implications. *Hlth. Affairs, 19*(2), 110–128.

Wilkinson, G., Piccinelli, M., et al. (1997). Lunar cycle and consultations for anxiety and depression in general practice. *Inter. J. Soc. Psychiat., 43*(1), 29–34.

Will, O. A. (1961). Paranoid development and the concept of self: Psychotherapeutic intervention. *Psychiatry, 24*(2), 516–530.

Will, O. A. (1967). Psychological treatment of schizophrenia. In A. M. Freedman & H. I. Kaplan (Eds.), *Comprehensive textbook of psychiatry.* Baltimore: Williams & Wilkins.

Williams, C. C. (1983). The mental foxhole: The Viet Nam veterans' search for meaning. *Amer. J. Orthopsychiat., 53*(1), 4–17.

Williams, J. (2003). Dementia and genetics. In R. Plomin, J. C. DeFries, I. W. Craig, & P. McGuffin (Eds.), *Behavioral genetics in the postgenomic era* (pp. 503–527). Washington, DC: American Psychological Association.

Williams, N., & Leiblum, S. L. (2002). Sexual dysfunction. In G. M. Wingood & R. J. DiClemente (Eds.), *Handbook of women's sexual and reproductive health: Issues in women's health* (pp. 303–328). New York: Kluwer Academic/Plenum.

Williams, R. B. (2001). Hostility (and other psychosocial risk factors): Effects on health and the potential for successful behavioral approaches to prevention and treatment. In A. Baum, T. A. Revenson, & J. E. Singer (Eds.), *Handbook of health psychology* (pp. 661–668). Mahwah, NJ: Erlbaum.

Williams, R. B., Barefoot, J. C., & Schneiderman, N. (Eds.). (2003). Psychosocial risk factors

for cardiovascular disease: More than one culprit at work. *JAMA, 290*(16), 2190–2192.

Willick, M. S. (2001). Psychoanalysis and schizophrenia: A cautionary tale. *J. Amer. Psychoanal. Assoc., 49*(1), 27–56.

Willick, M. S., Milrod, D., & Karush, R. K. (1998). Psychoanalysis and the psychoses. In M. Furer, E. Nersessian, & C. Perri (Eds.), *Controversies in contemporary psychoanalysis: Lectures from the faculty of the New York Psychoanalytic Institute.* Madison, CT: International Universities Press.

Willis, L. A., Coombs, D. W., Cockerham, W. C., & Frison, S. L. (2002). Ready to die: A postmodern interpretation of the increase of African-American adolescent male suicide. *Soc. Sci. Med., 55*(6), 907–920.

Wills, T. A., McNamara, G., Vaccaro, D., & Hirky, A. E. (1996). Escalated substance use: A longitudinal grouping analysis from early to middle adolescence. *J. Abnorm. Psychol., 105*(2), 166–180.

Wilson, G. T. (1994). Behavioral treatment of obesity: Thirty years and counting. *Adv. Behav. Res. Ther., 16,* 31–75.

Wilson, G. T. (2005). Psychological treatment of eating disorders. *Ann. Rev. Clin. Psychol., 1*(1), 439–465.

Wilson, G. T., Becker, C. B., & Heffernan, K. (2003). Eating disorders. In E. J. Mash & R. A. Barkley (Eds.), *Child psychopathology* (2nd ed., pp. 687–715). New York: Guilford Press.

Wilson, G. T., Heffernan, K., & Black, C. M. D. (1996). Eating disorders. In E. J. Mash & R. A. Barkley (Eds.), *Developmental psychopathology.* New York: Guilford Press.

Wilson, K. A., & Hayward, C. (2005). A prospective evaluation of agoraphobia and depression symptoms following panic attacks in a community sample of adolescents. *J. Anx. Dis., 19*(1), 87–103.

Wilson, K. A., Chambless, D. L., & de Beurs, E. (2004). Beck anxiety inventory. In M. E. Maruish (Ed.), *The use of psychological testing for treatment planning and outcomes assessment: Volume 3: Instruments for adults* (3rd ed., pp.399–419). Mahwah, NJ: Lawrence Erlbaum Associates.

Wilson, S. J., & Nutt, D. J. (2005). Sleep research and affective disorders. In C. Faravelli, D. J. Nutt, J. Zohar, & Griez, E. J. L. (Eds.), *Mood disorders: Clinical management and research issues* (pp. 449–465). New York: Wiley.

Wincze, J. P., Richards, J., Parsons, J., & Bailey, S. (1996). A comparative survey of therapist sexual misconduct between an American state and an Australian state. *Profess. Psychol.: Res. Pract., 27*(3), 289–294.

Winerman, L. (2004). Criminal profiling: The reality behind the myth. *Monitor Psychol., 35*(7), 66–69.

Winerman, L. (2005). A virtual cure. *Monitor Psychol., 36*(7), 87–89.

Wing, L. (1976). *Early childhood autism.* Oxford, England: Pergamon Press.

Wing, L., & Potter, D. (2002). The epidemiology of autistic spectrum disorders: Is prevalence rising? *Ment. Retard. Disabil. Res. Rev. Special Issue: The Epidemiology of Neurodevelopmental Disorders, 8,* 151–161.

Winick, B. J. (1983). Incompetency to stand trial: Developments in the law. In J. Monahan & H. J.

Steadman (Eds.), *Mentally disorded offenders.* New York: Plenum Press.

Winick, B. J. (2001). The civil commitment hearing: Applying the law therapeutically. In L. E. Frost & R. J. Bonnie (Eds.), *The evolution of mental health law* (pp. 291–308). Washington, DC: American Psychological Association.

Winick, B. J. (2002). The expanding scope of preventive law. *Florida Coastal Law Journal 189, 3.*

Winick, B. J., & La Fond, J. Q. (Eds.). (2003). *Protecting society from sexually dangerous offenders: Law, justice, and therapy.* Washington, DC: American Psychological Association.

Wink, P. (1996). Narcissism. In C. G. Costello (Ed.), *Personality characteristics of the personality disordered.* New York: Wiley.

Winn, B. D., Skinner, C. H., Allin, J. D., & Hawkins, J. A. (2004). Practicing school consultants can empirically validate interventions: A description and demonstration of the non-concurrent multiple-baseline design. *J. Appl. School Psychol., 20*(2), 109–128.

Winslade, W. J., & Ross, J. (1983). *The insanity plea.* New York: Scribner's.

Winson, J. (2004). To sleep, perchance to dream. *Learn. Memory, 11*(6), 659.

Winstead, B. A., & Sanchez, J. (2005). Gender and psychopathology. In B. A. Winstead & J. E. Maddux (Eds.), *Psychopathology: Foundations for a contemporary understanding* (pp. 39–61). Mahwah, NJ: Lawrence Erlbaum Associates.

Winston, A. S. (Ed.). (2004). *Defining difference: Race and racism in the history of psychology.* Washington, DC: American Psychological Association.

Winton, M. A. (2000). The medicalization of male sexual dysfunction: An analysis of sex therapy journals. *J. Sex Educ. Ther., 25*(4), 231–239.

Wirz-Justice, A., Graw, P., Kräuchi, K., Sarrafzadeh, A., et al. (1996). "Natural" light treatment of seasonal affective disorder. *J. Affect. Disord., 37,* 109–120.

Wise, R. A. (1996). Neurobiology of addiction. *Curr. Opin. Neurobiol., 6,* 243–251.

Wiseman, C. V., Gray, J. J., Mosimann, J. E., & Ahrens, A. H. (1992). Cultural expectations of thinness in women: An update. *Inter. J. Eat. Disorders, 11*(1), 85–89.

Wisner, K. L., Perel, J. M., Peindl, K. S., Hanusa, B. H., Findling, R. L., & Rapport, D. (2001). Prevention of recurrent postpartum depression: A randomized clinical trial. *J. Clin. Psychiat., 62*(2), 82–86.

Witkiewitz, K., & Marlatt, G. A. (2004). Relapse prevention for alcohol and drug problems. *Amer. Psychologist, 59*(4), 224–235.

Wituk, S. A., Shepherd, M. D., Warren, M., & Meissen, G. (2002). Factors contributing to the survival of self-help groups. *Amer. J. Comm. Psych., 30*(3), 349–366.

Witztum, E., Maragalit, H., & Van-der-Hart, O. (2002). Combat-induced dissociative amnesia: Review and case example of generalized dissociative amnesia. *J. Traum. Stress, 3*(2), 35–55.

Wolberg, L. R. (1967). *The technique of psychotherapy.* New York: Grune & Stratton.

Wolchik, S. A., West, S. G., Sandler, I. N., Tein, J. Y., Coatsworth, D., Lengua, L., et al. (2000). An experimental evaluation of theory-based mother and mother-child programs for children of divorce. *J. Cons. Clin. Psychol., 68,* 843–856.

Woldt, A. L., & Toman, S. M. (Eds.). (2005). *Gestalt therapy: History, theory, and practice.* Thousand Oaks, CA: Sage Publications.

Wolfe, B. E. (2005). The application of the integrative model to specific anxiety disorders. In B. E. Wolfe, *Understanding and treating anxiety disorders: An integrative approach to healing the wounded self* (pp. 125–153). Washington, DC: American Psychological Association.

Wolfe, D. A., Edwards, B., Manion, I., & Koverola, C. (1988). Early intervention for parents at risk for child abuse and neglect: A preliminary investigation. *J. Cons. Clin. Psychol., 56,* 40–47.

Wolfe, J. L., & Russianoff, P. (1997). Overcoming self-negation in women. *J. Rat.-Emot. & Cog.-Behav. Ther., 15*(1), 81–92.

Wolff, S. (1991). Schizoid personality in childhood and adult life I: The vagaries of diagnostic labeling. *Br. J. Psychiatry, 159,* 615–620.

Wolkowitz, O. M., & Reus, V. I. (2002). Dehydroepiandrosterone as a neurohormone in the treatment of depression and dementia. In D. Mischoulon & J. F. Rosenbaum (Eds.), *Natural medications for psychiatric disorders: Considering the alternatives* (pp. 62–82). Philadelphia: Lippincott, Williams & Wilkins.

Wolpe, J. (1958). *Psychotherapy by reciprocal inhibition.* Stanford, CA: Stanford University Press.

Wolpe, J. (1969). *The practice of behavior therapy.* Oxford, England: Pergamon Press.

Wolpe, J. (1987). The promotion of scientific psychotherapy: A long voyage. In J. K. Zeig (Ed.), *The evolution of psychotherapy.* New York: Brunner/Mazel.

Wolpe, J. (1990). *The practice of behavior therapy* (4th ed.). Elmsford, NY: Pergamon Press.

Wolpe, J. (1995). Reciprocal inhibition: Major agent of behavior change. In W. T. O'Donohue & L. Krasner (Eds.), *Theories of behavior therapy: Exploring behavior change.* Washington, DC: American Psychological Association.

Wolpe, J. (1997). From psychoanalytic to behavioral methods in anxiety disorders: A continuing evolution. In J. K. Zeig (Ed.), *The evolution of psychotherapy: The third conference.* New York: Brunner/Mazel.

Wolpe, J. (1997). Thirty years of behavior therapy. *Behav. Ther., 28*(4), 633–635.

Wong, Y., & Huang, Y. (2000). Obesity concerns, weight satisfaction and characteristics of female dieters: A study on female Taiwanese college students. *J. Amer. Coll. Nutr., 18*(2), 194–199.

Wood, J. M., Garb, H. N., Lilienfeld, S. O., & Nezworski, M. T. (2002). Clinical assessment. *Annu. Rev. Psychol., 53,* 519–543.

Woods, S. J. (2005). Intimate partner violence and post-traumatic stress disorder symptoms in women: What we know and need to know. *J. Interpers. Violence, 20*(4), 394–402.

Woodside, D. B., Bulid, C. M., Halmi, K. A., Fichter, M. M., Kaplan, A., Berrettini, W. H., et al. (2002). Personality, perfectionism, and attitudes towards eating in parent of individuals with eating disorders. *Inter. J. Eat. Disorders, 31*(3), 290–299.

Woodside, M. R., & Legg, B. H. (1990). Patient advocacy: A mental health perspective. *J. Ment. Hlth. Couns., 12*(1), 38–50.

Woody, G. E., McLellan, A. T., Luborsky, L., & O'Brien, C. P. (1998). Psychotherapy with opioid-dependent patients. *Psychiatr. Times, XV*(11).

Wooley, S. C., & Wooley, O. W. (1985). Intensive outpatient and residential treatment for bulimia. In D. M. Garner & P. E. Garfinkel (Eds.), *Handbook of psychotherapy for anorexia nervosa and bulimia.* New York: Guilford Press.

Work Group on Borderline Personality Disorder. (2001). Practice guideline for the treatment of patients with borderline personality disorder. *Amer. J. Psychiat., 158*(Suppl.), 1–52.

Wright, J. (1984). EAP: An important supervisory tool. *Supervisory Management, 29*(12), 16–17.

Wright, N. R., & Thompson, C. (2002). Withdrawal from alcohol using monitored alcohol consumption: A case report. *Alcohol Alcoholism, 37*(4), 344–346.

Wroble, M. C., & Baum, A. (2002). Toxic waste spills and nuclear accidents. In A. M. La Greca, W. K. Silverman, E. M. Vernberg, & M. C. Roberts (Eds.). *Helping children cope with disasters and terrorism* (pp. 207–221). Washington, DC: American Psychological Association.

Wu, J., Kramer, G. L., Kram, M., Steciuk, M., Crawford, I. L., & Petty, F. (1999). Serotonin and learned helplessness: A regional study of 5–HT-sub(1A), 5–HT-sub(2A) receptors and the serotonin transport site in rat brain. *J. Psychiatr. Res., 33*(1), 17–22.

Wu, L. T., Pilowsky, D. J., Schlenger, W. E. (2005). High prevalence of substance use disorders among adolescents who use marijuana and inhalants. *Drug Alc. Dep., 78*(1), 23–32.

Wunderlich, U., Bronisch, T., & Wittchen, H. U. (1998). Comorbidity patterns in adolescents and young adults with suicide attempts. *Eur. Arch. Psychiat. Clin. Neurosci., 248*(2), 87–95.

Wurtele, S. K., & Schmitt, A. (1992). Child care workers' knowledge about reporting suspected child sexual abuse. *Child Abuse Negl., 16*(3) 385–390.

Wylie, K. R., Jones, R. H., & Walters, S. (2003). The potential benefit of vacuum devices augmenting psychosexual therapy for erectile dysfunction: A randomized controlled trial. *J. Sex Marital Ther., 29*(3), 227–236.

Yalom, I. (1960). Aggression and forbiddenness in voyeurism. *Arch. Gen. Psychiat., 3,* 305–319.

Yamasaki, A., Chinami, M., Morgenthaler, S., Kaneko, Y., Nakashima, K., & Shirakawa, T. (2004). Enterprise failures correlate positively with suicide rate for both sexes in Japan. *Psychol. Rep., 95*(3, Part 1), 917–920.

Yamasaki, A., Sakai, R., & Shirakawa, T. (2005). Low income, unemployment, and suicide morality rates for middle-age persons in Japan. *Psychol. Rep., 96*(2), 337–348.

Yang, B., & Lester, D. (1995). Suicidal behavior and employment. In S. S. Canetto & D. Lester (Eds.), *Women and suicidal behavior.* New York: Springer.

Yarmey, A. D. (2004). Eyewitness recall and photo identification: a field experiment. *Psychol. Crime Law, 10*(1), 53–68.

Yen, H. (2005). High Court to review assisted suicide law. *Associated Press (Washington)/Yahoo!News.*

Yen, S., Sr., Shea, M. T., Battle, C. L., Johnson, D. M., Zlotnick, C., Dolan-Sewell, R., et al.

(2002). Traumatic exposure and posttraumatic stress disorder in borderline, schizotypal, avoidant and obsessive-compulsive personality disorders: Findings from the Collaborative Longitudinal Personality Disorders Study. *J. Nerv. Ment. Dis., 190*(8), 510–518.

Yewchuk, C. (1999). Savant syndrome: Intuitive excellence amidst general deficit. *Dev. Disabil. Bull., 27*(1), 58–76.

Yin, S. (2002, May 1). Coming up short. *Amer. Demog.*

Yoder, K. A., Hoyt, D. R., & Whitbeck, L. B. (1998). Suicidal behavior among homeless and runaway adolescents. *J. Youth Adolescence, 27*(6), 753–771.

Yolken, R. H., Karlsson, H., Yee, F., Johnston-Wilson, N. L., & Torrey, E. F. (2000). Endogenous retroviruses and schizophrenia. *Brain Res., 31*(2–3), 193–199.

Yontef, G., & Jacobs, L. (2005). Gestalt therapy. In R. Corsini & D. Wedding (Eds.). *Current psychotherapies* (7th ed., pp. 299–336). Belmont, CA: Brooks/Cole–Thompson Learning.

Yoshimasu, K., Kiyohara, C., & Ohkuma, K. (2002). Efficacy of day care treatment against readmission in patients with schizophrenia: A comparison between out-patients with and without day care treatment. *Psychiat. Clin. Neurosci., 56*(4), 397–401.

Young, J. (2002). Morals, suicide, and psychiatry: A view from Japan. *Bioethics, 16*(5), 412–424.

Young, K. S. (1996). Cited in: middle-aged women are more at risk for Internet addiction. *APA Monitor, 27*(10), 10.

Young, K. S. (1996). Psychology of computer use: XL. Addictive use of the Internet: A case that breaks the stereotype. *Psychol. Rep., 79*(3, Pt 1), 899–902.

Young, K. S. (1998). Internet addiction: The emergence of a new clinical disorder. *CyberPsychol. Behav., 1*(3), 237–244.

Young, K. S. (1999). Evaluation and treatment of Internet addiction. In L. VandeCreek & T. L. Jackson (Eds.), *Innovations in clinical practice: A source book* (Vol. 17, pp. 19–31). Sarasota, FL: Professional Resource Press/Professional Resource Exchange.

Young, M., Benjamin, B., & Wallis, C. (1963). Mortality of widowers. *Lancet, 2,* 454–456.

Yu, D. L., & Seligman, M. E. P. (2002). Preventing depressive symptoms in Chinese children. *Prev. Treat., 5,* [np].

Zal, H. M. (1999). Agitation in the elderly. *Psychiatr. Times, XVI*(1).

Zanarini, M. C., Frankenburg, F. R., Hennen, J., Reich, D. B., & Silk, K. R. (2005). Psychosocial functioning of borderline patients and Axis II comparison subjects followed prospectively for six years. *J. Pers. Disorders, 19,* 19–29.

Zanelli, J., Simon, H., Rabe-Hesketh, S., Walshe, M. McDonald, C., Murray, R. M., & MacCabe, J. H. (2005). Eye tracking in schizophrenia: Does the antisaccade task measure anything that the smooth pursuit task does not? *Psychiat. Res., 136*(2–3), 181–188.

Zarin, D. A., Young, J. L., & West, J. C. (2005). Challenges to evidence-based medicine: A comparison of patients and treatments in randomized controlled trials with patients and treatments in a practice research network. *Soc. Psychiat. Psychiatr. Epidemiol., 40*(1), 27–35.

Zec, R. F., Zellers, D., Belman, J., Miller, J., Matthews, J., Ferneau-Belman, D., & Robbs, R. (2001). Long-term consequences of severe closed-head injury on episodic memory. *J. Clin. Exp. Neuropsychol., 23*(5), 671–691.

Zec, R. F., Zellers, D., Belman, J., Miller, J., Matthews, J., Ferneau-Belman, D., & Robbs, R. (2002). "Long-term consequences of severe closed-head injury on episodic memory": Erratum. *J. Clin. Exp. Neuropsychol., 24*(1), 130.

Zelkowitz, P., Paris, J., Guzder, J., & Feldman, R. (2001). Diathesis and stressors in borderline pathology of childhood: The role of neuropsychological risk and trauma. *J. Amer. Acad. Child Adol. Psychiat., 40,* 100–105.

Zerbe, K. J. (1993). *The body betrayed: Women, eating disorders, and treatment.* Washington, DC: American Psychiatric Press.

Zerbe, K. J. (2001). The crucial role of psychodynamic understanding in the treatment of eating disorders. *Psychiatr. Clin. N. Amer., 24*(2), 305–313.

Zhao, M., Hao, W., Yang, D., Zhang, Y., & Li, L. (2001). A prospective study of factors related to relapse in heroin addicts. *Chin. J. Clin. Psychol., 9*(2), 81–83, 89.

Zhou, J.-N., Hofman, M. A., Gooren, L. J. G., & Swaab, D. F. (1995). A sex difference in the human brain and its relation to transsexuality. *Nature, 378,* 68–70.

Zhou, S., Chan, E., Pan, S. Q., Huang, M., & Lee, E. J. D. (2004). Pharmacokinetic interactions of drugs with St John's wort. *J. Psychopharmacol., 18*(2), 262–276.

Ziedonis, D., Williams, J., Corrigan, P., & Smelson, D. (2000). Management of substance abuse in schizophrenia. *Psychiatr. Ann., 30*(1), 67–75.

Zilboorg, G., & Henry, G. W. (1941). *A history of medical psychology.* New York: Norton.

Zimbardo, P. (1976). Rational paths to madness. Presentation at Princeton University, Princeton, NJ.

Zimmermann, G., Favrod, J., Trieu, V. H., & Pomini, V. (2005). The effect of cognitive behavioral treatment on the positive symptoms of schizophrenia spectrum disorders: A meta-analysis. *Schizo. Res., 77*(1), 1–9.

Zivin, J. (2000, April). Understanding clinical trials. *Scientif. Amer.,* p. 69.

Zoellner, T. (2000, November). "Don't get even, get mad." *Men's Health, 15*(9), 56.

Zohar, J., Kennedy, J. L., Hollander, E., & Koran, L. M. (2004). Serotonin-1D hypothesis of obsessive-compulsive disorder: An update. *J. Clin. Psychiat., 65*(Suppl. 14), 18–21.

Zohar, J., & Pato, M. T. (1991). Diagnostic considerations. In M. T. Pato & J. Zohar (Eds.), *Current treatments of obsessive-compulsive disorder.* Washington, DC: American Psychiatric Press.

Zonana, H., Roth, J. A., & Coric, V. (2004). Forensic assessment of sex offenders. In R. I. Simon & L. H. Gold (Eds.), *The American Psychiatric Publishing textbook of forensic psychiatry* (pp. 349–376). Washington, DC: American Psychiatric Publishing.

Zucker, K. J. (2005). Gender identity disorder in children and adolescents. *Ann. Rev. Clin. Psychol., 1*(1), 467–492.

Zuckerman, M. (1996). Sensation seeking. In C. G. Costello (Ed.), *Personality characteristics of the personality disordered.* New York: Wiley.

Zygmunt, A., Olfson, M., Boyer, C. A., & Mechanic, D. (2002). Interventions to improve medication adherence in schizophrenia. *Amer. J. Psychiat., 159*(10), 1653–1664. ⋘

[name index]

[subject index]

Note: Page numbers followed by f, t, and b indicate figures, tables, and boxed text, respectively.

family dynamics in, 430, 432–433, 447–448
fingerprints in, 429
gender and, 412
genetic factors in, 423–425, 424f
geographic aspects of, 412–413, 412f
hallucinations in, 419–420
hebephrenic, 422
historical perspective on, 411
infections and, 52
insanity test and, 562
media depictions of, 412, 414b
in Minnesota Multiple Personality
    Inventory, 94
overview of, 411–413, 433–434
paranoid, 422, 423
perceptual changes in, 418–420
poverty of speech in, 420
premorbid functioning and, 422
prevalence of, 411, 424, 424f
prodromal phase of, 422
psychodynamic view of, 429–430
psychological views of, 429–431
as psychosis, 411
race/ethnicity and, 412
recovery from, 422
residual, 422, 423
smooth pursuit eye movements in, 418–419
social labeling in, 431–432
social withdrawal in, 421–422
societal impact of, 411–412
sociocultural views of, 431–433
sociocultural-existential view of, 433
substance abuse and, 362–363, 450, 453b
symptoms of
    negative, 416, 420–422
    positive, 416–420
    psychomotor, 416, 422
treatment of, 437–459
    community approach in, 449–457
    drug therapy in, 442–446. *See also*
        Antipsychotics
    historical perspective on, 438–439
    institutional, 438–442
    overview of, 437, 457
    psychotherapy in, 446–449
undifferentiated, 423
viral infections and, 429
Schizophreniform disorder, 425t
Schizophrenogenic mother, 430
Schizotypal personality disorder, 462, 463f,
    468–469
School(s). *See also* Education; Learning
    bullying in, 502b–503b
    for mentally retarded, 528
School problems
    attention deficit/hyperactivity disorder and,
        508
    in autism, 521
    bullying and, 502b–503b
    learning disabilities and, 520–521, 523, 524b
School shootings, 502b–503b
Scientific method, 28. *See also* Clinical research;
    Experiment(s)
Screening, for dementia, 550
Seasonal affective disorder, 227, 231b
Seasonal bipolar disorder, 243
Second messengers, 274
Secondary prevention, 79

Sedative-hypnotics, 125, 125t
    abuse of, 344–347, 346t
Seizures, interictal personality disorder and, 87b
Selective amnesia, 204
Selective norepinephrine reuptake inhibitors,
    267–268, 267t. *See also* Antidepressants
Selective serotonin reuptake inhibitors,
    267–268, 267t. *See also* Antidepressants
Self theory, 57
Self-actualization, 66
Self-blame theory, of female depression, 241b
Self-help groups, 75, 76, 78b
    for substance abuse, 370–372, 371b
Self-hypnosis, 213–214. *See also* Hypnosis
Self-instruction training
    for hypoactive sexual desire, 392
    for pain, 183
Self-monitoring, 100
Semantic memory, 205
Semihospital crisis centers, 450
Senile plaques, 545–546
Sensate focusing, 390–391
Sentence-completion test, 91
Separation anxiety disorder, 140b
September 11 attack, stress disorders and,
    164b–165b, 167t
Serial killers, 578b
Seroquel, 445
Serotonin, 50. *See also* Neurotransmitters
    aggression and, 296
    antidepressant action and, 266–267
    antipsychotics and, 428
    in bipolar disorder, 245
    in borderline personality disorder, 478
    in depression, 229–231
    in eating disorders, 324
    in Ecstasy abuse, 355b
    in obsessive-compulsive disorder, 148
    in suicide, 296
Serotonin-norepinephrine reuptake inhibitors,
    267. *See also* Antidepressants
Sex history, 390, 391f
Sex hormones
    for gender identity disorder, 405
    for paraphilias, 397
    sex drive and, 380
Sex therapy, 389–396
    current trends in, 395–396
    for dyspareunia, 395
    for erectile disorder, 393
    for female orgasmic disorder, 395
    for female sexual arousal disorder, 395
    for hypoactive sexual desire, 392
    for male orgasmic disorder, 393
    for premature ejaculation, 393–395
    principles and techniques in, 390–391
    for sexual aversion, 392–393
    for vaginismus, 395
Sex-change surgery, 406–407
Sexism. *See also* Gender
    in insurance coverage, 394b
Sex-offender statutes, 566
Sex-role myths, 392t
Sexual abuse, 400–401. *See also* Child abuse
    borderline personality disorder and, 478
    pedophilia and, 400–401
    repressed memories of, 206b, 211
    sexual dysfunction and, 382, 388, 392

stress disorders and, 161–163
suicide and, 287
Sexual addiction, 396
Sexual arousal disorder, 382, 382t
    treatment of, 395
Sexual assault victims, stress disorders in,
    161–163
Sexual attitudes, gender differences in, 387f,
    391f
Sexual aversion, 379–382, 379t
    treatment of, 392–393
Sexual behavior
    gender differences in, 387f, 391f
    lifetime patterns of, 381b
Sexual desire, hypoactive, 379–382, 379t
    treatment of, 392–393
Sexual dysfunction, 377–396, 378
    antidepressants and, 386, 391
    classification of, 378
    definition of, 377
    diagnostic criteria for, 379t, 382t, 387t, 388t
    disorders of desire, 378–382
    disorders of excitement, 382–384
    disorders of orgasm, 384–388
    disorders of sexual pain, 388–389
    treatment of, 389–396. *See also* Sex therapy
Sexual intercourse, painful, 388–389, 388t, 395
Sexual masochism, 401–402
Sexual organs
    female, 379f
    male, 384f
Sexual pain, sadomasochistic, 401–403
Sexual pain disorders, 388–389
    treatment of, 395
Sexual reassignment surgery, 406–407
Sexual relationships, with clients, 579–580
Sexual response cycle, 378, 378f
    anatomic changes in, 379f, 384f
    in female, 378f, 379f
    in male, 378f, 384f
Sexual sadism, 403
Sexuality, myths about, 392t
Shamans, 8
Shared psychotic disorder, 425t
Sheltered workshops, 452, 521, 530–531
Shen-k'vei, 118t
Shock therapy. *See* Electroconvulsive therapy
Short-term hospitalization, 17, 450. *See also*
    Hospitalization/institutionalization
Short-term memory, 546
Short-term psychodynamic therapy, 59
Shuttle box, 237, 237f
Sick role, enmeshed families and, 322
Sildenafil, 393, 394b
Simultaneous communication, 521
Single-subject experiments, 42–43
Situational anxiety, 158
Skillful frustration, 69
Sleep
    circadian rhythms and, 230, 539b
    paradoxical, 538b
    penile erections during, 383–384, 383f
    REM, 230, 538
Sleep apnea, 538b
Sleep problems, 174–175, 538b–539b
    in depression, 230b
    in elderly, 538b–539b
    melatonin for, 265b